Education for Sustainability

Volume 7

Education and sustainability remain two of the most important topics at this inflection point in human history. As multiple intertwined crises challenge the creation of a sustainable, just, peaceful future, education for sustainability remains ever more critical. This series builds on a variety of international efforts. As part of the United Nations Sustainable Development Goals (SDGs 2015-2030) and as echoed by the Aichi-Nagoya Declaration on Education for Sustainable Development (2014), education must speak to climate change, biodiversity, sustainable consumption and production, and the urgency of the civilizational crisis we face. Supporting this aim, there is a call for research and coordinated actions with an emphasis on the principles of human rights, gender equality, democracy, and social and environmental justice. There is also a great need for attention to the importance and relevance of traditional knowledge and indigenous wisdom in all geographical, socio-cultural, and educational contexts. While the Decade of Education for Sustainable Development (DESD) (2005-2014) has been completed, the status and advocacy of education for sustainable development remains prominent. The United Nations goals of Education for All (2000) and the Millennium Development Goals (MDGs 2000-2015) were complementary and provided a rationale for the critical importance of environmental education and education for sustainable development. The United Nations Educational, Scientific and Cultural Organization's (UNESCO) Muscat Agreement in 2014 advocated seven global education targets, one of which was to cultivate skills for global citizenship and environmental sustainability. Many of these lofty aims remained unrealized and are ever more urgent as the predicted social and environmental crises of the twenty-first century unfold dramatically before our students' eyes.

With this background, and in light of UNESCO's Education 2030 Agenda (2017) and their world-wide consultations on Futures of Education: Learning to Become (2019), this Education for Sustainability Book Series was launched. Its purpose is to echo and enhance the global importance of education for a sustainable future as an educational vision. We hope the Series will provide insights on a broad range of issues related to the intersection of, and interaction between, sustainability and education. The Series will showcase innovative practice, discusses salient theoretical topics, and use cases as examples.

For further information on this important book series, to become involved, or to propose a manuscript, please contact any of the co-editors. We are interested in new approaches; humanistic, socially-critical, and radical perspectives; examples that tell a larger story; and manuscripts that speak to the crisis and challenges we face in education and in sustainability.

John Chi-Kin Lee
The Education University of Hong Kong
Hong Kong SAR, China
Rupert Maclean
University of Tasmania, Hobart, Australia
and RMIT University, Melbourne, Australia
Peter Blaze Corcoran
Florida Gulf Coast University
Fort Myers, FL, USA

Kim Beasy · Caroline Smith · Jane Watson
Editors

Education and the UN Sustainable Development Goals

Praxis Within and Beyond the Classroom

Editors
Kim Beasy
School of Education, College of Arts, Law,
and Education
Launceston, TAS, Australia

Caroline Smith
School of Education, College of Arts, Law,
and Education
Burnie, TAS, Australia

Jane Watson
School of Education, College of Arts, Law,
and Education
Hobart, TAS, Australia

ISSN 2367-1769   ISSN 2367-1777 (electronic)
Education for Sustainability
ISBN 978-981-99-3801-8   ISBN 978-981-99-3802-5 (eBook)
https://doi.org/10.1007/978-981-99-3802-5

This Springer imprint is published by the registered company Springer Nature Singapore Pte Ltd.
The registered company address is: 152 Beach Road, #21-01/04 Gateway East, Singapore 189721,
Singapore

We present this book, with hope, as a contribution from the various fields of education towards enacting sustainable and harmonious human and more-than-human flourishing.

Foreword

World leaders from United Nations (UN) member states have unanimously embraced sustainable development as the overarching future paradigm both to cope with massive interwoven social, environmental, and economic global issues confronting humanity and to fulfil the aspirations of the people for a better future for all. Achieving this aspired vision of our shared futures will demand concerted action by all countries. The most pressing global sustainability challenges comprise the 17 *UN Sustainable Development Goals (SDGs)* at the core of the *2030 Agenda for Sustainable Development* (UN, 2015).

Adopted in 2015, the *2030 Agenda* emphasized the importance of quality education through SDG4. More specifically, access to education, reorienting education systems, public awareness, and training, collectively referred to as *Education for Sustainable Development (ESD)*, are stated in target 4.7:

> By 2030, ensure that all learners acquire the knowledge and skills needed to promote sustainable development, including, among others, **through education for sustainable development** and sustainable lifestyles, human rights, gender equality, promotion of a culture of peace and non-violence, global citizenship and appreciation of cultural diversity and of culture's contribution to sustainable development. (UN, 2015)

At a time when the world's education systems are trying to recover from the devastating impacts of a global pandemic, while facing an unpredictable climate future and myriad serious conflicts including an unprovoked war that has struck Europe, education systems are confronted with unprecedented levels of uncertainty. Yet, most education systems are not strategically prepared for continuous change, nor do they have the resources to rise to these non-negotiable challenges. For manifold reasons, our education systems are not equipped to deliver an education that will contribute to the more caring, inclusive, and equitable societies that are so needed. Now, there are new calls for collective action to transform education and move towards seeing education as a social contract to unite all of us (United Nations Educational, Scientific and Cultural Organization [UNESCO], 2021). So, how can our educators successfully cope with these high expectations and make education become a unifying strength? How can they possibly prepare the generations of tomorrow without the foreseeability of life as we know it?

Education for Sustainability/Education for Sustainable Development (EfS/ESD) can unfold the potential to respond to these challenges when embedded holistically in education and training systems. Recognized by the UN General Assembly on three occasions as not only an integral element of quality education but also a key enabler of all 17 SDGs, ESD "empowers learners with knowledge, skills, values and attitudes to take informed decisions and make responsible actions for environmental integrity, economic viability and a just society empowering people of all genders, for present and future generations..." (UNESCO, 2020).

Education and the UN Sustainable Development Goals: Praxis Within and Beyond the Classroom is a most welcomed, comprehensive, and easily read publication for education leaders and practitioners to engage successfully with these challenges in a cohesive, synergistic, ethical, and most of all, practical manner. Many publications focus on the "why" of education or the "what" that education can potentially contribute to sustainability, as the need for knowledge and science are undisputed for any preventative, adaptive, or restorative sustainability effort.

This book goes beyond the "why/what" to also address the "how" and shares concrete evidence and stories of good practice and praxis to provide further guidance. It builds upon research and the experience of others, to provide insight and examples of how the SDGs are being taken up by ministries, institutions, and educators in both the developed and developing world. It shares the implementation strengths of others by providing examples and case studies that can be readily adapted to local situations. Chapters cover different perspectives and whether from a more discipline-oriented or systemically driven perspective, they all have aspects of ESD at their core.

The belief that it is difficult to embed sustainable development into education contexts without having exposure to how this has been done, and is working elsewhere, has guided the development of the book. It is widely accepted that having exposure to how others have not only coped but are benefitting economically and socially, enhancing their reputations, and greatly contributing to their students and communities, is extremely helpful in mounting one's own initiatives.

As a result, *this book* serves as an excellent implementation guide that not only is built upon UNESCO's universal four pillars of education for the twenty-first century (Delors, 1996): learning to know, learning to do, learning to be, and learning to live together, but does so in a novel context of today of education as a *common good*. This new context, which suggests the co-generation of knowledge, skills, and a context of action creates the new form of transformative learning that is called for by UNESCO and the UN as a whole (UN, 2022).

Education and the UN Sustainable Development Goals is an excellent guide to assist in the implementation of both current and emerging approaches in reorienting education towards sustainability. Its content is future-oriented, serving the education mandates of twenty-first-century attributes, such as critical thinking, questioning, and preparing students and their communities for the challenges and opportunities inherent in the pursuit of sustainability today and tomorrow.

This book escapes the trap of simply accepting the currently accepted concept of sustainable development without critical analysis. It rises above being an indoctrination tool by questioning the dichotomies between sustainable development's inherent conceptual framework and its current global implementation, an implementation that seemingly ignores ecological realities and continues to prioritize economic growth above social and environmental justice. Authors also question the lack of alternative sources of knowledge, such as traditional and Indigenous wisdom. Thoughtful discussions are found on the rights of nature, rights of future generations, and the emergence of anthropocentric values now taken as the norm. Many questionable aspects of colonization are brought forward, such as of knowledge and culture, but perhaps the greatest that is suggested by the book is the overarching colonization of the entire planet and nature itself.

As it is often our most educated societies that have created the deepest ecological footprints, it is not only essential that countries acquire dynamic learners who comprise the core of their societies, but also that learning be based on co-creating a sustainable future and considering others when making decisions. This book is a guide to help education leaders and practitioners, especially those in pre- and in-service teacher education, better understand the concept of sustainability, the contexts, roles of ESD, and how to create their own paths forward in embedding ESD in their practices, programmes, and policies, now and into the future. Educators who are primarily concerned with achieving better results in their teaching of the core disciplines of language and mathematics will also find chapters of great interest and how foundations can be taught in a meaningful context of the SDGs.

As we have delayed and postponed many of the truly necessary steps to tackle the most pressing sustainability issues of our time comprehensively, the path forward must go much further than simple acceptance of and compliance with corrective or adaptive measures, to the creation of thriving societies within planetary boundaries, with justice for all in diverse, peaceful settings. This will take a tremendous shift in the purpose and practices of education systems, to prepare future, globally knowledgeable citizens adequately, equipped with the knowledge, skills, ethics, and values necessary to build such a peaceful, just, and sustainable world in a purposeful and collaborative manner. This book contributes a sizable, well-balanced collection of existing knowledge and experiences, collected from around the world, and wonderfully encased in thoughtful provocations to further the quest of a sustainable future.

December 2022

Charles Hopkins
UNESCO Chair in Reorienting
Education towards Sustainability
York University
Toronto, Canada

Acknowledgments This book has been compiled in *lutruwita* (Tasmania), on *palawa* and *pakana* (Tasmanian Aboriginal) land, sea, sky, and waterways Country.

We acknowledge with deep respect the Traditional Owners of this Country the *palawa* and *pakana* peoples who have never ceded their sovereignty. We pay our respects to Elders past and present and to all *palawa* and *pakana* communities; all of whom have survived invasion and dispossession and continue to maintain their identity and culture.

References

Delors, J. (1996). *Learning: The treasure within—Report to UNESCO of the International Commission on Education for the Twenty-first Century.* UNESCO. https://unesdoc.unesco.org/ark:/48223/pf0000109590

United Nations. (2015). *Transforming our world: The 2030 agenda for sustainable development.* https://sdgs.un.org/2030agenda

United Nations. (2022). *Transforming education summit.* https://www.un.org/en/transforming-education-summit/

United Nations Educational, Scientific and Cultural Organization. (2020). *Education for sustainable development: A roadmap.* https://unesdoc.unesco.org/ark:/48223/pf0000374802

United Nations Educational, Scientific and Cultural Organization. (2021). *Reimagining our future together: A new social contract for education.* https://unesdoc.unesco.org/ark:/48223/pf0000379707

Series Editors Introduction

This is an important book on an important subject.

Education and the UN Sustainability Goals: Praxis Within and Beyond the Classroom, edited by Kim Beasy, Caroline Smith, and Jane Watson, all of whom are based in the School of Education at the University of Tasmania, Australia, is the VIIth volume to be published to date in the Springer book series *Education and Sustainability.*

The United Nations 17 Sustainable Development Goals, adopted by all 193 UN Member States in 2015, are a comprehensive plan to achieve a better future for all. The goals provide a blueprint for eliminating extreme poverty, reducing inequalities, rehabilitating the natural environment, ensuring access to justice, improving wellbeing, and building global partnerships needed to achieve sustainable development—all by 2030.

The contributors to the book examine how best to achieve these Sustainable Development Goals with particular reference to education and schooling.

In specific terms, the SDG's focus on achieving: no poverty; zero hunger; good health and wellbeing; quality education; gender equality; clean water and sanitation; affordable and clean energy; decent work and economic growth; industry, innovation, and infrastructure; reduced inequalities; sustainable cities and communities; responsible consumption and production; climate action; life below water; life on land; peace, justice, and strong institutions; and, partnerships to achieve the goals. There are 169 goal targets set to achieve the SDG's, some of which are examined in this book.

The chapters in this book examine, illustrate, and probe the close relationship between education and the United Nations Sustainable Development Goals (SDG's), if the Sustainable Development Goals are to be achieved. On three separate occasions (2017, 2019, and 2021) the UN General Assembly declared that Education for Sustainable Development (ESD) was and is the key enabler to achieve all of the SDG's.

Contributors examine what social, economic, and political action is necessary to achieve the SDG's goals through all forms of education, whether this be formal, non-formal, or informal, and in university practice and university systems.

The 40 chapters in the book are divided into seven sections, which examine: histories and critical perspectives; challenges to implementation from around the world; SDG implementation and assessment in university systems; enacting sustainable development goals in university practice; engagement in schools and classrooms; community initiatives; and alternative perspectives in moving the sustainable development goals forward.

Although the scope of this volume is international in nature, very many contributors come from the University of Tasmania (UTAS), a clear indication of just how fundamentally important sustainable development is to UTAS. Of the 77 authors contributing to the 40 chapters of the book, 58 are based at the University of Tasmania. Of these, 30 are from the School of Education, 7 from other Schools in the College of Arts, Law and Education, and 21 from other departments in UTAS. This extensive coverage indicates high recognition of the importance of addressing the Sustainable Development Goals within the University of Tasmania, not only in the School of Education, but also through courses in many other Colleges and by the UTAS organization as a whole, through various ongoing initiatives. In addition, with some authors having multiple associations, there are 11 authors linked to other Australian universities, as well as 11 authors from other countries of the world, including Canada, Singapore, Nepal, Italy, and the US. Further, the authors from within UTAS provide significant perspectives from Ghana, Uganda, Pakistan, Afghanistan, and Trinidad & Tobago.

We are delighted to publish this particular title in the Springer "Education for Sustainability" Book Series. The purpose of the book series is to echo and enhance the global importance of education for a sustainable future, as an educational vision. We hope the Series will provide insights on a broad range of issues related to the intersection of, and interaction between, sustainability and education. The series showcases innovative practice, discusses salient theoretical topics, and uses case studies as examples.

The Series adopts international, environmental education, and lifelong learning perspectives and explores connections with the agenda of education for sustainable development and promoting learning societies. The intended audience includes university academics and students in educational studies, environmental education, climate change education, geography education, science education, curriculum studies, comparative education, educational leadership, and teacher education; the staff of international agencies with responsibilities for education; and schoolteachers in primary and secondary schools.

Supported by the expertise of a distinguished and diverse International Advisory Board, this Series features authoritative and comprehensive global coverage, as well as diversified local, regional, national, and international perspectives. As a complement to the "Schooling for Sustainable Development" Book Series, it explores issues that go beyond primary and secondary schooling into university, vocational, and community education settings. These educational issues involve multiple stakeholders ranging from international agencies, governmental and non-governmental organizations, education and business leaders to teachers, parents, and, critically, students and youth. Research topics covered include global themes related to environment, such as climate change prevention, mitigation, and adaptation; disaster prevention and risk reduction; biodiversity education and ecological education. They also include human ecological issues such as global citizenship, peace education, childhood development, arts education, intergenerational equity, women's and gender studies, and human rights education. Further, they include society-orientated issues such as governance, green skills for sustainable development, and patterns of applied learning and leadership for a sustainable future.

The authors and co-editors of books in the Series are responsible for the choice and presentation of information and views contained in their particular volume, and for the opinions expressed therein, which are not necessarily those of the universities where the co-editors of this book series are employed, and so do not commit these respective organizations.

In terms of the Springer Book Series in which this volume is published, the various topics dealt with in the series are wide ranging and varied in coverage, with an emphasis on cutting edge developments, best practices, and educational innovations for development. More information about this book series is available at https://www.springer.com/series/15237.

We believe this book series makes a useful contribution to knowledge sharing about Education and Sustainability. Any readers of this or other volumes in the series who have an idea for writing or editing their own book, on any aspect of Education and Sustainability, are encouraged to approach the series editors either directly or through Springer to publish their own volume in the series. The Series Editors are always willing to assist prospective authors shape their manuscripts in ways that make them suitable for publication in this series.

April 2023

John Chi-Kin Lee
The Education University of Hong
Kong
Hong Kong SAR, China

Rupert Maclean AO
University of Tasmania
Hobart, CL, Australia

The Education University of Hong
Kong
Hong Kong, China

Peter Blaze Corcoran
Florida Gulf Coast University
Fort Myers, FL, USA

University of the Sunshine Coast
Queensland, QLD, Australia

Contents

Part I   Histories and Critical Perspectives

**1   Setting the Scene: The Sustainable Development Goals
and the Importance of Education**   3
Kim Beasy, Caroline Smith, and Jane Watson

**2   Sustainable Development Goals and UNESCO World
Heritage Sites in Australia and the Pacific: The Role
of Education**   11
Colin Power

**3   The United Nations Sustainable Development Goals
in a Neoliberal World**   29
Lyn Carter and Caroline Smith

**4   On the Right to a Sustainable Education: Philosophical
Perspectives and Moral Imperatives**   49
David Moltow and Cassandra Thoars

**5   Decolonising the Sustainable Development Agenda: Bitin'
Back at the Establishment Man**   63
Jennifer Evans

**6   Decolonising the Sustainable Development Agenda: The Voice
of Country and Treaty**   83
Jennifer Evans

**7   Future Lawyers, Future Laws: Reimagining Legal Education
for Sustainability in a World "Governing Through Goals"**   105
Phillipa C. McCormack and Michelle Lim

Part II   Challenges to Implementation from Around the World

8   **(Re)Conceptualizing the Role and Actions of Higher
    Education Through Excellence Discourse: Perspectives
    of University Management and Academics** 131
    Emmanuel Intsiful and Kim Beasy

9   **The Challenge of Meeting Sustainable Development Goal 4
    in a Developing Country: The Case of Ugandan Secondary
    Education** 147
    Gilbert Arinaitwe and John Williamson

10 **Enacting the Sustainable Development Goals in Nepalese
    Schools and Teacher Education** 169
    Peter Brett, Ganga Gurung, Rabi Shah, Krishna Kumar Yogi,
    and Jiwan Dhungana

11 **Exploring the Challenges Schoolteachers Are Facing
    in Promoting Sustainable Development Goal 4: The Case
    of Pakistan** 185
    Humaira Akhter, Andy Bown, and Yang Yang

12 **The Construction of Gender Identities Through Pakistani
    Curriculum Textbooks** 203
    Nousheen Naz, Steve Drew, and Kim Beasy

13 **A Trinidad and Tobago Case Study of One Response
    to the Equity Challenge in Education Within the Digital Era** 223
    Seeta Jaikaran-Doe, Ian Hay, Andrew Fluck, and David Moltow

**Part III   SDG Implementation and Assessment in University
          Systems**

14 **Designing for a Better World: Learning Systemic Design
    for the Sustainable Development Goals** 245
    John Fien

15 **From Climate Literacy to Climate Policy: Interrogating
    a University's Role as a Climate Change Thought Leader** 259
    Gabi Mocatta and Rebecca Harris

16 **Universities as Exemplars of Climate Action** 279
    Gabi Mocatta and Rob White

17 **Shooting for the STARS: Implementation of the Sustainable
    Development Goals at a University Through a Whole
    of Organisation Approach** 295
    Corey Peterson, Catherine Elliott, Caroline Smith, and Jane Watson

Part IV   Enacting Sustainable Development Goals in University Practice

18 **The Role of Arts and Crafts in Promotion of Students' Awareness About Environment and Sustainable Development Goals: The Case of Tabriz Islamic Art University, Iran** 315
Morteza Mirgholami

19 **Where Health Professional Education and Sustainability Collide** 335
Nick Towle

20 **Sustainability in a Bachelor of Engineering with Honours Degree** 375
Anna Wrobel and Sarah Lyden

21 **Encountering Sustainable Development Goal SDG13, Climate Justice, and Emotions While Role-Playing an International Forum on Climate Change-Induced Migration** 391
Malcolm S. Johnson, Charlotte A. Jones, Andrew Harwood, Vishnu N. Prahalad, and Aidan Davison

22 **Reducing Inequity Through Teacher Education: Reflection on a Teacher Education Subject on Classroom Management** 411
Si Fan and Jeffrey Thomas

23 **Realising the Sustainable Development Goals to Enrich Teacher Education for Children, Young People, and Lifelong Learners with Disabilities** 427
Judith Hudson

Part V   Engagement in Schools

24 **Answering Children's Questions on Climate Change: Curious Climate Schools** 445
Rachel Kelly, Kim Beasy, Chloe Lucas, Gabi Mocatta, and Gretta T. Pecl

25 **Tasmanian Secondary Students' Experiences of Education for Sustainability** 459
Peter Brett and Ian Ayre

26 **Strategies for Encouraging Children to Be Physically Active to Improve Health for Life** 473
Vaughan Cruickshank and Brendon Hyndman

27 **The Importance of Health Literacy for Sustainable Development** 491
Vaughan Cruickshank, Claire Otten, Jack Evans, Melissa Jarvis, and Rosie Nash

28 Genre-Based Literacy and Collaboration: Promoting Social
    Justice and Quality Education 507
    Emily Morgan and Vinh To

29 Developing Academic Language in Young Children to Support
    Sustainability 525
    Natasha Williams, Greg Oates, Vinh To, and Bronwyn Reynolds

30 Using the Practice of Statistics to Enhance Education Through
    UN Sustainable Development Goal 13, Climate Change 539
    Caroline Smith and Jane Watson

Part VI Community Initiatives

31 Sustainable Wellbeing and Learning Communities
    for Achieving the Sustainable Development Goals 559
    Robin Krabbe, Merete Schmidt, and Caroline Smith

32 People, Pets and Art: A Model of Creative and Cultural
    Enterprise for Connecting Communities 579
    Niklavs Rubenis, Meg Keating, Steven Carson, and Andy Terhell

33 Participatory Capacity Building for Sustainable Development:
    Community Skills Cafes 601
    Sherridan Emery, Kim Beasy, and Di Nailon

34 New Hope/*Omid Now* (امید نو): Supporting Afghan
    Women to Access Higher Education by Reimagining
    the Sustainable Development Goals 619
    Barbara Kameniar, Gali Weiss, and Mursal Nazari

35 Platforms of Skills Ecosystems: A Lifelong Learning System
    Model in Which TVET Can Lead Local Communities
    to Achieve the Sustainable Development Goals 637
    Filippo Del Ninno and Giovanni Crisonà

Part VII Moving the Sustainable Development Goals Forward:
          Alternative Perspectives

36 The Sustainable Development Goals and STEM Education:
    Paradoxes and Reframings 655
    Mellita Jones and Caroline Smith

37 Towards the Sustainable Development Goals: Building
    Capacity for Action via a Participation Income 673
    Robin Krabbe

38   **For an Education that Contributes to Heal the World: The
     Role of Buddhist Education** 691
     Marie-Laure Mimoun-Sorel

39   **Ethical and Spiritual Values for Transformative Sustainable
     Development: The Earth Charter Vision** 709
     Richard M. Clugston and Peter Blaze Corcoran

40   **The Closing Challenge for a Flourishing and Sustainable
     Future** 733
     Kim Beasy, Caroline Smith, and Jane Watson

Index 737

Part I
Histories and Critical Perspectives

Chapter 1
Setting the Scene: The Sustainable Development Goals and the Importance of Education

Kim Beasy, Caroline Smith, and Jane Watson

1.1 Introduction

Humanity's footprint on our planet can no longer be ignored. We are in the Age of the Anthropocene, where human impact is the largest force determining the fate of life on Earth. Our species has succeeded in co-opting Earth's resources for our own needs and desires, to the detriment of the planetary systems that sustain us and the whole Earth community. Direct impacts include the interconnected crises of climate change, biodiversity loss, desertification, pollution and declining soil fertility. As well, unacceptable inequalities and power asymmetries exist across the different regions of our planet; the gap between rich and poor widens, and we are far from achieving gender equality (Zewde, 2021). Continuing in this way makes sustaining a flourishing life for all members of the Earth community increasingly difficult. Instead, we are on the way to creating a world where, in Thomas Berry's words, "our supposed progress toward an ever-improving human situation is bringing us to a waste world instead of a wonderworld" (Berry, 1988, p. 17).

We now recognise that our impact is global in reach. As well as the appalling impact on humans, climate and biodiversity, the massive 2019 bushfires in Australia influenced weather patterns and air quality across the Pacific in New Zealand, and cities in South America (United Nations Environment Programme [UNEP], 2020).

K. Beasy (✉)
School of Education, College of Arts, Law, and Education, Launceston, TAS, Australia
e-mail: Kim.Beasy@utas.edu.au

C. Smith
School of Education, College of Arts, Law, and Education, Burnie, TAS, Australia
e-mail: Caroline.Smith1@utas.edu.au

J. Watson
School of Education, College of Arts, Law, and Education, Hobart, TAS, Australia
e-mail: Jane.Watson@utas.edu.au

© The Author(s), under exclusive license to Springer Nature Singapore Pte Ltd. 2023   3
K. Beasy et al. (eds.), *Education and the UN Sustainable Development Goals*, Education for Sustainability 7,
https://doi.org/10.1007/978-981-99-3802-5_1

This, and numerous other ecological disasters, bring into sharp focus our interconnection as one planet, and the recognition that solutions to our dilemmas must be conceptualised and addressed at all levels from local to global.

While humanity's impact on our life support systems has been recognised in (some) circles for more than 50 years (e.g., Meadows et al., 1972), little has been attempted globally to address and mitigate the negative environmental and social impacts until relatively recently. It has only been in the last few decades that humans have meaningfully attempted to come together to conceptualise more sustainable ways forward. The United Nations Earth Summits were the first forums to bring together world leaders to deliberate on our collective futures; the first of these being held in Rio in 1992. The first attempt to develop a blueprint for global sustainability through international cooperation came in 2000, with the formulation of the United Nations Millennium Development Goals (MDGs). Leaders of 189 countries signed the historic Millennium Declaration in which they committed to achieving a set of eight measurable goals, ranging from halving extreme poverty and hunger to promoting gender equality, and reducing child mortality, by 2015. The United Nations Sustainable Development Goals (SDGs) (United Nations, 2022) build on the MDGs and expand their scope from eight to 17 goals. Unlike the MDGs which only targeted countries of the Global South ("developing countries"), the SDGs apply to all (United Nation, 2021). They are nationally owned and led, providing a framework for each country to establish its own agenda for their achievement.

Yet, sustainability continues as a term that has multiple meanings and interpretations. The most widely used definition is "development which meets the needs of the present without compromising the ability of future generations to meet their own needs," from the so-called Brundtland commission report, *Our Common Future* (United Nations Secretary General, 1987). The SDGs themselves refer to sustainability as: "a shared blueprint for peace and prosperity for people and the planet, now and into the future." More recent considerations view the term "sustainability" as implying retaining a steady state and consider that this will not go far enough in rebuilding the Earth community's life support systems. Our preferred concept is "flourishing" (or "thriving") to indicate a positive development from where we are now. Examples of flourishing would be an increase in biodiversity in an ecosystem, improved water quality in a river, agriculture that regenerates and protects healthy soil, and a child thriving on education and loving to learn.

Given the vast scope and reach of the SDGs, critiques are to be expected. Although there have been some gains, in the view of a number of commentators, seven years after their formulation, the SDGs have not yet met their potential, and may even be going backwards. In an address to the United Nations Economic and Social Council (ECOSOC), the United Nations Secretary-General, António Guterres (2022) remarked that "[i]n a world in crisis, rescuing the Sustainable Development Goals is more important than ever. And I mean what I said. When we see most of the SDGs moving backwards by the accumulation of crises we are facing, to rescue them must be our highest common priority."

One key issue, as a number of authors in this volume discuss, is that the SDGs are largely a reflection of the habits of centuries of Western economic models and political institutions, which have promoted a version of human flourishing synonymous with the growth of material wealth through sustained economic growth. This is even enshrined in the framework as a separate goal (SGD8) as "decent work and economic growth" (Bendell, 2022; Hickel, 2019). Showcasing models and examples of human and non-human flourishing within and beyond such framings and the enabling role of education is the work of this book.

Despite their many detractors, the SDGs remain one of the key formulations and guiding documents for sustainability policy and practice in decision-making forums around the world, from local to global contexts. We recognise and pay tribute to the enormous effort and time that has gone into their conceptualisation, and their significant contribution to planetary sustainability. Whatever their flaws, they provide a beacon of hope, without which we risk sinking into despair. At the same time, we believe that a deeper understanding and critique of the SDGs' genealogy, history, underpinning values and gaps, are particularly important for those engaged in education to be able to consider and apply the SDGs, and hope that this book will provide educators and others with a range of useful perspectives on the SDGs, that will inform their thinking and practice in rich and nuanced ways.

1.2 Education and the SDGs

The SDGs cover all aspects of life on Earth, so why does this book focus specifically on "Education"? Very simply, because education is one of the most significant vehicles through which messages about sustainability can be discussed, debated and promoted. The crucial role of education in achieving sustainable development was noted at the 1992 United Nations Earth Summit, and, as well as being critical to meeting all 17 goals, it has its own specific goal within the SDGs in SDG4: "Ensure inclusive and equitable quality education and promote lifelong learning opportunities for all."

However, the world still faces the dual challenges of meeting the unfulfilled promise to ensure the right to quality education for all, and of fully realising the transformational potential of education in pathways to flourishing futures (Zewde, 2021). One goal of this book is to provide background and insights that face education across the many aspects of sustainability, for readers who want to understand more deeply the vast challenges facing our planet. Readers are introduced to a number of initiatives within the broad field of education that are taking place at all levels that address and consider the various SDGs. These need to be appreciated and publicised in order for the education community and beyond, to be able to support pro-sustainability initiatives from local to global. These perspectives and initiatives are wide ranging in their scope and draw on a range of SDGs in their discussion of how education can be mobilised to address and achieve the goals.

Education is the focus of this volume because it has been at the heart of human pursuits and interactions for millennia. The act of education is broadly conceived as the affordance of an experience of mind that in some way, changes one's thoughts from the way they once were. In this book, we recognise the vast array of institutional and non-institutional ways in which education "happens" and do not pretend to set one against the other; rather, we embrace the possibilities that all forms of education delivery offer in pursuing flourishing futures. With this in mind, readers will find in this volume examples of educational practice across the spectrum of education sectors, including tertiary, secondary and primary, as well as that which exists more informally in community. The authors themselves come from a diversity of backgrounds and disciplines, and exhibit a range of writing styles.

In the first instance, our considerations begin at the tertiary level with the universities, both within the educational offerings provided, and the physical organisations themselves as they endeavour to be models of sustainable practice. In particular, we acknowledge the key role of universities in providing education of teachers who become knowledge custodians for children from early childhood to upper secondary education within schools.

1.3 Structure of the Book

This book is divided into seven parts. The first part offers an overview of the history and genealogy of the SDGs, alongside the moral, ethical and political tensions that provide the context in which the SDGs are bound. An overview of how the SDGs evolved in relation to other international agreements is discussed in Chapter 2 by Colin Power, while in Chapter 3, Lyn Carter and Caroline Smith consider how liberalism and neoliberalism are permeated through the genealogy of the goals. In Chapter 4, David Moltow and Cassandra Thoars share their views on the moral obligation that we *all* have to ensure children receive sustainable education. Jennifer Evans then challenges us to consider the colonial framing of the goals, and presents her Aboriginal perspective from *lutruwita* (Tasmania) through theorising the notion of "Establishment Man." In Chapter 6, Jennifer Evans goes on to explore in depth the silences that exist in the Sustainable Development Goals with particular reference to Indigenous cultures. This part concludes with a reminder from Phillipa McCormack and Michelle Lan about how the SDGs are featured in an international legal framework, and draw on law education to make recommendations on what is needed in the future.

The authors in the second part remind us that implementation of the SDGs in education cannot be through a "one-size-fits-all" approach. Each of the chapters presents challenges and targeted actions required from different social and geographical contexts. Emmanuel Intsiful and Kim Beasy in Chapter 8 consider the influence of international discourses within the Ghanaian university system, and its impact on implementing actions for the SDGs. In Chapter 9, Gilbert Arinaitwe and John Williamson explore the impact of rurality and economic disparity on quality education in Uganda. Next, Peter Brett and colleagues show how the lack of financial resourcing (among other aspects), influence the ability of education systems to deliver quality (and sustainable) education in Nepal. In Chapter 11, Humaira Akhter and colleagues show the impact that language barriers have on implementing SDG4 in Pakistan's education system. Nousheen Naz and colleagues provide a compelling analysis of Pakistan's school textbooks, exploring their representations of gender, and conclude that they reproduce gender stereotypes to the detriment of girls and women. This part closes with Chapter 13 from Trinidad and Tobago by Seeta Jaikaran-Doe and colleagues, which reflects on the way access to technology can improve participation in learning and quality of teaching.

In Part III, we turn our attention to the higher education sector and explore how university systems are implementing and assessing progress on SDGs. In Chapter 14, John Fien shares an example of how the SDGs can be used as a vehicle for drawing on the expertise of students to solve complex problems. Gabi Mocatta and Rob White consider the various ways universities can and should take up actions for sustainable development, and argue that institutions need to engage in sustainable institutional practice. Gabi Mocatta and Rebecca Harris in Chapter 16 advocate for universities as climate change thought leaders, and explore one university's attempts to achieve this. In Chapter 17, Corey Peterson and colleagues consider how universities can be held accountable for their commitments and learn of one university's attempts to implement a universal whole-of-organisation framework (STARS) to measure and document progress towards the SDGs.

In Part IV, we look more closely at university educational practice from a range of geographical and disciplinary contexts, to discover creative and innovative means of embedding SDGs in higher education. Morteza Mirgholami shares the story of an arts university in Tabriz, Iran, and reflects on its contributions to creating impact towards SDGs 7, 11 and 13. In Chapter 19, Nick Towle argues the case for a shift in the education of health professional educators and for the health disciplines to take up the broader challenges of planetary health. Two examples of teaching in practice follow: In Chapter 20, Anna Wrobel-Tobiszewska and Sarah Lyden explore how the SDGs can be embedded throughout an engineering degree, and, in Chapter 21, Malcolm Johnson and colleagues provide an example of how SDG13 was introduced into the geography curricula of their institution, using role-play to explore the complex issues of human migration in the era of the climate crisis.

Also in this part, we acknowledge the important role that universities play in our society, specifically in relation to preparing teachers to nurture and educate future generations of young people. We include two chapters that explore pre-service teacher education. In Chapter 22, Frances Fan and Jeff Thomas consider how, through pre-service teacher education, classroom teachers can be prepared to create positive classroom environments, and the role that this has in achieving SDG4 (United Nations, n.d.). We conclude this part with a chapter from Judith Hudson, who argues that people with disability have less opportunity to achieve the SDGs, and as a response, reflects on the elements of pre-service teacher education that need to change to ensure children with disabilities in schools are afforded positive life opportunities.

In Part V, we turn our gaze towards schools themselves. We start this part with Chapter 24 from Rachel Kelly and colleagues, who review literature on the Australian schooling system before referring to SDG13 through describing their programme that connects children in schools with climate change experts in the community.

In Chapter 25, Peter Brett and Ian Ayre remind us of the critical importance of Education for Sustainability (EfS) and the SDGs, but that they remain somewhat neglected in schools. They share the voices of young people and their lived experiences of learning and engaging with EfS in school. Next, Vaughan Cruikshank and Brendon Hyndman advocate the importance of safe, healthy and well-educated children, and consider the role of health education in schools in support of SDG3 and SDG5. In Chapter 27, Vaughan Cruikshank and colleagues explore international health literacy programmes, and the ways in which schools can implement actions in support of SDG3 and SDG10. Next, Emily Morgan and Vinh To showcase the ways that genre-based models of learning can support SDG10 in an English as a Foreign Language context. In Chapter 29, Natasha Williams and colleagues argue that limited vocabulary is a barrier to learning about and for sustainability, specifically in science, technology, engineering and mathematics (STEM) education, and share a practice example from the classroom. This is followed in Chapter 30 by Caroline Smith and Jane Watson who introduce the importance of the Practice of Statistics in education using the example of SDG13, and showcase examples of what this might look like in the classroom.

In Part VI, we step out into the broader community, and explore programmes and projects that seek to embed the SDGs in their educational work. Robin Krabbe and colleagues describe the importance of collaborative informal learning within community to achieve the participatory discussions essential for considering the SDGs, and report on a case study of a Community of Practice that exemplifies the attributes of community-based learning. In Chapter 32, Niklavs Rubenis and colleagues also invoke the notion of a Community of Practice as they reflect on a community-based project that advances SDG4 by using people's pets as the context in arts-based methods to bring the community together. Sherridan Emery and colleagues share their experiences of working to deliver sustainability skills cafés in one community to achieve SDGs, and explain how they used a theory of change to conceptualise and advance the project. In Chapter 34, Barbara Kameniar and colleagues provide insights into the dire gender inequity situation in Afghanistan, and describe a programme in support of enabling Afghan women's access to higher education. The final chapter in this part, from Filippo Del Ninno and Giovanni Crisonà, considers a Technical and Vocational Education and Training (TVET) model from the European context, which advances local SDG initiatives through advanced manufacturing with implications for the whole of the education system.

In the final part, we consider alternative perspectives to advance the SDGs and development in education more broadly. In Chapter 36, Mellita Jones and Caroline Smith build on discussions from Part I to argue that the SDGs and formal education, including STEM education, are problematically underpinned by neoliberalism. They advocate for an eco-social justice perspective as the principle needed to guide STEM education for sustainability. In Chapter 37, Robin Krabbe discusses why is it so difficult for humans to reduce our footprint and take care of the world, and offers participation income as an alternative economic initiative that would enable a more prosocial, meaningful and purposeful existence to support achieving the SDGs. Marie-Laure Mimoun-Sorel argues that humanity needs to let go of consumerism, in order to obtain happiness and sustainability, and reports on a school that draws on the wisdom of Buddhism as a means of achieving this. Finally, in Chapter 39, Richard Clugston and Peter Blaze Corcoran invite us to participate in a conversation aimed at deepening the understanding of the spiritual or "inner"dimensions of sustainability that a number of authors, in particular, Jennifer Evans, Marie-Laure Mimoun-Sorel and Robin Krabbe, have alluded to. The authors consider that this is a missing dimension of the SDGs, and compare it with the Earth Charter which, they argue, includes these dimensions. We close the book with a short conclusion that draws together the themes of the book, and share the Editors' perspectives on the ways forward for the advancement of the SDGs in and through education.

The authors of this book hope that their writings will raise questions, suggest ways forward and resonate with readers. They hope they will motivate and challenge them to reflect and consider the actions they can take in their own communities and beyond, to engage with the vast scope and opportunities for education offered by the 17 SDGs.

References

Bendell, J. (2022). Replacing sustainable development: Potential frameworks for international cooperation in an era of increasing crises and disasters. *Sustainability, 14*(13), 8185. https://doi.org/10.3390/su14138185

Berry, T. (1988). *The dream of the earth.* Sierra Club.

Hickel, J. (2019). The contradiction of the sustainable development goals: Growth versus ecology on a finite planet. *Sustainable Development, 27*(5), 873–884. https://doi.org/10.1002/sd.1947

Meadows, D. H., Meadows, D. L., Randers, L., &. Behrens, W. W. (1972). *The limits to growth: A report for the Club of Rome's project on the predicament of mankind.* Universe Books.

United Nations. (n.d.). Department of Economic and Social Affairs. *Sustainable Development Goal 4: Ensure inclusive and equitable quality education and promote lifelong learning opportunities for all.* https://sdgs.un.org/goals/goal4

United Nations. (1992, June 3–14). *Conference on environment and development.* Rio de Janeiro, Brazil. https://www.un.org/en/conferences/environment/rio1992

United Nations. (2015). *Millennium development goals.* https://www.un.org/millenniumgoals/?

United Nations. (2021). *Our common agenda—Report of the Secretary-General.* https://www.un.org/en/common-agenda

United Nations. (2022). *Sustainable development goals.* https://sdgs.un.org/goals

United Nations Economic and Social Council. (2022). *Secretary-General's remarks to ECOSOC segment on operational activities for development [as delivered].* https://www.un.org/sg/en/content/sg/statement/2022-05-17/secretary-generals-remarks-ecosoc-segment-operational-activities-for-development%C2%A0-delivered%C2%A0

United Nations Environment Programme. (2020). *Ten impacts of the Australian bushfires.* https://www.unep.org/news-and-stories/story/ten-impacts-australian-bushfires

United Nations Secretary-General. (1987). *Report of the world commission on environment and development: Our common future* [Brundtland report]. https://sustainabledevelopment.un.org/content/documents/5987our-common-future.pdf

Zewde, S.-W. (2021). *Reimaging our futures together: A new social contract for education.* Foreword. Report from the International Commission on the Futures of Education, United Nations Educational, Scientific and Cultural Organization. https://unesdoc.unesco.org/ark:/48223/pf0000379707.locale=en

Chapter 2
Sustainable Development Goals and UNESCO World Heritage Sites in Australia and the Pacific: The Role of Education

Colin Power

2.1 Introduction

Concerns about the impact of human activities on the environment and cultural heritage led to the establishment of the United Nations Environment Programme (UNEP), the Joint UNESCO-UNEP International Environmental Education Programme, and the World Heritage Convention in the early 1970s. Subsequently, the Report of the World Commission on Environment and Development (Brundtland, 1987) argued that to assure "our common future" development must be sustainable not only from the ecological, but also from social, economic, and cultural points of view. In 2015, UN Member States agreed on 17 Sustainable Development Goals (SDGs) to be met by 2030. The SDGs cover global challenges, such as poverty, inequality, assuring good health and wellbeing, inclusive quality education, climate change, global citizenship, and the environment.

The UN Framework Convention on Climate Change and the Intergovernmental Panel on Climate Change (IPCC) provide the legal and scientific framework for climate action. At Conferences of Parties (COP) to the climate change agreement, governments set national targets and make commitments to meet them. IPCC Reports (IPCC, 2013, 2019) draw on the expertise and work of over 11,000 scientists from 153 nations. The latest Reports warn that the planet faces a climate crisis threatening the survival of all species unless urgent and decisive action is taken. The 2015 Paris Agreement on climate change sets legally binding emission reduction targets. According to the International Energy Agency (IEA), the major sources of

C. Power (✉)
School of Education, University of Queensland, St Lucia, QLD 4072, Australia
e-mail: c.power1939@gmail.com

© The Author(s), under exclusive license to Springer Nature Singapore Pte Ltd. 2023   11
K. Beasy et al. (eds.), *Education and the UN Sustainable Development Goals*, Education for Sustainability 7,
https://doi.org/10.1007/978-981-99-3802-5_2

emissions are electricity and heat (31%), transport (15%), agriculture (11%), manufacturing (12%), and forestry (6%); energy production and consumption across all sources account for 72% of greenhouse emissions (IEA, 2020).

At the most recent Conference of the Parties (COP) to the climate change agreement (COP26 in Glasgow), governments reported on what they had done and how they plan to achieve their targets. Although carbon dioxide levels continue to rise, modest progress is being made towards cutting greenhouse gas emissions as nations reduce their dependence on fossil fuels and invest in renewable energy. Nonetheless, the scientific community insists that few, if any, nations are moving fast enough. If they are right, the planet faces a ghastly future, much of the Earth being rendered uninhabitable (Wallace-Wells, 2019). Sadly, the damage to the environment stemming from unsustainable human activities is compounded by the claims being made by climate science deniers, and by the spin and disinformation stemming from the fossil fuel industry, media and mining corporations, and politicians (Bowen, 2008). The reality is that ignorance, indifference, and the "ruthless pursuit of wealth and political interests are still stymieing the action that is crucial for survival" (Bradshaw et al., 2021, p. 5).

The scientific evidence is clear: the planet is warming, greenhouse gas emission and pollution levels are rising, the climate is changing, and humans are responsible for much of the damage being done to the planet. Governments, industry, the media, schools, universities, communities, and families will be forced to make significant changes, difficult as they may be, or suffer the consequences. Although there may be uncertainties about the cost-effectiveness of proposed courses of action, governments must act quickly and decisively based on the best expert advice, putting in place economic, environmental, health, cultural, and education policies, then funding priorities, and implementing programmes consistent with the scientific evidence. Now that US President Biden has re-signed the Paris Agreement and the agenda has been set at COP26 on the action to be taken to tackle climate change, the pressure is on the governments of countries like Australia to do more to meet their moral and international legal responsibilities as set out in the SDGs and allied international agreements.

2.2 UNESCO Environmental and World Heritage Programmes

Within the UN system, UNESCO plays a key role in supporting education, science, and cultural programmes focusing on the SDGs. For example, the Culture Sector houses the World Heritage Centre (SDG 11.4), and the Science Sector focuses on SDGs 13 to 15 and is responsible for the Intergovernmental Oceanographic Commission (IOC) and Man and the Biosphere (MAB) (www.unesco.org). The Education Sector works on the education SDGs and Targets, especially SDG 4 (Inclusive and

Quality Education for All), that is, assuring that "all learners acquire the knowledge and skills needed to promote sustainable development by 2030" (UNESCO, 2021).

The period 2005–2014 was designated as the UN Decade for Education for Sustainable Development (ESD) with UNESCO as the lead agency. The data from all countries on Education SDGs are collected by the UNESCO Institute of Statistics, and progress reports can be found in UNESCO publications (e.g., Global Education Monitoring (GEM) Reports, 2020, 2021; UNESCO, 2021). UNESCO continues to work with the United Nations Development Programme (UNDP), Member States and non-government organisations to embed the principles of sustainable development in policies, programmes, and daily life of schools, higher education, non-formal education, and community-based initiatives. UNESCO also works in co-operation with the World Health Organization (WHO) on health education for all, school and community health education programmes playing a key role in prevention, be it malaria or Covid-19 crises.

The World Heritage Convention is an international normative instrument adopted by the governments of the Member States of UNESCO. UNESCO's World Heritage Committee and the World Heritage Centre (WHC) are responsible for policy, management, assessment, information, and dissemination at the international level. National governments are responsible for the identification, protection, and conservation of natural and cultural heritage sites listed according to their outstanding value to humanity. States Party to the Convention are also required to develop

> educational and information programmes to strengthen appreciation and respect by their peoples of the cultural and natural heritage...keep the public informed of dangers threatening this heritage...contribute to and comply with the sustainable development objectives...in their heritage conservation and management system. (UNESCO-WHC, 2019, p. 12)

The most serious threats to WHC sites are those on which the SDGs and the Climate Change Agreements are focused.

Developing and implementing education programmes that help assure the sustainability of life on the planet and that help protect, conserve, and transmit World Heritage have long been a significant part of the work of UNESCO. In implementing the UN Decade for Education for Sustainable Development (ESD), UNESCO has encouraged governments to embed the principles of ESD in their national education policies, curricula, and teaching programmes. A notable example of publications on ESD is UNESCO's multi-media teacher education programme *Teaching and Learning for a Sustainable Future* (UNESCO, 2010). The programmes include 27 modules covering sustainable development across the curriculum, contemporary issues, and teaching–learning strategies. At the higher education level, the UNITWIN-UNESCO Chairs programme (UNESCO, 2020) aims to strengthen teaching and research through knowledge sharing and joint ventures. Within this programme, 131 UNESCO Chairs play a key role in the UNESCO Global Programme on ESD.

Over the years, many education authorities and teachers have asked UNESCO to provide resources for schools on World Heritage sites. The Associated Schools Project (ASP) team in the Education Sector of UNESCO joined forces with the

WHC to prepare a multi-media kit for teachers. Entitled *World Heritage in Young Hands* (UNESCO, 2002), the kit has been published in 37 languages, and several countries have produced supplementary materials on their heritage sites. For example, *Our Pacific Heritage* (New Zealand National Commission for UNESCO, 2004) has chapters and resource materials on WHC sites in New Zealand, Fiji, Samoa, Solomon Islands, and Australia.

World Heritage in Young Hands is an excellent example of what is meant by "good practice" and "international co-operation." The Kit consists of five thematic chapters: The World Heritage Convention, Identity, Tourism, The Environment, and a Culture of Peace. It suggests both classroom and extra-curricular activities and provides a rich array of materials and compact discs on the world's major cultural and natural heritage sites for use in schools. Students learn, for instance, how distinctive building styles and materials express cultural identity; for example, how the Great Zimbabwe National Monument became a symbol of Zimbabwe, and how wood has influenced Norwegian culture. World Heritage education then helps build identity, mutual respect, and solidarity, and strengthens action in favour of preserving and protecting the world's natural and cultural heritage (UNESCO, 2002, pp. 88–89).

The story of the Associated Schools Project (ASP) and *World Heritage in Young Hands* is consistent with research (Power, 2015) confirming the value of the co-operative learning taking place in the arts, science, environmental, and cultural projects grounded in the community of which the school is a part. Such programmes have been found to help promote good quality, inclusive education, and the development of life skills. Moreover, they help indigenous and "at risk" students to discover who they are and to tackle problems of marginalisation and exclusion, while promoting mutual respect and understanding (Power, 2015, pp. 112–116).

The ASP was one of the first measures taken by UNESCO to transform its global educational, scientific, and cultural goals into reality in the day-to-day work of schools. Educational institutions that are part of the ASP network are expected to be innovative and to engage collaboratively in efforts to provide inclusive and equitable quality education for all (SDG4), one that ensures learners acquire the knowledge and skills needed to promote sustainable development (SDG4.7), including human rights, global citizenship, and climate action (UNESCO-ASP, 2016). Over 11,500 schools and colleges in 180 countries are members of ASP network. Network members join forces to prepare and distribute teaching–learning materials, and to organise international and regional workshops and youth festivals. At the national level, developing and supporting the ASP network is the responsibility of the National Commissions of UNESCO in co-operation with education authorities. Whereas the National Commission in New Zealand plays a significant role in nominating and supporting ASP schools in New Zealand, in Australia that responsibility has now been abandoned. Schools in Australia and many parts of the Pacific cannot be part of the ASP network, and thus they are being denied the opportunities that the ASP network provides to support ESD and World Heritage education and to forge links with ASP schools in other countries.

Involvement in UNESCO programmes like the ASP network is important for schools and students. For example, UNESCO organised a Global Children's Summit in 2000 at Disney World Florida. It brought together 2000 students from ASP schools in 90 countries (including New Zealand and Australia): young people who were "Millennium Dreamers." Empowered and supported by their schools, they made a difference. Many of their projects focused on the protection and conservation of natural and cultural heritage. An example was Jesus Mahoreo, a 15-year-old from Brazil. Jesus, a member of the ancient and nearly extinct Xavantes tribe, came from deep in the heart of Brazil's rainforest. Concerned that his 500-year-old culture was slipping away, he created a CD-ROM that recorded aspects of his tribe's history, culture, and unique language. The CD-ROM has been used widely by schools throughout Brazil. Jesus continues his fight to preserve his heritage, to promote respect for indigenous cultures, and to halt the ruthless clearing of what is left of the Amazonian forests (Power, 2015, pp. 121–122).

The ASP Youth Forum on World Heritage Cities in Bergen (Norway) was attended by over 100 students and their teachers from Associated Schools in 25 countries. The Forum was designed to coincide with the World Heritage meeting of the mayors of World Heritage-listed cities. Students attending the Forum developed multi-media kits for schools on the rich cultural heritage of the city from which they had come. Their kits were based on their cities' histories and rich cultural heritage. The ASP students insisted that the voice of youth be represented on the World Heritage Task Forces set up by the mayors of their cities, and young people now play an active role in protecting their heritage cities. Two years after the Youth Forum, the UNESCO Latin American and Caribbean Ministers' Conference was held in Kingston, Jamaica. Near Kingston are the ruins of Port au Prince, the Heritage-listed ancient pirate town. The students from Jamaica who attended the Bergen Forum told UNESCO: "We came from a tough part of Kingston, and spraying graffiti on public buildings was part of our life. In developing our kit, we learned who we were and are now very proud of our city and its heritage. So now, no one dares to deface it" (Power, 2015, pp. 118–119). These young people were in danger of becoming part of the violent underclass of Kingston, but now they have a passion and a purpose in life. Rather than dropping out of education, they went on to develop the expertise needed to protect and preserve their roots and what they have now become: responsible young people dedicated to serving the communities in which they live.

Protecting the environment, sustainability, and intercultural understanding are key goals in ESD and World Heritage education, quality education for all that is inclusive and empowering for all in the sense set out in *The Power of Education* (Power, 2015). It is what good teachers, early childhood centres, schools, colleges, and universities have always done as they build the pillars of learning throughout life. As reviews of the research on ESD indicate, well-designed environmental education programmes develop a sense of global outlook and civic responsibility: they build the knowledge base, skills, and values needed to make informed decisions about what needs to be done (O'Flaherty & Liddy, 2017; Power & Hogan, 1986). But to what extent are countries like Australia moving to address the challenges posed by climate change and to protect the environment? Is the education being provided empowering? Does it help both individuals and communities to make the informed decisions and to assume the responsibilities needed to address the challenges facing them?

2.3 Protecting the Australian Environment

Australia is the driest continent and is particularly vulnerable to climate change. A major report issued by the Australian Academy of Science (2021) lays out the potential damage to Australia and the Pacific posed by global warming and climate change. The Report, authored and reviewed by 21 experts, concludes that the damage is already evident: Australia's surface temperature has warmed by 1.4 °C and its open ocean by 1 °C. Extreme weather events are becoming more frequent and severe. Australia has just had the hottest years on record, a Great Barrier Reef is in serious trouble, unprecedented extreme weather events, prolonged droughts, and record floods and cyclones are now common. Between September 2019 and March 2020, horrific bushfires burned out over 18.6 million hectares of land, killing or severely injuring three billion native animals, destroying the habitats of many of Australia's most endangered species, and damaging indigenous cultural sites. The Report reveals why the outlook for the Great Barrier, for koalas, and for other endangered species is "very poor." It also points to the multiple and rising human, environmental, and economic costs of climate change and human activity, the need to take seriously the scientific evidence, and to scale up and to meet Australia's emission and SDG targets.

The Australian Environment Protection and Biodiversity Protection Act (EPBC Act) serves as the legal framework for protection of the Australian environment, including national and World Heritage sites. The Department of Agriculture, Water, and Environment (DAWE) in collaboration with State and Territory Environment authorities, is responsible for its implementation. The 2020 statutory independent review of the Act concluded that the laws created to protect unique species and habitats are "ineffective," their administration has been "poorly handled," and conflicts of interest are "not well-managed" (Samuel, 2020, p. 5). The review expresses concern about impact of climate change on ecosystems, land clearing, coal and coal-seam gas industry, grazing and invasive species, insufficient resources for environmental research and protection, and a lack of national co-ordination. It includes 38 recommendations, proposing a framework of legislated national environment standards with legally enforceable rules, and the establishment of an independent body to monitor compliance with environmental laws. Thus far, it seems that the Federal and State governments are reluctant to make all the legislative and administrative changes that the review has concluded are crucial to the protection of Australia's environment and biodiversity.

Faced with the health crisis created by the Covid-19 pandemic, Australian Federal and State governments have, for the most part, introduced the measures recommended by medical experts. As a result, Australian infection, hospitalisation, and death rates have been relatively low. The same cannot be said when it comes to the environment and heritage sites. Over the past five years, Australia has moved further and further away from the international consensus in its position on climate change (IPCC, 2022). At COP26, Australia was accused of setting very low emission reduction targets and downplaying the impact of climate change, warming oceans, land clearing, pollution, and mining as key factors behind the increasing intensity and frequency of environmental disasters. Australia has been slower than other OECD countries to take the hard steps needed to dramatically reduce greenhouse emissions. The Australian government has been reluctant to set more stringent standards for fuel and energy efficiency, to cut back on fossil fuel subsidies, to introduce a carbon or an air pollution tax, or to increase funding and incentives for research, development, and utilisation of renewable energy technologies.

In Paris, Australia set a 2030 target of just 28% reduction in emissions compared with 2005, but UN projections indicate that the actual reduction will be of the order of 16%. Reports (UNDP, 2019) on progress towards the SDGs show that although Australia performs well on most goals, it has one of the highest rates of carbon emissions per person. Australia rates poorly on clean energy and climate change, and has very high levels of solid waste, land clearing and loss of biodiversity. Studies undertaken at the Global Change Institute at the University of Queensland (Bell-James, 2020) have focused on whether the EPBC Act is achieving its objective of safeguarding Australia's biodiversity. Since the Act came into force in 2000, over 8 million hectares of potential habitat have been cleared, 93% of which was not referred to the Federal government for assessment, and 1390 threatened species suffered habitat loss.

In many countries, inconvenient truths are hidden or ignored by governments and industry. Australia is no exception. Roughly half of the university, industry, and government scientists working on the environmental impact of logging, mining, or climate change surveyed by the Ecological Society of Australia (Driscoll et al., 2021) reported that their findings were being suppressed or unduly modified, and their advice ignored by decision makers, especially when it comes to the plight of endangered species.

2.4 World Heritage in Australia

Australia has 20 World Heritage sites: four cultural (e.g., Sydney Opera House, Australian Convict sites), 12 natural sites (e.g., the Great Barrier Reef, Blue Mountains, Queensland wet tropics), and four both natural and cultural sites (e.g., Kakado, Uluru, Budj Bin Cultural Landscape). Information on over 20,000 natural, historic, and indigenous places in Australia, and lists of threatened species drawn up under the Act are available online on the website of the Australian DAWE (2021).

UNESCO-WHC has been critical of Australia's lack of planning and action on climate change, and the level of protection provided for threatened natural and cultural sites such as the Great Barrier Reef, Kakado, the Tasmanian wilderness, Gondwana rainforest, the Greater Blue Mountains, and the wet tropics. In addition, inadequacies in the protection of the basic rights of Australia's indigenous peoples and their cultural heritage sites have left a shameful stain on the nation. Recent examples include the threats to the Nigaloo Coast posed by oil and gas industrialization, and, most dramatically, when Rio Tinto blew up one of the oldest and most significant indigenous sites in the world, the 46,000-year-old heritage site in the Juukan Gorge. It did so to expand its very profitable iron ore development, contravening international norms as set out in the 2007 UN Declaration on the Rights of Indigenous Peoples and the World Heritage Convention. One can only hope that the Australian government implements in full, the recommendations of the 2020 Samuel Review.

In 2013, Australian non-governmental organisations, such as the Australian Conservation Foundation, Earth Charter Australia and the Wilderness Society, wrote to the Director-General of UNESCO warning that the Australian WHC sites are in more danger than ever before. They have urged UNESCO-WHC to oppose government plans to devolve the project approval process to the states and territories and have asked UNESCO to seek clarification from the government on how it will meet its international obligations under the World Heritage Convention. These obligations include the "strengthening of efforts to protect and safeguard the world's cultural and natural heritage" (SDG 11.4), ensuring that "all learners acquire the knowledge and skills necessary to promote sustainable development" (SDG 4.7), and that "people everywhere have the relevant information and awareness for sustainable development…including the mainstreaming of global citizenship education, education for sustainable development and climate change education in national education policies, curricula, teacher education and student assessment" (SDG 12.8.1).

2.5   World Heritage Education and ESD in Australia

In Australia, the provision of education at the pre-tertiary level is the responsibility of the States and Territories. Their policies and programmes are developed within national education frameworks generated in co-operation with the Federal government. The Australian Curriculum Assessment and Reporting Authority (2021) is responsible for setting the national curriculum framework for primary and secondary education. Topics like cultural heritage and climate change are embedded into the organising ideas of each of the three "cross-curriculum" priorities: Aboriginal and Torres Strait Islanders' histories and cultures, Asia and Australia's engagement with Asia, and Sustainability. In practice, this means that ESD and heritage education should form an essential component of the curriculum and teaching in schools in traditional subject areas like science, geography, history, and the arts, and as interdisciplinary projects and courses. However, Australia's National Assessment Programme (NAPLAN) and government funding policies ensure that the priority in schools is given to the areas tested, to English, Mathematics, and Science as the keys to economic development, sidelining other areas including ESD and the protection of Australia's environment and cultural heritage (Smith & Watson, 2019).

Studies undertaken by Fien et al. (2002) and Tilbury et al. (2005) concluded that the environmental education being provided by schools in Australia is inadequate in both quantity and quality, and that ESD is not being implemented according to international, national, or state guidelines in many schools. Year 10 students performed poorly on test questions relating to ecology, the precautionary principle, and sustainable development. The most important sources of the information about the environment come from outside the classroom, a tidal wave of claims and counter claims, hype and spin, stories and myths, facts and fiction. Young people want to enjoy the fruits of economic development but also worry as the planet warms, oceans acidify, coral reefs die, waterways are polluted, droughts, fires and cyclones become more frequent, and endangered species are wiped out.

ESD and World Heritage Education have struggled to find a place not only in an overcrowded curriculum but also in national and state education policy, assessment systems, and in schools and classrooms. A review commissioned by the Australian government concluded that education for sustainable development "struggles for acceptance in the mainstream curriculum in Australia" (Australian Research Institute in Education for Sustainability, 2006). Student protests over logging in Tasmanian forests, the bleaching of the Great Barrier Reef, denial of the rights of Aboriginal and Torres Straight Islanders, and the Adani coal mine are classic examples of issues that governments and education authorities seek to avoid—but they cannot. In 2019, over 7.8 million students from 40 countries, including Australia, marched in protest over the shortcomings in the action taken by governments to tackle climate change (Australian Association for Environmental Education, 2022; Wikipedia, 2020). Whereas governments and corporations try to hide "inconvenient truths," young people and the public need and want to know what is really happening, and how best to assure their future. As Peter Doherty (2015) insists, education and training programmes should help them to take a balanced, evidence-based view of the world, and to distinguish between genuine arguments based on sound information on the one hand, and propaganda and spin on the other.

Slowly but surely the reality of climate change and the threats to health, the environment, and natural and cultural heritage are having an impact. For example, most Australian schools are now engaged in a variety of waste management programmes, focusing mainly on recycling (Cutter-Mackenzie-Knowles & Siegel, 2019). Throughout Australia, Environmental Education and Outdoor Centres, cultural centres, zoos, museums, and the Australian Broadcasting Commission (ABC) continue to provide programmes and materials for schools and the community on the protection of natural and cultural sites, indigenous cultures, and intercultural understanding. The Sustainable Schools Network Australia (2021) seeks to encourage the greening of schools, with school planning, design, facilities, management, and teaching programmes consistent with ecologically sustainable principles. Examples include the Greener Government School Buildings Program and the Sustainable Facility: Policy in Victoria and the Queensland Environmentally Sustainable Schools initiative.

Technical colleges and non-formal community-based programmes for youth and adults also play an important role in tailoring their programmes to accommodate the skills and practices needed to protect vulnerable heritage buildings, habitats, and cultural sites. Australian Technical Colleges that are part of the global UNESCO International Project on Technical and Vocational Education network are sharing experience and teaching materials focussing on SDG Targets 4.3, 4.4, and 13.3, that is, on sustainable technical, work, and lifelong learning skills, climate change mitigation, and early warning systems (Maclean et al., 2013; Power, 2015).

Universities play a vital role in undertaking the research needed to provide the information needed by international organisations and governments to develop policy and implement programmes to assure sustainability. International reviews and assessments of the Greening of Universities reveal that both New Zealand and Australian universities are performing well on measures of SDG performance like the Times Impact Ratings and the Green Report Card (Lee & Power, 2021). However, government support for independent university research has been falling, the cuts in grants for Centres and projects focusing on environmental issues being far deeper than most. Increasingly, Australian environmental and climate scientists report that the results of their work are being ignored, distorted, and/or censored by policy makers and climate science deniers in government, industry, and the media (Driscoll et al., 2021). Estimates of the reductions in funding for environmental teaching and research are of the order of 30% (Gleeson, 2020).

As the section that follows indicates, all countries in the Pacific region need to give greater priority to ESD and World Heritage Education at all levels of their education system as they seek to address the environmental and cultural challenges facing them.

2.6   World Heritage and ESD in New Zealand and the Pacific

The Pacific region has an enormous wealth of cultural and marine biodiversity in an ocean that covers one-third of the Earth's surface. Oceans are home to most species living on the planet, and a prerequisite to the possibility of life on Earth. However, the Pacific Ocean, Pacific Island Countries (PICs) and their inhabitants are endangered by climate change, rising sea levels, the exploitation of resources, and pollution. In the absence of decisive collective action, more parts of the Pacific will become uninhabitable. Therefore, UNESCO has called for the inclusion of ocean education in school curricula (UNESCO, 2022).

The Pacific Island Forum plays a key role in facilitating intergovernmental co-operation in facing the environmental, cultural, and economic challenges facing its 18 Member States. The UNESCO Regional Office in Bangkok and its Pacific sub-regional office in Apia work with Pacific Island governments, UNESCO National Commissions, and non-government organisations to build capacity and implement ESD programmes. An Action Plan for 2016–2020 was developed to strengthen efforts to protect and safeguard the region's cultural and natural heritage, and a regional facility has been established at the University of the South Pacific to build the capacity of Pacific peoples to safeguard their heritage (UNESCO, 2021).

Twelve PICs have ratified the World Heritage Convention, and there are 37 World Heritage sites, of which 20 are in Australia and three are in New Zealand. However, global forces pose a threat, not only to the environment, but also to the very fabric of the indigenous cultures of the Pacific, their languages, norms, and values. At the heart of the social and educational problems facing young people in the Pacific is the loss of cultural identity.

It is difficult to provide a clear overall picture of ESD and World Heritage education in the Pacific, given the gaps in data and research. For the most part, it seems that most young people in the Pacific are not being empowered with the environmental and cultural knowledge, skills, and confidence they need to tackle the challenges facing them and the communities in which they live (Fien et al., 2002; UNESCO, 2021).

A new UNESCO Monitoring and Evaluating Climate Communication and Education Project is being undertaken by the UNESCO Institute of Statistics (UNESCO-UIS) and the Global Education Monitoring Report (2021). The project is generating a new evidence base of national profiles on ESD, climate change education, and communication policy and practice. The aim is to provide a comparative perspective towards the realisation of the sustainable development and climate change goals. The first 20 national ESD profiles were launched on the GEM Report's website in time for COP26. They included two from Oceania: New Zealand and Tuvalu. Thus far, although the mapping suggests that PICs are concerned about the impact of climate change, only a minority have national education laws, strategies, plans, and budget allocations that explicitly refer to climate change or heritage education.

In New Zealand, the Resource Management Act (New Zealand, 1991) and amendments embody the principles of sustainable development, providing the legal framework setting the nation's economic, social, cultural, and environmental policies, standards and rules relating to the use of land, air, and water, and the protection of New Zealand's natural and cultural heritage. The Act is administered by the Environment Protection Authority within the Ministry for the Environment. New Zealand is on track in terms of achieving most of its SDG and emission targets. For example, emission levels are relatively low, 80% of its energy coming from renewable sources. In response to the Covid-19 pandemic, New Zealand (2021) is investing significant amounts in creating "jobs for nature" to support a "greener recovery." The Ministry of Culture and Heritage is responsible for assuring the conservation of New Zealand's three World Heritage sites (Tongariro, Wahipounamu, and Sub-Antarctic Islands), its 18 National Parks, and for the preservation and promotion of Maori culture.

New Zealand's current Education for Sustainability policy, strategy, and action plan (2017–2021) includes learning about:

- the environment: water, food, ecosystems, waste, urban living, transportation,
- the interactions between the natural environment and human activities, and their consequences, and
- action to prevent, reduce or change activities harmful to the environment.

Sustainability is a key element in Maori-medium education. It aims to enable young Maori students to participate in the Maori world, advancing a Maori understanding of their roles within their communities and the wider society. Maori culture and heritage are very much part of New Zealand identity. A framework for developing a whole school approach to sustainability is set out as part of the New Zealand Teaching and Learning Research Initiative. In a sustainable school:

- people work collaboratively and are reflective of the nation's bicultural heritage and diversity
- students are involved in sharing decisions regarding programmes that focus on learning about the interaction between people and the environment
- students develop attitudes and behaviours for a more sustainable future
- activities help students discover why sustainability matters and how to make it a reality in their school and wider community
- sustainable practices are part of school culture instigated by students and staff to make a more resilient community for the future
- students and the community work together to reduce their impact on the planet for future generations (New Zealand, 2021).

The Global Education Monitoring Report (2021) profile for New Zealand indicates that although there is some support for schools to engage with climate change and sustainable development education, the onus to take action rests with individual educational institutions, teachers, and students. It concludes that environmental education policy is not reaching all schools and that there is a lack of coherent messaging from the top. There are, however, pockets of flourishing practice where school and community leadership prioritise and support sustainability, climate education, and inclusion, ensuring that the funding, staffing, resourcing, and programmes needed are directed towards achieving clear goals. The profile also highlights shortcomings in teacher education programmes, there being no requirement that they provide the training needed by teachers and principals. In New Zealand, as in other nations in the Pacific, the inclusion of ESD and climate change in teacher education and professional development programmes is patchy (New Zealand, 2021).

Tuvalu (population 11,000) is a classic example of a small, low-income PIC. Like most PICs, Tuvalu has signed and ratified climate change and emission protocols and agreements (Kyoto, Paris, Glasgow). It has one of the world's lowest levels of greenhouse emissions but is extremely vulnerable to climate change and associated disasters, due to its geography, limited resources, and technological capacity. With an average height above sea level of under two metres, Tuvalu faces rising sea levels, increasingly extreme weather events, coastal erosion, food and water insecurity, and damage to coral reefs and fisheries. For the education system, sustainability is a continuing issue, including the difficulties that students will face in daily life as they struggle to make the adaptations needed to live sustainably. They will also need to learn how to act as global citizens in preparation for a time when they may be forced to live outside of Tuvalu (Global Education Monitoring Report, 2021).

The Tuvalu Education Sector Plan (2021–2030) covers ESD goals, strategies, and outcomes, including the development of educational resources and training programmes to ensure that the provision of quality education for sustainable living is improved for all (Tuvalu, 2020). The intention is to mainstream climate change and disaster risk reduction in the curriculum, and to develop and implement relevant curriculum and teaching materials and resources. Although Tuvalu devotes 14% of its national budget to education, as in other low-income PICs, budgetary and capacity constraints have made it difficult to implement many of its education climate change and ESD policies and programmes (Global Education Monitoring Report, 2021).

In ten Pacific Island countries, Overseas Development Aid (ODA) is the highest in the world as a proportion of national income. As Dorman and Pryke (2017) note, the Pacific Islands region is one of the most aid-dependent in the world. With that, the extent to which low-income countries in the Pacific can address the challenges posed by climate change and the threat to their heritage is shaped by the amount and form of aid provided. ODA from major donors like Australia and China has fallen significantly in the past three years, and there has been a shift from project to programme-based approaches for delivering development assistance. Most of the aid going to Papua New Guinea, Solomon Islands, Niue, and Tokelau comes from Australia, and most low-income Pacific countries are involved in its Pacific Partnership for Development programme. For example, the Climate Connection initiative seeks to build the capacity of Pacific Island nations to provide remote climate change education via a series of workshops organised by education ministries in Fiji, Kiribati, Tuvalu, and Samoa in collaboration with the Australian National University.

Over 60% of New Zealand's ODA goes to its Pacific neighbours, reflecting shared concerns about stability in the region and the impact of climate change. The New Zealand National Commission for UNESCO also works in co-operation with indigenous education leaders of the Pacific Island nations. For example, the Handbook entitled *Caring in the Pacific* was developed with support from the New Zealand National Commission for UNESCO and Korea. It focuses on ESD and indigenous cultures, specifically on "learning to care for oneself, family, community, country and our Pacific" (Asia–Pacific Centre for International Understanding, 2009).

2.7 Conclusion

Concerns about the impact of global warming, climate change, and human activities on the environment led to the establishment of international goals and targets focusing on sustainable development (the SDGs), protecting World Heritage sites, and climate change. The SDGs, the World Heritage Convention, and climate change agreements recognise the crucial role that education must play in ensuring that all learners acquire the knowledge and skills needed to assure "our common future."

The scientific evidence is clear: global warming, climate change, and unsustainable human activities pose a serious threat to the survival of all species, to all nations, and to the world's natural and cultural heritage. In the Pacific, extreme weather events have become ever more destructive and frequent. Low-lying coastal areas and some PICs (e.g., the Marshall Islands, Tuvalu) are likely to become uninhabitable in the foreseeable future. For the Pacific, achieving the sustainable development goals and addressing the challenges posed by climate change are matters of life or death—environmentally, economically, culturally, politically, and socially.

UNESCO is an intergovernmental organisation, one that is governed by, serves, and reports to national governments. It is responsible for facilitating international co-operation in education, science, and culture needed to reach agreement on SDG goals and implement the programmes approved by Member States to help achieve them.

Based on the evidence set out in this chapter and the work of UNESCO, the following measures need to be taken by governments to protect the environment and cultures of the Pacific and to:

- take the legislative, policy, and budgetary steps needed to meet their education SDG goals and targets (SDG4, especially 4.7, and 12.8), and support professional development and capacity-building programmes (SDG13.3).
- involve all key stakeholders as partners in the development, revision, and co-ordination and implementation of environmental and cultural legalisation policy and programmes.
- ensure educational institutions, students, teachers, and the public have the "relevant information and awareness for sustainable development and lifestyles in harmony with nature" (SDG 12.8.1) being provided by the UN, UNESCO, and professional organizations via reports, publications, toolkits, and capacity-building opportunities.
- encourage the private sector to support school, youth, and community activities designed to "protect and safeguard cultural and natural heritage" (SDG 11.4), and to adopt the International Code of Corporate Social Responsibility (Munro, 2020).

This chapter has focused on the extent to which Australia, New Zealand, and small Pacific Island nations have introduced the ESD and World Heritage education programmes needed to assure our common future. The Pacific region includes many of the world's most vulnerable environments and indigenous peoples, and as such, may prove to be an early warning system as temperatures rise, and when education authorities fail to act decisively to provide ESD and cultural heritage programmes that are of high quality and inclusive. Challenging the market-based thinking that dominates the policies of many governments and corporations will not be easy. Governments are likely to act only if there are strong pressures within and from international and local communities to do so. It will be "people power" that forces governments and the private sector to introduce the tough measures needed to reduce greenhouse emissions, and to meet their SDG targets and commitments. The challenge is to focus attention on the kind of education, research, and public information programmes that are empowering, that equip learners and communities with the knowledge, skills, and determination needed to assure sustainability and to protect the Pacific's natural and cultural heritage. Governments, the private sector, and communities must not lose sight of what lies at the core of what it means to be sustainable, and of the key role that education and training must play in laying the foundations for sustainable development.

Author Note: Emeritus Professor Colin POWER, AM, Ph.D., FACE is Chair of the Commonwealth Consortium for Education and Adjunct Professor at the Universities of Queensland and New England. As Deputy Director-General and head of the Education Sector of UNESCO, he has been "a major figure on the world education stage playing a key role in major education initiatives such as Education for All, the reform and reconstruction of national systems of education, World Heritage and education for sustainable development."

References

Asia-Pacific Centre of Education for International Understanding. (2009). *Caring in the Pacific*. Asia-Pacific Centre of Education for International Understanding.

Australian Academy of Science. (2021). *The risks to Australia of a 3 °C warmer world*. Australian Academy of Science.

Australian Association for Environmental Education. (2022). Special issue: School strikes. *Australian Journal of Environmental Education, 38*(1).

Australian Curriculum, Assessment and Reporting Authority. (2021). *The Australian curriculum (Version 8.4)*. https://www.australiancurriculum.edu.au

Australian Department of Agriculture, Water and Environment. (2021). *Australia: State of the environment 2021*. https://soe.dcceew.gov.au/

Australian Research Institute in Education for Sustainability. (2006). *Whole-school approaches to sustainability*. Macquarie University.

Bell-James, J. (2020). Ecosystems for services as a metaphor in environmental law. *University of Queensland Law Journal, 39*(2), 525–548.

Bowen, M. (2008). *Censoring science*. Dutton.

Bradshaw, C., Ehrlich, P., & Blumstein, D. (2021). *Frontiers in conservation science*. https://www.frontiersin.org/articles/103389/fcosc.2020615419

Brundtland, G. (1987). *Our common future* (Report of the Brundtland World Commission on Environment and Development). Oxford University Press.

Cutter-Mackenzie-Knowles, A., & Siegel, L. (2019). A critical cartography of waste education in Australia. Turning to a post-humanist framing. In W. W. W. So, J. C. K. Lee, & C. F. Chow (Eds.), *Environmental sustainability and education for waste management*. Springer Nature. https://doi.org/10.1007/978-981-13-9173-6_12

Doherty, P. (2015). *The knowledge wars*. Melbourne University Press.

Dorman, M., & Pryke, J. (2017). Foreign aid to the Pacific: Trends and development in the 21st century. *Asia and Pacific Policy Studies, 4*(5), 386–404.

Driscoll, D., Garrad, G., & Kusmanoff, A. (2021). Consequences of information suppression in ecological and conservation sciences. *Conservation Letters, 14*(1), e12757. https://doi.org/10.1111/conl.12757

Fien, J., Yencken, D., & Sykes, H. (Eds.) (2002). *Young people and the environment: An Asian-Pacific perspective*. Kluwer Academic Publishers.

Gleeson, D. (2020, October 14). Environmental science hit with severe funding cuts in Coalition universities overhaul. *The Guardian*. https://www.theguardian.com/australia-news/2020/oct/14/environmental-science-hit-with-severe-funding-cuts-in-coalition-universities-overhaul

Global Education Monitoring Report. (2020). *Inclusion and education*. UNESCO. https://www.unesco.org/en/education/inclusion

Global Education Monitoring Report. (2021). *Environmental education policy*. UNESCO. https://www.gemreportunesco.wpcomstaging.com/2021/11/12/environmental-education-policy

International Energy Agency. (2020). *Global energy review: CO2 emissions in 2021*. https://www. iea.orgf/reports/global-energy-review-CO2-emissions-in-2021-2

Intergovernmental Panel on Climate Change. (2013). *Climate change: The physical science basis*. Cambridge University Press.

Intergovernmental Panel on Climate Change. (2019). *Special report on the oceans and cryosphere in a changing climate*. https://www.ipcc.ch/srocc/

Intergovernmental Panel on Climate Change. (2022). *Climate change 2022: Impacts, adaptation and vulnerability. Contribution of Working Group to the Sixth Assessment Report of the Intergovernmental Panel on Climate Change*. Cambridge University Press.

Lee, J., & Power, C. (2021). Building a green and sustainable university: An international review. In K. Lone, S. Komisar, & E. Everham (Eds.), *Making the sustainable university* (pp. 269–286). Springer Nature.

Maclean, R., Jagnnathan, S., & Sarvi, J. (Eds.). (2013). *Skills for inclusive and sustainable growth in developing Asia-Pacific*. Springer.

Munro, V. (2020). *CSR for purpose, shared value and deep transformation*. Emerald Publishing.

New Zealand. (1991). *Resource management act*. https://www.leglisltion.gov.nz

New Zealand (2021). *Education for sustainability policy*. https://environment.gov.nz

New Zealand National Commission for UNESCO. (2004). *Our Pacific heritage*. New Zealand Department of Education.

O'Flaherty, J., & Liddy, M. (2017). The impact of development education and Education for Sustainable Development interventions. *Environmental Education Research, 24*(7), 1031–1049.

Power, C. (2015). *The power of education: Education for all, development, globalisation and UNESCO*. Springer.

Power, C., & Hogan, R. (1986). Achieving the goals of environmental education: Ethics and affective outcomes. In M. Frazer & A. Kornhauser (Eds.), *Ethics and social responsibility in science education*. ICSU Press & Pergamon Press.

Samuel, G. (2020). *Final report: Independent review of the environment protection and biodiversity conservation act*. https://epbcactreview.environment.gov.au/resources/final-report

Smith, C., & Watson, J. (2019). Does the rise of STEM mean the demise of sustainability? *Australian Journal of Environmental Education, 35*(1), 1–13.

Sustainable Schools Network Australia. (2021). *Sustainable Schools Network Journal*. https://ssn. org.au/journal/

Tilbury, D., Coleman, V., & Garlick, D. (2005). *A National review of environmental education and its contribution to sustainability in Australia*. Australian Government Department of Environment and Heritage.

Tuvalu. (2020). *National strategy for sustainable development—Te Kete 2021–2030*. Government of Tuvalu.

United Nations Development Programme. (2019). *Sustainable Development Goals Report*.

United Nations Educational, Scientific and Cultural Organisation. (2002). *World heritage in young hands. To know, cherish and act: an educational resource kit for teachers*. UNESCO.

United Nations Educational, Scientific and Cultural Organisation. (2010). *Teaching and learning for a sustainable future: A multi-media teacher education programme*. https://www.unesco.org/en/education/tisf.

United Nations Educational, Scientific and Cultural Organisation. (2020). *UNITWIN-UNESCO Chairs Programme*. https://www.unesco.org/en/unitwin

United Nations Educational, Scientific and Cultural Organisation. (2021). *Learn for our planet: A global review of how environmental issues are integrated in education*.

United Nations Educational, Scientific and Cultural Organisation. (2022). *New blue curriculum: A tool kit for policy makers*. https://www.unesco.org/en/10C/2022/mg/90

United Nations Educational, Scientific and Cultural Organisation, & UNESCO-Associated Schools Project. (2016). *Getting climate ready: A guide for schools on climate action*.

United Nations Educational, Scientific and Cultural Organisation. UNESCO-World Heritage Centre. (2019). *Operational guidelines for the implementation of the world heritage convention (WHC.19/01—10 July 2019)*. https://whc.unesco.org/en/documents/178167
Wallace-Wells, D. (2019). *The uninhabitable earth*. Allen Lane.
Wikipedia. (2020). *Climate strikes*. https://en.wikipedia.org/september-2019-climatestrikes

Chapter 3
The United Nations Sustainable Development Goals in a Neoliberal World

Lyn Carter⊙ **and Caroline Smith**⊙

How did we end up in a world when a child should govern an old man an imbecile should lead a wise man and a handful of people should gorge themselves with superfluities while the hungry multitude goes in want of necessities?

Jean-Jacques Rousseau, A Discourse on the Origin of Inequality (1755/2018, p. 137). (Translated by G. D. H. Cole)

3.1 Introduction

At a special session of the German Bundestag on February 27, 2022, newly minted Chancellor Olaf Scholz declared that we had arrived at a *zeitenwende*, or a change of era (Borchert et al., 2022). While the specific context was a radical alteration to German foreign policy consequent to Vladimir Putin's invasion of Ukraine, essayist Jason Cowley (2022) believes it also refers to a new moral seriousness in humanity's approach to the profound intellectual and ethical anxieties of our times. Steger and James (2020, p. 188) have described our present moment as "the Great Unsettling"— a time where the "intensifying dynamics of instability, disintegration, insecurity, dislocation, relativism, inequality, and degradation … (are) unprecedented in their compounding confluence of events." After years of accelerating climate change, rampant neoliberalism, inequality, democracy's retreat in the face of authoritarianism, the decline of liberalism, post truth populism, algorithms, chat bots, data mining, and a devastating pandemic—what economic historian Adam Tooze (2021)

L. Carter (✉)
National School of Education, Faculty of Education and Arts, Australian Catholic University, Fitzroy, VIC 3065, Australia
e-mail: lyncarter333@gmail.com

C. Smith
School of Education, College of Arts, Law, and Education, Burnie, TAS 7320, Australia
e-mail: Caroline.Smith1@utas.edu.au

© The Author(s), under exclusive license to Springer Nature Singapore Pte Ltd. 2023   29
K. Beasy et al. (eds.), *Education and the UN Sustainable Development Goals*, Education for Sustainability 7,
https://doi.org/10.1007/978-981-99-3802-5_3

calls a "polycrisis" in its all-encompassing relentlessness—a *zeitenwende* surely proffers hope. Certainly, the war in Ukraine seems to have galvanised our attention on global instability, fossil energy dependence, food security, and suffering and destruction in a way the 2021 Glasgow climate change Conference of the Parties (COP 26) failed to achieve.

3.2   The United Nations Sustainable Development Goals

A recent attempt to focus our awareness on our profound problems has been the 2015 adoption by United Nations (UN) member states of the 2030 Agenda for Sustainable Development. The Agenda for Sustainable Development aims to provide "a blueprint for peace and prosperity for people and planet." Characterised as an urgent call for action by all countries in a global partnership, it centres on 17 intimately interconnected Sustainable Development Goals (SDGs) (UN, n.d.). Member states are expected to commit to aligning their national development efforts to promote prosperity while protecting the environment and use the SDGs to frame their political policies and agendas over the period 2015–2030. The SDGs claim that ending global poverty and improving environmental sustainability cannot be achieved without improvements in health and education, reducing inequality, and developing sustainable economies, all while tackling climate change and preserving biodiversity. Each of the 193 signatories contract to a voluntary national review report on implementation of the SDGs at least twice over the lifetime of the Agenda, reflecting the efforts and achievements of key national sectors such as business, civil society, academia, communities, and individuals, measured against the SDGs (e.g., The Australian Government's Department of Foreign Affairs and Trade, 2018).

However, it is against the increasing instability of third phase neoliberalism, elaborated on below, that the SDGs were adopted in 2015—a world in "polycrisis" to reiterate Tooze (2021). In a major critique of the SDGs, McCloskey (2019) wonders how they can "square the circle of combating climate change while enabling poor and middle-income countries to higher levels of growth with the enhanced global consumption of carbon which that implies?" (p. 156). We go further and wonder also about the polarising geopolitical consequences of failed rampant unchecked capital accumulation, further amplified by neoliberal accumulation and its consequences for the natural environment. Those like Belda-Miguel et al., (2019, p. 2) argue that as "the SDGs do not overcome the depoliticisation of aid discourses and policies and as they still frame development problems as technical, managerial and measurable problems, then issues of power and key political issues such as redistribution" will remain difficult to overcome. The new global Agenda and SDGs "reproduce(s) the status quo and (doesn't) address the causes of impoverishment created by the existing dominant (neoliberal) capitalist and developmentalist model" (p. 2). So, while the SDGs are to be welcomed as global recognition of the critical need to steer the human impact on the planet towards sustainability, a closer examination of their philosophical assumptions and inherent values is required to consider fully their viability as ways forward, especially their implications for education curricula and pedagogies.

This in turn, necessitates a better understanding of the SDGs' instigating organisation—the UN—and its ideological, political, and economic framings as well as its institutions and processes that find expression in the SDGs. Hence, in order to explore and understand these and other critiques of the UN and the SDGs, we first turn to consider their often fraught and lengthy genealogy.

3.3 The Genealogy of the United Nations and SDGs

The US President Theodore Roosevelt first suggested the name *United Nations* to refer to the allies in 1941, the idea being strengthened at the New Hampshire town of Bretton Woods, and ultimately charted in 1945. The Bretton Woods conference held towards the end of World War II sought to determine the world's macro structures going forward, particularly economic processes and structures, but also ideological and governance. Although there were 44 nations represented at the summit, the agreement forged a US-dominated liberal democratic capitalism that has held in spirit, though not organisation, until the present. Consequently, the UN has sought to implement liberal ideals of rule-based international law and peacemaking, multilateralism, humanism, and economic and social development, and in its more recent iteration, neoliberalism and globalisation. It has pursued an agenda of professed universal truths in relation to human rights and individual freedoms, health and education, and humanitarian aid. As the profoundly wicked problems of life on earth have become more apparent, sustainability and climate action have been added to the UN's spheres of responsibility.

Liberalism and neoliberalism are the axiomatic truths behind the UN and consequently, the SDGs. As liberalism and neoliberalism are fragile and faulty constructs—responsible for much human flourishing and emancipation but at the same time being rife with severe contradictions, inequalities, fractures, and intolerances—it is perhaps unsurprising that the Agenda and the SDGs have been subject to critiques from a number of areas. Adelman (2018) for example, traces the framing and trajectory of the SDGs to the idea of sustainable development articulated in the 1987 World Commission on Environment and Development (WECD) document *Our Common Future* (the so-called "Brundtland Commission"). For Adelman, *Our Common Future* represents an anthropocentric position which is "a neoliberal form of green capitalism" (p. 1). The SDGs do provide a (limited) structural analysis of how poverty and unsustainability are grounded historically in corporatism, colonialism, and other egregiousness of (neo)liberal global capitalism (Belda-Miguel et al., 2019). However, Kopnina (2020) argues that they fit within the wider sustained and inclusive economic growthist strategies promoted as solutions to the other SDGs objectives of improving health, alleviating poverty, reducing child mortality, and tackling climate change.

Irwin and Scali (2007) concur, demonstrating the impact of neoliberalism on global health initiatives; see also Towle, Chapter 19 in this volume.

Adelman (2018), Hickel (2019), and Kopnina (2020) all argue that the SDGs are unlikely to lead to greater social equality and economic prosperity, but rather, to further problematic economic growth through unsustainable production and consumption that has exacerbated the many environmental problems of unsustainability. Indeed, given that unlimited economic growth is not possible on a finite planet, this is essentially an oxymoronic position (Hamilton, 2015; Hickel, 2019; Smith & Watson, 2018).

Education is seen as critical to achieving the goals, and indeed has its own Goal (SDG4) where the aim of Target 4.7 is that "by 2023 ensure that all learners acquire knowledge and skills needed to promote sustainable development…" (UN Department of Economic and Social Affairs Sustainable Development [n.d.], Goal 4, p. 8). Education, of course, is also permeated with liberal and neoliberal ideologies and values that can be traced from Rousseau (1755/2018) and John Dewey through to contemporary settings. Education for Sustainable Development (ESD) (also referred to as Education for Sustainability [EfS]),[1] is the mainstream vehicle for achieving sustainability. ESD has been part of education in various countries since the Tbilisi Declaration of 1977, though waxing and waning in importance. The most wide-ranging and rigorous manifestation of ESD has been the UN Decade of Education for Sustainable Development (UNDESD) (UN Educational, Scientific, and Cultural Organization [UNESCO], 2002), which operated from 2005 to 2014. The Decade aimed to "empower learners to take informed decisions and responsible actions for environmental integrity, economic viability and a just society for present and future generations" (p. 7). Informed by the UNDESD, UNESCO, the United Nations' specialised agency for education, is charged with leading and coordinating the Education section of 2030 Agenda through the SDGs.

Given that the SDGs are likely to be important in guiding ESD, we believe that if educators are to make informed decisions about SDGs and their educational intentions, a fuller understanding of SDGs' historicity, genealogy, and orientations could be helpful. Hence, this chapter aims to provide an overview of their liberal and neoliberal constructions. After all, Rousseau's questioning in the opening quote of "how did we end here," together with Mirowski's (2020) more recent call to "look to the antecedents to understand how our moment may have developed and how it could be otherwise," entreats a closer inspection of historical trajectories. This means mapping a somewhat simplified, and necessarily perspectival, genealogy of liberalism and neoliberalism over time and their permeation of sustainable development discourses, practices, and processes.

In the next two sections of this chapter, we consider liberalism as the ascendant intellectual current in the West since the Enlightenment (with antecedents in the Renaissance and the Reformation). Complex in its component beliefs and ideas, liberalism encompasses moral philosophy, politics, economics, methodologies, and legal

---

[1] Although often used interchangeably, ESD and EfS are ideologically different; see Sterling (2001) for a full discussion of this.

and civic infrastructures, that fracture into theoretical critiques from both progressive and reactionary orientations. Early liberals were by and large, polymaths, as interested in nature and science as they were in moral philosophy, politics, religion, history, languages, and the classics. Well-educated, often aristocrats, leisured or patronised, they were a small elite circulating between Britain and Continental Europe. Liberals took from the Renaissance's intellectual ferment, individual expression, tolerance, and a certain notion of human dignity the fingerprints of which are clearly apparent in today's UN, executed through scepticism, reason, and empiricism. From the Reformation, and particularly from the early English Reformation's intolerant and punitive form, they took a desire to stabilise social chaos (Simpson, 2019). Secondly, as neoliberalism has been the most dominant form of twentieth- and twenty-first-century liberalism, we consider its genesis, sedimentation, and effects. Thirdly, as an example of neoliberalism's colonisation of sustainability and sustainable development that arguably find expression in the SDGs, we review some of the influence of the little-known E. Bruce Harrison, the putative father of "green washing," through the 1970s, 1980s, and 1990s (Aronczyk & Espinoza, 2021). And finally, we close the chapter with a call for other ways of animating the coming *zeitenwende*, especially within education.

3.4 The Contradictory Impulses of Liberalism

Runciman (2020) is among those who date early liberalism to Thomas Hobbes' 1651 publication of *Leviathan*. Primarily a political treatise, *Leviathan* is now regarded as one of the foundational texts of the Western canon and is, for Runciman, the organising principle and institution of contemporary politics throughout the world. Against the turmoil of the English Civil War (1642–1651), Hobbes developed the concept of the modern representative State by arguing that in the natural state of humans before society (the primal state of nature where "the life of man is solitary, poor, nasty, brutish, and short"), all are equal in their fragility to death, desirous of peace, but essentially in a war of all against all. As individual desires necessarily conflict, a right to life and stability occurs when people empower a sovereign, the metaphorical Leviathan, to make decisions to which they will defer. Representation through the State and law becomes the unity of the collective, without which Hobbes argues, ensues the political breakdown of war and death. However, it remains that life away from that governed by law still enables humans to pursue their individual interests (engendering the liberal constructs of freedom and individualism), be they religious, economic, or something other, in a peaceful, unhindered way.

A generation after Hobbes, John Locke further advanced liberal thinking with his *Two Treatises of Government* (1689–1690), examining rights (principally property rights), as well as slavery, freedom of expression, tolerance, and the separation of powers (church and state). For McManus (2020), Locke's understanding of property rights was an odd mix of his science and theology; Locke believed God's provision of all nature was available for man's (sic) appropriation and use (a religious legit-imisation for extraction and exploitation of nature). This was justified by "a man having property in his own person, he is therefore entitled to his labour and all with which he mixes his labour" (that is, material entities), which then become his own property. Thus, work justified property acquisition and protection and the use of nature to one's own ends. While Locke did not sanction greed per se and saw God's natural resources as available to all, his construct of property rights became the crux of liberalism going forward.

With Hobbes, Locke, and others then, early liberalism inscribed the State as preserving its citizen's rights to *life, liberty*, and *property*, punishing any violations of these, and pursuing the public good for *peace* and *stability*. These principles are clearly, fundamental conceptions within the contemporary UN and the SDGs. Early liberalism later bifurcated into political and economic branches, the latter emerging with British economist and philosopher Adam Smith and his 1776 *The Wealth of Nations*. Smith sought to replace mercantilist (preferential contracts) and physio-cratic (wealth is land and agriculture) economic theories, which were becoming less relevant with the onset of the Industrial Revolution, with ideas of laissez faire markets self-regulating through competition, supply and demand, and self-interest—the famous (or infamous) "invisible hand" metaphor. Capitalism and its desire for surpluses, rather than goods exchange mechanisms for sustenance, was now firmly settled in the West and became inexorably intertwined liberalism through discourses of property rights and freedom. With the contributions of Smith and later liberal economists, the three pillars of liberal thought, that is, the political, the economic, and the social, were now in place.

Hobbes' notion of the State was an artificial construction whose success has become so normalised and naturalised that there is now no other way of organising human affairs. We all live in nation-states, the collective of which is the UN. Like all human constructs, it is necessarily imperfect, permeated with inconsistencies and flaws. Hobbes was well aware of his State's own inherit paradox, that is, to be peaceful and free enough from conflict to pursue one's individual concerns (freedom), meant surrendering a great part of that freedom to the State. Thus, liberalism encodes only small perimeters of freedoms that vary with time and circumstance while *Leviathans* (States) exercise power that, in contemporary Western settings and the UN, are in rules-based organisations and institutions. Moreover, the legal rights and ideological tolerance espoused by Locke were also contingent, not extending for example, to religions beyond Protestantism, or to women, non-propertied men, or, in a time of expanding imperialism, to the racialised Other.

Liberalism has always been open to critique. Philosopher and educator, Jean-Jacques Rousseau saw liberalism and capitalism's accumulation as privileging the few. In his 1755 *Discourse on the Origin and Basis of Inequality Among Men* (also known as the *Second Discourse*), Rousseau argues that political settlements like Hobbes' State and Locke's property rights, obfuscate their embedded power and hier-archies while providing illusory solutions (Runciman, 2021). Rousseau concluded that private property, be it land or other natural resources, is the basis of all inequality:

The first man who, having enclosed a piece of ground, to whom it occurred to say this is mine, and found people sufficiently simple to believe him, was the true founder of civil society. How many crimes, wars, murders, how many miseries and horrors Mankind would have been spared by him who, pulling up the stakes or filling in the ditch and crying to his fellows, Beware of listening to this imposter; … (as) the fruits of the earth belong to us all, and the earth itself to nobody. (1755/2018, p. 161)

Taken as read, liberalism's long trajectory seems to have justified exploitation of planetary resources and their allocation to the few.

More contemporary critiques like Deneen (2018) argue that liberalism's three foundational principles are deeply contradictory. Liberalism trumpets equal rights while fostering capitalism's material inequality, and liberalism's legitimacy rests on the ostensibly freely given consent (of the people to the State). At the same time, it also discourages communitarianism and civic commitments in favour of private property and economic individualism. Jahn (2021) extends these points to argue that liberalism's successes were underpinned by a domestic and international divide, in which oppression was externalised into the non-Western international sphere, particularly to the imperial powers' colonies, along with political conflicts and other costs. Prosperity, political freedom, and human rights were also able to mature in the metropole, thus justifying the civilisational and developmental superiority of the West that embedded racism, nationalism, and imperialism. Bhambra (2021) agrees, arguing that colonialism provided the material wealth that enabled liberalism to thrive in the West. If colonial and other spaces could not be "liberal," it was believed, it was due to their own civilisational failures, like poor governance and corruption or just being "black" (Jahn, 2021). Perversely, many of these former colonies are spaces in which the SDGs now seek to improve education, health, poverty, and equity denied by their former liberal masters, and remediate environmental devastation caused by imperial extraction. Further, they potentially reinforce global structural conditions fostered by neoliberalism to maintain conditions of poverty, injustice, and environmental exploitation, through trade agreements, which weaken efforts to improve environmental standards and working conditions.

We turn now to consider the late twentieth- and early twenty-first-century iteration of liberalism—neoliberalism. More than 350 years on from Hobbes, Locke, and Smith, the twentieth century has seen liberalism expand into what has become known as the global liberal world order, the apex of which arguably, is the UN. The failure of Smith's nineteenth-century laissez faire liberal capitalism helped seed the two devastating world wars of the twentieth century. Post World War II (WW2), the chartering of the UN, and the Bretton Woods agreement responsible for establishing the World Bank and the International Monetary Fund (IMF), facilitated the growth of the global liberal world order. The World Bank monitors world currencies, stabilises the international monetary system, and aims to work to reduce poverty and increase shared prosperity, while the IMF keeps track of the economy globally. The UN, the World bank, and the IMF together with other multilateral organisations like the World Trade Organisation (WTO), the security-focussed North Atlantic Treaty Organization (NATO), and others, provide the pillars of modern liberalism in the political, economic, and social domains: (i) government regulated capitalism with a social contract embedded within (preferentially) democracy, though not always, for example, the former Soviet Bloc, China, and so on, (ii) the pursuit of evidence-based rational truth underpinning civil society(ies) organised multilaterally into rules-based organisations and practices, and (iii) freedom as self-determination with human rights underpinned by responsibilities (Duncombe & Dunne, 2018). The stagflation in the 1970s, along with global oil shocks, technological development, and emerging economies of previous colonies offering real competition, though, tested the government interventionist liberalism in train since the end of WW2. Keynesianism, named after its founder British economist John Maynard Keynes, otherwise known as welfarism that promoted strong social policies, had not successfully grappled with these challenges. Consequently, the West turned to the new iteration of liberalism—neoliberalism—that was already finding favour among many in the Western world.

3.5   The Rise, Rise, and Rise Again of Neoliberalism

One of neoliberalism's main progenitors, Friedrich von Hayek was an Austrian free-market economist who joined the London School of Economics (LSE) in 1931. Hayek was a protégé of fellow Austrian aristocrat, strident antisocialist, and free marketeer, Ludwig von Mises—one of the most influential conservative economic and political thinkers of the twentieth century. Hayek's famous 1944 book, *The Road to Serfdom*, argued for market-based, rather than interventionist or welfarist, political and social organisation. Fearing the totalitarianisms he had seen first-hand in Germany and the Soviet Union, Hayek believed liberalism's hallmark was freedom rather than human dignity. For Hayek, the market was the definitive instrument able to generate the knowledge required to run complex modern societies. Technocrats and experts (state planners, engineers, public health officials, and so on), pejoratively Hayek's second-hand dealers in ideas, "possess too much power in circulating ideas which, when coupled to the state…believe they know what is in the interests of all, and then set about establishing plans through which to pursue this" (Davis, 2017, p. 236). Hayek was also against extreme *laissez faire* approaches as he believed, left to its own devices, the market could ultimately cannibalise itself. Enough state regulation was required (ironically, by experts) to run the market without a regulated welfarist economy. What was new in Hayek's brand of liberalism, a "neo" liberalism, was that it was neither socially inclined nor *laissez faire*, but as he and his followers believed, something completely different (Innset, 2020).

Still teaching at the LSE in 1947, Hayek organised a meeting in Mont Pèlerin, Switzerland with notable attendees Ludwig von Mises, American economic and social commentator Walter Lippmann, Chicago School economists George Stigler and Milton Friedman, and science philosophers Karl Popper and Michael Polanyi. The meeting was to continue the work of the 1938 *Colloque Walter Lippmann (WLC)* organised in Paris by science philosopher Louis Rougier, centred on Walter Lippmann's 1937 book, *The Good Society*. Michel Foucault's 1979 Collège de France lectures, published later as *The Birth of Biopolitics* (Foucault, 2008), identified the lesser known WLC as important in neoliberalism's genesis. The WLC believed the State must:

> first, protect the *price mechanism*, … second, put in place and guarantee a *legal order* to safeguard the market's development and legally justify any intervention. Third, *political liberalism* must embrace law as the cornerstone of legitimacy, … Fourth, such a legal regime constitutes the liberal method to "*control the social*"; and fifth, a liberal state is responsible for continuously providing society with five essential elements, for which taxes could be imposed: *national defence, social insurance, social services, education, and scientific research*. (Schulz-Forberg, 2020, p. 171)

While traditionally liberal, but embryonically neoliberal in its privileging of the free market, the WLC promoted the rule of law as the best way to guarantee the inviolability of the human person, even though there are no binding treaties that guarantee this in the 2030 Agenda. Here again, we see antecedents which later find expression in the UN, Bretton Woods, and ultimately, the SDGs. Innset (2020) notes that WLC's progressiveness appeals to contemporary centre-left or progressive neoliberals, compared with the later Mont Pèlerin group's more right-wing orientation. Significantly, Slobodian and Plehwe (2020) contend that the WLC platform indicates again, that neoliberals did not believe in a "free" free market, even as the term had taken root. Neoliberals, as we have already seen, were still government interventionists, but different from welfarists, and were comfortable with authoritarianism when warranted by the neoliberal market programme. The term "neoliberalism," first proposed at the WLC by Alexander Rüstow, an admirer of the prominent Nazi party member Carl Schmitt, was formally adopted at the Mont Pèlerin Society meeting (MPS).

Various streams of thought were brought together at the MPS, from von Mises and his Austrian School's more *laissez faire* market ideologues to the Freiburg School German Ordoliberals, which included Hayek, who promoted some state market intervention. In doing so, they anticipated the *Third Way* politics of US President Bill Clinton and UK Prime Minister Tony Blair 60 years into the future. Also represented was the famous Chicago School, concerned with monopolistic tendencies created by unfettered markets. Contemporary neoliberalism's wide penetration is partly explained by the variability of these strands, allowing it to be more attractive to diverse audiences (Mirowski, 2020). Its emerging dominance over welfarism in the 1970s, argues Davies (2016, p. 132), followed a classical "rhythm of crisis in line with Thomas Kuhn's model of a paradigm shift." Even as the MPS promoted competitive markets and entrepreneurship, significantly, the MPS' ideological project never wished to be troubled by the real economic and political world, apparent in their stance on market-inducing inequality. Unlike some of their libertarians who believed inequality virtuously reflected true human nature, Hayek's consequentialism understood that market conditions produce tolerable inequality as everyone ultimately benefits (McManus, 2020). This "trickle down" or "all boats rise" economics, often associated with 1980s US President Ronald Reagan's policies, also influenced UK Prime Minister Margaret Thatcher, who is reported to have said, "it doesn't matter if the rich get richer as long as everyone benefits." Hayek did believe, nevertheless, that humans could be ranked by utility: "The requirement of preserving the maximum number of lives," he wrote, "is not that all individual lives be regarded as equally important" (Hayek, 1988, p. 132). Moreover, Hayek did not believe in universal suffrage, believing only older people with "skin in the game" deserved to vote. Such views remain an inconvenient truth for many involved with the UN and the SDGs.

Neoliberalism today is not the neoliberalism of the WLC, or even the more conservative MPS. Since its genesis in the 1930s and 1940s with Hayek and von Mises, neoliberalism has evolved, even as its leitmotif of the markets' supremacy over human cognition remained constant. This single point, for Mirowski (2020), explains contemporary neoliberalism's adaptability and resilience across economic and political history, ideology, affect, philosophy, imagination, epistemology, and any one of a number of other precepts scholars assign (for example, Gilbert, 2013; Peck et al., 2018). Neoliberalism's epistemological convictions and organisational structures cross a range of schools such as Austrian School, Ordoliberals from the Freiburg School, Chicago School, and Virginia School. These, Mirowski (2020) argues, provided further unity, able to feed into a variety of reconcilable political and cultural orientations making up our contemporary world and our multivariate UN, which include progressive, socially liberal, right-wing, cosmopolitan, authoritarian, internationalist, democratic, and populist forms. Neoliberalism now remains the preternatural.

While describing contemporary neoliberalism as always fraught, Steger and Roy (2021) are among those suggesting a reading describing various facets and phases. Their first facet, similar to Mirowski's (2014) Neoliberal Thought Collective (NTC), is ideology, meaning the development and dissemination of a coherent belief and value system as *the* only way to know the world. Secondly, neoliberalism is a mode of governmentality (after Foucault), remaking subjectivity around entrepreneurism, competitiveness, and self-interest. Governments no longer act for the public good, but for efficiency and profit, modelled on free-market corporatisation. The third facet is concrete public policy to privilege the market actively, promoting economic and institutional deregulation, trade liberalism, and privatisation of enterprises, which includes union busting, social welfare reduction, and tax cuts for the wealthy. Finally, neoliberalism is epoch, that is, it follows welfarism as the next phase of capitalism in a normative evolutionary sequence. Birch's (2015) neoliberal categories include Steger and Roy's (2021), but expand them into six approaches, paraphrased as: (i) a Foucauldian approach of neoliberalism as a form of governmentality, (ii) a Marxist approach as a class-based project privileging capital at the expense of labour, (iii) an ideological approach from Hayek and others, (iv) an epochal history and philosophy of economics approach, (v) an institutional approach expounding the multifarious articulations of restructuring with deregulation and new regulatory regimes, and (vi) a geographical approach, characterising neoliberalism as always emerging, inherently uneven and variably enacted. (See also Flew, 2014, for his six meanings of neoliberalism).

Although renderings of neoliberalism may vary, there seems to be more agreement on its temporal phases. Davies (2016) and Steger and Roy (2021) identify three distinct phases from the late 1970s through to today. The first phase roughly parallels the decade-long term of conservatives Margaret Thatcher, Ronald Regan, and Deng Xiaoping to the end of the 1980s. Steger and Roy see this phase as a reaction against welfarism, which parallels a growing right-wing base, particularly in the US, horrified by the civil and gender rights movements of the 1960s, culminating in the 1965 Voting Rights Act outlawing racial discrimination (Cooper, 2017), and the 1970 creation of the US Environmental Protection Agency (EPA) consequent to increasing environmental awareness. The second phase, known as the progressive or golden age of neoliberalism, dates from the late 1980s through to the first decade of the twenty-first century. Here, Tony Blair and Bill Clinton presided over a centre-left iteration of neoliberalism, dubbed the *Third Way*, that attempted to reintroduce some socially liberal policies back into the free-market mix. At the same time, Jiang Zemin (1993–2003) in China continued the liberalising policies that began under Deng, including hosting visits from Hayek and other prominent neoliberals.

Unlike the shorter and partly rhetorical first phase, much of the real neoliberal reconstruction in privatisation, decentralisation, competitive marketisation, and so on, occurred during this second stage. Davies (2016) argues the centre left was spectacularly successful in its interventions, remaking government with greater public spending—once the hallmark of welfarism, now used to construct neoliberalism's two infrastructures. The accelerating financialised markets increased wealth creation with, for example, the financial sector's GDP share increasing between 1970 and 2007 from 13 to 20% and its share of total US corporate profits increasing from 14 to 40% between 1981 and 2006 (Morrow, 2010). The wealthy became much happier. The golden age also saw Fukuyama (1992) proclaim a Western triumphal "end of history," while Chinese-fuelled, consumer-based globalisation flourished with its attendant environmental catastrophes (see Steger & James, 2020).

The first and second stage neoliberalism was also manifest within the UN and its agencies, policies, and programmes after its earlier welfarist or Keynesian orientation, by virtue of neoliberalism's world dominance, and the UN's reliance on nation-state funding. If the principal funders of the UN are neoliberal, so is the UN. Hence, while the UN may not explicitly be a supranational institution designed to protect the free flow of capital, it implicitly functions as a defender of the economic status quo. Rashid (2019) argues that the UN is just like the original League of Nations, a forum where countries could discuss global problems, but were ultimately powerless to prevent the kind of totalitarian fascism and expansion that characterised the 1930s. As Slobodian (2018) suggests, neoliberals like Ludwig von Mises viewed the League of Nations as an ideal supranational institution to protect the free market, "an iron glove for the invisible hand of the market"—faint praise indeed. During the 1980s and 1990s, the Bretton Woods institutions of the World Bank and IMF required many of the developing countries dependent on UN programmes to restructure on market-based (Adam Smith), privatised (John Locke) lines. A key example is the deficit construction of health as a lack or disease, and whose remedies are to be sought through technologies (Irwin & Scali, 2007; Towle [this volume]). These supranational entities are the new *Leviathans* in Hobbesian terms, where freedoms (in this case nation-states and the UN) are ceded to their orthodoxies to gain participation in the global economy.

. The third phase neoliberalism—late neoliberalism—came to prominence with the Global Financial Crisis (GFC) of 2007–2008 and beyond. Market and regulatory failures were a major cause of the GFC. Transformed second phase neoliberal financial systems enabled profit-focussed but faulty financial products, to pass credit risk down through complex and speculative securities. Credit rating agencies, whose own profits depended on their inflated values, favourably scored risky products. Regulators trusted private actors to self-regulate. Bill Clinton had allowed banks in the US to reduce capital reserves, and while there was some bank regulatory oversight, investment banks, newly dominant asset managers, insurance companies, and hedge funds sat outside these frameworks. Market-valued risk and assets produced a wealth-friendly bubble that ultimately burst. Centre-left politicians—Gordon Brown in the UK and Barack Obama in the US—oversaw the enormous public sector bailouts, paid to the "too big to fail" wealthy and financial sectors, despite rising unemployment and spiralling household debt. This dispelled any lingering doubt about the left's collusion with neoliberalism.

The GFC justified government cutbacks or "austerity" measures, systematically dismantling any institutional social protections left after previous neoliberal reforms, and further creating generalised socioeconomic and environmental insecurity. At the same time, corporate profits rose (Davies, 2016). This phase, perversely neoliberalism's renewed intensification even as it failed and frailed (Peck & Theodore, 2019), is characterised by three somewhat incommensurable tendencies: firstly, a blaming of the emerging precariat's economic circumstances on their own moral failure—a punitive meritocracy giving rise to the gig economy or the *Uberisation* of work; secondly, rising profits and anti-competitive regulation leading to oligopolies and a politics of plutocracy; and thirdly, the "left behinds" attraction to right-wing populist (RWP) movements. RWPs helped install conservative authoritarian politicians like Brazil's Jair Bolsanaro, Viktor Orbán in Hungary, Narendra Modi in India, Rodrigo Duterte in the Philippines, Poland's Andrzej Duda, Boris Johnston in the UK, and Donald Trump in the White House. RWPs reject middle class technocrats/experts as elites, even as they admire the real elites' wealth and power. They leverage culture war issues like racism, environmentalism, gender freedoms, abortion, and other human rights critical to the UN agendas. They look instead to strong charismatic anti-establishment leaders offering simple solutions to complex issues.

RWP movements have bled into authoritarian neoliberalism—a neo-illiberalism—while cleverly managing to not look like it, argues Bruff (2014). Authoritarian neoliberalism involves dominant groups excluding others through legally engineered means within supposed democratic institutions (see for example, the creation of "LGBTI+-free" zones in the "liberal democratic" Poland, the persecution of Muslims in Modi's Hindu India, the nationalist curriculum in Hungary, and the denial of climate change in Trump's US even as California burnt in record wildfires—the examples go on and on). Havertz's (2018, p. 3) research on the German RWP party Alternative for Germany (AfD) shows how RWPs seek to ensure inequality as society's organisational principle: "it is authoritarian because it recognises neither the legitimacy of any opposition to its positions nor any interests outside of what it claims to be the interests of 'the people'."

As an example of how neoliberalism is deeply entrenched in issues of sustainability, we now turn to sketch a specific example, the work of the little-known E. Bruce Harrison Jr (1932–2012). Harrison was a journalist and later a corporate communications or public relations (PR) specialist who is putatively thought of as the "father of greenwashing," and who helped develop the contemporary economic (neoliberal) construction of the term "sustainability" (Aronczyk & Espinoza, 2022). That Harrison's name is so unfamiliar within the public arena is testament to how business interests work successfully behind the scenes. Temporally, Harrison parallels first and second stage neoliberalism, whereas the publication of the SDGs coincides with its third phase.

3.6 Neoliberalism at Large: The Economy of Sustainable Development

While recognition of the massive and increasing impact of human settlement on the natural world has been recognised for centuries (Worster, 1977), the first protection of wildlife conference was not held until 1933 (Jepson & Blythe, 2020). It then took the 1962 publication of Rachael Carson's book *Silent Spring*, which provided the definitive link between commercial pesticides to numerous health dangers, to animate the modern environmental movement. The book alerted the public to environmental concerns and industry disinformation, and ultimately led to the creation of the Environment Protection Authority (EPA) responsible for government regulation of industry and business. Westervelt (2019) argues it also helped launch the 1972 UN Conference on the Human Environment responsible for the Stockholm Declaration (UN Environment Programme, 1972). He notes that "[t]his ground-breaking document made environmental issues global, emphasizing conservation, the redistribution of resources, and state responsibility for environmental damage both within and beyond their borders. It also had zero concern for business." That was to change over the next two decades with the assistance of people like E. Bruce Harrison.

As a young man believing vigorously in business and private enterprise, Harrison joined the Manufacturing Chemists Association (now American Chemistry Council) in 1960, and led the industry's campaign to discredit Carson personally and professionally. Though unsuccessful at both, Harrison learnt that stakeholder partnerships would be better mechanisms to further corporate business interests. He formed the E. Bruce Harrison & Co. public relations firm in 1973, as the first company specialising in green politics, and aimed at advising corporate clients about environmental issues and activist groups. It became one of the top ten PR firms in the US and counted among its clients General Motors, BP America, Monsanto, Ford Motor, American Petroleum Institute, RJ Reynolds Tobacco, Union Carbide, Phillips Petroleum, Philip Morris, Unocal, and Uniroyal Chemical.

Harrison's modus operandi was developing ostensibly public interest programmes of diverse stakeholders, a partnership of labour, agriculture, industry, and the polity, apparently working for better environmental solutions together. Aronczyk and Espinoza (2022) argue that Harrison positioned corporate environmentalism as a pragmatic alternative to environmentalists' "hot-headed" rhetoric. He was adept at reframing the issues or "changing the conversation," something he did so effectively when, following the global oil shocks, he "reframed the 1970s auto emissions debate from one of fuel efficiency to one of consumer preferences" (Aronczyk, 2022). Another example was his creation of the National Environment Development Association (NEDA), which although purportedly pro-environmental, was actually a coalition of chemical, mining, oil, gas, and agricultural companies, industry-friendly politicians, and unions. The NEDA worked to embed Harrison's reframed view of the environment as a balancing of environmental, health, and economic growth, rather than as something in need of conservation and protection (Aronczyk, 2022). NEDA's stated mission was to "gather and disseminate information relating to environment and economic policy issues; inform policy makers and the general public on the need for the balancing of environmental and economic policy." The ultimate goal was to foster soft commitments to sustainability instead of succumbing to environmental regulations policed by government like the EPA's Clean Air Act of 1975—which incidentally, it continues to fight today. By appearing to extend the olive branch in contentious environmental disputes, Harrison believed business could take the role of the reasonable and rational party, while counterposing antagonistic responses by environmentalists as unreasonable and extreme. Recycling campaigns, Environmental Social and Governance (ESG) performance metrics, and eco-friendly consumer products preserved free-market neoliberal optimism in the face of mounting pollution and greenhouse gas emissions. Harrison's critics believe he actively derailed environmentalism for more than four decades, and the approach he pioneered has come to be known as "greenwashing." Aronczyk and Espinoza (2021) argue that he is one of the principal actors responsible for embedding growthist economics into sustainability such that sustainable development is now an unqueried orthodoxy, all while greenhouse gas emissions continue to rise and biodiversity continues to decline.

As the climate crisis became more acute towards the late 1980s, Harrison used his familiar modus operandi to help develop the Global Climate Coalition (GCC) (1989–2001), the largest US industry group of fossil fuel producers and users. It was formed in response to the creation in 1988 of the UN's Intergovernmental Panel on Climate Change (IPCC). Harrison's PR firm ran the GCC, which included Exxon Mobil, The American Petroleum Institute, the National Coal Association, United States Chamber of Commerce, and the American Forest & Paper Association as its founding members among many others. At the same time, he partnered with Brussels-based public affairs consultancy, Andersson Elffers Felix (AEF) to form AEF/Harrison International; later the name was changed to EnviroComm in 1994. The agency created an international network of PR firms to use the same corporate messaging on environmental problems and aimed to provide "an early warning system" of the European Union's environmental policy for client companies (Aronczyk & Espinoza, 2021; Westervelt, 2021). The GCC questioned the climate science, sowing doubt, and strategised ways to contain and limit government environmental legislation, in much the same way as the tobacco companies had for so long thrown doubt on the links between smoking and lung cancer (Oreskes, 2010). The GCC registered as a non-governmental organisation to attend United Nations Climate Change Conferences and were well represented at the 1992 United Nations Conference on Environment and Development (UNCED)—the Earth Summit in Rio de Janeiro. Here, the GCC and Harrison himself (invited to attend by Rio Conference Secretary, oil man Maurice Strong, as an international PR consultant to the major corporations also in attendance), helped shape the primary international, intergovernmental forum for negotiating the global response to climate change, the UN Framework Convention on Climate Change (UNFCCC) (Aronczyk & Espinoza, 2021).

The UNFCCC sought to reduce atmospheric concentrations of greenhouse gases to prevent dangerous anthropogenic interference with Earth's climate system, at the same time promoting adaption and mitigation of climate change and calling for ongoing scientific research and regular meetings (the COPs) and policy agreements (including the Kyoto Protocol and the Paris Agreement). Harrison worked to see that targets and timetables were kept out of the treaty so that economic growth could continue to proceed relatively unhindered. Westervelt (2021) argues that the 20 years between the Stockholm Declaration in 1972 and the 1992 UN conference in Rio saw business, through Harrison's advocacy (and that of others), fully integrate neoliberal economics into the international approach to climate and environmental issues:

> At the Rio summit, there was none of the urgency or directness of the Stockholm Declaration. Gone, too, was the emphasis on government regulation—replaced by a sort of big-tent approach that included business interests and prioritized compromise. (Westervelt, 2021)

Conservation and protection were out, and business success was in. This is also apparent in Adelman's (2018) claim made above, that the idea of sustainable development was already articulated in the 1987 WCED document *Our Common Future* (the so-called "Brundtland Commission"), five years prior to Rio. The Rio conference also created the Business Charter for Sustainable Development (BCSD) at the direct suggestion of Maurice Strong. Harrison was centrally involved in the events leading up to the conference as well as the preparation of the BCSD. The BCSD elaborated a voluntary code of conduct for environmental management (the Charter) adherence to which was promoted as the international business community's commitment to environmental sustainability. Of the 203 companies and business organisations worldwide that had signed on to the Charter by March 1991, 37 were US companies; and of these 37, more than half were clients of E. Bruce Harrison & Co. (Aronczyk & Espinoza, 2021).

Interestingly, SDG13 aims to "take urgent action to combat climate change and its impact." One of its five targets is implementing the UNFCCC. Given the discussion above, it must be concluded that business (and hence, neoliberalism), and E. Bruce Harrison, have their fingerprints all over the SDGs. It is also important to recognise that post the GFC, business and industry involvement in the SDGs have become private–public partnerships aimed at leveraging the enormous financial reserves of asset managers like BlackRock Inc. as mechanisms for their achievement, the so-called "green finance." For example, Gabor (2020) argues that the shift in the development agenda can be conceptualised as the Wall Street Consensus (WSC), an emerging "Development as Derisking" paradigm that reframes the (Post) Washington Consensus…in the language of the Sustainable Development Goals, and identifies global finance as *the* actor critical to achieving the SDGs (p. 3).

Derisking here means governments guaranteeing enormous quantities of (largely Western) asset management funds against any risks incurred while investing in SDG projects in the Global South and other developing sites. In the same year as the release of the SDGs, the 2015 United Nations Financing for Development (FfD) conference in Addis Ababa sought ways to finance them. Confronted with daunting projections of trillions of dollars required, and the inability of the developing public sectors to raise such funds, agreement was reached for private funding: Neoliberalism again! The Global Infrastructure Forum was established and led by the multilateral development banks (MDBs) and the UN. In 2017, securitisation or derisking was adopted by the forum as the new financing model for MDB SDG infrastructure projects. The FfD Action Agenda became the "Billions to Trillions" strategy, which aims to deploy billions of dollars of public resources to mobilise trillions in private finance to achieve the SDGs.

Gabor (2020) (also Dafermos et al., 2021) believe this approach increases financial vulnerability in the Global South, while doing little to achieve the SDGs and climate-aligned development. More likely, they argue, it will accelerate the structural transformation of local financial systems towards neoliberal, market-based finance. It is also a harbinger of another neoliberal aim, that is, the net transfer of wealth from the public to the private sector. Dafermos et al. (2021) also warn that under the promise of "building a private finance system for net zero," COP26 hardwires the WSC regime of "derisking" into global climate initiatives. For Wainwright and Mann (2018), this means a blatant attempt to re-orient the institutional mechanisms of the State towards protecting the political order of financial neoliberal capitalism against climate justice movements and Green New Deal initiatives. Not only does the WSC become the new hegemonic approach to sustainable development, Gabor (2022) believes, it is potentially the new form of capitalism. Much work remains to be done to map, and understand better, such developments to evaluate the consequences, and to consider alternative approaches to economics that take planetary limits into account, e.g., Kate Raworth's "doughnut" model (Raworth, 2017).

3.7   *Zeitenwende*: Ways Forward for the New Era

Something is not functioning properly if humanity has changed the conditions for life to thrive, where multitudes of species are dying out and the climate is rapidly changing. Something is very wrong if we are continuing to educate children to continue to "conquer" nature. (Smith & Watson, 2020, p. 7)

Education is one of the key vehicles for delivering and enacting the SDGs, and the intention of this chapter has been to uncover their historicity and genealogy so that educators understand the liberal and neoliberal structures that permeate them.

Education is, of course, permeated in the same way, as a number of other chapters in this volume point out. We are not advocating that educators ignore or abandon the SDGs. Rather, that they are aware of these deeper structures if they are to reflect on critically, and make informed decisions about referring to, and using, the SDGs in their work.

With this understanding, educators can use the SDGs in more nuanced ways that also take account of and include perspectives that move towards a more inclusive, earth-centred perspective for education. For example, the framework offered by EfS (Australian Government Department of the Environment Water Heritage & the Arts, 2009; Sterling, 2001) provides an alternative underpinning. EfS is not centred in an ideology that promotes continued technology-mediated economic growth enabled by the free market as the solution to sustainability. Although EfS acknowledges that technology has an important role to play, it needs to be used in the service of a wider ecological framework, and that the continued flourishing of life cannot be achieved through technological solutions alone. Rather than merely reproductive of neoliberalism (Smith & Watson, 2019), it is explicitly critical, activist, and socially transformative. The principles of EfS link the environmental, social, cultural, and economic spheres with an expanded emphasis on integrated and holistic thinking, futures, and ecological and social justice. They are enacted through systems thinking, collaboration, ethics and values, critical thinking, and life-long learning. They actively encourage reflection and critique of the assumptions, worldviews, myths, and metaphors underpinning business-as-usual education and its contribution to unsustainability through promoting over-consumption (Smith, 2007; Smith & Watson, 2018). A key document that aligns with EfS principles and offers a clear way forward is the *Earth Charter* [n.d.], discussed by Clugston and Corcoran in this volume. Formulated over 20 years ago, the *Earth Charter* is based on sixteen principles that seek to inspire a new sense of global interdependence and shared responsibility for the wellbeing of the whole of humanity, the greater community of life, and future generations. It is a vision of hope and a call to action. Scholz's *zeitenwinde* is long overdue.

References

Adelman, S. (2018). The sustainable development goals, anthropocentrism and neoliberalism. In D. French & L. Kotzé (Eds.), *Sustainable Development Goals: Law, theory and implementation* (pp. 15–40). Edward Elgar.

Aronczyk, M. (2022, March 15). *New books in critical theory: An interview with Melissa Aronczyk.* https://newbooksnetwork.com/a-strategic-nature

Aronczyk, M., & Espinoza, M. (2021). Sustainable communication: Green PR and the export of corporate environmentalism, 1989–1997. *Environmental Sociology, 5*(3), 308–322. https://doi.org/10.1080/23251042.2018.1564455

Aronczyk, M., & Espinoza, M. (2022). *A strategic nature: Public relations and the politics of American environmentalism.* Oxford University Press.

Australian Government Department of the Environment Water Heritage and the Arts. (2009). *Living sustainably: The Australian Government's national action plan for education for sustainability*. Commonwealth of Australia. http://www.environment.gov.au/system/files/resources/13887ab8-7e03-4b3e-82bb-139b2205a0af/files/national-action-plan.pdf

Australian Government Department of Foreign Affairs and Trade. (2018). *2030 agenda for sustainable development*. https://www.dfat.gov.au/aid/topics/development-issues/2030-agenda/Pages/sustainable-development-goals/

Belda-Miguel, S., Boni, A., & Calabuig, C. (2019). SDG localisation and decentralised development aid: Exploring opposing discourses and practices in Valencia's aid sector. *Journal of Human Development and Capabilities, 20*(4), 386–402. https://doi.org/10.1080/19452829.2019.1624512

Bhambra, G. (2021). A polity divided: Empire, nation, and the construction of the British welfare state. *The Annual British Journal of Sociology Lecture*. London School of Economics and Politics. https://www.lse.ac.uk/lse-player?id=cd669ce6-f06c-4cfa-aa1e-e5d497df9fcd

Birch, K. (2015). Neoliberalism: The whys and wherefores … and future directions. *Sociology Compass, 9*(7), 571–584.

Borchert, H., Schütz, T., & Verbovszky, J. (2022, October 18). "Unchain my heart." A defense industrial policy agenda for Germany's zeitenwende. *Z Außen Sicherheitspolit, 15*(4), 429–451. https://doi.org/10.1007/s12399-022-00926-4. Epub ahead of print. PMCID: PMC9579649.

Bruff, I. (2014). The rise of authoritarian neoliberalism. *Rethinking Marxism, 26*(1), 113–129.

Carson, R. (1962). *Silent spring*. Houghton Mifflin Harcourt.

Cooper, M. (2017). *Family values: Between neoliberalism and the new social conservatism*. Princeton University Press.

Cowley, J. (2022, March 29). *What Is "Britishness"—And does it still matter?* [Audio podcast]. New Statesman. https://www.newstatesman.com/podcasts/new-statesman-podcast/2022/03/what-is-britishness-and-does-it-still-matter-with-gary-younge-jeremy-deller-and-jason-cowley

Dafermos, Y., Gabor, D., & Michell, J. (2021). The Wall Street consensus in pandemic times: What does it mean for climate-aligned development? *Canadian Journal of Development Studies/Revue Canadienne D'études du Développement, 42*(1–2), 1–14. https://doi.org/10.1080/02255189.2020.1865137

Davies, W. (2016, September/October). The new neoliberalism. *New Left Review*. https://newleftreview.org/issues/ii101/articles/william-davies-the-new-neoliberalism

Davis, W. (2017). Elite power under advanced neoliberalism. *Theory, Culture & Society, 34*(5–6), 227–250.

Deneen, P. J. (2018). *Why liberalism failed*. Yale University Press.

Duncombe, C., & Dunne, T. (2018). After the liberal world order. *International Affairs, 94*(1), 25–42.

Earth Charter. (n.d.). https://earthcharter.org/

Flew, T. (2014). Six theories of neoliberalism. *Thesis Eleven, 122*(1), 49–71.

Foucault, M. (2008). *The birth of biopolitics*. Lectures at the Collège de France 1978–1979. Palgrave Macmillan.

Fukuyama, F. (1992). *The end of history and the last man*. Free Press.

Gabor, D. (2020). *The Wall Street consensus*. SocArXiv wab8m, Center for Open Science. https://doi.org/10.31219/osf.io/wab8m

Gabor, D. (2022, February 4). *Financial empire* [Audio podcast]. The Dig podcast. https://www.listennotes.com/podcasts/the-dig/financial-empire-w-daniela-_ZIsRgN2QWu/

Gilbert, J. (2013). What kind of thing is neoliberalism? *New Formations, 80–81*, 7–22.

Hamilton, C. (2015). The technofix is in: A critique of "An Ecomodernist Manifesto". *Earth Island Journal*. http://clivehamilton.com/the-technofix-is-in-a-critique-of-an-ecomodernist-manifesto/

Havertz, R. (2018). Right-wing populism and neoliberalism in Germany: The AfD's embrace of Ordoliberalism. *New Political Economy, 24*(3), 385–403. https://doi.org/10.1080/13563467.2018.1484715

Hayek, F. (1944). *The road to serfdom*. Routledge Press.

Hayek, F. (1988). *The fatal conceit*. University of Chicago Press.

Hickel, J. (2019). The contradiction of the Sustainable Development Goals: Growth versus ecology on a finite planet. *Sustainable Development, 27*(5), 873–884. https://doi.org/10.1002/sd.1947

Jahn, B. (2021, February 16). *"World on the Edge": The crisis of the Western liberal order* [Audio podcast]. London School of Economics and Politics. https://www.lse.ac.uk/lse-player?id=168 d8077-b7df-4eea-92c3-2767407d020

Jepson, P., & Blythe, C. (2020). *Rewilding: The radical new science of ecological recovery*. Icon Books.

Innset, O. (2020). *Reinventing liberalism. The politics, philosophy and economics of early neoliberalism (1920–1947)*. Springer.

Irwin, A., & Scali, E. (2007). Action on the social determinants of health: A historical perspective. *Global Public Health, 2*(3), 235–256. https://doi.org/10.1080/17441690601106304

Kopnina, H. (2020). Anthropocentrism: Problem of human-centered ethics in sustainable development Goals. In W. L. Filho, P. G. Özuyar, P. J. Pace, A. M. Azul, L. Brandli, U. Azeiteiro, & T. Wall (Eds.), *Encyclopedia of the UN Sustainable Development Goals. Life on land* (pp. 48–57). Springer Major Reference Works. https://link.springer.com/referenceworkentry/10.1007/978-3-319-71065-5_105-1

McCloskey, S. (2019). The Sustainable Development Goals, neoliberalism and NGOs: It's time to pursue a transformative path to social justice. *Policy and practice: A development education review, 29*, 152–159. https://www.developmenteducationreview.com/sites/default/files/Full%20Issue%2029%20final-1.pdf#page=155

McManus, M. (2020). *A critical legal examination of liberalism and liberal rights*. Palgrave Macmillan.

Mirowski, P. (2014). *The political movement that dared not speak its own name: The neoliberal thought collective under erasure*. Institute for New Economic Thinking. https://www.ineteconomics.org/uploads/papers/WP23-Mirowski.pdf

Mirowski, P. (2020). Never let a serious crisis go to waste politics. *Politics Theory Other #85*. https://soundcloud.com/poltheoryother/85-never-let-a-serious-crisis-go-to-waste-w-philip-mirowski

Morrow, R. (2010). A critical analysis of the US causes of the Global Financial Crisis of 2007–2008. *Australian Marxist Review, 53*. https://archive.cpa.org.au/amr/53/index.html

Oreskes, N. (2010). *Merchants of doubt: How a handful of scientists obscured the truth on issues from tobacco smoke to global warming*. Bloomsbury Press.

Peck, J., Brenner, N., & Theodore, N. (2018). Actually existing neoliberalism. In D. Cahill, M. Cooper, M. Konings, & D. Primrose (Eds.), *The Sage handbook of neoliberalism* (pp. 3–15). Sage.

Peck, J., & Theodore, N. (2019). Still neoliberalism? *South Atlantic Quarterly, 118*(2), 245–265.

Rashid, L. (2019). Entrepreneurship education and Sustainable Development Goals: A literature review and a closer look at fragile states and technology-enabled approaches. *Sustainability, 11*(19), 5343. https://doi.org/10.3390/su11195343

Raworth, K. (2017). *Doughnut economics: Seven ways to think like a 21st-century economist*. Random House.

Rousseau, J.-J. (2018). The discourses and other early political writings. In V. Gourevitch (Ed.), *Cambridge texts in the history of political thought*. Cambridge University Press (Original work published 1755).

Runciman, D. (2020). Hobbes on the state [Audio podcast]. *Talking politics: The history of ideas*. https://play.acast.com/s/history-of-ideas/hobbesonthestate

Runciman, D. (2021). Questions and answers [Audio podcast]. *Talking politics: The history of ideas*. https://play.acast.com/s/history-of-ideas/historyofideasqanda

Schulz-Forberg, H. (2020). Embedded early neoliberalism: Transnational origins of the agenda of liberalism reconsidered. In D. Plehwe, Q. Slobodian, & P. Mirowski (Eds.), *Nine lives of neoliberalism* (pp. 169–196). Verso.

Simpson, J. (2019). *Permanent revolution: The reformation and the illiberal roots of liberalism.* Belknap Press of Harvard University Press.

Slobodian, Q. (2018). *Globalists: The end of empire and the birth of neoliberalism.* Harvard University Press.

Slobodian, Q., & Plehwe, D. (2020). Introduction. In D. Plehwe, Q. Slobodian, & P. Mirowski (Eds.), *Nine lives of neoliberalism* (pp. 1–19). Verso.

Steger, M., & James, P. (2020). Disjunctive globalization in the era of the great unsettling. *Theory, Culture & Society, 37*(7–8), 187–203. https://doi.org/10.1177/0263276420957744

Steger, M., & Roy, R. (2021). *Neoliberalism: A very short introduction.* Oxford University Press.

Sterling, S. R. (2001). *Sustainable education: Re-visioning learning and change.* Schumacher Briefings Book 6.

Smith, C. (2007). Education and society: The case for ecoliteracy. *Education and Society, 25*(1), 25–37.

Smith, C., & Watson, J. (2018). STEM: Silver bullet for a viable future or just more flatland? *Journal of Futures Studies, 22*(4), 25–44.

Smith, C., & Watson, J. (2019). Does the rise of STEM education mean the demise of sustainability education? *Australian Journal of Environmental Education, 35*(1), 1–11.

Smith, C., & Watson, J. (2020). From streams to streaming: A critique of the influence of STEM on students' imagination for a sustainable future. *Journal of Applied Teaching and Learning, 3*(1), 21–29.

Tbilisi Declaration. (1977). https://www.gdrc.org/uem/ee/tbilisi.html

Tooze, A. (2021). *Shutdown: How COVID shook the world's economy.* Viking.

United Nations. (n.d.). *Sustainable Development Goals.* https://www.un.org/sustainabledevelopment/sustainable-development-goals/

United Nations. (2015). *Transforming our world: The 2030 agenda for sustainable development.* https://www.refworld.org/docid/57b6e3e44.html

United Nations Conference on Environment and Development. (1992). *Earth summit.* https://sustainabledevelopment.un.org/milestones/unced

United Nations Department of Economic and Social Affairs Sustainable Development. (n.d.). *Goal 4. Ensure inclusive and equitable quality education and promote lifelong learning opportunities for all.* https://sdgs.un.org/goals/goal4Uniter

United Nations Educational, Scientific and Cultural Organization. (2002). *UN decade of ESD.* https://en.unesco.org/themes/education-sustainable-development/what-is-esd/un-decade-of-esd/

United Nations Environment Programme. (1972). *Stockholm Declaration: Declaration on the human environment.* https://wedocs.unep.org/20.500.11822/29567

Wainwright, J., & Mann, G. (2018). *Climate Leviathan: A political theory of our planetary future.* Verso Books.

Westervelt, A. (2019). The case for climate rage. *Popula.* https://popula.com/2019/08/19/the-case-for-climate-rage/

Westervelt, A. (2021, November 17). You can't beat climate change without tackling disinformation. *The Nation.* https://www.thenation.com/article/environment/climate-disinformation-pr/

World Commission on Environment and Development. (1987). *Our common future.* Oxford University Press.

Worster, D. (1977). *Nature's economy: The roots of ecology.* Sierra Club Books.

Chapter 4
On the Right to a Sustainable Education: Philosophical Perspectives and Moral Imperatives

David Moltow and Cassandra Thoars

Abstract It is in the interests of all children everywhere, we wish to say, that they have access to every opportunity to flourish in their childhood. It is also in their interests to have the opportunity to grow into adults who may flourish not only as individuals, but as citizens who are able and disposed to contribute to the sustained (and sustainable) flourishing of their communities, both local and global, including at ecosystemic and planetary levels.

4.1 Introduction

It is in the interests of all children everywhere, we wish to say, that they have access to every opportunity to flourish in their childhood. It is also in their interests to have the opportunity to grow into adults who may flourish not only as individuals, but as citizens who are able and disposed to contribute to the sustained (and sustainable) flourishing of their communities, both local and global, including at ecosystemic and planetary levels. This duality of interests, one might say their inseparability, is embedded in the necessarily symbiotic relation between individuals and their communities, which in turn follows naturally from the self-evidently true proposition that the flourishing of either depends crucially on the flourishing of the other, and that the sustained flourishing of both depends crucially on the ecosystem's capacity to sustain flourishing more generally. It would seem odd to argue that an individual can truly thrive in a moribund society, or that a society can be said truly to be flourishing when its individual members' lives are miserable. It would seem similarly

D. Moltow (✉) · C. Thoars
School of Education, College of Arts, Law, and Education, University of Tasmania, Hobart, TAS 7005, Australia
e-mail: David.Moltow@utas.edu.au

C. Thoars
e-mail: Cassandra.Thoars@utas.edu.au

K. Beasy et al. (eds.), *Education and the UN Sustainable Development Goals*, Education for Sustainability 7,
https://doi.org/10.1007/978-981-99-3802-5_4

odd to suggest that the sustained flourishing of future individuals is a given, considering an ecosystem's declining capacity to sustain their flourishing. However, unless symbiotic decline is intelligently and collectively addressed by present individuals and their societies, the prospects for sustained flourishing seem rather dim.

In light of this, we wish also to say that human flourishing, properly so called, including in terms of symbiosis, is impossible without access to forms of learning that allow humans effectively to navigate the social, moral, political, and environmental complexities of modern living. Such forms of learning also allow them to consider the very idea of flourishing in ways meaningful to their lives, such as to render sensible their approaches to a well lived life. Moreover, through both the depth and breadth of what is known, and via more sophisticated understandings of what is knowable, forms of knowledge have become more complex. It seems unlikely, therefore, that sufficiently elaborate forms of learning can be acquired by children and emerging citizens without access to a cohesive body of contemporary factual, technical, and ethical knowledge.

These forms of knowledge must be synthesised into the application of practical wisdom necessary for flourishing to be obtained for individuals, communities, and ecosystems. This holds, insofar as *human* beings, being the most agentic impactors on global flourishing, can choose, and must choose wisely, how their actions impact ecosystems, not just for their own and their communities' self-interested preservation, but also by reference to the minimal conception of moral goodness entailed in the consideration of all those who stand to be affected by their actions. The application of practical wisdom to relevant forms of flourishing for all organisms that are capable of flourishing is of global importance. It is unlikely, however, that a critical mass of human beings will cultivate sufficient knowledge without organised learning processes. These learning processes are most efficiently deployed via formal education.

4.2 Education as a Human Right and Force for Sustainable Development and Peace

The imperative to sustain flourishing, especially human flourishing, informs the enactment of UNESCO's 2015 17 Sustainable Development Goals (SDGs), which constitute the plan "agreed to by all world leaders to build a greener, fairer, better world by 2030" (UN Women, 2019). The fourth goal (SDG4) centres on education's role in realising this outcome, its realisation serving to "Ensure inclusive and equitable quality education and promote lifelong learning opportunities for all" (United Nations Educational Scientific and Cultural Organization, 2014). According to UNESCO,

> Education liberates the intellect, unlocks the imagination and is fundamental for self-respect. It is the key to prosperity and opens a world of opportunities, making it possible for each of us to contribute to a progressive, healthy society. Learning benefits every human being and should be available to all.

Education is deemed to be important for the protection and promotion of children's interests, and their interests as emerging adults and the inseparable interests of the communities and ecosystems that sustain their potential for flourishing. In articulating its rationale for SDG4, UNESCO considers education to be a "human right and force for sustainable development and peace."

This account of education's moral status that underpins SDG4 entails two values. First, given its universal benefit to "every human being" and the imperative that it be made "available to all," the provision of education is conceived as an entitlement couched in terms of a "human right," which gives rise to duties to ensure its provision. Second, as a "force for sustainable development and peace," education is implied to give rise to corresponding duties on the part of the educated, to direct the benefits of the education to which they are entitled to the realisation of the SDGs more generally. As discussed above, the increasing importance of education in promoting peaceable flourishing through sustainable development seems self-evident. Sustainable development is a global imperative that demands the contribution of active and informed emerging global citizens. It is difficult to see how their efforts to contribute to the sustained achievement of the SDGs can succeed without the careful and deliberate application of the forms of practical wisdom available only through education. Education, therefore, as articulated in SDG4, is itself an imperative upon the realisation of which all flourishing depends. The duty to ensure all children, as emerging citizens who will share the obligations to contribute to the realisation of the SDGs, are given access to quality education is thus a global imperative. Moreover, given the interests it serves to protect and foster, it is a global *moral* imperative.

4.3   Rights, Interests, and Moral Duties

The assumption that education is a *right*, however, connected to the interests of the rights-holders, is less evident. That education promotes the interests of the educated is a notion that underpins the *Convention on the Rights of the Child* [hereafter referred to as the *Convention*] (United Nations, 1989), which codifies children's interests in terms of their "rights." In so doing, it spells out its signatories' agreed duties concerning the opportunities they provide to children in terms of their access to the benefits of education consistent with SDG4. It is important to note that the rights considered in this chapter are not legal rights as such, but *moral* rights, entitlements that derive from interests and which give rise to someone else's moral duty to identify, protect, and promote them on the grounds that the rights-holder is not, or not yet, in a position to do this him- or herself. Legal rights, on the other hand, as H. L. A. Hart argues, are posited under law, and give rise to legal obligations to respect them (Hart, 2012). However, in being posited, the argument here is that their moral underpinning by the rights-holder's interests becomes redundant, except perhaps in arguments that rely on the law's *spirit* to support a judgement. The rights-holder's moral status also becomes redundant as it is superseded by his or her *juridical* status as the recipient of benefit from another who owes a legislated duty to the state, rather than directly in relation to the recipient's legal entitlements. This is an important point which will be explored in detail below. Suffice to say for now that it highlights the difference between one person engaging in a distinctly *moral* relationship with another, in which duties to protect each other's interests are to each other, and the *legal* relationship one has with another, in which one's duties in relation to the other's interests are incidental to one's duty to obey the law.

Education legislation informed by the rights approach entailed in the *Convention* and which underpins SDG4, does just this. The incidental relation between one's duties and another's interests in relation to the distinction between perfect and imperfect duties (O'Neill, 1988). A state that acts in relation to children because it recognises a legal obligation (a "perfect" duty) to protect their rights is operating from a different premise from the state that acts from the motivation to protect or foster those children's interests (an "imperfect" duty). Even when both states may perform the same action which yields the same consequences, each has differently configured moral relationship with those children. This first approach, which treats education as a child's right, also says little about the interests served by a child's education, such as those embedded in the SDGs, and to which states have a more general duty to protect and foster.

Now, this does not mean that, while one has a self-evident legal duty to obey the law, one cannot nevertheless prioritise moral reasoning and choose to recognise and act on a *moral* duty to obey or disobey the law, irrespective of legal imperatives and prospective redress. That is to say, while legally posited and moral duties are, along Hart's (2012) lines, separable, they are not necessarily *separate*. One's motivation to respect another's legal right may be informed, at least in part, by reference to one's recognition of a moral duty to act in accordance with their interests. As discussed below, the implications for education of this distinction are significant. Moreover, instruments such as the *Convention*, which codify the alignment between interests and duties via a system of rights, and whose precepts inform the moral authority of SDG4, render interests vulnerable to the threat of moral redundancy. Which is not to say that they are not worthy of consent and enforcement in the child's interests; only that, in moral terms, the child's interests become redundant. That is to say, when one is motivated to act in relation to a legal or conventional duty to protect a child's right *because the child bears that right*, one's moral duty to protect the child's *interests* are rendered surplus to the action-guiding process. Conversely, as argued below, were one to recognise and exercise a *moral* duty to protect a child's interests, it is the right that becomes morally superfluous. This latter implication informs the chapter's conclusion.

The assumption remains, however, given the significance of education as a right to SDG4, and a key informant of its moral validity, that rights are the moral progeny of their holders' interests, and that duties to protect them are derived therefrom. Arguments concerning the alignment between interests, rights, and duties are seminally encapsulated in legal philosopher Joseph Raz's (1994) position, according to which rights play a mediating role between interests and duties. Raz's argument, grounded on the assumption that the moral relation between interests and duties must be configured via rights, offers a compelling reason to accept the moral probity of arguments concerning children's rights to an education. It appears thus to justify the moral underpinnings of UNESCO's position on children's rights, their codification in the *Convention* (1989), and their reinforcement of SDG4's moral force.

4.4   Are Rights Necessary?

It is the function of philosophy to question such assumptions and arguments such as those advanced by Raz (1994). Analytic moral and political philosophers are interested in interrogating claims concerning the constitution of an organism's best interests, and what moral duties arise from a rationally defensible account of these. Such moral duties can arise either on the part of the organism itself or, more commonly, on the part of other suitably capable organisms whose actions stand to affect its interests either individually, in the case of moral agents or, socio-politically, in the case of moral agencies. Moral agents or agencies are, by definition, free to choose to identify their duties and decide how to enact them in relation to those whose interests stand to be affected by them. It is this freedom that defines their agency and the extent to which it is justified for them to be held morally responsible for their actions. The United Nations Department of Economic and Social Affairs (2015) position on children's rights identifies human beings as the principal rights-holders and the agents through whom the SDGs are to be realised. As such, here we will focus on the moral status of human organisms, notwithstanding the assumption that all organisms are symbiotically interdependent and, in virtue of having interests, are worthy of moral consideration.

In this chapter, we examine the moral status of children's interests insofar as they relate to education, and their connection to children's rights. Beginning with an interrogation of Raz's (1994) implicit justification of the moral status of children's rights, a discussion of Hart's (2012) opposing view of the moral status of rights and of those who bear them, is followed by an examination of Onora O'Neill's (1988) distinction between perfect and imperfect duties. This seems to go to the heart of what matters in terms of one's justification of the moral duty to protect children's interests, and interests more generally, independently of any *right* they have to one's protection. We conclude that the acknowledgement of children's rights to education implied in SDG4, and formalised in instruments such as the *Convention*, offer compelling and legislatively useful codifications of duties associated with children's interests. However, we find that their codification gives rise only to perfect institutional, conventional, or legal duties towards children, and thus fosters a *transactional* rather than a moral relationship between children and those endowed with the capacity, and hence the obligation, to identify, protect, and promote interests that they cannot (yet) themselves identify, protect, and promote.

4.5   Children's Rights and the Interests They Protect

In terms of societal approaches to children's interests, insofar as they can be protected and promoted through education, this may mean, minimally, that institutional barriers to educational opportunities are absent or be removed, so that children are free to access them. For example, inclusive education principles are enacted in schools and education systems such that all children in a jurisdiction have access to at least the minimal benefits afforded by schooling, such that the state of "being a child" (Archard, 2003) is the only requisite. More comprehensively, it may mean not just that barriers to opportunity are minimised or removed, but that these opportunities are created and that children's access to them is *facilitated* by whatever means. Thus, a child's opportunity to develop the ability and disposition to flourish, and so to emerge as a moral agent freely capable of contributing to sustainable flourishing more generally, is not dependent merely on the removal of barriers to access. Rather, the access itself is created by the institutional provision of opportunities intended to further their interests. These opportunities may be afforded by, for example, transport to and from school, specific subject content, targeted skills development, attendance standards, the provision of education-related welfare resources, and so on. Children, we wish to say in relation to what might be called the provision account, are not just free to take up the opportunities to flourish where they exist. Given that it is in their interests to flourish and, on the assumption that not all children are always capable of identifying, protecting, and promoting their own best interests, these opportunities are provided for them by reference to their having a right to them, or to others having a duty to provide them, or to both.

The idea that children be provided with opportunities to flourish, on the assumption that they are not all capable of identifying and protecting their best interests, gives rise to questions of society's duties in relation to children's interests. That is to say, the standard assumption is that those who can identify, protect, and promote their interests have a moral duty to do so (Archard, 2003; Brighouse & McAvoy, 2010; Griffin, 2009). This is because, while all interests are worthy of moral consideration, moral duties of a special character are owed to those unable in a morally relevant way to choose how best to protect their own interests. Hart (1955), as we shall see, supports this, and identifies "animals and babies" (p. 181) as examples of morally significant beings whose vulnerability gives rise to special duties of proper treatment by others. However, because babies and young children have interests that give rise to others' moral duties to protect or treat them with special consideration, does this mean they have a *right* according to which they are entitled to this treatment? Legally, perhaps, if the law posits this right. However, the question remains: what gives such rights their moral authority? By definition, a person who acts morally acts out of the recognition of an obligation to choose to act in a particular way because it is morally right (however construed), not because the law compels him or her to do so. What might ground a child's right such that it legitimises one's moral obligation to protect it?

4.6   Raz and the Moral Status of Rights

As noted earlier, Raz's (1994) argument supports the position according to which the possession of interests constitutes sufficient reason to treat children as rights-holders. According to Raz (1994), rights:

> indicate intermediate conclusions between statements of the right-holder's interests and another's duty. To say that a person has a right is to say that an interest of his is sufficient grounds for holding another to be subject to a duty, i.e., a duty to take some action which will serve that interest, or a duty the very existence of which serves such interest. One justifies a statement that a person has a right by pointing to an interest of his and to reasons why it is to be taken so seriously. One uses the statement that a right exists to derive … conclusions about the duties of other people towards the right-holder. (p. 243)

For Raz (1994), therefore, rights are the key progenitors of duties. As opposed to Hart's view, which as we shall see justifies a moral agent's duties to others by direct reference to those others having interests, rather than being mediated through rights, Raz first connects interests directly to rights and only then, transitively, to duties. Thus, for Raz, one has relevant duties because others have rights, and they have rights because they have interests. Rights thus *mediate* between interests and duties; they are "intermediate conclusions between statements of the right-holder's interests and another's duty" (p. 243). Here, Raz is making a point of logic. From the statement: *One has a relevant interest*, we can draw the conclusion: *Therefore, one has a corresponding right*. This statement serves as an intermediate conclusion when the further conclusion can be drawn: *One is therefore owed a (corresponding) duty.*

It is important to note here that Raz (1994) is developing the groundwork for an argument supporting the moral authority of legal rights, for their moral integrity, as it were, from which derives our obligation to obey. On Raz's account, rights serve a principally jurisprudential purpose in connecting duties to interests through the device of the intermediate conclusion between them. Interests are thus protected by the legal enforcement of connected rights which others have a legal duty to respect. That is to say, the right is the entity which is protected by a law, the moral justification of the enforcement of which is legitimised by the moral worthiness of the interest it protects.

In this way, Raz's (1994) account of the duty-compelling character of rights, given their juridical status, is consistent with a naturalistic account of the law's moral authority. According to natural law theory, a law commands our compliance if its demands are consistent with a moral precept that gives rise to our obligation to obey it (Finnis, 2011; Freeman, 2014). A law's authority, therefore, one's moral obligation to obey it as opposed to its power to compel one to obey it, is derived from its relation to objective morality. For example, a morally decent person refrains from killing an innocent other because it is morally wrong to do so, and not because he or she fears legal sanction were he or she, as it were, to be caught in the act. That such a law is consistent with such a moral principle, however, is what legitimises the sanction were someone caught breaking it. Tying the argument back to interests, a naturalistic transitive relation can be discerned between interests and legal rights: because one has interests, one has a natural right to have them protected; natural rights inform the duty-compelling authority of legal rights; therefore, one's interests are protected by others having a legal duty to protect them. Were we to replace *legal* duty with *conventional* duties, we can see how Raz's account grounds in children's interests the codification of their educational rights such as those that underpin SDG4. Thus, while parties to such instruments have a quasi-legal obligation to do what they agreed in principle to do (protect the children's rights nominated therein), rights so codified derive their authority from the signatories' compulsion to honour the terms of an agreement, rather than directly in relation to each other's interests or to the distinctly moral duties to which they give rise.

4.7 Freedom and Hart's Rejection of Natural Rights

The question remains, however: their legal status aside, are rights as such *morally* necessary? It must be noted here, that any acceptance of the force of arguments such as that crafted by Raz (1994) is not the product of an unruffled consensus. Raz's account of the interest-derived status of rights and their duty-guiding power operates in dialectical opposition to perhaps the most compelling counterargument in relation to moral rights presented by Hart (1955). Hart argues that there are no natural moral rights, holding the position that rights, as entitled claims on others' duties properly so called, are posited and, as such, are legal or conventional. However, if there were such things as natural moral rights, there are compelling reasons not to confer them on children. This is because children fall into the category occupied by those unable or not yet capable of protecting their own interests, such as "animals and babies" (Hart, 1955, p. 180). For Hart, operating in a liberal context, freedom is a basic moral value, and he sees it as the only *natural* entitlement worthy of protection and which underlies consideration of all further rights which, for their legitimacy, would be posited under law. According to Hart (1955),

> Any human being capable of choice (1) has the right to forbearance on the part of all others from the use of coercion or restraint against him save to hinder coercion or restraint and (2) is at liberty to do any action which is not coercing or restraining or designed to injure other persons. (p. 175)

In other words, consistent with liberal values that characterise Western democracy, Hart (1955) argues that human beings' freedom to live as they choose, or as they consent to be governed, is the most fundamental idea that underpins moral and legal consideration of entitlements that are to be protected under law as rights. While these legal rights may be consistent with the moral principles that inform their being posited, their authority is derived from their juridical status rather than their relation to those moral principles. For Raz (1994), any right derives its moral integrity and authoritative claim on duty by reference to the interests it protects, and applies equally to all holders of that right. For Hart, on the other hand, given the fundamental value of freedom, and his denial of natural rights and the necessity of moral integrity, rights are posited under law and derive their authority by reference to the integrity of the judicial or legislative process according to which they were created or conferred. As we saw above, however, not everyone is entitled to the fundamental right to freedom, irrespective of their interests.

For Hart (1955), "rights are essentially guarantees of various freedoms to direct one's own life, but not those of others" (as cited in Brighouse & McAvoy, 2010, p. 75). Given that rights-holders' freedoms are so protected, it follows that they are also guaranteed under law the freedom to waive their rights were they to choose another value that overrides them. For example, a mortally ill person may have the posited right to medical care; but if freedom is the "trumping" right, and he or she has retained the capacity for informed decision making, he or she may choose to waive the right to medical intervention and be allowed to die naturally, or to commit suicide. Waiving the right to intervention thus also waives the duty for those who can intervene to do so. Moreover, given the inseparability of freedom and responsibility, a person who freely acts so as unlawfully to impede another's rights may be found, in being held responsible for his or her actions, to have forfeited his or her right to freedom (if charged with a relevant crime, and sentenced accordingly).

Hart's (1955, 2012) argument rests on the premise that those who are entitled to the most basic right to freedom are those who are capable of recognising, protecting, and promoting their own interests. Given freedom's status as a basic value, however, it also constitutes a capable person's most basic interest, and they must be afforded the freedom to choose which other interests, if any, they seek to protect or promote, or to be protected and promoted by others. As shown in the example above, this means that they remain free to waive the duties of others to protect interests on their behalf. This is consistent with the premise that grounds John Stuart Mill's (1974) argument that constitutes the foundation for modern liberalism:

> If a person possesses any tolerable amount of common sense and experience, his own mode of laying out his existence is the best, not because it is the best in itself, but because it is his own mode. (pp. 132–133)

It is here that Hart's (1955) caveat concerning the attributes of those on whom rights ought to be conferred is brought into sharp focus. If the conferral of the most basic right is due only to those who can for themselves recognise, protect, and promote their interests in ways of their choosing, independently of any objective measure of "best," what of those who cannot (e.g., "animals and babies")? Hart (1955) argues that they are not entitled to this right, on the grounds that it makes no moral sense to allow relevant freedoms, especially the freedom to waive other's duties of care towards them, to those who have not yet developed, or who may have lost, the capacity to recognise and protect their own interests. Children who have not yet developed this capacity fall into this category and, as such, are not to be regarded as rights-holders. As Brighouse and McAvoy (2010) put it, on Hart's view, "the inappropriateness of considering children rights-bearers is obvious: crucially, this is because they are not competent choosers, are vulnerable, and are dependent" (p. 75). They are, therefore, not capable of making well-informed, rationally defensible decisions about which rights to claim or waive. They are incapable of exercising "the discretion that rights-as-freedom give in ways that enhance the quality of their lives" (Brighouse & McAvoy, 2010, p. 75). On this argument, children lack autonomy properly so called: they do not yet possess the moral agency required either to waive the duties others owe to their care, or to be held responsible for their actions.

While some philosophers argue against this premise (e.g., the "child liberationists" informed by the work of Cohen, 1980), it is not inconsistent with institutional views that dominate some Western societies. For example, in Australia, children cannot be held criminally responsible for their actions if they are under the age of fourteen (Moltow & Thoars, 2019). This is entailed in the legal principle of *doli incapax* (literally, "incapable of evil"), according to which children under a certain age are assumed to be incapable of evil intent (*mens rea*) and, so, cannot be held legally responsible for their actions, the motivations that informed them, or their consequences. The exception is where the principle can be rebutted, if the child is older than ten years and it can be proven that he or she possessed relevant knowledge of their conduct's moral significance, and understood that it was "seriously and morally wrong" so to have acted at the time of the offence (Moltow & Thoars, 2019). Along these lines, children (rebuttably under fourteen, but unconditionally ten years or under), lack the moral agency required for them to be held responsible for their choices, and so their freedom to exercise relevant discretion is withheld.

However, does a child's lack of moral agency, on the basis of which his or her basic moral right is withheld, undermine that child's moral status? That is to say, if children are to be denied rights on the grounds that they are not in a position to be held morally responsible for their free choices, is their moral status also undermined? Recall that, for Raz (1994), the duty one owes to protect the interests of another derives from the other having a right according to which the claim on one's duty is legitimised. In the case of children, this is uncontroversial and Raz's account dovetails neatly with the reasoning that underpins the *Convention* and which informs the rights approach embedded in SDG4. For Hart, (2012) on the other hand, rights are accorded only to those who are granted freedom on the basis of their moral agency. For Raz, therefore, the locus of duty is in the right; but if on Hart's view children have no rights, from where does one's duty to them derive? Crucially, as we saw above, Hart argues that children ought not to be given the freedom, thus the right, to waive our duties to recognise, protect and promote their interests on their behalf, given that they are incapable of doing this themselves. One's duties to children, then, must arise from their moral status, their worthiness of moral consideration, rather than from any notion of rights that may be posited on their behalf.

4.8 Moral Status Derives from Morally Relevant Interests

The possession of moral status, worthiness of moral consideration, is not limited to moral agents with the capacity to make autonomous, well-informed, reasonable decisions concerning what to believe, do, and feel, and to act accordingly. Rather, moral status is conferred on someone by reference to them having interests, and thus by being owed consideration of how those interests are affected by the beliefs, actions, and attitudes of others.

Moral status is possessed independently of moral agency. Moral agency is the capacity freely to make morally relevant decisions concerning what to believe, do, and feel. This capacity renders one accountable for the impact on others' interests of those decisions, at least in part because the agent understands or can imagine, or has the capacity to understand or to imagine, how others may be affected by them. Moral agency is thus connected to freedom and bound tightly with responsibility. This is because it makes no sense to hold a person responsible, in other words to blame or to praise her, for actions or consequences the control over which, for whatever reason, she has no capacity and, hence, can exercise no agency. But does this mean that such a person is not owed moral consideration of his or her interests? It is by having interests, and being owed moral consideration thereby, that confers moral status. As we have seen, children who lack moral agency cannot reasonably be held responsible for their actions and are therefore denied by Hart (1955) the moral right to freedom. However, this does not affect their non-agentic moral status, which grounds all arguments in relation to moral duties owed to them, including Hart's own. Freedom is thus not a necessary condition of moral status in the way having interests is, and so the absence of the relevant right to freedom, as argued by Hart, does not render children ethically marginalised. They have interests, some or all of which they cannot themselves recognise, foster, or protect, and it is on this basis that moral status is conferred and from which duties to them are derived.

Moral status gives rise to more than the duty to others merely to *consider* the impact on their interests of our beliefs, actions, and attitudes. Where the moral agent can choose whether and how to *act* in respect of others' interests, it seems uncontroversial to argue that they have a moral duty to choose to perform the "most right" action (this is entailed in the definition of moral action as "that which one ought to do"). The recognition of moral status thus carries normative implications concerning what one ought or ought not to do in consideration of others' interests (in other words, the duties one owes them).

Take, for example, an unconscious person, who is incapable of acting freely in a morally relevant way, and thus while unconscious he may be said to lack moral agency (or indeed any relevant form of freedom). The unconscious person has interests even though he is not aware of them at the time and cannot exercise agency to act in their respect. However, the absence of moral agency does not imply that he is not owed a moral duty of consideration by whomever is able positively or negatively to affect his interests. In other words, his lack of agency does not entirely diminish his interests, nor does it forfeit his entitlement to moral consideration, even while unconscious.

For instance, in terms of negative effects on interests, if we consider stealing to be morally wrong because it deprives a person of their property against their will, or because it contradicts a personal value, or breaches a universal moral principle, we could hardly deem it to be morally praiseworthy to steal the unconscious person's expensive watch, merely because he cannot autonomously make a well-informed, rationally defensible decision concerning how to feel or what to do about it being stolen.

We are not excused from moral disapprobation, simply because the person from whom we are stealing the watch cannot express his will to keep it, or because he is are not in a position to waive our moral duty to refrain from stealing it from him. On the other hand, in terms of the positive effects of our actions on their interests, if the unconscious person is in no position to recognise, protect, and foster his own interests, but we are in a position to do so, then our moral duty to consider them when deciding whether and how best to act obtains despite his lack of agency. If in his presence, for example, we notice that he is having breathing difficulties because of the way he is lying, and if we have the knowledge and capacity to ease his breathing and perhaps save his life by placing him in the recovery position and summoning medical assistance, we could hardly deem it morally praiseworthy to refrain from doing so, all other things being equal, merely because he cannot autonomously make a well-informed, rationally defensible decision concerning how to feel or what to do about his imminent danger. Importantly, the unconscious person is incapable of making a well-informed, rationally defensible, and morally acceptable decision to waive our duty to refrain from stealing his watch, or to reposition him, or to summon medical assistance and save his life if we can. A moral duty is a moral duty, whether or not we are forgiven by the recipient our obligation to discharge it.

Thus, we may say that a person who is owed any form of moral consideration by reference to their having interests has moral status thereby. Irrespective of their incapacity to perform morally relevant actions for which they can reasonably be held accountable, therefore, what confers moral status upon them is the fact that morally relevant actions may be performed by those who do have the capacity to make well-informed, rationally defensible, morally appropriate decisions to recognise, protect, and foster their interests on their behalf.

Thus it must be with children. On Hart's (1955) view, we would not confer upon a child the basic right to self-determination, either because of her status as a child, or because she has not yet reached a point at which she can reasonably be expected to make autonomous, well-informed, rationally defensible, morally appropriate decisions about what is in her best interests to believe, do, or feel (Archard, 2003). However, this does not mean, and Hart does not imply, that her best interests ought not to be recognised, protected, and fostered by those who are able, and so have a duty, to do so.

4.9 Moral Relations Rather Than Legal or Conventional Transactions

Revisiting the example above, we can see that, for Raz (1994), our moral duty to consider and attend to the unconscious person's medical interests is justified by his having the right, to be entitled, to have his interests considered and attended to. It is his *right*, not our duty, that derives from his moral status (as an interest bearer), and any moral duty he is owed by others derives from, and corresponds to, this right. However, were the locus of duty to be in the unconscious person's interests, then the relationship between his interests and our duties becomes one of moral directness. In strictly moral terms, we engage directly with him rather than through his rights.

Our moral conscience thus informs how we act and, rather than merely *transacting* a duty in relation to a codified imperative to obey a law or comply with a convention. To transact a duty risks impoverishing the nature of our relational duties to children, rendering actions compliant rather than moral. Rights, as discussed above, render the moral imperative to protect interests redundant. Contrariwise, recognising and acting directly out of care for another's interests renders rights superfluous. Hart's (1955) account retains the moral value of interests and centres the locus of duty on the agent's will to act morally in relation to those interests. Moreover, this seems to avoid the reductive transactionalism entailed in arguments for rights. The transaction implied in the exchange: "Why are you looking after me?" "Because I am simply discharging a duty to do so" seems to omit something essentially humane from the relationship between the interlocutors. Focussing on interests and the duties to which they give rise rather than rights leaves open the consideration of richer and more humanely appealing accounts of moral relations, such as those embedded in theories of character (e.g., Slote, 1983, 1992, 2007) and care (e.g., Noddings, 1984, 1992, 1995, 2006). It also allows further consideration of the nature of the more general duties one owes to those whose interests one has an obligation to protect.

Onora O'Neill (1988) refers to actions performed out of a symmetrical relation between rights and duties as the results of "perfect" obligations (p. 187). Were we to limit our understandings of duties, say, to those forms of compliance which derive from the codified rights in the *Convention* and, by implication, those which underpin SDG4, we would be acting in order to fulfil perfect obligations that apply to all rights-holders nominated therein, because the rights have been thus posited. The reduction to transactionalism here is clear. However, O'Neill identifies "imperfect" obligations (p. 189) as grounding the special moral relationship one has with others whose interests are worthy of one's moral consideration, independent of the requirements entailed in perfect obligations such as those identified by rights. A rights approach to SDG4, in compliance with other instruments such as the *Convention*, a teacher's employment contract, education legislation, and so on, may give rise to a perfect obligation to help a child acquire knowledge or learn and apply a skill. This obligation may be derived, along Raz's (1994) lines, from consideration of the interests of the child, as rights-holder. However, the child's interests exist in an interpenetrative, inclusive, symbiotic system of interests to which we all have imperfect obligations that cannot be codified by reference to individual rights.

4.10   Conclusion

The moral premises that underpin SDG4 are not limited to children's rights as entitlements derived from their education-relevant interests alone. They entail consideration of our duties to protect and foster the interests of all who stand to be affected by the goal's enactment. By displacing rights from the locus of moral duty, Hart's (2012) view, informed by O'Neill's (1988) account, centres the locus of moral duty on the relationship between the agent and the interest bearer, and on interests more generally. This allows a broader and deeper consideration of the global interest-derived reasons that underpin the imperative for sustainable education and its necessity for sustainable development in line with SDG4. It also places the onus on the moral agent to act in accordance with these in a manner compatible with the kind of creatures we are as humans, according to which freedom is an essential attribute, and with moral action, in which care and responsibility are the necessary correlatives to freedom.

References

Archard, D. (2003). Children. In H. Lafollette (Eds.), *The Oxford handbook of practical ethics* (pp. 91–111). Oxford University Press.

Brighouse, H., & McAvoy, P. (2010). Do children have any rights? In *Introduction to philosophy in education*. Continuum.

Cohen, H. (1980). *Equal rights for children*. Littlefield, Adams & Co.

Finnis, J. (2011). *Natural law and natural rights*. Oxford University Press.

Freeman, M. D. (2014). *Lloyd's introduction to jurisprudence* (9th ed.). Sweet & Maxwell.

Griffin, J. (2009). *On human rights*. Oxford University Press.

Hart, H. L. A. (1955). Are there any natural rights? *The Philosophical Review, 64*(2), 175–191.

Hart, H. L. A. (2012). *The concept of law* (3rd ed.). Oxford University Press.

Mill, J. S. (1974). *On liberty*. Penguin.

Moltow, D., & Thoars, C. (2019, 10–13 December). *The doli incapax rebuttal and its meta-ethical complications*. Presentation, Australian and New Zealand Society of Criminology Conference.

Noddings, N. (1992). Shaping an acceptable child. In A. Garrod (Ed.), *Learning for life: Moral education, theory and practice* (pp. 47–70). Praeger.

Noddings, N. (1995). Caring [1984]. In V. Held (Ed.), *Justice and care* (pp. 7–30). Routledge.

Noddings, N. (2006). *Critical lessons: What our schools should teach*. Cambridge University Press.

O'Neill, O. (1988). Children's rights and children's lives. *Ethics, 98*(3), 445–463.

Raz, J. (1994). *Ethics in the public domain: Essays in the morality of law and politics*. Oxford University Press.

Slote, M. A. (1983). *Goods and virtues*. Clarendon.

Slote, M. A. (1992). *From morality to virtue*. Oxford University Press.

Slote, M. (2007). *The ethics of care and empathy*. Routledge.

UN Women. (2019). *Progress on the sustainable development goals: The gender snapshot*.

United Nations. (1989). *Conventions on the rights of the child*. https://www.ohchr.org/en/instruments-mechanisms/instruments/convention-rights-child

United Nations Department of Economic and Social Affairs. (2015). *Sustainable Development Goals*. https://sdgs.un.org/goals

United Nations Educational Scientific and Cultural Organization (UNESCO). (2014). *UNESCO roadmapfor implementing the global action programme on education for sustainable development*.

Chapter 5
Decolonising the Sustainable Development Agenda: Bitin' Back at the Establishment Man

Jennifer Evans

5.1 Introduction

5.1.1 Bitin' Back

> They think that when they have your fork they think they have your land.
> (Bunda in Bunda, 2007, p. 76)

I am bitin' back (Cleven in Bunda, 2007) at the colonising agenda of the Sustainable Development Goals (SDGs). In her exploration of Indigenous sovereignty, Bunda uses the fictional work Bitin' Back by Cleven (2001) to illustrate how the Black sovereign warrior woman can challenge "the colonisers' representations of who we are," and expand understandings of sovereign acts through writing (Bunda, p. 75). In this chapter, I argue that the SDGs perpetuate colonisation, driven by White male hegemony, and thus require Black sovereign warrior woman acts to expose their negative impacts. As I am bitin' back in this decolonising work, I call on the power of strong Indigenous female governance (see Dudgeon & Bray, 2019), engage with racial debates (see Moreton-Robinson, 2016) around the SDGs, and highlight their White possession (see Moreton-Robinson, 2015). This chapter aims to define the theoretical frame of the Establishment man as a utility term, and his colonising behaviours through the SDGs. It explores concepts of Whiteness, Blackcuriousity, and faux-wokeness, which are later deployed in my following chapter (Chapter 6), in the form of a case study regarding the voice of country and treaty in *lutruwita* (Tasmania).

J. Evans (✉)
College of Health and Medicine, University of Tasmania, Burnie, TAS 7320, Australia
e-mail: jen.evans@utas.edu.au

© The Author(s), under exclusive license to Springer Nature Singapore Pte Ltd. 2023   63
K. Beasy et al. (eds.), *Education and the UN Sustainable Development Goals*, Education
for Sustainability 7,
https://doi.org/10.1007/978-981-99-3802-5_5

5.2   The Colonising Agenda of the SDGs

"Liberalism and colonialism are historically entwined" (Strakosch, 2015, p. 17). Indigenous People are being excluded from liberal citizenship by settler states and denied substantive decolonisation on the basis of "incapacity" (Strakosch, 2015). Colonial entities and corporations use "sustainable development" as a façade for their dominant free market, allowing them to weaken Indigenous People's resurgence (Corntassel, 2012). These shape-shifting colonial entities use a dirty politics of deception and distraction (Jamieson, 1993) to separate Indigenous Peoples from their homelands, cultures, and communities, away from decolonising movements towards state-centric co-optation and assimilation (Corntassel, 2012; Smith, 2000). Under the banner of sustainability, the global expansion of renewable energy development has been labelled as "green colonialism," reigniting "historical processes of dispossession and subjugation" of Indigenous Peoples, and is revitalising colonial legacies (Normann, 2021, p. 81). For example, Sammi herders are being dispossessed of their pasture lands by large-scale wind power developments, which in turn are reducing the resilience of reindeer herding, all whilst being framed as a positive climate change mitigation strategy (Normann, 2021).

Racial discrimination continues to be a global crisis, promoting poverty, and hindering equitable sustainable development (Ahmed et al., 2020). I am not arguing about sustainability altogether, but rather that inequitable sustainability (framed as sustainable *development*) subordinates the lives of Indigenous Peoples. For example, Indigenous Peoples endure displacement, dispossession, and cultural and physical genocide as a consequence of industrialisation and sustainable development (see Howitt, 2001a). Indigenous sustainable practices, Indigenous "wealth" and Indigenous entrepreneurship are fundamentally misunderstood, and the self-determining authorities of Indigenous Nations are not recognised by state-centric international forums (Corntassel, 2014; Downing et al., 2002; Tengeh et al., 2022). The tired narrative of development "aggression," that economic growth and mainstream development will bring increased production, technological progress, and alleviate poverty and inequity, is alive and well (Gilbert & Lennox, 2019). Although Barras (2004) proposed the "life project" as an alternative to the development project, Indigenous Peoples are still subordinate to the state, nation, and international system and its western cultural frame (Blaser et al., 2004; Stavenhagen, 1996; Tully, 2000).

5.3   Debut of Establishment Man

In *lutruwita* (Tasmania), like elsewhere in the world, colonisation is "a process that continues unabated, despite the West's pretence of civility" (Lehman, 2021, p. 161). As Tuck and Yang (2012) put it, the colonial settler gaze is firmly focussed on *palawa*[1] (Tasmanian Aboriginal People), through the eyes of continuous White patri-archal state Governments (see Vanderfeen, 2022), that, in spite of having been led by a woman, and including a majority of women in the current parliament, remains staunchly White and patriarchal.

Senior *trawlwulwuy* woman Emma Lee[2] recognised this gaze as one that belongs to "Establishment men." Writing about White tourism research, *tebrakunna* and Lee define Establishment men as "academics, researchers and policy makers who cause harm or exploit our Black female bodies in privileging western epistemologies" (*tebrakunna* & Lee, 2017, p. 96). They are men who, "create harms as simply as perpetuating colonial stereotypes" (Lee, 2018, p. 4), and "defend their privilege and epistemologies by reducing the value of our localised and place-based connections to country" (Lee, 2018, p. 5). Lee uses performance theory (see Schechner, 2003) to expose the sensual Othering of Black female bodies, by Establishment men, so as to "avert the gaze away from exploitation or harm" (*tebrakunna* & Lee, p. 97).

I build on *tebrakunna* and Lee's (2017) characterisation of Establishment men, towards a variant: *Establishment man*. I use the term *man* as it represents the gendered historical hegemony of colonisation as a singular archetype, an individualised and personalised entity of powerful global collectiveness, the embodiment of a mass movement of neoliberal colonisers (see Bargh, 2007; Goodman, 2021), and a symbol of the Global North (see Mosoetsa et al., 2016). This male archetype represents the veiled ideals of sustainability (see Alexander, 2007) through the SDGs and large corporations, who profit from pro-poor growth (Kakwani & Pernia, 2000). Pro-poor growth refers to growth that reduces poverty and decreases inequity (see Ravallion, 2004; Zepeda, 2004). I am amplifying the maleness of *tebrakunna* and Lee's *men* towards the singular, as an all-pervasive male collective power. Although it is often the singular *man* that we Blaks[3] encounter in our everyday interactions, who demonstrate their individual colonising powers (see Rose, 1996), these individuals are merely the latest "acceptable"[4] embodiment of the tendrils that extend from the unchanging centre of Establishment Man.

My argument for this new variant of Establishment man, to whom I give a singular pronoun of *man* as a collective, is a subtle one. *tebrakunna* and Lee (2017) describe their Establishment men as dangerous universalisers, who hold a paternal view of Black female bodies, dissect us, and "highlight our singularities" (p. 100). I am turning the mirror onto Establishment men, whilst I dissect them and highlight them as singular males and use the same colonising modes that they use on Blak female bodies in our defence. Whilst *tebrakunna* and Lee encountered men in the plural,

---

[1] The term *palawa* is used by some to refer to Tasmanian Aboriginal People.

[2] Lee locates herself as a *"trawulwuy* woman from *tebrakunna* country, north-east Tasmania, Australia" (*tebrakunna* country & Lee, 2022, p. 137) and co-authors with her ancestral *tebrakunna* country.

[3] I use the term "Blak" as defined by Ku Ku/Erb/Mer visual artist Destiny Deacon as a "vehicle to express identity and subvert the racist notion that Aboriginal People are 'black', or rather identifiable as having 'black' skin" (Baylis, 2015, p. 16; Evans, 2022).

[4] I use the term "acceptable" as referring to being palatable to White society, as opposed to being "acceptable" to Blaks.

they were confronted by a particular type of men (academics, researchers, and policy makers, regardless of colour[5]). It could be argued that by restricting Establishment men to this grouping, other men can be "let off the hook" and ceased to be seen as White colonisers, by not identifying themselves in this grouping. As Establishment *men* may have the capability of switching out of their grouping and being shape shifters, I prefer to use the term Establishment *man*, as a utility term, as it holds the individual man and his individual acts to account. Ultimately, we (Evans et al., 2017) are all referring to a male collective power, however, I am casting the net wider in order to problematise colonising behaviours of men within the SDGs globally.

Performative tourism was one of the latest "acceptable" versions of Establishment man. However, he is no longer satisfied with performative tourism and its offerings of "bodily performance that needs to please, seduce, or entertain especially visually" (Larsen & Urry, 2011, p. 1119). He is bored with the "Indigeneity [that] is only useful as a function of the workers who create the performance stage" (*tebrakunna* & Lee, 2017, p. 98). Despite having consumed the sensual Othering of Blak female bodies, and attempting to remove our "placed connections away from country" (*tebrakunna* & Lee, p. 97), Establishment man's appetite and curiosity of Indigeneity persists. He turns his attention to using the SDGs as another colonising armoury to keep Blaks off country.[6] Sustainability becomes framed with Blackcuriosity (see Crawford in Brown et al., 2014) and faux-wokeness (see Kaskazi & Kitzie, 2021; Rapley, 2021) (these terms are described in the next section), whereby Blaks are required to demonstrate the impossible task of delivering SDGs outcomes, whilst being denied sovereignty and without voice. This way, country remains in the hands of Establishment man, allowing non-sustainable use of resources from country for the benefit of the colonising settler and their corporates. Establishment man not only denies Black female bodies from access to country, but Blak and Blaq[7] (see Evans, 2022) bodies too.

---

[5] In their description of Establishment men, *tebrakunna* & Lee state "only characterising white males inhibits understanding that Establishment men are defending a class structure against Black female bodies and not solely confined by their colour or gender" (2017, p. 96).

[6] The term "country" is used to describe the homelands (Kingsley et al., 2013), traditional estate[s] (Langton, 2020), and places of belonging (Moreton-Robinson, 2003) of Aboriginal and Torres Strait Islander Peoples in Australia, co-created with Aboriginal and Torres Strait Islander Peoples (Bawaka Country et al., 2015, 2016; Suchet-Pearson et al., 2013) having powerful agency independent from colonisation (Evans, 2022). I chose not to capitalise the word "country" in acknowledgement that there is not one specific singular place of country, but many and diverse places of Aboriginal country, and diverse language terms and conventions for its use, thus I do not consider the term a proper noun requiring capitalisation.

[7] As I use the term "Blaq," I do so "whilst respectfully acknowledging that 'BlaQ/BlaQueer' is used by 'people of Black/African descent and/or from the African diaspora who recognize their Queerness/LGBTQIA+ identity as a salient identity attached to their Blackness and vice versa' (Petersen et al., 2020, p. 3). Recently in Australia, the term 'BlaQ/balq' is being used by some Aboriginal and Torres Strait Islander LGBTQ+ people to define their identity (see Sullivan, 2020), with hashtags such as '#blaqMobs #blaqAs #BQmob #BlaqOut' emerging in social media (see BlaQ, 2021). When I use the term 'Blaq' I am doing so in the context of belonging to my Queer Blak Aboriginal mob in Australia" (Evans, 2022, p. 34).

5.3.1 Background: Blakcuriosty and Faux-Wokeness —Weapons for the Establishment Man

In popular culture, *Blackcurious* is described as "the act of another race, other than African American that wants to be Black and is curious as to the Black culture" (Urban Dictionary, 2020). This definition is distinct from the sexual definition of Blackcurious, to which I am not referring. Although the *Urban Dictionary* has been criticised as a linguistic tool for ideological weaponising (Turton, 2021), it is used to explain and define non-standard phrases and emerging word forms (Nguyen et al., 2018). The term "Blackcurious" is rarely used in scholarly work. One fleeting reference defines Blackcuriosity as "thinking about what it means to be black-interested … complex arrangement of interests and alignments around blackness and black collectivity" (Crawford in Brown et al., 2014, p. 96), regarding African Americans and the African diaspora. I am engaging with the term Blackcurious here, as it is helpful in exposing the hypocritical interests of colonising settler states, their denial of Indigenous sovereignty and *faux-woke* reporting on the progress of the SDGs, particularly in *lutruwita*. As I do so, I am not conflating or appropriating the term "Blackcurious," "nor try[ing] to introduce a characterisation of Indigeneity as "Black" (Evans & *tebrakunna* country and Lee, 2022, p. 2). Rather, I am situating the term "Black" that has "given rise to our rights to exist as Indigenous Peoples in Australia" (Evans & *tebrakunna* country and Lee, p. 2). I am nuancing the term "Blackcurious" to "Blakcurious" so as to make space for *Blaks* and Indigenous Peoples who may wish to use the term, so that a greater understanding of the extent and nature of White possession of the SDGs can be explored. As I define and use the term "Blakcurious." I respectfully acknowledge the original term "Blackcurious" and its established meaning for African Americans and the African diaspora. I acknowledge that Indigenous Peoples and communities will have their own ways, preferences and terms for explaining this phenomenon, however, I am using "Blakcurious" in the context of Australia, and how it may be applied. My intent is to emphasise that the terms "Blackcurious" and "Blakcurious" may be useful for Indigenous Peoples, African Americans, and the African diaspora, when combating the colonising behaviours of Establishment man.

I go further to define "*Blakcuriosty*" as a narrow interest in Australian Aboriginal culture by non-Aboriginal people, particularly relating to their (non-Aboriginal) consumption of Aboriginal culture in curatorial arts, and in romanticised notions of Indigenous People's biological conservation of country. I use the term "*Blak*" as defined by K'ua K'au/Kuku and Erub/Mer artist Destiny Deacon, who states that "growing up, white people called us 'little black c…s' and it still gets shouted at us today. I decided to take the 'c' out of black in 1990 for my titles. I'm glad that 'Blak' is now used for Indigenous People and events in Australia" (Deacon, 2020). The de-weaponising of the insult "black cunt" is an act of Blak womanist resistance and is gaining recognition (see Balla, 2020).

As I use my definition of Blakcuriosity, I focus on the coloniality of settler fascination with Aboriginal culture, from the situatedness of the settler, and the hypocrisy it entails. The Blakcurious has a level of interest in Aboriginal culture and affairs that is confined to the bounds of aspects that do not unsettle the settler, for example, popular consumptive outputs, such as art, cultural performances, welcomes, and statements on what country they live or work on. The Blakcurious does not want to be Blak, but wants to know what it might be like to have Blak culture: making baskets, stringing shell necklaces or owning them, and being distinct to their White counterparts. Further, the Blakcurious is not curious about country, notions of country, agency, nor sovereignty of country. By ignoring country, the Blakcurious can also ignore their settler occupation of country. These boundaries help to maintain their un-wokeable status, ensuring that their curiosity does not lead to becoming actively woke.

Wokeness is defined as "critical consciousness to intersecting systems of oppression" and "to be a woke person is to hold an unretractable embodied consciousness and political identity acknowledging the oppression that exists in individual and collective experiences" (Ashlee et al., 2017, p. 90). Wokeness is rooted in Black activism, and a state of learning and growing (Whiteout, 2018). A woke person "must be aware of structural epistemic injustice and ensure that [their] beliefs do not contribute to that injustice" (Atkins, 2020, p. 12). In contrast, *woke-washing* is a term that describes *white saviours* who "uphold neoliberal 'colour blind' and 'post-racial' ideologies," and "connotes hierarchical colonial relations" (Sobande, 2019). Adolescents of colour have defined *fake woke* as "engagement in politics for the sake of impressing other people or appearing to be interested and knowledgeable about a political issue" (Kaskazi & Kitzie, 2021, p. 15). The term *faux-woke* has been used to describe organisations that "publicly take a stance against systemic racism and then in practice, they do not do any of the things they promised in their public statement" (Rapley, 2021). Similarly, *performative wokeness* is defined as "a disingenuous demonstration of an acute awareness of social issues that affect marginalized populations" (Watson, 2020, p. 241), whilst promoting a self-image of being socially conscious, and endorsing social justice irrespective of personal levels of activism and beliefs, but failing to acknowledge anti-Blackness (see Gray, 2018; Watson). Some argue that performative wokeness is pernicious, widespread, not only confined to corporate and government arenas (see Rhodes, 2021), but also fervently maintaining power structures in academia (Ezell, 2021).

I further define *faux-woke* as an individual attitude and behaviour regarding Aboriginal rights and affairs, that are seemingly supportive, but fall short of recognising their settler White possessiveness, by denying complete Aboriginal sovereignty and land rights. Being faux-woke is a desirous state for those who wish to be seen as informed and aware of Indigenous and Aboriginal concerns, having acquired the cultural capital and authority of wokeness, whilst only interested in partial Aboriginal rights. In this state, the faux-woke individual gains credibility and status in the eyes of others (excluding Blaks), as they use their wokeness as a tradeable commodity, which they can monetise and use to gain personal benefit, particularly in academia and bureaucracy. In the production of the newest "acceptable" man-infestation of the Establishment man, treaty, truth telling, and reconciliation becomes his new playground. For example, in *lutruwita*, the Establishment man uses faux-woke smokescreens as weapons, pretending to engage in real treaty considerations with *palawa* Peoples, yet shapeshifts processes and puts identity contestation as a barrier to participation, thus feeding lateral violence (see Chapter 6 for a discussion of this).

5.3.2 Racial Discrimination and Ongoing Colonialism in the SDGs

According to Iqtadar et al., (2021), "the binary between the Global South-Global North gives impetus for and further reifies the global racist and ableist hegemony of western cultural norms, domination, and violence identified within human rights discourses" (p. 19). This binary is present in the stark difference in the outcomes of the SDGs in Africa compared with Europe, where the goals are suited to the "highest priorities of the European region" (Salvia et al., 2019, p. 848). In Africa, the SDGs focus on poverty, hunger, water access and sanitation, and reduction of inequalities; whereas in Europe, the focus is education, industry, innovation, infrastructure, and sustainable consumption and production (Salvia et al.). The privilege of the Global North and the inequality of the Global South are entrenched by the SDGs. For example, the rapacious green economies and zero-carbon lifestyles of the Global North (see Jerez et al., 2021), require extraction of raw materials in the Global South, such as lithium and nickel mining. This can lead to abuse of customary lands and conflict, as Indigenous Peoples attempt to defend their ancestral homelands (see Kowasch, 2018; Shipton & Dauvergne, 2021). Others describe this phenomenon as "green crime," where local people end up working in these exploitative projects, losing their Indigenous ontologies of nature to consumerism and commodification (Goyes et al., 2021).

The SDGs are "disturbingly silent about the eradication of systemic racism and racial and ethnic discrimination" (The Society for the Physiological Study of Social Issues [SPSSI], 2020, p. 1), which continues to be a global phenomenon, allowing human rights violations as a means to rationalise hierarchical domination of Africans, people of African descent, Asians, people of Asian descent, and Indigenous Peoples (Society for the Psychological Study of Social Issues, 2020). According to the United Nations Human Rights Council (2021), people of African descent continue to face systematic racism, "interconnected, intersectional and compounded forms of racial discrimination, marginalisation and exclusion" (p. 6). The United Nations Department of Economic and Social Affairs (2021a) report found that civic space was closed, repressed, or obstructed in the participating countries of the Global South, and that this limited their participation in the SDGs. The report emphasised that some of the governments of the Global South lacked interest in dialogue with Indigenous Peoples and did not recognise them as legitimate actors.

Racial discrimination and ongoing colonialism are embedded in reporting on the outcomes of the SDGs in Africa. Agozino (2021) argues that United Nations reporting on all 17 SDGs fails to recognise the impacts of "enslavement, colonization, apartheid and neo-colonialism" that has allowed surplus value "to be expropriated from the labour of Africans by the international community" (p.45). Also, White supremacy and its colonial heritage continue to create endemic discrimination in global health (Olusanya et al., 2021). The voice of Black African and African diaspora researchers is excluded in formal submission processes regarding programmes relating to good health and wellbeing (SDG3). For example, non-Black WHO and UNICEF officials in their publication *Nurturing care handbook* (World Health Organisation, 2021), chose White South African academics over Black Academics to represent the interests of sub-Saharan Africa (Olusanya, 2021). This document, which is branded and aligned with the SDGs, uses imagery of *poor Africans* to "appeal to philanthropists in high income countries" (Olusanya, 2021, p. e1051), whilst lacking honest commitment to vulnerable and marginalised Africans. This focus on *poor Africans* reflects the colonising behaviours of the Global North, as it allows them to ignore SDGs outcomes that relate to pan-African communities (particularly women), in Latin America, the Caribbean, Central America, and the United States, where "extraordinarily higher rates of hunger and poverty" are being witnessed (Walker-Smith, 2020, p. 145).

5.4   Methodologies: Bitin' Back at the Establishment Man

Blaq bodies can disrupt colonising behaviours and challenge binaries (see Evans, 2022). As I work through this investigation, I am calling on my own Aboriginal Sovereign Warrior Woman (Bunda, 2007) and aligning my Blaq body with country, whilst responding to the matriarchy and power of *palawa* women (Burt, 2022; Matson-Green & Cameron, 1994) through kinship, who are the leaders and decision makers in *lutruwita* (Matson-Green & Cameron). I use "clubs" as a metaphor for my Indigenous and decolonising methodologies (see Evans, 2022). This is how I conceptualise my warrior act of speaking out, as I expose the Establishment man at work in his implementation of SDGs. I am "bitin' back" (Cleven in Bunda, 2007), "talkin' up to" (Moreton-Robinson, 2000), and "researching back" (Smith, 2021). These are the clubs I use to decolonise the discourse regarding SDGs. I am not "love-bombing" (*tebrakunna* country & Lee, 2019), nor using "loving critiques" (Paris & Alim, 2014, p. 417), rather, I am engaging in discomfort and unsettling the settler (see Brigg et al., 2011), whilst "reclaim[ing] space for Indigenous women's rage" (Flowers, 2015, p. 33), as an anticolonial act. Further, I am responding to the call of Nakata and Maddison (2019, p. 407) to "engage more comprehensively in research that considers the dynamics and structures of Indigenous-settler relations as a matter of priority," and to contribute to the "fracturing of the hegemony of Western/settler knowledge" (Nakata & Maddison, p. 408).

I power my clubs in this investigation with *Australian Indigenous Woman's Standpoint Theory* (Moreton-Robinson, 2013) and *Queer Indigenous Standpoint Theory*

(Sullivan & Day, 2019). Our Indigenous and decolonising methods are performative (see Swadener & Mutua, 2008) for our benefit as a means to keep us safe (see Evans, 2019). As we dance in our methods, we control the flow of cultural information, deciding how we reveal our cultural authority and meaning in our methods as we "research back" (Smith, 2021) to the Western academic canon and norms. It is ours to form and create to our advantage. This is our decolonising work; how we choose to do it. Through using *Australian Indigenous Woman's Standpoint Theory* (Moreton-Robinson, 2013) and *Queer Indigenous Standpoint Theory* (Sullivan & Day) in combination, this investigation honours *palawa* matriarchy (see Burt, 2022; Matson-Green & Cameron, 1994) and brings Blaq power to assist in decolonising work as it busts binaries (see Evans, 2022), and counters hegemony (Logan & Ciszek, 2022).

5.4.1 Faux-Woke Reporting Progress of SDGs

Under the banner of *Indigenous Peoples and the Post-2015 Development Agenda*, The United Nations Department of Economic and Social Affairs, Indigenous Peoples (UN DESA, 2022), reported that:

> The process to formulate the 2030 Agenda is described as one of the most inclusive in the history of the United Nations. Indigenous peoples were one of the nine "major groups" that were involved in consultations and discussions in the lead-up to the adoption of the 2030 Agenda and Indigenous Peoples have been engaged in multiple ways in the journey from the MDGs to the new post-2015 framework.

However, little progress has been made to ensure that the voices of Indigenous Peoples have been reflected in the ongoing reporting of progress of the SDGs, despite the ongoing efforts of Indigenous People to be equitably included in the SDG agenda. The UN DESA (2022) reporting fails to disclose that, despite their claim of conducting engagement processes that are the "most inclusive in the history of the United Nations," Indigenous voices have been largely ignored. This is an example of faux-woke reporting on the progress of the SDGs at the highest level. In 2017, the United Nations Permanent Forum on Indigenous Issues, held panels recommending ways forward from lessons learned since 2015 (UN PFII, 2017). Panel moderator and Indigenous human rights activist Joan Carling stated that the panel had concluded that "governments and corporations must be held to account for their violations of our collective rights [and] trumping up on our dignity as peoples and our wellbeing." She added "… an intergenerational approach should be a major consideration because otherwise the young people will not have any future if this destructive development paradigm continues to destroy not only our lands but actually our people" (UN PFII, 2017, 17:04 mins).

In addition, the UN report *5th volume State of the World's Indigenous Peoples' Rights to Land, Territories and Resources* (UN DESA, 2021b), provides comprehensive criticism of the 2030 Agenda for Sustainable Development (including the

SDGs), stating that it does not recognise collective rights, lacks cultural sensitivity, does not reflect free prior informed consent, and self-determination for Indigenous Peoples (UN DESA, 2021b).[8] Despite this condemnatory review, the report also states that Indigenous Peoples "advocacy and participation in intergovernmental processes contributed to the design of a framework that incorporates explicit references to Indigenous peoples and that is based on their core priorities, including the principles of universality, human rights, equality and environmental sustainability" (UN DESA, 2021b, p. 152). This statement could be interpreted as a claim that *all* Indigenous Peoples share *core* priorities of "universality, human rights, equality and environmental sustainability" as defined by the UN. However, this may be cast in doubt, given that the SDG Agenda has been disparaged as lacking free prior informed consent from Indigenous Peoples (UN DESA, 2021b).

There is no evidence that these faux-woke sentiments of "advocacy and participation" and "universality" have translated into action or reporting on the progress of the SDGs. For example, in the *UN The Sustainable Development Goals Report 2021* (UN SDG, 2021) the report makes one reference to "Indigenous" under the heading "leveraging the power of collaboration and partnerships," reporting that,

> … for the first time, intersex persons, persons with albinism, Indigenous peoples and stateless populations were all counted in the census. This enabled the Government to tailor services, but it also demonstrated to members of these groups that they count. "I asked the enumerator to show me the 'I' mark [for intersex]. I saw it, and I got emotional," recalls one census respondent, the parent of an intersex child from Kajiado. "This is the beginning of a long journey, and it's going in the right direction" (UN SDG, 2021, p. 6)

This narrative erases Indigenous People as just another census category, lumped in with intersex and albinism persons, and stateless populations. The disrespect given to Indigenous Peoples in this report is breathtaking. The report has many images of Indigenous People and Africans throughout to portray, conveniently, some level of inferred Indigenous and Black content. In the section that reports on life on the land (SDG15), an image with the title "A boy walks through Argentina's biodiverse terrain. The Sustainable Natural Resources Management project aims to improve management of forest resources and conserve biodiversity in protected areas and forest landscapes" (UN SDG, 2021, p. 56), prompts many questions. For example, how does the reader know if this boy is Indigenous and is walking through his homelands in order to protect it, or not? Why is this information not disclosed? The term *biodiverse terrain* nullifies the possibility that the place may be someone's ancestral lands.

This method of communication could be construed as an erasure of *potential* Indigeneity of people and place, an effort to make Indigenous People invisible. Further, this section of SDG15 focuses on biodiversity decline, the IUCN Red List, sustainable forest management, and responding to alien species. It fails to address the realities

---

[8] Although this report is a United Nations publication, it contains a note that "the views expressed in the present publication do not necessarily reflect those of the United Nations" (UN DESA, 2021b, n.p.). It could be argued that this demonstrates a level of hypocrisy in their claim of historically inclusive engagement with Indigenous Peoples by creating distance from the recommendations.

of Indigenous life in caring for and protecting homelands; for example, the murders of Indigenous environmental defenders (McVeigh, 2022) and 14-year-old Breiner David Cucuñame, a Colombian boy and Indigenous activist, who was killed whilst defending his Indigenous territories (Daniels, 2022).

The faux-woke reporting and marketing of the SDGs continues in the report on the *Progress towards the Sustainable Development Goals* (UN, 2022). This report has no single reference to "Indigenous" but instead refers to "traditional knowledge" without any indication if it is referring to Indigenous traditional knowledge. It states that "[a]t the end of 2021, 68 countries had at least one legislative, administrative or policy measure in place to ensure the fair and equitable sharing of benefits arising from the use of genetic resources and associated traditional knowledge in accordance with the Nagoya Protocol" (UN, p. 24). One can assume that it is referring to Indigenous traditional knowledge (see Secretariat of the Convention on Biological Diversity Montreal [SCBDM], 2011). However, it repeats the same erasure of Indigenous Peoples as the previous report (see UN SDG, 2021), by evading any recognition of Indigenous Peoples. This is the Establishment man at work, with his consumptive attitude of the Global North regarding Indigenous People's traditional knowledge and genetic resources. I ask, what has changed and been delivered for the benefit of Indigenous Peoples in the SDGs since the rhetoric of the post-2015 development agenda? My answer is "very little."

5.5   The White Australian SDG Fantasy

At the national level, the Australian Government, in its reporting on the progress of the SDGs, deploys a different kind of faux-wokeness that narrates a blatantly dishonest version of reality. Their faux-wokeness is one that is tied to romantic ideals about Aboriginal People caring for country and providing a sustainable future for the nation, with no apparent disadvantage in outcomes of the SDGs for them. For example, in the *Report on the Implementation of the Sustainable Development Goals 2018*, under the heading of Aboriginal and Torres Strait Islander Peoples' the following statement was made:

> "The rich history of Australia's First Peoples stretches back at least 65,000 years and is celebrated as one of the longest living civilisations on earth. This endurance of human life and caring for country is both profound and inspiring. The Australian Government is committed to recognising Aboriginal and Torres Strait Islander peoples in our constitution. Whilst there is no SDG specific to Indigenous peoples, all 17 SDGs are significant for Aboriginal and Torres Strait Islander peoples. The Aboriginal and Torres Strait Islander concept of 'caring for country' incorporates not just environmental and landscape management, but also the socio-political, cultural, economic, and physical and emotional wellbeing of Aboriginal and Torres Strait Islander peoples." (Australian Government, 2018, p. 7)

This faux-woke reporting is disconnected from the realities of Aboriginal life, and is representative of non-recognition of Aboriginal sovereignty and silencing of Blak voices. It is a cultural colonialist rendering of country as a place for ecological restoration, subjugated by ethnonationalist White nativism (see Campion, 2019). By using the terms "profound and inspiring," the report promotes idealised notions of First Nations Peoples' caring for country whilst ignoring colonisation, and sugar coating our survival. This narrative exemplifies cultural imperialism and its ability to generate romantic nostalgia and sentimental renderings of Aboriginal Peoples as primitive noble savages, and utopian mythic memorialising of Aboriginal culture and country as fixed and non-dynamic (O'Brien, 2006). The report can be considered a political statement in support of nativism, a standpoint which "runs deep in Australian politics" (Kleinfeld & Dickas, 2020, p. 33). It supports the position of "the white Australian as a harmonious and native figure in the spiritual and physical landscape … living in unity with nature … essential to the racial landscape and mythos" (Campion, p. 214)—faux-wokeism at its best.

Further, the posit that Australia's First Peoples are "celebrated as one of the longest living civilisations on earth," is a hollow statement, an attempt to hide the dishonesty of the declaration that the "Australian Government is committed to recognising Aboriginal and Torres Strait Islander peoples in our constitution." The Uluru *Statement from the Heart* was rejected on @@26 October 2017 (Thorpe, 2017), by the same government that authored the *Report on the Implementation of the Sustainable Development Goals 2018* (Australian Government, 2018), before its publication. This deceit mimics what Rose (1999, p.177) termed "monologue development," whereby Aboriginal People and country are rendered absent in White statements, allowing White power to deny coexistence, and make way for frontier development. Thus, Australia becomes a geography of hegemonic exclusion, where the imperial project plays out in White Australian imaginations, denying the possibility of cultural diversity (Howitt, 2001b).

The *Report on the Implementation of the Sustainable Development Goals 2018*, states that "While there is no SDG specific to Indigenous peoples, all 17 SDGs are significant for Aboriginal and Torres Strait Islander peoples" (Australian Government, 2018, p. 7), then quickly moves on to concepts of caring for country, so as to avoid the reality of Australia's failure to deliver outcomes for Aboriginal Peoples regarding the SDGs. The Australian Government's report is thick with faux-woke inscriptions, and is evasive on the actual implementation and outcomes of the SGDs for Aboriginal and Torres Strait Islander Peoples. For example, the report states that for good health and wellbeing (SDG6), the Government is "assist[ing] countries in Indo-Pacific by sharing our experience and expertise in water sanitisation" (Australian Government, 2018, p. 51), despite lack of safe drinking water and sanitation in remote Indigenous communities in Australia itself (Hall et al., 2020). On reduced inequality (SDG10), the report stated in context to *Closing the Gap*[9] that "of the seven targets … three are on track … the Closing the Gap agenda is being refreshed" (Australian Government, 2018, p. 70), although the program has been failing for some time (Altman, 2018). Since 2018, only two of the Closing the Gap targets are on track to being met (Australian Government, 2020). For climate action

---

[9] *Closing the Gap* is a response to a call for Australian governments to commit to achieving equality for Aboriginal and Torres Strait Islander people in health and life expectancy, within a generation.

(SDG13), the report says that an Aboriginal Carbon Fund was created to "support greater Aboriginal and Torres Strait Islander community participation in carbon markets" (Australian Government, 2018, p. 86), and that "Aboriginal and Torres Strait Islander peoples are using traditional knowledge and practices … to undertake Emissions Reduction Fund projects … Savannah burning projects … improving biodiversity and the conservation of threatened species" (Australian Government, 2018, p. 87). Again, this relegates Blaks to fixing climate change impacts through co-opting cultural knowledges. All the while, the voices of Aboriginal and Torres Strait Islander Peoples are excluded from reporting processes (Moggridge et al., 2022).

Regarding "protect, restore and promote sustainable use of terrestrial ecosystems" (SDG15), the report states that "Aboriginal and Torres Strait Islander peoples … contribute to positive biodiversity outcomes" (Australian Government, 2018, p. 96), in the context of looking after the land—an affirmation of White possession whereby Blaks must act as subservient ecological restorers for the benefit of the Establishment man. Also poignant, are the misleading reports of Native Title determinations (see Australian Government, 2018, p. 97), and their failings (Audit Office of New South Wales, 2022; Torre, 2022). Under this section of their report, the Government notes that 75 Indigenous Protected Areas (IPAs) exist (Australian Government, 2018, p. 98). No mention is made of the difficulties and pitfalls being faced by Aboriginal Peoples, despite others calling out IPAs as problematic. For example, Lee (2015) has criticised IPAs as not reflective of Indigenous Peoples' relational values to country, as they embed a nature–culture dualism that undermines Indigenous power and authority. Finally, under "peace, justice and strong institutions" (SDG16), the report provides a master class in deficit discourse and structural racism, portraying Aboriginal Peoples as "victims of violence … more likely to be subject to substantiated child protection notifications … overrepresented in criminal justice system" (Australian Government, 2018, p. 102). This mode of language that frames Aboriginal Peoples as deficient, is "embedded within the race paradigm," influences stereotyping, prejudice, and discrimination, and can be linked to outcomes for Indigenous Peoples (Fforde et al., 2013, p. 162). It restates the Establishment man's fantasy of being the saviour of Indigenous Peoples, and Indigenous Peoples as Rudyard Kipling's "White Man's burden" (Kipling, 1899). Under this fundamental SDG, the report brings deafening silence to the rejection of the *Uluru Statement from the Heart* (see Fredericks & Bradfield, 2021), and has nothing to say about an Indigenous Voice to parliament, or recognition of the agency and sovereignty of country.

5.6 Conclusion: The Establishment Man's Hold on the SDGs

I have called the entire enterprise of the SDGs developed by the United Nations into question. In doing so, I am underscoring the nonsense of developing sustainable development goals without serious, equitable, and respectful engagement with Indigenous Peoples and their homelands as equal sovereigns. Not only are the SDGs unrepresentative, but they constitute further examples of Global North, neoliberal, colonial weasel words that give an appearance that something is being done to repair harm, when in reality, the general acceptance of a Westphalian worldview means that little will/can be achieved. The denial of White possession in the SDGs is deep, substantiated by the reporting of progress which is rife with faux-woke inscriptions, and in Australia, topped up with Blakcuriosty. I have used the Establishment man as a utility term to headline the colonising attributes amongst the SDGs, their misrecognition and misrepresentation of Indigenous Peoples, and the resultant maldistribution of rights and resources.

In this chapter, through my actions of bitin' back at the Establishment man, I have demonstrated the inescapability of the White possessiveness of the SDGs, and their consistent occlusion and silencing of Indigenous Peoples. I have held a mirror to the Global North's agenda to keep the Global South, Indigenous Peoples, African Peoples, and the African diaspora in place of *lesser than*, by characterising the Establishment man. In this decolonial act, I have lifted the veil of White privilege inherent in the SDGs. I have racialised the SDG agenda, and highlighted shown how Indigenous voices and demands are ignored. Thus, I have evidenced how the SDGs are producing, protecting, and perpetuating ongoing colonisation, White privilege, and White possession, and ultimately harming Indigenous Peoples, their countries, and homelands.

References

Agozino, B. (2021). Maintaining law and order or maintaining conditions ideal for the exploitation of Africa? A counter-colonial critique of colonial development assumptions. In F. Allen & L. Amadi (Eds.), *Decolonizing colonial development models in Africa* (pp. 43–64). Lexington Books.

Ahmed, U. A., Aktar, M. A., & Alam, M. M. (2020). Racial discrimination and poverty reduction for sustainable development. In W. Leal Filho et al. (Eds), *No poverty: Encyclopedia of the UN sustainable development goals* (pp. 1–11). Springer International Publishing.

Alexander, J. (2007). Environmental sustainability versus profit maximization: Overcoming systemic constraints on implementing normatively preferable alternatives. *Journal of Business Ethics, 76*(2), 155–162.

Altman, J. (2018). Indigenous Australia. In Academics Stand Against Poverty Oceania (Ed.), *Australia, poverty, and the sustainable development goals: A response to what the Australian Government writes about poverty in its report on the implementation of the sustainable development goals* (pp. 19–23). University of Wollongong.

Ashlee, A. A., Zamora, B., & Karikari, S. N. (2017). We are woke: A collaborative critical autoethnography of three "womxn" of color graduate students in higher education. *International Journal of Multicultural Education, 19*(1), 89–104.

Atkins, J. S. (2020). Moral encroachment, wokeness, and the epistemology of holding. *Episteme, 20*(1), 86–100.

Audit Office of New South Wales. (2022). *Facilitating and administering Aboriginal land claim processes.* https://www.audit.nsw.gov.au/our-work/reports/facilitating-and-admini stering-aboriginal-land-claim-processes.

Australian Government. (2018). *Report on the implementation of the sustainable development goals 2018.* https://www.dfat.gov.au/sites/default/files/sdg-voluntary-national-review.pdf.

Australian Government. (2020). *Closing the gap report 2020.* https://ctgreport.niaa.gov.au/sites/def ault/files/pdf/closing-the-gap-report-2020.pdf.

Balla, P. (2020). *Disrupting artistic terra nullius: The ways that first nations women in art & community speak blak to the colony & patriarchy* (Doctoral dissertation, Victoria University, Melbourne).

Bargh, M. (Ed.). (2007). *Resistance: An indigenous response to neoliberalism.* Huia Publishers.

Barras, B. (2004). Life projects: Development our way. In M. Blaser, H. Feit, & G. McRae (Eds.), *In the way of development: Indigenous peoples, life projects and globalization* (pp. 47–51). Zed Books.

Bawaka Country, Wright, S., Suchet-Pearson, S., Lloyd, K., Burarrwanga, L., Ganambarr, R., Ganambarr-Stubbs, M., Ganambarr, B., & Maymuru, D. (2015). Working with and learning from Country: Decentring human authority. *Cultural Geographies, 22*(2), 269–283.

Bawaka Country, Wright, S., Suchet-Pearson, S., Lloyd, K., Burarrwanga, L., Ganambarr, R., Ganambarr-Stubbs, M., Ganambarr, B., Maymuru, D., & Sweeney, J. (2016). Co-becoming Bawaka: Towards a relational understanding of place/space. *Progress in Human Geography, 40*(4), 455–475.

Baylis, T. (2015). Introduction: Looking into the mirror. In D. Hodge (Ed.), *Colouring the rainbow blak queer and trans perspectives: Life stories and essays by First Nations People of Australia* (pp. 1–17). Wakefield Press.

Blaser, M., Feit, H. A., & McRae, G. (Eds.). (2004). *In the way of development: Indigenous peoples, life projects, and globalization.* Zed Books.

BlaQ (2021, March 15). *Blaq mail, tropical fruits.* Blaq Aboriginal Corporation Redfern Sydney. https://www.blaq.org.au/media.

Brigg, M., Maddison, S., & Altman, J. (2011). *Unsettling the settler state: Creativity and resistance in Indigenous-Settler state governance.* The Federation Press.

Brown, R. M., Copeland, H., Crawford, R., Gates, T., Lax, T., Lowe, R., & Tancons, C. (2014). Question & answer. *Nka: Journal of Contemporary African Art, 34*(1), 94–96.

Bunda, T. (2007). The sovereign Aboriginal woman. In A. Moreton-Robinson (Ed.), *Indigenous sovereignty matters: Sovereign subjects* (pp. 75–85). Allen & Unwin.

Burt, A. (2022). A spoke in the wheel: Ancestral women's legacies. In *tebrakunna* country and E. Lee & J. Evans (Eds.), *Indigenous women's voices: 20 years on from Linda Tuhiwai Smith's decolonizing methodologies* (pp. 107–119). Zed Books, Bloomsbury Publishing.

Campion, K. (2019). Australian right wing extremist ideology: Exploring narratives of nostalgia and nemesis. *Journal of Policing, Intelligence and Counter Terrorism, 14*(3), 208–226.

Cleven, V. (2001). *Bitin' back.* University of Queensland Press.

Corntassel, J. (2014). Our ways will continue on: Indigenous approaches to sustainability. In *The internationalization of Indigenous rights: UNDRIP in the Canadian context* (pp. 65–71). Centre for International Governance Innovation.

Corntassel, J. (2012). Re-envisioning resurgence: Indigenous pathways to decolonization and sustainable self-determination. *Decolonization: Indigeneity, Education & Society, 1*(1), 86–101.

Daniels, J. (2022, 19 January). Shock in Colombia over murder of 14-year-old indigenous activist. *The Guardian.* https://www.theguardian.com/global-development/2022/jan/18/colombia-indigenous-activist-murdered-14-breiner-david-cucuname

Deacon, D. (2020). 'Blak': Destiny Deacon uncovers the histories of Indigenous trauma. *ArtReview*. https://artreview.com/destiny-deacon-blak/

Downing, T. E., Moles, J., McIntosh, I., & Garcia-Downing, C. (2002). Indigenous peoples and mining encounters: Strategies and tactics. *International Institute for Environment and Development, 57*, 1–41.

Dudgeon, P., & Bray, A. (2019). Indigenous relationality: Women, kinship and the law. *Genealogy, 3*(2), 23.

Evans, J. (2019). Giving voice to the sacred black female body in *takayna* country. In J. Liljeblad & B. Verschuuren (Eds.), *Indigenous perspectives on sacred natural sites* (pp. 15–31). Routledge.

Evans, J. (2022). Can men weave baskets in Queer country? In *tebrakunna* country and E. Lee, & J. Evans (Eds.), *Indigenous women's voices: 20 years on from Linda Tuhiwai Smith's decolonizing methodologies* (pp. 33–50). Zed Books, Bloomsbury Publishing.

Evans, J., & *tebrakunna* country, & Lee, E. (2022). Introduction: Indigenous women's voices: 20 years on from Linda Tuhiwai Smiths' decolonizing methodologies. In *tebrakunna* country and E. Lee, & J. Evans (Eds.), *Indigenous women's voices: 20 years on from Linda Tuhiwai Smith's decolonizing methodologies* (pp. 1–14). Zed Books, Bloomsbury Publishing.

Ezell, J. M. (2021). "Trickle-down" racial empathy in American higher education: Moving beyond performative wokeness and academic panels to spark racial equity. *Journal of Education, 0*(0), 1–8. https://doi.org/10.1177/00220574211053586

Fforde, C., Bamblett, L., Lovett, R., Gorringe, S., & Fogarty, B. (2013). Discourse, deficit and identity: Aboriginality, the race paradigm and the language of representation in contemporary Australia. *Media International Australia, 149*(1), 162–173.

Flowers, R. (2015). Refusal to forgive: Indigenous women's love and rage. *Decolonization: Indigeneity, Education & Society, 4*(2), 32–49.

Fredericks, B., & Bradfield, A. (2021). "Seeking to be heard": The role of social and online media in advocating for the Uluru Statement from the Heart and constitutional reform in Australia. *Journal of Alternative & Community Media, 6*(1), 29–54.

Gilbert, J., & Lennox, C. (2019). Towards new development paradigms: The United Nations declaration on the rights of Indigenous Peoples as a tool to support self-determined development. *The International Journal of Human Rights, 23*(1–2), 104–124.

Goodman, J. (2021). Three worlds of climate imperialism?: Prospects for climate justice. In *The Routledge handbook of transformative global studies* (pp. 301–314). Routledge.

Gray, J. (2018). Performing wokeness. *The Harvard Crimson*. https://www.thecrimson.com/column/better-left-unsaid/article/2018/10/1/gray-performing-wokeness/

Goyes, D. R., South, N., Abaibira, M. A., Baicué, P., Cuchimba, A., & Ñeñetofe, D. T. R. (2021). Genocide and ecocide in four Colombian Indigenous communities: The erosion of a way of life and memory. *The British Journal of Criminology, 61*(4), 965–984.

Hall, N. L., Creamer, S., Anders, W., Slatyer, A., & Hill, P. S. (2020). Water and health interlinkages of the sustainable development goals in remote Indigenous Australia. *NPJ Clean Water, 3*(1), 1–7.

Howitt, R. (2001a). *Rethinking resource management: Justice, sustainability and Indigenous peoples*. Routledge.

Howitt, R. (2001b). Frontiers, borders, edges: Liminal challenges to the hegemony of exclusion. *Australian Geographical Studies, 39*(2), 233–245.

Iqtadar, S., Hernández-Saca, D. I., Ellison, B. S., & Cowley, D. M. (2021). Global conversations: Recovery and detection of Global South multiply-marginalized bodies. *Race, Ethnicity and Education, 24*(5), 719–736.

Jamieson, K. H. (1993). *Dirty politics: Deception, distraction, and democracy*. Oxford University Press on Demand.

Jerez, B., Garcés, I., & Torres, R. (2021). Lithium extractivism and water injustices in the Salar de Atacama, Chile: The colonial shadow of green electromobility. *Political Geography, 87*, 102382.

Kakwani, N., & Pernia, E. M. (2000). What is pro-poor growth? *Asian Development Review, 18*(1), 1–16.

Kaskazi, A., & Kitzie, V. (2021). Engagement at the margins: Investigating how marginalized teens use digital media for political participation. *New Media & Society, 25*(1), 72–94.

Kingsley, J., Townsend, M., Henderson-Wilson, C., & Bolam, B. (2013). Developing an exploratory framework linking Australian Aboriginal peoples' connection to country and concepts of wellbeing. *International Journal of Environmental Research and Public Health, 10*(2), 678–698.

Kipling, R. (1899). *The white man's burden: A poem*. Doubleday and McClure Co.

Kleinfeld, R., & Dickas, J. (2020). *Resisting the call of nativism: What US political parties can learn from other democracies*. Carnegie Endowment for International Peace.

Kowasch, M. (2018). Nickel mining in northern New Caledonia—A path to sustainable development? *Journal of Geochemical Exploration, 194*, 280–290.

Langton, M. (2020). Welcome to country: Knowledge. *Agora, 55*(1), 3–10.

Larsen, J., & Urry, J. (2011). Gazing and performing. *Environment and Planning D: Society and Space, 29*(6), 1110–1125.

Lee, E. (2018). Black female cultural safety in *tebrakunna* country. In B. S. R. Grimwood, H. Mair, K. Caton, & M. Muldoon (Eds.), *Tourism and wellness: Travel for the good of all* (pp. 1–20). Lexington Books.

Lee, E. (2015). Protected areas, country and value: The nature–culture tyranny of the IUCN's protected area guidelines for Indigenous Australians. *Antipode, 48*(2), 355–374.

Lehman, G. (2021). The tense of place. In J. Gough (Ed.), *Past tense* (pp. 153–172). Tebrikunna Press.

Logan, N., & Ciszek, E. (2022). At the intersection of race, gender and sexuality: A queer of color critique of public relations habitus. *Journal of Public Relations Research, 33*(6), 487–503.

McVeigh, K. (2022, March 2). More rights defenders murdered in 2021, with 138 activists killed just in Colombia. *The Guardian*. https://www.theguardian.com/global-development/2022/mar/02/more-human-rights-defenders-murdered-2021-environmental-indigenous-rights-activists

Matson-Green, V., & Cameron, P. (1994, June). Pallawah women: Their historical contribution to our survival [Paper presented at the Tasmanian Local History Societies' Biennial Seminar (2nd: 1993: Launceston)]. In *Papers and Proceedings: Tasmanian Historical Research Association, 41*(2), 65–70.

Moggridge, J., Pecl, G., Lansbury, N., Creamer, S., & Mosby, V. (2022, March 4). IPCC reports still exclude Indigenous voices. Come join us at our sacred fires to find answers to climate change. *The Conversation*. https://theconversation.com/ipcc-reports-still-exclude-indigenous-voices-come-join-us-at-our-sacred-fires-to-find-answers-to-climate-change-178045.

Moreton-Robinson, A. (2000). *Talkin' up to the white woman: Aboriginal women and feminism*. University of Queensland Press.

Moreton-Robinson, A. (2003). I still call Australia home: Indigenous belonging and place in a white postcolonizing society. In S. Ahmed, A. M. Fortier, M. Sheller, & C. Castaneda (Eds.), *Uprootings/regroundings questions of home and migration* (pp. 23–40). Routledge.

Moreton-Robinson, A. (2013). Towards an Australian indigenous women's standpoint theory: A methodological tool. *Australian Feminist Studies, 28*(78), 331–347.

Moreton-Robinson, A. (2015). *The white possessive: Property, power, and Indigenous sovereignty*. University of Minnesota Press.

Moreton-Robinson, A. (2016). Race and cultural entrapment: Critical Indigenous studies: Engagements in first world locations. In A. Moreton-Robinson (Ed.), *Critical Indigenous studies: Engagements in first world locations [Critical Issues in Indigenous Studies]* (pp. 102–115). The University of Arizona Press.

Mosoetsa, S., Stillerman, J., & Tilly, C. (2016). Precarious labor, south and north: An introduction. *International Labor and Working-Class History, 89*, 5–19.

Nguyen, D., McGillivray, B., & Yasseri, T. (2018). Emo, love and god: Making sense of Urban Dictionary, a crowd-sourced online dictionary. *Royal Society Open Science, 5*(5), 172320.

Nakata, S., & Maddison, S. (2019). New collaborations in old institutional spaces: Setting a new research agenda to transform Indigenous-settler relations. *Australian Journal of Political Science, 54*(3), 407–422.

Normann, S. (2021). Green colonialism in the Nordic context: Exploring Southern Saami representations of wind energy development. *Journal of Community Psychology, 49*(1), 77–94.

O'Brien, W. (2006). Exotic invasions, nativism, and ecological restoration: On the persistence of a contentious debate. *Ethics, Place and Environment, 9*(1), 63–77.

Olusanya, B. O. (2021). Systemic racism in global health: A personal reflection. *The Lancet Global Health, 9*(8), e1051–e1052.

Olusanya, B. O., Mallewa, M., & Ogbo, F. A. (2021). Beyond pledges: Academic journals in high-income countries can do more to decolonise global health. *BMJ Global Health, 6*(5), e006200.

Paris, D., & Alim, H. S. (2014). What are we seeking to sustain through culturally sustaining pedagogy? A loving critique forward. *Harvard Educational Review, 84*(1), 85–100.

Petersen, D. L., Barber, M. E., Nix Zelin, M. D., & Yarbrough, E. (2020). The L in LGBTQ2 IAPA. In P. Levounis & E. Yarbrough (Eds.), *Pocket guide to LGBTQ mental health: Understanding the spectrum of gender and sexuality* (pp. 1–6). American Psychiatric Association Publishing.

Rapley, L. (2021). Faux statements and fake love: On performative activism and faux-woke organisations. *Community Centric Fundraising.* https://communitycentricfundraising.org/2021/07/14/faux-statements-and-fake-love-on-performative-activism-and-faux-woke-organizations/

Ravallion, M. (2004). *Pro-poor growth: A primer. IPC-IG collection of one pagers* (p. 1). International Policy Centre for Inclusive Growth.

Rhodes, C. (2021). *Woke capitalism: How corporate morality is sabotaging democracy.* Policy Press.

Rose, D. B. (1996). Land rights and deep colonising: The erasure of women. *Aboriginal Law Bulletin, 3*(85), 6–13.

Rose, D. B. (1999). Indigenous ecologies and an ethic of connection. In *Global ethics and environment* (p. 175). Routledge.

Salvia, A. L., Leal Filho, W., Brandli, L. L., & Griebeler, J. S. (2019). Assessing research trends related to Sustainable Development Goals: Local and global issues. *Journal of Cleaner Production, 208*, 841–849.

Secretariat of the Convention on Biological Diversity Montreal. (2011). Nagoya protocol on access to genetic resources and the fair and equitable sharing of benefits arising from their utilization to the convention on biological diversity. *Convention on Biological Diversity United Nations Environmental Programme.* https://www.cbd.int/abs/doc/protocol/nagoya-protocol-en.pdf

Schechner, R. (2003). *Performance theory.* Routledge.

Shipton, L., & Dauvergne, P. (2021). The politics of transnational advocacy against Chinese, Indian, and Brazilian extractive projects in the Global South. *The Journal of Environment & Development, 30*(3), 240–264.

Smith, G. H. (2000). Protecting and respecting Indigenous knowledge. In M. Battiste (Ed.), *Reclaiming Indigenous voice and vision* (pp. 209–224). UBC Press.

Smith, L. T. (2021). *Decolonizing methodologies: Research and indigenous peoples.* Bloomsbury Publishing.

Sobande, F. (2019). Woke-washing: "Intersectional" femvertising and branding "woke" bravery. *European Journal of Marketing, 54*(11), 2723–2745.

Society for the Psychological Study of Social Issues. (2020). Beyond the human rights rhetoric on the "leaving no one behind" integrating the elimination of systemic racism, and racial and ethnic discrimination into the implementation of the SDGs. *The Society for the Psychological Study of Social Issues.* https://www.spssi.org/index.cfm?fuseaction=document.viewdocument&ID=3F28EB86AE4CA3BB2EE025BE0093BF048C8F7052AE83D097C0BECCF091EC4D6C8A419D9A5BFC2C3737450814D3839CB6

Strakosch, E. (2015). Neoliberal colonialism. In *Neoliberal indigenous policy* (pp. 17–32). Palgrave Macmillan.

Stavenhagen, R. (1996). Self-determination: Right or demon? In D. Clark & R. Williamson (Eds.), *Self-determination international perspectives* (pp. 1–11). Palgrave Macmillan.

Suchet-Pearson, S., Wright, S., Lloyd, K., Burarrwanga, L., & Country, B. (2013). Caring as country: Towards an ontology of co-becoming in natural resource management. *Asia Pacific Viewpoint, 54*(2), 185–197.

Sullivan. C. (2020). *Launching the "preliminary report to community" sharing the stories of #lgbtiq+ #blaq youth @the NICE @westernsydney @westernduics @blaq blah.org.au*, Twitter. https://twitter.com/rin_sullivan/status/1325592317441445890

Sullivan, C., & Day, M. (2019). Queer(y)ing indigenous Australian higher education student spaces. *The Australian Journal of Indigenous Education, 50*(1), 2–9.

Swadener, B. B., & Mutua, K. (2008). Deconstructing the global postcolonial. In N. K. Denzin, Y. S. Lincoln, & L. T. Smith (Eds.), *Handbook of critical and indigenous methodologies* (pp. 31–43). Sage.

tebrakunna country, & Lee, E. (2017). Performing colonisation: The manufacture of Black female bodies in tourism research. *Annals of Tourism Research, 66*, 95–104.

tebrakunna country, & Lee, E. (2019). 'Reset the relationship': Decolonising government to increase Indigenous benefit. *Cultural Geographies, 26*(4), 415–434.

tebrakunna country, & Lee, E. (2022). Reclaiming the first person voice. In *tebrakunna* country and E. Lee & J. Evans (Eds.), *Indigenous women's voices: 20 years on from Linda Tuhiwai Smith's decolonizing methodologies* (pp. 137–150). Zed Books, Bloomsbury Publishing.

Tengeh, R. K., Ojugbele, H. O., & Ogunlela, O. G. (2022). Towards a theory of indigenous entrepreneurship: A classic? *International Journal of Entrepreneurship and Small Business, 45*(1), 1–15.

Thorpe, N. (2017, October 26). The Turnbull government has officially rejected the referendum council's proposal for an Indigenous voice to parliament. *NITV.* https://www.sbs.com.au/nitv/nitv-news/article/2017/10/26/turnbull-government-rejects-proposal-indigenous-voice-parliament

Torre, G. (2022, May 2). Decades-long claims backlog highlights NSW native title failure. *National Indigenous Times.* https://nit.com.au/decades-long-claims-backlog-highlights-nsw-native-titlefailure/?fbclid=IwAR0HVoeptlWSgvB8kcnX3TSDpDBZusUze35mynLD6HN28jVf7sqWW04kSCs

Tuck, E., & Yang, K. W. (2012). Decolonization is not a metaphor. Decolonization: Indigeneity. *Education & Society, 1*(1), 1–40.

Tully, J. (2000). The struggles of Indigenous peoples for and of freedom. In D. Ivison, P. Patton, & W. Sanders (Eds.), *Political theory and the rights of Indigenous peoples* (pp. 36–59). Cambridge University Press.

Turton, S. (2021). Deadnaming as disformative utterance: The redefinition of trans womanhood on Urban dictionary. *Gender & Language, 15*(1), 42–64.

United Nations. (2022). Progress towards the Sustainable Development Goals report of the *Secretary-General. United Nations Economic and Social Council.* https://sustainabledevelopment.un.org/content/documents/29858SG_SDG_Progress_Report_2022.pdf

United Nations Department of Economic and Social Affairs. (2021a). *Strengthening the multi-stakeholder dimension of national development planning and SDG mainstreaming—A follow up report.* https://sdgs.un.org/stakeholders/strengthening-multi-stakeholder-dimension-national-development-planning-and-sdg

United Nations Department of Economic and Social Affairs. (2021b). *5th Volume state of the world's Indigenous Peoples: Rights to lands, territories, and resources.* https://www.un.org/development/desa/indigenouspeoples/wp-content/uploads/sites/19/2021/03/State-of-Worlds-Indigenous-Peoples-Vol-V-Final.pdf

United Nations Department of Economic and Social Affairs. (2022). *Indigenous peoples and the post-2015 development agenda.* https://www.un.org/development/desa/indigenouspeoples/focus-areas/post-2015-agenda/the-sustainable-development-goals-sdgs-and-indigenous/post2015.html

United Nations Human Rights Council. (2021). Promotion and protection of the human rights and fundamental freedoms of Africans and of people of African descent against excessive use of force and other human rights violations by law enforcement officers. *Report of the United Nations High Commissioner for Human Rights.* https://www.ohchr.org/en/documents/reports/ahrc4753-promotion-and-protection-human-rights-and-fundamental-freedoms-africans

United Nations Permanent Forum on Indigenous Issues. (2017). *Panel on ways forward: Lessons learned since 2015—Priorities to take forward.* https://www.facebook.com/unpfii/videos/160 8748162471543

United Nations Sustainable Development Goals. (2021). *The Sustainable Development Goals report 2021.* https://unstats.un.org/sdgs/report/2021/.

Urban Dictionary. (2020). *Blackcurious.* https://www.urbandictionary.com/define.php?term=bla ckcurious.

Vanderfeen, J. (2022). Black panopticon: Who wins with lateral violence? In *tebrakunna* country and E. Lee, & J. Evans (Eds.), *Indigenous women's voices: 20 years on from Linda Tuhiwai Smith's decolonizing methodologies* (pp. 53–68). Zed Books, Bloomsbury Publishing.

Walker-Smith, A. (2020). Pan-African women of faith: Lifting our voices and votes to end hunger and poverty. In J. Stevenson-Moessner (Ed.), *Women with 2020 vision: American theologians on the voice, vote and vision of women* (pp. 139–156). Fortress Press.

Watson, T. N. (2020). A seat at the table: Examining the impact, ingenuity, and leadership practices of Black women and girls in PK-20 contexts. *Journal of Educational Administration and History, 52*(3), 241–243.

Whiteout, S. (2018). Popularizing wokeness. *Harvard Journal of African American Public Policy,* 63–70.

World Health Organisation. (2021). *Nurturing care handbook: World Health Organisation.* https://nurturing-care.org/handbook/

Zepeda, E. (2004). *Pro-poor growth: What is it? IPC-IG collection of one pagers* (p. 4). International Policy Centre for Inclusive Growth.

Chapter 6
Decolonising the Sustainable Development Agenda: The Voice of Country and Treaty

Jennifer Evans

Abstract In my previous chapter (see Evans, Chapter 5, this volume) I defined the theoretical frame of the Establishment man as a utility term and his colonising behaviours through the SDGs. I also explored concepts of Whiteness, Blackcuriosity, and faux-wokeness, and illustrated how the Establishment man weaponises these in his pursuits of perpetual colonisation globally.

6.1 Introduction

6.1.1 Silencing Aboriginal Voices and Reporting on the SDGs

In my previous chapter (see Evans, Chapter 5, this volume) I defined the theoretical frame of the Establishment man as a utility term and his colonising behaviours through the SDGs. I also explored concepts of Whiteness, Blackcuriosity, and faux-wokeness, and illustrated how the Establishment man weaponises these in his pursuits of perpetual colonisation globally. In this chapter I use a case study regarding the voice of country[1] and treaty in *lutruwita* (Tasmania), to demonstrate how Establishment man uses the SDGs at national and local levels to tighten his grip on White possession

---

[1] The term "country" is used to describe the homelands (Kingsley et al., 2013), traditional estate[s] (Langton, 2020) and places of belonging (Moreton-Robinson, 2003) of Aboriginal and Torres Strait Islander Peoples in Australia, co-created with Aboriginal and Torres Strait Islander Peoples (Bawaka Country et al., 2015, 2016; Suchet-Pearson et al., 2013) having powerful agency independent from colonisation (Evans, 2022). I chose not to capitalise the word "country" in acknowledgement that there is not one specific singular place of country, but many and diverse places of Aboriginal country, and diverse language terms and conventions for its use; thus I do not consider the term a proper noun requiring capitalisation.

J. Evans (✉)
College of Health and Medicine, University of Tasmania, Burnie, TAS 7320, Australia
e-mail: Jen.Evans@utas.edu.au

© The Author(s), under exclusive license to Springer Nature Singapore Pte Ltd. 2023   83
K. Beasy et al. (eds.), *Education and the UN Sustainable Development Goals*, Education for Sustainability 7,
https://doi.org/10.1007/978-981-99-3802-5_6

and excuse his disrespect and disregard of Indigenous voices with whom no treaty has been made.

Australia has a poor track record of its performance in meeting the SDG targets, particularly relating to outcomes for Australian Indigenous Peoples (see Evans, Chapter 5, this volume). For example, although the Australian Government has reported success in meeting targets for quality and access to safe drinking water and sanitation (SDG6), it is not the case for remote Indigenous communities, where the goal of good health and wellbeing (SDG3) is also not being met (Hall et al., 2020). The Australian Government has been criticised as being selective in their reporting of SDG targets and producing documents that read like "propaganda for international consumption rather than serious reporting" (Altman, 2018, p. 18). Closing the Gap aims to "overcome the inequity experienced by Aboriginal and Torres Strait Islander People" (Australian Government, 2020) and reduce inequality (SDG10). It is a long-term action plan for achieving equality of health status and life expectancy between Aboriginal and Torres Strait Islander Peoples and non-Indigenous Australians (see Lowitja Institute, 2022) funded by the Australian Government. However, Closing the Gap is failing (Altman, 2018). Systematic defunding of Indigenous-controlled community health organisations (Pha, 2020), lack of appropriate, genuine, and stable engagement with Aboriginal Peoples throughout all stages of the program (Fitz-patrick, 2018), and ongoing racism are preventing Aboriginal Peoples from receiving optimal health care (Milroy & Bandler, 2021). All of these factors are contributing to the failure of Closing the Gap and make the claims that Australia is succeeding in meeting the SDGs disingenuous.

Indigenous voices of Aboriginal and Torres Strait Islander Peoples are excluded in Australia's reporting processes on the Intergovernmental Panel on Climate Change, which has direct links to outcomes for the goal of climate action (SDG13) (Moggridge et al., 2022). These failings are ever-present under the backdrop of the govern-ment ignoring the voice of Aboriginal and Torres Strait Islander Peoples. The Uluru Statement from the Heart calls for First Nation Voice to be enshrined in the Australian constitution (Uluru Statement from the Heart, 2017). The White, pater-nalistic Government (Fredericks & Bradfield, 2021) led by Prime Minister Malcom Turnbull (2015–2018), rejected the Uluru Statement from the Heart, whose action in this decision has been described as "a despicable act of mean-spirited bastardty" (Wahlquist, 2017). Although the current Prime Minister, Anthony Albanese has committed in full to the Uluru Statement of the Heart (Kildea & Synot, 2022), others warn that "Australian nation-state sovereignty is a doxa composed of colonial foun-dations that are ill equipped for Indigenous-led truth-telling or social justice fixes" (tebrakunna country et al., 2020, p. 35). To date, treaty processes and outcomes in Australia vary, with the states of Victoria (Dunstan, 2021), Northern Territory (Wellington, 2018), Western Australia (Higgins & Collard, 2019), Tasmania (Black-wood, 2021), Queensland (Siganto, 2019) and South Australia having held conversa-tions or embarked on treaties. South Australia abandoned treaty talks in 2018 (ABC News, 2018), however, there has been recent action to restart the treaty process (McLoughlin & Boisvert, 2022). Regardless of progress, Indigenous participation in conversations and negotiations continues to be fraught with difficulty and political inaction (Davis, 2022; Harley, 2015).

Despite being named up, structural racism, misogyny, and Whiteness (see Fredericks & Croft, 2002; Moreton-Robinson, 2000) continue to impact Indigenous voices, particularly Indigenous women's voices being heard in Australia (see Burt, 2022; Clark et al., 2021; Moodie et al., 2022; Sullivan, 2018). For example, Fredericks and Croft (2002) argue that patriarchy, and racial and economic oppression, overlap, and are not fully recognised by white feminism, thus cutting off Aboriginal women from discourses. Further, Moreton-Robinson (2000) puts the case that white women have a sense of superiority that is informed by white masculine values, and therefore are implicated in gendered racial oppression of Aboriginal women, both consciously and subconsciously. Forums regarding the progress of the SDGs are not immune to the same silencing of Indigenous and Aboriginal women that takes place in treaty talks, decision-making tables, and bureaucratic processes (see Redolfi et al., 2019; Simpson, 2017).

As I navigate my way through this investigation, I use my Blaq[2] body with kinship connections with *palawa*[3] and *palawa* country, to critique the role of Establishment man in the deployment of the SDGs in *lutruwita*. As I do this decolonising work, I listen to the wisdom of *trawlwoolway* woman and scholar Julie Gough, who describes her response to the colonisation of her family: "I deploy my suspension of belief as a secret weapon, a radar of anxiety and responsibility to those who came before me, to not let their lives, evading a culture not their own, render them lost in time" (Gough, 2021, p. 255). I place my focus on the relevance of the SDGs in current decolonising debates and decisions around *palawa* access to and control of their country.

In *lutruwita*, the Tasmanian Government has initiated a pathway to Truth-telling and treaty (Tasmanian Government, 2022; Warner et al., 2021). I use the treaty process in *lutruwita* as a case study, to tease out what progress is being made towards the implementation of the SDGs locally and their relevance to *palawa* and Indigenous Peoples beyond *lutruwita*. In this investigation I am seeking answers to questions such as "who is the burden of sustainability being placed on? Is Establishment man genuinely interested in healing country? Do the SDGs need to be decolonised? and are the SDGs able to be decolonised?".

As I commence this investigation, I situate myself in this enquiry as a Queer Dharug woman, who has kinship with *palawa*, living with and responding to the

---

[2] As I use the term "Blaq", I do so "whilst respectfully acknowledging that 'BlaQ/BlaQueer' is used by people of Black/African descent and/or from the African diaspora who recognize their Queerness/LGBTQIA+ identity as a salient identity attached to their Blackness and vice versa (Petersen et al., 2020, p. 3). Recently in Australia, the term 'BlaQ/balq' is being used by some Aboriginal and Torres Strait Islander LGBTQ + people to define their identity (see Sullivan, 2020), with hashtags such as '#blaqMobs #blaqAs #BQmob #BlaqOut' emerging in social media (see BlaQ, 2021). When I use the term 'Blaq' I am doing so in the context of belonging to my Queer Blak Aboriginal mob in Australia" (Evans, 2022, p. 34).

[3] The term *palawa* is used by some to refer to Tasmanian Aboriginal People.

agency of *lutruwita* country, with dual connections to Dharug (Sydney Basin,[4] New South Wales, Australia) and *palawa* country. I come to this critique I am making, as a Blaq person representing my Indigenous ancestors who were colonised. Whilst I do not have authority to speak on behalf of *palawa* and *palawa* country, I do however have the authority to speak on behalf of myself as a Blaq, and my familial ancestors. I do so with the utmost respect, giving over authority to those in each of these realms. Thus, colonisation and decolonisation are both personal and collective to me, my family, my ancestors, and my *palawa* kin.

6.2 Background

6.2.1 Indigenous Voice and Sovereignty in the SDGs

The voice of Indigenous Peoples has not been heard in the 2030 Agenda for Sustainable Development, and the Agenda has been criticised as lacking cultural sensitivity, being void of free, prior, and informed consent, and ignoring the concept of Indigenous People's self-determination (United Nations Department of Economic and Social Affairs [UNDESA], 2021). The SDG indicators are borne from the power structures that have, and continue to undermine, self-determination of Indigenous People and their aspirations for development (Yap & Watene, 2019). Indigenous People have voiced their concerns that the 2030 Agenda "risks undermining Indigenous People's holistic development approaches" due to focus being placed on domestic product growth, increased production, and industrialisation (UNDESA, 2021, p. 154). This focus is emanating from the Global North, where an obsession with economic growth and markets that can achieve such growth is rife (Khosravinik, 2017). Indigenous voices are naming up transnational corporates from the Global North for their abusive practices and "their ability to control governments and develop policies that favour their monopolisation of resources, their take-over of land, and their profits and the way they exclude Indigenous voices" (Yazzie in UNDESA, 2017, 14:57 min), particularly in the Global South (see Shipton & Dauvergne, 2021). Indigenous Peoples are calling for Governments and the private sector to be held accountable for respecting the rights of Indigenous Peoples in the implementation of the SDGs (UNDESA, 2021).

Indigenous women play central roles in the delivery of sustainable management of natural resources and conservation of biodiversity (UNDESA, 2021). Further, Indigenous women are the holders and transmitters of traditional knowledges (see Burarrwaŋa et al., 2019; Rose, 1996; *tebrakunna* country and Lee & Evans, 2022), that sustain not only their families and communities, but also the wellbeing of their homelands. Therefore, their voice requires respect and their actions recognition,

---

[4] I acknowledge that the geographical boundary of Dhaurg Ngurra (country) is contested as not confined to Western Sydney, therefore I chose to refer to the larger Sydney Basin as Dharug Ngurra to be respectful of varying Dharug views (see Darug Custodian Aboriginal Corporation, 2022).

which has been lacking (Krauss, 2021). Even though in some places the representation of Indigenous Peoples in policy and legislative bodies is mandatory, Indigenous women continue to face numerous hurdles to have a seat at the table, let alone be heard (see Pasimio, 2020).

The notion of sovereignty of Indigenous People is ignored within the context of SDGs. Sovereignty has been framed only from the perspective of "food sovereignty," particularly for poor farmers in the Global South (United Nations [UN], 2015). In the document, promoted under "protect, restore and promote sustainable use" (SDG15), *Making Peace with Nature a Scientific Blueprint to Tackle the Climate, Biodiversity and Pollution Emergencies* (United Nations Environment Programme [UNEP], 2021), there is no mention of "sovereign" or "sovereignty." Instead, Indigenous Peoples are othered as "actors," stuck in "power asymmetries" (UNEP, 2021, p. 25). "Custodial traditions and knowledges" of Indigenous Peoples are referred to as being important for biodiversity restoration (UNEP, 2021, p. 32) without recognition of custodial rights or sovereignty. The report frames Indigenous Peoples' homelands as "land…less impacted" with "very low human intervention" (UNEP, 2021, p. 62). Such a glib interpretation of country, tribal lands, and homelands, feeds into nature-culture dualism (see Lee, 2015), the othering of country as wilderness, devoid of Indigenous histories and ongoing relationships (see Evans, 2019; Ross, 2017), and ignores the agency and sovereignty of country itself. The same document lumps Indigenous communities in the same category as "unique and threatened systems" including "tropical glaciers [and] coral reefs" (UNEP, 2021, p. 48).

6.2.2 Land Rights and Treaty in Lutruwita

Sovereignty has never been ceded by *palawa* People in *lutruwita* (see Aboriginal Land Council Tasmania [ALCT], 2021; Mansell, 2003; Pratt, 2003; *tebrakunna* country & Lee, 2022). The fight for the return of land to the Tasmanian Aboriginal[5] People continues (see ALCT, 2021). In *lutruwita*, less than one per cent of the total land area of the Island is Indigenous owned or controlled (Australian Institute of Aboriginal and Torres Strait Islander Studies [AIATSIS], 2016). This is in stark contrast to the Australian Government report on the implementation of protection, restoration, and promotion of the sustainable use of terrestrial ecosystems (SDG15), stating that "native title determinations cover approximately 34 percent of that land area of Australia, with a further 26 percent of Australia subject to application" (Australian Government, 2018, p. 97). However, a recent report found that Native Title and Aboriginal land claim processes in NSW are fundamentally failing (Audit Office of New South Wales, 2022; Torre, 2022). Despite more than 25 years having passed since the 1992 High Court Mabo decision, no determinations of Native

---

[5] I use the terms "Aboriginal" to refer to the First Peoples of Australia, including Tasmania and the mainland of Australia, but excluding the Torres Strait. I use the term "Indigenous" to refer to all First Peoples of Australia and for First Peoples globally.

Title have been made in *lutruwita* (AIATSIS, 2016). Tasmanian Aboriginal activist Heather Sculthorpe explains

> unfortunately, the way the Native Title was interpreted became that people in Tasmania couldn't even claim Native Title because it said that the tide of history had washed away our continuing connection with the land. So bad luck, you got invaded, you got done over, you haven't been on your land, you've been separated from your land for too long, you don't have native title. (Sculthorpe in Shine, 2017)

Uncle Graeme Gardner, a Tasmanian Aboriginal Elder, states that "in most cases we pretty much have to beg the government for it and justify ourselves as to why we want that land" (Gardner in Hosier, 2019).

Adrill (2013, p. 318) explains that "there is a discernible gulf between the narratives of First Peoples of Australia and the narratives of other scholars concerning sovereignty." White settler researchers who write about Indigenous sovereignty risk being complicit in ongoing racism and colonialism in their vain quests to make contributions to antiracist and decolonising struggles (Macoun, 2016). "When Indigenous People refuse settler benevolence...and assert political agency, good white people's response is not pity but a self-defensive anxiety" (Slater, 2018, p. 3). Sullivan (2014, p. 3) goes further, stating that "white people generally don't know how to live their racial identities in ways that promote racial justice," that they (white people) are ignorant and hold racial hierarchy and dominance over mixed-raced and light-skinned Asians, Latinos, and more so dark-skinned peoples, and those they count as black including African Americans. Nicoll (2004, p. 19) argues that white Australians have a compulsory investment in White sovereignty, that they circumscribe Indigenous sovereignty and "deny the collective rights of Indigenous Australians" as "white know-all[s]" (Moreton-Robinson, 2003, p. 127). Thus, the role of white settlers in Indigenous research must be questioned (see Smith, 2021). Even though some outsiders (white settler researchers) squirm "in the discomfort from a lack of legitimacy" (Evans, 2022, p. 6) in their attempts to engage in Indigenous research, others defiantly blame identity politics and culturalism (see Pybus & Moore, 2019), enabling White possessiveness of Indigenous research agendas free of White guilt. This also occurs in White engagement with Indigenous Australians among governments, agencies of government, and private industries and enterprises that make moves to appear "race cognizant" (Frankenburg, 1993), even whilst they fail to ask questions of themselves, their intentions, and the impact of their decisions on the very Indigenous Australians with whom they claim to be engaging.

6.3 Methodology

6.3.1 Queer Indigenous Standpoint Theory

It is important to demonstrate how decolonising and Indigenous methodologies can be deployed for the benefit of Blaks and Indigenous Peoples when challenging the White representation of us in the SDGs. This deployment is also useful for challenging the SDGs in their entirety, as some may otherwise see them as justifiable mechanisms for alleviating poverty and inequities globally (see Fukuda-Parr, 2016). In this investigation I chose to use my Blaq body with kinship (see Evans, 2022), to critique the Establishment man, his White possession of the SDGs, and call out the violence that he perpetuates towards country. "Body sovereignty is inseparable from sovereignty over our lands and waters" (Wilson in, Wilson & Laing, 2019, p. 135), thus it is appropriate for me to use my Blaq body to disrupt power dynamics and structures whilst challenging and inverting hegemony (see Wilson & Laing, 2019). As I tackle the weaponisation of faux-wokeness[6] and Blakcuriosity,[7] I am responding to the provocation that Indigenous studies needs to "Queer itself up" to challenge entrenched binaries and hierarchies, gender, and sexuality (Wilson in, Wilson & Laing, 2019, p. 139).

In their debut of a Queer Indigenous Standpoint Theory, Sullivan and Day (2019, pp. 4–5) describe their framework as "centring the lived realities of Queer Gender Diverse Indigenous people in a heteronormative colonial society," whilst providing a "decolonising model of inquiry" that is "transferable to other spaces and settings which require critique and reform." Sullivan and Day (2019) have created a methodology specific to Queer Indigenous Peoples, that furthers the work of Indigenous Standpoint Theory (Nakata, 2007) and Indigenous Women's Standpoint Theory (Moreton-Robinson, 2000, 2013). Given that their work is an introduction to the theory, rather than a deep theoretical dive, space exists for the preliminary development of Queer Indigenous Standpoint Theory and its application. What interests me most is the invitation of Queer Indigenous Standpoint Theory to "offer the possibility of producing alternative knowledges with the 'dual imperatives' (Monaghan, 2015) of queer(ing) and decolonial goals" (Sullivan & Day, 2019, p. 4). Binaries can be confronted, and settlers unsettled by combing queer theories with Indigenous and decolonising methodologies (see Clark, 2015; Evans, 2022; Finley, 2011). In this way, I am using Queer Indigenous Standpoint Theory to tackle the binary

---

[6] I use the term "faux-woke" (see Evans, Chapter 5, this volume) to refer to an individual attitude and behaviour regarding Aboriginal rights and affairs, that are seemingly supportive, but fall short of recognising their settler White possessiveness by denying complete Aboriginal sovereignty and land rights.

[7] I am using the term "Blakcuriosity" (see Evans, Chapter 5, this volume) to define interest in Aboriginal culture in Australia by non-Aboriginal People whilst respectfully acknowledging that the term "Black curiosity" is used to define a "complex arrangement of interests and alignments around blackness and black collectivity" (Crawford in Brown et al., 2014, p. 96) regarding African Americans and the African diaspora.

between the Global South-Global North (see Iqtadar et al., 2021) and the colonising behaviours of the Global North towards Indigenous Peoples in the SDGs (see Evans, Chapter 5, this volume). I also use Queer Indigenous Standpoint Theory to disrupt the power dynamics and hierarchical dominance of the Establishment man and his SDG agenda and his disregard for the sovereignty of country.

6.4 Case Study

6.4.1 A White Treaty

In 2021 the Tasmanian Government appointed two non-Aboriginal academics to conduct consultations with Tasmanian Aboriginal People "to learn from Tasmanian Aboriginal people their thoughts on and aspirations for treaty, truth-telling and reconciliation" (Warner et al., 2021, p. 8). Since then, the Tasmanian Government has decided to co-design Truth-telling and Treaty processes with Tasmanian Aboriginal representatives, in response to feedback from Tasmanian Aboriginal organisations (Tasmanian Government, 2022). The Tasmanian Aboriginal Centre has criticised this decision as one that "might end up being a treaty between white government and white people" (Mansell in Holmes, 2022), as the issue of who can or cannot claim to be Tasmanian Aboriginal is back on the agenda, despite the government stating that it will not determine Aboriginality or eligibility (Tasmanian Government, 2022). The Aboriginal Land Council of Tasmania has blamed the decision as "right-wing influence" within government (Mansell, 2022). Identity contestation in *lutruwita*, whereby *palawa* communities determine Aboriginality has been labelled as "government-aided lateral violence" (Vanderfeen, 2022, p. 61). Certain Tasmanian Aboriginal People are being denied their Aboriginal identity and enduring identity judgements by both Blaks[8] and Whites (see Vanderfeen, 2022). Some Whites deny the Aboriginality of others through arguments of false extinction, whilst some Blaks deny the Aboriginality of others based on organisational membership and affiliation, and familial and political alignments (see Vanderfeen, 2022). Those that are rejected are rendered as "paper blacks" (Gough in Marks, 2013, p. 185) and/or belonging to a "bunch of whites wanting to be Aboriginal" (Mansell in Marks, 2013, p. 184). The latter are those to which Mansell may be referring to as being the "white people" that may end up negotiating a treaty with the government (see Mansell in Holmes, 2022).

---

[8] I use the term "Blak" as defined by Ku Ku/Erb/Mer visual artist Destiny Deacon as a "vehicle to express identity and subvert the racist notion that Aboriginal People are 'black', or rather identifiable as having 'black' skin" (Baylis, 2015, p.16; Evans, 2022).

6.4.2 Settler Smokescreens

Faux-wokeness and Blakcuriosity combine as settler smokescreens, providing safe backdrops for the Establishment man in his quest to protect co-exiting sovereignty and non-recognition of country. In *lutruwita*, White historians (see for example Clements, 2014; Cox, 2021; Pybus, 2020; Ryan, 2012; Taylor, 2017), and White historical novelists (see Broinowski, 2019; Kneale, 2000; Wilson, 2011) consume and profit from the colonisation of *palawa* and memorialise racism as a historical event: an inevitable consequence of colonisation. Meanwhile, arts and curatorial movements co-opt *palawa* culture (Evans, 2022) whilst indulging in Blakcuriosity. Among this colonising masquerade is the Truth-telling and Treaty process, which has been received with both positivity and negativity (see Blackwood, 2021). Some predict that it will take two or more generations to settle a treaty (see Dillon in Blackwood, 2021), whilst others question if the treaty will be realised due to people's discomfort and genuine interest in moving on (see Cameron in Blackwood, 2021).

6.4.3 The Colonising Trap of Coexisting Sovereignty

In the personal acknowledgements section of the report Pathway to Truth-Telling and Treaty, the White authors recognise that Tasmanian Aboriginal People[9] "never ceded nor extinguished [their] sovereignty" (Warner et al., 2021, p. 4), but their sentiments do not translate into statements nor recommendations directly within the body of the report to recognise the Indigenous sovereignty of *palawa* People specifically. Rather, the report states that a treaty between the state and Tasmanian Aboriginal People should include "recognition that Aboriginal sovereignty has not been extinguished but that it coexists with that of the Crown" (Warner et al., 2021, p. 9). Coexistence and its implied togetherness is a white invention. Notions of coexistence between Indigenous and non-Indigenous Australians is fragile, messy, and discordant with the lived experiences of Australian Aboriginals (Howitt, 2006). Coexisting sovereignty is a colonising trap where "Indigenous people [are] incorporated into mainstream political administration on European-Australian terms" (Murphy et al., 2017, p. 2). A coexisting sovereignty implies that White sovereignty has subsumed a portion of Indigenous sovereignty and that a portion of Indigenous sovereignty has been given over to White possession. Neither of these happened or is happening. Indigenous sovereignty has never been ceded; therefore, it still exists within its own absolute right (see Moreton-Robinson, 2007; Murphy et al., 2017). Consequently, a coexisting sovereignty is only made possible under the conditions of the myth of patriarchal White sovereignty and White possession (see Moreton-Robinson, 2006).

There are debates about whether a treaty was made in *lutruwita* in 1831 (see Cameron in Mansell, 2016; Cameron et al. in Cooper, 2020; Harman, 2018). Cameron

---

[9] I also use the term *palawa* and Tasmanian Aboriginal interchangeability, whilst acknowledging and respecting that it is not a term that is used by all Tasmanian Aboriginal Peoples.

(2019) argues that a treaty was made in 1831, when "Robinson, his Aboriginal guides, and the Big River and Oyster Bay people, arrived in Hobart Town on the 7 January 1832. Holding spears in their hands and accompanied by 100 dogs, the warriors, women and child, walked to Government House and met the Governor." This account contrasts Harman's (2018) suggestion that it was a negotiated exodus, where Robinson had "paraded the remnants of the Big River and Oyster Bay tribes through the streets of Hobart" as an orchestrated event for colonial purposes and resultant exiling. Even so, the fact remains that "the British Government failed to negotiate a formally recognised treaty when deciding to set up colonies in... Van Dieman's Land" (Warner et al., 2021, p. 40), and consent to share sovereignty was never given. The proposition that Tasmanian Aboriginal sovereignty coexists with the Crown (Warner et al., 2021) without consent from *palawa*, perpetuates avoidance of recognition of invasion and colonisation by the British Government. It also fails to distinguish between the sovereignty of different Indigenous nations.

It could be argued that the report has faux-woke inscriptions through the inconsistent messaging regarding absolute and coexisting sovereignty. I suggest such an inscription is representative of the Establishment man at work. In this context the Establishment man is acting as a powerful regime, where "patriarchal White sovereignty operates ideologically, materially and discursively to reproduce and maintain its investment in the nation as a white possession" (Moreton-Robinson, 2007, p. 88). Whilst some hold out hope for popular modes of sovereignty in multi-people settler states, genuine sovereignty requires conditions that allow Indigenous Peoples to be able to negotiate and determine their constitutional order with states on equal terms (Beckman et al., 2022). Whyte (2018) argues that reconciliation in the form of treaties between Indigenous Peoples and parasitic settler nations are illusionary and create "additional empowerment [of settler nations] to exercise something like a right to judge whether Indigenous Peoples are good or bad dependents, sovereigns, or citizens" (Whyte, 2018, p. 282). In this context, the Establishment man is able to maintain absolute sovereignty whilst he remains "extremely busy reaffirming and reproducing this possessiveness" (Moreton-Robinson, 2015, p. xi), through inconsistent faux-woke messaging whilst refusing independent *palawa* sovereignty and offering piecemeal concessions.

6.4.4   Treaty in Lutruwita and Its Relevance to the SDGs

The Pathway to Truth-Telling and Treaty report (Warner et al., 2021) provides insights into the reality of how the SDGs are implemented on the ground in *lutruwita*. The Report reinforces the hypocritical and faux-woke approach of Australian Governments (see Evans, Chapter 5, this volume) and the Tasmanian state to caring for country,[10] whereby statements of acknowledgement of the value of Indigenous caring for country are not supported by return of Aboriginal lands. The Report references national legalisation (Environment Protection and Biodiversity Conservation Act 1999) (Australian Government, 2022) as a central legal framework to protect and manage country, and whilst it highlights the reforms required to address the lack of Indigenous Voice in the legalisation, it falls short of addressing the relationship between Indigenous sovereignty and caring for country. That is, Aboriginal People's knowledges of biodiversity are to be "promoted," particularly in its "role in the conservation and ecologically sustainable use of Australia's biodiversity" (Warner et al., 2021, p. 83). However, actually placing country in the hands of *palawa* to care for country is not part of the treaty narrative. Even the "vexed issue of identity" is used to excuse the impasse of land handbacks to *palawa* (Warner et al., 2021, p. 11).

A new category of "Aboriginal Protected Areas" has been mooted whereby "lease-hold or lease-back arrangements and funded healthy Country plans/management plans [are] a requirement" (Warner et al., 2021, p. 11). The report suggests that Aboriginal Protection Areas "serve as a model and would serve as a test of local management and access," whereby "capacity building [is] a step towards return of title to land" (Warner et al., 2021, p. 11). Aboriginal People's practices are frequently faced with the double burden of being both model and test. This approach to concepts of Aboriginal Protection Areas is founded in Blakcuriosity, as a means to model "Blak country" as defined by Whites for the benefit and entertainment of Whites. Then this notion of "Blak country" is tested using faux-wokeness, by non-genuine non-trusting White interests, to determine if Blaks can make it appealing and real enough before considering handing the land back.

Further faux-woke sentiments are evident in the Pathway to Truth-Telling and Treaty report (Warner et al., 2021) where the authors reflect on their time on country with *palawa*. For example, "The way in which Country continues to be cared for is a gift to all of us that share in the beauty of this place," and "talking to us about Country, showing us these unique and culturally significant places. There are memories and special experiences from these visits that will stay with us forever" (Warner et al., 2021, p. 27). In my criticism here, I am not denying the deep emotions and sentiments that the authors felt in response to being on country with *palawa*, rather I am highlighting the disconnect between these sentiments and the recommendations in the report as a faux-woke action. The report infantilises *palawa* capacity to care for country and resists full recognition of *palawa* sovereignty and return of Aboriginal land. In this way, Establishment man can silence country and *palawa* sovereignty, whilst maintaining power and control over Blak ownership and access to country.

The relevance of the SDGs in *lutruwita* regarding treaty narratives is problematic. A gulf exists between the ontologies of country as a sovereign entity and as a land asset for development within the sustainable development agenda. There is an absence of literature regarding notions of country as a sovereign entity. However, it

---

[10] I use the term "caring for country" to include notions of environmental sustainability as framed by the SDGs, whilst arguing that the SDGs do not reflect nor respect Indigenous concepts of caring for country.

is important to raise this concept that country may be its own sovereign body and have powers of supreme legitimate authority over its own territories of life. I do this so as to counter development tropes that are harmful to Indigenous Peoples and their traditional estates, and to push back on the sustainable development agenda. The dominant model of sustainable development is seen as hypocritical and disrespectful by many Indigenous Peoples and their homelands globally (Vásquez-Fernández & Ahenakew pii tai poo taa, 2020). The SDGs reflect this gulf between notions of sustainability within the SDGs and caring for country, by being silent about Indigenous sovereignty and sovereignty of country. When country is cared for appropriately, it can be recognised as a fundamental action of a sustainable relationship (see Vásquez-Fernández & Ahenakew pii tai poo taa, 2020). However, the axiological, epistemological, and ontological relationship between caring for country and the sustainable development agenda remains at odds. Caring for country as a sovereign entity is absent within the SDGs. The problem with the relevance and implementation of the SDGs, is that they are predicated on White possession, and do not recognise coloniality's ambivalence and epistemic violence towards country and settler axiological retreat from country (see Kearney, 2021). By this I mean for example, the affluent Global North is pursuing green economies and zero-carbon lifestyles, which includes an expansion of electric car production (Jerez et al., 2021). A key element in this production is lithium batteries, yet nickel mining by European corporates in the Global South is leaving customary lands commodified and abused and is widening social disparities within Indigenous communities (Kowasch, 2018).

I argue that Indigenous knowledges are being co-opted in the absence of recognising Indigenous sovereignty, such that sustainability is framed as the work of Blaks in servitude to the state without ownership and full access to country. This is an act of infantilisation (see Nakata, 2018), whereby Indigenous Peoples are expected to contribute to sustaining land that they do not own, on behalf of others, as Blak performance, whilst the Establishment man watches on with his scorecard. In this performance, neoliberal colonisation is centre stage, country is seen as "land" belonging to the state requiring management not healing, and Blaks must perform cultural acts of magic to maintain biodiversity whilst demonstrating capability and being denied sovereignty. Country becomes othered, seen as a cultural construct, thus no responsibility is required by Establishment man and his state to care for it. For the Establishment man in *lutruwita*, the SDGs are no threat, as they support White possession and promote faux-woke inscriptions in their reporting progress. Indigenous participation in the SDGs requires performances to suit White possession. Thus, the SDGs are relevant to Establishment man, but not Blaks.

6.4.5 The Sovereign Body of Country and Sustainable Development Tropes

Country is a life force and being (see Bawaka Country et al., 2016; Evans, 2019, 2022; Fisher, 2022; Neidjie et al., 1985; Rose, 1996), "one big living thing" (Yolŋu in Bawaka Country et al., 2019, p. 684) and is a sovereign entity within itself. Yankunytjatjara Elder Uncle Bob Randall explains that "the land owns us" (Randall, 2006). Country is sentient, a place of relationality (Brigg & Graham, 2020a), where "the Indigenous sense of belonging, home and place [are] incommensurable [in their] difference" (Moreton-Robinson, 2020). In country, "The Dreaming and Law, operating through Country… invite lawfulness through proportional behaviour…of mutual obligation" (Brigg & Graham, 2020b), where humans and country are in a state of embodiment (Moreton-Robinson, 2020). "Country is alive for us, it cares for us, communicates with us, and we are part of it" (Burarrwaŋa et al., 2019, p. ix). Indigenous sovereignty is distinct from and challenges state sovereignty and is not constrained by White possession or the myth of patriarchal White sovereignty (Moreton-Robinson, 2006). Thus, country is sovereign, through The Dreaming, Lore, mutual obligation, and the relationality between country, Indigenous Peoples, and other-than-human beings. Whilst integral to the sovereignty of Indigenous Peoples, country has feelings, and its own requirements for healing, being cared for, and care giving (see Brigg & Graham, 2020c; Darug Ngurra et al., 2019; Neidjie, 1989; Ngaanyatjarra Pitjantjatjara Yankunytjatjara Women's Council Aboriginal Corporation, 2013; Suchet-Pearson et al., 2013). Country is a "source of health, wellbeing and renewal" (Marshall, 2019, p. 238) providing deep connections with Indigenous Peoples (see Burarrwaŋa et al., 2019; Everett, 2014, 2017; Rose, 1996) and does not require human development. It requires human respect and care (see Darug Ngurra et al., 2020; Magulagi Yarmirr, 1997). It commands, invites, and holds relationships with humans (see Bawaka Country et al., 2019; Evans, 2022; Yunupingu & Muller, 2009).

Country in its diverse forms around the world, should be spared from the tropes of sustainable development (seeIsar, 2017; Santamarina et al., 2015; Shah, 2009), as it harms the sovereign body of country. In particular, the imprecise and contested new development trope (Saiz & Donald, 2017) of leave no one behind (SDG10), in fact does leave country behind by concentrating on humans only. Thus, the SDGs fundamentally ignore the sovereignty of country, as country is seen as land, resources, places for extraction, and human benefit, for the coffers of the Global North. This ignorance parallels and reinforces the disregarding of the voice and sovereignty of Indigenous Peoples in the SDGs, as Indigenous Peoples are of country and place. It is no surprise then, that Indigenous Peoples are pushing back on the sustainable development agenda, calling out its parasitic neoliberal settler colonialism (see Haebich, 2015; Whyte, 2018). Indigenous Peoples speak on behalf of their country, homelands, traditional estates, and tribal lands (see Feodoroff, 2022; Fisher, 2022; Marshall, 2019; Ramírez et al., 2018). Therefore, their voice and sovereignty are paramount in any agenda, policy, law, and debate regarding how country should be respected, cared for, and kept safe from sustainable development tropes.

6.5   Conclusion

As I work through this investigation, it has become apparent that both the Tasmanian and Australian Governments continue to disrespect Aboriginal and Torres Strait Islander Peoples, their culture and country, through their actions of Blakcuriosity and faux-wokeness. These governments are not acting alone but are blindly mimicking the perpetual colonising behaviours of the Global North. Under the banner of the SDGs and its agenda, the Establishment man is able to work fluidly across geographies, domains of government, corporations, and society, uninterruptedly exercising his White possession of country, control of sovereignty, and ongoing racism against Blaks and Indigenous Peoples. Through his domination, Establishment man renders Blaks and Indigenous Peoples invisible, irrelevant, or incapable, only to be acknowledged when their plight becomes a marketable brand for the Global North to attract neoliberal and philanthropic investors in their schemes to develop the Global South. The Establishment man does his colonising work so that he can keep Blaks off their country. This way the SDGs are rendered something that goes on "over there," an othered place where the poor Blacks in Africa (see Evans, Chapter 5, this volume) and the Indigenous Peoples of the Global South eek out an existence and are infantilised in servitude as ecological restorers. The SDGs are profoundly colonising, rooted in cultural imperialism and create conditions whereby structural racism, stalling of meaningful treaties with Indigenous Peoples and denial of Indigenous Voice to parliament, can flourish.

It is not clear if there is an antidote for decolonising the SDGs. To suggest that the SDGs need to be decolonised, or could be decolonised is naive and simplistic, as the values of the SDGs are representative of global society, capitalism, and the consumption of country for benefit of some humans. If decolonisation of the SDGs were to be entertained, work would need to start with a focus on the Global North. This would require "deep decolonisation," whereby hegemony would have to be stripped to the bone, development tropes eradicated, and White possession given up. This would require a fundamental overturning in power relations, a reversing of the domination and control exercised over the Global South by the Global North. This would not be a straightforward "refresh" of the SDGs, but rather a fundamental rebuild, based on the dismantling of White possession. In this fantasy, Blaks and Indigenous Peoples would be required to cease their support for the privileged lifeworlds of the Global North and resist subjugation.

Alternatively, the SDGs and the sustainable development agenda needs to be called out as colonising, along with its faux-woke reporting and the scourge of Blakcuriosity and the White privilege it upholds. Further, Establishment man needs to be held to account as a significant colonising force and his neoliberal agenda and binarism of Indigenous Peoples of the Global South requires challenging. Most importantly, country as an entity in its own right, with its own sovereignty, and shared sovereignty with First Peoples must be respected. Only then, can all Peoples share the responsibility to heal and care for country.

References

ABC News. (2018, June 8). *SA Government decides not to go ahead with Aboriginal treaties.* https://www.abc.net.au/news/2018-06-08/sa-govt-decides-not-to-go-ahead-with-aboriginal-treaty/9851166

Aboriginal Land Council Tasmania. (2021, March 31). *Submission from ALCT: Reservation of future potential production forest land in the Tasmanian Wilderness World Heritage Area.* https://nre.tas.gov.au/Documents/71%20FPPF%20Land%20Submission%20-%20Aboriginal%20Land%20Council%20Tasmania.pdf

Adrill, A. (2013). Australian sovereignty, indigenous standpoint theory and feminist standpoint theory: First peoples' sovereignties matter. *Griffith Law Review, 22*(2), 315–343.

Altman, J. (2018). Indigenous Australia. In Academics Stand Against Poverty Oceania (Eds.), *Australia, poverty, and the sustainable development goals: A response to what the Australian Government writes about poverty in its report on the implementation of the sustainable development goals* (pp. 19–23). University of Wollongong.

Audit Office of New South Wales. (2022). *Facilitating and administering Aboriginal land claim processes.* https://www.audit.nsw.gov.au/our-work/reports/facilitating-and-administering-aboriginal-land-claim-processes

Australian Government. (2018). *Report on the implementation of the sustainable development goals 2018.* https://www.dfat.gov.au/sites/default/files/sdg-voluntary-national-review.pdf

Australian Government. (2020). *Closing the gap report 2020.* https://ctgreport.niaa.gov.au/sites/default/files/pdf/closing-the-gap-report-2020.pdf

Australian Government. (2022). *About the EPBC Act.* https://www.awe.gov.au/environment/epbc/about

Australian Institute of Aboriginal and Torres Strait Islander Studies. (2016). *Native title information handbook Tasmania 2016.* https://aiatsis.gov.au/sites/default/files/research_pub/native_title_information_handbook_2016_tas_2.pdf

Bawaka Country, Suchet-Pearson, S., Wright, S., Lloyd, K., Tofa, M., Sweeney, J., Burarrwanga, L., Ganambarr, R., Ganambarr-Stubbs, M., & Maymuru, D. (2019). Goŋ Gurtha: Enacting response-abilities as situated co-becoming. *Environment and Planning D: Society and Space, 37*(4), 682–702.

Bawaka Country, Wright, S., Suchet-Pearson, S., Lloyd, K., Burarrwanga, L., Ganambarr, R., Ganambarr-Stubbs, M., Ganambarr, B., & Maymuru, D. (2015). Working with and learning from Country: Decentring human authority. *Cultural Geographies, 22*(2), 269–283.

Bawaka Country, Wright, S., Suchet-Pearson, S., Lloyd, K., Burarrwanga, L., Ganambarr, R., Ganambarr-Stubbs, M., Ganambarr, B., Maymuru, D., & Sweeney, J. (2016). Co-becoming Bawaka: Towards a relational understanding of place/space. *Progress in Human Geography, 40*(4), 455–475.

Baylis, T. (2015). Introduction: Looking in to the mirror. In D. Hodge (Ed.), *Colouring the rainbow. Blak Queer and trans perspectives: Life stories and essays by first nations people of Australia* (pp. 1–18). Wakefield Press.

Beckman, L., Gover, K., & Mörkenstam, U. (2022). The popular sovereignty of Indigenous peoples: A challenge in multi-people states. *Citizenship Studies, 26*(1), 1–20.

Blackwood, F. (2021, October 10). Tasmanian treaty to navigate complex path of truth-telling, Aboriginal identity and land return. *ABC News.* https://www.abc.net.au/news/2021-10-10/aboriginal-treaty-tasmania-talks-underway/100492656

BlaQ. (2021). *Blaq Mail*. BlaQ Aboriginal Corporation. www.blaq.org.au/media.

Brigg, M., & Graham, M. (2020a, May 24). The relevance of Aboriginal political concepts (1): The current pandemic and the importance of ancient wisdom. *ABC Religion & Ethics*. https://www.abc.net.au/religion/coronavirus-and-aboriginal-political-concepts-morgan-brigg-and/12281304

Brigg, M., & Graham, M. (2020b, August 13). The relevance of Aboriginal political concepts (4): how "proportionality" can help close the gap. *ABC Religion & Ethics*. https://www.abc.net.au/religion/morgan-brigg-and-mary-graham-aboriginal-political-concepts-prop/12553830

Brigg, M., & Graham, M. (2020c, October 26). The relevance of Aboriginal political concepts (5): Country, place and territory. *ABC Religion & Ethics*. https://www.abc.net.au/religion/aboriginal-political-concepts-country-place-territory/12815608

Broinowski, I. (2019). *The pakana voice: Tales of a war correspondent from lutruwita (Tasmania) 1814–1856*. Lulu.com.

Brown, R. M., Copeland, H., Crawford, R., Gates, T., Lax, T., Lowe, R., & Tancons, C. (2014). Question & Answer 3. *Nka: Journal of Contemporary African Art, 34*(1), 94–96. https://muse.jhu.edu/article/548195/pdf

Burarrwaṇa, L., Ganambarr, R., Ganambarr-Stubbs, M., Ganambarr, B., Maymuru, D., Wright, S., Suchet-Pearson, S., & Lloyd, K. (2019). *Songspirals: Sharing women's wisdom of Country through songlines*. Allen & Unwin.

Burt, A. (2022). A spoke in the wheel: Ancestral women's legacies. In *tebrakunna* country and E. Lee & J. Evans (Eds.), *Indigenous women's voices: 20 Years on from Linda Tuhiwai Smith's decolonizing methodologies* (pp. 107–119). Zed Books, Bloomsbury Publishing.

Cameron. P. (2019, August 26). *Trick or treaty? Tasmania's unfinished business inaugural lecture for World Indigenous People's Day*. TRACA, Tasmanian Regional Aboriginal Communities Alliance. https://traca.com.au/blog/2019/08/26/trick-or-treaty-tasmanias-unfinished-business/

Clark, M. (2015). Indigenous subjectivity in Australia: Are we queer? *Journal of Global Indigeneity, 1*(1), 7.

Clark, T., Dodson, S., Guivarra, N., & Widders Hunt, Y. (2021). "We're not treated equally as Indigenous people or as women": The perspectives and experiences of Indigenous women in Australian public relations. *Public Relations Inquiry, 10*(2), 163–183.

Clements, N. (2014). *The black war: Fear, sex and resistance in Tasmania*. University of Queensland Press.

Cooper, E. (2020, November 15). The hopes for a Tasmanian Aboriginal treaty focus on a diary entry from 1831. *ABC News*. https://www.abc.net.au/news/2020-11-15/tasmanian-aboriginal-treaty-push-renewed/12883932

Cox, R. (2021). *Broken spear: The untold story of black Tom Birch, the man who sparked Australia's bloodiest war*. Wakefield Press.

Darug Custodian Aboriginal Corporation. (2022). *Darug boundaries*. https://darugcorporation.com.au/about/

Darug Ngurra, Dadd, U. L., Glass, P., Norman-Dadd, A. C., Hodge, P., Suchet-Pearson, S., Graham, M., Judge, S., Scott, R., & Lemire, J. (2020). Yanama Budyari Gumada, walk with good spirit as method: Co-creating local environmental stewards on/with/as Darug Ngurra. In A. Campbell, M. Duffy, & B. Edmondson (Eds.), *Located research* (pp. 15–37). Palgrave Macmillan.

Darug Ngurra, Dadd, L., Glass, P., Scott, R., Graham, M., Judge, S., Hodge, P., & Suchet-Pearson, S. (2019). Yanama budyari gumada: Reframing the urban to care as Darug Country in western Sydney. *Australian Geographer, 50*(3), 279–293.

Davis, M. (2022). Speaking up: The truth about truth-telling. *Griffith Review, 76*, 25–35.

Dunstan, J. (2021, March 9). Victoria announces landmark truth and justice royal commission as part of Aboriginal treaty talks. *ABC News*. https://www.abc.net.au/news/2021-03-09/victoria-truth-and-justice-royal-commission-aboriginal-treaty/13226116

Evans, J. (2019). Giving voice to the sacred black female body in takayna country. In J. Liljeblad & B. Verschuuren (Eds.), *Indigenous perspectives on sacred natural sites* (pp. 15–31). Routledge.

Evans, J. (2022). Can men weave baskets in Queer country. In *tebrakunna* country and E. Lee & J. Evans (Eds.), *Indigenous women's voices: 20 Years on from Linda Tuhiwai Smith's decolonizing methodologies* (pp. 33–50). Zed Books, Bloomsbury Publishing.

Everett, J. (2014). Savage nation first nations' philosophy and sovereignty. *Southerly, 74*(2), 27–42.

Everett, J. (2017). *The First Tasmanian: Our story* [Exhibition]. Queen Victoria Museum and Art Gallery.

Feodoroff, P. (2022). What form can an atonement take? In *tebrakunna* country and E. Lee & J. Evans (Eds.), *Indigenous women's voices: 20 Years on from Linda Tuhiwai Smith's decolonizing methodologies* (pp. 169–188). Zed Books, Bloomsbury Publishing.

Finley, C. (2011). Decolonizing the queer native body (and recovering the native bull-dyke). Bringing 'Sexy Back' and Out of Native Studies' Closet. In Q-L. Driskill, C. Finley, B. J. Gilley, & S. L. Morgensen (Eds.), *Queer Indigenous studies: Critical interventions in theory, politics, and literature* (pp. 31–42). University of Arizona Press.

Fisher, K. (2022). Decolonizing rivers in Aotearoa New Zealand. In *tebrakunna* country and E. Lee & J. Evans (Eds.), *Indigenous women's voices: 20 Years on from Linda Tuhiwai Smith's decolonizing methodologies* (pp. 17–31). Zed Books, Bloomsbury Publishing.

Fitzpatrick, S. (2018). Closing the gap: Coming to terms with a decade of failure. *The Australian.* http://www.kooriweb.org/foley/news/2000s/2018/aust12feb2018a.pdf

Frankenburg, R. (1993). *White women, race matters: The social construction of whiteness.* Routledge.

Fredericks, B., & Bradfield, A. (2021). 'Seeking to be heard': The role of social and online media in advocating for the Uluru Statement from the Heart and constitutional reform in Australia. *Journal of Alternative & Community Media, 6*(1), 29–54.

Fredericks, B. L., & Croft, P. (2002). Book review of "Talkin'Up to the White Woman," Aileen Moreton-Robinson, University of Queensland Press. *IDIOM 23, 14*(1), 117–119.

Fukuda-Parr, S. (2016). From the Millennium Development Goals to the Sustainable Development Goals: Shifts in purpose, concept, and politics of global goal setting for development. *Gender & Development, 24*(1), 43–52.

Gough, J. (2021). The progress of disclosure. In J. Gough (Ed.), *Past tense* (pp. 253–280). Tebrikunna Press.

Haebich, A. (2015). Neoliberalism, settler colonialism and the history of Indigenous child removal in Australia. *Australian Indigenous Law Review, 19*(1), 20–31.

Hall, N. L., Creamer, S., Anders, W., Slatyer, A., & Hill, P. S. (2020). Water and health interlinkages of the sustainable development goals in remote Indigenous Australia. *NPJ Clean Water, 3*(1), 1–7.

Harley, A. (2015). What value does a treaty have in Australia? *Indigenous Law Bulletin, 8*(16), 17–19.

Harman, K. (2018). 'As much as they can gorge': Colonial containment and Indigenous Tasmanian mobility at Oyster Cove Aboriginal Station. In R. Standfield (Ed.), *Indigenous mobilities: Across and beyond the antipodes* (pp. 145–165). ANU Press.

Higgins, I., & Collard, S. (2019, November 29). WA Indigenous group's $290 billion compensation claim could become one of the world's biggest payouts. *ABC News.* https://www.abc.net.au/news/2019-11-29/$290-billion-wa-native-title-claim-launched/11749206

Holmes, A. (2022, March 5). Tasmanian treaty and truth-telling faces Aboriginality issue as TAC threatens to walk away from process. *The Advocate.* https://www.theadvocate.com.au/story/7645359/could-vexed-issue-scuttle-tasmanian-treaty-talks-at-the-start/

Hosier, P. (2019, February 21). Tom and Jane own 220 hectares—Today they're handing back half to the Aboriginal community. *ABC News.* https://www.abc.net.au/news/2019-02-21/tasmanian-private-land-handed-back-to-aboriginal-community/10825984

Howitt, R. (2006). Scales of coexistence: Tackling the tension between legal and cultural landscapes in post-Mabo Australia. *Macquarie Law Journal, 6*, 49–64.

Iqtadar, S., Hernández-Saca, D. I., Ellison, B. S., & Cowley, D. M. (2021). Global conversations: Recovery and detection of Global South multiply-marginalized bodies. *Race Ethnicity and Education, 24*(5), 719–736.

Isar, Y. R. (2017). 'Culture', 'sustainable development' and cultural policy: A contrarian view. *International Journal of Cultural Policy, 23*(2), 148–158.

Jerez, B., Garcés, I., & Torres, R. (2021). Lithium extractivism and water injustices in the Salar de Atacama, Chile: The colonial shadow of green electromobility. *Political Geography, 87*, 102382.

Kearney, A. (2021). To cut down the dreaming: Epistemic violence, ambivalence and the logic of coloniality. *Anthropological Forum, 31*(3), 312–334.

Khosravinik, M. (2017). Right wing populism in the west: Social media discourse and echo chambers. *Insight Turkey, 19*(3), 53–68.

Kildea, P., & Synot, E. (2022, May 26). We keep hearing about a First Nations Voice to Parliament, but what would it actually look like in practice? *The Conversation.* https://theconversation.com/we-keep-hearing-about-a-first-nations-voice-to-parliament-but-what-would-it-actually-look-like-in-practice-183718

Kingsley, J., Townsend, M., Henderson-Wilson, C., & Bolam, B. (2013). Developing an exploratory framework linking Australian Aboriginal peoples' connection to country and concepts of wellbeing. *International Journal of Environmental Research and Public Health, 10*(2), 678–698.

Kneale, M. (2000). *English passengers.* Penguin Books.

Kowasch, M. (2018). Nickel mining in northern New Caledonia—A path to sustainable development? *Journal of Geochemical Exploration, 194*, 280–290.

Krauss, J. E. (2021). Decolonizing, conviviality and convivial conservation: Towards a convivial SDG 15, life on land? *Journal of Political Ecology, 28*(1). https://doi.org/10.2458/jpe.3008

Langton, M. (2020). Welcome to country: Knowledge. *Agora, 55*(1), 3–10.

Lee, E. (2015). Protected areas, country and value: The nature–culture tyranny of the IUCN's protected area guidelines for Indigenous Australians. *Antipode, 48*(2), 355–374.

Lowitja Institute. (2022). *Close the Gap: Transforming power: Voices for generational change, Close the Gap campaign report 2022.* Lowitja Institute for the Close the Gap Steering Committee, Australia.

Macoun, A. (2016). Colonising white innocence: Complicity and critical encounters. In S. Maddison, T. Clark, & R. de Costa (Eds.), *The limits of settler colonial reconciliation* (pp. 85–102). Springer.

Magulagi Yarmirr, M. (1997). Women and land rights: Past, present and future. In G. Yunupingu (Ed.), *Our land is our life: Land rights—Past, present and future* (pp. 80–83). University of Queensland Press.

Mansell, M. (2003). Citizenship, assimilation and a treaty. In *Treaty: Let's get it right!* (pp. 5–17). Aboriginal Studies Press.

Mansell, M. (2016). *Treaty and statehood: Aboriginal self-determination.* Federation Press.

Mansell, M. (2022, March 3). Statement—Michael Mansell, Chairman, Aboriginal Land Council of Tasmania. *Tasmanian Times.* https://tasmaniantimes.com/2022/03/on-pathway-to-truth-telling-and-treaty/?fbclid=IwAR0-oncPn3qNp3SoJ6HUdhGATZrvCvAMsLLbUv04CuqhkEyrG6ipqojw3Wo

Marks, K. (2013). Channelling Mannalargenna: Surviving, belonging, challenging, enduring. *Griffth Review, 39*, 174–192.

Marshall, V. (2019). Removing the veil from the 'Rights of Nature': The dichotomy between First Nations customary rights and environmental legal personhood. *Australian Feminist Law Journal, 45*(2), 233–248.

McLoughlin, C., & Boisvert, E. (2022, June 13). Consultation to start on SA Indigenous voice to parliament ahead of 2023 launch. *ABC News.* https://www.abc.net.au/news/2022-06-13/consultation-to-start-on-sa-voice-to-parliament/101147480

Milroy, T., & Bandler, L. G. (2021). Closing the Gap: Where to now? *Medical Journal of Australia, 214*(5), 209–210.

Moggridge, J., Pecl, G., Lansbury, N., Creamer, S., & Mosby, V. (2022, March 4). IPCC reports still exclude Indigenous voices. Come join us at our sacred fires to find answers to climate change. *The Conversation.* https://theconversation.com/ipcc-reports-still-exclude-indigenous-voices-come-join-us-at-our-sacred-fires-to-find-answers-to-climate-change-178045

Monaghan, O. (2015). Dual imperatives: Decolonising the queer and queering the decolonial. In D. Hodge (Ed.), *Colouring the rainbow. Blak queer and trans perspectives: Life stories and essays by first nations people of Australia* (pp. 195–207). Wakefield Press.

Moodie, D., Menzell, K., Cameron, L., & Moodie, N. (2022). Blak & salty: Reflections on violence and racism. In *tebrakunna* country and E. Lee & J. Evans (Eds.), *Indigenous women's voices: 20 Years on from Linda Tuhiwai Smith's decolonizing methodologies* (pp. 69–85). Zed Books, Bloomsbury Publishing.

Moreton-Robinson, A. (2000). *Talkin' Up to the White woman: Aboriginal women and feminism.* University of Queensland Press.

Moreton-Robinson, A. (2003). I still call Australia home: Indigenous belonging and place in a white postcolonizing society. In S. Ahmed, A. M. Fortier, M. Sheller, & C. Castaneda (Eds.), *Uprootings/regroundings questions of home and migration* (pp. 23–40). Routledge.

Moreton-Robinson, A. (2006). Towards a new research agenda? Foucault, whiteness and indigenous sovereignty. *Journal of Sociology, 42*(4), 383–395.

Moreton-Robinson, A. (2007). Introduction: Sovereign subjects. In A. Moreton-Robinson (Ed.), *Indigenous sovereignty matters: Sovereign subjects* (pp. 1–11). Allen & Unwin.

Moreton-Robinson, A. (2013). Towards an Australian Indigenous women's standpoint theory: A methodological tool. *Australian Feminist Studies, 28*(78), 331–347.

Moreton-Robinson, A. (2015). *The white possessive: Property, power, and indigenous sovereignty.* University of Minnesota Press.

Moreton-Robinson, A. (2020, November 9). "Our story is in the land": Why the Indigenous sense of belonging unsettles white Australia. *ABC Religion & Ethics.* https://www.abc.net.au/religion/our-story-is-in-the-land-indigenous-sense-of-belonging/11159992

Murphy, L., Graham, M., & Brigg, M. (2017, June 22). The Uluru Statement: We never ceded sovereignty, but can we join yours? *NITV News.* https://www.sbs.com.au/nitv/nitv-news/article/2017/06/22/uluru-statement-we-never-ceded-sovereignty-can-we-join-yours#:~:text=2017%20%2D%203%3A14pm-,The%20Uluru%20Statement%3A%20We%20never%20ceded,but%20can%20we%20join%20yours%3F&text=Comment%3A%20The%20Uluru%20statement%20from,but%20in%20fact%2C%20enshrines%20it

Nakata, M. (2007). *Disciplining the savages: Savaging the discipline.* Aboriginal Studies Press.

Nakata, S. (2018). The infantilisation of indigenous Australians: A problem for democracy. *Griffith Review, 60*, 104–116.

Neidjie, B. (1989). *Story about feeling.* Magabala Books.

Neidjie, B., Davis, S., & Fox, A. (1985). *Kakadu man—Bill Neidjie.* Mybrood P/L Incorporated.

Ngaanyatjarra Pitjantjatjara Yankunytjatjara Women's Council Aboriginal Corporation. (2013). *Traditional healers of Central Australia: Ngangkari.* Magabala Books.

Nicoll, F. (2004). Reconciliation in and out of perspective: White knowing, seeing, curating and being at home in and against Indigenous sovereignty. *Whitening Race: Essays in Social and Cultural Criticism, 1*, 17–31.

Pasimio, J. A. (2020). A snapshot of the lives of Indigenous women. In R. P. Ofreneo & J. F. I. Illo (Eds.), *Philippine NGO Beijing+25 Report* (pp. 405–417). University of the Philippines Center for Women's and Gender Studies.

Petersen, D. L., Barber, M. E., Nix Zelin, M. D., & Yarbrough, E. (2020). The L in LGBTQ[2] IAPA. In P. Levounis & E. Yarbrough (Eds.), *Pocket guide to LGBTQ mental health: Understanding the spectrum of gender and sexuality* (pp. 1–6). American Psychiatric Association Publishing.

Pha, A. (2020, February 24). Closing the Gap more than rhetoric required. *The Workers' Weekly Guardian.* https://search.informit.org/doi/epdf/10.3316/ielapa.023403030526751

Pratt, A. M. (2003). *"Indigenous sovereignty-never ceded": Sovereignty, nationhood and whiteness in Australia* [Doctoral thesis, University of Wollongong].

Pybus, C. (2020). *Truganini journey though the apocalypse*. Allen & Unwin.

Pybus, C., & Moore, T. (2019). White guilt, Aboriginal culturalism and the impoverishment of tertiary education in Australia. *Journal of the European Association for Studies on Australia, 10*(1), 59–77.

Ramírez, A. P. V., Aragón, Ú. G., Ulisse, A., Cerami, D., & de la Cruz Carillo, S. (2018). Sacred Heart of Mexico: Pueblo Wixárika (Huichol). In J. Liljeblad & B. Verschuuren (Eds.), *Indigenous perspectives on sacred natural sites: Culture, governance and conservation* (pp. 155–166). Routledge.

Randall, B. (2006). *The land owns us* [Video]. Global Oneness Project. Hogan, M. (Producer), Randall, B. & Hogan, M. (Directors). https://www.youtube.com/watch?v=w0sWIVR1hXw&t=17s

Redolfi, G., Pikramenou, N., & Algora, R. G. (2019). Raising Indigenous women's voices for equal rights and self-determination. *New England Journal of Public Policy, 31*(2), Article 9.

Rose, D. B. (1996). Land rights and deep colonising: The erasure of women. *Aboriginal Law Bulletin, 3*(85), 6–13.

Ross, D. (2017). Black country, white wilderness: Conservation, colonialism, and conflict in Tasmania. *Journal for Undergraduate Ethnography, 7*(1), 1–24.

Ryan, L. (2012). *Tasmanian Aborigines: A history since 1803*. Allen & Unwin.

Saiz, I., & Donald, K. (2017). Tackling inequality through the Sustainable Development Goals: Human rights in practice. *The International Journal of Human Rights, 21*(8), 1029–1049.

Santamarina, B., Vaccaro, I., & Beltran, O. (2015). The sterilization of eco-criticism: From sustainable development to green capitalism. *Anduli Revista Andaluza de Ciencias Sociales, 14*, 13–28.

Shah, E. (2009). *Manifesting utopia: History and philosophy of UN debates on science and technology for sustainable development* (STEPS working paper 25). STEPS Centre. https://opendocs.ids.ac.uk/opendocs/handle/20.500.12413/2451

Shine, R. (2017, June 3). Mabo anniversary: Aboriginal Tasmanians say land handback fight far from over. *ABC News*. https://www.abc.net.au/news/2017-06-03/what-did-mabo-mean-for-aboriginal-tasmanians/8585452

Shipton, L., & Dauvergne, P. (2021). The politics of transnational advocacy against Chinese, Indian, and Brazilian extractive projects in the Global South. *The Journal of Environment & Development, 30*(3), 240–264.

Siganto, T. (2019, July 14). Queensland Government announces 'conversation' to formalise Indigenous treaty. *ABC News*. https://www.abc.net.au/news/2019-07-14/queensland-government-indigenous-treaty-process-promise/11307682

Simpson, L. B. (2017). *As we have always done: Indigenous freedom through radical resistance*. University of Minnesota Press.

Slater, L. (2018). *Anxieties of belonging in settler colonialism: Australia, race and place*. Routledge.

Smith, L. T. (2021). *Decolonizing methodologies: Research and indigenous peoples*. Bloomsbury Publishing.

Suchet-Pearson, S., Wright, S., Lloyd, K., Burarrwanga, L., & Country, B. (2013). Caring as Country: Towards an ontology of co-becoming in natural resource management. *Asia Pacific Viewpoint, 54*(2), 185–197.

Sullivan, C. T. (2018). Indigenous Australian women's colonial sexual intimacies: Positioning indigenous women's agency. *Culture, Health & Sexuality, 20*(4), 397–410.

Sullivan. C. (2020). Launching the "Preliminary Report to Community" Sharing the stories of #lgbtiq+ #blaq youth @the NICE @westernsydney @westernduics @blaq blah.org.au. *Twitter*. https://www.twitter.com/rin_sullivan/status/1325592317441445890

Sullivan, C., & Day, M. (2019). Queer (y) ing Indigenous Australian higher education student spaces. *The Australian Journal of Indigenous Education, 50*(1), 2–9.

Sullivan, S. (2014). *Good white people: The problem with middle-class white anti-racism*. Sunny Press.

Tasmanian Government. (2022, March 1). *Next steps on pathway to truth-telling and treaty.* https://www.premier.tas.gov.au/site_resources_2015/additional_releases/next_steps_on_pathway_to_truth-telling_and_treaty

Taylor, R. (2017). *Into the heart of Tasmania.* Melbourne University Press.

tebrakunna country and Lee. E (2022). Reclaiming the first person voice. In *tebrakunna* country and E. Lee & J. Evans (Eds.), *Indigenous women's voices: 20 Years on from Linda Tuhiwai Smith's decolonizing methodologies* (pp. 137–150). Zed Books, Bloomsbury Publishing.

tebrakunna country, Lee, E., & Evans, J. (2022). Indigenous women's voices: 20 Years on from Linda Tuhiwai Smith's decolonizing methodologies. In *tebrakunna* country and E. Lee & J. Evans (Eds.), *Indigenous women's voices: 20 Years on from Linda Tuhiwai Smith's decolonizing methodologies* (pp. 1–14). Zed Books, Bloomsbury Publishing.

tebrakunna country, Lee, E., Richardson, B. J., & Ross, H. (2020). The 'Uluru Statement from the Heart': Investigating Indigenous Australian sovereignty. *Journal of Australian Indigenous Issues, 23*(1–2), 18–41.

Torre, G. (2022, May 2). Decades-long claims backlog highlights NSW native title failure. *National Indigenous Times.* https://nit.com.au/decades-long-claims-backlog-highlights-nsw-native-title-failure/?fbclid=IwAR0HVoeptlWSgvB8kcnX3TSDpDBZusUze35mynLD6HN28jVf7sqWW04kSCs

Uluru Statement from the Heart. (2017). *The statement.* https://ulurustatement.org/the-statement/

United Nations. (2015, June 24). *Farmers, food security and sovereignty—Interactive dialogue.* https://sdgs.un.org/sites/default/files/statements/15013farmers.pdf

United Nations Department of Economic and Social Affairs. (2017). *United Nations Permanent Forum on Indigenous Issues.* https://www.facebook.com/unpfii/videos/1608748162471543

United Nations Department of Economic and Social Affairs. (2021). *5th Volume: State of the world's Indigenous peoples: Rights to lands, territories, and resources.* https://www.un.org/development/desa/indigenouspeoples/wp-content/uploads/sites/19/2021/03/State-of-Worlds-Indigenous-Peoples-Vol-V-Final.pdf

United Nations Environment Programme. (2021). *Making peace with nature a scientific blueprint to tackle the climate, biodiversity and pollution emergencies.* https://www.unep.org/resources/making-peace-nature

Vanderfeen, J. (2022). Black panopticon: Who wins with lateral violence? In *tebrakunna* country and E. Lee & J. Evans (Eds.), *Indigenous women's voices: 20 Years on from Linda Tuhiwai Smith's decolonizing methodologies* (pp. 53–68). Zed Books, Bloomsbury Publishing.

Vásquez-Fernández, A. M., & Ahenakew pii tai poo taa, C. (2020). Resurgence of relationality: Reflections on decolonizing and indigenizing 'sustainable development.' *Current Opinion in Environmental Sustainability, 43*, 65–70.

Wahlquist, C. (2017, October 26). Turnbull's Uluru Statement rejection is 'Mean-Spirited Bastardry'—Legal expert. *The Guardian.* https://www.theguardian.com/australia-news/2017/oct/26/turnbulls-uluru-statement-rejection-mean-spirited-bastardry-legal-expert

Warner, K., McCormack, T., & Kurnadi, F. (2021). *Pathway to truth-telling and treaty: Report to Premier Peter Gutwin.* https://www.dpac.tas.gov.au/__data/assets/pdf_file/0029/228881/Pathway_to_Truth-Telling_and_Treaty_251121.pdf

Wellington, S. (2018, June 8). Indigenous treaty a step closer after NT Government makes historic pledge. *ABC News.* https://www.abc.net.au/news/2018-06-08/indigenous-treaty-a-step-closer-after-nt-government-pledge/9848856

Whyte, K. P. (2018). On resilient parasitisms, or why I'm skeptical of Indigenous/settler reconciliation. *Journal of Global Ethics, 14*(2), 277–289.

Wilson, A., & Laing, M. (2019). Queering indigenous education. In L. T. Smith, E. Tuck, & K. W. Yang (Eds.), *Indigenous and decolonizing studies in education* (pp. 131–145). Routledge.

Wilson, R. (2011). *The roving party.* Allen & Unwin.

Yap, M. L. M., & Watene, K. (2019). The Sustainable Development Goals (SDGs) and Indigenous peoples: Another missed opportunity? *Journal of Human Development and Capabilities, 20*(4), 451–467.

Yunupingu, D., & Muller, S. (2009). Cross-cultural challenges for Indigenous sea country management in Australia. *Australasian Journal of Environmental Management, 16*(3), 158–167.

Chapter 7
Future Lawyers, Future Laws: Reimagining Legal Education for Sustainability in a World "Governing Through Goals"

Phillipa C. McCormack and Michelle Lim

7.1 Introduction

> The practice of the law and the essential role of the lawyer in society is, after all, about very much more than knowing the law. (The Hon. Michael Black AC QC in Black, 2017, p. 12)

Current cohorts of law students are preparing to enter the legal profession in a very, very different world to the one that their academic instructors, and earlier generations of lawyers, encountered. As reflected in the comment above by the Hon. Michael Black (2017), practising law requires more than *knowing* the law. Now, more than ever, legal academics need to be mindful that we are training lawyers for *their* future. That is, for futures that *they* are moving towards and have the opportunity to influence—not for the future we had imagined for ourselves. The world is changing rapidly. Emerging social, technological, and ecological challenges are changing and complicating the task of educating the next generation of legal graduates. When updating an edited collection on the topic of changes in legal education, first published 20 years ago, Twining (2018) noted that even he had "underestimated the acceleration of the pace of change in education, legal services, information technology, globalisation and so on" (p. 250) (see also Roper et al., 2020).

P. C. McCormack (✉)
Adelaide Law School, The University of Adelaide, Adelaide, SA 5005, Australia
e-mail: phillipa.mccormack@adelaide.edu.au

Centre for Marine Socioecology, Taroona, TAS 7053, Australia

M. Lim
Yong Pung How School of Law, Singapore Management University, Singapore, Singapore
e-mail: michellel@smu.edu.sg

© The Author(s), under exclusive license to Springer Nature Singapore Pte Ltd. 2023
K. Beasy et al. (eds.), *Education and the UN Sustainable Development Goals*, Education for Sustainability 7,
https://doi.org/10.1007/978-981-99-3802-5_7

In a broader sense, legal educators—like educators in other professional degree programs—are in a powerful position to influence not just how our students understand the rules of their profession and their roles as members of it, but also their expectations and perspectives on the world and their futures. We also have the honour and challenge of influencing our students' expectations of the health and adaptive capacity of future institutional structures, communities, and environments; and we can help our students to see more clearly their own capacity to influence what futures are possible.

Implementation and achievement of the Sustainable Development Goals (SDGs) depends, at least in part, on effective global and domestic laws and policies. For example, at the heart of achieving SDG13 ("Take urgent action on climate change and its impacts") is the Paris Agreement, a global (legal) agreement that will be implemented through regional and domestic legislation and policies, under which governments will seek to rapidly reduce global carbon emissions, facilitate climate adaptation, and respond to climate-related loss and damage. Many of the people that will help to design, draft, and implement those laws and policies will have legal training: the kind of training that can help them to understand legal and political constraints (and opportunities) and use law-making processes to their greatest effect. Similarly, SDG16 ("Peace, justice, and strong institutions") includes a focus on access to justice and building effective, accountable, and inclusive institutions. Concepts of peace and justice are core business for lawyers, advocates, and legal researchers, including through the implementation and enforcement of legal instruments such as anti-discrimination laws, through institutions such as anti-corruption and integrity bodies, and long-established sub-disciplines in law such as administrative, constitutional, criminal, and human rights law (see Rigney, 2020).

In addition to the significance of law for implementing and achieving certain specific SDGs, the structure of the SDG framework as a whole also mirrors the existing architecture of international agreements. The siloed nature of goals and targets about climate, oceans, and biodiversity on land, for example, reflect corresponding conventions that pre-date the SDGs by decades (Kim, 2016).

Legal research and practice will both be needed to enhance humanity's opportunities to promote, critique, and ultimately achieve the healthy, flourishing, and equitable world contemplated by the SDGs. Furthermore, our contribution allows us to offer a governance-focused critique of legal education and the SDGs. We highlight both weaknesses and opportunities, including equipping law graduates to reconceive the global governance envisioned in the SDGs, in a way that enhances our capacity to realise more equitable and effective governance of complex socio-ecological systems.

With interdisciplinary expertise in climate and biodiversity law and combined teaching experience at five different Australian law schools in four Australian states, our contribution to this book reflects our shared interest in analysing and promoting reform of legal frameworks to support the pursuit of desirable global futures (e.g. Lim, 2019; Lim & Allan, 2016; McCormack, 2018, 2020; Wyborn et al., 2020). We also share a keen desire to equip the next generation of law graduates to pursue those desirable futures and to build in them the capacity to adapt, professionally and personally, to the complexity of a rapidly changing world.

Recognising the conceptual complexity inherent in the term, we have not adopted a definition of "sustainability" for this chapter (Wals & Jickling, 2008). Like Wals and Jickling, we acknowledge that the concept of sustainability can mask deep and irreconcilable differences "under the false pretence of a shared understanding, set of values and common vision of the future." accepting that there is no "single right vision or best way to sustain the earth" and, that underneath the concept of sustainability lie "norms, values and interests that are in conflict," while at the same time, "shallow consensus" about the concept can, itself, "also serve specific prevailing norms, values, and interests" (pp. 223–224).

Even so, "when handled with care," the concept of sustainability may yet have the potential to bring very different people together, providing a common language to discuss environmental and other issues shaping our future (Jickling & Wals, 2008; Wals & Jickling, 2008, p. 222). We argue that, if we are to achieve this richer, deeper goal, of creating a common language to resolve complex challenges, we will need more than the SDGs can offer, at least as they are currently articulated.

With that in mind, our chapter proceeds as follows. First, we set the context for our discussion by highlighting a series of important social, technological, and environmental changes that are growing in speed and scale, making the world more complex and less predictable for both future legal graduates and sustainability institutions. We then look specifically at the SDGs, the ways in which they are operationalised in law and their significant weaknesses. We use the SDGs as a practical example of the need for profound disruption of global governance systems, in recognition of corresponding changes in society, technology, and environments across the world. Next, we consider legal education in Australia and the need for legal educators to foster "transformative, transgressive social learning" (Lotz-Sistitka et al., 2015), alongside delivering core, legal content, to build in legal graduates the resilience and capacity to *be* disruptive practitioners and citizens in pursuit of a healthy, flourishing world. We conclude by drawing from our broader discussion about governance, disruption, and rapid change, to underpin a series of provocations to legal educators and the *academe*, inviting law schools and educators to equip law graduates better with the resources they need to make their future a better place.

7.2 Global Governance Regimes Are Poorly Adapted for This Period of Extreme Disruption

Rapid global changes have important implications for existing governance structures, and for how we understand the roles, possibilities, and constraints of global and domestic governance for the future. However, as the world changes rapidly, global governance structures have proved difficult to reform. In fact, many governance structures retain features that actively obstruct our capacity to adapt and flourish. For example, even as globalisation drives the development of instant, technological networks and consumption across vast distances and populations, governance regimes continue to silo policies and regulations of separate topics such as biodi-versity management, trade, pollution control, and human movement. Dividing the complex and hyperconnected challenges that face us into discrete governance regimes will not help us to understand or resolve them. As other global changes proceed apace, it is now the global governance system that is most in need of disruption. In this section, we briefly highlight three areas of important, rapid, and large-scale change: social, technological, and environmental. Each of these areas profoundly influences governance regimes and global sustainability. These three areas of change also have significant implications for legal education, if we want to enhance the capacity of our law graduates to interact with and influence governance structures and improve sustainability for the future.

The first area of rapid global change with significant implications for legal educa-tion is socio-political change. We define socio-political change broadly to include changes to the way that humans define themselves, individually and in groups, and interact in communities and polities across time and space. Socio-political change is driving, and being driven by, the impacts of globalisation (Sexson & Wilson, 2021), political and social fragmentation, and a decline in shared understandings about truth, transparency, and accountability. Drivers of fragmentation include the individualisation of new media, including social media, and ideological bundling, where groups of people coalesce around shared identities, often defined by political parties or ideological "opponents" rather than a cohesive set of shared values (e.g. Fielding et al., 2012). Social changes with particularly important implications for law and legal education include the emergence of "post-truth" politics (Hannan, 2018; Suiter, 2016), in which effective accountability is difficult to define, allocate, and enforce; a decline in the authority of the rule of law; and a "hollowing out" of the accountability reforms that emerged in Australia in the 1970s (e.g. Australian Public Law, 2021; Krieger et al., 2019). Future legal graduates will almost certainly need to grapple with rapidly changing ideas about the role, influence, and legitimacy of law itself, even as they work to effect change and promote sustainability.

The second critically important area of change with wide-ranging implications for law, legal education, and sustainability is technology (Caserta & Madsen, 2019; Goldsworthy, 2020; Legg et al., 2020; Webb, 2019). Technology is accelerating unsustainability, with technological "solutions" to political and physical bound-aries allowing communication, consumerism, and industrial supply chains to rapidly expand and intensify (Adger et al., 2009; Carrasco et al., 2017; Liu et al., 2013). These same technological developments have shifted environmental degradation from extractive and manufacturing industries from local to far-distant environments. That is the environmental impacts of manufacturing new goods and disposing of waste, such as clothing and electronics, are experienced in one location, typically in the Global South, while the benefits of accessing and using those goods accrue elsewhere, typically in the Global North. Examples include the clearing of primary forests in South East Asia to make way for oil palm plantations. Oil palm is then used in products ranging from biofuels to cosmetics and confectionery and sold to markets around the world (Rulli et al., 2019). Similarly, the clearing of the Amazon rainforest in Latin America is linked to the production of soybeans for food and feed in distant

Asian markets (Liu et al., 2013). This separation of the benefits and harms of excessive consumption and economic growth is driving, exacerbating, and "locking in" both unsustainability and inequality across time and enormous distances.

Some of the implications of advances in technology are positive, promoting more equitable and effective rule-making and supporting the global enforcement of these rules. Hyperconnected flows of information can also result in opportunities for regulation and corporate social responsibility, bringing international consumer pressure to bear on corporate and government interests (Carrasco et al., 2017, pp. 1–5; Lim, 2021, p. 180). Meanwhile, block chain technologies that underpin crypto currencies are being used to track products along extremely complex and opaque supply chains to reveal the (un)sustainability of industries such as fishing and fashion (Paliwal et al., 2020; United Nations Conference on Trade and Development, 2021). Developments in block chain technologies, and legal advisors with expertise in these technologies, create new opportunities for sustainability, including through the enforcement of illegal fishing prohibitions and informing and enhancing the power of consumers to make sustainable choices.

New technologies such as artificial intelligence (AI) and machine learning are also affecting the legal profession, lawyers, and the law (Bell et al., 2020; Caserta, 2021). AI is being deployed to improve efficiency in private, government, and court decision-making processes, changing our understanding of "who" made, and can therefore be held accountable for, particular decisions (Bell et al., 2020). AI and machine learning technologies can also directly affect SDG measures such as access to justice (Zalnieriute et al., 2019), procedural fairness in the fair (and lawful) calculation of welfare entitlements (Ng et al., 2020), unbiased and transparent character assessments for determining whether a person is eligible for parole or likely to reoffend after serving a criminal sentence (Bennett Moses, 2017; Sourdin, 2018), and opportunities for individual citizens to review government decisions and to hold decision-makers to account (Ng et al., 2020).

Technology is now at the heart of *how* we teach and, increasingly, *what* we teach: "not only mediat[ing] the way society operates; [but changing] the very nature of social arrangements and therefore what is substantively the concern of law" (Goldsworthy, 2020, p. 262). Goldsworthy notes that "[t]echnology will likely render the pedagogical practices of many law schools and instrumental approach of equipping graduates with the skills required for a career in law today…outdated, if not obsolete, tomorrow" (p. 260). Although a small number of Australian law schools have integrated law units, modules, or a curricula-wide focus on technology-related innovations, trends, and challenges, all law degree programs are expected to follow suit in the coming years (Goldsworthy, 2020).

The third significant area of rapid global change, intimately connected with the first two, is environmental change. Ecological harms and greenhouse gas (GHG) emissions from power generation and industry often now occur far from their source, driven primarily by technology and consumption patterns in the most-developed parts of the world. Just as ecological harms are typically having the most profound and damaging impacts on those least responsible and least able to address their cause, many of the effects of climate change, such as sea level rise and extreme heatwaves, are being experienced earlier and most severely by those least able to affect GHG emissions and adapt to those changes (World Meteorological Organization [WMO], 2020).

International reports from authoritative sources such as the Intergovernmental Panel on Climate Change (IPCC), the Intergovernmental Science-Policy Platform on Biodiversity and Ecosystem Services (IPBES), and from non-governmental global actors such as the World Bank and World Wide Fund for Nature, have repeatedly demonstrated the scale of ongoing biodiversity loss and ecological decline and its inextricable connection to climate change and trends of unsustainable development (e.g. IPBES, 2019; World Bank, 2008). Decades of international reporting have emphasised the urgent need to address climate change rapidly, prepare more effectively for catastrophic natural disasters, reverse biodiversity loss, and alleviate human suffering.

However, in response, global commitments—including in law and policy—continue to lack sufficient ambition and speed to guarantee a liveable future. Repeated failure, particularly by the most-developed countries, to address emphatically the challenges of climate change and biodiversity loss has already had catastrophic effects on marginalised communities in Australia and around the world (see United Nations Human Rights Committee [UNHRC], 2019). Already-disadvantaged groups face greatly increased risks from climate-driven changes to extreme weather such as bushfires and flooding, sea level rise, health insecurity, and social and economic disruption, as well as from biodiversity loss and ecological change. These impacts will be exacerbated by existing inequalities and co-morbidities (see IPCC, 2012).

Australia's domestic governance offers a microcosm in which we can see local examples of these broader global failings. Despite clear evidence of climate-driven changes to extreme events, Australia has spent the last decade in political deadlock about climate law and policy. Despite long-established laws for conservation and environmental management, fundamental concerns about their operation and failings have been repeatedly ignored, side-stepped, or neglected (Samuel, 2020) and conservation laws remain ill-prepared for emerging climate-related challenges (McCormack, 2018). It is well-past time to address these failings, including in the content and enforcement of legal frameworks, and in the political and institutional area, where legal and policy instruments are negotiated and implemented.

The deeply interconnected biophysical and socio-economic systems crisscrossing the planet, which we have described here, mean that global shock and rapid changes reverberate around the world, with both local and far-distant impacts. Alongside the need for greater social and scientific creativity, tackling the magnitude and complexity of these interacting social, technological, and environmental changes will require creative and novel forms of governance, designed and championed by creative, adaptable people who understand law and policy (Adger et al., 2009). We urgently need to rethink siloed approaches within existing legal frameworks to avoid harm to humans and nature, while adopting anticipatory approaches to law (Lim, 2021).

7.3   Critically Examining the SDGs in Their Legal and Institutional Context

Legal education that seeks to engage students through the concept of sustainability and, more specifically, the SDGs, must first acknowledge the normative or values-based foundation of those goals and the world order over which they have been laid. Doing so will reveal core problems with the assumptions of the SDGs themselves, including the ways in which they replicate the status quo, and reinforce global narratives and trends about continual growth and consumerism, anthropocentrism, and colonialism. While the SDGs reflect, on the one hand, entrenched dominant worldviews and structures perpetuated by multilateral environmental agreements, on the other hand, they fail to engage sufficiently with advances in the international legal principle of sustainable development in the last few decades.

The SDGs centre around the concept of sustainability, which is deeply embedded in international and domestic environmental laws around the world. As noted above, the concept has the potential to be a useful starting point for conversations and teaching about institutions, governance frameworks, and nature, but the concept of sustainability has also been heavily criticised. Key criticisms include its lack of clarity (see Wals & Jickling, 2008), and its resounding failure to arrest biodiversity decline, achieve equitable development outcomes, and moderate the excesses of capitalism and consumerism (see Beckerman, 1994; Howes et al., 2017). The framing of sustainability as a "balancing" process for competing values has been criticised for justifying decision-makers considering, and then discounting, environmental losses in the face of economic gain (Macintosh, 2015; Ong, 2016). The concept has also been criticised as seeking to maintain a mediocre status quo instead of requiring governments, corporations, and communities to enhance human and non-human flourishing, including by grappling with the complexity and trade-offs needed to achieve deep emissions cuts, climate-adapted conservation, and effective environmental stewardship (e.g. Harm Benson & Kundis Craig, 2017).

The SDGs are not law. Rather, they are statements of ambition, intended to create norms to guide behaviour change (Fukuda-Parr, 2014; Macintosh, 2015; UN, 2015). The SDGs are also an example of developments in international governance to "govern through goals" (Kanie & Biermann, 2017). Other examples include the temperature target of the Paris Agreement under the United Nations Framework Convention on Climate Change (UNFCCC) and the Aichi and post-2020 targets of the Convention on Biological Diversity. However, the legal status of the SDGs is different to these others, as the SDGs do not sit under a legally binding Convention. Nevertheless, as Kim (2016) highlights, the SDGs have neither emerged from nor have been inserted into, a legal vacuum. Instead, the goals reflect the architecture of existing agreements. For example, the goals separate out terrestrial conservation or "life on land" (SDG15) from "life below water" (SDG14) in the same way that agreements such as the United Nations Convention on the Law of the Sea (UNCLOS) and its subsidiary protocols separate out marine conservation and management from the

Convention on Biological Diversity, with each instrument being governed and implemented under separate international secretariats, governmental organs, and domestic legal instruments. Similarly, the SDGs separate the environmental goals from goals about health, justice, and climate action, in the same way that multilateral governance separates the work of the World Health Organisation from climate governance under the UNFCCC and even-more fragmented arrangements focusing on peace and justice.

Although the SDGs reflect existing, fragmented international governance architectures, international legal instruments themselves are only incorporated into the SDGs in a haphazard and inconsistent manner. For example, only three conventions are explicitly named in the SDGs themselves: the UNFCCC in SDG13; the UNCLOS in Target 14©, and perhaps unexpectedly, the Framework Convention on Tobacco Control was deemed worthy of inclusion in Target 3(a). There is also a non-specific reference to "World Trade Organisation agreements" in Target 10(a). This is not to say that the content of other Conventions is not implicitly incorporated. For example, the Secretariats of biodiversity-related international laws have studiously integrated a range of issues reflecting the objectives of existing environmental agreements. However, referring to some Conventions by name and not others risks prioritising named Conventions at the expense of the multitude of other, internationally recognised values, objectives, and priorities.

There have been repeated calls to address the interactions and links across the social, economic, and environmental issues contained within the Goals and Targets of the SDGs (Deacon & St Clair, 2015; Lim et al., 2018; Weitz et al., 2014). Even the then-UN Secretary-General, Ban Ki Moon, emphasised that recognition of the inter-relationships between Goals and Targets would be key to achieving transformations towards sustainable development (Ban, 2014). Others have argued that internal inconsistencies in the SDGs could undermine the ultimate goal of sustainable development (Kundis Craig & Ruhl, 2021; Nilsson & Costanza, 2015).

The lack of explicit linkages across the Goals and Targets creates the risk that governments and other actors will "cherry pick" elements of the SDGs that align with existing priorities (Stafford-Smith et al., 2016). For example, global leaders have explicitly prioritised quality education, peace and justice, and decent work and economic growth, as the three most important SDGs (Kundis Craig & Ruhl, 2021). In contrast, the environmental SDGs are ranked 17th (SDG14, Life in Water), 15th (SDG13, Climate Action), and 13th (SDG15, Life on Land) in terms of importance, three of the lowest rankings of all of the SDGs (Kundis Craig & Ruhl, 2021); but, as Kundis Craig and Ruhl have argued, "the environment is the boundary of, not co-equal to, development, constraining potential progress both economically and socially" (p. 1).

Without truly integrative and systems-based approaches to interpreting and applying the SDGs, their capacity to transform environmental governance is limited. These limitations are exacerbated when governments and multi-national corporations claim to be applying the SDGs when, in reality, they are doing nothing more than business as usual (a concept known as "additionality," see Kotzé et al., 2022).

Shortfalls in additionality are compounded by the central position of neoliberal narratives—premised on individualism and continued economic growth—which are key drivers of continued unsustainability. For example, governments continue to prioritise economic growth despite unrestrained economic growth being a core component of "the problem" of ecological unsustainability and environmental decline. Wals and others have argued that, if the world's governments were truly committed to the SDGs, including for example, eradicating poverty (SDG1), an excellent place to start might have been an additional SDG dedicated to eradicating extreme wealth (Wals, 2021; see Kundis Craig & Ruhl, 2021).

Genuinely transformative approaches towards sustainability require a serious reckoning with the false equivalence drawn between economic growth and gross domestic product on the one hand and human wellbeing on the other. Similarly, we need to challenge the narrative that equates thriving human futures as a necessary trade-off with securing the ecological integrity of the planet.

Even though the corporate sector will need to play a key role if we are to achieve the ambition of the SDGs, corporations only explicitly feature in the SDGs in Target 12.6 in relation to waste reduction. Whether by design (Brewer, 2015) or oversight, the limited attention paid to corporations is a missed opportunity to address the socioeconomic restructuring required for a sustainable and equitable planet (Lim et al., 2018). In contrast, domestic legal frameworks are increasingly employing corporate regulation as a means to reduce unsustainability.

Although international law has been at the forefront of shaping our understanding of sustainable development (French, 2010), the SDGs do not sufficiently engage with legal developments surrounding the principle. The content of the principle of sustainable development is difficult to pin down, even in international law scholarship, given the broad nature of the concept and limited jurisprudence. Nevertheless, four key components can be distilled from the literature: (1) integration, (2) intergenerational equity, (3) intragenerational equity, and (4) governance imperatives, such as the duty to cooperate, common but differentiated responsibilities, and public participation. Alongside these key components of the principle, the 2030 Agenda (of which the SDGs are a part) demonstrates an explicit commitment to integration with other aspects of international law, using phrases such as "full respect for international law" (United Nations [UN], 2015, para.10) and "consisten[cy] with" and a "commitment to" international law (UN, 2015, para.18). However, these expressions of commitment are not supported by practical interactions within and across heavily fragmented international governance regimes for each of the environmental, social and economic "pillars" of sustainable development. As a result, despite developments in international legal scholarship and repeated commitments to integrate the SDGs with existing international laws, integration across the pillars of sustainable development remains superficial at best.

More needs to be done to bring about practical and effective integration in international laws. The most significant gap is in relation to intergenerational equity, which has long been considered central to the legal conception of sustainable development. However, not only do the terms "intergenerational equity" and "the precautionary principle" *not* appear anywhere in the SDGs or in the broader 2030 Agenda, the term "future generations" appears only in the preamble of the Agenda and once in paragraph 18. Achieving intergenerational equity will certainly require explicit references to generations not yet born along with a far longer-term vision for the SDGs and the 2030 Agenda than the 15 years that the Goals cover.

*Intra*generational equity, on the other hand, is clearly in focus across the SDGs and in the broader 2030 Agenda. SDGs 4 (Education), 6 (Water), and 9 (Infrastructure), each emphasise the importance of equity; by inference, equity amongst those currently alive. SDG5 (Gender Equality) explicitly points to the need for equity across genders for those currently alive, and SDGs 1 (No Poverty) and 2 (Zero Hunger) imply similar equity considerations. However, unless we address the kinds of structural and systemic issues with the equitable redistribution of wealth, described above, it will remain very difficult to make meaningful progress on either *intra*generational or *inter*generational equity.

To some extent, these critiques of the SDGs are mirrored in legal education in Australia. Legal education is similarly siloed, with law degrees designed to prepare graduates for legal practice by conveying the historical development and current deployment of legal theories, principles, and processes within neatly defined sub-disciplines (Barker, 2014, 2017; Goldsworthy, 2020; Keyes & Johnstone, 2004). Discrete legal topics are typically taught in separate units. For example, environmental law is often an elective unit, separate from core, mandated units such as criminal, administrative, corporate, and property law, despite the fact that these areas are deeply interwoven and overlapping in the context of environmental management and disputes. In teaching environmental law in this way, a legal academic may introduce students to, for example, SDGs about life underwater and life on land, without expressly connecting the imperative to conserve nature with the need to govern industry and economic activity, and to foster reconciliation and Indigenous Peoples' ownership and connection with Country. Siloed approaches imply to law students that, for example, environmental legal issues can be separated in simplistic ways from other legal sub-disciplines; but no such separation exists in the "real world."

Teaching siloes in law *may* fail to prepare graduates for the kinds of legal issues they will encounter in practice, but *certainly* fail to prepare graduates to understand and resolve the wicked problems that societies across the world face and will face in future as, for example, climate change continues. System-wide, deeply complex, wicked problems demand more holistic and integrated forms of learning (Doran, 2016). In the face of socio-political, technological, and environmental change, the nature of these emerging challenges provides an important reason to tackle and dismantle siloes in legal education and disrupt the narrow and siloed approaches that have been embedded into global governance regimes such as the SDGs.

7.4   Legal Education in Australia

To overcome the complications and failings of the SDGs, we need to be able to think beyond the strictures of disciplinary and sub-disciplinary boundaries. That is, we will need negotiators, politicians, and civil society actors who can think about problems in their systemic context and engage in productive ways with complexity and uncertainty. We consider whether legal education is equipped to contribute to graduates who have begun to build this capacity, noting that, at present, siloed legal curricula and teaching units replicate the status quo embedded in the SDGs and environmental governance instruments internationally and in Australia. We argue that disrupting legal education may be necessary to help future graduates reimagine their roles as lawyers and citizens in a way that promotes a better future.

7.4.1   Trends in Legal Education in Australia

Australian legal education has changed a great deal, from its early focus on Greek, Latin, and ancient history and English history in the late 1800s, to its current professionalised, neoliberal form (Harrison, 2014; Lücke, 2010, p. 110). Legal education has also expanded its reach dramatically, with a proliferation of law schools across the country (from just six in 1927, to 38 Australian law schools and thousands of graduates, annually, by 2018; e.g. Council of Australian Law Deans [CALD], 2018; McNamara, 2018).

There are broad pressures and trends affecting the higher education sector generally that also influence the form and delivery of legal education in important ways. Neoliberal values, in particular, have come to dominate the political and economic context for higher education in Australia and around the world. Burdon defines neoliberalism as a "mode of reason that economizes all things and moulds human conduct to a model of the market" (Burdon, 2019, p. 31, drawing on Brown and others; Hudson, 2021; Roper et al., 2020; Thornton, 2019). This neoliberal "mode of reason" has increased regulation by university management of academics and their work and simultaneously increased all aspects of academic workloads, from administration and teaching, to obligations to publish and win grant money (Roper et al., 2020; Thornton, 2020). Heavy workloads and tighter school and faculty budgets have had negative effects on academic and student wellbeing (James et al., 2020), exacerbating already-high rates of depression, anxiety, and other mental illness. Neoliberal trends, including shifts in government funding, have caused universities (and students themselves) to reconceive students as "consumers" and legal education as a service or product to be bought and sold, rather than as a public good (Burdon, 2019; Thornton, 2020). Thornton argues that these trends, in workloads, managerialism, consumerism, and neoliberalism have "significantly affected the quality of legal education" (Thornton, 2020), and limited the time, energy, and capacity for educators to design and deliver the kinds of transgressive and transformative educational opportunities that might produce resilient, curious, and civic-minded graduates.

There are also pressures operating on law schools that derive from their professional accreditation status in relation to the legal profession. The specific structure and content of law degrees in Australia vary between universities, but all Australian law curricula are loosely guided by the Australian Law Schools Standards Committee, under the auspices of the Council of Australian Law Deans (CALD) (Black, 2017). Although there is no requirement or objective in the overarching standards that relates to sustainability in legal education in Australia, the "CALD Standards for Australian Law Schools" require law schools to articulate their mission and objective in providing legal education, including by committing "to the rule of law, the promotion of the highest standards of ethical conduct, professional responsibility, and community service" (CALD, 2009, Standard 1.3.3; Black, 2017). As in other jurisdictions, an Australian law degree is a professional accreditation, which means that law schools are required to produce technically competent professionals. The National Law Admissions Consultative Committee works with legal accreditation bodies in each state and territory to achieve national consensus about accreditation standards, or "academic requirements for admission," and this oversight likely weighs against law schools setting curricula-wide priorities such as sustainability and reflexive and transgressive pedagogies that fall outside of formal accreditation standards and mandates (Galloway, 2017; Goldsworthy, 2020; Reid, 2016).

To achieve accreditation in Australia, law schools must deliver a curriculum that includes the "Priestly 11": eleven topics that are prerequisites for legal practice in Australia. Among other things, these topics include core areas of legal practice such as administrative, Constitutional, criminal, and property law. Cross-cutting themes such as sustainability and the SDGs are not included in these mandatory topics and, as a result, must compete for the limited remaining space in the law curriculum. Non-mandatory topics are sometimes perceived as receiving less recognition and support from law schools, professional bodies, and employers (Reid, 2016), as well as from students themselves, who may consider concepts such as sustainability, less immediately relevant and important to their education as core legal competencies (Ong, 2016).

Although Australian law degrees provide a pathway to a career in legal practice, more than one third of law graduates in Australia never work as practising lawyers (CALD, 2021; McNamara, 2018). Tensions between the different, underlying purposes for legal education (Barker, 2017, p. 239; Goldsworthy, 2020, pp. 245–246)—which include producing "practice-ready lawyers," producing "tomorrow's lawyers" (Arthurs, 2014), and equipping students as practitioners and future citizens, whatever career path they take (Goldsworthy, 2020, pp. 245–250)—resonate across similar jurisdictions (Reid, 2016). However, in some places, the law school's mission is expressed in broader terms than in Australia's CALD Standards. For example, the Law Professors' Working Group on Law School Accreditation in Canada states that, "[i]n many ways, our most important job... is to educate graduates who will become sensitive, thoughtful, creative, generous, ethical, professional, and bright members of civil society, regardless of what career path they choose" (Pue, 2008; cf. Sexson & Wilson, 2021). This statement suggests a broad conception of the purpose of legal education and readily accommodates that aspect of legal education that is most interested in sustainability—not just as content but as an expression of values such as critical inquiry; reflexive, democratic, and student-led learning; and engagement with a full diversity of perspectives from the individual through to whole-of-community (Wals & Jickling, 2008).

Nevertheless, some of the CALD Standards do contemplate approaches to teaching that have been identified, in Australia and elsewhere, as excellent tools for embedding sustainability training in legal education. For example, the CALD Standards emphasise the benefits of experiential and legal practice-based learning, "including through clinical programs, internships, workplace experience and pro bono community service" (CALD, 2009, Standard 2.2.4; Black, 2017). Similarly, Black (2017) notes that law schools and staff are encouraged to "engage with the wider community" and, use their knowledge and skills for the benefit of the community in outreach programs including, for example, and as far as is practicable, clinical programs, law reform, public education, and other forms of pro bono community service [Standard 9.6.2].

These practical learning approaches offer valuable opportunities to overcome existing siloes in legal education while also promoting access to justice (Obuka & Ukwueze, 2020). For example, in practice-based learning contexts, an educator can introduce a range of different legal topics in a single task, or allow students to grapple with the task of defining a real-world problem *before* equipping and supporting them to respond to that problem. Student surveys demonstrate the value law students gain from putting their skills into practice in these kinds of learning contexts, including helping real people to access justice and understand their rights (Roper et al., 2020, p. 457). Neoliberal forces in the university sector, in particular, risk undermining opportunities to deliver precisely these kinds of practical and clinic-based programs by reducing available funding and increasing academic workloads.

The pressures and trends described here influence legal education across the common law world and are accelerating rapidly. They illuminate a mismatch between diverse and shifting roles and expectations of educators, and the next generation of lawyers and legal graduates in society, as well as the opportunities and constraints that both will face in the future.

7.4.2 Using Systems-Thinking to Re-Imagine Legal Education for a Very Different Future

After the UN Decade of Education for Sustainable Development from 2005, sustainability in education was the focus of a host of policy and scholarly work (Ong, 2016) but sustainability has still only been implemented in legal curricula in limited ways, and with varying levels of success (Barth et al., 2016; Filho, 2015; Ong, 2016). As we approach 20 years since the UN Decade began, we argue that there is a need to rethink and reimagine how we teach law in the context of the rapid and complex disruptive trends described above, particularly through an improved "capacity to think critically about why we think what we do—and then to think and act differently" (Raskin, 2008, p. 469).

Many scholars have highlighted the challenges of "systemic global dysfunction" and disruption for education practice, and we join those that argue for a move beyond the "double think and newspeak" of education *for* sustainability, which is slippery and open to abuse, towards broader concepts such as "regenerative education" (Wals, 2021; Wals & Jickling, 2008), "transformative" education, and "transgressive social learning" (Lotz-Sistitka et al., 2015). These concepts seek, at least in part, to overcome shallow and fragmented ways of thinking about hyperconnected social-ecological challenges such as those captured by the SDGs. These proposed education paradigms resemble systems-thinking, which we argue provides a useful framework for thinking about legal education as a complex system of connected actors, expectations, changing backdrops, and shifting pressures. Systems-thinking can help us to examine how we might teach law students to move past "simple answers," including for sustainability, to a point where they can cope with complexity and navigate future challenges that we, as educators, may not foresee.

Systems-thinking is a concept that emerged in the ecological sciences, and has since been applied by environmental and climate scholars, among others, to complex social-ecological governance systems. Systems-thinking is a useful lens for interrogating complex governance challenges and tools (Lim et al., 2018), though its application may be complicated if, indeed, "resistance to holistic thinking stems from an 'arrogant and obsessively anthropocentric worldview' which is nowhere 'more apparent than in law'" (Cullinan, 2011; Sterling, 2003).

We do not propose to synthesise systems-thinking in education scholarship (this has been done expertly by others; see, e.g. Sterling, 2003). Rather, we draw on the following key components of systems-thinking to inform our principles (below) for reimagining education for future legal graduates. First, the "essential quality" of systems-thinking is that of "relation," seeking to understand connections, interactions, and relationships between elements in a system (Sterling, 2003, p. 102). Second, systems-thinking creates a space and openness to recognising difficult realities, such as the extraordinary scale and speed at which transformation is required to meet the challenges of the future (Randers et al., 2018). Finally, education in a systems-thinking paradigm requires frequent and ongoing feedback so that learning can be iterative and adjusted when necessary (Habron et al., 2012). When applied to legal education, these aspects of systems-thinking offer insights about the role that the SDGs *could* play in teaching law, and the normative foundations of the global status quo that we hope future graduates will be inspired to disrupt.

We propose the following three principles as provocations, to underpin urgently needed conversations about legal education for an uncertain future: (1) law graduates must be equipped to interrogate the human context for law; (2) law schools must embrace "almost-transformative" approaches to teaching; and (3) legal educators must be equipped to transcend traditional sub-disciplinary siloes so that students can glimpse something of the legal system's "whole" and the relationships between its components.

First, law schools need to equip graduates to interrogate the interconnected and complex human context for law.

The study and practice of law is an inherently socially contextual activity. For law degrees to remain relevant as technologies rapidly change the legal and social context, and geopolitical upheaval challenges international rule-making and the rules-based order, understanding context will be more crucial than it has ever been. Goldsworthy makes this point, arguing that the purpose and role of a law degree in a world that is being rapidly transformed by new technology should be understood by identifying the kinds of tasks "that require creativity, complex reasoning or social intelligence (such as the ability to negotiate complex social relationships effectively)," because these tasks will "remain the province of human beings" (2020, p. 264). Goldsworthy suggests that legal curricula *cannot* keep pace with the ways that technology is fundamentally changing law and the legal profession, so legal graduates of the future will "require a broad and liberal education that enables interdisciplinary insights, creativity and social intelligence" (2020, p. 264). This first principle highlights the need for more attention on the purposes and relative value of relying on goal-based approaches in law rather than enforceable instruments. The SDGs reinforce trends in international law towards malleable, opaque, and unenforceable mechanisms for achieving widely supported goals such as ending poverty, but have demonstrably failed to achieve that goal, despite it being identified as the first priority among the SDGs, by global leaders.

Second, law schools need to embrace an "almost-transformative" approach in teaching, pushing the boundaries of professional accreditation requirements and constraints.

As we have explained above, law schools cannot readily undertake a transformative overhaul of the law degree program because they are constrained by professional accreditation requirements and standards committees. Despite deeply entrenched, conservative, and neoliberal forces operating against re-imagining what legal education might achieve, legal academics can nevertheless engage in transformative thinking at smaller scales, within units and unit groupings, as well as in what we describe as "almost-transformative" reforms across the law degree that, for example, embed future-oriented, socially, and ecologically focused modules or themes across multiple law units and whole degree programs (e.g. see Graham, 2014; Lowther & Sellick, 2016; Ong, 2016; Varnava et al., 2010).

This second principle could be implemented in a number of different ways. For example, to prompt an almost-transformative approach, law schools could consider adopting a new core competency for graduates that focuses on teaching students to "think critically about *why* we think what we do," but crucially, then taking the next step of taking that critical process as the basis for thinking, *and* acting, differently (drawing on Raskin, 2008). Ecological principles ought to be embedded into non-environmental law units. Embedding ecological principles in this way would help students to understand that sustainable economies and communities need governance principles and relationships, including in corporate, criminal, and property contexts, that have firmly integrated social-ecological goals embedded at their heart (on the pre-conditions for such a transformation; see e.g. Boström et al., 2018). At a unit level, students can be taught and then assessed on their competency in interrogating legal frameworks for those frameworks' capacities to produce sustainability outcomes rather than simply reflecting sustainability language (Lowther & Sellick, 2016). Finally, this second principle ought to prompt law schools to advocate for changes to professional accreditation standards within degree programs (Reid, 2016); and for changes to enforceable ethics standards in the legal profession—given the implications those standards have for the skills that employers seek in legal graduates. For example, in Canada, Rules of Professional Conduct and Ethical Standards require legal practitioners to act with "competence," which is defined to include a requirement for the skills and training to consider climate change in all legal decision-making (e.g. Law Society of Ontario, 2022), a call that has been echoed by the International Bar Association's *Climate Crisis Statement* (2020). Advocacy to change professional rules and standards in Australia should include a strong emphasis on the need for more flexibility, so that the content and structure of law degrees and professional training can be adapted—as emphasised by systems-thinking scholars—in iterative and innovative ways, over time (Goldsworthy, 2020).

Third, legal educators need to be equipped and resourced to transcend sub-disciplinary siloes in their teaching.

A narrow focus on sub-disciplinary content and principles risks missing the crucial backdrop to a legal education, which is the large-scale dysfunction of global and domestic governance, across environmental, health, social, and economic measures. Narrowly focusing on sub-disciplinary subjects also obscures or ignores the radical and rapid discipline-wide transformations that we need, to address governance dysfunction. To understand the necessary transformations, students must be equipped to see the complexity and hyper-connected nature of problems and the system in which they occur. Interdisciplinary teaching is far from the norm in Australian law degrees, though we have identified surprisingly early contributions to legal scholarship on interdisciplinarity in law degree programs internationally and in Australia (e.g. Godden & Dale, 2000; Priest, 1993).

Interdisciplinarity can help to build skills in empathy, communication, collaboration, and negotiation across diverse knowledges, values, and experiences. In a teaching context, interdisciplinary approaches can involve assessment tasks marked against criteria from two different (combined) degree programs such as science and law (e.g. Godden & Dale, 2000), or within individual practical and experiential legal units, can bring together scientific, industrial, political science, and psychology expertise to foster creativity and broaden the scope of information available to students as they undertake a particular task (Foerster, 2022). For example, legal academics at Queen's University, Belfast, have designed an Environmental Law and Sustainable Development unit (explicitly drawing on systems-thinking objectives) in which students negotiate a hypothetical climate agreement with a computer model feeding the students information about the real-world consequences, such as increasingly frequent weather extremes, sea level rise, and long term global climate change, of their negotiated outcomes, in real time (Doran, 2016). The unit helps students to appreciate that they are not simply negotiating to solve a legal problem but affecting and *creating* social, economic, and climatic conditions with implications for the short, medium, and long-term future of the planet (Doran, 2016). There are also recent, profoundly disruptive examples of legal practitioners bridging the "bright-line" boundaries between legal sub-disciplines such as torts and administrative law (Sharma, 2021), and corporations or consumer laws and climate law (Grantham Research Institute, 2021), to force action on climate change in the absence of effective national law and policy. Future legal graduates ought to be equipped to feel confident in bridging sub-disciplinary and disciplinary divides to challenge the status quo and respond to complex challenges, including through the novel application of existing legal instruments; and further they could be fostered through interdisciplinary and cross-sub-disciplinary teaching in Australian law degrees.

7.5   Conclusion: Training Lawyers for *Their* Future, Not Ours

The SDGs were developed with the ambition of responding holistically to a multitude of intersecting global challenges such as poverty, environmental degradation, and ill-health. However, in practice, the SDGs have replicated and reinforced both existing *horizontal* sectoral and governance siloes, for example, by separating out human and environmental health and economies from biodiversity loss, and *vertical* priorities, continuing to prioritise economic growth over community goals and ecological restoration. As such, the SDGs represent the opposite of the disruptive force that is necessary in international and domestic laws, to achieve social and ecological health and flourishing.

Our central argument is that legal educators must be equipped to teach their students how to pick apart the "masquerade" of sustainability so that they can identify the basis for the problems that we face; that is, that the legal graduates of the future must be able to interrogate that which is stopping us from understanding and solving the big problems of our time, including climate change, poverty, biodiversity loss, and inequality. Legal education must, itself, be disrupted if we are to produce lawyers and legal graduates that have the capacity to disrupt unsustainable governance regimes and foster more holistic visions of future sustainability and flourishing.

This demands of us that we go beyond asking how to improve or enhance the 17 SDGs themselves, but also that we investigate how the framework itself is represented, because the SDG framework is the masquerade that protects the status quo. With that in mind, we end with a call to upscale advocacy and disruptive teaching paradigms as a starting point for challenging and disrupting the system that the SDGs represent. We present three provocations for pushing legal degree programs forwards, including that law schools must equip graduates to interrogate interconnected and complex human contexts for law; embrace "almost-transformative" approaches to teaching; and equip legal educators to transcend sub-disciplinary siloes in their teaching. In sum, we argue that legal graduates are perfectly suited, and ought to be better-equipped, as citizens and practitioners of law, to work to achieve a better version of *their* future, for the benefit of us all.

Author Note We are grateful to the editors for the opportunity to contribute to this important work. We also extend our thanks to our research assistant, Sarah Vanderfield, and to an anonymous reviewer for the feedback on an earlier draft.

References

Adger, W. N., Eaken, H., & Winkels, A. (2009). Nested and teleconnected vulnerabilities to environmental change. *Frontiers in Ecology and Environment, 7*(3), 150–157. https://doi.org/10.1890/070148

Arthurs, H. W. (2014). The future of law school: Three visions and a prediction. *Alberta Law Review, 51*(4), 705–716. https://doi.org/10.29173/alr33

Australian Public Law. (2021). Special series: 50 Years after the Kerr report. *Australian Public Law.* https://www.auspublaw.org/50-years-after-the-kerr-report

Ban, K. M. (2014). *The road to dignity by 2030: Ending poverty, transforming all lives and protecting the planet—synthesis report of the Secretary-General on the Post-2015 Agenda.* https://www.un.org/disabilities/documents/reports/SG_Synthesis_Report_Road_to_Dignity_by_2030.pdf

Barker, D. (2014). The Pearce Report—Does it still influence Australian legal education? *Journal of the Australasian Law Teachers Association, 7*(1&2), 77–86.

Barker, D. (2017). *A history of Australian legal education.* Federation Press.

Barth, M., Michelsen, G., Rieckmann, M., & Thomas, I. (Eds.). (2016). *Routledge handbook of higher education for sustainable development.* Routledge.

Beckerman, W. (1994). "Sustainable development": Is it a useful concept? *Environmental Values, 3*(3), 191–209.

Bell, F., Rogers, J., & Legg, M. (2020). Artificial intelligence and lawyer wellbeing. In M. Legg, P. Vines, & J. Chan (Eds.), *The impact of technology and innovation on the wellbeing of the legal profession* (pp. 239–266). Intersentia.

Bennett Moses, L. (2017). Artificial intelligence in the courts, legal academia and legal practice. *Australian Law Journal, 91*(7), 561–574.

Black, M. (2017, August). The CALD standards for Australian law schools: Much more than course content. In *The future of Australian legal education conference.* Australian Academy of Law. https://academyoflaw.org.au/event-2428669

Boström, M., Andersson, E., Berg, M., Gustafsson, K., Gustavsson, E., Hysing, E., Lidskog, R., Löfmarck, E., Ojala, M., Olsson, J., Singleton, B. E., Svenberg, S., Uggla, Y., & Öhman, J. (2018). Conditions for transformative learning for sustainable development: A theoretical review and approach. *Sustainability, 10*(12), 4479. https://doi.org/10.3390/su10124479

Brewer, J. (2015). *Who framed global development? Language analysis of the sustainable development goals.* [PowerPoint Slides]. http://www.slideshare.net/joebrewer31/who-framed-global-development

Burdon, P. D. (2019). Neoliberalism in legal education research. In B. Golder, M. Nehme, A. Steel, & P. Vines (Eds.), *Imperatives for legal education research: Then, now and tomorrow* (pp. 31–49). Taylor & Francis Group.

Carrasco, L. R., Chain, J., McGrath, F. L., & Nghiem, L. T. P. (2017). Biodiversity conservation in a telecoupled world. *Ecology and Society, 22*(3). https://doi.org/10.5751/ES-09448-220324

Caserta, S. (2021). Review essay: The legal profession in the digital age. *Sydney Law Review, 43*(3), 411.

Caserta, S., & Madsen, M. R. (2019). The legal profession in the era of digital capitalism: Disruption or new dawn? *Laws, 8*(1). https://doi.org/10.3390/laws8010001

Council of Australian Law Deans. (2009). *The CALD standards for Australian law schools.* https://cald.asn.au/wp-content/uploads/2017/11/CALD-Standards-As-adopted-17-November-2009-and-Amended-to-March-2013-1.pdf

Council of Australian Law Deans. (2018). *Data regarding law school graduate numbers and outcomes.* https://cald.asn.au/wp-content/uploads/2017/11/Factsheet-Law_Students_in_Australia.pdf

Council of Australian Law Deans. (2021). *Legal education in Australia.* https://cald.asn.au/slia/legal-education/

Cullinan, C. (2011). *Wild law: A manifesto for earth justice* (2nd ed.). Chelsea Green Publishing.

Deacon, B., & St Clair, A. (2015). Goal 1—End poverty in all its forms everywhere. In *Review of the sustainable development goals: The science perspective* (pp. 15–18). International Council for Science & International Social Science Council. https://council.science/wp-content/uploads/2017/05/SDG-Report.pdf

Doran, P. (2016). Head, hand and heart: Immersive learning for a demanding new climate at Queen's University Belfast's School of Law. *The Law Teacher, 50*(3), 341–351. https://doi.org/10.1080/03069400.2016.1241049

Fielding, K. S., Head, B. W., Laffan, W., Western, M., & Hoegh-Guldberg, O. (2012). Australian politicians' beliefs about climate change: Political partisanship and political ideology. *Environmental Politics, 21*(5), 712–733. https://doi.org/10.1080/09644016.2012.698887

Filho, W. (Ed.). (2015). *Transformative approaches to sustainable development at universities.* Springer. https://doi.org/10.1007/978-3-319-08837-2

Foerster, A. (2022, February). *Teaching corporate sustainability regulation to business students* [Paper presentation]. The 8th Frontiers in Environmental Law Colloquium. https://www.youtube.com/watch?v=OIRCDEzWQl4

French, D. (2010). Sustainable development. In M. Fitzmaurice, D. Ong, & P. Merkouris (Eds.), *Research handbook on international environmental law* (pp. 51–68). Edward Elgar Publishing.

Fukuda-Parr, S. (2014). Global goals as a policy tool: Intended and unintended consequences. *Journal of Human Development and Capabilities, 15*(2–3), 118–131. https://doi.org/10.1080/19452829.2014.910180

Galloway, K. (2017). A rationale and framework for digital literacies in legal education. *Legal Education Review, 27*(1), 117–142.

Godden, L., & Dale, P. (2000). Interdisciplinary teaching in law and environmental science: Jurisprudence and environment. *Legal Education Review, 11*(2), 239–251.

Goldsworthy, J. (2020). The future of legal education in the 21st Century. *Adelaide Law Review, 41*(1), 243–267.

Graham, N. (2014). This is not a thing: Land, sustainability and legal education. *Journal of Environmental Law, 26*(3), 395–422. https://doi.org/10.1093/jel/equ020

Grantham Research Institute on Climate Change and the Environment and the Centre for Climate Change Economics and Policy. (2021). *Global trends in climate change litigation: 2021 snapshot policy report.* https://www.lse.ac.uk/

Habron, G., Goralnik, L., & Thorp, L. (2012). Embracing the learning paradigm to foster systems thinking. *International Journal of Sustainability in Higher Education, 13*(4), 378–393. https://doi.org/10.1108/14676371211262326

Hannan, J. (2018). Trolling ourselves to death? Social media and post-truth politics. *European Journal of Communication, 33*(2), 214–226. https://doi.org/10.1177/0267323118760323

Harm Benson, M., & Kundis Craig, R. (2017). *The end of sustainability: Resilience and the future of environmental governance in the Anthropocene.* University Press of Kansas.

Harrison, R. (2014). The legal profession in colonial Victoria: Information in records of admission held by Public Record Office Victoria. *Provenance: The Journal of Public Record Office Victoria, 13.* https://prov.vic.gov.au/explore-collection/provenance-journal/provenance-2014/legal-profession-colonial-victoria

Howes, M., Wortlet, L., Potts, R., Dedekorkut-Howes, A., Serrao-Neumann, S., Davidson, J., Smith, T., & Nunn, P. (2017). Environmental sustainability: A case of policy implementation failure? *Sustainability, 9*(2), 165. https://doi.org/10.3390/su9020165

Hudson, A. (2021). Two futures for law schools. *The Law Teacher, 55*(1), 101–104. https://doi.org/10.1080/03069400.2020.1862616

Intergovernmental Panel on Climate Change. (2012). *Managing the risks of extreme events and disasters to advance climate change adaptation.* Cambridge University Press. https://www.ipcc.ch/report/managing-the-risks-of-extreme-events-and-disasters-to-advance-climate-change-adaptation/

Intergovernmental Science-Policy Platform on Biodiversity and Ecosystem Services. (2019). *Global assessment report on biodiversity and ecosystem services of the Intergovernmental Science-Policy Platform on Biodiversity and Ecosystem Services.* https://doi.org/10.5281/zenodo.3831673

International Bar Association. (2020, May 5). *International Bar Association climate crisis statement.* [Press Release]. www.ibanet.org/Article/NewDetail.aspx?ArticleUid=cac6e15d-ec80-4669-9025-2773e9019519

James, C., Stevens, C., & Field, R. (2020). Law teachers speak out: What do law schools need to change? In M. Legg, P. Vines, & J. Chan (Eds.), *The impact of technology and innovation on the wellbeing of the legal profession.* Intersentia.

Jickling, B., & Wals, A. E. J. (2008). Globalization and environmental education: Looking beyond sustainable development. *Journal of Curriculum Studies, 40*(1), 1–21. https://doi.org/10.1080/00220270701684667

Kanie, N., & Biermann, F. (Eds.). (2017). *Governing through goals: Sustainable development goals as governance innovation.* MIT Press.

Keyes, M., & Johnstone, R. (2004). Changing legal education: Rhetoric, reality, and prospects for the future. *Sydney Law Review, 26*(4), 537–564.

Kim, R. (2016). The nexus between international law and the sustainable development goals. *Review of European, Comparative & International Environmental Law, 25*(1), 15–26. https://doi.org/10.1111/reel.12148

Kotzé, L. Kim, R., Glass, L. M., Du Toit, L., Kashwan, P., Liverman, D., Montesano, F., Senit, C. A., Treyer, S., & Villavicencio-Calzadilla, P. (2022). Planetary integrity. In F. Biermann, T. Hickmann, & C. A. Sénit (Eds.), *The political impact of the Sustainable Development Goals—Transforming governance through global goals* (pp. 140–171). Cambridge University Press.

Krieger, H., Nolte, G., & Zimmerman, A. (Eds.). (2019). *The international rule of law: Rise or decline?* Oxford University Press.

Kundis Craig, R., & Ruhl, J.B. (2021). New realities require new priorities: Rethinking Sustainable Development Goals in the Anthropocene. In J. Owley & K. Hirokawa (Eds.), *Environmental law beyond 2020.* ELI Press.

Law Society of Ontario. (2022). *Rules of professional conduct.* https://lso.ca/about-lso/legislation-rules/rules-of-professional-conduct

Legg, M., Vines, P., & Chan, J. (Eds.). (2020). *The impact of technology and innovation on the wellbeing of the legal profession.* Intersentia.

Lim, M. (Ed.). (2019). *Charting environmental law futures in the Anthropocene.* Springer. https://doi.org/10.1007/978-981-13-9065-4

Lim, M. (2021). Pandemics and unprecedented biodiversity loss in a telecoupled world-what role for law? *Australian Environment Review, 35*(7/8), 179–184.

Lim, M., & Allan, A. (2016). The use of scenarios in legal education to develop futures thinking and sustainability competencies. *The Law Teacher, 50*(3), 321–340. https://doi.org/10.1080/03069400.2016.1241048

Lim, M., Søgaard Jørgensen, P., & Wyborn, C.A. (2018). Reframing the sustainable development goals to achieve sustainable development in the Anthropocene—A systems approach. *Ecology and Society, 23*(3). https://doi.org/10.5751/ES-10182-230322

Liu, J., Hull, V., Batistella, M., DeFries, R., Dietz, T., Fu, F., Hertel, T. W., Izaurralde, R. C., Lambin, E. F., Li, S., Martinelli, L. A., McConnell, W. J., Moran, E. F., Naylor, R., Ouyang, Z., Polenske, K. R., Reenberg, A., de Miranda Rocha, G., Simmons, C. S., …, Zhu, C. (2013). Framing sustainability in a telecoupled world. *Ecology and Society, 18*(2). https://doi.org/10.5751/ES-05873-180226

Lotz-Sistitka, H., Wals, A. E. J., Kronlid, D., & McGarry, D. (2015). Transformative, transgressive social learning: Rethinking higher education pedagogy in times of systemic global dysfunction. *Current Opinion in Environmental Sustainability, 16*, 73–80.

Lowther, J., & Sellick, J. (2016). Embedding sustainability literacy in the legal curriculum: Reflections on the Plymouth model. *The Law Teacher, 50*(3), 307–320. https://doi.org/10.1080/03069400.2016.1240919

Lücke, H. (2010). Legal history in Australia: The development of Australian legal/historical scholarship. *Australian Bar Review, 34*(1), 109–147.

Macintosh, A. (2015). The impact of ESD on Australia's environmental institutions. *Australasian Journal of Environmental Management, 22*(1), 33–45. https://doi.org/10.1080/14486563.2014.999724

McCormack, P. C. (2018). The legislative challenge of facilitating climate change adaptation for biodiversity. *Australian Law Journal, 92*(7), 546–562.

McCormack, P. C. (2020). Climate change, wildfires and wetland ecosystem services: Governing transformation. *Queensland University Law Review, 39*(3), 417–447.

McNamara, M. (2018). University legal education and the supply of law graduates: A fresh look at a longstanding issue. *Flinders Law Journal, 20*(2), 223–255.

Ng, Y., O'Sullivan, M., Paterson, M., & Witzleb, N. (2020). Revitalising public law in a technological era: Rights, transparency and administrative justice. *UNSW Law Journal, 43*(3), 1041–1077. https://doi.org/10.53637/YGTS5583

Nilsson, M., & Costanza, R. (2015). Overall framework for the sustainable development goals. In *Review of the sustainable development goals: the science perspective* (pp. 7–12) International Council for Science & International Social Science Council.

Obuka, B. O., & Ukwueze, F. O. (2020). Challenges and strategies for sustainable clinical legal education in Nigeria. *The Law Teacher, 54*(3), 385–399. https://doi.org/10.1080/03069400.2019.1690343

Ong, D. M. (2016). Prospects for integrating an environmental sustainability perspective within the university law curriculum in England. *The Law Teacher, 50*(3), 276–299. https://doi.org/10.1080/03069400.2016.1262988

Paliwal, V., Chandra, S., & Sharma, S. (2020). Blockchain technology for sustainable supply chain management: A systematic literature review and a classification framework. *Sustainability, 12*(18), 7638. https://doi.org/10.3390/su12187638

Priest, G. L. (1993). The growth of interdisciplinary research and the industrial structure of the production of legal ideas: A reply to Judge Edwards. *Michigan Law Review, 91*(8), 1929–1944.

Pue, W. W. (2008). Legal education's mission. *Law Teacher, 42*(3), 270–290. https://doi.org/10.1080/03069400.2008.9959788

Randers, J., Rockström., Stoknes, P. E., Golüke, U., Collste, D., & Cornell, S. (2018). *Transformation is feasible: How to achieve the Sustainable Development Goals within planetary boundaries.* Stockholm Resilience Centre and BI Norwegian Business School. https://www.stockholmresilience.org/download/18.51d83659166367a9a16353/153967 5518425/Report_Achieving%20the%20Sustainable%20Development%20Goals_WEB.pdf

Raskin, P. (2008). World lines: A framework for exploring global pathways. *Ecological Economics, 65*(3), 461–470. https://doi.org/10.1016/j.ecolecon.2008.01.021

Reid, C. T. (2016). Education for sustainable development and the professional curriculum. *The Law Teacher, 50*(3), 300–306. https://doi.org/10.1080/03069400.2016.1262986

Rigney, S. (2020). Creating the law school as a meeting place for epistemologies: Decolonising the teaching of jurisprudence and human rights. *The Law Teacher, 54*(4), 503–516. https://doi.org/10.1080/03069400.2020.1827821

Roper, V., Dunn, R., & Rasiah, S. (2020). Revisiting "Pressing problems in the law: What is the law school for?" 20 years on. *The Law Teacher, 54*(3), 455–464. https://doi.org/10.1080/03069400.2020.1745004

Rulli, M. C., Casirati, S., Dell'Angelo, J., Frankel Davis, K., Passera, C., & D'Odorico, P. (2019). Interdependencies and telecoupling of oil palm expansion at the expense of Indonesian rainforest. *Renewable and Sustainable Energy Reviews, 105*, 499–512. https://doi.org/10.1016/j.rser.2018.12.050

Samuel, G. (2020). *Independent review of the EPBC act—Final report.* Australian Department of Agriculture, Water and Environment. https://epbcactreview.environment.gov.au/resources/final-report

Sexson, W. R., & Wilson, M. J. (2021). The university's fragile role in fostering societal resilience by facilitating the development of community-engaged professionalism. *The Law Teacher, 55*(1), 88–100. https://doi.org/10.1080/03069400.2021.1872882

Sharma v Minister for the Environment (No 2) [2021] FCA 744.

Sourdin, T. (2018). Judge v Robot? Artificial Intelligence and Judicial Decision-Making. *UNSW Law Journal, 41*(4), 1114–1133.

Stafford-Smith, M., Griggs, D., Gaffney, O., Reyers, B., Norichika, K., Shrivastava, P., Ullah, F., Stigson, B., Leach, M., & O'Connell, D. (2016). Integration: The key to implementing the sustainable development goals. *Sustainability Science, 12*(6), 911–919. https://doi.org/10.1007/s11625-016-0383-3

Sterling, S. (2003). *Whole systems thinking as a basis for paradigm change in education* [PhD thesis]. University of Bath.

Suiter, J. (2016). Post-truth politics. *Political Insight, 7*(3), 25–27.

Thornton, M. (2019, June 17). *What are law schools for in a neoliberal milieu?* [Keynote Address]. Modern Law Review Symposium, Revisiting "Pressing Problems in the Law: What is the Law School for?" 20 years on, Northumbria School of Law and Nottingham Law School, United Kingdom.

Thornton, M. (2020). The challenge for law schools of satisfying multiple masters. *Australian Universities Review, 62*(2), 5–13.

Twining, W. (2018). Rethinking legal education. *The Law Teacher, 52*(3), 241–260. https://doi.org/10.1080/03069400.2018.1497260

United Nations. (2015). *Transforming our world—The 2030 agenda for sustainable development.* https://sustainabledevelopment.un.org/content/documents/21252030%20Agenda%20for%20Sustainable%20Development%20web.pdf

United Nations Conference on Trade and Development. (2021). *Harnessing blockchain for sustainable development: Prospects and challenges.* https://unctad.org/system/files/official-document/dtlstict2021d3_en.pdf

United Nations Human Rights Committee. (2019). *Petition of Torres Strait Islanders to the United Nations Human Rights Committee alleging violations Stemming from Australia's inaction on climate change.*

Varnava, T., Lowther, J., & Payne, S. (2010). Sustainability, Is it legal? The benefits and challenges of introducing sustainability into the law curriculum. In P. Jones, D. Selby, & S. Sterling (Eds.), *Sustainability education: Perspectives and practice across higher education* (pp. 133–154). Earthscan.

Wals, A. E. J. (2021). *Transformative learning in education.* Learning for Sustainability. https://transformativelearning.education/about/

Wals, A. E. J., & Jickling, B. (2008). "Sustainability" in higher education: From doublethink and newspeak to critical thinking and meaningful learning. *International Journal for Sustainability in Higher Education, 3*(3), 221–232. https://doi.org/10.1108/14676370210434688

Webb, J. (2019). Information technology and the future of legal education: A provocation. *Griffith Journal of Law & Human Dignity* [Special Issue: Law & Human Dignity in the Technological Age], 72–104.

Weitz, N., Nilsson, M., & Davis, M. (2014). A nexus approach to the post-2015 agenda: Formulating integrated water, energy, and food SDGs. *SAIS Review of International Affairs, 34*(2), 37–50. https://doi.org/10.1353/sais.2014.0022

World Bank. (2008). *Biodiversity, climate change, and adaptation: Nature-based solutions from the world bank portfolio.* https://openknowledge.worldbank.org/bitstream/handle/10986/6216/467260WP0REPLA1sity1Sept020081final.pdf?sequence=1&isAllowed=y

World Meteorological Organization. (2020). *State of the global climate 2020 provisional report.* https://library.wmo.int/doc_num.php?explnum_id=10444

Wyborn, C., Davila, F., Pereira, L., Lim, M., Alvarez, I., Henderson, G., Luers, A., Harms, M. J. M., Maze, K., Montana, J., Ryan, M., Sandbrook, C., Shaw, R., & Woods, E. (2020). Imagining Transformative Biodiversity Futures. *Nature Sustainability, 3*(9), 670–672.

Zalnieriute, M., Moses, L. B., & Williams, G. (2019). The rule of law and automation of government decision-making. *Modern Law Review, 82*(3), 425–455. https://doi.org/10.1111/1468-2230.12412

Part II
Challenges to Implementation from Around the World

Chapter 8
(Re)Conceptualizing the Role and Actions of Higher Education Through Excellence Discourse: Perspectives of University Management and Academics

Emmanuel Intsiful and Kim Beasy

Abstract Higher education institutions are recognised as a key agent because they play a significant role in society through their contributions to generating new knowledge and training. In Universities' quests to contribute to SDG 4 (specifically target 4.7), a flagship University in Ghana has employed excellence discourse in its strategic mission. This chapter explores how management and academic staff interpret excellence discourse in the context of SDG 4 and what actions are being taken to realise it. Semi-structured interviews were conducted among five university management staff and five academics, and Foucauldian critical discourse analysis was used as an analytic frame to understand how excellence discourse was constructed and strategic actions were implemented.

The findings reveal actors' understandings of excellence discourse relating to the SDG focused on global and international benchmarks of ending poverty in all its forms everywhere, generating quality research in solving problems, creating an inclusive, equitable and affordable access to higher education and preparing/training quality manpower relevant for both national and global citizenship. In addition, the study reveals that standardised models for restructuring of academic programs/curriculum and establishment of technology transfer centres are some of the actions that are being taken to promote SDG 4. Furthermore, the findings show a broad intersection of SDG 4 and SDGs 8, 10 and 11. The study recommends that university stakeholders in developing countries critically consider operationalizing SDGs

E. Intsiful (✉) · K. Beasy
School of Education, College of Arts, Law and Education, University of Tasmania, Launceston, TAS 7248, Australia
e-mail: Emmanuel.Intsiful@utas.edu.au

K. Beasy
e-mail: Kim.Beasy@utas.edu.au

K. Beasy et al. (eds.), *Education and the UN Sustainable Development Goals*, Education for Sustainability 7,
https://doi.org/10.1007/978-981-99-3802-5_8

within their local context. The study contributes to a critical and ongoing engagement among higher education actors concerning how universities serve as a fulcrum to achieve SDGs in enhancing social justice and transformation.

Keywords Excellence · Research · Higher Education · Sustainable Development Goals

8.1 Introduction

Since the inception of the Sustainable Development Goals (SDGs), there have been calls by supranational, national and local policymakers in both developed and developing countries, for higher education institutions to play a major role in helping contribute to the attainment and measurement of the SDGs (Siegel & Batos Lima, 2020). The SDGs urge institutions to strive for environmental, social and economic sustainability. Many higher education institutions have taken up the SDGs (to varying degrees), evident in strategy and policy documents. Within SDG aspirations, institutions communicate a striving for excellence in their commitments, with commitments measurable across international comparative frameworks. For example, the University STARS rating measures institution performance, awarding bronze, silver, gold and platinum ratings—discussed in this volume in Chapter 17. In 2019, the Times Higher Education (THE) introduced the University Impact Rankings to measure universities' socio-economic impacts. The ranking recognizes over seven hundred higher education institutions across the globe for their work on confronting the grand challenges facing humanity and the planet and have included celebrating the University of São Paulo (Brazil) for their work on ending poverty, the Tongji University (China) for their work on affordable and clean energy and the University of Auckland (New Zealand) for their research on sustainable use of terrestrial ecosystems (THE, 2020).

Within the African context, the University of Pretoria (South Africa) and Ahfad University for Women (Sudan) are two examples of universities working to help solve local challenges. The University of Pretoria strategy emphasises its research activities to address food security, while the Ahfad University for Women has restructured its academic, research and community outreach services to assist women as change agents and future leaders (Chankseliani & McCowan, 2021). Ahfad University for Women's ambition is linked with SDG5 that seeks to ensure gender equality and empower all women and girls (United Nations [UN], 2020). As a result, these two universities together with a further fifteen other universities, have been selected as SDG centres to extend their continued efforts to address SDGs and educate future generations about the biggest global challenges (UN, 2018). The establishment of the SDG centres within these universities is an attestation of improving the analytical and empirical understanding of how SDGs can be achieved through higher education (Chankseliani & McCowan, 2021).

A flagship University in Ghana, University of Alpha (pseudonym), in its quest to contribute to the SDG's, has included ambitions to achieve excellence in its strategic vision. However, the question that begs answers is what excellence discourse means within the context of SDGs and what actions are being taken to accomplish the SDGs in varying contexts?

In this chapter, we consider universities pursuit of excellence in the context of SDG Target 4.7:

> By 2030 ensure all learners acquire knowledge and skills needed to promote sustainable development, including among others through education for sustainable development and sustainable lifestyles, human rights, gender equality, promotion of a culture of peace and non-violence, global citizenship, and appreciation of cultural diversity and of culture's contribution to sustainable development.

We recognize that SDG Target 4.7 evokes critical and challenging questions. What are the "knowledge and skills needed to live sustainably", and who decides which ones are the most important? What sort of education programmes are needed to build the required knowledge and skills for sustainable living and global citizenship? And how will we know if these programmes are working? These questions have become very important in current higher education contexts because higher education institutions feel pressured to balance their academic core activities of ensuring local relevance (i.e., solving the challenges of society) while at the same time, achieving global indicators of becoming world-class universities (McCowan, 2019; Oketch et al., 2014; Salvia et al., 2019).

However, while there are prevalent projects that demonstrate how higher education institutions can support SDG achievement, coupled with a growing number of universities streamlining their academic activities with the SDGs, there remains further opportunity to extend knowledge and evidence from a range of contexts. There is a need to explore the activities related to sustainable development being undertaken by universities, particularly in low- and middle-income countries, who are underrepresented in the literature. Furthermore, rigorous research is needed to gauge the impact in practice of these activities beyond intentions or assumptions. In this chapter, we focus on the uptake of SDGs in one middle-income country, Ghana, and consider the ways in which a discourses of excellence influence the pursuit and interpretation of SDGs.

8.2 Literature Review: Role of Higher Education in Achieving SDGs

Over the last two decades, scholarly literature has documented the significant role higher education can play in ensuring the achievement of SDGs (Chankseliani et al., 2021; Fehlner, 2019; Findler et al., 2019a; Leal Filho et al., 2021; Leal Filho et al., 2019; Littledyke et al., 2013). This is predicated on institutions of higher learning being regarded as "catalysts" and "change agents" in the advancement of SDGs

(Shields, 2019). A study conducted by Fehlner (2019) showed a positive link between higher education and sustainability related development issues. Institutions of higher education contribute substantially to graduates having well-paid jobs and building stable and prosperous societies. In addition, higher education promotes the creation of new ideas and technologies that are the basis of initiatives that support sustainability. Despite this, Fehlner (2019) suggests that higher education institutions' contributions to society are likely underestimated.

Universities can lead by example and influence university members as well as other institutions and publics in society more broadly (Ferrer-Estévez & Chalmeta, 2021; Littledyke et al., 2013). The development of a sustainability culture can be developed through activities carried out on campus, including through embedding philosophies in institutional frameworks and assessment, through research and education, and in operations and outreach; all of which have been found to positively contribute to the environment, economy, society and to community awareness of sustainability (Findler et al., 2019b; Leal Filho & Brandli, 2016; Meadows, 2020).

The investment in higher education is crucial in the development of a culture of sustainability because higher education contains valuable academic knowledge, pursues and identifies research interest and demonstrates a willingness to adopt research advancements, including those related to SDGs (Mbah et al., 2021; Rosati & Faria, 2019). By embedding sustainability principles in research and academic programs, university students (undergraduates and postgraduates) and staff actively work towards a sustainable world (UNESCO, 2015).

Nevertheless, there are some challenges that are essential for consideration in the future of higher education. For example, multidisciplinary and interdisciplinary approaches are required in different disciplinary domains for effective implementation and adoption of SDGs (Chankseliani & McCowan, 2021). The integration of diverse disciplines improves students' problem-solving capacities and can broaden their minds to create solutions for different challenges (Annan-Diab & Molinari, 2017). Some knowledge disciplines such as geography, consider social, economic, natural, and political dimensions that can help in understanding the complexity of sustainability and the solutions needed for their correct implementation (Meadows, 2020).

A study conducted by Franco et al. (2019) identified that there exist different gaps and approaches in higher education for sustainable development policy, curriculum, and practice across continents. For example, in the Americas, the biggest gaps were observed in SDGs 1, 5 and 14, while in Europe they were identified in SDGs 1, 2, 3, 5, 8 and 10 (Franco et al., 2019). In Asia and the Pacific, the most significant gaps were found in SDGs 2, 3, 9, 10 and 16. Finally, in Africa, except for SDGs 5, 7, 11, 12 and 15, gaps were identified in all other SDGs. Hence, understanding how university actors interpret and implement SDGs in the global south will decrease knowledge gaps and ultimately support the achievement of sustainable development worldwide.

8.3 Methods

The purpose of the study reported here was to explore how managers and academics in higher education institutions interpret excellence discourse in the context of SDG4, and to understand their actions to realizing SDG4 in Ghana. Ghana and the higher education system are experiencing a unique moment in two specific ways. Firstly, Ghana has been rated with lower-middle-income status, while being one of the fastest-growing economies in sub-Saharan Africa, and this has occurred in the context of successive governments championing the discourse of "the Golden Age of Business" (Asante, 2012, p. 12). The underlying motive is to stimulate entrepreneurial mind-sets and wealth creation across all institutions and organizations, including higher education institutions (Gyamera & Burke, 2018). Secondly, analysis indicates that Ghana made substantial gains in achieving Millenium Development Goals (MDGs) 1,2,3,4,5 6, 7 and 8 (Sakyi, 2019). With this background, it is significant to explore how higher education institutions mandated to become entrepreneurial and granted institutional autonomy are responding to global mandates such as SDGs within a country characterized as a gateway to Sub-Saharan Africa.

The first author interviewed ten respondents including five management and five academic staff of one University in Ghana. Participants were recruited using a purposive sampling technique. During data collection, participants were assured that all data obtained would be treated with strict confidentiality and that identities would not be disclosed. Pseudonym codes of participants are used throughout to protect anonymity. Interviews with each participant lasted on average 1 h 20 min and all interviews were conducted in English. Participants (i.e., management and academic staff) were asked how they interpreted excellence discourse and what actions are being taken to realize SDGs. Thematic analysis (Teddlie & Tashakkori, 2009) was used to identify common concepts and ideas in the data. The process of the qualitative analysis included six steps (Creswell, 2013). The steps included (1) organizing and preparing the data for analysis and transcribing interviews; (2) reading through all the data line by line to guarantee that the transcript was sound and credible; (3) a detailed analysis with a coding process (Johnson & Christensen, 2013, p. 592); (4) utilizing the codes to develop larger themes; 5) connecting the codes, topics and implications of the qualitative data to the review of the literature; and 6) the interpretation and making meaning of the data (Creswell, 2013). Analysis forefronted the research focus, study context, and research questions in the identification of themes (Tashakkori & Teddlie, 2003). The study was approved by the Tasmania Social Science Research Ethics Number H0020376.

Participants comprised six males and four females. The gender composition of management staff included two females and three males, while the academic staff included two females and three females. All participants interviewed held doctorate degrees; and four and six participants belonged to the social sciences/humanities and sciences respectively. On average, participants interviewed had ten years of experience in teaching, research, consultancy, and managerial experiences at local and global levels.

8.4 Findings

In this section, we detail how management staff and academics perspectives of excellence, in the context of their institution, supported the pursuit of SDGs, and find evidence of SDG1, SDG8.2 and SDG4.3.

8.4.1 SDG 1: End Poverty in All Its Forms Everywhere

Interviews with participants suggested that there was a strong belief that education has a ripple effect which contributes to ending poverty in Ghana and features in students' ability to gain employable skills after completing school. Participants argued that the curricula of the university are designed for job-ready courses that allow students to develop analytical minds, entrepreneurial abilities and to get a job after completing university. A participant asserted that "some courses have been introduced in the curriculum that are termed as University Required Courses at the undergraduate and postgraduate levels include but are not limited to numeracy skills, academic writing, practical reasoning, information technology and critical thinking" (Management 01). The rationale underpinning the introduction of new courses into the curricula according to participants' interviewed was "to enhance broadminded and critical thinkers among students" (Academic, 01).

According to participants, these attributes contribute to a reduction of poverty, captured in the following participant assertion:

> You see, we want to produce graduates who can compete with other graduates from other top western universities in USA, UK, Canada, Australia, and other countries for the same job. For us to do this we have to make sure our curricula are restructured in meeting both global and national needs. So, I think there is no other option for us than to adapt our curriculum to ensure market-driven or economic courses for students to be job ready. This I believe has a strong relationship in reducing poverty levels in Ghana. (Management, 03)

The above participant's views show how the rationale for the changing curricula is underpinned by socio-economic motives, thereby enabling students to gain employable jobs and skills after completion, which they perceive, has a ripple effect on reducing poverty levels. This was further revealed by participants when they noted that by graduating from higher education, incomes rise, and graduates get decent and well-paid jobs. Hence, they can take care of themselves and families. In connection with reducing poverty levels, the participants spoke about how supporting systems have been implemented by the university to enable marginalized groups of students access to higher education, as the following participant's view suggests:

> We have established the Student Financial Aid Office that grant Scholarships for students who have good academic records but do not have the financial means to go through the university education. This is in the right direction if we want to develop highly skilled labour towards national development. I am of the view that your brains will take you to places where money cannot afford, hence such schemes are there to make brilliant students' dreams come

true. We have and are sponsoring student pharmacists, medical doctors, engineers, and lots more professionals. Through these initiatives we are contributing to reducing poverty levels by educating and contributing to the human resource base of the country. (Academic 08)

The above participant's assertion showcases one of the ways in which the university is contributing to ending poverty levels: by helping sponsor students from lower socio-economic status who could not afford university education. Overall, the findings within this theme suggest two vital issues are contributing towards reducing poverty levels. First, it is evident that there is an emphasis of the curricula from a vocational perspective in securing employment and developing entrepreneurial skills, hence having an economic imperative agenda, which contributes to reducing poverty levels. Second, to provide scholarship schemes to brilliant but financially constrained students to pursue higher education may have a ripple effect of contributing to reducing poverty levels.

8.4.2 *SDG4.3: By 2030, Ensure Equal Access for All Women and Men to Affordable and Quality Technical, Vocational and Tertiary Education, Including University*

Findings suggested that participants were conscious of the need for higher education to address issues of social equity. In line with SDG4.3, participants recognized that universities have a responsibility to ensure that women have equal access to opportunities, and reflected on cultural reasons that can inhibit this. The interviews suggested that because education is a right and not a privilege, access to higher education should not be for the privileged few. According to respondents, if Ghana wants to achieve the SDGs, access for all to higher education is needed. According to respondents, this will be essential, not only to enhancing social justice and transformation, but also to promoting sustainable development.

> You see we should be committed to issues of gender, marginalized people in society and give them support to have access to the university; because, for such people from poor backgrounds, having access to higher education provides them a platform to break the poverty cycle of their families. (Academic, 03)

Although participants recognized that policy was needed in addressing gender equity, others viewed gender as well as access to Higher Education for other marginalised groups as important.

> Affirmative action needs to be implemented to ensure that there is gender equity, because of cultural reasons. We need to take a critical look at the context and develop such policies if we want to achieve SDGs. Admission policy or quota policy should also be implemented. (Management, 02).

Here, we see participants recognize the connection between addressing issues of equity (SDG4.3) and efforts to reduce poverty (SDG1). The above respondents' assertions make recommendations about how universities in Ghana can enhance inclusive and equitable access to, and participation in, higher education. The quest to increasing access through widening participation polices especially for women, seem to be a priority focus for institutions of higher education. For instance, some universities in their quest to promote SDG4.3 are implementing affirmative policies relating to admissions to academic disciplines/programmes that are male-dominated such as STEM (Science, Technology, Engineering and Mathematics) disciplines. Besides, scholarship packages are made available for women in such disciplines to pursue higher studies. Respondents emphasized that an enabling environment has been provided through women in STEM mentorship programs that role model for young women and work on challenges to solve problems in the society. According to participants, not only are these provisions made for women in STEM disciplines, but also in non-STEM disciplines. Some participants asserted that, government is also playing a key role through ensuring access at the secondary level of education. To ensure equitable access, technical and vocational education and training is made free for both male and female students to support sustainable development.

8.4.3   SDG8.2: Achieve Higher Levels of Economic Productivity Through Diversification, Technological Upgrading and Innovation, including through a Focus on High-value Added and Labour-intensive Sectors

Findings revealed that respondents viewed excellence as university research activities centred on technology and innovation. With regard to technology advancement, respondents argued the establishment of Technology Development and Transfer Centre (TDTC), as an avenue to ensure a stronger relationship/link between university-industry. Participants suggested that management had become chief advocates for collaborations and alliances in universities, which had led to the establishment of a Technology Transfer Office (TTO), with the main goal of identifying suitable industry research. Furthermore, participants emphasized that the TTO provides opportunities that enable processes for commercialization (licenses, contracts and dealing with patents) which supports university and industry collaboration.

According to respondents, a TDTC has also been established to deal with research problems or issues that have a monetary value. Most importantly, the Centre provides support to researchers, industries, and companies to map their challenges and needs, to find solutions. A respondent suggested that "the main goal of TDTC is to bridge the space between industry and the University of Alpha" (Academic, 03). However, some respondents were of the view that the centre is highly regulated by the institution's research themes and spearheaded by SDGs which, to some extent, are linked to foreign donors' research interests. In addition to the TDTC, an intellectual property unit has also been established to protect and safeguard academics' novelty and discoveries. Participants viewed this as a good initiative because the research development officers liaise with other corporate and donor agencies both in Ghana and across the globe for possible funding for their research within the Ghanaian context. These two arguments were related:

> I must emphasize that the creation of Technology Development and Transfer Centre coupled with research development officers at every faculty has been very good since it has helped academics connect their research to the corporate world to solve real challenges. At the same time, they have provided them with prospective funding agencies to apply for funds for their research. In fact, this was not possible initially but now I think the University is making great strides in enhancing research activities connected to issues of technological advancement, digitalization, and innovation. We are on track to become an excellent university like top universities in the western world. (Academic, 05)

Respondents' views above explain how excellence is embedded in discourses of technological advancement through ground-breaking research, recognizing this as a way to solve societal problems. One respondent claimed, "that scholars research gets featured in the University Research Report and the University quarterly news if academics or research groups pursue research that is related to technology, nanotechnology and climate change" (Management, 10). The above respondent's assertions suggest institutional factors that motivate academics' conduct of research to support SDG 8.2. Furthermore, some respondents also highlighted that the close relationship between the university and industry has given birth to innovation. Innovation is viewed as an aspect of excellence from the respondents' perspectives. Becoming innovative through research is a marker of excellence for the University of Alpha.

Overall, according to participants, excellence is producing meaningful and innovative contributions to knowledge that aid in solving local challenges. One respondent's comment enumerates their interpretations of excellence as innovation:

> I believe excellence is using our research from our faculties and research centers to help find innovative solutions to problems. For instance, the Centre for Crop Science, is almost done with a prototype testing of maize, rice, banana, coconut, and other food varieties which can withstand insects and harsh weather condition and climate change conditions. This I believe and I agree will be the way forward to make a difference to the agriculture sector, create sustainable innovation in the long term and enhance social transformation. (Management, 05)

The conceptualization of excellence as innovation is strongly connected to innovation within the agricultural sector in Ghana. Some respondents in support of the above assertion, highlighted the fact that agriculture contributes to about 50% of the Ghana's Gross Domestic Product. Hence considering such contribution to the country's development and supporting the sustainable agricultural sector, the University of Alpha has established a Centre for Climate Change and Sustainability Studies. According to a respondent, "the aim of the Centre is to work towards organizing and promoting interdisciplinary research on climate change and sustainability and to contribute to the development of sustainable and resilience strategies for coping with present and future environmental change" (Academic, 04). Hence, respondents emphasized that "as a result of cross-disciplinary research innovation academics are encouraged to undertake their research projects around climate change and biodiversity;

climate change and food security, green economy, climate and water sustainability, economics and environment, climate change and health, and renewable energy" (Academic, 02).

8.5   Discussion

How does this interpretation of excellence sit within international SDG mandates? It could be argued that the interpretations of excellence made by participants in this study, to some extent, sit within the global mandates of SDGs. The strong contributions and responses to SDG1, SDG4.3 and SDG8.2 provide some evidence of the role that universities have to ensure their academic core activities align with the targets and indicators of the SDGs. However, as observed through this study, there are intersections and interrelationships between SDGs.

The interpretation of excellence as contributing to ending poverty in various forms as the results revealed, emphasizes the university as a change agent to end poverty aligned with SDG1 (Bloom et al., 2014; Canning et al., 2014). Specifically, at the University of Alpha, providing training to students is perceived as a strategic way to help contribute to eradicating poverty levels. Similarly, the university has established financial support systems to help marginalized students who do not have the financial capacity to access university and pursue higher education. This, according to participants, has a ripple effect of reducing poverty levels in the long term. The findings corroborate with a study conducted at the Open University of Tanzania which acknowledged that providing financial support to students for their higher education contributes to reducing the marginalization and poverty of its students (Chankseliani & McCowan, 2021). For this reason, they have supported the training of disadvantaged students as a strategy to fight poverty (Collins & Kalehua-Mueller, 2016; UN, 2020). Therefore, this study further encouraged the training of marginalized, poor, or disadvantaged students. In addition, the findings of the study demonstrated how access to training promoted economic development and employment opportunities for students from low socio-economic backgrounds. Participants similarly discussed that reducing poverty is enabled by transferring skills in the field of training. The University of Alpha has and is contributing to the training of world-class professionals who can compete with other university graduates across the globe for the same job positions. Some studies have documented how higher education qualifications contribute substantially to graduates general wellbeing through a sustainable job and build stable and prosperous societies in the long-term. The findings align with studies conducted by Small et al. (2018, p. 4) that interpreted higher education institutions as contributing to higher employability from an instrumental perspective and the ability to compete for jobs.

Another international mandate within which the interpretation of excellence falls, is aligned with SDG4.3, which stresses access and affordability. Access and affordability are complex concepts which, like quality and public good, need to be understood in relation to particular contexts. What does affordable university education mean, and is it compatible with universal or even rising access to higher education in countries that have not managed to adequately fund universal primary education? The SDG Target 4.3 suggests affordability is a facet of quality but does not make clear whether university education is to be affordable for individuals, countries, or communities. Under what terms of social contract and evaluation of the public good are these assessments made? The inclusion of affordability in Target 4.3 is laudable, as it challenges the idea that university education is only a private good for those who can afford it (Aarts et al., 2020; Castells, 1994; Richardson, 2019; Teixeira & Queirós, 2016). However, many countries (including Ghana) are shifting to "user fees" for university education, which place affordability under scrutiny. For some, this is a result of neoliberal policy orientations and the shift away from universal, free service provision, but for all countries, funding mass higher education is a very different fiscal prospect compared to funding a small, elite higher education sector (Marginson, 2016). The findings in this study indicate that tensions exist for university leadership to position an institution as globally competitive but locally relevant.

At the same time, university leaders are constantly pushing for commercialization of research activities, establishing patenting offices, technology transfer offices and trademarks, all of which are various avenues that university leaders seek to promote academic capitalism (Marginson & Vander Wende, 2007). Another dominant interpretation of excellence discourse within SDG8.2 that emerged from the data, included research innovation and emphasis on technological advancement through research. The findings highlighted academic research functions as a key ingredient to research innovation and technological advancement. That is, the uses of research to help solve environmental problems in society, climate change and greenhouse effects were explicitly emphasized by participants and indicate a belief that universities should seek to advance scientific knowledge in current times (Mbah et al., 2021; Newman, 2008).

In this study, we also wondered, what did the actors' perspectives on excellence limit in terms of progressing SDGs? For instance, it seems that they were very much making comparisons internationally and wanting to be globally competitive. This makes sense from Ghana's positioning, but what does it mean for the local context? The advent of higher education globalization, internationalization and the knowledge economy, seek to regulate the actions of the university and confine them within a particular action (Altbach, 2013). For instance, most universities use global academic rankings as a yardstick to measure performance of their universities and use indicators to measure key performance in their university strategic plans (Ball & Olmedo, 2013). The power of the global ranking system (for instance, THE impact ranking system) has diffused through the institutional field to influence key actors in HE decision-making. The phenomenon implicitly serves as a surveillance that regulates universities' strategic actions and choices with respect to SDGs.

However, some global policies do not seek to cause change in society or contribute to socio-economic development from a social justice perspective, but rather have a negative effect of exacerbating the already existing inequalities embedded in some global policies and agendas (Aarts et al., 2020). Some universities in Ghana (both private and public) are in a hurry to introduce and collaborate with other universities in Europe, Australia, and the United Kingdom with the aim of introducing what they term "world-class programmes". We argue that most of these academic programmes and their course contents are mismatched with local needs and problems. For local benefits, SDG targets and programmes should be localized to make students aware of the problems within their environment; this could be done through problem-posing questions and case studies (Sakyi, 2019). This in effect would develop students' critical thinking skills and increase critical engagement with cultural and social norms that exacerbate and/or sustain inequalities (Annan-Diab & Molinari, 2017).

There is a growing debate in the higher education literature on the seemingly hegemonic influence of institutional isomorphism or differentiation. This is a result of the seeming convergence and transplanting of global policies including notions of excellence from one context to the other to enhance organizational legitimacy.

8.6 Implications

It would appear that an emphasis on being excellent internationally is still viewed in economic growth/capitalist terms—that is, the production of productive workers. Although this is great for some aspects of the SDGs, it does not seem to aspire to develop "self" or have any real consideration for the environment. So perhaps an implication is that the interpretations of excellence are insightful in identifying what is prioritized in institutions and identifying what needs changing within discourse, to better reflect what excellence *should* be about.

Excellence in the university contexts of Ghana is based upon the extent to which qualifications and skills acquired by graduates are globally competitive. It appears that pursuing excellence in the higher education context relates to the production of quality human capital, specifically related to producing graduates that are in high demand in the global knowledge market and the world of work (Salmi, 2011). A dominant theme that emerged from this study was the actors' conceptualization of excellence discourse in training or producing quality human capital for national and global needs. The findings suggest that one of the ancient functions of the university has been to train and develop the workforce for both society and other areas of the economy. The study indicated that in the higher education sector, because of the global knowledge economy, the competitiveness of a country is highly dependent on the intellectual capabilities of its citizens rather than physical resources (UN, 2018; World Bank, 2002). They argue that to promote a sustainable future, which is a strategic aim of the SDGs, there is a need for universities to produce and train human resources that can contribute to sustainable development. Some scholars have also argued that by training human resources in order to promote education for SDGs emphasis should be placed on critical pedagogies and student-centred learning (Misiaszek, 2015). Against this background Chisholm and Leyendecker (2008) note that in heavily donor-led sub-Saharan African policy contexts "learner-centred education is considered *the* vehicle to drive societies and economies from mainly agricultural bases into modern and knowledge-based societies with the attendant economic benefits" (p. 202). Following this line of thought, the current debate on enhancing competency in universities is to ensure that the SDGs are embedded in the curriculum (Findler et al., 2019b). Most importantly, some scholars have recommended that multidisciplinary and interdisciplinary approaches are required for effective implementation and adoption of SDGs (Chankseliani & McCowan, 2021). This approach would help students to gain competencies such as teamwork, critical thinking skills, problem-solving capacities and could broaden their minds to create sustainable solutions for different challenges (Annan-Diab & Molinari, 2017).

Finally, an implication from this study is the belief of higher education staff that higher education can lift marginalized groups out of oppression and poverty. To ensure an all-inclusive, equal, and equitable Ghanaian society, the study revealed that education is a right and not a privilege; hence access to higher education should not be for the privileged few. It was observed that excellence discourse aims to promote a socially just society by helping students from underprivileged regions, and senior high school gain equitable space and access to higher education. In addition, there were calls for an affirmative policy that would allow equal access and participation to higher education irrespective of gender and socio-economic status. Working within a discourse of excellence saw participants recognize and value the contributions of higher education to social equity, this is a learning that could be transferred to other contexts.

References

Aarts, H., Greijn, H., Mohamedbhai, G., & Jowi, J. O. (2020). The SDGs and African higher education. In M. Ramutsindela & D. Mickler (Eds.), *Africa and the Sustainable Development Goals* (pp. 31–242). Springer International Publishing.

Altbach, P. (2013). Advancing the national and global knowledge economy: The role of research universities in developing countries. *Studies in Higher Education, 38*(3), 316–330. https://doi.org/10.1080/03075079.2013.773222

Annan-Diab, F., & Molinari, C. (2017). Interdisciplinarity: Practical approach to advancing education for sustainability and for the sustainable development goals. *International Journal of Education Management, 15*, 73–83. https://doi.org/10.1016/j.ijme.2017.03.006

Asante, E. A. (2012). *The case of Ghana's President's Special Initiative on Oil Palm (PSI-oil palm)* (DISS working paper).

Ball, S. J., & Olmedo, A. (2013). Care of the self, resistance and subjectivity under neoliberal governmentalities. *Critical Studies in Education, 54*(1), 85–96. https://doi.org/10.1080/17508487.2013.740678

Bloom, D. E., Canning, D., Chan, K., & Luca, D. L. (2014). Higher Education and economic growth in Africa. *International Journal of African Higher Education, 1*(1). https://doi.org/10.6017/ijahe.v1i1.5643

Canning, D., Chan, K. J., & Luca, D. L. (2014). *Higher Education and economic growth in Africa.* Social Science Research Network.

Castells, M. (1994). The university system: Engine of development in the new world economy. In J. Salmi & A. M. Verspoor (Eds.), *Revitalising higher education* (pp. 14–40). Pergamon.

Chankseliani, M., & McCowan, T. (2021). Higher education and the Sustainable Development Goals. *Higher Education, 81*(1), 1–8. https://doi.org/10.1007/s10734-020-00652-w

Chankseliani, M., Qoraboyev, I., & Gimranova, D. (2021). Higher education contributing to local, national, and global development: New empirical and conceptual insights. *Higher Education, 81*(1), 109–127. https://doi.org/10.1007/s10734-020-00565-8

Chisholm, L., & Leyendecker, R. (2008). Curriculum reform in post-1990s sub-Saharan Africa. *International Journal of Educational Development, 28*(2), 195–205. https://doi.org/10.1016/j.ijedudev.2007.04.003

Collins, C. S., & Kalehua-Mueller, M. (2016). University land-grant extension and resistance to inclusive epistemologies. *The Journal of Higher Education, 87*(3), 303–331. https://doi.org/10.1080/00221546.2016.11777404

Creswell, J. W. (2013). *Qualitative inquiry & research design: Choosing among five traditions* (3rd ed.). Sage.

Fehlner, W. (2019). Educating for sustainability: The crucial role of the tertiary sector. *Journal for Sustainable Development, 12*(2), 18–28. https://doi.org/10.5539/jsd.v12n2p18

Ferrer-Estévez, M., & Chalmeta, R. (2021). Integrating Sustainable Development Goals in educational institutions. *The International Journal of Management Education, 19*(2), 1–19. https://doi.org/10.1016/j.ijme.2021.100494

Findler, F., Schonherr, N., Lozano, R., Reider, D., & Martinuzzi, A. (2019a). The impacts of higher education institutions on sustainable development: A review and conceptualization. *International Journal for Sustainability in Higher Education, 20*(1), 23–38. https://doi.org/10.1108/IJSHE-07-2017-0114

Findler, F., Schönherr, N., Lozano, R., & Stacherl, B. (2019b). Assessing the impacts of higher education institutions on sustainable development—An analysis of tools and indicators. *Sustainability, 11*(1), 59. https://doi.org/10.3390/su11010059

Franco, I., Saito, O., Vaughter, P., Whereat, J., Kanie, N., & Takemoto, K. (2019). Higher education for sustainable development: Actioning the global goals in policy, curriculum and practice. *Sustainable Science, 14*, 1621–1642. https://doi.org/10.1007/s11625-018-0628-4

Gyamera, G. O., & Burke, P. J. (2018). Neoliberalism and curriculum in higher education: A postcolonial analyses. *Teaching in Higher Education, 23*(4), 450–467. https://doi.org/10.1080/13562517.2017.1414782

Johnson, B., & Christensen, L. B. (2013). *Educational research: Quantitative, qualitative, and mixed approaches* (5th ed.). Sage.

Leal Filho, W., & Brandli, L. (2016). *Engaging stakeholders in education for sustainable development at university level* (1st ed.). Springer.

Leal Filho, W., Frankenberger, F., Salvia, A., Azeiteiro, U., Alves, F., Castro, P., Will, M., Platje, J., Lovren, V., Brandli, L., Price, E., Doni, F., Mifsud, M., & Ávila, L. (2021). A framework for the implementation of the Sustainable Development Goals in university programmes. *Journal of Cleaner Production, 299*. https://doi.org/10.1016/j.jclepro.2021.126915

Leal Filho, W., Shiel, C., Paço, A., Mifsud, M., Ávila, L., Brandli, L., Molthan-Hill, P., Pace, P., Azeiteiro, U., Vargas, V., & Caeiro, S. (2019). Sustainable Development Goals and sustainability teaching at universities: Falling behind or getting ahead of the pack? *Journal of Cleaner Production, 232*, 285–294. https://doi.org/10.1016/j.jclepro.2019.05.309

Littledyke, M., Manolas, E., & Littledyke, R. A. (2013). A systems approach to education for sustainability in higher education. *International Journal of Sustainability in Higher Education, 14*(4), 367–383. https://doi.org/10.1108/IJSHE-01-2012-0011

Marginson, S. (2016). The worldwide trend to high participation higher education: Dynamics of social stratification in inclusive systems. *Higher Education, 72*(4), 413–434. https://doi.org/10.1111/j.1468-2273.2011.00496.x

Marginson, S., & van der Wende, M. (2007). *Globalisation and higher education* (OECD Education Working Papers, 8). OECD Publishing.

McCowan, T. (2019). Higher Education for and beyond the Sustainable Development Goals. *Palgrave Studies in Global Higher Education.* https://doi.org/10.1007/978-3-030-19597-7_1

Mbah, M., Johnson, A. T., & Chipindi, F. (2021). Institutionalizing the intangible through research and engagement: Indigenous knowledge and higher education for sustainable development in Zambia. *International Journal of Educational Development, 82.* https://doi.org/10.1016/j.ije dudev.2021.102355

Meadows, M. E. (2020). Geography education for sustainable development. *Geography and Sustainability, 1*(1), 88–92. https://doi.org/10.1016/j.geosus.2020.02.001

Misiaszek, G. W. (2015). Ecopedagogy and citizenship in the age of globalisation: Connections between environmental and global citizenship education to save the planet. *European Journal of Education, 50*(3), 280–292. https://doi.org/10.1111/ejed.12138

Newman, J. H. (1852/2008). *The idea of a university defined and illustrated in nine discourses delivered to the Catholics of Dublin.* Project Gutenberg. https://www.gutenberg.org/ebooks/24526

Oketch, M., McCowan, T., & Schendel, R. (2014). *The impact of tertiary education on development: A rigorous literature review.* Department for International Development. http://r4d.dfid.gov.uk/

Richardson, C. W. (2019). Obstacles to implementation of the SDGs: Feelings over facts. In J. M. Vilalta, A. Betts, V. Gómez, M. Cayetano, & M. J. Villacís (Eds.), *Implementing the 2030 agenda at higher education institutions: Challenges and responses* (pp. 54–65). Global University Network for Innovation. www.guninetwork.org

Rosati, F., & Faria, L. G. D. (2019). Addressing the SDGs in sustainability reports: The relationship with institutional factors. *Journal of Cleaner Production, 215*, 1312–1326. https://doi.org/10.1016/j.jclepro.2018.12.107

Sakyi, E. K. (2019). A post-mortem of the progress and problems of achieving millennium development goals in Ghana: Perspectives of the Ada East Local government managers. *International Journal of Sustainable Development, 12*(2), 27–40.

Salmi, J. (2011). *The challenge of establishing world-class universities.* World Bank.

Salvia, A. L., Leal Filho, W., Brandli, L. L., & Griebelera, J. S. (2019). Assessing research trends related to Sustainable Development Goals: Local and global issues. *Journal of Cleaner Production, 208*, 841–849. https://doi.org/10.1016/j.jclepro.2018.09.242

Shields, R. (2019). The sustainability of international higher education: Student mobility and global climate change. *Journal of Cleaner Production, 217*, 594–602. https://doi.org/10.1016/j.jclepro.2019.01.291

Siegel, K. M., & Bastos Lima, M. G. (2020). When international sustainability frameworks encounter domestic politics: the sustainable development goals and agri-food governance in South America. *World Development, 135.* https://doi.org/10.1016/j.worlddev.2020.105053

Small, L., Shacklock, K., & Marchant, T. (2018). Employability: A contemporary review for higher education stakeholders. *Journal of Vocational Education and Training, 70*(1), 148–166. https://doi.org/10.1080/13636820.2017.1394355

Tashakkori, A., & Teddlie, C. (2003). *Handbook of mixed methods in social and behavioral research.* Sage.

Teddlie, C., & Tashakkori, A. (2009). *Foundations of mixed methods research: Integrating quantitative and qualitative approaches in the social and behavioral sciences.* Sage.

Teixeira, A. A. C., & Queirós, A. S. S. (2016). Economic growth, human capital and structural change: A dynamic panel data analysis. *Research Policy, 45*(8), 1636–1648. https://doi.org/10.1016/j.respol.2016.04.006

Times Higher Education. (2020). *Impact Rankings 2020.* https://www.timeshighereducation.com/rankings/impact/2020/overall#!/page/0/length/25/sort_by/rank/sort_order/asc/cols/undefined

UNESCO. (2015). *Rethinking education: Towards a global common good.* UNESCO.

United Nations. (2018). *SDG Hubs.* https://academicimpact.un.org/content/sdg-hubs

United Nations. (2020). *The Sustainable Development Goals Report 2020.* https://unstats.un.org/sdgs/report/2020/

World Bank. (2002). *Constructing knowledge societies: New challenges for tertiary education.* World Bank.

Chapter 9
The Challenge of Meeting Sustainable Development Goal 4 in a Developing Country: The Case of Ugandan Secondary Education

Gilbert Arinaitwe and John Williamson

9.1 Introduction

In most countries, academic education has had a higher status than vocational/technical education (Brunello & Rocco, 2017). Throughout the world, secondary education is becoming synonymous with mass education, and this has led to an increased interest in secondary education by researchers, policymakers, and international agencies such as the United Nations. The United Nation's SDG4 contained the first reference in this organisation's development goals to lower secondary education as part of the basic education cycle. SDG4 suggests that by 2030, all countries should 'ensure inclusive and equitable quality education and promote lifelong learning opportunities for all' (Boeren, 2019, p. 281). The goal aims to address all forms of exclusion and marginalization, disparity, vulnerability, and inequality in education access, participation, retention and completion, and in learning outcomes. This agenda pays particular attention to gender-based discrimination as well as to vulnerable groups, and to ensuring that no one is left behind (United Nations Educational, Scientific and Cultural Organization [UNESCO], 2015). Although 'quality education' is a goal in itself, it is important to avoid regarding the 17 SDGs as fragmented 'work packages'. Many of the goals can, in fact, be interpreted as compounding with each other. For example, research on the benefits of educational attainment shows that achieving SDG4 may support the achievement of another seven of the

G. Arinaitwe (✉) · J. Williamson
School of Education, College of Arts, Law and Education, University of Tasmania, 2 Invermay Rd, Launceston TAS 7248, Australia
e-mail: gilbert.arinaitwe@utas.edu.au

J. Williamson
e-mail: John.Williamson@utas.edu.au

© The Author(s), under exclusive license to Springer Nature Singapore Pte Ltd. 2023   147
K. Beasy et al. (eds.), *Education and the UN Sustainable Development Goals*, Education for Sustainability 7,
https://doi.org/10.1007/978-981-99-3802-5_9

17 SDGs including (SDG1) eradication of poverty, (SDG5) achievement of gender equality, (SDG3) ensuring good health and wellbeing, (SDG10) reducing inequalities among countries, (SDG8) promoting sustained, inclusive and sustainable economic growth and decent work for all, (SDG9) building resilient infrastructure and foster innovation and (SDG16) promoting peaceful and inclusive societies (Frey, 2017; Psacharopoulos & Patrinos, 2018; Schuller et al., 2004).

SDG4 contains two targets relevant to secondary education with a total of 14 corresponding pre-defined set of indicators used to measure progress. The SDG4.1 target challenges all countries to 'ensure that all girls and boys complete free, equitable and quality primary and secondary education leading to relevant and effective learning outcomes'. The corresponding indicators relate to conditions (i) the proportion of children at each of the major year transitions, e.g., from primary to secondary, (ii) that minimum standards have been reached in reading and mathematics, (iii) that girls are represented equally across all age and grade levels, (iv) that there is a national achievement standards assessment exercise at the major year transitions, and (v) that schooling is free and compulsory up until the end of secondary school (Organisation for Economic Co-operation and Development [OECD], 2019; UNESCO, 2016). The SDG4.c target challenges all countries to 'substantially increase the supply of qualified teachers, including through international cooperation for teacher training in developing countries, especially least developed countries and small island developing States'. The corresponding broad indicators relate to (i) minimally qualified teachers for the classroom level and curriculum they teach, (ii) that the professional training of teachers be recognised in working conditions and salary, and (iii) that there be appropriate professional development for the teaching workforce, and this be recognised in salary (UNESCO, 2016). In this chapter, not all of the specific targets are discussed; however, several of the broader categories are referred to while examining the case of Uganda's progress in aspiring to implement SDG4.1 and SDG4.c.

9.2   Case Study Context: Uganda

Uganda is a landlocked low-income country in Sub-Saharan Africa in the eastern region surrounded by Tanzania, Rwanda, Democratic Republic of Congo, South Sudan, and Kenya. In 2020, GDP per capita (current US$) was $860, with annual income growth contracting by 2.1%.

Uganda's education system has four levels: seven years of primary education, followed by four years of lower (ordinary level) and two years of upper (advanced level) secondary education and three to five years of university education. There is a vocational/technical pathway parallel to secondary education in which graduates may proceed to university or join the labour market. This chapter does not discuss the vocational/technical pathway; the focus is on secondary education.

In Uganda schools may be owned and operated by the government or the private sector. The government schools comprise approximately one-third of the schools and includes privately founded schools that receive government funding (termed government-aided) and those solely established and operated by the government. Most government-aided schools were established by religious bodies, and they exert influence over staffing and curricula; in practice, limiting the government's mandate to provide an inclusive secondary education as promulgated in SDG4. In 2017, 34% of the academic secondary schools received government funding and comprised 6% government established and 28% government-aided private schools. The remaining 66% of the academic secondary schools, which are owned by the private sector, do not receive government funding (Arinaitwe et al., 2020) and hence sit outside a tight coupling with Government policy and implementation.

Uganda's population is predominantly rural with an average growth rate of 2.7% for the period between 2008 and 2018, although the proportion of rural population has decreased from 81 to 76% over this period. In this context, the attainment of SDG4 is heavily influenced by provision of education in rural areas. The rural areas are characterised by hindered access to services and public utilities that are available in urban areas, including regular electricity supply, piped safe water, teacher training institutions, banks, and referral hospitals. The rural areas in the western and eastern regions are heavily forested, with low population densities and mountainous terrain, and experience weather temperatures that fall below the usual Ugandan tropical climate. The rural areas in districts located along the international borders experience security challenges, including cattle rustling and rebel insurgencies due to the Government's inability to exercise authority over vast distances (Agade, 2010; Day, 2019). The rural areas in the central and eastern parts of Uganda are an amalgamation of tiny island areas within Lake Victoria. They experience travel difficulties and the environment promotes a myriad of diseases less common in mainland Uganda (Kabatereine et al., 2011). In 2010, rural areas in 24 districts of the 111 districts in Uganda, had consistently failed to attract and retain quality teachers (Ministry of Public Service [MoPS], 2010).

In 2007, the Ugandan Government introduced Universal Secondary Education (USE) at lower secondary and, in 2012, into upper secondary, which was aimed at increasing access to secondary education. Although the implementation of USE is not universal, it is in at least one public secondary school at every sub-county level (Molyneaux, 2011). In sub-counties (a smaller local government unit in a district) without public secondary schools, the Government partners with private school owners to provide a level of public education (Crawfurd, 2017).

As a result, the public secondary school system has in the past two decades been categorised into non-tuition fee paying, also called Universal Secondary Education (USE) schools and tuition fee paying (non-USE) schools. The Ministry of Education (MoE) data indicates that most public USE schools are in areas demarcated as rural, while most public non-USE schools are in urban areas.

In the most recent statistics (2017), there were 314 academic secondary schools in 22 districts with rural areas that the government categorised as hard-to-staff and 2261 academic secondary schools in 86 districts that were easier-to-staff (MoE, 2019, p. 2).

9.3 Methodology

The chapter presents relevant data for the two SDG 4 targets and a number of corresponding indicators relating to secondary education from the most recent available official UN SDG Indicator Global Database (UNESCO Institute for Statistics, 2020, 2021, 2022) and Ugandan government sources (MoE, 2019), including: the 2014 UN SDG Indicator Global Database for literacy and numeracy proficiency; the 2017 over-age students, gross-intake ratio, qualified teachers and student–teacher ratio (STR) indicators; and the 2016 data for completion and out-of-school indicators. Because of the missing trend data and school-level data from the official sources, complementary sources from an empirical case study of two Ugandan rural districts conducted in 2018 are used (Arinaitwe, 2021). As indicated, the country's relatively poor data availability affects the chapter's cross-country comparisons and trend analysis but nonetheless provides a snapshot to understand the challenges towards the attainment of SDG4.

9.4 Free, Equitable, and Quality Secondary Education

9.4.1 Free and Compulsory Secondary Education

The idea of universal and free access to basic education for all children is not new, being formally recognised as a basic right in the *Universal Declaration of Human Rights* in 1948. Article 28 of the *Convention on the Rights of the Child* states that secondary education should be available and accessible to every child (Opoku et al., 2020). In 2015, the United Nations set a 2030 agenda for countries to ensure that 12 years of free, publicly funded, inclusive, equitable, quality primary and secondary education—of which at least nine years are compulsory, leading to relevant learning outcomes—be ensured for all, without discrimination (UNESCO, 2015). In response to this global agenda, some African countries introduced some form of fee-free lower and/or upper secondary education. including Kenya in 2008 (Milligan, 2011), Ethiopia in 2010 (Gbre-eyesus, 2017), Rwanda in 2012 (Williams et al., 2015), Tanzania in 2016 (Brandt & Mkenda, 2020), and Ghana in 2017 (Salifu, 2020). In 2007, Uganda introduced Universal Secondary Education (USE) in selected schools, usually one school per sub-county and, hence, this implementation was not universal (Chapman et al., 2010; Huylebroeck & Titeca, 2008). By 2017, USE was implemented in 89% of the schools that are part of the 34% schools that receive government funding (MoE, 2017). The remaining 11% of the schools that receive government funding and 66% of the schools that do not receive any government funding operate without any assistance to parents whose children attend those schools. Therefore, contrary to SDG4 goal of the government to provide a free secondary education, parents must be able and willing to pay. In Uganda, currently 271 sub-counties are without either a public or private academic secondary school (Kakuba et al., 2021).

This has major implications for educational access for many children whose parents cannot afford to send them to schools in other locations. Although reports suggest that USE has increased enrolment, in the context of the limited selective implementation described above, it is likely that most students attend schools without Government support. As stated in the Government's USE policy, tuition was to be free and schools were not to levy any fees for education. The Government was to provide schools with a capitation grant of 41,000 Uganda shillings (approx. USD11.00) per child per school term, educational materials, and other capital development inputs, and to pay the salaries of all teaching and non-teaching staff. The abolishment of school fees presents one of the clearest efforts on the part of countries at expanding access. However, as shown in Uganda, the announcement of 'removal' of school fees is an important but insufficient step towards the elimination of material and structural barriers to educational enrolment and completion. Even where school fees have officially been 'removed', families are asked or required to finance their children's education directly in different ways, which act as barriers to access and completion rates of children (Arinaitwe et al., 2020; Williams et al., 2015). In addition, under the Ministry's policy, schools were permitted to collect voluntary contributions from parents 'for emergencies' (Education Act, 2008) but in doing so, were not to exclude any student for failure to contribute. These contributions, in practice, are compulsory and typically higher than the government's tuition subsidy. Recent data show that for the schools under the Universal Secondary Education arrangement, the parents' contribution maybe three to four times that of government (Arinaitwe et al., 2020). In these schools, children whose parents delay or fail to pay these 'emergency' contributions may be excluded from the school, which clearly acts against the national policy and also the SDG goal of inclusivity and education as a right of every child (Arinaitwe et al., 2020). These on-ground practices highlight the significant gap between the announced policy and the implementation in a large majority of schools; it separates those who can afford to attend school and those who cannot.

9.4.2 Gross Intake, Over-Age, and Completion Rates

The introduction of USE has undoubtedly increased student enrolment (Asankha & Takashi, 2011). However, the intertwined challenges of high rates of grade repetition, low completion rates, and multi-age classrooms are barriers to the realisation of the sustainable development targets in Ugandan secondary education. Access to secondary education is extremely limited and those who manage to reach it both self-regard and are regarded by others as the brightest and ableist of the Ugandan population (Namubiru, 2017). Despite the official Ugandan secondary schooling ages being 13–18 years old, in practice, Ugandan schools have flexible school starting ages and completion of grades. In 2017, only 18.8% of the new entrants to academic secondary school were the Ministry suggested age of 13 years (MoE, 2017). This sets up a vicious cycle as older students are likely to drop out of school (Wells, 2009) as they need to help support their families financially. Children from urban areas and the wealthiest households have much higher attendance rates in both lower and upper secondary education, with the gap growing wider at the upper academic secondary level (MoE, 2017).

Over-age is also an outcome of grade repetition with its detrimental socio-emotional effects on student retention and costs for the education system (Ikeda & García, 2014; Martorell & Mariano, 2018). Like most developing countries, grade repetition in Uganda starts at the primary school level (Kabay, 2016) and contributes to a high student–teacher ratio (Jones, 2016) and multi-age grade classrooms at the same grade (Ronksley-Pavia et al., 2019). These factors in concert result in students from low-SES backgrounds discontinuing their education.

9.4.3   Out-Of-School Rate

Uganda's out of secondary school adolescent numbers increased from 40.3% to 48.8% at lower secondary level and 74.4–75% at the upper secondary school level between 2012 and 2017 (UNESCO Institute for Statistics, 2021). In terms of gender, females are predominantly out-of-school with a growth during 2012–2017 from 42.1% to 49.0% at lower secondary level and a very small decrease from 77.6 to 77.5% at upper secondary level over this period. This in-school minority and out-of-school majority of adolescents is a result of the combination of poverty, school governance, and socio-cultural barriers. Reasons for such a large school dropout include early marriages (Schlecht et al., 2013; Wells, 2009; Wodon et al., 2016), girls' involvement in self-employment (Gavigan et al., 2020) and domestic chores (Tuyizere, 2017).

9.5   The Challenge of Covid-19 on SDG4 in Uganda

In response to the outbreak of covid-19 pandemic, the Ugandan government closed secondary schools on March 20, 2020. The government issued standard operating procedures for a phased reopening of schools. On October 15, 2020, schools were reopened for final year students and on March 1, 2021, schools reopened for third-year students and second-year students on April 6, 2021, and reclosed on June 4, 2021. From March 2020 until February 2022, when all schools were reopened, first-year students were not permitted to attend school. This was the world's longest school closure (Gudel, 2022).

During school closures, students were asked to study from home and the government was to distribute printed study materials and selected teachers were to teach using radio, television, newspapers, telephone, and the internet. The uncertain measures of schools reopening and then closing was a very disruptive stop–go period and threatened to reverse years of educational progress in Uganda, with children out of school indefinitely while the country's education system is still confronting three key challenges: access to, quality of, and relevance of education (Human Rights Watch, 2021; Sserwanja et al., 2021; Tumwesige, 2020). The prolonged lockdown adversely reduced parents' incomes and, therefore, it is likely that large numbers of children may not return to school due to parents' poverty. Media reports indicate that as children were out of school, there was an increasing risk of violence, child labour, teenage pregnancies, and sex work (Daily Monitor, 2021). International studies show that full school closures enforced over a long period disadvantage a significant proportion of students from more vulnerable backgrounds through a range of barriers: long-term educational disengagement, digital exclusion, poor technology management, and increased psychosocial challenges (Drane et al., 2021).

9.5.1 National Standardised Examinations

Since 1980, proficiency in all curriculum areas has been monitored by the Uganda National Examinations Board (UNEB) at the end of primary, lower secondary, and upper secondary educational cycles by conducting national examinations. National testing of individual student performance on basic skills is a fundamental tool to measure both individual performance and the performance of schools. Predominantly, their social capital as well as the quality of educational provision by the school is measured (Chen et al., 2018; Mphafe et al., 2014).

The publication of schools' performance data has resulted in the ranking of schools and sifting of students to progress in the Ugandan education system. A consequence of this ranking of schools has been the discontinuation in education of many students in schools ranked poorly (Synnott, 2017) and the growth of a small number of elite schools, i.e., non-USE private and public boarding academic secondary schools, which are often expensive and hence admit mostly children of the middle class (Kakuba et al., 2021), with highly restrictive admissions criteria to match their reputations. These schools admit only the top academic students from primary school level examinations or those from wealthy families and consequently, they perform better in the subsequent national examinations at the end of the education cycle. For example, in 2017, the ranking of Ugandan schools' performance in lower academic secondary national exams (percentage total students with highest grade) indicates the stark contrast across different categories of schools. In Uganda, the percentage of students with the highest score (D1) at the end of lower academic secondary is a useful tool to determine fairness and inclusion in accessing quality education (Fig. 9.1).

Both USE public and USE private schools in-hard-to-staff and easier-to-staff districts were the worst-performing schools and that both non-USE public and non-USE private schools in hard-to-staff and easier-to-staff districts from all regions were the best-performing. In short, the elite schools (non-USE urban public schools) are not located in the hard-to-staff districts of the northern, eastern, and central regions and so restrict the attainment of SDG targets across the whole education system.

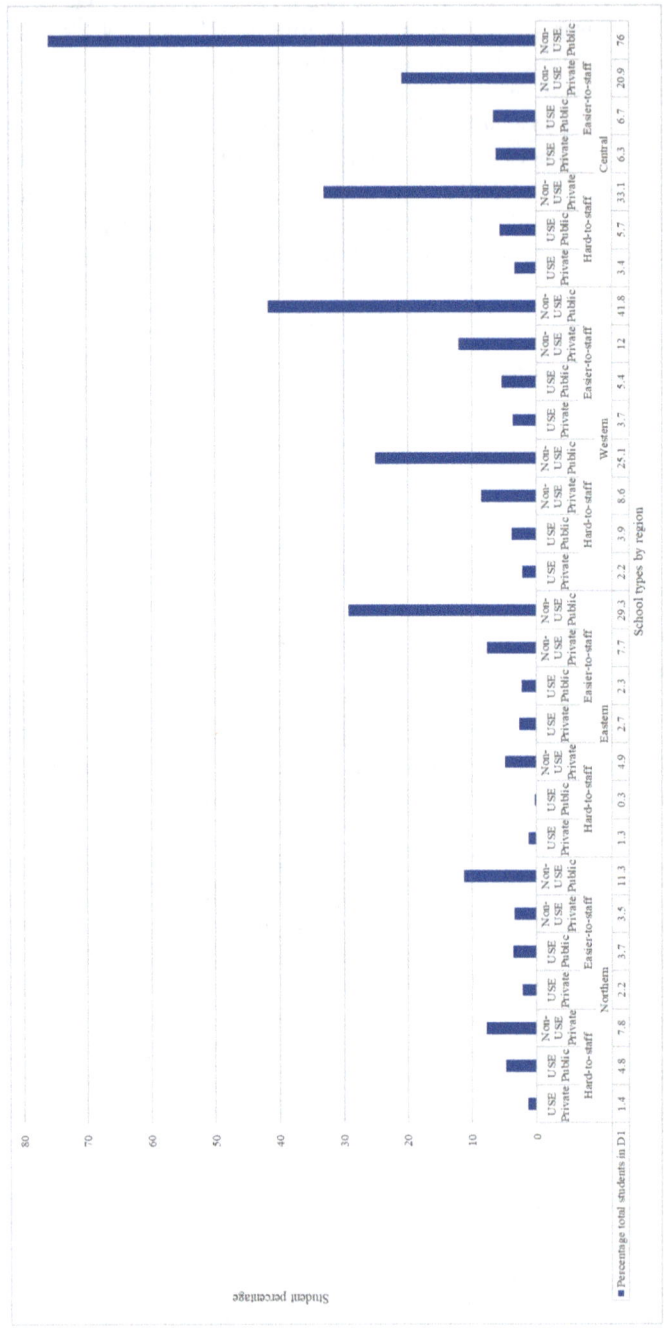

Fig. 9.1 D1 data used to inform fairness and inclusion (*Source* Namubiru 2017)

The student performance in national examinations across districts shows extreme inequalities across regions and within different categories of districts (Namubiru, 2017). The performance show patterns of entrenched inequality where most districts at the bottom level of student performance are located along the international borders and mostly from the northern and eastern regions; whereas the top ranked districts are mostly internal, especially those located in the central region. Within each region, top ranked districts comprise mostly the largest towns (cities) whereas those at the bottom level of performance are mostly (remote) districts in the region. In respect of gender performance, female students trail male students across all regions and across/within districts.

The inequalities in 'quality' education across regions and across/within districts further limits the realisation of Sustainable Development Goal 4 target to ensure quality education for all. In the bid to implement a policy of equitable education opportunity across the nation, the reality of outcomes is not just a geographical/location inequality but importantly, also a gendered inequality.

9.5.2 Proficiency Level in Reading and Mathematics

SDG4 challenges countries to attend to the quality of education and the attainment of students and as a result, UNESCO has developed a global framework for reading and mathematics for countries to measure progress. As outlined in the *Education 2030 Framework for Action (FFA)*, all countries are to ensure that:

> Upon completion of the full cycle of primary and secondary education, all children should have established the building blocks of basic literacy and numeracy skills and achieved an array of relevant learning outcomes as defined by and measured against established curricula and official standards, including subject knowledge and cognitive and non-cognitive skills, that enable children to develop to their full potential. (UNESCO, 2015)

The goal suggests that access to secondary education should result in meaningful and assessed learning outcomes (Ahmed et al., 2019). Like other countries that set national benchmarks (that vary from international proficiency frameworks) appropriate to their contexts, Uganda since 2008 has had a national assessment of progress in education (NAPE) to grade 9 (S2) students administered by Uganda National Examinations Board (UNEB). NAPE draws a select number of schools across the country and administers a standardised test to students who are present at school on the day of the assessment. In 2014, less than 50% of students reached the minimum proficiency level in both reading and mathematics, that is, 41.5% in mathematics and 49.3% in reading. In terms of gender, in mathematics, only 48.7% of male and 33.7% female, and in reading only 49.8% male and 48.5% female achieved a minimum proficiency level (UNESCO Institute for Statistics, 2021). This level of performance indicates that the target for all students to possess a high level of understanding of concepts and use relevant skills in numeracy and literacy is likely not to be realised by 2030. This is particularly the case for females.

9.6 Supply of Qualified Teachers

The second major focus of this chapter concerns the SDG4.c—the aspiration that developing countries increase the supply of qualified teachers for secondary education. International literature shows that teacher qualifications enhance self-efficacy (Williams, 2009) and contributes to improved students' performance in academic secondary schools (Koedel et al., 2015; Lee & Lee, 2020). Quality education begins with qualified teachers (Croninger et al., 2007; Manning, 2017). The distribution of qualified teachers is an issue for an equitable secondary education (Luschei & Chudgar, 2017). Rural schools have a great need of experienced and highly qualified teachers, and this is especially the case in largely rural Africa (Mulkeen, 2005).

9.6.1 Teacher Qualifications

In Uganda minimum academic qualification standards are set by the MoE for teaching levels, i.e., a Diploma in Education (Grade V) is the minimum qualification to teach at lower academic secondary and a degree of Bachelor of Education (Graduate teacher) is the minimum qualification to teach at upper academic secondary level. In 2017, however, 16.5% of the teachers did not possess the minimum qualifications to teach at the secondary level. These included licenced teachers, teachers with other training and those who did not state their qualifications. Even with the staff that met the minimum requirements, less than half of teachers (46.2%) possessed the minimum qualifications to teach at the upper secondary level (Bachelor of Education degree, described as Graduate teachers) and just over one in three (37.3%) were qualified to teach at lower secondary level (Diploma in Secondary Education, described as Grade V). These data also show a significant gender disparity as the majority teachers available at both lower and upper secondary are male, comprised of 72.1% Graduate and 78.4% Grade V (Fig. 9.2).

However, the official statistics also hide the inequitable distribution of qualified teachers among different school types, such as rural versus urban, or USE versus non-USE. Accordingly, this results in schools engaging in 'a game of buying talent' (Drew, 2015; Nair, 2019) as schools struggle to hire highly qualified teachers and parents look for schools with the potential to hire qualified teachers. As a result, the distribution of qualified teachers across school types and locations reveals high inequalities in access to qualified teachers, especially for schools located in rural areas and schools that serve low Socioeconomic status populations. Although there is a lack of Ugandan published school-level data, a sample from 2018 of 22 rural hard-to-staff schools provides a snapshot of the distribution of qualified teachers among these schools and this allows for an examination of the progress of SDG4 targets and attainments (Table 9.1).

There are intertwined complexities of (i) unequal teacher distribution across schools within the sampled districts, (ii) much higher percentages of male teachers

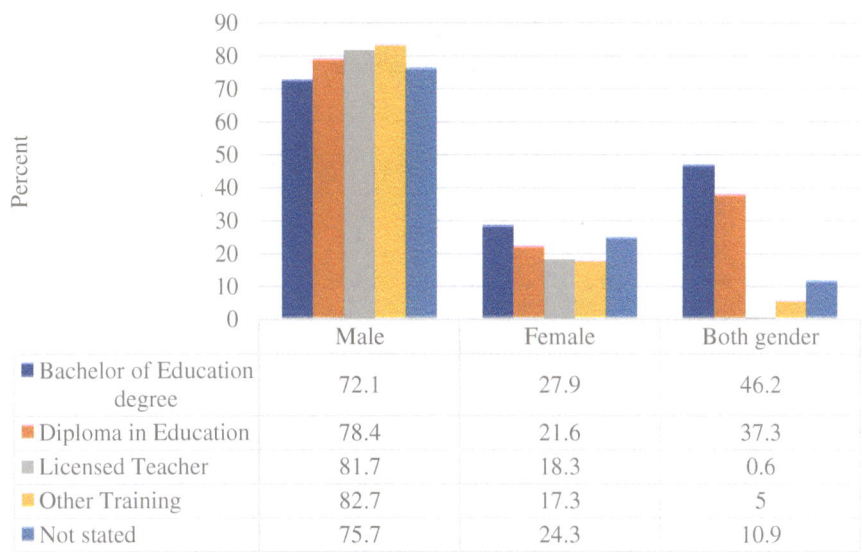

	Male	Female	Both gender
■ Bachelor of Education degree	72.1	27.9	46.2
■ Diploma in Education	78.4	21.6	37.3
■ Licensed Teacher	81.7	18.3	0.6
■ Other Training	82.7	17.3	5
■ Not stated	75.7	24.3	10.9

Fig. 9.2 Gender and qualification breakdown of teachers in Uganda (Sourced from MoE 2017, p. 196)

than female teachers at school level distribution, and (iii) a significant proportion of teachers who do not meet the minimum teaching requirement for upper secondary level (that is, teachers with a qualification below Bachelor degree level). This pattern is likely to be typical for the supply of appropriately qualified teachers to all Ugandan rural schools and therefore affects the realisation of SDG4.c to supply appropriately qualified teachers to all schools.

9.6.2   Student–Teacher Ratio: The Rosy Picture Versus On-Ground Experiences

The 2013–2017 Ugandan MoE data and UNESCO data reported a student–teacher ratio (STR) of 22:1 (MoE, 2019; UNESCO, 2020). This STR is a simple headcount formula dividing the total student population by the number of teachers (regardless of their teaching assignment and individual school deployments) within the country. The Ugandan and UNESCO's cited STR gives a much more positive view of classroom life than the actual school-level experience. Rather than providing individual-level data, the MoE data gathers data at macro-level, from a limited number of people providing answers to a set of questions. In practice, student enrolment varies across schools and within a school across different grades.

The on-ground STR formula is based on the interplay between (a) the number of hours per week required for each subject, (b) the maximum number of students per

Table 9.1 Percentage of teachers in 22 rural schools by gender and qualifications in 2018

School	Graduate teachers		Grade V teachers		Unlicenced teachers	
	Male	Female	Male	Female	Male	Female
A	75	12.5	12.5			
B	33.33	8.33	58.33			
C	48.38	19.35	29.03	3.23		
D	40.91	13.64	18.18	22.73		4.45
E	56.67	6.67	30	3.33	3.33	
F	52.95	11.76	29.41	5.88		
G	18.18	18.18	40.91	18.18	4.55	
H	29.41	11.76	35.29	23.53		
I	61.54		30.77	7.69		
J	30.77		46.15	15.39	7.69	
K	28.57	9.52	57.14	4.77		
L	20.83		66.67	8.33	4.17	
M	42.86	14.29	35.71	7.14		
N	25		66.67	8.33		
O	50		50			
P	61.54	7.69	30.77			
Q	68.75		18.75	12.5		
R	50	9.09	31.82	9.09		
S	40.91	13.64	45.45			
T	23.81		66.67	9.52		
U	12.5	6.25	75	6.25		
V	46.15		38.46	15.39		

Sourced from Arinaitwe (2021, p. 114)

grade, (c) the teacher's teaching load per week in a single specialty, and (d) whether or not the subject specialty is crosscutting, compulsory or elective for a specific grade. Therefore, when these intricate school-level experiences are put into consideration, the STR at individual schools, is significantly different from the above-cited STR in Ugandan and UNESCO reports.

Due to the lack of nationally published school-level data, a closer look at the sample of schools provides a snapshot of the distribution of students and teachers among schools to illustrate intricate school-level experiences with the progress of SDG 4 targets and indicators (Table 9.2).

Student enrolment varies across schools and within a school across different grades. In such situations, because of understaffing of schools, most teachers are assigned to teach an extra subject (Arinaitwe et al., 2020), raising issues similar to international literature of teaching out-of-field (McConney & Price, 2009; Sharplin, 2014) and work overload (Bartlett, 2004; Butt & Lance, 2005), affecting effective

Table 9.2 Selected schools' number of teachers and students by gender in 2018

School	Teachers			S1		S2		S3		S4		S5		S6		Total		Total
	M	F	Total	M	F	M	F	M	F	M	F	M	F	M	F	M	F	
A	11	1	12	33	35	25	25	26	13	26	11					110	84	412
B	24	7	31	81	89	92	98	98	90	124	91	25	12	29	17	449	397	1754
C	13	9	22	27	38	24	36	20	34	24	35	7	3	3	7	105	153	560
D	27	3	30	53	59	60	54	48	51	44	56	41	59	49	51	295	330	1310
E	14	3	17	24	26	27	31	32	25	37	32					120	114	502
F	14	9	23	21	25	32	39	25	21	29	31					107	116	492
G	11	6	17		60		45		51		43		28		18		245	524
H	12	1	13	32	29	39	25	37	35	40	23					148	112	546
I	11	2	13	23	32	29	41	37	32	35	31					124	136	546
J	18	3	21	35	15	30	12	40	13	45	10					150	50	442
K	22	2	24	29	37	17	24	23	20	11	20					80	101	410
L	20	8	28	80	83	72	71	79	69	73	57	18	7	15	1	337	288	1306
M	22	2	24	160	123	107	96	85	70	74	69	5	5	12	0	443	363	1660
N	13	1	14	19	22	18	21	19	22	22	20					78	85	354
O	12	1	13	50	37	47	25	36	15	20	27	7	2	6	0	166	106	570
P	14	2	16	48	57	45	45	47	43	30	35					170	180	732
Q	18	4	22	75	62	18	20	22	10	12	9					127	101	500
R	19	3	22	28	30	44	45	41	41	26	25	9	3	10	1	158	145	650
S	19	2	21	76	79	44	36	41	30	50	49					211	194	852
T	14	2	16	57	47	62	42	47	41	46	32					212	162	780

(continued)

Table 9.2 (continued)

School	Teachers			S1		S2		S3		S4		S5		S6		Total		
	M	F	Total	M	F	M	F	M	F	M	F	M	F	M	F	M	F	Total
U	11	2	13	35	55	37	52	40	45	32	62					144	214	742
Total	339	73	412	986	1040	869	883	843	771	800	768	112	119	124	95	3734	3676	15,644

Note Abbreviations in the table include M for Male, F for Female and S for grade level

Data sourced from Arinaitwe (2021, p. 115)

teaching, quality education, and school management (Steyn & Plessis, 2007). In addition, most schools choose only elective subjects whose teachers are readily available, and do not require expensive resources (Arinaitwe et al., 2020). Faced with such on-ground experiences, elective subjects that are inherently more expensive and technical to teach than others (e.g., the vocational and technical sciences rather than the humanities), are not offered to students. Consequently, this denies many students the full range of subjects, which limits their choices and ultimately their career options.

9.6.3 The Challenge of Teacher Salary in Uganda

Government teachers are paid differently according to individual teacher's experience, rank, and subject specialty (Yuyou & Wenjing, 2018); that is, positions of headteachers and deputy headteachers are paid relatively higher than the highest-paid teacher and these positions are obtained through promotion out of the classroom teaching position. Also, there are salary differentials according to subject specialty, with science teachers earning more than non-science teachers to attract and retain science teachers. Furthermore, the Government suspended teachers' incremental salary progression in 2012 and as a result, most teachers who upgrade their qualifications (for example, from Diploma to Bachelor degree) remain earning the same salary on which they commenced. When salary increments are made for a select category of teachers, they are usually small in size, and the opportunity cost is often deemed not worth the effort as it is not linked to a well-structured salary progression scale and hence not supporting the SDG targets.

As described above the percentage of Government schools is approximately one-third of the total number of schools and there are variations in remuneration within districts, occurring more often between rural and urban districts. The development of the so-called 'elite schools' in urban areas has exacerbated this issue of salary difference. In turn, the location advantage, coupled with salary increase, means that schools that cannot afford to pay more—or to pay to attract staff—have problems in attracting and retaining suitably qualified teachers.

Pay parity is an issue: in relation to other professionals and occupations (Findlay et al., 2014; Woessmann, 2011), teachers' pay is significantly less than people who hold equivalent qualifications and similar experience. In addition to the salary differentials other occupations enjoy benefits and allowances which teachers do not receive.

One consequence of low salaries is the withdrawal of labour (i.e., strikes) and Uganda regularly experiences teacher strikes (Namara & Kasaija, 2016). Another consequence has been persistent teacher absenteeism (Chaudhury et al., 2006) partly because of 'teacher moonlighting', that is, having multiple teaching appointments across several schools to earn a reasonable salary (Gilpin, 2020; Molyneaux, 2011). Other reasons include a high number of cases of teachers leaving schools in the form of transfers to other schools (lateral transfer), transfers to non-teaching roles (vertical transfer), job abandonment (with unknown reasons), resignation, and dismissal

(Arinaitwe et al., 2020; Bennell, 2004). These cases of resignation, dismissal, and job abandonment signal important issues related to ethics and teacher's behaviour, career choices and decisions, and job satisfaction. These breaks in classroom teaching have a disruptive effect on student learning (Abadzi, 2009; Summers, 2006), and hence exacerbate the challenge of quality teacher shortages for the realisation of SDG targets.

9.7 Conclusion

Uganda is a country that has committed to the SDG4 goals; however, as described, at present the national aspirations are not on track for goal attainment. The chapter argues that despite the stated goal, the data suggest that structural issues in school governance, the challenges of teacher recruitment and retention, competing national financial needs, and the lack of a truly national policy push, achievement of the two targets of SDG 4 are unlikely to be attained by 2030. A combination of geography, economic conditions, and history have provided numerous ongoing challenges. These have been severely impacted recently by the Covid-19 pandemic. The examination of the broad goals of ensuring that all girls and boys complete free, equitable, and quality secondary education, and of the aspiration to increase substantially the supply of qualified teachers, are adversely affected by structural challenges that government reports and UNESCO data often present more positively than the on-ground realities demonstrate.

   The data presented in this chapter highlight in different ways of how the aspirations of the SDG4 were interpreted in Uganda, a resource-constrained developing country context in three ways. First, minority elite schools, that is, schools not under USE arrangement, are not accessible in most rural districts and have instituted highly restrictive admissions criteria to match their reputations. Students who attend elite schools perform better in national examinations than their counterparts who attend schools under USE arrangements, hence resulting in education inequalities. Second, the majority of the students attending USE schools are over the expected age due to grade repetition and late school entry (Kabay, 2016; Yuko et al., 2010) and, this leads to a low net completion rate. One consequence is the school non-completion rate, especially for female students, due to teenage pregnancies, early marriages, and girl-unfriendly school structures, which undermines the realisation of SDG targets. Third, less than half of teachers in USE schools meet the minimum qualification level for teaching upper secondary curricula. This is especially so for female teachers, who are also under-represented in the school staffing profile. The consequences of lack of qualified teachers include schools assigning the available teachers to teach a high number of students and assigning teachers to teach out-of-field (McConney & Price, 2009; Sharplin, 2014; Steyn & Plessis, 2007). These decisions result in increased teachers' workloads, a decrease in students' classroom discipline, and students' low academic performances (Filges et al., 2018). The combination of policy and practical factors described in this chapter has resulted in the achievement of SDG4 not being met. However, while the Government has not achieved the goals of SDG4 to date, there are initiatives that could be implemented to improve quality education in Uganda including a greater focus on policies such as: making schools more female-friendly, increased female teacher employment in rural schools, and the provision of ongoing paid teacher professional development.

References

Abadzi, H. (2009). Instructional time loss in developing countries: Concepts, measurement, and implications. *World Bank Research Observer, 24*(2), 267–290. https://doi.org/10.1093/wbro/lkp008

Agade, K. M. (2010). Complexities of livestock raiding in Karamoja. *Nomadic Peoples*, 87–105.

Ahmed, A. Y., Miller, V. W., Gebremeskel, H. H., & Ebessa, A. D. (2019). Mapping inequality in access to meaningful learning in secondary education in Ethiopia: Implications for sustainable development. *Educational Studies, 45*(5), 554–581. https://doi.org/10.1080/03055698.2018.1509777

Arinaitwe, G. (2021). *Teacher engagement and retention in rural public secondary schools in Uganda* [Unpublished Doctoral Dissertation]. University of Tasmania, Launceston, Tasmania, Australia.

Arinaitwe, G., Williamson, J., & Kilpatrick, S. (2020). 'Birds of a feather flock together!': Rural teacher recruitment policy and retention in and for hard-to-staff Ugandan schools. In J. Fox, C. Alexander, & T. Aspland (Eds.), *Teacher education in globalised times: Local responses in action* (pp. 295–310). Springer Singapore.

Asankha, P., & Takashi, Y. (2011). Impacts of universal secondary education policy on secondary school enrolments in Uganda. *Journal of Accounting, 1*(1), 16–30.

Bartlett, L. (2004). Expanding teacher work roles: A resource for retention or a recipe for overwork? *Journal of Education Policy, 19*(5), 565–582. https://doi.org/10.1080/0268093042000269144

Bennell, P. (2004). *Teacher motivation and incentives in Sub-Saharan Africa and Asia.* Department for International Development. https://assets.publishing.service.gov.uk/media/57a08be640f0b652dd000f9a/ResearchingtheIssuesNo71.pdf

Boeren, E. (2019). Understanding sustainable development goal (SDG) 4 on "quality education" from micro, meso and macro perspectives. *International Review of Education, 65*(2), 277–294. https://doi.org/10.1007/s11159-019-09772-7

Brandt, K., & Mkenda, B. (2020). *The impact of eliminating secondary school fees: Evidence from Tanzania* (Development Economics Research Group Working Paper). https://doi.org/10.2139/ssrn.3748754

Brunello, G., & Rocco, L. (2017). The effects of vocational education on adult skills, employment and wages: What can we learn from PIAAC? *Series, 8*(4), 315–343. https://doi.org/10.1007/s13209-017-0163-z

Butt, G., & Lance, A. (2005). Secondary teacher workload and job satisfaction: Do successful strategies for change exist? *Educational Management Administration & Leadership, 33*(4), 401–422. https://doi.org/10.1177/1741143205056304

Chapman, D. W., Burton, L., & Werner, J. (2010). Universal secondary education in Uganda: The headteachers' dilemma. *International Journal of Educational Development, 30*(1), 77–82. https://doi.org/10.1016/j.ijedudev.2009.08.002

Chaudhury, N., Hammer, J., Kremer, M., Muralidharan, K., & Rogers, F. H. (2006). Missing in action: Teacher and health worker absence in developing countries. *The Journal of Economic Perspectives, 20*(1), 91–116.

Chen, Q., Kong, Y., Gao, W., & Mo, L. (2018). Effects of socioeconomic status, parent–child relationship, and learning motivation on reading ability. *Frontiers in Psychology, 9*, 12–97. https://doi.org/10.3389/fpsyg.2018.01297

Crawfurd, L. (2017). School management and public–private partnerships in Uganda. *Journal of African Economies, 26*(5), 539–560. https://doi.org/10.1093/jae/ejx021

Croninger, R. G., Rice, J. K., Rathbun, A., & Nishio, M. (2007). Teacher qualifications and early learning: Effects of certification, degree, and experience on first-grade student achievement. *Economics of Education Review, 26*(3), 312–324. https://doi.org/10.1016/j.econedurev.2005.05.008

Daily Monitor. (2021). We need concerted effort to curb teenage pregnancies. *Daily Monitor.* https://www.monitor.co.ug/uganda/oped/editorial/we-need-concerted-effort-to-curb-teenage-pregnancies-3536526

Day, C. R. (2019). "Survival mode": Rebel resilience and the Lord's Resistance Army. *Terrorism and Political Violence, 31*(5), 966–986. https://doi.org/10.1080/09546553.2017.1300580

Drane, C. F., Vernon, L., & O'Shea, S. (2021). Vulnerable learners in the age of COVID-19: A scoping review. *The Australian Educational Researcher, 48*(4), 585–604. https://doi.org/10.1007/s13384-020-00409-5

Drew. (2015). How to win the game of talent. *Journal of accountancy, 220*(4), 28–52.

Education Act. (2008). *The Education (pre-primary, primary and post-primary) Act, 2008.* Government of Uganda. http://www.unesco.org/education/edurights/media/docs/5d1b721a509097c2833561341ead3d788906cf4a.pdf

Filges, T., Sonne-Schmidt, C. S., & Nielsen, B. C. V. (2018). Small class sizes for improving student achievement in primary and secondary schools: A systematic review. *Campbell Systematic Reviews, 14*(1), 1–107. https://doi.org/10.4073/csr.2018.10

Findlay, J., Findlay, P., & Stewart, R. (2014). Occupational pay comparisons–easier said than done? *Employee Relations, 36*(1), 2–16. https://doi.org/10.1108/ER-05-2013-0056

Frey, D. F. (2017). Economic growth, full employment and decent work: The means and ends in SDG 8. *The International Journal of Human Rights, 21*(8), 1164–1184. https://doi.org/10.1080/13642987.2017.1348709

Gavigan, S., Ciprikis, K., & Cooney, T. (2020). The impact of entrepreneurship training on self-employment of rural female entrepreneurs in Uganda. *Small Enterprise Research, 27*(2), 180–194. https://doi.org/10.1080/13215906.2020.1769715

Gbre-eyesus, M. T. (2017). Achieving universal general secondary education in Ethiopia in line with the middle-income country vision: A reality or a dream? *Africa Education Review, 14*(1), 171–192. https://doi.org/10.1080/18146627.2016.1224570

Gilpin, G. (2020). Policy-induced school calendar changes and teacher moonlighting. *Southern Economic Journal, 86*(3), 989–1018. https://doi.org/10.1002/soej.12402

Gudel, H. (2022). *After a 2-year lockdown, schools in Uganda have reopened–but for many it may be too late.* http://eprints.lse.ac.uk/113964/

Human Rights Watch. (2021). *"I must work to eat": Covid-19, poverty, and child labor in Ghana, Nepal, and Uganda.* https://www.hrw.org/sites/default/files/media_2021/05/crd_childlabor0521_web.pdf

Huylebroeck, L., & Titeca, K. (2008). Universal secondary education (USE) in Uganda: Blessing or curse? The impact of USE on educational attainment and performance. *Journal of Educational Development, 28*, 161–175.

Ikeda, M., & García, E. (2014). Grade repetition: A comparative study of academic and non-academic consequences. *OECD Journal: Economic Studies, 2013*(1). https://doi.org/10.1787/eco_studies-2013-5k3w65mx3hnx

Jones, S. (2016). How does classroom composition affect learning outcomes in Ugandan primary schools? *International Journal of Educational Development, 48*, 66–78. https://doi.org/10.1016/j.ijedudev.2015.11.010

Kabatereine, N. B., Standley, C. J., Sousa-Figueiredo, J. C., Fleming, F. M., Stothard, J. R., Talisuna, A., & Fenwick, A. (2011). Integrated prevalence mapping of schistosomiasis, soil-transmitted helminthiasis and malaria in lakeside and island communities in Lake Victoria, Uganda. *Parasites & Vectors, 4*(1), 232. https://doi.org/10.1186/1756-3305-4-232

Kabay, S. (2016). Grade repetition and primary school dropout in Uganda. *Harvard Educational Review, 86*(4), 580–606. https://doi.org/10.17763/1943-5045-86.4.580

Kakuba, C., Nzabona, A., Asiimwe, J. B., Tuyiragize, R., & Mushomi, J. (2021). Who accesses secondary schooling in Uganda; Was the universal secondary education policy ubiquitously effective? *International Journal of Educational Development, 83*, 102–370. https://doi.org/10.1016/j.ijedudev.2021.102370

Koedel, C., Mihaly, K., & Rockoff, J. E. (2015). Value-added modeling: A review. *Economics of Education Review, 47*, 180–195. https://doi.org/10.1016/j.econedurev.2015.01.006

Lee, S. W., & Lee, E. A. (2020). Teacher qualification matters: The association between cumulative teacher qualification and students' educational attainment. *International Journal of Educational Development, 77*, 102–218. https://doi.org/10.1016/j.ijedudev.2020.102218

Luschei, T. F., & Chudgar, A. (2017). Demand-side explanations for inequitable teacher distribution. In T. F. Luschei & A. Chudgar (Eds.), *Teacher distribution in developing countries* (pp. 43–85). Palgrave Macmillan.

Manning, M. (2017). The relationship between teacher qualification and the quality of the early childhood education and care environment. *Campbell Systematic Review, 13*(1), 1–82. https://doi.org/10.4073/csr.2017.1

Martorell, P., & Mariano, L. T. (2018). The causal effects of grade retention on behavioral outcomes. *Journal of Research on Educational Effectiveness, 11*(2), 192–216. https://doi.org/10.1080/19345747.2017.1390024

McConney, A., & Price, A. (2009). Teaching out-of-field in Western Australia. *Australian Journal of Teacher Education, 34*(6), 86–100. https://doi.org/10.3316/aeipt.181569

Milligan, L. (2011). Global influences in educational policymaking: Free secondary education in Kenya. *Research in Post-Compulsory Education, 16*(3), 275–287. https://doi.org/10.1080/13596748.2011.601924

MoE. (2017). *Education Abstract*. Education Policy and Planning Department, Ministry of Education. https://www.education.go.ug/wp-content/uploads/2019/08/Abstract-2017.pdf

MoE. (2019). *Statistics abstract*. Ministry of Education. http://www.education.go.ug/statistics-abstract/

Molyneaux, K. J. (2011). Uganda's universal secondary education policy and its effect on empowered women: How reduced income and moonlighting activities differentially impact male and female teachers. *Research in Comparative and International Education, 6*(1), 62–78. https://doi.org/10.2304/rcie.2011.6.1.62

MoPS. (2010). *Payment of the hardship allowance in the public service*. Ministry of Public Service. https://www.publicservice.go.ug/policy?page=1.

Mphafe, O., Miruka, O., & Pelser, T. G. (2014). The impact of cost sharing and parental participation on secondary school performance in Botswana. *South African Journal of Higher Education, 28*(1), 180–196.

Mulkeen, A. G. (2005). *Teachers for rural schools: A challenge for Africa*. Paper presented at the Ministerial Seminar on Education for Rural Peoples in Africa: Policy lessons, options and priorities, Addis Ababa.

Nair. (2019). Winning the talent game: HR gamification experience for Generation Z. *International Journal on Leadership, 7*(1), 44–62.

Namara, R. B., & Kasaija, J. (2016). Teachers' protest movements and prospects for teachers improved welfare in Uganda. *Journal of Education and Training Studies, 4*(5), 149–159. https://doi.org/10.11114/jets.v4i5.1482

Namubiru, L. (2017). *UCE results by school 2011–2016*. Open Data in Uganda, African Centre for Media Excellence. http://catalog.data.ug/dataset/uce-school-results-2011-2016

OECD. (2019). *Sustainable results in development: Using the SDGs for shared results and impact.* OECD Publishing.

Opoku, M. P., Asare-Nuamah, P., Nketsia, W., Asibey, B. O., & Arinaitwe, G. (2020). Exploring the factors that enhance teacher retention in rural schools in Ghana. *Cambridge Journal of Education, 50*(2), 201–217. https://doi.org/10.1080/0305764X.2019.1661973

Psacharopoulos, G., & Patrinos, H. A. (2018). Returns to investment in education: A decennial review of the global literature. *Education Economics, 26*(5), 445–458. https://doi.org/10.1080/09645292.2018.1484426

Ronksley-Pavia, M., Barton, G. M., & Pendergast, D. (2019). Multiage education: An exploration of advantages and disadvantages through a systematic review of the literature. *Australian Journal of Teacher Education, 44*(5). https://doi.org/10.14221/ajte.2018v44n5.2

Salifu, I. (2020). State-funded secondary education policy: Implications for private school management in Ghana. *Leadership and Policy in Schools.* https://doi.org/10.1080/15700763.2020.1823997

Schlecht, J., Rowley, E., & Babirye, J. (2013). Early relationships and marriage in conflict and post-conflict settings: Vulnerability of youth in Uganda. *Reproductive Health Matters, 21*(41), 234–242. https://doi.org/10.1016/S0968-8080(13)41710-X

Schuller, T., Preston, J., Hammond, C., Brassett-Grundy, A., & Bynner, J. (2004). *The benefits of learning: The impact of education on health, family life and social capital.* Routledge.

Sharplin, E. D. (2014). Reconceptualising out-of-field teaching: Experiences of rural teachers in Western Australia. *Educational Research, 56*(1), 97–110. https://doi.org/10.1080/00131881.2013.874160

Sserwanja, Q., Kawuki, J., & Kim, J. H. (2021). Increased child abuse in Uganda amidst COVID-19 pandemic. *Journal of Paediatrics and Child Health, 57*(2), 188–191. https://doi.org/10.1111/jpc.15289

Steyn, G. M., & Plessis, d. E. (2007). The implications of the out-of-field phenomenon for effective teaching, quality education and school management. *Africa Education Review, 4*(2), 144–158. https://doi.org/10.1080/18146620701652754

Summers, C. (2006). Subterranean evil' and 'tumultuous riot' in Buganda: Authority and alienation at King's College, Budo, 1942. *The Journal of African History, 47*(1), 93–113.

Synnott, M. G. (2017). *The half opened door: Discrimination and admissions at Harvard, Yale, and Princeton, 1900–1970.* Routledge.

Tumwesige, J. (2020). *COVID-19 educational disruption and response: Rethinking e-Learning in Uganda.* https://www.kas.de/en/web/uganda/single-title/-/content/covid-19-educational-disruption-and-response

Tuyizere, A. P. (2017). Determinants of students' career choices in secondary schools from southwestern Uganda; Insights from a domestic chores Perspective. *International Journal of Science and Research, 6*(9), 1810–1816. https://doi.org/10.21275/ART20176939P

UNESCO. (2015). *Incheon declaration and framework for action for the implementation of sustainable development goal 4.* Paris.

UNESCO. (2016). *Education 2030: Incheon declaration and framework for action for the implementation of sustainable development goal 4.* http://unesdoc.unesco.org/images/0024/002456/245656e.pdf

UNESCO. (2020). *Technical cooperation group on the indicators for SDG 4 country data table.* UNESCO Institute for Statistics (UIS): Technical cooperation group. http://tcg.uis.unesco.org/data-resources/.

UNESCO Institute for Statistics. (2020). *Literacy rate, adult total (% of people ages 15 and above)—Uganda.* https://data.worldbank.org/indicator/SE.ADT.LITR.ZS?locations=UG

UNESCO Institute for Statistics. (2021). *SDG country data table.* http://tcg.uis.unesco.org/data-resources/

UNESCO Institute for Statistics. (2022). *Education and literacy: Uganda.* http://uis.unesco.org/en/country/ug

Wells, R. (2009). Gender and age-appropriate enrolment in Uganda. *International Journal of Educational Research, 48*(1), 40–50. https://doi.org/10.1016/j.ijer.2009.03.002

Williams, R. (2009). Gaining a degree: The effect on teacher self-efficacy and emotions. *Professional Development in Education, 35*(4), 601–612. https://doi.org/10.1080/19415250903059558

Williams, T. P., Abbott, P., & Mupenzi, A. (2015). 'Education at our school is not free': The hidden costs of fee-free schooling in Rwanda. *Compare: A Journal of Comparative and International Education, 45*(6), 931–952. https://doi.org/10.1080/03057925.2014.938611

Wodon, Q., Nguyen, M. C., & Tsimpo, C. (2016). Child marriage, education, and agency in Uganda. *Feminist Economics, 22*(1), 54–79. https://doi.org/10.1080/13545701.2015.1102020

Woessmann, L. (2011). Cross-country evidence on teacher performance pay. *Economics of Education Review, 30*(3), 404–418. https://doi.org/10.1016/j.econedurev.2010.12.008

Yuko, N. T., Loaiza, E., & Engle, P. L. (2010). Late entry into primary school in developing societies: Findings from cross-national household surveys. *International Review of Education, 56*(1), 103–125.

Yuyou, Q., & Wenjing, Z. (2018). What does professional rank mean to teachers? A survey of the multiple impacts of professional rank on urban and rural compulsory education teachers. *Chinese Education & Society, 51*(2), 117–132. https://doi.org/10.1080/10611932.2018.1433412

Chapter 10
Enacting the Sustainable Development Goals in Nepalese Schools and Teacher Education

Peter Brett, Ganga Gurung, Rabi Shah, Krishna Kumar Yogi, and Jiwan Dhungana

10.1 Introduction

Issues around sustainable development are central to Nepal's progress and wellbeing as a developing nation. After a long period of being largely isolated from the rest of the world, Nepal has cautiously embraced globalisation and, with flooding threats from the effects of global warming on the Himalayas, is on the front line of climate change. Nepal committed itself to the Incheon Declaration of the World Education Forum and its Universal Declaration on Education by 2030 agenda (UNESCO, 2015): "To transform lives through education, recognizing the important role of education as a main driver of development and in achieving the other proposed SDGs…[through]…

P. Brett (✉)
School of Education, College of Arts, Law and Education, University of Tasmania, 2/8 Bass Hwy, Burnie, TAS 7320, Australia
e-mail: peter.brett@utas.edu.au

G. Gurung
SOS Children's Villages Nepal, Bhaktapur, Nepal
e-mail: Ganga.Gurung@sosnepal.org.np

R. Shah
School of Education, College of Arts, Law and Education, University of Tasmania, Newnham Drive, Newnham, TAS 7248, Australia
e-mail: rabis.shah@utas.edu.au

K. K. Yogi
School of Education, College of Arts, Law and Education, University of Tasmania, Churchill Ave, Hobart, TAS 7005, Australia
e-mail: krishnakumar.yogi@utas.edu.au

J. Dhungana
Mahendra Multiple Campus, Tribhuvan University, Kathmandu, Nepal

© The Author(s), under exclusive license to Springer Nature Singapore Pte Ltd. 2023   169
K. Beasy et al. (eds.), *Education and the UN Sustainable Development Goals*, Education for Sustainability 7,
https://doi.org/10.1007/978-981-99-3802-5_10

a renewed education agenda that is holistic, ambitious and aspirational, leaving no one behind" (p. 1). Commendably, the United Nations Sustainability Development Goals (UN SDGs) were referenced centrally in Nepal's School Sector Development Plan [SSDP] of 2016–2023. This document envisaged a vision of Prosperous Nepal, Happy Nepali by a target date of 2043, with ten national goals, including the goal of a healthy and balanced environment designed for environmental resilience (National Planning Commission, 2020). Specifically, in addressing SDG4 Quality Education, Target 4.7, calls for "all learners to acquire the knowledge and skills (and mindsets) to promote sustainable development" (Government of Nepal, 2019a, p. 6).

Presenting at the Conference of the Parties (COP26) environmental summit in Glasgow in November 2021, Nepalese Prime Minister Sher Bahadur Deuba called for recognition of the Himalayas' climate vulnerability, highlighting that around 80 per cent of Nepal's population is at risk from natural and climate-induced hazard (Ghimire, 2021). Himalayan glaciers and permafrost are melting. Nepal has experienced changes in temperature faster than the global average and millions of Nepalese are estimated to be at risk from the impacts of climate change, including reductions in agricultural production, food insecurity, strained water resources, loss of forests and biodiversity, and damaged infrastructure (Sapkota & Rijal, 2016). In Kathmandu, the capital city of Nepal, local communities are dealing with daily environmental challenges such as air pollution, burning of plastics, and poorly managed waste disposal systems. In terms of its contribution to combatting climate change, Nepal has made impressive commitments to emit no net carbon between 2022 and 2045 and to become carbon negative after this. Nepal has also committed to halting deforestation and increasing forest cover to 45 per cent and ensuring that all vulnerable people are protected from climate change by 2030 (Government of Nepal, 2021). In these circumstances, there is a need for educational efforts to promote an informed citizenry supportive of climate policies.

Nepal has set aside more than 30,000 square kilometres, almost a quarter of the country's total area, as national parks, wildlife reserves, and conservation areas. Community forests, in particular, have conservation-friendly management as a focus in order to nurture biodiversity and support local livelihoods in environmental corridors (Government of Nepal, 2018). These protected areas cover wetlands and grasslands areas in the south, temperate forests in the mid-mountain region and alpine meadows, and the glacial tundra of the Himalayas. Biological diversity is also mirrored in the cultural diversity of Nepal with ethnic groups from the high mountains like the Sherpas, to the mid-mountain groups like the Gurungs and the Tamangs, and the dwellers of tropical flatlands like the Tharus and the Dhimals. Education has a key role to play in raising community awareness of the values of both biodiversity and cultural diversity in Nepal and the conservation of these elements for future generations.

In 2019, the Government of Nepal endorsed a National Climate Change Policy, which aimed to support measures that will "mainstream or integrate climate change issues into policies, strategies, plans and programs at all levels of State and sectoral areas" (Government of Nepal, 2019b, p. 7). Specifically, within education, objectives were articulated in the following areas:

- Subject matters related to causes and impacts of climate change and climate-friendly traditional knowledge, skills and practices will be incorporated into formal and non-formal educational curricula.
- Youth human resources will be mobilized by developing their capacity for raising awareness about climate change.
- The focal point of schools will be provided with climate change-related training in addition to the formation of Eco Clubs in secondary schools to carry out activities pertaining to climate change (Government of Nepal, 2019b, pp. 17–18).

These commitments clearly raise implementation challenges and opportunities across all levels of education in Nepal. The purpose of this paper is to explore the implications of the SDGs for Nepalese educational leaders, schools, and teachers.

10.2 Roots, Reflexivity, and Structure

This chapter has its roots in data and reflections from three recent University of Tasmania doctoral theses on Nepalese education complemented by observations, and interviews from an in-country teacher educator based at Nepal's largest provider of initial teacher education. Distinctive sections of the paper reflect upon implications of the SDGs for: policy, school leadership, and curriculum change in general; reforms to the curriculum and textbooks in particular, and possible changes that might occur at the level of whole school culture, values, and ethos. A final section of the paper suggests implications for revisions in approaches to teachers' professional learning that might be prompted by a focus on the SDGs. Four teacher educators from Tribhuvan University were interviewed to understand their perspectives on existing programs and units in relation to sustainable development-related content and skills. The paper touches upon four of the SDGs: SDG4 (Quality education); SDG11 (Sustainable cities and communities), SDG13 (Climate action), and SDG15 (Life on land). Each of the contributors submitted draft text for their assigned sections. The lead writer was a supervisor across all three doctoral projects and assumed a coordination role in facilitating the collaboration of the past and present doctoral students and in framing the chapter's observations.

Gurung's (2018) mixed methods study explored the perceptions of key stakeholders around the school curriculum and its relationship to teaching and learning in Nepal. He conducted individual and focus group interviews with teachers, parents, curriculum advisers, and secondary school leaders across three schools from different districts of Nepal (Parbat, Myagdi, and Chitwan). He also immersed himself in schools, exploring student-generated representations as a pedagogical intervention. He concluded that the lived experiences of teachers and students in the schools that he sampled reflected a lack of capacity to shape learning experiences to particular contexts. He also highlighted gaps in teachers' capacity to implement curriculum initiatives.

Shah's (2020) study was titled Exploring Civics and Citizenship Education in Nepal: From Policy to Practice. Bowe et al.'s (1992) policy cycle approach (with modifications by Ledger et al., 2015) provided a conceptual framework for the study. The thesis analysed notions of national identity and democracy, cultural diversity, and global education that were embodied within three units of analysis: curriculum policy documents, Social Studies textbooks, and teachers' perspectives. Sixteen middle years teachers across six schools in the Kathmandu area of Nepal were interviewed. Of the four public schools, two were in rural settings and two in urban settings. The study found that the analysed textbooks depicted relatively idealised and theoretical models of Nepalese politics and society. It also identified how Nepalese teachers can be constrained by issues such as their beliefs, preferred teaching methodologies, interpretations of the curriculum and textbooks, and diverse and challenging cohorts of students, all of which could serve as obstacles in the effective enactment of civics and citizenship curriculum policy.

Yogi's (2022, forthcoming) study investigates the place of values and virtues in Nepalese secondary education and specifically the potential role of gratitude as perceived and conceptualised by Nepalese educators. Interviews with educators of different levels of age and experience from two schools (a public school and a private school) helped to provide an understanding of the perspectives of educators working in different contexts as to the importance and role of gratitude. Reeves' (2006) education design-based research (EDR) framework provided a structure for deploying the ideation and sense-making, design and construction, and enactment and reflection phases. Data analysis generated conceptualisations of gratitude and identified links between gratitude and a positive school culture which served to inform the development of draft gratitude education frameworks (see Howells, 2012). The construction and refinement cycles of the EDR frameworks were illuminated, framed, and shaped by interviews and focus group discussions.

The shared focus for contributors emerged out of us collectively identifying questions that would enable lessons to be drawn from our work, linked to the SDGs, which can inform the thinking of relevant Nepalese stakeholders—policymakers, advisers, school leaders, teacher education institutions, and teachers. The SDGs were not a central focus of the data collected for the authors' theses or the research questions which were addressed. Nevertheless, all three authors, in terms of their post-study reflection around the implications of their studies (Brookfield, 1995), were of the view that their findings illuminated key policy and practice themes that are germane to the effective enactment of the SDGs in Nepal.

10.3   Implications of the SDGs for Policy Implementation and School Leaders—the Challenges

It will be important that Nepalese school leaders and teachers feel a sense of ownership over policies related to the enactment of the SDGs, but this has proved to be a challenge in implementing earlier curriculum initiatives. Considerable involvement by foreign actors in developing education in Nepal has influenced nearly all policy decisions in recent years. For example, the World Bank, UNESCO, the Asian Development Bank, and the European Union have all supported education initiatives in Nepal (Bhattarai, 2016; Regmi, 2019). As Galegher et al. (2019) observed, "Nepalese policymakers are still grappling with making imported policies best suit the needs of the country" (p. 127). This comparative sense of powerlessness can also be felt further down the educational policy chain. Nepalese schools and teachers mostly perceive themselves as implementers of the curriculum and transmitters of textbook perspectives when teaching about Nepal and the world. Subedi (2020) found that many Nepalese classroom teachers feel a lack of agency over their curriculum choices and planning.

To counteract impulses towards uncritical policy borrowing, there is an aspiration—in incorporating the SDGs—that "oriental philosophies serve as the foundation for setting Nepal's agenda of education drawing on local cultures, knowledge systems, history, indigenous skills and cosmologies" (Government of Nepal, 2019a, p. ix). In theory, following the adoption of a new national constitution in 2015, education policy for basic and secondary education has been devolved to regional levels of government. There are opportunities to shift towards more autonomy for individual localities in relation to the interpretation and implementation of educational aspirations, including the SDGs (Chaudhary, 2019; Daly et al., 2020). However, a Principal from the Karnali Province, interviewed for the fourth author's doctoral study, articulated a concern that this philosophy was not recognised in reality:

> The preparation of the mechanistic *Orientation Manual for Local Curriculum Development* (2020) for the government institutions in local governments to draft the curriculum for local subjects, which has been developed and printed by the Asian Development Bank (ADB) in collaboration with the European Union and British Council is a clear example of the donor-driven top-down approach of curriculum development.

As Fanon (2004) observed several decades ago, any educational policy initiative and implementation should be "geared to the production, invention and creation of work" (p. 98) that values local epistemologies.

Nepal has long had a centralised mechanism that defines the curriculum and publishes the textbooks to be used in its schools. The national curriculum is intended to provide the overarching design for education in schools and sets out what is to be learned through formal education. However, as in all jurisdictions globally, there is a complex relationship between the intended, the implemented, and the enacted or attained curriculum (Kurz et al., 2010). Naturally, these dynamics will all be at play in the efforts to assign the SDGs a more central place in schools' and teachers' thinking. Gurung (2018) concluded that a greater degree of control over curriculum and textbook content selection could usefully be assigned to the local level, thereby aligning it with the recent political restructuring of Nepal into seven different federal states to better cater to the needs of diverse ethnic/indigenous cultures.

Another area that will benefit from fresh thinking in implementing the SDGs (especially Goal 4, Quality Education) is the dominant pedagogical practices. Teaching–learning activities and classroom practices are mostly teacher-centred, examination-oriented, and focus on the transmission of knowledge (UNESCO, 2008). In an evaluation, the World Bank (2009) found that "teachers mainly lectured, using the blackboard, and asked students fact-related questions" (p. 11). This traditional teaching approach is often criticised for making students passive. Education for sustainability (EfS) benefits from the application of open, discursive, and active teaching and learning approaches, so there will be pedagogical, as well as administrative and curriculum content challenges for the Nepalese education system in incorporating the SDGs.

Sustainable development-related issues are currently taught with the help of textbooks, teacher guidebooks, whole school campaigns for environmental protection, and some climate change-related videos. The types of resources available in schools depend upon their initiative and commitment. The curriculum aspires to be increasingly region and place-specific. For example, teaching in the hilly, mountainous areas might focus on protecting forests, with the success of community forests highlighted so that the local needs of fodder and wood are protected and sources of drinking water ensured. Conversely, in the food-predominant Terai rural economy, protecting the fertility of the soil, and measures against soil erosion might have priority. In Kathmandu, the priorities might be on waste disposal or combatting pollution. A secondary headteacher commented that in the dense urban areas schools are developing detailed plans to make their schools green zones and are seeking financial support from different organisations to support Eco Club programs in secondary schools. However, the activities of Eco Clubs in secondary schools in rural areas have generally been less effective as rural area-based schools are seen as located within natural green zones and are thus, to a certain extent, taken for granted.

There are problems about educational access and equity in Nepal, which link to some of the social sustainability challenges embedded within the SDGs. Although education is free at public schools, where around two-thirds of students attend (Teach for Nepal, 2017), sending children to school means parents and villages losing someone to work for them in the fields or in household work that directly or indirectly affects families' financial situations. There are issues of unequal access to school education across social, economic, gender, regional, ethnic, and marginalised groups (Mathema, 2007). For example, the Dalits—one of the least privileged caste groups of Nepal—and Muslims have the lowest rates of completing basic education (Bennett, 2006). Children who belong to marginalised communities, and lower-status ethnic and indigenous groups, have a significantly lower academic achievement (Parajuli & Das, 2013). Stronger recognition of cultural, ethnic, religious, geographical, and social diversity is among the biggest challenges in achieving the SDGs in Nepal. Awareness of past policy implementation challenges may serve to highlight opportunities to think in more bottom-up, dialogical, and inclusive ways when it comes to weaving the SDGs into Nepalese education.

10.4   Implications of the SDGs for Reforms to Textbooks

Many teachers (and the general public) consider textbooks to be the definitive guide to the curriculum and most teaching is tied to these books. Nepali textbooks inevitably play a key role in developing young people's perceptions about democracy, participation, civic engagement, identities, and social and political rights and responsibilities (Curriculum Development Centre [CDC], 2007). The same textbooks are used in public schools throughout the country regardless of geographical and cultural differences. This can be a policy and pedagogical obstacle given the imperative that high-quality Education for Sustainability (EfS) responds to local place-based circumstances and contexts. The texts and contents too often only support knowledge-centric and surface understanding of the subject matter, leaving limited space for students to generate deeper understandings of subjects and topics or to engage in more participative active citizenship projects.

Having said this, there is some worthwhile and purposeful content in the student textbooks. For example, the Grade 7 and 8 Science and Environment textbooks each include units on environmental degradation, conservation, and sustainable development. The Grade 7 textbook highlights the importance of natural resource conservation, and how humans should use it in a more effective way to avoid wastage. The texts start to educate students on climate change. "Climate change is defined as a change in climate in long-term shifts due to human activities and natural imbalance" (CDC, 2020, p. 215). The Grade 8 textbook highlights the interrelationship and dependency between humans and natural resources and how living beings are benefited from natural resources. An emphasis is placed on making students aware of the importance of national parks and conservation areas for the preservation of natural resources, flora, and fauna. Consequences, such as air pollution, water pollution, land pollution, and contribution to the greenhouse effect, are highlighted as some of the effects of human activities on the environment. Effects of climate change such as rising temperatures, rising sea levels, an increase in heavy precipitation, a decrease in agricultural production, and degradation of biodiversity, are discussed. The Grade 8 textbook also includes text educating students about the role of national and international organisations in environmental conservation. Nevertheless, the textbooks could do more to link the individual units with sustainability and social justice.

Many teachers report a relative lack of training in social studies (including facets of EfS) as one of the prominent barriers inhibiting the effectiveness of their civics and citizenship teaching, which likely contributes to their reliance upon textbooks (Shah, 2020). The need for reinvigorating teacher education and enhancing teachers' subject knowledge in the social sciences has long been discussed to improve the effectiveness of teaching and learning and promote quality education in Nepal (Ham, 2020). One teacher put it thus, in an interview as part of a recent doctoral study (Shah, 2020):

> Social studies includes disciplines ranging from community to international relations. Thus, social studies teachers must act as a lawyer, economist, historian and a geographer to deliver the respective contents. We have not received subject-specific training and orientation on implementing the curriculum and textbooks.

The treatment of curriculum content related to global education and key SDGs is limited at the basic level of education. Much content about the world beyond Nepal is pushed into secondary education. Essential elements of citizenship education such as the environment and sustainability, social justice, the human rights of minority groups, and interdependence and globalisation are reserved for Grades 8, 9, and 10. The deferral of content to higher grades for educating about the SDGs will have consequences for students making sense of the world around them and in developing the knowledge, skills, values, and worldviews necessary for people to take action for sustainability because a large proportion of Nepalese students will have exited education at the end of Grades 7 or 8.

Policymakers might want to reflect upon what steps they can take to empower Nepalese textbook writers to open up classroom discussions on contested contemporary issues that will interest Nepalese young people and develop opportunities for more critical thinking and consideration of different points of view. Sometimes it will be about learning that sustainability challenges are nuanced and complex. For example, there are dilemmas around human and environmental interactions in mountain cultural landscapes in the Himalayas. Prioritising wild landscape in landscape management policies, which is favoured by both tourism values and the claims of climate change responsiveness, has affected indigenous communities and local people adversely, including yak-cow cheesemakers (Bennett et al., 2015; Campbell, 2018). Kadiwal and Jain (2020) have recently observed about civics textbooks in India and Pakistan that "the lack of a critical lens in civics textbooks [is] inimical to the development of citizenship in a democracy" (p. 6). This mirrors the situation in Nepal. Students will benefit from opportunities for a more in-depth discussion about the meaning of sustainable living patterns, and valuing diversity and social justice as essential elements for achieving sustainability. Moreover, it is crucial to link the experiences at personal and local levels to individual and community actions for sustainability.

10.5 Implications of the SDGs for the Whole School Culture and Ethos

Nepalese schools might view the SDGs as a catalytic opportunity to generate awareness in local communities about a more sustainable and eco-friendly future, and model good practice in contributing to sustainable living and sustainable society-making. Nepal has a proud record of stewardship of the environment as something to be reflected upon via whole school involvement and eco-clubs (Bhandari & Osamu, 2003; Gurung & Shrestha, 2003). The recent UNESCO Berlin Declaration on Education for Sustainable Development (2021) envisages education as the foundation for transforming values and attitudes. This section of the chapter, drawing upon interview data with Nepalese school leaders and teachers, posits that a gratitude-based approach to education for sustainability might contribute to bridging gaps "between articulating values and then knowing what to do to make them come alive in practice" (Wilbur, 1998, p. 139).

A focus on attitudes and values can play a crucial part in the preparation of environmentally sensitive and conscious citizens. A co-curricular activity [CCA] co-ordinator at a Kathmandu-based secondary school, who participated as an interviewee in an investigation into gratitude education in Nepal (Yogi, 2022), observed that:

> Values, attitudes, and gratitude can have a great inter-linkage to sustainability because they enrich a personal values system. It is a major component of developing a culture of sustainable living. Many values and virtues, such as gratitude and social justice, cannot completely show their results in a limited life span or time frame, but they are in a continuum showing some progression in a gradual pattern.

The underlying logic of nurturing integrity (extending to environmental awareness and sensitivity) in students may support raising a generation who can act responsibly against environmental evils. As a leading international NGO has observed, "Exploring, developing and expressing values and opinions supports learners to make informed choices about how they engage with SDG issues" (Oxfam, 2019, p. 9).

Gratitude can be an essential ingredient of a human value system that contributes to building a sustainable mindset in students. For example, a Kathmandu-based secondary teacher articulated a sense of heartfelt gratitude to the environment:

> To realise the power of gratitude, we need to listen to our hearts and equally to nature and give back for what we have received. Look at mother nature, she is not asking anything from us. Seeing this, it is our responsibility to feel the reality on the earth and drive ourselves accordingly. If we do something in this direction that is a kind of gratitude that we are practising. It is our responsibility to hear the cry of mother earth.

Generating a sense of gratitude, care, responsibility, and respect towards nature and the planet can contribute to shaping the values of future generations, redirecting societal preferences and inclinations, and instilling the empowering skills to enact them (Gautam & Shyangtan, 2020; UNESCO, 2013). A local case study exemplifies the power of such a philosophy. The Tamang, an indigenous community of Nepal, has a traditional institution, Choho, which—in terms of governance—has particular norms, values, beliefs, and practices for looking after the forest and school (Parajuli et al., 2019). These communities work closely with nature through their norms and values, perceiving nature as a teacher, and rather than exploiting nature, there is the presence of spiritual connection, worship, and wise use of natural resources. The deeper the human relationships with nature, the better and more assured the future existence of the planet.

In a similarly collaborative manner, a respectful approach is adopted in a Nepali school based in the Kathmandu valley whose CCA proudly shared:

> We run classes based on teamwork where students and teachers support and collaborate, practising politeness, sympathy, and empathy without jealousy. It is teachers' first responsibility to treat students respectfully. So, teachers use polite language with humble vocabulary to students and everyone within classrooms and across the school premises. The respect system is based on Eastern philosophy, and its inevitable element is Namaste (a Nepali greeting and welcoming) culture. For its sustainability, we train, motivate and support teachers in their every step. This can be useful in building themselves as caring and responsible citizens.

Nepalese schools, as exemplified in this example, can showcase how values and virtues related to sustainability, including teamwork and responsible citizenship, can be enacted through classrooms and throughout the school premises.

It would be wrong to suggest that the change agenda is not challenging related to a values transformation across Nepalese schools. Referring to the challenges, a monitoring officer from an international organisation working closely with Nepalese community schools in the Kathmandu area reflected that:

> The focus upon values such as gratitude in schools to promote sustainability is much needed. There is a difference between knowledge, skills, and values relating to sustainability. For example, if we ask teachers to talk about sustainable development, they can talk fluently and give a long lecture because it is in the school's course content. But when it comes to a sustainability practice, they are void because sustainability cannot be practised until it is internalised with their personal values system. When values cannot be exemplified at the personal level with broader linkages to societal developmental practices, sustainable practices can be difficult to execute since people aren't driven by their hearts.

As this educator's perspective indicates, the deep and felt commitment by teachers and schools to deliver fully upon the transformationist goals of the SDGs remains a work in progress.

Other students and teachers interviewed for the fourth author's project expressed scepticism about the quality of the consultation around making a reality of the SDG goals and whether the expected progress was achievable. There has been a little tradition of responding to student voices in Nepal. A Grade 10 student in a Kathmandu secondary school noted:

> Although government bodies, particularly those who are assigned to develop and revise/ update curriculum, claim that multiple consultations have taken place, I hardly find students' voices given due space in this process. Some representations from us might have been formally sought, but that is very limited. My understanding is that when any new international policies are formulated, government agencies are fast to respond and show their commitment without proper consultations with us.

A teacher from the same school offered similar doubts:

> I believe whether it is about SDGs or anything, the government wants to show that they are proactive in showing that they are really concerned. However, in real practice, nothing much has been done. They take years to update the school curriculum.

Nevertheless, the practice of sustainability, focusing on what ought to be, can be generated in school classrooms that nurture a sense of appreciation based on mutual respect and empathy. Such approaches can be instrumental in building sustainable values in students, leading to a more sustainable future adult life. Students learn to share, interact, respect, and live together, appreciating mutual cooperation. There is congruence here with elements of the Nepalese government's sustainability targets, strategies, and key interventions servicing Nepal's focus upon SDG4, Quality Education.

10.6   Implications of the SDGs for Initial Teacher Education and Teachers' Professional Development

Education within Nepal is considered a foundational base for preparing all types of human resources for the country, including a citizenry conscious of responding to climate change (Ministry of Education, Science and Technology, 2019). As detailed above, the subject matter related to the causes and impacts of climate change and climate-friendly traditional knowledge, skills, and practices, is being incorporated into formal and non-formal educational curricula in Nepal. Additionally, Tribhuvan University (TU), Nepal's primary provider of beginning teachers, is in the process of reviewing its initial teacher education programs through the lens of sustainable development perspectives and the challenges of climate change.

There is an acknowledgement that the existing four-year Bachelor of Education (B.Ed.) program will benefit from being revised to give greater prominence to education for sustainability and climate change. The B.Ed. course seeks to develop language competency through English and Nepali as core courses, which are seen as incorporating a range of sustainable development-related content and skills. The current structure of the B.Ed. course consists of 2200 credits, including a language course of 200 credits, a pedagogy core course assigned 400 credits, a major subject specialisation of 1000 credits, a minor subject specialisation worth 500 credits, and practice teaching assigned 100 credits (Faculty of Education [FOE], 2021). The program recognises the importance of preparing teachers who are literate in sustainable development-related issues and problems. Course leaders argue that the knowledge, skills, and abilities required for sustainable development understanding can be integrated into the existing course structure rather than creating a new and separate subject domain.

There are professional-pedagogical units offered in the B.Ed., such as the philosophical and sociological foundations of education, educational psychology, curriculum and evaluation, and classroom instruction within which social equity, human rights, social transformation, and social empowerment-related concepts are being critically discussed, but the concept of environmental protection and sustainable development are not included yet. The pedagogical courses are regarded as the foundation of the teacher education program and are all required to be oriented towards sustainable development issues. The subject committee head of the Foundation of Education under the Faculty of Education (FOE) of TU noted in an interview that sustainable development and climate change issues are touched upon in various subject specialisation courses and that the TU is planning to incorporate them further into pedagogical competencies units as part of an upcoming revision of the curriculum.

Two contributing lecturers to the B.Ed. program at TU were interviewed to understand their perspectives on existing units in relation to the sustainable development-related content and skills. A lecturer of Nepali education observed that a module on creative writing and reading has incorporated a range of social equity, human rights, sustainable development, and environment protection-related issues. Likewise, a lecturer of English education commented that although there is little content on environmental protection and climate change, there are plenty of issues such as diversity, marginalisation, and social justice, which are being critically discussed in the context of English. However, both tutors acknowledged that language courses could be enhanced by ensuring the greater inclusion of sustainable development-related content than currently exists in the units.

A content audit has indicated that the major subject specialisation course structure of B.Ed., apart from the environment-related major subjects, is also light on sustainability-linked content. Elements of environmental education currently included in the Bachelor of Education subsist within the major subject specialisations of Population Education and Science Education and an optional minor specialisation. Moreover, within a new minor subject specialisation, an environment-related subject can be chosen. However, other major and minor subject specialisations will review their content for opportunities to link to sustainability themes.

The FOE also operates a professional learning program as a Master of Education (M.Ed.) for teachers, teacher educators, educational administrators, system analysts, and education experts (FOE, 2021). It has revised its M.Ed. curriculum by adding an area called Education and Development as the core subject to prepare sustainable development literate teachers, teacher educators, and other educational leaders. The course aims to align with the concept of sustainable development, an emphasis on the importance of education for sustainability, and developing a framework of education that ensures prominence for the SDGs within a responsive education system.

Consistent with the emphasis of the Nepal government, the school curricula will include more content related to sustainable development and climate change-related issues. Accordingly, teacher preparation courses will be required to prepare teachers with a more robust knowledge and awareness of climate issues and a repertoire of possible classroom activities to undertake with young people. Educational intermediaries such as curriculum development centre and textbook writers should play a catalytic role in bridging between school curricula and teacher preparation programs. Teachers are a vital link in the chain to help to nurture sustainability-conscious young people who will be critical participants in mobilising societal engagement as educational projects develop their capacity for raising awareness about climate change at the broader community level.

The in-service teacher training programs are designed to mirror and support the course structure of school education. The concepts of sustainable development and climate change are discussed in the core subjects of Social Studies and Science and Environment, within which some more specific content is provided. Similarly, following the needs of the school curriculum, there is in-service Teacher Professional Development (TPD), Refreshment Training, and education for aspiring and in-role for school headteachers. An in-service professional learning course designer and instructor of TPD noted in one of the TU interviews that there are two sessions for sustainable development-related competencies development: one for sustainable development and the second for climate change, as a mandatory training package for all levels and all subjects related to schoolteachers.

A range of efforts has thus commenced in initial and continuing teacher education to endeavour to deliver upon the ambitious policy intentions of the Nepalese government. Both have commenced the journey of preparing sustainability and climate change literate schoolteachers. However, there perhaps needs to be a more vital awareness that this will involve conceiving of sustainability as incorporating social and environmental sustainability, including the SDGs of reduced inequality, diversity, sustainable cities and communities, life on land and justice, and strong institutions. Teacher education will also need to encompass the deployment of more active and experiential pedagogic approaches than have generally been the norm within Nepalese tertiary education. Both teachers and students will need to be able to do sustainability as well as learn about it.

10.7 Conclusion

This chapter has highlighted that there is much work to undertake in several areas if the SDGs are to be genuinely embedded within Nepalese education, including leadership and curriculum envisioning, changes to both the content and pedagogical use of textbooks, the place of EfS within whole school cultures, and the preparation and support for teachers in educating school children and community members about environmental and climate change issues. The monitoring and reporting of progress by provincial governments and their implementing agencies concerning accountability for the attainment of the SDGs will also be crucial, if they are to translate from aspiration into practice.

Nevertheless, there are countervailing reasons to be optimistic about the possibilities of exploring and living the SDGs in Nepalese schools. The policy and rhetorical commitments among Nepalese educational stakeholders to realise the SDGs are encouraging. Teacher education institutions are aware of their responsibilities. The Nepalese people (and young people) can see the effects of climate change and the perils of unsustainability around them. There is a national environmental culture and heritage to be proud of. The challenge lies in implementing and foregrounding the SDGs in locally tailored and pedagogically engaging ways and in empowering teachers to harness actively the enthusiasm and commitment of their students and local community stakeholders.

References

Bennett, L. (2006). *Citizens: Gender, caste and ethnic exclusion in Nepal.* World Bank/DFID.
Bennett, E. M., Cramer, W., Begossi, A., Cundill, G., Dıaz, S., Egoh, B. N., Geijzendorffer, I. R., Krug, C. B., Lavorel, S., & Lazos, E. (2015). Linking biodiversity, ecosystem services, and human wellbeing: Three challenges for designing research for sustainability. *Current Opinion in Environmental Sustainability, 14*, 76–85.

Bhandari, B. B., & Osamu, A. (2003). *Education for sustainable development in Nepal: Views and visions.* International Institute for Global Environmental Strategies.

Bhattarai, B. (2016). Educational development and improving the quality of education in Nepal. *American Journal of Educational Research, 4*(4), 314–319.

Bowe, R., Ball, S., & Gold, A. (1992*). Reforming education and changing schools: Case studies in policy sociology.* Routledge.

Brookfield, S. (1995). *Becoming a critically reflective teacher.* Jossey-Bass.

Campbell, B. (2018). Biodiversity, livelihoods and struggles over sustainability in Nepal. *Landscape Research, 43*(8), 1056–1067.

Chaudhary, D. (2019). The decentralization, devolution and local governance practices in Nepal: The emerging challenges and concerns. *Journal of Political Science, 19,* 43–64.

Curriculum Development Centre. (2007). *National curriculum framework for school education in Nepal.*

Curriculum Development Centre. (2017). *Social studies and population education: Grade 7.*

Curriculum Development Centre. (2020). *Social studies and population education: Grade 8.*

Daly, A., Parker, S., Sherpa, S., & Regmi, U. (2020). Federalisation and education in Nepal: Contemporary reflections on working through change. *Education 3–13, 48*(2), 163–173.

Faculty of Education. (2021). *Tribhuvan University Faculty of Education.* http://tufoe.edu.np/introduction

Fanon, F. (2004). *The wretched of the earth.* Grove Press. (Original work published 1963).

Galegher, E., Park, M., Cheng, A., Davidson, P., & Wiseman, A. (2019). A comparative analysis of educational policy for citizenship following political transitions: A case study of Egypt, Nepal, and Hong Kong. In J. A. Pineda-Alfonso, N. De Alba-Fernández, & E. Navarro-Medina (Eds.), *Handbook of research on education for participative citizenship and global prosperity* (pp. 108–132). IGI Global.

Gautam, S., & Shyangtan, S. (2020). *From suffering to surviving, surviving to living: Education for harmony with nature and humanity.* UNESCO.

Ghimire, A. (2021, November 12). COP26 and Nepal's climate commitments, *Kathmandu Post.* https://kathmandupost.com/climate-environment/2021/11/12/cop26-and-nepal-s-climate-commitments

Government of Nepal. (2018). *Nepal's Sixth national report to the convention on biological diversity.*

Government of Nepal. (2019a). *Sustainable development goal 4: Education 2030: Nepal national framework.* Ministry of Education, Science and Technology.

Government of Nepal. (2019b). *National Climate Change Policy.* https://mofe.gov.np/downloadfile/climatechange_policy_english_1580984322.pdf

Government of Nepal. (2021). *Nepal's long-term strategy for net-zero emissions.*

Gurung, C. P., & Shrestha, N. (2003). School-based environmental clubs: An initiative towards education for sustainable development in Nepal. In B. B. Bhandari & O. Abe (Eds.), *Education for sustainable development in Nepal: Views and visions* (pp. 199–204). International Institute for Global Environmental Strategies.

Gurung, G. (2018). *Perceptions of key stakeholders about the school curriculum and its relationship to teaching and learning in Nepal* [Doctoral dissertation, University of Tasmania].

Ham, M. (2020). Nepali primary school teachers' response to national educational reform. *Prospects, 50*(2), 1–21.

Howells, K. (2012). *Gratitude in education: A radical view.* Springer.

Kadiwal, L., & Jain, M. (2020). Civics and citizenship education in India and Pakistan. In P. M. Sarangapani & R. Pappu (Eds.), *Handbook of education systems in South Asia* (pp. 1–27). Springer.

Mathema, K. B. (2007). Crisis in education and future challenges for Nepal. *European Bulletin of Himalayan Research, 31,* 46–66.

Kurz, A., Elliott, S. N., Wehby, J. H., & Smithson, J. L. (2010). Alignment of the intended, planned, and enacted curriculum in general and special education and its relation to student achievement. *Journal of Special Education, 44*(3), 131–145.

Ledger, S., Vidovich, L., & O'Donoghue, T. (2015). International and remote schooling: Global to local curriculum policy dynamics in Indonesia. *The Asia-Pacific Education Researcher, 24*(4), 695–703.

Ministry of Education, Science & Technology. (2019). *Sustainable development goal 4: Education 2030: Nepal national framework.* Government of Nepal.

National Planning Commission. (2020). *National review of sustainable development goals.* Government of Nepal.

Oxfam. (2019). *The sustainable development goals: A guide for teachers.*

Parajuli, D. R., & Das, T. (2013). Performance of community schools in Nepal: A macro level analysis. *International Journal of Scientific and Technology Research, 2*(7), 148–154.

Parajuli, N. M., Rai, M. I., Bhattarai, C. P., & Gautam, S. (2019). Local values in governance: Legacy of choho in forest and school management in a Tamang Community in Nepal. *Journal of Indigenous Social Development, 8*(7), 35–55.

Reeves, T. C. (2006). Design research from a technology perspective. In J. van den Akker (Ed.), *Design methodology and developmental research in education and training* (pp. 86–109). Kluwer.

Regmi, K. D. (2019). Educational governance in Nepal: Weak government, donor partnership and standardised assessment. *Compare: A Journal of Comparative and International Education, 33*(1), 185–197.

Sapkota, R., & Rijal, K. (2016). *Climate change and its impact in Nepal.* Tribhuvan University.

Shah, R. (2020). *Exploring civics and citizenship education in Nepal: From policy to practice* [Doctoral dissertation, University of Tasmania].

Subedi, K. R. (2020). Fostering the local curriculum conceptualizations: Empowerment and decentralization. *Pragya Manch, 32*(16), 52–63.

Teach for Nepal. (2017). *Education in crisis.* https://www.teachfornepal.org/tfn/education-in-crisis/

UNESCO. (2021). *Berlin Declaration on Education for Sustainable Development.* https://en.unesco.org/sites/default/files/esdfor2030-berlin-declaration-en.pdf

UNESCO. (2008). *Building UNESCO national education support strategy (UNESS) Nepal 2008–2013.*

Wilbur, G. (1998). Schools as equity cultures. *Journal of Curriculum and Supervision, 13*(2), 123–147.

World Bank. (2009). *Nepal: BPEP II, project performance assessment report.* World Bank.

Yogi, K. K. (2022). *Possibilities for enacting gratitude education in Nepalese schools* [Manuscript in preparation]. School of Education, University of Tasmania.

Chapter 11
Exploring the Challenges Schoolteachers Are Facing in Promoting Sustainable Development Goal 4: The Case of Pakistan

Humaira Akhter, Andy Bown, and Yang Yang

Abstract Sustainable Development Goal (SDG) 4 aims to "Ensure inclusive and equitable quality education and promote lifelong learning opportunities for all" (Ferguson, T., Iliško, D., Roofe, C., & Hill, S. (2018). SDG4-Quality education: Inclusivity, equity and lifelong learning for all. Emerald Group Publishing.).

11.1 Introduction

Sustainable Development Goal (SDG) 4 aims to "Ensure inclusive and equitable quality education and promote lifelong learning opportunities for all" (Ferguson et al., 2018). Education quality is core to the overarching SDG4 and is referred to directly in three of the 10 targets within SDG4. The concept is embedded in other targets of SDG4 without actual use of the term (Sayed & Moriarty, 2020). Although education impacts stakeholders at the global, regional, local, and individual levels, measures designed to achieve SDG4 have proven to be the most difficult to implement, as mentioned by Franco and Derbyshire (2020). The challenge does not lie in the promotion or reflection of quality education in policies and plans. The real challenge is to implement the quality education indicators by addressing grass-roots issues, especially at the school level (Farooq, 2018). In particular, this chapter focuses

H. Akhter (✉) · A. Bown
School of Education, College of Arts, Law and Education, University of Tasmania, Launceston, TAS, Australia
e-mail: Humaira.Akhter@utas.edu.au

A. Bown
e-mail: Andy.Bown@utas.edu.au

Y. Yang
School of Education, College of Arts, Law and Education, University of Tasmania, Hobart, TAS, Australia
e-mail: Yang.Yang@utas.edu.au

on selected targets of SDG4, namely, 4.a, build and upgrade the education facilities for the effective learning outcomes for all, and 4.c, increase the supply of qualified teachers through international cooperation of the teachers' training (Department of Economic and Social Affairs [DESA], 2015).

This chapter reports the findings of a qualitative study into the challenges faced by primary school teachers, master trainers, and school principals tasked with improving the quality of English language instruction in Sindh Province, Pakistan.

11.2   Literature Review

In Pakistan, the government is taking measures to promote quality education in schools, such as the development of minimum standards for quality education, joining the UNESCO Associated Schools Project Network (ASPnet), and introducing courses on sustainability education or Education for Sustainable Development (ESD) as a part of master's programmes in Educational Sciences. In line with these, more than 60 ASPnet schools have developed peace and sustainable development education programmes to share contextualised knowledge on respect and cultural diversity with teachers, students, parents, and the community at large. Furthermore, a pedagogical initiative on ESD was proposed by the Institute of Education, Lahore College for Women University (Kalsoom & Qureshi, 2019).

As a developing country with the sixth largest population in the world and 60% of its population comprised of young people (between 15 and 29), Pakistan desperately needs a widely accessible, quality, and equitable education system. The country is currently spending around 2.2% of its Gross Domestic Product on education against the required minimum target of four per cent, despite the 2009 National Education Policy recommending that seven per cent of Gross Domestic Product be spent on education. After several years, provincial governments are still struggling to make any notable progress in the education sector as highlighted by a report from the Ministry of Planning, Development and Reform (MPDR, 2019).

Although there are individual or institutional efforts related to the implementation of SDGs in teacher education, SDGs are only tentatively entering Pakistan's education policy. The analysis of various documents, such as national education policies (Government of Pakistan, 2009), provincial education sector plans (Government of Balochistan, 2013; Government of Punjab, 2013–2017), the Bachelor of Education (B.Ed) Honours curriculum (Higher Education Commission, 2023), and National Professional Standards for Teachers (Ministry of Education, 2009), do not reveal education for sustainable development as a national priority. For more details on the background of Pakistan (see Naz et al., Chapter 12 of this volume).

Kalsoom, Qureshi, and Khanam (2018) analysed a database of research-based articles written by Pakistani authors on the subject of Education for Sustainable Development (ESG). The databases consulted were Springer, Taylor, and Francis, as well as four national educational journals. They found more than 2,500 articles on ESD, but no empirical studies on ESD have been conducted by Pakistani authors. They analysed 353 articles published in national journals from 2004 to 2016 and concluded that no articles had been published on Pakistani ESD. Pakistani researchers conducted research in this field to some extent but there was limited empirical research related to the concepts of sustainable development and education for sustainable development. Despite the efforts of some, there are many challenges to quality education, from the training of the teachers to the curriculum.

This chapter mainly focuses on the two targets of SDG4 due to their particular relevance to the educational context of Pakistan. These targets are explored in detail below.

11.2.1 SDG4.a: Build and Upgrade Education Facilities

Many developing countries still lack the basic infrastructure and facilities needed to provide effective learning environments. Sub-Saharan Africa faces the biggest challenges—at the primary and lower-secondary levels, less than half of all schools have access to electricity, the Internet, computers, and basic drinking water described in the document on the High Level Political Forum (HLPF) on sustainable development (2019). Another study by Pandey (2018) in India found that long distances from schools, infrastructural facilities, poor access to safe drinking water and sanitation facilities, and corporal punishment are the biggest barriers to inclusiveness in education systems.

Inadequate facilities are one of the main challenges to achieve quality education. Osamwonyi (2016) also highlighted the inadequate educational facilities in Nigerian schools, including the lack of laboratories, classrooms, and boarding facilities to accommodate a large number of students. Similarly, Mupa and Chinooneka (2015) reported that Zimbabwean schools suffer from inadequate facilities in terms of textbooks, teaching resources, and revision books, which would help enhance student learning. Najumba (2013), in his studies of school achievement, discovered that schools that are well equipped with relevant educational facilities and instructional materials, such as textbooks, libraries, and laboratories, do much better in standardised examinations than those who do not have such resources.

In Pakistan poor facilities, such as no drinking water, inadequate water supplies, furniture, and electricity supplies, adversely affect the studies of school children. Thirty-seven per cent of Pakistani schools do not have basic sanitation or toilet facilities, according to Martínez (2018). Indeed, none of Pakistan's education indicators compare favourably with other countries in the region, let alone globally. This is a consequence of decades of government under-investment in the education and the social sectors, which has led to the dilapidated physical condition of public schools, limited access to educational facilities, high dropout rates, and low literacy rates across the country (Richter, 2019).

As mentioned by the MPDR (2019), teachers, physical facilities, and school environments were the principal causes of low performance at the school level. More than 70% of respondents thought that teachers were primarily responsible for good or bad performance, while almost 15% thought physical facilities were responsible for low performance, particularly in girls' schools. The remainder thought that the school environment (comprising teachers, physical facilities, teaching methodologies, and parents' role combined) had the most impact on performance.

As seen above, a major factor in the success of primary schools is the availability of adequate resources and instructional materials. However, pupils' progress is still adversely affected if teachers lack the pedagogical skills required to use those resources that are available effectively.

11.2.2 SDG4.c: Supply of Qualified Teachers

Improving teacher quality through certification and training can lead to the best outcomes in terms of student performance in developing countries (Pugatch, 2017), as insufficient, unqualified, and uncertain teachers have a detrimental effect on learning. In fact, as Holmqvist (2019) mentioned globally, many countries are facing the challenge of qualified teachers and very few studies are considering teacher education.

A study conducted in Saudi Arabia found that the barriers to effective teaching are mainly working environment factors, such as ineffective line management and a lack of incentives and authority to implement skills acquired in training (Almannie, 2015). In South Africa, the Department of Education working on the support of teachers' professional development (Holmqvist, 2019) also mentioned that poor material conditions of learning, wage structures, and pupil learning issues adversely affect the training of teachers. Alrabea (2011) mentioned that a lack of incentives and support from school principals, along with inadequate equipment and training creates hurdles in applying new skills and knowledge at school. Other researchers (e.g., Gilley et al., 2002) mentioned that insufficient support from management is the primary barrier to transforming teaching practices. Likewise, the study conducted by Almannie (2015) mentioned that 72% of teachers and principals faced a lack of cooperation from school leadership and management, and 64% faced a lack of cooperation from colleagues in the implementation of the training practices.

Chan (2009) identified some challenges faced by teachers in New Zealand. He argued for the need to provide focused ICT, literacy, numeracy, and language training for the teachers. Mohammad et al. (2018) also highlighted some factors that impact the provision of quality education: poor infrastructure, the lack of monitoring systems, high teacher workloads, overcrowded classrooms, and the lack of language courses for teachers' professional development. Teachers having a low proficiency in English does not allow them to use the different interactive methods rather relying mostly on translation methods for English teaching.

Although the challenges may be more acute in the developing world, even developed countries, such as the United States and Sweden, are facing a shortage of qualified teachers in their schools (García & Weiss, 2019; Holmqvist, 2019).

Teachers need support through an analysis of their needs, training programmes, learning materials, financial assistance, and proper systemised monitoring if countries are to achieve their SDG4 targets. Almannie (2015) mentioned that a proper accountability system for training programmes, training needs of the teachers, and investment in training programmes could be useful for the promotion of training practices and producing qualified teachers in Saudi Arabia. Mupa and Chinooneka (2015) also indicated that schools need to employ qualified and well-trained teachers who can play their role in enhancing effective teaching strategies. School leadership also needs to support teachers in lesson planning, teaching methods, and instructional materials.

Regarding the situation in Pakistan, Nadeem (2007) stated that there is a gap between teachers' theoretical knowledge and the application of their pedagogical skills. It was also found that the lack of an accountability system and the poor alignment among textbooks, the curriculum, and learners' needs are the main issues for English language development at primary Schools in Punjab. Another major issue is that many teachers are not getting proper and continuous training in Pakistan (Pugatch, 2017). The *National Professional Standards for Teachers* mentioned above are intended to help address the problem of inadequate pedagogical skills among teachers in Pakistan (Ministry of Education, 2009). The three domains of the Standards (knowledge, disposition, and pedagogy) align with the Pedagogical Content Knowledge (PCK) framework developed by Shulman (1986). The PCK model incorporates content knowledge, pedagogical knowledge, and pedagogical content knowledge, and emphasises the combination of knowledge and pedagogy (Jing-Jing, 2014). It was selected as the theoretical framework for this current study, as it provides a means for analysing teachers' knowledge, attitudes, and pedagogical skills.

There is no doubt that training and continuous professional development help to prepare qualified teachers in this technological era. As mentioned by Tariq et al. (2020), knowledge alone cannot play its role; teaching demands more comprehensive support via investments related to quality inputs and teacher training that leads to better outcomes. Shaukat and Chowdhury (2020) stated that teacher education programmes supplied qualified teachers nationwide, as mentioned by the scholarly literature, as well as in reports of foreign donors and international organisations operating in Pakistan. However, training alone is not enough to supply qualified teachers as the education system is shifting from knowledge to PCK. Quality education needs to consider the teachers' competencies and the educational facilities to accelerate the students' learning (Khan & Islam, 2015). This situation is mirrored in other countries. For example, Mupa and Chinooneka (2015) also reflected on the importance of teachers' PCK in their study by stating that teachers are mainly focused on textbooks and syllabuses instead of applying the different teaching methods and instructional media to bring improvements in students in Zimbabwe schools. Teachers also lack confidence, content knowledge, and English proficiency, all of which impact the learning process. This interpretation was supported by Garcia (2018), who argued that ineffective teaching methods and inadequate training for English language teachers were the main hurdles towards achieving effective learning outcomes.

Given the difficulties faced in Pakistan in achieving its SDG4-related targets, this study explored the following research question:

- What challenges are teachers of English facing in promoting quality education (SDG4) at the primary school level in Pakistan?

11.3 Method

11.3.1 Research Design

This study employed a qualitative research design, taking an interpretivist stance to explore the perspectives of the participants (Creswell, 2014). The interpretivist stance was selected, as it would facilitate the gathering of rich, contextually situated understandings (McChesney & Aldridge, 2019), leading to a greater understanding of the challenges faced by the participants in Pakistani primary schools.

11.3.2 Participants

Having received ethics approval from the University of Tasmania's research committee (Project ID S0023264), 10 primary school teachers of English, four principals, and four master trainers1 from Sindh Province, Pakistan, were recruited to take part in semi-structured interviews.

11.3.3 Data Collection and Analysis

The semi-structured interviews each lasted 30 to 40 min and included questions such as: What training have you received and delivered in relation to the National Professional Standards? What support do you require for the implementation of the continuous professional development activities? Interviews were conducted using telephone or Zoom® communications software and the framework discussed above. The codes and themes that emerged from the analysis were reviewed and cross-checked by the research team to ensure their validity and reliability.

11.4   Results

From the thematic analysis of the interview data, four themes emerged: *design and delivery of training, PCK, barriers to quality education,* and *support to enhance quality education.* These themes are presented below in relation to SDG4 targets 4.a and 4.c. In order to preserve the anonymity of the participants, the following abbreviations are used, along with an identifying participant number: MT (master trainer), T (teacher), P (school principal). Furthermore, in order to represent the perspectives and voices of the participants as accurately as possible, direct quotations are presented in their original form, without editorial modifications to grammar or vocabulary.

11.4.1   Theme 1: Design and Delivery of Training

This theme covers the nature and types of training provided. Trainers highlighted that they gave training to teachers on different topics, including lesson planning, teaching methodologies, assessment methods, collaborative learning, student learning outcomes, and confidence-building among students. As MT4 mentioned, "the content knowledge, teaching methods, assessment methods, commitment and loyalty to the profession, teaching skills, and leadership were part of the training." Other areas of training were noted by teachers, including T1, who noted that: "the main focus of the training sessions was interpersonal communication, child's health and development, teaching methods, language development, and language barrier." Most of the participants stated that usually they received formal training, which was sponsored by the government and which they were paid to attend. In addition, school leadership and management also arranged some informal training during their regular work hours, and trainers also sent teachers to different government and international organisations for the trainings. For example; Sindh Teacher Education Development Authority and Provincial Institute of Education are the two main authorities who arranged and organised training for the government. Apart from that, some training courses were funded by the British Council and other organisations for teachers. For instance, P1 mentioned that "I send to the teachers in various programs and teacher's training. These programs are based on the U.S. Aid program." However, the type of training was not always decided by the principals or master trainers. MT3 also mentioned that it "depends on the government, whenever they want, they send teachers for training, the government decides and selects the teachers for training in our institute."

Regarding the delivery of training, master trainers reported that they utilise pre- and post-tests, classroom observations, daily diaries, and lesson plans from the teachers to estimate their effectiveness. They also practise micro-teaching among teachers. For example, MT2 stated, "I gave a test to the teachers in a form of a questionnaire, sometimes ask direct questions or visit the classroom and their lesson plans."

11.4.2   Theme 2: PCK

Under this theme, both trainers and teachers highlighted the existing and required PCK of the teachers, and teachers also reflected their self-efficacy regarding confidence, English proficiency, and managing complex situations. This theme is divided into three categories: existing PCK, required PCK, and teachers' self-efficacy, as detailed below.

11.4.2.1   Existing PCK

Trainers mentioned that teachers who have both academic and professional degrees had a much better understanding of the materials and teaching methods when compared to those who have only academic degrees, supported by the P1 that "in my school, out of seven teachers, only three have a professional degree (B.Ed and M.Ed.) and I think those who have professional degrees understand the teaching standards." It was also highlighted by the trainers that teachers mostly used lectures or other more traditional methods in their teaching, and that they used the same teaching methods for all subjects, rather than differentiating between content-based subjects and language instruction. MT2 mentioned, "I see that teachers have enough content knowledge, but they do not deliver it in the right way by using different teaching methods." MT1 mentioned that "they even don't have the knowledge about the authentic text and basic concepts about the language development." MT1 also stated that "teachers have a huge syllabus to cover so they can't deliver quality education in the classroom." Another master trainer argued that teachers lacked sufficient subject matter (language) knowledge and only focused on reading the lessons aloud in the classroom. It was also mentioned by the majority of the master trainers and principals that teachers mainly employed outdated reading-translation methods. In contrast, teachers mentioned that they were trying to use the other innovative methods in the classrooms but faced difficulties. For example, T10 said, "I used the lecture method due to the strength of the students, 90% weightage given to lecture and 10% to other methods," and T9 said, "I do not know about the content knowledge, I focused on reading and writing, as completion of copy work is more important." Some teachers reported they attempted to use other methods, but also faced challenges, partly due to inadequate PCK, as described below.

11.4.2.2   Required PCK

Trainers mentioned that teachers need to be well-prepared, know about their students' learning outcomes and intellectual abilities, and be capable of simplifying concepts for students. MT4 mentioned that teachers should "involve students into interactive activities and avoid lecture method." Teachers should have command of the subject matter knowledge and the way they convey the content being taught. This was supported by MT3, who mentioned that "the teachers before class must under-stand the subject matter or content." Overall, master trainers indicated that teachers should use discussions, dialogues, role-play methods, and learning tools in their teaching. Regarding inadequacies in teachers' PCK, MT4 stressed that "there is a need to bring changes in teachers' pedagogies." However, teachers offered a different perspective on the challenges associated with employing a range of teaching methods. For instance, T7 said, "we can use different methods, but it also depends on the mood and results we are getting from the students," whereas T2 said, "the main focus of the teaching should be on students' psyche, and based on that, we should select the teaching method." In other words, although the level of teachers' PCK had an influ-ence on the teaching methods employed, learner variables were another determining factor.

11.4.2.3   Teachers' Self-Efficacy

The majority of the teachers mentioned that they did not have enough confidence in their fluency in English, which created another hurdle for them in their teaching. As T3 noted, "our English is so weak, we can't speak and communicate in English; if we try, then students' can't understand, so we use Urdu (national language)." The majority of the teachers mentioned that they had an interest in the teaching and learning of the English language, but due to a lack of confidence, lack of vocabulary, grammar knowledge, and pronunciation issues, and the multicultural background of the students, they faced difficulties. However, teachers were able to manage the complex learning and behavioural problems of their students by giving them extra time to cope and making allowances for them. T1 said, "I gave leniency to my students first," and T7 said, "I identified the reasons for the disruptive behaviour and give counselling sessions alone after class." Teachers suggested that they needed to adjust their techniques according to the skillset and level of the students. The majority of the teachers mentioned that they were trying to transition from a teacher-centred approach to a more student-centred one, where students would feel confident and ask anything from the teacher. The advantages of this are described by T8, who stated: "We give them the confidence to speak even they are wrong. Then students' behaviour changes also, and they come too close to the teacher and talk openly."

11.4.3   Theme 3: Barriers to Quality Education

From the data, interviewees mentioned two different types of barriers to quality education, which were categorised as *training-related* and *resource-related barriers.*

11.4.3.1 Training-Related Barriers

Master trainers considered that time was a constraint on the provision of adequate training and suggested that it was not possible to train the teachers in two or three days, especially with all the areas that needed to be covered, such as teaching styles, lesson planning, and professional standards. All of this required time and continuous training but, unfortunately, as mentioned by MT4, "the frequency of the training is very low. We cannot prepare or trained or prepared professional teachers in three days." This opinion was supported by teachers, such as T2, who stated that there was a lack of continuous professional workshops and training: "We learned from our experiences and our senior teachers/headmasters."

It was further noted that government schoolteachers only received one mandatory training course at the start of their careers, in the form of induction training. This was highlighted by T5, who stated: "I started my teaching at Government school in 2014, and from 2015 to 2021, I only received one training." A majority of the participants mentioned that they received only one initial training at the start of their careers from the government. Furthermore, it was reported that there was no specific timeframe or hard and fast rules for the continuous training of the schoolteachers. This depended on the government; whenever they had funds or felt it necessary, they offered the training to the selected teachers regardless of their need, age, level, and professional competencies.

Usually, teachers were not ready to bring changes to the system due to some factors, such as the lack of a proper monitoring system, lack of continuous training, and the lack of competition among teachers. The attitude of the teachers towards learning and training can be evident by this response of P3,

> In simple, I disturb their smooth and easy-going teaching and life. They were not responding and rejected my ideas. They were saying that I was imposing the private system on them. If I gave an example of a lesson plan, they just said that it is just a formality and paperwork. There is no need to teach according to the lesson plans.

It was mentioned by many participants that training and implementation of the training practices need support from the government, but in Pakistan, there was a lack of support from the government to the trainers and schoolteachers. As mentioned by MT4, "School leadership and administration are not supportive, so gradually they came to the same approach due to the challenges." Another response from P1 also demonstrated this: "We do not have any kind of support from the government to design and conduct activities." The government just focused on the paperwork to give a clear and smooth picture to the audience that they were supporting and funding in the education sector. Somehow, they did, but many times it was only done on paperwork like mentioned by P3, "the things are only done on paperwork in Pakistan, especially at the Government level. All is well and rules, commission, training, etc. all are on paperwork not practically executed." Teachers views, however, that they had, were pressure from the school to focus more on the completion of the syllabus and copy work of the students. Government gave them the content in the shape of a book rather providing the other learning resources, technology, and support to make the learning conducive. As mentioned by a T7, "Government do not concern about the resources; they are just concerned that these are our outlines and student learning outcome and this our students should be taught."

11.4.3.2 Resources-Related Barrier

The majority of the trainers mentioned in their interviews that teachers tried to implement the teaching methods and the learning material learnt from the trainings in their practical classrooms. Teachers also demonstrated that they learned many fruitful strategies from training, but without proper resources and facilitation, they could not implement those elements in the classroom, as demonstrated by T9: "training we received are not applicable in my school as it requires many things which are not covered by the management." As mentioned by T7, "I learned lesson planning and time management skills from training, now I manage 40 min of my class into different elements like activities, feedback, assessment, summary and all." T10 demonstrated that "we cannot use the training practices into the classroom due to the conditions of the schools. We only apply those techniques which can be easily applicable."

The majority of the participants mentioned the lack of resources in terms of physical and human resources, i.e., teaching aids, resource material, electricity, furniture, drinking water, fans, cleaners, and funding issues. As described by P3,

> The first thing is that we do not have benches, furniture for the students, we do not have drinking water, we do not have fans, proper washrooms and sweepers are not available. Sometimes, I am bound as I cannot provide everything.

P1 also stated that,

> Lack of facilities (Internet, projector, laptop), lack of master trainers, lack of teachers like 2 teachers for 5 or 6 classes, lack of teachers and facilities to divide the students into the sections, lack of the desired environment for the delivery of the lesson plans and activities.

The above statements also show the worst conditions of the resources for the quality education in the schools. T3 said, "We only have one blackboard and white chalk in every class because we are government teachers. We do not have any other resources for teaching." This also demonstrated the condition of the available teaching aids in the classroom, which boosts the quality of education in the educational system. When a school does not have the necessities, the delivery of quality education is difficult, as described by T6, that "Government provided carpet for sitting, we do not have chairs. Some schools have desks and chairs." Another major issue highlighted by the participants was the student–teacher ratio. Many schools have more students and fewer teachers. As the standard, the student–teacher ratio is 25:1, described by the World Bank, but the conditions in Pakistani primary schools are different. As mentioned by teachers they cannot apply different methods due to the class size of 80 students per teacher without any teacher assistant. T2 stated that "student strength as class size is very large and it is difficult to accommodate all students for a single teacher."

11.4.4   Theme 4: Support to Enhance Quality Education

Interviewees discussed the support they were receiving, such as mentoring sessions and informal support delivered via social media platforms, which were intended to improve their teaching and to enhance the education system more generally. For example, One MT4 said that "teachers usually asked in a WhatsApp group, and they can also call us with any kind of problem, and we support them in every issue." On the contrary, T9 said, "lack of support from management, they asked us to focus on copy work, we do not have any sessions with [the principal] to discuss our issues or problems." The government is not supporting the headmasters to give the training and brush up the skills of the teachers as P3 stated that "I did not get any support from the government. If I need any kind of support, then I have to hire a person on my own like from Greenwich University for training sessions of the teachers." On the other hand, some teachers get the support from the headmasters and master trainers in their teaching or pedagogical problems. As P2 mentioned that "I visited their class and give demo teaching to the teachers. If teachers made any mistakes, then I discuss those mistakes with teachers." And P1 said, "we maintain the daily diary in which teachers mentioned their lesson plans and I checked the daily diary on a daily basis." In contrast, T10 said, "no support is provided from senior teachers and [the principal]." Teachers also facilitate the students by giving them extra time in breaks or vacations to minimise the learning difficulties as T3 said, "I give them an incentive if they work well even if it has some mistakes. I ask the whole class to clap for them. This is the way I increase their learning level." T9 also stated, "I provide support with the help of the tutorial method and textbook. I give them extra class and time." Interviewees also mentioned that they required support from the government, in the form of continuous training, accountability systems to support teachers, and the provision of additional learning materials. They also stated that schools required more teachers and staff to balance the student–teacher ratios. They stressed that this support could assist in meeting the Quality Education's indicators set by the United Nations in 2015, as mentioned by the P3, "If government wants to apply the policies and frameworks, then first you need to work on teachers, and they should be up to the mark." T2 said, "government should revise the student–teacher ratio by providing more staff or teachers."

11.5   Discussion

The results of this study indicated that, while Pakistan has the stated intention of improving the quality of its education systems in line with SDG4, teachers' efforts to help achieve this are hampered by a range of factors. Insufficient training, outdated teaching methods, a lack of resources for teaching and training, and inadequate monitoring and accountability systems all create barriers to a more effective, higher quality education system.

This study found that the training offered to teachers usually focused on teaching methods, classroom management, and lesson planning. Although this focus is helpful, the lack of continuity of the training hampered efforts to produce more suitably qualified and well-trained teachers. As Pugatch (2017) mentioned, teachers in developing countries are facing the issue of continuous training. Another researcher, Holmqvist (2019), supported the same findings by stating that lack of continuous training for in-service teachers impacts the quality of the education system. Similar findings by Pugatch (2017), García and Weiss (2019), and Holmqvist (2019) underline the importance of ongoing, quality training, which, according to Tariq et al. (2020), would lead to better-quality outcomes. The government of Pakistan needs to emphasise the continuous training of the teachers by spending funds on the teachers' training and by asking the training institutes to modify the policies and training materials as per the requirement of the SDGs.

Another finding of the study was that teachers were relying on traditional methods due to their inadequate knowledge of the content appropriate teaching methods and poor language skills. Furthermore, it was found that too much emphasis was given to the completion of the training syllabus in a required timeframe at the expense of developing teachers' PCK. This aligns with the findings of Mupa and Chinooneka (2015), Khan and Islam (2015), McNamee and Hansen (2014), who also noted that insufficient time is spent on enhancing the pedagogical content knowledge of the teachers. In contrast, Chan (2009) and Mohammad et al. (2018) mentioned that teachers need language courses, familiarity with information communication technology, and literacy training for the contribution of effective pedagogies. Therefore, it may be a practical step for the teachers and for promoting quality education if school leadership encourages teachers to develop and demonstrate the skills of modern technology in their teaching.

Another significant finding reveals that teachers cannot implement the training practices due to the lack of resources and support from the government and school leadership. Often, they do not even have basic facilities in their schools, such as teaching aids, resource materials, electricity, furniture, drinking water, and basic equipment. Pandey (2018), Martínez (2018), Osamwonyi (2016), and Mupa and Chinooneka (2015) also found that inadequate facilities and a lack of support from the management constrain the effectiveness and quality of teaching. Furthermore, Najumba (2013) mentioned that schools perform better when they have adequate resources and facilities, compared with those that do not. Support from the management and school leadership also plays a vital role in quality education; studies by Alrabea (2011), Gilley et al. (2002), and Almannie (2015) all support the findings of this study that a lack of support makes it challenging to implement quality teaching skills and methods in the classroom.

Every education system faces difficulties and barriers; however, if the existing barriers in education can be handled with care and proper support, then the outcome can be effective, as another significant finding of this study reveals that the teachers are getting informal support in the form of regular meetings, mentors, peer-observation, team teaching, and connecting with other teachers. A survey conducted by the National Centre for Tertiary Teaching Excellence (NCFTTE, 2009) supports the finding of informal support by mentioning that peer support, mentoring, and micro-teaching would help reduce the difficulties of the schoolteachers in boosting quality education. McNamee and Hansen (2014) also supported the findings by stating that the teachers can perform better in different aspects of teaching if they get the proper guidance and support from the school leaders. At the same time, challenges can be overcome if the government and school leaders work on the welfare of the teachers by offering support and training to them.

Efforts and supports implemented in schools are useless if systems do not have corresponding accountability and monitoring systems. This study found that there is no monitoring system to assess the implementation of training practices or the pitfalls of quality education in schools. Nadeem (2007) also mentioned in his study that Pakistani schools lack accountability systems. On the other hand, Almannie (2015) mentioned that a proper accountability system for training programmes and practices could be a reasonable effort to promote training practices and produce qualified teachers. Therefore, the Pakistani government is encouraged to introduce proper mechanisms for the ongoing monitoring of the teachers, which can be a constructive step towards increasing the quality of education at the school level.

11.6   Conclusion

Based on the results and findings, this study suggests that from a broader perspective, for quality education, all stakeholders need to work collaboratively and provide facilities and resources to the schools and teachers. In addition, teachers also need continuous training through the planning and training programmes, and refresher courses that align with the aims of SDG4.

Institutes, teachers, students, management, and administration all are responsible for the quality assurance in the education system of Pakistan. Therefore, there is a need for practical and theoretical interventions such as pedagogical support, resources and facilities, and monitoring systems to ensure of the implementation of the indicators set under SDG4.

Given the circumstances, to enhance the quality of teacher education, the Pakistani government should take the following initiatives:

1. Create awareness of SDG4 as part of training materials and curriculum.
2. Make a central policy for all training institutes in which every prospective teacher practises the same skills and follows the same modified curriculum to achieve the SDGs.
3. Support and implement the use of modern technology.
4. Set criteria for the selection and hiring of teachers.
5. Implement a proper system monitoring and evaluation.
6. Provide adequate funds for teacher training.
7. Pay greater attention to the welfare of teachers.

Pakistan is a developing country, facing many issues, but other issues should not distract the government's attention from the primary issue of "quality education." The government of Pakistan set the 4% of Gross Domestic Product target for the education sector, but this target is not being met as reported by the UNDP and Ministry of Planning, Pakistan (2019). Therefore, all people with the collaboration of government should carry out their duties or responsibilities. In order to achieve SDG4, governments need to formulate a collective and strategic approach to engage all the stakeholders because in education, there is no one person show, and it is a collective responsibility of the nation to promote quality education.

References

Almannie, M. (2015). Barriers encountered in the transfer of educational training to workplace practice in Saudi Arabia. *Journal of Education and Training Studies, 3*(5), 10–17.

Alrabea, B. I. (2011). *Using Learning Transfer System Inventory (LTSI) to determine the status quo application of experiences gained from training by female school principals in performing their jobs* [Unpublished PhD dissertation]. King Saud University.

Chan, S. (2009). Perspectives of new trades tutors: Towards a scholarship of teaching and learning for vocational educators. *National Centre for Tertiary Teaching Excellence.* http://citeseerx.ist.psu.edu/viewdoc/download?doi=10.1.1.606.3968&rep=rep1&type=pdf

Creswell, J. W. (2014). *Research design: Qualitative, quantitative and mixed methods approaches* (4th edn.). SAGE.

Department of Economic and Social Affairs. (2015). *Transforming our world: The 2030 agenda for sustainable development.* https://sdgs.un.org/2030agenda.

Farooq, M. S. (2018). Millennium development goals (MDGs) and quality education situation in Pakistan at primary level. *International Online Journal of Primary Education, 7*(1), 1–23.

Ferguson, T., Iliško, D., Roofe, C., & Hill, S. (2018). *SDG4-Quality education: Inclusivity, equity and lifelong learning for all.* Emerald Group Publishing.

Franco, I. B., & Derbyshire, E. (2020). SDG4 quality education. In I. Franco, T. Chatterji, E. Derbyshire, & J. Tracey (Eds.), *In actioning the global goals for local impact* (pp. 57–68). Springer.

García, E., & Weiss, E. (2019). *The teacher shortage is real, large and growing, and worse than we thought.* The perfect storm in the teacher labor market series. Economic Policy Institute. https://eric.ed.gov/?id=ED598211

Gilley, J., Eggland, S., Gilley, A. M., & Maycunich, A. (2002). *Principles of human resource development.* Basic Books.

Government of Balochistan Policy Planning Implementation Unit, Education Department. (2013). *Balochistan education sector plan.* http://emis.gob.pk/Uploads/Balochistan%20Education%20Sector%20Plan.pdf

Government of Pakistan. (2009). *National Educational Policy.* http://library.aepam.edu.pk/Books/National%20Education%20Policy%202009.pdf.

Government of Punjab. (2013). *Punjab school education sector plan (2013–2017).* http://aserpakistan.org/document/learning_resources/2014/Sector_Plans/Punjab%20Sector%20Plan%202013-2017.pdf

Higher Education Commission. (2023). Curriculum of Education-B.Ed (Hons) Elementary ADE (Associate Degree in Education), Electronic, 484.

High Level Political Forum on Sustainable Development. (2019). *Review of SDG implementation and interrelations among goals Discussion on SDG 4—Quality education.* https://sustainabledevelopment.un.org/content/documents/23669BN_SDG4.pdf

Holmqvist, M. (2019). Lack of qualified teachers: A global challenge for future knowledge development. In R. B. Monyai (Ed.), *Teacher education in the 21st century.* (pp. 53–65). IntechOpen.

Jing-Jing, H. (2014). A critical review of pedagogical content knowledge components: Nature, principle, and trend. *International Journal of Education and Research, 2*(4), 411–424.

Kalsoom, Q., & Qureshi, N. (2019). Teacher education for sustainable development in Pakistan: Content analysis of teacher education curriculum and standards. *Journal of Research and Reflections in Education, 13*(1), 20–33.

Kalsoom, Q., Qureshi, N., & Khanam, A. (2018). Perceptions of the research scholars regarding education for sustainable development (ESD) in Pakistan. In Leal Filho, W., J. Rogers, U. Lyer-Raniga (Eds). *Sustainable development research in the Asia-Pacific region* (pp. 165–179). Springer.

Khan, R., & Islam, S. (2015). An evaluation of national professional standards of public sector schoolteachers at primary level in district Peshawar. *The Dialogue, 10*(4), 365–376.

Maldonado García, M. I. (2018). Improving university students writing skills in Pakistan. *The European Educational Researcher, 1*(1), 1–16. https://doi.org/10.31757/euer.111

Martínez, E. (2018). *Shall I feed my daughter or educate her? Barriers to girls' education in Pakistan.* Human Rights Watch. https://www.hrw.org/report/2018/11/12/shall-i-feed-my-daughter-or-educate-her/barriers-girls-education-pakistan

McChesney, K., & Aldridge, J. (2019). Weaving an interpretivist stance throughout mixed methods research. *International Journal of Research and Method in Education, 42*(3), 225–238. https://doi.org/10.1080/1743727X.2019.1590811

McNamee, T., & Hansen, C. (2014). *Teacher effectiveness training. Inducting industry trainers for success.* National Centre for Vocational Education Research. https://www.voced.edu.au/content/ngv:65098

Ministry of Education. (2009). *National professional standards for teachers.* Government of Pakistan.https://www.nacte.org.pk/assets/download/NationalProfessionalStandardsforTeachersinPakistan.pdf

Ministry of Planning, Development, and Reform. (2019). *Structural bottlenecks in mainstreaming quality in the existing education system in Pakistan.* https://www.sdgpakistan.pk/uploads/pub/Structural_Bottlenecks_Quality_Education_System_Pakistan1.pdf

Mohammad, N., Masum, R., Ali, Z., & Baksh, K. (2018). Teaching practices of English language in the schools of Lasbela District, Pakistan. *International Journal of Experiential Learning & Case Studies, 2*(2), 34–39.

Mupa, P., & Chinooneka, T. I. (2015). Factors contributing to ineffective teaching and learning in primary schools: Why are schools in decadence? *Journal of Education and Practice, 6*(19), 125–132.

Nadeem, M. (2007). *Status of English language teaching at primary level in Punjab.* Unpublished doctoral dissertation, University of Education.

Najumba, J. (2013). *The effectiveness of teaching and learning in primary schools.* Sage Publication.

National Centre for Tertiary Teaching Excellence. (2009). *Survey of literature relating to tertiary teacher development and qualifications.* https://ako.ac.nz/assets/Knowledge-centre/Qualifications-Literature-review/REPORT-Survey-of-teacher-development-qualifications.pdf

Osamwonyi, E. F. (2016). In-service education of teachers: Overview, problems, and the way forward. *Journal of Education and Practice, 7*(26), 83–87.

Pandey, B. (2018). *Achieving SDG 4 in India: Moving from quantity to quality education for all.* Research and Information System for Developing Countries.

Pugatch, T (2017). Does the official certification of teachers lead to better educational outcomes in developing countries? *IZA World of Labor*, evidence-based policy making. https://doi.org/10.15185/izawol.349. https://wol.iza.org/articles/is-teacher-certification-an-effective-tool-for-developing-countries/lang/de

Richter, S. (2019). A system dynamics study of Pakistan's education system: Consequences for governance. *The Electronic Journal of Information Systems in Developing Countries, 85*(1). https://doi.org/10.1002/isd2.12065

Sayed, Y., & Moriarty, K. (2020). SDG 4 and the 'education quality turn': Prospects, possibilities, and problems. In Wulff, A. (Ed). *Grading goal four* (pp. 194–213). Brill Sense. https://doi.org/10.1163/9789004430365_009

Shaukat, S., & Chowdhury, R. (2020). Teacher educators' perceptions of professional standards: Implementation challenges in Pakistan. *Issues in Educational Research, 30*(3), 1084–1104.

Shulman, L. S. (1986). Those who understand: Knowledge growth in teaching. *Educational Researcher, 15*(2), 4–14.

Tariq, T. M., Hina, K., & Arshad, A. M. (2020). National professional standards for teachers: Awareness, perspective & implementation in Pakistan. *Research Journal of Social Sciences and Economics Review, 1*(4), 242–249.

Chapter 12
The Construction of Gender Identities Through Pakistani Curriculum Textbooks

Nousheen Naz, Steve Drew, and Kim Beasy

12.1 Introduction

With the 2030 agenda of transforming the world by ensuring wellbeing, economic prosperity, and a protected climate for humanity and by taking a multifaceted and holistic view of human development, United Nations sustainability development goals (SDGs) address many challenges faced by humanity (Pradhan et al., 2017). SDG5 aims to "achieve gender equality and empower all women and girls" (Bernstein, 2017; Franco et al., 2020). Gender equality is influenced by everyday discourses in societies, for example in the media and places of worship (Akdemir, 2020), which are informed by religious and cultural values and beliefs. This chapter focuses upon the articulation of educational discourse within textbooks. It argues that considering SDG5 in relation to educational discourse illuminates taken for granted societal assumptions, which contribute to normalising the exploitation of women in the name of religious and cultural values and beliefs, consequently becoming a hindrance to achieving SDG5. This chapter contends that empowering women and girls through the provision of equitable education can bring attention to the issues of gender inequality in terms of construction of gender identities through

N. Naz (✉)
School of Education, College of Arts, Law and Education, University of Tasmania, Churchill Ave, Hobart, TAS, Australia
e-mail: Nousheen.Naz@utas.edu.au

S. Drew
Academic Division, University of Tasmania, Churchill Ave, Hobart, TAS, Australia
e-mail: Steve.Drew@utas.edu.au

K. Beasy
School of Education, College of Arts, Law and Education, University of Tasmania, Newnham Dr, Launceston, TAS, Australia
e-mail: Kim.Beasy@utas.edu.au

© The Author(s), under exclusive license to Springer Nature Singapore Pte Ltd. 2023
K. Beasy et al. (eds.), *Education and the UN Sustainable Development Goals*, Education for Sustainability 7,
https://doi.org/10.1007/978-981-99-3802-5_12

educational discourses and helps to determine ways to address gender inequalities, which is a topic of great interest to academic scholars around the globe (Cooray & Potrafke, 2011; Durrani, 2008; ur Rahman et al., 2018).

According to Subrahmanian (2005), "to achieve gender equality in and through education," it is important to achieve "rights within education," which involve supporting a gender aware educational environment, processes, and outcomes. Focusing on the constituent elements of a gender aware educational environment, this chapter explores ways in which curriculum textbooks are used to perpetuate gender identities in students regarding the contemporary gender order. This study is contextualised in Pakistan, which is one of the first countries where the SDG agenda was passed in parliament with unanimous support (Javeed et al., 2021). The country has prioritised its interests regarding SDGs to enable itself to join "the league of upper middle-class countries" by 2030 (Kousar & Brett, 2020). Therefore, investigating the barriers and potential opportunities for improving opportunities for girls and women are important considerations for the coming decade.

Women constitute almost half of the total population of Pakistan (Abbasi et al., 2019; Khan & Mahmood, 1997), yet because of the patriarchal structure of society, various forms of violence, social inequality, and marginalisation against women prevail (Raza & Murad, 2010). In terms of gender inequality, Pakistan currently has the fourth largest overall gender gap among 156 countries by index (Lohana et al., 2021; Sharma et al., 2021). Ahmad and Anwar (2018) are of the view that this gender-based inequity and discrimination in Pakistani society is the result of the perpetuation of gender identities for both men and women. In Pakistani society, women are discriminated against compared to men in many ways (Hadi, 2017; Niaz, 2003) resulting in consequential challenges (Farooq & Tayyab, 2019; Yunis et al., 2019). Domestic violence, early forced marriages, poor quality of housing, family restrictions, sexual harassment, rape and sexual assault, stereotyping, and traditional practices are guised in social values and religious and beliefs and are examples of discriminatory attitudes towards women in Pakistan (Bhattacharya, 2014; Durrani et al., 1995; Hadi, 2017; Raza & Murad, 2010; Winkvist & Akhtar, 2000). The social, cultural, contemporary, and political contexts also influence the attitudes and treatment of women (Bhattacharya, 2014) and contribute to gender-based discrimination (Durrani et al., 1995; Saeed, 2012).

Provision of gender equity in ensuring equal representation in, and opportunities to have access to, education for girls has always been a mandatory part of the educational policies of Pakistani governments (Durrani & Halai, 2020; Ullah & Skelton, 2013). Despite the claims of government to change the conditions for women, the country so far remains unsuccessful in achieving the goal (Bhattacharya, 2014; Islam & Asadullah, 2018). A contributing factor to the failure in reaching gender equity in educational attainment may be attributed to perpetuation of gender stereotypes and inequities in educational discourse. Analysis of compulsory texts written in Urdu reveals that these textbooks promote gender stereotypes making classrooms places where stereotypes are nurtured, instead of challenged (Blumberg, 2007). Both males and females are represented in stereotypical roles in textbooks (Agha et al., 2018; Jat et al., 2018) despite the revision of the content of books by the authorities to ensure gender equity and empowerment of women follow SDG5 aims (Jabeen & Ilyas, 2012; Waqar & Ghani, 2019). Male dominance is both legitimised as well as naturalised in depictions of gender roles through the content of textbooks. Gender stereotypes are conveyed both through pictorial images as well as in the use of language (Shahnaz et al., 2020).

This chapter provides qualitative assessment of the compulsory textbooks used at primary level in the schools of Pakistan. It utilises a critical post structuralist stance to explore the construction of gender identities. This chapter also delineates the ideological power of curriculum textbooks in shaping gender identities of students. It contends that the Pakistani curriculum textbooks in their current form maintain, reproduce, and reinforce gender hierarchies, which creates obstacles in attaining SDG5 aims. The chapter concludes by opening space for further research to review critically the Pakistani government's claim of eliminating all kinds of gender biased content within educational resources.

12.2 Gender Identities, Religion, and Education

Each society constructs gender according to its own customs and traditions, which means that different gender identities are observable. The characteristics of these identities are defined by the respective social, cultural, and religious norms of the society in question. Our understanding of social, cultural, and religious norms refers to the beliefs about "what other people do and approve of" (Cislaghi & Heise, 2020).

Pakistani society is characterised by patriarchal values that subjugate the position of women socially, politically, and economically (Hadi, 2017). Patriarchy refers to a gendered hierarchy (Hunnicutt, 2009). It is characterised by an unequal distribution of power in favour of men (Facio, 2013; Sultana, 2010). Unlike western societies Pakistani society treats gender in a "very traditional way" (Kousar & Brett, 2020), where the world outside of the home is considered a man's domain (Yasmin, 2021). Males are the centre of Pakistani society. They participate in all professions, in outdoor activities and sports and their work is valued, unlike women. They are presented as head of families and as bread winners. Contrary to this, most women in Pakistan undertake (unpaid) domestic work. As a consequence of their lower economic participation and lesser employment opportunities, women's contributions are relatively undervalued by society generally (Yasmin, 2021). Women, in general, do not undertake professional roles, and for those women who are working in paid jobs, there is a limited career specification (Raza & Murad, 2010). Women are generally dependent on men in all affairs of everyday life (Jejeebhoy & Sathar, 2001; Malik & Aamir, 2017). Home making is associated with women and the home is considered their domain (Yasmin, 2021). The religious (Islamic) teachings, as well as the cultural norms, second the notion that the focus of attention and action for women should be their home. In the 33rd line of the Chapter 33 of the Quran, while addressing the wives of Prophet Muhammad, Allah says, تَبَرَّجْنَ تَبَرُّجَ الْجَاهِلِيَّةِ الْأُوْلَى

وَ قَرْنَ فِىْ بُيُوْتِكُنَّ وَ لَا And stay in your houses and refrain from displaying yourselves as (was) the custom of the former times of ignorance (verse 33, Surah Ahzab).

Owing to this religious and cultural belief, a woman is generally presented in the role of a carer and nurturer (Bhattacharya, 2014; Islam & Asadullah, 2018). These kinds of socio-cultural perceptions and beliefs about women form the basis of the constructs, on which the society devises its definition of a good woman.

Adherence to religion and gender views cannot be separated from each other (Cassese & Holman, 2017; Predelli, 2004). In various parts of the world, it is common to observe that in many religious traditions, cultural and religious continuity depends on gender practices (Avishai et al., 2015). One cannot ignore or negate the influence of religion on (gender) identity construction, especially when one talks about a country such as Pakistan that was founded because of a religious conflict (Michael, 2018). The customs of a country also play a significant role and determine the extent to which religion shapes (and perpetuates) gender identities.

Islam is the religion of 96% of the population in Pakistan (Yilmaz & Ahmed, 2018). It recognises different but equal roles and responsibilities for both men and women (Darakchi, 2018) so that the existence of a balanced and harmonised society can be made possible. Contrary to this aim, the religious groups in patriarchal Pakistani society, use religion as a "toolkit" (Bartkowski & Read, 2003; Shahnaz et al., 2020) to promote an unbalanced distribution of duties and responsibilities such that women are represented as weaker and of less value than their male counterparts. One of the reasons for this portrayal according to Bhattacharya (2014) is that men in Islam are given the status of *Qawwam,* which means the carer and provider. It suggests that men, being providers enjoy a dominant position over women. In the case of women, their image of "submissive wife" is hailed through different discourses including through media discourses. Their motherhood is glorified in such a way that the only purpose of a woman seems to be to raise her children in a supportive way (Nasir, 2017). This portrayal reinforces women's stereotypical image. An ideal and model woman is portrayed as one who is subordinated to males and follows patriarchal traditions, unlike western women who are presented as "insecure, vulnerable and pervert Western women" (Rashid, 2006). Gender roles are defined with various prohibitions in the name of religious exhortations that have confined women's role in society. Men generally do not participate in any domestic chores and are traditionally projected in "business like financial affairs" (Nasir, 2017). This deeply rooted ideology in Pakistani society hierarchically divides the society, representing men as superior to women.

Jinnah, the founder of Pakistan, himself being secular, never stated that the country would be an Islamic state (Ispahani, 2017), yet it is represented as a country that was founded in the name of Islam and is an ideological state (Grünenfelder, 2013; Shaikh, 2018; Zaman, 2018). Jinnah envisioned a country where there would be equality for all citizens, but modern Pakistan has become more intolerant in many practices

(Ispahani, 2017). Shah (2012) on the other hand, holding a different opinion, argued that the country was established in the name of Islam, but politically Islam was first institutionalised by General Zia who came to power because of coup d'état on July 5th, 1977. To legitimise his dictatorship, General Zia used the name of Islam and laid the foundation of Islamising the country. Islamisation developed strong roots in General Zia's tenure in the country (Shah, 2012) and the religious groups started dominating the lives of common Pakistanis, especially women. The effect of Islamisation introduced by Zia is evident from his first television speech that he delivered after assuming the control of the country. The speech stated: "Pakistan, which was created in the name of Islam, will continue to survive only if it sticks to Islam. That is why I consider the introduction of [an] Islamic system as an essential prerequisite for the country" (cited in Din, 2014). Based on this context, it can be stated that in today's Pakistan the roles and responsibilities of men and women, apart from having social and cultural influence, are also greatly influenced by Islam.

Ashraf and Hafiza (2016) argue that the political, cultural, social, and economic life of a nation is promoted and improved by its educational institutions. In the case of Pakistan, there are also differences in the provision of equal opportunities of education for girls and boys in the country (Mehmood et al., 2018), with boys being more privileged (Saeed, 2012; Winkvist & Akhtar, 2000). Overall, Pakistan has low literacy levels, and it has the lowest female literacy rates among all other western and Muslim countries across the globe (Latif, 2009; Mehmood et al., 2018; Qureshi & Rarieya, 2007). The education statistics in Pakistan reveal an unsatisfying and discouraging situation for the education sector (Ashraf & Hafiza, 2016; Shah, 2003). According to the Global Gender Gap Index 2021, Pakistan currently has the 13th largest overall educational attainment gap by the index when compared against 156 countries of the world (Malik & Marwah, 2021).

One of the factors that contribute to the poor performance of the education sector is gender discrimination by society and culture (Hadi, 2017; Niaz, 2003), which is due to observance of patriarchal social norms in the country (Ahmad & Anwar, 2018; Rana, 2016). Almost half of the population of women are completely illiterate, which is a major hindrance in the development of the country's economy (Hadi, 2017; Latif, 2009). Education is very important for girls/women. Education of women ensures higher economic return rates as compared to any other investment (Mehmood et al., 2018). The findings of a study conducted by Le and Nguyen (2021) suggest that education of a woman strengthens her position as a decision-maker within the family. Education empowers women and educates them about the world around them (Malik & Courtney, 2011). It is important for better parenting (Rasool, 2007). It is also widely believed that investment in education for women benefits society in a variety of economic and non-economic ways (Islam & Asadullah, 2018).

12.3   Methodology and the Study

A critical post structuralist stance is utilised to approach analysis of compulsory curriculum textbooks to understand the ways textbooks construct gender identities of students. Foucault's concept of discourse and "discursive power" is utilised to theorise curriculum textbooks (including visual images) as socially constructed texts that constitute knowledge in relation to "social practice, forms of subjectivity and power relations" (Weedon, 1996, p. 106). From a Foucauldian perspective, curriculum textbooks construct knowledge and students actively shape their subjectivities by taking subject positions within available discourses. It is reiterated that the basic presupposition of this study is that gender, being a social category, is a social construction that is not fixed. Exploring the content of the compulsory curriculum textbooks, this study highlights the ways that textbooks maintain and naturalise the gender hierarchy in a way that continues to reflect male hegemony.

In this study thematic analysis of textbooks is undertaken to discern how gender is portrayed (Braun & Clarke, 2006). The data for this chapter comes from the primary level compulsory textbooks of Urdu taught in schools of Pakistan. The curriculum textbooks that are the focus for this study were produced by the PCTB (Punjab Curriculum and Textbook Board) and approved by the curriculum wing of the Ministry of Federal Education, Islamabad. Curriculum textbooks of PCTB were chosen because Punjab is the most populous province of Pakistan and people of almost all ethnicities live there. Hence, a study conducted using the curriculum textbooks taught in Punjab is representative of Pakistan. The curriculum textbooks of "Urdu" were chosen for analysis for two reasons. First because, "Urdu" is the national language of Pakistan, which is spoken and understood by the majority of people all over the country (Mahmood et al., 2022). Second, Urdu is taught as a compulsory subject from primary through higher secondary level in schools. Language is a powerful medium that plays a significant role in shaping the identities of the nation (Qazi & Shah, 2019). The language textbooks are the only compulsory texts for all students in the region, therefore generalisations of potential impact for the whole population can be made. The compulsory language texts, as a group, are clearly an educational discourse as well as a cultural discourse that have power to influence all students.

For this study SDG5 Target 5.1 was considered, which aims to "end all forms of discrimination against all women and girls everywhere." The main theme of the study, "stereotypical representation of men and women," is discussed regarding the contemporary gender order in Pakistani society, using religious discourse as a boundary marker, claiming that religion, apart from unifying groups of people in the name of belief, also marks boundaries, divides, and discriminates.

12.4 Findings

12.4.1 Relative Positioning of Religion and Gender in Textbooks

Findings revealed a connection between religion and gender in analysed textbooks. The textbooks analysed in this study construct gender identities of characters in alignment with religious identities. Religious discourses were present in the texts and embedded within them were gender identities and roles. Themes observed included the use of meanings and signs signalling segregation/division of society into good muslim-bad muslim, good man-bad man, good woman-bad woman, good muslim man-bad muslim man, good muslim woman-bad muslim woman, and so on. Non-Muslims living in Pakistani society are automatically seen/judged from the muslim perspective in the texts.

The following sections discuss the level of association of Islamic values with the stereotypical representation of women presented through their representation and dress code in the content of Urdu textbooks taught from grade 1 to 5 at primary level in schools of Pakistan.

12.4.2 Dress Code

Dress code has a symbolic significance (Sandborg, 2021) and has the potential to shape experiences as well as construct identity (Buse & Twigg, 2018). The dress code of the children in the images presented in textbooks attracts the attention of the readers where both girls and boys are shown wearing traditional dresses in almost all pictures e.g., in the image presented at the top of each page from book I to book IV, the girl is shown wearing *shalwar kameez* and *dupatta* (piece of cloth used to cover one's body). She is shown having long hair tied in two ponytails and the boy is shown wearing *shalwar kameez*, the national dress of males in Pakistan. The images of young children wearing traditional dresses worn by the elders reflect that right from the beginning of the academic journey, girls and boys both are prepared to look at each other and others from the lens of religious and cultural values and societal norms (Figs. 12.1 and 12.2). This implicitly sets the reader up to appreciate the socio-cultural values and norms of Pakistan and how they are interwoven into the fabric of everyday life. Both characters are presented in such a way that the local reader immediately identifies/relates oneself with the characters.

In Pakistan, covering of a woman's body is related to religious identity. Because most of the population of Pakistan is Muslim, their religious identity is also conveyed through their dress code. The dress code presented in pictures in the textbooks helps the reader identify the religious identity of the characters also. A few instances from each book are seen in Figs. 12.3, 12.4, 12.5, 12.6, and 12.7.

Fig. 12.1 Imagery of students in national dress (*Source* Urdu textbooks for class I, II, III, PCTB)

Fig. 12.2 Imagery of students in national dress (*Source* Urdu textbooks for class IV, PCTB)

Fig. 12.3 Having a meal (*Source* Urdu textbooks for class I, PCTB, 106)

Fig. 12.4 Storytelling to children (*Source* Urdu textbooks for class II, PCTB, 149)

Fig. 12.5 Family time (*Source* Urdu textbooks for class III, PCTB, 197)

Fig. 12.6 Helping children study together (*Source* Urdu textbooks for class V, PCTB, 71)

Fig. 12.7 Madre Millat
Fatima Jinnah (*Source* Urdu
textbooks for class V, PCTB,
19)

Fig. 12.8 Dress as representative of religious identity (*Source* Urdu textbooks for class II, PCTB, 157)

On page 158 of book II (see Fig. 12.8), two non-Muslim female characters are shown in the images of a lesson. The females are shown wearing a different dress code than the ones described earlier, which reinforces the idea of associating dress code with religion and religious belief in a Pakistani context.

The significance of dress and its relation to religious identity can be understood with the dialogue of the child mentioned in the pictured story on page 157 of book II (see Fig. 12.9). Looking at the dress of the teachers, the child shouts, Aery, ye to musalman nhi, mujhey to ye Parsi lgti hain! (Oh, they are not Muslims, they look Zoartist to me!).

The analysis of the textbooks reveals an attempt also to relate religious identity to cultural identity. Where on one side the dress code of the characters is used to represent the religious identities, on the other side it is associated with their cultural

Fig. 12.9 Dress of Miss Roopa and of Miss Bina as representative of their religious identity (*Source* Urdu textbooks for class IV, PCTB, 157)

Fig. 12.10 Representing religious and cultural identity using dress code of Eric's teacher (*Source* Urdu textbooks for class IV, PCTB, 69)

identities, too. In the Eric ki Urdu (Eric's Urdu) on page 69 of book IV, the dress code of the woman teacher and the dress code of Eric's mother are different, revealing their different cultural and religious identities. Eric is a Pakistani child living with his parents in New York, America. His teacher is shown wearing a western dress—revealing her cultural identity (see Fig. 12.10), while Eric's mother is shown wearing a dupatta exhibiting her cultural as well as her religious identity (see Fig. 12.11).

Images of three female characters from three generations (Fig. 12.12) and another in a later textbook (Fig. 12.13) reveal the women wearing a dupatta to cover their

Fig. 12.11 *Representing religious and cultural identity* using dress code (*Source* Urdu textbooks for class IV, PCTB, 71)

Fig. 12.12 Representing religion through dress code of women (*Source* Urdu textbooks for class IV, PCTB, 88)

bodies, which differentiate them from the non-Muslim images represented in Eric's teacher (Fig. 12.10), of Miss Roopa and of Miss Bina (Fig. 12.9).

Strategically, dress code (employed in the textbooks through presentation of images) facilitates the authors construction of the "ideal image" of a Pakistani woman (Baulch & Pramiyanti, 2018; Ramírez, 2015). The appropriateness of the physical appearances also helps in drawing boundaries within groups of women, i.e., Muslim women and non-Muslim women, Pakistani women and western women, and so on. The images also reflect the influence of religion on the cultural values of society where covering body parts is treated as much a religious act as a cultural act in Pakistani society.

A good woman is one who dresses modestly, and the first thing that counts as being modest is that the dress she wears should cover her body properly. On the other hand,

Fig. 12.13 Representing religion through dress code of women (*Source* Urdu textbooks for class IV, PCTB, 90)

males do not have any specific dress code that qualifies them to be a Muslim/non-Muslim, good man/indecent man. Pictures in the textbooks help children see what is being talked about and puts "more ideas" in the readers' minds (Faisal Elhussien et al., 2020; Hibbing & Rankin-Erickson, 2003). The way dress code is presented through pictorial images shows both differentiation and discrimination between men and women, which becomes a hurdle in empowering women as equal to men. The textbooks discourses seem to perpetuate the discourse of the powerful by reinforcing the cultural and religious beliefs through their content.

12.5 Stereotypical Representation of Gender

Through its findings, the analysis of textbooks suggests that the textbooks endorse the idea by presenting women in domesticated roles (e.g., house makers), implicitly appreciating and encouraging the image of good women as good house makers, as constructed through the perspective of the religious and cultural discourse. The story *Ami ko kia hua?* (What happened to mother?) on page 83 of book I starts with *Ami ko bukhar hae* (mother has a fever). With mother having a fever, a range of questions is raised:

Ab kia hoga? (What will happen next?)

*Sabko nashta kon de ga? (*Who will serve breakfast?)

School ka kam non kerwaye ga? (Who will help with schoolwork?)

And then *sham hui to abu daftar se ghar aye- wo ami ko doctor k pass le* gai (In the evening father came from office and took mother to the doctor). *Nani jee* (the grandmother) served food to everyone, and *dada jee* (the grandfather) helped with school homework.

In this lesson, a woman is shown in a traditional role of a mother who should ideally remain indoors taking care of the family. With mother falling sick, a range of questions arise, like who will serve breakfast and help the children in doing schoolwork. Because stereotypically, it is assumed that all the house chores are the responsibility of women (the mother), with her sickness the balance of the family gets disturbed. The roles ascribed to the female gender in examples throughout book II put her in the stereotypical role of one who takes care of the family and helps with household. She is assigned the religiously and culturally approved role of one who fits best within the boundaries of the house. The unpaid household activities are not valued or recognised as work. A few examples have been randomly selected from book II to support this point:

> *Ami ne halwa banaya* (Mother cooked Halwa, a traditional dessert made of semolina). (p. 71)
>
> *Sarah ne sabzi kaati* (Sarah cut the vegetable). (p. 72)
>
> *Ami ne phal kaatey* (Ami cut the fruit). (p. 9)
>
> *Maria se aam* lo (Take mangoes from Maria). (p. 78)

Similar to book I and book II, men and women in book III are presented in stereotypical roles where there is segregation between the roles and responsibilities of both men and women in society, religiously, as well as culturally.

> *Ami wahan khana pakati hain* (Mother cooks food there). (p. 11)
>
> *Baji kaprey dhoti hai* (Elder sister washes clothes). (p. 17)
>
> *Sajid Bazar se sabzi laya* (Sajid brought vegetables from market). (p. 17)

In the lesson titled *Cheen* (China) (book-IV, p. 80), Umer's *mamu* (maternal uncle) was coming from abroad, "China." In Pakistani society, males, being the money-earning members of the family are independent to make decisions including to stay abroad and live on their own in foreign lands, unlike women who are not permitted to travel alone within the country. Women can only move openly when they are accompanied by male members of the family. To receive *mamu* (maternal uncle), only the male members went to the airport. This again reflects the common practice of the society where men mostly go to receive their friends and family members coming from airports, stations, etc.

> *Umer key mamu paanch saal bad Cheen sey Pakistan wapis aye they. Umer apney nana key sath mamu ko Lahore key hawaii addey sey leney gaya* (Umer's uncle returned to Pakistan from China after five years. Umer accompanied by his grandfather had gone to receive his uncle from the airport).

The allotment of segregated roles by society to both men and women continues in book IV, where again household chores are shown as the responsibility of women.

> *Ami ne Ali ko parhaya* (Mother taught Ali). (p. 24)
>
> *Ami khana pakati hain* (Mother cooks food). (p. 26)

The story *Ahsan ki Eid* (Ahsan's Eid) (book-IV, p. 143) also puts women into the stereotypical role of being responsible for the household chores. *Baji* (elder sister) and *Begam Hameed* (Hameed's wife) are both shown cooking in the kitchen while *Ahsan* (male) remains busy in *gupshup* (chatting) with *Hameed sahib* (Mr. Hameed).

Baji ne ek plate mae gosht dala aur Hameed sahib k ghar ja kar inki begam key sath kitchen mae hath bataney lagien. Ahsan, Hameed sahib key sath gupshup mae masroof hogaya. Baji aur Hameed sahib ki begam khana tayyar ker key ley ayen (Elder sister put meat on the plate and started helping Mrs. Hameed in the kitchen while Ahsan remained busy chatting with Mr. Hameed. Elder sister and Mrs. Hameed brought food after preparing it). (p. 145)

In the lesson Quomi parcham (national flag) on page 167, Ami's (mother) duty is to get the children ready, displaying child-rearing as a woman's role alongside representations of chores that are performed within the four walls of the house, and are her unsaid and naturally assumed responsibility. A few examples from book IV are:

Basim, Tayyab aur Qurat-ul-Ain ko aj unki ami ne khas taur per tayyar kia tha (Basim, Tayyab and Qurat-ul-Ain's mother got them ready in a special way today). (p. 167)

Ami ne Ali ko parhaya (Mother taught Ali). (p. 24)

Ami khana pakati hain (Mother cooks food). (p. 26)

The image in lesson *ache Kam* (book-I, p. 104) (Fig. 12.14) draws the attention of the reader to the mother, who is cooking something on the fire, again reflecting stereotypical tasks performed by women.

In *Khewara ki sair* (visit to Khewara) in book V (p. 51), where Saad and his father are busy exchanging useful information about the salt mine, *Khewara*, his mother likes the decoration pieces made from salt extracted from the mine. The attention of the mother is focused not on the information delivered but on the objects of beauty. By exhibiting women's inclination to decorating their houses, the text implicitly suggests that women support home making. It also implicitly constructs a woman's image as one who is involved in the home-making role by choice and by her virtue of being a woman. This is presented in such a subtle way that it appears natural for women only to fit into the role of home making. This relates to the famous concept of *ghar and ghar dari* (home and home making) in Pakistani society. Apart from this, it also constructs the image of a good woman as one who is involved in *ghar* (house), and all affairs related to the house within the four walls of the home. Through the character of Saad's mother, the qualities of a good woman are highlighted:

Fig. 12.14 Woman in domestic role (*Source* Urdu textbooks for class I, PCTB, 104)

Saad ki ami ko namak sey bani sajawati ashiya bohat pasanda ayen (Saad's mother liked the decoration pieces made of salt). (book-V, p. 51)

Similarly, males are presented performing chores outside the house. Nowhere in the textbooks are men show to perform any household tasks. They go to market without any restriction whenever they want; e.g., in *Pakistan ka tohfa* (the present of Pakistan) (book-II, p. 93) *Zahid aur Shahid ki ami ney inko bazar se pakorey laney ka kaha* (Zahid and Shahid's mother asked them to bring fritters from market). The segregation of roles for men and women displayed in the texts implicitly legitimises them as social norms. This stereotypical segregation of roles and responsibilities between men and women within textbooks suggests the association of authority and power is held by men only. This kind of stereotyping of gender roles in the text reflects a prejudiced approach of the authors towards women and in practice, this approach contributes to the marginalisation and exclusion of women from mainstream society.

12.6   Conclusion

This chapter unveils the ways curriculum, through the content of textbooks, reflects "cultural artefacts," which reproduces existing relations of power (Gray, 2013; Qin, 2020). This chapter has explored the ways curriculum textbooks act to construct gender identities of students in a particular way based on the differences of dress code and the cultural and religious roles assigned to each gender. This differentiation emphasises disparate expectations and reinforces cultural boundaries in relation to gender identity. Through representation of gender identities, the textbooks prioritise subject positions, which results in the reproduction of power and patterns of gender-based inequality. The current textbooks used in the schools of Pakistan present a homogenous representation of women. The dress code serves as a marker to construct their religious identity. The ideal spaces of women as presented through the textbooks are their respective domestic spheres where their roles are to nurture and care for the needs of family. In the case of participation of women in professional jobs, there is limited career specification for them. The findings of the study indicate that instead of supporting the government's claim to achieve the sustainable goal of empowering all girls and women, the content of the textbooks naturalises and maintains the gender hierarchy through acceptance and promotion of a religious discourse that continues to exhibit male hegemony. To achieve SDG5, it would be of benefit if the curriculum were revised with a gender equity lens. The findings of this study can serve as a foundation step in making the case of proposing revisions to the curriculum.

References

Abbasi, A. M., Abbas, I., & Malik, S. (2019). Exploring the problems of women at workplace. *Journal of Social Sciences and Media Studies, 3*(1), 17–27.

Agha, N., Syed, G. K., & Mirani, D. A. (2018). *Exploring the representation of gender and identity: Patriarchal and citizenship perspectives from the primary level Sindhi textbooks in Pakistan.* Paper presented at the Women's Studies International Forum.

Ahmad, A., & Anwar, H. N. (2018). Femininity, patriarchy and women political representation in Pakistan. *Pakistan Journal of Peace and Conflict Studies, 3*(1), 23–37.

Akdemir, A. (2020). The construction of gender identity in Alevi organisations: Discourses, practices, and gaps. *Ethnography.* https://doi.org/10.1177/1466138120924435

Ashraf, M. A., & Hafiza, I. (2016). Education and development of Pakistan: A study of current situation of education and literacy in Pakistan. *US-China Education Review B, 6*(11), 647–654.

Avishai, O., Jafar, A., & Rinaldo, R. (2015). A gender lens on religion. *Gender & Society, 29*(1), 5–25.

Bartkowski, J. P., & Read, J. N. G. (2003). Veiled submission: Gender, power, and identity among evangelical and Muslim women in the United States. *Qualitative Sociology, 26*(1), 71–92.

Baulch, E., & Pramiyanti, A. (2018). Hijabers on Instagram: Using visual social media to construct the ideal Muslim woman. *Social Media+Society, 4*(4), https://doi.org/10.1177/2056305118800308

Bernstein, S. (2017). The United Nations and the governance of sustainable development goals. In N. Kanie & F. Biermann (Eds.), *Governing through goals: Sustainable development goals as governance innovation* (pp. 213–239). MIT Press.

Bhattacharya, S. (2014). Status of women in Pakistan. *Journal of the Research Society of Pakistan, 51*(1), 179–211.

Blumberg, R. L. (2007). *Gender bias in textbooks: A hidden obstacle on the road to gender equality in education.* UNESCO Paris.

Braun, V., & Clarke, V. (2006). Using thematic analysis in psychology. *Qualitative Research in Psychology, 3*(2), 77–101.

Buse, C., & Twigg, J. (2018). Dressing disrupted: Negotiating care through the materiality of dress in the context of dementia. *Sociology of Health & Illness, 40*(2), 340–352.

Cassese, E. C., & Holman, M. R. (2017). Religion, gendered authority, and identity in American politics. *Politics and Religion, 10*(1), 31–56.

Cislaghi, B., & Heise, L. (2020). Gender norms and social norms: Differences, similarities and why they matter in prevention science. *Sociology of Health & Illness, 42*(2), 407–422.

Cooray, A., & Potrafke, N. (2011). Gender inequality in education: Political institutions or culture and religion? *European Journal of Political Economy, 27*(2), 268–280.

Darakchi, S. (2018). *Gender, religion, and identity: Modernization of gender roles among the Bulgarian Muslims (Pomaks).* Paper presented at the Women's Studies International Forum.

Din, N. U. (2014). Islamization of laws in Pakistan during the rule of General Zia Ul Haq.

Durrani, N. (2008). Schooling the 'other': The representation of gender and national identities in Pakistani curriculum texts. *Compare, 38*(5), 595–610.

Durrani, N., & Halai, A. (2020). Gender equality, education, and development: Tensions between global, national, and local policy discourses in postcolonial contexts. In *Grading goal four* (pp. 65–95). Brill Sense.

Durrani, T., Hoffer, W., & Hoffer, M. (1995). *My feudal lord.* Random House.

Facio, A. (2013). *What is patriarchy?* (M. Solis, Trans.) International Women's Human Rights Institute. http://www.learnwhr.org/wp-content/uploads/D-Facio-What-is-Patriarchy.pdf

Faisal Elhussien, A., Mohammed, A., & Hassan Elhafyan, M. (2020). *Using pictures based activities in developing oral skills of basic school pupils.* http://repository.sustech.edu/handle/123456789/24868

Farooq, M. Y., & Tayyab, M. (2019). Impacts of psychological and domestic violence on women in Pakistan: Problems & solutions in the light of islamic teachings. *ĪQĀN, 1*(02), 1–16.

Franco, I. B., Meruane, P. S., & Derbyshire, E. (2020). SDG 5 Gender equality. In *Actioning the global goals for local impact* (pp. 69–83): Springer.

Gray, J. (2013). *Critical perspectives on language teaching materials*. Springer.

Grünenfelder, J. (2013). Discourses of gender identities and gender roles in Pakistan: Women and non-domestic work in political representations. *Women's Studies International Forum, 40*, 68–77. https://doi.org/10.1016/j.wsif.2013.05.007

Hadi, A. (2017). Patriarchy and gender-based violence in Pakistan. *European Journal of Social Science Education and Research, 4*(4), 297–304.

Hibbing, A. N., & Rankin-Erickson, J. L. (2003). A picture is worth a thousand words: Using visual images to improve comprehension for middle school struggling readers. *The Reading Teacher, 56*(8), 758–770.

Hunnicutt, G. (2009). Varieties of patriarchy and violence against women: Resurrecting "patriarchy" as a theoretical tool. *Violence against Women, 15*(5), 553–573.

Islam, K. M. M., & Asadullah, M. N. (2018). Gender stereotypes and education: A comparative content analysis of Malaysian, Indonesian, Pakistani and Bangladeshi school textbooks. *PLoS ONE, 13*(1), e0190807.

Ispahani, F. (2017). Pakistan's descent into religious intolerance [Essay]. *Current Trends in Islamist Ideology, 21*, 69.

Jabeen, S., & Ilyas, A. (2012). Gender role modelling in textbooks: Case study of Urdu textbooks of Sindh province. *Pakistan Journal of Women's Studies, 19*(1), 75–93.

Jat, A. R. L., Pathan, H., & Shah, S. W. A. (2018). Representation of national heroes in English language textbooks taught at government higher secondary schools of Sindh Pakistan. *Education and Linguistics Research, 4*(2), 25. https://doi.org/10.5296/elr.v4i2.13612

Javeed, A., Khan, M. Y., Rehman, M., & Khurshid, A. (2021). Tracking sustainable development goals–a case study of Pakistan. *Journal of Cultural Heritage Management and Sustainable Development*. https://doi.org/10.1108/JCHMSD-04-2020-0052

Jejeebhoy, S. J., & Sathar, Z. A. (2001). Women's autonomy in India and Pakistan: The influence of religion and region. *Population and Development Review, 27*(4), 687–712.

Khan, A. H., & Mahmood, N. (1997). Education in Pakistan: Fifty years of neglect [with Comments]. *The Pakistan Development Review, 36*(4), 647–667.

Kousar, R., & Brett, P. (2020). Citizenship education and gender in Pakistan teachers' and students' perspectives. *The Social Educator, 38*(2), 27–40.

Latif, A. (2009). A critical analysis of school enrollment and literacy rates of girls and women in Pakistan. *Educational Studies, 45*(5), 424–439. https://doi.org/10.1080/00131940903190477

Le, K., & Nguyen, M. (2021). How education empowers women in developing countries. *The BE Journal of Economic Analysis & Policy, 21*(2), 511–536.

Lohana, K., Alizai, S. H., & Ahmed, P. (2021). Gender equality as a sustainable development goal analytical study of gender issues in Pakistan. *Pakistan Journal of International Affairs, 4*(1). https://doi.org/10.52337/pjia.v4i1.161

Mahmood, Q. K., Jafree, S. R., & Qureshi, W. A. (2022). The psychometric validation of FCV19S in Urdu and socio-demographic association with fear in the people of the Khyber Pakhtunkhwa (KPK) Province in Pakistan. *International Journal of Mental Health and Addiction, 20*, 426–436. https://doi.org/10.1007/s11469-020-00371-4

Malik, A. A., & Aamir, M. (2017). Hurdles in women development in Pakistan. *Margalla Papers, 21*(1), 61–72.

Malik, H., & Marwah, S. (2021). Prospects of women empowerment under the pretext of Indonesia and Pakistan. *Indonesian Journal of Interdisciplinary Islamic Studies, 5*(1), 24–44. https://doi.org/10.20885/ijiis.vol5.iss1.art2

Malik, S., & Courtney, K. (2011). Higher education and women's empowerment in Pakistan. *Gender and Education, 23*(1), 29–45. https://doi.org/10.1080/09540251003674071

Mehmood, S., Chong, L., & Hussain, M. (2018). Females higher education in Pakistan: An analysis of socio-economic and cultural challenges. *Advances in Social Sciences Research Journal, 5*(6). https://doi.org/10.14738/assrj.56.4658

Michael, A. (2018). Realist-constructivism and the India-Pakistan conflict: A new theoretical approach for an old rivalry. *Asian Politics & Policy, 10*(1), 100–114.

Nasir, M. H. (2017). *Subscription or subversion: Gender representation in Pakistani television commercials.* Corpus ID: 197693205.

Niaz, U. (2003). Violence against women in South Asian countries. *Archives of Women's Mental Health, 6*(3), 173–184.

Pradhan, P., Costa, L., Rybski, D., Lucht, W., & Kropp, J. P. (2017). A systematic study of sustainable development goal (SDG) interactions. *Earth's Future, 5*(11), 1169–1179.

Predelli, L. N. (2004). Interpreting gender in Islam: A case study of immigrant Muslim women in Oslo. *Norway. Gender & Society, 18*(4), 473–493.

Qazi, M. H., & Shah, S. (2019). Discursive construction of Pakistan's national identity through curriculum textbook discourses in a Pakistani school in Dubai, the United Arab Emirates. *British Educational Research Journal, 45*(2), 275–297.

Qin, K. (2020). Curriculum as a discursive and performative space for subjectivity and learning: Understanding immigrant adolescents' language use in classroom discourse. *The Modern Language Journal, 104*(4), 842–859.

Qureshi, R., & Rarieya, J. F. (2007). *Gender and education in Pakistan.* Oxford University Press.

Ramírez, Á. (2015). Control over female 'Muslim' bodies: Culture, politics and dress code laws in some Muslim and non-Muslim countries. *Identities, 22*(6), 671–686.

Rana, A. (2016). Listen to this silence: Women in higher education in Pakistan. In B. Taylor (Ed.), *Listening to the voices: Multi-ethnicb women in education* (pp. 119–128). University of San Francisco.

Rashid, T. (2006). Radical Islamic movements: Gender construction in Jamaat-i-Islami and Tabligh-i-Jamaat in Pakistan. *Strategic Analysis, 30*(2), 354–376.

Rasool, G. R. (2007). Education in Pakistan: The key issues, problems and the new challenges. *IBT Journal of Business Studies, 3*(1).

Raza, A., & Sohaib Murad, H. (2010). Gender gap in Pakistan: A socio-demographic analysis. *International Journal of Social Economics, 37*(7), 541–557. https://doi.org/10.1108/030682 91011055478

Saeed, S. (2012). *Modeling Son Preference In Pakistan.* Doctoral dissertation, University of Texas. https://rc.library.uta.edu/uta-ir/handle/10106/11020

Sandborg, K. (2021). Malay dress symbolism. In T. Bleie, V. Broch-Due, & I. Rudie (Eds.), *Carved flesh/cast selves* (pp. 195–206). Routledge.

Shah, D. (2003). *Country report on decentralization in the education system of Pakistan: Policies and strategies.* Academy of Educational Planning and Management (Islamabad), Ministry of Education.

Shah, J. (2012). Zia-ul-Haque and the proliferation of religion in Pakistan. *International Journal of Business and Social Science, 3*(21), 310–323.

Shahnaz, A., Fatima, S. T., & Qadir, S. A. (2020). 'The myth that children can be anything they want': Gender construction in Pakistani children literature. *Journal of Gender Studies, 29*(4), 470–482.

Shaikh, F. (2018). *Making sense of Pakistan.* Oxford University Press.

Sharma, R. R., Chawla, S., & Karam, C. M. (2021). Global gender gap index: World economic forum perspective. In E. S. Ng, C. L. Stamper, A. Klarsfeld, & Y. J. Han (Eds.) *Handbook on diversity and inclusion indices.* Edward Elgar Publishing. https://doi.org/10.4337/978178897 5728.00017

Subrahmanian, R. (2005). Gender equality in education: Definitions and measurements. *International Journal of Educational Development, 25*(4), 395–407.

Sultana, A. (2010). Patriarchy and women's subordination: A theoretical analysis. *Arts Faculty Journal, 4*, 1–18. https://doi.org/10.3329/afj.v4i0.12929

Ullah, H., & Skelton, C. (2013). Gender representation in the public sector schools textbooks of Pakistan. *Educational Studies, 39*(2), 183–194.

ur Rahman, S., Chaudhry, I. S., & Farooq, F. (2018). Gender inequality in education and household poverty in Pakistan: A case of Multan District. *Review of Economics and Development Studies, 4*(1), 115–126.

Waqar, S., & Ghani, M. (2019). Gender exclusion in textbooks: A comparative study of female representation in provincial ELT textbooks of Pakistan. *International Journal of English Linguistics, 9*(5), 377–391.

Weedon, C. (1996). *Feminist practice & poststructuralist theory* (2nd ed.) Blackwell Publishers.

Winkvist, A., & Akhtar, H. Z. (2000). God should give daughters to rich families only: Attitudes towards childbearing among low-income women in Punjab. *Pakistan. Social Science & Medicine, 51*(1), 73–81.

Yasmin, M. (2021). Asymmetrical gendered crime reporting and its influence on readers: A case study of Pakistani English newspapers. *Heliyon, 7*(8), e07862.

Yilmaz, I., & Ahmed, Z. S. (2018). *Islam and Women Rights in Pakistan.* https://doi.org/10.2139/ssrn.3229025

Yunis, M. S., Hashim, H., & Anderson, A. R. (2019). Enablers and constraints of female entrepreneurship in Khyber Pukhtunkhawa, Pakistan: Institutional and feminist perspectives. *Sustainability, 11*(1), 27. https://doi.org/10.3390/su11010027

Zaman, M. Q. (2018). *Islam in Pakistan: A history.* Princeton University Press.

Chapter 13
A Trinidad and Tobago Case Study of One Response to the Equity Challenge in Education Within the Digital Era

Seeta Jaikaran-Doe, Ian Hay⬤, Andrew Fluck⬤, and David Moltow⬤

13.1 Introduction

Previous and contemporary Trinidad and Tobago leaders have recognised that to achieve sustainable economic and social development, a quality education system is essential (Kalloo et al., 2020; Oxford Business Review, 2020). A skilled and educated workforce is considered vital for the effective functioning of an economy, for wealth creation, and for the wellbeing of a country's citizenship (Ministry of Education [MoE], 2012; Warner et al., 2021). There is also an extensive body of accumulated evidence that testifies to the strong correlation between educational attainment and economic outcomes, both for the country as a whole and for individuals (Lange et al., 2018; Spring, 2008). In addition, countries that have a history of investing more of their resources into developing a quality education system, to enhance the "human capital" of its citizenship, over time were associated with greater economic and social developments within that country (Lange et al., 2018).

According to human capital theory (Coleman, 1988) an equity focussed investment into individuals expands their capabilities to make a positive long-term contribution to their own financial, psychological, and social wellbeing, and the wellbeing

S. Jaikaran-Doe · I. Hay (✉) · D. Moltow
School of Education, College of Arts, Law and Education, University of Tasmania, Churchill Ave, Hobart, TAS 7005, Australia
e-mail: Ian.Hay@utas.edu.au

D. Moltow
e-mail: David.Moltow@utas.edu.au

A. Fluck
School of Education, College of Arts, Law and Education, University of Tasmania, Launceston, TAS 7248, Australia
e-mail: Andrew.Fluck@utas.edu.au

© The Author(s), under exclusive license to Springer Nature Singapore Pte Ltd. 2023
K. Beasy et al. (eds.), *Education and the UN Sustainable Development Goals*, Education for Sustainability 7,
https://doi.org/10.1007/978-981-99-3802-5_13

of their community and country. This is particularly the situation for those individuals and groups who historically have had limited access and opportunities to participate in quality education, because of one or more of these factors; discrimination, poverty, oppression, gender, race, location, and social disadvantage (Aitken et al., 2018; Becker, 2009). For these individuals from marginalised groups, additional support and interventions represent enhanced equity, social justice, fairness, and opportunity (Freire, 2018, 2021). Paulo Freire (2018) emphasised that the effective economic and social advancement and development of a country must involve the participation of all its citizenship, including those individuals and groups historically marginalised. This case study of an education equity initiative acknowledges Freire's argument that to assist marginalised students to access and benefit from education, they need ongoing support and schooling that is useful and relevant to them, delivered by teachers who are knowledgeable, sympathetic, and responsive to their needs.

The target equity groups in this study were teachers and students in Trinidad and Tobago who have had limited access to and participation with information and communication technology (ICT) in their classrooms. Before focussing on this ICT education concern, it is important to place it in its historical and contemporary contexts. The government of Trinidad and Tobago is operating an educational system that was initially constructed during the time of British colonial rule that mirrored the British "home" curriculum and structures (Coates, 2012; Laurence, 1963). One of the challenges within the post-British colonialism context is improving and increasing the quality of education and teaching to all Trinidad and Tobago citizens, a challenge that increasingly finds resonance in the twenty-first-century technology era (Brissett, 2021). For Trinidad and Tobago to prosper, it needs more of its citizenship to participate and to operate within a global, digital, and e-connected world (Ministry of Public Administration, 2019; Roztocki et al., 2019). This chapter uses a case study methodology to investigate how Trinidad and Tobago teachers reacted to the government's equity initiative of providing free computers to students. Teachers were the focus of the data collection because quality education in Trinidad and Tobago is dependent on having qualified and competent teachers (Ministry of Education [MoE], 2010a, 2010b, 2017).

13.2   Understanding the Context of the Equity Challenge

Understanding why equity and the UNESCO SDGs of quality education (SDG4), reduced inequalities (SDG10), and sustainable development (SDG16) are important to Trinidad and Tobago requires some knowledge of its people, its resources, and its history. Trinidad and Tobago is a dual-island Caribbean nation near Venezuela, with Trinidad occupying 4,828 square kilometres and Tobago an area of 300 square kilometres. The official language is English, but there is an extant rich body of dialects originating from the multi-ethnic groups who settled in the country.

Historically and politically, the country has undergone many changes since Christopher Columbus landed in 1498, including the granting of its independence in 1962, and its transition to republic status in 1976. The country changed hands from the Spanish, to the French, then to the Dutch, and eventually to the British. To underpin its economy, African slaves were brought in to work on the sugar cane, cocoa, coffee, and cotton plantations. With the abolition of slavery in 1834 (Brereton, 2007), Indians, and a small number of Chinese, Syrians, and residents from the Middle East were brought to the island to provide labour for agriculture (Reddock, 1986).

With a population of 1.39 million people, Trinidad and Tobago has to date, one of the higher Gross National Incomes Per Capita (GNIPC) in Latin America and the Caribbean (World Bank, 2020a, 2020b), principally due to its petroleum and natural gas wealth. The distribution of this wealth across the society is, however, uneven, with some 20% of the Trinidad and Tobago population living well below the poverty line (United National Congress, 2010).

13.3 Equity Challenges and Education

The education system in Trinidad and Tobago has evolved from the British model. The four-tiered education system commences with pre-school (3–5 years of age), followed by primary (5–12 years of age), secondary (12–17/19 years of age), and finally tertiary levels (>17 years). Formal education in government schools is free from early childhood to an undergraduate degree. The Trinidad and Tobago Ministry of Education (MoE) oversees all public and private schools, which in 2017 included: 900 early childhood care and education (ECCE) institutions; 540 primary schools, of which 477 were public and 63 were private; around 190 secondary schools, with 134 public and 56 private; and 74 tertiary institutions (Oxford Business Review, 2020). University education is obtained from two universities, the University of the West Indies (UWI) and the University of Trinidad and Tobago (UTT). This is supplemented by a total of nine local and international private institutions, along with an established Technical Vocational Education and Training college structure.

As a result of the ethnic diversity within the country, school types consist of denominational, government, private, and international schools. Whereas denominational schools are under the management of a religious board (e.g., Hindu, Muslim, or Christian), government schools are managed by the MoE (Steinbach, 2012). Denominational schools receive government funds. Privately owned schools and international schools are independently financed and controlled by their own managerial boards. Whereas the government, denominational, and privately owned schools deliver the national curriculum, the international schools offer the curriculum from their home countries, such as Canada, USA, and England. Some denominational schools are single gender (either male or female students).

13.3.1   Equity Challenges and Youth

The Trinidad and Tobago policymakers have worked to achieve the UNESCO SDGs, but challenges remain. This is particularly so for the youth cohort aged 16–19 (International Labour Organisation [ILO], 2018; World Bank, 2013). Student attrition rates in the Trinidad and Tobago vocational and training sector are high, in some cases 20–25%. These attrition rates have been associated with an inability of teachers to provide relevant teaching and instruction at the students' levels of ability and interest (Mack & White, 2019). This is not to suggest that the Trinidad and Tobago governments have not been mindful of the need to support education and youth programmes. Based on 2020 data, education in Trinidad and Tobago received one of the largest allocations of funding from the national budget, at 14% (Oxford Business Group, 2020). Even so, youth unemployment in Trinidad and Tobago is twice as high as the total unemployment rate, especially for females 15–19 and youth from poor, rural, and ethnic minority communities (ILO, 2018). There are also elevated levels of under-employment, with more than 50% of youth and young adults estimated not to be in education, employment, or training (NEET) (Caribbean Development Bank, 2015). The concern is that employment insecurity has a direct and indirect negative influence on individuals' overall wellbeing, and that of their families and communities (Abbas & Raja, 2019).

Many of these youth employment problems can be linked back to educational concerns, poverty, and inequalities, such that only half of the high school students in Trinidad and Tobago sit for the end of high school Caribbean Secondary Examinations Certificate (CSEC) (MoE, 2021). Low levels of secondary school graduation are a concern because higher levels of secondary school graduation are associated with higher levels of economic and social development, due to higher rates of "human capital" within the citizenship (Allen et al., 2018; Hanushek & Woessmann, 2015). Thus, a significant portion of school leavers find themselves in low paid, casual employment with a limited future (United National Congress, 2010) and typically join the upwards to 60% of the Trinidad and Tobago workforce that is unskilled and in vulnerable and insecure employment (ILO, 2018). In addition, retaining boys in school to the completion of secondary education remains a challenge. For example, of the students who sat the end of high school (CSEC) 45% were males compared to 55% females. Of those who sat the exam, only 61% of males achieved a passing grade in the CSEC, compared to 69% of females (MoE, 2021).

13.4   Initiatives to Achieve Greater Equity in Education

To try to facilitate higher levels of secondary school graduation, the Trinidad and Tobago government has made ongoing initiatives and investments in education and schooling. As noted in the Trinidad and Tobago MoE (2017) planning documents, the purpose was to implement programmes and strategies aimed at providing a higher quality of education to more students, and to improve the skills and competencies of teachers. The objective was to work towards reducing educational inequalities and to enhance the access and participation of students from disadvantaged and marginalised backgrounds. The following summarises some key MoE initiatives (2010a, 2010b, 2017):

- No school fees for government schools.
- Free breakfast and lunch programmes in government schools.
- Books and related school resources provided at no cost to the family in government schools.
- Transportation to and from school provided at no cost to the family.
- Refocus the school curriculum to enhance all students' engagement with schooling and make it more future focussed.
- Improve the quality of teaching by enhancing teacher preparation programmes and providing more opportunities for teachers to reskill.

To address better the equity needs of students in the post-secondary education sector, the following initiatives were activated by the MoE (UNESCO, 2010).

- Develop a National Qualifications Framework (NQF) to facilitate greater horizontal and vertical student mobility and incorporate non-formal student learning experiences into the NQF.
- Improve the quality of teaching and student learning across the whole education sector.
- Develop additional post-secondary programmes that make graduates more employable.
- Accelerate the further development of alternative student learning systems, i.e., distance learning programmes.
- Develop and implement student capacity building initiatives.
- Encourage e-management and e-resources across the educational sector.

Thus, as part of the equity agenda and the need to skill more of its citizenship for a digital economy and world, the Trinidad and Tobago MoE has focussed on promoting ICT in schools. The following is a summary of some of these ICT initiatives (Government of the Republic of Trinidad and Tobago [GORTT], 2012; MoE, 2010a, 2010b; Mohammed, 2014).

- Promote high-speed internet services, dialup, broadband, and wireless hosting for businesses, residences, and schools.
- Promote ICT infrastructure upgrading across the country with a focus on rural areas to enhance access.
- Promote e-education across schools with free internet connections and computers.
- Offer teachers a four-year part-time ICT professional development course.
- Provide ICT services and e-resources to all students with a disability.
- Provide free personalised laptop computers to all students transitioning from primary schools to secondary schools.

13.5 Education as the Way Forward

The above initiatives have a strong focus on improving the quality of education by improving the quality of the teaching and teachers. There have been some positive developments within the country that can be traced back to these initiatives. Most noticeable, at the primary school level, the student enrolment rate has increased to 95% (MoE, 2017).

Even so, concerns remain about the quality of the teaching and often the lack of specific and relevant qualifications of teachers (Oxford Business Review, 2020; Warner et al., 2021). About 12% of Trinidad and Tobago primary school students fail the secondary entry examination (MoE, 2021), with concerns that students with learning difficulties and special needs are over-represented in this number. This along with high rates of youth unemployment, particularly from rural and disadvantaged communities (Caribbean Development Bank, 2015), has led to the recognition that additional resources are needed to address equity and educational concerns, especially at the start of secondary school education.

13.6 Equity and Technology

In terms of the Trinidad and Tobago equity initiatives, a core initiative was the eConnect and Learn program, to provide free personalised laptop computers to all students transitioning from primary schools to secondary schools (MoE, 2010a). The following section reports on the teachers' reactions to the equity initiative and their knowledge and teaching practices linked to this ICT initiative. The teacher surveys used in this case study were adapted from the relative literature related to teachers' Technological Knowledge (TK), and their Technological Pedagogical Content Knowledge (TPACK); see Jaikaran-Doe (2016) for additional information on these measures. The TK survey was an adaption of the Williams et al. (2000) survey investigating teachers' confidence and knowledge to use digital devices. The TPACK survey reported in this chapter was developed by Jamieson-Proctor et al. (2013) and has been shown to be a reliable and valid instrument.

TPACK surveys were introduced into the educational research field as a method for understanding teachers' knowledge for the integration of ICT into their teaching practices (Mishra & Koehler, 2009). The teacher surveys were conceptualised from Shulman's (1987) Pedagogical Content Knowledge (PCK) research. Shulman maintained that in addition to teachers' subject content knowledge, teachers also needed specific pedagogical knowledge about how to teach that content to their students. The TPACK teacher surveys aimed then to identify teachers' levels of understanding and knowledge of the different types and forms of ICT, along with when, how, and why teachers incorporated ICT into their teaching practices (Schmidt et al., 2009; Voogt et al., 2012). Thus, it provides a "snapshot" of how teachers were responding to the provision of free computers to their students, and the teachers' level of competencies in teaching with ICT.

13.7   Case Study of an Initiative to Enhance Equity

In total, 226 secondary school teachers from Trinidad and Tobago participated in the two teacher surveys involved in the evaluation of the eConnect and Learn initiative; 173 (77%) were full time teachers employed in 12 high schools and 53 (23%) were final year pre-service teachers. The ratio of female to male participants for full time teachers was 3:1, and the ratio for pre-service teachers was 4:1. Ethical permission to conduct the research was provided by the relevant university and school authorities. The first author administered the two teacher surveys at each school, and after this, entered the data into an SPSS (IBM, 2016) spreadsheet for statistical analysis. The findings of this analysis are reported below.

13.7.1   Technological Knowledge (TK) Survey

The pattern in the Technological Knowledge (TK) survey data is that "newer" teacher graduates, compared to "older" and more experienced full time teachers were more confident and knowledgeable about ICT devices (see Table 13.1). The full time teachers were more confident with devices of a more general nature, such as using word processing, spreadsheets, the world wide web, and multi-media devices, such as a camera. The Trinidad and Tobago full time teachers' confidence and knowledge dropped away when more specific classroom devices were considered. This reduction in confidence was associated with the use of white boards and video editing, and webpage construction and design. These last devices are often used in developed countries as part of their secondary school English and communication curriculum (Thomas & Thomas, 2022). The teachers also reported reduced confidence with Personal Computers (PCs), software programmes and devices, which are typically related to science, technology, engineering, and mathematics (STEM) education in high schools in developed countries (Banks & Barlex, 2020). This lack of teacher confidence with some devices and programmes in the survey is more of a reflection that when the survey was conducted, some programmes and devices, often used in developed countries were still unavailable in many of the Trinidad and Tobago schools.

13.7.2   Technological Pedagogical Content Knowledge (TPACK) Survey

Similar to the technology knowledge and confidence survey, "newer" pre-service teachers had a greater understanding of how ICT could be infused and incorporated into their teaching practices, compared to the full time teachers (see Table 13.2). The TPACK teaching practice survey used a 6-point scale, with "older" full time teachers

Table 13.1 Technological Knowledge and Confidence (TK) Survey: PS = pre-service, FT = full time teachers. Rating scale 1–6; 6 = highly confident, $N = 226$

How confident are you to use the following ICT devices?	Teacher	M	sd	t	P
Computer	PS	5.25	1.00	5.77	0.001
	FT	4.27	1.15		
World Wide Web	PS	5.25	1.04	5.58	0.001
	FT	4.21	1.22		
Multi-media devices	PS	5.13	1.00	7.02	0.001
	FT	3.78	1.28		
Word processing	PS	5.06	1.25	4.77	0.001
	FT	4.12	1.26		
Digital camera/document camera	PS	4.85	1.29	4.57	0.001
	FT	3.88	1.37		
Spreadsheet	PS	4.47	1.37	4.83	0.001
	FT	3.42	1.39		
Databases	PS	4.38	1.40	5.31	0.001
	FT	3.24	1.35		
Digital video for production and editing	PS	4.32	1.53	5.90	0.001
	FT	2.98	1.42		
Interactive whiteboard	PS	3.79	1.79	3.39	0.001
	FT	2.88	1.46		
Webpage design	PS	3.71	1.61	5.69	0.001
	FT	2.45	1.33		
PC provided software	PS	3.69	1.54	3.51	0.001
	FT	2.93	1.30		
Additional Installed PC software	PS	3.68	1.49	3.34	0.001
	FT	2.86	1.33		

typically scoring above the midpoint range of 3 (moderately confident). This pattern suggests that full time teachers were developing an appreciation of the worth and value of ICT to inform their teaching. The teachers recognised that software and ICT programmes had a role in students' engagement with learning and they gave a higher rating to teaching practices that related to students' developing an understanding of the world, by using the world wide web.

Table 13.2 TPACK survey: PS = pre-service, FT = full time teachers. Rating scale 1–6; 6 = highly confident, $N = 226$

How confident are you to use ICT to support your students' learning with ICT in the following?	Teachers	M	sd	t	p
To provide motivation for curriculum tasks	PS	3.14	0.77	2.58	0.011
	FT	2.79	0.88		
To develop competencies in your subject area/s	PS	4.40	0.98	5.14	0.001
	FT	3.62	0.96		
To actively construct knowledge that integrates curriculum areas	PS	4.32	0.98	5.50	0.001
	FT	3.44	1.02		
To actively construct their own knowledge in collaboration with their peers and others	PS	4.38	1.10	5.82	0.001
	FT	3.41	1.04		
To analyse their knowledge	PS	4.00	1.02	3.67	0.001
	FT	3.41	1.03		
To synthesise their knowledge	PS	3.96	1.02	3.55	0.001
	FT	3.38	1.05		
To demonstrate what they have learnt	PS	4.25	1.05	4.92	0.001
	FT	3.51	0.93		
To acquire the knowledge, skills, abilities, and attitudes to deal with ongoing technological change	PS	4.15	1.08	5.04	0.001
	FT	3.29	1.09		
To integrate different digital media to create appropriate projects	PS	4.72	0.97	7.62	0.001
	FT	3.45	1.07		

(continued)

Table 13.2 (continued)

How confident are you to use ICT to support your students' learning with ICT in the following?	Teachers	M	sd	t	p
To develop rich understanding about a topic of interest relevant to the curriculum area/s being studied	PS	4.40	0.88	6.11	0.001
	FT	3.45	1.01		
To engage in activities of the learning process	PS	4.70	0.95	7.27	0.001
	FT	3.56	1.00		
To develop understanding of the world	PS	4.52	0.96	6.39	0.001
	FT	3.48	1.05		
To plan and/or manage assigned curriculum projects	PS	4.21	1.07	5.08	0.001
	FT	3.37	1.06		
To engage in sustained involvement with curriculum activities	PS	4.02	0.95	4.18	0.001
	FT	3.32	1.09		
To undertake formative and/or summative assessment	PS	4.54	0.70	8.91	0.001
	FT	3.41	1.06		
To engage in independent learning through access to education at a time, place, and pace of their own choosing	PS	4.16	1.05	5.43	0.001
	FT	3.27	1.00		
To gain intercultural understanding	PS	4.53	0.85	7.60	0.001
	FT	3.33	1.05		
To acquire awareness of the global implications of ICT-based technologies on society	PS	4.33	0.99	6.50	0.001
	FT	3.23	1.08		
To communicate with others locally and globally	PS	4.64	1.09	6.46	0.001
	FT	3.55	1.07		

(continued)

Table 13.2 (continued)

How confident are you to use ICT to support your students' learning with ICT in the following?	Teachers		M	sd	t	p
To understand and participate in the changing knowledge economy	PS		4.15	1.06	5.62	0.001
	FT		3.22	1.05		
To critically evaluate their own and society's values	PS		4.11	1.01	5.53	0.001
	FT		3.18	1.09		
To facilitate the integration of curriculum areas to construct multidisciplinary knowledge	PS		3.91	0.97	4.27	0.001
	FT		3.18	1.12		
To critically interpret and evaluate the worth of ICT-based content for specific subject area/s	PS		4.00	1.04	5.00	0.001
	FT		3.12	1.14		
To gather information and communicate with a known audience	PS		4.68	1.01	7.34	0.001
	FT		3.41	1.13		

13.8   Implications of the Equity Initiative

The two ICT teacher surveys were highly correlated ($r = 0.77$). This implies that Trinidad and Tobago teachers' knowledge of and confidence with ICT devices influenced and informed the teachers' abilities to incorporate ICT into their pedagogical practices.

The two tables revealed that the "older" Trinidad and Tobago teachers were in transition, in terms of their knowledge of and confidence to use ICT in their teaching practices. Most of these teachers rated their knowledge and skills in the moderate range, around 3.5 on the 1–6 scale. In contrast, most of "newer" teacher graduates rated their knowledge and skills to use ICT in the confident range, around 4.5 on the 1–6 scale. These results suggest that both the "older" and the "newer" teachers were aware of what that they needed to understand now to incorporate digital resources into their teaching. The evidence is that as teachers become more knowledgeable and confident with their content and how to teach it, the more positive the educational outcomes are for their students (Callingham et al., 2019; McKlin et al., 2019). In addition, as teachers become more interested and motivated in using ICT in their teaching, this interest and motivation, in turn, typically transfers to their students (Hay et al., 2015). The surveys used in this study were originally developed for teachers in more developed ICT classrooms. Thus, the findings of this study suggest that, at the time of the data collection, in comparison to teachers in more developed countries, the Trinidad and Tobago teachers still lacked many classroom based digital resources and infrastructures. Providing free PCs to secondary students was a start, but based on the teacher survey findings, more digital resources and infrastructures were still required in Trinidad and Tobago classrooms and schools.

This case study supports the notion that when implementing new initiatives into schools, teachers also need to receive meaningful professional development, along with adequate and appropriate ongoing support and resources (Apple Classrooms for Tomorrow—Today, 2008; Hargreaves, 2005). The findings of the teacher surveys also reinforce the claim that effective education requires a multidimensional focus, because there are teacher factors, student factors, and factors external to the school that impact on students' educational process and achievement (Monie & Hay, 2019). The reality is, schooling is embedded within a complex social network involving a range of variables and a range of stakeholders who may operate from different political, cultural, social, historical, philosophical, and economic perspectives (Bronfenbrenner, 1989; Nikel & Lowe, 2010). Consequently, policies that are "top down" directives, such as providing free PCs to students without adequately considering the other stakeholders, means that the implementation is likely to be problematic (Carlyon & Branson, 2018; Hargreaves, 2005). As noted, in this case study the needs of the teachers were not adequately considered, with the teachers often having to peer learn and self-learn how to incorporate additional digital resources into their teaching. In addition, they had limited access to specific PC devices and software that may have assisted their students.

The strong interrelationship between teachers' knowledge and confidence of ICT devices and incorporating ICT devices into their teaching practices is evident in the high correlation between the two variables ($r = 0.77$). This interrelationship highlights that teachers need resources and support when new initiatives are being introduced into schools (Ball et al., 2008). As this study has demonstrated, as the teachers' knowledge of ICT devices increased, so too did their knowledge of how to incorporate ICT into their teaching and into their students' learning. Acquiring this pedagogical and content knowledge takes time, resources, and teacher engagement (Park et al., 2011). The evidence is, students' learning increases when their teachers have the content knowledge and can confidently manipulate and modify it, to accommodate the needs of all their students (Gess-Newsome et al., 2019; Hay et al., 2015).

13.9   Knowledge Is Cumulative

This chapter has used the implementation of one equity intervention in schools to illustrate that educational change is both possible and a challenge. As noted in this case study, teachers' capacity to change practices may be incremental and uneven, but engaging with change helped the teachers to understand the problem more and it helped them incorporate more ICT into their teaching. The evidence is, as a consequence of past experiences, acquired knowledge, and confidence with digital technology in the classroom, teachers become more able to use and extend their knowledge into the future (John & Wheeler, 2015). This assertion that teachers' digital knowledge is acquired, cumulative, and adaptable, is illustrated in how the Trinidad and Tobago teachers responded to the COVID-19 pandemic. George (2020) reported that at the start of the pandemic and school closures, some 60,000 Trinidad and Tobago students did not have access to either PCs or internet data in their homes, again reflecting issues of poverty, inequality, and the difficulties of providing a quality education to all Trinidad and Tobago students. Even so, teachers worked to provide digital learning to a greater number of their at-home students, through the use of a variety of ICT devices and PC software (George, 2020). These devices included PCs, mobile phones, and television, with the teachers developing skills and knowledge related to using online software programmes, such as Notes Master, the Big Blue Button (a Moodle platform), and Google Classroom (George, 2020; Kalloo et al., 2020).

The pandemic provided teachers with new challenges and opportunities to rethink their pedagogical practices and consequently transition into using more ICT devices in their teaching (UNESCO, 2020). It also suggests that although the Trinidad and Tobago equity initiative of providing free PCs to students had its limitations, it seems to have assisted many of the teachers to develop the confidence and skills to meet better the new challenge associate with COVID-19. This illustrates that developing teachers' confidence and capabilities in the domain of digital technology, assisted them to extend and apply it when new challenges arose. It also recognises that education interventions alone are unlikely to "cure" or to solve social and resource problems, particularly complex and entrenched social problems (Homel et al., 2001). Rather, interventions help to change the participants' trajectory from a downward spiral to a more positive trajectory, on a curve related to school achievement and social and economic wellbeing (Cranston et al., 2016; Farrington, 2005; Pallas, 2003). Equipping teachers and students with additional competences, support, and resources contributes to their development of protective and resilience factors, which in turn, help the teachers and students countenance and mitigate against risk factors, such as poverty and disadvantage at the individual, school, and community levels (Jaikaran-Doe et al., 2016; Mansfield et al., 2016; Tomaszewska-Pękała et al., 2020).

13.10 Limitations of This Equity Case Study

In terms of limitations, this case study research had a strong equity focus and hence it needs to be interpreted in the context of a developing country at a particular time with a particular set of economic and social challenges.

The teacher data were collected before the COVID-19 pandemic and although the results were reflective of this period, the teachers' knowledge and confidence with ICT may have changed since the start of COVID-19. On this point, Kalloo et al. (2020) identified that the Trinidad and Tobago teachers had, because of the pandemic become more confident with ICT devices and more knowledgeable of how to adapt and incorporate ICT into their teaching practices. A future research direction would be to conduct follow-up research, using the same or related surveys, to identify if and how the Trinidad and Tobago teachers' ICT knowledge and practices has altered since COVID-19.

Although the surveys selected in this research had context validity and strong psychometric properties (Jaikaran-Doe, 2016), other researchers using related survey measures may produce somewhat different results. An extension activity could be to consider comparing the findings based on the survey instruments used in this study, with more recent ones develop by Lázaro-Cantabrana et al. (2019) and Tondeur et al. (2017).

13.11 Reflecting on Change

Trinidad and Tobago has many challenges that pertain to enhancing participation and equity for its citizenship because of underlying inequality, poverty, and social disadvantage issues. Even so, it is working on the UNESCO SDGs of quality education (SDG4), reduced inequalities (SDG10), and sustainable development (SDG16), with an emphasis on digital and technology development. This focus is because in a contemporary digital society, being technologically literate is an essential skill for both work and personal use.

This chapter investigated the initiative of providing free PCs to first year Trinidad and Tobago high school students, from their teachers' perspective. This perspective was selected because the quality of students' learning is highly correlated with and dependent on the quality of the teachers' knowledge and ability to teach (Ball et al., 2008; Hargreaves, 2005). This free PC initiative was one of a range of initiatives aimed at providing greater equity and a more sustainable and quality education system within the country. The evidence from this case study research with teachers was that, compared with the "newer" graduates, the "older" teachers typically had less confidence and knowledge of ICT devices. This was, in part, because when the surveys were conducted the schools had limited PC software programmes and related devices provided to the schools. The teachers were, however, aware of their limitations and recognised that they needed more support and resources. They also understood the possibilities of incorporating more ICT into their classroom practices and assisting more of their students to connect to digital resources.

Reflecting on the study, the following are observations related to the challenges associated with implementing educational change in Trinidad and Tobago. Change is a complex process and in this study involved building capabilities and competences with different stakeholders. Change was uneven across the teacher cohort in this study, and in part, it was dependent on the teachers' prior knowledge, qualifications, and current settings. The PC intervention identified new challenges as it progressed. The target concern was identified to be nested within an array of related concerns and in this study many of these related concerns were connected to poverty and disadvantaged communities. Change that just involves providing physical resources (PCs to student) is thus considered less effective, compared to change that involves providing ongoing services and support, as well as physical resources to a range of stakeholders (Carlyon & Branson, 2018).

In this investigated initiative, policymakers gave less consideration to the teachers and to those students whose home settings were less able to support the PCs, because of a lack of internet connections and in some home's electricity. In this study, the intervention was more of a "top down" directive, and additional consultation with stakeholders may have assisted in the implementation of the intervention. This study also highlighted that the first step involved in enacting change involves recognising the full and extended problem and its contexts, then recognising who are the intended targets for the intervention, who is going to do the implementation, and how are they going to be supported over time.

As noted already, change is multidimensional and so one set of interventions is not expected to solve the fundamental social problems of poverty, particularly for students in disadvantaged communities. In this study the intervention contributed to teachers obtaining and accumulating new skills related to digital technology. In reality, change is less about "curing" the underlying problems, but rather, it is more about changing and moving the participants' long-term trajectory in a more positive direction (Farrington, 2005; Homel et al., 2001). This movement in trajectory was demonstrated when the teachers were more able to extend and adapt their digital and ICT knowledge when the country was faced with the COVID-19 pandemic. When considering the outcomes of any intervention, the danger is to expect too much too soon, and so ignore the latent effects associated with an intervention (Reynolds et al., 2001). In the Reynolds et al. study, many of the strongest latent effects of an education intervention for students from a disadvantaged community only became evident some 15 years after the intervention was finished.

This recognition that there are latent effects associated with an intervention is illustrated when reviewing how the teachers responded to the unexpected pandemic challenge. Providing free PCs to secondary school students required their teachers to begin the process of up-skilling their ICT competencies and so improving their confidence and knowledge with digital technology. The latent effect of their experiences with the free PC intervention better enabled the teachers to apply, adapt, and extend their acquired ICT skills, as they had to shift their teaching to an online digital framework, when schools closed because of the COVID-19 pandemic.

Achieving greater equity and a more sustainable quality education is an ongoing challenge for both developed and developing countries. Responding to that challenge requires educational policymakers to engage in a continuous process of reviewing, targeting, resourcing, implementing, and re-evaluating responses and adapting over time. For counties like Trinidad and Tobago, a quality education system is essential if it is going to achieve greater equity and more positive long-term social and economic trajectories for all its citizenship and the country.

Acknowledgements Dr. Peter Doe, University of Tasmania, contribution to the conceptualising of this chapter (Peter.Doe@utas.edu.au).

References

Abbas, M., & Raja, U. (2019). Challenge-hindrance stressors and job outcomes: The moderating role of conscientiousness. *Journal of Business and Psychology, 34*(2), 189–201. https://doi.org/10.1007/s10869-018-9535-z

Aitken, M., Shaw, M., Crowther, J., Martin, I., Ledwith, M., Hall, B. L., ... & Johnston, B. (2018). Special anniversary issue: Pedagogy of the oppressed. *Pedagogy, 54,* 64.

Allen, J. M., Wright, S., Cranston, N., Watson, J., Beswick, K., & Hay, I. (2018). Raising levels of school student engagement and retention in rural, regional and disadvantaged areas: Is it a lost cause? *International Journal of Inclusive Education, 22*(4), 409–425.

Apple Classrooms for Tomorrow—Today. (2008). *Apple classrooms of tomorrow—Today: Learning in the 21st century.* http://ali.apple.com/acot2/global/files/ACOT2_Background.pdf

Ball, D. L., Thames, M. H., & Phelps, G. (2008). Content knowledge for teaching: What makes it special? *Journal of Teacher Education, 59*(5), 389–407.

Banks, F., & Barlex, D. (2020). *Teaching STEM in the secondary school: Helping teachers meet the challenge.* Routledge.

Becker, G. S. (2009). *Human capital: A theoretical and empirical analysis, with special reference to education.* University of Chicago Press.

Brereton, B. (2007). *Emancipation in Trinidad and Tobago.* http://sta.uwi.edu/resources/speeches/2007/EMANC_LECT.pdf

Bronfenbrenner, U. (1989). Ecological systems theory. In R. Vasta (Ed.), *Six theories of development: Revised formulations and current issues* (pp. 187–249). JAI Press.

Brissett, N. (2021). A critical appraisal of education in the Caribbean and its evolution from colonial origins to twenty-first century responses. *Oxford Research Encyclopedia of Education.* https://doi.org/10.1093/acrefore/9780190264093.013.1650

Callingham, R., Oates., G., & Hay, I. (2019). Mathematics teachers' work: Identifying what teachers do and how they do it. *The Australian Mathematics Education Journal, 1*(3), 4–8.

Caribbean Development Bank. (2015). *Youth are the future: The imperative of youth employment for sustainable development in the Caribbean.* https://www.caribank.org/publications-and-resources/resource-library/thematic-papers/study-youth-are-future-imperative-youth-employment-sustainable-development-caribbean

Carlyon, T., & Branson, C. (2018). Educational change: A view from the bottom up. *New Zealand Journal of Teachers' Work, 15*(2), 105–123.

Coates, C. O. (2012). Educational developments in the British West Indies: A historical overview. *Bulgarian Comparative Education Society.* ERIC No. ED567093.

Coleman, J. S. (1988). Social capital in the creation of human capital. *American Journal of Sociology, 94,* S95–S120.

Cranston, N. C., Watson, J. M., Allen, J. M., Wright, S. E., Hay, I., Beswick, K., Smith, C., Roberts, W., & Kameniar, B. (2016). Overcoming the challenge of keeping young people in education: A wicked problem with the implication for leadership policy, and practice. *Leading and Managing, 22,* 1–18.

Farrington, D. P. (2005). Conclusions about developmental and life-course theories. In D. P. Farrington (Ed.), *Integrated developmental and life-course theories of offending.* Advances in criminological theory (Vol. 14, pp. 247–256). Transaction Press.

Freire, P. (2018). *Pedagogy of the oppressed.* Bloomsbury Publishing.

Freire, P. (2021). *Pedagogy of hope: Reliving pedagogy of the oppressed.* Bloomsbury Publishing.

George, K. (2020, June 1). TTUTA Tobago: Learning platforms ineffective. *Newsday.* https://newsday.co.tt/2020/06/01/ttuta-tobago-learning-platforms-ineffective/

Gess-Newsome, J., Taylor, J. A., Carlson, J., Gardner, A. L., Wilson C. D., &. Stuhlsatz, M. A. (2019). Teacher pedagogical content knowledge, practice, and student achievement. *International Journal of Science Education, 41*(7), 944–963. https://doi.org/10.1080/09500693.2016.1265158

Government of the Republic of Trinidad and Tobago. (2012, January 5). *Education sector strategic plan: 2011–2015.* Approved by Cabinet Minute No. 38. Ministry of Education, Trinidad and Tobago. https://planipolis.iiep.unesco.org/sites/default/files/ressources/trinidad_and_tobago_strategic_plan_2011-2015.pdf

Hargreaves, A. (2005). Pushing the boundaries of educational change. In A. Hargreaves (Ed.), *Extending educational change: International handbook of educational change* (pp. 1–14). Kluwer Academic Publishers.

Hanushek, E. A., & Woessmann, L. (2015). Universal basic skills: What countries stand to gain. *Organisation for Economic Co-Operation and Development Publishing.* https://doi.org/10.1787/9789264234833-en

Hay, I., Callingham, R., & Carmichael, C. (2015). Interest, self-efficacy, and academic achievement in a statistics lesson. In K. A. Renninger, M. Nieswandt, & S. Hidi (Eds.), *Interest in mathematics and science learning and related activity* (pp. 173–188). American Educational Research Association.

Homel, R., Elias, G., & Hay, I. (2001). Developmental prevention in a disadvantaged community. In R. Eckersley, J. Dixon, & R. Douglas (Eds.), *The social origins of health and wellbeing: From the planetary to the molecular* (pp. 269–279). Cambridge University.

IBM. (2016). *IBM SPSS statistics for windows.* Version 24.0. IBM Corp.

International Labour Organisation. (2018). *Mapping of youth employment intervention in Caribbean countries.* https://www.ilo.org/wcmsp5/groups/public/---americas/---ro-lima/---sro-port_of_spain/documents/publication/wcms_632706.pdf

Jaikaran-Doe, S. (2016). *Teachers' confidence with technology and perceptions of the impact of a student laptop computer program in Trinidad and Tobago.* [Unpublished doctoral dissertation], University of Tasmania. https://eprints.utas.edu.au/22927/

Jaikaran-Doe, S., Fluck, A., & Hay, I. (2016). *Exploring teachers' confidence to integrate technology in Trinidad and Tobago.* [Referred paper presentation]. Australian Association for Research in Education Conference. http://ecite.utas.edu.au/113101

Jamieson-Proctor, R., Albion, P., Finger, G., Cavanagh, R., Fitzgerald, R., Bond, T., & Grimbeek, P. (2013). Development of the TTF TPACK Survey Instrument. *Australian Educational Computing, 27*(3), 26–35.

John, P., & Wheeler, S. (2015). *The digital classroom: Harnessing technology for the future of learning and teaching.* David Fulton Publishers.

Kalloo, R. C., Mitchell, B., & Kamalodeen, V. J. (2020). Responding to the COVID-19 pandemic in Trinidad and Tobago: Challenges and opportunities for teacher education. *Journal of Education for Teaching, 46*(4), 452–462.

Lange, G. M., Wodon, Q., & Carey, K. (Eds.) (2018). *The changing wealth of nations 2018: Building a sustainable future.* World Bank Publications.

Laurence, K. O. (1963). Colonialism in Trinidad and Tobago. *Caribbean Quarterly, 9*(3), 44–56.

Lázaro-Cantabrana, J., Usart-Rodríguez, M., & Gisbert-Cervera, M. (2019). Assessing teacher digital competence: The construction of an instrument for measuring the knowledge of pre-service teachers. *Journal of New Approaches in Educational Research, 8*(1), 73–78.

Mack, A. J., & White, D. (2019). Challenges affecting technical vocational education and training in Trinidad and Tobago: Stakeholders' perspective. *Journal of Technical Education and Training, 11*(3). https://publisher.uthm.edu.my/ojs/index.php/JTET/article/view/4080

Mansfield, C. F., Beltman, S., Broadley, T., & Weatherby-Fell, N. (2016). Building resilience in teacher education: An evidenced informed framework. *Teaching and Teacher Education, 54*, 77–87. https://doi.org/10.1016/j.tate.2015.11.016

McKlin, T., Lee, T., Wanzer, D., Magerko, B., Edwards, D., Grossman, S., ... & Freeman, J. (2019, July). Accounting for pedagogical content knowledge in a theory of change analysis. *Proceedings of the 2019 ACM conference on international computing education research* (pp. 157–165). https://doi.org/10.1145/3291279.3339412

Ministry of Education, Trinidad and Tobago. (2010a). *E-connect and learn programme policy: Trinidad and Tobago.* http://moe.edu.tt/laptop_info/eConnect_and_Learn_Policy.pdf

Ministry of Education, Trinidad and Tobago. (2010b). *Education @ Work: E-connect and learn takes off.* https://paperless11blog.files.wordpress.com/2012/01/eaw_issue201.

Ministry of Education, Trinidad and Tobago (2012). *Education sector strategic plan: 2011–2015.* https://planipolis.iiep.unesco.org/sites/default/files/ressources/trinidad_and_tobago_strategic_plan_2011-2015.pdf

Ministry of Education, Trinidad and Tobago. (2017). *Draft education policy paper 2017–2022.* https://trinihomeschooling.files.wordpress.com/2018/10/Abridged-Education-Policy-Paper-2017-2022-final.pdf

Ministry of Education, Trinidad and Tobago. (2021). *Trinidad and Tobago student performance at CSEC and CAPE 2021.* https://www.moe.gov.tt/news-release-230921-3-2-2-2-2/

Ministry of Public Administration, Trinidad and Tobago. (2019). *ICT Blueprint: National ICT plan 2018–2022.* https://data.gov.tt/dataset/ict-blueprint-national-ict-plan-2018-2022

Mishra, P., & Koehler, J. M. (2009). Introducing technological pedagogical content knowledge. *Contemporary Issues in Technology and Teacher Education, 9*(1), 60–70.

Mohammed, S. (2014, February 2). ICT centre launched. *Trinidad and Tobago Express.* http://www.i-policy.org/2014/02/ict-centrelaunched-in-penal.html

Monie, K. B., & Hay, I. (2019). Secondary school and beyond. In A. Ashman (Ed.), *Education for inclusion and diversity* (6th ed., pp. 365–399). Pearson Australia.

Nikel, J., & Lowe, J. (2010). Talking of fabric: A multi-dimensional model of quality in education. *Compare, 40*(5), 589–605.

Oxford Business Group. (2020). *Diversification and high-value exports encourage sustainable economic growth in Trinidad and Tobago.* https://oxfordbusinessgroup.com/overview/road-recovery-diversification-and-emphasis-high-value-exports-encourage-sustainable-economic-growth

Oxford Business Review. (2015). *Overview: Trinidad and Tobago's education system: Multi-faceted and well-funded.* https://oxfordbusinessgroup.com/overview/trinidad-and-tobagos-edu cation-system-multi-faceted-and-well-funded

Oxford Business Review. (2020). *Skills gap creates a need for educational diversification in Trinidad and Tobago.* https://oxfordbusinessgroup.com/overview/sustainability-challenge-rapid-expans ion-creates-need-diversification-higher-levels

Pallas, A. M. (2003). Educational transitions, trajectories, and pathways. In J. T. Mortimer & M. J. Shanahan (Eds.), *Handbook of the life course* (pp. 165–184). Kluwer Academic/Plenum Publishers.

Park, S., Jang, J. Y., Chen, Y. C., & Jung, J. (2011). Is Pedagogical content knowledge (PCK) necessary for reformed science teaching? Evidence from an empirical study. *Research in Science Education, 41*(2), 245–260. https://doi.org/10.1007/s11165-009-9163-8

Reddock, R. (1986). Indian woman and indentureship in Trinidad and Tobago, 1845–1917: Freedom denied. *Caribbean Quarterly, 32*(3), 27–49. https://doi.org/10.1080/00086495.1986.11671699

Reynolds, A. J., Temple, J. A., Robertson, D. L., & Mann, E. A. (2001). Long-term effects of an early childhood intervention on educational achievement and juvenile arrest: A 15-year follow-up of low-income children in public schools. *Journal of the American Medical Association, 285*(18), 2339–2346.

Roztocki, N., Soja, P., & Weistroffer, H. R. (2019). The role of information and communication technologies in socioeconomic development: Towards a multi-dimensional framework. *Information Technology for Development, 25*(2), 171–183. https://doi.org/10.1080/02681102.2019. 1596654

Schmidt, D. A., Baran, E., Thompson, A. D., Mishra, P., Koehler, M. J., & Shin, T. S. (2009). Technological pedagogical content knowledge (TPACK). *Journal of Research on Technology in Education, 42*(2), 123–149. https://doi.org/10.1080/15391523.2009.10782544

Spring, J. (2008). Research on globalization and education. *Review of Educational Research, 78*, 330–363.

Steinbach, M. (2012). Obstacles to change in teacher education in Trinidad and Tobago. *The International Education Journal: Comparative Perspectives, 11*(1), 69–81.

Shulman, L. (1987). Knowledge and teaching: Foundations of the new reform. *Harvard Educational Review, 57*, 1–22.

Thomas, D., & Thomas, A. (Eds.) (2022). *Teaching and learning primary English.* Oxford University Press.

Tomaszewska-Pękała, H., Marchlik, P., & Wrona, A. (2020). Reversing the trajectory of school disengagement? Lessons from the analysis of Warsaw youth's educational trajectories. *European Educational Research Journal, 19*(5), 445–462. https://doi.org/10.1177/1474904119868866

Tondeur, J., Aesaert, K., Pynoo, B., van Braak, J., Fraeyman, N., & Erstad, O. (2017). Developing a validated instrument to measure preservice teachers' ICT competencies: Meeting the demands of the 21st century. *British Journal of Educational Technology, 48*(2), 462–472.

United National Congress. (2010). *Prosperity for all: Manifesto of the people's partnership for a united people to achieve sustainable development for Trinidad and Tobago.* http://www.trinid adandtobagonews.com/articles/UNC-manifesto-2010.pdf

United Nations Educational, Scientific and Cultural Organization. (2010). *Trinidad and Tobago: Policy on tertiary education, Technical Vocational Education and Training and lifelong learning.* UNESCO Institute for Lifelong Learning. https://uil.unesco.org/document/trinidad-and-tobago-policy-tertiary-education-technical-vocational-education-and-training

United Nations Educational, Scientific and Cultural Organization. (2015). *Sustainable development goals (SDGs).* https://en.unesclosco.org/sustainabledevelopmentgoals

United Nations Educational, Scientific and Cultural Organization. UNESCO Educational Sector (2020, April). *Distance learning strategies in response to COVID-19 school closures.* UNESCO COVID-19 Education Response, Education Sector Issue Note n 2.1. https://unesdoc.unesco.org/ark:/48223/pf0000373305

Voogt, J., Fisser, P., Pareja, N., Tondeur, J., & van Braak, J. (2012). Technological pedagogical content knowledge (TPACK): A review of the literature. *Journal of Computer Assisted Learning, 29*(2), 109–121.

Warner, S. C., Malik, M. A., & Mohammed, J. H. (2021). ICT professional development workshops and classroom implementation challenges: Perceptions of secondary school teachers in Trinidad and Tobago. *International Journal of Innovation in Teaching and Learning, 7*(1), 1–19.

Williams, D., Coles, L., Wilson, K., Richardson, A., & Tuson, J. (2000). Teachers and ICT: Current use and future needs. *British Journal of Educational Technology, 31*(4), 307–320. https://doi.org/10.1111/1447-8535.00164

World Bank. (2013). *How to improve quality of education in the Caribbean for the next generation?* https://www.worldbank.org/en/news/feature

World Bank. (2020a). *Trinidad and Tobago overview.* https://www.worldbank.org/en/country/trinidadandtobago/overview#1

World Bank. (2020b). *Economy profile of Trinidad and Tobago. Doing business 2020b.* https://openknowledge.worldbank.org/handle/10986/32845. License: CC BY 3.0 IGO.

Part III
SDG Implementation and Assessment in University Systems

Chapter 14
Designing for a Better World: Learning Systemic Design for the Sustainable Development Goals

John Fien

14.1 Introduction

"Sustainable Development Goals (SDGs): Real-World Strategies and Solutions" is a core course in the Master of Disaster, Design and Development (MoDDD) degree at RMIT University in Australia as well as a university wide masters level elective. MoDDD differs from traditional degrees in disaster management in several ways. Two are relevant in the context of this chapter. The first is a focus on development, through which students investigate critiques of the processes of maldevelopment such as inequality, poverty, and land degradation that turn extreme environmental events, such as cyclones or earthquakes, into disasters (e.g., see Kelman, 2020; Tierney, 2014, 2019). The focus on development also involves student exploration of the desirable ends of recovery and rebuilding after disasters, such as alignment with the kind of world envisaged in the SDGs. The second is a focus on design, especially the development of skills in using systemic design as a strategy for dealing with the complexity and uncertainties of disaster risk management. Hence, the inclusion of "Sustainable Development Goals (SDGs): Real-World Strategies and Solutions" as a core course in the MoDDD programme.

Designers have a particular responsibility in helping to deliver the SDGs because they turn people's visions and aspirations into tangible landscapes, homes, products, and services. This reflects the definition of design as a process for "changing existing situations into preferred ones" (Simon, 1996, p. 111). Designing for a "better world" is thus the translation of the SDGs into a world of sustainable living and sustainable livelihoods. However, achieving any of the targets in the SDGs is the sort of wicked problem that cannot be addressed through traditional linear problem-solving

J. Fien (✉)
School of Architecture and Urban Design, RMIT University, 240 La Trobe Street, Melbourne, VIC 3182, Australia
e-mail: john.fien@rmit.edu.au

© The Author(s), under exclusive license to Springer Nature Singapore Pte Ltd. 2023   245
K. Beasy et al. (eds.), *Education and the UN Sustainable Development Goals*, Education for Sustainability 7,
https://doi.org/10.1007/978-981-99-3802-5_14

methods (Bron & Bron, 2018). Rather, given the complexity and uncertainties of all sustainability challenges, an understanding of systemic processes and the creative skills of design thinkers are needed. Linking systems thinking and design thinking is a process known as "systemic design."

This chapter outlines how skills for systemic design are taught in "Sustainable Development Goals (SDGs): Real-World Strategies and Solutions," outlining the rationale and scope of studies in the course and the nature of the learning experiences provided. It also provides examples of the work produced by students and explores the outcomes and challenges of teaching for a better world through systemic design.

The course is taught wholly online through the Canvas learning platform with student learning supported by weekly webinars that provide course guidance, the review of key concepts, and presentations by, and discussions with, guest speakers working in the SDG space. The course begins with students completing an online university micro-credential titled "Sustainability 101" to ensure all students have a common starting point in an understanding of the integrated social, economic, environmental, cultural, and political dimensions of sustainability, and how attitudes towards sustainability are influenced by different worldviews and cultural practices. From there, the course is divided into three parts. These are, firstly, an introduction to the SDGs; secondly, the development skills in systems thinking, design thinking, and systemic design; and thirdly, the application of these skills in planning a way of attaining one or more SDG targets.

14.2 Part 1: An Introduction to the Sustainable Development Goals (SDGs)

The first part of the course involves a series of written mini-lectures, videos, readings, and guest speakers that introduce the SDGs; their origins are in the Millennium Development Goals and publication of *The Future We Want* (United Nations General Assembly [UNGA], 2012); planetary boundaries and "doughnut economics" (Raworth, 2017); the scope of the 17 goals, 169 targets, and 232 indicators; progress towards the targets and goals; short case studies of organisations using the SDGs in their planning; and the SDGs in action at RMIT University. Developing this basic understanding of the SDGs could make for a dull, didactic approach to teaching and learning. Instead, students process the online resources through five workshop exercises that require them to apply the provided materials and develop arguments to support their opinions of key issues. The five exercises are presented in a workbook that contains choices from alternative activities and modes or genres of reporting, and that may be completed individually or in small [need to define] ITC-supported teams. The five exercises include the following:

1. Completion of a second RMIT micro-credential on "Sustainable Change" that develops skills in change management for integrating the SDGs in an organisation.

2. Writing a blog debating Stephen Pinker's arguments about how conditions in the world have never been as good as they are now and, therefore, why we need or really do not need the SDGs (Pinker, 2018a, 2018b).
3. Writing a film review of the UN-produced movie, *Urgent Solutions for Urgent Times* (UN, 2020).
4. Producing a mini-Pecha Kucha (an iMovie based upon 10 slides × 20s narration each) on the relevance of the SDGs to students' chosen or anticipated professions.
5. Writing a review of the "SDGs in Action" app, which was developed through a partnership between the telecommunications industry and an NGO to share news of SDG action projects from around the world (see https://sdgsinaction.com/).

Students post their reports, blogs, reviews, and Pecha Kuchas on the Canvas site for the course for all members of the class to see—and to provide each other feedback and to discuss and debate the views expressed. The text in Fig. 14.1 is taken from a discussion among Catherine, Steven, and Rosa (not their real names) regarding Steven's review of the "SDGs in Action" app. The dialogue illustrates the interactivity and level of engagement the workshop and exercise workbook approach to learning is able to engender.

14.3 Part 2: Developing Tools and Skill Sets for Systemic Design

The second part of the course seeks to develop student familiarity with some of the processes and problem-solving tools used in systemic design for working on the kinds of problems that the SDGs seek to address: in effect, developing the skills that will be required to complete the SDG challenge project in the third part of the course. This section briefly outlines the rationale for including these skill sets in the course and their significance in addressing the "wickedness" of the challenges posed by seeking to attain the SDGs.

Many of the problems that the SDGs are addressing are what are known as wicked problems. These are the sorts of problems that are difficult to solve because there is no one right answer, people's opinions and values are often in conflict, and today's solutions are very often tomorrow's new problem. Examples of such problems include:

- How can we solve global poverty (SDG1)?
- How can we end discrimination against women and girls everywhere (SDG5)?
- How can cities become sustainable (SDG11)?
- How do we overcome opposition to actions that reduce carbon emissions (SDG13)?

These are very *broad* concerns but, even if we *localise* them, they remain very difficult to address. For example:

- How can low-income families in Sydney get access to affordable homes (**SDG1**)?

Catherine

Hi Steven,

Thank you for your post. You did an excellent job providing an overview of the app and its purpose. You really explained the merits of the app and I felt encouraged to use it after reading your post. Was there anything about the app that you particularly felt could be improved?

Reply to Comment (4 likes)

Steven

Hi Catherine

Thank you for your response.

Perhaps the content could be better as some of it was quite a bit old.

Once everything loads it is easy to use.

I like the tab with the goals, targets under each one. It is simple and good information.

Reply to Comment (2 likes)

Rosa

Hi Steven,

Thank you for such an uplifting perspective on the app! Our views are polar opposites, but your introduction to the app in your blog is exactly what I feel is missing. Using an atavar to personify the positive impact one can create by taking on an Action is a strong motivator.

I agree, it is a great resource although it does not inspire me to take this particular form of 'Action'. I am doubtful that it encourages people to act and as a result misses a chance to operationalise the SDGs through a bottom-up approach at the individual and community levels.

Reply to Comment (7 likes)

Fig. 14.1 Student online discussion of a review of the "SDGs in Action" app

- Levels of domestic violence, more likely to be perpetrated against women, always increase in a crisis, e.g., after a natural disaster or during the COVID-19 pandemic. How should local organisations prepare to prevent this from recurring in future crises (**SDG5**)?
- How can flooding from storm surges around the Elwood canals in Melbourne be prevented (**SDG11**)?
- How can we shield low-income families from the increased energy prices that come by using smart metres that increase electricity costs during peak-demand periods (SDG13)?

If, as argued in the Introduction to this chapter, design is a process for "changing existing situations into preferred ones," why is it seen as preferable to analytical ones?

Fig. 14.2 The integration of systems thinking and design thinking in systemic design (Allen, n.d.)

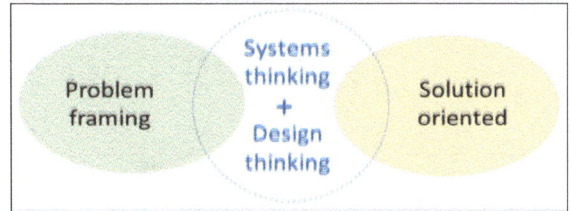

The proposition underlying the case for systemic design is that wicked problems reflect the complexity of relationships within and across these types of problems and their interconnected nature with other problems. For example, poverty is linked with education, nutrition with poverty, the economy with nutrition, and so on. Yet these SDG challenges—poverty, sustainability, equality, health, and discrimination—cannot be solved by scientific reasoning or experimentation alone. These are important skills for *framing* problems but, by themselves, are not sufficient for *resolving* them. The scientific method requires a tightly defined problem and a search for the single correct solution. However, neither of these—a tightly defined problem or a single correct solution—is possible with a wicked problem. Indeed, working out how to address a wicked problem is a wicked problem in itself! This is where systemic design—as a process for both *framing* problems (through systems thinking) and *resolving* them (through design thinking)—is important to the SDGs (cf. Fig. 14.2).

14.4 Systems Thinking

In learning about systemic design, students in the course are first introduced to systems thinking and associated tools. This is done through exploring the ideas of Donella Meadows (1992, 2008) and Leila Acaroglu (2017). The key idea taken from Meadows relates to her concept of leverage points. Although her seminal work in this area identified twelve levels for systemic interventions, students focus on the simplified version she depicted in her "iceberg model" (Fig. 14.3), which shows that change agents are more effective if they focus on the values and beliefs that underpin systemic structures and processes than if they seek to address only everyday events and patterns of behaviour. This means focussing on the root causes of problems rather than their visible "symptoms."

This is then related to Daniel Kim's (1994/2000) argument that the points of intervention reflect four levels of understanding problems (Fig. 14.4):

1. Shared visionsWhat are the stated or unstated visions that generate structures and systems?
2. Systemic structure What are the mental models that create the patterns?
3. Patterns of events   What are the trends or patterns of events that seem to be occurring?
4. Events   What is the fastest way to respond to this event NOW?

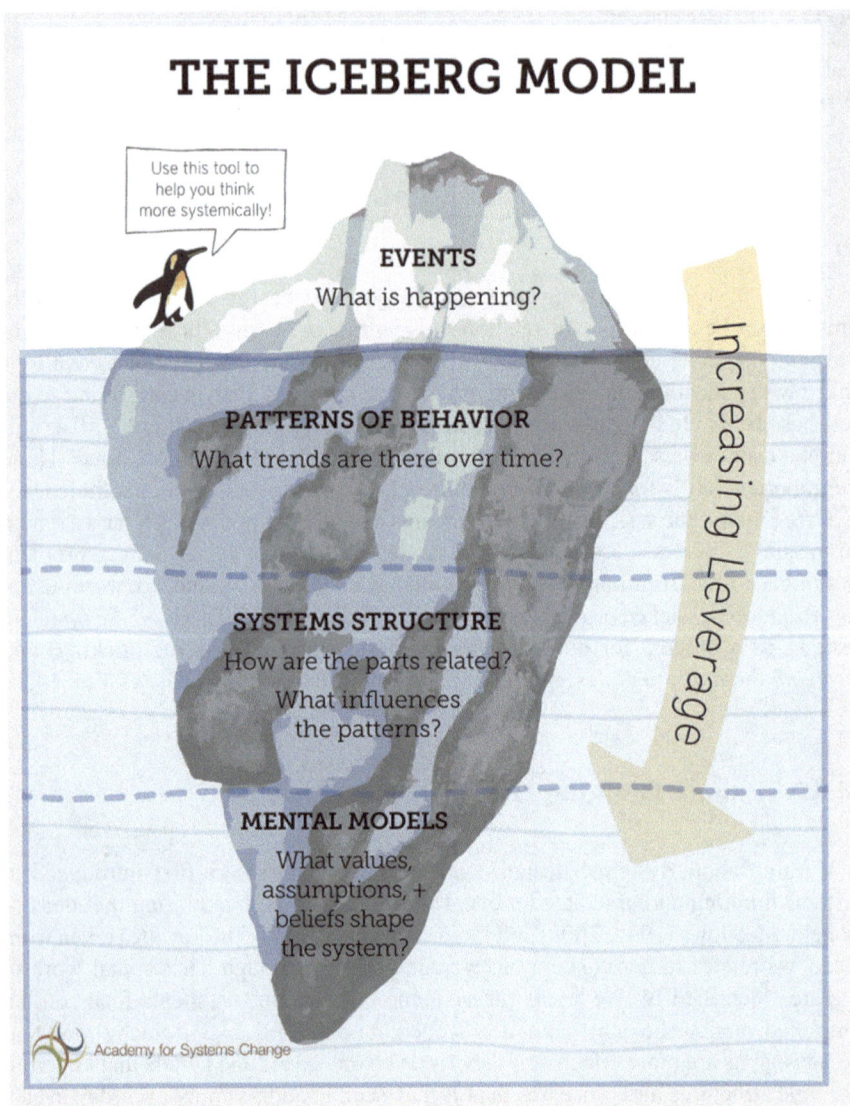

Fig. 14.3 Donella Meadows' Iceberg model of leverage points for sustainability (Meadows, 1992)

Students develop their understanding of these ideas through two case studies related to Target 4 of SDG2, Zero Hunger: one about the ineffectiveness of using pesticides alone to counter agricultural pests rather than the systems-based approaches of integrated pest management, and the other about the Reimagined Futures project in Catalonia, which developed a locally based sustainable food system (see https://www.reimaginedfutures.org/). Students are asked to use Acaroglu's six basic concepts

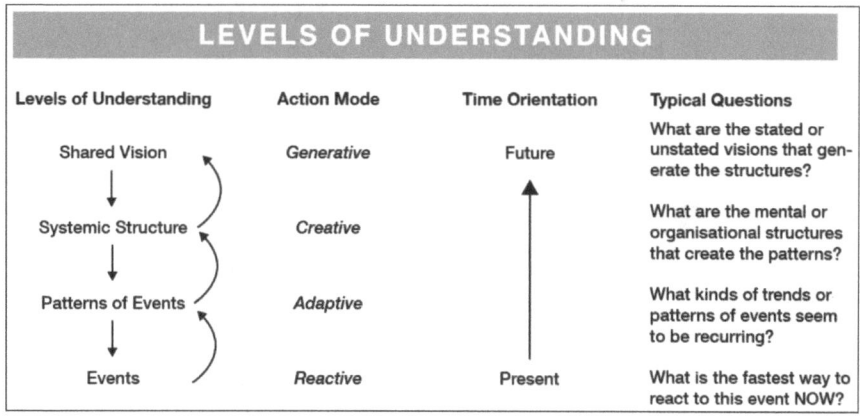

Fig. 14.4 Four levels of understanding and, therefore, framing a problem (Klim, 1994/2000)

in systems thinking (interconnectedness, synthesis, emergence, feedback loops, causality, and systems mapping) to analyse the case studies—and also to identify different approaches to systems mapping that are used in the case studies, such as the iceberg model, behaviour-over-time graphs, and causal loop diagrams (Acaroglu, 2017). Students who wish to develop a deeper understanding of systems thinking are referred to the readings and online courses at Acaroglu's *UNSCHOOL Disruptive Design* programme (see www.disruptdesign.co/disrupt-home).

14.5 Design Thinking

The second part of systemic design is design thinking. Design thinking has become popular in many activities, from industrial and service design to leadership and organisational change. In contrast to the linear, input-process-outcome thinking of "rationalist" approaches to problem solving, design thinking involves sequences of observation (to understand the needs of users through their participation and collaboration), rapid concept prototyping and testing, design, assessing, and refining of preliminary solutions, and then full project implementation and evaluation.

Design thinking was popularised in the 1990s by David M. Kelley and Tim Brown, the founders of IDEO Design Company, who described it as a designing methodology for solving problems and fulfilling human needs (Brown, 2008). They divided the design thinking process into several stages:

1. Empathise < – > 2. Define < – > 3. Ideate < – > 4. Prototype < – > 5. Testing

Importantly, these stages are **not** linear, and each stage can be done multiple times, with the multiple iterations aiming continuously to improve the design solution. The five stages of design thinking and their iterative nature are shown in Fig. 14.5.

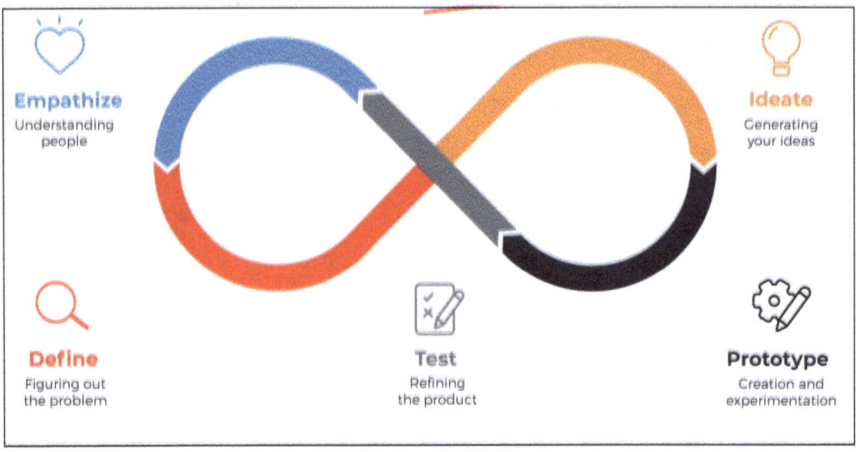

Fig. 14.5 The five iterative stages of design thinking (MAQE, 2020)

Students analyse a case study related to Target 11.5 of SDG11 on sustainable cities and communities. Target 11.5 is:

> By 2030, significantly reduce the number of deaths and the number of people affected and substantially decrease the direct economic losses relative to global gross domestic product caused by disasters, including water-related disasters, with a focus on protecting the poor and people in vulnerable situations. (UN Department of Economic and Social Affairs, n.d.)

Students first read a short article on "how design thinking can help beat a crisis" (Tregloan, 2020), applying it to a case study of the use of design thinking to develop an app (called CaredJP) after the "triple disaster" of earthquake, tsunami, and consequent nuclear meltdown that occurred in Japan on March 11, 2011 (Hanif, 2020). The CaredJP app provides localised disaster reports, helps people find family and friends, and communicates with disaster management authorities. Students are asked to analyse what was done in each of the five design thinking phases, the iterations, and which stage/s they believed to have been most successful. Most identified the importance of empathy to see the needs and problems from the perspective of local people, and iterations between prototyping, testing, and back to empathising.

14.6 Systemic Design

With this appreciation of the value of design thinking, the course then helps students develop skill in integrating it with systems thinking, i.e., to begin to practise systemic design. The Design Council in the United Kingdom has been proactive in promoting systemic design and has developed a key tool for this called the Double Diamond technique (Design Council, 2019, 2020). Rather than five stages as in the IDEO

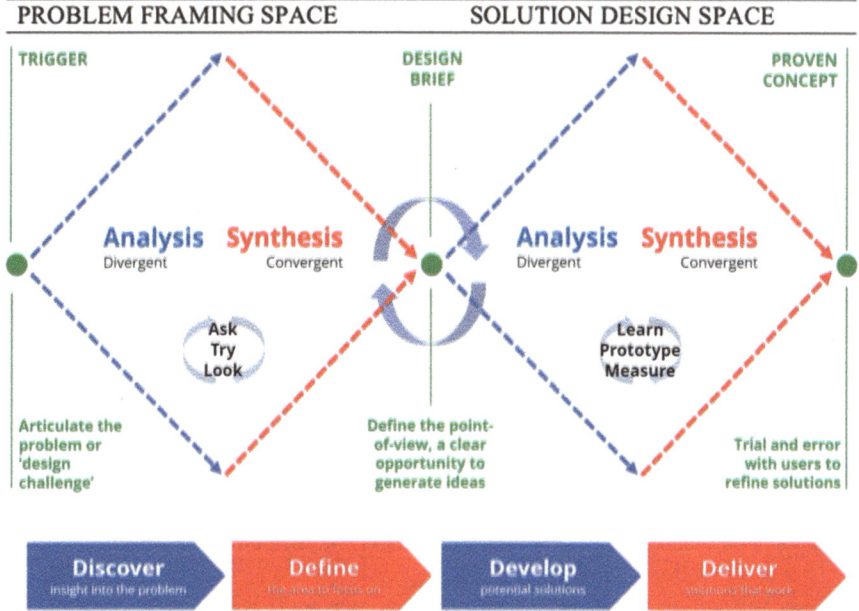

Fig. 14.6 The double diamond technique (Adapted from Eklund, 2021, after Design Council, 2019)

model, the Double Diamond technique has four: Discover, Define, Develop and Deliver, as in Fig. 14.6.

The Double Diamond technique sees the design process as comprising a problem framing space for systems analysis (Diamond 1) and a solution space for design thinking (Diamond 2). The problem framing space is where the problem can be broken into its systemic elements, relationships, drivers, and impacts so that it can be defined clearly (Discover and Define) whereas the solution space is where designs are generated, visualised, and prototyped and tested prior to delivery (Develop and Deliver). As Fig. 14.6 is complex, the course materials encourage students to read it from the bottom–up, and ask them to think critically about it, for example:

- Start at the bottom with the four "D Stages": Discover, Define, Develop and Deliver. *How do these relate to the IDEO model?*
- There is a trigger and then two milestones in the four "D Stages" (the brief and the proven concept). *What happens at each of these?*
- The Double Diamond sits between these three milestones. Each of the diamonds has a divergent (analysis) and a convergent (synthesis) phase. *What does this mean and why is it important?*
- The three iteration "cyclones" emphasise the non-linear or iterative nature of the Double Diamond tool. *Why does the Design Brief sit as the middle cyclone?*

The course materials then start to steer students to the major project in the course. This is to select a problem of concern to people in their neighbourhoods and to identify an SDG and Target relevant to addressing the problem. The assignment then asks them to use the Double Diamond technique, or other systemic design tools such as the Systemic Design Toolkit (Jones & van Ael, 2022), to develop a strategy that could contribute to addressing the problem.

To prepare for this project, students analyse a case study of the way the Madrid bus system was revitalised using the Double Diamond technique (Gimenez, 2018). Target 11.2 of SDG11 on Sustainable Cities and Communities calls for improved "access to safe, affordable, accessible and sustainable transport systems for all, improving road safety, notably by expanding public transport, with special attention to the needs of those in vulnerable situations, women, children, persons with disabilities and older persons." Madrid had a fleet of 2,000 buses that ran over 200 different bus routes (totalling 3,000 km in length) and over 10,000 stops. Yet, surveys showed that many passengers were disappointed with the bus service and passenger numbers were declining for many years. The Double Diamond technique was used to address the problem. From street interviews, an online survey, and desk research, it was found that:

- Older people used the bus most often, usually out of habit or because they lived close to a bus stop.
- Buses were often overcrowded, and standing was a serious problem for most.
- It was difficult to exit from the back of the bus in the short time the busses were stationary at a stop.
- The Metro was the most used mode of public transport method because it was fast, and passengers could always get a seat and felt safe using it.

Following this discovery stage, the problem was defined as a faulty design of the seating and the placement of doors. A range of prototype designs was developed, and additional passenger consultations were undertaken. The revised designs were then tested until there was consensus among the passengers, designers, and bus service managers and staff. The new bus designs resulted in 25% more seats than in the old busses even though 12 seats were made 10% larger than regular seats and there was more space between seats. Passenger numbers began to increase. The part of the case study that the students have often found most helpful was a statement by the designer-consultant that the systemic design process is a flexible one.

> It did help us to start with a clear structure, but something important to remark is that you might be willing to adapt the strategy to your own point of view and use or re-adapt what suits you the most for every individual project. And that is totally okay, because there is no rule that has to be obeyed. As long as you empathize with the user, [and] apply the strategy that you found is helpful for you! (Gimenez, 2018)

Students always take a lot of confidence from this statement.

14.7 Part 3: SDG Challenge Projects

A great many schools, colleges, universities, businesses, and community organisations host an SDG Challenge for their students, members, and local communities. Some are competitions between organisations, while others seek partnerships between educational institutions and local businesses. Some are even international in scope and require participants to work in cross-national teams. Some emphasise the competition aspect, offering significant prizes, while others use recognition, certificates, and support to continue the challenge projects. What all have in common, however, is encouragement for people, especially university students, to take action towards achieving targets for one or more of the SDGs and to write reports or visual presentations on their project. All such efforts are very commendable and have resulted in significant contributions to the sustainability of many communities, businesses, and ecosystems.

We had originally planned for our course, "Sustainable Development Goals (SDGs): Real-World Strategies and Solutions," to include such an SDG Challenge project. However, we found a number of barriers to this. For example, we thought of allotting half the semester to these projects, but discussions with students indicated that this would be insufficient time for them to do impactful projects, especially as most are working full-time and have busy family lives and responsibilities. Also, the course first started during the COVID-19 pandemic and, with students spread across most Australian states—and with several working overseas—the significant differences in lockdown restrictions would have made assessment based upon the potential projects unfair for many.

We resolved the dilemma in the first offering of the course by asking students to use systemic design just to *plan* a project rather than plan and implement one, and the plans that were produced for addressing various SDG-related problems were excellent; in particular, in relation to being able to explain the relevance of SDG Targets to issues of local concern, empathise and work with local interest groups to scope the root causes and impacts of problems, and develop skills in integrating different approaches to systems mapping and design thinking in the problem framing and solution design spaces of the Double Diamond. Some students found the Double Diamond approach limiting and decided to adopt the more open approach of the Systemic Design Toolkit (Jones & van Ael, 2022). Others criticised the exercise because it put too much effort on planning and not enough on *doing*, reporting that the step-by-step nature of the systemic design process did not take account of the value of intuition in problem solving or their personal stakes in particular issues or outcomes from their research. However, these students were reassured by Gimenez's (2018) advice (above) that it is important to "adapt the strategy" and that this "is totally okay, because there is no rule that has to be obeyed." Among the SDG Challenge reports that were developed were plans for addressing almost all of the SDGs. Table 14.1 provides a flavour of the projects that were planned by illustrating the SDG challenges, research questions, SDG targets, and the systemic design tools in student projects in 2020–2021.

Table 14.1 Sample SDG challenge questions and targets and systemic design tools for student projects, 2020–2021

SDG challenge question	SDG target	Systemic design tools employed[a]
How can the relatively high rates of substance use and subsequent disproportionate contact with the criminal justice system by Australian Indigenous communities be reduced?	3.5	Causal loop diagram Influence diagram Jones and van Ael's systemic design toolkit (7 steps)
How can my university ensure that low socioeconomic (SES) student enrolment numbers at universities in Melbourne reach population parity (25%)?	4.3	Causal loop diagram Stakeholder mapping Probable vs. preferable futures Backcasting
How can sustainability education be implemented in schools and ensured to all the children in Switzerland?	4.7	Causal loop diagram Structure-behaviour pairing Jones and van Ael's systemic design toolkit (7 steps)
How can governments and communities stop child marriage so that children can live the lives they deserve?	5.3	Meadow's iceberg diagram Causal loop diagram Backcasting
How can farm waste be used to produce renewable, reliable, and affordable energy for rural farmers at Henderson, Solomon Islands?	7.2	Stakeholder mapping Influence diagram Double Diamond
How can small businesses be supported to develop resilience to continue operating following disasters in South Australia?	8.3	Cause and effect diagram Actor mapping Community visioning Backcasting
How can the financial industry leverage their products and services to create a more climate resilient built environment for Australian cities?	9.3	Causal loop diagram Stakeholder mapping Jones and van Ael's systemic design toolkit (7 steps)
How could the precinct structure plan for the Melbourne Eastfield Regeneration Project be designed on "20-min Neighbourhood" principles?	11.6	If–then diagram Program logic Strategic planning
How can the occurrence of illegal dumping (fly-tipping) be decreased to improve waste management systems in the boroughs of Greater London?	11.6	Drifting goals diagram Behaviour-over-time graph Graphical function diagram Double Diamond
How can integrating "Cities Fighting Diabetes" principles for the Eastfield Regeneration Project contribute to health and wellbeing in the region?	11.8	Stakeholder mapping Causal loop diagram Double Diamond

(continued)

Table 14.1 (continued)

SDG challenge question	SDG target	Systemic design tools employed[a]
How can fashion designers and retailers encourage consumers to purchase sustainable fashion products?	12.6	Stakeholder mapping Probable vs. preferable futures Backcasting
What can alternatives to incarceration can be promoted for young offenders from rural and remote settlements in Australia?	16.2	Causal loop diagram Stakeholder mapping Double Diamond

[a]Definitions and strategies for using these systems thinking, design thinking, and systemic design tools may be found at: Acarolglu (2017), CoLab (2016), Design Council (2019), FSG (2017), Jones and van Ael (2022), Kim (1994, 2000), Namahm, MaRS and Shiftn (2021)

14.8 Conclusion

The course, "Sustainable Development Goals (SDGs): Real-World Strategies and Solutions," is now in its fourth iteration and continuing to draw students in strong numbers. Its offering as a wholly online course was attractive to students during the COVID-19 years but word has spread among students about its self-paced nature, assignment workbook approach, and weekly webinars with experts on the SDGs from government, business, and NGO agencies, as well as its focus on systemic design as a problem framing and design solutions process. Hence, our hope is that the course will continue to provide students with opportunities to develop systems analysis and design thinking skills to use in their current and prospective careers, and to find ways of reorienting their workplaces and careers around the UN Sustainable Development Goals.

References

Acarolglu, L. (2017). *Tools for systems thinkers: The 6 fundamental concepts of systems thinking.* https://medium.com/disruptive-design/tools-for-systems-thinkers-the-6-fundamental-concepts-of-systems-thinking-379cdac3dc6a

Allen, W. (n.d.). *Systemic co-design.* https://learningforsustainability.net/systemic-design/

Bron, K., & Bron, P. (2018). Sustainability: A wicked problem needing new perspectives. In H. Borland, A. Lindgreen, F. Maon, V. Ambrosini, B. Palacios Florencio, & J. Vanhamme (Eds.), *Business strategies for sustainability* (pp. 1–18). Routledge.

Brown, T. (2008). *Change by design.* Harper Business.

CoLab. (2016). *Follow the rabbit: A field guide to systemic design.* https://oecd-opsi.org/toolkits/follow-the-rabbit-a-field-guide-to-systemic-design/

Design Council. (2019). *Framework for innovation: Design Council's evolved double diamond.* https://www.designcouncil.org.uk/our-work/skills-learning/tools-frameworks/framework-for-innovation-design-councils-evolved-double-diamond/

Design Council. (2020). *System-shifting design: An evolving practice explored.* www.designcouncil.org.uk/fileadmin/uploads/dc/Documents/Systemic%2520Design%2520Report.pdf

Eklund, A. (2021). *Common words and phrases of design thinking.* https://andyeklund.com/com mon-words-phrases-design-thinking/

FSG. (2017). *Systems thinking toolkit: Putting systems thinking into practice in your organization.* https://www.fsg.org/resource/systems-thinking-toolkit-0/

Gimenez, M. (2018). *Double-diamond strategy for Madrid´s public citybus.* https://uxdesign.cc/double-diamond-strategy-for-madrid-s-public-citybus-e73b0a0374d8

Hanif, D. (2020, April 28). Design thinking in disaster management: A case study on CaredJP. *Medium.* https://medium.com/learning-with-prodev/design-thinking-in-disaster-man agement-a-case-study-on-caredjp-cd67c1d5ece

Jones, S., & van Ael, K. (2022). *Design journeys through complex systems: Practice tools for systemic design.* BIS Publishers.

Kelman, I. (2020). *Disaster by choice: How our actions turn natural hazards into catastrophes.* Oxford University Press.

Kim, D. (2000). *Systems think tools: A user's reference guide.* Pegasus Communications (Original work published 1994).

MAQE. (2020). *The design thinking process: How does it work?* www.maqe.com/insight/the-des ign-thinking-process-how-does-it-work/

Meadows, D. (1992). *Leverage points: Places to intervene in a system.* http://donellameadows.org/archives/leverage-points-places-to-intervene-in-a-system/

Meadows, D. (2008). *Thinking in systems: A primer.* Chelsea Green Publishing.

Namahm, MaRS, & ShiftN. (2021). *Systemic design toolkit.* https://www.systemicdesigntoolkit.org/

Pinker, S. (2018a). *Enlightenment now: The case for reason, science, humanism, and progress.* Viking.

Pinker, S. (2018b). *Is the world getting better or worse? A look at the numbers.* https://www.ted.com/talks/steven_pinker_is_the_world_getting_better_or_worse_a_look_at_the_numbers/tra nscript

Raworth, K. (2017). *Doughnut economics: Seven ways to think like a 21st century economist.* Random House Business.

Simon, H. (1996). *The sciences of the artificial* (3rd ed.). MIT Press.

Tierney, K. (2014). *The social roots of risk, producing disasters, promoting resilience.* Stanford University Press.

Tierney, K. (2019). *Disasters.* Polity Press.

Tregloan, K. (2020). *How design thinking can help beat a crisis.* www.unimelb.edu.au/professio nal-development/insights/society/design-thinking-beat-crisis

United Nations. (2020). *Urgent solutions for urgent times.* https://www.youtube.com/watch?v=xVWHuJOmaEk

United Nations Department of Economic and Social Affairs. (n.d.). *Goal 11: Make cities and human settlements inclusive, safe, resilient and sustainable.* https://sdgs.un.org/goals/goal11

United Nations General Assembly. (2012). *The future we want.* Resolution 66/288. https://digitalli brary.un.org/record/731519?ln=en

Chapter 15
From Climate Literacy to Climate Policy: Interrogating a University's Role as a Climate Change Thought Leader

Gabi Mocatta and Rebecca Harris

15.1 Introduction

The impact of a university's activities has traditionally been assessed using metrics such as the number of publications by its researchers and citations of their work. However, such simple measures offer a limited understanding of a university's true impact on society. Activities beyond research, including learning, teaching, operationalisation of research findings, and other outreach and engagement activities must also be taken into account to gain a more holistic understanding of a university's effectiveness. This may be particularly so in relation to a university's work on climate change: an area in which rapid action on the ground is needed both for adaptation and mitigation initiatives.

This chapter investigates how a university's work in this *holistic* sense can engage with, and influence its surrounding community on the issue of climate change. We draw on Sustainable Development Goals (SDGs) SDG4 and SDG13 (United Nations Department of Economic and Social Affairs) to discuss how a university can both deliver lifelong learning opportunities (SDG4), and spread the knowledge needed at all levels of society to catalyse urgent action on climate change (SDG13). In doing this, we outline ways in which a university can be a climate change thought leader: motivating and enabling climate action, and establishing itself as a trusted information source on the science and solutions of climate change.

G. Mocatta (✉) · R. Harris
Climate Futures, School of Geography, Planning and Spatial Sciences, College of Sciences and Engineering, University of Tasmania, Private Bag 76, Hobart, TAS 7001, Australia
e-mail: gabi.mocatta@utas.edu.au

G. Mocatta
School of Communication and Creative Arts, Deakin University, 221 Burwood Highway, Burwood, VIC 3125, Australia
e-mail: gabi.mocatta@deakin.edu.au

© The Author(s), under exclusive license to Springer Nature Singapore Pte Ltd. 2023   259
K. Beasy et al. (eds.), *Education and the UN Sustainable Development Goals*, Education for Sustainability 7,
https://doi.org/10.1007/978-981-99-3802-5_15

To interrogate the role and the potential possibilities for higher education institutions in climate change thought leadership, we use as a case study the University of Tasmania, a medium-sized university and the only higher education institution in Australia's southern island state, which has a population of 558,000 (ABS, 2022). This regional university has an identified strategy to be impact-focused and orientated towards *place*: that is, concerned with the ways it can both serve and positively influence its surrounding community, offering education that responds closely to its unique location. The University of Tasmania is also a globally recognised centre for climate science, climate modelling, Antarctic research, oceanographic research and climate change impacts, and adaptation research. It is also an emerging global centre of climate literacy education. In recognition of this climate focus, the university is home to several lead authors for the Intergovernmental Panel on Climate Change, and has won many climate-related accolades, including being ranked first in the world in the 2022 and 2023 Times Higher Education impact rankings for "climate action."

In this chapter, using the University of Tasmania as a case in point, we investigate what a university's impact and influence on climate change within its community can look like. We argue that to promote necessary action on climate change at all levels of a community, universities must firstly understand community climate literacy, and then actively work to enhance it. Universities must also seek to bring the research findings of fundamental climate science and climate solutions to the attention of policymakers in a way that enhances their climate decision-making. We also discuss here what a university's "community" actually means, in the current un-emplacing context of digital learning. We note that, though until recently, a university's community was genuinely place-based, today, online study extends this community nationally and even globally. We consider, therefore, how a university can be a thought leader on climate change, both in its immediate geographical location, and more broadly.

In the sections below, we appraise the current literature on climate literacy and climate thought leadership, and then we lay out our three cases of university climate thought leadership—two of which are locally emplaced, and one that allows the university to extend such leadership, via online learning, more broadly. In the final section, we offer a brief framework for university climate leadership that responds to both SDG4 and SDG13, and tends to enabling societal knowledge of climate change in the broadest sense, with the aim of contributing towards meaningful climate action.

15.2   Climate Literacy and Thought Leadership

A climate-literate public has been identified as an essential prerequisite for taking effective action on climate change (Tobler et al., 2012; United Nations Educational, Scientific and Cultural Organization [UNESCO], 2022). Basic comprehension of climate science, as well as the impacts of and solutions to climate change, can empower ordinary citizens and policymakers to contribute to the urgent task of acting on climate. It is essential, if we are to address climate change with the urgency and commitment now required on a global scale, that citizens at all levels of society have adequate climate literacy. The United Nations' SDGs explicitly acknowledge this, linking education and sustainability in SDG7.4, and education and climate action in SDG13.3.

Climate literacy has been defined as: "an understanding of your influence on climate and climate's influence on you and society" (United States Global Change Research Program [USGCRP], 2009, p. 4). Differently described, it is also the set of competencies necessary "to understand how climate change happens, its impacts, and relevant mitigation approaches" (UNESCO, 2022). Azevedo and Marques (2017) have offered a systematic review of climate literacy, and a model to describe this area of research, engagement, and educational practice. As an overall synthesis of the field, their review of 22 papers in the subject area established that to be climate literate, a person must have competencies in three areas, including: "knowledge of climate science, the ability to access and assess relevant information on climate change," and to "communicate it in a meaningful way". A climate-literate person should also possess a set of attitudes that lead to "conception and/or implementation of adaptation and mitigation strategies" (Azevedo & Marques, 2017, p. 9).

Educating for climate literacy accordingly commonly seeks to ensure that learners understand basic climate science, that individuals and organisations have the knowledge to make informed decisions, and that this results in behaviour change to reduce anthropogenic influence on the climate (Johnston, 2020). Formal education in school and higher education can be a setting for such climate learning, as can media coverage of climate change—the source of climate information for many (Newman et al., 2020). Understanding the basic science of climate and the social responses now urgently needed also requires information, media, and technological literacies. This is especially so in the digital age, where mediatised misinformation on climate has become prevalent, especially in online discourse. However acquired, climate literacy, backed up by information competencies, is arguably an essential skill for *everyone*, from top-level policymakers right through to individual householders. To ensure a safer climate, each has a role to play.

With the accelerating imperative to take action on climate change has come a surge of research interest in public climate literacy. Research has sought to describe in what sense the public needs to understand climate change (for example, Bord et al., 2000); it has also tried to establish the extent of existing public climate knowledges (Dupigny-Giroux, 2008), and the challenges and barriers to enhancing public understanding of climate change (Dupigny-Giroux, 2010; Lorenzoni et al., 2007). Other research has investigated the most useful ways to address public misconceptions on climate change (for example, McCaffrey & Buhr, 2008), and to "inoculate" people against climate misinformation (van der Linden et al., 2017). Different studies have sought to establish the efficacy of community-based climate literacy initiatives (Schapiro Ledley et al., 2014). Climate literacy research has likewise investigated public understanding of energy production and consumption (McCaffrey, 2015). Crucially, climate literacy research has established that a good understanding of the climate problem is important for engendering climate concern (for example, Guy et al., 2014; Stoutenborough & Vedlitz, 2014), although ideology also has a strong influence on people's objective levels of climate literacy (see, for example, Bedford, 2016).

Despite these detailed and extensive efforts in both describing and *prescribing* climate literacy as a crucial intervention in efforts to promote climate action, there has been limited research examining the role that universities as institutions can play as thought leaders in their communities on climate change literacy and action. The bulk of related research is focused on curriculum content for students. Molthan-Hill et al. (2019), for example, have examined the disparate ways that universities currently introduce climate change into their curricula, arguing that addressing climate change should be mainstream and transdisciplinary at universities. Cooper et al. (2019) examined climate change courses in particular and found these to be relatively limited to teaching climate science, neglecting a "broader array of inter-disciplinary topics, place-based information, communication strategies, and mitigation and adaptation solutions to bridge the gap between climate science, literacy, and action" (p. 102). Leal Filho et al. (2018) have suggested changing approaches to research, outreach, and teaching at universities to better support education for sustainability and promote climate action. They found that a transformation of higher education curricula was needed to promote sustainability, and that, if enacted, this could develop the "transformative potential of students as agents of a sustainable future". They also found that by fostering sustainability learning, universities could serve as "models of social justice and environmental stewardship" (p. 286). Such university leadership would allow these institutions to maximise their potential climate impact "outside the campus walls and beyond the end of formal university study" (Molthan-Hill & Blaj-Ward, 2022).

It is in this context that we examine how a university can make efforts to gauge what its community already knows about climate change, and how it might evaluate its own impact on its community in this sphere. We also discuss how a university can be a thought leader in working with its students and with external stakeholders, to promote climate literacy and action. We then appraise pathways that a university can follow to guide government policy, leading climate "thinking" and decision-making. Finally, we offer a framework for cross-disciplinary university climate leadership that responds to both SDG4 and SDG13, with the aim of contributing towards meaningful climate action.

15.3 Measuring a University's Societal Impact

In this first case under examination, we describe a study undertaken by the University of Tasmania (UTAS) and the Dutch publishing and analytics company, Elsevier. In 2020, UTAS and Elsevier partnered in the study, *Measuring Societal Impact: Climate Change in Tasmania*. The objective of this study was to design a conceptual framework for understanding a university's impact on society that could be extended to research in almost any sphere. Tasmania, with its single university and research strength in climate change, was chosen as the case study context. The study sought to understand how research on climate was translated, understood, and implemented in the university's immediate, place-based community. UTAS researchers (including this chapter's authors) partnered with Elsevier to co-design the study. The global research consultancy and polling firm, Ipsos, was engaged to conduct public surveys and stakeholder interviews, working with the UTAS and Elsevier teams to develop the content and approach. Here, we present baseline community understanding of climate change, and results that best demonstrate the university's impact on climate literacy, as well as data on community expectations around university climate action leadership.

In this study, impact of UTAS research and teaching was assessed in two ways. Firstly, a public survey ($n = 575$) gauged the Tasmanian community's climate knowledge. Then the survey delved into awareness of the university's climate-related activities, and to what extent participants expected the university to contribute to solving the problem of climate change. Survey participants were recruited from Ipsos' research Access Panels, consisting of population-representative individuals who have volunteered to take part in market research surveys (Elsevier/Ipsos 2020). Secondly, semi-structured interviews ($n = 25$) were deployed to identify the views of key stakeholders who use the knowledge the university generates to inform climate change adaptation and responses. Interview participants included emergency service workers, local business/industry representatives, and those in local and state government climate decision-making positions. Interviews identified participants' views on climate change in general, their perceptions of the university's role in influencing climate response, and the actual societal impact of the university. The data generated will form the baseline for longitudinal measurement, to understand change over time in UTAS' impact on climate change adaptation and literacy within the state of Tasmania.

The findings from the Ipsos public survey showed that the Tasmanian public feels well informed about climate change (72%) (Fig. 15.1), and those who feel more informed are more likely to see it as an urgent issue (77% of the informed, compared to 22% uninformed). Level of education had a significant influence on concern. Those with a university-level qualification were more likely to feel very or fairly well informed and concerned (81%), compared with those with a lower education level (vocational college, 68%, and Year 10 school level-usually obtained at around 16 years old-at 60%). This is consistent with global findings in this regard, where high levels of climate concern and calls for action were found to be strongly associated with having a post-secondary education (Flynn et al., 2021).

When climate change was ranked against other issues, however, respondents expressed less concern about a changing climate. Economic, employment, and housing worries exceeded concern about the environment and climate change in the survey, with 60% ranking environment and only 55% ranking climate change as urgent or very urgent in comparison with other issues. This may have been influenced by the timing of the survey in May 2020 at the height of the first wave of the COVID-19 pandemic: a time—when especially in Tasmania, Australia's most socio-economically disadvantaged state—materialist values, rather than more post-materialist ones were paramount. Another survey in Australia, including Tasmania,

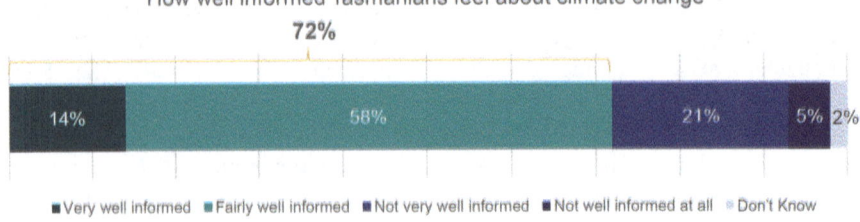

Fig. 15.1 How well informed do you feel about climate change? Base: All respondents ($n = 575$) 2020 (*Source* Elsevier/Ipsos,)

has since shown that Australians are markedly more worried about climate change than COVID-19, or even the employment consequences of the COVID pandemic. This survey was conducted just a few months after the Ipsos survey referred to above, in November and December 2020 (Patrick et al., 2021). Despite the relative magnitude of issue concern in relation to the environment that was gauged at the time of the Tasmanian survey, participants in this survey clearly understood the currency, seriousness, and anthropogenic nature of climate change, as the following responses indicate (Fig. 15.2).

Participants were then asked who or what entity they most relied on for advice or information about climate change. The survey found that 59% of participants in all age cohorts, saw universities and research organisations as key sources of information on climate change, while, for comparison, only 13% saw government or politicians as a key source, and only 12% relied on social media/blogs/forums or newspapers/ magazines (Fig. 15.3).

Not only were universities seen as key sources, but they were also regarded as the most *trusted* sources, scoring highest for trust (48%) and reliability (67%) (versus

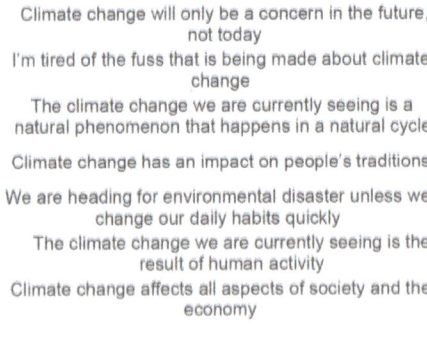
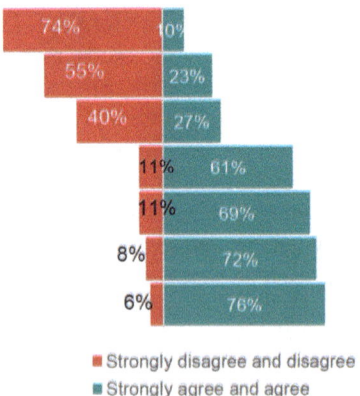

Fig. 15.2 Please indicate the extent to which you agree or disagree with the following statements. Base: All respondents ($N = 575$) (*Source* Elsevier/Ipsos, 2020)

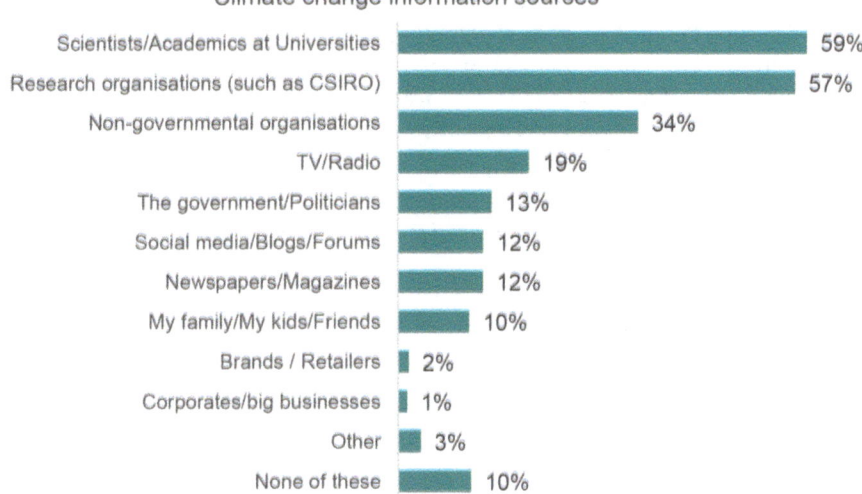

Fig. 15.3 When it comes to climate change, which of the following do you take advice or information from? Base: All respondents ($n = 575$) (*Source* Elsevier/Ipsos, 2020)

government: trust 14%, reliability 13%; media: trust 5%, reliability 6%). Responses to another question indicated that universities, as key information sources, were also regarded as being responsible for taking action on climate change: 54% of participants believed scientists and academics at universities were responsible for major action; 35% were responsible for small actions. This perceived position on taking major action put the expectation of universities ahead of individual responsibility (major action 35%; small actions 57%), but behind government (major action 73%, small actions 18%), and business/corporations (63% major action, 24% small actions). It is clear from these results, that universities are regarded as authoritative and trustworthy in terms of purveying accurate information on climate change, and as climate change thought leaders; they are also strongly regarded as being responsible for meaningful action.

Results from other questions showed, however, that there is still work to be done to ensure individuals are aware of the most important and impactful actions they themselves can take to mitigate environmental harm. Although 62% of respondents said they took action out of consideration for future generations, the top three actions that the Tasmanian respondents reported taking out of concern for climate change, were relatively less impactful for mitigating greenhouse gas emissions. These included recycling (73%) and buying/using less plastic (59%). In contrast, fewer respondents reported taking the most impactful actions: only 25% said they travelled by car less, 24% reported eating less meat/dairy products; 21% chose to fly less, and only 9% engaged in political action. It is these areas where UTAS could have an influence on action, both by enhancing communities' understanding of impactful climate mitigation actions, and by working with government to plan policy frameworks that better "nudge" people towards pro-environmental behaviours. The survey additionally showed that in terms of research, a university must make its community constituents sufficiently *aware* of its work. While 72% of survey respondents agreed that UTAS specifically had a positive impact on society, around a quarter of respondents were neutral or unaware about UTAS' interaction with the public, its research, and its relationship with local organisations on the issue of climate change. Overall, the findings of the public survey confirm that the university has an important role to play in facilitating urgent action to combat climate change and its impact (SDG13), and that one of the most effective mechanisms for doing this is through SDG4, ensuring inclusive and equitable quality education, and promoting lifelong learning opportunities for all.

The interviews with stakeholders from private and public sectors clearly demonstrated the direct impact of UTAS' research and engagement on Tasmanian society. UTAS research, particularly modelling by the university's Climate Futures climate science and science translation programme, has been applied to understanding climate impacts on natural resource management, water, hydroelectricity, fire and emergency management, engineering and local government planning, biosecurity, and future planning in the wine and alpine snow industries. Tasmanian stakeholders are increasingly focusing on adaptation, and the interviews showed that adaptation actions are becoming more formal, strategic, and proactive, although the climate-focused operations of many organisations remain reactive. For example, a large proportion of available resources in the Tasmanian Parks and Wildlife Service is currently spent minimising bushfire damage to natural ecosystems and cultural heritage, but this agency is also using UTAS' regional climate projections for future fire danger and vegetation changes to plan where hazard reduction burning is carried out. Into the future, understanding the increase in fire danger that is expected with ongoing climate change, is also important in order for organisations to plan for increased resource requirements and greater coordination with fire agencies on the Australian mainland.

There is an accelerating appetite for an evidence-led approach, with UTAS seen as a trusted, primary player in providing climate projections, clarifying climate change impacts, and informing adaptation planning for the future. One interviewee from the State Emergency Service expressed this trust in the university as follows: "There is that level of trust in the community that they are working for a societal value". An interview respondent from the Tasmanian Parks and Wildlife Service explained that:

> The past 10 years we talked about climate change, but we actually didn't have hard data. Now the work that UTAS did has actually produced gridded climate data, that we can implement into process.

Workshops and conversations facilitated by UTAS have helped in communicating the impacts of climate change to a broad audience, providing "another form of communication and another, deeper way of assessing the impact" (interviewee from engineering firm, Pitt & Sherry). Importantly, UTAS' provision of industry-specific climate data has been influential with stakeholders. As an interview participant from the State Emergency Service commented, "industry specific, targeted practical research" from UTAS was "foundational" for setting up new climate-appropriate systems.

The interviews for this study also identified areas where the uptake and impact of UTAS' research outputs could be improved. For example, the proven-successful approaches identified above are not always applied; funding rounds do not always allow for theoretical research to be continued through to producing operational or practical conclusions; new knowledge may not be communicated in an accessible way, and more operational and policy-relevant outputs may be needed to increase the usability of research for immediate application. An interview participant from the (then) Tasmanian Climate Change Office in the state government's Department of Premier and Cabinet, noted that: "to get that relationship, government has got to be willing to spend the funds to bring [the university] into the policy making or policy development cycle". Finally, one interviewee (an indigenous artist and Knowledge Holder) pointed to the crucial importance of incorporating Indigenous perspectives in work on climate change. He particularly noted "respect and understanding" within UTAS of "traditional practices on the island," and the university's efforts towards continuous relationship-building with Indigenous people.

Overall, then, the *Measuring Societal Impact: Climate Change in Tasmania* study provided many valuable insights into community climate literacy, and a university's role in enhancing understanding of climate change in a variety of societal contexts. It demonstrated that communities can look up to their local university as a thought leader and leader of action on climate change. It showed also that business and government are keen to work directly with university-based researchers, to discover and implement climate research outputs to facilitate forward planning. It also suggested some ways that universities could better serve their communities on all these fronts.

In the next case study, we direct our enquiry specifically towards university teaching and learning on climate change, to discuss how a university's role in educating students can promote climate action, both locally and, in an online context, even globally.

15.4 Building Climate Literacy Through University Teaching

As discussed above, it is clear that knowledge of the causes and consequences of climate change increases concern about climate, and is more likely to translate into effective action than general concerns about the environment (Bord et al., 2000). Lack of climate literacy is therefore an important barrier to personal engagement on the issue of climate change (Lorenzoni et al., 2007). Studies in Australia (Dawson & Carson, 2013), and elsewhere (Libarkin et al., 2018), indicate that undergraduate students' knowledge of climate science concepts is limited and inaccurate in some aspects (Kuthe et al., 2020). Despite this, there remain few studies from a critical pedagogical perspective of university teaching of climate change, to allow researchers to gauge such understanding in students, and to critically evaluate the role of teaching in enhancing such knowledge (Beck et al., 2013; Bush et al., 2017). For a university to be a climate thought leader ultimately requires that university graduates understand scientific consensus on climate, and that they be actively engaged as part of the solution to it (Wachholz et al., 2014).

In August 2020, UTAS launched the first of a sequence of two 13-week undergraduate study offerings: *Introduction to the Science of Climate Change* and *Responding to Climate Change,* launched in February 2021. The units were written and taught by a small interdisciplinary group of climate change lecturers and researchers—including this chapter's authors—and, studied sequentially, the units provide an essential overview of climate science, climate impacts on natural and human systems, global climate governance, climate communication and misinformation, decarbonisation, and climate justice. The units conclude with a discussion of climate change and system change. Tellingly, when the university posted about this new climate change study offering on its social media pages, there was strong reaction—best described as "trolling"—which included climate change denial and attacking the university for teaching about climate change. This clearly reinforces the need for more and better climate teaching and learning. At the time of writing, the two units had educated almost 1,200 students on climate change. The majority of students take both units, which gives them 26 weeks of climate change learning, and a total of six assessments on the science and social science of climate change.

To understand students' interest, prior knowledge, change intentions, and thought leadership in relation to studying climate science and human responses to climate change, we applied for and were given ethics clearance to survey our students pre- and post-study with a voluntary, anonymous survey. By collecting data on students' perspectives, we intend to contribute to improved practice in climate literacy learning and climate change pedagogy. We likewise aimed to generate a better understanding of how higher education teaching and learning can contribute to improved climate change knowledge, and confidence in sharing knowledge. The survey is ongoing (412 students have participated to date), but preliminary results demonstrate that students have gained markedly in their knowledge of the causes and consequences of climate change, and that, having completed the units, they feel significantly more confident to share their climate knowledge with others. For example, a comparison between the pre- and post-surveys shows that the number of students who felt "very well informed" about climate change increased from 4.2% pre-study to 41.5%. Having studied the units, 95.8% of students felt either "very well informed" or "fairly well informed" about climate change (up from 59.2% pre-study). This pre-study percentage is somewhat similar to the figure that the UTAS/Elsevier/Ipsos study (2020) discussed in the section above found for self-reported climate knowledge, suggesting that a course of formal study on climate change can significantly elevate the base level of self-reported climate literacy in the community (Fig. 15.4).

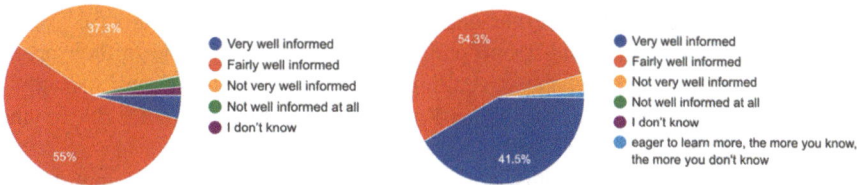

Fig. 15.4 How well informed do you feel about climate change? Pre- (Left) and post-study (Right) ($N = 412$)

In addition to this, students reported feeling more confident to discuss climate change with others due to their new skills in climate literacy, and to call out misinformation when they encountered it. In the qualitative answer sections, students said:

> I'm now more likely to bring up the issue of climate change, now that feel I can speak more knowledgeably and positively about it, particularly around people who aren't convinced or concerned about climate change impacts.

> This unit has given me the knowledge to confidently talk about climate change to others.

> Let's just say that I am no longer a skeptic and will be spreading the climate change message wherever and whenever I can.

> I think that I am less inclined to be silent and disengaged when hearing misinformation from others.

Of course, climate literacy skills are only one component of being empowered to take action on climate change. Climate literacy can motivate citizens to work in a bottom–up way to reduce their own environmental impacts, however, the study units also emphasise that top–down societal transformation is needed in response to climate change. So, while some students reported more awareness of individual responsibility in their survey responses, others emphasised the importance of political action. For example, one student commented:

> I'm more determined to find ways personally to contribute to less CO_2 emissions. I would like to create a balance between emissions and mitigation - my own personal zero!

Others, however, noted:

> I am more keen to engage in community awareness and political action.

> It has changed how involved I have become in political activity – I have recently started to chat with a local political climate action group.

> In the election I changed my traditional vote and voted for the candidate with strongest climate policy.

Results from the student survey also show, however, that even when students well understand what behaviours in their own lives make the most meaningful difference to their environmental impact, they are not always able and empowered to take those actions. For example, several students responded that they were not easily able to reduce their own car travel, as no public transport was available in their areas. Advocating for structural change and calling for policy to enable citizens' individual changes better, is therefore crucial—and a nuance that students better understand after studying the two units under examination.

In this chapter, we have written a lot about "community." Though community is usually considered to be geographically proximate, it is important to note how the community established in an online unit of study may be both proximate and distant. Geographically dispersed communities are enriching in the context of discussing climate, because they bring many different experiences of a changing climate into discussion. Students engaged in vibrant asynchronous conversations in both units, often around locally distinct climate impacts, adaptation strategies, and mitigation actions. Online study as a virtual community is a surprisingly ideal site for addressing the global phenomenon of climate change in locally relevant ways. Though environmental education pedagogy research emphasises the importance of learning "in place" (Ballantyne & Packer, 2009) the "un-emplacing" online space as a learning context (Hawley et al., 2023) also simulates the kind of global community of solidarity needed to confront global climate change. Speaking from an arguably peripheral geographical location in Tasmania to a potentially global online learning community has also allowed the university to extend its thought leadership on climate change. To extend further this community, the university is now planning a rapid expansion of its climate education offerings, including online undergraduate and postgraduate certificates, and online micro-credential type units, orientated towards professionals.

Finally, university study of climate change needs to be considered through the lens of mental health. Laying bare for students the current facts and projected trajectories of Earth's future climate is a sobering exercise. On conclusion of their study, 89.4% of students felt "very concerned" about the climate issue, and many reported feeling "anxious", "worried", "overwhelmed", "terrified", "doomed", "sad". They felt "helpless", "angry" and "enraged at those who turn a blind eye". Many reported being "scared for the future" or "frightened for [their] children" and "future generations". This makes it clear that a university engaged in climate pedagogy must address how confronting the issue is for students: part of a university's broad responsibility to its community and society. In these units, we offered a forum for discussion of eco-anxiety, and included an interview with a psychologist who specialises in environmental grief. We also notified students how to access the university's counselling services. As research into eco-anxiety notes, however, the best way to counter the justified grief many of us feel about climate change is to take action to counter it (Baudon & Jachens, 2021). Climate literacy learning at its best—the kind of lifelong learning described in SDG4—can indeed be the start of that journey of action.

15.5   Influencing Government Policy

As noted in the section above, widespread community understanding of climate will not be sufficient to effect the transformative change now needed to mitigate climate change. Research indicates that climate-orientated policy settings by government at every level are needed to offer a framework for helping individual households make meaningful change in terms of climate mitigation (Dubois et al., 2019). Likewise, business needs the certainty and nudging of pro-climate policy settings to undertake transformative change. Government policies to enable adaptation to the changes already occurring must also be enacted. In this final case study, we turn, therefore, to the ways that a university might use its expertise to work for impact on climate policymaking. Again, we use the example of UTAS, and we discuss the university's work both with local and state government in the Australian island state of Tasmania.

Tasmania can credibly claim to be among the few jurisdictions globally that have achieved and exceeded net zero. Tasmania's net emissions in 2020 were negative 3,733 kt CO_2-e, meaning that the state currently absorbs more carbon from the atmosphere than it emits (Johnson et al., 2022). In 2020, land use and forest uptake of carbon dioxide exceeded gross emissions, resulting in this net-negative emission figure. This is assisted by the fact that most of Tasmania's power comes from hydroelectricity. While this is a nationally and internationally significant achievement, this is not the full story, and work must be done to ensure that Tasmania retains and even improves on this status. Tasmanian emissions from transport, non-transport energy, agriculture, industrial processes, and waste have not reduced for 30 years, and by as soon as 2030, climate change itself may make Tasmania a net positive emitter, for example, through projected increases in fire changing the ability of the island's forests to absorb carbon dioxide. Tasmania must therefore carefully consider and act on both adaptation and mitigation policy.

Tasmania was an early adopter in terms of Australian subnational climate change policy. The state government's first climate policy body, the Tasmanian Climate Change Office (TCCO) was established in 2008, when the state's Climate Change Act (www.legislation.tas.gov.au/view/html/inforce/current/act-2008-036) passed and the state's Framework for Action on Climate Change was released (www.stors.tas.gov.au/au-7-0020-00419). Climate research from the university provided the science foundation of the work the TCCO (now Renewables, Climate and Future Industries Tasmania: www.recfit.tas.gov.au). Key to the Tasmanian government's early development of climate adaptation policy has been a university programme in climate science and modelling that was established in 2011, and continues today. The Climate Futures programme (www.climatefutures.org.au) is a UTAS research group that specialises in downscaled regional climate modelling and science translation. Climate Futures' work to understand climate in Tasmania to 2100 provided the state with the first comprehensive future climate information of any state in Australia in 2011. Effective, sector-specific science translation has also enhanced climate literacy among government decision-makers, to enable better climate policy. This and subsequent Climate Futures' work has now been used to inform the state's adaptation initiatives, across a number of agencies, including the emergency services for natural disaster risk assessment, the management of Tasmania's World Heritage Area, and in agriculture, biosecurity, forestry, aquaculture, hydropower, energy transmission, and other infrastructure. Climate science work generated at UTAS has also closely informed climate polices of *local* government. Regionally specific climate projections have been prepared for many council authorities, to inform adaptation planning. UTAS research is also currently being used to inform bushfire adaptation policy by local government in Hobart, Tasmania's capital, one of the most bushfire-prone cities in the world.

Interview data from the Elsevier/Ipsos/UTAS (2020) study discussed in the first section provided several insights into the university's influence on government climate policy. One local council leader, referring to climate modelling data from the Climate Futures group, stated that: "all the climate change policies in local governments were based on that original UTAS data." Another interview participant, an emergency services representative, noted that UTAS climate researchers were:

> genuinely interested in how we are using this information to make decisions. They are genuinely interested in understanding what are the challenges we face in emergency response. There is a genuine desire to be doing research that is adding value to public policy.

This close collaboration between university climate researchers and the end users of their work needs to be one of the hallmarks of successful university-government relationships in the climate sphere. These kinds of collaborations are sites where a university can additionally contribute towards SDG11, particularly 11b, which attends to cities' mitigation and adaptation to climate change and their resilience to disasters.

The nexus between a university's climate and political science expertise is another key location for impactful outreach to government policymaking. In 2021, led by political scientists at the university's public policy research institute, the Tasmanian Policy Exchange, UTAS contributed a detailed *Blueprint for a climate-positive Tasmania: a submission to Tasmania's climate change Act and Climate Action Plan* (Tasmanian Policy Exchange, 2021). This document, to which both this chapter's authors contributed details the kinds of policy needed to establish a nation-leading emissions target by 2030, as well as adaptation policies to manage current and future impacts. Although the new climate change Act had not been submitted for parliamentary debate at time of writing, preliminary feedback suggests that this expert-led and research-based submission has been influential. The independent review of the Act has closely followed many of the recommendations in the *Blueprint* document.

15.6   Conclusion: A Framework for University Thought Leadership on Climate Through Incorporating the SDGs

The case studies presented here provide snapshots of the pathways via which a university can be influential in relation to climate change in its local community and beyond. Understanding and enhancing students' and wider publics' climate literacy, and providing place-relevant climate science information and translation for high-level decision-making, clearly serves towards addressing several SDG goals and targets. Applied university research and thought leadership in this space addresses SDG4, by enabling urgent action on climate change and its impacts. Climate education at all levels of society, including within and beyond a university, addresses the scope of SDG4, particularly target 4.7: "providing education for sustainable development and sustainable lifestyles". In Table 15.1, in summary, we offer the outline of a framework of some of the expertise a university can offer in promoting broad community understanding of climate change. We also summarise the kinds of collaborations needed for the shared task of mitigating and adapting to climate change, as well as possible success markers for this process, and the SDGs addressed. This table is not comprehensive in terms of disciplines (it includes just core climate science and science translation, education, and communication roles), as clearly the number of university disciplines and roles connected at least in *some* aspect to climate is very large.

Universities in many places around the world are well equipped to disseminate their research-informed expertise on climate broadly in their communities in order to serve the task of addressing climate change. Though this task is urgent and necessary, it is not without challenges. An important challenge to overcome is the kind of disciplinary silos that can sometimes characterise work within universities, and interaction with professions beyond universities. Evaluating a university's impact in this sphere requires an acknowledgement that social change does not automatically occur as a result of conducting quality research. Many different players need to be engaged before quality research can be incorporated into action. Indeed, the kind of societal transformation that is called for in the face of climate change will take decades and will not be dependent on one institution. Though many of the impacts discussed here are quite clearly evident, the influence of a large institution on its community in terms of climate may not always be clearly defined. Likewise, to be effective, university-empowered climate action in any jurisdiction must be sustained over time.

The task at hand—perhaps the most crucial and demanding that universities everywhere have ever been confronted with—demands depth and breadth of knowledge and willingness to step outside normal professional roles and boundaries for knowledge translation. Guided by the SDGs, universities are well placed to work with their communities towards the world-changing challenge at hand.

Table 15.1 A basic framework for University Science Translation for Societal Impact

University role or discipline	Climate change expertise	Collaborates with…	Information provided	Success markers	SDGs addressed
Climate science researcher/future climate modeller	Current climate systems, local climate impacts, and future climate projections	Climate educators Government (local, state, national) Industry	Climate science information and data visualisation for climate literacy Industry-specific climate indices provided	Better climate information and climate literacy for decision-making at all levels of society Climate change mitigation policies enacted	SDG 4 SDG13
Climate educator	Broad climate knowledge, climate change pedagogy, understanding of climate literacy requirements	University students Non-university learners for industry-specific learning (e.g. microcredentials)	Comprehensive climate literacy Industry-relevant information for decision-making	Learners are empowered for individual decision-making and collaborative action Learners are empowered for pro-environmental policymaking	SDG4, 4.7 SDG 13, 13.3

(continued)

Table 15.1 (continued)

University role or discipline	Climate change expertise	Collaborates with…	Information provided	Success markers	SDGs addressed
Climate science translation/climate communication expert	Knowledge of climate science, impacts and adaptation pathways, and knowledge of optimal group-specific modes of climate communication to catalyse action	University students Climate educators Community groups Government (local, state, national) Industry	Audience specific messaging on climate change, globally and locally, impacts, projections, and adaptation	Climate literacy becomes ubiquitous and mainstream Climate misinformation loses relevance Climate change is depoliticised	SDG4 SDG13
Climate adaptation specialist	Knowledge of current climate impacts and future projected impacts and optimal adaptation pathways	Climate educators Community groups Industry Government (local, state, national) Industry	Local climate impacts and options for adaptation actions	All levels of society have the necessary understanding of adaptation pathways to reduce climate risk Government/industry decision-makers enact policy to facilitate climate adaptation	SDG4 SDG 11, 11b

15.7   Dedication to Dr. Rebecca Harris

Co-author of this chapter, Dr. Rebecca (Bec) Harris lost a battle with cancer at the end of 2021. She contributed to this chapter until shortly before her death. This chapter stands as testimony to her career-long focus on the parallel tasks of both climate science and science translation, for the betterment of humanity and the planet. Her strength, sharp intellect, kindness, and sense of fun are sorely missed by her colleagues at Climate Futures, the University of Tasmania, and the Intergovernmental Panel on Climate Change (IPCC). Vale Bec.

References

Australian Bureau of Statistics. (2022). *Snapshot of Tasmania.* Avia. https://www.abs.gov.au/art icles/snapshot-tas-2021

Azevedo, J., & Marques, M. (2017). Climate literacy: A systematic review and model integration. *International Journal of Global Warming, 12*(3–4), 414–430.

Ballantyne, R., & Packer, J. (2009). Introducing a fifth pedagogy: Experience-based strategies for facilitating learning in natural environments. *Environmental Education Research, 15*(2), 243–262.

Baudon, P., & Jachens, L. (2021). A scoping review of interventions for the treatment of eco-anxiety. *International Journal of Environmental Research and Public Health, 18*(18), 9636.

Beck, A., Sinatra, G. M., & Lombardi, D. (2013). Leveraging higher-education instructors in the climate literacy effort: Factors related to university faculty's propensity to teach climate change. *International Journal of Climate Change: Impacts & Responses, 4*(4), 1–17.

Bedford, D. (2016). Does climate literacy matter? A case study of US students' level of concern about anthropogenic global warming. *Journal of Geography, 115*(5), 187–197.

Bord, R., O'Connor, R., & Fisher, E. (2000). In what sense does the public need to understand global climate change? *Public Understanding of Science, 9*(3), 205–218. https://doi.org/10.1088/0963-6625/9/3/301

Bush, D., Sieber, R., Seiler, G., & Chandler, M. (2017). University-level teaching of anthropogenic global climate change via student inquiry. *Studies in Science Education, 53*(2), 113–136.

Cooper, O., Keeley, A., & Merenlender, A. (2019). Curriculum gaps for adult climate literacy. *Conservation Science and Practice, 1*(10), 102.

Dawson, V., & Carson, K. (2013). Australian secondary school students' understanding of climate change. *Teaching Science, 59*(3), 9–14.

Dubois, G., Sovacool, B., Aall, C., Nilsson, M., Barbier, C., Herrmann, A., Bruyère, S., Andersson, C., Skold, B., Nadaud, F., & Dorner, F. (2019). It starts at home? Climate policies targeting house-hold consumption and behavioral decisions are key to low-carbon futures. *Energy Research & Social Science, 52*, 144–158.

Dupigny-Giroux, L.-A. (2008). Introduction: Climate science literacy: A state of the knowl-edge overview. *Physical Geography, 29*(2008), 483–486. https://doi.org/10.2747/0272-3646.29.6.483

Dupigny-Giroux, L.-A. (2010). Addressing the challenges of climate science literacy: Lessons from students, teachers and lifelong learners. *Geography Compass, 4*(9), 1203–1217.

Elsevier/Ipsos. (2020). *Measuring societal impact: Climate change in Tasmania, in maximizing universities' societal impact. Project results* (Unpublished).

Flynn, C., Yamasumi, E., Fisher, S., Snow, D., Grant, Z., Kirby, M., Browning, P., Rommerskirchen, M., & Russell, I. (2021). *Peoples' climate vote*. United Nations Development Programme and University of Oxford.

Guy, S., Kashima, Y., Walker, I., & O'Neill, S. (2014). Investigating the effects of knowledge and ideology on climate change beliefs. *European Journal of Social Psychology, 44*(5), 421–429.

Hawley, E., Mocatta, G., & Milstein, T. (2023). The place of the teacher: Environmental communication and transportive pedagogy. *Environmental Communication, 17*(4), 339–352.

Johnson, L., Langridge, M., & Eccleston, R. (2022, August). *Tasmanian greenhouse gas emissions update annual progress report for the 2020 reporting year.*. Tasmanian Policy Exchange, University of Tasmania.

Johnston, J. D. (2020). Climate change literacy to combat climate change and its impacts. *Climate Action*, 200–212.

Kuthe, A., Körfgen, A., Stötter, J., & Keller, L. (2020). Strengthening their climate change literacy: A case study addressing the weaknesses in young people's climate change awareness. *Applied Environmental Education & Communication, 19*(4), 375–388.

Leal Filho, W., Morgan, E. A., Godoy, E. S., Azeiteiro, U. M., Bacelar-Nicolau, P., Ávila, L. V., Mac-Lean, C., & Hugé, J. (2018). Implementing climate change research at universities: Barriers, potential and actions. *Journal of Cleaner Production, 170*, 269–277.

Libarkin, J. C., Gold, A. U., Harris, S. E., McNeal, K. S., & Bowles, R. P. (2018). A new, valid measure of climate change understanding: Associations with risk perception. *Climatic Change, 150*(3), 403–416.

Lorenzoni, I., Nicholson-Cole, S., & Whitmarsh, L. (2007). Barriers perceived to engaging with climate change among the UK public and their policy implications. *Global Environmental Change, 17*(3–4), 445–459.

McCaffrey, M. S. (2015, January). The energy-climate literacy imperative: Why energy education must close the loop on changing climate. *Journal of Sustainability Education, 8*.

McCaffrey, M. S., & Buhr, S. M. (2008). Clarifying climate confusion: Addressing systemic holes, cognitive gaps, and misconceptions through climate literacy. *Physical Geography, 29*(6), 512–528.

Molthan-Hill, P., & Blaj-Ward, L. (2022). Assessing climate solutions and taking climate leadership: How can universities prepare their students for challenging times. *Teaching in Higher Education, 27*(7), 943–952. https://doi.org/10.1080/13562517.2022.2034782

Molthan-Hill, P., Worsfold, N., Nagy, G. J., Leal Filho, W., & Mifsud, M. (2019). Climate change education for universities: A conceptual framework from an international study. *Journal of Cleaner Production, 226*, 1092–1101.

Newman, N., Fletcher R., Schultz, A., Andi, S., & Rasmus, K. (2020). *Reuters Institute digital news report 2020*. https://reutersinstitute.politics.ox.ac.uk/sites/default/files/2020-06/DNR_2020_FINAL.pdf

Patrick, R., Garad, R., Snell, T., Enticott, J., & Meadows, G. (2021). Australians report climate change as a bigger concern than COVID-19. *The Journal of Climate Change and Health, 3*, 100032. https://doi.org/10.1016/j.joclim.2021.100032

Schapiro Ledley, T., Gold, A. U., Niepold, F., & McCaffrey, M. (2014). Moving toward collective impact in climate change literacy: The climate literacy and energy awareness network (CLEAN). *Journal of Geoscience Education, 62*(3), 307–318.

Stoutenborough, J. W., & Vedlitz, A. (2014). The effect of perceived and assessed knowledge of climate change on public policy concerns: An empirical comparison. *Environmental Science & Policy, 37*, 23–33.

Tasmanian Policy Exchange. (2021). *Blueprint for a climate-positive Tasmania: A submission to Tasmania's climate change act and climate action plan*. University of Tasmania.

Times Higher Education (THE) Impact Rankings. (2022). *Top universities for climate action (2022)*. https://www.timeshighereducation.com/student/best-universities/top-universities-climate-action

Tobler, C., Visschers., M., & Siegrist, M. (2012). Consumers' knowledge about climate change. *Climatic Change, 114* (2), 189–209. https://doi.org/10.1007/s10584-011-0393-1

United Nations Department of Economic and Social Affairs. *Sustainable development.* https://sdgs.un.org/

United Nations Educational, Scientific and Cultural Organization. (2022). *Climate change education.* https://www.unesco.org/en/education/sustainable-development/climate-change

United States Global Change Research Program. (2009). *Climate literacy: The essential principles of climate science [eBook].* Global Change Research Program.

van der Linden, S., Leiserowitz, A., Rosenthal, S., & Maibach, E. (2017). Inoculating the public against misinformation about climate change. *Global Challenges, 1*(2), 1600008.

Wachholz, S., Artz, N., & Chene, D. (2014). Warming to the idea: University students' knowledge and attitudes about climate change. *International Journal of Sustainability in Higher Education, 15*(2), 128–141.

Chapter 16
Universities as Exemplars of Climate Action

Gabi Mocatta and **Rob White**

16.1 Introduction

This chapter discusses the systematic role of universities in engaging with sustainable development. Specifically, this chapter maps out the ways in which universities, as publicly significant large institutions, act to meaningfully address climate change, particularly in terms of mitigating their own environmental impacts. This frequently occurs in contexts where action by governments on climate change is either lacking or not sufficiently rapid to fit the timeframe for keeping global temperature rise under the 1.5 degree goal of the Paris Agreement. As this chapter points out, not only are universities vital hubs for research and teaching on climate change, but as large organisations, they also have significant emissions profiles, thereby contributing to the climate crisis. As such, they have significant responsibilities to address sustainability issues. If they do this credibly and visibly, communicating with their communities their efforts to minimise their environmental impacts, they can indeed be exemplars of climate action, thereby contributing meaningfully to SDG13 concerning climate action.

This chapter surveys some of the efforts higher education institutions have been making, singly and in coalition, to meet sustainability and emissions reductions

G. Mocatta (✉)
Climate Futures, School of Geography, Planning and Spatial Sciences, College of Sciences and Engineering, University of Tasmania, Private Bag 76, Hobart, TAS 7001, Australia
e-mail: gabi.mocatta@utas.edu.au; gabi.mocatta@deakin.edu.au

School of Communication and Creative Arts, Deakin University, 221 Burwood Highway, Burwood, VIC 3125, Australia

R. White
School of Social Sciences, College of Arts, Law and Education, University of Tasmania, Churchill Ave, Hobart, TAS 7005, Australia
e-mail: R.D.White@utas.edu.au

© The Author(s), under exclusive license to Springer Nature Singapore Pte Ltd. 2023   279
K. Beasy et al. (eds.), *Education and the UN Sustainable Development Goals*, Education for Sustainability 7,
https://doi.org/10.1007/978-981-99-3802-5_16

targets. We argue that although many universities have been on the leading edge of climate science research for decades, these same universities have only more recently begun to take climate action within their own operations. Some indeed, operating as neoliberal institutions, have used sustainability credentials as "greenwashing" to enhance their brands. As Borgermann et al. (2022) note, universities should not be "preaching water while drinking wine". As these authors argue, it is high time for universities to "practice what they preach" and move to a position where they are leading at the "frontline of climate action". This chapter maps out some of the ways universities are acting on that front line, and points to other areas where the requisite action is lacking.

The chapter begins with general remarks about the SDGs in relation to action on climate change. We discuss how all the SDGs fundamentally depend on systemic climate action in order to be achieved by the 2030 target date. We point out, however, that given current inadequate action on climate, progress towards many or all of the SDGs may be hindered. We argue that transformative change is needed to enable the SDGs, and that universities are well placed to be catalysts and exemplars of such change. We then go on to examine multiple examples of global and local university-based climate action initiatives that attend to the climate impacts of universities as institutions, and we explore what authentic university *climate action leadership* can look like. We also point out that universities indeed want to act as climate action role models for other organisations and communities—and that universities want to be seen to be doing this. The universities we point to in our examples are illustrative of many of the aspirations—and also challenges—of university climate leadership. We conclude that for university-based climate action to be credible, it must be much more than a brand-building exercise. Instead, it should be truly system wide and sustained over the long term, with a university's community at every level (including management, staff, and students) engaged in taking action.

16.2   Sustainable Development and Climate Change

The UN Sustainable Development Goals are intrinsically intertwined with each other, particularly if viewed from the perspective of social justice and ensuring better conditions of life for the maximum number of people. They are also connected to the key conduits of global power, because how (or if) nations pursue the SDGs has a ripple effect throughout the world community. If some nations lead on implementing the SDGs in their jurisdictions, other nations are more easily brought along on this journey. These same principles apply to large institutions in terms of action on sustainability, which we explore in the chapter: exemplary action by some towards sustainability can provide the impetus for others to follow suit.

However, regardless of fine words and positive pronouncements, the UN SDGs themselves, and how to make progress towards them, is contested. The goals are questioned for their imperative for continued economic growth (for example, by Bendell, 2022). As noted by Jones and Smith in this volume, this objective is unsustainable within planetary boundaries. The SDGs are also manifestly undermined by the relative lack of transformative intentional action on the part of many nation-states and corporations. Progress towards the SDGs has also been eroded by circumstance—namely, current interrelated crises of economy, war, and pandemic, interwoven with the overarching threat of climate change. As UN Secretary General António Guterres noted in 2021, the world is "tremendously off track" to meet the SGDs by 2030 (UN News, 2021).

Though addressing climate change is accepted as fundamental to achieving the SGDs, current analysis of climate change and progress towards mitigating it points to stark trends. First, global average temperatures continue to rise with each passing year and greenhouse gas emissions also increase, despite scientific warnings urgently to curb emissions, and political commitments to do so (Goal 13 of the SDGs, and also the UN Framework Convention on Climate Change). As greenhouse gas emissions continue to rise (IEA, 2022); extensive subsidies are still being provided by governments to fossil fuel industries (Campbell et al., 2021; Watts et al., 2019). Global heating and the extreme weather events it precipitates continue to have profound social, economic, and health consequences (IPCC, 2021; World Meteorological Organization, 2020), which go to the heart of most—if not all of—the SDGs. Many aspects of life are getting worse for increasing numbers of people as climate disruption intensifies existing problems (UNHRC 2019).

Second to this, each failure to act decisively and immediately exacerbates the unfolding catastrophe of global warming. Among the key producers of greenhouse gas emissions, and those with the most responsibility for planet-warming emissions are the hegemonic nation-states. This includes especially the colonising nations of the Global North, which have had the greatest historical impact on Earth's climate (Ritchie et al., 2020). So too, large corporations bear significant responsibility for climate-damaging emissions (Kramer, 2020; White, 2018; Whyte, 2020). It is also clear that the industry most responsible for global climate change, the purveyors of fossil fuels, has deployed concerted efforts to deny climate change and postpone action (Brulle, 2018). Delayed cuts in greenhouse gas emissions mean deeper cuts are needed, even as we run out of time.

It is clear that mitigation and adaptation strategies required to curb the worst impacts of global warming are fundamental to any possibility of meaningful achievement of the SDGs. The increasingly urgent warnings of the meticulous science underpinning current understandings of climate recommend "overarching and economy-wide climate actions" (UNEP, 2019, p. 31) towards achieving zero emissions. These will need to entail carbon pricing, an end to fossil fuel subsidies, 100% renewable energy production, ending fossil fuel exploration and production, low-carbon or zero-emission industry, transport, and buildings; and reversing deforestation (UNEP, 2019, p. 31). Closing the emissions gap this way could, with proper design, also serve directly towards advancing the United Nations 2030 Agenda and the 17 SDGs. In other words, addressing climate change properly and holistically would have the additional benefit of enhancing quality of life for people everywhere (UNEP, 2019). Our argument, then, is that achieving SDG 13 fundamentally underpins achievement of all the other UN SDGs, and action towards them will be undermined without action on climate also.

16.3 Who Will Lead Climate Action?

In the face of the urgency described above—and, given the tendency of some governments to deliberately obfuscate to delay action—a few national governments, as well as state and local administrations, institutions, social movements, communities, and individuals at all levels of society have been taking climate action into their own hands. For example, while national climate action in the US—historically the largest source of planet-warming emissions—has been slow, some of its jurisdictions *are* acting on climate. The State of California, for example, has legislated to enable carbon-free transport, renewable energy, carbon cap-and-trade, habitat restoration, and climate adaption (CalEPA, 2022). In Australia, where a recent decade of conservative government mired in politicised "climate wars" (Hornsey et al., 2022) led to the country being labelled internationally as a "climate laggard" (Christoff & Eckersley, 2021), community initiated and owned renewable energy projects have been appearing, serving to decentralise and democratise clean energy production—in spite of national policy. Then there are small countries leading the way, like carbon neutral Bhutan, also aiming to be waste free by 2030, which offers "big lessons on climate change" for the world (Dixon, 2015). And, perhaps the greatest impetus for current action on climate change, the wave of young people's climate protests that make up the international School Strike 4 Climate movement—demonstrating that collective direct action, in global solidarity, can influence climate policy. Given the global cooperation needed for climate solutions, it is imperative that such climate leadership at all levels of society and in every national context, keep forging and inspiring a way forward.

What is the role of universities in this context? For decades universities have been the expert purveyors of the science and solutions of the climate crisis. Academics within universities have warned about the escalating seriousness of the present situation and carefully mapped out pathways for responding. They have advised that there is little time to act: deep change is urgent, now. Contributions have come from multiple disciplines including the physical and natural sciences, humanities, education, law, social sciences, and the creative arts. Across many specialisations and fields of inquiry, there has been common cause to acknowledge and address climate change and climate justice. A small but growing literature, both in scholarly and public media outputs, attests to universities' efforts to use their autonomy to make pro-active decisions in the face of climate change. This literature shows that universities are increasingly doing so, both individually and collectively.

Several scholars have noted universities' potential leadership role in impelling society-wide sustainability, which Velazquez et al. (2006) have described as "stewardship" and Omrcen et al. (2018) discuss as being in the position of a societal "role model". Robinson et al. (2013) similarly call university action a "societal testbed for sustainability". Other scholars have provided concrete examples of a single university's climate leadership, for use as a template for others to follow. Knuth et al. (2007) for example, use Pennsylvania State University as a case study to illustrate how universities can be climate exemplars by working both to reduce their own emissions profiles, and by collaborating at grassroots level with regional actors to develop climate mitigation programmes. Ormcren et al. (2018) have also investigated universities' capacities as "living laboratories" for climate action. They lay out the results of implementing within a university an institution-wide climate strategy—presenting the experiences of a 5-year programme of climate and sustainability actions at the University of Gothenburg as a blueprint for other universities to follow. Other university actions documented in the literature have a more symbolic dimension, like the initiative taken by Bristol University in 2019 when it became the first United Kingdom university to declare a climate emergency, prompting 36 other UK universities to follow suit (Latter & Capstick, 2021). Of course, like countries' fine words and stated intentions on climate (and indeed on the SDGs) any university declaration of "climate emergency" must be accompanied by appropriate action in response. As Sterling (2013) argues, the action now required of universities goes beyond both the symbolic and even the operational, and needs to be thought of as their guiding purpose, not an "add-on". Importantly, many academics looking at their own (or other) universities in terms of institutional sustainability note the moral obligation to take meaningful climate action, given universities' multi-disciplinary expertise, and the potential to serve the public good on an issue that is truly universal.

As Kilkis (2014) argues, universities can be influential on climate in at least three key spheres of action, these being in research, in education, and in outreach. How action in these three spheres might look for a single university is addressed in detail by Mocatta and Harris in this volume. This current chapter, however, mainly addresses a fourth sphere for action: that is, how a university might attend to its own environmental footprint, and in doing so, how it might act as an exemplar for other institutions. In the sections below, we lay out some of the ways universities are attending to their own environmental impacts, and we discuss how, in doing so, they can act as examples towards more widespread progress on SDG13.

16.4   Operationalising Climate Leadership

16.4.1   Carbon Accounting

Universities are significant consumers and emitters—some spheres and disciplines more than others—and, through detailed carbon accounting, this impact can be measured in terms of CO_2 equivalent of heating potential contributed to the Earth's atmosphere. Carbon accounting is a first step, something many universities have been doing for almost a decade at time of writing, to understand their greenhouse gas (GHG) emissions profiles. A university GHG inventory must account for direct

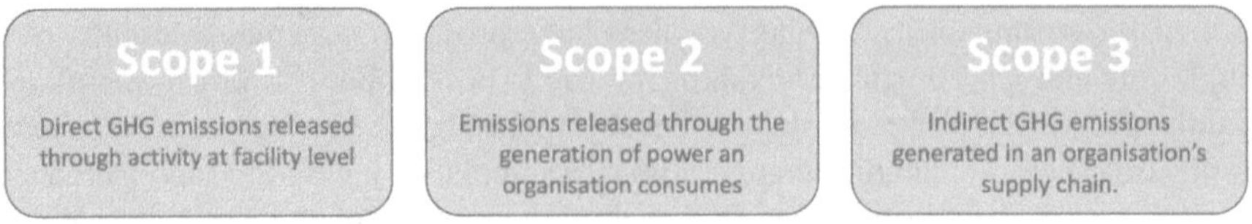

Scope 1	Scope 2	Scope 3
Direct GHG emissions released through activity at facility level	Emissions released through the generation of power an organisation consumes	Indirect GHG emissions generated in an organisation's supply chain.

Fig. 16.1 Emission types by scope

emissions, indirect emissions across the supply chain, and carbon credits or emissions offsets. Carbon accounting designates emissions as Scope 1–Scope 3 as seen in Fig. 16.1.

Scope 1 emissions include those from the use of natural gas, transport fuels, stationary fuels, refrigerants, and waste incineration. Scope 2 emissions come from purchased electricity generated off-site, whereas Scope 3 emissions include a broad range of other supply chain GHG emissions, including equipment manufacture, employee and student commuting, flights, waste disposal, and other utilities. Many universities now undertake annual public reporting of carbon accounting figures. For example, a large public university like the University of Melbourne in Australia with some 50,000 students, accounted for 195,795.8 tonnes of carbon dioxide equivalent emissions (tCO2-e) in 2019 (Endean, 2019). Of this, the largest source of emissions was from electricity generation (59.6%). Carbon accounting provides a vital baseline for understanding GHG emissions—and universities everywhere are now seeking to acknowledge and rachet down their emissions. Each university will seek to do this by a slightly different pathway depending on a host of variables including location, size, alternative energy availability, and ultimately, an institution's financial means. For some, this may mean energy use reduction, for others, switching to their own, or purchased, renewable energy; others may choose emissions offsetting (discussed in further detail below).

For example, University College London (ULC) in the UK has committed to becoming a net zero emissions institution by 2030 for all emissions, including the most difficult to tackle, Scope 3 emissions, with a pathway guided by a 40% reduction in institutional energy use by 2024 (UCL, 2021). In Australia, the University of New South Wales (UNSW) aims to take a leadership position by converting to 100% renewable energy (as it did in 2020), comprehensively reporting all emissions, and committing to a 1.5°C-aligned target. For UNSW this translates into a 30% emissions reduction by 2025, 50% by 2030, and net zero by 2050 (UNSW, 2021). Alignment with the Paris Agreement targets also ensures that an institution is moving on SDG13—and thereby supporting the achievement of all the other SDGs, as discussed above. It is important, though, also to think critically about university carbon accounting. As Helmers et al. (2021) remind us, there is limited consistency between universities' self-reported emissions profiles, because their analyses tend to use a range of methods, measures, and definitions. We apply a critical lens to university sustainability work later in this chapter.

16.4.2   Energy Reduction and Generation

Given that electricity generation from a carbon-intensive grid tends to the most significant source of emissions, some universities have begun generating their own energy on campus or nearby to reduce these Scope 2 emissions. Universities have shown that they can be nimble in this regard and quickly pivot to generating low-emissions energy. For example, in Australia, Deakin University has developed an industrial-scale microgrid: a 14.5 hectare, 23,000 panel solar energy farm with a 2 megawatt hour central battery, accompanied by a 0.25 megawatt distributed rooftop solar generation and storage system at the university's Waurn Ponds regional campus. The project is intended to supply over half the campus' energy demand and reduce CO_2 emissions by 12,000 tonnes each year (Deakin, 2021). Similarly, also in Australia, the University of Queensland (UQ) has set up an A\$125 million solar farm just outside the town of Warwick, which now provides the university with 100% of its own electricity needs (UQ, 2020). Of course, not all universities have the physical space required to house such energy infrastructure. Projects like Boston University's BU Wind, which sources power generated by off-site through the US Environmental Protection Agency (EPA) Green Power Partnership programme, allow this university to meet its energy needs with 100% wind power (BU, 2021).

Importantly, as all large institutions should be doing, universities are also attending to *reducing* their energy consumption. As Gui et al. (2021) report, energy use to power buildings accounts for 80–90% of total electricity demand for most universities. Using avenues like smart building technology so that heating/cooling/lighting only kick in when the relevant part of the building is occupied, and by being responsive to the fluctuating energy demands of teaching versus non-teaching periods on campus, Gui et al. (2021) underscores universities' capacity to make significant energy reductions. Researchers at Covenant University in Nigeria (Oyedepo et al., 2021) have written about energy auditing campus buildings, finding changes to lighting infrastructure alone that would save that university US\$81,000 annually, with the initial cost recouped within 6 years, and a saving of 500 tons of CO_2 emissions annually. Thermal performance and energy efficiency of new university buildings, alongside low-carbon design and construction of new university buildings, is clearly imperative to underpin this kind of reduction in energy use, and can also be added to some degree through retrofitting.

16.4.3   Divesting from Fossil Fuels

Large universities globally have significant investments and endowments that have historically supported the extraction of planet-heating fossil fuels, while profits enhance university wealth. Divestment from fossil fuels has therefore been seen as a crucial aspect of university climate action—and an important component of Scope 3 emissions. Many universities are now making divestment the core of their

Negative screening	Positive screening	Withdrawal
no new investments in fossil-fuel-related industries	investment in renewable energy and ecologically sustainable industries	phased withdrawal of existing investments in fossil-fuel-related industries and activities

Fig. 16.2 The three key elements of university fossil fuel divestment

climate action, with such initiatives often driven by their own students. Divestment initiatives must consider exposure to investment in companies that own coal, oil, and gas reserves, and all of this industry's supply chain, including entities that refine and sell fossil fuel products, and provide equipment and services to the fossil fuel industry. Divesting for climate action also reduces climate risk exposure: that is, the longer-term declining value of fossil fuel-related assets in a decarbonising global economy. Additionally, it may help universities to avoid litigation risk and reputational risk given the mounting social costs of carbon. Fossil fuel divestment is a process of transition, usually including the three elements as seen in Fig. 16.2.

In the US West, already an epicentre of climate impacts, one of the largest university divestment efforts has come from the University of California Berkley, which in 2019 announced it would divest completely from fossil fuels in its US$126 billion investment portfolio and $70 billion pension fund, a process it said it had completed in 2020 (Watabe, 2020). Such efforts can be contested, however, given the complicated supply chains and "long tail" of fossil fuel industries. The "Fossil Free UC" campaign claimed in mid-2022 that the university may still have funds invested in the fossil fuel industry and had divested mainly to minimise its climate risk (Fossil Free UC, 2022).

University pension funds are another sphere where university students and staff themselves are campaigning for decarbonisation. In Australia, for example, the largest university superannuation scheme, UniSuper, which has 450,000 members, encompassing the vast majority of the nation's university employees, has been subject to a campaign to divest from fossil fuels. As of August 2021, this had been partly successful—resulting in the fund withdrawing AU$2 billion in investments—but still, significant investments remain (UniSuper Divest, 2021). As noted in this chapter's first section, only initiatives that result in authentic action—meaningfully communicated—as opposed to action that is perceived as being taken perhaps more for public relations purposes, or action that is publicly perceived as not going far enough, constitutes the kind of exemplary institutional climate action that we are pointing to here.

Box 16.1: A university climate and sustainability case study
One of the most celebrated universities in advancing policies and practices towards climate action and sustainability is the University of Tasmania (UTAS) with which the authors of this chapter are associated. This is a smaller, regional university and the

only higher education institution in the Australian southern island state of Tasmania. In 2022 and 2023, UTAS was named the leading university in the world for Climate Action by the Times Higher Education Awards, which are aligned with the UN SDGs. It was also named Sustainability Institution of the Year in the 2021 Green Gown Awards Australasia. The Green Gown Awards aim to support change towards best practice sustainability within the operations, curriculum, and research of the tertiary education sector.

Climate action leadership at UTAS has several interrelated dimensions. The university is already a leader on climate in the spheres of research and teaching. It punches above its weight with many climate change research groups and more Intergovernmental Panel on Climate Change (IPCC) authors than any other Australian university. As well, it leads in research and teaching on climate change in science, social sciences, law, education, and humanities. It hosts leading climate impacts and adaptation research, particularly by its Climate Futures research programme, and prominent public outreach activities, like the Curious Climate Schools projects (described elsewhere in this volume, by Kelly et al.).

The University of Tasmania is additionally one of only two universities in Australia that is certified carbon neutral. This means it has closely audited and reduced emissions from all aspects of its operations. It uses almost 100% renewable energy (most sourced from the state hydroelectric-powered grid) and rooftop solar, and has offset its remaining emissions. A critique of university emissions offsetting follows below. UTAS has held carbon neutral status since 2016 and in 2020, announced it had divested from fossil fuels.

UTAS' support for climate action is evident in other ways as well. The university's Sustainability Committee is engaged in a wide range of pro-environmental initiatives. It is currently developing guidelines for a climate sustainable food culture at UTAS covering procurement, preparation, waste management, growing, vending, and food systems education. "Education for sustainability" principles are also being integrated across all areas of the university. UTAS' sustainability policy will provide a strategic framework for actions into the future, guiding, for example, what the university does in regard to air travel carbon emissions, how it embodies the SDGs through both operations and education, and how it implements a circular economy action plan.

Located in cities that are subject to significant flood and bushfire risk—which will worsen under a changing climate—the university's campuses will need to prepare better for such risks in a way that makes them exemplar of climate-safe campuses. More generally, however, UTAS will also need to look to its carbon and environmental footprints in its built environment. The university is currently planning a complete relocation of its Hobart campus from its current green-space campus in a suburban location to the city centre. It is crucial that climate change be factored into the location, design, and build—potentially a great source of GHG emissions—if the university is to retain its internationally recognised sustainability status.

Looking ahead, the best "green" credentials for UTAS will also include considerations such as generating its own renewable energy on site, enabling sustainable transport, and ensuring its purchasing also aligns with the SDGs.

16.4.4 Food on Campus

Food systems have a well-documented climate impact, with an estimated 23% of total global anthropogenic GHG emissions derived from Agriculture, Forestry, and other Land Use. Although food systems are deeply intertwined with our carbon-based economy, they are also one of the systems where rapid change is possible. Individual choices around diet can be made rapidly, at will, and the collective weight of individual dietary choices has potential for significant impacts on GHG emissions (e.g., Kwasny et al., 2022; Verfuerth et al., 2021), although consumers in some socio-economic settings and national contexts have been shown to be more open to reducing, for example, meat consumption, than in others (Hielkema & Lund, 2021).

For universities, making climate-orientated changes to food on campus is a pathway both for reducing especially Scope 3 GHG emissions, and providing their communities—students and staff—with learning around what sustainable, lower-emissions eating looks like. Just one example is the University of Maryland (UMD), which in 2019 became the first university to join the World Resources Institute's Cool Food Pledge, to cut food-related greenhouse gas emissions by 25% by 2030, in line with the goals of the 2015 Paris Agreement. GHG emissions from food arise from its production and transport, waste and farming related land-use change. The University of Maryland is therefore cutting emissions with mainly plant-based foods on campus, a campus farm that provides 300,000kg of produce annually, reducing food transport emissions, and reducing waste by redistributing unused food (UMD, 2019). Signatories to the Cool Food Pledge programme announce progress annually and call on other organisations to put sustainability on the table—again offering opportunities to take demonstrable leadership on emissions reduction in a way that other organisations can emulate.

16.4.5 Offsetting

Having reduced Scope 1 and 2 emissions particularly, those most amenable to reduction by an institution's own policy and action, what are universities to do about remaining—often Scope 3—GHG emissions? Some of these, an institution may not have much power to influence, for example, emissions from essential staff air travel on university business (having replaced non-essential travel with video conferencing), or indeed the daily commutes of staff and students. Carbon offsets are a strategy that contributes (usually financially) to avoidance of emissions in one place, to allow equivalent warming emissions in another. This is a key concept underlying the much-used terms "carbon neutral" and also "net zero." Offsetting is not without critique (for example, Lovell & Liverman, 2010; Watt, 2021)—avoiding the emissions completely is naturally preferable, and simply displacing emissions has been questioned as a form of "carbon colonialism" which makes little sense in the face of the truly global phenomenon of anthropogenic climate change (Bumpus & Liverman,

2010; Dehm, 2016). However, carbon offsetting is a pathway that many universities are now using to bring their emissions closer to "zero."

In 2018 American University, Washington D.C., for example, became the first university in the US to achieve "carbon neutral" status. It did this by investing in on- and off-campus renewable energy and buying "strategic" carbon offsets, which it calls "thoughtful alternatives to reducing emissions that are difficult to reduce by other means" (American University, 2022). The university reports that its carbon neutral status is the equivalent of taking 10,000 internal combustion engine cars off the road each year. Of interest here, are the offsetting technologies. American University (2022) reports using:

- Efficient cookstoves in Kenya, in partnership with The Paradigm Project, offset study abroad air travel and decrease deforestation, which is a major contributor to climate change. They also improve indoor air quality.
- Planting trees in D.C. helps offset GHG emissions from commuting, and helps the District move towards its tree canopy goals. Homeowners also benefit from onsite stormwater management.
- Landfill methane projects offset natural gas use and landfill waste, decreasing the GHG emissions from landfill.

Like many other higher education institutions pointed to in this chapter, American University expresses why this work is being undertaken in terms of the institution being a role model in its community. On the university's online information pages related to sustainability, it states: "We have a responsibility to be a role model for how communities should respond to some of the great challenges of today, which includes climate change". It also says: "We hope that our work will become a model and show how one community can make a real impact". (American University, 2022).

16.4.6 Collective Action

Finally, universities well understand that by joining together with allied higher education institutions and other organisations taking exemplary climate action, their initiatives can have more impact than they might singly. There are now myriad groupings, associations, and events that bring universities together in this shared task. The International Universities Climate Alliance is one of these: an association of 56 universities across five continents dedicated to catalysing collaboration in climate research and action and serving as a knowledge hub for climate action initiatives. Over 1000 universities in twenty countries now also take part in the UN-backed global campaign, Race to Zero. This campaign brings together all kinds of businesses and organisations, plus local and regional governments and investors to lead net zero initiatives—the largest ever alliance committed to decarbonisation by 2050, which it claims, accounts for 25% global CO_2 emissions and over 50% GDP (UN, 2022). Various regional university sustainability groupings also exist. In the southern part of the planet, there is ACTS (Australasian Campuses Towards Sustainability) and the Green Impact programme that supports university staff and students to take impactful actions towards sustainability. An international universities climate action event, Global Climate Change Week, brings climate action under focus for a week each year. Universities are asked to use this week as an opportunity to lift their ambition on climate and sustainability targets, and report progress year on year.

Collective action offers universities an avenue to share—and indeed compete—with each other and other organisations on climate action, and to be seen to be doing so. This is a positive thing, which should contribute to a ratcheting up of climate ambition. As we contend at the start of this chapter, taking authentic action and being *seen* to be doing so is crucial: leadership by example necessarily includes such visibility. In the next section (Sect. 16.5), however, we turn to a brief critique, pointing to some of the obstacles along the pathways to true organisational sustainability.

Box 16.2: International comparisons as a sustainability incentive

Universities are compared and ranked internationally for their sustainability efforts via measures such as the Sustainable Campus Index (SCI), which highlights innovative and high-impact initiatives from colleges and universities. The SCI is published by the Association for the Advancement of Sustainability in Higher Education (AASHE). Central to these comparisons is the Sustainability, Tracking, Assessment & Rating System (STARS). This consists of specific performance measures organised into four categories: Academics, Engagement, Operations, and Planning & Administration. STARS is detailed and specific. It includes a number of benchmarks and targets against which universities can plot their performance and aspirations. These range from waste reduction (e.g., reducing waste production, recycling waste, applying circular economy model to waste management) through to pedagogical initiatives (e.g., introducing a generic sustainability induction module for students; establishing "applied" majors in sustainability). Peterson et al. in this volume, explain how The University of Tasmania uses STARS to move its sustainability agenda forward.

16.5   Climate Action at Universities—Virtue Signalling?

Higher education in many national settings has undoubtedly taken a neoliberal turn in recent times. Universities as market-driven institutions, it would seem, may hold some paradoxes when it comes to meaningful climate action. Orientated towards growth, and competing against each other for students in the crowded higher education marketplace, universities must use sophisticated marketing strategies to distinguish themselves from competitors. Given that the young people who are universities' key constituents are among those calling loudest for climate action, universities would be remiss not to use green credentials as a marketing opportunity. Though students themselves may be quick to distinguish authentic "green" from "greenwashing," sometimes the line between meaningful action and virtue signalling is not clear. Indeed, media reporting increasingly points to universities "talking up" climate action, while at the same time maintaining sponsorships and partnerships with the fossil fuel industry responsible for global climate disruption—even, absurdly, for climate science research (Harvey, 2022). This tendency has been described as "betraying" a commitment to young people and their futures (Coleman, 2022). Such potential for greenwashing is clear at every level of university sustainability initiatives. To give just a few examples: the use of biomass energy as "renewable," when this energy source often accelerates forest clearing; the building of new "green" university infrastructure, when retrofitting of older buildings would have avoided more emissions; the fierce competition for lucrative foreign students, whose international flights contribute to the climate crisis; and the use of carbon offsets that are "questionable at best" (Kingdollar, 2022). Climate action that is seen as calculated, not sincere, undermines not just *universities*' potential to be exemplars, but invites public cynicism around climate action in every sector.

So too, university climate action should not neglect the need for *adaptation* initiatives—perhaps less visible and less "marketable" than mitigation, but equally crucial. Universities seem to publicise comparatively little the ways they are adapting to become "climate ready" or "climate safe," though extreme events, driven by climate change, have already been shown to impact universities' core operations. Rickards (2022) notes that the academic sector is one of the slowest to act when it comes to climate adaptation. This is, then, a key area for university attention and action.

16.6   Conclusion

As we argued at the beginning of this chapter, action on climate change is now so urgent, it underpins the attainment of sustainable development of all kinds, and in all sectors, in local and global settings. Many efforts made by the higher education sector towards mitigating its environmental impacts are indeed laudable. They give impetus to the growing global climate action movement, and jointly, they contribute towards significant change. At the same time, they can orientate minds: students learning on campuses that are authentically climate active come to understand what climate action looks like in practice and can take such learning into their own professional futures. To support and advance the attainment of the SDGs, the university sector must deepen its efforts in exemplary climate leadership. It should even look beyond "net zero," seeking to become a "climate positive" exemplar—as the University of Melbourne says it intends to do by 2050 (University of Melbourne, 2021). With the expertise, independence, and in many cases, the financial means to act—and the reputational advantages that flow from genuine climate leadership—universities must be at the forefront of creating a climate-safe future. In this way, they can most genuinely support the eventual attainment of the UN's SDGs, which, without climate action and justice, may never be realised.

References

American University. (2022). *American University is carbon neutral.* https://www.american.edu/about/sustainability/carbon-neutrality.cfm

Bendell, J. (2022). Replacing sustainable development: Potential frameworks for international cooperation in an era of increasing crises and disasters. *Sustainability, 14*(8185). https://doi.org/10.3390/su14138185

Borgermann, N., Schmidt, A., & Dobbelaere, J. (2022). Preaching water while drinking wine: Why universities must boost climate action now. *One Earth, 5*(1), 18–21.

Boston University Sustainability. (2021). *BU wind.* https://www.bu.edu/sustainability/projects/bu-wind/

Brulle, R. J. (2018). The climate lobby: A sectoral analysis of lobbying spending on climate change in the USA, 2000 to 2016. *Climatic Change, 149*(3), 289–303.

Bumpus, A. G., & Liverman, D. M. (2010). 10: Carbon colonialism? Offsets, greenhouse gas reductions, and sustainable development. In R. Peet, P. Robbins, & M. Watts (Eds.), *Global political ecology* (pp. 203–224). Routledge.

Campbell, R., Littleton, E., & Armistead, A. (2021). Fossil fuel subsidies in Australia: Federal and state government assistance to fossil fuel producers and major users 2020–21, *The Australia Institute*, available at: https://australiainstitute.org.au/wp-content/uploads/2021/04/P1021-Fossil-fuel-subsidies-2020-21-Web.pdf

Christoff, P., & Eckersley, R. (2021). Convergent evolution: Framework climate legislation in Australia. *Climate Policy, 21*(9), 1190–1204.

Coleman, Z. (2022, June 22). Why elite universities like Cambridge must ditch big oil funding. *New Scientist.* https://www.newscientist.com/article/mg25433920-100-why-elite-universities-like-cambridge-must-ditch-big-oil-funding/

Deakin University. (2021, April 20). *Deakin unveils largest-ever solar farm at an Australian university.* https://www.deakin.edu.au/about-deakin/news-and-media-releases/articles/deakin-unveils-largest-ever-solar-farm-at-an-australian-university

Dehm, J. (2016). Carbon colonialism or climate justice: Interrogating the international climate regime from a TWAIL perspective. *Windsor YB Access Just, 33*, 129.

Dixon, A. (2015). *Big lessons on climate change from a small country.* World Bank. https://blogs.worldbank.org/endpovertyinsouthasia/big-lessons-climate-change-small-country

Endean, J. (2019). *Greenhouse gas assessment for the University of Melbourne.* Pangolin Associates. https://sustainablecampus.unimelb.edu.au/__data/assets/pdf_file/0004/3556300/UoM-CY2019-GHG-Report-V2-ExecSummary.pdf

Fossil Free UC. (2022, May). *Fossil free or de-risked?* https://fossilfreeuc.net/

Gui, X., Gou, Z., & Lu, Y. (2021). Reducing university energy use beyond energy retrofitting: The academic calendar impacts. *Energy and Buildings, 231*, 110647.

Harvey, F. (2022, May 21). Universities must reject fossil fuel cash for climate research, say academics. *The Guardian.* https://www.theguardian.com/science/2022/mar/21/universities-must-reject-fossil-fuel-cash-for-climate-research-say-academics

Helmers, E., Chang, C. C., & Dauwels, J. (2021). Carbon footprinting of universities worldwide: Part I—Objective comparison by standardized metrics. *Environmental Sciences Europe, 33*(1), 1–25.

Hielkema, M. H., & Lund, T. B. (2021). Reducing meat consumption in meat-loving Denmark: Exploring willingness, behavior, barriers and drivers. *Food Quality and Preference, 93*, 104257.

Hornsey, M. J., Chapman, C. M., Fielding, K. S., Louis, W. R., & Pearson, S. (2022). A political experiment may have extracted Australia from the climate wars. *Nature Climate Change,* 1–1.

International Energy Agency. (2022). *Global energy review: CO_2 emissions in 2021.* IEA. https://www.iea.org/reports/global-energy-review-co2-emissions-in-2021-2

IPCC. (2021). *Climate change 2021: The physical basis.* IPCC, Cambridge University Press.

Kilkis, S. (2014). Comparative sustainable campus analyses: Case studies from ISCN, Turkey and the Netherlands. *Proceedings of the 9th conference on sustainable development of energy, water and environment systems*. Center, Zagreb, Croatia, SDEWES2014.0133, 1–35.

Kingdollar, B. (2022, June 22). Harvard, MIT students denounce schools' push to use global carbon offsets to satisfy proposed city requirement. *The Harvard Crimson*. https://www.thecrimson.com/article/2022/6/22/harvard-mit-student-letter-carbon-offsets/

Kramer, R. (2020). *Carbon criminals, climate crimes*. Rutgers University Press.

Knuth, S., Nagle, B., Steuer, C., & Yarnal, B. (2007). Universities and climate change mitigation: Advancing grassroots climate policy in the US. *Local Environment, 12*(5), 485–504.

Kwasny, T., Dobernig, K., & Riefler, P. (2022). Towards reduced meat consumption: A systematic literature review of intervention effectiveness, 2001–2019. *Appetite, 168*, 105739.

Latter, B., & Capstick, S. (2021). Climate emergency: UK universities' declarations and their role in responding to climate change. *Frontiers in Sustainability, 2*, 660596.

Lovell, H., & Liverman, D. (2010). Understanding carbon offset technologies. *New Political Economy, 15*(2), 255–273.

Omrcen, E., Lundgren, U., & Dalbro, M., 2018. Universities as role models for sustainability: A case study on implementation of University of Gothenburg climate strategy, results and experiences from 2011 to 2015. *International Journal of Innovation and Sustainable Development, 12*(1-2), 156–182.

Oyedepo, S. O., Anifowose, E. G., Obembe, E. O., & Khanmohamadi, S. (2021). Energy-saving strategies on university campus buildings: Covenant University as case study. In *Energy Services Fundamentals and Financing*, 131–154.

Rickards, L. (2022, March 17). *Universities and climate change adaptation: Climate change risk to universities*. https://www.monash.edu/msdi/news-and-events/events/events/2022/climate-change-risks-to-universities

Ritchie, H., Roser, M., & Rosado, P. (2020). *CO_2 and greenhouse gas emissions. Our world in data*. https://ourworldindata.org/co2-and-other-greenhouse-gas-emissions

Robinson, J., Berkhout, T., Cayuela, A., & Campbell, A. (2013). Next generation sustainability at the University of British Columbia: The university as societal test-bed for sustainability. In A. Konig (Ed.), *Regenerative sustainable development of universities and cities* (pp. 27–48). Edward Elgar Publishing Inc.

State of California Environmental Protection Agency. (2022). *Climate action*. https://calepa.ca.gov/climate-action/

Sterling, S. (2013). The sustainable university: Challenge and response. In S. Sterling, L. Maxey, & H. Luna (Eds.), *The sustainable university: Progress and prospects* (pp. 17–50). Routledge.

UN News. (2021, July 12). 'Tremendously off track' to meet 203 SDGs: UN chief. *UN News*. https://news.un.org/en/story/2021/07/1095722

United Nations. (2022). *Race to net zero, United Nations framework convention on climate change*. https://unfccc.int/climate-action/race-to-zero-campaign

United Nations Environment Programme. (2019). *Emissions gap report*. Geneva: UNEP.

United Nations Human Rights Council. (2019). *Climate change and poverty: Report of the special rapporteur on extreme poverty and human rights, A/HRC/41/39-24 June–12 July 2019, Agenda item 3, 1–19*.

University of Maryland. (2019, August 27). *Cool food pledge to reduce UMD's 'foodprint'*. https://today.umd.edu/cool-food-pledge-reduce-umds-foodprint-ffb19773-f30a-4bd7-8006-188c81894a0f

Unisuper Divest. (2021). *UniSuper is investing our retirement savings in climate destruction*. Available at: https://unisuperdivest.org/

University of Melbourne. (2021, November 10). *University of Melbourne joins race to net zero*. https://www.unimelb.edu.au/newsroom/news/2021/november/university-of-melbourne-joins-race-to-zero

UNSW. (2021). *Environmental sustainability report 2020*. https://www.sustainability.unsw.edu.au/sites/default/files/documents/UNSW-2020-Environmental-Sustainability-Report-FINAL.pdf

UQ News. (2020, July 17). *Warwick solar farm: $125m warwick solar farm powers UQ to 100 per cent renewable.* https://stories.uq.edu.au/news/2020/warwick-solar-farm-powers-uq-100-cent-renewable/index.html

Velazquez, L., Munguia, N., Platt, A., & Taddei, J. (2006). Sustainable university: What can be the matter? *Journal of Cleaner Production, 14,* 810–819.

Verfuerth, C., Gregory-Smith, D., Oates, C. J., Jones, C. R., & Alevizou, P. (2021). Reducing meat consumption at work and at home: Facilitators and barriers that influence contextual spillover. *Journal of Marketing Management, 37*(7–8), 671–702.

Watabe T., (2020, May 19). UC becomes nation's largest university to divest fully from fossil fuels. *Los Angeles Times.* https://www.latimes.com/california/story/2020-05-19/uc-fossil-fuel-divest-climate-change

Watts, N., Amann, M., Arnell, N., Ayeb-Karlsson, S., Belesova, K., Boykoff, M., Byass, P., Cai, W., Campbell-Lendrum, D., Capstick, S., & Chambers, J. (2019). The 2019 report of The Lancet Countdown on health and climate change: Ensuring that the health of a child born today is not defined by a changing climate. *The Lancet, 394*(10211), 1836–1878.

Watt, R. (2021). The fantasy of carbon offsetting. *Environmental Politics, 30*(7), 1069–1088.

White, R. (2018). *Climate change criminology.* Policy Press.

Whyte, D. (2020). *Ecocide: Kill the corporation before it kills Us.* Manchester University Press.

WMO. (2020). *State of the global climate 2020 WMO,* Geneva, Switzerland.

Zero Carbon Plan for UCL. (2021). https://www.ucl.ac.uk/sustainable/sites/sustainable/files/a_zero_carbon_plan_for_ucl_0.pdf

Chapter 17
Shooting for the STARS: Implementation of the Sustainable Development Goals at a University Through a Whole of Organisation Approach

Corey Peterson⊙, Catherine Elliott⊙, Caroline Smith⊙, and Jane Watson⊙

17.1 Introduction

In understanding the imperative to address the complexities of the environmental, sociocultural, and economic challenges facing our global civilisation, universities often take a leading role given their focus on educating people for the future and through their research into the most salient issues of our time. It is also related to the operational impact they have, often as anchor institutions in their communities. In line with this understanding, the University of Tasmania (UTAS) has a firm and ambitious commitment to be a leading "sustainable university." This understanding and commitment arises from extensive consultation with the University's wider community, whose members wish for it to be a sustainable, innovative, and global

C. Peterson (✉)
University of Tasmania, Churchill Ave, Hobart, TAS 7005, Australia
e-mail: Corey.Peterson@utas.edu.au

C. Elliott
Student Services and Operations, University of Tasmania, Churchill Ave, Hobart, TAS 7005, Australia
e-mail: Catherine.Elliott@utas.edu.au

C. Smith
School of Education, College of Arts, Law and Education, University of Tasmania, 2/8 Bass Hwy, Burnie, TAS 7320, Australia
e-mail: Caroline.Smith1@utas.edu.au

J. Watson
School of Education, College of Arts, Law and Education, University of Tasmania, Churchill Ave, Hobart, TAS 7005, Australia
e-mail: Jane.Watson@utas.edu.au

K. Beasy et al. (eds.), *Education and the UN Sustainable Development Goals*, Education for Sustainability 7,
https://doi.org/10.1007/978-981-99-3802-5_17

295

university (e.g., Sustainability Surveys, UTAS, 2016–2022). This includes staff and students who also expect the University to incorporate sustainability into all decisions and actions (e.g., *Strategic Framework for Sustainability 2019–2024 [Framework]*, UTAS, 2020). The Framework considers that current and future students, as well as staff and the broader community, want a university that has a strong sustainability focus across all areas of activity because the mission of any university must be to enrich its community with a conscience, and imbue it with hope for the future. The University's Vice-Chancellor has championed inclusion of sustainability as one of the University's strategic priorities, a "mission integrator," noting that the University indeed has an ethical obligation to do so, while acknowledging the inherent opportunities for the University by making sustainability a focal point. The aim of the University Executive Team and its Sustainability Working Group, comprising the Vice-Chancellor, Head of Student Services and Operations, Deputy Vice-Chancellor (Research), Deputy Vice-Chancellor (Education), Chief Sustainability Officer, Executive Director Campus Services, and a lead academic, is for UTAS to be recognised as one of the most sustainable universities and institutions on the planet.

There is support in the literature for this holistic approach that can lead to success, both for the institution and for broader sustainability outcomes such that sustainability in higher education institutions can serve a significant role as a culture change agent for sustainable development (Dziminska et al., 2020). This role is best supported through a transformative approach (Ferreira & Tilbury, 2012). There is also recognition that the most successful higher education institutions share a sustainability vision, with university leaders playing a pivotal role in the affirmation and dissemination of a sustainability culture (Salvioni et al., 2017). Further, the literature recognises value in the use of numerous tools to benchmark and assess sustainability in higher education institutions (Caeiro et al., 2020).

Increasing sophistication of students, staff, and the community about what constitutes sustainability outcomes in the higher education sector has required clear, understandable, and agreed upon approaches and metrics to monitoring and reporting. After significant and wide-reaching consultation, UTAS made the decision to adopt an approach that brings together the United Nations (UN) *Sustainable Development Goals: the 17 goals* (SDGs) (UN, n.d.), the *Learning in Future Environments* (LiFE, 2014) Index model, and the *Sustainability Tracking, Assessment & Rating System (STARS, 2022)*, to guide and measure its performance as a sustainable institution. Although the SDGs were designed for nation-states, colleges and universities have increasingly sought to orient their sustainability efforts towards the SDGs. This has led to the creation in 2019 of the *THE Impact Rankings* (Times Higher Education, 2022) system, which is entirely based on university activity within the 17 SDGs and is an annual comparison against all other participating universities. The University of Tasmania also participates in the STARS rating, which has alignment with the SDGs. In contrast to a ranking approach, STARS is an assessment of sustainability outcomes on a set scale rather than a comparison to other universities. Using both systems underpins success as defined by being a sustainability leader among peers (ranking) and by delivering holistic sustainability outcomes (rating). As the University seeks to operate in the most sustainable way, the STARS rating is the primary tool to guide actions and monitor achievement.

17.2 The Sustainability Tracking, Assessment and Rating System (STARS)

STARS is a holistic, transparent, self-reporting framework for colleges and universities that enables them to measure their sustainability performance across all higher education activity areas. Originating in North America, STARS now operates internationally with hundreds of institutions using it, and since 2020, several Australasian universities have taken up the system. The STARS criteria are open for review and feedback every three years. Feedback is open for staff and students at participating universities. STARS is specifically designed for and by the higher education sector to describe the sector's collective agreement about what a sustainable university should look like, in contrast to other frameworks such as the Global Reporting Initiative's *Universal Standards* (2021), that need to be adapted for use in the higher education sector. STARS is based on a points system that encompasses long-term sustainability goals, designed both for already high-achieving institutions as well as for providing entry points for institutions taking their first steps towards sustainability. Essentially, the STARS framework provides an excellent benchmarking tool for universities to be able to design their own principles-based governance, policies, and practices.

STARS describes the four quadrants of activity of a higher education organisation: Planning and Administration, encompassing leadership and governance; Engagement, encompassing internal and external communities and partnerships; Academics, including teaching, learning, and research; and Operations. An institution seeking a rating pursues credits in these four quadrants with the resulting total categorised as a Bronze, Silver, Gold, or Platinum level. There are over a thousand universities using STARS to guide their sustainability efforts, with 572 earning a rating. Currently, only 11 institutions have reached Platinum. The *STARS Technical Manual* (n.d.) describes and explains each credit, defines relevant terminology, and explains which data are required and how points are calculated.

17.2.1 STARS and the Sustainable Development Goals

Sustainable Development: the 17 Goals (SDGs) (UN, n.d.) recognises that integration of environmental, economic, and sociocultural aspects is essential for achieving sustainable development in all its dimensions at all levels from local to global. With the aim of being a leading global, sustainable, and responsible institution, and in recognising the global importance of the SDGs, the University has committed to demonstrating how it contributes to achieving the SDGs and using STARS to guide and monitor University activities.

However, given that STARS predates the SDGs by a decade and that the SDGs go well beyond the higher education sector, it would not be expected that there would be perfect alignment between them (Association for the Advancement of Sustainability in Higher Education [AASHE], 2020). The latest iteration of the STARS tool (version 2.2) provides a guide for using STARS to report contributions to the SDGs as well as demonstrate alignment between the two systems and how to use STARS effectively to communicate impacts towards achieving the SDGs.

Notwithstanding the imperfect alignment between STARS and the SDGs, there is significant alignment among STARS, the SDGs, and many of the University's activities; and further, the University's institutional goals are based on the underpinning rationale of the SDGs and are specifically named as a focus in the University *Strategic Plan 2019–2024: Sustainability Development Goals* (UTAS, 2019). The challenge for University leadership, then, is to demonstrate to the University community and beyond, that using STARS and other means shows how the SDGs are enacted in the University context to increase positive environmental and social impact. Figure 17.1 illustrates how the University has aligned STARS and the SDGs within the Framework. In conjunction with Fig. 17.2, it can be seen which areas of the University have primary leadership roles in activities delivering on the SDGs in line with the strategic intent.

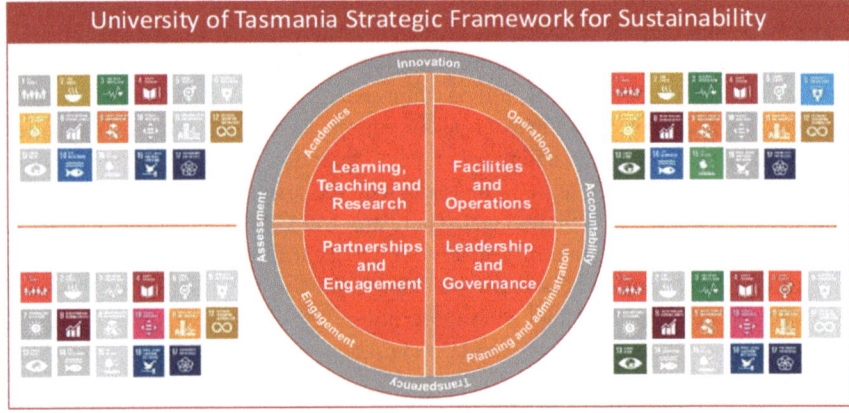

Fig. 17.1 *Aligning STARS with the SDGs in the UTAS strategic framework for sustainability* (*Source* https://www.utas.edu.au/__data/assets/pdf_file/0014/1302422/UOTBR200122-UTAS-Str ategic-Framework-For-Sustainability-2020_vWeb_R.pdf)

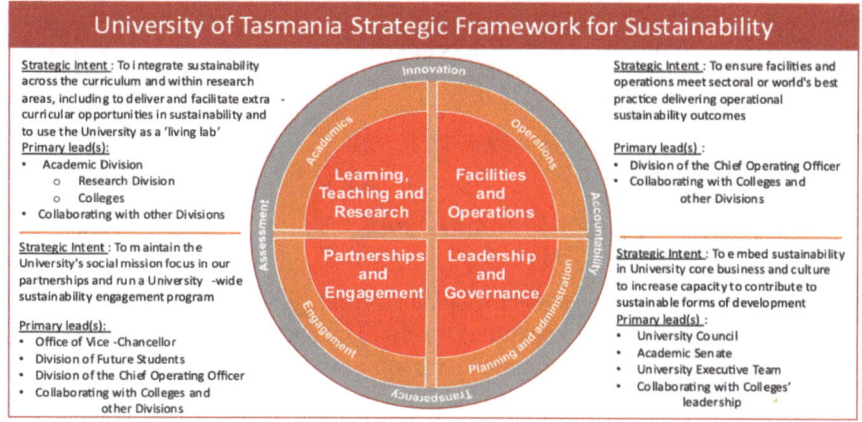

University of Tasmania Strategic Framework for Sustainability

Strategic Intent : To integrate sustainability across the curriculum and within research areas, including to deliver and facilitate extra-curricular opportunities in sustainability and to use the University as a 'living lab'
Primary lead(s):
- Academic Division
  - Research Division
  - Colleges
- Collaborating with other Divisions

Strategic Intent : To maintain the University's social mission focus in our partnerships and run a University-wide sustainability engagement program

Primary lead(s):
- Office of Vice-Chancellor
- Division of Future Students
- Division of the Chief Operating Officer
- Collaborating with Colleges and other Divisions

Strategic Intent : To ensure facilities and operations meet sectoral or world's best practice delivering operational sustainability outcomes
Primary lead(s) :
- Division of the Chief Operating Officer
- Collaborating with Colleges and other Divisions

Strategic Intent : To embed sustainability in University core business and culture to increase capacity to contribute to sustainable forms of development
Primary lead(s) :
- University Council
- Academic Senate
- University Executive Team
- Collaborating with Colleges' leadership

Innovation / Academics / Operations / Accountability / Assessment / Engagement / Planning and administration / Transparency

Learning, Teaching and Research | Facilities and Operations
Partnerships and Engagement | Leadership and Governance

Fig. 17.2 The University of Tasmania's strategic framework for sustainability (*Source* https://www.UTAS.edu.au/__data/assets/pdf_file/0014/1302422/UOTBR200122-UTAS-Strategic-Framework-For-Sustainability-2020_vWeb_R.pdf)

17.3 Documenting Sustainability at UTAS Using STARS

STARS enables UTAS to deliver an approach to sustainability that is robust, comprehensive, fully transparent, and within a comparable framework to gauge where the University is on a "sustainability maturity scale" as measured by the rating level achieved. This approach allows for the determination of the University's authenticity and impact as a sustainable organisation. It is also key in supporting a gap analysis to be undertaken through a process of assessing, tracking, and monitoring whether UTAS is achieving its targets, goals, and relevant key performance indicators. The gap analysis is critical for guiding future action across the four quadrants of the University's activities.

Aligning with STARS and hence the SDGs, the four quadrants of the University's *Strategic Framework for Sustainability, 2019–2024* (UTAS, 2020) are shown in Fig. 17.2. Each quadrant or activity area has a Strategic Intent and identified Primary leads and collaborating areas to ensure that sustainability is included in all University strategies and activities, which are underpinned by requiring innovation, accountability, transparency, and assessment. The Strategic Intent includes detail of current and future activities and how they will be progressed by the four quadrants.

17.3.1 Leadership and Governance

The Strategic Intent of the Leadership and Governance quadrant is to embed sustainability in UTAS core business and culture to increase the capacity to contribute to sustainable forms of development. This includes embedding sustainability into the policy and strategy frameworks, ensuring high level focus and support are maintained, and monitoring and reporting undertaken. This quadrant is led by the University Council, University Executive Team, and the Academic Senate, in collaboration with the Colleges' leadership.

17.3.2 Partnerships and Engagement

The Partnerships and Engagement quadrant's Strategic Intent is to maintain the University's social mission focus and to develop and deliver a university-wide sustainability engagement programme for all staff and students. This includes sustainability-focused outcomes in internal and external partnerships designed to deliver broader community impact. This quadrant is overseen by the Office of the Vice-Chancellor, the Division of the Chief Operating Officer, and the Division of Future Students, in collaboration with the Colleges.

17.3.3 Teaching, Learning, and Research

The Strategic Intent for UTAS Academic endeavours is to integrate sustainability across all curricula and research, including the delivery and facilitation of extra-curricular learning opportunities in sustainability. The quadrant is led by the Academic Division, Research Division, and the Colleges. UTAS already has an excellent track record in climate, water, land, forestry, and agriculture research, as well as offering sustainability-focused degrees at the Certificate, Diploma, and Bachelor levels. Mapping curricula to embed sustainability into teaching in all courses and units across all Colleges of the University is a significant undertaking currently in progress. Here, gap analysis has shown both where excellent work is being done, as well as where focus is still needed. STARS provides recommendations about sustainability in curricula that the University can translate into course descriptions and outcomes. This has the potential to embed change in significant ways, so that staff and students can understand what is expected of them, and to ensure that course and units are either sustainability-focused or sustainability-inclusive.

17.3.4 Facilities and Operations

Facilities and Operations are charged with meeting sectoral world's best practice in delivering operational sustainability outcomes. Led by the Division of the Chief Operating Officer, this quadrant covers all operational areas from energy and transport, waste and cleaning management, facilities maintenance, construction project management, and procurement, to workplace health and safety, health and well-being, and contributions to student experience. It is an area that provides considerable opportunity to develop and add to the STARS rating. Procurement policy is a critical element in this quadrant. The University provides information around sustainability, so staff engaged in procurement can understand how it fits into their decision-making, and that it needs to be a priority. For example, the procurement process requires staff to look at the Procurement Policy and Principles that relate to issues such as modern slavery commitments, environmental impact, social impact, and buying locally, all of which align with the Sustainability Policy.

17.4   Going for Platinum

Recognising that STARS as a reporting mechanism signals a higher education institution's level of commitment to sustainability, thereby legitimating it as well as resulting in improved performance (Minutolo et al., 2021), as a university with a global focus, UTAS was the first to use STARS in the Australasian region. At the beginning of the process, information submitted for rating by the University resulted in a Silver rating in 2020 with just over 50% of available points—the "low hanging fruit." One reason was that not enough data were received for a complete assessment, which highlighted that a higher rating was achievable if more areas of the University were engaged in the process. Although unreported data had contributed to this average rating, it was also clear that major strategic work was still required so that all staff realised that they were encouraged and supported to participate in meeting the high priority placed on sustainability by the University. The first set of data was also highly motivating for the University leadership as it demonstrated that in some areas, Gold and even Platinum level activity were already underway or already achieved, while in others, more work was needed. The successes could be celebrated, while other areas clearly needed more focus and support to improve. Although the Silver rating may have been enough for some staff, it was clearly well below the expectations and goals of the University leadership, who established a timeframe for achieving an overall Gold and Platinum rating that was quite ambitious, including Gold in 2022 and Platinum by 2025.

The aim to achieve a STARS Gold rating motivated work to address the findings in the STARS Silver rating gap analysis. Guided by the new Sustainability Policy, in late 2020, a first tranche of 39 co-designed initiatives by the Sustainability Team and staff accountable for desired outcomes were implemented. These initiatives built on the foundation already in place (those "low hanging fruit"), including filling gaps in data availability with new approaches allowing for consultation across the Framework's activity quadrants to enable more initiatives to emerge and milestones to be set to ensure achievement. With these efforts, the journey of fully implementing the Framework and guiding the University towards achieving a Gold rating and setting a goal for Platinum took a great leap forward, where the concept of sustainability became an embedded holistic approach to deliver on the broader institutional mission.

The success of this mission integration approach delivered a STARS Gold status in 2022 by achieving over 73% of available points (where greater than 65% was the required threshold) and a renewed commitment to a Platinum rating that will require achieving over 85% of available points by 2025. These goals and the initiatives required to achieve them also underline the powerful role that STARS can play, by enabling people to recognise that what they are doing contributes to being a sustainable University: everyone matters to the bigger picture.

17.5   Sustainability is Everyone's Business

Having principles, policies, initiatives, and the STARS rating system in place with the imprimatur of the Leadership team are all critical to success, but successful implementation also requires operationalisation that translates to action and ownership at all levels. STARS has enabled robust conversations with key stakeholders about the intent of credits and credit requirements, which has promoted the understanding of the relevance and importance of the role everyone needs to play to help deliver a sustainable university. Key to this is an understanding and a sense of responsibility about sustainability for all stakeholders. Hence, a mission of the Leadership team is to ensure that sustainability is understood by everybody at every level, and that all staff and students see themselves as having an active role in promoting sustainability, however small. One example is the placement of colour-coded and labelled bins and signage in workspaces to avoid contamination of the recycling and compost streams. Providing the bins is a facilities function, but everyone still needs to make the decision to use them properly. To lead this new holistic approach and facilitate policy into action, a goal to motivate staff was needed. In response, the University established the concept of a "sustainability mission integrator" in late 2019, which has evolved both as a description for the approach as well as a key role within the University.

17.6   STARS at the University of Tasmania and the Role of the Sustainability Mission Integrator

The University's *Framework* (UTAS, 2020) is the context-setting and framing document. The Framework is a comprehensive, holistic document that includes sociocultural, environmental, and financial sustainability elements, as well as intergenerational equity and student experience. The Framework implementation process was part of a broader University project to condense 150 policies to 30 principles-based policies, of which sustainability is one. The Sustainability Policy comprises nine principles, designed to be mutually exclusive but interrelated, which were ratified by the Vice-Chancellor, the University Executive Team, and the University

Council in 2019. With sustainability included as one of the 30 policies, it has clear institutional imprimatur as a priority. The Framework document is key to consolidating the University's direction and to providing a baseline for its STARS rating. The broad base of STARS provided guidance on measuring the University's performance on issues of wider community concern, such as equity, access, providing opportunities for all, strategies for inclusion of students from low SES backgrounds, and support for students who may be the first in their families to attend a university, as well as retention and graduation rates.

The role of the Sustainability Mission Integrator at the University is to guide implementation of what has been agreed at the leadership level, and to encourage and facilitate all staff and students to participate in achieving the mission. There are two Mission Integrators at the University: Sustainability, and Antarctic and Southern Oceans. Of interest here, the Sustainability Mission Integrator (SMI) is both an approach and a role. To take on the SMI role, Corey Peterson was appointed Associate Director—Sustainability in late 2020, with a direct team of three full-time equivalent staff. The team is charged with implementing the SMI approach and reports directly to the Vice-Chancellor and the University Executive Team, as well as the broad membership-based *Sustainability Committee* (UTAS, 2022a). The SMI meets with the Leadership team every two months to review initiatives and progress and to address any continuing hurdles.

The SMI's role is one of facilitation, but success depends on the leadership in each quadrant being able to motivate and enable individual staff members and students to embed sustainability in all they do. The process seeks to emulate the model used to embed appropriate workplace health and safety compliance behaviour to ensure it becomes standard workplace practice. To ensure the University successfully achieves its sustainability mission, the SMI approach is framed by the four key mission integration characteristics: it is a top priority for the University; it is externally focused; it spans the University; and student and staff objectives are clearly defined (Fig. 17.3).

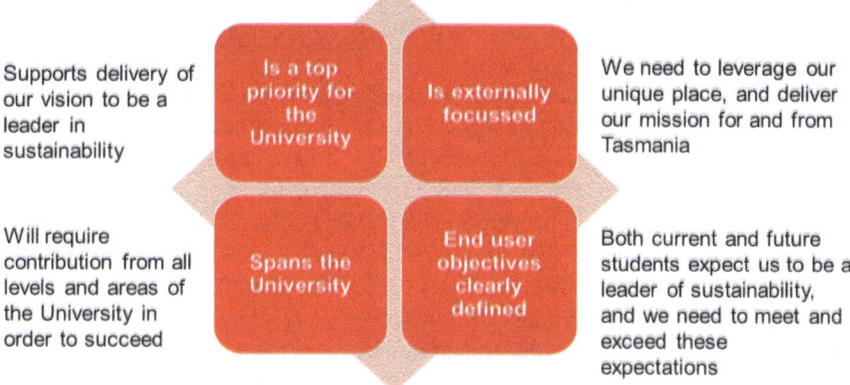

Fig. 17.3 The key roles of the sustainability mission integrator

17.7 Operationalising the Governance Framework: Guiding the Journey to Embedding Sustainability

The STARS tool is now firmly in place at UTAS, but being a whole of system approach, the journey to embed sustainability remains complex and far from straightforward. Looking back over the process, significant progress has been made. For example, a decade ago there were no recycling bins on the campuses, and very limited bicycle parking at the University—elements now considered base level environmental sustainability requirements. Previously, the institution was environmental and risk compliance-based with few internal stakeholders really understanding the broader concept of holistic sustainability. Although sustainability research and teaching were happening within pockets of the University, these activities were siloed from operations. However, environmental management provided a useful starting point for the Sustainability team to provide a more positive impact focus, instead of just minimising negative impacts, and this was able to evolve into a broader understanding of a holistic concept of sustainability. Through continued consultation and targeted presentations to the Leadership, the Sustainability team has been able to ensure that sustainability is maintained as key focus at the highest level.

Genuine progress in embedding sustainability at all levels and areas of an institution represents a major challenge. A full discussion of the enablers and barriers is beyond the scope of this chapter, but two main insights emerge from the literature. The first emphasises the critical importance of the Leadership team in setting the policy directions and making these binding. There are many examples of institutions that appear to reap benefits from being signatories to agreements (e.g., University Leaders for a Sustainable Future, 1990), but unless they follow through with binding policies, they are not likely to be successful (Bekessy et al., 2007). With binding support mechanisms including the SDGs and broader sustainability referencing in the overall University strategy document, the University Council-approved *Framework* (UTAS, 2020) and Sustainability Policy, use of the STARS rating system and participation in THE *Impact Rankings* (2022), and inclusion in strategic and operational Key Performance Indicators, the University Leadership has empowered the sustainability mission at the University.

The second insight, while relying on the first, relates to what Adlong (2013) describes as the recognition of the many social and cultural processes that are essential aspects of achieving change towards sustainability. This requires individuals not only to have knowledge about the issues, but also to recognise their root causes in the production and consumption patterns in society, as well as challenging deeply held assumptions about progress and success. This requires ongoing opportunities for collaborative reflection and discussion at all levels of the institution.

Biennial data collected through the University's *Sustainability Surveys* in 2016, 2018, 2020, and 2022 demonstrate the importance of leadership support for sustainability culture (UTAS, 2016–2022), as well as gaining insight into organisational sustainability culture. These findings have allowed the University to identify an increase over time and a clear shift in staff and student perceptions of leadership support for the sustainability mission, coinciding with the change in senior leadership and mission priorities from 2018.

Here, STARS and the SDGs can have an impact to suggest ways to address some of the issues identified above and further embed sustainable thinking and action. For example, a practical level of commitment that would add further impetus for deep and long-lasting outcomes is inclusion of sustainability in staff performance frameworks, position descriptions, and staff (and student) agreements. For academic staff specifically, mapping of all curricula has been able to show where gaps are, but remediation and/or development of new units depend both on deep understanding of sustainability as well as knowledge of appropriate pedagogies for those engaged in teaching. It also requires the recognition that as a holistic concept, a systems approach is needed to ensure that sustainability is embedded across all aspects of teaching and learning.

In addition, a key tool for staff at all levels to enable understanding of the University's approach to sustainability is the introduction of a Sustainability Induction Module, which is being piloted at the time of writing. This module, written by way of a collaboration of staff with backgrounds in sustainability theory, practice, and pedagogy, is like the workplace behaviour module that all staff are currently required to complete. The purpose of the Sustainability Induction Module is for all staff to gain a common understanding of the University's implementation of sustainability and their personal roles in how it is being implemented and embedded. However, the question of whether the Sustainability Induction Module will be sufficient to educate to the level needed for change and action remains to be answered. For some staff it will be an important first step on the path to more widespread understanding of embedding sustainability intrinsically into thoughts and actions, whereas for others it will enable them to take their sustainability journey further.

Other specific examples of how UTAS is using the SDGs and STARS to strengthen sustainability messaging and outcomes include the Sustainability Integration Program for Students (SIPS) (SDG4) and addressing climate action (SDG13). These are explored below.

17.7.1 SDGs in Action 1: The University's Sustainability Integration Program for Students (SIPS)

An important way of understanding and contributing to sustainability, for both staff and students, is through participation in the SIPS (UTAS, n.d.), a national and international award-winning example of place-based student engagement and sustainability education (International Green Gown Awards, 2022). SIPS relates directly to several SDGs, both for the students themselves, and the University and its broader communities. Specifically, SIPS delivers directly on SDG4: Quality Education, as well as through SIPS projects that cover most of the SDGs and all STARS quadrants. The Sustainability team use the SDGs to ensure there is diversity in the programme each year. Projects are mapped to the SDGs and then the project list is evaluated, with a gap analysis used to prompt creative thinking about ways to tackle or learn more about SDGs not included in the initial annual planning. During their introductory workshop students are invited to think broadly about the SDGs. For example, if a project is to host a bike education workshop, the student is invited to think about who the stakeholders could be, how to design the workshop for a disadvantaged group and if so, what could the workshop be working towards outside of transport education? In a previous project to create a new marine biodiversity trail, the student worked with Riawunna, the University Aboriginal education centre, to identify place names that could be used in the trail in palawa kani (Tasmania Aboriginal language). Students are made aware not only of how their projects may relate to an SDG but also of the relationship between SDGs and a broader awareness of current challenges to create richer, more meaningful projects.

SIPS also links directly to and is evaluated on achievement of goals in the Strategic Plan 2019–2024: Sustainable Development Goals (UTAS, 2019) that explicitly include a commitment to "provide unique learning and teaching experiences for our students, which in turn enables them to make significant contributions to the island and to the world." SIPS also relates to the *Framework* (UTAS, 2020), which aims to "engage students and staff as creative partners who understand and support sustainability as an integral aspect of University endeavours." Given the challenges the world faces are serious and can be isolating and overwhelming, a central value of SIPS is the ability to bring people together, to share experiences, and to feel hope through the creative and meaningful contributions they make.

SIPS has three key aims. First, it provides valuable opportunities for students to apply their learning to real-world sustainability challenges, and to be paid or gain course credit while doing so. Second, it assists the University to deliver positive impacts and to demonstrate leadership as a sustainable university, thus contributing to the STARS rating. Third, it provides opportunities for academic engagement with sustainability. Uniquely, SIPS fuses interdisciplinary academic inquiry, values diverse expertise and passion, and promotes a culture of continued learning to address complex sustainability challenges by allowing students to make meaningful sustainability contributions. The structure of SIPS enables the University to respond efficaciously to new challenges affecting students and the University as they arise.

Completed SIPS projects to date have contributed to strategic decision-making for sustainability policies, resource allocations, infrastructure provision, and operational activities. Programme outcomes are reviewed regularly by the University *Sustainability Committee* (UTAS, 2022b), with collaborative feedback and evaluation used to strengthen the programme pedagogically and operationally. Accordingly, SIPS students and their mentors have contributed significantly to the University strategic direction and governance of sustainability and to the University STARS rating.

Focusing on the university experience described as a "living lab," the University enables on-campus research and learning opportunities for a diverse range of students to be part of the SIPS programme. The potential for university campuses to be "living labs" for sustainability has been well documented (Rivera & Savage, 2020; Verhoef et al., 2019).

In collaboration with academic and professional staff from across the University, SIPS provides students with mentoring, support, and opportunity to bring their passions to life through leading tangible projects as part of a team comprising paid interns, students studying for course credit, and research candidates. It also enables an increasing number of students to participate in societies and clubs as collaborators bringing together expertise and skills from different areas of the University.

The most distinctive feature of SIPS is its scale and diversity. Since its inception in 2010, the programme has continually supported thousands of students to engage meaningfully with sustainability in a manner that complements their academic learning and prepares them for implementing sustainability in their lives and future workplaces. Further, SIPS has involved hundreds of staff across academic and professional areas, facilitating personal and professional growth. Without SIPS, these opportunities for students and staff to be engaged in progressing sustainability at the University in such an impactful way would not exist. To date, there have been more than 248 projects involving over 2,550 students and 108 staff from 12 academic and professional areas. SIPS projects have direct or indirect environmental, social, operational, and financial benefits, including resource efficiency (e.g., energy, transport, water, and waste), better data collection to help identify problematic areas and sustainability opportunities (e.g., mobile apps tailored for the University data collection), and infrastructure design (e.g., bicycle hubs). SIPS projects have also involved on-campus biodiversity, such as developing the Natural Values Scavenger Game and the Marine Biodiversity Discovery Trail, and running the first University "BioBlitz" on campus in 2021 that identified 178 plant, animal, and fungal species. SIPS interns also facilitate the UN SDG Tasmania network, a network of over 100 Tasmanian organisations. SIPS students contribute to and participate in several *Sustainability Committee* (UTAS, 2022b) working groups, including Plastics Minimisation, Education for Sustainability (EfS) Community of Practice, and Students for Sustainability.

The popularity of the programme is very evident, as it received 143 applications in 2021, for 17 positions available in 2022, making it one of the top three most popular paid student jobs on campus, which all receive equivalent application numbers. The programme has also increased its impact through contributions to both student experience and operational sustainability. Recognition of these benefits has manifested in increased resourcing being allocated to it, wherein the SIPS coordination role within the Sustainability team has grown from a part-time contract position when it was created in 2016, to a full-time ongoing senior officer position, with additional budget allocated to support student projects more directly.

SIPS students and mentors have consistently provided positive feedback about their experiences. They have identified benefits including the opportunity for networking, flexibility, feeling supported, meaningfulness of the projects, and learning new skills and knowledge of sustainability. Financial benefits are achieved in terms of avoided costs for consultant fees, and in addition, some projects result in financial benefits from savings derived from reduced resources use and disposal, such as through energy efficiency projects and waste reduction programmes and education campaigns. Developing internal partnerships harnesses UTAS community knowledge, allowing SIPS to deliver cost efficiency for sustainability initiatives. Savings can also be achieved, as projects requiring funding now access budgets used for outsourcing. Instead, students are provided an academically relevant experience while delivering a "work force" to advance the sustainability agenda. For many projects, only low levels of funding are required to ensure a project can progress (e.g., purchase of personal protective equipment or transport), with low labour costs or overheads. The return on investment is substantial when considering gains in staff and student knowledge, positive changes towards sustainability behaviours and practices, and the contribution of project findings to operational sustainability and capital works projects.

17.7.2   STARS in Action 2: Addressing SDG13: Climate Action

The University's leading role in climate action is also evident in its focus on the SDGs in general and SDG 13: Climate Action, in particular; this is monitored through STARS. The University's carbon neutral certification, research impact, and emission reduction efforts contributed to UTAS being ranked #1 globally out 674 universities in the THE *Impact Ranking* (2022) for SDG13 Climate Action.

Climate Action at UTAS has made steady progress for well over a decade, encompassing activities in operations, research, and community outreach. University students have demonstrated strong leadership in this space over the past ten years, and with broad-based staff support. This is a unique aspect of the University's commitment to climate action, in that students have been critical catalysts throughout the University's journey to carbon neutrality and emissions reduction. The University encourages students to share their voices as demonstrated by student-led forums, workshops, rallies, and petitions (e.g., "Go Fossil Free") in relation to Climate Action (e.g., Fossil Free UTAS, 2019; Sinclair, 2017). Furthermore, students lead or participate in various sustainability projects, including climate action-related projects. The 2019 Green Gown Awards Australasia highly commended "Repower the Tasmanian University Union" project as an outstanding example of students' engagement and students and University staff collaboration for sustainability (http://www.greeng ownawards.org/2019-winners2). The project delivered the first 100% student-funded on-site renewably powered Australasian student union, highlighting to students that renewable energy is a viable climate change response that leveraged the opportunity to support student leaders. Furthermore, SIPS has seen 495 students involved in climate-related projects across energy, waste, transport, food, and gardens between 2017 and 2022.

An example of holistic climate action focus and sectoral leadership was demonstrated when UTAS announced its commitment to certified carbon neutrality from 2016. Although several universities have established a target to become "carbon neutral" in the next few years or decades, carbon neutral certification requires annual reporting and actions to address all material emissions sources. These include scope 1 (direct emissions, e.g., from burning fossil fuels for heating and transport), scope 2 (indirect emissions from use of grid-based electricity), and scope 3 (all other material emission sources such as staff business travel, construction activity, procurement activities). Without certification, carbon neutral claims may only focus on scope 1 and scope 2, with limited, if any, scope 3 sources included (Open Sourced Workplace, 2022). Although a good start, in contrast, UTAS has included all material emissions across all three scopes as required for carbon neutral certification by the Commonwealth Climate Active (2021) programme. In 2017, and starting for calendar year 2016, UTAS became one of only two carbon neutral certified universities in Australia. The University has chosen to become (and remain) certified carbon neutral to support a strong focus on progressively reducing emissions. Climate Active publishes the University's Public Disclosure Statements in its certified organisations webpage (Climate Active, 2022), and the latest, more detailed University's Greenhouse gas emissions data (UTAS, 2021) is published on the University's website.

Since 2014, University staff and student bodies, such as Fossil Free UTAS, have advocated for divestment from fossil fuels; in 2018 UTAS was fully divested in the direct investment portfolio and achieved full divestment from fossil fuels in the remaining portfolios in 2021. Additional positive screening for direct investments was also introduced for broader environmental, social, and governance outcomes. Building on the carbon neutral and investment policy changes, the University also joined the Global Universities Climate Alliance in 2019 and made the "Race to Zero" commitment in 2021. The Vice-Chancellor's direct support and encouragement via bulk emails to staff and students to attend the Schools Strikes for Climate (Climate Council, 2019) over the past few years are other examples of the University's commitment to being open and public about the climate emergency.

Although emissions reduction has been a focus of individual action plans for transport, energy, and waste for many years, a detailed "all in one place" Emissions Reduction Strategic Plan (UTAS, 2022a) across all current emission sources was approved by UTAS leadership in early 2022. Examples of emissions reduction range from achieving a greater than 30% reduction in embodied carbon emissions in two new buildings in Launceston and directly avoiding over 6,000 tCO2-e through various initiatives since 2006, including fuel source changes, energy efficiency, sustainable transport, air conditioning control upgrades, waste management, and renewable energy installations.

The University also has several areas with a significant applied research focus in climate. For example, the University's Climate Futures group leads the nation in impact mapping at a fine scale, winning the 2012 Resilient Australia Award from Emergency Management Australia (Climate Futures, 2012). This project was an Australian leader and one of the first of its kind internationally due to its localised projections. Data from the project are now being made available to many sectors of the community including state and local government, emergency services, water authorities, power companies, farmers, graziers, fruit growers, vignerons, and researchers. Academic staff regularly present to company Boards and CEOs.

Other groups engaged in activities relating to climate action include the Centre for Renewable Energy and Power Systems (CREPS), the Blue Economy Cooperative Research Centre led by the University, the Centre for Marine Socioecology, and the Global Climate Change Week committee, as well as a number of groups researching ecological restoration in the face of climate change.

17.8   Conclusion

The challenge of understanding and embedding holistic sustainability is difficult and complex for many organisations, including the higher education sector, not only given its remit to fulfil its community and knowledge building obligations, but also its necessity to remain financially viable while doing so. As an example of a higher education institution that has progressed rapidly through various stages of a sustainability maturity scale, the University of Tasmania has successfully applied a governance structure, guiding framework, and monitoring and reporting systems to guide and document the effort, as well as the resources and leadership imprimatur required. The UNSDGs, the LiFE Index, and the STARS have been used to inform the University's approach as documented in the *Framework* (UTAS, 2020). These tools and the *Framework* provide the accountability and transparency required to meet staff, student, peer, and community expectations.

The University has parlayed its efforts into becoming a leading sustainable university both in its region and globally, with examples including a Gold STARS rating, international award-winning programmes such as SIPS, and recognition for holistic efforts in specific areas of endeavour, such as achieving the #1 *THE Impact Ranking* in SDG13—Climate Action in 2022 and 2023, including advancing from #25 in 2022 to #5 in 2023 for overall work on the SDGs. With these successes, the stage has been set to underpin the additional work required to achieve further positive impacts across the SDGs and achieve a Platinum STARS rating. The STARS rating system, aligned with the SDGs, provides a strong, workable, implementable framework within which all stakeholders can continue to develop policies, strategies, and procedures to enable UTAS to achieve its mission to be a leading sustainable, innovative, global university.

References

Adlong, W. (2013). Rethinking the talloires declaration. *International Journal of Sustainability in Higher Education, 14*(1), 56–70. https://doi.org/10.1108/14676371311288958

Association for the Advancement of Sustainability in Higher Education. (2020). *Can we use STARS to report on our contributions to the United Nations Sustainable Development Goals (SDGs)?* https://stars.aashe.org/resources-support/help-center/the-basics/can-we-use-stars-to-report-on-our-contributions-to-the-united-nations-sustainable-development-goals-sdgs/

Bekessy, S. A., Samson, K., & Clarkson, R. E. (2007). The failure of non-binding declarations to achieve university sustainability: A need for accountability. *International Journal of Sustainability in Higher Education, 8*(3). https://doi.org/10.1108/14676370710817165

Caeiro, S., Hamon, L. A. S., Martins, R., & Aldaz, C. E. B. (2020). Sustainability assessment and benchmarking in higher education institutions—A critical reflection. *Sustainability, 12*(2), 543. https://doi.org/10.3390/su12020543

Climate Active. (2021). *Australia's collective action.* http://www.climateactive.org.au/

Climate Active. (2022). *University of Tasmania.* https://www.climateactive.org.au/buy-climate-active/certified-members/university-tasmania

Climate Council. (2019). *Australian students strike for climate action.* https://www.climatecouncil.org.au/australian-students-strike-for-climate-action/

Climate Futures. (2012). *ACE CRC team wins national award.* https://climatefutures.org.au/news/ace-crc-team-wins-national-award/

Dziminska, M., Fijalkowska, J., & Sulkowski, L. (2020). A conceptual model proposal: Universities as culture change agents for sustainable development. *Sustainability, 12*(11), 4635. https://doi.org/10.3390/su12114635

Ferreira, J., & Tilbury, D. (2012). Higher education and sustainability in Australia: Transforming experiences. In Global University Network for Innovation (Ed.), *Higher education in the world 4, higher education's commitment to sustainability: From understanding to action* (pp. 96–99). Palgrave Macmillan.

Fossil Free UTAS. (2019). https://www.facebook.com/fossilfreeUTAS/?business_id=10152592499697447

Global Reporting Initiative. (2021). *Universal standards.* https://www.globalreporting.org/standards/standards-development/universal-standards/

International Green Gown Awards. (2022). *University of Tasmania, Australia winner: Creative and critical inquiry leads change: The sustainability integration program for students.* https://www.greengownawards.org/university-of-tasmania-australia1

Learning in Future Environments. (2014). *About LiFE.* https://life.acts.asn.au/about-LiFE/

Minutolo, M. C., Ivanova, A., & Cong, M. (2021). Signaling sustainability: Impact that learning how to report has on enrolment, endowment and emissions of North American higher education institutions. *Sustainability Accounting, Management and Policy Journal, 12*(5), 1140–1158. https://doi.org/10.1108/SAMPJ-06-2020-0224

Open Sourced Workplace. (2022). *What are the three scopes of carbon emissions?* https://opensourcedworkplace.com/news/what-are-the-three-scopes-of-carbon-emissions

Rivera, C. J., & Savage, C. (2020). Campuses as living labs for sustainability problem solving: Trends, triumphs and traps. *Journal of Environmental Studies and Sciences, 10*(3), 334–340.

Salvioni, D. M., Franzoni, S., & Cassano, R. (2017). Sustainability in the higher education system: An opportunity to improve quality and image. *Sustainability, 9*(6), 914. https://doi.org/10.3390/su9060914

Sinclair. A. (2017). *Investigation into the University of California system approaches to achieving carbon neutrality by 2025: A student perspective.* University of Tasmania. https://www.utas.edu.au/__data/assets/pdf_file/0014/804020/US-Mission-Report-Student-Perspective.pdf

STARS. (n.d.). *Technical manual.* https://stars.aashe.org/resources-support/technical-manual/

STARS. (2022). *Sustainability tracking, assessment and rating system.* https://stars.aashe.org/

Times Higher Education. (2022). *Impact rankings 2022.* https://www.timeshighereducation.com/impactrankings#!/page/0/length/25/sort_by/rank/sort_order/asc/cols/undefined

United Nations. (n.d.). *Sustainable development: The 17 goals.* https://sdgs.un.org/goals

University Leaders for a Sustainable Future. (1990). *Talloires declaration.* http://ulsf.org/talloires-declaration/

University of Tasmania. (n.d.). *Sustainability integration program for students.* https://www.theUniversity.edu.au/infrastructure-services-development/sustainability/SIPS

University of Tasmania. (2016–2022). *Sustainability surveys.* https://www.utas.edu.au/sustainability/performance/sustainability-surveys

University of Tasmania. (2019). *Strategic plan 2019–2024: Sustainable development goals (SDGs)*. https://www.theUniversity.edu.au/__data/assets/pdf_file/0004/1255234/THE UNIVERSITY-Strategy-Document-2019.pdf

University of Tasmania. (2020). *Strategic framework for sustainability 2019–2024*. https://www.theUniversity.edu.au/__data/assets/pdf_file/0014/1302422/UOTBR200122-THE UNIVERSITY-Strategic-Framework-For-Sustainability-2020_vWeb_R.pdf

University of Tasmania. (2021). *Greenhouse gas emissions data*. https://www.theUniversity.edu. au/infrastructure-services-development/sustainability/greenhouse-gas-emissions/gas-accord ion/our-progress

University of Tasmania. (2022a). *Greenhouse gas emissions reduction strategic plan 2022a–2030*. https://www.utas.edu.au/__data/assets/pdf_file/0006/1583250/UTAS-Emissions-Reduct ion-Strategic-Plan-2022-2030.pdf

University of Tasmania. (2022b). *Sustainability committee*. https://www.THEUNIVERSITY.edu. au/sustainability/governance/sustainability-committee

Verhoef, L. A., Bossert, M., Newman, J., Ferraz, F., Robinson, Z. P., Agarwala, Y., Wolff III, P. J., Jiranek, P., & Hellinga, C. (2019). Towards a learning system for university campuses as living labs for sustainability. In W. L. Filho, A. L. Salvia, R. W. Pretorius, L. L. Brandli, E. Manolas, F. Alves, U. Azeiteiro, J. Rogers, C. Shiel, & A. Do Paco (Eds.), *Universities as living labs for sustainable development* (pp. 135–149). Springer. https://doi.org/10.1007/978-3-030-156 04-6_9

Part IV
Enacting Sustainable Development Goals in University Practice

Chapter 18
The Role of Arts and Crafts in Promotion of Students' Awareness About Environment and Sustainable Development Goals: The Case of Tabriz Islamic Art University, Iran

Morteza Mirgholami

18.1 Introduction

Universities and Higher Educations Institutes (HEI) are drivers of development and knowledge transfer, as well as of innovative solutions for social, economic, and environmental problems. The role and mission of universities, however, is dynamic and evolving, based on the transformation of societies from industrial to post-industrial, network, and knowledge-based economies. Universities are classified based on this evolution and upgrading into several generations known as first and second generation (teaching and research centres), respectively, to more recent models of third, fourth, and fifth generation (Lukovics & Zuti, 2013; Taylor, 2001). Since the beginning of the twenty-first century, there has been a shift in Western economies from a linear innovation model to a nonlinear, interactive paradigm and knowledge-based economy, in which research, innovation, and economic growth dynamically interact with industry, policymakers, and HEIs (De la Poza et al., 2021; Florinda & Gaetani, 2020).

Despite huge progress in terms of technology, including SMART and Nano technologies, artificial intelligence, life expectancy, medical equipment, and overall improvement in global welfare, new challenges such as poverty and injustice, climate change, pollution, and environmental degradations call for new responsibilities for universities. These conditions necessitate a revision of universities' vision and mission to integrate sustainability goals into their research, curriculum,

M. Mirgholami (✉)
Centre for Urban Research, RMIT University, 124 La Trobe St, Melbourne, VIC 3000, Australia
e-mail: moretza.mirgholami@rmit.edu.au

and campus design in order to be able to combat such problems and adapt themselves to the Sustainable Development Goals (SDGs) to play more effective roles as leading centres of society (Bhowmik et al., 2018; Čiegis & Gineitienė, 2006; ISCN Report, 2014). Art Universities can have a critical role in incorporating SDGs in their research, campus environment, and curriculum, and especially using art, not just as a visual and aesthetic phenomenon, but also as an inspiring element and driving force through which environmental awareness and attention of students, staff, and communities to sustainability can be triggered and internalised. In neoliberal economies, as systems in Habermas's (1987) term, universities encounter the challenge of commodification that threatens their lifeworld, reducing them from places of civil discourse and students' self-actualisation to centres of wealth creation and technocratic-bureaucratic rationality. Universities in developing countries such as Iran face both commodifications of knowledge via producing college qualifications in exchange for money, and also ideological subjection and homogenisation by central policies that ignore the geographical diversity of different provinces.

This chapter explores the actions taken by Tabriz Islamic Art University across two separate sections: (1) the official aspects in terms of research, curriculum, campus design and governance, and external leadership to integrate SDGs, in its mission towards an innovative and entrepreneur university in art and craft; and (2) the informal and innovative approaches employed by some of the staff in practical teaching to internalise sustainable goals in students' views that would inspire them in their future lifestyles and practice, and push the SDGs beyond the campus boundaries, and with greater influence.

Observation, archival records, and interviews with students and academic staffs have been used as methods to collect data and delve into the university's contribution to SDGs (Table 18.1).

Table 18.1 Some characteristics of first, second, and third-generation universities (Lukovics & Zuti, 2013)

Aspect	First generation universities	Second generation universities	Third generation universities
Goal	Education	Education and research	Education, research and utilization of knowledge
Role	Protection of truth	The cognition of nature	Creation of added value
Output	Professionals	Professionals and scientists	Professionals, scientists and entrepreneurs

18.2   Art Universities as Inspirational Environments for Contributing to Sustainable Development Goals in Iran: Limits and Opportunities

Development with economic progress is a driving force. It is an engine that has motivated many governments and mobilised their actions towards investment in knowledge and technology transfer, and establishing industries, R&D activities, research centres, and universities to provide more prosperity, welfare, and happiness for their societies (Lukovics & Zuti, 2013). Florinda and Gaetani (2020) highlight the universities' role as a key source of talent, and a key driver of innovation and economic growth, in a knowledge-based economy. The superiority of a technocratic and economic interpretation of development, in neoliberal economies and some developing countries, however, has prioritised the economy over the social, cultural, and environmental aspects of development, resulting in unsustainable development. Therefore, the 2030 Agenda for Sustainable Development was adopted by all UN members in 2015, which introduced 17 global goals to tackle the world's challenges, and gave a critical role to universities to take action and find solutions in this regard. The irony is that universities were part of the problem themselves because they had been transformed from centres of teaching, thinking, and inspiration (first generation) to economic enterprises that turn knowledge into wealth and power, and endorse consumerism. This issue is reflected in the writings of some scholars such as Readings (1997), Fazeli (2017), and Lewis (2007). Lewis is a professor and the previous dean of Harvard University. In his book, *Excellence without a Soul: Does liberal education have a future?*, Lewis has criticised the way Harvard, as a leading education centre in America, has forgotten that the fundamental purpose of undergraduate education is to turn young people into adults who will take responsibility for society.

In developing countries such as Iran, with centralised political and economic systems, universities that should be symbols of development and leadership, are elitist and bureaucratic centres with little role in integrating and inspiring local communities or providing local solutions and preparing students for social and environmental challenges. They are faced with two challenges dependent on the ownership model: non-public universities such as Azad and Gheire-Entefai universities (nearly 840 out of 2569[1] total campuses) are commodified education centres that reduce universities to economic agencies, which create their finances via tuition fees, and produce large numbers of graduate students without guaranteeing their future employment. Public universities (141 campuses), as financially dependent state centres, also have to conform to the state's ideological and political values and follow the curriculum that is dictated by the Ministry of Science, Research and Technology (MSRT) (Fazeli, 2003). Fazeli (2017) criticises this hierarchical system and the bias towards technology and science over educational, inspirational, and social roles of universities, which is reflected in the title of the ministry itself (previously known as the Ministry of

---

[1] This consensus only represents universities under the Ministry of Science, Research and Technology (MSRT). Medical science universities are under another ministry called Ministry of Health and Medical Education.

Culture and Higher Education). He introduces a concept called "university culture", which is about enabling stakeholders, i.e., students and staff, to teach, learn, discover, and innovate independently without any subordination to consumerism and academic commodification or ideological homogenisation. An academic member in this view is not just a staff member with an affiliation, a human resource, ranking enabler, research producer, or grant catcher, but also an independent individual with abilities, skills, and intuition who can criticise, innovate, teach, and train responsible citizens.

Fazeli (2017) criticises what he calls the "researchism policy" of the Ministry, developed after the 1980s that encouraged the production of more research projects, papers, and books by universities (known as second generation), without increasing the quality of the applied research and fulfilling the more primary task of universities, i.e., educating students as skilled, self-actualised, esteemed, and responsible citizens.

Art universities in Iran, including fine arts and traditional arts and crafts, are no exception to these conditions. Therefore, universities, especially those with social science and art curricula, should revise their missions and characters to go beyond the roles that are defined by the Ministry to become centres for entrepreneurship and innovation, not just for wealth creation, but also for community engagement, environmental awareness, and problem-solving. They should take effective action by integrating new strategies and objectives into their vision plans to be able to act more ethically, socially, and environmentally, and to integrate sustainable goals into their environment. But how this might happen?

18.2.1 How Universities in General and Art Universities in Particular Can Contribute to the SDGs

Some scholars, including Kestin and her colleagues, in a report produced by the Sustainable Development Solutions Network (SDSN), and Bhowmik et al. (2018), suggest different areas that universities can contribute towards SDGs. These include the four areas of education, research, organisation, and external leadership (Bhowmik et al., 2018; Kestin et al., 2017; Fig. 18.1).

- **Learning and teaching**: through Education for Sustainable Development (ESD) that provides in-depth academic or vocational expertise to implement SDG solutions.
- **Research**: through facilitating the implementation of the SDGs by the global community through research, evidence-based studies, and facilities; providing capacity building for developing countries in undertaking and using research; and assisting innovative companies to implement SDG solutions.
- **Organisational**: through governance structures and operational policies and decisions, such as employment, finance, campus services, facilities, and student administration, help to implement the principles of the SDGs.

Research on the SDGs
Interdisciplinary and transdisciplinary research
Innovations and solutions
National & local implementation
Capacity building for research

RESEARCH

EDUCATION

Education for sustainable development
Jobs for implementing the SDGs
Capacity building
Mobilising young people

Governance and operations aligned with SDGs
Incorporate into university reporting

OPERATIONS & GOVERNANCE

EXTERNAL LEADERSHIP

Public engagement
Cross-sectoral dialogue and action
Policy development and advocacy
Advocacy for sector role
Demonstrate sector commitment

Fig. 18.1 An overview of university contributions to SDGs (Kestin et al., 2017)

- **External leadership**: through encouraging community engagement and participation in implementing SDGs; cross-sectoral interchange and action; and representation of higher education in national implementation.

Luna-Krauletz et al. (2021) also stressed the role of Higher Education Institutions (HEI) in the transition towards Environmental Education for Sustainability (EEfS). They developed an instrument to assess the level of incorporation of EEfS into the environmental agenda of HEIs, and considered five dimensions for their assessment, including institutional identity, teaching, research, extension/dissemination, and linkage.

Art universities have a more challenging role in contributing to SDGs, because a knowledge-based economy driven by technologies and industries, they have to compete with scientific disciplines that are responsible for some of the environmental crises. There is also an aesthetic bias towards art that defines it as an elitist cultural product to be presented in the realm of galleries, concert halls, and museums. Such definition of art, however, has been revised and new forms of environmental art and aesthetics such as "eco-art" and "sustainable aesthetics" have emerged from the 1990s onwards. Eco-art is a form of art that acts more ethically and responsibly towards environmental crises such as climate change, deforestation, water shortage, pollution, war, nuclear threats, and economic recession (Weintraub, 2012).

Eco-art is not limited to galleries and can be installed in public environments such as campuses, urban spaces, and natural environments (see Fig. 18.2, for example).

Fig. 18.2 A firing sculpture built in the central campus with students' participation

Some types of eco-art such as public firings encourage public engagement and participation in the process of artwork creation (Mirgholami & Fallah, 2021). Traditional arts and crafts such as pottery, woodwork, architecture, and carpet weaving are rich sources of inspiration for modern and contemporary eco-artists to transmit environmental messages to the public and contribute to the SDGs.

Heather Leier, the winner of the 2020 Sustainability Teaching Award and an art professor at Calgary University, believes that art universities can integrate SDGs into their curricula and research programs, not as separate goals but as interconnected ones. She uses the term "global citizens" to highlight the role of students as responsible actors with worldwide influencing impacts, not limited to their campuses, cities, or even countries (Crossland, 2020).

Therefore, with evolving new approaches to art, art universities can contribute more effectively to SDGs, especially via re-inviting people and students to think critically about nature, and the impacts of unsustainable developments on the environment. Exploring all of the 17 SDGs seems unfeasible in one chapter, so the focus here is only on SDGs 11, 13, and part of Goal 7. SDG 11 relates to creating sustainable, inclusive, and resilient cities and settlements. Urban design and planning approaches such as urban regeneration, child-friendly cities, pedestrian-oriented and biophilic cities fulfil this goal. SDG 13 calls for mitigating climate change and its impacts, via a collective responsibility to support flexible capacity and resilience to environmental crises related to climate change. Mitigation, adaptation, impact reduction, and early warnings are different strategies that universities can define in their vision plans. Increasing public awareness and training responsible students, staff, and citizens, who are ready to follow, and encourage more sustainable lifestyles including using public transport, recycling, wise use of energy and food, and less consumerism, are ways in which art universities can contribute to this goal. SDG 7 seeks the provision of affordable, reliable, sustainable, and clean energy for all. Integrating such features in a university's curricula and campus design can make this goal operational.

18.3 Tabriz Islamic Art University and Contribution to SDGs Through Official and Non-official Procedures

This section explores Tabriz Islamic Art University in Iran as a case study to assess its contribution to SDGs 7, 11, and 13, using Fazeli's (2017) concept of "university culture" as its critical approach and observation, with interviews and archival records as its methods. Four areas of assessment, including 1: governance and campus design; 2: research; 3: teaching; and 4: external leadership (community engagement), are used as the criteria for assessment of the university's contribution to the SDGs.

It should be noted that Iran's Ministry of Science, Research and Technology (MSRT) has not introduced the SDG agenda to universities as an official policy to be integrated, implemented, or embedded in their strategies, policies, and plans as yet, but a number of universities have taken reasonable steps towards some of these goals voluntarily. Tabriz Islamic Art University is one university that has taken some effective steps towards integrating SDGs 7, 11, and 13, to promote students' awareness of environmental challenges and sustainable solutions for cities, due to its specific context, operational policies, and curriculum. These actions are explored across two categories of official and non-official actions. Here, "official" includes the vision and mission statement that are reflected on the university's website and through curriculum, reporting, and policies, as well as the institutional structures that are defined under the central state's policies. This is similar to what Habermas (1987) calls "System". "System", in his view, is composed of formal organisations, such as governments, unions, institutions, and parties. The members of such organisations have official roles and must follow the pre-defined objectives of the system. Non-official actions cover what is taken on by staff and students voluntarily, innovatively, and individually, through their life worlds, which are experiential, lived, and meaningful. The Lifeworld, in Habermas's communicative action theory, means the background of ordinary life, which is mainly private, but authentic and essential to people's satisfaction as human beings.

Tabriz is a metropolitan city in the north-east of Iran, best known for its historical grand bazaar, carpets, and brick architecture. Tabriz Islamic Art University was founded in 1999 with three disciplines of architecture, carpet, and handicraft. The first campus was in fact a complex of three decayed traditional houses in a historical neighbourhood that were restored and turned into a small university. With the increase in students and establishment of new degrees, disciplines, and faculties, such as urban design, architecture and energy, industrial design, applied art, and multimedia art, four other traditional houses in the neighbourhood were bought and an old abandoned leather factory was also donated to the university to materialise the second campus and a successful urban regeneration project in Tabriz. New facilities and services such as a library, sports facilities, amphitheatre, museum and an art exhibition, mosque, administration offices, workshops, and laboratories were added gradually.

The leather factory was founded in 1934. The electric generator of this plant was the first Iranian industrial generator in history, built in 1935 in Leningrad, Russia, and its six-cylinder diesel provided electricity for some parts of Tabriz (see Fig. 18.3). The university provides a green and attractive campus for its 2934 students via preserving an urban heritage site and training students in traditional arts and crafts techniques such as pottery, carpet design, woodwork, glass art, and modern disciplines such as industrial design and multimedia art to create innovative and contemporary artworks. It consists of seven faculties including Architecture and Urbanism, Crafts, Fine Arts, Industrial Design, Multimedia Art, Carpet, and Applied Arts (heritage objects restoration). Some of the disciplines have a technological nature combined with art, which provides an interdisciplinary environment for students to learn, practise, and research at three academic levels from bachelor to Ph.D. (Tabriz Islamic Art University TIAU Booklet, 2018).

The contribution of the university to the SDGs can be categorised, based on the Kestin's et al. (2017) proposed model, into four areas as follows.

Fig. 18.3 One of the buildings of the leather factory before and after the restoration—sustainability in practice

18.3.1   Campus Design, Governance, and Institutional Structure

The design of the university campus exemplifies sustainable design practice, because it demonstrates how to reduce a carbon footprint by preventing the use of new materials and construction of buildings, reuse and recycling materials, and incorporating renewable energy technologies such as solar panels on the roofs of some buildings (SDGs 7, 11, and 13) (Fig. 18.4).

The central campus of the university, which used to be the Khosravi leather factory, was the first factory operated in the history of Iran's industry. Daily exposure to sustainability solutions in all aspects of campus design and planning, is a powerful teaching tool, and campus sustainability programs can also contribute to it. Both central and architecture campuses, as regenerated historical sites via restoration and reuse of materials, enable students, staff, and visitors to experience many aspects of sustainable environments such as adaptability, using renewable energy, vernacular materials, and water recycling. Traditional underground water storage at the central campus (the leather factory) and the architecture campus, save rainwater for irrigation of the green space. Both campuses exemplify urban sustainable features including improvement of environmental quality and green space, stimulating redevelopment of underdeveloped areas, attracting tourists, and preserving traditional urban identity. The university decided to turn a recently purchased residential building on the Architecture campus into a zero-carbon complex to accommodate students of Energy and

Fig. 18.4 Central university campus that incorporates five faculties: Crafts, visual arts, industrial design, carpet, and heritage objects restoration (applied art). The multimedia art and the architecture faculty are located in separated campuses

Architecture. Nevertheless, an energy audit of the campus buildings and improvement of the thermal insulation systems, using timed lamps and sensor faucets, and grey water treatment, are actions that are still needed to be taken by the university with respect to SDGs 11, 13, and 7 in the future.

In terms of governance, the mission statement of the university stresses its role as a third-generation university that is geared towards vocational teaching and practical training of students, helping them to run their businesses after graduation.

> The University pays special attention to students' relationship with traditional arts and bringing brilliant talents up, training well-educated students, and paying attention to work and entrepreneurship. The university, with the cooperation of talented professors, honorable staff and esteemed students tries to act as an entrepreneur university with a fully electronic administration system … (Tabriz Islamic Art University Booklet, 2018, Part of Mission Statement)

There is no specific and direct policy statement mentioning terms such as sustainable development or the SDGs in the mission statement, but issues such as entrepreneurship can be interpreted as a sustainable policy.

> The first third-generation university (entrepreneur in the field of art) … It [the university] is equipped with several art entrepreneurship workshops along with training and doing research with a special emphasis on entrepreneurship in the field of Islamic-technical artistic education at the academic level. The university is considered as the first third-generation in the field of art. To compete with Muslim artists of other nations, the graduates of the university produce and sell their innovative and creative products in the entrepreneurial workshops of the university. In another step, the university has provided a permanent exhibition of the artistic products in Campus No.1, with cooperation of private sector, to support the private entrepreneurs and housewives, in order to provide a practical opportunity to sell their products and attempt exhibition held in other countries. (Tabriz Islamic Art University Booklet, 2018; Fig. 18.5)

Based on the above extracts from the official university mission statement, it can be argued that even though these sorts of entrepreneurial workshops and exhibitions can help to promote students' practical and professional skills, they also may reduce the artworks to products, as marketable and "kitsch" outputs that do not transmit ethical or responsible messages expected from an artwork by the public.

The university's institutional charts allow for three vice president positions including education and innovation, research and entrepreneurship, and cultural-social-student affairs, and three sub-sectors including a centre for soft technologies, an entrepreneur centre, and an environment club that can contribute to sustainable goals. The centre for soft technologies and cultural industries includes eight pre-growth and nine post-growth units, working on innovative research-based ideas in areas such as furniture, art, tourism, and industrial products which can be turned into marketable products. The entrepreneur centre, founded in 2009, offers more than 50 workshops, providing workspace, loans, and technical advice for about 77 students in support of their connection with the industries and urban community. Students can exhibit their products at the university's art exhibition and shops for selling. Some of the students, supported by these two centres, also present their ideas and innovations at annual state or national exhibitions such as the Rinotex innovation and technology

Fig. 18.5 Faculty of architecture and urbanism's campus contains six traditional Qajari houses with vast open and green yards at the heart of the city

exhibition.[2] There are 13 students clubs under the university cultural sector, mostly for the cultural, religious, and health affairs of students. The only club relevant to SDGs 11 and 13 is the environment club that acts as a campus monitoring unit to encourage sustainable behaviour, such as recycling, reuse, and prevention of plastic use in the campus. According to the interview with the president of this club, students made innovative proposals such as making clay mugs for students and staff to stop the use of disposable products, participating in campus arboriculture and planting, creating a pigeon house for campus birds to protect brick surfaces from acid excreta, designing recycling bins for the campus, reusing students' artworks waste materials and steel sculptures after their exhibition, and taking up a sterilisation program for stray dogs living around the campus. However, many of these ideas could not be materialised due to budget shortages and the university's bureaucracy.

---

[2] Rinotex is a knowledge-based business environment in Tabriz since 2005. https://rinotex.ir/.

18.3.2   External Leadership and Community Participation

Even though the open-door policy attracts citizens and other sectors to the university campuses during the research week every year, this connection should be expanded and promoted in institutional terms to increase the cross-sector and community engagement with the university. Voluntary engagement of some of the academic staff with local institutions and industries such as the municipality, the city council, and heritage organisation in terms of knowledge transfer and offering advice to reduce negative impacts of developments on natural environment and historical neighbourhoods, are other examples of the university's contribution to SDGs, especially SDG 11, via external leadership.

18.3.3   Research Areas and Activities

According to Kestin et al. (2017), research is an important area through which universities can contribute to the SDGs. Table 18.2 reports the number of SDG-oriented research projects across the faculties against the total number of projects conducted by each faculty's staff members. The author reviewed the university research projects to identify the integration and consideration of SDGs in their topics. It is evident that the number of research projects with respect to the SDGs are trivial (18 out of 142) and the university's research vision should direct and encourage more research activities towards SDGs. Research titles such as "the impact of colours used in the carpet industry on water pollution", "natural elements affecting the establishment of sustainable historical city of Tabriz", and "infill development in historical districts of Tabriz with conservation approach" exemplify the contribution of university's research projects to SDGs, especially SDG 11.

Table 18.2 Research projects and the SDGs at Tabriz Islamic Art University

Faculty	Number of conducted research projects	Number of related projects to SDGs 11, 13, 7
Architecture and urbanism	56	13
Crafts	18	0
Industrial design	16	0
Carpet	21	1
Heritage objects restoration	20	1
Multimedia art	11	3
Fine arts	0	0
Total	142	18

18.3.4   Teaching Curriculum and Students' Works

As the chapter aims to highlight the educational role of arts and crafts in promotion of students' environmental awareness and their contribution to SDGs, this section explores both official university curriculum and non-official teaching activities with regard to SDGs 11, 13, and 7. Table 18.3 illustrates the structure of faculty disciplines and curriculum (Bachelor, Master, and Ph.D. degrees) and the number of credits relevant to SDGs compared with the total number of modules. Again, the author's review of the taught materials and credits revealed the extent of SDG integration in their contents.

As is evident in the table below, the number of credits based on topics relevant to SDGs is marginal compared with the total number of credits, and a review of some of the faculties' curriculum, including carpet, heritage objects restoration, and fine arts, reveals that there are no modules included with regard to SDGs in their program. However, conducting extracurricular workshops and seminars such as LEED (Leadership in Energy and Environmental Design) in Iran, urban planning and climate change, and sustainable industrial design and waste management, are evidence of the university's sensibility towards environmental issues, although the number of such events needs to be increased.

Nevertheless, this is the official side of the teaching environment (as conceived by the system) and not the experiential side, the workshop experiences, and the real artworks and output of vocational teaching processes that can integrate SDGs innovatively and effectively into the curriculum. To enhance the "sustainability literacy" of their graduates, leading universities can use innovative approaches to reach students in novel and lasting ways, and to integrate sustainability subject matter across the curriculum. The following section reviews some samples of the practical outputs of design studios and workshops in two faculties, i.e., architecture and crafts, with regard to the SDGs.

In Urban Design and Energy Workshop 3 (semester 1, 2021), for example, Master of Architecture and Energy students selected an abandoned residential site in Tabriz as their topic and provided innovative solutions to rehabilitate the buildings, use

Table 18.3 University curriculum and the SDGs

Faculty	Number of credits taught	Number of related credits to SDGs 11, 13, 7
Multimedia art	202	3
Architecture and urbanism	544	41
Crafts	636	12
Industrial design	205	5
Carpet	270	0
Heritage objects restoration	238	0
Fine arts	316	0

sustainable energy, water, and waste management, and encourage a more sustainable lifestyle through designing a low-carbon emission complex. This workshop exemplifies the innovative role of an instructor in inserting SDGs 11 and 13 in urban design education without any inquiry by the official curricula. Similarly, undergraduate students of architecture in their design studio (school design), with the support of their lecturer (the author), decided to design a school for parentless children. The students visited a real school in Tabriz, talked to children, and engaged actively to understand the social problems in the city to propose sustainable and innovative design solutions for these groups and design an inclusive, resilient, and sustainable school (SDG 11). Eventually, they designed some interior decorations for the children as an exercise, using recycled materials, and donated them to the school. These are not integrated into the official curriculum and studio objectives but can be pursued depending on the lecturer's will and interest.

Similarly, students of arts and crafts in their pottery workshop and an external exhibition called Enbesat in Tehran, presented successful forms of eco-art collections entitled Negaran (Solicitous), addressing several environmental crises, such as water shortages, air pollution, animal extinctions, sea pollution, etc., with the objective of promoting environmental awareness.

Artworks in Figs. 18.6–18.8 illustrate the water crises in Iran and the world. The first artwork shows how a small hole in a bowl can put the life of the two fish at risk silently and gradually. Visitors are invited to engage actively in this challenge and pour the leaking water back in the bowl again. It is a simple work but very impressive.

The second artwork (Fig. 18.7) illustrates Aquarius, a water bearer character in mythology with a dammed jug in his arm, criticising the impact of dam development in Iran. The third work also cautions about the water crisis, showing people standing with containers in a queue for water. This image is familiar to Iranians and reminds them of the kerosene queues during the war period with Iraq, when there was a shortage of this heating source, and people, with barrels in their hand, had to line in queues to buy it from tankers.

In the fourth artwork (Fig. 18.9), the artist has calculated the amount of dust in different cities of the southwestern Iranian Province of Khoozestan, which has

Fig. 18.6 Artwork by Hani Taj. Pour the leaking water back into the bowl to save the fish

Fig. 18.7 Artwork by Samaneh Marhaba. Aquarius, with a dammed jug. The 11th astrological sign in the zodiac, the mythological symbol of the water bearer

Fig. 18.8 Artwork by Zahra Amani. Water queue. Clay sculptures for Teheran exhibition

struggled with air pollution for years, and used the same weight of dust in each cubic metre of air to build a stamp out of clay. This work has a more powerful effect on visitors' perceptions of the crises than any documentary or scientific measurement because it materialises the catastrophe and the pollution that is experienced by citizens of that province.

Another impressive artwork has created clay whistles in the shape of Iranian extinct animals' heads (Fig. 18.10). Visitors can pick an animal, whistle, and scan the QR to know more about each species. This is an interactive and informative piece of art that stresses the importance of taking actions to save endangered species. It also suggests the Israfil (Raphael) mythology, the angel who blows the trumpet to announce the day of resurrection and injects life into the dead bodies. Other

Fig. 18.9 Artwork by Forough Noei. A stamp made of dust and air pollution in Khoozestan

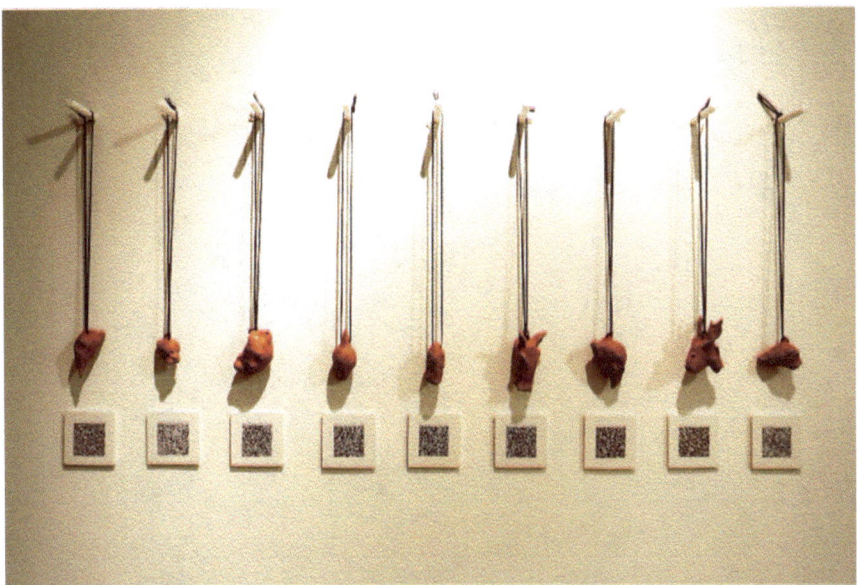

Fig. 18.10   Artwork by Milad Azizi. Whistle to bring the extinct animals back to life

artworks also symbolise the environmental crises, such as sea pollution and climate change (Figs. 18.11 and 18.12). These bottom-up educational art experiences can be considered as efforts made by lecturers and instructors to contribute to SDGs 7 and 11 to promote students' awareness about climate change and sustainable, resilient cities.

18.4   Discussion and Conclusion

This chapter has explored the contribution of Tabriz Islamic Art University to the SDGs across four areas of governance and campus design, external leadership and participation, research, and especially art and crafts teaching. Although the SDGs, as a global agenda, have not been incorporated in the MSRT's national policies, Tabriz Islamic Art University has taken effective steps to reduce environmental impacts via energy efficiency, water-sensitive strategies and reducing pollution, and heritage preservation and restoration in its campus planning. These policies have effectively incorporated SDGs 7, 11, and 13 into the university campus plan and physical infrastructure. However, these actions are not enough, and the university needs to integrate the SDGs more effectively in its different areas of influence, especially teaching and research activities.

The national bias towards entrepreneurship and third-generation universities has encouraged many universities, including Tabriz Islamic Art University, to shift from

Fig. 18.11 Clay penguins in the central campus

Fig. 18.12 Artwork by Zahra Ghaffari Touran. Sea pollution tragedy

their teaching tasks towards knowledge-based activities and economic gains. Art and especially crafts, with their practical aspects, have a powerful potential for involving students in understanding environmental crises and pursuing the SDGs in their academic and professional life. Therefore, it is argued that Tabriz Islamic Art University should invest more in quality education, not just as formal curriculum imposed by the institutional bureaucracy, but as innovative and bottom-up interaction between students and motivated lecturers at the life-world scale. The university needs to take a holistic approach towards the SDGs to make them fully integrated into its four areas of influence and should avoid soulless and quantity-driven policies. Instead, it should adopt and outline more policies in the area of environmental sustainability and community engagement. It should also practically declare that the university is a place for independent thinking and protection of the truth, self-actualisation, innovation, and self-confidence, that act responsibly towards local and global crises, and is not just an economic agency or physical campus with high-tech buildings and facilities.

Acknowledgements I would like to thank Dr. Majid Ziai, Assistant Professor of the Faculty of Crafts, for his generous provision of students' artwork images in the Enbesat Exhibition, and for his thoughtful comments on the topic.

References

Bhowmik, J., Selim, S., & Huq, S. (2018, Feb). *The role of universities in achieving the Sustainable Development Goals.* CSD-ULAB and ICCCAD Policy Brief. ULAB. http://www.icccad.net/wp-content/uploads/2015/12/Policy-Brief-on-role-of-Universities-in-achieving-SDGs.pdf

Crossland, M. (2020, May 19). *Can art help to achieve the United Nations sustainable development goals? Interview with Heather Leier.* University of Calgary. https://ucalgary.ca/news/can-art-help-achieve-united-nations-sustainable-development-goals

Čiegis, R., & Gineitienė, D. (2006). The role of universities in promoting sustainability. *Engineering Economics, 3*(48), 56–62. https://inzeko.ktu.lt/index.php/EE/article/view/11373

De la Poza, E., Merello, P., Barberá, A., & Celani, A. (2021). Universities' reporting on SDGs: Using the impact rankings to model and measure their contribution to sustainability. *Sustainability, 13*(4), 20–38. https://doi.org/10.3390/su13042038

Fazeli, N. (2003). A comparative study of Iranian and British academic cultures: An anthropological investigation into the inefficiency of Iranian academic education. *Iranian Journal of Anthropology, 1*(3), 93–132. https://www.sid.ir/paper/66351/en

Fazeli, N. (2017). *Culture and university.* Sales Publication.

Florinda, R., & Gaetani, R. (2020). The university's Janus face: The innovation-inequality nexus. *Managerial and Decisions Economics, 41*(6), 1097–1112. https://doi.org/10.1002/mde.2938

Habermas, J. (1987). *The theory of communicative action, Volume 2. Lifeworld and system: A critique of functionalist reason* (Translated by Thomas McCarthy). Beacon Press. chrome-extension://efaidnbmnnnibpcajpcglclefindmkaj/https://teddykw2.files.wordpress.com/2012/07/jurgen-habermas-the-theory-of-communicative-action-volume-2.pdf

ISCN. (2014). *Best practice in campus sustainability, Latest examples from ISCN and GULF* Schools. https://icap.sustainability.illinois.edu/files/projectupdate/2236/ISCN%202014%20B est%20Practices%20in%20Campus%20Sustainability%20Report.pdf

Kestin, T., Van den Belt, M., Denby, L., Ross, K., Thwaites, J., & Hawkes, M. (2017). *Getting* started *with the SDGs in universities (A guide for universities, higher education institutions, and the academic sector).* Sustainable Development Solutions Network, Australia/Pacific. https://ap-unsdsn.org/wp-content/uploads/University-SDG-Guide_web.pdf

Lewis, H. (2007). *Excellence without a soul: How a great university forgot education.* Public Affairs Books.

Lukovics, M., & Zuti, B. (2013). Successful universities towards the improvement of regional competitiveness: Fourth generation universities. *53rd Congress of the European Regional Science Association: Regional integration: Europe, the mediterranean and the world economy,* Palermo, Italy. https://doi.org/10.5281/zenodo.227202

Luna-Krauletz, M. D., Juárez-Hernández, L. G., Clark-Tapia, R., Súcar-Súccar, S. T., & Alfonso-Corrado, C. (2021). Environmental education for sustainability in higher education institutions: Design of an instrument for its evaluation. *Sustainability, 13*(13). https://doi.org/10.3390/su1 3137129

Mirgholami, M., & Fallah, Z. (2021). Firing sculptures and its public interaction. In L. Joubert (Eds.), *Craft shaping society: Educating in the crafts—The global experience* (pp. 135–152). Springer. https://doi.org/10.1007/978-981-16-9472-1

Readings, B. (1997). *The university in ruins.* Harvard University Press.

Tabriz Islamic Art University. (2018), *TIAU booklet.* https://en.tabriziau.ac.ir/Uploads/User/1/hafa/University%20Booklet.pdf

Taylor, J. C. (2001). *Fifth generation distance education.* Higher Education Series. http://www.c3l.uni-oldenburg.de/cde/media/readings/taylor01.pdf

Weintraub, L. (Ed.). (2012). *To life! Eco art in pursuit of a sustainable planet.* University of California Press.

Chapter 19
Where Health Professional Education and Sustainability Collide

Nick Towle

19.1 Introduction

It is true, the twentieth and early twenty-first centuries have seen many impressive gains in human health and advances in medical technologies. However, such gains have not been fairly distributed and the impact of our collective human endeavour on the biosphere threatens to erode future prospects for good health.

A wide literature exists around the social determinants of health, that is, the conditions into which we are born, grow, work, live, and age (World Health Organisation [WHO], n.d.), and the efforts to incorporate these within health curricula. Yet, there remains considerable lag in acknowledging and incorporating our understanding of the ecological determinants of health (Parkes et al., 2020).

After considering our current health trajectory, I bring attention to critical societal context which serves to narrow the perspective and practices of current and future health professionals, such that we are unknowingly complicit in reproducing the conditions of social injustice and ecological decline. This forms a compelling argument to adopt a greatly expanded definition of health, that of planetary health. Planetary health provides a holistic focus to advance the SDGs and reorient health professional education to become deeply conscious and engaged in the complex transformations required for a sustainable future.

N. Towle (✉)
Tasmanian School of Medicine, College of Health and Medicine, University of Tasmania, Burnie, TAS 7320, Australia
e-mail: Nick.Towle@utas.edu.au

Considerable global momentum is building around planetary health, and in subsequent sections, I share part of my journey and draw on the experience and insights of many others in creating planetary health curricula. Specific opportunities and potential pitfalls in seeking to create transformative pedagogy are then considered. I conclude with an emphasis on key challenges for educators and institutional leaders to ensure we and future graduates are resilient in the face of emerging challenges and equipped to contribute meaningfully to shared aspirations for a sustainable future.

19.2 Pulse of the Planet

The latter part of the twentieth and early twenty-first centuries saw impressive gains in many indices of health, with increasing longevity, a rapid reduction in childhood deaths under 5 years, reductions in maternal mortality, and significant progress in tackling many neglected tropical diseases. For some, these are triumphs of modern medical science (Whitty, 2017). Others (e.g., Horton et al., 2014) claim such gains are not irreversible and will be easily lost if we fail to address broader global trends in which they are made possible.

Indeed, COVID-19 has highlighted the precarious trajectory of these continued health gains, and we are enhancing the conditions for even deadlier pandemics (Carlson et al., 2022; Settele et al., 2020). For the first time since records began in 1950, global longevity has declined, falling by 1.5 years between 2019 and 2021 (Heuveline, 2022).

Furthermore, COVID-19 has shone a spotlight on the grossly unequal and unjust nature of our global society. The celebrated milestone of lifting a billion of the global population out of absolute poverty has obscured the decade-on-decade trend of widening wealth inequality. In relative terms, the wealth of the world's poor has fallen, with the wealth of the most affluent 1% approximating that of the poorest half of the global population (Shorrocks et al., 2021). Poverty defined as less than $2/day, is a convenient though arbitrary reporting metric, and says nothing of what is required for achieving a dignified life and the foundations for a functional society (Wilkinson & Pickett, 2009).

Global ecosystems are in serious decline, with 82% declines in biomass and species abundance, and 25% of species threatened with extinction in the next three decades. Already, environmental conditions contribute to approximately 23% of all annual global deaths (WHO, 2016). Global environmental change from human activity, such as climate change, pollution of air, soil, and water, and depletion of fish stocks has accelerated in recent decades and threatens to undermine progress towards 80% (35 out of 44) of the assessed targets of goals related to poverty, hunger, health, water, cities, climate, oceans, and land (Sustainable Development GoalsSustainable Development Goals (SDGs) 1, 2, 3, 6, 11, 13, 14, and 15) (Diaz et al., 2019, p. 15).

Those impoverished, dispossessed, and displaced populations who have contributed the least to such widespread ecological destruction, face a disproportionately heavy burden (Haines & Ebi, 2019; Watts et al., 2019), thus compounding the harm created by a grossly unequal and unjust social order.

The health gains of the past century have been impressive, though unevenly distributed and our increasingly detrimental human impacts on the biosphere threatens to erode such gains.

Given the current state of the world it is no longer tenable to profess to be part of a caring profession and not be alarmed by it.

In acknowledging the threats posed by converging social and ecological crises, it is necessary to revisit the way we define health, as importantly, this shapes our perspectives on the purpose and goals of health professional education and establishes the boundaries of our consideration of sustainable development.

19.3 (Re)Defining Health

The definition of health within the original WHO Constitution has remained remarkably consistent in its adoption over several decades:

> Health is a state of complete, physical, mental and social wellbeing and not merely the absence of disease. The enjoyment of the highest attainable standard of living is one of the fundamental rights of every human being without distinction of race, religion, political belief, economic or social condition. (WHO, 1948)

Since then, declarations from several globally significant conferences have impressed the need for a more expansive definition of health.

The Declaration of the Alma-Ata (1978) conference advocated health for all through universal primary healthcare and the necessity to couple health and social development. The Ottawa Charter for Health Promotion (WHO, 1986), advanced the need to adopt a socio-ecological approach to health, noting the inextricable links between people and environment. Key foundations for health such as peace, shelter, education, social justice, and equity were framed as priorities for action, as was addressing societal structures known to undermine health. Less than a decade later, the Rio Declaration on Environment and Development (United Nations, 1992) reaffirmed the importance of the integrity of the natural world for sustaining and advancing human health.

The insights and intentions of these global declarations are encompassed within the Sustainable Development Goals, where health is both a beneficiary and requirement for advancing many goals (Nunes et al., 2016; Rosa et al., 2019).

To advance the SDGs requires an even wider view of people within the biosphere. Today, a more holistic concept of "planetary health" is gaining traction, succinctly defined by the *in*VIVO Planetary Health network as "the interdependent *vitality* of all natural and anthropogenic ecosystems (social, political, and otherwise)" (Prescott et al., 2018, p. 1). Thus, health is moved from a population-based concept to encompass people and biosphere (Brand et al., 2021); as Stranger (2011) argues, a necessary re-centring of socio-ecological models to an "eco-sociological model" (p. 167).

A longer, more widely adopted definition is offered by Whitmee et al. (2015, p. 1978):

> The achievement of the highest attainable standard of health, wellbeing, and equity worldwide through judicious attention to the human systems—political, economic, and social—that shape the future of humanity and the Earth's natural systems that define the safe environmental limits within which humanity can flourish. Put simply, planetary health is the health of human civilization and the state of the natural systems on which it depends.

The recognition of our critical dependence on ecosystems, from a healthy gut microbiome through to a stable global biosphere, distinguishes planetary health from earlier notions of environmental health (Parkes et al., 2020). This is not a new concept; Prescott and Logan (2019) trace more recent historical origins, showing it is an essential recognition of traditional knowledges, which "emphasize that relationality and interconnectedness with all things is not a willed choice—it is a reality" (Redvers, 2018 cited in McKimm et al., 2020, p. 1124).

Although advancing the SDGs requires a planetary view of health, current societal influences and trends in health professional education remain aligned weakly with the concept or may even conflict with aspirations to improve planetary health. Our endeavours to create change must include a deeper awareness of the wider societal influences that shape the perspectives of our students and may enhance or resist our pursuit of planetary health.

19.4 Where Health Professional Education and Sustainability Collide

An historical critique by Irwin and Scali (2007) is instructive in how successive global attempts to foreground and address the social determinants of health, with its "health for all" approach, have been derailed by waves of geopolitical influence, colonial domination, economic doctrines, and technological change. These influences have also narrowed the perspective and engagement of health professionals in addressing ecological decline and in understanding its link to health. Neoliberal ideology has been one of the most profound influences on health (and indeed all) education over the past forty years.

19.5   Neoliberal Forces

Neoliberal ideology has profoundly reoriented the contributions of healthcare delivery and the purpose of health professional education. When enacted, neoliberalism seeks to limit the perceived interference of democratic institutions in the operation of competitive globalised markets, where individuals and corporations are liberated to act according to values of individualism, competition, consumerism, and material accumulation. It is a worldview that regards economic growth as a "universal and unquestionable precondition for sustainability" (Gale et al., 2015, p. 255) in stark contrast to a large body of contemporary research (Wilkinson & Pickett, 2009) demonstrating wealth inequality within and between nations harms health. Conversely, Gross Domestic Product (GDP) growth per capita bears little relationship to the important measures of health and wellbeing.

Emerging globally in the 1980s, health policy leaders adopting the underpinning ideology were successful in reframing emerging concern for social and ecological determinants of health as a matter of personal choice and responsibility (Irwin & Scali, 2007), or natural and largely unchangeable attributes of contemporary human society (Sharma et al., 2018). This has manifested in health professional practice as a shift in attitude and culture towards blaming individuals for their poor health, assuming the health and social status of individuals are predominantly a consequence of "lifestyle" choices made over their lifetimes (Cavanagh et al., 2019). It is not surprising, then to see the fingerprints of neoliberalism appearing in many areas of health professional education. For example, Hubinette et al. (2017) documented a shift in the intended focus of health advocacy in Canadian medical curricula away from systems-level advocacy to individual behaviour-focussed intervention. This has given rise to a situation where high-level sustainability declarations and aspirations are in competition with a relentless drive to commodify all aspects of our daily lives, including the necessary foundations for good health. The distorting influence of this economic doctrine is compounded by subconscious beliefs and hopes of technological advances providing solutions to our human problems (Irwin & Scali, 2007; Johnston et al., 2005). At the heart of this perspective is the abundance of cheap, high-density fossil fuel energy that has enabled technological approaches to health to flourish and dominate.

19.6   The Subconscious Privilege of Our High Technology and Energy Intensive Lives

What kind of health service could we create and sustain if timber or animal manure was our primary source of energy? It is a rhetorical question I ask my students as we explore the seriously underappreciated role of energy (not money) in shaping the historical trajectory of health gains, health systems, widening inequalities, and escalating threats to health.

We are living in an unprecedented era of exponential rise in energy and material consumption, to which most of us owe our very existence (Goodman, 2016; Mahli & Raworth, 2018). This trajectory gave rise to major technical breakthroughs in the 1940s and 1950s, with apparent successes derived from new medicines, antibiotics, and vaccines displacing calls for greater attention to addressing the social and ecological determinants of health (Irwin & Scali, 2007).

A strongly reductionist epistemological approach to refining further our knowledge of the pathophysiology and treatment of specific diseases continues to reinforce this biomedical orientation in students. This manifests as a predominantly linear thinking perspective where the solutions to poor health are considered largely technical and health system-centric. Though far from delivering widely shared improvements to health, the strong influence of neoliberal ideology has ensured such advances have accrued to less than one third of the global population (Benatar et al., 2018).

The unjust distribution of economic power is a proxy for material consumption, with just 20% of the global population consuming approximately 80% of available resources (Benatar et al., 2018). Health students often display limited insight into the extent to which such extreme privilege has, until now, buffered them from the worst effects of global environmental change and social upheaval, and distances them from the plight of the global majority.

For health services in affluent countries and regions, the great acceleration in energy and material consumption has also enabled and sustained an explosion of specialised disease care, with graduates displaying a mental drift from healthcare to disease care specialisation (Anåker et al., 2021; MacNeill et al., 2021) and a greater readiness to fill roles around treating ill health rather than preventing harm (Walpole et al., 2016). In this context, having regard for the messy and complex social and ecological conditions necessary for planetary health is perceived as someone else's speciality and not relevant to their intended career aspirations (Griffiths et al., 2021; Nunes et al., 2016).

The pace of technological advances in affluent society feeds a compelling cultural story centred on technology optimism. In this story, technology gains will enable a radical decoupling of ecologically destructive material consumption and ever-rising economic growth. The benefits will trickle down enabled by increasing flows of capital and technology transfer and usher in a new dawn of progress to solve the problems of global society (Raworth, 2017). It is a compelling story, though with little empirical support (Eisenmenger et al., 2020; Hickel, 2019) it has earth systems scientists fearing we are greatly underestimating "the challenges (and our role) of avoiding a ghastly future" (Bradshaw et al., 2021, p. 1). High hopes and expectations for future health gains fueled by technological advances and expansion need to be tempered with a consideration of the impact of health systems predicated on a continued trajectory of high energy and material consumption.

19.7 The Footprint of Global (North) Health Systems

Health systems are not benign actors in the decline of planetary ecosystems and social exploitation. The collective global healthcare enterprise is estimated to account for 1/10th of global economic activity (Xu et al., 2018), and of this, relatively small amounts are directed to prevention and primary healthcare (MacNeill et al., 2021).

The greatest ecological impacts are predominantly associated with tertiary-level hospital care and pharmaceuticals. Healthcare contributes an estimated 4.4% of global greenhouse gas emissions (Karliner et al., 2019), with the Australian health sector accounting for 7% of national greenhouse gas emissions (Malik et al., 2018). Broader ecological impacts such as air pollution through waste incineration, or water pollution through pharmaceutical waste, have been estimated by Lenzen et al. (2020) to be between 1 and 5%, and greater for some national environmental impacts.

For comparison, estimates for how much of our lifetime health may be attributed to access to health services, range from 25% to as little as 10% (Kaplan & Milstein, 2019; McGovern et al., 2014). This is not to downplay the need for and valuable contribution of accessible healthcare services, but to acknowledge that the majority of our lifetime health and wellbeing is contingent on what occurs outside the four walls of the hospital or clinic.

In operating within a neoliberal paradigm, the goals of our global healthcare endeavours have clearly departed from being of service to and advancing "Health for All" (Declaration of Alma-Ata, 1978). Training of health professionals today is now more aligned to maintaining a multibillion-dollar industry with advances and greatest benefit accruing to the most affluent (Johnston et al., 2005) and centred on personalised disease management, as the most profitable area for research and investment (Benatar et al., 2018).

We urgently need to ask: are our students, educators, and practitioners ready to change course and assume a more prominent role in advancing planetary health to enable them to meet the SDGs? In the following sections I consider what perspectives and vision, directions in curriculum and pedagogy, and educational leadership may be necessary to enable future health professionals to see themselves as responsible for and as leaders for sustainability.

19.8 Disposition of Students, Educators, and Clinicians Towards Engaging with Sustainability

In a qualitative exploration of nursing students' perceptions of climate change and sustainability, Anåker et al. (2021) describe a "mismatched discourse" (p. 4). The students' general awareness appears to give rise to a pessimistic "gloomy" view of the future, while simultaneously conveying an ethical predisposition towards inter-generational justice and recognition of nurses having a shared responsibility for sustainability. Ultimately, many still struggle to see the relevance and application of sustainability within the professional nursing role, a struggle common to many other health disciplines (Blum et al., 2019; Tun, 2019).

Anåker et al. (2021) suggest that such findings reflect a failure of our current courses in preparing students as actors and leaders for sustainability within a rapidly changing world. This sentiment is supported by a landmark review of global health professional education conducted by Frenk et al. (2010), which found health professional education to be static, with limited adaptation to changing sociopolitical and technological contexts, thereby failing to deliver on rising expectations around social accountability (Boelen et al., 2016; Jacobs et al., 2020). These findings underscore a persistent tension between those calling for health professionals to embrace the SDGs through a more holistic scope of practice (Rosa et al., 2019) and the views of clinicians firmly committed to the biomedical disease care paradigm (Jacobs et al., 2020).

Given the deep-seated ideological underpinnings that have given rise to current health professional education, it would be naïve to assume that in the future it will naturally align with sustainability. If we are to accept responsibility for advancing a greatly expanded view of health, that of planetary health, there is a compelling need to transform health professional education from a system that is largely complicit in reproducing the conditions of social injustice and ecological decline, to one that is deeply conscious and engaged in the complex task of societal transformation.

19.9 A Vision for Health Professional Education for People and Planetary Health

Several international collaborations are rising to the challenge of creating frameworks, vision statements, and principles intended to guide educators, institutional leaders, and students in the task of reimagining and redesigning health professional education. Some of these are:

- AMEE Consensus Statement: Planetary health and education for sustainable healthcare (Shaw et al., 2021),
- Cross-cutting principles for planetary health education (Stone et al., 2018),
- The Canmore Declaration: Statement of Principles for Planetary Health (Prescott et al., 2018), and
- The Planetary Health Education Framework (Guzman et al., 2021b).

Various terminology reflects different emphases, from "Sustainable Healthcare Education," more weighted toward sustainable practices in delivering care, to "Education for Sustainable Healthcare" and "Planetary Health Education." These latter concepts, considered synergistic (Prescott et al., 2018) and at times used interchangeably, are envisaged as more encompassing of the required skills, values, and competencies for health professional students to become leaders and advocates for societal-level change (Shaw et al., 2021). Guzman et al. (2021b) have employed a broader transdisciplinary perspective in developing a Planetary Health Education Framework (PHEF) (Fig. 19.1), describing five interlinked domains of inquiry. These are intended to capture foundational knowledge, values, and practice to support transformative change to embed planetary health education within higher education curricula. The domains are: (1) Interconnection with Nature; (2) The Anthropocene and Health; (3) Systems Thinking and Complexity; (4) Equity and Social Justice; and (5) Movement Building and Systems Change, and include related concepts to support exploration and action.

A particular conceptual model that holds great appeal is the "doughnut economics model," created by UK economist Kate Raworth (2017) Fig. 19.2. The inner circle is derived from the SDGs, capturing essential conditions for health and wellbeing (the social foundation), with the outer circle reflecting the work of earth system scientists in defining safe planetary boundaries (Steffen et al., 2015). The interdependence of social and ecological dimensions reflects the holistic goal of planetary health. As is discussed later, the model has broad application, inclusive of a wide range of students, and may be applied to transdisciplinary curriculum development. Importantly, it repositions economics in service of people and planet.

Common to these frameworks is the holistic intent of the SDGs, remaining open to contested meanings of sustainability (Gale et al., 2015), and adaptable to local context and needs. The SDGs may either be integrated or offer a valuable overlay

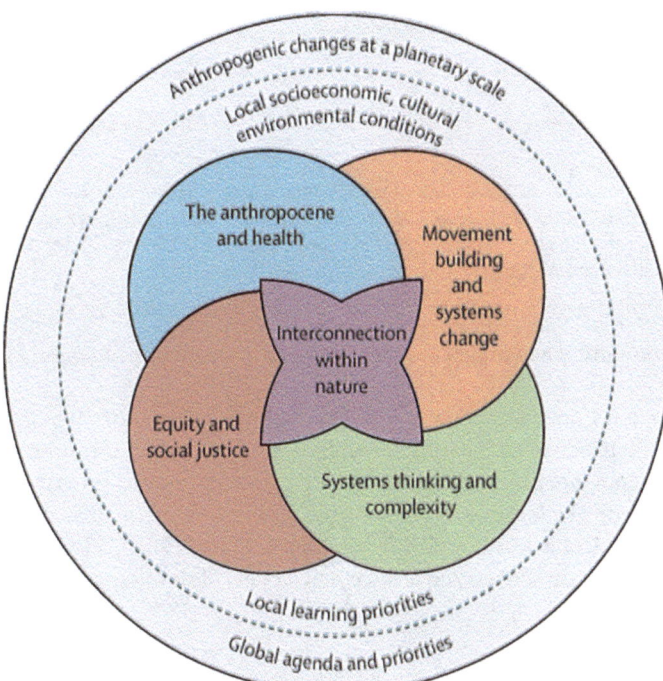

Fig. 19.1 Planetary health education framework (*Source* Guzman et al., 2021b)

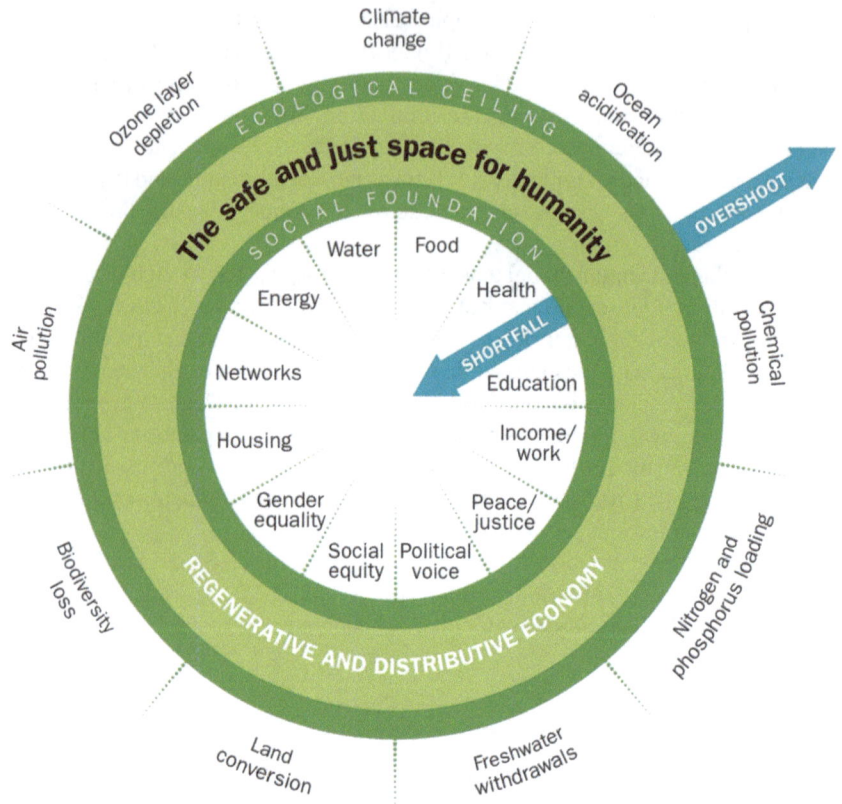

Fig. 19.2 The Doughnut of social and planetary boundaries. Credit: Kate Raworth and Christian Guthier. CC-BY-SA 4.0 (*Source* The developers of the Doughnut image have requested a specific attribution, found here:https://web.archive.org/web/20220427141346/https:/doughnutecon omics.org/license Raworth, 2017)

for others, providing a compass for global aspiration with corresponding metrics of progress.

At this point, I draw attention to original research by Tun (2019) that articulated the interplay between several barriers, enablers, influences such as institutional ethos/ideology, and potential solutions to advancing planetary health. Tun's primary study was around medical education, though the broad, systems-oriented analysis is highly relevant and applicable to many health disciplines (Fig. 19.3). This is a valuable point of reference as we move to consider the practical task of developing planetary health curricula.

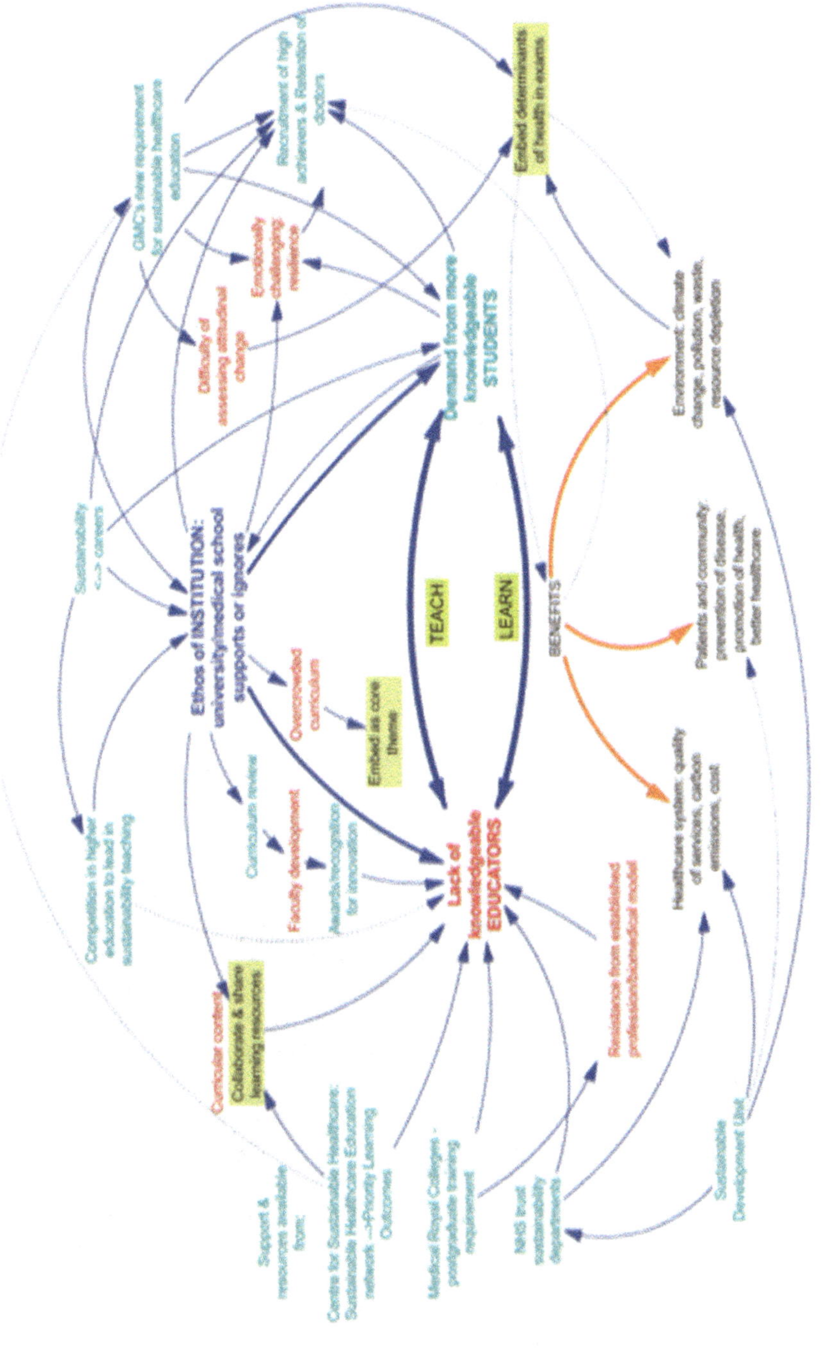

Fig. 19.3 Barriers (red), enablers (light blue), solutions (yellow highlight), and benefits (black) for Education for Sustainable Healthcare (Tun, 2019)

19.10   Moving from Big Ideas to Practice

19.10.1   What Do Students Need for the Critical Decades Ahead?

Significant efforts have been made to define and refine specific learning objectives for planetary health and education for sustainable healthcare; see for example, Teherani et al. (2017). Frameworks such as those referenced above bring coherence to these potentially large and expansive sets of learning objectives, though rather than moving to create an exhaustive list of learning objectives, I advocate consideration of what are the broad competencies and transferable skills that will enable current and future students to interrogate the breadth of ecological, sociopolitical, and economic dimensions of planetary health.

Within the field of health professional education, there is convergence around developing competencies in resource stewardship, social and environmental justice (Parker et al., 2020), and most prominently, systems thinking (Gruenberg et al., 2017; Maxwell & Blashki, 2016; Parker et al., 2020; Schwerdtle et al., 2020a), and advocacy and activism (McKimm & McLean, 2020; Teherani et al., 2017). Logically, resource stewardship is concerned with reducing the ecological and social footprint of health services, and the nexus between awareness of social and environmental justice and leadership being advocacy.

19.10.2   Seeing and Acting on the Big Picture

Systems thinking skills are an essential foundation for appreciating the holistic nature of planetary health, recognising the interdependent complex causal relationships and the need to simultaneously address multiple goals to advance health. As a counter to reductionist, linear ways of thinking, seeing the world from a systems perspective will enable students to identify potential leverage points, beyond the clinical encounter, where their actions may contribute to more enduring and widely shared health gains.

Complementing systems thinking, the imperative for health professionals to engage in advocacy is greater than ever. Despite a proud history of leading important social and policy change (Haines & Ebi, 2019), many health professionals still hold narrow conceptualisations of health advocacy (Hubinette et al., 2017). Educators and clinicians typically having only a rudimentary development of relevant skills leaves students with few role models of advocacy (Griffiths et al., 2021; Hubinette et al., 2017). Introducing the concept of planetary health brings an opportunity to instil a greater understanding of the scope and rationale for engaging in advocacy and activism (McKimm & McLean, 2020). Student surveys have shown that the development of advocacy skills would ideally be skills-based, with hands-on opportunities that may involve NGO partnerships (SDG17) and the non-physician community (Griffiths et al., 2021).

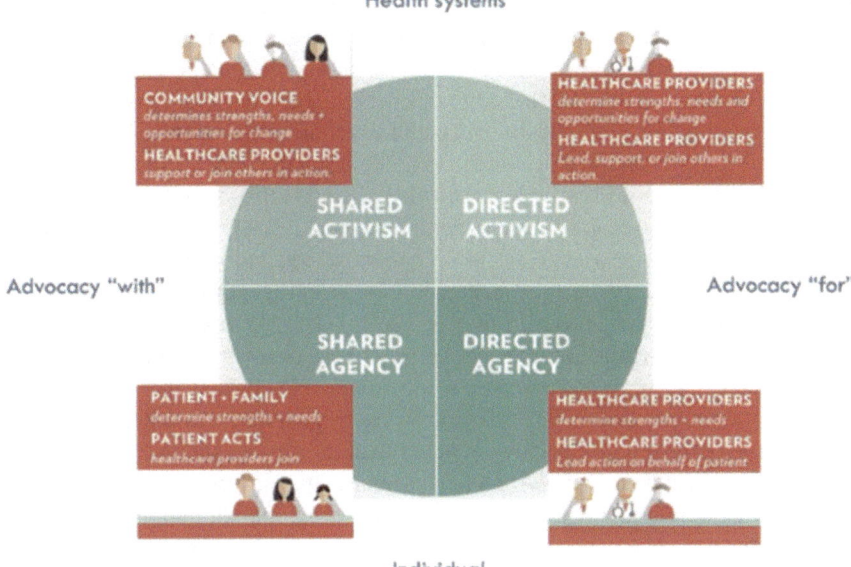

Fig. 19.4 UBC health advocacy model (*Source* Hubinette et al., 2017)

For our purposes, a model of advocacy developed by Hubinette et al. (2017) has application to a wide range of health professional curricula. The model defines two axes, one representing the spectrum of focus from the individual to the structural societal conditions, and the other acting on behalf of, or with, those affected. This establishes four quadrants presenting a much wider spectrum of health advocacy and activism opportunities (Fig. 19.4).

19.11   Resilience

With the prospect of an increasingly volatile and uncertain future, the prevalence of eco-anxiety (Shaw et al., 2021) is on the rise. Deepening our understanding and engagement in tackling existential threats in the process of developing health advocacy competencies may bring further anxiety. With this comes an obligation for educators and institutions to embed strategies to build greater resilience for both our students and ourselves (Tun, 2019). For me, resilience is a place of conscious and empowered engagement that sits between the poles of denial and despair.

Despite having limited examples to share, I urge educators and institutions to pursue resilience-building strategies, either in parallel or integrated within curriculum development efforts. For example, in my own institution, colleagues within Social Sciences have empowered social work students to deliver climate café sessions. In essence, these students provide a safe, non-judgemental space for fellow students and staff to share the breadth of emotions that can arise. This contribution helps to legitimise the awareness and lived experience of participants and build a sense of community. Others suggest that our courses should encourage and enable time in nature (Guzman et al., 2021b), citing robust evidence of such activity reducing anxiety, among many other physiological and psychological benefits.

Resilience, however, must be more than moderating the internal state. Advancing planetary health requires motivation, knowledge, and skills to confront the societal conditions that feed this growing anxiety. Many persuasively argue that the development of advocacy knowledge and skills can move educators and students beyond despair (Walpole et al., 2016), enhancing motivation and agency to address the conditions leading to poor health (Griffiths et al., 2021). The SDG targets and indicators may be used as an anchor for advocacy efforts (Rosa et al., 2019) and the development of practical projects around these could do much to enhance morale in the face of an uncertain future (Tun, 2019). To borrow a poignant quote from Harald Zindler (1989): "The optimism of the action is better than the pessimism of the thought."

Drawing on my own journey and that of many others, I now consider in more detail the curriculum and pedagogic approaches being applied by those seeking to advance planetary health.

19.12   How: Curriculum and Pedagogy

Not surprisingly, if a strong agreement exists among scholars and educators to establish the relevance of and engagement with planetary health, it needs to be integrated as a cross-cutting theme (Schwerdtle et al., 2020a; Tun, 2019), spanning specialities, with multiple points of exposure through each year of training (Shaw et al., 2021). In other words, a relevant spiral curriculum needs to operate (Schwerdtle et al., 2020b; Walpole et al., 2017).

The goal for such comprehensive renewal is transformative learning, engaging both cognitive and affective domains to move sustainability (and thus health) beyond a mere technical fix (Johnston et al., 2005) and create learning "that challenges established perspectives, leading to new ways of being in the world" (Van Schalkwyk et al., 2019, p. 547). To this end, the curriculum and pedagogic approaches described in health professional education curricula are very diverse (McLean et al., 2020; Shaw et al., 2021 [in Appendix]), and there is currently very limited empirical evidence around what works (Upvall & Luzincourt, 2019). Therefore, I have chosen to explore several differing approaches to encourage more critical reflection on the merits and cautions to apply in developing planetary health curricula.

19.12.1 Curriculum: Embed or Add On?

The SDGs offer many crucial and rich areas of focus for content development. One approach is to draw on them as a set of topics, or syllabus within the broader theme of sustainability. For example, climate change (SDG13) is recognised as the biggest health threat and opportunity of the twenty-first century (Watts et al., 2015), and is now arguably the most prominent focus for planetary health curriculum development within health professional education (McKinnon et al., 2022).

A common strategy has been to infuse topic-specific content into existing biomedical disciplines (Fadadu et al., 2020). A recently completed initiative included comprehensively mapping and incorporating climate change content to organ systems within formative medical subjects (Burch et al., 2021), such as linking the effect of bushfires (wildfires) on respiratory health within microbiology and pathophysiology lectures.

Curriculum crowding is a legitimate and widespread concern in all of education (Tun, 2019), therefore, infusing content into an established curriculum may ameliorate this to some extent (Tun, 2019), though potentially impractical if replicated for several SDGs. Infusing content may enhance the perceived clinical relevance and awareness of issues (Walpole & Mortimer, 2017), though others caution that there is a risk of unintentionally reinforcing the so-called hard sciences of biomedicine (Cavanagh et al., 2019), thus detracting from efforts to develop systems thinking competencies.

Drawing on specific SDGs has also formed the basis for developing new lectures or dedicated workshops enabling opportunistic inclusion of sustainability concepts and testing new delivery formats (Walpole & Mortimer, 2017). Countering such benefits, "add on" elements may be perceived as less relevant, even devalued if not able to be assessed. Such content may also be vulnerable to neglect or omission (Schwerdtle et al., 2020b). In practice, Nunes et al. (2016) note that curriculum development approaches to date mostly have used a blended approach, embedding content into existing learning activities, as well as delivering additional elements. Learning objectives have also gravitated towards awareness raising more than action or advocacy. Although small reforms are important for establishing a sense of progress, educators must remain mindful of the need to pursue the larger goal of transformative pedagogies. Changes in curriculum alone will not bring about a student body empowered to advocate for sustainability. Transformative, participatory, and problem-based pedagogies that engage students in deep and reflective learning are required to achieve this (Cavanagh et al., 2019; Lopez-Medina et al., 2019).

19.12.2 Transformative Pedagogy

A notable and enabling shift in the pedagogy of many health professional courses is from didactic, transmissive forms of teaching, towards more constructivist approaches, as employed within case-based or problem-based learning (Lopez-Medina et al., 2019). Problem-posing approaches can enable the development of critical reflection, as a means to teach environmental and structural causes of poor health (Cavanagh et al., 2019).

There are a number of useful emerging examples of innovative evidence-based approaches to developing transformative pedagogy in health education. Janet Richardson and her team embedded a scenario within a series of skills stations, addressing the critical dependency of healthcare delivery on fossil fuels. A facilitated discussion, fostering critical enquiry, examined the consequences of potential interruption to the supply of key items used in everyday clinical practice (Richardson et al., 2014).

As reported by Grose and Richardson (2016), this active learning approach valued the contextual knowledge of students, while challenging subconscious assumptions. The clinical focus enhanced the perceived relevance of sustainability to the profession and the desire to translate new learning into practice. Another initiative involved bringing design students into clinical skills sessions to observe and discuss common healthcare procedures. Instrumental to the success of this endeavour was a focus on fostering a transdisciplinary approach to identifying problems and opportunities to improve existing systems (Plymouth University, 2014). These examples demonstrate a commitment to a transformative pedagogy (Plymouth University, 2014).

Integration of sustainability themes into case-based learning and clinical scenarios opens up the potential for more transformative learning. However, Sharma et al. (2018) present one of the most important critical reflections on the way social determinants of health have been introduced. They raise the prospect that this approach might actually reinforce current worldviews if framed within the biomedical paradigm. Students may be encouraged to develop a greater awareness of social disparities, but without sufficient exploration of the structural conditions giving rise to them, the critical social context may be lost in the endeavour of mastering biomedical learning objectives. Translating this to concern for sustainability, social or ecological contexts are at risk of becoming issues "to 'recognize' or 'acknowledge' as opposed to a site of possible professional intervention or advocacy" (Cavanagh et al., 2019, p. 40). The knowledge, skills, and mental models of educators are thus critical if new pedagogic approaches are to achieve their transformative potential, a point I return to.

19.12.3   Bringing Competencies and Themes Together: The Case of the Global Tobacco Industry

The following case study from my own practice illustrates my early endeavours in integrating topics as a tangible focus to develop broad competencies, drawing on the example of the impact of the tobacco industry on health from a systems perspective.

Within a fourth-year medical student workshop I reframe familiar topics, such as the effect of tobacco on health (SDG3.a.1) and explore them in a way that moves beyond the pathophysiology and engages in practices of systems thinking and advocacy. Using Kate Raworth's (2017) Doughnut Economics concept discussed above, we explore the health consequences of the tobacco industry through the four lenses of (1) local ecological; (2) local social; (3) global ecological, and (4) global social impacts (Doughnut Economics Action Lab [DEAL], 2020).

Critical interrelated issues of social and environmental justice emerge. For example, cigarette butts constitute the largest single source of marine pollution locally (SDG14); globally the production of tobacco contributes to significant land clearing (SDG15), thereby exacerbating climate change (SDG13). The tobacco industry exploits child labour in global supply chains (SDG8), while tobacco smoking remains the single biggest preventable cause of premature death and disease for our local population (SDG3). This demonstrates that smoking is much more than a direct health problem, with the goals of the industry being irreconcilable with aspirations to achieve the SDGs.

To complete the systems thinking exercise, students draw on the iceberg model (Academy for Systems Change, n.d.), looking at the underlying worldviews, structures, and patterns that are mostly invisible from view. The exercise can reveal the subconscious beliefs of separation from nature and each other, which allow the exploitation of others to become accepted practice and protected through neoliberal political and economic structures.

The session concludes with a focus on applying the Hubinette et al. (2017) model of health advocacy. The exercise is inclusive as students can identify with advocacy efforts that align with their current journey. Some emerge with a renewed commitment to support individuals to quit smoking. Others, inspired by leading health activists, such as Dr. Bronwyn King (TEDxSydney, 2017), seek out more ambitious avenues to leverage change. In the absence of formal evaluation, evidence for the transformative potential has emerged through students' volunteering actions, such as collecting details of superannuation/pension funds and comparing how their personal values and company investment practices align. However, as in all education, assessment is a key driver of motivation, as well as acting as a gatekeeper. So as new teaching approaches are developed, particularly in areas of transdisciplinary learning, new approaches to assessment must also be considered (Prideaux, 2007).

19.13   Approaches to Assessment in Transformative Pedagogies

Many recommendations have been developed for planetary health assessment items (see for example, Shaw et al., 2021, p. 279), with some novel proposals, such as engaging students in developing a personal action plan for sustainability (Goodman, 2011). However, measuring the effect of new pedagogic approaches in developing desirable competencies is still at an early stage (Upvall & Luzincourt, 2019) with most published work evaluating a change in awareness and attitudes, and few works around a change in practice or advocacy (Nunes et al., 2016).

The goal of creating transformative pedagogy is an ambitious endeavour, requiring significant curriculum renewal. These examples and many more reflect the concerted efforts of health professional educators around the world to respond to the challenges of planetary health. Building momentum and enhancing the transformative potential of our curricula and institutions requires knowledgeable and dedicated educators and committed, supportive leadership.

19.13.1   Focus on Educators

The process of curriculum mapping needs to be embraced as an exercise in critical reflection, working alongside students and fellow educators to interrogate course design and structures that favour or discourage transformative learning for sustainability.

Hence, an important and rarely elaborated entry point for educators seeking to engage others in the challenges of planetary health is to cultivate an awareness of our own mental models, incorporating worldviews, values, beliefs, and biases (Meadows, 2008; Stone et al., 2018). For many of us, there is a discomfort in discovering our personal and professional identities are rooted in the practices of a cultural paradigm that is ecologically destructive and socially unjust (Tun, 2019). We must confront the present reality that our higher education institutions are deeply embedded within a neoliberal paradigm (Gale et al., 2015) and work to reorient the purpose of health professional education to be in service of planetary health.

Reflection on our personal interpretation of sustainability is essential. If we hold too narrow or perhaps a weak concept of sustainability (Gale et al., 2015), we are likely to convey this narrow view to colleagues and students (Christie et al., 2015; Reid & Petocz, 2006). Building educator knowledge and expertise is a critical enabler for advancing planetary health.

19.14   Developing Educator Knowledge and Expertise

Planetary health is not the domain of any one discipline (Prescott et al., 2018; Shaw et al., 2021), and as an evolving field of endeavour it is widely recognised that health professional educators currently lack much of the foundational knowledge, skills, experience, or confidence to engage and adopt it within current practice (Brand et al., 2021; Richardson et al., 2016; Tun, 2019; Walpole et al., 2019). However, there is convergence around three responses considered more effective for building educator expertise: educator/learner partnerships, collaborative curriculum development, and transdisciplinary collaborations.

19.14.1   Educator/Learner Partnerships

As Anåker et al. (2021) have illustrated, many students have insight into global environmental change (climate change and biodiversity loss) and persistent social injustice (poverty, regional conflict, and war). Many have committed to developing their personal knowledge and engaging in related advocacy efforts. The humility to acknowledge we are all learners opens opportunities for the collaborative development of planetary health curricula.

Formative development of a planetary health curriculum within our school has been advanced through partnerships between faculty, recent graduates and current students, a strategy shared by many (Burch et al., 2021; Huss et al., 2020; Slimings et al., 2022). This collaboration produced a planetary health lecture for all final year students and an optional five-week immersion in health system sustainability with an SDG focus, for example, exploring the health consequences of energy systems (SDG7), and conducting a workplace energy audit, culminating in the production of a written report on avenues to enhance sustainability.

19.14.2   Collaborative Curriculum Development

A collaborative curriculum project across eight UK medical schools demonstrated the potential to accelerate the development and implementation of new content and enhance educator confidence in the process (Walpole & Mortimer, 2017). Health professional education shares several core domains of competency: scholarship, clinical expertise, advocacy, professionalism, communication, and leadership, providing ample scope to extend this to interdisciplinary collaboration. Collaborative development of case studies can allow each discipline to introduce and broaden the pool of available expertise (Huss et al., 2020; Lopez-Medina et al., 2019).

19.14.3   Transdisciplinary Collaboration

The complex nature of sustainable development and striving for planetary health compels us to move beyond the confines of the particular ontological and epistemological orientation of our discipline or profession, towards transdisciplinary engagement. Transdisciplinarity involves a "higher level of integrated study…concerned with the unity of intellectual frameworks beyond the disciplinary perspectives" (Stember, 1991, p. 4, as cited in Schwertdle et al., 2020a). Critically this is where we can challenge and broaden personal concepts of sustainability. In grappling with this challenge Noy et al. (2021, p. 859) have developed a framework (Sustainability Wheel of Fortune), which has enabled them to collaborate across their own disciplinary boundaries and develop transformative learning opportunities for students who share similarly diverse epistemological backgrounds. At an institutional level, the opportunity to engage and contribute to an Education for Sustainability Community of Practice (Salter et al., 2013) has revealed the richness of diverse perspectives, challenged biases, and evolved into practical collaboration in the development and delivery of transdisciplinary sustainability focussed units.

The nature of converging social and ecological crises requires leaders, and planetary health practitioners, prepared to reshape personal and professional identities, reimagine and redesign our institutions, and look beyond institutional boundaries, to engage in urgent societal transformation.

19.15   Leading for Planetary Health

There is reason for hope as leadership is emerging in all quarters and in myriad forms. Students themselves are shining a spotlight on where curricula fail to address the most urgent health challenges of our time (El Omrani et al., 2020) and developing dedicated learning materials (International Federation of Medical Students Associations, 2016). Institutional leaders, such as Madden et al. (2022), are calling for a revision of graduate outcome statements of course-accrediting bodies. Professional Colleges from all disciplines are voicing the urgency of advancing the SDGs and tackling major health threats, such as climate change (Rosa et al., 2019; Royal Australian College of Physicians, 2016). Clearly the message is being received; the translation into action is pending.

The capabilities and qualities required of those seeking to lead such transformation include higher level systems thinking skills, and the capacity to build and translate vision into action through personal action and enabling others (McKimm et al., 2020).

19.16   Reflection on the Ideology and Goals of Health Professional Education

As leading systems thinker, Donella Meadows (2008) reminds us, the deep leverage for transformative change occurs when we examine and redefine the paradigms and mental models that give rise to the goals of the system(s) and structures we create. The importance of this cannot be overstated, as the invisible ideological positions and implied goals of health professional courses fundamentally shape everything from curriculum design, the suite of assessment tasks, and faculty reward structures, through to the relationships with communities in which they are embedded.

Leading necessary change will require deeper reflection on competing ideological positions and goals that give rise to course and institutional structures. Frenk et al. (2010) characterised three broad functions of health professional education and the related purpose or goals. First, health professional education may provide informative learning, where acquiring knowledge and skills relates to the purpose of producing experts. Second, formative learning is about socialising students around values, to produce professionals. Instrumentalism, as an underpinning ideology, stresses the utility and value of the course in providing trained professionals for the health workforce. A third function is around developing leaders, as enlightened change agents. An ideological foundation of reconstructivism seeks to equip students for changing societal roles and is critical to advancing sustainability, challenging orthodoxy and existing power structures. Courses will require all three functions, though moving them towards the necessary transformative learning pedagogy will require an explicit reevaluation of the worldviews and assumptions on which they are founded.

19.17   Are First Nations Voices Being Heard?

A provocation to initiate such reflection is to consider the position of the institution in relation to First Nations people. Graduating First Nations people in Western health traditions is often cited as a metric of success. The question must be asked, are our institutions inadvertently a force for colonisation, replicating colonial power relationships by simply teaching First Nations people to become better competitors in a neoliberal world? (See Chapters 5 and 6 in this volume). Dr. Nicole Redvers, a member of the Deninu K'ue First Nation asks about the other side of this equation: "What about the training of conventional, technologically-minded healthcare providers by Indigenous peoples so that the former can better understand how to simultaneously protect health and biodiversity through age-old mind–body-spirit connections to the land and its life?" (Prescott & Logan, 2019, p. 101).

19.18   Frameworks for Building Vision and Guiding Action

The planetary health frameworks outlined above have the potential to provide educational leaders with a holistic lens to support the process of curriculum renewal. Guzman et al. (2021a) suggest significant benefits of providing a common foundational language for the transdisciplinary endeavour and a dynamic representation of the breadth of planetary health. Again, the SDGs provide a valuable overlay in bringing specific challenges and global aspirations into view. Shaw et al. (2021, p. 282) propose a roadmap for institution, course, and curriculum transformation, defining several areas requiring leadership, the actors involved, and suggested targets for measuring progress. However, the particular tool or framework adopted may be less important than the process. The University of Tasmania's experience with the STARS (Sustainability Tracking and Assessment Rating System) (see Chapter 17 in this volume) highlights that the process may be in danger of being reduced to a mere technical checklist, inviting very little scrutiny or institutional learning.

In regard to process, I again refer to the doughnut economics concept (Raworth, 2017), which communicates an intrinsic and compelling vision of meeting the needs of all within planetary boundaries. As a specific example, it is being applied in a multifaceted (process-enabling) way, capturing a picture of the present, a "selfie," vision building, and as a decision support tool, which is scalable and sensitive to local context and need (see for example, DEAL, 2020).

Ultimately, leadership is most critical in bringing multiple actors together around a shared vision and mutually agreed goals.

19.19   Transdisciplinary Coalitions

Advancing the sustainable development agenda is clearly beyond the capacity of individual disciplines or professions. Fostering transdisciplinary coalitions presents the most challenging, yet widely called for (Gale et al., 2015; Parkes et al., 2020; Schwerdtle et al., 2020a) transformation in higher education, requiring radical and unfettered collaboration (Schwerdtle et al., 2020a) beyond disciplinary (and professional) siloes. The solutions and "responsibility for planetary health requires us to relinquish conventional professional, societal, and cultural partitions and to develop contextual coalitions based both on science and broader cultural narratives" (Prescott & Logan, 2019, p. 102).

In itself, the work to create global consensus statements around planetary health is a manifestation of inter and transdisciplinary coalitions. However, the capacity to maintain such collaborations is not guaranteed, often sustained by transient "side of the desk" efforts. As such, institutional leaders must support contributions to transdisciplinary endeavours through new metrics linked with career recognition (Gale et al., 2015; Shaw et al., 2021; Tun et al., 2020). Leadership is more important than ever if health professions are to move from a position of being complicit in replicating unsustainable futures to becoming active contributors to advancing planetary health.

19.20   Conclusion

The past century saw impressive gains in human health, but the future trajectory is far less certain. COVID-19 has shone a spotlight on grossly unjust and widening global social inequalities, and the pressure of our collective human endeavour is pushing ecosystems upon which we all depend towards collapse. Countering forces that currently narrow our perspective and diminish our sense of responsibility requires leadership committed to deep learning, that is, "… a process of unlearning—that is, deconstructing and uprooting long-held ideas, beliefs, values, and practices" (Guzman et al., 2021b, p. 9).

Embracing global ambitions for sustainable development, through a holistic planetary health perspective, presents us with a unique opportunity to reorient the goals of health professional education. Health professional education must overcome the influences and vested interests that narrow the perspective and practice of future health professionals. We require the humility to recognise health professions cannot lead this transformation alone and must embrace opportunities for transdisciplinary collaboration and partnerships. A renewed curriculum that is ethically aligned, inclusive, and transformative, will be our most valued contribution to producing planetary health leaders. Graduates equipped with the skills and commitment to engage in the urgent task of societal transformation will be more adaptable and resilient in the face of an uncertain future.

Appendix

Curriculum opportunities for transdisciplinary engagement (*Source* Shaw et al., 2021, pp. 279–280; See Table 19.1)

Table 19.1 Examples of learning activities, opportunities and possible assessment approaches that promote transdisciplinary, action‑based learning and the involvement of multiple stakeholders (SDSN, 2020)

Learning activity	Examples	Opportunities	Possible formative and summative assessments
			Rubrics for all assessments can be developed based on intended learning outcomes and enhance validity of assessment
Activities with a clinical focus			
Environmental history in communication skills training	In a role play, take a history from a patient who has been affected by bushfire smoke or has diarrhea as a result of limited or no access to clean water	• Promote attention to ecological and social determinants of health • Practise sensitive enquiry about risk factors • Integrate sustainability with history taking skills • Address SDG3 (promotion of health and well-being for all)	Formative—observed role play Summative—OSCE history station; MCQs & SAQs regarding environmental risk factors
Lifecycle analysis of common medical resources	Investigate using peer reviewed literature and/or grey literature (e.g. product information, health system data) the social, environmental and financial costs of equipment and medications commonly used in healthcare. Discuss the implications of these costs for healthcare planning and healthcare practice	• Create awareness of the ecological footprint of medical equipment from manufacture to disposal • Raise discussion about ethical issues related to consumption, e.g. mining for metals/elements and dismantling of medical devices often happens in low and low-middle income countries • Address SDGs 12 (sustainable consumption and production), 14 (life below water) and 15 (land and biodiversity protection)	Formative—observation of group activity, oral assignment, discussion in clinical practice Summative—written or oral assignment, MCQs or SAQs about measurement methods or relative costs

(continued)

Table 19.1 (continued)

Learning activity	Examples	Opportunities	Possible formative and summative assessments
			Rubrics for all assessments can be developed based on intended learning outcomes and enhance validity of assessment
Concept mapping exercise, individual or group, may be transdisciplinary	Research the environmental impacts of care provided within one healthcare specialty. Use graphical tools to demonstrate where environmental change may alter disease burden and healthcare seeking and where healthcare may impact on ecosystems. Consider how causes and effects interact and varied drivers of costs such as greenhouse gas emissions and negative impacts on patients' employment or social support	• Promote understanding of ecological and social determinants of health • Apply systems thinking • Creative activity engages learners and facilitates active learning • Address SDGs 3, 12, 13 (climate action), 14 and 15	Formative—assessment of process, reflections, or the concept map produced Summative—assessment of the concept map produced using a rubric based on key learning outcomes

(continued)

Table 19.1 (continued)

Learning activity	Examples	Opportunities	Possible formative and summative assessments
Practicing communicating with patients about environmental sustainability and health promotion in communication skills training	In a role play, discuss with a patient a more environmentally sustainable intervention that can provide equivalent (or greater) health benefits than the alternative, e.g.: • Options with lower environmental impact, e.g. dry powder inhalers over metered dose inhalers (asthma pumps) • Lifestyle changes and the co-benefits, i.e. reducing environmental footprint and improve health, e.g. reducing meat intake and increasing grain and vegetable intake; walking or cycling rather than driving	• Facilitate learning about health co-benefits of sustainable lifestyles, e.g. sustainable diets, increased exercise • Facilitate learning about environmental impacts of healthcare interventions • Develop motivational interviewing skills • Address SDGs 3 and 12	*Rubrics for all assessments can be developed based on intended learning outcomes and enhance validity of assessment* Formative—Direct observation of role play Summative—OSCE communication skills station; MCQs & SAQs about relevant evidence, e.g. health co-benefits, carbon impacts of healthcare interventions, and/or related ethical issues

(continued)

Table 19.1 (continued)

Learning activity	Examples	Opportunities	Possible formative and summative assessments *Rubrics for all assessments can be developed based on intended learning outcomes and enhance validity of assessment*
Healthcare pathway analysis activity	Explore one patient pathway (e.g. that taken by a patient presenting to primary care with abdominal pain and referred to secondary care), and consider how to apply principles of sustainable healthcare, including: • Avoiding investigations that do not add value, (e.g. imaging not recommended for low back pain unless neurological damage is suspected) • Avoiding interventions where a conservative approach is beneficial or equivalent and lower financial or social cost (e.g. watch and wait approach for hernias can be preferable) • Choosing lower carbon options which are equivalent in health benefits, e.g. anaesthetic gases with less global warming potential	• Calculate (or apply calculations of) the financial, social and environmental costs of healthcare provision • Understand the integration (or lack of integration) of different healthcare services • Consider patient's experiences of accessing healthcare and take this into account when evaluating a healthcare pathway • Identify strategies to achieve both sustainability gains and improvements in healthcare • Address SDGs 12, 13, 14 and 15	Formative—Observed group work, group presentation, individual reflective practice assignment Summative—group presentation, written assignment (group or individual)

(continued)

Table 19.1 (continued)

Learning activity	Examples	Opportunities	Possible formative and summative assessments
			Rubrics for all assessments can be developed based on intended learning outcomes and enhance validity of assessment
Quality improvement projects in primary or secondary or higher levels of care	Apply the SusQI (Sustainability in Quality Improvement) framework (Mortimer et al. 2018) to plan and deliver a project, e.g. about medicines waste	• SusQI framework can be applied in different contexts to focus on local needs and resources • Clearly link environmental topics to clinical practice • Integrate environmental, social, cultural, financial and ethical perspectives • May address any or all SDGs	Formative—supervisor's report, learner's reflective report Summative—report, poster, oral or other presentation
Activities which may have a clinical, public health or wider sustainability focus			
Literature-based individual or group research project and presentation	Research and communicate best evidence on a planetary health topic. The SDGs offer a useful framework which could inform the choice of topic or approach to addressing it. Learners may choose to produce a video to communicate on their topic or use another format	• Practise and demonstrate effective communication with colleagues or the public about planetary health • Learners may choose a topic of personal interest • If video presentation is used, learners may develop digital technology skills • May address any or all of the SDGs	Formative or summative—Assessment of the presentation may be carried out using a rubric based on key learning outcomes

(continued)

Table 19.1 (continued)

Learning activity	Examples	Opportunities	Possible formative and summative assessments
			Rubrics for all assessments can be developed based on intended learning outcomes and enhance validity of assessment
Written assignment, informed by a literature review	Design an assignment question or select from a list of questions addressing any planetary health topic. Construct a written argument in response to the question	• Develop skills for evidence based practice, including critical appraisal and synthesizing complex and / or diverse information • Demonstrate effective written communication about a planetary health topic • In-depth learning on a chosen planetary health topic	Formative or summative—A rubric for marking assignments may include understanding of topic, development of argument and written communication. This assessment may, however, be time-consuming with large cohorts
Research assignment involving local or global communities, preferably transdisciplinary	A scenario or challenge that allows learners to explore the relationship between one or more ecological crises, social determinants of health and inequality, e.g. exploring how marginalized Indigenous communities experience these issues, or investigating gender inequality Participatory research (*with* not *about* communities) would be an ideal way to achieve deeper learning if time and structures to support ethical research are in place	• Develop qualitative research skills • Participatory research may promote empathy and advocacy • Learners may focus on an area of personal interest • Learners may form lasting connections with students from other disciplines; they may mutually support each other to implement positive change • Mirrors teamwork in clinical practice • Learner may explore several SDGs, e.g. 1 (alleviation of poverty), 5 (gender equality) and 13 (climate action)	Formative—observation of team working, learners provide feedback on other presentations, written reflections on learning Summative—research project write-up as conference presentation or journal article

(continued)

Table 19.1 (continued)

Learning activity	Examples	Opportunities	Possible formative and summative assessments
Debate, preferably transdisciplinary	Prepare an argument and debate a motion, which could be about: • Professional duty—the role of health professionals in advancing sustainable development through resource stewardship, • An ecological justice issue such as the impact of rising sea levels on Small Island Nations • Responding to a sustainability challenge, e.g. the link between pandemics and environmental factors • An ethical issue, e.g. single-use items in health care, or the global burden of disease caused by the health sector emissions	• Practice developing an evidence-based viewpoint • Engaging format to encourage engagement • Promotes communicating effectively with colleagues from different health professions and addressing resistance or conflict • Allows engagement with emotionally challenging, ethical and/or political issues • Learners may form lasting connections with students from other disciplines; they may mutually support each other to implement positive change • May address various SDGs depending on debate topic	*Rubrics for all assessments can be developed based on intended learning outcomes and enhance validity of assessment* Formative—observation of team working in preparation or during debate Summative—observation of debate presentations and contributions using assessment rubric, essay around the debate question, MCQs or SAQs on the debate topics

(continued)

Table 19.1 (continued)

Learning activity	Examples	Opportunities	Possible formative and summative assessments *Rubrics for all assessments can be developed based on intended learning outcomes and enhance validity of assessment*
Small group public health learning scenario, preferably interprofessional or transdisciplinary	Use systems thinking to design a public health strategy for a scenario (individual patient or community) addressing an ecological event or crisis and its impacts on health and/or healthcare facilities, e.g.: • Respiratory disease linked to local air pollution • Forced migration due to sea level rise • Bush fire causing destruction of a local health post • Climate-induced drought and food insecurity • Ecological crisis causing eco-anxiety*, grief, depression and suicide, particularly among youth	• Stimulates discussion about health professionals' roles in, e.g. reducing healthcare's environmental footprint and advocacy • Scenarios can be designed based on local ecological and public health challenges to promote engagement • Systems thinking explores interactions between different parts of a system and potential unintended consequences of a given response. Learners can then apply it to other settings and challenges • Opportunity to promote transdisciplinary collaboration	Formative—observation of discussion or presentation by small group Summative—using rubric to assess small group work or a group presentation of discussion and solutions identified, written report of learning

(continued)

Table 19.1 (continued)

Learning activity	Examples	Opportunities	Possible formative and summative assessments
			Rubrics for all assessments can be developed based on intended learning outcomes and enhance validity of assessment
Reflective assignment	Explore personal, professional and/or ethical challenges, e.g. single-use plastic equipment in terms of sustainable lifestyles and global citizenship or in relation to healthcare practice. Read relevant articles, consider how the issues are faced in your day to day life and may affect current or future choices. Write an essay or collection of short reflections on this process	• Facilitate engagement with personal values, feelings and attitudes, which may lead to mindset and behavioural changes • Identify and explore tensions which may enhance ability to understand diverse perspectives • Practice written communication regarding challenging and sensitive issues • May address any or all SDGs	Formative—portfolio entries Summative—portfolio entries or essay to meet particular domain requirements, e.g. professional, advocacy

References

Academy for Systems Change. (n.d.). *Leverage points and the iceberg model in economic development.* https://www.academyforchange.org/2019/12/07/leverage-points-iceberg-model-economic-development/

Anåker, A., Spante, M., & Elf, M. (2021). Nursing students' perception of climate change and sustainability actions—A mismatched discourse: A qualitative, descriptive exploratory study. *Nurse Education Today, 105*, 105028. https://doi.org/10.1016/j.nedt.2021.105028

Benatar, S., Upshur, R., & Gill, S. (2018). Understanding the relationship between ethics, neoliberalism and power as a step towards improving the health of people and our planet. *The Anthropocene Review, 5*(2), 155–176. https://doi.org/10.1177/2053019618760934

Blum, N., Berlin, A., Isaacs, A., Burch, W. J., & Willott, C. (2019). Medical students as global citizens: A qualitative study of medical students' views on global health teaching within the undergraduate medical curriculum. *BMC Medical Education, 19*(1), 175. https://doi.org/10.1186/s12909-019-1631-x

Boelen, C., Pearson, D., Kaufman, A., Rourke, J., Woollard, R., Marsh, D. C., & Gibbs, T. (2016). Producing a socially accountable medical school: AMEE guide no. 109. *Medical Teacher, 38*(11), 1078–1091. https://doi.org/10.1080/0142159X.2016.1219029

Bradshaw, C. J. A., Ehrlich, P. R., Beattie, A., Ceballos, G., Crist, E., Diamond, J., Dirzo, R., Ehrlich, A. H., Harte, J., Harte, M. E., Pyke, G., Raven, P. H., Ripple, W. J., Saltré, F., Turnbull, C., Wackernagel, M., & Blumstein, D. T. (2021). Underestimating the challenges of avoiding a ghastly future. *Frontiers in Conservation Science, 13.* https://doi.org/10.3389/fcosc.2020.615419

Brand, G., Collins, J., Bedi, G., Bonnamy, J., Barbour, L., Ilangakoon, C., Wotherspoon, R., Simmons, M., Kim, M., & Schwerdtle, P. N. (2021). "I teach it because it is the biggest threat to health": Integrating sustainable healthcare into health professions education. *Medical Teacher, 43*(3), 325–333. https://doi.org/10.1080/0142159X.2020.1844876

Burch, H., Watson, B., Simpson, G., Beaton, L. J., Maxwell, J., & Winkel, K. (2021). *Mapping climate change and health into the medical curriculum: Co-development of a "planetary health-organ system map" for graduate medical education.* Doctors for the Environment Australia. https://dea.org.au/educational-resource-mapping-climate-change-and-health-into-the-medical-curriculum/

Carlson, C. J., Albery, G. F., Merow, C., Trisos, C. H., Zipfel, C. M., Eskew, E. A., Olival, K. J., Ross, N., & Bansal, S. (2022). Climate change increases cross-species viral transmission risk. *Nature, 607*(7919), 555–562. https://doi.org/10.1038/s41586-022-04788-w

Cavanagh, A., Vanstone, M., & Ritz, S. (2019). Problems of problem-based learning: Towards transformative critical pedagogy in medical education. *Perspectives on Medical Education, 8*(1), 38–42. https://doi.org/10.1007/s40037-018-0489-7

Christie, B. A., Miller, K. K., Cooke, R., & White, J. G. (2015). Environmental sustainability in higher education: What do academics think? *Environmental Education Research, 21*(5), 655–686. https://doi.org/10.1080/13504622.2013.879697

Declaration of Alma-Ata International. (1978). Conference on primary health care, Alma-Ata, USSR, 6–12 September. *WHO Chron, 32*(11), 428–430.

Diaz, S., Settele, J., Brondízio, E. S., Ngo, H. T., Guèze, M., Agard, J., Arneth, A., Balvanera, P., Brauman, K., Butchart, S. H., Chan, A., Garibaldi, L. A., Ichii, K., Liu, S., Subramanian, S. M., Midgley, G. F., Miloslavich, P., Molnar, Z., Obura, D., … Zayas, C. N. (2019). *Summary for policymakers of the global assessment report on biodiversity and ecosystem services of the intergovernmental science-policy platform on biodiversity and ecosystem services.* Intergovernmental Science-Policy Platform on Biodiversity and Ecosystem Services. https://doi.org/10.5281/zenodo.3553579

Doughnut Economics Action Lab (DEAL). (2020). *Downscaling the doughnut to the city* [Video]. *YouTube.* https://www.youtube.com/watch?v=YCqGf7T9ABo&t=603s

Eisenmenger, N., Pichler, M., Krenmayr, N., Noll, D., Plank, B., Schalmann, E., Wandl, M.-T., & Gingrich, S. (2020). The sustainable development goals prioritize economic growth over sustainable resource use: A critical reflection on the SDGs from a socio-ecological perspective. *Sustainability Science, 15*(4), 1101–1110. https://doi.org/10.1007/s11625-020-00813-x

El Omrani, O., Dafallah, A., Paniello Castillo, B., Amaro, B., Taneja, S., Amzil, M., Sajib, M., & Ezzine, T. (2020). Envisioning planetary health in every medical curriculum: An international medical student organization's perspective. *Medical Teacher, 42*, 1–5. https://doi.org/10.1080/0142159X.2020.1796949

Fadadu, R. P., Jayaraman, T., & Teherani, A. (2020). Climate and health education for medical students. *The Clinical Teacher, 18*(4), 362–364. https://doi.org/10.1111/tct.13317

Frenk, J., Chen, L., Bhutta, Z. A., Cohen, J., Crisp, N., Evans, T., Fineberg, H., Garcia, P., Ke, Y., Kelley, P., Kistnasamy, B., Meleis, A., Naylor, D., Pablos-Mendez, A., Reddy, S., Scrimshaw, S., Sepulveda, J., Serwadda, D., & Zurayk, H. (2010). Health professionals for a new century: Transforming education to strengthen health systems in an interdependent world. *The Lancet, 376*(9756), 1923–1958. https://doi.org/10.1016/s0140-6736(10)61854-5

Gale, F., Davison, A., Wood, G., Williams, S., & Towle, N. (2015). Four impediments to embedding education for sustainability in higher education. *Australian Journal of Environmental Education, 31*(2), 248–263. https://www.jstor.org/stable/26422897

Goodman, B. (2011). The need for a 'sustainability curriculum' in nurse education. *Nurse Education Today, 31*, 733–737. https://doi.org/10.1016/j.nedt.2010.12.010

Goodman, B. (2016). Developing the concept of sustainability in nursing. *Nursing Philosophy, 17*(4), 298–306. https://doi.org/10.1111/nup.12143

Griffiths, E. P., Tong, M. S., Teherani, A., & Garg, M. (2021). First year medical student perceptions of physician advocacy and advocacy as a core competency: A qualitative analysis. *Medical Teacher, 43*(11), 1286–1293. https://doi.org/10.1080/0142159x.2021.1935829

Grose, J., & Richardson, J. (2016). Can a sustainability and health scenario provide a realistic challenge to student nurses and provoke changes in practice? An evaluation of a training intervention. *Nursing and Health Sciences, 18*(2), 256–261. https://doi.org/10.1111/nhs.12241

Gruenberg, K., Apollonio, D., MacDougall, C., & Brock, T. (2017). Sustainable pharmacy: Piloting a session on pharmaceuticals, climate change, and sustainability within a U.S. pharmacy curriculum. *Innovations in Pharmacy, 8.* https://doi.org/10.24926/iip.v8i4.929

Guzmán, C. A. F., Aguirre, A. A., Astle, B., Barros, E., Bayles, B., Chimbari, M., El-Abbadi, N., Evert, J., Hackett, F., Howard, C., Jennings, J., Krzyzek, A., LeClair, J., Maric, F., Martin, O., Osano, O., Patz, J., Potter, T., Redvers, N., … Zylstra, M. (2021a). A framework to guide planetary health education. *The Lancet Planetary Health, 5*(5), e253–e255https://doi.org/10.1016/S2542-5196(21)00110-8

Guzman, C., Potter, T., Aguirre, A. A., Astle, B., Barros, E., Bayles, B., Chimbari, M., El-Abbadi, N., Evert, J., Hackett, F., Howard, C., Jennings, J., Krzyzek, A., LeClair, J., Maric, F., Martin, O., Osano, O., Patz, J., Redvers, N., & Zylstra, M. (2021b). *The planetary health education framework.* https://doi.org/10.13140/RG.2.2.27505.20320

Haines, A., & Ebi, K. (2019). The imperative for climate action to protect health. *New England Journal of Medicine, 380*(3), 263–273. https://doi.org/10.1056/NEJMra1807873

Heuveline, P. (2022). Global and national declines in life expectancy: An end-of-2021 assessment. *Population and Development Review, 48*(1), 31–50. https://doi.org/10.1111/padr.12477

Hickel, J. (2019). The contradiction of the sustainable development goals: Growth versus ecology on a finite planet. *Sustainable Development, 27*(5), 873–884. https://doi.org/10.1002/sd.1947

Horton, R., Beaglehole, R., Bonita, R., Raeburn, J., McKee, M., & Wall, S. (2014). From public to planetary health: A manifesto. *The Lancet, 383*(9920), 847. https://doi.org/10.1016/S0140-6736(14)60409-8

Hubinette, M., Dobson, S., Scott, I., & Sherbino, J. (2017). Health advocacy. *Medical Teacher, 39*(2), 128–135. https://doi.org/10.1080/0142159X.2017.1245853

Huss, N., Ikiugu, M. N., Hackett, F., Sheffield, P. E., Palipane, N., & Groome, J. (2020). Education for sustainable health care: From learning to professional practice. *Medical Teacher, 42*(10). https://doi.org/10.1080/0142159X.2020.1797998

International Federation of Medical Students' Associations (IFMSA). (2016). *Training manual: Climate & health. Enabling students and young professionals to understand and act upon climate change using a health narrative.* https://ifmsa.org/wp-content/uploads/2017/03/Final-IFMSA-Climate-and-health-training-Manual-2016.pdf

Irwin, A., & Scali, E. (2007). Action on the social determinants of health: A historical perspective. *Global Public Health, 2*(3), 235–256. https://doi.org/10.1080/17441690601106304

Jacobs, C., Van Schalkwyk, S. C., Blitz, J., & Volchenk, M. (2020). Advancing a social justice agenda in health professions education. *CriSTaL, 8*(2). https://doi.org/10.14426/cristal.v8i2.272

Johnston, N., Rogers, M., Cross, N., & Sochan, A. (2005). Global and planetary health: Teaching as if the future matters. *Nursing Education Perspectives, 26*(3), 152–156.

Kaplan, R. M., & Milstein, A. (2019). Contributions of health care to longevity: A review of 4 estimation methods. *Annals of Family Medicine, 17*(3), 267–272. https://doi.org/10.1370/afm.2362

Karliner, J., Slotterback, S., Boyd, R., Ashby, B., & Steele, K. (2019). *Health care's climate footprint: How the health sector contributes to the global climate crisis and opportunities for action.* Health Care Without Harm & Arup. https://noharm-global.org/sites/default/files/documents-files/5961/HealthCaresClimateFootprint_092319.pdf

Lenzen, M., Malik, A., Li, M., Fry, J., Weisz, H., Pichler, P. P., Chaves, L. S. M., Capon, A., & Pencheon, D. (2020). The environmental footprint of health care: A global assessment. *The Lancet Planetary Health, 4*(7), e271–e279. https://doi.org/10.1016/s2542-5196(20)30121-2

Lopez-Medina, I. M., Álvarez-Nieto, C., Grose, J., Elsbernd, A., Huss, N., Huynen, M., & Richardson, J. (2019). Competencies on environmental health and pedagogical approaches in the nursing curriculum: A systematic review of the literature. *Nurse Education in Practice, 37*, 1–8. https://doi.org/10.1016/j.nepr.2019.04.004

MacNeill, A. J., McGain, F., & Sherman, J. D. (2021). Planetary health care: A framework for sustainable health systems. *The Lancet Planetary Health, 5*(2), e66–e68. https://doi.org/10.1016/s2542-5196(21)00005-x

Madden, D. L., Horton, G. L., & McLean, M. (2022). Preparing Australasian medical students for environmentally sustainable health care. *Medical Journal of Australia, 216*(5), 225–229. https://doi.org/10.5694/mja2.51439

Mahli, Y., & Raworth, K. (2018, May 3) *Planetary health: Does our planet have boundaries?* [Video]. YouTube. https://www.youtube.com/watch?v=OYceZqVsrEo

Malik, A., Lenzen, M., McAlister, S., & McGain, F. (2018). The carbon footprint of Australian health care. *The Lancet Planetary Health, 2*(1), e27–e35. https://doi.org/10.1016/S2542-5196(17)30180-8

Maxwell, J., & Blashki, G. (2016). Teaching about climate change in medical education: An opportunity. *Journal of Public Health Research, 5*(1), 673. https://doi.org/10.4081/jphr.2016.673

McGovern, L., Miller, G., & Highes-Cromwick, P. (2014). *Health policy brief: The relative contribution of multiple determinants of health outcomes.* https://www.healthaffairs.org/do/https://doi.org/10.1377/hpb20140821.404487

McKimm, J., & McLean, M. (2020). Rethinking health professions' education leadership: Developing 'eco-ethical' leaders for a more sustainable world and future. *Medical Teacher, 42*(8), 855–860. https://doi.org/10.1080/0142159X.2020.1748877

McKimm, J., Redvers, N., El Omrani, O., Parkes, M. W., Elf, M., & Woollard, R. (2020). Education for sustainable healthcare: Leadership to get from here to there. *Medical Teacher, 42*(10), 1123–1127. https://doi.org/10.1080/0142159X.2020.1795104

McKinnon, S., Breakey, S., Fanuele, J. R., Kelly, D. E., Eddy, E. Z., Tarbet, A., Nicholas, P. K., & Ros, A. M. V. (2022). Roles of health professionals in addressing health consequences of climate change in interprofessional education: A scoping review. *The Journal of Climate Change and Health, 5*, 100086. https://doi.org/10.1016/j.joclim.2021.100086

McLean, M., Madden, L., Maxwell, J., Schwerdtle, P. N., Richardson, J., Singleton, J., MacKenzie-Shalders, K., Behrens, G., Cooling, N., Matthews, R., & Horton, G. (2020). Planetary health:

Educating the current and future health workforce. In D. Nestel, G. Reedy, L. McKenna, & S. Gough (Eds.), *Clinical education for the health professions: Theory and practice* (pp. 1–30). Springer. https://doi.org/10.1007/978-981-13-6106-7_121-1

Meadows, D. H. (2008). *Thinking in systems: A primer*. Chelsea Green Publishing.

Mortimer, F., Isherwood, J., Wilkinson, A., & Vaux, E. (2018). Sustainability in quality improvement: Redefining value. *Future healthcare journal, 5*(2), 88–93. https://doi.org/10.7861/future hosp.5-2-88

Noy, S., Capetola, T., & Patrick, R. (2021). The wheel of fortune as a novel support for constructive alignment and transformative sustainability learning in higher education. *International Journal of Sustainability in Higher Education, 22*(4), 854–869. https://doi.org/10.1108/IJSHE-08-2020-0289

Nunes, A. R., Lee, K., & O'Riordan, T. (2016). The importance of an integrating framework for achieving the sustainable development goals: The example of health and wellbeing. *BMJ Global Health, 1*(3), e000068. https://doi.org/10.1136/bmjgh-2016-000068

Parker, G., Berta, W., Shea, C., & Milller, F. (2020). Environmental competencies for healthcare educators and trainees: A scoping review. *Health Education Journal, 79*(3), 327–345.

Parkes, M. W., Poland, B., Allison, S., Cole, D. C., Culbert, I., Gislason, M. K., Hancock, T., Howard, C., Papadopoulos, A., & Waheed, F. (2020). Preparing for the future of public health: Ecological determinants of health and the call for an eco-social approach to public health education. *Canadian Journal of Public Health, 111*(1), 60–64. https://doi.org/10.17269/s41997-019-00263-8

Plymouth University. (2014). *Nursing sustainability by design* [Video]. *YouTube*. http://youtu.be/zIFT2Dbg08o

Prescott, S. L., & Logan, A. C. (2019). Planetary health: From the wellspring of holistic medicine to personal and public health imperative. *Explore: The Journal of Science and Healing, 15*(2), 98–106. https://doi.org/10.1016/j.explore.2018.09.002

Prescott, S., Logan, A., Albrecht, G., Campbell, D., Crane, J., Cunsolo, A., Holloway, J., Kozyrskyj, A., Lowry, C., Penders, J., Redvers, N., Renz, H., Stokholm, J., Svanes, C., & Wegienka, G. (2018). The Canmore declaration: Statement of principles for planetary health. *Challenges, 9*(31). https://doi.org/10.3390/challe9020031

Prideaux, D. (2007). Curriculum development in medical education: From acronyms to dynamism. *Teaching and Teacher Education, 23*(3), 294–302. https://doi.org/10.1016/j.tate.2006.12.017

Raworth, K. (2017). *Doughnut economics: Seven ways to think like a 21st-century economist*. Random House Business.

Reid, A., & Petocz, P. (2006). University lecturers' understanding of sustainability. *Higher Education, 51*(1), 105–123. https://doi.org/10.1007/s10734-004-6379-4

Richardson, J., Grose, J., Doman, M., & Kelsey, J. (2014). The use of evidence-informed sustainability scenarios in the nursing curriculum: Development and evaluation of teaching methods. *Nurse Education Today, 34*(4), 490–493. https://doi.org/10.1016/j.nedt.2013.07.007

Richardson, J., Heidenreich, T., Álvarez-Nieto, C., Fasseur, F., Grose, J., Huss, N., Huynen, M., López-Medina, I. M., & Schweizer, A. (2016). Including sustainability issues in nurse education: A comparative study of first year student nurses' attitudes in four European countries. *Nurse Education Today, 37*, 15–20. https://doi.org/10.1016/j.nedt.2015.11.005

Rosa, W. E., Dossey, B. M., Watson, J., Beck, D.-M., & Upvall, M. J. (2019). The United Nations sustainable development goals: The ethic and ethos of holistic nursing. *Journal of Holistic Nursing, 37*(4), 381–393. https://doi.org/10.1177/0898010119841723

Royal Australasian College of Physicians. (2016). *Climate change and health position statement*. https://www.racp.edu.au/docs/default-source/advocacy-library/climate-change-and-health-position-statement.pdf

Salter, S., Murray, S., Davison, A., Fallon, F., & Towle, N. (2013). Establishing a community of practice and embedding education for sustainability at the University of Tasmania. *The International Journal of Social Sustainability in Economic, Social, and Cultural Context, 9*(1), 12. https://doi.org/10.18848/2325-1115/CGP/v09i01/55211

Schwerdtle, P. N., Horton, G., Kent, F., Walker, L., & McLean, M. (2020a). Education for sustainable healthcare: A transdisciplinary approach to transversal environmental threats. *Medical Teacher, 42*(10), 1102–1106. https://doi.org/10.1080/0142159X.2020.1795101

Schwerdtle, P. N., Maxwell, J., Horton, G., & Bonnamy, J. (2020b). 12 tips for teaching environmental sustainability to health professionals. *Medical Teacher, 42*(2), 150–155. https://doi.org/10.1080/0142159X.2018.1551994

Settele, J., Diaz, S., & Brondízio, E. S. (2020). *COVID-19 stimulus measures must save lives, protect livelihoods, and safeguard nature to reduce the risk of future pandemics.* https://ipbes.net/covid19stimulus

Sharma, M., Pinto, A. D., & Kumagai, A. K. (2018). Teaching the social determinants of health: A path to equity or a road to nowhere? *Academic Medicine, 93*(1), 25–30. https://doi.org/10.1097/acm.0000000000001689

Shaw, E., Walpole, S., McLean, M., Alvarez-Nieto, C., Barna, S., Bazin, K., Behrens, G., Chase, H., Duane, B., El Omrani, O., Elf, M., Faerron Guzmán, C. A., Falceto de Barros, E., Gibbs, T. J., Groome, J., Hackett, F., Harden, J., Hothersall, E. J., Hourihane, M., … Woollard, R. (2021). AMEE consensus statement: Planetary health and education for sustainable healthcare. *Medical Teacher, 43*(3), 272–286.https://doi.org/10.1080/0142159X.2020.1860207

Shorrocks, A., Davies, J., & Lluberas, R. (2021). *Credit suisse global wealth report 2021.* https://www.credit-suisse.com/about-us/en/reports-research/global-wealth-report.html

Slimings, C., Sisson, E., Larson, C., Bowles, D., & Hussain, R. (2022). Adaptive doctors in Australia: Preparing tomorrow's doctors for practice in a world destabilised by declining planetary health. *Environmental Education Research, 28*(5), 786–801. https://doi.org/10.1080/13504622.2021.2025343

Steffen, W., Richardson, K., Rockström, J., Cornell, S. E., Fetzer, I., Bennett, E. M., Biggs, R., Carpenter, S. R., de Vries, W., de Wit, C. A., Folke, C., Gerten, D., Heinke, J., Mace, G. M., Persson, L. M., Ramanathan, V., Reyers, B., & Sörlin, S. (2015). Planetary boundaries: Guiding human development on a changing planet. *Science, 347*(6223), 1259855. https://doi.org/10.1126/science.1259855

Stone, S. B., Myers, S. S., & Golden, C. D. (2018). Cross-cutting principles for planetary health education. *The Lancet Planetary Health, 2*(5), e192–e193. https://doi.org/10.1016/s2542-5196(18)30022-6

Stranger, N. (2011). Moving "Eco" back into socio-ecological models: A proposal to reorient ecological literacy into human developmental models and school systems. *Human Ecology Review, 18*(2), 167–173.

TEDxSydney. (2017). *Dr Bronwyn King: You may be accidentally investing in cigarette companies* [Video]. *TED.* https://www.ted.com/talks/bronwyn_king_you_may_be_accidentally_investing_in_cigarette_companies?language=en

Teherani, A., Nishimura, H., Apatira, L., Newman, T., & Ryan, S. (2017). Identification of core objectives for teaching sustainable healthcare education. *Medical Education Online, 22*(1), 1386042. https://doi.org/10.1080/10872981.2017.1386042

Tun, S. (2019). Fulfilling a new obligation: Teaching and learning of sustainable healthcare in the medical education curriculum. *Medical Teacher, 41*(10), 1168–1177. https://doi.org/10.1080/0142159X.2019.1623870

Tun, S., Wellbery, C., & Teherani, A. (2020). Faculty development and partnership with students to integrate sustainable healthcare into health professions education. *Medical Teacher, 42*(10), 1112–1118. https://doi.org/10.1080/0142159X.2020.1796950

United Nations. (1992). *Report of the United Nations conference on environment and development.* https://www.un.org/en/development/desa/population/migration/generalassembly/docs/globalcompact/A_CONF.151_26_Vol.I_Declaration.pdf

Upvall, M. J., & Luzincourt, G. (2019). Global citizens, healthy communities: Integrating the sustainable development goals into the nursing curriculum. *Nursing Outlook, 67*(6), 649–657. https://doi.org/10.1016/j.outlook.2019.04.004

Van Schalkwyk, S. C., Hafler, J., Brewer, T. F., Maley, M. A., Margolis, C., McNamee, L., Meyer, I., Peluso, M. J., Schmutz, A. M. S., Spak, J. M., Davies, D., & The Bellagio Global Health Education Initiative. (2019). Transformative learning as pedagogy for the health professions: A scoping review. *Medical Education, 53*(6), 547–558.https://doi.org/10.1111/medu.13804

Walpole, S., & Mortimer, F. (2017). Evaluation of a collaborative project to develop sustainable healthcare education in eight UK medical schools. *Public Health, 150*, 134–148. https://doi.org/10.1016/j.puhe.2017.05.014

Walpole, S. C., Barna, S., Richardson, J., & Rother, H. A. (2019). Sustainable healthcare education: Integrating planetary health into clinical education. *The Lancet Planetary Health, 3*(1), e6–e7. https://doi.org/10.1016/s2542-5196(18)30246-8

Walpole, S. C., Pearson, D., Coad, J., & Barna, S. (2016). What do tomorrow's doctors need to learn about ecosystems?—A BEME systematic review: BEME guide no. 36. *Medical Teacher, 38*(4), 338–352. https://doi.org/10.3109/0142159X.2015.1112897

Walpole, S. C., Vyas, A., Maxwell, J., Canny, B. J., Woollard, R., Wellbery, C., Leedham-Green, K. E., Musaeus, P., Tufail-Hanif, U., Pavão Patrício, K., & Rother, H. A. (2017). Building an environmentally accountable medical curriculum through international collaboration. *Medical Teacher, 39*(10), 1040–1050. https://doi.org/10.1080/0142159x.2017.1342031

Watts, N., Adger, W. N., Agnolucci, P., Blackstock, J., Byass, P., Cai, W., Chaytor, S., Colbourn, T., Collins, M., Cooper, A., Cox, P. M., Depledge, J., Drummond, P., Ekins, P., Galaz, V., Grace, D., Graham, H., Grubb, M., Haines, A., … Costello, A. (2015). Health and climate change: Policy responses to protect public health. *The Lancet, 386*(10006), 1861–1914.https://doi.org/10.1016/s0140-6736(15)60854-6

Watts, N., Amann, M., Arnell, N., Ayeb-Karlsson, S., Belesova, K., Boykoff, M., Byass, P., Cai, W., Campbell-Lendrum, D., Capstick, S., Chambers, J., Dalin, C., Daly, M., Dasandi, N., Davies, M., Drummond, P., Dubrow, R., Ebi, K. L., Eckelman, M., … Montgomery, H. (2019). The 2019 report of The Lancet countdown on health and climate change: Ensuring that the health of a child born today is not defined by a changing climate. *The Lancet, 394*(10211), 1836–1878. https://doi.org/10.1016/S0140-6736(19)32596-6

Whitmee, S., Haines, A., Beyrer, C., Boltz, F., Capon, A. G., de Souza Dias, B. F., Ezeh, A., Frumkin, H., Gong, P., Head, P., Horton, R., Mace, G. M., Marten, R., Myers, S. S., Nishtar, S., Osofsky, S. A., Pattanayak, S. K., Pongsiri, M. J., Romanelli, C., … Yach, D. (2015). Safeguarding human health in the Anthropocene epoch: Report of The Rockefeller Foundation–Lancet Commission on planetary health. *The Lancet, 386*(10007), 1973–2028. https://doi.org/10.1016/S0140-6736(15)60901-1

Whitty, C. J. (2017). Harveian oration 2017: Triumphs and challenges in a world shaped by medicine. *Clinical Medicine (London), 17*(6), 537–544. https://doi.org/10.7861/clinmedicine.17-6-537

Wilkinson, R. D., & Pickett, K. (2009). *The spirit level: Why more equal societies almost always do better*. Bloomsbury Publishing.

World Health Organisation (WHO). (n.d.). *Social determinants of health*. https://www.who.int/health-topics/social-determinants-of-health#tab=tab_1

World Health Organisation. (1948). *Constitution of the World Health Organisation*. https://www.who.int/about/governance/constitution

World Health Organisation. (1986). *Ottawa Charter for health promotion: First international conference on health promotion. Ottawa, 21 November 1986*. https://www.healthpromotion.org.au/images/ottawa_charter_hp.pdf

World Health Organisation. (2016). *An estimated 12.6 million deaths each year are attributable to unhealthy environments.* https://www.who.int/news/item/15-03-2016-an-estimated-12-6-million-deaths-each-year-are-attributable-to-unhealthy-environments

Xu, K., Soucat, A., Kutzin, J., Brindley, C., Dale, E., Van de Maele, N., Roubul, T., Indikadahena, C., Toure, H., & Cherilova, V. (2018). *New perspectives on global health spending for universal health coverage.* World Health Organisation. https://www.who.int/publications/i/item/WHO-HIS-HGF-HFWorkingPaper-18.2

Zindler, H. (1989). In M. H. Brown & J. May (Eds.), *The greenpeace story* (p. 158). Dorling Kindersley.

Chapter 20
Sustainability in a Bachelor of Engineering with Honours Degree

Anna Wrobel and Sarah Lyden

20.1 Introduction

Engineers are creative problem solvers who use their knowledge and skills in mathematics, science, and design to solve problems. This position means that engineers have an important role to play in the transition to a more sustainable future through their awareness of sustainable engineering design, and their advocacy for more sustainable solutions (Engineers Australia, 2017).

Although historically it can be argued that engineers have contributed towards our unsustainable consumption of resources through the continual development and improvement of technologies (Qureshi & Nawab, 2016), they are also uniquely placed to help move society towards more sustainable solutions, which balance economic, social, and environmental goals. Cruikshank (2003) argues that there are significant similarities between engineering activities and the fundamental elements of sustainable development, particularly regarding how the three systems of environment, society, and economics interact. She also argues that the perception of engineering work in recent years, as destroying the environment, contrasts significantly with the perception of engineers in earlier times as innovators. Perhaps engineers need to seek to regain their status as innovators in addressing the most pressing issues facing the world at present.

While engineering innovation has led to many developments including but not limited to nuclear technologies, lasers and fibre optics, oil, gas, and coal technologies, health technologies, space exploration, electrification, automation, and electronics,

A. Wrobel (✉) · S. Lyden
School of Engineering, College of Science and Engineering, University of
Tasmania, Churchill Ave, Hobart, TAS 7005, Australia
e-mail: Anna.Wrobeltobiszewska@utas.edu.au

S. Lyden
e-mail: Sarah.Lyden@utas.edu.au

K. Beasy et al. (eds.), *Education and the UN Sustainable Development Goals*, Education
for Sustainability 7,
https://doi.org/10.1007/978-981-99-3802-5_20

many of these technologies were developed and implemented without consideration for the potential impacts they could have socially, economically, and on the natural world (Qureshi & Nawab, 2016). A shift has occurred in recent years, with organisations such as the World Federation of Engineering Organisations having key goals around the promotion and integration of the United Nations Sustainable Development Goals (UN SDGs) (World Federation of Engineering Organisations, 2021). Closer to home, Engineers Australia include sustainability as one of the key requirements for accredited degrees and practicing professional engineers (Engineers Australia, 2019; Engineers Australia, 2021). Sustainability is also mentioned in the University of Tasmania Strategic Plan 2019–2024 (University of Tasmania, 2019), from the perspective of economic sustainability, as well as environmental sustainability aimed at addressing climate change issues.

De Graaff and Ravesteijn (2001) argued that engineering education needs to shift with the changing role of engineers in society, due to rapid changes in technology and knowledge required by engineers. More recently, the Barcelona Declaration for engineering education for sustainable development, suggested that a future engineer should be "one who has a long-term, systemic approach to decision-making, one who is guided by ethics, justice, equality and solidarity, and has a holistic understanding that goes beyond his or her own field of specialization" (University of British Columbia, 2004, p. 1). The Declaration goes on to highlight the importance of engineers being able to design solutions in complex social, economic, and environmental settings and that engineers need to be able to respond to the needs of society.

To address the increasingly complex social, economic, and environmental settings where engineers design solutions, engineering graduates need to be aware of the key challenges facing humanity and be capable of developing and delivering sustainable solutions. Due to the nature of engineering and the role of engineers in contributing to infrastructure and product development, the important role of sustainability as an element of engineering education is highlighted by Thürer et al. (2018). As such, a focus on sustainable solutions in engineering curricula is an important feature of emerging engineering curricula. One of the key approaches for integrating this focus on sustainability is through the inclusion of sustainability units in engineering curricula (Arefin et al., 2021). This can typically take the form of being embedded into standard engineering units, the design of a new unit, or the development of a specialisation dedicated to sustainable engineering practice (Thürer et al., 2018). Additionally, Arefin et al. advocate for the need to have design-based and active learning experiences for students to gain the intellectual maturity to apply sustainability concepts in their future engineering practice. Of particular focus in this chapter are undergraduate engineering students completing an entry to practice engineering degree.

The chapter outlines the degree program offered at an Australian regional university and describes and provides case studies of how sustainability, sustainable development, and the UN SDGs are embedded into the course. Following on from this baseline, the case for embedding sustainability further into the course is made, and recommendations are provided on how this could be achieved in similar courses.

20.2 Degree Outline

The Bachelor of Engineering with Honours degree is a four-year full-time undergraduate degree with five specialisations. These specialisations are within the three main fields of engineering—civil, mechanical, and electrical. From the course description, the degree seeks to educate engineers who are "committed to crafting modern engineered solutions that are sustainable, economically feasible, safe, and appropriate to context and purpose" (University of Tasmania, 2022).

The degree commences with a common year where students study eight foundational units including mathematics, statics, dynamics, circuits, programming, and design. At the start of year 2, students select their future specialisation from civil, mechanical, electronics and communications, electrical and electronics, or electrical power, which determines their remaining study plan. In years 2–4, all students engage in two design units (year 2), two work placement units (years 2 and 3), and a final year capstone honours unit, worth 50% of year 4.

The degree is accredited by Engineers Australia (EA), demonstrating that graduating students meet the competencies required for entry into practice at the end of their degree (Engineers Australia, 2021). Within these competencies, there are six indicators of attainment, which specifically mention sustainability or sustainable development (Table 20.1) and further indicators where sustainability is highly related.

Sustainability is considered a key foundational area for engineering practice, as engineers should integrate environmental, social, and economic factors into their designs and solutions. The EA code of ethics, which provides values to guide the engineering profession in Australia, highlights, as one of the four areas, the importance for engineers to "promote sustainability" (Engineers Australia, 2019, p. 2). This is through their engagement with stakeholders and community, how they practice engineering, and in line with the Brundtland report definition of sustainability—to ensure that there is a balance between the needs of the future and current needs in engineering work (United Nations, 2021).

Understanding the perception and meanings that teaching staff assign to the language of sustainability is important in working towards extending the delivery of sustainability across the whole curriculum. Koth and Woodward (2009) through a survey of staff teaching in engineering degrees found that, at an individual level, definitions of sustainability tended to be very individual and constrained to within specific fields covering one or two dimensions of sustainability. As such, a common understanding of what sustainability is, and how sustainable development is relevant to engineering professionals, essential for a cohesive student experience of this throughout a degree program.

Table 20.1 Engineers Australia competencies and indicators of attainment aligned with sustainability and sustainable development and names of the units in which they are achieved

	Unit
1.5 Knowledge of engineering design practice and contextual factors impacting the engineering discipline	
(b) Identifies and understands the interactions between engineering systems and people in the social, cultural, environmental, commercial, legal, and political contexts in which they operate, including both the positive role of engineering in sustainable development and the potentially adverse impacts of engineering activity in the engineering discipline	ENG102—Engineering design and sustainable development ENG201—Design and build A ENG437—Environmental engineering ENG401/402—Honours units
1.6 Understanding of the scope, principles, norms, accountabilities, and bounds of *sustainable engineering practice* in the specific discipline	
(c) Appreciates the social, environmental, and economic principles of sustainable engineering practice	ENG102—Engineering design and sustainable development ENG201—Design and build A ENG437—Environmental engineering
(e) Appreciates the formal structures and methodologies of systems engineering as a holistic basis for managing complexity and *sustainability in engineering practice*	ENG313—Fluid mechanics 1 ENG333—Power systems 1 ENG433—Renewable and sustainable energy
2.3 Application of systematic engineering synthesis and design processes	
(b) Addresses broad contextual constraints such as *social, cultural, environmental,* commercial, legal, political, and human factors, as well as health, safety, and *sustainability imperatives as an integral part of the design process*	ENG102—Engineering design and sustainable development ENG201—Design and build A ENG437—Environmental engineering ENG401/402—Honours units
(c) Executes and leads a whole systems design cycle approach including tasks such as: *systematically addressing sustainability criteria*	ENG437—Environmental engineering ENG203/303—Work placement
2.4 Application of systematic approaches to the conduct and management of engineering projects	
(f) Demonstrates commitment to sustainable engineering practices and the achievement of sustainable outcomes in all facets of engineering project work	ENG201—Design and build A ENG202—Design and build B ENG401/402—Honours units

20.3 Sustainability Throughout the Degree

20.3.1 Year 1

20.3.1.1 ENG102—Engineering Design and Sustainable Development

In this first-year core unit, students are exposed to sustainability in the context of the Engineers without Borders (EWB) Challenge. ENG102 involves students completing two design projects. The first is in humanitarian engineering with a focus on the EWB challenge or a partnership with a local community organisation. The second project involves human-centred design, with a focus on development of an electrical design and associated skills. Students are introduced to the idea of sustainable solutions and the concept of sustainable development through a lecture delivered by an engineer from industry. Throughout this lecture, the SDGs are introduced. Sustainability in this unit is aligned with Intended Learning Outcomes (ILOs) 1 and 3:

> ILO1: Design a solution for a societal problem using engineering design practice and principles in conjunction with project management within a team context;
>
> ILO3: Demonstrate individual responsible and accountable ethical work practice within my group.

Students are encouraged to identify sustainability considerations related to their design solutions to the EWB challenge, by addressing the design consideration on sustainability from EWB (below) in their team report, and through a series of questions in their individual ePortfolio.

20.3.2 Sustainability of Design

Students are asked to consider the long-term sustainability of their project proposal, and what measures could be put in place to ensure the successful continuation into the future (EWB, 2021). The EWB challenge can be aligned, depending on the project selected by students, with SDG 1 (no poverty), SDG 6 (clean water and sanitation), SDG 7 (clean and affordable energy), SDG 11 (sustainable cities and communities), SDG 12 (responsible consumption and production), or SDG 13 (climate action). Specifically, in their reports, students are assessed on their evaluations of the designs with respect to their suitability for the safety of people and protection of the environment, through the three lenses of sustainability—environmental, social, and economic.

The intention of the unit is to introduce students to these concepts of sustainability and encourage them to keep these in mind throughout their future studies. The level of engagement that students have with this can vary from a superficial understanding of planning how to make sure a proposed design solution lasts, to a comprehensive evaluation of the CO_2 emissions associated with a particular technology.

Through ENG102, students are introduced to sustainability and encouraged to consider how sustainability concepts can be embedded into their design projects. Although concepts of sustainability are well-embedded when students are engaging with the humanitarian engineering-based EWB challenge, further development of this unit could embed these principles more clearly in the electrical project that students also undertake in this unit. In particular, students could consider the choice of materials in the electrical design project and how they could repurpose other items in meeting their design challenges.

20.3.3 Year 2

20.3.3.1 ENG 201—Engineering Design and Build A

Engineering Design and Build A is a unit taught to all the engineering students in the first semester of second year. Although the ILOs do not specifically mention sustainability, the recent deliveries of the unit have been closely wrapped around some of the SDGs. This unit is dedicated to teaching students how to design and build properly, according to engineering standards and requirements, and it emphasises the need for rethinking the application of engineering designs, along with some of the principles listed in Desha et al. (2007). Learning outcomes dedicated to design and building skills are achieved in this unit by challenging students with a task to design a mobile kayaking device to be used by people with a disability, who can only use one arm. Sustainability is taught by encouraging students to reuse materials from a recycling shop located at a landfill, and include various components in their final design, to understand how the reused materials can be used in engineering design in addition to social sustainability connections.

The project on which this unit is based is very closely related to two major SDGs:

- SDG 9 (Industry, Innovation, and Infrastructure), where students research and develop innovative methods to provide a device equipped with a pivoting point, allowing a one-handed person to use a two-handed device, namely a kayaking paddle. Students must think "out of the box" and use their creativity to suggest optimal solutions.
- SDG 10 (Reduced Inequalities), via the project that is a pillar for the delivery. The mobile kayaking device ("pirate kayaker") was predominantly used to align the unit with the sustainability goals of the University of Tasmania and the SDGs and to address the sustainability requirements. In future deliveries, teaching staff might choose to include a lecture about UN SDGs and how specifically they are implemented in the kayaking project, and ask students to reflect on how they might align to SDGs in their reports.

20.3.3.2   ENG 202—Engineering Design and Build B

This second-year unit is a continuation of ENG 201, and the last of the set of design units delivered to students in the first two years of the degree. It is aimed at further developing skills related to engineering analysis, design knowledge, and skills within the discipline and multi-disciplinary contexts. Students work both on their own and in teams, to analyse an engineering problem in terms of its context, dilemmas, and objectives, prior to developing conceptual and technical design solutions.

There is a brief mention of sustainability in the unit's ILOs, in relation to evaluating the sustainability of the full cycle of the project. The actual sustainability related to particular SDGs is captured in the nature of the project on which the delivery of this unit is based. Sustainability is taught through in-project mentoring by engineering staff, using the vehicle of the Farmbot (https://farm.bot/). FarmBot is an open-source agriculture farming robot and one example of a project where sustainability is implemented into the engineering profession. All students have to complete a design project related to the open-source FarmBot project, to add novel functionality to the design of the equipment. The sustainability concept of this project is additionally reinforced by a guest lecture delivered by the FarmBot director. The concept of FarmBot is directly related to SDG 2 (Zero Hunger), SDG 4 (Quality Education), SDG 11 (Sustainable Cities and Communities), and SDG 12 (Responsible Consumption and Production) and introduces students to the idea of applying sustainability into engineered farming.

The second part of the unit is dedicated to students building a prototype/equipment to validate or invalidate a design concept they are working on. This is where sustainability links to the SDGs and is illustrated by the nature of the projects students are working on. Examples of projects chosen and completed by students, directly related to SDGs, include the following:

Plastic bottle recycling device—Students make a mobile device turning plastic bottles into plastic strips, to be further processed and eventually used as a feeder material for 3D Printers. This is directly related to SDG 12 (Responsible Consumption and Production) and challenges students to investigate methods for reusing certain materials in the production process.

Home automation systems—This project is based around developing an innovative system for controlling numerous devices around the home, related to SDG 9 (Industry, Innovation, and Infrastructure).

Universal and mobile water filter—Students build an adjustable device to be fixed to any standard plastic drinking bottle and filter the water "on the go." This project illustrates the principles of SDG 3 (Good Health and Wellbeing), SDG 6 (Clean Water and Sanitation), and SDG 11 (Sustainable Cities and Communities).

3D Printed turbine—The turbine is developed to convert compressed air into DC power and potentially be used to charge small mobile devices. This aligns with SDG 7 (Affordable and Clean Energy) and SDG 9 (Industry, Innovation, and Infrastructure).

The future development of this unit might include clearer guidelines delivered to students in a form of a report or tutorial, based on understanding and illustrating the project work with the SDGs.

20.3.4 Year 3

20.3.4.1 ENG 203 and ENG303—Work Placement

Work placement units are completed by students in the 2nd and 3rd years of the degree. The units are organised around students completing 12 weeks of work with an engineering company. The company can be the student's choice (approved by teaching staff), but students are also presented with a wide range of collaborating companies to choose from. In their work practice, students follow the steps of experienced engineers, learn how to operate in professional work environments, and how to apply their engineering skills to various projects. The unit's ILOs do not specifically mention sustainability; however, the nature of this unit is directly related to SDG 4 (Quality Education) by providing students with a different (practical) knowledge of the topic and teaching them the importance of practical work that augments their theoretical knowledge. Additionally, in being exposed to a real work environment, students learn about different aspects of sustainability in engineering, which in the past, has involved working in renewable energy development schemes or including sustainable approaches to stormwater management. Specific examples of work environments directly linked to the SDGs include the following:

Windfarm project: A student works in an energy networks company, on a project dedicated to supporting the connection enquiry for a new wind farm. This work exposes the students to sustainability covered in SDG 7 (Affordable and Clean Energy) and SDG 9 (Industry, Innovation, and Infrastructure), and teaches them the practical skills of assessing wind conditions and potential energy generation.

Neurotransmitters: A student is involved in laboratory work dedicated to gaining a greater understanding of the function of neurotransmitters and developing therapeutics to treat a variety of stress disorders. This work placement is directly related to SDG 3 (Good Health and Wellbeing).

Eco-friendly industry: A student is involved in the competitive tender to support a provincial government's project in enlarging an eco-friendly industrial region. This work experience is linked with SDG 13 (Climate Action) and gives students practical knowledge of the characteristics of the eco-friendly concept.

20.3.4.2 ENG313—Fluid Mechanics 1

Fluid Mechanics is a 3rd year unit for mechanical engineering students. Although not specifically mentioning sustainability in the ILOs or in its teaching content, there are tangential links through the topic area of renewable energy. In this unit, students learn about turbines and perform problem-solving assessments around turbine operation and performance. This has the potential to involve more explicit discussion of renewable energy and sustainability, and alignment with the SDGs. The most relevant SDG to material covered in this unit is SDG 7 (Affordable and Clean Energy), resulting from students learning about the theory of designing an alternative energy generation system.

20.3.4.3 ENG333—Power Systems 1

Power Systems 1 is a 3rd year unit for electrical power engineering students. A key underlying context in this unit is that power systems around the world are transitioning to systems that have a greater reliance on renewable energy, with implications for the operation and design of such systems. Although the learning outcomes do not specifically mention sustainability, this underlying context of renewable energy provides some degree of linkage to this field, which could be further developed. In future iterations, the importance of implementing SDGs, and the real-world examples already occurring in the engineering profession, could be made more explicit The most relevant SDG to material covered in this unit is SDG 7 (Affordable and Clean Energy).

20.3.5 Year 4

20.3.5.1 ENG 437—Environmental Engineering

Environmental Engineering is a 4th year unit for civil engineering students (about 1/3 of the whole engineering cohort). The unit introduces students to various concepts related to environmental and sustainable fields of engineering, including topics such as air pollution, water and waste management, soil and geotechnics, environmental risk management, circular economy, and solid waste and recycling. Students have lectures about practices involved in sustainable water management, incorporating the concept of a circular economy into engineering design and projects, and implementing sustainable approaches to designing water supply systems. They are exposed to testing those concepts in practice through class-based problem activities. Two out of three ILOs specifically mention sustainability:

ILO2. Design elements of geo-environmental, water supply, wastewater treatment, and air pollution control systems with a focus on system suitability, feasibility, and sustainability.

ILO3. Evaluate the effectiveness of Environmental Engineering solutions in the context of design, sustainability, monitoring, control, and remediation.

The first ILO is achieved by completing assignments. The most important one is Assignment 3, where students need to assess and design a dam and reservoir. This task is particularly important from the sustainability perspective, as students learn how to include elements of environmental and economic sustainability, energy supply safety and responsible consumption, and production into their engineering design. ILO3 is achieved by numerous tasks in the unit, but most significantly in Assignment 4. In that assignment, students need to evaluate various industry-related projects in terms of their environmental impact and create an environmental impact statement document for a particular project and site.

Other activities in this unit that contribute to broadening the sustainability approach among engineering students include the following:

1. Environmental sampling activity. Students are asked to measure levels of certain pollutants in indoor and outdoor air and suggest sustainable solutions to addressing problems and implementable mitigation strategies.
2. Field trip. One of the tasks for students when preparing a field trip report is to identify and comment on the sustainable aspect of how the plant operates (usually a wastewater treatment plant or water treatment plant).

In summary, various tasks in this unit are directly related to the following goals: SDG 6 (Clean Water and Sanitation), SDG 7 (Affordable and Clean Energy), SDG 8 (Decent Work and Economic Growth), SDG 11 (Sustainable Cities and Communities), and SDG 12 (Responsible Consumption and Production).

While the current delivery of the unit strongly supports the inclusion of the SDGs in higher education, there are opportunities to implement more sustainability in the delivery of this unit. These are discussed in the "looking forward" section of this chapter.

20.3.5.2 ENG433: Renewable and Sustainable Energy

Renewable and Sustainable Energy is a year 4 unit undertaken by students majoring in electrical power engineering and as an elective for students majoring in electrical and electronics. The unit introduces students to all forms of renewable energy with a particular focus on wind and solar. Sustainability is a key consideration in the renewable energy industry, and although renewable sources have lower associated emissions than fossil fuels, these are not negligible when the full life cycle of assets is considered. This point often challenges students to consider the industry beyond the simple assumption that renewable energy sources are better for the environment than conventional sources. Additionally, what happens to assets at the end of their lifetime is considered in this unit.

The learning outcome that aligns specifically with sustainability is ILO2: Describe and evaluate key factors of renewable energy integration, including operational issues and sustainability. This learning outcome is assessed through a design project, where students design a renewable-based energy system for a particular application and consider the full lifetime of these assets. Additionally, this learning outcome is assessed through an ePortfolio and individual interview task, where students are asked to reflect on their learning experiences in the unit, and the challenges and opportunities they see for the renewable energy industry.

As each source in the unit is introduced, the relevant sustainability considerations for that technology are described, however, these are not framed in the context of the UN SDGs. Long-term system sustainability considerations are also introduced in this unit through a series of lectures delivered by an engineer from industry.

Renewable energy links clearly to SDG 7 (Affordable and Clean Energy), and SDG 13 (Climate Action). Although these links are not explicitly made in the delivery of the unit, it is assumed that students have some foundational knowledge of the goals from their prior studies and are capable of making these connections themselves.

Future development of the unit will include more explicit connections to the SDGs throughout the lecture materials and within the student ePorfolio task.

20.3.5.3 Honours Units (ENG401, ENG402)

Honours (ENG401, ENG402) project units are two-semester units during which students complete their final year projects. The projects are experimental or theoretical research projects, which finish with a complete thesis at the end of the second semester. Although all of these units have seminars dedicated to different aspects of doing research and writing an academic paper, the most important task for students is to complete their research and write up their results in the form of a thesis.

Although there are no specific mentions of the word "sustainability" among the ILOs in this unit, ILO 1 (Select, adapt, and effectively apply research processes, methods, tools, and techniques to plan, conduct, and manage an independent related research project) and ILO 7 (Apply advanced engineering principles, techniques, computation, abstraction, and creative and critical thinking to solve a problem and evaluate the effectiveness of that solution), indirect application of SDGs applies through the way of thinking embedded in the engineering profession.

How sustainability is being taught within these units is dependent on the specific projects that students choose and the actual knowledge and skillset delivered by engineering staff mentors. Depending on their specialisations and interests, students usually have around 150 projects and 25 supervisors to choose from. Although some project proposals do not include sustainability explicitly, due to the nature of engineering, others might have a large component directly related to the SDGs. Some examples of the Honours and Masters projects involving sustainability include the following.

Microplastics in the Ocean—Tasmanian Contribution and Mitigation Strategies (2020)—This work investigated currently available mitigation strategies to address the microplastics entering the ocean, assessing the Tasmanian microplastics release, and adjusting the mitigation options to be applied in Tasmania. The project aligned closely with SDG 6 (Clean Water and Sanitation) and SDG 14 (Life Below Water).

Feasibility Study on the Implementation of Recycled Materials in Asphalt Mixtures (2019)—This project investigated the possibility, environmental and economic feasibility of using some solid waste materials (ceramics, tyres, plastics, glass) for building roads. SDG 9 (Industry, Innovation, and Infrastructure) and SDG 11 (Sustainable Cities and Communities) were embedded in this project.

Increasing Green Areas, Filtration and Water Reuse in the Context of Urban Water Metabolism (2021)—This project investigated installing the most appropriate biofiltration units to treat stormwater and adding green urban areas in the city of Launceston (northern Tasmania). The topic aligned with SDG 6 (Clean Water and Sanitation), SDG 11 (Sustainable Cities and Communities), and SDG 13 (Climate Action).

FarmBot Goes Polar (2021)—The project investigated a small-scale automated farming system and its applicability to commercial farming, and the adjustments to be made for making it work on the basis of different coordinates. The project aligned with SDG 2 (Zero Hunger), SDG 8 (Decent Work and Economic Growth), and SDG 9 (Industry, Innovation and Infrastructure).

Feasibility of Biogas Production from Urban Food Waste in Hobart (2019)— This project investigated the financial and operational feasibility of using bread food scraps for generating biogas in an urban anaerobic digester. The nature of this project aligned with SDG 7 (Affordable and Clean Energy) and SDG 13 (Climate Action).

Attracting Girls to Engineering (2021)—This project aimed to identify reasons why young women do not tend to choose engineering, and proposed strategies to encourage more girls to start an engineering degree. This topic was directly related to SDG 5 (Gender Equality).

Although sustainability is not specifically mentioned within the ILOs of honours units, the specifics of the final year projects often introduce the concept of sustainability, with much more depth, in comparison to any of the previous units. Students work on topics related to different aspects of sustainability over two semesters, and in this way, they investigate the complex issue of incorporating the sustainable pathway of thinking into their professional work in the future.

The topic of sustainability and its implementation in the engineering degree has become one of the major goals for the School of Engineering at the University of Tasmania. As illustrated in this chapter, there are many aspects of sustainability covered throughout the degree, some of which, similar to the examples outlined in Leifler and Dahlin (2020), need further commitment from University decision-makers and teaching staff. The concepts of sustainability and the link between UN SDGs and engineering work tasks are introduced for students in the first year of their degree. Although small tasks and concepts address this topic again in the 2nd and 3rd year of the Bachelor of Engineering, it is mostly in the final year of their studies that students have a real opportunity to embed and implement sustainability into their engineering approach. Table 20.2 provides a summary of which SDGs are currently addressed through the degree.

As expected from the engineering degree, SDG 7 (Affordable and Clean Energy), SDG 9 (Industry, Innovation, and Infrastructure), and SDG 13 (Climate Action) are covered the most extensively in the degree, and only two goals are not specifically currently covered in any of the units in the Degree. Currently, the School is working on introducing sustainability into more units that are taught throughout the degree and making engineering sustainability more visible for students and more applicable at the beginning of their professional engineering career.

20.4   Conclusions

This chapter has illustrated that there is wide coverage of the SDGs and concepts of sustainability throughout the current engineering program, however, in some places, this is not explicit or is very brief, and there is ample opportunity to extend this further into the future. Depending on the choices students make in their study plans,

Table 20.2 UN SDGs covered in particular units delivered as a part of the bachelor of engineering (with honours) degree, at University of Tasmania, at the end of the year 2021

SDGs	ENG102	ENG201	ENG202	ENG203/ENG303	ENG313	ENG333	ENG433	ENG437	Honours unit
1. No poverty	✓								
2. Zero hunger			✓						✓
3. Good health and wellbeing			✓	✓					
4. Quality education			✓	✓					
5. Gender equality	✓		✓						✓
6. Clean water and sanitation	✓		✓					✓	✓
7. Affordable and clean energy	✓		✓	✓	✓	✓			✓
8. Decent work and economic growth									✓
9. Industry, innovation, and infrastructure		✓	✓					✓	✓
10. Reduced inequalities		✓							
11. Sustainable cities and communities	✓		✓					✓	
12. Responsible consumption and production	✓		✓					✓	
13. Climate action	✓			✓			✓	✓	
14. Life below water							✓		✓
15. Life on land								✓	
16. Peace, justice, and strong institutions									
17. Partnership for the goals									

including specialisation and honours project topics, they may experience different levels of depth in their exposure to sustainability concepts and the SDGs. To deliver the educational goal of providing all students with a comprehensive understanding of sustainability and sustainable development, our approach to embedding these concepts in the curriculum needs further work. In looking forward, it is recommended that sustainability be defined in such a way that all staff have a clear understanding of it, and that, where necessary, professional development be provided to teaching staff to develop their skills and knowledge in this area. A clear understanding of the teaching staff's current attitudes and personal definitions around sustainability would be helpful to achieve this.

Embedding more content into an already crowded curriculum may create tensions with teaching staff, so identifying ways where sustainability and the SDGs can be embedded into units in efficient, consistent, and cohesive ways is essential. This will lead to an improved student awareness of sustainability and sustainable development and provide a clear thread throughout the degree.

Identifying opportunities for the extension of sustainability concepts throughout the curriculum is essential to achieve this goal. The guiding principles identified in Dodds and Venables (2005), and their range of case studies covering all fields of engineering, provide some insight into the range of potential topics available to include these concepts. Their examples include embedded sustainable development in organisations, chemical engineering in laundry cleaning products, building regeneration, and product design of mobile phones. As an example, third-year technical engineering subjects were identified in the School of Engineering work as lacking in explicit links to sustainability, and this presents an opportunity for a specialisation-related sustainability content to be embedded in this course. For example, in the Power Systems unit discussed, treatment of SDG 7 (Clean and Affordable Energy) and SDG 13 (Climate Action) could be made explicit by providing students with case studies of how the different elements of the power system are changing in a transition to a system based more on renewable energy. Another example of deepening the perception of SDGs among students could be a session delivered to first-year students, explicitly dedicated to explaining the goals. This would ideally be planned in the first year, and the goals could be reflected in the following years of the degree. Extending beyond this, relevant case studies, industry-informed teaching, and state-of-the art research work in different discipline areas, could all provide inspiration for sustainable development contexts to be embedded within engineering degrees and could be framed in the context of the SDGs.

The goal outlined above of increasing the coverage of sustainability and sustainable development in engineering curricula is aligned with the University of Tasmania's strategic plan (University of Tasmania, 2019). The strategic plan not only seeks to achieve sustainable outcomes for the University, but also addresses the challenges facing Tasmania. Engineers are well-placed to help address or contribute to developing solutions to many of the environmental, technical, and social challenges facing Tasmania, and as such, need a well-rounded education including consideration of sustainability.

Including more sustainability in any engineering degree and adapting to the needs of the changing work environment and engineering challenges requires work and commitment, both from the leaders and from the teaching staff (Desha et al., 2007). Although there are different approaches to address this issue, researchers agree that sustainability needs to be more evident throughout the learning pathway to engineering, and in a form that is readily applicable to graduate engineers.

References

Arefin, M. A., Nabi, M. N., Sadeque, S., & Gudimetla, P. (2021). Incorporating sustainability in engineering curriculum: A study of the Australian universities. *International Journal of Sustainability in Higher Education, 22*(3), 576–598.

Cruickshank, H. (2003). The changing role of engineers. *Engineering Management Journal, 13*(1), 24–29.

De Graaff, E., & Ravesteijn, W. (2001). Training complete engineers: Global enterprise and engineering education. *European Journal of Engineering Education, 26*(4), 419–427.

Desha, C. J. K., Hargroves, K. O., Sith, M. H., & Stasinopoulos, P. (2007). The importance of sustainability in Engineering education: A toolkit of information and teaching material. [Paper presentation]. In *Engineering training and learning conference*, Australasian Association for Engineering Education Conference.

Dodds, R., & Venables, R. (2005). *Engineering for sustainable development: Guiding principles.* The Royal Academy of Engineering.

Engineers Australia. (2017). *Implementing sustainability: Principles and practice.* https://www.engineersaustralia.org.au/sites/default/files/Learned%20Society/Resources-Guidelines%26Practice%20notes/Implementing%20Sustainability-Principles%20and%20Practice.pdf

Engineers Australia. (2019). *Code of ethics and guidelines on professional conduct.* https://www.engineersaustralia.org.au/sites/default/files/resource-files/2020-02/828145%20Code%20of%20Ethics%202020%20D.pdf

Engineers Australia. (2021). *Stage 1 competency standard for professional engineers.* https://www.engineersaustralia.org.au/sites/default/files/2019-11/Stage1_Competency_Standards.pdf

Engineers Without Borders. (2021). *Design considerations.* https://ewbchallenge.org/participant-resources/design-considerations/

FarmBot. (n.d.). https://farmbot.com.au/

Koth, B., & Woodward, M. (2009). *Civil engineering education for sustainability: Faculty perceptions and result of an Australian course audit.* Proceedings of the 20th Australasian Association of Engineering Education conference, 6–9 December, Adelaide, pp. 776–782.

Leifler, O., & Dahlin, J.-E. (2020). Curriculum integration of sustainability in engineering education—A national study of programme director perspective. *International Journal of Sustainability in Higher Education, 21*(5), 877–894.

Qureshi, A. S., & Nawab, A. (2016). *The role of engineers in sustainable development.* https://pecongress.org.pk/images/upload/books/10-311%20Role%20of%20Sustainable%20Dr.pdf

Thürer, M., Tomašević, I., Stevenson, M., Qu, T., & Huisingh, D. (2018). A systematic review of the literature on integrating sustainability into engineering curricula. *Journal of Cleaner Production, 181*, 608–617.

United Nations. (2021). *Sustainability.* https://www.un.org/en/academic-impact/sustainability

University of British Columbia. (2004). *EESD Barcelona declaration.* https://eesd15.engineering.ubc.ca/declaration-of-barcelona/

University of Tasmania. (2019). *University of Tasmania strategic plan 2019–2024.* https://www.utas.edu.au/__data/assets/pdf_file/0004/1255234/UTAS-Strategy-Document-2019.pdf

University of Tasmania. (2022). *Bachelor of engineering (specialisation) with honours (P4D)*. https://www.utas.edu.au/courses/cse/courses/p4d-bachelor-of-engineering-specialisation-with-honours

World Federation of Engineering Organisations. (2021). *About us*. http://www.wfeo.org/about-us/

Chapter 21
Encountering Sustainable Development Goal SDG13, Climate Justice, and Emotions While Role-Playing an International Forum on Climate Change-Induced Migration

Malcolm S. Johnson⊙, **Charlotte A. Jones**⊙, **Andrew Harwood**⊙, **Vishnu N. Prahalad**⊙, **and Aidan Davison**⊙

21.1 Introduction

Education for Sustainable Development (ESD) recognises the Sustainable Development Goals (SDGs) as frameworks for addressing global problems in interdisciplinary and solution-based ways (Franco et al., 2019; O'Byrne et al., 2015; Saito et al., 2017). ESD is less about educating *about* sustainable development, but rather cultivating competencies *for* sustainable development (Tilbury, 2004). These competencies include incorporating interdisciplinary skills in problem-solving, knowledge

M. S. Johnson (✉) · C. A. Jones · A. Harwood · V. N. Prahalad · A. Davison
School of Geography, Planning, and Spatial Sciences, University of Tasmania, Hobart, TAS 7005,
Australia
e-mail: malcolm.johnson@utas.edu.au

C. A. Jones
e-mail: ca.jones@utas.edu.au

A. Harwood
e-mail: andrew.harwood@utas.edu.au

V. N. Prahalad
e-mail: vishnu.prahalad@utas.edu.au

A. Davison
e-mail: aidan.davison@utas.edu.au

M. S. Johnson
Centre for Marine Socioecology, University of Tasmania, Hobart, TAS Battery Point, 7004,
Australia

© The Author(s), under exclusive license to Springer Nature Singapore Pte Ltd. 2023   391
K. Beasy et al. (eds.), *Education and the UN Sustainable Development Goals*, Education
for Sustainability 7,
https://doi.org/10.1007/978-981-99-3802-5_21

synthesis, value-based advocacy, and adaptative inquiry (Davidson & Lyth, 2012; Strachan et al., 2021). ESD is therefore predicated on educational approaches that invite an active and ethical engagement with the world, with the express purpose of seeking to increase the flourishing of human and non-human life (Hay, 2012; Solem et al., 2013).

SDG13 acknowledges that climate change and its emergent impacts pose an existential threat to current ways of existing within, relating to, and thinking about the world around us. The five overarching targets under this goal, to be achieved by 2030, demand literacy about the extraordinarily complex phenomenon of climate change, which integrates multiple social and physical systems and scales. Much existing education about climate change seeks to incorporate the facts of climate science into curricula. Such diffusion of scientific knowledge is critical. However, the goal of sustainable development also requires that education systems enable profound personal and societal transformation (Macintyre et al., 2018). This necessitates that climate change education "build capacities for critical thinking, reflexivity, systems thinking, collaboration, collective agency, and transformative practice" (Macintyre et al., 2018, p. 81). It also requires "creative, participatory, and technologically-mediated" pedagogies while enabling engagement "with climate change in ways that are culturally and regionally relevant" (Rousell & Cutter-Mackenzie-Knowles, 2020, p. 192).

The sustainability problem of climate change-induced migration provides a powerful focus for problem-based learning activities rooted in the lived complexities of climate change or how it acts as a wicked problem (Peters & Tarpey, 2019). SDG13 does not explicitly refer to climate displacement or migration (Jolly & Trivedi, 2020), and the United Nations refugee frameworks continue to neglect the existence of tens of million environmental refugees (McNamara, 2007; Myers, 2002). Without a legal definition of climate displacement and the outsized impact on marginalised communities (Gonzalez, 2018; Wilkinson et al., 2016), climate-induced migration is a climate justice issue that must be taught through both the lens of climate literacy and emotional literacy (Porter et al., 2020; Reid, 2019). Additionally, the climate-migration-development nexus is often approached through disconnected perspectives and disciplines (Gioli et al., 2016), further highlighting the importance of interdisciplinarity.

In this chapter, we present an interdisciplinary scenario and role-play activity on climate-induced migration embedded in geographical pedagogies that challenge preconceived understandings of geography, climate change, and knowledge systems. We first provide a summary of the relevance of the activity for interdisciplinary ESD before describing the specific structure of the activity. This offers educators an understanding of the historical development of the activity, its place in the wider curriculum, and the steps necessary for implementation. We then reflect on our experiences in delivering this learning activity over multiple years, with a focus on the importance of performance making, the challenge of identity bias, and the significance of emotional responses. We conclude with implications for educators interested in teaching SDG13 and our call for climate justice-forward transformative learning experiences that are creative, collaborative, and solution-based (Davidson et al., 2021).

21.2   Climate-Induced Migration Learning Activity

21.2.1   Interdisciplinary Teaching Team

There has been a growing demand for interdisciplinary and innovative teaching approaches that tackle climate change with problem-based pedagogies (Dobson & Bland Tomkinson, 2012). In recognition of this demand, faculty and staff members at the University of Tasmania (UTAS) partnered with the University of Wollongong, Murdoch University, and the University of New South Wales to develop a "cross-disciplinary peer network" with the broad aim of improving how complex problems are taught at the university level (Davison et al., 2012). The four institutions concentrated on climate change as an interdisciplinary "anchor" to further embed sustainability development education as "part of the core curriculum across all disciplines" based on the aims of the 2012 Rio+20 *Commitment to Sustainable Practices of Higher Education Institutions* (Pharo et al., 2014; The United Nations Conference on Sustainable Development, 2012).

Building on the existing difficulties of teaching complex problems in a meaningful way at universities (Harris et al., 2011), the first stage of the project sought to integrate interdisciplinary climate change activities into existing courses. Faculty and students at UTAS worked together to develop a teaching activity around the shared problem of climate change refugees, which resulted in a proposal to include a mock international summit as part of a redesigned first-year geography course available to both arts and science students (Davison et al., 2012). The international forum is based on two real-world issues, the increasing number of people displaced by environmental hazards every year and the lack of refugee status designation for climate-induced migrants from the United Nations High Commissioner for Refugees (Biermann & Boas, 2008, 2010). The purpose of the summit is for students to take on the task of representing four countries seeking to negotiate a collaborative approach to the issue of climate-induced migration. The central inquiry question for students during the activity is "who is responsible for climate change refugees?".

21.2.2   Locating the Activity

The activity is part of a required subject, *Global Geographies of Change*, in the first semester of a 3-year major in Geography and Environment at UTAS from within one of three different courses: Bachelor of Arts, Bachelor of Science, or Bachelor of Natural Environments and Wilderness. The class can also be taken as an elective within many other undergraduate courses. Students can take the class on-campus in Tasmania's two major population centers, and off-campus via online/distance learning. A high level of academic and demographic diversity characterises students studying this unit.

Global Geographies of Change is organised around seven modules and assesses students against four intended learning outcomes that integrate environmental science and social science curriculum (see Table 21.1). The first module (Mapping) conceptualises the processes, practices, and products of mapping as central to geographical and environmental inquiry, and hence as a means for describing and analysing global geographical change. Modules two (Natural Evolution) and three (Social Development) introduce core ideas associated with physical and human geographical processes respectively, ranging in breadth from landscape geomorphology to global population demographics. The design is based on the understanding that we need to develop the expertise to understand the relations amongst such diverse natural and social phenomena to apprehend patterns of global change. With this understanding, the remainder of the class provides students with opportunities to integrate social and physical processes to investigate contemporary challenges across four themes (modules 4–7): climate change, sustainability, vulnerability, and globalisation. The four Intended Learning Outcomes (ILOs) for the unit are in turn linked to specific learning objectives for the climate-induced migration activity and then in turn reflected in associated assessment criteria (see Table 21.1).

21.3 The Learning Activity

The climate-induced migration learning activity starts in Week 5 of a 13-week semester. It is spread across three consecutive calendar weeks, worth 10% of overall assessment, and is structured around four lectures and three three-hour interactive workshops. The mix of lecture content and workshop activities is designed with the characteristics of learning settings identified for effective sustainability education (e.g., Davidson et al., 2021). These include providing a learner-centred environment, employing a problem-based approach, encouraging peer collaboration, facilitating learning in both formal and informal settings, and engendering creative learning processes and outcomes. The learning activity seeks to develop students' skills in integrating diverse knowledge domains, working effectively within diverse teams, communicating creatively and empathetically, and thinking critically about geographical diversity in the context of global climate change. Below we link these pedagogical imperatives to the content and activities that comprise the lectures and workshops.

The group work embedded in the learning activity reflects the importance of professional skills of collaborative teamwork in addressing complex problems. Students are scaffolded to the development of teamwork skills through a trajectory from teacher-facilitation to self-directed leadership of groups. In Week 1, each group is provided with an experienced facilitator who helps to prompt and guide each group. This person leads a discussion on the benefits of groups and the nature of group dynamics, roles, and the characteristics of an effective group member. Students are encouraged to find out about, value, and build on their group's diverse understandings, abilities, experiences, and motivations. In Week 2, groups are mostly self-directed,

Table 21.1 Global geographies of change: MLOs; ILOs; structure of module 4 climate; and assessment criteria for the climate-induced migration learning activity

Geography and environment Major Learning Outcomes (MLOs)	Intended Learning Outcomes (ILOs)	Module 4: Climate	Assessment criteria for climate-induced migration learning activity
1. Evaluate and synthesise diverse perspectives, arguments, and knowledges to solve social and environmental problems and identify opportunities relevant to the integrated discipline of geography 2. Investigate and explain past, present, and future geographical processes that shape Tasmanian, Australian and other environments, places, and peoples at scales from the local to the global 3. Apply geographic and environmental techniques of communication, fieldwork, and spatial analysis to diverse contexts through ethical practices 4. Engage in ongoing intellectual and professional development as inquiry-based, self-reflexive, and lifelong learners	1. Describe spatial patterns and processes of global environmental and social change 2. Apply geographical skills of mapping to interpret and produce spatial information 3. Consider geographical arguments, contexts, and evidence in assessing global debates about the environment, development, and sustainability 4. Communicate critical, coherent, and evidence-based geographical thinking through writing, speaking, teamwork, and academic integrity	Four lectures 4.1 Earth's atmospheric structure 4.2 How climate works 4.3 Human impacts on the atmosphere 4.4. Climate change: a political geography Three workshops (3 h each)	1. Demonstrates self-directed and effective teamwork in the lead up to the forum 2. Offers a considered, well-researched and insightful understanding of diverse perspectives on the topic of climate change migrants in one national context 3. Presents a well-structured, well-articulated, engaging, and creative 15-min presentation, using effective strategies of oral and visual communication 4. Engages constructively and substantively in a cross-national dialogue 5. References all sources appropriately

although the facilitator checks in and provides any required guidance. In Week 3, groups are provided only guided facilitation. The importance of teamwork skill development is underscored by group assessment. This assessment includes provision for the adjustment of individual marks based on anonymous student feedback on their group dynamics as well as facilitator observations of group processes.

21.3.1 The Lecture Program

The lecture program provides students who come from varied educational backgrounds with an introduction to the geophysical attributes and socio-political processes that characterise the earth's changing climate. The first lecture introduces the structure of the earth's atmosphere. The second examines the processes of the earth's climate system, such as controls on temperature, rainfall, and winds, and how geographical differences lead to distinct regional climates. The third explores the manner and extent to which modern human society is now changing earth's atmosphere and some of the issues that this poses for humans, biota generally, and the physical landscape itself. The final lecture reviews the public and political debate about anthropogenic climate change, and explores the relationship between science, public concern, and politics. The uneven and contrasting geographies of the causes and consequences of climate change are presented and related to questions about equity and sustainability.

21.3.2 The Workshop Program

In the first workshop, students are introduced to the learning activity and the assessment task. In brief, the activity consists of students working together in groups or "delegations" of 6–10 to represent one of four allocated countries that face very different climate migration challenges. Students are encouraged to adopt individual roles within each of their delegations. This role play encourages students to reflect on the diversity of perspectives that may be important to consider, to empathise with the lived experience of others, and to employ creative and emotionally engaging forms of communication. While delegations are encouraged to incorporate government perspectives, they are not intended to represent governments. The task given to students is to represent these nations at an international forum with the aim of finding collaborative solutions to the issue of climate-induced migration. Each national delegation prepares and delivers a 15-min oral and visual presentation setting forth perspectives relevant to their country and offering arguments to the other nations present about opportunities for collaboration. The delegations then participate in 45 min of dialogue with representatives from other countries with the aim of pursuing collaborative international responses.

Having set out the rationale, structure, and assessment of the learning activity, students develop skills in numeracy and critical thinking through a series of activities with climate change data. They are encouraged to consider how climate change is measured, represented, and interpreted as well as what sorts of knowledge or expertise are involved in these practices. They are presented with information around migration, refugees, and the significance of environmental change as a driver of human movement—both within and across national borders—and encouraged to discuss and reflect on what they already know about the issue of human migration and climate change, including national responsibilities and collaborative solutions.

Following these discussions, each group is assigned one of the four countries to represent at the climate-induced migration forum. Groups are encouraged to start by pooling what information they already know in terms of how they might engage the issue of climate-induced migration. The four countries chosen are illustrative of the Global North and Global South divide (Roberts & Parks, 2007; Rosales, 2008). These countries offer a platform for the discussion of both "common but differentiated responsibility" and historically-embedded climate (in)justice (Bortscheller, 2009; Jamieson, 2010), with students quickly noting that the two countries most severely impacted by climate change, Bangladesh and Solomon Islands, have contributed significantly less to the cause of this problem. The existing national platforms on these issues and the roles these countries typically play in international negotiations introduce avenues for inquiry while, as is especially the case for students representing their own country (in this case Australia), compelling students to question assumptions about national responsibility and debates on climate change (Head, 2014).

Students are given time in the second workshop to prepare for their presentation at the forum, but they also need to spend several hours out of class gathering, analysing, and synthesising information, deliberating with their peers, and developing and rehearsing their presentation. Hence, groups are expected to allocate tasks such as researching, collating information, coordinating the group, planning the presentation, determining speaker roles, so that every member is an active participant. The creative and role-play elements of the task are emphasised, and groups are encouraged to consider a range of communication strategies, including exhibits, handouts, and performances—such as the perspective offered by a fictional personal account of a climate change migrant.

Students are asked to consider what perspectives their national delegation might pursue and are reminded there is no absolute *correct* or *incorrect* perspective. Indeed, their group may wish to present several different, and potentially conflicting, perspectives from within the national context (e.g., in addition to considering government perspectives, delegations may include scientific, religious, indigenous cultural, farmers', migrants', school-children's perspectives, and so on). Recognising that this is not a comprehensive list, discussion around alternative perspectives is typically quite fruitful (Perumal, 2018). However, students are encouraged to draw together these diverse perspectives within a coherent presentation to elicit collaboration from other nations. Likewise, groups are encouraged to consider in advance the perspectives and contexts of the other national delegations that they will be engaging in dialogue within the forum. At this point in the activity, students are expected to have developed a robust empirical understanding of their country's relationship with climate change (i.e., emission contributions and projected impacts) and anticipated movement of relevant populations of migrants and refugees, including in-migration, out-migration, and internal migration.

The third workshop is dedicated to the international climate-induced migration forum and runs on a tight schedule to maximise time for dialogue. Students are given an hour to finalise and practice their presentations (including resolving any potential technical difficulties). The order of country presentations is selected at random, and students are reminded to listen actively by taking notes to respond more meaningfully during the dialogue. In their presentations, groups are asked to introduce their country context and any roles being represented by the delegation. Groups are encouraged to put forward arguments in relation to what their country needs by way of support from other nations and what support they can offer in turn to others. Students are assessed on the delivery of the presentation and their understandings of diverse perspectives.

The first stage of the dialogue includes a two-minute response from each country, structured as an opportunity to endorse or rebut arguments, including clarifying matters of fact. The remainder of the dialogue is a combination of delegates probing each other on their stances, with moderation from facilitators as needed to keep the conversation purposefully on track. Reaching the stated goal of *agreements* between two or more countries on climate-induced migrants usually occurs during the last minutes of the dialogue, if at all. Students are also assessed on meaningful contributions to the dialogue and their ability to work in teams throughout the activity.

The last thirty minutes of the workshop invite students to drop their roles and to reflect on the learning activity. Voicing their thoughts and emotions about the experience, and on climate change and refugees more broadly, this final component of the activity is where many of our reflections as facilitators emerge. In discussion amongst ourselves, it is apparent that both this reflective period and the activity can play out differently based on who is facilitating and what backgrounds and interests students bring. Facilitators comprise academic and casual staff including Ph.D. candidates with enthusiasm for teaching climate change, geography, and sustainable development. Throughout the three weeks, they bring stories of their own life experiences to the table, which has included attendance at UN (United Nations) conferences, working with communities on the frontline of climate change, or engaging in climate change activism. These anecdotes tend to draw students into side discussions that inform their presentations and offer avenues for potential proactive responses to the wicked problems explored across the course and degree.

Students are a mix of various ages and backgrounds; while typically sharing an interest in geography, their knowledge of more complex concepts and theories are just being established. Over the 13 years that the learning activity has been running, a larger proportion of the classes have pre-existing awareness and understanding of the issue of climate change and its potential impacts (Wachholz et al., 2014). However, there is usually an expression of surprise when exploring the lived impacts of climate change and hearing stories from marginalised countries. Although this might be attributed to better science around the impacts and the acceleration of those impacts mixed with increased communication, the combination of research, role play, and dialogue offers a unique avenue to explore these uneven geographies of climate change.

There have been significant developments of the activity since its original conception in 2008, reflecting feedback from students and facilitators, the changing circumstances of climate change, changes in teaching staff, and pedagogical fine-tuning. First, in the early years, students were asked to imagine that the summit was taking place in 2025. However, as the issue of climate change migration is no longer a speculative concern but a lived reality, the activity was adapted to focus on present opportunities for action. Second, the dialogue during the final workshop was originally framed as a debate, which might have led to more antagonistic attitudes between the countries. Despite the shift in framing and regular reminder for collaboration, there still seems to be a tendency towards this behaviour. Third, the activity was adapted to online learning in the wake of COVID-19 and will likely maintain an integrated in-person/online format, despite the perceived value of the in-person dialogue experience. Lastly, we want to acknowledge the role facilitators play in shaping the activity based on their own positionalities. By bringing different experiences of and relationships with climate change to the table, facilitators can determine the perceived value of differing roles, the trajectory of the dialogue, and act as agents of change by encouraging values, responsibilities, and emotions for a more sustainable world (Bamber, 2019).

21.4   Facilitator Reflections on the Learning Activity

This activity provides students with a global understanding of sustainable development while offering a geographical engagement with differences between countries and regions (Meadows, 2020; Palacios et al., 2017). The interdisciplinary tasks of gathering information, taking on roles, presenting to the class, and engaging in dialogue requires students to consider the pragmatic constraints of national efforts while also demonstrating potential transformative pathways for international collaboration. Although we feel as though the role play aspect of the activity is essential for understanding and encountering "the other" (Hölscher & Grace Bozalek, 2012), we recognise that there is a precarious balance between embodying the unfamiliar versus stereotyping or romanticising other cultures. However, through the act of investigation and communication of the issues facing, in particular, the Global South countries of Bangladesh and the Solomon Islands, as well as the marginalised communities within Global North countries including Australian First Nations, this exercise can encourage students to recognise and engage with marginalised forms of localised knowledge (Pyy, 2021).

To date, more than 2000 students have participated in the climate-induced migration activity. As current and past facilitators and lecturers of the activity and course, we have made several key observations and detailed our lessons learned, which we have synthesised into three overarching concepts. Together, these concepts, amongst others not addressed here, contribute to the need for solution-based climate justice-forward transformative learning experiences in the face of climate change.

21.4.1 Performance Making

Early in the assignment students are encouraged to think outside traditional presentation formats, adopting various roles within their assigned countries, and challenging the dominant narratives around climate-induced migration. By encountering the activity through the act of performance making, students see themselves through different lenses, which presents an opportunity to engage with seemingly distant and complex problems (Harris et al., 2011). As the groups conduct research about their assigned countries, they often question how true to the stated policy lines they need to maintain. For example, the Global North countries will typically see their stated positions at odds with their own personal values (i.e., Australia's policies on migration) such that they begin to question how they will present proposals at the migration dialogue that are constructive and proactive. We typically remind the students that the goal of the dialogue is to collaborate based on the reality of the situation in each country and that within each country there are a diversity of values, worldviews, and opinions that can be at odds.

Taking this into account, groups tend to assign different roles to each group members. These include government ministers, climate change scientists, migration NGO workers, impacted community members, and human-rights activists, amongst many others. These various roles serve as pathways to better understand both the internal and external challenges around climate-induced migration, shifting the focus from purely a pro-/anti-migration stance between the North and South into a conversation around why, if, and how migration will occur. Both during each country's presentation and within the international dialogue, these roles begin to find solidarity with pleas for action directed at either, the most sympathetic member of a group, or disgruntled commentary pointed at a more statutory role-player. At the end of the dialogue, the groups are pressed on their choice of roles and the class is questioned to think of roles that may be missing from the dialogue.

Despite the encouragement to think outside of traditional presentation norms, the country presentations seem to follow a particular pattern: introduction of the country, maps around the projected climate change impacts, commentary on SDGs or other global goals, and either a request for action from countries or a statement of capability. Some presentations will also include a focus on historical injustice, commentary on adaptation, or other ideas typically based on individual interests. A noticeable exception to the norm involves the use of poetry, song, artwork, or more humanities-based techniques. During the lecture introducing the activity, a poem by Kathy Jetñil-Kijiner, presented at the United Nations Climate Summit Opening Ceremony in 2014 (Jetñil-Kijiner, 2014) is shown to the class, accompanied with an encouragement to think outside the expected framings of climate change. The likelihood of creativity in presentations depends on facilitator encouragement and tends to help uncover often unexplored attitudes, feelings, and ideas.

The activity finds itself aligned with existing literature on performance making and scenario-based learning (Lehtonen & Pihkala, 2021; Papadopoulos, 2019). For example, the process of embracing a country as their own, presenting their adopted reality, allows the participants to creatively explore representations of their role's lived experiences, while critically reflecting on their own relationships with climate change, migration, and policy action (Gallagher & Wessels, 2013). Participants often voice this self-reflection and internal conflict around personal, cultural, and political norms as a major takeaway from the experience. Similar to Lehtonen and Pihkala's (2021) findings, the performative aspects of the activity prompted questions around responsibility and powerlessness, which leads to questions about whether or not the activity alleviates eco-anxiety or induces it. However, there is significant individual variance, particularly with students who found the performative aspect of the activity to be at odds with their own learning style or constrained by the current state of politics of their own country (i.e., Australia) (Rasmussen, 2010).

21.4.2 Identity Bias

Representation or, in many cases, over-representation of specific identities within the activity risks reinforcing established policy and value platforms. Although not previously the case, scientists are currently the most adopted roles during the mock summit, with most individual group presentations dedicating significant time to the national impacts of climate change and the scientific facts guiding the decision of each country. Rather than representing the multitude of lived experiences within countries (Jaspal et al., 2014), students tend to use science as a justification for their national positions, with the Global South countries highlighting the existential threat of sea-level rise, floods, and droughts as a statement of need and the Global North countries exposing their own impacts of floods, fires, and sea level rise as a reason not to support migration.

Many students struggle with the task of scenario-based learning as they feel bound by the existing systems of governing. Each of the four countries has made well-established comments and commitments at UN conferences, which get synthesised by students during their research. Leaning into nationalistic commentary and commitments to the nation state as a form of representation (Conversi & Friis Hau, 2021), the dialogue often centers on questions of common but differentiated responsibility, the provision of financial, diplomatic, and technical support, and the challenge posed by climate change refugees. It is tricky for facilitators to know how to navigate this boundary as the scenario needs to build on a recognisable and shared state of play (e.g., the existence of nation-states and the UN's SDGs), while also encouraging students to imagine the possibility of radically different futures.

Students in the Australian and UK (United Kingdom) delegations are inclined to offer support for physical adaptation and accept responsibility for more mitigation, yet rarely do they consent to allowing an influx of refugees. Those representing Bangladesh and the Solomon Islands adopt more of a focus on the historical injustices perpetrated by Australia and the UK. Although this can be considered problematic, particularly because students are speaking on behalf of a group of people they do not belong to and have little personal experiences with, we believe that the act of researching, understanding, and performing on behalf of knowledges and cultures typically external from their own can lead to nuanced reflections on climate change impacts and migration more generally.

Arguments around commitment specifics, such as how many refugees or how much money, are quite common and in many ways reflect the international negotiations over the last decade (Downie, 2014). As such, many groups approach the dialogue more as a debate to be won, despite the transition away from that term in the unit outline. As facilitators, we are responsible for diffusing situations that get too antagonistic and questioning the entrenchment of policy stances, while encouraging students to seek collaboration across differences. For example, Australia at the international scale is considered a hinderance to global climate progress (Cass, 2008), with the students representing that country just as easily finding themselves as an obstacle towards progress during the dialogue, either intentionally or otherwise. Even with more divergent roles adopted in groups (e.g., climate activist, immigration advocate, local farmer, etc.), consensus is often not reached and commitments to the global community seem distant.

Climate change and climate-induced migration are thoroughly social problems that result from the dynamic and intersecting relationship between the climate system and policy systems (Keskitalo & Preston, 2019). By peering into the difficulties of policy to reach consensus and the reality of how international agreements are made, there is realisation that it often does not work effectively or efficiently, and that people are being actively harmed by the current systems. As educators, we need to encourage students to learn to embody and identify the complexities of action and inaction. In order to reduce the impacts of climate change on both humans and non-humans, we need to act in a fundamentally different way than we have before (Verlie, 2020). However, when presented with the inactivity of the existing political systems, the difficulty of reaching consensus, and the reality of impending climate disaster, students encounter a multifaceted web of emotional responses.

21.4.3 Emotional Responses

Employing problem-based and scenario-based learning approaches, facilitators and students engage with this task in intense, embodied, and emotional ways. The combination of asking students to role play in relation to an existential threat invited them to consider the interplay of facts and feelings in discussion of climate change. Through this activity we, as facilitators, challenged the dualistic notion of mind versus body, and rather purposefully tried to understand how knowledge is felt and embodied in both everyday life and in educational settings. We built on previous authors and educators, who have sought to disrupt the segmentation of the head from the heart, or mind from body, in our teaching practice of this activity (Ahmed, 2014; Head, 2016; Jones & Davison, 2021; Milton, 2005; Verlie, 2022).

As students researched the roles and lives of those they were going to perform, many came to be moved through and by their learnings. Previous research has demonstrated the affective significance of learning about wicked problems, such as climate change (Jones & Davison, 2021). In this learning activity we observed the emotional significance for students as they learnt about climate change. Part of the task is also bringing students into recognition of the urgency of climate change for climate-induced migration. Student learnings of the climate injustices experienced by those in the Global South, in particular, were affective experiences. Engagement with students' emotional experiences is a key component of educational engagement with climate change that needs to be brought to the forefront of pedagogical approaches (Ojala, 2012a). We join in other researchers and educators who seek to disrupt the persistent privileging of *positive* emotions over *negative* ones in climate change education. Rather, we acknowledge that difficult emotions, experienced by our students, about climate change are rational responses to such a crisis (Pihkala, 2021).

A central component of this task was the imaginative and empathetic one of adopting the positionality of others. This engagement is an emotional as well as an intellectual endeavour, as students grappled with and sought to replicate the emotions of others, and consequently themselves felt some shadow of those emotions. For some, this involved the embodiment of emotions such as fear, frustration, anger, and hope. For other students, this task involved an emotional incongruence of assuming a position that they themselves may not hold. Navigating this jump between belief and performance, we acknowledged as facilitators, had significant emotional impacts for students.

Through this mock summit, students often used emotions within their presentations to try and elicit responses and actions from other countries. Emotions were often present in presentations and frequently used communicative tools, as a way of moving others. Student emotions, therefore, played a significant role in moral exhortation and were entangled with the tellings of climate information. In this regard, the learning exercise was a replicate of the use of emotion that has been observed in real-life international summits (Farbotko & McGregor, 2010). The dialogue section of the activity has an affective atmosphere that changes (Anderson, 2009). Often the dialogue time is characterised by tension, as students seek to represent the concerns and needs of their assigned countries.

Previous research has demonstrated the importance of having spaces for young people to express their distressing emotions about climate change (Jones & Davison, 2021; Ojala, 2012b). There has been particular emphasis on the need to foster these spaces within formal educational frameworks (Zummo et al., 2020). Through including a dialogue at the end of this task, we seek as facilitators to create a place for students to express their emotional experiences with the activity. A further emotional significance of this task that we observed is the realisations from students (and from ourselves) of the problems and failures of current international diplomacy and dialogue for climate action. We noticed some students, at the conclusion of the activity, grappling with and sitting with the discomfort of an absence of a clean resolution. Teaching students to learn how to sit with not having "the answer", was a peripheral learning outcome of this task. Reckoning with the messiness of international dialogues, we noticed, moved many students through emotions of frustration, disappointment, resignation, disavowal, determination, and passion. As facilitators, we purposefully sought to recognise and name the embodiment of learnings through this activity and encourage students to recognise the role of emotions in their learnings of wicked problems.

The affective experience of the activity changed as we adapted the task for online learning. Now, the affective atmosphere was facilitated through devices, a different emotional experience and one which we are still learning to navigate. Students were experiencing the task with separate climatic atmospheres of the places within which they were situated, as well as the online atmosphere. Reading of emotion became challenged as the shared affective atmosphere was segmented (Kung-Keat & Ng, 2016).

21.5 Solution-Based Justice-Forward Transformative Learning Experiences

Our experience with this activity demonstrates the need to move beyond a knowledge-deficit approach that continues to shape education about wicked problems like climate change (Peters & Tarpey, 2019). Students will increasingly encounter wicked problems in their lives. This may be through direct encounters with impacts, embodied experiences through friends, or from the increasing visibility on social media. As other researchers have indicated (Cross & Congreve, 2021), responding to wicked problems requires competencies and practices, information and knowledges, understandings, and connections. Interdisciplinary, engaged, solution-based activities challenge students to learn widely applicable skills in advocacy, negotiation, affective practices, and empathy. The activity presented here offers an example of an interdisciplinary learning activity that integrates scientific literacy about climate change with empathetic learning about diverse political, economic, and cultural contexts. This therefore supports students in developing not only practical skills and critical knowledges, but also affective practices that encourage students to imagine otherwise and engage in activities that promote unlearning assumed ways of doing adaptation.

Climate change is an issue of climate justice (Schlosberg & Collins, 2014). At the core of the climate-induced migration activity, and our experiences facilitating it, is an omnipresent understanding of inequality, which takes the form of distributional justice, scales mismatches, and a growing concern around representation in decision-making (Svarstad, 2021). The complex maldistribution of impacts and the stark differences between adaptive capacities become the fundamental disagreement during the summit activity's quest for consensus. Although always at risk of perpetuating reductionist climate justice narratives of good versus bad or rich versus poor, particularly when students are speaking on behalf of other cultures, the activity helps to identify the historic, existing, and future injustices wrought by the intersection of exploitative systems and climate change (Sultana, 2021). Rather than shying away from the potentially uncomfortable reality of inequality, interdisciplinary and transformative learning, activities must adopt justice-forward frameworks that encourage students to critically examine their own countries and privileges. This is not easy, and only further highlights the importance of adopting new ways of teaching and feeling climate change.

Replicating a model closely based on the true formats of international summits around SDGs, the "real world" experience of the activity allows students to engage with current practices of international decision-making and action critically, constructively, and transformatively. This is reflected most acutely through our key takeaways from the experience. The performance making aspect seeks to challenge the spatial and temporal distancing from the impacts of climate change, which previous researchers have demonstrated occurs for many young people (McDonald et al., 2015), particularly those in the Global North who are yet to experience catastrophic impacts of climate change. The acknowledgement of the complexities of viewpoints within countries demonstrates that there is a different way to do things, while bringing in creative ways to communicate super wicked problems beyond just "the UN is hopeless". By allowing space to engage collectively with climate change in an embodied and emotional way, students and facilitators alike build new connections and languages around the shared experience of the lived problem. Although this transformation is not experienced by all students, as educators we must strive for learning activities that challenge existing paradigms while engaging with the personal, societal, and ecological implications of the projected climate change scenarios we will collectively experience in our lifetimes (Kagawa & Selby, 2010).

The climate-induced migration activity presented in this chapter aims to be as student-led, problem-based, and inquiry-based as possible, with students drawing on the four pillars of sustainability (society, culture, environment, and economy) and their connections to climate change and climate refugees. Students are confronted with multiple scales, stakeholders, and inequalities at the core of sustainable development (Dale & Newman, 2005). The need to *take urgent action to combat climate change and its impacts* (SDG13) is multidimensional, requiring international collaboration, national commitments, and local understandings (Leal Filho et al., 2018). By embedding the sustainable development goal into an interdisciplinary curriculum and focusing on the complex impact of climate-induced migration, we believe that students will think, feel, and relate to climate change differently, a vital step towards the development of novel solutions and the adoption of more sympathetic positionality in the face of wicked problems.

References

Ahmed, S. (2014). *The cultural politics of emotion* (2nd ed.). Edinburgh University Press. https://research.gold.ac.uk/id/eprint/13883/

Anderson, B. (2009). Affective atmospheres. *Emotion, Space and Society, 2*(2), 77–81.

Bamber, P. (Ed.). (2019). Introduction: Reconnecting research, policy and practice in education for sustainable development and global citizenship. In *Teacher education for sustainable development and global citizenship* (pp. 1–19). Routledge.

Biermann, F., & Boas, I. (2008). Protecting climate refugees: The case for a global protocol. *Environment: Science and Policy for Sustainable Development, 50*(6), 8–17. https://doi.org/10.3200/ENVT.50.6.8-17

Biermann, F., & Boas, I. (2010). Preparing for a warmer world: Towards a global governance system to protect climate refugees. *Global Environmental Politics, 10*(1), 60–88. https://doi.org/10.1162/glep.2010.10.1.60

Bortscheller, M. J. (2009). Equitable but ineffective: How the principle of common but differentiated responsibilities hobbles the global fight against climate change climate law reporter. *Sustainable Development Law & Policy, 10*(2), 49–69.

Cass, L. R. (2008). A climate of obstinacy: Symbolic politics in Australian and Canadian policy. *Cambridge Review of International Affairs, 21*(4), 465–482. https://doi.org/10.1080/09557570802452763

Conversi, D., & Friis Hau, M. (2021). Green nationalism: Climate action and environmentalism in left nationalist parties. *Environmental Politics, 30*(7), 1089–1110. https://doi.org/10.1080/09644016.2021.1907096

Cross, I. D., & Congreve, A. (2021). Teaching (super) wicked problems: Authentic learning about climate change. *Journal of Geography in Higher Education, 45*(4), 491–516. https://doi.org/10.1080/03098265.2020.1849066

Dale, A., & Newman, L. (2005). Sustainable development, education and literacy. *International Journal of Sustainability in Higher Education, 6*(4), 351–362. https://doi.org/10.1108/14676370510623847

Davidson, J., & Lyth, A. (2012). Education for climate change adaptation—Enhancing the contemporary relevance of planning education for a range of wicked problems. *Journal for Education in the Built Environment, 7*(2), 63–83. https://doi.org/10.11120/jebe.2012.07020063

Davidson, J., Prahalad, V., & Harwood, A. (2021). Design precepts for online experiential learning programs to address wicked sustainability problems. *Journal of Geography in Higher Education, 45*(3), 319–341. https://doi.org/10.1080/03098265.2020.1849061

Davison, A. G., Pharo, E. J., Warr, K., Aboudha, P., Boyd, D., Brown, P., Devereaux, P., Egan, A., Hart, G. D., & McGregor, H. V. (2012). *Demonstrating distributed leadership through cross-disciplinary peer networks: Responding to climate change complexity.* Final Report to the Australian Learning and Teaching Council.

Dobson, H. E., & Bland Tomkinson, C. (2012). Creating sustainable development change agents through problem-based learning: Designing appropriate student PBL projects. *International Journal of Sustainability in Higher Education, 13*(3), 263–278. https://doi.org/10.1108/14676371211242571

Downie, C. (2014). *The politics of climate change negotiations: Strategies and variables in prolonged international negotiations.* Edward Elgar Publishing.

Farbotko, C., & McGregor, H. V. (2010). Copenhagen, climate science and the emotional geographies of climate change. *Australian Geographer, 41*(2), 159–166. https://doi.org/10.1080/00049918003742286

Franco, I., Saito, O., Vaughter, P., Whereat, J., Kanie, N., & Takemoto, K. (2019). Higher education for sustainable development: Actioning the global goals in policy, curriculum and practice. *Sustainability Science, 14*(6), 1621–1642. https://doi.org/10.1007/s11625-018-0628-4

Gallagher, K., & Wessels, A. (2013). Between the frames: Youth spectatorship and theatre as curated, 'unruly' pedagogical space. *Research in Drama Education: The Journal of Applied Theatre and Performance, 18*(1), 25–43. https://doi.org/10.1080/13569783.2012.756167

Gioli, G., Hugo, G., Costa, M. M., & Scheffran, J. (2016). Human mobility, climate adaptation, and development. *Migration and Development, 5*(2), 165–170. https://doi.org/10.1080/21632324.2015.1096590

Gonzalez, C. G. (2018). Climate justice and climate displacement: Evaluating the emerging legal and policy responses. *Wisconsin International Law Journal, 36*(2), 366–396.

Harris, J., Brown, V. A., & Russell, J. (Eds.). (2011). *Tackling wicked problems: Through the transdisciplinary imagination.* Routledge. https://doi.org/10.4324/9781849776530

Hay, I. (2012). Over the threshold—Setting minimum learning outcomes (benchmarks) for undergraduate geography majors in Australian universities. *Journal of Geography in Higher Education, 36*(4), 481–498. https://doi.org/10.1080/03098265.2012.691467

Head, B. W. (2014). Evidence, uncertainty, and wicked problems in climate change decision making in Australia. *Environment and Planning c: Government and Policy, 32*(4), 663–679. https://doi.org/10.1068/c1240

Head, L. (2016). Hope and grief in the Anthropocene: Re-conceptualising human–nature relations. *Routledge.* https://doi.org/10.4324/9781315739335

Hölscher, D., & Grace Bozalek, V. (2012). Encountering the other across the divides: Re-grounding social justice as a guiding principle for social work with refugees and other vulnerable groups. *The British Journal of Social Work, 42*(6), 1093–1112. https://doi.org/10.1093/bjsw/bcs061

Jamieson, D. (2010). Climate change, responsibility, and justice. *Science and Engineering Ethics, 16*(3), 431–445. https://doi.org/10.1007/s11948-009-9174-x

Jaspal, R., Nerlich, B., & Cinnirella, M. (2014). Human responses to climate change: Social representation, identity and socio-psychological action. *Environmental Communication, 8*(1), 110–130. https://doi.org/10.1080/17524032.2013.846270

Jetñil-Kijiner, K. (2014). *Dear Matafele Peinem* [Statement and poem]. United Nations Climate Summit, New York, NY. https://www.youtube.com/watch?v=mc_IgE7TBSY

Jolly, S., & Trivedi, A. (2020). Implementing the SDG-13 through the adoption of hybrid law: Addressing climate-induced displacement. *Brill Open Law, 2*(1), 69–100. https://doi.org/10.1163/23527072-20191016

Jones, C. A., & Davison, A. (2021). Disempowering emotions: The role of educational experiences in social responses to climate change. *Geoforum, 118*, 190–200. https://doi.org/10.1016/j.geoforum.2020.11.006

Kagawa, F., & Selby, D. (2010). *Education and climate change: Living and learning in interesting times.* Routledge.

Keskitalo, E. C. H., & Preston, B. L. (2019). *Research handbook on climate change adaptation policy.* Edward Elgar Publishing.

Kung-Keat, T., & Ng, J. (2016). Confused, bored, excited? An emotion based approach to the design of online learning systems. In C. Y. Fook, G. K. Sidhu, S. Narasuman, L. L. Fong, & S. B. Abdul Rahman (Eds.), *7th International Conference on University Learning and Teaching (InCULT 2014) Proceedings* (pp. 221–233). Springer. https://doi.org/10.1007/978-981-287-664-5_19

Leal Filho, W., Azeiteiro, U., Alves, F., Pace, P., Mifsud, M., Brandli, L., Caeiro, S. S., & Disterheft, A. (2018). Reinvigorating the sustainable development research agenda: The role of the sustainable development goals (SDG). *International Journal of Sustainable Development & World Ecology, 25*(2), 131–142. https://doi.org/10.1080/13504509.2017.1342103

Lehtonen, A., & Pihkala, P. (2021). Encounters with climate change and its psychosocial aspects through performance making among young people. *Environmental Education Research, 27*(5), 743–761. https://doi.org/10.1080/13504622.2021.1923663

Macintyre, T., Lotz-Sisitka, H., Wals, A., Vogel, C., & Tassone, V. (2018). Towards transformative social learning on the path to 1.5 degrees. *Current Opinion in Environmental Sustainability, 31*, 80–87. https://doi.org/10.1016/j.cosust.2017.12.003

McDonald, R. I., Chai, H. Y., & Newell, B. R. (2015). Personal experience and the 'psychological distance' of climate change: An integrative review. *Journal of Environmental Psychology, 44,* 109–118. https://doi.org/10.1016/j.jenvp.2015.10.003

McNamara, K. E. (2007). Conceptualizing discourses on environmental refugees at the United Nations. *Population and Environment, 29*(1), 12–24. https://doi.org/10.1007/s11111-007-0058-1

Meadows, M. E. (2020). Geography education for sustainable development. *Geography and Sustainability, 1*(1), 88–92. https://doi.org/10.1016/j.geosus.2020.02.001

Milton, K. (2005). Emotion (or life, the universe, everything). *The Australian Journal of Anthropology, 16*(2), 198–211. https://doi.org/10.1111/j.1835-9310.2005.tb00034.x

Myers, N. (2002). Environmental refugees: A growing phenomenon of the 21st century. *Philosophical Transactions of the Royal Society of London. Series B: Biological Sciences, 357*(1420), 609–613. https://doi.org/10.1098/rstb.2001.0953

O'Byrne, D., Dripps, W., & Nicholas, K. A. (2015). Teaching and learning sustainability: An assessment of the curriculum content and structure of sustainability degree programs in higher education. *Sustainability Science, 10*(1), 43–59. https://doi.org/10.1007/s11625-014-0251-y

Ojala, M. (2012a). Regulating worry, promoting hope: How do children, adolescents, and young adults cope with climate change? *International Journal of Environmental and Science Education, 7*(4), 537–561.

Ojala, M. (2012b). Hope and climate change: The importance of hope for environmental engagement among young people. *Environmental Education Research, 18*(5), 625–642. https://doi.org/10.1080/13504622.2011.637157

Palacios, F. A., Oberle, A., Quezada, X. C., & Ullestad, M. (2017). Geographic education for sustainability: Developing a bi-national geographical thinking curriculum. In C. Brooks, G. Butt, & M. Fargher (Eds.), *The power of geographical thinking* (pp. 103–117). Springer International Publishing. https://doi.org/10.1007/978-3-319-49986-4_8

Papadopoulos, A. (2019). Integrating the natural environment in social work education: Sustainability and scenario-based learning. *Australian Social Work, 72*(2), 233–241. https://doi.org/10.1080/0312407X.2018.1542012

Perumal, N. (2018). "The place where I live is where I belong": Community perspectives on climate change and climate-related migration in the Pacific island nation of Vanuatu. *Island Studies Journal, 13*(1), 45–65. https://doi.org/10.24043/isj.50

Peters, B. G., & Tarpey, M. (2019). Are wicked problems really so wicked? Perceptions of policy problems. *Policy and Society, 38*(2), 218–236. https://doi.org/10.1080/14494035.2019.1626595

Pharo, E., Davison, A., McGregor, H., Warr, K., & Brown, P. (2014). Using communities of practice to enhance interdisciplinary teaching: Lessons from four Australian institutions. *Higher Education Research & Development, 33*(2), 341–354. https://doi.org/10.1080/07294360.2013.832168

Pihkala, P. (2021). Eco-anxiety. In *Situating sustainability: A handbook of contexts and concepts* (pp. 119).

Porter, L., Rickards, L., Verlie, B., Bosomworth, K., Moloney, S., Lay, B., Latham, B., Anguelovski, I., & Pellow, D. (2020). Climate justice in a climate changed world. *Planning Theory & Practice, 21*(2), 293–321. https://doi.org/10.1080/14649357.2020.1748959

Pyy, I. (2021). Developing political compassion through narrative imagination in human rights education. *Human Rights Education Review, 4*(3), 24–44. https://doi.org/10.7577/hrer.4482

Rasmussen, B. (2010). The 'good enough' drama: Reinterpreting constructivist aesthetics and epistemology in drama education. *Research in Drama Education: The Journal of Applied Theatre and Performance, 15*(4), 529–546. https://doi.org/10.1080/13569783.2010.512187

Reid, A. (2019). Climate change education and research: Possibilities and potentials versus problems and perils? *Environmental Education Research, 25*(6), 767–790. https://doi.org/10.1080/13504622.2019.1664075

Roberts, J. T., & Parks, B. C. (2007). *A climate of injustice: Global inequality, North-South politics, and climate policy.* The MIT Press.

Rosales, J. (2008). Economic growth, climate change, biodiversity loss: Distributive justice for the Global North and South. *Conservation Biology, 22*(6), 1409–1417. https://doi.org/10.1111/j.1523-1739.2008.01091.x

Rousell, D., & Cutter-Mackenzie-Knowles, A. (2020). A systematic review of climate change education: Giving children and young people a 'voice' and a 'hand' in redressing climate change. *Children's Geographies, 18*(2), 191–208. https://doi.org/10.1080/14733285.2019.1614532

Saito, O., Managi, S., Kanie, N., Kauffman, J., & Takeuchi, K. (2017). Sustainability science and implementing the sustainable development goals. *Sustainability Science, 12*(6), 907–910. https://doi.org/10.1007/s11625-017-0486-5

Schlosberg, D., & Collins, L. B. (2014). From environmental to climate justice: Climate change and the discourse of environmental justice. *Wires Climate Change, 5*(3), 359–374. https://doi.org/10.1002/wcc.275

Solem, M., Lambert, D., & Tani, S. (2013). Geocapabilities: Toward an international framework for researching the purposes and values of geography education. *Review of International Geographical Education Online, 3*(3), 214–229.

Strachan, S., Logan, L., Willison, D., Bain, R., Roberts, J., Mitchell, I., & Yarr, R. (2021). *Reflections on developing a collaborative multi-disciplinary approach to embedding education for sustainable development into higher education curricula*. Emerald Open Research. https://doi.org/10.35241/emeraldopenres.14303.1

Sultana, F. (2021). Critical climate justice. *The Geographical Journal, 188*(1), 118–124. https://doi.org/10.1111/geoj.12417

Svarstad, H. (2021). Critical climate education: Studying climate justice in time and space. *International Studies in Sociology of Education, 30*(1–2), 214–232. https://doi.org/10.1080/09620214.2020.1855463

Tilbury, D. (2004). Environmental education for sustainability: A force for change in higher education. In P. B. Corcoran & A. E. J. Wals (Eds.), *Higher education and the challenge of sustainability* (pp. 97–112). Springer Netherlands. http://link.springer.com/chapter/10.1007/0-306-485 15-X_9

United Nations Conference on Sustainable Development. (2012). *Commitment to sustainable practices of higher education institutions on the occasion of the United Nations Conference on Sustainable Development in Rio 2012*. United Nations. https://sdgs.un.org/sites/default/files/documents/1889HEI%2520Declaration%2520English%2520new%2520version.pdf

Verlie, B. (2020). From action to intra-action? Agency, identity and 'goals' in a relational approach to climate change education. *Environmental Education Research, 26*(9–10), 1266–1280. https://doi.org/10.1080/13504622.2018.1497147

Verlie, B. (2022). *Learning to live with climate change: From anxiety to transformation*. Taylor & Francis. https://doi.org/10.4324/9780367441265

Wachholz, S., Artz, N., & Chene, D. (2014). Warming to the idea: University students' knowledge and attitudes about climate change. *International Journal of Sustainability in Higher Education, 15*(2), 128–141. https://doi.org/10.1108/IJSHE-03-2012-0025

Wilkinson, E., Schipper, L., Simonet, C., & Kubik, Z. (2016). *Climate change, migration and the 2030 Agenda for Sustainable Development* (Shaping Policy for Development, p. 15) [ODI Briefing]. odi.org. https://odi.org/en/publications/climate-change-migration-and-the-2030-agenda-for-sustainable-development/

Zummo, L., Gargroetzi, E., & Garcia, A. (2020). Youth voice on climate change: Using factor analysis to understand the intersection of science, politics, and emotion. *Environmental Education Research, 26*(8), 1207–1226. https://doi.org/10.1080/13504622.2020.1771288

Chapter 22
Reducing Inequity Through Teacher Education: Reflection on a Teacher Education Subject on Classroom Management

Si Fan and Jeffrey Thomas

22.1 Introduction

Improving education is identified as an important strategy to achieve the Sustainable Development Goals (SDGs) (United Nations Department of Economic & Social Affairs, 2022a). Quality education and school completion have direct links to one's life opportunities and choices, as well as future earning and even life expectancy (Australian Institute of Health and Welfare (AIHW), 2021b). The Australian Commonwealth Government set a target to develop a schooling system that is of high-quality and highly equitable by international standards by 2025 (The Law Library, 2018).

Initial Teacher Education (ITE) programs are key players in producing teachers who have an equitable approach. ITE programs have the professional responsibility to equip pre-service teachers with the range of skills and knowledge that will allow them to perform as effective teachers in schools. The Australian Institute for Teaching and School Leadership (2022) defines the professional standards for teachers in Australia, with explicit indicators for high-quality and effective teaching that are required of classroom-ready teachers. Education for Sustainability (EfS) is reflected in many of these standards; for instance, Standard 1.4 requires an understanding of students with diverse linguistic, cultural, and socio-economic backgrounds and

S. Fan (✉)
School of Education, College of Arts, Law and Education, University of Tasmania, Launceston,
TAS 7250, Australia
e-mail: Si.Fan@utas.edu.au

J. Thomas
School of Education, College of Arts, Law and Education, University of Tasmania, Hobart,
TAS 7005, Australia
e-mail: jeffrey.thomas@utas.edu.au

Standard 1.5 requires the ability to differentiate teaching for students across the full range of abilities (Australian Institute for Teaching and School Leadership, 2022). In a broader sense, as stated by García-González et al. (2020) and supported by Odell et al. (2020), the aim of EfS "is not only for students to be successful in their future careers, it also seeks to provide them with skills, motivation, and a scale of values with which to contribute to the wellbeing of the global community" (p. 1).

Since the SDGs were launched, university ITE programs have made attempts to embed them in diverse ways, depending on the institutions' strategies and ways of operation (García-González et al., 2020). Some of the initiatives work to raise awareness about the SDGs among pre-service teachers. For instance, García-González et al. from the Faculty of Education at the University of Cadiz developed a sequence of activities to investigate changes in student perceptions and knowledge regarding the SDGs and how to incorporate them into the classroom. These activities resulted in an enhanced understanding and awareness of both what the SDGs involve and how to implement them in teaching practices.

This chapter focuses on SDG4, Quality Education, which aims to "ensure inclusive and equitable quality education and promote lifelong learning opportunities for all" (United Nations Department of Economic & Social Affairs, 2022c, para.1). The first key target within this SDG is to ensure free, equitable, and quality education in school education leading to positive learning outcomes (United Nations Department of Economic & Social Affairs, 2022b). The chapter discusses how this target can be addressed in one key area in Australian ITE programs: classroom management. In particular, it examines how a humanistic approach to classroom management can make a significant difference to children's schooling, and how an inclusive approach at a classroom level can help reduce disengagement and inequity in schools. This chapter uses examples of classroom management practices to explain how schooling experiences can be enhanced for three selected student groups: students from lower socio-economic backgrounds, students with learning disabilities, and students from diverse language and cultural backgrounds.

22.2   Inequality in Australian Schools

Inequity appears in Australian schools in many forms, and there are known student groups who are more likely to be disadvantaged. The Department of Education Employment and Training (1990) defines six equity groups in higher education, including students from lower socio-economic backgrounds, students with disabilities, and students from non-English speaking backgrounds. Although these equity groups are defined for higher education, many students who experience educational inequity in schools are from similar backgrounds. Adapted from these categories, this chapter uses three student groups as examples: students from lower socio-economic backgrounds, students with learning disabilities, and students from diverse language and cultural backgrounds. The chapter unpacks the demographics of these groups and examines gaps between the needs of these groups and insufficiency in school support that contributes to the inequity for these students.

22.2.1 Students from Low Socio-Economic Status (SES)

Students from lower socio-economic backgrounds are often recognised as a significant group correlated with educational disadvantages (Thomson, 2017). The Index of Community Socio-Educational Advantage (ICSEA) provides an indication of the socio-educational backgrounds of students (Australian Curriculum, Assessment and Reporting Authority (ACARA), 2016). There is a clear correlation between ICSEA and school achievement, retention, and attendance (Beswick et al., 2019), as well as with reported disengaged and disruptive behaviour (Peacock, 2015). For instance, school completion rates are significantly lower among low SES students (65%), as compared with students in medium (78%) and high SES areas (87%) (Buddelmeyer et al., 2011).

Numerous factors contribute to students from lower SES being at risk of educational disadvantages, including characteristics of the students, characteristics of the schools, and other cultural and financial factors such as family aspirations (Buddelmeyer et al., 2011). Students from disadvantaged areas statistically achieve lower academic performance and have lower educational aspirations compared to their high SES counterparts (Buddelmeyer et al., 2011). To add to these factors, differences in school characteristics, including the lack of school resources and peer influences, also contribute to the low school completion rates of this student group (Buddelmeyer et al., 2011). For those who remain learning at school, students from low SES areas experience more challenges in achieving some targets than their high SES counterparts, for instance, physical fitness (Peralta et al., 2019) and emotional health (Arslan, 2018). Some of these gaps have been further widened during the COVID pandemic (Drane et al., 2021).

22.2.2 Students with Learning Disabilities

Apart from the socio-economic factors, students with learning disabilities are another significant group that experiences inequity. Australian schools have students with diverse needs. According to the AIHW (2021a), 1 in 10 school students in Australia aged 5–18 have some level of disability, with intellectual, sensory, and speech disabilities as the most common types. In 2018, 338,000 (89%) children with disabilities attended school. Some student groups present higher dropout rates from school. For instance, male students who live with Attention Deficit Hyperactivity Disorder (ADHD) are reportedly ten times more likely to leave school early than students who are considered typically developing and without a learning disability (Kent et al., 2011). Perhaps even more concerningly, students with a disability are over-represented in school suspensions and exclusions (Grasley-Boy et al., 2019) and are also much more likely to be enrolled in schools and programs for disengaged youth (Graham et al., 2020).

Research calls for a better recognition of the relationship between students' learning disabilities and disengagement in schools (Thomas & Rayner, 2021). Better support and understanding of these students' needs are crucial for their school participation and attainment. Learning disabilities are not always identified, formally diagnosed, or properly treated. The process of obtaining support can also be more challenging for some of these student cohorts. For instance, in Australian public schools, children with ADHD may not get additional school support if they do not have other types of impairments (Boon, 2020). There is also a reported lack of knowledge among schools and teachers in addressing the needs of children with ADHD (Anderson et al., 2017). These negative factors lead to real challenges for these students' schooling and cause "… the collateral damage to a child's sense of confidence and competence that can come from years of unabated stress …" (Schultz, 2011, p. 7).

Experiences of trauma can also cause learning disabilities. Traditionally, working with trauma-affected students has been approached from the medical and judicial perspectives; however, the awareness of its impacts has become more widespread in education (Davidson, 2017). Up to 40% of the student population in Australian schools has been exposed to or witnessed traumatic events (Australian Bureau of Statistics, 2011; Bailey & Brunzell, 2019). Students who have been impacted by trauma similarly are more highly represented in the statistics of early school leaving, school refusal, and exclusion (Hobbes et al., 2019). One significant group who may be trauma-affected are students from a refugee background, who often have a combination of learning needs. Most of these students come from other language and cultural backgrounds, and many have had interrupted schooling (Miller et al., 2018). Research has identified experiences of discrimination, racism, and inappropriate pedagogies as impeders to positive schooling experiences (Correa-Velez et al., 2017).

22.2.3 Students from Diverse Language and Cultural Backgrounds

Another identified group that experiences inequity in schools is students from culturally and linguistically diverse backgrounds. This is again a diverse group and could include multiple sub-groups, such as Aboriginal and Torres Strait Islander students, students with a refugee background, students from homes where English is not spoken, and international students from non-English speaking countries (ACARA, 2022). In Australia, students come from over 2,000 different ethnic backgrounds (ACARA, 2022), with over 600,000 students learning English as an additional language or dialect in Government and Catholic schools (Australian Council of TESOL Associations, 2020). Despite the growth in this student population, not all of these students receive the support they require. Research identifies the lack of funding for schools to support these students, unpreparedness of teachers to teach them, and insufficient consideration of their needs, as main challenges in supporting this student group (Australian Council of TESOL Associations, 2014). In Australian schools, 5.7% of students are identified as Aboriginal and/or Torres Strait Islanders, yet, this student group appears to be less likely to complete their compulsory education, and more likely to face disciplinary action than their non-indigenous peers (Schwab, 2018). Inappropriate teaching materials, which do not include enough Aboriginal lives and history, a lack of cultural awareness among teachers, and missing role models are some major barriers to the education of this student group (Korff, 2022).

The groups identified above are by no means considered homogenous, nor exhaustive. In this chapter, these groups are used as examples to illustrate systemic inequalities, rather than the individual circumstances of students in Australia's schooling system. It is recognised that neither the disadvantages nor the strategies proposed to address these issues could represent the experiences of all students from these groups. However, a common link among these student groups is their overrepresentation in the statistics of early school leaving, poor achievement, and involvement with school behaviour management systems. These statistical outcomes are the result of a prolonged disengagement with education. In a system where inequalities in educational outcomes persist among specific demographic groups, identifying strategies that are based on increasing student engagement for all students is paramount.

The following section uses these key student groups as examples to discuss how quality and inclusive education can be achieved through fostering student engagement and promoting a positive classroom environment. More specifically, these are achieved through creating a sense of belonging, a sense of competence, and a sense of value in schooling.

22.3 Addressing Inequality Through Classroom Management

In the area of classroom management, pre-service teachers explore the theoretical and practical issues concerned with establishing and maintaining positive learning environments, and strategies that allow all students to participate fully in educational opportunities, including those in the mentioned student groups. The following educational philosophy should be key to the teaching of classroom management strategies:

- Classroom management practices should be based on a humanist and inclusive approach that recognises and respects individual differences; and
- Behaviours should be viewed as indicators of student engagement, which is an interplay between the student and educational experiences.

A humanist and inclusive approach starts with recognising individual differences. An awareness that students are unique individuals, with their own sets of strengths, needs, abilities, and aspirations, is fundamental to a humanist and inclusive approach. Teachers who recognise individual differences and have a humanist and inclusive approach are more likely to perceive their students from a strength-based, rather than a deficit perspective. The focus of classroom management then can be placed on meeting students' needs, building on their strengths, and thereby fostering their engagement with education.

Where a behaviour is observed, either positive or undesirable, it should be seen as an indicator of student engagement with education. Positive behaviour indicates student engagement with learning, and negative behaviour is a reflection of disengagement. Student engagement is an interplay between the student and the educational experience that happens every day at school (McMahon & Zyngier, 2009). If students have positive interactions in the school environment, feel safe, see the value in their learning, and have a sense of belonging, they are more likely to attend school, actively participate, and display productive learning behaviours (Thomas, 2019). Unfortunately, the converse is also true, if students have poor relationships with education, created by a series of negative interactions, these are also likely to be reflected in their behaviour (Reichenberg, 2018).

Research identifies teacher–student relationships as one of the most significant factors impacting student engagement (Walker & Graham, 2021). As the people interacting with students on a daily basis, teachers have a direct impact on students' attitudes towards education and schooling. Therefore, teachers must create interactions that promote and foster student engagement in order to build a positive classroom (Nagro et al., 2019). The following sections discuss some strategies that can be used to promote such interactions and foster higher learner engagement. Examples of inclusive classroom management practices are provided, with particular references to support the key student groups, as identified in the previous section.

22.3.1 Creating a Sense of Belonging

First, classroom management strategies need to create a sense of belonging for every student (K. Allen et al., 2018). Students who feel like they do not fit in schools are more likely to disengage. Belonging can largely be achieved through preventative strategies that target individual students' strengths and promote positive interactions in the classroom (K.-A. Allen et al., 2021). For students to feel like they belong, they need to understand, and to be part of, the culture of the class. Traditionally, behaviour expectations are expressed through a hidden curriculum, with comments such as, "you need to have good manners" or "we don't speak that way here." In many cases, students from different language or cultural backgrounds to the teacher may find themselves having difficulty understanding or following such instructions because they do not share the same behavioural expectations. To overcome this, behaviour should be seen as a curriculum and taught explicitly. Expected behaviours should be discussed with the class, taught, modelled, and practised (Bennett, 2017; De Nobile et al., 2021). The concept of a "behaviour agreement" where students and the teacher work collaboratively to identify behaviours to be used in the class, such as those suggested by Rogers (2015), can enhance the student's sense of belonging and ownership of the class.

In addition to understanding and accepting the behavioural norms of the class, students need to see explicitly that they are part of the class. There are several ways this can be achieved, the most powerful being strategies such as "check and connect," where every student is greeted personally every day by the teacher (Goulet et al., 2018). Students need to see that their teacher sees them, and cares for them as individuals. Students also need to be able to see themselves as students—especially if they come from educationally disadvantaged backgrounds. One way to address this in a diverse class is to ensure that there is the representation of many types of people displayed and celebrated. In a science class, for example, posters can be displayed on the walls showing successful scientists from different genders, ages, and ethnic and cultural backgrounds. Inviting Aboriginal elders into the classroom to share stories about Aboriginal history is a great way to engage students with an Aboriginal and/ or Torres Strait Islander background. Designing a culturally responsive classroom is seen as a key component of student motivation (Kumar et al., 2018). As such, teaching content should not always favour the dominant culture. Relating teaching to the culture and lived experiences of students from other cultural backgrounds has proven to be beneficial in enhancing the retention of these students in science education and chemistry education (Spencer et al., 2022).

In terms of students living with a disability and trauma-affected students, the physical design of the classroom can change how students feel and their sense of belonging. Various seating options, such as wobble chairs, standing desks, and couches, can send the message to students with diverse needs that the school welcomes them and respects who they are (Gochenour & Poskey, 2017). Spaces for students to go to when they are feeling overwhelmed, anxious, or triggered can also be useful for those with mental health conditions, including those being trauma-affected (Schwartz-Henderson, 2016) and those living with Autism Spectrum Disorder (ASD) (McAllister, 2010). Having such spaces purposefully designed can create a sense of calmness for these students. Equipping the spaces to reduce sensory overloads, such as noise cancelling headphones, low lighting, and self-regulation mantra can help students learn that the school accepts them, including when they are struggling to cope. Similarly, simple strategies of material inclusion need to be considered when thinking about students who come from lower socio-economic backgrounds. For example, if uniforms are compulsory, the school should have a system of providing uniforms to families that cannot afford them (Sabic-El-Rayess et al., 2019).

22.3.2   Creating a Sense of Competence

Secondly, students must feel like they are competent in the class. Disengaged behaviour may often emanate from students feeling like they do not have the skills or knowledge to be able to succeed, and sometimes students are punished for not understanding the correct way of being a student, further disengaging them (Skiba et al., 2014). The key to building a student's perception of competency is to ensure clear differentiation. Teachers are generally aware of differentiating between different academic abilities by varying content, assessment, or delivery methods. When it comes to behaviour support, teachers also need to differentiate behaviourally. This idea is the antithesis of the no excuses approach common in many charter schools in the United States, where highly structured and standardised discipline has been associated with poorer social and behavioural outcomes (Golann & Torres, 2020). It is best illustrated through the use of an example. With the no excuse approach, a class might have a rule that everyone must sit in their chairs for the duration of the lesson and only speak when invited to do so by the teacher. This class might also have a consequence of detention if the class rules are broken. Most students would be able to abide by this rule, but a student with unmedicated ADHD would find it impossible. In a scenario like this, differentiating behaviourally would allow this student to have altered behavioural expectations, similar to academic differentiation providing altered academic expectations. Rather than a class rule, there might be an agreement that everyone will try their best to stay on task (DuPaul et al., 2011). The teacher might, for example, allow a student to sit on a wobble chair, use a fidget spinner, get up and walk around the class at set times, and understand that the student might need regular reminders not to call out. In this way, these students understand that their personal needs are being catered for, and opportunities are created for them to engage in learning activities.

Students who do not meet the behaviour agreement or expectations would still be required to work with the teacher. Some corrective strategies follow the behaviourist concept of providing an unpleasant experience or removing the desired activity, to deter future poor behaviour (De Nobile et al., 2021). These negative reinforcements or punishments typically include strategies such as detentions, writing lines, or removal of privileges. Each of these methods deliberately makes the school experience less enjoyable for the student, which is by definition, affectively disengaging. At the same time, these methods are not addressing the underlying cause of the behaviour and as such are found to predict, rather than prevent, problematic behaviour (Skiba & Losen, 2016; Way, 2011). Educative or solution-focussed strategies should aim to raise the student's awareness of why the behaviour is unacceptable, to understand the reasons behind the behaviour, and to co-construct ways of improving that behaviour in the future. Using these strategies, the aim is for students to understand the impact of their behaviours, and feel empowered to change them, leading to a greater sense of competency.

Personalised, humanistic behaviour management approaches are even more important when considering students who may exhibit highly challenging behaviour due to being trauma-affected (Hobbes et al., 2019). Trauma responses are characterised by the "flight, fight or freeze" responses exhibited by a person in a state of terror. For trauma-affected students, these responses may occur in situations where there is no objective danger, hence being described by the term maladapted (Solomon & Heide, 2005). In a school situation these responses may be perceived and described as unacceptable behaviour in many policy documents: shouting, fighting, hitting, running away, noncompliance, or disengagement in the work program planned by teachers. For these students, the main objective in responding to these behaviours should be de-escalation—or calming the student through removing the perceived threat (Berger & Martin, 2021). Active listening, a calming tone, and playful interactions are key in de-escalating the situation and building healing relationships (Purvis et al., 2013). Teachers need to be skilled in working with the students after an escalation, so the students will know and feel that they are safe and understood, and they are not defined by their behaviour that was triggered by an event.

22.3.3 Creating a Sense of Value in Schooling

Finally, to maximise engagement, students must enjoy the experience and see the worth of schooling. Students who can see the relevance of learning to their future life are more likely to participate, and less likely to display disruptive behaviour (De Nobile et al., 2021). This can often be a struggle for teachers who need to satisfy the requirements of a crowded curriculum but has been achieved through approaches such as project-based learning (Big Picture Learning Australia, 2021). More importantly, perhaps, is the need for students to see school as a safe and enjoyable place. For students to be engaged in schooling they need to feel physically, culturally, socially, and emotionally free from harm, and in this situation, teachers' approaches to classroom management are paramount.

Safety relies on teachers creating a culture of respect in the class, and one which celebrates diversity among the peer group. At a class level, this relies on the implicit and explicit teaching of acceptance of difference and individuality. Bullying emanates from the power imbalances within groups and thrives in cultures where the power differential is celebrated (Rigby, 2012). Students who are perceived as different from their peers are more likely to face bullying and harassment from other students (Rigby, 2017). Student groups who have higher vulnerability to bullying victimisation include those who have a disability (Moffat et al., 2019) and those from other language and cultural backgrounds (Mishna et al., 2020).

Schools can promote inclusiveness by shifting the cultures of who is celebrated in a school (Rigby, 2017). For example, traditional school prizes are given for academic and sporting achievements, which promotes the most able-minded and able-bodied to a higher status. This leaves students who are less likely to be celebrated for their physical prowess or academic brilliance, publicly disempowered. One way to reduce this power differential is for teachers to ensure that they celebrate students for attitudes and values that are not based on genetic accidents. For example, all students can be in the equal running for prizes in courage, kindness, persistence, and conscientiousness. Students who have learning disabilities can be acknowledged for their efforts in completing a major task. Students from other language and cultural backgrounds can be celebrated for helping their peers in a group project.

Some key aspects of affective engagement, enjoyment, and worth, can be achieved through careful lesson planning. In addition to learning objectives and curriculum links, lesson plans should consider aspects that promote student participation. This can be accommodated in a variety of ways, and of course, depends on the students and the context of learning. Students see value in attending class because it is relevant to their future and is an enjoyable experience—hopefully, both! To have future value, teachers can make the learning outcomes explicit to real-life learning, future vocational opportunities, or academic stepping stones (Orthner et al., 2013). To support students from low SES backgrounds, teachers can show students what success looks like, break down learning to small steps, and support them in every step through explicit teaching (New South Wales Government, 2021). Enjoyable lessons are also, unsurprisingly, required for increasing affective engagement. This enjoyment can be achieved through games, social interactions, achieving challenges, curious facts, and working as a team. Alternating low-appeal and high-appeal activities can help motivate students who have ADHD.

It is worth noting that certain teaching techniques can make the lesson experience less enjoyable for some students and can be easily avoided. For example, any strategy that puts a student on the spot can be very stressful for students who suffer from anxiety disorders or those with lower cognitive abilities. Group activities can be unenjoyable for students who are introverted or who have ASD, as they may find such social interactions confronting (Symes & Humphrey, 2010). Sitting still for long periods will likely be unenjoyable, or even intolerable, for students with ADHD. Therefore, through careful lesson planning, pedagogical approaches and activities should take into consideration the characteristics and needs of the students in class.

22.4   Bringing It Together

In order to achieve equity in education, at a classroom level students need to be respected and supported as uniquely different individuals. The previous section discussed practical approaches that can be used in the area of classroom management, to support individual differences and learning needs. In particular, these are achieved through the promotion of three key characteristics in students: their sense of belonging, their sense of competency in themselves, and their sense of value in schooling. The development of these desired characteristics in children is critical for a positive schooling experience. To achieve this, it is vital that teachers take a humanist approach, through differentiating teaching practices for individual students in different curriculum areas, including behaviour support.

Positive learning environments and relationships are fundamental for any productive classroom, and teachers play a key role in building these. Every classroom has its climate, and teachers are the ones who make the weather, as stated by the American educator Ginott (1972), "I am the decisive element in the classroom. It is my personal approach that creates the climate. It is my daily mood that makes the weather. As a teacher I possess tremendous power to make a child's life miserable or joyous" (p. 15). A positive learning environment and climate can only be achieved through recognising students as valuable individuals and through positive relationships between the teacher and the students and among students themselves.

It is recognised that there are increasing pressures experienced by teachers on compliance, standardisation, and a crowded curriculum, and these may bring challenges when teachers try to personalise learning approaches for individual students. With recognition of these challenges, the authors of this chapter advocate for a classroom management style that is guided by the principles of engagement and humanism. This key message responds directly to the first key target within SDG4, which is to ensure free, equitable, and quality education in school education, leading to positive learning outcomes (United Nations Department of Economic & Social Affairs, 2022b). Through this engagement and humanist approach, to the largest extent possible, all student groups can be treated with understanding, respect, and compassion, and thereby allowing them to have an equal opportunity for participation and success in education.

22.5   Conclusion

In this chapter, we acknowledge that the schooling system in Australia has perpetuated inequalities, including the very way in which schoolwork has continued to disadvantage students from diverse language and cultural backgrounds, those living with learning disabilities, and perhaps most consistently, students from lower SES backgrounds. The structures in schools result in students from these groups being much less likely to receive the benefits of a full and complete education, which can result in lifelong disadvantages. Although these inequalities stem from larger factors in society, this chapter suggests that how schools are managed at a classroom level can provide some balance for the traditionally disadvantaged students. The way that teachers set behavioural expectations, address unproductive behaviour, create learning experiences, and even how they present their classrooms, can all be factors that keep a student's relationship with school strong. Through a humanistic and engagement-driven approach to classroom management, teachers can create classroom environments that promote a sense of belonging, competence, and value of education, and thereby promote inclusive and equitable education for all students.

References

Allen, K.-A., Jamshidi, N., Berger, E., Reupert, A., Wurf, G., & May, F. (2021). Impact of school-based interventions for building school belonging in adolescence: A systematic review. *Educational Psychology Review, 34*, 229–257.

Allen, K., Kern, M. L., Vella-Brodrick, D., Hattie, J., & Waters, L. (2018). What schools need to know about fostering school belonging: A meta-analysis. *Educational Psychology Review, 30*(1), 1–34.

Anderson, D. L., Watt, S. E., & Shanley, D. C. (2017). Ambivalent attitudes about teaching children with attention deficit/hyperactivity disorder (ADHD). *Emotional and Behavioural Difficulties, 22*(4), 332–349.

Arslan, G. (2018). Understanding the association between school belonging and emotional health in adolescents. *International Journal of Educational Psychology, 7*(1), 21–41.

Australian Bureau of Statistics. (2011). *Australian social trends, March 2011 (Cat. No. 4102.0).* ABS.

Australian Council of TESOL Associations. (2014). *State of EAL/D in Australia 2014.* Hindmarsh. https://tesol.org.au/wp-content/uploads/2019/01/562_ACTA_2014_Survey_Report_Final.pdf

Australian Council of TESOL Associations. (2020). *How many English as an Additional Language or Dialect (EAL/D) learners are there in Australian Schools?* https://tesol.org.au/how-many-english-as-an-additional-language-or-dialect-eal-d-learners-are-there-in-australian-schools/

Australian Curriculum, Assessment and Reporting Authority. (2016). *Guide to understanding ICSEA (Index of Community Socioeducational Advantage) values.* https://docs.acara.edu.au/resources/Guide_to_understanding_icsea_values.pdf

Australian Curriculum, Assessment and Reporting Authority. (2022). *Meeting the needs of students for whom English is an additional language or dialect.* https://www.australiancurriculum.edu.au/resources/student-diversity/meeting-the-needs-of-students-for-whom-english-is-an-additional-language-or-dialect/#:~:text=Across%20Australia%2C%20around%2025%20per,high%20as%2090%20per%20cent

Australian Institute for Teaching and School Leadership. (2022). *Australian professional standards for teachers.* https://www.aitsl.edu.au/docs/default-source/national-policy-framework/australian-professional-standards-for-teachers.pdf

Australian Institute of Health and Welfare. (2021a). *Australian's children.* https://www.aihw.gov.au/reports/children-youth/australias-children/contents/data-sources/survey-data-sources

Australian Institute of Health and Welfare. (2021b). *Secondary education: School retention and completion.* https://www.aihw.gov.au/reports/australias-welfare/secondary-education-school-retention-completion

Bailey, B., & Brunzell, T. (2019). *A new approach to trauma-informed teaching: Teacher practice with the Berry Street Education Model.* https://aifs.gov.au/cfca/2019/08/22/new-approach-trauma-informed-teaching-teacher-practice-berry-street-education-model

Bennett, T. (2017). *Creating a culture: How school leaders can optimise behaviour.* Department for Education.

Berger, E., & Martin, K. (2021). Embedding trauma-informed practice within the education sector. *Journal of Community & Applied Social Psychology, 31*(2), 223–227.

Beswick, K., Wright, S., Watson, J., Hay, I., Allen, J., & Cranston, N. (2019). Teachers' beliefs related to secondary school completion: Associations with socio-educational advantage and school level. *The Australian Educational Researcher, 46*(5), 751–774.

Big Picture Learning Australia. (2021). https://www.bigpicture.org.au/about-us/big-picture-education-australia

Boon, H. J. (2020). What do ADHD neuroimaging studies reveal for teachers, teacher educators and inclusive education? *Child & Yourth Care Forum, 49*, 533–561. https://doi.org/10.1007/s10566-019-09542-4

Buddelmeyer, H., Hanel, B., & Polidano, C. (2011). *The effect of schools in retaining disadvantaged youth in education.* Melbourne Institute of Applied Economic and Social Research.

Correa-Velez, I., Gifford, S. M., McMichael, C., & Sampson, R. (2017). Predictors of secondary school completion among refugee youth 8 to 9 years after resettlement in Melbourne, Australia. *Journal of International Migration and Integration, 18*(3), 791–805.

Davidson, S. (2017). *Trauma-informed practices for postsecondary education: A guide.* Education Northwest.

De Nobile, J., Lyons, G., & Arthur-Kelly, M. (2021). *Positive learning environments: Creating and maintaining productive classrooms* (2nd ed.). Cengage AU.

Department of Education Employment and Training. (1990). *A fair chance for all.* AGPS.

Drane, C. F., Vernon, L., & O'Shea, S. (2021). Vulnerable learners in the age of COVID-19: A scoping review. *The Australian Educational Researcher, 48*(4), 585–604.

DuPaul, G. J., Weyandt, L. L., & Janusis, G. M. (2011). ADHD in the classroom: Effective intervention strategies. *Theory into Practice, 50*(1), 35–42.

García-González, E., Jiménez-Fontana, R., & Azcárate, P. (2020). Education for sustainability and the Sustainable Development Goals: Pre-service teachers' perceptions and knowledge. *Sustainability, 12*(18), 7741.

Ginott, H. (1972). *Teacher and child: A book for parents and teachers.* Macmillan.

Gochenour, B., & Poskey, G. A. (2017). Determining the effectiveness of alternative seating systems for students with attention difficulties: A systematic review. *Journal of Occupational Therapy, Schools, & Early Intervention, 10*(3), 284–299.

Golann, J. W., & Torres, A. C. (2020). Do no-excuses disciplinary practices promote success? *Journal of Urban Affairs, 42*(4), 617–633.

Goulet, M., Archambault, I., Janosz, M., & Christenson, S. L. (2018). Evaluating the implementation of check & connect in various school settings: Is intervention fidelity necessarily associated with positive outcomes? *Evaluation and Program Planning, 68*, 34–46.

Graham, L., McCarthy, T., Killingly, C., Tancredi, H., & Poed, S. (2020). *Inquiry into suspension, exclusion and expulsion processes in South Australian Government schools.* QUT, The Centre for Inclusive Education. https://eprints.qut.edu.au/206791/1/Inquiry_into_Suspension_Exclusion_and_Expulsion_Processes_in_South_Australian_Government_Schools.pdf

Grasley-Boy, N. M., Gage, N. A., & Lombardo, M. (2019). Effect of SWPBIS on disciplinary exclusions for students with and without disabilities. *Exceptional Children, 86*(1), 25–39.

Hobbes, C., Paulsen, D., & Thomas, J. (2019). *Trauma-informed practice for pre-service teachers.* Oxford University Press.

Kent, K. M., Pelham, W. E., Molina, B. S., Sibley, M. H., Waschbusch, D. A., Yu …, J., & Karch, K. M. (2011). The academic experience of male high school students with ADHD. *Journal of Abnormal Child Psychology, 39*(3), 451–462.

Korff, J. (2022). *Barriers to aboriginal education.* https://www.creativespirits.info/aboriginalculture/education/barriers-to-aboriginal-education

Kumar, R., Zusho, A., & Bondie, R. (2018). Weaving cultural relevance and achievement motivation into inclusive classroom cultures. *Educational Psychologist, 53*(2), 78–96.

McAllister, K. (2010, July 7–9). The ASD friendly classroom—Design complexity, challenge and characteristics. In D. Durling, R. Bousbaci, L. Chen, P. Gauthier, T. Poldma, S. Roworth-Stokes, & E. Stolterman (Eds.), *Design and complexity—DRS International Conference 2010*, Montreal, Canada. https://dl.designresearchsociety.org/drs-conference-papers/drs2010/researchpapers/84

McMahon, B., & Zyngier, D. (2009). Student engagement: Contested concepts in two continents. *Research in Comparative and International Education, 4*(2), 164–181. https://doi.org/10.2304/rcie.2009.4.2.163

Miller, E., Ziaian, T., & Esterman, A. (2018). Australian school practices and the education experiences of students with a refugee background: A review of the literature. *International Journal of Inclusive Education, 22*(4), 339–359.

Mishna, F., Sanders, J. E., McNeil, S., Fearing, G., & Kalenteridis, K. (2020). "If somebody is different": A critical analysis of parent, teacher and student perspectives on bullying and cyberbullying. *Children and Youth Services Review, 118*, 105366.

Moffat, A. K., Redmond, G., & Raghavendra, P. (2019). The impact of social network characteristics and gender on covert bullying in Australian students with disability in the middle years. *Journal of School Violence, 18*(4), 613–629.

Nagro, S. A., Fraser, D. W., & Hooks, S. D. (2019). Lesson planning with engagement in mind: Proactive classroom management strategies for curriculum instruction. *Intervention in School and Clinic, 54*(3), 131–140.

New South Wales Government. (2021). *Effective strategies for supporting students from low socio-economic backgrounds.* https://education.nsw.gov.au/teaching-and-learning/school-exc ellence-and-accountability/school-excellence-in-action/effective-improvement-measures-and-strategies/excellent-for-students-from-low-socio-economic-backgrounds/effective-strategies-for-supporting-students-from-low-socio-econ#Effective0

Odell, V., Molthan-Hill, P., Martin, S., & Sterling, S. (2020). Transformative education to address all sustainable development goals. In W. Leal Filho (Ed.), *Quality education* (pp. 905–916). Springer Nature Switzerland.

Orthner, D. K., Jones-Sanpei, H., Akos, P., & Rose, R. A. (2013). Improving middle school student engagement through career-relevant instruction in the core curriculum. *The Journal of Educational Research, 106*(1), 27–38.

Peacock, D. (2015). Widening participation as behaviour management: An ethnography of student equity outreach in one Australian low SES school. *International Studies in Widening Participation, 2*(2), 20–28.

Peralta, L. R., Mihrshahi, S., Bellew, B., Reece, L. J., & Hardy, L. L. (2019). Influence of school-level socioeconomic status on children's physical activity, fitness, and fundamental movement skill levels. *Journal of School Health, 89*(6), 460–467.

Purvis, K. B., Cross, D. R., Dansereau, D. F., & Parris, S. R. (2013). Trust-based relational intervention (TBRI): A systemic approach to complex developmental trauma. *Child & Youth Services, 34*(4), 360–386.

Reichenberg, O. (2018). Student behavioural disengagement, peer encouragement and the school curriculum: A mechanism approach. *Educational Studies, 44*(2), 147–166.

Rigby, K. (2012). Bullying in schools: Addressing desires, not only behaviours. *Educational Psychology Review, 24*(2), 339–348.

Rigby, K. (2017). Bullying in Australian schools: The perceptions of victims and other students. *Social Psychology of Education, 20*(3), 589–600.

Rogers, B. (2015). *Classroom behaviour: A practical guide to effective teaching, behaviour management and colleague support.* Sage.

Sabic-El-Rayess, A., Mansur, N. N., Batkhuyag, B., & Otgonlkhagva, S. (2019). School uniform policy's adverse impact on equity and access to schooling. *Compare: A Journal of Comparative and International Education, 50*(8), 1122–1139.

Schultz, J. J. (2011). *Nowhere to hide: Why kids with ADHD and LD hate school and what we can do about it?* Wiley.

Schwab, R. (2018). *Why only one in three? The complex reasons for low indigenous school retention.* Centre for Aboriginal Economic Policy Research.

Schwartz-Henderson, I. (2016). Trauma-informed teaching and design strategies: A new paradigm. *Exchange.* http://www.brightspaces.org/wp-content/uploads/Trauma-informed-Tea ching-and-Design-Strategies-Ileen-Henderson.pdf

Skiba, R. J., Chung, C.-G., Trachok, M., Baker, T. L., Sheya, A., & Hughes, R. L. (2014). Parsing disciplinary disproportionality: Contributions of infraction, student, and school characteristics to out-of-school suspension and expulsion. *American Educational Research Journal, 51*(4), 640–670.

Skiba, R. J., & Losen, D. J. (2016). From reaction to prevention: Turning the page on school discipline. *American Educator, 39*(4), 4.

Solomon, E. P., & Heide, K. M. (2005). The biology of trauma: Implications for treatment. *Journal of Interpersonal Violence, 20*(1), 51–60.

Spencer, J. L., Maxwell, D. N., Erickson, K. R. S., Wall, D., Nicholas-Figueroa, L., Pratt, K. A., & Shultz, G. V. (2022). Cultural relevance in chemistry education: Snow chemistry and the Iñupiaq community. *Journal of Chemical Education, 99*(1), 363–372. https://doi.org/10.1021/acs.jchemed.1c00480

Symes, W., & Humphrey, N. (2010). Peer-group indicators of social inclusion among pupils with autistic spectrum disorders (ASD) in mainstream secondary schools: A comparative study. *School Psychology International, 31*(5), 478–494.

The Law Library. (2018). *Australian Education Act 2013 (Australia)*. CreateSpace Independent Publishing Platform.

Thomas, J. (2019). *Managing behaviour or promoting engagement?* Oxford University Press.

Thomas, J., & Rayner, C. (2021). A preliminary study of students with disabilities in 'flexi' education settings. *Australasian Journal of Special and Inclusive Education, 45*(1), 76–89.

Thomson, S. (2017). The effects of inequity in Australian schools. *Professional Learning, 12*(1), 29–39.

United Nations Department of Economic and Social Affairs. (2022a). *Expert group meeting on SDG 4 (Quality education) and its interlinkages with other SDGs*. https://sdgs.un.org/events/expert-group-meeting-sdg-4-quality-education-and-its-interlinkages-other-sdgs-46165

United Nations Department of Economic and Social Affairs. (2022b). *Goal 4 ensure inclusive and equitable quality education and promote lifelong learning opportunities for all—Targets and indicators*. https://sdgs.un.org/goals/goal4

United Nations Department of Economic and Social Affairs. (2022c). *Goal 4 overview*. https://sdgs.un.org/goals/goal4

Walker, S., & Graham, L. (2021). At risk students and teacher–student relationships: Student characteristics, attitudes to school and classroom climate. *International Journal of Inclusive Education, 25*(8), 896–913.

Way, S. M. (2011). School discipline and disruptive classroom behavior: The moderating effects of student perceptions. *The Sociological Quarterly, 52*(3), 346–375.

Chapter 23
Realising the Sustainable Development Goals to Enrich Teacher Education for Children, Young People, and Lifelong Learners with Disabilities

Judith Hudson

23.1 Introduction

Equity across societies is a utopian notion (Anthony, 2017; Davis, 2017). Its principles at the global level should be embedded in the education systems of signatories to the United Nations (UN) 17 Sustainable Development Goals (SDGs) of the 2030 Agenda for Sustainable Development (UN, n.d.). Although the term disability may not be directly cited in the goals, realising, and advancing efforts to remove barriers and empower persons with a disability underpins the aims of several goals, and is referenced in several parts (UN, 2018). Specifically, it is referenced in those parts of the goals relating to growth and employment, equality, accessibility of homes and settlements, and the focus of this chapter—disability, and inclusive quality education for all, including those engaged in teacher training and teacher education institutions. These all offer relevance to ensure the inclusion and development for persons with disabilities.

For the purposes of this chapter, "persons with disability" refers to those with physical, psychosocial, intellectual, or sensory impairments, who are presented with numerous barriers in society, and that will often impact on general health, mental health, and wellbeing (SDG3). The inherent philosophies of the social model of disability (Shakespeare, 2010) are described here, and for context, the former widely used medicalised model of disability (Triano, 2000), that once prevailed, is also discussed. So too is the 2030 Agenda for Sustainable Development that adopted the comprehensive, far-reaching, and people-centred set of universal and transformative 17 SDGs and targets (UN, 2018).

J. Hudson (✉)
School of Education, College of Arts, Law and Education, University of Tasmania, Hobart, TAS, Australia
e-mail: dr.jhudson@btinternet.com

© The Author(s), under exclusive license to Springer Nature Singapore Pte Ltd. 2023   427
K. Beasy et al. (eds.), *Education and the UN Sustainable Development Goals*, Education for Sustainability 7,
https://doi.org/10.1007/978-981-99-3802-5_23

It has been reported that worldwide, there are nearly 240 million children with disabilities (United Nations Children's Fund [UNICEF], 2021), and disability experience varies greatly and will change over the life span of the individual. Outcomes will depend on the type of disability, on where the child, young person, or adult lives, and on what services and support systems they have available to them that they can access.

In this chapter, I focus on education and consider pre-service teacher education, thinking through how this could impact positively on the life opportunities for children and young people with a disability. To maximise the impact of SDGs, and break down barriers that can, and do, impact on those with disability, SDG4 "quality, inclusive education" must be an integral part of any sustainable development plan. Disability and poverty (SDG1) are closely linked, and rates of poverty are higher than for people without disability (Hughes, 2013). Globally, people with disabilities have poorer health outcomes (SDG3) (World Health Organization [WHO], 2021); lower educational achievements (SDG10) (Ainscow & Miles, 2008; Singal, 2017), and may fall into juvenile delinquency and a criminal life trajectory (Grigorenko et al., 2019; McCarthy et al., 2015). In terms of education, many disabilities can, and do, impact on learning, and I briefly introduce disabilities that teachers are highly likely to face daily in the classroom. This issue is briefly elaborated on with clarification of the terms "high frequency" and "low frequency" learning disabilities (Hudson, 2014). Those with disabilities have fewer options in employment (SDG8) (Adams & Oldfield, 2012); have less opportunity for economic participation (SDG10) (Hughes, 2013); are more likely to experience poverty, disadvantage, and human rights violations compared with those without disability (Frohmader, 2019).

Ensuring children, young people, and lifelong learners have equal and unrestricted access to education is indeed an enormous challenge, but education is paramount, and significant, in effecting change. It has the power to lift people out of chronic poverty (Hanushek & Woessmann, 2021), and quality "inclusive" education allows for all children and young people with disabilities to be educated so they can achieve their academic, creative, and social potential. Ultimately, this can lead to improved learning outcomes, improved employment, improved income opportunity, and better health outcomes.

Relating to the SDGs, at the macro level, learning disabilities impact across genders (SDG5), socioeconomic status (SDG8), and race and ethnicity (SDG10). Providing quality "inclusive" education (SDG4), is the primary device through which to effect positive change, not only for individuals, but for their families and their wider communities. The links to other SDGs are drawn into the discussion here that examines how disability legislation has been interpreted and needs-led action adopted. Through the chapter, I identify connective routes and potential partnerships that might transform not only the education experience, but also the lives of those children, young people, and lifelong learners with disability.

For those countries who are signatories to the Convention on the Rights of Persons with Disabilities (CRPD) (Centre for Studies on Inclusive Education [CSIE], 2021), this has introduced a new right in international human rights law—the right to "inclusive" education. This is not always seen as the best option for all children with disability, however, and the issue is often contentious and politically challenged. A valid examination of the concept of inclusive education is offered elsewhere (de Beco, 2014) with questioning of whether special schools should still be available as the school of choice for those who want or require them. I return to this further when discussing what the "inclusive" right actually stands for and/or what segregated education entails. First, I consider interpretations of disability and their implications in policy and practice.

23.2 The Social Model of Disability

The Social Model of Disability as a political ideology has evolved over the past four decades. It acknowledges that barriers operating in society disable people who have disabling impairments, and, that such barriers exclude and discriminate against them. This model replaced the "medical" model of disability universally used previously. The "medical" model sees "disability" as synonymous with illness, sickness, and suffering that should be cured or remediated, and sees individuals as being disabled by their impairments or differences (Wendell, 2017). The social model has moved away from blaming factors within the disabled individual and makes explicit that it is barriers in the social setting wherein a person is placed that disadvantage disabled people.

Broadly speaking, these barriers can be the physical environment, attitudes, expressive language used, and the ways in which people communicate through policies, organisations, and institutions. In other words, barriers include anything that discriminates against those with disability that may be disadvantaging them, and/ or barring them from full access and effective participation in society. The concept of "ableism" (Lewis, 2006) is also relevant here. Ableism refers to discrimination and social prejudice against people with disabilities that are perceived as disabled, or characterised and defined by their disability. Ableism can manifest as a lack of compliance with disability rights laws, using discriminatory language, or segregating adults or children with disabilities in institutions, away from those who are "able" bodied. Equally, discrimination can be in the physical environment, taking the form of designing buildings that are inaccessible, failure to provide accessibility routes or support to access information; and failure to make reasonable adjustments, or accommodate the needs of the persons with a disability. Many children and young people face multiple barriers to access education, including school infrastructure, the use of materials that have not been adapted to accommodate their disability, and a lack of specialism and/or disability awareness in the teaching workforce.

I use the internationally adopted understanding of the social model of disability in this chapter; however, I acknowledge that it is critiqued as being a model that implicitly aims for a "barrier free utopia (…) impossible to realise" (Shakespeare, 2017, p. 195). Thus, disability can be considered as a cultural and historical phenomenon, that makes the distinction between disabled people as an oppressed group and, as Shakespeare suggests, non-disabled people as the oppressors who can both cause, and contribute, towards that oppression. While the social model has dominated internationally for several decades, as with all conceptual models, rarely will one provide a full description.

It could be argued that conceptualising disability as unilaterally socially caused, the social model presents a partial but, to a certain extent, flawed understanding of the relationship between impairment, disability, and society. Although I concur that it has limitations, this model was never designed to be a perfect theory of disability. Rather, it seeks to explain the experience of the disabled within our communities, and more importantly, creates a tool for social change. Thus, for the purposes here, fundamental philosophical underpinnings of the social model of disability assume that the barriers that operate in society exclude and/or discriminate against disabled people with physical, or mental impairment. If we are to reduce inequalities then, encumbering barriers need to be identified and circumvented. So too, do the tensions that exist between surface compliance and meaningful engagement, and the enactment of policies and advocacy for change.

23.3 Educational Reform for People with Disability

Mandated conditions affecting education reform, and that embrace neurodiversity and the idea of inclusivity in each jurisdiction are identified. The term "neurodiversity" refers to the diversity of all people, a concept developed in the 1990s by Australian sociologist Judy Singer (2016) to promote equality and inclusion across all neurological differences, and often contextualises neurological and developmental conditions such as Autism, Attention Deficit Hyperactivity Disorder (ADHD), and dyslexia among others. Those who advocate for neurodiversity, encourage inclusive, non-judgemental language, and view disabilities as differences, not deficits (Chapman & Carel, 2022).

Neurodevelopmental difficulties, both congenital (present from birth), or acquired (through trauma, disease, or injury), frequently create functional limitations that manifest as learning disabilities, and their prevalence has been reported as up to 15% of populations in global north countries (Ogundele & Morton, 2022). This includes, for example, neurodevelopmental, emotional, behavioural, and intellectual disorders, the prognosis of which, in some cases, will depend very much on early identification, quality intervention teaching, and additional learning support.

In what follows, I argue that quality education, which is fundamentally inclusive, can only be achieved if teachers thoroughly understand the underlying concepts of inclusive education, are informed, know what they are looking for, and know what they can do about it. In an ideal world training about neurodiversity and disabilities should be undertaken prior to entering the teaching workforce. Here, universities have a role to play, and thus contribute towards enriching the quality of education (SDG4); the reduction of inequalities (SDG10), and the building of strong institutions (SDG16). Teachers with limited, or no, knowledge and understanding of learning disabilities, are profoundly constrained in their professional practice, and without appropriate professional training, the learning outcomes for their students can have lifelong repercussions.

23.4 Policies and Policy Enactment

When the global context of activated charters and treaties are examined, it is possible to trace their influence on national policies and their enactment. This then becomes a window on the progressing of the human rights of persons with disabilities in their developmental and life setting. The CRPD, with 184 ratifications and 164 signatories, offers a comprehensive international treaty of a legally binding nature. The Optional Protocol is an additional agreement that establishes a mechanism for complaints for when individual disabled people make allegations of discrimination, or regarding the denial of their rights under the Convention (UN, 2006).

Signing this treaty signifies the intention to comply with the terms of the treaty, but an expression of intent is, by itself, not binding, and at this stage, the rhetoric does not have to become a reality. Once the treaty has been signed, its conditions need to be enacted through administration within each nation and across states, and through its own distinctive national procedures. For example, this will require gaining the respective country's parliamentary approval, and seeking approval for the adoption of the treaty. Once gained, all other parties in the treaty are notified, and this ratification means the treaty is now officially sanctioned by that state, territory, or nation. At this stage, the rhetoric does become reality, and presents a binding legal instrument, which includes a specific emphasis on the right to education for those with disability. The CRPD comprises 50 such Articles that interact with each other. Under Article 4, the stated obligations require each country to develop, and carry out, policies and laws, and effect administrative changes. The aims of the obligations are to secure the rights as recognised in the Convention, and abolish laws, regulations, customs, and practices that constitute discrimination.

The fundamental rights for all people with disabilities for access to education and employment are regulated in two defining Articles of the CRPD: Article 24 and Article 27. Article 24 covers education and requires a commitment to recognise the right of persons with disabilities to education, without discrimination and with equal opportunity, in an inclusive education system. This is opposed to segregation, or integration where children with disability must fit into a largely unchanged mainstream school environment. The process must therefore involve "…a transformative system change process. This process entails changing the structure, organisation, learning, curriculum, and assessment of the education system to accommodate the diversity of pupils" (Farkas, 2014).

This process has marked a paradigm shift from the deficit/medical model of disability described earlier, to one of social/human rights, which underlies the UN CRPD. Article 8 also applies and underpins inclusive education policies that can enable children with disabilities to attend school, keeping them in school, and supporting them to become successful, both socially and academically. As such, this

Article aims to foster and respect the rights of persons with disabilities, to reduce inequalities in schools and institutions across all levels of the education system. These aims underpin directly, and embrace, the aims of the SDGs of quality education (SDG4) and reduced inequalities (SDG10).

In each country, administration and due process of incorporating the Articles in both the CRPD and the Universal Declaration of Human Rights (UDHR) (UN, 1948) differ quite broadly, as do the eventual outcomes in each of the jurisdictions within countries. To achieve the rights as set out in such Conventions as the CRPD, requires effective enactment management. How the implementation and monitoring of treaty obligations vary is examined here through the lens of Australia's enactment systems. The wealth of information that stems from the UN Conventions, treaties, and initiatives, form a huge corpus of documentation, reports, directives, instructions, and regulations. An exposition for Australia presents examples of due process, to demonstrate how their response is translated into practice.

The CRPD (CSIE, 2021) and the 17 UN SDGs (UN, n.d.) were adopted by Australia, alongside major UN Human Rights treaties including, the *International Covenant on Economic, Social and Cultural Rights* (UN, 1966b) ratified in October 1975 (Australian Government Department of Foreign Affairs & Trade [DFAT], 2009), the *International Covenant on Civil and Political Rights* (UN, 1966a) ratified in 1980 and the CRPD, ratified in 2008, thus creating obligations in accordance with international human rights values.

To ensure that agreements are being followed in accordance with all member states, a special committee on the rights of disabled people is elected and based at the UN. Each member country is required to submit a written report to the UN every four years and the committee can ask for more information, give advice about issues, and make all reports available to all member countries, as well as give open access to members of the public. The committee, in response, has a duty to write a report every two years and submit this to the General Assembly and Economic and Social Council. The Equality and Human Rights Commission (EHRC) publishes the UN findings and the UN committee examines each report (Adams & Oldfield, 2012).

The committee then addresses its concerns and recommendations, to the "State Party" which refers to any nation that has ratified, accepted, or is a signatory to United Nation's Convention on Treaties (UN, 2022). The UN committee of scrutinisers also responds with recommendations. Evidence from the outcome of reported assessments, and the degree or "level of compliance" to obligations, is also given (McCallum, 2020). This due process aims to substantiate the progress or otherwise, that has occurred since the last review cycle. The range and internationality of all member nations are enormous, and no claims are made here that the impact of directives on the education system is in any way typical of the enactment of policy, or education reforms, of all member nations.

23.5 The Australian Case

Ratification, accession, and succession to the CRPD were completed by Australia in July 2008. Thus, Australia has made a commitment to protect and promote the rights of those citizens who have disabilities. Administration and implementation of the CRPD across Australia is organised through comparable geophysical and jurisdictional organisation features. Jurisdiction in Australia is given to the six states: New South Wales, Queensland, Victoria, Western Australia, South Australia, and Tasmania; and two territories: Northern Territory (NT), and Australian Capital Territory (ACT). Each interprets the demands of the Convention for their administration and action but do so under the umbrella authority of the Federal Government.

A mechanism is in place that allows those Australians with disabilities, through their representative bodies, associations, and/or not-for-profit support organisations, to report to the UN committee that reviews Australia's performance. Representation from disability groups is strongly encouraged and aims to guide and strengthen engagement and representation of those with disabilities, with policy makers. This report is known as a civil society Shadow Report, and reports on what has been achieved in terms of Australia's compliance with its obligations under the convention. First reviewed in September 2013, the most recent review and report in 2019 (Frohmader, 2019) was compiled with an input from Australian Disabled People's Organisations (DPOs) and disability advocacy organisations. This report noted positive reforms had been initiated since the first review, but also found that people in Australia with disability still experienced poverty, disadvantage, and violations of human rights. This was reported as being particularly so among Indigenous disabled people, and a further failing was also expressed in "the over-representation of people with disability in the criminal justice system", and a call to "end the unwarranted use of prisons for the management of un-convicted people with disability" (Frohmader, 2019, p. 10).

Shadow reporting is an important conduit for advocacy and through which Non-Government Organisations (NGOs) can give those with disability a voice. The shadow report channels supplementary, or alternative information, to that of the government report required under Human Rights treaty obligations. NGO advocacy then can present opinions of civil society on government action, or inaction, and present them to the UN Committees. This due process aims to help reduce inequalities (SDG10) as well as raising public awareness of disability through advocacy and education (SDG4). The route can also support the development of peace, justice, and strong institutions (SDG16), and through education, promote peaceful and inclusive societies and develop stronger partnerships (SDG17), particularly with disability community members. Through these channels, NGOs shadow the government report and provide an analysis, and often a critique, of the State report and that is usually published after, or in response to, the government report.

One example of improved initiatives at the Federal level of government in Australia, is the National Disability Insurance Scheme (NDIS), formed through legislated practice at the Federal Government level, and "rolled out" nationally, to meet the needs of the nation's disabled citizens (Australian Government, 2013). This can fund support within the education system, providing physical and practical initiatives that can promote the mainstreaming of disability and the implementation of the SDGs. Delivered in each state or territory through the National Disability Insurance Agency (Australian Government, 2013), this then engages with the disability community to make decisions about eligibility to access funds to support individual need. This puts a finite level of resource allocation on the table, awarded to the individual according to specified criteria. These resources can include support for schools to make "reasonable adjustments" and accommodate students with disability within the mainstream or regular classroom. "Reasonable adjustments" can balance everyone's need, the student with disability, other students, the staff, and the education provider. It can involve a physical adjustment such as providing ramps for a wheelchair user, or a human resource, such as providing a teacher aide to support a student in class. In short, any adjustment made to comply with the obligations under the Disability Standards for Education (DSE) can be considered a reasonable adjustment.

To raise the quality of education standards, the Australian government developed a joint project—the Rights, Education, and Protection (REAP) project, with UNICEF (2010). This aimed to enhance education and child protection systems, and to ensure sensitive, responsive, and inclusive education of children with disability, not only in Australia, but also as a joint nations project, globally. The extensive literature review undertaken by the study identified many issues worldwide, but generally found that children who identified as the most disadvantaged, were children with a disability, and who were among the most stigmatised, excluded, and marginalised group within community, school, and wider society. A significant outcome from this joint venture, however, was the provision of strengthened guidance to all countries, including Australia. This led to the development and implementation of new programmes and responses regarding the inclusion of those students with disability, giving all children an inclusive mainstream education (UNICEF, 2010).

In Australia's education system, children and young people with disability have the right to go into a mainstream school, under the government or state system, independent or Catholic school, regardless of their disability. Alternatively, a child may be eligible for a special school, depending on the nature of need, services, or level of support required. Under the Disability Discrimination Act (DDA) (Australian Human Rights Commission [AHRC], 2015) schools are required to eliminate discrimination against those with disability in terms of access to premises, services, and education. Formulated under section 31 of the DDA is the DSE (Australian Government Department of Education [AGDE], 2005). This sets out the lawful rights of the student with disability and clarifies the obligations of education or training providers and teachers. It is unlawful to contravene a disability standard and it is also a code of conduct by which teachers must have a professional regard. Although the main aim of the DSE is to make clear the rights of students with disability and determine the same educational opportunities and choices as all other students (Section 32), it also makes clear that education providers must consult, make reasonable adjustments, and eliminate harassment and victimisation. Importantly too, the standards cover the lifetime of a person's engagement with the schooling system, including further education, a training course, or higher education.

Nuanced here however, is a caveat that under both the DDA Act (Section 11) and the DSE, namely that schools, organisations, or institutions are not required to make a reasonable adjustment if the making of the adjustment would impose "unjustifiable hardship" on another person. The DSE caveat states "it is not unlawful for an education provider to fail to comply with a requirement of the standards, if compliance would impose unjustifiable hardship on the provider" (AGDE, 2005, Subsection 10.2). In determining "unjustifiable hardship", all circumstances of the specific case need to be considered and the burden of proof falls with the institution to demonstrate the unjustifiable hardship. If the institution is unable to make reasonable adjustment because unjustifiable hardship has been proved (e.g., insufficient financial funds, unable to make necessary adaptations to building, unable to fund additional human resources), it must ensure that students are made aware of the reasons and are helped to find an alternative provider and/or course that will meet their needs and capabilities. It should be noted here that each case is tried with its own particular facts. There are no norms.

All schools in Australia are required to collect data annually in a Nationally Consistent Collection of Data (NCCD) about students who are receiving reasonable adjustments, and there is an assumption made that data are collected in a reliable and consistent way across Australia (https://www.nccd.edu.au/). All schools and approved authorities in Australia participate in the NCCD annually, and it applies across all educational settings and contexts, including mainstream schools and classes, special schools, and special classes that cater for students with needs related to their disability. These data enable schools, education authorities, and governments to understand better, the needs of students with a disability, and how best they can be supported at school. The data are used as an evidence base, to give teachers, schools, and parents, information about students with disability and the level, and nature, of educational adjustment being provided. Data inform policy development and capture the work of schools under the obligations of the DDA and DSE. Students affected by trauma and students with disability undertaking learning from home are also included in the data collection. This collection of data is a major mandate for schools to undertake, but since its mandatory inception in 2018, for many children and young people in Australia, it has recognised their disabilities formally for the first time. In addition, law also documents the provision of resources and support strategies offered by the school. Schools Census Day is the date on which schools identify the student population to count for the Census, which includes the NCCD. Unless otherwise determined by a state's Minister of Education, a school's Census Day is the first Friday in August each year. Also important is the anonymity in data that must not disclose details of any individual student.

In Australia, laws exist to raise awareness and promote equity in education and employment that safeguard disability legislative obligations. However, at best, disability laws only serve as prohibiting active discrimination. Anti-discrimination legislation can offer some redress for anyone that believes they have been discriminated against in their education, but with insufficient clarity around the term "learning disability", or, even establishing that the nature of an individual's difficulties concurs with WHO terminology of a "disability" (Woods et al., 2005), action against a discriminator, has rarely been demonstrated through Australian law. Living with a disability in Australia is frequently challenging, and each year, the AHRC receives more complaints about disability discrimination than any other form of discrimination (44% of all complaints) (Australian Institute of Health and Welfare [AIHW], 2020).

23.6   Teacher Education, Learning Disabilities, and Realising Sustainable Development Goals

A snapshot of Australian surveys has indicated that 10–16% of students are perceived by their teachers to have learning difficulties, with an estimated 4% of children recognised as learning disabled (AIHW, 2020). Without scrutiny of type, nature, and differences in diagnosis and assessment, the figures given indicate the likelihood that teachers will meet many children with learning needs and/or a learning disability. In terms of education, many disabilities impact on learning, with some disabilities regarded as "high frequency" or highly likely to present daily in the mainstream classroom. Other learning disabilities are "low frequency" or less common but more complex (Hudson, 2014). High frequency disabilities are those most commonly occurring, such as Dyslexia, Dyspraxia, or ADHD, and can present the teacher with challenges, if not challenges to a whole school community. At the very least, awareness training of the high frequency of learning difficulties described here should be a part of the initial teacher education curriculum, otherwise it can become stressful for mainstream teachers to know how to best serve such learners (Forlin, 2010; Rouse, 2008).

Education as a right for all children has been enshrined in international instruments since the UDHR (UN, 1948), but that "right" does not imply inclusion. The right to inclusive education has been established as a legal right and has evolved through the UN CRPD and the SDGs. Realising sustainable goals through teacher education and training requires a whole-of-community response to inclusion for people with disability. Educating teachers for meeting quality inclusive education, however, must first make very clear what the concept of inclusion means. Placement in the mainstream school is increasingly referred to by terms such as "special needs", "integration", or even attendance in a mainstream school, but taught within a special unit, which is not the same thing as "inclusive education". Integration does not support a whole school community ethos of inclusivity. The key issue concerning the definition of inclusive education is based on rights and the social model of disability discussed earlier in this chapter. It involves a process of changing the school, what is taught, how it is taught, and how it is assessed. Primarily, the system needs to be adapted to the child, and *not* the child to the system, and to challenge the status quo, which is imperative if society overall is to become inclusive and benefit all of its citizens. An inclusive education system identifies barriers, be they physical, social, or academic, finds effective solutions by consultation with expertise, and is underpinned by key values, beliefs, and principles of inclusion within the community wherein a school is situated.

Inclusive education also requires not only teaching techniques, or appropriate methods, that support learning for the individual. Rather, it is a wider context of disability awareness, and the challenges and opportunities to address the needs of all children. Paucity of knowledge about disability must be addressed. Teacher education pre-service courses frequently are offered as an "elective" component, offering modules concerned with identifying and meeting specific needs, and as a part of a "pick and mix" option. Sadly, too, the pedagogy and practical teaching methods, skills, and knowledge necessary to implement inclusive education in the classroom, are not always taught to all prospective new entrants to the teaching workforce. If we are to achieve aims within quality inclusive education that will "ensure inclusive and equitable quality education and promote lifelong learning opportunities for all" (SDG4), I raise the question, "how are teachers being educated to achieve the general commitment to inclusion?" Models of teacher education need to be examined, as does course delivery, to ensure accordance with the UN CRPD Article 24(4):

> ...Parties shall take appropriate measures to employ teachers, including teachers with disabilities, who are qualified in sign language and/or Braille, and to train professionals and staff who work at all levels of education. Such training shall incorporate disability awareness and the use of appropriate augmentative and alternative modes, means and formats of communication, educational techniques, and materials to support persons with disabilities. (UN, 2019)

There is evidence that by providing all teachers with some grounding in disability studies, and with the cooperation and involvement of DPOs, teachers can develop strong empathy, and it opens discussion and debate around disability that serves an instructive function (Rieser, 2013). Research from around the world has also shown that if teachers are educated to include children with disabilities, then the level and standard of learning for children with disabilities rises, but significantly, so do the learning levels of their non-disabled peers (MacArthur, 2009). The development of schools for all children, where the learning and participation of all children are valued, not only supports disability equity within the school community but also makes sound economic and social sense.

Although there may be support for inclusion at a philosophical level, there are also concerns that the policy of inclusion is difficult to implement because teachers are not sufficiently well prepared and supported to work in inclusive ways (Rouse, 2008). Educating teachers about inclusive education requires different skills from those required for classroom teaching, and it may be difficult to find teachers with the knowledge to teach about inclusion, because many do not have experience or preparation themselves (UNICEF, 2014). Yet, research suggests that teachers are stressed, by the issues around the behaviour of the child with moderate or severe intellectual disability in the regular mainstream classroom, but not as much by practices of inclusion (Forlin, 2010). To advance inclusive education there is a need to educate and prepare teachers and ensure that those institutions who educate teachers, will train a workforce with preparedness about diverse disabilities, and ability to implement effective practices required for inclusive education (Zagona et al., 2017).

If there is to be a shift towards an inclusive and transformative pedagogy, one of the first challenges will be to address the nuances of the concept of "inclusion", with teacher understanding often incongruent with what "inclusive education" entails. Teachers have been found to have a pre-occupation with children with special learning needs as a group that requires a special or different way of teaching, rather than focusing on overcoming the barriers to learning for the individual and including full participation within the whole-school community (Stubbs, 2008). As Stubbs recognised, "creating ownership and changing attitudes is the life blood of an inclusive education programme" (p. 76), but it is important to understand also how to combat the "cycle of oppression" (Shakespeare, 2017, p. 12), oppression that Tom Shakespeare recognised as being dealt by non-disabled people. Thus, the non-disabled people were emerging as the "oppressors" of the disabled.

23.7   To Conclude

Models of how education can be transformed is a focus for the UN, which seeks to drive political ambition and action, to transform universal education, to share good practice, and to revitalise national and global efforts to achieve SDG4. Teacher educators and the institutions wherein they are situated, need to base course content on evidence-based best practice regarding education for students with disability.

As a result of the REAP initiative (UNICEF, 2014), UNICEF agreed to develop guidance, grounded in evidence-based theories and existing knowledge, for teachers' education about disabled children. This was to cover: initial teacher training, in-service training and professional development for current serving teachers, advanced and leadership training for principals and school leaders, as well as for the college and university teacher trainers themselves (Rieser, 2013). Further, a series of five advocacy guides *Promoting Inclusive Teacher Education* (Kaplan & Lewis, 2013, p. 4) challenge barriers to inclusive education, for policymakers, teachers, and trainee teachers. However, unless institutions responsible for delivering teacher education courses also adopt the principles of quality inclusive education, incorporate these principles in the degrees that teachers receive, and examine the content of courses and their teaching syllabi, while furthermore ensuring the principles are addressed *before* validating *all* teaching qualifications, there will be a conflict, or a disconnect, between policy enactment and practice.

I close this chapter with an all-embracing statement concerning the due process of inclusive education.

> Inclusive education is a dynamic process of change and improvement through which the education system, and individual schools, school managers and teachers address the education needs of *all* (italics added) children without discrimination. It is an ongoing process, not a fixed model or goal that can be achieved by following specific instructions over a predetermined period of time. (Kaplan & Lewis, 2013, p. 4)

References

Adams, L., & Oldfield, K. (2012). *Equality and human rights commission research report 77 opening up work: The views of disabled people and people with long-term health conditions.* https://www.equalityhumanrights.com/sites/default/files/research_report_77_opening_up_work.pdf

Ainscow, M., & Miles, S. (2008). Making education for all inclusive: Where next? *Prospects, 38*(1), 15–34. https://doi.org/10.1007/s11125-008-9055-0

Anthony, C. (2017). *The idea of a realistic Utopia* [Doctoral dissertation, University of Pennsylvania]. https://repository.upenn.edu/cgi/viewcontent.cgi?article=3954&context=edissertations

Australian Government. (2013). *National disability insurance scheme act 2013 (Amended July 2018).* https://www.legislation.gov.au/Details/C2018C00276

Australian Government Department of Education. (2005). *Disability standards for education 2005 plus guidance notes.* https://www.education.gov.au/swd/resources/disability-standards-education-2005-plus-guidance-notes

Australian Government Department of Foreign Affairs & Trade. (2009). *International covenant on civil and political rights.* https://www.info.dfat.gov.au/Info/Treaties/treaties.nsf/AllDocIDs/CFB1E23A1297FFE8CA256B4C000C26B4

Australian Human Rights Commission. (2015). *Disability discrimination.* https://humanrights.gov.au/our-work/employers/disability-discrimination

Australian Institute of Health and Welfare. (2020). *People with disability in Australia.* https://www.aihw.gov.au/getmedia/7005c061-1c6e-490c-90c2-f2dd2773eb89/aihw-dis-77.pdf.aspx?inline=true

Centre for Studies on Inclusive Education. (2021). *The UN convention on the rights of persons with disabilities.* http://www.csie.org.uk/inclusion/rights-persons-disabilities.shtml#:~:text=(4)%20In%20order%20to%20help

Chapman, R., & Carel, H. (2022). Neurodiversity, epistemic injustice, and the good human life. *Journal of Social Philosophy.* https://doi.org/10.1111/josp.12456

Davis, L. J. (2017). *The disability studies reader.* Routledge.

de Beco, G. (2014). The right to inclusive education according to Article 24 of the UN convention on the rights of persons with disabilities: Background, requirements and (remaining) questions. *Netherlands Quarterly of Human Rights, 32*(3), 263–287. https://doi.org/10.1177/016934411403200304

Farkas, A. (2014). *Conceptualizing inclusive education and contextualizing it within the UNICEF mission—Companion technical booklet webinar 1.* https://www.unicef.org/lac/media/35101/file/Ingl%C3%A9s.pdf

Forlin, C. (2010). Inclusion: Identifying potential stressors for regular class teachers. *Educational Research, 43*(3), 235–245. https://doi.org/10.1080/00131880110081017

Frohmader, C. (2019). *Disability rights now 2019 Australian Civil Society shadow report to the United Nations Committee on the rights of persons with disabilities.* https://www.afdo.org.au/wp-content/uploads/2019/08/CRPD-Shadow-Report-2019-English-PDF.pdf

Grigorenko, E. L., Hart, L., Hein, S., Kovalenko, J., & Naumova, O. Y. (2019). Improved educational achievement as a path to desistance. *New Directions for Child and Adolescent Development, 2019*(165), 111–135. https://doi.org/10.1002/cad.20290

Hanushek, E. A., & Woessmann, L. (2021). Education and economic growth. *Oxford Research Encyclopedia of Economics and Finance.* https://doi.org/10.1093/acrefore/9780190625979.013.651

Hudson, J. P. (2014). *A practical guide to congenital developmental disorders and learning difficulties.* Routledge.

Hughes, C. (2013). Poverty and disability. *Career Development and Transition for Exceptional Individuals, 36*(1), 37–42. https://doi.org/10.1177/2165143413476735

Kaplan, I., & Lewis, I. (2013). *Promoting inclusive teacher education: Introduction.* United Nations Educational, Scientific and Cultural Organisation. https://en.unesco.org/inclusivepolicylab/sites/default/files/learning/document/2017/1/221033e.pdf

Lewis, B. (2006). A mad fight: Psychiatry and disability activism. In L. J. Davis (Ed.), *The disability studies reader* (pp. 3–16). Psychology Press.

MacArthur, J. (2009). *Learning better together: Working towards inclusive education in New Zealand schools.* IHC New Zealand. https://inclusive.tki.org.nz/assets/inclusive-education/res ource-documents/learning-better-together.pdf

McCallum, R. (2020). *The United Nations convention on the rights of persons with disabilities: An assessment of Australia's level of compliance.* https://apo.org.au/node/308792

McCarthy, J., Chaplin, E., Underwood, L., Forrester, A., Hayward, H., Sabet, J., Young, S., Asherson, P., Mills, R., & Murphy, D. (2015). Characteristics of prisoners with neurodevelopmental disorders and difficulties. *Journal of Intellectual Disability Research, 60*(3), 201–206. https://doi. org/10.1111/jir.12237

Ogundele, M. O., & Morton, M. (2022). Classification, prevalence and integrated care for neurodevelopmental and child mental health disorders: A brief overview for paediatricians. *World Journal of Clinical Pediatrics, 11*(2), 120–135. https://doi.org/10.5409/wjcp.v11.i2.120

Rieser, R. (2013). *Teacher education for children with disabilities: Literature review for UNICEF REAP project.* https://www.eenet.org.uk/resources/docs/Teacher_education_for_children_dis abilities_litreview.pdf

Rouse, M. (2008). *Developing inclusive practice: A role for teachers and teacher education?* University of Aberdeen. https://www.abdn.ac.uk/education/documents/journals_documents/issue16/ EITN-1-Rouse.pdf

Shakespeare, T. (2010). The social model of disability. In L. J. Davis (Ed.), *The disability studies reader* (pp. 266–273). Routledge. http://thedigitalcommons.org/docs/shakespeare_soc ial-model-of-disability.pdf

Shakespeare, T. (2017). The social model of disability. In L. J. Davis (Ed.), *The disability studies reader* (5th ed., pp. 195–203). Routledge.

Singal, N. (2017, November 13). *Children with disabilities are being denied equal opportunities for a quality education across the world, including in the UK.* University of Cambridge. https://www.cam.ac.uk/research/news/children-with-disabilities-are-being-denied- equal-opportunities-for-a-quality-education-across-the

Singer, J. (2016). *Neurodiversity: The birth of an idea.* Kindle eBook.

Stubbs, S. (2008). *Inclusive education: Where there are few resources.* https://www.academia.edu/ 12577906/Inclusive_Education_Where_there_are_few_resources_2008

Triano, S. L. (2000). Categorical eligibility for special education: The enshrinement of the medical model in disability policy. *Disability Studies Quarterly, 20*(4). https://doi.org/10.18061/dsq.v20 i4.263

United Nations. (n.d.). *The 17 goals.* https://sdgs.un.org/goals

United Nations. (1948). *Universal declaration of human rights.* https://www.un.org/en/about-us/ universal-declaration-of-human-rights

United Nations. (1966a). *International covenant on civil and political rights.* https://www.ohchr. org/en/instruments-mechanisms/instruments/international-covenant-civil-and-political-rights

United Nations. (1966b). *International covenant on economic, social and cultural rights.* https:// www.ohchr.org/en/instruments/mechanisms/instruments/international-covenant-economic-soc ial-and-cultural-rights

United Nations. (2006). *Optional protocol to the convention on the rights of persons with disabilities.* https://www.ohchr.org/en/instruments-mechanisms/instruments/optional-protocol-conven tion-rights-persons-disabilities

United Nations. (2018). *Sustainable Development Goals (SDGs) and disability.* https://www. un.org/development/desa/disabilities/about-us/sustainable-development-goals-sdgs-and-disabi lity.html

United Nations. (2019). *Disability: Article 24—Education.* https://www.un.org/development/desa/ disabilities/convention-on-the-rights-of-persons-with-disabilities/article-24-education.htm

United Nations. (2022). *United Nations Human Rights Committee (HRC).* Retrieved November 2022, from https://www.refworld.org/publisher,HRC,CASELAW,,,,0.html#SRTop21

United Nations Children's Fund. (2010). *Rights, Education and Protection (REAP) A project proposal.* https://www.dfat.gov.au/sites/default/files/unicef-reap-proposal.pdf

United Nations Children's Fund. (2014). *Educating teachers for children with disabilities: Mapping, scoping and best practices exercise in the context of developing inclusive education.* http://worldofinclusion.com/v3/wp-content/uploads/2014/01/UNICEF-Educating-Teachers-for-Children-with-Disabilities_Lo-res.pdf

United Nations Children's Fund. (2021). *Nearly 240 million children with disabilities around the world, UNICEF's most comprehensive statistical analysis finds.* https://www.unicef.org/press-releases/nearly-240-million-children-disabilities-around-world-unicefs-most-comprehensive

Wendell, S. (2017). Unhealthy disabled: Treating chronic illnesses as disabilities. In L. J. Davis (Ed.), *The disability studies reader* (5th ed., pp. 160–194). Routledge.

Woods, A., Wyatt-Smith, C., & Elkins, J. (2005). Learning difficulties in the Australian context: Policy, research and practice. *Curriculum Perspectives, 25*(3), 1–14. https://eprints.qut.edu.au/19646/

World Health Organization. (2021, November 24). *Disability and health.* https://www.who.int/news-room/fact-sheets/detail/disability-and-health

Zagona, A. L., Kurth, J. A., & MacFarland, S. Z. C. (2017). Teachers' views of their preparation for inclusive education and collaboration. *Teacher Education and Special Education: The Journal of the Teacher Education Division of the Council for Exceptional Children, 40*(3), 163–178. https://doi.org/10.1177/0888406417692969

Part V
Engagement in Schools

Chapter 24
Answering Children's Questions on Climate Change: Curious Climate Schools

Rachel Kelly, Kim Beasy, Chloe Lucas, Gabi Mocatta, and Gretta T. Pecl

24.1 Introduction

Climate change significantly impacts the futures of children. Children's lives are already being affected and the changing climate will continue to have lifelong effects on their health, wellbeing, opportunities, and experiences. Children and young people are currently inheriting climate change impacts they have had little to no influence in creating (Abate, 2020; Cutter-Mackenzie & Rousell, 2019). Under current climate action pledges, those born in the year 2020 can expect to experience up to seven times more extreme events than people born in 1960 will experience in their lifetimes (Thiery et al., 2021). For the first time in history, current leaders are knowingly bestowing children with the burden of climate change and its impacts (Intergovernmental Panel on Climate Change [IPCC], 2021).

Present Address:
R. Kelly (✉) · K. Beasy · C. Lucas · G. T. Pecl
Centre for Marine Socioecology, University of Tasmania, Hobart, TAS, Australia
e-mail: r.kelly@utas.edu.au

K. Beasy
School of Education, College of Law, Arts and Education, University of Tasmania, Launceston, TAS, Australia

C. Lucas
School of Geography, Planning, and Spatial Sciences, University of Tasmania, Hobart, TAS, Australia

G. Mocatta
Climate Futures, School of Geography, Planning and Spatial Sciences, University of Tasmania, Hobart, TAS, Australia

School of Communication and Creative Arts, Deakin University, Burwood, VIC, Australia

R. Kelly · G. T. Pecl
Institute for Marine and Antarctic Studies, University of Tasmania, Hobart, TAS, Australia

445

Many children feel overwhelmed by the enormity of the climate problem and frustrated at their limited voice and power in today's decision-making on climate (Jones & Davison, 2021). A recent global study showed that 75% of children and young people surveyed (aged 16–25 years) think that their futures are frightening (Hickman et al., 2021). Furthermore, children are more at risk for the mental health impacts associated with climate change including anxiety (Clayton et al., 2014). Climate anxiety describes the feelings of overwhelm and helplessness related to the global climate crisis and threat of environmental disaster (Clayton, 2020), feelings that approximately two-thirds of young people report experiencing (Hickman et al., 2021).

There is an immense need to support and equip children with the knowledge, hope, and agency to deal with climate change. Further, given the rise of climate anxiety, there is a growing need for active dialogue-based learning on climate that is accurate, realistic, and optimistic (Kelly et al., 2022; McAfee et al., 2019). Yet, approaches to climate education in many national curricula (including in Australia) tend to position climate change as a scientific phenomenon, with inquiries mostly limited to understandings of climate change science. These science-focused learning opportunities fail to provide a moral vision or ethical position for how children can engage with and act on emerging climate issues (Hulme, 2020). Research suggests that young people feel disempowered by their experiences of climate change education (Jones & Davison, 2021), and more participatory and active models of learning and engagement on climate change are needed. Consequently, there are calls for climate education to be holistically integrated into curricula to engage and empower young people as emerging political citizens (Cutter-Mackenzie & Rousell, 2019).

Here, we highlight that not only does the climate crisis cause alarm among children, but also educating children about climate can generate understanding and action. The influence of leading youth voices on climate, for example, School Strikes 4 Climate movement (Verlie & Flynn, 2022), demonstrates the huge potential for children and young people to shape more positive climate futures for themselves (Kelly et al., 2022). In this chapter, we outline the potential for educational initiatives that can engage children in learning about climate change to (i) establish their knowledge base of accurate climate science information (and where to find it), and (ii) enable conversations that can empower children to articulate their climate worries and questions, as well as (iii) support children experiencing climate anxiety and grief. Such initiatives can advance broader objectives that seek to enhance children's knowledge and skills, to enable them to participate as global citizens in adapting to (and mitigating) the impacts of climate change. These efforts align to specific targets as set by the United Nations (UN) Sustainable Development Goals (SDGs), including SDG4.7 (Ensure that all learners acquire the knowledge and skills needed to promote sustainable development…) and SDG13.3 (Improve education, awareness-raising, and human and institutional capacity on climate change mitigation, adaptation, impact reduction, and early warning).

In this chapter, we look first at the Australian policy and education context for climate literacy. Specifically, we consider how climate change education is supported by the international and national policy context of Australia and reflect on literature that discusses barriers and enablers of climate change education. Then we outline how climate education can be delivered to facilitate climate literacy in classrooms, by exploring the case study of the researcher-led climate engagement initiative: Curious Climate Schools in Tasmania, Australia. The aim of this chapter is to provide insights and lessons for developing climate change education that is student-led, holistic, transdisciplinary, and action-focused.

24.2 Teaching Climate Change in the Australian Context

Widespread climate literacy is essential for informed decision-making at every level of society. Examples from the literature evidence that climate literacy is a precursor to climate concern and action (Tobler et al., 2012). At an international level, the Paris Agreement (UN, 2015, Article 12) commits parties "to enhance climate change education, training, public awareness, public participation and public access to information" (p. 16). However, Australia's latest (2021) Nationally Determined Contributions update did not include reference to children or to climate change education as part of its ongoing commitment to the Agreement (Australian Government, 2021). Although education for sustainability is a key component of Australian education policies, details on how climate change is specifically addressed by formal education are absent from these policies. As a result, the Australian policy context has weak ability to support climate change education (Colliver, 2017). Reference to climate change in the *Australian Curriculum* (Australian Curriculum, Assessment and Reporting Authority [ACARA], 2019)—the overarching curriculum framework that all teachers must use to guide their teaching practice—is limited, not appearing at all in the primary curriculum, and dominated by a science focus (Beasy et al., 2022).

Due to this relative "invisibility" of climate change in the *Australian Curriculum* (ACARA, 2019), climate change education delivery is largely underpinned by educators' personal beliefs and values. Consequently, only educators who are personally motivated to teach about climate change tend to do so. The broader literature suggests that educator beliefs may also influence their view of the purpose of climate change education. For example, teachers in Ireland viewed climate change education as a geographical process necessitating individual private action (Waldron et al., 2016). In contrast, teachers of environmental studies viewed climate change education as a means of motivating political, social, and economic action at the societal level (Waldron et al., 2016). These views would suggest that the perceived purpose of climate change education varies among those engaged in teaching it. Other barriers to climate change education are also prevalent. For instance, researchers in the USA found that the complexity of the topic, educators' lack of personal knowledge on the subject, and their fear of accusations of advancing a political agenda, influence if and how climate change is taught (Anchondo, 2019). Professional development for in-service teachers is shown to improve teacher self-efficacy in teaching about climate change and when equipped with appropriate teaching tools, teachers are more likely to teach about climate change in classrooms (Li et al., 2021).

Historically, climate change education has been considered within select disciplines and fields, and predominantly within science (Busch et al., 2019; Stevenson et al., 2017). Climate change education and the approaches used to teach it in schools vary across these disciplines. To date, interdisciplinary teaching in secondary school contexts remains challenging due to the siloed nature of the curriculum (Beach et al., 2017), however, some recent research reports examples of climate change education incorporated in diverse discipline areas and in interdisciplinary ways (Siegner & Stapert, 2020).

Effective climate education approaches should emphasise climate action competence, and not only climate knowledge, directing students beyond critical thinking to critical action, by both learning to know and learning to do (Vaughter, 2016). Recent research has emphasised the importance of dialogue in teaching climate change and assisting young people to make sense of the complexity of the climate crisis (Rousell & Cutter-Mackenzie-Knowles, 2020). Pedagogical approaches that give voice to students and engage them in learning beyond fact-giving are increasingly recommended in climate change education, although arguably, these approaches remain teacher-centric (Lawler & Patel, 2012; Rousell & Cutter-Mackenzie-Knowles, 2020; Tanner, 2010).

Conversations about climate change among young adults and with their teachers, friends, and family support their development of concern about climate change and adaptive climate change behaviour (Goldberg et al., 2019; Valdez et al., 2017). Still, these conversations can be disempowering, if accompanied by a sense of lack of action on climate change. In Tasmania, for example, young people's educational experiences of climate change were found to be frequently disempowering and contributed to their feelings of abandonment and betrayal by older generations (Jones & Davison, 2021). Therefore, educators should support student emotional wellbeing when engaging them in conversations about climate change (Baker et al., 2020).

The literature to date on climate change and education has primarily focused on knowledge and understanding of climate change science (Boon, 2009, 2010), effective learning strategies (Monroe et al., 2019; Sezen-Barrie et al., 2019), as well as educator experiences (Lombardi & Sinatra, 2012). This research suggests that effective climate education strategies include providing students with opportunities to interact with scientists, in order to address their climate understanding and discuss their opportunities to participate in climate action projects (Monroe et al., 2019). Climate change education that is delivered in accessible ways, where connections between people and climate change are made clear, can have a lasting impact on the everyday decisions that students make, and prompt them to consider how their decisions may impact climate change (Cordero et al., 2020). In the next section, we consider society-level climate literacy as the goal, and effective climate change education—beginning in schools—as a method for achieving this and supporting SDGs 4.7 and 13.3.

24.3 Project Background

As leaders of the future, young people need to be engaged in programs and initiatives that support their climate literacy. To help prepare young people with enhanced knowledge, skills, and experiences, and to strengthen their agency, ideally these literacy initiatives would include (1) diverse voices, (2) active dialogue-based science learning, (3) connection to nature, (4) critical thinking skills, and (5) co-created visions of a sustainable future (Kelly et al., 2022). This need for dialogue-based learning on climate change resulted in the development of the parent project to Curious Climate Schools: Curious Climate Tasmania[1] (Nettlefold & Pecl, 2020). Building on evidence of the value of climate conversations, Curious Climate Tasmania invited local people (in Tasmania, Australia), through extensive dissemination by the local radio station, to submit questions on any aspect of climate change about which they were curious. The project team (including several co-authors of this chapter) then conducted a geographically specific thematic analysis of all submitted questions and collated teams of researchers to deliver answers to those most popular questions at public presentations around the state (Kelly et al., 2020). The project was highly successful. A follow-up survey (conducted two years after the project ran) revealed that 82% of participants learned something new about climate change, 70% felt empowered to take climate action, and 81% shared the information they learned with family and friends. Based on this success, the project format was modified to engage specifically with school children on their climate questions and Curious Climate Schools was conceived.

Knowledge about climate change is closely associated with climate concern among young people, and concern is a precursor to pro-environmental behaviours (Stevenson & Peterson, 2016). As researchers, our motivation for this project stemmed from the recognition that climate change is not systematically or holistically addressed in the school education system in Australia, and that fundamental knowledge of climate change is crucial for all people, including young people, if we are to take the actions urgently required of us to mitigate and adapt to our changing climate. On a personal level, four out of five of us are also parents of children in this school system. We see our children's worries about climate change at home and we know that, alongside the relative silences on climate change in the national curriculum, our children's feelings about climate change are neither discussed nor addressed at school. Given the politicisation of climate change and its scant treatment in the current school curriculum, we were motivated to provide children with the opportunity to engage with interdisciplinary climate experts, and to access climate science knowledge firsthand. In doing this, we also aimed to address the holistic social context of climate change, including the mental health implications for young people.

---

[1] Curious Climate Schoolswww.curiousclimate.org.au/schools/ and Curious Climate Tasmania—www.curiousclimate.org.au.

24.4   Curious Climate Schools: A Case Study

The Curious Climate Schools project is an engagement and research project that aims to address children's unanswered questions and concerns about climate change (Fig. 24.1). This case study focuses on the first year of the project, launched in 2021, which involved over one thousand Tasmanian school students between the ages of 9 and 18.

Teachers across Tasmania were invited to register their classes for the project and were provided with guidelines to facilitate brainstorming sessions where each class formulated questions about any aspect of climate change. The local classes then voted on up to ten questions they most wanted to be answered and submitted these to the project website with their teachers' assistance. A total of 280 student questions were submitted, of which 273 were "unique" questions (i.e., questions only asked once using the same words). Many of the questions that were submitted were complex, and often included multiple sub-questions. The Curious Climate Schools team harnessed the collective knowledge of 57 experts from the University of Tasmania, Commonwealth Scientific and Industrial Research Organisation (CSIRO), and other research organisations, who volunteered to answer student questions. These experts included climate scientists, climate communicators, conservation biologists, fire scientists, chemists, lawyers, engineers, ecologists, psychologists, oceanographers, Indigenous knowledge holders, and health scientists. Each student question was answered either in video or webpage format. The project and the Curious Climate Schools website (containing expert answers and other climate information) were launched at the beginning of the UN COP26 Climate Summit (UN, n.d.). As an enduring resource, the website provides information for children and teachers on how to handle feelings

Fig. 24.1 Overview of the curious climate school project

about climate change, what people of all ages can do to be part of the solution, and how young people's questions are part of a larger global conversation about climate action, including work led by the UN and the Intergovernmental Panel on Climate Change (IPCC).

24.5 Cultivating Curiosity in the Classroom

Teachers were asked to think about climate change in its broadest sense when facilitating question brainstorming sessions with their classes—i.e. not to consider it as belonging to a particular discipline or subject area. To help teachers consider some of the different perspectives from which questions might emerge, they were advised to consider Political, Economic, Social, Technological, Legal, and Environmental perspectives (the PESTLE framework). In addition, the teachers were asked to avoid framing questions for students, or suggesting specific topics, as it was important for the process of inquiry to be led by students themselves (see the project's pedagogical principles, Table 24.1) and not confined to what might be useful for teaching to curriculum or exams. The classroom discussions were guided by suggestions for teachers to ask their students:

- What words or images come to mind when you hear "climate change"?
- What do we know about climate change?
- What do we know about the causes of climate change?
- What do we know about solutions?
- What don't we know?
- What are the past, present, and future aspects of climate change?
- What is something we want to learn about climate change?

The children were encouraged to consider conversations about climate change they may have had with friends or family, and to ponder what questions arose from these encounters. They were also prompted to think about questions they might have about climate change impacts occurring from local to global scales. Teachers were asked to emphasise that there were no right or wrong questions, and to encourage their students to be curious and open to asking all kinds of questions. The students wrote their questions on index cards, and once all students had contributed as many questions as they wanted, the index cards were gathered and examined by the class. Teachers then gave students the opportunity to reflect on the kinds of questions asked, and to add additional questions if they liked. Students then assigned the questions on index cards into categories of similar questions, so that they could see which were most often asked and compare the wording of similar questions. Finally, the students were asked to vote for the questions they would most like to be answered by climate researchers. Up to ten questions were voted "most wanted" by each class and were then submitted to the Curious Climate Schools website by the teacher. Some classes submitted these as text, while other students created artworks or videos for their questions. Teachers were also asked to debrief with the class following the

Table 24.1 Five pedagogical principles underpinning curious climate schools

1. Student-led inquiry
Curious Climate Schools aims to respond directly to what students themselves say they want to know. This means that in facilitating brainstorming sessions, teachers are encouraged not to preempt questions in any way, to pose questions themselves, or to limit the types of questions students could ask. By enabling student-led inquiry, the project helps to build critical thinking skills, as well as empowering students by taking their concerns and questions seriously, and ensuring they feel heard
2. Holistic approach to climate literacy
We see climate literacy as fundamental to good citizenship. Climate change is a wicked problem that involves profound changes to the environment and society. It is important to learn about all aspects of such change, and not to silo information into certain subjects or disciplines. This means students are free to ask about anything related to climate change and are not limited to questions about scientific processes or impacts
3. Acknowledging feelings
Climate change places a burden on all of us, including children. It is vital for mental health to acknowledge the feelings that this can generate. Talking about climate change, and getting support from others, is important and should be encouraged in schools. Curious Climate Schools provides psychology-informed resources for teachers and students dealing with, and sharing about, climate feelings including anxiety and grief
4. Empowering individual and system change
Children can be powerful actors and advocates for climate action. Curious Climate Schools helps students to think about what they can do to act on climate, in a way that celebrates the things they can do, acknowledges the structural changes that are also necessary, and avoids judging individuals for the things that they do not (or cannot) do. While acting on climate change can be individually and collectively motivating, and help assuage feelings of powerlessness and hopelessness, it is important not to place undue responsibility on individuals
5. Being part of a global conversation
Curious Climate Schools creates connections—between students in a class, between classes across Tasmania, between children and experts, and between conversations happening in Tasmanian schools and those occurring at a global level. The project aims to show Tasmanian students that they can be part of a global movement for climate action and adaptation

activity, including discussing any feelings of anxiety or concern it may have generated. Students were encouraged to research answers to the questions not submitted themselves.

24.6 Curating Questions and Communicating Answers

Once the submitted questions were received by the Curious Climate Schools team, these were transcribed into a spreadsheet (see abridged example, Table 24.2) and each question was allocated subject(s) based on the disciplinary areas suitable to address it. Keywords were then assigned to help group the questions. Together, the subjects and keywords were used to sort questions, and to identify similar questions that could be addressed in the same answer; for example, "Can climate change be reversed and go back to the way it was?" was grouped with "How long do we have left before it is irreversible?" and "Is it possible to reverse the effects of climate change?" and six similarly phrased questions asked by different classes. The subjects and keywords were then matched against the expertise of available experts and questions were allocated to these experts to be answered. The spreadsheet approach also enabled the project team to ensure that each class had their group of questions answered by a range of different experts, via a mix of video and written text formats. For some questions, this need extended beyond the existing pool of expertise, and the project team sought other expert volunteers via professional networks (e.g., questions about pangolins, plastics, and the earth exploding). The expert responses were reviewed by the project team to ensure that they were understandable and accessible for school-age children (e.g., addressed jargon or lengthy responses) and engaging images were added to text responses where relevant.

The expert responses to student questions were uploaded to the Curious Climate Schools website where they could (and still can) be explored by students and their teachers (as well as the wider public) in multiple ways:

- through a school class webpage—where classes could review answers to their own questions and see what other classes asked;
- through an interactive Google map—which identifies where each question came from;
- through a set of themed webpages—including *most asked* questions (and their responses), questions about *looking ahead* to the future, and questions on *taking action* and what needs to happen to limit or stop climate change, and what we can all do to help;

Table 24.2 Extract from the spreadsheet used for curating student questions

Question	Subject	Keywords	Grade (student ages)
With rising sea temperatures, will the current fishing industry in Tasmania be sustainable?	Marine science	Fisheries Temperature Sustainability Tasmania	9/10 (14–16)
What would have happened if we had never had the Industrial Revolution?	Social science	History	5 (10–11)
How will climate change affect our generation in the future?	Social science	Future Social impacts Intergenerational	8 (13–14)
Are there any positives from climate change, including benefits for animals?	Conservation	Wildlife Benefits	5 (10–11)
Does being vegan really reduce emissions?	Agriculture social science	Diet	10 (15–16)

- by typing key terms or phrases into a search bar.

Finally, in addition to providing answers to student questions on the website, the project also coordinated expert visits to 33 classrooms (online and in person) across Tasmania. The purpose of these visits was not only to answer student questions about climate change, but also to demonstrate how many different types of learning are involved in climate research, and to offer real-life examples of how different people are working to mitigate and adapt to climate change.

24.7 Reflections

A key outcome of the Curious Climate Schools project is the climate literacy it supports, by providing a body of expert knowledge conveyed accessibly for school students in video, image, and short texts. Much of this information addresses questions with no straightforward, or "easily google-able," answers. In addition, the project provides children with opportunities to see and meet experts working on climate change, and to connect more readily with the science. Thus, the project has capacity to give students agency over their own learning about climate change by connecting them personally with researchers working in diverse fields of climate research. Fostering this direct connection with researchers both validates student concerns and critical thinking, and can inspire them with local role models who have dedicated their careers to working on this issue. The project involves students from different geographical areas facing varied climate risk and socio-economic challenges. By viewing questions from other classes across the state on the project website, students can also recognise their shared concerns and consider a sense of solidarity towards action. For classes where climate change was a new topic of discussion, these peer questions may open new directions of thinking and exploration.

In the project, we felt it was crucial to recognise the climate impacts unfolding around the world, as well as the very real and personal impacts that learning about climate change can have. The timing of the project to coincide with COP26 in Glasgow in 2021 enabled Tasmanian students to make connections between their own questions and concerns and those being negotiated concurrently on the world stage. The resources we provided helped to situate a global issue that can sometimes feel abstract into their everyday lives. The learning material provided also helped students and teachers to navigate conversations about their emotional responses to climate change, something that is absent from school curricula. It also helped them to channel strong feelings into action at a local level. To make a project like this even more student-led, one innovation could be to involve a team of student editors in ensuring the clarity of the expert answers for their fellow students at different age levels.

Conducting this project underscored several challenges for climate literacy in the Australian education system. Although the curriculum is full for students of all ages, the specific requirements of the curriculum for students in their upper high school years mean that there is little opportunity for them to participate in initiatives like Curious Climate Schools. We found that we had the greatest participation from classes in upper primary and lower high school grades. The project also relies on interested teachers to sign up—meaning that the students of teachers who feel that they lack knowledge or confidence to teach climate, or those who do not see climate change as a relevant or important issue, are excluded from participating. To address this challenge, our experience with this project suggests that teachers could usefully undertake climate literacy learning as part of their pedagogical training or through professional development. Additionally, a project of this nature demands a great deal of time from both organisers and the experts involved. This makes projects like this one unsustainable in the longer term. This underscores the fact that climate literacy must be embedded in the curriculum if school students are to finish their schooling possessing a holistic understanding of the climate challenge.

In the absence of state-mandated climate learning in school curricula, a project like Curious Climate Schools could fruitfully be implemented in almost any jurisdiction. As it did in the Tasmanian context, this would bring the benefit of connecting young people with local experts to answer questions relevant to students' place-based climate experiences. The program addressed a gap in school curricula around the teaching of and availability of expert knowledge on climate change. In alignment with SDG13.3, the program increased the capacity of students in their agency and knowledge of climate change, and also increased the capacity of teachers and schools to teach about climate change through the provision of a website with validated expert information, delivered through student-derived questions and pitched to engage young people.

The success of such a project relies on the existence of local climate expertise and extensive researcher networks, which may not be available in all areas. Adapted to other local contexts, a project like this could be universally valuable for addressing the SDGs. Curious Climate Schools is particularly helpful for addressing SDGs 4.7 and 13.3, enabling sustainable development and global citizenship by building capacity, climate literacy, and action. However, in our experience teaching about climate change, many other SDGs are also considered through the range of questions posed by students and through the holistic and poignant responses by experts.

In this chapter, we have outlined our experiences of delivering the Curious Climate Schools project as an ongoing initiative and have shared key insights and lessons. We have also identified several specific recommendations for other groups and projects that seek to deliver more interactive and immersive forms of climate change education to/with young people, which include:

- providing students, teachers, and experts alike space and opportunity to reflect on their feelings about climate change;
- supporting students' self-efficacy and agency to take climate action by encouraging them to engage in climate dialogue with climate experts as well as their classroom peers; and
- suggesting that students are involved as "editors" in future projects, to ensure clarity/relevance of climate information to young people and their peers.

As researchers who are committed to catalysing action on climate change, this is a project close to our hearts. We are concerned about the unmet need for children to have their climate questions listened to and respected with adequate responses. As a research team, we also felt the gravity and painfulness of providing children with answers that are sometimes hard truths. We shed tears over some of the questions students put to us. Some commentators have questioned the suitability of sharing climate knowledge for children, but we feel that when children ask big questions about climate change, they deserve our utmost attention—and they deserve the truth.

References

Abate, R. S. (2020). Climate change and the voiceless: Protecting future generations, wildlife and natural resources. *Cambridge University Press*. https://doi.org/10.1017/9781108647076

Anchondo, C. J. (2019). Lukewarm response to climate change: Across Texas, teachers face obstacles to covering a politicized subject in their classrooms [Doctoral dissertation, University of Texas]. https://repositories.lib.utexas.edu/handle/2152/86654

Australian Curriculum, Assessment and Reporting Authority. (2019). *F-10 Curriculum (Version 8.4)*. https://www.australiancurriculum.edu.au/f-10-curriculum/

Australian Government. (2021). *Australia's nationally determined contribution: Communication 2021*. Retrieved from https://www4.unfccc.int/sites/ndcstaging/Pages/Party.aspx?party=AUS&prototype=1

Baker, C., Clayton, S., & Bragg, E. A. (2020). Educating for resilience: Parent and teacher perceptions of children's emotional needs in response to climate change. *Environmental Education Research, 27*(5), 687–705.

Beach, R., Share, J., & Webb, A. (2017). Teaching climate change to adolescents: Reading, writing, and making a difference. *Routledge*. https://doi.org/10.4324/9781315276304

Beasy, K., Lucas, C., Mocatta, G., Pecl, G. T., & Kelly, R. (2022, May 23). How well does the new Australian Curriculum prepare young people for climate change? *The Conversation*. https://theconversation.com/how-well-does-the-new-australian-curriculum-prepare-young-people-for-climate-change-183356

Boon, H. (2009). Climate change? When? Where? *The Australian Educational Researcher, 36*, 43–64.

Boon, H. (2010). Climate change? Who knows? A comparison of secondary students and pre-service teachers. *Australian Journal of Teacher Education, 35*(1), 104–120.

Busch, K. C., Henderson, J. A., & Stevenson, K. T. (2019). Broadening epistemologies and methodologies in climate change education research. *Environmental Education Research, 25*(6), 955–971.

Clayton, S. (2020). Climate anxiety: Psychological responses to climate change. *Journal of Anxiety Disorders, 76*, 102263.

Clayton, S., Manning, C. M., & Hodge, C. (2014). Beyond storms and drought: The psychological impacts of climate change. *American Psychological Association and ecoAmerica*.

Colliver, A. (2017). Education for climate change and a real-world curriculum. *Curriculum Perspectives, 37*(1), 73–78.

Cordero, E. C., Centeno, D., & Todd, A. M. (2020). The role of climate change education on individual lifetime carbon emissions. *PLoS One, 15*(2), e0206266.

Cutter-Mackenzie, A., & Rousell, D. (2019). Education for what? Shaping the field of climate change education with children and young people as co-researchers. *Children's Geographies, 17*(1), 90–104.

Goldberg, M. H., van der Linden, S., Maibach, E., & Leiserowitz, A. (2019). Discussing global warming leads to greater acceptance of climate science. *PNAS, 116*(30), 14804–14805.

Hickman, C., Marks, E., Pihkala, P., Clayton, S., Lewandowski, E. R., Mayall …, E. E., & van Susteren, L. (2021). Climate anxiety in children and young people and their beliefs about government responses to climate change: A global survey. *Lancet Planet Health, 5*, e863-873. https://doi.org/10.2139/ssrn.3918955

Hulme, M. (2020). One earth, many futures, no destination. *One Earth, 2*(4), 309–311.

Intergovernmental Panel on Climate Change. (2021). *Climate change 2021: The physical science basis. Contribution of working group I to the Sixth Assessment Report of the Intergovernmental Panel on Climate Change.* Cambridge University Press.

Jones, C. A., & Davison, A. (2021). Disempowering emotions: The role of educational experiences in social responses to climate change. *Geoforum, 118*, 190–200.

Kelly, R., Elsler, L. G., Polejack, A., van der Linden, S., Tönnesson, K., Schoedinger, S. E., … Wisz, M. S. (2022). *Empowering young people with climate and ocean science: Five strategies for adults to consider* [Manuscript in preparation].

Kelly, R., Nettlefold, J., Mossop, D., Bettiol, S., Corney, S., Cullen-Knox …, C., & Pecl, G. T. (2020). Let's talk about climate change: Developing effective conversations between scientists and communities. *One Earth, 3*, 415–419. https://doi.org/10.1016/j.oneear.2020.09.009

Lawler, J., & Patel, M. (2012). Exploring children's vulnerability to climate change and their role in advancing climate change adaptation in East Asia and the Pacific. *Environmental Development, 3*, 123–136.

Li, C. J., Monroe, M., Oxarart, A., & Ritchie, T. (2021). Building teachers' self-efficacy in teaching about climate change through educative curriculum and professional development. *Applied Environmental Education and Communication, 20*(1), 34–48.

Lombardi, D., & Sinatra, G. M. (2012). Emotions about teaching about human-induced climate change. *International Journal of Science Education, 35*(1), 167–191.

McAfee, D., Doubleday, Z. A., Geiger, N., & Connell, S. D. (2019). Everyone loves a success story: Optimism inspires conservation engagement. *BioScience, 69*(4), 274–281. https://doi.org/10.1093/biosci/biz019

Monroe, M., Plate, R. R., Oxarart, A., Bowers, A. W., & Chaves, W. A. (2019). Identifying effective climate change education strategies: A systematic review of the research. *Environmental Education Research, 25*(6), 791–812.

Nettlefold, J., & Pecl, G. T. (2020). Engaging journalism and climate change: Lessons from an audience-led, locally focused Australian collaboration. *Journalism Practices, 16*(1), 19–34. https://doi.org/10.1080/17512786.2020.1798272

Rousell, D., & Cutter-Mackenzie-Knowles, A. (2020). A systematic review of climate change education: Giving children and young people a 'voice' and a 'hand' in redressing climate change. *Children's Geographies, 18*(2), 191–208.

Sezen-Barrie, A., Miller-Rushing, A., & Hufnagel, E. (2019). 'It's a gassy world': Starting with students' wondering questions to inform climate change education. *Environmental Education Research, 26*(4), 555–576.

Siegner, A., & Stapert, N. (2020). Climate change education in the humanities classroom: A case study of the Lowell school curriculum pilot. *Environmental Education Research, 26*(4), 511–531.

Stevenson, K., & Peterson, N. (2016). Motivating action through fostering climate change hope and concern and avoiding despair among adolescents. *Sustainability, 8*(6).

Stevenson, R. B., Nicholls, J., & Whitehouse, H. (2017). What is climate change education? *Curriculum Perspectives, 37*(1), 67–71.

Tanner, T. (2010). Shifting the narrative: Child-led responses to climate change and disasters in El Salvador and the Philippines. *Children & Society, 24*(4), 339–351.

Thiery, W., Lange, S., Rogelj, J., Schleussner, C.-F., Gudmundsson, L., Seneviratne …, S. I., & Wada, Y. (2021). Intergenerational inequities in exposure to climate extremes. *Science, 374*(6564), 158–160.

Tobler, C., Visschers, V. H., & Siegrist, M. (2012). Consumers' knowledge about climate change. *Climatic Change, 114*(2), 189–209.

United Nations. (n.d.). *COP26: Together for our planet.* https://www.un.org/en/climatechange/cop26

United Nations. (2015). *United Nations Paris Agreement.* https://unfccc.int/process-and-meetings/the-paris-agreement/the-paris-agreement

Valdez, R. X., Peterson, M. N., & Stevenson, K. T. (2017). How communication with teachers, family and friends contributes to predicting climate change behaviour among adolescents. *Environmental Conservation, 45*(2), 183–191.

Vaughter, P. (2016). Climate change education: From critical thinking to critical action. *Policy Brief, 4*(4), 1–4.

Verlie, B., & Flynn, A. (2022). School strike for climate: A reckoning for education. *Australian Journal of Environmental Education, 38*(1), 1–12. https://doi.org/10.1017/aee.2022.5

Waldron, F., Ruane, B., Oberman, R., & Morris, S. (2016). Geographical process or global injustice? Contrasting educational perspectives on climate change. *Environmental Education Research, 25*(6), 895–911.

Chapter 25
Tasmanian Secondary Students' Experiences of Education for Sustainability

Peter Brett and Ian Ayre

25.1 Introduction

They're preparing you for how life is at the moment, not how to change how life is at the moment (Student)

The 2021 report of the Intergovernmental Panel for Climate Change demonstrated that the speed of global warming is greater than anticipated, from even a few years ago. In November 2019, a group of more than 11,000 scientists from 153 countries named climate change as an "emergency" that would lead to "untold human suffering" if no big shifts in action take place:

> We declare clearly and unequivocally that planet Earth is facing a climate emergency. To secure a sustainable future, we must change how we live. [This] entails major transformations in the ways our global society functions and interacts with natural ecosystems. (Ripple et al., 2020)

The concomitant implication of this statement is that changes in approaches in education need to match the transformative scale of the climate emergency. Australia's *per capita* greenhouse gas emissions in 2021 are five times greater than the global average, and 40% higher than any other major coal power user (Morton, 2021), and the nation is increasingly affected by extreme weather events. Whilst formal schooling's and curriculum structures' limited responses to the challenge of

P. Brett (✉)
School of Education, College of Law, Arts and Education, University of Tasmania, Burnie,
TAS 7320, Australia
e-mail: peter.brett@utas.edu.au

I. Ayre
School of Education, College of Law, Arts and Education, University of Tasmania, Launceston,
TAS 7248, Australia
e-mail: ian.ayre@utas.edu.au

K. Beasy et al. (eds.), *Education and the UN Sustainable Development Goals*, Education
for Sustainability 7,
https://doi.org/10.1007/978-981-99-3802-5_25

459

the Anthropocene can be seen as inadequate, "[c]hildren and youth have, understand-ably, led some of the most forceful calls for action and delivered harsh rebukes to those who refuse to acknowledge the precarity of our moment and take meaningful corrective action" (United Nations Education, Scientific and Cultural Organization [UNESCO], 2021a, p.31).

In Australia, youth activism hit the news in November 2018, March and May 2019, with tens of thousands of students in more than 70 cities and towns across the country missing school to take part in the global "Strike 4 climate action" move-ment (Australian Broadcasting Corporation (ABC), 2018; Baker, 2019). The protest was initially inspired by Swedish schoolgirl Greta Thunberg, who went on strike in September 2018, ahead of a Swedish national election, demanding that the country's leaders do something about climate change. The movement has spread to 112 coun-tries. At the same time, climate anxiety has emerged as a substantial issue for young people (Ojala, 2016). A recent survey asked 10,000 young people in ten countries how they felt about climate change and government responses to it. The results revealed that most respondents were concerned about climate change, with nearly 60% saying they felt "very worried" or "extremely worried." Many associated negative emotions with climate change—the most commonly chosen were "sad," "afraid," "anxious," "angry," and "powerless" (Hickman, 2021, p. e863).

Fifty years ago, the first major international conference dedicated to the envi-ronmental crisis, the 1972 United Nations Conference on the Human Environment, produced a set of agreed principles. Principle 19 of the Conference declared that: "Education in environmental matters for the younger generation as well as adults … is essential" (cited in Palmer, 1998, p. 7). The importance of this area continues to be articulated through to the present day. The United Nations has incorporated many elements of the Sustainability Development Goals (SDGs) into the Education 2030 Incheon Declaration, to ensure, within the aspirations of SDG4 (Quality Education), that:

> All learners are provided with the knowledge and skills to promote sustainable development, including, among others, through education for sustainable development and sustainable lifestyles, human rights, gender equality, promotion of a culture of peace and non-violence, global citizenship and appreciation of cultural diversity and of culture's contribution to sustainable development. (UNESCO, 2021b)

This chapter, drawing upon data from a wider study (Ayre, 2022), highlights the frustrations and hopes of Tasmanian young people in relation to sustainability. The qualitative data indicate that the scope and breadth of the SDGs are scarcely reflected in Tasmanian secondary students' experiences of learning about sustain-ability. Specifically, the chapter underlines the inadequacy of secondary school responses to the imperative of Goal 13 of the SDGs in relation to "Climate Action" and throws light upon what a "Quality Education" in Education for Sustainability (EfS) might look like (Goal 4). Listening to the lived experiences of Tasmanian secondary school students in relation to EfS, and understanding learner perspec-tives, provides lessons for educators and policymakers to conceive how EfS might be reimagined. Consequentially, curriculum and extra-curricular re-thinking might encompass a more developed and holistic understanding of sustainability, as manifest across the breadth of the SDGs. The student voices highlight the imperative of improving the way that secondary school students experience sustainability in their education.

25.2 The Challenges for EfS in Schools

Some decades ago, Stevenson (1987, p. 73) argued that critical and action orientations create a challenging task for schools, and that schools were historically "not intended to develop critical thinkers, social inquirers and problem solvers, or active participants in environmental and political (or even educational) decision making." Indeed, the traditional educational system might be regarded as part of the problem, having effectively educated the population for "unsustainability" Orr (2004, p. 5), referred to the problem *of* education rather than problems *in* education, arguing that, "without significant precautions, education can equip people merely to be more effective vandals of the earth." Consequently, many researchers, such as Sterling (2014, p. 21), have concluded that, "[i]t may be optimistic to expect education to engage with and contribute towards resolving the modern crisis when mainstream culture and values of which education is both parent and child largely make an inadequate response." This scepticism about the capacity of schools to respond with requisite attention and urgency to the challenge of climate change, and broader unsustainability of governmental and industrial practices, has been proven accurate. In Australia, the implementation of EfS has largely been marginalised by a disproportionate focus upon the basics of literacy and numeracy, and positioned as a low priority, left to a few very dedicated teachers, or employed as an add-on to an already overcrowded curriculum (Barnes et al., 2019; Buchanan, 2021).

The educational policy rhetoric at both national and state levels in relation to EfS has seemed, at face value, to take the issue seriously. Sustainability potentially has a key position in the *Australian Curriculum* (Australian Curriculum, Assessment and Reporting Authority [ACARA], 2021) as a cross-curriculum priority [CCP]. In its Overview, the *F–10 Australian Curriculum* sets out its vision for the learning domain:

> Sustainability education is futures-oriented, focusing on protecting environments and creating a more ecologically and socially just world through informed action. Actions that support more sustainable patterns of living require consideration of environmental, social, cultural and economic systems and their interdependence. (ACARA, 2021)

This statement reinforces a focus upon sustainability not only as an environmental, but also as a social, cultural, and economic priority. Further, the statement links sustainability and social justice. Interdisciplinary approaches are encouraged, consistent with the SDGs, as prevailing orientations of EfS attempt to replace a narrow "green" focus on ecology and the protection of nature, with more of a focus on social justice and "the pedagogies of humans as agents for change" (Elliott &

Davis, 2009, p. 67). In Tasmania, EfS has had a presence in schools through projects such as the Australian Sustainable Schools Initiative (Rickinson et al., 2014). The Tasmanian state government's sponsored program aimed to help schools reduce their ecological footprints: "Participating Tasmanian schools are actively supported to include sustainable practices and processes across the curriculum and to integrate sustainability into all school operations" (Environment Protection Authority Tasmania, 2013).

Unfortunately, in practice the history of education for sustainability in schools is generally one of low status within the curriculum. Traditional subjects, in secondary schools especially, are clearly demarcated into different domains; spatially they happen in separate rooms; temporally they take place in different timeslots across a timetable; and cognitively they are guided by the disciplinary concepts of distinct subjects. "Horizontal," cross-curricular, multi-disciplinary, and whole school initiatives such as EfS struggle to find space in a "vertical" world of traditional disciplinary curriculum dominance (Bernstein, 1996, p. 171). Barnes et al. (2019) identified the clear disadvantage of positioning the cross-curricular priorities as "priorities" but spread across a number of learning areas in that, "there is no explicit requirement (or accountability) for whether and how to teach them, nor are there specific metrics to determine how successfully teachers have implemented them." Salter and Maxwell (2016, p. 14) explain this further by stating:

> The construction of the priorities as (optional) solutions to problems, rather than intrinsically worthwhile content, has meant that bodies such as ACARA could respond to stakeholder demands that such content be included or excluded as politically expedient. Rather than being developed with the interests of school communities in mind, the priorities have been engineered to address the interests of others.

In practice, in Australian secondary schools in particular, the research evidence suggests that EfS is not a "priority" at all (Kennelly et al., 2011).

Although there are outlier positive stories of Australian schools implementing sustainability initiatives (ARTD Consultants, 2010), the enactment of EfS remains patchy across school systems (Nayler, 2011). In 2014, the Australian Education for Sustainability Alliance (AESA), in partnership with the Australian government, completed a large, multistate research project titled "The State of Education for Sustainability in Australia" (AESA, 2014). About 70% of the responses to the survey were from primary and secondary teachers; the rest were from principals and executive and support staff in schools. Ninety-two per cent of the individuals surveyed thought that sustainability education was important, of value to students, and should be integrated into curriculum. However, 80% of the respondents were either unaware of EfS or did not understand what it was. Perhaps not surprisingly, 91% of the same respondents reported they were yet to integrate sustainability into their teaching practices. Only 2% of respondents said that they used EfS teaching practices in their classrooms (AESA, 2014). The disappointing response of secondary schools to the invitation to innovate in the EfS curriculum space cannot be assigned to a lack of good practice examples (Colliver, 2017; Pettifer, 2019; Thorne & Whitehouse, 2018). There is no shortage of solutions to hand.

A study of the early stages of implementation of the sustainability cross-curricular priority in Tasmania concluded that, "much work is still to be done by schools and educators … to integrate the sustainability CCP in innovative ways which are true to the interdisciplinary intent of the CCP, and indeed sustainability discourse" (Dyment et al., 2014, pp. 1116–1117). A similar story was recorded in South Australia and Western Australia (Altman, 2019; Prabawa-Sear & Dow, 2018). A significant gap, or "blind spot" (Wagner, 1993), in the research into EfS relates to what Rickinson and Lundholm (2008, p. 341) refer to as "questions of learners and learning." In other words, there was limited research into students' experience of EfS. This has been borne out in a number of reviews of EfS research (Hart & Nolan, 1999; Rickinson, 2001), as well as being noted as a significant issue in other additions to the literature in the past decade (Lundholm et al., 2013; Wals & Dillon, 2013). Within our study, the participants were not considered as "adults in waiting," but young citizens with agency and a right to actively participate in shaping the world in which they live.

25.3 Methods

The study involved participants in Years 7–9 from secondary schools across northern Tasmania. The interviews with around thirty students who were between 12 and 15 years old, took place across four Tasmanian schools: one independent, one Catholic, and two government high schools. There was a relatively even distribution of students across the schools. This was the result of a deliberate decision to involve representation from all three secondary education sectors in Tasmania. The research was designed to allow learners to speak from, and be appreciated for, their own perspectives. The research addressed the question "What do the experiences of Tasmanian learners contribute to an understanding of the reality-rhetoric gap in relation to EfS in secondary schools?".

A suite of four qualitative data collection methods were employed with the participants in the context of the wider study. These were a short qualitative survey, a photo-elicitation task, and an individual interview, with pictures taken across a period of some weeks, and culminating in focus group interviews that included all of the participating students from the same school. In this chapter, the main data drawn upon are from the individual and focus group interviews, although we also include a summary of the findings of the photo-elicitation activity. Briggs et al. (2014) found that photo-elicitation activities can contribute to theorising and assessing children's sense of place-based education. Students were asked to take ten digital photographs as responses to the questions, "What does sustainability mean to you, and, how do you learn about it?" The focus group data collection method was selected because it allowed participants to share and compare their experiences of learning inside and outside the classroom (Breen, 2006). This method provided for multiple perspectives, and a stimulating environment to aid students in recalling their experience of learning about sustainability (Fontana & Frey, 1994).

In spite of efforts to be open, approachable and friendly, and establish a rapport with the adolescent participants, the second author found, as other educational researchers have experienced, that "encouraging a teenager to have a conversation in a semi-structured research interview is fraught with difficulties" (Bassett et al., 2008, p. 119). As Brinkmann and Kvale (2005) have observed, even a qualitative interview that is warm and empowering can conceal large power differences, with most of the power lying in the hands of the interviewer, who "initiates the interview, determines the topics to be discussed, controls the interview guide, and decides when to terminate the conversation" (p. 164). Speaking with the adolescents in an institutional setting where they are used to being "tested" through being asked questions by adults, the second author worked hard to satisfy the interviewing aim of "helping teens to see the situation less as an exercise in finding the 'right answers' to interview questions, and more as a two-way conversation" (Bassett et al., p. 129). Although ethnographic interactions with learners across the four sites revealed differences in types of student experiences with EfS between participating schools, there were also strong thematic similarities that allow us to consider the learners' experiences collectively.

25.4   Conceptions and Misconceptions

Analysis of students' photographs and subsequent photo-elicitation interviews confirmed a dominant association of sustainability with the environment. In total, 106 photographs from the photographic component of the data were collected with student participants, and of these, 101 contained some form of representation of the natural environment (the remainder were of built environments). Thematic analysis of the photographs, including in follow-up interviews with students (which allowed them to explain why they were directing their camera in particular ways), elicited a number of categories. These are presented in Table 25.1.

The student photographs, and the ways in which the students discussed and described them in interviews, revealed a number of different aspects of what might broadly be termed as environmental conceptualisations of sustainability. The first was a conceptualisation of environments as places that are "untouched" by humans. Students emphasised the subjective quality of beauty. A second sub-category within an environmental conceptualisation of sustainability was its association with natural environments that students regularly go to for activities such as camping or hiking. Again, students explained their understanding of this type of environment as a place to which one goes, rather than considering their daily lived surroundings to be "the environment." Another sub-category of the environment category was an association of sustainability with a "well-kept," neat, and managed local environment. Students, both in their photographs and interview conversations, drew references to gardens and well-ordered, litter-free surroundings. Practical actions that people can take to reduce their own environmental impacts constituted a fourth theme to emerge from students' interviews, surveys, and photographs. Consistent with the

Table 25.1 Student photographs' thematic focus

Food/vegetable gardens, productive home gardening	17
Actions/ways to reduce personal ecological footprint	16
"Untouched" natural environments	10
Conservation ethic/appreciation of nature	8
Trees	7
Neat, well-kept, "pretty" manicured environments	6
Metaphorical/symbolic images	6
Environment as a habitat for non-human species	5
Bringing nature into the urban setting	4
Climate change/air pollution	4
Agricultural/rural land use	4
Water and its sustainable use	3
Rubbish/litter	3
Panoramic landscapes/wilderness	3
Self-sufficiency	3
Local environmental issue	1
Efficiency	1
TOTAL	101

students' perceptions that sustainability is essentially about ecological matters, three individual students included a recycling bin image in their submitted photos.

Whether it was an idealised wilderness version of nature, a camping spot away from daily urban life, a neat and manicured garden, or individual commitments to recycling, the environment in all these forms was the dominant element of students' conceptualisations of sustainability. There was limited cognisance demonstrated by the students, that the sustainability challenge (as represented in the breadth of the SDGs) encompasses an interconnected web of social, economic, and political, as well as ecological factors (Gough, 2011). Beyond environmental concerns, the concept of sustainability includes, "aspects such as social justice; intergenerational justice; mental and physical wellbeing; social, economic and cultural transformation; and the flourishing of the diversity of life" (Stribbe & Luna, 2009, p. 14).

25.5 Frustrations

Nearly all of the interviewed students reported significantly more EfS experiences in primary schools than in their current secondary contexts. Oliver[1] observed that "[i]t definitely tapered off enormously" and Emily agreed that "[i]t cut back a fair

---

[1] All students' names are pseudonyms.

bit." Phoebe was representative of students who looked back wistfully on some rich primary school experiences:

> Yeah, I did a lot more of like sustainability and that kind of thing in primary school. Grade 6 was probably one of the biggest times that we had a look at that and did inquiries on that kind of thing. But I know there were different groups that would, you know, even art groups looking out at the wetlands and stuff and trying to encourage keeping that safe and protecting that kind of thing, like down at the wetlands and stuff. We even set up gardens and everything, and that was something that we really looked into, and creating different energy and, you know, solar power and wind turbines.

Liam agreed, noting that, "I felt like in Years 1, 2, 3, 4 we kind of … had a lot more of it than we do now." He went on to observe that by Years 7 and 8 it "slackened off," so "you didn't really think about it anymore." The students put this down to factors such as the more open-ended, project inquiries undertaken in primary schools, more extended opportunities to be involved in school vegetable garden or wetlands projects, and the busyness of a more crowded and unitised secondary curriculum. As Philip put it: "I think there's that much like packed into the curriculum that they have to get through that there's no flexibility for them to really change things." Aaliyah agreed that "a lot of things are kind of crammed into the curriculum," adding more provocatively that "I think that [secondary] schools are sausage factories and that we're all having the creativity smashed out of us."

A number of students expressed related frustrations about the piecemeal nature of their learning about sustainability, the relatively formal, knowledge-centric approaches that they experienced in Science and Geography secondary school curricular contexts, and the lack of opportunities to engage in active and authentic projects. Most participants struggled to identify specific contexts in which their understanding of sustainability had been developed and required plenty of prompting. Answers in the main expressed vagueness and uncertainty. Nick observed that "it kind of comes in in different subjects, even probably without the teachers actually focusing on it. It just drifts into what we're learning about." He added that "they're more educating you by telling you rather than the doing at primary school." Erin agreed—"all the work's been really theory, like in classroom work, like we haven't gotten out and done anything really." Philip observed, "[y]ou don't learn much more than like the basics. They like tell you to not litter and stuff, but they don't go much further than that." Aaliyah again pithily summarised a widely held perspective—"[i]t'd probably be good to find out more about how we're hurting the world and how we can help to fix it."

There was a common desire expressed for more active learning approaches. For example, Mark commented: "[w]e do assignments on it and things like that, but we don't really physically do anything about it. Like we learn about it, but we don't actually do anything." Philip echoed this perspective: "I think you just need to be able to make actual changes, not like talk about making changes and never following through with it," Molly expanded upon the issue of lack of student voice and agency, speculating upon why this might be the case:

> I just don't think that students get enough say. You know, people are probably thinking the same as us, you know, "we need to do more stuff," but they can't put it into action because

they don't have a voice. Everyone just shuts them down, you know, "you're teenagers, you're into drugs, social media, alcohol, partying," and all that sort of stuff. Who's going to listen to us?

This student's sense of their lack of agency as an adolescent was confirmed in the following exchange during the focus group with students from one of the schools. As we talked about sustainability issues, we asked, "what *can* you do as 15-year-olds?" and were met with a pessimistic attitude from all participants:

Aiden: There's not much, in all honesty.
Jennifer: I think we can care. That's it.
Aiden: Yeah, we can care, but like ...
Mark: We don't have any power at all really.
Jennifer: Nope.
Interviewer: No power at all?
              [group-wide agreement with that notion]
Jennifer: No one listens to teenagers.

The students participating in other focus groups expressed similar feelings of a lack of empowerment when it came to acting as active citizens and making a difference in sustainability matters. The students universally conveyed feelings of powerlessness and of being silenced as adolescents in what they considered to be an adult-controlled world.

25.6 Hopes

There was a powerful consensus among all of the interviewed students in their survey responses (even if several of them struggled to articulate it clearly) that sustainable development was a fundamental priority. This was confirmed in the students' interview responses. For example, Erin was adamant that "everybody needs to know about how we can make the world more sustainable, to help future generations." Freya expressed it thus:

There are all these big issues going on in the world ... and there are lots of issues that people look at, and they tend to focus on one and then they move on and focus on another...But then there's kinda like this big shadow looming over it, that you've got to try and keep things sustainable, otherwise you'll never get the opportunity to fix all these other problems.

Sienna was one of the most thoughtful, informed, and engaged participants throughout the project, but even her response, when invited to consider possible future solutions, was hesitant and struggling for coherence.

I think humans have like, ahh need to be a part of the solution. Like the way we act towards it, and how we contribute to the problems, umm, with pollution, which leads to global warming and ... so I think not only do we need to find a solution, we need to stop ... I think, I always think that instead of trying to find a solution you need to stop the problem, with things like this. Like, umm, with global warming, I think obviously it's very important to solve it, and people need to do that. Like it needs to be ... we need to find out how. But it's also, we need to be taking the small steps to stopping it, like stopping the whole thing, if you know what I mean. Like trying to get electric cars out faster, 'cause they're quite expensive.

Overall, the interview data cumulatively indicated across the four schools that the students had not generally been inducted into the systematic critical thinking and reflective futures thinking that the Australian Curriculum Sustainability cross-curricular priority aspires to promote, although the students' attitudes towards wanting to learn more about the issues were very evident.

A small number of outlier students reflected upon human responsibility (and lack of responsibility) for stewardship of the planet. For example, Nick commented that:

> I think it's important so that the landscapes and environments that we live in are kept liveable and pleasant to live in...If we don't sustain them now, then it's going to be a lot bigger job to try and fix it in the future. And that'll have to be other people doing it, and it won't be us, so kind of gives them a job that they shouldn't have to do 'cause it wasn't their problem in the first place. They're not the people that've ruined it.

Aiden developed the idea of essential human selfishness around issues of planetary sustainability:

> Deep down we're quite selfish as human beings. We're trying to make us good and we're trying to make sure we continue to live on. And even like the people, certain people who say like we need to save the planet, they know that in our minds we're actually doing it for the benefit of us. Like, it sounds terrible, but it's sort of just the way humans act. It's not like we're doing it all for the creatures, or for the environment, it always has to be something that can benefit us as well.

Some of the students were edging towards solutions, but typically these usually related more to technological progress rather than changes in human behaviour. Brandon expressed a hope that "if we do move towards the clean energy thing, I think we could still have quite a good future ahead of us." Oliver highlighted the issue of marine debris:

> That's coming to a head. Well, that has come to a head in the last year or so, so that's getting quite bad. And it's fixable is the only problem. Like we could stop giving out McDonalds toys and we could stop giving out plastic bags and we can stop making plastic drink bottles, that can't be reused.

He added the insightful observation that, "[o]ur consumption is the big thing. We can choose to grow our own food, but we can also choose to eat things from a sustainable source." Nick speculated that:

> I think we'll look a lot more at using resources we've got and, so say solar and water, hydroelectricity, instead of big power plants and that kind of thing. So, I think it's started already for companies to try and start looking at sustainability and preserving the environment a bit more than they have been, but I think it'll just increase, and with the new generation of kids coming through, I reckon they'll be a bit more mindful and want to act on it a bit more than probably the older generation has been.

Several students recognised (albeit often hazily, and without a sense of detail and certainty), that the world might look very different by 2050. Erin had a thoughtful bet each way.

Well, it could go two different ways. If people like pick up their act right now, I reckon we could have like nice green cities, and using clean energy, and it'd be all nice, but if it didn't, I reckon we could be in a depression and lots of people living in slums and stuff like that. Wouldn't be too good.

Aiden was not without some hope for the future:

I think people are getting more aware, which is great news. It's not like all doom and gloom, although it's pretty bad right now. I think with learning, with enlightenment on this subject, people will start to be more environmental, and especially like in politics and such, people will have that more as a main factor, and be taking that more in consideration to make the nation a lot better.

Emily broadly shared this optimism, commenting that "I kind of like to hope that people will get better and people will learn about it and they'll do something about it, so we'll still have what we have today, or even better."

25.7 Conclusion

The nature of ecologically oriented learning in schools has historically been upheld by the root metaphors of individualism (privileging self-interest), anthropocentrism (privileging humans), scientism (privileging scientific meta-narratives), and techno-logical change being equated with progress (Bowers, 2001). The student interview responses described above are representative of the broader data obtained in our project and demonstrate the dominance of these received ideas. High-quality educa-tion for sustainability requires a paradigm shift in schools. However, as Sterling (2004, p. 50) observed:

Sustainability does not simply require an 'add-on' to existing structures and curricula but implies a change of fundamental epistemology in our culture and hence also in our educa-tional thinking and practice. Seen in this light, sustainability is not just another issue to be added to an overcrowded curriculum, but a gateway to a different type of curriculum, of pedagogy, of organisational change, of policy and particularly of ethos.

If young people are to learn how to be the type of citizens the world needs to achieve the global SDGs (and in particular respond to the Goal 13 imperatives related to "Climate Action"), they need to possess a thoughtful view of contemporary global issues (and their resonance in local contexts), and be able to think critically and work effectively with others motivated by a sense of the common good. They also need to be given opportunities to examine problems and effect change in their own contexts.

Student voices highlighting a "thin" experience of EfS in Tasmanian secondary schools corroborate the scale of the transformational challenge, but also identify some ways in which things might be organised differently and demonstrate an enthusiasm to embrace more active and participatory problem-solving approaches to EfS within and beyond their communities. There are some solutions available for schools that are more prepared to take EfS seriously and listen to student voices. Trust in young people and their capacity and willingness to instigate and lead local and community projects in the service of wider global goals might serve to neutralise some of the conservative forces of inertia (Blanchet-Cohen, 2008; Cutter-Mackenzie & Rousell, 2018; Mackey, 2012).

The challenges in educating young people about the possibilities of envisioning a more optimistic ecological future are considerable. However, the SDGs themselves offer a framework around which to structure problem-based and project-based interdisciplinary learning that may help students to develop the capabilities to advance the full range of goals. The Tasmanian young people interviewed for our study recognised the change imperative. At the end of a long focus group discussion, Oliver observed that "[t]hey're preparing you for how life is at the moment, not how to change how life is at the moment." His friend Freya immediately added, "[o]r how it should be. Or could be."

References

Altman, L. (2019). Education for sustainability in SA schools: A call for local action. *SASTA Journal, 1*, 2–5.

ARTD Consultants. (2010). *Evaluation of operational effectiveness of the Australian Sustainable Schools Initiative (AuSSI)*. Department of Environment, Water, Heritage and the Arts.

Australian Broadcasting Corporation. (2018). *Students strike for climate change protests, defying calls to stay in school*. https://www.abc.net.au/news/2018-11-30/australian-students-climate-change-protest-scott-morrison/10571168

Australian Curriculum, Assessment and Reporting Authority. (2021). *Australian curriculum: Cross-curricular priorities*. http://www.australiancurriculum.edu.au/f-10-curriculum/cross-cur riculum-priorities/sustainability/

Australian Education for Sustainability Alliance. (2014). *The state of education for sustainability in Australia*. Australian Conservation Foundation.

Ayre, I. (2022). *Experiences of learners and learning with education for sustainability in Tasmanian secondary schools* (Unpublished Ph.D. thesis, University of Tasmania).

Baker, N. (2019). *Australian students join global strikes to demand urgent climate action*. https://www.sbs.com.au/news/australian-students-join-global-strikes-to-demand-urgent-cli mate-action

Barnes, M., Moore, D., & Almeida, S. (2019). Education for sustainability: A priority or an add-on? In M. Barnes, M. Gindidis, & S. Phillipson (Eds.), *Evidence-based learning and teaching: A look into Australian classrooms* (pp. 179–189). Routledge.

Bassett, R., Beagan, B., Ristovski-Slijepcevic, S., & Chapman, G. (2008). Tough teens: The methodological challenges of interviewing teenagers as research participants. *Journal of Adolescent Research, 23*(2), 119–131.

Bernstein, B. (1996). *Pedagogy, symbolic control and identity: Theory, research, critique*. Taylor and Francis.

Blanchet-Cohen, N. (2008). Taking a stance: Child agency across the dimensions of early adolescents' environmental involvement. *Environmental Education Research, 14*(3), 257–272.

Bowers, C. A. (2001). *Educating for eco-justice and community*. University of Georgia Press.

Breen, R. L. (2006). A practical guide to focus-group research. *Journal of Geography in Higher Education, 30*(3), 463–475.

Briggs, L. P., Stedman, R. C., & Krasny, M. E. (2014). Photo-elicitation methods in studies of children's sense of place. *Children, Youth and Environments, 24*(3), 153–172.

Brinkmann, S., & Kvale, S. (2005). Confronting the ethics of qualitative research. *Journal of Constructivist Psychology, 18*(2), 157–181.

Buchanan, J. (2021). Environmental trust? Sustainability and renewables practice in the school years. *Curriculum Perspectives, 41*(2), 163–173.

Colliver, A. (2017). Education for climate change and a real-world curriculum. *Curriculum Perspectives, 37*(1), 73–78.

Cutter-Mackenzie, A., & Rousell, D. (2018). Education for what? Shaping the field of climate change education with children and young people as co-researchers. *Children's Geographies, 17*(1), 90–104. https://doi.org/10.1080/14733285.2018.1467556

Dyment, J. E., Hill, A., & Emery, S. (2014). Sustainability as a cross-curricular priority in the Australian curriculum: A Tasmanian investigation. *Environmental Education Research, 21*(8), 1105–1126. https://doi.org/10.1080/13504622.2014.966657

Elliott, S., & Davis, J. (2009). Exploring the resistance: An Australian perspective on educating for sustainability in early childhood. *International Journal of Early Childhood, 41*(2), 65–77.

Environment Protection Authority Tasmania. (2013). *Sustainable schools: The Australian sustainable schools initiative.*

Fontana, A., & Frey, J. H. (1994). Interviewing—The art of science. In N. K. Denzin & Y. S. Lincoln (Eds.), *The handbook of qualitative research* (pp. 361–376). Sage.

Gough, A. (2011). The Australian-ness of curriculum jigsaws: Where does environmental education fit? *Australian Journal of Environmental Education, 27*(1), 9–23.

Hart, P., & Nolan, K. (1999). A critical analysis of research in environmental education. *Studies in Science Education, 34*(1), 1–69.

Hickman, C. (2021). Climate anxiety in children and young people and their beliefs about government responses to climate change: A global survey. *Lancet Planet Health, 5*, e863–e873.

Intergovernmental Panel on Climate Change. (2021). *Climate change 2021: The physical science basis.* Cambridge University Press. https://www.ipcc.ch/report/ar6/wg1/

Kennelly, J., Taylor, N., & Serow, P. (2011). Education for sustainability and the Australian curriculum. *Australian Journal of Environmental Education, 27*(2), 209–218.

Lundholm, C., Hopwood, N., & Rickinson, M. (2013). Environmental learning: Insights from research into the student experience. In R. Stevenson, M. Brody, J. Dillon, & A. Wals (Eds.), *International handbook of research on environmental education* (pp. 243–252). Routledge.

Mackey, G. (2012). To know, to decide, to act: The young child's right to participate in action for the environment. *Environmental Education Research, 78*(4), 473–484.

Morton, A. (2021). Australia shown to have highest greenhouse gas emissions from coal in world on per capita basis. *The Guardian*, November 11.

Nayler, J. (2011). Enacting Australian curriculum: Planning issues and strategies for P-12 multiple year level classrooms. *Queensland Studies Authority.* https://www.qcaa.qld.edu.au/downloads/p_10/ac_p10_multi_planning_issues.pdf

Ojala, J. (2016). Facing climate anxiety in climate change education: From therapeutic practice to hopeful transgressive learning. *Canadian Journal of Education, 21*, 41–56.

Orr, D. (2004). The learning curve. *Resurgence, 226*, 11–12.

Palmer, J. (1998). *Environmental education in the 21st century: Theory, practice, progress and promise.* Routledge.

Pettifer, L. (2019). Making sustainability happen: Activating environmental citizens and behaviour change in schools. *The Social Educator, 37*(2), 15–28.

Prabawa-Sear, K., & Dow, V. (2018). Education for sustainability in Western Australian secondary schools: Are we doing it? *Australian Journal of Environmental Education, 34*(3), 244–261.

Rickinson, M. (2001). Learners and learning in environmental education: A critical review of the evidence. *Environmental Education Research, 7*(3), 207–320.

Rickinson, M., Hall, M., & Reid, A. (2014). *ResourceSmart Schools Research Project Final Report* [Report commissioned by Sustainability Victoria]. Monash University.

Rickinson, M., & Lundholm, C. (2008). Exploring students' learning challenges in environmental education. *Cambridge Journal of Education, 38*(3), 341–353.

Ripple, W., Wolf, C., Newsome, T., Barnard, P., & Moomaw, W. (2020). World scientists' warning of a climate emergency. *BioScience, 70*(1), 8–12. https://doi.org/10.1093/biosci/biz088

Salter, P., & Maxwell, J. (2016). The inherent vulnerability of the Australian curriculum's cross-curriculum priorities. *Critical Studies in Education, 57*(3), 296–312.

Sterling, S. (2004). Higher education, sustainability, and the role of systemic learning. In P. Corcoran & A. Wals (Eds.), *Higher education and the challenge of sustainability: Problematics, promise, and practice* (pp. 49–70). Kluwer.

Sterling, S. (2014). Education in change. In J. Huckle & S. Sterling (Eds.), *Education for sustainability* (pp. 18–39). Earthscan.

Stevenson, R. (1987). Schooling and environmental education: Contradictions in purpose and practice. In I. Robottom (Ed.), *Environmental education: Practice and possibility* (pp. 69–82). Deakin University Press.

Stribbe, A., & Luna, H. (2009). Introduction. In A. Stribbe (Ed.), *The handbook of sustainability literacy*. Green Books.

Thorne, M., & Whitehouse, H. (2018). Environmental stewardship education in the Anthropocene (part two): A learning for environmental stewardship conceptual framework. *The Social Educator, 36*(1), 17–28.

United Nations Education, Scientific and Cultural Organization. (2021a). *Reimagining our futures together: A new social contract for education*. https://en.unesco.org/futuresofeducation/

United Nations Education, Scientific and Cultural Organization. (2021b). *What is global citizenship education?* https://en.unesco.org/themes/gced/definition

Wagner, J. (1993). Ignorance in educational research: Or, how can you not know that? *Educational Researcher, 22*(5), 15–23.

Wals, A., & Dillon, J. (2013). Conventional and emerging learning theories: Implications and choices for educational researchers with a planetary consciousness. In R. Stevenson, M. Brody, J. Dillon, & A. Wals (Eds.), *International handbook of research on environmental education* (pp. 252–290). Routledge.

Chapter 26
Strategies for Encouraging Children to Be Physically Active to Improve Health for Life

Vaughan Cruickshank⬥ and Brendon Hyndman⬥

26.1 Introduction

Over recent decades, the importance of encouraging physical activity participation for both children and adults has emerged as a major international public health objective. The United Nations (UN, 2015) stated that people need to develop lifelong physical activity habits for the benefit of all of society. Physical activity is defined as "any bodily movement produced by skeletal muscles that results in energy expenditure" (World Health Organisation [WHO], 2020, p. 15). Being physically active is a crucial component in maintaining health across the life course (Pedersen et al., 2017), with the WHO (2020) stating that regular physical activity is an important strategy for the prevention and management of non-communicable diseases (NCDs) such as cardiovascular disease, diabetes, osteoporosis, and obesity. Additionally, other researchers (e.g., Bangsbo et al., 2019; Macpherson et al., 2017) have stated that physically active older adults have improved cognitive and brain health, mental health, and mobility, and are at less risk of pain, depression, and falls. The projected increases in the percentage of the population aged 50 years and over in many countries around the world mean that physical activity has the potential to make a substantial difference to global health.

In addition to the many physical benefits of undertaking physical activity, there is emerging evidence over the past 20 years that physical activity participation can

V. Cruickshank (✉)
School of Education, College of Law, Arts and Education, University of Tasmania, Newnham Drive, Newnham, TAS 7248, Australia
e-mail: v.j.cruickshank@utas.edu.au

B. Hyndman
Faculty of Arts and Education, Charles Sturt University, Elizabeth Mitchell Drive, Thurgoona, NSW 2640, Australia
e-mail: bhyndman@csu.edu.au

© The Author(s), under exclusive license to Springer Nature Singapore Pte Ltd. 2023   473
K. Beasy et al. (eds.), *Education and the UN Sustainable Development Goals*, Education for Sustainability 7,
https://doi.org/10.1007/978-981-99-3802-5_26

aid in cognitive functioning (Hyndman et al., 2020). Until very recently, there has been a segregation in educational contexts between considering the body and the mind in relation to how they can intersect and influence each other. For instance, physical activity movements have often been considered as a lesser focus or status for educational attention, as movement had been more associated as the "non-thinking thing" (Cruickshank et al., 2021a; Dodd, 2015). Yet researchers are continuing to unpack and explore the interlinking nature of the body and mind, discovering that "biological processes can influence cognitive processes and vice versa...an integrated individual with a mind and body that are interdependent" (Santrock, 2011, p. 16). For instance, the brain requires a constant flow and nourishment of nutrients such as glucose and oxygen to meet its many cognitive demands and this accounts for one-fifth of the body's total metabolism (Ogoh & Ainslie, 2009). If people are inactive, they may have insufficient movement to ensure sufficient flow from the body's cardio-respiratory systems to support brain functioning (Falck et al., 2017). In essence, if a person is experiencing more regular and vigorous physical activities, this can further activate and fuel healthy brain performance such as attention, perception, concentration, and memory (Dodd, 2015). The brain is unable to keep itself self-sufficiently functioning to an optimal level without a body that is adequately moving.

The benefits from physical activity participation can also be described as "human capital": a resource that can provide future gains, value, and returns (Dodd, 2015). For instance, by undertaking sufficient physical activity, this can lead to individual capital (build individual character), emotional capital (mental/psychological health), work capital (improved work efficiency, performance, and attendance), and intellectual capital (improved academic/cognitive gains). Increasing physical activity is one way to contribute to SDG3 (Good Health and Wellbeing) and might also contribute to achieving many of the 2030 Sustainable Development Goals (SDGs). This chapter highlights how schools, particularly through curricular, co-curricular, and non-curricular Health and Physical Education (HPE) strategies to develop children's physical activity, can contribute to understanding of, and action towards realising SDG3 (Good Health and Wellbeing), SDG4 (Quality Education), and SDG5 (Gender Equality).

26.2 Physical Activity Guidelines

The WHO (2020) defines physical inactivity as not meeting minimum global recommendations on physical activity for health. For adults these recommendations are for at least 150–300 min of moderate intensity aerobic physical activity, or at least 75–150 min of vigorous intensity aerobic physical activity, throughout the week. The WHO estimates that one in four adults globally do not meet these recommendations, and that up to five million deaths a year could be prevented if the global population was more physically active. Their data also highlight that women are less active and that there is significant difference in physical activity levels between countries and regions. Although one in four adults being defined as physically inactive is concerning, the figure is far worse for the 5–17-year-old age group, where the WHO (2020) estimates physical inactivity to be approximately 80%. This figure is extremely troubling considering that patterns of physical activity set in childhood usually form the basis for physical activity levels later in the lifespan (MacNamara et al., 2015; United Nations Educational, Scientific and Cultural Organisation [UNESCO], 2003).

The WHO (2020) recommends that "children and adolescents should do at least an average of 60 min per day of moderate- to vigorous-intensity, mostly aerobic, physical activity, across the week" (p. 25). Consequently, this 60-min recommendation can be seen in many national physical activity guidelines worldwide, particularly in developed Western countries (Table 26.1), to support healthy growth and development and help prevent non-communicable diseases such as obesity, cardiovascular disease, and diabetes. Researchers from countries such as the United States, the United Kingdom, Qatar, and Australia have found that many children are falling well short of this 60-min recommendation (Abarca-Gómez et al., 2017; Aspetar Orthopaedic, 2014; Guthold et al., 2020). These countries were also included in a report by the Active Healthy Kids Global Alliance (Active Healthy Kids Australia, 2021) that compared 49 countries from six continents to assess global trends in childhood physical activity in developed and developing nations. Active Healthy Kids Australia (2021) stated that children around the world are not moving enough to maintain healthy growth and development and said 75% of countries they reported on had failing physical activity grades.

Although there are many physical activity opportunities for children to pursue, the evidence suggests that there is continued growth in more sedentary opportunities that are capturing children's attention and reducing their physical activity participation levels (Hesketh et al., 2017). Comprehensive evidence has established that children across the world are not meeting national physical activity guidelines to be able to optimise their health and prevent chronic diseases (e.g., Dentro et al., 2014; Schranz et al., 2014), alongside exceeding recommended screen time quotas (Houghton et al., 2015).

26.3 Physical Activity and the Sustainable Development Goals (SDGs)

Physical activity has numerous health, social, and economic benefits. Investing in policies to promote physical activity such as walking, cycling, sport, active recreation, and play will directly contribute to SDG3 and has the potential to contribute to the achievement of many of the SDGs (WHO, 2018). Some examples of these potential contributions are presented in Table 26.2.

Table 26.1 Examples of national physical activity and sedentary behaviour guidelines for children across developed western countries

Country	Guidelines
Australia (Department of Health, 2017)	Encourage young people to participate in at least one hour of moderate to vigorous daily physical activity per day (up to several hours), activities that strengthen bones and muscles, and a variety of aerobic-type activities (some being vigorous).
Canada (Canadian Society for Exercise Physiology, 2012)	Encourage young people to engage in at least one hour of moderate-to-vigorous physical activity each day over at least three days, and to engage in activities which will bolster the development of muscles and bones.
UK (UK Chief Medical Officers Physical Activity Guidelines, 2019)	Encourage young people to engage in at least one hour of daily moderate to vigorous physical activity (spread across the day), with multiple days across the week dedicated to vigorous activities which bolster the development of muscles and bones.
US (Department of Health & Human Services, 2018)	Encourage young people to participate in at least one hour of daily moderate to vigorous physical activity, with at least three days dedicated to engaging in resistance-type physical activities to bolster the development of muscles and bones. Activities are also recommended to be enjoyed by the participants.

Given the potential contribution of physical activity towards achieving the SDGs, the UN (2015) has stated that it is time to invest in physical activity across the globe, not just for its direct health benefits, but also because of the role physical activity can have on the development of a more equitable, sustainable, and prosperous world. In addition to enhancing human health and wellbeing across the lifespan, Lawson (2005) stated that within a North American context, sport and exercise programs can contribute to sustainable development through reducing social exclusion, social isolation, and inter-group conflict, contributing to human capital development and fostering social networks. As childhood physical activity habits and perceptions are closely related to adult physical activity levels (MacNamara et al., 2015; UNESCO, 2003) it is important to encourage children to develop a lifelong love of being physically active. Schools, particularly HPE classes, are a key setting for this work to occur.

Table 26.2 Examples of connections between physical activity and the SDGs

SDG	Target	Pathway
3	3.4—Reduce one third premature mortality from non-communicable diseases (NCDs) through prevention and treatment to promote mental health and wellbeing	Physical activity and sedentary behaviour are key risk factors for NCDs. Increased participation in physical activity contributes to the prevention and treatment of NCDs in the general population and at-risk individuals. Increased rates of physical activity in children will also reduce the subsequent disease burden (on the health system) and overall mortality, promoting wellbeing and mental health for all.
3	3.6—Halve the number of global deaths and injuries from road traffic accidents	Half of road fatalities involve pedestrians and cyclists, including children. Reducing traffic volumes and speeds and improving infrastructure that enables equitable access to safe walking, cycling, and use of public transport contributes to a reduction in road traffic accidents while promoting increased physical activity participation.
4[a]	4.1—Ensure that all girls and boys complete free, equitable and quality primary and secondary education leading to relevant and effective learning outcomes	Quality physical education and physical activity opportunities in schools contribute to increased physical activity participation. Increased physical activity participation in all girls and boys can lead to greater ability to concentrate and improved cognitive function, thereby resulting in better academic outcomes.
5	5.1—End all forms of discrimination against all women and girls everywhere	In most countries there is a gender bias in physical activity participation, with boys more likely to be active than girls. Increased access and opportunities for physical activity for women and girls across the life course contribute to ending discrimination and can help enable women and girls to develop transferable skills that enable a more self-reliant life and lead to income-generating activities as well as economic participation.
10[b]	10.2—Empower and promote the social, economic, and political inclusion of all, irrespective of age, sex, disability, race, ethnicity, origin, religion, economic, or other status	Physical activity programs and sports promote values such as fairness and inclusion that can help reduce inequities such as boys being more active than girls. These activities can empower participants, regardless of their individual traits. A greater sense of empowerment can encourage greater contribution to the social, economic, and political domains.

[a]SDG4 (Quality Education)
[b]SDG10 (Reduced Inequalities)
Adapted from WHO (2018)

26.4   The Role of Schools in Encouraging Physical Activity

Children are key to sustainable development, with the United Nations International Children's Emergency Fund (UNICEF, 2013) stating that "sustainable development starts and ends with safe, healthy and well-educated children" (p. 7). Quality educational opportunities via school (SDG4) are seen as a major key for promoting and contributing to children meeting international physical activity requirements (SDG3) as they provide multiple opportunities such as physical education (PE) classes, after-school sport, and recess and lunch breaks. Schools are recognised as one of the most powerful influencers in establishing children's physical activity participation (Hills et al., 2015). This is exemplified by a comprehensive review of 25 years of physical activity studies (from predominantly developed Western contexts) that found positive, strong links between children's attendance at school and their physical activity participation (Ferreira et al., 2007). For instance, children are often spending the majority of weekdays (often >30 h) attending schools, with a multitude of strategies in schools introduced that can encourage physical activity (Naylor et al., 2015). The quality of educational settings such as within schools can be seen as even more vital when considering that there are reports of greatly reduced home and neighbourhood play opportunities for children (e.g., safety considerations, reduced spaces for play) (Hand et al., 2018; Holt et al., 2015).

School HPE classes are key locations for developing positive physical activity habits, with UNESCO (2015) stating that they can be considered the entry-point for lifelong participation in physical activity. A high-quality HPE program (SDG4) aims to promote lifelong engagement in physical activity (SDG3) and give students opportunities to experience a range of sports and activities through which they can lead active and healthy lives (Humphrey & Cruickshank, 2018). In their survey of 52 countries around the world, Bailey and Dismore (2006) found that the promotion of lifelong physical activity was a universal aim of PE. This finding has been supported more recently by research in the United Kingdom (e.g., MacNamara et al., 2011) and the inclusion of lifelong physical activities is one of the 12 focus areas of the *Australian HPE Curriculum* (Australian Curriculum Assessment and Reporting Authority, 2021). This aim aligns closely with UNESCO's (2015) challenge for HPE teachers "to help young people develop lifelong participation in physical activity, for the benefit of all society" (p. 8). UNESCO (2003) states that school HPE education is an effective means of promoting physical activity among young people and also helps students "respond to many of the challenges faced by young people, including the threat of HIV/AIDS and other sexually transmitted diseases, and the dangers of tobacco and drugs" (p. 9). Along with the promotion of physical activity to help achieve SDG Target 3.4 (Table 26.2), this health knowledge is key to reducing the spread of communicable diseases (SDG Target 3.3) and harmful use of drugs and alcohol (SDG Target 3.5) and illustrates the importance of school HPE towards achieving SDG3.

26.5   Strategies for Developing School Children's Lifelong Physical Activity Habits and How They Can Contribute to Understanding of, and Action Towards Realising SDG3, SDG4, and SDG5

26.5.1   Curricular HPE Strategies

Quality education strategies (SDG4) to develop physical activity in children for lifelong skills and habits (SDG3) can be undertaken within schools via curricular, non-curricular, and co-curricular programs. School PE programs (within a combination of Health & PE in some countries) are the main "curricular" methods for children developing physical activity habits and skills (Cruickshank et al., 2021b). UNESCO (2015) stated that it is crucial that all children are given equal opportunities to participate actively in quality physical education as this "quality education, particularly for girls, generates immediate, intergenerational payback across all dimensions of sustainable development" (p. 36). The PE curriculum is used to guide educators to provide opportunities to engage in physical activities via a safe, positive, and supportive class context (Kirk, 2014). It is within this curricular time in which children develop Fundamental Movement Skills (FMS) that can last a lifetime. The types of FMS include both locomotion skills (e.g., running, jumping, hopping, leaping) and object control (e.g., throwing, catching, kicking, striking). Tactical and decision-making strategies can also be developed across such movement situations (Miller et al., 2015).

Quality pedagogical approaches (SDG4) commonly used by teachers to develop young people's movement habits (SDG3) include game-based approaches (guided exploration of game problems within a context of physical activity problem solving), sport education model approaches (including key features of sporting competitions within PE lessons), teaching personal and social responsibility (TPSR) approaches (prioritising the "affective domain" of PE teaching), and cooperative learning (tasks set up aligned to group members, encourage face to face interaction, open dialogue, and include accountability) (Hyndman et al., 2020). From these selected approaches to PE curricula delivery, game-based approaches have emerged in recent decades as a favoured choice of PE delivery (Miller et al., 2015). Such game-based approaches involve physical activities that are organised according to striking/fielding (cricket, baseball), invasion (hockey, basketball), target-based (bocce, lawn bowls), and net/wall (badminton, volleyball). The games are used to scaffold according to guided, open-ended questions and can be modified according to the coaching method of scoring, how scoring occurs, the size and dimensions of the playing area, number of players, game rules, equipment, inclusion for learning needs, and time of the games (Pill et al., 2017). These quality student-centred approaches to developing children's physical activity skills (SDG4) can increase student enjoyment, and consequently engagement, in PE classes and help them establish positive physical activity habits that can last throughout their lives (SDG3).

26.5.2 Co-Curricular HPE Strategies

Quality co-curricular strategies (SDG4) can also be implemented within school grounds to develop school children's skills for lifelong physical activity (SDG3). These approaches include the provision of accessible, safe, and supervised strategies outside scheduled classes within school grounds, which allow children often to have more autonomy to explore chosen physical activity pursuits in the spaces around them. Strategies that schools and educators have implemented with physical activity increases include the provision of "activity cards" that detail games and activities for children to engage with, digitally interactive games to encourage physical activity, training staff to deliver recess games, themed activity weeks (e.g., fitness circuits, obstacle courses, frisbee weeks), fitness-focused recess periods, the provision of loose equipment for children to direct their own physical activities, and developing zones within spaces for different physical activity types (Hyndman et al., 2020).

26.5.3 Non-Curricular HPE Strategies

There is also a diverse range of quality non-curricular physical activity strategies (SDG4) that can be trialled within schools to develop and encourage the development of long-term physical activity habits in young people (SDG3), such as summer camps, active transportation to/from school and before/after-school physical activity programs. Summer camp physical activities are most common in countries such as the USA and Canada, which can involve and develop (Seal & Seal, 2011) a range of outdoor recreational practical activities with specialised performing arts, sports, and religious activity focus for young people (Baker et al., 2017). Such camp approaches suggest an improved likelihood for young people to meet the recommended amounts of physical activity participation (Brazendale et al., 2017; Hinton & Buchanan, 2015).

26.5.4 Active Transportation

Active transportation can be facilitated and encouraged by schools, encouraging young people to walk or bike/scooter to school, which helps develop more "incidental" physical activity habits into school children's lives (Brown et al., 2017). Researchers suggest that quality active transport strategies provided to children (SDG4) can decrease obesity, increase cardiovascular fitness, and support the development of long-term routines in sustainable physical activity behaviour (SDG3) (Faulkner et al., 2004; Pucher et al., 2010). Despite some declining active transportation trends in school-aged children across the world (Begum et al., 2012; Van Kann et al., 2015), there is scope to reinvigorate active transportation programs across many jurisdictions. This includes improving socialisation on active transport routes, ensuring teacher professional development for active transportation, developing community partnerships, and increasing safety messages (Larouche et al., 2018; Villa-Gonzáleza et al., 2018). One idea includes the "walking school bus" concept, which has an adult leading an active transport team, and has been implemented across the world to reduce safety concerns with the physical activity strategy (TravelSmart Australia, 2005).

26.5.5 After-School Strategies

After-school strategies are another approach to non-curricular school delivery of physical activity (SDG4), which are often collaborative, and draw upon community resources for meaningful, inclusive physical activities for school children (SDG3) (Hyndman et al., 2020). Community resources that schools can draw upon are facilities, personnel, and equipment that are available in the neighbourhood. After-school programs can be coordinated by school physical education teachers for leisure or competitive sport, and they can also involve partnerships between schools and national sporting organisations. After-school programs that collaborate with national sporting organisations can consist of school children being connected with major sporting organisations within their communities, with the goal and hope of the children pursuing sports participation in those areas beyond curricular school programs (Hogan & Stylianou, 2018). An example of schools connecting with major sporting organisations is through the Sporting Schools programs in Australia, in which schools apply for funding from the Australian Government, and representatives from the schools align with selected sports and programs they wish to be delivered at their schools (Australian Sports Commission, 2015). This approach has been recognised as an effective way to bridge school children into local community sport from the school contexts to continue to enhance the possibilities for sustained physical activity participation into the future.

26.5.6 School Uniforms

In developed Western countries, research (e.g., McCarthy et al., 2020; Norrish et al., 2012) has suggested that one of the reasons children, particularly girls, may not be active enough at school is due to the impracticability of their school uniforms (SDG5). Many school children are expected to wear traditional uniforms, usually consisting of leather shoes with shirts and pants for boys, and a dress, or skirt and shirt, with leather shoes and socks or stockings for girls (McCarthy et al., 2020). This attire can reduce the likelihood of children being physically active during break times, especially for girls in dresses. Some schools allow students to wear their sports uniforms on days they have PE classes, whereas other schools expect students to change into their sports uniforms for PE and then change back into their traditional uniforms at the end of their classes. The McCarthy et al. (2019) survey of 832 primary school students found that 61.6% of students would prefer to wear their sports uniform every day and 62.1% of students believed that they would be more active if they did.

Changing school policies to allow students to wear sports uniforms everyday could be an inexpensive and effective strategy for increasing children's physical activity. This would be especially important for girls, as international research (e.g., Guthold et al., 2020; Kwon et al., 2011; Olds et al., 2011; van Stralen et al., 2014; Zimmo et al., 2017) has consistently noted a gender-based disparity in physical activity among youth (SDG5), whereby girls are less physically active than boys. This gender-based disparity is also evident in school break times, with research identifying uniform as a key contributor. For example, Norrish et al. (2012) compared the school recess and lunchtime physical activity of 64 primary school children over four weeks and found that girls, but not boys, were significantly more active when wearing their sports uniforms compared to their traditional uniforms. Similarly, the Watson et al. (2015) focus groups with 15 adolescent girls found that uniforms could either be the strong facilitator (if an activity-promoting uniform) or a strong barrier (if not an activity-promoting uniform) for lunchtime physical activities in both high and low socioeconomic status schools. Additionally, Stanley et al. (2012) noted that girls stated that uniforms restricted them from playing some types of activities, whereas no boys in the study mentioned uniforms.

26.5.7 Strategies to Increase Girls' Physical Activity Levels

Another uniform-related issue related to low physical activity levels is that research (e.g., Victoria University, 2021) has indicated girls want school sports uniforms that are designed for them, rather than unisex uniforms, which can be uncomfortable and ill-fitting, particularly around areas such as their hips. In terms of competitive sport, where uniforms are different for males and females, Slater and Tiggemann (2010) noted that sport uniforms that show greater skin and body detail for girls versus boys, were also an inhibiting factor in teenage sport participation due to body image concerns (SDG5). These concerns and the resultant reduction in active play and activity are highly relevant in the context of long-term health and current obesity rates, as well as realisation of SDG5. A recent Australian study of girls' sports uniform preferences (Victoria University, 2021) found similar results. It stated that girls need to be provided with flexible options of uniform styles that are made from comfortable material (SDG5). Specifically, girls stated they wanted a range of choices including shorts and t-shirts that hid sweat, were stretchy, dark-coloured, and designed for girls rather than being unisex. Girls noted that their male peers got to wear looser clothing whereas they were often expected to wear tight outfits that showed off their curves. This trend can also be seen at the elite level, with recent high-profile pushback from athletes such as the Norwegian women's beach handball team at the 2021 Tokyo Olympic Games (Goodwin, 2021).

The level of physical activity between genders (SDG5) has been the most common demographic variable that has been investigated within school recess periods across the international literature (Hyndman et al., 2016; Ridgers et al., 2012). A review of 31 recess studies from over a decade (Ridgers et al., 2012) revealed that girls were consistently less active than boys and this further reinforced previous international reviews across age groups (Hinkley et al., 2008; Sallis et al., 2000; Van Der Horst et al., 2007). Researchers have suggested that girls can often view school playgrounds more as a place to socialise (Pellegrini & Bohn, 2005), an important consideration within schools better to accommodate girls' play behaviour (SDG5). Other researchers have found that girls tend to possess higher levels of enjoyment for creating/making things, using their imagination and some of the lighter intensity activities during school recess, such as walking (Hyndman, 2017). These findings were further reinforced when a school recess intervention was implemented, which was designed to enhance creative and imaginative play through "loose parts" play in primary schools (Hyndman, 2017). Teachers reporting on the intervention found girls to be more engaged, and the play had more inclusive options to meet gender needs from introducing loose parts into school grounds during recess (SDG5). Focus group discussions with primary and secondary school students have identified that girls have also suggested ideas such as dog-walking programs and excursions to meet their physical activity needs (Hyndman, 2017). Such trends can be further considered for physical activity strategies within schools to ensure that the physical activity needs for girls are better accommodated during this foundational stage to establish positive physical activity habits to enact across the lifespan (SDG5).

In addition to noting girls are less active than boys, research (e.g., Cowley et al., 2021) has also noted that influences on youth participation in physical activity often differ by gender (SDG5). For example, competition and muscle gain are often considered motivators for boys' participation in physical activity but are considered a barrier for girls (Casey et al., 2016; Flintoff & Scranton, 2001). Additionally, research such as Pawlowki et al. (2018) has observed that girls are more likely to cite low self-esteem, low perceived competence, and poor body image as deterrents to being physically active. UNESCO (2015) stated that quality school PE (SDG4) is the ideal way to reach large numbers of girls (SDG 5) and equip them with the information, skills, and confidence necessary for lifelong engagement with physical activity and sport (SDG3). However, this physical-activity-related engagement and enjoyment is unlikely to occur if PE teachers do not understand the differences in how boys and girls approach and experience sport, so that they can ensure a mix of activities and sports that are relevant and enjoyable to all students. Traditional, technique-focused, sport-based PE, where predominantly masculine values of over competitiveness and aggression take precedence over values such as fair play and co-operation, have been identified as a barrier to girls' participation (Kirk, 2012). UNESCO (2015) argued that this form of PE only caters for "a minority of already sport competent children, typically boys, resulting in confirmation of incompetence and failure for the majority" (p. 36). To encourage "regular, beneficial and sustainable participation by girls in physical education" (Kirk, 2012, p. 7), schools need to ensure their PE programs are designed to encourage lifelong physical activity engagement for all students. This move could assist in the achievement of SDG3 and SDG5, as well as align with the global strategy for women's, children's, and adolescents' health (2016–2030) (UN, 2016) and the "Every Women Every Child" initiative launched by the former UN Secretary-General Ban Ki-moon in 2010.

26.6 Conclusion

Increased physical activity participation via quality educational strategies worldwide (SDG4) is a key strategy to improve global health and wellbeing, help achieve SDG3, and contribute to the attainment of SDG5 and other SDGs. UNESCO (2003) noted that physical activity is critical for the holistic development of young people; yet, the WHO (2020) estimates that approximately 80% of 5–17-year-olds across the world do not meet minimum physical activity guidelines. This is concerning given that childhood physical activity habits and perceptions formed via educational strategies (SDG4) usually form the basis for lifelong activity (SDG3) (MacNamara et al., 2015) and are especially problematic for girls, who are often given fewer opportunities to be active than boys (SDG5).

Schools are key educational sites for promoting lifelong physical activity engagement to young people, particularly through HPE classes. While school HPE is focused on much more than just physical activity, high-quality and well-designed school curricular, co-curricular, and non-curricular HPE programs can deliver positive experiences and opportunities for active recreation, sports, and play for girls and boys (SDG4). These experiences can assist in meeting the objectives of sustainable human development, by strengthening human capabilities, creating connections between individuals, and improving social cohesion (UNESCO, 2003). Programs targeting young people need to have a whole-of-school approach (Nash et al., 2021) to promoting the enjoyment of, and participation in, physical activity (WHO, 2018), to ensure that they are effective in establishing and reinforcing lifelong health and physical activity habits regardless of capacity and ability (SDG3).

References

Abarca-Gómez, L., Abdeen, Z. A., Hamid, Z. A., Abu-Rmeileh, N. M., Acosta-Cazares, B., Acuin, C., Adams, R. J., Aekplakorn, W., Afsana, K., Aguilar-Salinas, C. A., Agyemang, C., Ahmadvand, A., Ahrens, W., Ajlouni, K., Akhtaeva, N., Al-Hazzaa, H. M., Al-Othman, A. R., Al-Raddadi, R., Al Buhairan, F., ... Ezzati, M. (2017). Worldwide trends in body-mass index, underweight, overweight, and obesity from 1975 to 2016: A pooled analysis of 2416 population-based measurement studies in 128.9 million children, adolescents, and adults. *The Lancet, 390*(10113), 2627–2642.
Active Healthy Kids Australia. (2021). *Report cards.* https://www.activehealthykidsaustralia.com.au/report-cards/

Aspetar Orthopaedic and Sport Medicine Hospital. (2014). *State of Qatar national physical activity guidelines.* https://www.aspetar.com/AspetarFILEUPLOAD/UploadCenter/637736948034 432931_QATAR%20NATIONAL%20PHYSICAL%20ACTIVITY%20GUIDELINES_ENG LISH.pdf

Australian Curriculum, Assessment and Reporting Authority. (2021). *Australian curriculum: Health and physical education.* https://www.australiancurriculum.edu.au/f-10-curriculum/health-and-physical-education/structure/

Australian Sports Commission. (2015). *Play sport Australia.* https://www.ausport.gov.au/__data/assets/pdf_file/0006/625902/PlaySportAustralia_brochre_MARCH_15_web.pdf

Bailey, R., & Dismore, H. (2006). The nature and function of sport pedagogy: International review. *International Journal of Physical Education, 63*(4), 144–147.

Baker, B. L., McGregor, A., Johnson, L. G., & Taylor, M. (2017). Summer day camp attendance facilitates some children meeting physical activity recommendations: Differences by gender and weight status. *Journal of Applied Biobehavioral Research, 22*(4), e12097.

Bangsbo, J., Blackwell, J., Boraxbekk, C. J., Caserotti, P., Dela, F., Evans, A. B., Jespersen, A. P., Gliemann, L., Kramer, A. F., Lundbye-Jensen, J., Mortensen, E. L., Lassen, A. J., Gow, A. J., Harridge, S. D. R., Hellsten, Y., Kjaer, M., Kujala, U. M., Rhodes, R. E., Pike, E. C. J., ... Viña, J. (2019). Copenhagen consensus statement 2019: Physical activity and ageing. *British Journal of Sports Medicine, 53*(14), 856–858.

Begum, N., Abernethy, P., Clemens, S., & Harper, C. (2012). Physical activity and school active transport behaviours of Queensland school children. *Journal of Science and Medicine in Sport, 15*, S212.

Brazendale, K., Beets, M. W., Weaver, R. G., Chandler, J. L., Randel, A. B., Turner-McGrievy, G. M., Moore, J. B., Huberty, J. L., Ward, D. S. (2017). Children's moderate to vigorous physical activity attending summer day camps. *American Journal of Preventive Medicine, 53*(1), 78–84.

Brown, V., Moodie, M., Herrera, A. M., Veerman, J. L., & Carter, R. (2017). Active transport and obesity prevention–A transportation sector obesity impact scoping review and assessment for Melbourne, Australia. *Preventive Medicine, 96*, 49–66.

Canadian Society for Exercise Physiology. (2012). *Canadian 24-hour movement guidelines for children and youth.* http://csepguidelines.ca/children-and-youth-5-17/

Casey, M., Mooney, A., Smyth, J., & Payne, W. (2016). Power, regulation and physically active identities: The experiences of rural and regional living adolescent girls. *Gender and Education, 28*(1), 108–127.

Cowley, E. S., Watson, P. M., Foweather, L., Belton, S., Thompson, A., Thijssen, D., & Wagenmakers, A. J. (2021). "Girls aren't meant to exercise": Perceived influences on physical activity among adolescent girls—The HERizon Project. *Children, 8*(1), 31.

Cruickshank, V., Hyndman, B., Patterson, K., & Kebble, P. (2021a). Encounters in a marginalised subject: The experiential challenges faced by Tasmanian Health and Physical Education teachers. *Australian Journal of Education, 65*(1), 24–40.

Cruickshank, V., Pill, S., & Mainsbridge, C. (2021b). 'Just do some physical activity': Exploring experiences of teaching physical education online during Covid-19. *Issues in Educational Research, 31*(1), 76–93.

Dentro, K. N., Beals, K., Crouter, S. E., Eisenmann, J. C., McKenzie, T. L., Pate, R. R., & Katzmarzyk, P. T. (2014). Results from the United States' 2014 report card on physical activity for children and youth. *Journal of Physical Activity and Health, 11*(s1), S105–S112.

Department of Health. (2017). *Australia's physical activity and sedentary behaviour guidelines for children.* http://www.health.gov.au/internet/main/publishing.nsf/content/health-pubhlth-strateg-phys-act-guidelines#apa512

Department of Health and Human Services. (2018). *Physical activity guidelines for Americans.* https://health.gov/paguidelines/pdf/paguide.pdf

Dodd, G. D. (2015). The unrealised value of human motion–'moving back to movement!' *Asia-Pacific Journal of Health, Sport and Physical Education, 6*(2), 191–213.

Falck, R. S., Davis, J. C., & Liu-Ambrose, T. (2017). What is the association between sedentary behaviour and cognitive function: A systematic review. *British Journal of Sports Medicine, 51*(10), 800–811.

Faulkner, G., Reeves, C., & Chedzoy, S. (2004). Nonspecialist, preservice primary-school teachers: Predicting intentions to teach physical education. *Journal of Teaching in Physical Education, 23*(3), 200–215.

Ferreira, I., Van Der Horst, K., Wendel-Vos, W., Kremers, S., Van Lenthe, F. J., & Brug, J. (2007). Environmental correlates of physical activity in youth: A review and update. *Obesity Reviews, 8*(2), 129–154.

Flintoff, A., & Scraton, S. (2001). Stepping into active leisure? Young women's perceptions of active lifestyles and their experiences of school physical education. *Sport, Education and Society, 6*, 5–21.

Goodwin, S. (2021). *Broadcasters take action against sexualisation of female Olympians.* https://au.sports.yahoo.com/olympics-2021-broadcasters-act-sexualisation-female-athletes-223357779.html

Guthold, R., Stevens, G. A., Riley, L. M., & Bull, F. C. (2020). Global trends in insufficient physical activity among adolescents: A pooled analysis of 298 population-based surveys with 1.6 million participants. *The Lancet Child & Adolescent Health, 4*(1), 23–35.

Hand, K. L., Freeman, C., Seddon, P. J., Recio, M. R., Stein, A., & van Heezik, Y. (2018). Restricted home ranges reduce children's opportunities to connect to nature: Demographic, environmental and parental influences. *Landscape and Urban Planning, 172*(April), 69–77.

Hesketh, K. R., Lakshman, R., & Sluijs, E. M. (2017). Barriers and facilitators to young children's physical activity and sedentary behaviour: A systematic review and synthesis of qualitative literature. *Obesity Reviews, 18*(9), 987–1017.

Hills, A. P., Dengel, D. R., & Lubans, D. R. (2015). Supporting public health priorities: Recommendations for physical education and physical activity promotion in schools. *Progress in Cardiovascular Diseases, 57*(4), 368–374.

Hinkley, T., Crawford, D., Salmon, J., Okely, A. D., & Hesketh, K. (2008). Preschool children and physical activity: A review of correlates. *American Journal of Preventive Medicine, 34*(5), 435–441.

Hinton, V., & Buchanan, A. M. (2015). Positive behavior interventions and support in a physical activity summer camp. *Physical Educator, 72*(4), 660–676.

Hogan, A., & Stylianou, M. (2018). School-based sports development and the role of NSOs as 'boundary spanners': Benefits, disbenefits and unintended consequences of the Sporting Schools policy initiative. *Sport, Education and Society, 23*(4), 367–380.

Holt, N. L., Lee, H., Millar, C. A., & Spence, J. C. (2015). 'Eyes on where children play': A retrospective study of active free play. *Children's Geographies, 13*(1), 73–88.

Houghton, S., Hunter, S. C., Rosenberg, M., Wood, L., Zadow, C., Martin, K., & Shilton, T. (2015). Virtually impossible: Limiting Australian children and adolescents daily screen-based media use. *BMC Public Health, 15*(1), 1–11.

Humphrey, A., & Cruickshank, V. (2018). Encouraging students to be active and healthy for life. *Active and Healthy Journal, 25*(1), 10–13.

Hyndman, B., Benson, A., & Telford, A. (2016). Active play: Exploring the influences on children's school playground activities. *American Journal of Play, 8*(3), 325–344.

Hyndman, B. (Ed.). (2017). *Contemporary school playground strategies for healthy students.* Springer.

Hyndman, B., Winslade, M., & Wright, B. (2020). Physical activity and learning. In R. Midford, G. Nutton, B. Hyndman, & S. Silburn (Eds.), *Health and Education Interdependence* (pp. 179–204). Springer.

Kirk, D. (2012). *Empowering girls and women through physical education and sport: Advocacy brief.* https://www.un.org/sport/sites/www.un.org.sport/files/ckfiles/files/UNESCO_Advocacy_Brief_Empowering-Girls_2012_EN.pdf

Kirk, D. (2014). *Physical education and curriculum study: A critical introduction.* Routledge.

Kwon, S., Janz, K. F., Burns, T. L., & Levy, S. M. (2011). Effects of adiposity on physical activity in childhood: Iowa Bone Development Study. *Medicine and Science in Sports and Exercise, 43*(3), 443.

Larouche, R., Mammen, G., Rowe, D. A., & Faulkner, G. (2018). Effectiveness of active school transport interventions: A systematic review and update. *BMC Public Health, 18*(206), 1–18.

Lawson, H. A. (2005). Empowering people, facilitating community development, and contributing to sustainable development: The social work of sport, exercise, and physical education programs. *Sport, Education and Society, 10*(1), 135–160.

Macpherson, H., Teo, W. P., Schneider, L. A., & Smith, A. E. (2017). A life-long approach to physical activity for brain health. *Frontiers in Aging Neuroscience, 9*, 147.

McCarthy, N., Hope, K., Sutherland, R., Campbell, E., Wolfenden, L., & Nathan, N. (2020). Australian primary school principals', teachers', and parents' attitudes and barriers to changing school uniform policies from traditional uniforms to sports uniforms. *Journal of Physical Activity and Health, 1*, 1–6.

McCarthy, N., Nathan, N., Hope, K., Sutherland, R., & Hodder, R. (2019). Australian secondary school student's attitudes to changing from traditional school uniforms to sports uniforms. *Journal of Science and Medicine in Sport, 22*, S94–S95.

MacNamara, A., Collins, D., Bailey, R., Toms, M., Ford, P., & Pearce, G. (2011). Promoting lifelong physical activity and high-level performance: Realising an achievable aim for physical education. *Physical Education & Sport Pedagogy, 16*(3), 265–278.

MacNamara, A., Collins, D., & Giblin, S. (2015). Just let them play? Deliberate preparation as the most appropriate foundation for lifelong physical activity. *Frontiers in Psychology, 6*, 1548.

Miller, A., Christensen, E. M., Eather, N., Sproule, J., Annis-Brown, L., & Lubans, D. R. (2015). The PLUNGE randomized controlled trial: Evaluation of a games-based physical activity professional learning program in primary school physical education. *Preventive Medicine, 74*(May), 1–8.

Nash, R., Cruickshank, V., Pill, S., MacDonald, A., Coleman, C., & Elmer, S. (2021). HealthLit4Kids: Dilemmas associated with student health literacy development in the primary school setting. *Health Education Journal, 80*(2), 173–186.

Naylor, P. J., Nettlefold, L., Race, D., Hoy, C., Ashe, M. C., Higgins, J. W., & McKay, H. A. (2015). Implementation of school based physical activity interventions: A systematic review. *Preventive Medicine, 72*(March), 95–115.

Norrish, H., Farringdon, F., Bulsara, M., & Hands, B. (2012). The effect of school uniform on incidental physical activity among 10-year-old children. *Asia-Pacific Journal of Health, Sport and Physical Education, 3*(1), 51–63.

Ogoh, S., & Ainslie, P. N. (2009). Cerebral blood flow during exercise: Mechanisms of regulation. *Journal of Applied Physiology, 107*(5), 1370–1380.

Olds, T., Maher, C. A., & Ridley, K. (2011). The place of physical activity in the time budgets of 10-to 13-year-old Australian children. *Journal of Physical Activity and Health, 8*(4), 548–557.

Pawlowski, C. S., Schipperijn, J., Tjørnhøj-Thomsen, T., & Troelsen, J. (2018). Giving children a voice: Exploring qualitative perspectives on factors influencing recess physical activity. *European Physical Education Review, 24*(1), 39–55.

Pedersen, S. J., Cooley, P. D., & Cruickshank, V. (2017). Caution regarding exergames: A skill acquisition perspective. *Physical Education and Sport Pedagogy, 22*(3), 246–256.

Pellegrini, A. D., & Bohn, C. M. (2005). The role of recess in children's cognitive performance and school adjustment. *Educational Research, 34*(1), 13–19.

Pill, S., Harvey, S., & Hyndman, B. (2017). Novel research approaches to gauge global teacher familiarity with game-based teaching in physical education: An exploratory Twitter analysis. *Asia-Pacific Journal of Health, Sport & Physical Education, 8*(2), 161–178.

Pucher, J., Buehler, R., Bassett, D. R., & Dannenberg, A. L. (2010). Walking and cycling to health: A comparative analysis of city, state, and international data. *American Journal of Public Health, 100*(10), 1986–1992.

Ridgers, N. D., Salmon, J., Parrish, A.-M., Stanley, R. M., & Okely, A. D. (2012). Physical activity during school recess: A systematic review. *American Journal of Preventive Medicine, 43*(3), 320–328.

Sallis, J. F., Prochaska, J. J., & Taylor, W. C. (2000). A review of correlates of physical activity of children and adolescents. *Medicine and Science in Sports and Exercise, 32*(5), 963–975.

Santrock, J. W. (2011). *Life-span development* (13th ed.). McGraw-Hill.

Schranz, N., Olds, T., Cliff, D., Davern, M., Engelen, L., Giles-Corti, B., & Lubans, D. (2014). Results from Australia's 2014 report card on physical activity for children and youth. *Journal of Physical Activity and Health, 11*(s1), S21–S25.

Seal, N., & Seal, J. (2011). Developing healthy childhood behaviour: Outcomes of a summer camp experience. *International Journal of Nursing Practice, 17*(4), 428–434.

Slater, A., & Tiggemann, M. (2010). "Uncool to do sport": A focus group study of adolescent girls' reasons for withdrawing from physical activity. *Psychology of Sport and Exercise, 11*(6), 619–626.

Stanley, R. M., Boshoff, K., & Dollman, J. (2012). Voices in the playground: A qualitative exploration of the barriers and facilitators of lunchtime play. *Journal of Science and Medicine in Sport, 15*(1), 44–51.

TravelSmart Australia. (2005). *Walking school bus: A guide for parents and teachers*. Australian Greenhouse Office in the Department of the Environment and Heritage.

UK Chief Medical Officers. (2019). *UK Chief Medical Officers physical activity guidelines*. http://www.bristol.ac.uk/sps/research/projects/physical-activity/uk-cmo-physical-activity-gui delines-2019/

United Nations. (2015). *Transforming our world: The 2030 agenda for sustainable development*. http://www.un.org/en/development/desa/population/migration/generalassembly/docs/glo balcompact/A_RES_70_1_E.pdf

United Nations. (2016). *Global strategy for women's, children's and adolescents' health (2016–2030)*. https://www.who.int/life-course/partners/global-strategy/globalstrategyreport2016-2030-lowres.pdf

United Nations Educational, Scientific and Cultural Organisation. (2003). *Sport for development and peace: Towards achieving the Millennium Development Goals*. https://digitallibrary.un.org/record/503601?ln=en

United Nations Educational, Scientific and Cultural Organisation. (2015). *Quality physical education: Guidelines for policy-makers*. http://www.unesco.org/new/en/social-and-humansciences/themes/physical-educationand-sport/policy-project/

United Nations International Children's Emergency Fund. (2013). *Sustainable development starts and ends with safe, healthy and well-educated children*. https://sustainabledevelopment.un.org/content/documents/3372SD_children_FINAL.pdf

Van Der Horst, K., Paw, M. J., Twisk, J. W., & Van Mechelen, W. (2007). A brief review on correlates of physical activity and sedentariness in youth. *Medicine and Science in Sports and Exercise, 39*(8), 1241–1250.

Van Kann, D. H., Kremers, S. P., Gubbels, J. S., Bartelink, N. H., De Vries, S. I., De Vries, N. K., & Jansen, M. W. (2015). The association between the physical environment of primary schools and active school transport. *Environment & Behavior, 47*(4), 418–435.

Van Stralen, M. M., Yıldırım, M., Wulp, A., Te Velde, S. J., Verloigne, M., Doessegger, A., Androutsos, O., Kovács, É., Brug, J., Chinapaw, M. J. M. (2014). Measured sedentary time and physical activity during the school day of European 10- to 12-year-old children: The ENERGY project. *Journal of Science and Medicine in Sport, 17*(2), 201–206.

Victoria University. (2021). *What girls want in sport uniforms*. https://www.vu.edu.au/sites/default/files/girl-sport-uniforms-national-study.pdf

Villa-González, E., Barranco-Ruiz, Y., Evenson, K. R., & Chillón, P. (2018). Systematic review of interventions for promoting active school transport. *Preventive Medicine, 111*, 115–134.

Watson, A., Eliott, J., & Mehta, K. (2015). Perceived barriers and facilitators to participation in physical activity during the school lunch break for girls aged 12–13 years. *European Physical Education Review, 21*(2), 257–271.

World Health Organisation. (2018). *Global action plan on physical activity 2018–2030: More active people for a healthier world*. https://apps.who.int/iris/bitstream/handle/10665/272722/978924 1514187-eng.pdf

World Health Organisation. (2020). *WHO guidelines on physical activity and sedentary behaviour.* https://www.who.int/publications/i/item/9789240015128

Zimmo, L., Farooq, A., Almudahka, F., Ibrahim, I., & Al-Kuwari, M. G. (2017). School-time physical activity among Arab elementary school children in Qatar. *BMC Pediatrics, 17*(1), 1–7.

Chapter 27
The Importance of Health Literacy for Sustainable Development

Vaughan Cruickshank⑩**, Claire Otten, Jack Evans, Melissa Jarvis, and Rosie Nash**

27.1 Introduction

Sustainable development was first described in 1987 as "development that meets the needs of the current generation without compromising the ability of future generations to meet their own needs" (World Commission on Environment & Development, 1987, p. 16). Achieving the Sustainable Development Goals (SDG) requires success in realising six major transformations. They are Quality Education (SDG 4), access to good quality and affordable health care (SDG 3), renewable energy and a circular economy (SDGs 7, 12, and 13), sustainable land and marine management (SDGs 2, 14, and 15), sustainable urban infrastructure (SDGs 6, 9, and 11), and universal access to digital services (SDG 9). Each of the six transformations requires a significant increase in public investments.

V. Cruickshank (✉)
School of Education, College of Law, Arts and Education, University of Tasmania, Newnham Drive, Newnham, TAS 7248, Australia
e-mail: v.j.cruickshank@utas.edu.au

C. Otten · R. Nash
Tasmanian School of Medicine, College of Health and Medicine, University of Tasmania, Liverpool Street, Hobart, TAS 7000, Australia
e-mail: claire.otten@utas.edu.au

R. Nash
e-mail: rmcshane@utas.edu.au

J. Evans
Menzies Institute for Medical Research, University of Tasmania, Liverpool Street, Hobart, TAS 7000, Australia
e-mail: jack.evans@utas.edu.au

M. Jarvis
Edinburgh, Scotland

© The Author(s), under exclusive license to Springer Nature Singapore Pte Ltd. 2023   491
K. Beasy et al. (eds.), *Education and the UN Sustainable Development Goals*, Education for Sustainability 7,
https://doi.org/10.1007/978-981-99-3802-5_27

The World Health Organisation (WHO, 2021c) seeks to enhance people's well-being and reduce their health risks associated with tobacco use, alcohol consumption, and physical inactivity, thereby contributing to improved population health. The development and implementation of cross-cutting normative, fiscal, and legal measures, and capacity development tools will be used to support these goals. Global health improvements will be achieved through key strategies including widespread awareness and adoption of Health Literacy (HL), community engagement strategies, and good governance for health (WHO, 2021b). Improving HL increases understanding of health and disease as well as the available services; hence people can make decisions to take care of their own selves and others (Budhathoki et al., 2017).

Given the current health, social, and political challenges experienced internationally in recent years, further action is required to promote health and encourage people to make healthy choices. However, people are only equipped to make such choices if they understand their implications (Budhathoki et al., 2017). The Shanghai Declaration on health promotion, endorsed at the 9th Global Conference on Health Promotion to support the SDGs, identified HL as a key driver to achieve sustainable development (Budhathoki et al., 2017). This endorsement strengthens the view that sustainable development requires more than just health education, it also involves enabling individuals to "gain access to, understand and use information in ways which promote and maintain good health for themselves, their families and their communities" (Menabde, 2017, p. 31). Although many, often overlapping, definitions of HL exist (Sørensen et al., 2012), this definition is appropriate given that it acknowledges that HL is an interacting and complex model that fundamentally extends beyond the competencies of an individual.

HL relies on the responsiveness of community and health services (Trezona et al., 2017, 2018) and the distributed HL available to individuals through their social networks (Edwards et al., 2015). Distributive HL has been described by Edwards et al. as:

> individuals benefit from the distribution of health literacy within their social network whatever their level of health literacy. Friends, family, colleagues and even acquaintances mediate the development and practice of health literacy by sharing knowledge, facilitating learning, contributing their own skills and supporting decision making. (p. 9)

Developing HL can therefore be employed as a strategic approach to empower people to improve their health and the health of those around them. HL has recently been recognised as a social determinant of health in its own right (Bröder et al., 2018). The social determinants of health can be defined as the "conditions in which people are born, grow, work, live, and age, and the wider set of forces and systems shaping the conditions of daily life" (WHO, 2021a, p. 1). Pelikan et al. (2018) sought to determine if HL was a determinant, moderator, or mediator of health. Their research concluded that comprehensive (interactive and critical) HL is a direct determinant of health and therefore has the potential to improve population health and reduce health inequities.

The WHO acknowledge there is no specific target on HL within SDGs; however, they recognise that efforts to raise HL will be crucial in whether the social, economic, and environmental ambitions of the 2030 Agenda for Sustainable Development are fully realised (WHO, 2021a). For example, within a Nepali context, Budhathoki et al. (2017) noted that there are currently few mechanisms in place for HL to impact positively on the SDGs, yet they state that increased HL could impact on the SDGs by helping to reduce inequalities and increase health system responsiveness. A life course approach addresses the SDGs by including children from an earlier stage, therefore, equipping them with HL tools to utilise throughout their development. Strengthening participatory and representative decision-making about HL development and equity at all levels will promote individual and community action for health. Although HL interventions are likely to be highly context-specific, the process and impact of implementing them can enable decision-makers from different government sectors to understand better the significance of HL, both to health and to their sectors' core objectives. This can scale up commitment to work across sectors, especially to achieve the SDGs (WHO, 2021b). Although SDG3 (Ensure healthy lives and promote wellbeing at all ages) is the only specific health goal among the SDGs, other goals (e.g., SDG1 (No Poverty), SDG2 (Zero Hunger), SDG4 (Quality Education), SDG8 (Decent Work and Economic Growth), and SDG10 (Reduced Inequalities)) are all linked to health and will contribute to improvements in population health globally (Murthy, 2014). In the WHO (2021c) Health promotion strategy, related to HL, mandated key areas in reducing population's health risks include reducing health inequities while empowering citizens, which would be natural outcomes of the success of the SDGs. This chapter focuses on how the granular intersections between SDGs 3, 4, and 10 make HL essential for sustainable development (Budhathoki et al., 2017).

27.2 SDG3: Ensure Healthy Lives and Promote Wellbeing for All at All Ages

Good health is the key to productive societies (Menabde, 2017). When people are healthy, they are better able to go to school and work, flourish, and contribute to their local community. This understanding is reflected in the central placement of health in the 2030 Agenda for Sustainable Development (United Nations [UN], 2015). Ensuring healthy lives and promoting wellbeing at all ages is essential to sustainable development, however, the recent COVID-19 pandemic has reversed recent progress in health by disrupting health services, reducing life expectancy, and increasing stress on healthcare workers (UN, 2021). The UN noted that the full toll of COVID-19 on health is not yet known as many people may have long-term health effects from lung scarring, heart damage, and mental health issues. The building back better initiative (Organisation for Economic Co-operation and Development [OECD], 2020; WHO, 2013) seeks to insert more sustainable strategies to address the mental health consequences of disasters on communities and their economies. HL is essential in these efforts.

Health is a vital component of SDG3; however, health and its social determinants cut across all SDGs (Menabde, 2017). SDG3 incorporates 13 targets focused on key health concerns globally. These targets focus on various aspects of wellbeing and healthy lifestyles. Various agencies such as the WHO, United Nations International Children's Emergency Fund (UNICEF), and OECD are responsible for reporting on the key indicators of progress towards these targets.

The WHO has positioned HL as one of three key pillars for achieving sustainable development and health equity in the Shanghai Declaration on Health Promotion (Trezona et al., 2018). HL has been linked to achieving good health within societies around the world (e.g., Budhathoki et al., 2017; Popoola, 2019), and its improvement in both developing and developed economies could aid in the achievement of SDG3. Popoola (2019) noted that low literacy rates in developing countries are a key barrier to the success of health programmes and that "increased access to information and knowledge, underpinned by universal literacy, is an essential pillar of sustainable development" (p. 112). Basic numeracy and literacy levels are foundational to an individual's functional HL assets (Nutbeam, 2000). Within the Nigerian context, libraries have been recommended as a key community knowledge hub to improve HL. More specifically Popoola (2019) stated that "libraries in developing countries can counteract the effect of the low resource status of their health care system on health literacy by proactively facilitating access to quality information, literacy skills and lifelong learning for individuals, community and practitioners" (p. 111). This statement aligns with the findings of Murthy (2014) who noted that HL levels are dependent upon more general levels of literacy. Poor literacy can affect people's health directly by limiting their personal and social development, as well as restricting the development of HL. Amoah and Phillips (2018) similarly noted that low HL in Ghana is linked with "poor judgements regarding decisions about the use of health services and difficulty in interpreting and using health information" (p. 41). Consequently, people who experience HL challenges are likely to spend more on health because of the increased use of emergency room services and the flow on effects of uninformed or unsupported health choices.

Strong evidence exists that HL skills are limited even in wealthy, developed countries (Vamos et al., 2020). For example, the results of the European HL Survey showed that 47% of respondents (from Austria, Bulgaria, Germany, Greece, Ireland, Netherlands, Poland, and Spain) reported limited HL skills (Palumbo et al., 2016). This figure was above 50% for respondents from Bulgaria (62.1%), Spain (58.3%), Austria (56.4%), and Italy (54.6%). Studies from the United States and Canada have shown similar results (Vamos et al., 2020). Palumbo et al. also stated within an Italian context, that while patients who faced HL challenges reported higher hospitalisation rates and greater use of health services, HL is routinely overlooked by policymakers and health care practitioners as a strategy for improving the health system. Moreover, they believe that healthcare settings in Italy are usually designed assuming that patients have "limitless health literacy skills" (p. 1093), when their research indicates this is not the case for many people. Budhatoki et al. (2017) made similar observations about recent health research paying:

little attention to health literacy, that is, how people and the community might be empowered to engage in recognising health needs, how to improve knowledge about the health system, and enabling people to regard access to health services as a right. (p. 2)

These individual and community attributes are key elements of HL and vital components of any actions to strengthen the health system, improve health outcomes, and, ultimately, to meet the SDG3 around the world.

Low HL leads to poor health outcomes and health inequalities. Certain population groups experience worse health outcomes due to lower HL levels (Murthy, 2014). These groups include women, rural residents, and immigrants, and can have higher incidence of communicable and non-communicable diseases such as cancer, diabetes, and HIV/AIDS. Incorporating HL into educational programmes for these groups is vital. An example of an innovative HL project is the Global Initiative on Education and HIV and AIDS (EDUCAIDS). This collaboration between stakeholders such as the United Nations Educational Scientific and Cultural Organization (UNESCO) and the Joint United Nations Programme on HIV/AIDS (UNAIDS) has been highly successful since being implemented in schools in countries such as Angola, Vietnam, Moldova, and Mexico (Murthy, 2014; Preckler Galguera, 2018). Better HL has also been associated with a lesser likelihood of becoming over- or underweight, as well as positive health behaviours such as increased physical activity, less use of alcohol, and less smoking (Okan et al., 2020).

Good health is essential to sustainable development and the 2030 Agenda. Considering the global pandemic of COVID-19, there is a need to give significant attention towards the realisation of good health and wellbeing on a global scale. This will involve governments implementing and enforcing health-focused policies, improving health systems, and ensuring equity in terms of access and opportunities for health. However, Menabde (2017) stated that we need higher levels of HL internationally if these policies and decisions are to have a positive impact on health. This caution aligns with the International Union for Health Promotion and Education (2019) statement on HL:

higher levels of health literacy in a population support a wide range of health actions to improve health, prevent and better manage ill-health, including greater capacity to change personal behaviours, take social actions for health, and influence others towards healthy decisions. (p. 15)

To ensure higher levels of HL within the community health systems need to support clear, accurate, appropriate, and accessible information for diverse audiences. This information should be accompanied by context and age-specific education that helps people choose healthy options where those choices exist. Health education is more likely to improve HL when the delivery is customised to the specific needs of individuals and populations across their life course.

27.3   SDG4: Ensure Inclusive and Equitable Quality Education and Promote Lifelong Learning Opportunities for All

Promoting health and education are international priorities. The UN including Good Health and Wellbeing and Quality Education as fundamental Sustainable Development Goals for the twenty-first century (UN, 2015) and as key rights for children (UN, 1989) and adults (UN, 1948) evidences their importance. HL has been acknowledged as a lifelong skill that must be maintained over time (Kickbusch et al., 2013). An imperative exists to support health and education. Improving HL could help to meet this imperative.

A bidirectional relationship exists between health and education (Fig. 27.1) (Pérez-Rodrigo et al., 2001). Improving people's health increases their ability to engage with education (Cummings & Obel-Omia, 2016). For example, a child who is well-fed and has had an appropriate amount of sleep is more likely to engage in higher order thinking skills and learn new concepts, than a child who is hungry and lacks sleep. Similarly, improving education supports positive health outcomes (Jackson, 2009). For instance, a child who has been educated about nutrition may be more likely to make positive nutritional choices than one who has not been. These relationships create a self-perpetuating cycle whereby one's health and educational attainment continuously affect each other.

HL can influence health and educational outcomes. An inextricable link exists between HL and educational attainment; this is because core competencies (e.g., literacy, numeracy) are fundamental to achieving both outcomes (educational attainment and HL). HL is also associated with health (Svendsen et al., 2020). Like education, increasing HL impacts people's understanding and ability to think critically about the factors that impact their health, thus, understand their realms of choices (Cummings & Obel-Omia, 2016). Supporting HL can, therefore, help to promote positive health outcomes and educational outcomes (Fig. 27.1).

Childhood is a key time to promote the development of HL, with many health attitudes, beliefs, and behaviours formed during this period and childhood HL being a predictor for adult HL (Bröder & Carvalho, 2019). Although clinical outcomes

Fig. 27.1 The associations between health outcomes, educational attainment, and health literacy

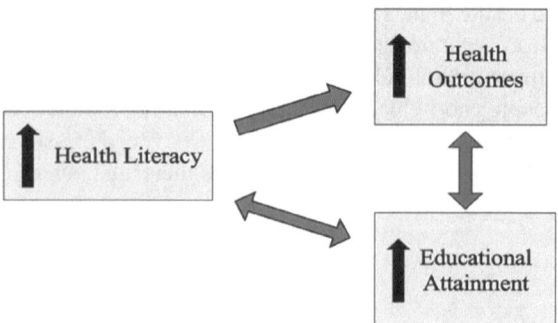

of chronic diseases (e.g., type 2 diabetes, heart disease) typically occur later in life, their onset can be prevented with primary intervention; for example, by providing children with the assets necessary to manage their health (HL, access to services, etc.) from an early age. Consequently, children should have access to education that can support the development of HL.

Primary schools provide an optimal setting to support HL development for several reasons. First, the students that attend school are children. Second, teachers should be equipped with the pedagogical knowledge and skills to educate students appropriately, including supporting HL development (Bröder & Carvalho, 2019). Third, schools are generally equitable settings (Sykes & Wills, 2019). Given that education is supported by many governments internationally (OECD, 2015) and is a right of the child (UN, 1989), it should be broadly accessible.

Despite the acknowledgement of schools as optimal settings to support HL development, barriers exist to implementing HL education. The UN (2015) has recognised access to education as a major barrier to health education. More needs to be done to promote access to health education, particularly in low-resourced countries and where gender disparities in educational outcomes exist. In regions/countries where schools are accessible, teachers need to be supported to develop the skills to promote HL development. Evidence suggests that many teachers lack the confidence/ability to teach HL (Deal et al., 2010; Nash et al., 2020a). Including HL as a larger component in tertiary education for preservice educators could help to overcome this barrier, as well as provide more professional development for practicing teachers (Nash et al., 2018).

Two approaches to supporting HL development in schools are professional development programmes such as HealthLit4Kids (Cruickshank et al., 2022) and mandating HL into areas of the curriculum such as media literacy (Schulenkorf et al., 2021). HealthLit4Kids (https://www.utas.edu.au/hl4k/home) is a professional development programme run in Australian primary schools to support teachers and primary school-aged students to incorporate health literacy into the classroom and to encourage schools to embrace health literacy across their curriculum (Nash et al., 2021a). The purpose of the programme is to improve teachers' competence and confidence to develop HL in students (Nash et al., 2021b). Teachers are encouraged to create lesson plans that are adapted to the HL needs of their students and provide them with opportunities to develop HL artefacts (e.g., artwork) and share these with their families and school community (MacDonald et al., 2021). The programme has been recognised by the WHO (2019b) as a demonstration project. Another example of how HL development has been supported is in Germany where a programme for digital education and digital literacy has been recently introduced in schools (Schulenkorf et al., 2021). The programme provides a framework for teachers and multiple opportunities for HL to be integrated into the curriculum (Schulenkorf et al., 2021). Although existing HL programmes are likely to have been tailored to the context in which they were developed, key principles (e.g., the strength of integrated learning) can be effectively applied to multiple settings to support learning.

Schools have the potential to improve not only the HL of their pupils but also that of the greater community via distributive HL. It has been shown that students who develop HL in a school context share their health knowledge and skills with members of their families and communities (Flecha et al., 2011; Nash et al., 2020b). It can, therefore, be suggested that educating students can act as a protective factor, not only for their health individually but also for the health of others around them. This positive influence can perpetuate beyond the individuals directly associated with the student and into the broader community with the sharing of information.

As well as impacting the existing community, improving HL in young people has the potential to halt intergenerational inequalities (Flecha et al., 2011). Along with teachers, parents are among the greatest influencers of child education and success (Dubow et al., 2009). By equipping today's youth with the skills necessary to navigate information and systems and form educated choices, we might be able to influence positively the HL trajectory of future generations. It is, therefore, imperative that quality education (including HL education) becomes a focus for the twenty-first century.

27.4 SDG10: Reduce Inequality Within and Among Countries

Inequality presents in many forms; however, a selection that may be redressed with HL is considered in this section. Inequality within and among nations is an issue of significant concern (UN, 2021). The term health inequality refers to the unjust nature of health differences between social groups. Often generated by social conditions, health inequalities may be observed by their patterns of effect, in which those from economically and socially poorer backgrounds experience higher risks of premature death and both communicable and non-communicable diseases (Farrell et al., 2008).

Targets and indicators for SDG 10 are primarily centred around ideas of fiscal and migratory equality (UN, 2015). Despite efforts to close the divide between both countries and classes, clear disparities in opportunity and capital remain. These social, political, and economic imbalances manifest in alarming country health inequalities. For many, health is directly reflective of an individual's position on the social gradient (Gibney et al., 2020). As such, the most socio-economically disadvantaged individuals are hit the hardest, with the lowest levels of health most prevalent among the poor. This effect is exponentially magnified among those that also reside in low-income countries (WHO, 2021b) As the sustainable development of one country may influence the development and wellbeing of people in another, a cooperative global response to inequalities within and between nations is imperative (Schmidt-Traub et al., 2019).

HL is well established as a modifiable factor that contributes to the promotion and maintenance of good health and wellbeing across the life course (Gibney et al., 2020). In addition, HL can make an impact on lower social status groups by reducing the effect of social disparities on health outcomes. Further, HL can educate those of a higher class as to the disparities in health that exist within their system, facilitating those in power to become a voice for the voiceless (Gibney et al., 2020). Previous research has established that comprehensive HL (interactive and critical) is a direct determinant of health and therefore has the potential to improve population health and tackle health inequities (Bröder et al., 2018; Pelikan et al., 2018). Therefore, HL must be recognised for its ability to reduce inequities in health and beyond (WHO, 2021b).

Education and resultant increases in HL have the capacity to help empower and promote the social, economic, and political inclusion of all, irrespective of age, sex, disability, race, ethnicity, origin, religion, economic, or other status (SDG target 10.2). To care most optimally for one's own health and the health of others, it is crucial that an individual be health literate (Batterham et al., 2016). This fact is compounded by the complex processes and information presented within healthcare and political systems. Without HL the individual would not possess the capacity to participate in health negotiations and decision-making processes that lead to the best outcomes for all (Budhathoki et al., 2017). Further yet, health education crucially allows those who become literate to comprehend the circumstances afforded the minority groups (whether they be racially, sexually, physically, or mentally different) and create understanding and inclusion from what was once stigma. One example of a potential pathway through which improvements in HL can contribute to the reduction of inequality is the education of young women. By increasing sexual and reproductive HL, young women of socio-economic disadvantage are more likely to remain in school (reducing gender gaps in education and contributing the gender equality (SDG5)) and as a result, experience improved economic opportunities. By advancing access to better jobs and by delaying pregnancy, sexual and reproductive HL may help to break chains of intergenerational poverty.

While supporting the development of an individuals' HL needs is important, there have been consistent and increasingly urgent calls for greater emphasis on the responsibility of service providers to examine and improve the HL responsiveness of their healthcare and community services (Pelikan et al., 2018; Trezona et al., 2017, 2018). This call must also extend to wider communities, private organisations, not-for-profits, government, and political systems. Those with higher levels of HL are empowered to hold their governments accountable, whether for access to essential medicines, universal health coverage, removing environmental air pollutants, or tearing down discriminatory laws and practices. Thus, countries need to be held to account, to ensure equal opportunities and to reduce inequalities of outcome, including by eliminating discriminatory laws, policies, and practices, and promoting appropriate legislation, policies, and action in this regard (SDG target 10.3). However, this is only likely to be effective if governments take steps to increase and sustain their own HL and they understand the complex, moving, and interacting parts that contribute to the construct. This is essential to ensure inequality is not further perpetuated through poor policy and decision-making. For example, some large-scale capital projects (ignorant to the local wisdom, culture, and contextual elements at play) have been shown to increase health risks in surrounding communities, with the potential to widen economic inequities—rather than to bring intended inclusive economic growth (Ballard & Banks, 2003). This is not acceptable, justifiable, or equitable if the benefits from these projects only flow to a few.

Health education is a key means through which social protection policies can be implemented and greater equality achieved. Corporations propagate the non-communicable diseases pandemic. Low and middle-income countries, and poor people in all countries, are disproportionately exposed to health-harming messaging (Kickbusch & Franz, 2016). They are targeted by industry marketing of products such as tobacco, alcohol, and sugar-sweetened foods and beverages. Investments in raising HL in poorer populations can counter this pressure, to prevent the widening of inequities both within and between countries (WHO, 2021b). Commercial determinants of health are defined as "strategies and approaches used by the private sector to promote products and choices that are detrimental to health" (Kickbusch & Franz, 2016). This single concept unites several others: at the micro level, these include consumer and health behaviour, individualisation, and choice; at the macro level, they include the global risk society, the global consumer society, and the political economy of globalisation. The tobacco industry is an example of an institution that influences an individual's commercial determinants of health by disproportionately targeting those from low and middle-income countries and those of low socioeconomic regions, to expand markets (Kickbusch & Franz, 2016). To combat the marketing campaigns and commercial determinants that yield negative health effects perpetuated via tobacco consumption, well-designed health warnings and messages on tobacco product packages have been implemented. These warnings act to increase public awareness of the health harms of tobacco use, reduce tobacco consumption, and address inequities in health.

Without strengthening HL (particularly among the most disadvantaged and marginalised societies) poverty and inequality will persist. Poor health reduces people's ability to work and earn income, while burdening individuals and families with medical expenses, or even forcing them to forego care. Developing HL can be used as a tool to support individuals and communities to make health-promoting choices. As a result, this is likely to lead to improved health outcomes, bridging the gap between advantaged and disadvantaged individuals, within and between countries.

27.5   Conclusion

The SDG agenda offers a new opportunity to involve multiple stakeholders to ensure that all people can fulfil their potential—to live in health and with dignity and equality (WHO, 2021b). A Community of Practice of WHO national HL demonstration projects was convened on November 2nd, 2021, to share knowledge and resources to overcome their common challenges (Nash, 2021). These challenges included limited community awareness of HL and its importance to health outcomes, minimal ministerial and government support, the diverse needs of stakeholders, difficulty accessing priority populations, and lack of resourcing and funding. The Community of Practice, with the support of the WHO, will aim to identify solutions to each of these challenges and work at a global level to ensure the solutions reduce inequality. Additionally, as there are currently limited existing systems to measure HL, developing these is a key step in supporting sustainable development.

HL has contributed to global health improvements in part by empowering participation in negotiations concerning health and social care. It is an essential tool that allows competent addressing of health needs by providing skills to think critically about health choices. Consideration must be given to how the concept of HL is applied in theory and in policy to prevent individualisation and thus erasure of the strengths and challenges that have contributed to existing HL competences.

Fulfilling the SDG agenda will require advocating and facilitating cross-sectoral integration of HL and promoting HL in all phases of the life course. Introducing the concept earlier in the life course allows HL to inform children's habits, beliefs, and behaviours, which are then able to be maintained and developed as they age. Future policies, strategies, and actions should take advantage of opportunities and motivation for HL development. HL must be promoted and included in all policies through a multisectoral approach, involving a range of stakeholders to create environments favourable to better outcomes (WHO, 2019a). HL can make a sustained impact on marginalised parts of the population by reducing the effect of social disparities on their health outcomes by incorporating HL into existing education projects.

Cross-sectoral, global, and inter-institutional partnerships must be formed to develop and improve methods to measure HL, collate and distribute examples of best practice in HL intervention development, and provide evidence of what works, in which contexts, and why. Underpinning these roles are some critical strategies to enable better synergies in health and development planning. It will be important to extend HL measurement beyond health-related reading ability and numeracy in clinical populations (Beauchamp et al., 2015). This extension will involve building on recent attempts to develop valid and reliable tools that aim to measure more completely the broader HL concept in a range of populations that includes, for example, interaction with the health care system and critical appraisal of health information (WHO, 2021b).

Recent study has shown that addressing SDGs can have both positive and negative knock-on effects for other SDGs (Pradhan et al., 2017). There is a noted almost symbiotic relationship between good health and educational attainment. HL can help to achieve quality education (SDG 4); however, it should not be considered in isolation from other sustainable development goals. Additionally, basic needs must be met successively before higher needs can be achieved. For example, at an individual level no poverty (SDG 1), zero hunger (SDG 2), promoting good health and wellbeing (SDG 3), gender equality (SDG 5), clean water and sanitation (SDG 6), and reduced inequalities (SDG 10), must be met prior to ensuring quality education (SDG 4) (UN, 2015). Developing HL is critical as it supports quality education concurrently with other Sustainable Development Goals.

As the WHO (2021b) stated, if the SDG are to be achieved by 2030, governments must invest now and take a strong leadership role in the development and implementation of HL promotion policies by providing sustained funding, setting up special projects, coordinating action across sectors, and conducting HL surveillance regularly. Improving and measuring HL (both strengths and needs) is particularly important in poorer areas. Vulnerable populations must be prioritised and empowered to engage in early and sustained health-promoting actions, whether to prevent acute and chronic conditions or to promote active and curative treatments. There is a real need to develop, implement, and evaluate interventions that improve knowledge, understanding, and capacity to act on social, economic, and environmental determinants of health.

References

Amoah, P. A., & Phillips, D. R. (2018). Health literacy and health: Rethinking the strategies for universal health coverage in Ghana. *Public Health, 159*, 40–49. https://doi.org/10.1016/j.puhe.2018.03.002

Ballard, C., & Banks, G. (2003). Resource wars: The anthropology of mining. *Annual Review of Anthropology, 32*(1), 287–313. https://doi.org/10.1146/annurev.anthro.32.061002.093116

Batterham, R., Hawkins, M., Collins, P., Buchbinder, R., & Osborne, R. (2016). Health literacy: Applying current concepts to improve health services and reduce health inequalities. *Public Health, 132*, 3–12. https://doi.org/10.1016/j.puhe.2016.01.001

Beauchamp, A., Buchbinder, R., Dodson, S., Batterham, R., Elsworth, G., McPhee, C., Sparkes, L., Hawkins, M., & Osborne, R. (2015). Distribution of health literacy strengths and weaknesses across socio-demographic groups: A cross-sectional survey using the Health Literacy Questionnaire (HLQ). *BMC Public Health, 15*, Article 678. https://doi.org/10.1186/s12889-015-2056-z

Bröder, J., & Carvalho, G. (2019). Health literacy of children and adolescents: Conceptual approaches and developmental considerations. In O. Okan, U. Bauer, P. Pinheiro, & K. Sørensen (Eds.), *International handbook of health literacy: Research, practice and policy across the life-span* (pp. 39–49). Bristol Press.

Bröder, J., Chang, P., Kickbusch, I., Levin-Zamir, D., McElhinney, E., Nutbeam, D., Okan, O., Osborne, R., Pelikan, J., Rootman, I, Rowlands, G., Nunes-Saboga, L., Simmons, R., Sørensen, K., Van den Broucke, S., Velardo, S., Wills, J. (2018). IUHPE position statement on health literacy: A practical vision for a health literate world. *Global Health Promotion, 25*(4), 79–88.https://doi.org/10.1177/1757975918814421

Budhathoki, S., Pokharel, P., Good, S., Limbu, S., Bhattachan, M., & Osborne, R. (2017). The potential of health literacy to address the health related UN sustainable development goal 3 (SDG3) in Nepal: A rapid review. *BMC Health Services Research, 17*, Article 237. https://doi.org/10.1186/s12913-017-2183-6

Cruickshank, V., Pill, S., Williams, J., Nash, R., Mainsbridge, C. P., MacDonald, A., & Elmer, S. (2022). Exploring the 'everyday philosophies' of generalist primary school teacher delivery of health literacy education. *Curriculum Studies in Health and Physical Education*. https://doi.org/10.1080/25742981.2022.2059384

Cummings, C., & Obel-Omia, C. (2016). Healthy reading: Teaching strategies for integrating health and literacy education. *Childhood Education, 92*(6), 455–464. https://doi.org/10.1080/00094056.2016.1251794

Deal, T., Jenkins, J., Deal, L., & Byra, A. (2010). The impact of professional development to infuse health and reading in elementary schools. *American Journal of Health Education, 41*(3), 155–166. https://doi.org/10.1080/19325037.2010.10598857

Dubow, E., Boxer, P., & Huesmann, L. (2009). Long-term effects of parents' education on children's educational and occupational success: Mediation by family interactions, child aggression, and teenage aspirations. *Merrill-Palmer Quarterly, 55*(3), 224–249. https://doi.org/10.1353/mpq.0.0030

Edwards, M., Wood, F., Davies, M., & Edwards, A. (2015). 'Distributed health literacy': Longitudinal qualitative analysis of the roles of health literacy mediators and social networks of people living with a long-term health condition. *Health Expectations, 18*(5), 1180–1193. https://doi.org/10.1111/hex.12093

Farrell, C., McAvoy, H., & Wilde, J. (2008). *Tackling health inequalities: An all-Ireland approach to social determinants.* Combat Poverty Agency.

Flecha, A., Garcia, R., & Rudd, R. (2011). Using health literacy in school to overcome inequalities. *European Journal of Education, 46*(2), 209–218. https://doi.org/10.1111/j.1465-3435.2011.01476.x

Gibney, S., Bruton, L., Ryan, C., Doyle, G., & Rowlands, G. (2020). Increasing health literacy may reduce health inequalities: Evidence from a national population survey in Ireland. *International Journal of Environmental Research and Public Health, 17*(16), 5891. https://doi.org/10.3390/ijerph17165891

International Union for Health Promotion and Education. (2019). *IUHPE Position statement on health literacy: A practical vision for a health literate world.* https://www.iuhpe.org/images/IUHPE/Advocacy/IUHPEHealth_Literacy_2018.pdf

Jackson, M. I. (2009). Understanding links between adolescent health and educational attainment. *Demography, 46*(4), 671–694. https://doi.org/10.1353/dem.0.0078

Kickbusch, A. L., & Franz, C. (2016). The commercial determinants of health. *The Lancet Global Health, 4*(12), e895–e896. https://doi.org/10.1016/S2214-109X(16)30217-0

Kickbusch, I., Pelikan, J., Apfel, F., & Tsouros, A. (2013). *Health literacy: The solid facts.* World Health Organization.

MacDonald, A., Cruickshank, V., Nash, R., & Patterson, K. (2021). Contemplating [en] active curriculum: Becoming health literate through Arts and HPE interconnection. *Curriculum Perspectives, 41*(1), 119–124.

Menabde, N. (2017). *Health literacy and the SDGs.* https://www.sustainablegoals.org.uk/health-literacy-and-the-sdgs/

Mõttus, R., Johnson, W., Murray, C., Wolf, M. S., Starr, J. M., & Deary, I. J. (2014). Towards understanding the links between health literacy and physical health. *Health Psychology, 33*(2), 164–173. https://doi.org/10.1037/a0031439

Murthy, P. (2014). *Health literacy and sustainable development.* https://www.un.org/en/chronicle/article/health-literacy-and-sustainable-development

Nash, R. (2021, November 2). *World Health Organisation National Health Literacy Demonstration Program CoP meeting 1.*

Nash, R., Cruickshank, V., Flittner, A., Mainsbridge, C., Pill, S., & Elmer, S. (2020a). How Did parents view the impact of the curriculum-based HealthLit4Kids program beyond the classroom? *International Journal of Environmental Research and Public Health, 17*(4), 1449–1462. https://doi.org/10.3390/ijerph17041449

Nash, R., Cruickshank, V., Pill, S., MacDonald, A., Coleman, C., & Elmer, S. (2021a). HealthLit4Kids: Dilemmas associated with student health literacy development in the primary school setting. *Health Education Journal, 80*(2), 173–186.

Nash, R., Elmer, S., Thomas, K., Osborne, R., MacIntyre, K., Shelley, B., Murray, L., Harpur, S., Webb, D. (2018). HealthLit4Kids study protocol; crossing boundaries for positive health literacy outcomes. *BMC Public Health, 18*(1), 690–690. https://doi.org/10.1186/s12889-018-5558-7

Nash, R., Otten, C., Pill, S., Williams, J., Mainsbridge, C., Cruickshank, V., & Elmer, S. (2021b). School leaders reflections on their school's engagement in a program to foster health literacy development. *International Journal of Educational Research Open, 2,* 100089. https://doi.org/10.1016/j.ijedro.2021.100089

Nash, R., Patterson, K., Flittner, A., Elmer, S., & Osborne, R. (2020b). School based health literacy programs for children (2–16 years): An international review. *Journal of School Health, 91*(8), 632–649. https://doi.org/10.1111/josh.13054

Nutbeam, D. (2000). Health literacy as a public health goal: A challenge for contemporary health education and communication strategies into the 21st century. *Health Promotion International, 15*(3), 259–267. https://doi.org/10.1093/heapro/15.3.259

Okan, O., Paakkari, L., & Dadaczynski, K. (2020). *Health literacy in schools: State of the art.* Schools for Health in Europe.

Organisation for Economic Co-operation and Development. (2015). *Education at a glance 2015.* https://www.oecd-ilibrary.org/education/education-at-a-glance-2015_eag-2015-en

Organisation for Economic Co-operation and Development. (2020). *Building back better: A sustainable, resilient recovery after COVID-19.* OECD Publishing.

Paakkari, L., & George, S. (2018). Ethical underpinnings for the development of health literacy in schools: Ethical premises ('why'), orientations ('what') and tone ('how'). *BMC Public Health, 18*(1), 1–10.

Palumbo, R., Annarumma, C., Adinolfi, P., Musella, M., & Piscopo, G. (2016). The Italian Health Literacy Project: Insights from the assessment of health literacy skills in Italy. *Health Policy, 120*(9), 1087–1094. https://doi.org/10.1016/j.healthpol.2016.08.007

Pelikan, J. M., Ganahl, K., & Roethlin, F. (2018). Health literacy as a determinant, mediator and/or moderator of health: Empirical models using the European Health Literacy Survey dataset. *Global Health Promotion, 25*(4), 57–66. https://doi.org/10.1177/1757975918788300

Pérez-Rodrigo, C., Klepp, K., Yngve, A., Sjöström, M., Stockley, L., & Aranceta, J. (2001). The school setting: An opportunity for the implementation of dietary guidelines. *Public Health Nutrition, 4*(2), 717–724. https://doi.org/10.1079/phn2001162

Popoola, B. (2019). Involving libraries in improving health literacy to achieve sustainable development goal-3 in developing economies: A literature review. *Health Information & Libraries Journal, 36*(2), 111–120. https://doi.org/10.1111/hir.12255

Pradhan, P., Costa, L., Rybski, D., Lucht, W., & Kropp, J. P. (2017). A systematic study of Sustainable Development Goal (SDG) interactions. *Earth's Future, 5*(11), 1169–1179. https://doi.org/10.1002/2017EF000632

Preckler Galguera, M. (2018). *Human rights in global health: Rights-based governance for a globalizing world.* Springer.

Schmidt-Traub, G., Hoff, H., & Bernlöhr, M. (2019, July 15). *International spillovers and the Sustainable Development Goals (SDGs): Measuring how a country's progress towards the SDGs is affected by actions in other countries.* http://www.jstor.org/stable/resrep25834

Schulenkorf, T., Krah, V., Dadaczynski, K., & Okan, O. (2021). Addressing health literacy in schools in Germany: Concept analysis of the mandatory digital and media literacy school curriculum. *Frontiers in Public Health, 9,* Article 687389. https://doi.org/10.3389/fpubh.2021.687389.

Sykes, S., & Wills, J. (2019). Critical health literacy for the marginalised: Empirical findings. In O. Okan, U. Bauer, P. Pinheiro, & K. Sørensen (Eds.), *International handbook of health literacy: Research, practice and policy across the life-span* (pp. 167–178). Bristol Press.

Sørensen, K., Van den Broucke, S., Fullam, J., Doyle, G., Pelikan, J., Slonska, Z., & Brand, H. (2012). Health literacy and public health: A systematic review and integration of definitions and models. *BMC Public Health, 12,* Article 80. https://doi.org/10.1186/1471-2458-12-80

St Leger, L. (2001). Schools, health literacy and public health: Possibilities and challenges. *Health Promotion International, 16*(2), 197–205.

Svendsen, M. T., Bak, C. K., Sørensen, K., Pelikan, J., Riddersholm, S. J., Skals, R. K., Mortensen, R. N., Maindal, H. T., Bøggild, H., Nielsen, G., Torp-Pedersen, C. (2020). Associations of health literacy with socioeconomic position, health risk behavior, and health status: A large national population-based survey among Danish adults. *BMC Public Health, 20,* Article 565. https://doi.org/10.1186/s12889-020-08498-8

Trezona, A., Dodson, S., & Osborne, R. (2017). Development of the organisational health literacy responsiveness (Org-HLR) framework in collaboration with health and social services professionals. *BMC Health Services Research, 17*, Article 513. https://doi.org/10.1186/s12913-017-2465-z

Trezona, A., Rowlands, G., & Nutbeam, D. (2018). Progress in implementing national policies and strategies for health literacy–What have we learned so far? *International Journal of Environmental Research and Public Health, 15*(7), 1554. https://doi.org/10.3390/ijerph150 71554

United Nations. (1948). *Universal declaration of human rights.* https://www.un.org/en/about-us/universal-declaration-of-human-rights

United Nations. (1989). *Convention on the rights of the child.* https://www.unicef.org.au/united-nations-convention-on-the-rights-of-the-child?

United Nations. (2015). *Transforming our world: The 2030 agenda for sustainable development.* United Nations, Department of Economic and Social Affairs.

United Nations. (2021). *The Sustainable Development Goals Report 2021.* https://unstats.un.org/sdgs/report/2021/The-Sustainable-Development-Goals-Report-2021.pdf

Vamos, S., Okan, O., Sentell, T., & Rootman, I. (2020). Making a case for "Education for health literacy": An international perspective. *International Journal of Environmental Research and Public Health, 17*(4), 1436. https://doi.org/10.3390/ijerph17041436

World Commission on Education & Development. (1987). *Our common future.* Oxford University Press.

World Health Organisation. (2013). *Building back better: Sustainable mental health care after emergencies.* World Health Organization.

World Health Organisation. (2019a). *Draft WHO European roadmap for implementation of health literacy initiatives through the life course.* Retrieved from https://www.euro.who.int/__data/assets/pdf_file/0003/409125/69wd14e_Rev1_RoadmapOnHealthLiteracy_190323.pdf

World Health Organisation. (2019b). *WHO independent high-level commission on NCDs report of working group 1.* https://www.who.int/ncds/governance/high-level-commission/HLC2-WG1-report.pdf?ua=1

World Health Organisation. (2021a). *Health literacy: The mandate for health literacy.* https://www.who.int/teams/health-promotion/enhanced-wellbeing/ninth-global-conference/health-literacy

World Health Organisation. (2021b). *Health promotion: Health literacy.* https://www.who.int/teams/health-promotion/enhanced-wellbeing/ninth-global-conference/health-literacy

World Health Organisation. (2021c). *Preventing noncommunicable diseases.* https://www.who.int/activities/preventing-noncommunicable-diseases

Chapter 28
Genre-Based Literacy and Collaboration: Promoting Social Justice and Quality Education

Emily Morgan and Vinh To

28.1 Introduction

Education for sustainable development is crucial for the achievement of the Sustainable Development Goals (SDGs) (Agbedahin, 2019) and must be empowering, participatory, and liberating (Sterling & Huckle, 2014). The importance of social justice and inclusiveness, the idea of leaving no one behind, is a strong theme running throughout all the SDGs, not just SDG10—Reduced Inequalities (United Nations [UN] Department of Economic and Social Affairs, n.d.b), and it is the role of all nations, both developed and developing, to enable this (Leal Filho et al., 2018). With the SDGs, higher education has now been recognised as playing a key role for the achievement of SDG4: Quality Education (UN, n.d.a). This chapter considers the context of English as a Foreign Language (EFL) and the learning of reading and writing literacy, with a focus on practical support for teachers and pre-service teachers to incorporate principles of sustainable development within their teaching. Language classes are an ideal place for discussing sustainability issues as they are well placed to facilitate globalised citizenship thinking and discourse (Tavakkoli & Rashidi, 2020). EFL teachers have been found to have low levels of sustainability literacy (Tavakkoli & Rashidi, 2020) and to require more support to incorporate sustainability into their English teaching (Nkwetisama, 2011). They have also registered concerns that their current curricula are not delivering on sustainability and internationalisation (Badawi, 2019). As dedicated professionals, EFL teachers want to contribute to this area. After all, English has a major influence in global discourse,

E. Morgan (✉) · V. To
School of Education, College of Arts, Law and Education, University of Tasmania, 2 Invermay Road, Launceston, TAS 7248, Australia
e-mail: emily.morgan@utas.edu.au

V. To
e-mail: vinh.to@utas.edu.au

and English teachers therefore play an important role in promoting sustainable action among societies (Nkwetisama, 2011) and in the nurturing of a peaceful world (Birch, 2009; Langlois & Vibulphol, 2019).

However, sustainability need not pose a great additional burden on English language teachers. Alongside Burns' (2011) model of sustainable pedagogy, well-studied pedagogical models for English teaching exist already, which may be easily adapted to education for sustainability in the English language classroom. This chapter focuses on two of these, the content-driven model of genre-based education (Martin, 1993) and the collaborative model of Gradual Release of Responsibility (Fisher & Frey, 2014).

We therefore consider two of the SDGs in this chapter, which are of relevance to English language education: SDG4—Quality Education and SDG10—Reduced Inequalities. We consider these goals in reverse order, for we wish to discuss first *what* to teach, which may support the attainment of SDG10, and then *how* to teach it, which may contribute towards attaining SDG4.

First, SDG10 aims to reduce inequality for vulnerable groups and populations including women and girls, people with disability, and people living in poverty (UN, n.d.b). Among its targets are the empowerment and promotion of social, economic, and political inclusion of all, ensuring equal opportunities and reduced inequalities of income through changes to discriminatory laws, policies, and practices, and adoption of positive and progressive alternatives, ensuring enhanced representation and voice of underrepresented developing countries in global institutions (UN, n.d.b). In order to achieve these elements of social justice, we argue that teachers of English and other disciplines can contribute through the incorporation of *genre-based teaching*. This pedagogy and its potential to address social inequality are explored in the first part of the chapter.

Second, SDG4 includes among its targets to ensure relevant and effective learning outcomes, to turn out learners with relevant employment-focused skills, to significantly improve literacy rates for adults and children, and to increase the supply of qualified teachers, especially in least developed countries (UN, n.d.a). We argue that these targets can be supported by the scaffolded integration of collaborative learning activities and the development of collaborative skills in the classroom. Sustainability in higher education should be experiential and include diverse and non-dominant perspectives (Burns, 2013). Collaborative learning models are ideal for including such perspectives and for bringing authentic problem-solving into the classroom at all levels. The pedagogical model that we suggest as the means to achieve this is the *Gradual Release of Responsibility framework* from Fisher and Frey (2014), which we explore in detail in the second half of the chapter.

Throughout the chapter, we provide examples from a recent study of a Japanese university English language class. Japan was selected because of its traditionally teacher-centred educational system in which students have little experience with collaborative work and tend to have poor attitudes towards it (Araki & Raphael, 2018; DeBoer, 2018). This disadvantages students, like those in this study, who wish to study in overseas universities where student-centred learning is the norm (Freimuth, 2016). In the study, collaborative, genre-based activities, scaffolded through the use of the Gradual Release of Responsibility framework (Fisher & Frey, 2014), helped students to improve their English language and collaborative skills and to develop an appreciation of collaboration for learning. Students were able to move past their initial concerns about group work and to recognise its benefits to their learning, and its enjoyability as an activity when well scaffolded. Attitudes towards learning have been shown to affect learning outcomes (Chen & Yu, 2019; Lai et al., 2016) and this has implications for the role of English learning as a driver for a sustainable future, such as when students' attitudes towards English learning improved once they understood its benefits to sustainability (Elsakka, 2019; Langlois & Vibulphol, 2019). The study we use for our examples here also provided further evidence of the efficacy of the genre-based teaching model for improved English outcomes in writing persuasive genres, a text type that plays a vital role across society, including in politics, news, opinion, and academia (Crosswhite, 2012; Macken-Horarick et al., 2018) and is considered to be writing with power (Crosswhite, 2012).

28.2   Genre and Social Justice

A major aspect of sustainability is the development of equity among nations (Odum & Odum, 2001). Social justice and ecological sustainability must be integrated, and education can be the medium for change (Sterling, 2014b). However, education as an agent for transformation towards a more sustainable society must itself be transformed (Sterling, 2014b). Education for sustainability needs to be, among other things, contextual, holistic and human, systemic and connective, and critical (Sterling, 2014b). These characteristics will support learners in their journey towards becoming agents of change for a sustainable, empowered, and just global society. Educational change can promote sustainability through the public choices of "effective institutions of governance and a well-informed, democratically engaged citizenry" (Orr, 2002, p. 1459). New approaches are needed to ensure that education supports social justice, social equity, and a global mindset (United Nations Educational Scientific and Cultural Organisation [UNESCO], 2015). When these concepts are embedded into education, they can support the attainment of SDG4, the reduction of inequalities throughout the world. With this in mind, we recommend the genre-based teaching model as a practical method for embedding the principles of social justice to reduce inequalities within English teaching, one classroom and one curriculum at a time.

28.2.1   Genre-Based Teaching

Genre theory stems from systemic functional linguistics and considers all texts as staged, goal-oriented social processes (Martin & Rothery, 1993): staged, in that individual genres are comprised of stages that combine to create meaning; goal-oriented, in that texts from individual genres aim to achieve particular communicative goals; and social processes, in that communication is an interactive phenomenon, in which meaning is socially determined. Genre theory can be used to categorise all texts and text types (Martin, 2012), and can also be used to examine the stability and dynamic variation between texts, as well as concepts of power and interactive relationships (Kress, 1993). Genres evolve with their societies in order to remain functional and purposeful (Derewianka & Jones, 2016). Critical and systemic thinking skills are crucial for sustainability (Tilbury, 2007). Genre-based learning offers a pathway to develop these skills through a deep exploration of high-value genres of dominant cultures, and the content and systems within them.

In the context of education, genre-based education involves teaching students to identify the genre of a text by considering its communicative purpose or message (known as Field), its interpersonal purpose and relationships (known as Tenor), and its mode of transmission (known as Mode). Students discover the language features and structures that characterise typical texts of a particular genre, and through deconstructing these genres, learn how to interpret, create, and manipulate them to achieve specific communicative goals. For example, students may be introduced to the genre family of persuasive texts and learn how these texts achieve their persuasive purpose through the language features, moves, and structures they use. Teaching genres ensures that, regardless of social standing or disadvantage, all students are given the opportunity to become familiar with genres of power and dominant ways of expressions within their societies (Veel, 2006). The inability to write these genres excludes individuals from participating in social conversations and social change, and the inability to comprehend and analyse these genres ensures they cannot even understand what is happening in the first place (Martin, 1993). Fluency in genres of power provides individuals with the ability to engage in conversations of power and promotes social justice (Martin, 2012). Additionally, if we are to promote a sustainability culture within the media, we must develop an active and critical audience (Howson & Cleasby, 2014; Tilbury, 2007), who must be, fundamentally, an informed audience. If sustainability is to be reached through the actions of "governments acting with an informed public" (Orr, 2002, p. 1458), genre fluency offers a medium by which the public can be purposefully informed. "Sustainability, in short, is constituted by a series of public choices that require effective institutions of governance and a well-informed, democratically engaged citizenry" (Orr, 2002, p. 1459).

Since the earliest genre-based programmes in primary and secondary schools in Australia, the weight of evidence in support of genre-based education has grown consistently, across increasingly diverse educational contexts, including first language (L1) and foreign language (L2) English teaching across the age groups (e.g., Kerfoot & Van Heerden, 2015; Lee, 2012; Rose & Martin, 2012; Wang, 2013) to the extent that it is now embedded in national curricula in countries including Australia, Singapore, and the United States (Derewianka, 2015; Gebhard & Harman, 2011; Munandar, 2020). Genre-based teaching has brought social equality within the grasp of students in Australia and elsewhere by improving educational outcomes through ensuring students, regardless of background, are empowered confidently to write and read texts of importance in genres of power (Martin, 2012; Veel, 2006).

28.2.2   Genre-Based Teaching for Social Justice

The ecosocialist, or radical democratic, view of education for sustainability promotes the ideas of participation, social justice, and equity (Huckle, 2014; Sterling, 2014b), within which genre-based education plays an important role. Genre-based learning has the added advantage of being cross- or trans-disciplinary, in that genres often span multiple subjects, or disciplines, as the education system calls them. Persuasive texts and information report genres, for example, can be found in science journalism as often as in literature studies (contrast the "book report" with the "animal habitats report" or contrast an op-ed on the benefits of vaccination with an essay on the benefits of reading aloud to children). Genre-based teaching, then, has the opportunity to disrupt the "vertical fragmentation of knowledge into subjects and their associated defences" (Sterling, 2014b, p. 31).

Additionally, genre-based teaching can promote critical literacy. Advertisers and those who use the media for their own purposes (i.e., everyone from marketers to government) are experts at exploiting people's weaknesses, particularly those who are most vulnerable, such as children and young people (Orr, 2016). If we take climate change, for example, it is clear that "attitudes and opinions about climate change reflect the distribution of power and wealth" (Orr, 2016, p. 41). A study of opinion pieces about the impacts of climate change written from a variety of perspectives and seen through the lenses of Field, Tenor, and Mode could offer students a valuable insight into how genre-specific features can have significant effects and ultimately promote significantly different messages when manipulated for different purposes. When students learn about how these texts are designed through their language features for these specific purposes, it decodes the mystery and opens up opportunities for critical discussion and understanding, leading to empowered engagement with these and other texts in the future (Tilbury, 2007).

Sterling (2014b) argues that education should be "process oriented and empowering rather than product oriented" (p. 23); however, we argue that learning to create and analyse the products of the dominant culture is the first step towards independent manipulation and creative evolution of these products: one cannot disrupt the status quo without first understanding it. This, we argue, is a path to empowerment. A problem from earlier conceptions of education as demonstrated in Australian schools in the 1980s (Martin, 2012) was the expectation of students to write nothing but "stories," and for little or no instruction to be provided on how this might be successfully achieved. Genre-based teaching overcomes this problem by providing explicit explanations and examples of genres, and how the individual features of a genre act within it to achieve its purpose, appeal to its audience, and fit into its context. It then allows for a more critical and nuanced investigation into how genres change and evolve over time, just as their cultural contexts do, and how to appropriate genres and genre features for new purposes.

In a recent study at a Japanese university, students were taught two English persuasive genres, the exposition and discussion genres, to support students in their pursuit of high standardised test scores and future English-medium academic studies (Morgan, 2022). Students learned about the typical structure of these genres, including the stages and sub-stages they tended to include. For an exposition, the stages and sub-stages, following Martin and Rose (2008), included a *Thesis* stage, a series of *Argument* stages, and a *Restatement of Position* final stage, with accompanying sub-stages. This is illustrated using a student essay from the final week of our Japan study in Table 28.1.

This example represents a significant improvement in the overall structure of student essays following the teaching programme, with all main and sub-stages included, contributing to higher overall scores of coherence, logical structure, and task response. That is, the student's text was more persuasive through its carefully structured arguments, such that this student was able to achieve a higher essay score and potentially a higher International English Language Testing System (IELTS) grade through a targeted look at structuring key genres for specific purposes.

Table 28.1 Student exposition essay with genre staging present (Morgan, 2022)

Student essay example	Main Stages	Sub-stages
Today, more and more people choose to speak English instead of their mother tongue	Statement of Position/Thesis	Issue
…because communicating is easier by using English when we talk with foreign people		Background Information
However, I think this has a strong negative effect on our society		Appeal/Statement of Position
In this essay, I will examine how the common global language influences our daily lives		Preview of Arguments
First, other discarded languages are forgotten and lost if people stop talking in them	Argument 1	Point
If the languages are forgotten, people cannot read books written in the language, which leads to the loss of knowledge in the world. It is a serious problem, and people should try hard to avoid it		Elaboration
Second, people in the same country lose a sense of unity as a country member	Argument 2	Point
So far, most people in one country have shared the same language, and it makes them feel closer as members of the country. However, if they choose to talk other foreign language, this sense of connection will be lost forever		Elaboration
Based on the terrible effects above, I believe that using the same global language is a negative thing. It is clear that we have to stop this trend…	Restatement of Position	Review of Arguments

However, this student did not allow the modelled and taught structure to limit her creative writing choices, as we will see in a moment.

An example of how students need not be limited or constrained by the explicit teaching of genre characteristics was identified in this and other students' essays. In both genres, a new sub-stage was identified, which was given the name "Solution," and in which students, after giving their arguments and summing up their position, offered solutions to the problems outlined in their arguments, as a way of further consolidating their conclusions, or offered ways to implement their recommendation (Morgan et al., 2022). For example, the student whose essay is featured in Table 28.1, who was not in favour of a global language and was concerned at the disappearance of languages wrote after the Restatement of Position: "…and here is a solution: every countries [sic] should teach their mother tongue properly to children, rather than focusing on other language education" (Morgan, 2022). Another student discussed the pros and cons of a global language in her essay using a discussion genre format. She concluded that a global language was a good thing, which nonetheless had some negative points. Then she wrote: "To solve this problem, they should save other language. For example, they should learn and educate that there are a variety of languages and they should promote people to use other languages" (Morgan, 2022). Her argument did not require this information; she had already argued persuasively in favour of the global language. However, its inclusion added additional weight to her argument.

These examples demonstrate some critical thinking on the part of the students, and a willingness to consider the various consequences of a decision for those affected, even though the argument structure they had been taught did not mandate the inclusion of such considerations. The new sub-stage had not been taught or modelled, and yet it appeared. It is likely that the concept was familiar to students from earlier studies or other models of appropriate essay responses for the IELTS, for which all students were studying, but the point remains that they did not feel limited or constrained by the teaching of the genre structure but rather used it as a foundation or platform from which to make independent, informed decisions in their text creation. Their essays were more coherent and logically constructed, adding power to their arguments, and yet they were not carbon copies of each other or of the model texts included in the teaching programme. All language education should primarily ensure that students can take the knowledge and skills they have learned and transform that knowledge for new contexts and purposes (Mahboob, 2015). In this classroom, students were encouraged to consider carefully the question and identify the most appropriate genre and structure to address it. In cases such as these, where students structured their responses differently to the models they had seen during teaching, it helped them to improve the overall quality of their essays, through their improved understanding and manipulation of persuasive genre structures.

Genre-based teaching, then, has the potential to foster critical literacy, promote fluency in the comprehension and production of texts in the genres considered powerful or dominant, and support the development of an informed and critically aware and active public for sustainable change. The examples here come from the English classroom, either English as the first language or English as a foreign language, but genre-based teaching can encompass multiple disciplines and interdisciplinary education as well.

We can now move to the second question that this chapter seeks to address, which is how should we go about teaching genre? We next investigate SDG4, Quality Education, and how the Gradual Release of Responsibility framework may support the acquisition of this goal.

28.3   Collaboration and Quality Education

SDG4 focuses on access to education and equity of education rather than type, particularly as regards research into education and sustainability (Jickling & Sterling, 2017). One target speaks of ensuring students acquire the knowledge and skills needed to promote sustainable development (UN, n.d.a); however, these are not explicitly identified. We argue that collaborative skills have a crucial place in any such skill set.

Transformative educational experiences are those in which students are exposed to influences and people who disrupt their mental status quo and promote fundamental changes in perspective, and ultimately, action (Jickling, 2017). Although many students in the same class will have many of the same experiences, the opportunity for transformative events and changes in thinking is still there; and the experience of this kind of collaborative work may make additional transformative experiences more available and accessible to students outside of the classroom.

Education has been and remains in many ways a market-driven entity in which students and parents are consumers and the main purpose of the institution is to improve the economy through jobs and profit-making expertise (Sterling, 2017). A change of fundamental purpose of education at all levels is needed (Sterling, 2017)— a belief echoed in UNESCO's 2015 publication *Rethinking Education: Towards a Global Common Good?* (UNESCO, 2015)—and collaborative education offers a practical way forward for educators, while they wait for institutional and political processes to catch up. The systemic or radical ecologic view (Sterling, 2017) promotes the ideas of networks, interdependence, and connectedness, all of which are enabled through collaboration, and where better to begin than in education? Indeed, transformative, interconnected, and collaborative activities are very important for sustainable education (Frisk & Larson, 2011), and it need not take too great a shift in educators' thinking. Dewey's democratic, skills-based pedagogy, for example, remains a sound model for education for sustainability, with its emphasis on adaptive and integrated learning, and offers a way to approach the development of key skills for sustainability including critical and systems thinking skills, communication skills, and collaboration skills (Tarrant & Thiele, 2016). Collaborative work promotes the development of understanding, empathy, and compassion, characteristics that are needed to solve the problems presented by the transition to a sustainable world, problems described by Orr (2002) as divergent, forming from "the tensions between competing perspectives that cannot be solved but can be transcended" (p. 1459).

Children and young people have the potential to become social actors and to identify and collaborate to solve problems in their immediate environments and contexts (Sauvé, 2017). This can be enabled by educators who help to promote the concept of the common good, and cooperative co-construction of meaning and action (Sauvé, 2017). Teachers can and do facilitate bottom-up approaches and practical initiatives for sustainability, driving change from the classroom outward (Sauvé, 2017). Humanising education and focusing on the common good (UNESCO, 2015) includes bringing social learning to the fore and promoting collective, intentional agency (Lotz-Sisitka, 2017). This supports the argument for using and teaching collaboration in education. Collaborative activities in which the students lead in the creation and analysis of content can be truly inspiring and stimulating for students and teachers both. During a recent study in Japan, English language students worked together to create persuasive texts on topics of relevance to them, including why their university was the best or worst (the teacher offered "best" as the topic, but students overruled the teacher and created the text about why it was the "worst"!), and the creative process was educational and entertaining for all involved.

Social learning for sustainability encompasses three key ideas: the need to challenge mental models of unsustainability by questioning and reflecting on actions and social dispositions and rethinking and redesigning our actions; the need to develop new learning approaches and build skills that enable change such as facilitation, participative inquiry, and action learning; and the need to make use of pluralism and diversity in imagining sustainable actions (Tilbury, 2007; UNESCO, 2002). The promotion and development of productive group work and true collaborative skills are practical ways for teachers to incorporate these ideas into the classroom. Tilbury's learning-based change approach to sustainability "encourages collaborative learning environments which [sic] do not merely impart knowledge but build capacity of the learner. Negotiation, evaluation and action are essential parts of this process" (Tilbury, 2007, p. 120). These concepts are fundamental to constructive or transformative models of education, which are essential to education for sustainable development (Sterling, 2014a). The acquisition of key competencies aligned with transformational learning, such as collaborative skills, will be required along with other knowledge and skills for education for sustainable development (Giangrande et al., 2019).

Collaboration, then, is a key skill that supports sustainable futures and is an important part of education for sustainable development. At the tertiary level, students are transitioning out of the education system and into the workforce, and it is here that collaborative skills become even more crucial. Additionally, language classrooms are an ideal environment for the development of these skills because of their focus on culture, global perspectives, and peer support in learning. Ver Steeg (2019) argues that education for sustainable development should be a specific focus area in university English as a Foreign Language courses, through the use of place-based education and collaborative action projects to develop the attitudes and skills critical to sustainability discourse. Engaging students by making connections between a local place and personal identity stimulates personal agency within a global sustainable development discourse and improves awareness and attitudes around global issues. When writing English short persuasive essays, Japanese university-level students were able to make local connections to global issues with little prompting from the teacher, when they discussed the potential advantages and disadvantages of a global language and considered the implications for themselves and their communities as well as for the wider world (Morgan, 2022). For example, one student looked at the wider global context before offering a local example.

> Speaking the same global language implies a tremendous loss of diversity to the world's culture. As languages have a strong link to how cultures and traditions function, people will lose their cultures and traditions along with the loss of language if they choose to speak the same language as the rest of the world does. Take an example of Japanese language. Imagine Japanese is no longer spoken and gradually disappears, instead Japanese people take up English as their native language, there is a high chance that their behaviour and attitude will also change with the change of spoken language. (Morgan, 2022)

One of the advantages of the language classroom is that students engage with a wide variety of topics that offers excellent opportunities for deeper and sustainable thinking. For example, in answer to the same question on a global language, another student considered the context of developing nations' education systems.

> Next, all children in the world can be offered good level education. Children in developing countries often do not have access to nice education. On the other hand, a lot of developed countries offer much better education than that of developing countries. Children from poor countries have less chances to have good job because of this difference. If children can use the same language, nicer education of rich countries become available to poor children by using internets. Then, they may get good job. (Morgan, 2022)

Universities need to be collaborative and act as models for their students for sustainable learning and sustainable futures (Leal Filho et al., 2018). Education for sustainability is, in its essence, reflecting on and taking action on types of political economy that would enable us to live sustainably with one another and the rest of nature (Huckle, 2014). The language classroom, shown in these student work examples, is an environment in which this type of thinking follows naturally from the diverse topics that students read, write, and talk about. One way in which teachers can support students to engage with sustainability principles is through group work. At the same time, students can discover how group work as an activity can help them learn about the effectiveness of collaboration for sustainability (Oxenswärdh & Persson-Fischier, 2020).

Let us now consider a pedagogical model that promotes the acquisition of collaborative skills, which has demonstrated success in English classes and is beginning to be recognised as beneficial across more diverse learning contexts. The Gradual Release of Responsibility framework offers a way to scaffold collaborative skills while also promoting content-specific knowledge and skills acquisition, not only for writing and literacy but also for all types of teaching.

28.3.1   The Gradual Release of Responsibility Framework

The Gradual Release of Responsibility framework (GRRF) is a pedagogical model for teaching that involves a gradual and staged move from teacher-focused to student-focused activities (Fisher & Frey, 2014). It is flexible, in that a class or group or individual can enter the framework at any stage and move between stages according to the level of scaffolding they need for a given learning topic. For example, in one lesson in our study in Japan, in which it was felt that some of the content may already be familiar to students, the teacher commenced the class with a group work activity, rather than a content delivery stage, to evaluate the students' existing knowledge prior to adjusting the learning activities, to ensure students gained the most from the class time. Using the GRRF, teachers are able to work with whole classes, small groups, or individuals, while others are getting on with student-focused collaborative or independent activities, providing needs-based learning for each individual.

The GRRF has its foundations in the concepts of scaffolding (Wood et al., 1976) and sociocultural theory (Vygotsky, 1978), and was developed originally for teaching reading and comprehension in first language (L1) English classes (Pearson & Gallagher, 1983). Since its early stages, it has evolved in complexity, and has begun to be used in many more contexts. Its efficacy for English teaching in L1 has been demonstrated in primary and secondary education (e.g.,Grant et al., 2012; Slater & Groff, 2017; Webb, et al., 2019) and some studies have begun to demonstrate its efficacy in second-language (L2) English contexts (e.g., Hu et al., 2018; Kim, 2010), as well as other disciplines (e.g., Grant et al., 2012, in science; McIntosh & Bowman, 2019, in teacher training; Nyachae et al., 2019, in social justice). In Fisher and Frey's (2014) model, the intent of the GRRF is gradually to transfer responsibility for learning from the teacher to the students in systematic and scaffolded ways that ensure that students ultimately acquire the knowledge and skills they need to complete tasks independently, promoting student agency and responsibility for their own learning. The GRRF's stages include teacher-focused Context-Setting and Focused Instruction stages, a teacher-facilitated Guided Instruction stage, and student-focused Collaborative Learning and Independent Work stages (Fig. 28.1). Collaborative work is scaffolded through teacher-facilitated activities in which the teacher assists students to work collaboratively on a task that they will later practice in small groups. This Guided Instruction stage has the advantage of allowing the teacher to evaluate students' understanding and facilitate deeper acquisition of knowledge, while also providing a model for student-led group work that students can later attempt on their own, with the teacher taking a step back.

Throughout the course in Japan, students were asked about their perceptions of whole-class and small-group work (Morgan, 2022). Students expressed trepidation about group work prior to the course, and during the early weeks, their feedback was mixed, with many comments about their shyness and lack of fluency and their dislike of working with partners of lower skill. However, as the programme continued, students' weekly reflections became increasingly positive. In the final week, students completed a questionnaire in which they were clear about the many benefits of group

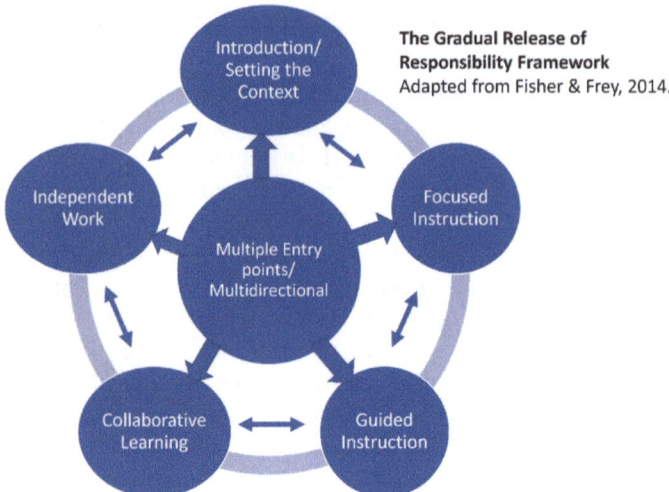

Fig. 28.1 The stages of the GRRF (Adapted from Fisher & Frey [2014])

work, from networking and relationship-building to ideas and knowledge sharing and skills development. Here is a sample of student comments (Morgan, 2022).

- Discussing and countering other groups' opinions are really helpful to improve my writing skills.
- Throughout the group works, I often encountered the situations where I had to talk. I got used to it and felt more comfortable to speak.
- I can keep the motivation of studying English by group work.
- Friends show [sic] new points I've never thought of, so it inspired me a lot.

These comments suggest that the careful scaffolding of the overall programme and individual activities supported students to come to recognise and appreciate collaboration as a beneficial learning strategy that they could engage with successfully.

Additionally, students compared the teaching style to their accustomed educational system in a positive light:

> The class style is quite different. In high school or university, lecture is very passive. So, during the majority of time, only a teacher is talking. Students hesitate to ask questions or state their opinions if they want to do so. To make matters worse, some students don't listen to a teacher and they are looking at smartphones, sleeping, or doing other stuffs because all they need to do is to go to the class, sit down and pretend to listen the teacher. On the other hand, this teacher's class is very interactive. She always asks questions and students have more opportunities to express themselves in English. (Morgan, 2022)

The emphasis on scaffolded collaboration and student-centred learning in this model offers a strong argument for its use in L2 English education, especially for students who are accustomed to an authority-driven, teacher-focused education system but wish to study or work in contexts where collaboration and student-centred learning are preferred. For example, students in many Asian countries are more likely to experience teacher-focused passive styles of learning (DeWaelsche, 2015) instead of the increasingly prevalent inquiry-based, student-focused pedagogies in Western settings. A lack of opportunity to develop collaboration skills may put students at a disadvantage in a globalised world in which they may seek to work in English-medium, Westernised companies, or study in Westernised universities (Freimuth, 2016; Ruegg, 2018). As the number of displaced people in the world grows (UN Department of Economic and Social Affairs, n.d.b), the ability to collaborate across cultures and contexts becomes increasingly important. Collaboration skills must also be explicitly taught in L1, and much investigation has looked into what effective collaboration looks like and what its diverse benefits to learning can be (e.g., Gillies, 2019; Johnson & Johnson, 2017; Slavin, 2020). The GRRF offers a model that can be used effectively across educational contexts, both to teach knowledge and skills and to scaffold and develop collaborative skills that students may use to advantage throughout their lives. This makes it an ideal model to promote SDG4, Quality Education.

28.4   Conclusion

The SDGs include a goal to reduce inequalities and a goal for quality education (UN Department of Economic and Social Affairs, n.d.a). For quality education for sustainable development, Sterling advocates for "a learning-based breakthrough to a changed worldview which [sic] is both *collective* and *connective*" (Sterling, 2007, p. 64). He argues that *first-order learning*, which takes place within a consensually accepted framework and is effectively maintenance of a status quo of what is and is not right and true, needs to give way, and is gradually giving way, to *second-order learning*, in which a deep questioning of assumptions occurs such that the system in which the learners are embedded also changes. Genre-based learning offers this opportunity, from where learners can eventually aspire to *third-order learning* in which an individual's consciousness, perceptions, and actions are permanently and drastically changed (Sterling, 2007). To promote social justice and reduce inequalities, it is essential that all individuals are given the opportunity to become fluent in the genres of power and dominance in their societies. Genre-based teaching, which teaches the key elements and structures of living and evolving genres within individual cultures and societies, is well-placed to support this.

The will of an informed public is essential to create stable and effective governments (Orr, 2016). Bottom-up, local-to-international approaches to sustainability are needed, which can be supported through genre-based teaching and collaborative learning in which students learn about, discuss and take action on local, regional, and state issues as a prelude to taking on greater national and ultimately international issues. Key competencies and skills such as collaborative skills, cooperation, and empathy are needed within education for sustainable development if we wish to develop a world that is durable and just, inclusive, and fair. The GRRF supports both content learning (such as the teaching of genres) and collaborative skills development and is flexible enough to be used across disciplines and age groups, supporting both new and experienced teachers to offer more sustainability-focused teaching. This chapter has offered some practical tools for teachers in the English language space to promote education for sustainable development within their classes, in the hopes of building momentum and change, one classroom at a time.

References

Agbedahin, A. V. (2019). Sustainable development, education for sustainable development, and the 2030 agenda for sustainable development: Emergence, efficacy, eminence, and future. *Sustainable Development, 27*(4), 669–680. https://doi.org/10.1002/sd.1931

Araki, N., & Raphael, J. (2018). Firing the imagination: Process drama as pedagogy for 'melting' EAP speaking anxiety and increasing Japanese university students' confidence in speaking. In R. Ruegg & C. Williams (Eds.), *Teaching English for academic purposes (EAP) in Japan: Studies from an English-medium university* (pp. 41–58). Springer.

Badawi, M. F. A. B. (2019). The development of a suggested internationalized curriculum for Egyptian prospective EFL teachers. *CDELT Occasional Papers in the Development of English Education, 66*(2), 5–42. https://doi.org/10.21608/OPDE.2019.126872

Birch, B. M. (2009). *The English language teacher in global civil society.* Routledge.

Burns, H. (2011). Teaching for transformation: (Re)Designing sustainability courses based on ecological principles. *Journal of Sustainability Education, 2.* https://pdxscholar.library.pdx.edu/elp_fac/20/

Burns, H. (2013). Meaningful sustainability learning: A study of sustainability pedagogy in two university courses. *International Journal of Teaching and Learning in Higher Education, 25*(2), 166–175. https://www.isetl.org/ijtlhe/pdf/IJTLHE1509.pdf

Chen, W., & Yu, S. (2019). Implementing collaborative writing in teacher-centered classroom contexts: Student beliefs and perceptions. *Language Awareness, 28*(4), 247–267. https://doi.org/10.1080/09658416.2019.1675680

Crosswhite, J. (2012). *The rhetoric of reason: Writing and the attractions of argument.* University of Wisconsin Press.

DeBoer, M. (2018). Expansive learning: Assessment recapitulates experience. In R. Ruegg & C. Williams (Eds.), *Teaching English for academic purposes (EAP) in Japan: Studies from an English-medium university* (pp. 141–166). Springer.

Derewianka, B. (2015). The contribution of genre theory to literacy education in Australia. In J. Turbill, G. Barton, & C. Brock (Eds.), *Teaching writing in today's classrooms: Looking back to looking forward* (pp. 69–86). Australian Literary Educators' Association.

Derewianka, B., & Jones, B. (2016). *Teaching language in context* (3rd ed.). Oxford University Press.

DeWaelsche, S. (2015). Critical thinking, questioning and student engagement in Korean university English courses. *Linguistics and Education, 32*(B), 131–147. https://doi.org/10.1016/j.linged.2015.10.003

Elsakka, S. M. F. E. (2019). Emotional intelligence—Enhanced instruction to develop EFL students' critical reading skills and their attitudes towards English learning as a sustainable development process. *CDELT Occasional Papers in the Development of English Education, 68*(1), 359–381. https://doi.org/10.21608/opde.2019.132679. Accessed 10 December 2021.

Fisher, D. & Frey, N. (2014). *Better learning through structured teaching: A framework for the gradual release of responsibility* (2nd ed.). ASCD.

Freimuth, H. (2016). Revisiting the suitability of the IELTS examination as a gatekeeper for university entrance in the UAE. In L. Buckingham (Ed.), *Language, identity and education on the Arabian Peninsula: Bilingual policies in a multilingual context* (pp. 161–175). Multilingual Matters.

Frisk, E., & Larson, K. L. (2011). Educating for sustainability: Competencies & practices for transformative action. *Journal of Sustainability Education, 2.* http://www.jsedimensions.org/wordpress/content/educating-for-sustainability-competencies-practices-for-transformative-action_2011_03/

Gebhard, M., & Harman, R. (2011). Reconsidering genre theory in K–12 schools: A response to school reforms in the United States. *Journal of Second Language Writing, 20*(1), 45–55. https://doi.org/10.1016/j.jslw.2010.12.007

Giangrande, N., White, R. M., East, M., Jackson, R., Clarke, T., Coste, M. S., & Penha-Lopes, G. (2019). A competency framework to assess and activate education for sustainable development: Addressing the UN Sustainable Development Goals 4.7 Challenge. *Sustainability, 11*(10), 2832. https://doi.org/10.3390/su11102832

Gillies, R. M. (2019). Promoting academically productive student dialogue during collaborative learning. *International Journal of Educational Research, 97*, 200–209. https://doi.org/10.1016/j.ijer.2017.07.014

Grant, M., Lapp, D., Fisher, D., Johnson, K., & Frey, N. (2012). Purposeful instruction: Mixing up the "I", "we", and "you." *Journal of Adolescent & Adult Literacy, 56*(1), 45–55. https://doi.org/10.1002/JAAL.00101

Howson, J., & Cleasby, A. (2014). Towards a critical media. In S. Sterling & J. Huckle (Eds.), *Education for sustainability* (pp. 149–164). Routledge.

Hu, R., Liu, X. M., & Zheng, X. (2018). Examining meaning making from reading wordless picture books in Chinese and English by three bilingual children. *Journal of Early Childhood Literacy, 18*(2), 214–238. https://doi.org/10.1177/1468798416643357

Huckle, J. (2014). Realizing sustainability in changing times. In S. Sterling & J. Huckle (Eds.), *Education for sustainability* (pp. 3–17). Routledge.

Jickling, B. (2017). Education revisited: Creating educational experiences that are held, felt, and disruptive. In B. Jickling & S. Sterling (Eds.), *Post-sustainability and environmental education: Remaking education for the future* (pp. 15–30). Palgrave Macmillan.

Jickling, B., & Sterling, S. (2017). Post-sustainability and environmental education: Framing issues. In B. Jickling & S. Sterling (Eds.), *Post-sustainability and environmental education: Remaking education for the future* (pp. 1–11). Palgrave Macmillan.

Johnson, D. W., & Johnson, R. T. (2017). The use of cooperative procedures in teacher education and professional development. *Journal of Education for Teaching, 43*(3), 284–295. https://doi.org/10.1080/02607476.2017.1328023

Kerfoot, C., & Van Heerden, M. (2015). Testing the waters: Exploring the teaching of genres in a Cape Flats primary school in South Africa. *Language and Education, 29*(3), 235–255. https://doi.org/10.1080/09500782.2014.994526

Kim, Y. (2010). Scaffolding through questions in upper elementary ELL learning. *Literacy Teaching and Learning, 15*(1&2), 109–137.

Kress, G. (1993). Genre as social process. In B. Cope & M. Kalantzis (Eds.), *The powers of literacy: A genre approach to teaching writing* (pp. 22–37). The Falmer Press.

Lai, C., Lei, C. L., & Liu, Y. (2016). The nature of collaboration and perceived learning in wiki-based collaborative writing. *Australasian Journal of Educational Technology, 32*(3), 80–95. https://doi.org/10.14742/ajet.2586

Langlois, G., & Vibulphol, J. (2019). Using a workshop to raise awareness of the role of English in promoting sustainable development. *English Teaching Forum, 57*(2), 12–23.

Leal Filho, W., Raath, S., Lazzarini, B., Vargas, V. R., de Souza, L., Anholon, R., Quelhas, O. L. G., Haddad, R., Klavins, M., & Orlovic, V. L. (2018). The role of transformation in learning and education for sustainability. *Journal of Cleaner Production, 199*, 286–295. https://doi.org/10.1016/j.jclepro.2018.07.017

Lee, I. (2012). Genre-based teaching and assessment in secondary English classrooms. *English Teaching-Practice and Critique, 11*(4), 120–136.

Lotz-Sisitka, H. (2017). Education and the common good. In B. Jickling & S. Sterling (Eds.), *Post-sustainability and environmental education: Remaking education for the future* (pp. 63–76). Palgrave Macmillan.

Macken-Horarick, M., Love, K., Sandiford, C., & Unsworth, L. (2018). *Functional Grammatics: Re-conceptualizing knowledge about language and image for school English*. Routledge.

Mahboob, A. (2015). Identity management, language variation, and English language textbooks. In D. Djenar, A. Mahboob, & K. Cruickshank (Eds.), *Language and identity across modes of communication* (pp. 153–178). Walter de Gruyter.

Martin, J. R. (1993). A contextual theory of language. In B. Cope & M. Kalantzis (Eds.), *The powers of literacy: A genre approach to teaching writing* (pp. 116–136). The Falmer Press.

Martin, J. R. (2012). Grammar meets genre: Reflections on the 'Sydney School'. *Arts: The Journal of the Sydney University Arts Association, 22*, 47–95.

Martin, J. R., & Rose, D. (2008). *Genre relations: Mapping culture*. Equinox.

Martin, J. R., & Rothery, J. (1993). Grammar: Making meaning in writing. In B. Cope & M. Kalantzis (Eds.), *The powers of literacy: A genre approach to teaching writing* (pp. 137–153). The Falmer Press.

McIntosh, N. A., & Bowman, C. L. (2019). Reflections: Professional development using a gradual release model to facilitate culturally responsive strategies in a rural secondary school curriculum in Malawi. *International Journal of Educational Reform, 28*(3), 235–252. https://doi.org/10.1177/1056787919858147

Morgan, E. (2022). *An investigation into genre-based content and collaborative pedagogy in a Japanese tertiary teaching program* [manuscript in preparation]. College of Arts, Law and Education, University of Tasmania.

Morgan, E., To, V., & Thomas, A. (2022). Using genre-based pedagogy to teach structural staging of short persuasive essays in a Japanese university context. *English as a Foreign Language International Journal, 26*(6).

Munandar, I. (2020). A critical review of the Singapore English language syllabus as an advance syllabus in English language teaching (ELT). *Jurnal as-Salam, 4*(1), 46–60. https://doi.org/10.37249/as-salam.v4i1.172

Nkwetisama, C. M. (2011). EFL/ESL and environmental education: Towards an eco-applied linguistic awareness in Cameroon. *World Journal of Education, 1*(1), 110–118. https://doi.org/10.5430/wje.v1n1p110

Nyachae, T. M., McVee, M. B., & Boyd, F. B. (2019). Gradually releasing responsibility in justice-centred teaching: Educators reflecting on a social justice literacy workshop on police brutality. In M. B. McVee, E. Ortlieb, J. S. Reichenberg, & P. D. Pearson (Eds.), *The gradual release of responsibility in literacy research and practice (literacy research, practice and evaluation)* (Vol. 10, pp. 103–118). https://doi.org/10.1108/S2048-045820190000010007

Odum, H. T., & Odum, C. E. (2001). *A prosperous way down*. University Press of Colorado.

Orr, D. W. (2002). Four challenges of sustainability. *Conservation Biology, 16*(6), 1457–1460. https://www.jstor.org/stable/3095399. Accessed 10 December 2021.

Orr, D. W. (2016). *Dangerous years: Climate change, the long emergency, and the way forward*. Yale University Press.

Oxenswärdh, A., & Persson-Fischier, U. (2020). Mapping master students' processes of problem solving and learning in groups in sustainability education. *Sustainability, 12*(13), 5299. https://doi.org/10.3390/su12135299

Pearson, P. D., & Gallagher, M. C. (1983). The instruction of reading comprehension. *Contemporary Educational Psychology, 8*(3), 317–344. https://doi.org/10.1016/0361-476X(83)90019-X

Rose, D., & Martin, J. R. (2012). *Learning to write, reading to learn: Genre, knowledge and pedagogy in the Sydney School*. Equinox.

Ruegg, R. (2018). Increasing autonomy in learners of EAP writing: An exploratory study. In R. Ruegg & C. Williams (Eds.), *Teaching English for academic purposes (EAP) in Japan: Studies from an English-medium university* (Vol. 14, pp. 99–122). Springer.

Sauvé, L. (2017). Education as life. In B. Jickling & S. Sterling (Eds.), *Post-sustainability and environmental education: Remaking education for the future* (pp. 111–124). Macmillan.

Slater, W. H., & Groff, J. A. (2017). Tutoring in critical thinking: Using the stases to scaffold high school students' reading and writing of persuasive text. *Reading & Writing Quarterly, 33*(4), 380–393. https://doi.org/10.1080/10573569.2017.1294516

Slavin, R. E. (2020). Co-operative learning: What makes group-work work? In H. Dumont, D. Istance, & F. Benavides (Eds.), *The nature of learning: Using research to inspire practice* (pp. 161–178). OECD Centre for Educational Research and Innovation.

Sterling, S. (2007). Riding the storm: Towards a connective cultural consciousness. In A. E. J. Wals (Ed.), *Social learning: Towards a sustainable world* (pp. 63–82). Wageningen Academic Publishers.

Sterling, S. (2014a). Developing strategy. In S. Sterling & J. Huckle (Eds.), *Education for sustainability* (pp. 197–211). Routledge.

Sterling, S. (2014b). Education in change. In S. Sterling & J. Huckle (Eds.), *Education for sustainability* (pp. 18–39). Routledge.

Sterling, S. (2017). Assuming the future: Repurposing education in a volatile age. In B. Jickling & S. Sterling (Eds.), *Post-sustainability and environmental education: Remaking education for the future* (pp. 31–45). Palgrave Macmillan.

Sterling, S., & Huckle, J. (2014). Introduction. In S. Sterling & J. Huckle (Eds.), *Education for sustainability* (pp. xiii–xxv). Routledge.

Tarrant, S. P., & Thiele, L. P. (2016). Practice makes pedagogy—John Dewey and skills-based sustainability education. *International Journal of Sustainability in Higher Education, 17*(1), 54–67. https://doi.org/10.1108/IJSHE-09-2014-0127

Tavakkoli, Z., & Rashidi, N. (2020). A study on the status of sustainability education among Iranian EFL instructors: Developing a glocalized model. *Journal of Teacher Education for Sustainability, 22*(2), 66–89. https://doi.org/10.2478/jtes-2020-0017

Tilbury, D. (2007). Learning based change for sustainability: Perspectives and pathways. In A. E. J. Wals (Ed.), *Social learning: Towards a sustainable world* (pp. 117–131). Wageningen Academic Publishers.

United Nations. (n.d.a). *Goal 4 Quality education.* https://www.un.org/sustainabledevelopment/education/

United Nations. (n.d.b). *Goal 10: Reduce inequality within and among countries.* https://www.un.org/sustainabledevelopment/inequality/

United Nations Department of Economic and Social Affairs (n.d.a.). *The 17 goals.* https://sdgs.un.org/goals

United Nations Department of Economic and Social Affairs (n.d.b). *Goal 10 reduce inequality within and among countries.* https://sdgs.un.org/goals/goal10

United Nations Educational Scientific and Cultural Organisation. (2002). *Education for sustainability: From Rio to Johannesburg: Lessons learnt from a decade of commitment.* Report presented at the Johannesburg World Summit for Sustainable Development.

United Nations Educational Scientific and Cultural Organisation. (2015). *Rethinking education: Towards a global common good?* http://unesdoc.unesco.org/images/0023/002325/232555e.pdf

Veel, R. (2006). The write it right project—Linguistic modelling of secondary school and the workplace. In R. Whittaker, M. O'Donnell, & A. McCabe (Eds.), *Language and literacy* (pp. 66–92). Continuum.

Ver Steeg, J. (2019). Developing a public voice: Place-based education as an approach to education for sustainable development in the EFL classroom. *PUPIL: International Journal of Teaching, Education and Learning, 3*(1), 71–87. https://doi.org/10.20319/pijtel.2019.31.7187

Vygotsky, L. S. (1978). *Mind in society—The development of higher psychological processes.* Harvard University Press.

Wang, C. (2013). A study of genre approach in EFL writing. *Theory & Practice in Language Studies, 3*(11), 2128–2135. https://doi.org/10.4304/tpls.3.11.2128-2135

Webb, S., Massey, D., Goggans, M., & Flajole, K. (2019). Thirty-five years of the gradual release of responsibility: Scaffolding toward complex and responsive teaching. *Reading Teacher, 73*(1), 75–83. https://doi.org/10.1002/trtr.1799

Wood, D., Bruner, J. S., & Ross, G. (1976). The role of tutoring in problem-solving. *Journal of Child Psychology and Psychiatry and Allied Disciplines, 17*, 89–100. https://doi.org/10.1111/j.1469-7610.1976.tb00381.x

Chapter 29
Developing Academic Language in Young Children to Support Sustainability

Natasha Williams⑩, Greg Oates, Vinh To, and Bronwyn Reynolds

29.1 Introduction

It is commonly accepted that language and vocabulary form the foundation for understanding and engaging with the world around us (Mercer, 2002). However, many students from low Socio-Economic-Status (SES) areas begin school with low vocabulary and language skills (Fernald et al., 2013; Goldstein et al., 2017). Hart and Risley (1995) identified a 30-million-word gap in the number of words young children from low SES areas were exposed to compared to students from higher SES areas. Further international research has acknowledged the impact of low SES on the development of young children's oral language and vocabulary development (Fernald et al., 2013; Ginsborg, 2006). These insights suggest that the effects of generational poverty, including cognition and behavioural problems, are cumulative (Duncan & Brooks-Gunn, 1994; Payne, 2013).

Research has also demonstrated that there is a connection between oral language and the acquisition of reading and writing skills (Locke et al., 2002; Scarborough et al., 2009). Such studies have provided evidence that the oral language skills of young children from low SES areas place them at a disadvantage when learning to read and write (Ginsborg, 2006; Locke et al., 2002). Halliday (1993) suggests

N. Williams (✉) · G. Oates · V. To · B. Reynolds
School of Education, College of Arts, Law and Education, University of Tasmania, Newnham Drive, Newnham, TAS 7248, Australia
e-mail: nh.williams@utas.edu.au

G. Oates
e-mail: greg.oates@utas.edu.au

V. To
e-mail: vinh.to@utas.edu.au

B. Reynolds
e-mail: bronwyn.reynolds@utas.edu.au

that language is the foundation of learning because it is through language that meaning is derived. Beimiller (2005) supports these claims, identifying vocabulary as essential for students' reading comprehension and access to higher education. An academic language is a specific form of language identified as the language used by teachers and students in the acquisition of new knowledge (Snow & Uccelli, 2009). Within any language, vocabulary may be categorised into three "tiers" of word types (Beck et al., 2008). Tier One comprises basic vocabulary, words that rarely require direct instruction and typically do not have multiple meanings. Academic vocabulary, however, includes a combination of Tier Two words, more sophisticated high-frequency, multiple-meaning words often found in picture books, and Tier Three words, lower frequency words which are subject-specific and occur in domains such as Science, Technology, Engineering and Mathematics (STEM), for example, photosynthesis. Tier Three words are central to understanding concepts within various academic subjects and should be integrated into content instruction (Beck et al., 2008, 2013).

Education for Sustainable Development (ESD) identifies the important role education plays in paving the way to a sustainable future. Early childhood is acknowledged as the starting point for ESD, as young children are the citizens of the future (United Nations [UN] Decade of Education for Sustainable Development [DESD], 2014). Two of the four major thrusts for the DESD were *"Improving access and retention in quality basic education"* and *"Increasing public understanding and awareness of sustainability"* (p. 17). It is fundamental to such aspirations that children have access to the vocabulary and conceptual understanding that underpins sustainability and the Sustainable Development Goals (SDGs). The teaching of STEM has been acknowledged to be of great importance in developing a sustainable economic future in many countries around the world (Buchter et al., 2017; Education Council, 2015). Skills and capabilities linked to STEM subjects, such as problem-solving, reasoning and scientific skills, have been identified as those needed for career opportunities in the future (Blums et al., 2017). Students from low SES areas, however, have been shown to disengage from STEM studies (Cooper et al., 2020; Thomson et al., 2017).

There appears to be a consensus as to the importance of low SES students developing academic vocabulary for access to and engagement with STEM subjects, and the concepts of sustainability, and that this needs to occur in early childhood to be most effective (Buchter et al., 2017; Cooper et al., 2020; Goldstein et al., 2017). Siraj-Blatchford et al. (2010) concur with this viewpoint, stressing that it is during early childhood when children start to develop their attitudes and values towards sustainability, and it is vital to support them in building a strong foundation in this area. Given such evidence and imperatives, clear connections may be drawn between developing young children's academic vocabulary in STEM and their effective engagement with the SDGs. Consider, for example, the wording of Goal 14, *Life Below the Water,* elaborated as "Conserve and sustainably use the oceans, seas, and marine resources for sustainable development", and Goal 15, *Life on Land,* "Protect, restore and promote sustainable use of terrestrial ecosystems, sustainably manage forests, combat desertification, and halt and reverse land degradation and halt biodiversity loss" (United Nations General Assembly, 2015).

This chapter reports on preliminary findings from a wider research study that aims to explore the gap in the literature with respect to how we might strengthen young children's academic vocabulary and to identify further what types of experience, are most effective in supporting young children's learning of academic language. The study aims to support teachers assisting young children from low SES areas who begin school with lower vocabulary levels and reduced conceptual understanding. This chapter will describe the types of experiences that have initially been found to be successful in encouraging the use and understanding of targeted academic vocabulary, and how this might link to and support effective engagement with the goals of sustainability.

29.2 Academic Vocabulary and the Sustainable Development Goals

Academic vocabulary is important for young children to participate equitably in STEM subjects and understand the language necessary to engage with the SDGs. This is a critical issue for students from low SES areas, who have been shown to have lower vocabulary levels. Thus, developing their academic vocabulary is essential to ensure inclusive and equitable opportunities for all students to receive a quality education and achieve academic success.

Goal 4 of the SDGs explicitly references education to ensure "inclusive and equitable quality education to promote lifelong learning opportunities." The significance for young children from low SES backgrounds is exemplified in the UN agenda, which pledges "no one is left behind" and the "goals will be met for all segments of society" (UN General Assembly, 2015). Multiple targets and indicators, used to identify progress towards Goal 4, suggest access to quality and equitable education should begin in early childhood (Elfert, 2019). Vladimirova and Le Blanc (2016) explored the links between education and the SDGs and emphasise the recommendation in the UN flagship reports that children are developmentally ready for learning and able to progress in areas like reading, mathematics and ICT from an early age. The UN reports also suggest the importance of children potentially developing the different skills necessary to access vocational opportunities in the future (Vladimirova & Le Blanc, 2016). Webb et al. (2017) advise that although much of the focus on this goal has been on supporting underdeveloped countries, the importance of quality education is equally relevant for disadvantaged students in developed countries. Merton (1968) coined the term "The Matthew Effect," which refers to the idea that students with an advantage will always maintain an advantage over those more disadvantaged students. This effect remains contemporary, as echoed by Boeren (2019), who emphasises that the socio-economic and socio-demographic characteristics of families significantly impact a child's opportunity to receive a quality education.

Elliott and Young (2016) suggest intentional teaching experiences can help children make connections and links with the concept of sustainability. Research has demonstrated children from low SES areas are often hampered by limited language, vocabulary and concept knowledge in receiving equitable access to quality education across the curriculum (Aikens & Barbarin, 2008; Considine & Zappalà, 2002; Feza, 2018; Goldstein et al., 2017). Zevenbergen (2002) suggests that for some students to be able to participate with their learning, they must be able to participate with the discourse and practices of the community of learning with which they wish to engage. Elliott and Young propose that through engagement with intentional teaching experiences, children can make meaningful connections and links with the concept of sustainability, and Elliott and Davis (2009) suggest the early years are a pivotal time in this respect, when concept-construction and ethical understandings of sustainability can be first formed. Arlemalm-Hagser and Elliott (2017) identified that quality education in early childhood must form part of a multifaced approach to sustainability arguing that because it is children who will be most negatively impacted in the future by any global inequities linked to non-sustainable development, it is therefore an ethical responsibility for sustainable futures to be an essential component of early childhood education. Samuelsson and Park (2017) support the need for sustainability to be an early childhood focus, explaining that to achieve the SDGs, the focus must shift from education to learning so that children are able to achieve their full potential.

The importance of quality education for everyone to promote the goal of lifelong learning has been widely identified in the literature (Arlemalm-Hagser & Elliott, 2017; Boeren, 2019; Elfert, 2019; Samuelsson & Park, 2017). The emergence and growth in popularity internationally of the Forest Schools movement has led to a wealth of research demonstrating the importance for opportunities for children to connect with outdoor spaces (Cumming & Nash, 2015; Harris, 2017; MacEachren, 2013; Mitchell et al., 2016). Proponents of the Forest Schools movement argue that through spending additional time outside children forge a greater sense of belonging and connection to nature and community. Allowing students to engage in experiences like cubby building, tree climbing and using the outside space to support the teaching of STEM subject helps children make a more authentic connection to the SDGs (Cumming & Nash, 2015; Harris, 2017; MacEachren, 2013). Harris claims that the importance of outdoor time in learning is especially vital for students from low SES environments who tend to have a greater disconnect from nature.

In identifying what constitutes as quality education in early childhood, The Australian Government's Department of Education and Workplace Relations (DEEWR) (2018) identified play-based learning as the best practise for learning in the early years. This perspective has been well-supported in the literature, where play is commonly defined as a voluntary and enjoyable experience that provides children with a framework to make connections with the world around them (Dockett & Fleer, 1999; Hohmann et al., 1995; Mellou, 1994; Samuelsson & Carlsson, 2008). Using play-based learning to support teaching of academic vocabulary and concepts through an enriched STEM programme has thus formed the focus of this current study.

29.3 The Current Study

The research project from which this chapter is drawn focussed on providing the students in a prep (preparation) class (first year of schooling in Australia, for students aged five), who come from a low SES area, with an equitable opportunity to access and understand some of the subjects they would be required to engage with in later years. Many of the children in the project school begin classes with low vocabulary levels. Therefore, the aim was to develop an enriched STEM programme, utilising both the indoors and outdoors environments of the school, to enhance the young children's range and understanding of academic vocabulary and the connected concepts. Through this approach, the hope was to enhance their opportunity to engage in the subject matter and provide them with a firm foundation to build on in future years. There were 28 students in the class, all of whom were involved in the study, and the lessons were taught by the main classroom teacher (who was also the researcher), accompanied by two teacher aides who assisted in the observations (one was the classroom fulltime aide and another assisted in the morning block).

29.4 Research Design

The methodology chosen for this project was action research using a mixed methods approach encompassing quantitative and qualitative tools (Efron, 2013). Action research was an appropriate design for the study, as the enriched STEM programme was implemented in a cyclical manner as a part of a whole class programme. The cyclic approach of action research incorporates planning, implementation, analysis and reflection, which allows for each cycle to build on the discoveries of the first cycle and adapt the future cycles based on these understandings (Kember & McKay, 1996; Pine, 2009). The timing allowed for some pretesting to be done at the end of Term Four, 2020, in readiness to begin the first research cycle in Term One, 2021. The project involved three cycles, taught over three terms, with a new cycle commencing at the start of each new term (see Fig. 29.1).

29.5 Research Procedure

The research approach and the topics and experiences explored in each research cycle are summarised in Fig. 29.1 (three topics based on the science themes of *Living Things,* "Properties of Materials" and "Forces and Motion"). The choice of topics provided an opportunity to raise awareness of and build connections to several of the SDGs, for example, the first cycle dealt with living things including plants and animals (SDG14—*Life Below Water* and SDG15—*Life on Land*). Within Cycle One, the children not only looked at classifying parts of plants and their life cycles but

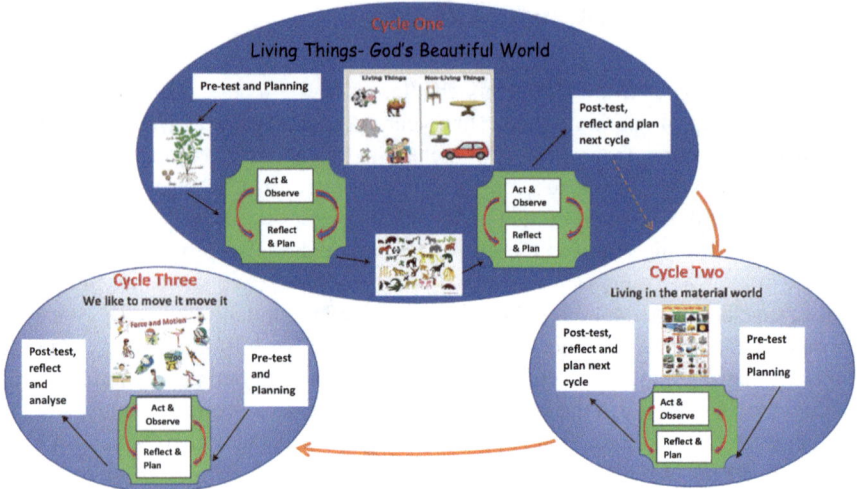

Fig. 29.1 The three cycles of the study

also learned about animal classification and how plants, animals and ecosystems are interconnected. This discussion focuses on preliminary findings from the first cycle, with the other cycles given to provide a more complete picture of the complete study. A baseline of the students' conceptual knowledge and vocabulary level was gained by administering pre-tests in Term Four of the previous year and was then used to guide the planning of how to introduce the cycle, group the words, and develop the sequence for learning.

Cycle One began with the word *living*, introduced through YouTube video clips and books. The students were taken outside to explore what things they could find and identify if they were living or non-living. In the classroom, the students sorted, drew and constructed objects that were living, non-living, or had never been living, and observational data were taken to monitor their growing understandings and provide guidance in judging what additional experiences were needed to consolidate their understandings. It was important to start with the word *living*, as it underpinned the focus of the entire cycle. Next, the students moved onto learning about plants. The focus words planned for this part of the cycle included *seed, root, stem, and photosynthesis*. This section of the cycle was introduced with the book *The Tiny Seed* (Carle, 1970).

For the next few weeks of the lesson cycle, the children engaged in many rich activities within their indoor and outdoor environments, aimed at reinforcing their language development. They set up a plant nursery in their dramatic play space, used their wooden blocks to create gardens and build towering trees, and explored different sorts of seeds in the sensory tubs. Through art, they created collages of the different parts of a plant and used bee-bots (small bee-shaped robots with arrows that are pressed to get them to move in different directions) to go through the life cycle of a plant. They also conducted an experiment requiring them to plant seeds in damp paper towels, place them in zip-lock bags and hang them in the window of the classroom to observe the life cycle process. Throughout these experiences, the children were encouraged to repeat the focus words or were prompted to respond with them when questioned about the activities. When doing the seed experiment, the children's interests and questions prompted the teachers to introduce additional words not on the pre-tested list, this included *sprout* and *germinate*, which became words with which the children are really connected. As we observed and checked the seeds and the children were asked about what they were observing with their seeds, they would shout out that their seeds had started to *germinate*.

As the cycle progressed and the students moved on to learning about animals and habitats, they continued to care for their plants and garden beds. They were overcome with excitement when some of the plants started producing peas and bean pods. The nursery dramatic play world continued and expanded. Our focus story *The Tiny Seed* (Carle, 1970) was read many times over this period and became part of the dramatic play, with children taking on the roles of seeds, birds, mice and people. Although it had not been planned as a conceptual play world (Fleer, 2018), through the children's engagement with the play it did evolve into one. Vygotsky (1966) believed that when imaginary play is a leading activity, it is the stimulus for child development, helping them make connections through their play. This perspective is supported by Fleer, who suggests it is through play that children integrate new concepts and vocabulary.

29.6 Data Collection

Data were collected using primarily qualitative tools during Cycle One. These included photos, audio recordings, videos and written anecdotal observations. The observations encompassed whole class discussions, small group and individual conversations, mainly during the experiences as they occurred. Checklists were used in this cycle to monitor which words were said. The checklist helped the researchers identify whether the word was repeated or used due to prompting by a teacher through questioning, or was heard being used independently and spontaneously in their play.

Groupings were used to ensure that all students had the opportunity to experience all of the activities and share their time between both play spaces. The planned experiences provided opportunities for the students to be prompted and scaffolded into using and repeating the vocabulary, as well as encouraging independent use of the vocabulary once the students became more familiar with the words. On completing the cycle, the quantitative vocabulary screener was repeated along with the inclusion of additional words which had been added throughout the cycle, to measure their progress in identifying the words from a visual stimulus and using the words in a sentence.

29.7   Data Analysis

The Boehm 3 Test of basic concepts (Boehm, 2001), which was administered in the pre-test phase of the cycle, includes 50 pre-selected basic concepts that have been identified by the creator as being helpful in identifying students at risk of academic delays. For the study, we used the percentage of responses to the different concept types to identify which concepts needed direct instruction, and ongoing explanations when introducing the different experiences.

In the vocabulary pre-tests, simple word counts were used to identify words that students were familiar with, and those they struggled with. The results of the pre- and post-test analysis are summarised in the results and discussion section. For the qualitative data (for example, observations and collected word samples), the frequency of word use and the contexts in which they were used or appeared, were examined and compared by the classroom teacher, with the assistance of the teacher aides. For example, each observed spontaneous use of vocabulary was noted against the experience in which it was generated: did it happen because of think-a-loud or hands-on-activities such as sorting and block-building or during dramatic play?

29.8   Results and Discussion

The preliminary analysis of Cycle One for this chapter appears promising. In the test of their concept knowledge before the commencement of the first cycle (Boehm 3), only three concepts were answered correctly by all 28 students. This suggested that the students had reasonably low levels of conceptual understanding at the start of the cycle. When comparing the results of the pre- and post-vocabulary screen tests for the 14 words initially created by the teacher, with the four additional words added, student responses demonstrate visible improvements in the identification of the words from the pictures. Gains were also made across all words for the number of children who were able to explain the words or use the words in a sentence in the correct context. The largest gains were closely associated with the level of picture recognition. For example, all 28 students correctly identified the word *seed* from the picture and could use the word in context in the post-test. The excitement of planting seeds and the value of the activity in supporting vocabulary development is clearly evidenced in the use of *germinate* (added to the list in response to students' usage), with 26 students correctly identifying the picture and being able to use the word in context in the post-test.

The observations of the experiences during Cycle One support the gains seen in the pre- and post-vocabulary screener and provide some insight into the nature of how each activity contributes to vocabulary development. The checklists showed that the use of books, particularly with accompanying think-a-loud questioning, was an effective strategy to introduce the target vocabulary and make explicit the meaning of words. An example of this was in the first week of the cycle when the teacher read the story *A year on our farm* (Matthews & McLean, 2002). During the story, the teacher and students started discussing the pictures and identifying which pictures were of living things and which were non-living things. As the reading progressed, the teacher would point to a picture and the students would call out "living" or "non-living" in response.

Some themes emerged as to the types of play-based learning that best supported the development of academic vocabulary in the early years. Hands-on-activities such as sorting, block-building and small-world creations offered the most frequent opportunities to prompt the students into repeating or using the vocabulary in context. As the children learnt more about animals (phase three of Cycle One, animals and habitat, see Fig. 29.1), they were able to build on their understandings and make connections that habitats for animals need to include plants and water. This understanding was particularly evident when the children were using loose materials to make small-world habitats, and included representations of these things within their habitat creations. When questioned about what they had built, several of the children were able to articulate their understanding that plants and water are important to include, even if the animal is a carnivore, as they will provide shelter and food for the other animals the carnivore eats, as witnessed from the following observational notes:

> Two students (codes LC and AA) were creating zoo habitats for the plastic animals. LC asked AA for some glass pebbles and scallop shells, when AA asked why, LC replied that they had to make sure each habitat for the different animals must all include water or they will die.

As the children engaged in the second phase of Cycle One (plants, see Fig. 29.1), their interest provoked many different conversations comparing the size of the different sprouts over time, offering explanations and introducing or using new vocabulary, such as one student who said during dramatic playtime that:

> this tiny seed is a flower seed it might take longer to germinate and grow its roots and stem and the bean and pea seeds are much bigger so they might germinate faster and grow bigger.

The use of academic language, emerging from such engagement with the intentional teaching experiences, supports the findings cited earlier in helping children make connections and links with the concept of sustainability (Elliott & Davis, 2009). As the students' engagement with the plants grew, they asked to be able to plant their sprouts and construct a raised garden bed in their outdoor space. The planting of the sprouts took place in their dramatic playtime, with the children taking the roles of plant nursery shop keepers, horticulturalists as well as customers learning about how to plant and look after the sprouts, which became another important time to reinforce the vocabulary.

The dramatic play appeared to be the type of provocation most effective in generating the students' spontaneous, contextual and voluntary use of the targeted academic vocabulary. During our outside free play time, building on the conceptual play world, the children often used the vocabulary in an authentic way, which indicated they were integrating this vocabulary into their lexicons, and even expanding on it. A compelling example came from their engagement with the book *The Tiny Seed* (Carle, 1970). We created a conceptual play world (Fleer, 2018), acting out roles as different seeds landing in varied environments, with the accompanying elements such as wind, rain and sun. It was from this play that the word *germinate* was introduced and added to their vocabulary. It was evident that words that had received the most repetition, and had become part of their imaginary play, were best understood by the students.

Data from both the pre- and post-tests and the qualitative observations paint the picture of the importance of a diverse range of experiences and point to the types of experiences the study found most effective for developing the students' understanding of the vocabulary. While our school is not part of the Forest School movement, we are certainly supportive of the importance of providing our students plenty of outside time and using our outdoor spaces to support our curriculum. The results from the project have supported the research from the Forest School movement (Cumming & Nash, 2015; Harris, 2017; MacEachren, 2013; Mitchell et al., 2016). They demonstrate that young children can connect to the goals of sustainability and are supported in building a connection to the world around them by engaging in authentic outdoor experiences as part of an enriched STEM programme. The varied approaches adopted here, which were developed based on research (e.g., Elley, 1989; Penno et al., 2002), provided opportunities to repeat words, respond appropriately with the correct vocabulary when prompted and elicit spontaneous and independent use of the vocabulary during their play. However, as positive as the results found in previous studies are, they have not been proved powerful enough to overcome the Matthew Effect (Boeren, 2019; Merton, 1968) and were similarly echoed in our project, where those more capable students made greater gains than those students with language and learning difficulties and those with frequent absences.

While the full results of the project are still being analysed and interpreted, it seems clear from the results of Cycle One that an enriched STEM programme can be created to provide students with the valuable foundation language concepts and skills necessary to access these curriculum areas, as they progress through their education. Future research would be valuable to see whether this foundation of vocabulary and the engagement with the SDGs can be effectively built upon as they progress through school. Additional promising outcomes arising from the project include an increased understanding of the impact of the environment on living things, and this has magnified the attention they place on reducing their carbon footprint, for example, with anecdotal observations of improved recycling (all litter is sorted into various bins, items like cardboard, pouch lids and yoghurt containers are cleaned and used to create and for constructing things); the students indicate they are using less packaging in their lunch boxes; and where possible, reuse paper to reduce the number of trees used for paper production.

29.9 Summary

Education is at the heart of the SDGs. For these goals to be achieved, it is important for today's children, as the ones who will be most affected in the future, that sustainability is a central focus of their learning from early childhood. Young children are naturally curious and full of wonder about the world around them and how it works. Their engagement and fascination with nature opens all manner of possibilities for their imaginations to soar and new ideas to be nurtured and grow. The focus of this chapter has been the design of rich experiences to support young children from low SES areas to receive a quality education, by building a foundation of STEM vocabulary and concepts that would open opportunities for accessing these curriculum areas in the future. We have demonstrated that a varied range of activities and experiences are effective in developing students' vocabulary and that sizeable gains in their familiarity with words and ability to use them in authentic contexts can be found from an appropriate mix of hands-on and play-based experiences.

Sustainability was not the primary focus of this project in its initial conception. However, we have seen from the preliminary findings of the first cycle discussed here, that there are clear connections to the SDGs among the selected topics and the academic language developed during the cycle, as a result of the selected activities and topic themes. In particular, explicit links between the academic vocabulary and SDG14 and SDG15 may be seen to underpin all areas of learning in this approach. The connections between the vocabulary and sustainability have heightened students' awareness of sustainability in general and have helped lead the students to think about sustainability in other areas. For example, there have been real changes in the types of lunchboxes and the number of packaged goods they use and bring to school, increased recycling of rubbish, conserving of water and caring for their school environment. This awareness of the importance of sustainability will not only affect their lives but also affect the school as a whole and their families. We anticipate similar positive results from Cycles Two and Three, informed and designed in response to the findings reported here, but these remain to be analysed.

References

Aikens, N. L., & Barbarin, O. (2008). Socioeconomic differences in reading trajectories: The contribution of family, neighborhood, and school contexts. *Journal of Educational Psychology, 100*(2), 235–251.

Ärlemalm-Hagsér, E., & Elliott, S. (2017). Special issue: Contemporary research on early childhood education for sustainability. *International Journal of Early Childhood, 49*(3), 267–272.

Australian Government: Department of Education and Workplace Relations (Producer). (2018). *Belonging, being & becoming. The early years learning framework for Australia.* https://www.acecqa.gov.au/sites/default/files/acecqa/files/National-Quality-Framework-Resources-Kit/educators_guide_to_the_early_years_learning_framework_for_australia_2.pdf

Beck, I. L., McKeown, M. G., & Kucan, L. (2008). *Creating robust vocabulary: Frequently asked questions and extended examples.* The Guilford Press.

Beck, I. L., McKeown, M. G., & Kucan, L. (2013). *Bringing words to life: Robust vocabulary instruction*. Guilford Press.

Beimiller, A. (Ed.) (2005). *Size and sequence in vocabulary development: Implications for choosing words for primary grade vocabulary instruction*. Laurence Erlbaum.

Blums, A., Belsky, J., Grimm, K., & Chen, Z. (2017). Building links between early socioeconomic status, cognitive ability, and math and science achievement. *Journal of Cognition and Development, 18*(1), 16–40.

Boehm, A. (2001). *Boehm test of basic concepts* (3rd ed.). Pearsons Education.

Boeren, E. (2019). Understanding Sustainable Development Goal (SDG) 4 on "quality education" from micro, meso and macro perspectives. *International Review of Education, 65*(2), 277–294.

Buchter, J., Kucskar, M., Oh-Young, C., Welgarz-Ward, J., & Gelfer, J. (2017). Supporting STEM in early childhood education. *Policy Issues in Nevada Education, 2*, 1–12. https://digitalschol arship.unlv.edu/co_educ_policy/2/

Carle, E. (1970). *The tiny seed*. Simon and Schuster.

Considine, G., & Zappalà, G. (2002). Factors influencing the educational performance of students from disadvantaged backgrounds. In *Competing visions: Refereed proceedings of the national social policy conference* (Vol. 2001, pp. 91–107).

Cooper, G., Berry, A., & Baglin, J. (2020). Demographic predictors of students' science participation over the age of 16: An Australian case study. *Research in Science Education, 50*(1), 361–373.

Cumming, F., & Nash, M. (2015). An Australian perspective of a forest school: Shaping a sense of place to support learning. *Journal of Adventure Education and Outdoor Learning, 15*(4), 296–309.

Dockett, S., & Fleer, M. (1999). *Play and pedagogy in early childhood: Bending the rules*. Harcourt Pty Ltd.

Duncan, G. J., & Brooks-Gunn, J. (1994). Economic deprivation and early childhood development. *Child Development, 65*(2), 296–318.

Education Council. (2015). *National STEM school education strategy: A comprehensive plan for science, technology, engineering and mathematics education in Australia*. https://www.educat ion.gov.au/education-ministers-meeting/resources/national-stem-school-education-strategy

Efron, S. E. (2013). *Action research in education: A practical guide* [electronic resource].

Elfert, M. (2019). Lifelong learning in Sustainable Development Goal 4: What does it mean for UNESCO's rights-based approach to adult learning and education? *International Review of Education, 65*(4), 537–556.

Elley, W. B. (1989). Vocabulary acquisition from listening to stories. *Reading Research Quarterly,* 174–187.

Elliott, S., & Davis, J. (2009). Exploring the resistance: An Australian perspective on educating for sustainability in early childhood. *International Journal of Early Childhood: Journal of OMEP: L'organisation Mondiale Pour L'education Prescolaire, 41*(2), 65.

Elliott, S., & Young, T. (2016). Nature by default in early childhood education for sustainability. *Australian Journal of Environmental Education, 32*(1), 57–64.

Fernald, A., Marchman, V. A., & Weisleder, A. (2013). SES differences in language processing skill and vocabulary are evident at 18 months. *Developmental Science, 16*(2), 234–248.

Feza, N. N. (2018). The Socioeconomic status label associated with mathematics. In *Global ideologies surrounding children's rights and social justice* (pp. 186–203). IGI Global.

Fleer, M. (2018). Conceptual playworlds: The role of imagination in play and learning. *Early Years,* 1–12.

Ginsborg, J. (Ed.). (2006). *The effects of socioeconomic status in children's language*. John Willey and Sons Ltd.

Goldstein, H., Ziolkowski, R. A., Bojcyk, K. E., Marty, A., Schneider, N., Harping, J., & Haring, C. D. (2017). Academic vocabulary learning in first through third grade in low-income schools: Effects of automated supplemental instruction. *Journal of Speech, Language and Hearing Research, 60*, 3237–3258.

Halliday, M. A. (1993). Towards a language-based theory of learning. *Linguistics and Education,* *5*(2), 93–116.

Harris, F. (2017). The nature of learning at forest school: Practitioners' perspectives. *Education* *3–13, 45*(2), 272–291.

Hart, B., & Risley, T. R. (1995). The early catastrophe: The 30 million word gap by age 3. *American* *Educator, 27*(1), 4–9.

Hohmann, M., Weikart, D. P., & Epstein, A. S. (1995). *Educating young children: Active learning* *practices for preschool and child care programs.* High/Scope Press.

Kember, D., & McKay, J. (1996). Action research into the quality of student learning: A paradigm for faculty development. *Journal of Higher Education, 67*(5), 528–554.

Locke, A., Ginsborg, J., & Peers, I. (2002). Development and disadvantage: Implications for the early years and beyond. *International Journal of Language & Communication Disorders, 37*(1), 3–15.

MacEachren, Z. (2013). The Canadian forest school movement. *Learning, 7*(1), 219–233.

Matthews, P., & McLean, A. (2002). *A year on our farm.* Omnibus Books.

Mellou, E. (1994). Play theories: A contemporary review. *Early Child Development and Care,* *102*(1), 91–100.

Mercer, N. (2002). *Words and minds: How we use language to think together.* Routledge.

Merton, R. K. (1968). The Matthew effect in science: The reward and communication systems of science are considered. *Science, 159*(3810), 56–63.

Mitchell, D., Tippins, D. J., Kim, Y. A., Perkins, G. D., & Rudolph, H. A. (2016). Last child in the woods: An analysis of nature, child, and time through the lens of eco-mindfulness. In *Mindfulness and educating citizens for everyday life* (pp. 135–158). Brill Sense.

Payne, R. K. (2013). *A framework for understanding poverty: A cognitive approach* (5th ed.). Aha! Process Inc.

Penno, J. F., Wilkinson, I. A., & Moore, D. W. (2002). Vocabulary acquisition from teacher explanation and repeated listening to stories: Do they overcome the Matthew effect? *Journal of* *Educational Psychology, 94*(1), 23.

Pine, G. J. (2009). *Teacher action research: Building knowledge democracies.* Sage.

Samuelsson, I. P., & Carlsson, M. A. (2008). The playing learning child: Towards a pedagogy of early childhood. *Scandinavian Journal of Educational Research, 52*(6), 623–641.

Samuelsson, I. P., & Park, E. (2017). How to educate children for sustainable learning and for a sustainable world. *International Journal of Early Childhood, 49*(3), 273–285.

Scarborough, H. S., Neuman, S., & Dickinson, D. (2009). Connecting early language and literacy to later reading (dis) abilities: Evidence, theory, and practice. In F. Fletcher-Campbell, J. Solar, & G. Reid (Eds.), *Approaching difficulties in literacy development: Assessment, pedagogy and* *programmes* (pp. 23–38). Sage.

Siraj-Blatchford, J., Smith, K. C., & Samuelsson, I. P. (2010). *Education for sustainable development* *in the early years.* OMEP, World Organization for Early Childhood Education.

Snow, C. E., & Uccelli, P. (2009). The challenge of academic language. In D. R. Olson & N. Torrance (Eds.), *The Cambridge handbook of literacy* (pp. 112–133). Cambridge University Press.

Thomson, S., De Bortoli, L., & Underwood, C. (2017). *PISA 2015: Reporting Australia's results.* Australian Council for Educational. https://research.acer.edu.au/ozpisa/22/?__hstc=227787 458.1bb630f9cde2cb5f07430159d50a3c91.1496361600072.1496361600073.1496361600074. 1&__hssc=227787458.1.1496361600075&__hsfp=1773666937

United Nations Decade of Education for Sustainable Development (2005–2014). (2014). *Final* *report. Shaping the future we want.* https://en.unesco.org/themes/education-sustainable-develo pment/what-is-esd/un-decade-of-esd

United Nations General Assembly. (2015). *Transforming our world: The 2030 agenda for* *sustainable development.* https://www.refworld.org/docid/57b6e3e44.html

Vladimirova, K., & Le Blanc, D. (2016). Exploring links between education and sustainable development goals through the lens of UN flagship reports. *Sustainable Development, 24*(4), 254–271.

Vygotsky, L. S. (1966). Igra i ee rol v umstvennom razvitii rebenka, voprosy psihologii [Play and its role in the mental development of the child]. *Problems of Psychology, 12*(6), 62–76.

Webb, S., Holford, J., Hodge, S., Milana, M., & Waller, R. (2017). Lifelong learning for quality education: Exploring the neglected aspect of Sustainable Development Goal 4. *International Journal of Lifelong Education, 36*(5), 509–511.

Zevenbergen, R. (2002). Mathematics, social class, and linguistic capital: An analysis of mathematics classroom interactions. In B. Atweh, H. J. Forgasz, & B. Nebres (Eds.), *Sociocultural research on mathematics education* (pp. 201–215). Lawrence Erlbaum Associates.

Chapter 30
Using the Practice of Statistics to Enhance Education Through UN Sustainable Development Goal 13, Climate Change

Caroline Smith⬥ and Jane Watson⬥

30.1 Introduction

The uncertainty of our times raises questions about how mathematics education can assist students to engage meaningfully with critical global issues. Over the past decades, a number of authors have called for mathematics education to align with critical analyses of sociocultural, economic and political issues and movements for change (e.g., D'Ambrosio, 1990; Frankenstein, 2012; Skovsmose, 1994). Skovsmose called for a "critical mathematics education" that expands traditional mathematical skills to include competence in model building and reflection in evaluating the applications of mathematics to social issues. As statistics has become prominent in school curricula since the 1990s (e.g., Australian Education Council, 1991; National Council of Teachers of Mathematics, 1989), more opportunities exist for analysing data to address social issues.

Data and statistics are critical to a deep understanding and interpretation of the world's sustainability issues, both for professionals and the citizenry in general. Hence, statistics education provides a powerful opportunity and motivation for educators to engage in preparing and equipping the next generation for informed decision-making in the uncertain contexts they will encounter now and into the future. For example, Watson and Smith (2022) show how the complexity and volume of

C. Smith (✉)
School of Education, College of Arts, Law and Education, University of Tasmania, 2/8 Bass Hwy, Burnie, TAS 7320, Australia
e-mail: caroline.smith1@utas.edu.au

J. Watson
School of Education, College of Arts, Law and Education, University of Tasmania, Churchill Ave, Hobart, TAS 7005, Australia
e-mail: jane.watson@utas.edu.au

© The Author(s), under exclusive license to Springer Nature Singapore Pte Ltd. 2023   539
K. Beasy et al. (eds.), *Education and the UN Sustainable Development Goals*, Education for Sustainability 7,
https://doi.org/10.1007/978-981-99-3802-5_30

data produced throughout the COVID-19 pandemic have provided a highly relevant context for students to engage in the Practice of Statistics.

Referring to climate change as our context, we draw on the United Nations (UN) Sustainable Development Goals (SDGs) (UN, 2020a), and specifically Goal 13, *Climate Change*, to explore how statistics education can strengthen understanding of this context (United Nations Framework Convention on Climate Change ([UNFCCC], 2020). We are given further impetus by the interest of many school students in the global School Strike 4 Climate Action (SS4C, 2022) movement that emerged in response to Greta Thunberg's activism in 2019.

30.2   Education and the Sustainable Development Goals

Education is considered an essential strategy in the pursuit and achievement of the SDGs and one of the SDGs, Goal 4, *Quality Education,* states in Target 4.7 that "by 2023 ensure that all learners acquire knowledge and skills needed to promote sustainable development..." (UN, 2020a, p. 8). A key document supporting education in the SDGs is *Education for Sustainable Development Goals: Learning Objectives* (United Nations Education, Scientific and Cultural Organisation [UNESCO], 2017). This is intended to guide educators and allied professionals to support and promote learning about the SDGs. It includes education-related targets and Learning Objectives written for the overarching platform of the SDGs in general, as well as specific details targeted towards each goal, with suggested topics and learning activities. The document also includes implementation methods at different levels, from course design to national strategies. Central to the document are eight Competencies that learners should develop (UNESCO, 2017, p. 10), among which are the following three:

C1. Systems thinking competency: the abilities to recognize and understand relationships; to analyse complex systems; to think of how systems are embedded within different domains and different scales; and to deal with uncertainty.

C6. Critical thinking competency: the ability to question norms, practices and opinions; to reflect on one's own values, perceptions and actions; and to take a position in the sustainability discourse.

C8. Integrated problem-solving competency: the overarching ability to apply different problem-solving frameworks to complex sustainability problems and develop viable, inclusive and equitable solution options that promote sustainable development, integrating the above-mentioned competences.

30.3 Data and Statistics in the Learning Objectives and Competencies

Although both the *UN Decade of ESD* (Education for Sustainable Development) (UNESCO, 2020) and the SDGs rely on collecting a wide range of data for monitoring and evaluation of their own impact and success, it is quite disappointing that they do not include data and statistics as a central component of their educational programs. In its critique of the SDGs, the Trinity College Dublin Future Learn (2020) course *Achieving Sustainable Development* identified lack of data as one of its five top concerns. It states that "[T]he data that we do have is not enough for us to use the goals either as a way to guide our management of easing poverty or as a way to report on progress. If we don't have this data, how useful can the goals be for those people making policy?" This lack of data is also noted in a review commissioned by the Partnership in Statistics for Development in the 21st Century (Rogerson & Calleja, 2019), which notes that in order to implement and monitor the SDGs, better data are urgently needed, but statistical and administrative systems, especially in poor countries, remain seriously underfunded.

Obtaining and using data, and the application of statistics, are critical to the ability to recognise and understand relationships, analyse complex systems, discover how they are embedded within different domains and different scales, and deal with uncertainty. We argue, then, that statistical literacy is fundamental to prepare a generation of global citizens with the ability to interpret the data and arguments surrounding them to make the critical decisions required for humanity to flourish. The competencies themselves clearly suggest the importance of statistics. Competency C1, *Systems thinking competency*, implies the importance of the role of data and statistics in understanding the complexity and interrelated nature of the SDGs, whereas statistical analysis is able to provide a powerful problem-solving framework called for in Competency C8, *Integrated problem-solving competency.*

Statistics as it specifically relates to education, however, is only mentioned once throughout all 17 SDG Learning Objectives, in the Cognitive Learning Objective C1 of SDG10: *Reduced Inequalities*. It states: "The learner knows different dimensions of inequality, their interrelations and applicable statistics" (UNESCO, 2017, p. 35). We argue that data and statistics can be addressed through all the educational competencies included in the Learning Objectives.

Before turning to explore specifically how the Practice of Statistics can be applied to the SDGs, and in particular SDG13, we first discuss the importance of variation and its relationship to learning, as foundational to the Practice.

30.4 Variation and the Importance of the Practice of Statistics

A dictionary definition for "vary" might seem straightforward, with synonyms such as "to be different, to diversify, to alter, to deviate, to change, perhaps to increase or decrease" (Dictionary.com, n.d.). In other words, variation can occur and be named in many ways depending on the context. However, in order to appreciate the importance of variation for the building of statistical understanding to answer questions arising from data, and hence its role in relation to sustainability, four steps are necessary:

1. Consideration of basic mathematical skills that are necessary to appreciate variation
2. Examination of descriptions of data that can assist in clarifying variation
3. Linking variation to the Practice of Statistics in order to answer questions about data
4. Linking this Practice to learning more generally with the potential to contribute to decision-making in sustainability contexts involving variation

Innabi (2018) is helpful in this regard by pointing to research findings relating to the first two steps. She argues that three hierarchical mathematical skills are required when dealing with sampling tasks (Noll & Shaughnessy, 2012): additive skills to give information in the form of frequencies to allow for basic comparisons; proportional reasoning understanding, e.g., percentages and relative frequencies, as required for difference in sample size; and distributional appreciation, e.g., centre, shape and measures of variability to make possible suggestions about underlying populations.

Further, Konold et al. (2015) add a perspective on variation to the second step by noticing how learners view numerical data as pointers to issues from the context producing the data, as particular case values such as extreme values, as classifiers related to frequency of data with the same attributes, and as aggregates summarising overall distribution characteristics such as centre and spread. Next, utilising these basic skills and using the Practice of Statistics, Watson et al. (2018) provide a process for answering questions involving data. The Practice involves the following steps, all of which acknowledge the importance of variation (Franklin et al., 2007):

• Formulating questions, anticipating variability;
• Designing and implementing a plan to collect data, acknowledging variability;
• Analysing data with appropriate graphical and numerical methods, accounting for variability; and
• Interpreting the results of the analysis in relation to the original question, allowing for variability.

At the school level, learners follow the pathway shown in Fig. 30.1.

Finally, it is this pathway where contact with the "real world" becomes important, because conclusions drawn from data via the Practice of Statistics can potentially contribute to solving problems in science and society, including our focus here, questions relating to sustainability. As well as the significance of variation at every stage of

Fig. 30.1 Pathway for the Practice of Statistics (Franklin et al., 2007)

I. Formulate Questions

→   clarify the problem at hand

→   formulate one (or more) questions that can be answered with data

II. Collect Data

→   design a plan to collect appropriate data

→   employ the plan to collect the data

III. Analyze Data

→   select appropriate graphical and numerical methods

→   use these methods to analyze the data

IV. Interpret Results

→   interpret the analysis

→   relate the interpretation to the original question

the Practice, when samples are based on populations, for example, confidence in the answer obtained must be reported including a level of uncertainty based on previous stages of the investigation. Bulmer and Haladyn's (2011) application of the Practice of Statistics provides a powerful example of this approach. They used an online simulation of activities of a human population restricted to an island to develop innovative activities for teaching statistics through data investigations, aligned with the Statistics and Probability strand of the *Australian Mathematics Curriculum* (Australian Curriculum Assessment and Reporting Authority [ACARA], 2022).

Having mastered the Practice of Statistics, the next step is to be able to use this understanding when encountering reports on related investigations that make claims using statistics in other contexts. This is termed "statistical literacy" in these situations where there are no data to carry out the investigation (Watson, 2006). It is important for either accepting or questioning claims and requires understanding of:

- The terminology and representation used—what does it mean statistically?
- The context—what does the terminology and representation mean in the context where it is presented?
- Critical thinking—what is the precise claim being made and is it reasonable?

An example of these requirements can be seen in a classroom activity for Years 7–10 suggested by Watson and Callingham (2020), motivated by the graph shown in Fig. 30.2 reporting the results of a poll on Global Warming by Fox News. In terms of *the terminology and representation*, students need to understand percentage and realise that the figures add to 120%, which contradicts understanding that 100% should represent the whole sample collected. *The context* is Global Warming but there is no description of the people sampled or how many responded. Would

Fig. 30.2 Report showing results of poll on global warming (*Source* https://www.businessinsider.com/top-ten-dubious-polls-2010-2)

students believe that 94% of Americans (or any group) would think it somewhat or very likely that scientists falsified their research to support their own theories on Global Warming? *Critical thinking* should lead students to ask, "Who was in the sample? How many were sampled? What exactly was asked and what alternatives were provided for responses?" Students might conduct a survey of their class to answer the question in the figure and compare with the results (after recalculating the reported results to add to 100%!).

The actual question asked in the survey was, "In order to support their own theories and beliefs about global warming, how likely is it that some scientists have falsified research data?" The difference in the actual question and the one in the figure should attract a critical discussion among students, including questioning language such as "some scientists." They also might ask what the choices of responses were. These are the kinds of issues expected to be raised by the statistically literate, who have not conducted a study themselves, but because of their experience with the Practice of Statistics can raise important issues when confronted with claims made in public. In fact, for the actual question asked, the results were: Very likely (35%), Somewhat likely (24%), Not very likely (21%), Not likely at all (5%), Unsure (15%). Presented with these figures, statistically literate students should be able to have a critical discussion about how the question was phrased, likely responses, and the purpose of the report in combining the figures as was done in Fig. 30.2.

30.5 Variation and Learning Theory

Innabi (2018) goes further by linking the concept of variation with the general learning theory proposed by Marton (2015), in which discerning critical aspects of the context contribute to successful learning. For Marton, learning occurs through systematic interactions between the learner and the object of learning, and the concept of variation is the means to generate the interaction. This is especially effective when learners experience variation based on the concepts that support building further understanding. Marton proposes four contexts for exploring patterns of variation: *contrast* between different and dissimilar aspects; *separation* of critical features and dimensions of variation; *generalisation* by exploring whether a pattern can occur while certain aspects vary, and *fusion* by integrating aspects or dimensions of variation into a whole. This moves beyond the specific use of the term "variation" within the Practice of Statistics to apply to the nature of learning more generally. As Marton suggests, this is about learning to learn. He asks: "[h]ow can learners be prepared for the unknown by means of the known?" (p. 67), which aligns well with SDG 4's call for learning itself to be sustainable, that is, be life-long (UN, 2020a). Innabi builds on this in statistics education with a focus on variation related to *students' awareness levels, dynamic visualisations*, and *complex real-life contexts*.

For learning to be effective, learners need to interact with patterns of variation and invariance, identifying both differences and similarities, which lead them to statistical questions and investigations. All statistical investigations begin with a context/situation involving variation, where data can be collected. Marton's (2015) view of learning acknowledges this variation in all learning situations.

30.6 Developing the Practice of Statistics at the Primary School Level

The importance and feasibility of introducing the Practice of Statistics early in children's education is beginning to be recognised by curriculum authorities around the world (e.g., ACARA, 2022, Content Descriptor AC9MFST01). It is now known that even very young children are able to ask questions about their world that require data to answer them, for example, about their own class at school. They are able to collect, record and create pictures of their data, answer a question about their class and speculate on what the answer might be for another class or the whole school, for example, "What is the favourite fruit in our class?" By the time learners reach middle school they are able to ask questions based in curriculum areas beyond mathematics, e.g., science, social sciences, geography, history, health, and digital and design technology. They can collect the data themselves and/or use data from other sources to make decisions.

In Australia, a program was developed over three years that introduced the Practice of Statistics to primary school learners. The first activity in Year 4 saw the learners engaged in a problem-posing activity based on developing multiple-choice questions for their fellow learners on improvements to their school playground (English & Watson, 2015a). The purpose of this activity was for the researchers to become acquainted with the learners and set the starting points for the study. The learners learned about variation through posing different multiple-choice questions, (e.g., Why?, What?, How? and When?), in contrasting a variety of answers to their questions, and in creating the rudimentary representations possible for the data collected. Together they were then able to use their data to consider a range of actions that could take place to improve the playground.

The second activity moved to obtaining measurement data with a focus on the difference in the variation when one learner's arm span was measured by all members of the class, and then all learners had their arm spans measured once (English & Watson, 2015b). Plotting the data by hand and using the software *TinkerPlots* helped create a transition from idiosyncratic data representation methods to more conventional methods, usually a stacked dot plot, as a way of showing the difference in the variation in the two measurement contexts (Konold & Miller, 2015). The third activity combined modelling the tossing of two coins theoretically with physical tossing and simulation of many trials with *TinkerPlots* (English & Watson, 2016). The focus this time was the relationship between variation and expectation, and for many learners, a consolidation of their understanding was that as the number of trials increased, the percentage value of results became closer to the expectation from the theoretical model.

Following Marton (2015), by the end of Year 4, these learners had experienced a *contrast* of different questions that required different data to answer. Each time they had experienced problem posing and appreciation of variation (and in one context, its relationship with formal expectation), developing data representation skills, and recognising the uncertainty of their conclusions from the data collected. Overall, they experienced a *separation* of techniques for handling features for different types of data and the *generalisation* of pattern through the varying contexts of measurement and coin tossing. This led to the decision that when they reached Year 5 it would be appropriate to introduce the learners "formally" to the complete Practice of Statistics by integrating and *fusing* these aspects and naming them.

The manner of enabling this consolidation illustrates some of the technicalities of combining the complexities of a realistic context with those of allowing the learners the freedom within the classroom to decide their own criteria for answering questions, but still to be able to relate and/or compare their conclusions with those of their classmates (Watson & English, 2015). It was decided that the "raw" data with which learners worked in the context would be the same, but they would set their own unique criteria for answering the general research question. This decision meant that there could be no supposition that the learners could agree on their conclusions (and potentially much variation). The context, which related to SDG13, arose because at that time, the Australian Bureau of Statistics (ABS) was cooperating with an international Census at School project (Davies et al., 2010). As part of this project, data were collected from thousands of Australian school students including five questions on their actions relating to environmental sustainability. The questions are shown in Fig. 30.3.

Fig. 30.3 Questions from ABS National Survey for school learners (Watson & English, 2015)

Am I environmentally friendly?	Yes	No
Our household has a water tank.		
I take shorter showers. (4 mins max)		
I turn the tap off while brushing my teeth.		
I turn off appliances (e.g., TV, computer, gaming consoles) at the power point.		
My household recycles rubbish.		

As well as consolidating the concepts learned from the previous activities, this introduced a new type of data—YES/NO categorical data—requiring the use of mathematical proportional reasoning skills. A general class discussion on climate change, sustainability and initiatives that learners and their families themselves could take, was followed by the introduction of the Census at School and its questions. This led to considering the question of whether learners in Year 5 in their class and in Australia generally were "environmentally friendly." Even further this led to the formal introduction of the term "sample" and the ownership of their class's answers to their survey as the sample to represent the "population" of Australia's Year 5 learners. Because of the nature of the general question, each learner was given the freedom to decide the percentage of YES answers to the five questions required in order to determine whether the class was environmentally friendly, and then to discuss their certainty of the decision for all Year 5 learners students in the country.

Again, reflecting Marton (2015), within the activity, the learners were taught how to collect random samples from a "population" of 1300 Australian Year 5 learners. This promoted much discussion relating to the *contrast* of the samples and their *separation* due particularly to the variation observed. Nine random samples were then *generalised* to look for patterns that would reflect the population values responding to the five questions (Watson & English, 2016). At each stage, learners were asked to make decisions about whether their class, a random sample, or a collection of random samples, satisfied their criteria for being environmentally friendly. They finally combined their results to integrate the components of the activity to make a decision about Australian Year 5 learners' level of environmental friendliness, expressing their levels of certainty based on their own criteria. This *fusion* was complex for about half of the learners but provided a starting point for further activities.

The above examples clearly show that the Practice of Statistics is possible and achievable with primary aged learners. By this, we refer to the framework developed by Franklin et al. (2007) as noted earlier, which describes the process of formulating a question to explore and anticipate variability (Are Year 5s environmentally friendly?), then designing and implementing a plan to collect data (first from the class and then across Australia), acknowledging variability, followed by analysing data with appropriate graphical and numerical methods (comparing percentages with their criteria), accounting for variability. Finally, it involves interpreting the results of the analysis in relation to the original question, allowing for variability (making a decision for Australia). This framework not only provides a structure for working with statistics but also incorporates the very foundation of statistics: variation (Cobb & Moore, 1997). Innabi (2018) agrees with regard to sustainable learning, contending that statistics should be taught not as an isolated discipline, but rather within a context of complex real-life issues.

This extended example illustrates the relationship of the concept of variation in sustainable learning (Marton, 2015) to its fundamental role in carrying out the Practice of Statistics (Watson et al., 2018), and to possibilities for its application with young children, given the appropriate pedagogical approach. It also illustrates Innabi's (2018) concerns, as *students' awareness levels* were seen in the detailed analysis of students' responses to the tasks (Watson & English, 2015, 2016), *dynamic visualisation* was experienced through viewing sample outcomes in *TinkerPlots*, and the *complex real-life context* related to the possibilities in the questions related to being environmentally friendly.

In the next section, we return to the SDGs and in particular, Goal 13, "take urgent action to combat climate change and its impacts," as the vehicle to explore in more detail how the Practice of Statistics can be used to highlight important elements of the Goal for school learners.

30.7 Sustainable Development Goal 13 and the Practice of Statistics

In Australia, the government departments of Environment and Energy, Agriculture and Water Resources and Home Affairs Emergency Management are responsible for input into reporting against SDG13 (Australian Government Department of Foreign Affairs and Trade, 2018). The wealth of information associated within Goal 13 provides a range of data in the form of graphics and statistics that illustrate the complexity of the issue, clearly showing the need for statistical literacy to be able to interpret and create meaning from them.

Reminding ourselves of Competency C1 (UNESCO, 2017), in particular, we now focus on the cognitive learning objectives and selected suggested topics of SDG13 (UN, 2020b, pp. 36–37) and indicate related data that could be used to develop the cognitive learning objectives (Table 30.1).

As noted earlier, all statistical investigations begin with a context/situation involving variation where data can be collected, and Marton's (2015) view of learning acknowledges this variation is a function of all learning situations. Table 30.2 summarises the parallels between Marton's view, the Practice of Statistics, and SDG13 as the context for learning.

30.8 Examples Relating to SDG13 Across the School Curriculum

In general, it is in Science and Geography curricula, as well as curricula based around ESD, where examples and contexts for exploring SDG13 are to be found. In the United States, the *Next Generation Science Standards* (National Research Council, 2013) mentions data 932 times and suggests using data in relation to the core idea *Earth and Human Activity*, which includes focus on "Human Impacts on Earth Systems" and "Global Climate Change." *Natural Resources* considers that "all forms of energy production and other resource extraction have associated economic, social,

Table 30.1 Cognitive learning objectives, suggested topics and examples of data in SDG13

SDG13 cognitive learning objectives	Suggested topics from SDG13	Examples of related sources of data
1. The learner understands the greenhouse effect as a natural phenomenon caused by an insulating layer of greenhouse gases	Greenhouse gases, their sources, emission levels and impact on biophysical systems	Greenhouse gases (GHG) and their levels in the atmosphere
2. The learner understands the current climate change as an anthropogenic phenomenon resulting from increased greenhouse gas emissions	Energy, agriculture and industry-related greenhouse gas emissions Future scenarios including alternative explanations for the global temperature rise, e.g., volcanic emissions and solar radiation fluctuations	GHG levels and global temperature changes over deep time Relative GHG emissions by sector
3. The learner knows which human activities—on a global, national, local and individual level—contribute most to climate change		Forest cover loss over time Glacier shrinkage over time Biodiversity loss over time Sea-level rise over time
4. The learner knows about the main ecological, social, cultural and economic consequences of climate change locally, nationally and globally and understands how these can themselves become catalysing, reinforcing factors for climate change	Climate change-related hazards leading to disasters like drought, weather extremes, etc. and their unequal social and economic impact within households, communities and countries and between countries Effects of and impacts on big eco-systems like forests, oceans, glaciers and biodiversity Sea-level rise and its consequences for countries (e.g., small island states)	Numbers and intensity of extreme weather events: drought, flooding, cyclones storm surges, bushfires over time
5. The learner knows about prevention, mitigation and adaptation strategies at different levels (global to individual) and for different contexts and their connections with disaster response and disaster risk reduction	Migration and flight related to climate change Prevention, mitigation and adaptation strategies and their connections with disaster response and disaster risk reduction Local, national and global institutions addressing issues of climate change Local, national and global policy strategies to protect the climate	Human and other species migration patterns Examples of adaptations to climate change—measurable changes, e.g., building design and city cooling through tree cover Impact of disasters and community responses

Table 30.2 Relationships between Marton's general learning theory, the Practice of Statistics and SDG13 as the learning context

Marton's general learning theory	The Practice of Statistics to answer a question	Context: Sustainable development goal 13 climate change
Contrast: different & dissimilar	Collected data displaying variation	Natural phenomena show variation: data on climate change
Separation: critical features, dimensions of variation	Multiple variables, use of distributions to view features	Impact of different phenomena, locations, risks on climate change
Generalisation: seek observed patterns within variation	Expectation arising from distribution: pattern, peaks, associations	Explanation of observations in terms of potential outcomes
Fusion: integrate aspects/ dimensions into a whole	Answer to statistical question acknowledging uncertainty	Promotion of policies to support action required with respect to climate change

environmental and geopolitical costs as well as benefits" (p. 126). In Australia, the curriculum includes *Sustainability* as a Cross-Curriculum Priority (ACARA, 2022):

> Young people require the knowledge and skills to engage with contemporary issues such as climate change, biodiversity loss, equitable access to resources, and preservation of cultural and language diversity. They are looking for social, economic and political models that provide solutions to these issues.

This priority is then recognised in the *Australian Science Curriculum* (ACARA, 2022) as an example of the integration of the three strands of that curriculum.

> The content of *Science understanding* can inform students' understanding of everyday phenomena, as well as contemporary issues such as use of resources, emerging technologies, climate change and protection of biodiversity. The importance of these areas of science can be emphasised through the content of *Science as a human endeavour*, and students can be encouraged to view historical and contemporary science critically through aspects of the *Science inquiry* strand, for example, by evaluating and communicating.

The strand *Science Inquiry* specifically includes "generating and analysing data; evaluating results; and drawing critical, evidence-based conclusions." These are precisely the aims of the Statistics strand of the Mathematics Curriculum, which provides the techniques required to carry out the Practice of Statistics across the years. In discussing the barriers and opportunities for teaching climate change science in senior classes, Bunten and Dawson (2014) not only provide an outline of lessons on the underlying topics, including analysis of temperature data from the pre-twentieth century, but also discuss averages, variation, likelihood and uncertainty at many points. All of these tools are built on statistical literacy that hopefully has been built across the earlier years as described above.

That these understandings are critical across the curriculum is further demonstrated by looking at the *Australian Geography Curriculum for Years 7 to 10* (ACARA, 2022):

Students develop a range of relevant questions about a geographical phenomenon or challenge. They collect, represent and compare relevant and reliable geographical data and information by using a range of primary research methods and secondary research materials, using appropriate formats. They interpret and analyse data and information to make generalisations and predictions, explain significant patterns and trends, and infer relationships. They draw evidence-based conclusions, based on relevant data and information, about the impact of the geographical phenomenon or challenge. They develop and evaluate strategies using criteria, recommend a strategy and explain the predicted impacts. Students use geographical knowledge, concepts, terms and digital tools as appropriate to develop descriptions, explanations and responses that synthesise research findings.

These criteria are implicit when Jones and Bagheri (2019) suggest using national data from across 18 geographical regions globally with a high school class to consider differences in relation to percentage change in carbon dioxide and methane for the regions, highlighting the impact of oil extraction and refining, agricultural production, population, fossil fuel energy consumption and renewable energy.

Related specifically to the Statistics and Probability part of the *Australian Mathematics Curriculum* (ACARA, 2022), Barnett (2001) suggested moving away from "balls in urns [and] drawing pins falling the wrong way up," to "'green' aspects of statistics" (p. 35). One example given included a bar graph of 10 plant species and the rate they consumed zinc per kilogram of soil in the context of remediating pollution in contaminated land. In much more detail, Fawcett and Newman (2017) had the same aim of making the subject more relevant than "pulling a green sock out of the drawer" by providing an extended activity on "The Storm of the Century" based on Hurricane Katrina and the Annual Maximum Wave Heights in the Gulf of Mexico for the preceding 50 years.

The National Aeronautics and Space Administration (NASA, n.d.a) at the middle school level provides learners (Years 5 to 8) with data to consider how the annual average temperature of the earth has changed over recent decades due to global warming. Detailed instructions are provided for teachers working with learners just beginning to be aware of graphs and their essential features (https://www.jpl.nasa.gov/edu/teach/activity/graphing-global-temperature-trends/).

Although provided in Excel, NASA *Global Land and Ocean Temperature Anomalies January-December* (n.d.b) data can be imported into either *TinkerPlots* or the Concord Consortium's CODAP (2020), to allow learners considerable freedom in the form of the presentation they wish to make. These can be discussed across the class in relation to questions about climate change, moving from the display of variation to the appreciation of time and temperature as linked variables, to examining patterns and associated expectation, and then suggesting answers to question acknowledging uncertainty regarding climate change (cf. Marton, 2015).

Using the NASA data, Fig. 30.4 shows four possible graphs created in *TinkerPlots* that learners might create, with the potential for classroom discussion about which graph tells the story most effectively. Although the horizontal axis is the same in each plot, the difference in the vertical scale and the use of icons or value bars presents different impressions of the data. Figure 30.5 shows the same data displayed in a NASA graph, adding another feature related to the warming impact of El Nino.

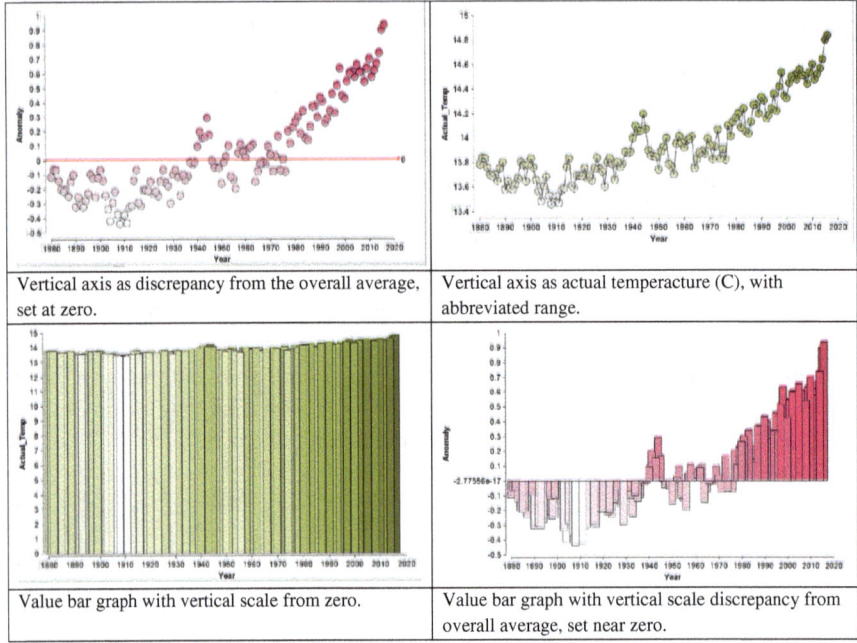

Fig. 30.4 TinkerPlots graphs created for the same data from NASA data by year

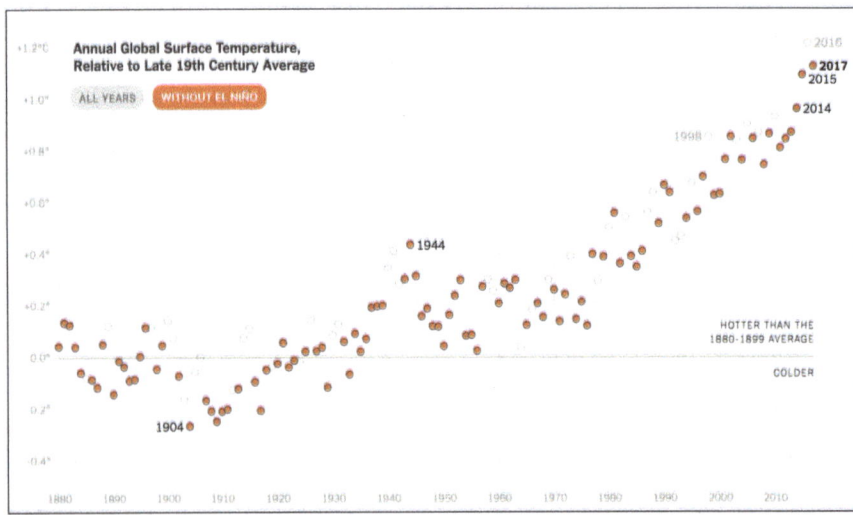

Fig. 30.5 The same data presented in a graph created by NASA distinguishing the occurrence of El Nino years in open circles

Further variations in contexts that relate to SDG 13, which learners might investigate using the Practice of Statistics, are provided by the Intergovernmental Panel on Climate Change (IPCC) (2018):

- From 1880 to 2012, average global temperature increased by 0.85 °C. For each 1 degree of temperature increase, grain yields decline by about 5%.
- From 1901 to 2010, the global average sea level rose by 19 cm as oceans expanded due to warming and ice melted.
- Given current concentrations and on-going emissions of greenhouse gases, it is likely that by the end of this century, the increase in global temperature will exceed 1.5 °C compared with the period from 1850 to 1900.
- Emissions grew more quickly between 2000 and 2010 than in each of the three previous decades.
- Australia's 2018–2019 summer was the hottest yet recorded, reaching a peak of 41.9 degrees centigrade on December 18.

The hottest recent day recorded, however, was 50.7 degrees centigrade on January 14, 2022, matching that of January 3, 1960 (https://www.bbc.com/news/world-australia-59977193).

30.9 Implications

The UN SDGs generally raise critical questions for educators about the form of education that should be provided to learners to engage meaningfully with issues that arise from the Goals. In particular, SDG13, Climate Change, places expectations on the school curriculum related to sustainability in and beyond the classroom. SDG13 presents educators with a plethora of actual problems that involve complexity and uncertainty, and that enable authentic opportunities to promote statistical literacy in the citizenry through the Practice of Statistics. The general public cannot perform the experiments that are reported in the media by scientists related to climate change, but those who are statistically literate can ask questions about the graphs presented, the data collected and the reasonableness of the claims made. Statistical literacy should be the aim of the school curriculum, as well as encouraging some students to pursue careers in applied statistics related to this or any of the SDGs (Watson et al., 2020).

The data and statistics implicitly embedded in SDG13 illustrate how the Practice of Statistics can be included in the associated school education at all levels when issues related to climate change are studied. This integrated approach is essential not only for moving towards a deeper understanding of the complexities of issues embedded in the SDGs, but also for preparing and equipping the next generation for informed decision-making in the uncertain contexts they will encounter now and into the future. In today's post-truth world of "fake news," where in some circles, facts are made up to support a particular point of view, or where everyone's opinion is regarded as equally valid, it is particularly critical that students develop the skills to discern and understand the collection and analysis of data. Recognising that even young children are able to engage in the Practice of Statistics in contextually meaningful ways, it is essential for the Practice to be given a central role across many subjects in the school curriculum as a critical part of a creating a better world. If this can create more "Greta Thunbergs," the curriculum will have succeeded even before students become statistically literate adults!

References

Australian Curriculum, Assessment and Reporting Authority. (2022). *Australian Curriculum v.9.0.* https://v9.australiancurriculum.edu.au/

Australian Education Council. (1991). *A national statement on mathematics for Australian schools.*

Australian Government Department of Foreign Affairs and Trade. (2018). *2030 Agenda for sustainable development.* Retrieved 11 November, 2020, from https://www.dfat.gov.au/aid/topics/development-issues/2030-agenda/Pages/sustainable-development-goals/

Barnett, V. (2001). Green statistics. *Teaching Statistics, 23*(2), 35–37.

Bulmer, M., & Haladyn, J. K. (2011). Life on an island: a simulated population to support student projects in statistics. *Technology Innovations in Statistics Education, 5*(1). https://doi.org/10.5070/T551000187

Bunten, R., & Dawson, V. (2014). Teaching climate change science in senior secondary school: Issues, barriers and opportunities. *Teaching Science, 60*(1), 10–18.

Cobb, G. W., & Moore, D. S. (1997). Mathematics, statistics, and teaching. *American Mathematical Monthly, 104*(9), 801–823. https://doi.org/10.2307/2975286

Concord Consortium. (2020). *CODAP: Common online data analysis platform.* https://codap.concord.org/

D'Ambrosio, U. (1990). The role of mathematics education in building a democratic and just society. *For the Learning of Mathematics, 10*(3), 20–23. https://www.jstor.org/stable/40247989?seq=1#metadata_info_tab_contents

Davies, N., Richards, K., Aliaga, M., & Nichols, R. (2010). Census at School. *Significance,* December, p. 175.

Dictionary.com. (n.d.). https://www.dictionary.com/browse/vary

English, L. D., & Watson, J. M. (2015a). Statistical literacy in the elementary school: Opportunities for problem posing. In F. Singer, N. Ellerton, & J. Cai (Eds.), *Problem posing: From research to effective practice* (pp. 241–256). Springer. https://doi.org/10.1007/978-1-4614-6258-3_11

English, L., & Watson, J. (2015b). Exploring variation in measurement as a foundation for statistical thinking in the elementary school. *International Journal of STEM Education, 2*(3). https://doi.org/10.1186/s40594-015-0016-x

English, L., & Watson, J. (2016). Development of probabilistic understanding in fourth grade. *Journal for Research in Mathematics Education, 47*(1), 28–62. https://doi.org/10.5951/jresematheduc.47.1.0028

Fawcett, L., & Newman, K. (2017). The storm of the century! Promoting student enthusiasm for applied statistics. *Teaching Statistics, 39*(1), 2–13.

Frankenstein, M. (2012). Quantitative form in arguments. In S. Mukhopadhyay & W.-M. Roth (Eds.), *Alternative forms of knowing (in) mathematics* (pp. 283–298). Sense Publishers.

Franklin, C., Kader, G., Mewborn, D., Moreno, J., Peck, R., Perry, M., & Scheaffer, R. (2007). *Guidelines for assessment and instruction in statistics education (GAISE) report: A pre-K-12 curriculum framework.* American Statistical Association. http://www.amstat.org/education/gaise/

Innabi, H. (2018). Teaching statistics for sustainability. In M. A. Sorto & K. Makar (Eds.), *Looking back, looking forward* (Proceedings of the 10th International Conference on the Teaching of

Statistics, Kyoto, Japan). International Statistical Institute. https://iase-web.org/icots/10/procee dings/pdfs/ICOTS10_1F3.pdf?1531364186

Intergovernmental Panel on Climate Change. (2018). *Global warming of 1.5°C. Special Report.* United Nations Environment Program. https://www.ipcc.ch/sr15/

Jones, R. C., & Bagheri, N. (2019). National warming: An exercise for world geography. *Geography Teacher, 16*(2), 68–83. https://doi.org/10.1080/19338341.2019.1579107

Konold, C., Higgins, T., Russell, S. J., & Khalil, K. (2015). Data seen through different lenses. *Educational Studies in Mathematics, 88*(3), 305–325. https://doi.org/10.1007/s10649-013-9529-8

Konold, C., & Miller, C. D. (2015). *TinkerPlots: Dynamic data exploration* [Computer software, Version 2.3.2]. Learn Troop.

Marton, F. (2015). *Necessary conditions of learning.* Routledge.

National Aeronautics and Space Administration. (n.d.a). *Graphing global temperature trends.* https://www.jpl.nasa.gov/edu/teach/activity/graphing-global-temperature-trends/

National Aeronautics and Space Administration. (n.d.b). *Global land and ocean temperature anomalies January-December.* https://www.jpl.nasa.gov/edu/pdfs/global_annual_mean_temp_anomalies_land-ocean_1880-2016.txt/

National Council of Teachers of Mathematics. (1989). *Curriculum and evaluation standards for school mathematics.*

National Research Council. (2013). *Next generation science standards: For states, by states.* The National Academies Press.

Noll, J., & Shaughnessy, J. M. (2012). Aspects of learners' reasoning about variation in empirical sampling distributions. *Journal for Research in Mathematics Education, 43*(5), 509–556. https://doi.org/10.5951/jresematheduc.43.5.0509

Rogerson, A., & Calleja, R. (2019). *Mobilising data for the SDGs: How could a data acceleration facility help, and how might it work?* https://paris21.org/sites/default/files/2019-01/Mobilising%20Data%20for%20the%20SDGs%20%28DP15%29_0.pdf

School Strike 4 Climate. (2022). https://www.schoolstrike4climate.com/

Skovsmose, O. (1994). Towards a critical mathematics education. *Educational Studies in Mathematics, 27*(1), 35–57. https://doi.org/10.1007/BF01284527

Trinity College Dublin Future Learn. (2020). *Achieving sustainable development.* https://www.futurelearn.com/courses/achieving-sustainable-development

United Nations. (2020a). *Sustainable development goals.* https://www.un.org/sustainabledevelopment/sustainable-development-goals/

United Nations. (2020b). *Sustainable development goals. Goal 13: Take urgent action to combat climate change and its impacts.* https://www.un.org/sustainabledevelopment/climate-change/

United Nations Education, Scientific and Cultural Organisation. (2017). *Education for sustainable development goals: Learning objectives.* https://www.sdg4education2030.org/education-sustainable-development-goals-learning-objectives-unesco-2017/

United Nations Educational, Scientific and Cultural Organization. (2020). *UN decade of ESD.* https://en.unesco.org/themes/education-sustainable-development/what-is-esd/un-decade-of-esd/

United Nations Framework Convention on Climate Change. (2020). *Paris agreement on climate change.* https://unfccc.int/process-and-meetings/the-paris-agreement/the-paris-agreement/

Watson, J. M. (2006). *Statistical literacy at school: Growth and goals.* Lawrence Erlbaum.

Watson, J., & Callingham, R. (2020). *A guide to statistical literacy in the classroom.* National Media Literacy Week 24–31 October. ABC Education. https://www.abc.net.au/education/media-literacy/a-guide-to-statistical-literacy-in-the-classroom/12789152

Watson, J., & English, L. (2015). Introducing the practice of statistics: Are we environmentally friendly? *Mathematics Education Research Journal, 27*(4), 585–613. https://doi.org/10.1007/s13394-015-0153-z

Watson, J., & English, L. (2016). Repeated random sampling in Year 5. *Journal of Statistics Education, 24*(1), 27–37. https://doi.org/10.1080/10691898.2016.1158026

Watson, J., Fitzallen, N., & Chick, H. (2020). What is the role of statistics in integrating STEM education? In J. Anderson & Y. Li (Eds.), *Integrated approaches to STEM education: An international perspective* (pp. 91–116). Springer. https://doi.org/10.1007/978-3-030-52229-2_6

Watson, J., Fitzallen, N., Fielding-Wells, J., & Madden, S. (2018). The practice of statistics. In D. Ben-Zvi, K. Makar, & J. Garfield (Eds.), *International handbook of research in statistics education* (pp. 105–137). Springer.

Watson, J., & Smith, C. (2022). Statistics education at a time of global disruption and crises: A growing challenge for the curriculum, classroom and beyond. *Curriculum Perspectives*. https://doi.org/10.1007/s41297-022-00167-7

Part VI
Community Initiatives

Chapter 31
Sustainable Wellbeing and Learning Communities for Achieving the Sustainable Development Goals

Robin Krabbe, Merete Schmidt, and Caroline Smith

31.1 Introduction

Richard Slaughter's (2010) book *The Biggest Wake Up Call in History* is just one of many recent texts sounding the alarm call that humanity faces its greatest challenge ever—a planetary emergency of interconnected, systemic polycrises (Tooze, 2021) that are deeply affecting all life on earth (Fuchs, 2004). These include the contested and thorny issue of a global human population estimated to be three times the number the earth can support (Ehrlich & Ehrlich, 2008). For Fuchs, we have reached a time of social chaos, instability, and global crisis, arising from and further contributing to many living in precarious conditions, whether in the Global South or Global North. Jem Bendell (2018), in a hugely controversial and much quoted paper, goes much further, arguing that accelerating climate change means that the time for winding back these crises to their previous state is essentially over, and that deep adaptation is all that is left to us in order to even survive on a ruined planet. As Kegan (1994) noted nearly 30 years ago, "we are in over our heads," pointing to the Human Gap, that is, the gap between our problems and our ability to solve them.

R. Krabbe (✉) · M. Schmidt
School of Social Sciences, College of Arts, Law and Education, University of Tasmania, 2/8 Bass Hwy, Burnie, TAS 7320, Australia
e-mail: robin.krabbe@utas.edu.au; rkrabbe@westnet.com.au

M. Schmidt
e-mail: Merete.Schmidt@utas.edu.au

R. Krabbe
Live Well Tasmania Coordinator, 28 Saunders Street, Wynyard, TAS 7325, Australia

C. Smith
School of Education, College of Arts, Law and Education, University of Tasmania, 2/8 Bass Hwy, Burnie, TAS 7320, Australia
e-mail: caroline.smith1@utas.edu.au

Bendell (2018) argues not only for the need for drastic action, but also for a need of deep understanding about the systems that have brought us to this moment in history. These are the political-economic systems and their attendant values, world-views, and beliefs that are actively preventing life from flourishing, and pointing to the critical need for working for a fully integrated sustainable development that involves simultaneously addressing the ecological crisis and improving the human condition (Vare & Scott, 2007). One response to Bendell's stark warning is to retreat into apocalyptic survivalism (Hoggett, 2011), which is the opposite of the collective, hopeful, and positive response needed. Better, surely, to work towards change, however hopeless it may seem at times.

The 17 United Nations (UN) Sustainable Development Goals (SDGs) offer useful insights and pathways towards a sustainable world (Sachs, 2012). However, the Goals tend to focus largely on the exterior world of process, indicators, metrics, and actions that position sustainability as largely a technological challenge rather than a human development challenge, that is, the challenge of the inner world of culture, values, beliefs, and worldviews that underpin our wellbeing (Langford, 2016). In this chapter, we first identify development in our inner world as a key concept that underpins the capacity to progress towards sustainable development as a goal of all human endeavour; that is, the development of the world of culture, values, beliefs, and worldviews. We contrast this with the still-dominant economism paradigm that focuses almost exclusively on economic growth as a measure of progress and which still largely underpins the SDGs. Second, we introduce the concept of sustainable wellbeing, and explore the links between sustainable wellbeing and education. We identify and discuss the concepts of lifewide (McKay, 2018) and lifedeep learning (Banks et al., 2007), which add new dimensions to the concept of lifelong learning (see for example, LifeWide Education UK [n.d.]), and progressive, informal notions of education. In particular, we discuss Learning Communities as supporting human development and sustainable wellbeing that have the potential to provide a strong foundation for the promotion of the SDGs. We end by providing a discussion of a Community of Practice as an example of a Learning Community that exemplifies these perspectives.

31.1.1   Dimensions of Development: The Inner World

Sustainability is commonly couched in terms of technoscientific concepts and measures such as biodiversity loss and increased greenhouse gas emissions leading to the climate emergency. Hence technological development is commonly posed as the solution. However the past decades have seen the emergence of a large body of literature that goes beyond these perspectives to attempt to address the root causes of our pathway to unsustainability (Wamsler, 2020). It is the inner world of human values, worldviews, and behaviours that have shaped the outer world of socio-economic systems and structures of society where we find the sources of unsustainability, and in turn, these systems shape our inner world (Eisenstein, 2011; Wilber, 1996). The structures and systems that we live by have become pathological, in that in many cases they are no longer able to satisfy basic human needs, and indeed, they are now actively undermining the socio-ecological systems that are necessary for flourishing of all life (Gray et al., 2021; Ives et al., 2020; Woiwode et al., 2021). Transforming values, worldviews, and behaviours is now an urgent requirement to challenge and change the often unexamined and unproblematised goals of our political-socio-economic systems (Göpel, 2016; Laininen, 2019; Witt, 2014; Woiwode et al., 2021) which, for Cook-Greuter (2004), is the ultimate meaning of appropriate, healthy development. As Thomas Berry (1999) reminds us,

> We see quite clearly that what happens to the nonhuman happens to the human. What happens to the outer world happens to the inner world. If the outer world is diminished in its grandeur then the emotional, imaginative, intellectual, and spiritual life of the human is diminished or extinguished. (p. 200)

Jacobs et al. (1997) provide a useful concept of social development as a complement to sustainable development. They contend that development is the outcome of the organisation of human energies and productive resources to address multiple and complex societal challenges, and that the basic mechanism of this process is increasing consciousness or awareness that can lead to better organisation. The corollary is that sustainable societies develop via a continuous process of learning and change, with a variety of actors involved in guidance and leadership (United Nations Economic Commission for Europe, 2012). This aligns with Scharmer's (2019) concept of Theory U, which includes the belief that the quality of the outcomes that we create in social systems depends on the quality of awareness, attention, or consciousness that the participants in the system possess (Monkelbaan, 2019). Inglehart and Welzel (in Witt, 2011) agree, viewing social change as a process of human development that results in more humanistic societies that place greater value on mutual freedom and self-actualisation.

Two recent areas of work explicitly highlight the need for a focus on inner development to align with and achieve the SDGs. These are the Inner Development Goals (Jordan, 2021) and the Good Life Goals (World Business Council for Sustainable Development, 2018). The Inner Development Goals were created to fill a perceived gap in identifying and promoting the abilities, qualities, and skills required to progress the SDGs. They recognise five categories of skills and qualities identified as important for inner growth and development in order to contribute to the SDGs. These are: (i) Being (relationship to self), (ii) Thinking (cognitive skills), (iii) Relating (caring for others and the world), (iv) Collaborating (social skills), and (v) Acting (driving change). One particular aspect of Being is the Inner Compass, which is characterised as "Having a deeply felt sense of responsibility and commitment to values and purposes relating to the good of the whole" (Jordan, 2021, p. 13).

The Good Life Goals are less about abilities, qualities, and skills, and more about everyday actions everyone can take to support the SDGs; essentially, the creators seek to send a message that everyone, both individually and collectively, can contribute to sustainable development (World Business Council for Sustainable Development, 2018).

31.1.2 The Sustainable Development Goals and Wellbeing

Within the SDGs, the focus of SDG3 (Health and Wellbeing) is to "[e]nsure healthy lives and promote wellbeing for all at all ages" (Pettigrew et al., 2016, p. 2119). The major targets of this Goal rightly focus on improving basic health outcomes in the countries of the Global South such as reproductive, maternal, and child health; communicable, non-communicable, and environmental diseases; universal health coverage; and access for all to safe, effective, quality, and affordable medicines and vaccines (Pettigrew et al., 2016). However, in the Global North, basic needs regarding communicable and infectious diseases and sanitation have largely been met. At the same time, these countries are witnessing a rise in autoimmune conditions thought to arise from unhealthy diets (Logan et al., 2016), while factors that impact the quality of life such as unemployment, loneliness, and poverty contribute to a crisis in mental health and wellbeing (Schumaker, 2001; Thoits, 2010). Wellbeing is foundational to any healthy, functioning society, and a good quality of life is critical to wellbeing (Delhey & Dragolov, 2016). However, the socio-economic foundations for wellbeing are far from being provided in many parts of the world (Benatar et al., 2018).

For Hirvilammi and Helne (2014), wellbeing is innately the ultimate goal of all species, and for humans, wellbeing is related to "[t]he meaning of life, and the joy we experience in living, [and is] enhanced through increased self-realization, that is, through the fulfillment of potentials that each of us has" (p. 2165). Wellbeing has been usefully defined as "a state of being with others, where human needs are met, where one can act meaningfully to pursue one's goals, and where one enjoys a satisfactory quality of life" (Pouw & McGregor, 2014, p. 16). Hsee and Hastie (2006) contend that we make all our decisions according to whether or not we think they will further our wellbeing.

A key determinant of wellbeing is quality education. The importance of education is recognised in SDG4, which seeks to "[e]nsure inclusive and equitable quality education and promote lifelong learning opportunities for all" (Wamsler, 2020, p. 112). Given that the ultimate goal of all the SDGs is human and planetary flourishing, then sustainable wellbeing and quality education are inextricably linked. We return to this later.

31.1.3 Social Pathologies and Economism

It is now accepted that the worldviews and actions of the Global North, in particular, are directly responsible for the damage inflicted on our world through a belief in economic growth as the measure of and means to progress, success, and human development. An important corollary is an increasing level of inequality both within and between countries (Freistein & Mahlert, 2016). However, up until recently, the now glaring contradiction between material growth and a finite planet was rarely taken into account (Jackson, 2009). The Marxist term, economism, describes this view well, referring to the exaggeration of the importance of the economic sphere in social and political relations, particularly governance, with a corresponding underestimation of the autonomy and integrity of the political sphere (Ashley, 1983; Göpel, 2016).

Given that this is now well understood, the question remains, why then do we seem to persist in these actions? The theory of social pathology (Freyenhagen, 2018) is useful to explain the tenacity of all human systems in supporting economic growth as the overriding goal of most political-socio-economic systems around the world. Social pathology explains and encapsulates the process whereby systems have evolved that are not able to satisfy basic human needs. Parallel concepts are structural violence (Christie, 1997) and cultural disintegration, which Sørensen et al. (2013) relate to the degeneration of social communication systems and processes of mutual assistance. In turn, all three theories relate to the tendency of capitalism to generate antagonistic relationships (Fuchs, 2004).

Brandt (1995) notes that any system that separates people into artificial groups, whereby some are classed as superior (the ruling elites) and charged with the right to dominate those classed as inferior (the peasant and working classes), will always be unstable, driven by the unmet needs of too many people. Further, Brandt describes how the dominant class spreads the narrative of "There Is No Alternative," referring to alternative ways of living that portray challenges to prevailing economic systems (usually forms of capitalism) as unacceptable, and in many cases impossible. For example, the idea of living with lower levels of consumption is referred to as going back to the cave (Tröger & Reese, 2021) or wearing hair-shirts (Snyder, 2009).

Delving even deeper and further back into the causes of the causes, theories of evolutionary health (Boyden, 2004) and evolutionary mismatch point to the massive changes caused by the Agricultural and then the Industrial Revolutions to the original physical, political, and psychosocial environment for which the Hunter-Gather environment adapted us (Brenner et al., 2015). Prescott and Logan (2016) see problems of mental health as the result of this mismatch. A final point about societal maladaptiveness is the failure to provide opportunities to reflect on and debate the hitherto goals of our collective lives (Hirvilammi & Helne, 2014), especially the opportunity for public debate on what gives our lives meaning and value.

The economism that has come to rule so many aspects of much of human existence can be seen as both a cause and an outcome of social pathology in its failure to reflect on and prioritise basic human needs. As noted earlier, not only is endless economic growth not possible on a finite planet (Jackson, 2009; Smith & Watson, 2018), but also economic growth has limited correlation with wellbeing (Costanza et al., 2013; Whiting et al., 2018). In fact, there is a consistent finding that there is a diminishing returns relationship between income and wellbeing, referred to as the Easterlin Paradox (Easterlin, 2005) once a certain level of consumption has been reached. Indeed, there is significant evidence that some 72% of greenhouse gas emissions are linked to consumer choices (Hertwich & Peters, 2009), whereby much of this consumption does not increase wellbeing. It is of course also important to note the intention behind the concept of contract and converge (Nelson & Timmerman, 2011), whereby over-consumption in some parts of the world needs to be reduced, but increased for those with sub-optimal levels of material needs. This points to the need to make changes, particularly in the Global North, to the way we travel, the food we eat, the clothes we wear, the houses we build, and so on (Grabs et al., 2016). Essentially, personal development in our inner world is required to overcome the adverse effects of economism.

31.2 Sustainable Wellbeing and Prefigurative Politics

We have argued that economism is incompatible with focusing human endeavour towards sustainability, and that wellbeing is the key. Sustainable wellbeing refers to the requirements for humans to function well, including collaborating effectively, and to supporting the functioning of thriving ecological systems. We propose the concept of sustainable wellbeing as a useful replacement for economism to guide personal growth. Personal growth is important; it is an end in itself, but it is also compelling enough to replace the economism paradigm as the ultimate goal of all human endeavours.

The concept of sustainable wellbeing draws from a large body of literature that clusters around core themes of flourishing, emancipation, justice, ecological rationality, and planetary health (Prescott & Logan, 2018). An underlying theme here is in relation to social change and innovation as drivers for societal improvement, and a belief in human knowledge and agency to change the world for the better (Avelino, 2021). Sustainable wellbeing recognises that as well as needing a certain (but not endless) level of material goods, as argued earlier, humans need satisfaction of their inner lives for physical and mental health, and to feel empowered to work collaboratively to help solve societal problems. Indeed, Costanza et al. (2013) have argued that the behaviours necessary to reduce ecological footprints are the same behaviours that generate human health and wellbeing. Sustainable wellbeing focuses on inner development and is fundamentally about transformative social learning, rather than on an exclusive focus on humanity's ecological footprints and other explicitly external environmental measures (Marshall, 2009).

It is also worth noting that the collective institutions that humans devise, including the quality and capacity of our institutions (including, crucially, the quality of our educational systems), are dependent on individual cognitive capacity. This is in line with the concept of agency structure duality (Jackson, 2005), also called Structuration Theory (Giddens, 1991), and is supported by Boyer (2018) in his book *Minds Make Societies: How Cognition Explains the World Humans Create*.

The concept of prefigurative politics is also useful here, highlighting the importance of personal growth as encapsulated in the slogans "Another World is Possible" and "Be the Change You Want to See" (Cornish et al., 2016). Prefigurative politics has been defined as: "[t]he embodiment, within the ongoing political practice of a movement, of those forms of social relations, decision-making, culture and human experience that are the ultimate goal" (Boggs, 1977, p. 6). Rather than a focus on opposing the dominant regime, prefigurative politics involves actions towards a vision of a better world (Swain, 2019). Prefigurative politics overlaps with other ideas relating to imagination, visioning, and Future Studies in general (Bai et al., 2016; Pouru-Mikkola & Wilenius, 2021; Slaughter, 2010). It involves a deep learning process and hence is profoundly educational, and is a significant means of personal growth. Essentially, we are arguing for an enhanced quality of life mediated through satisfying our inner lives (perhaps characterised as needs), as opposed to standard of living (which relates to accumulation of material goods, perhaps better characterised as wants). The notion of sustainable wellbeing, then, links directly to the idea of living with less, and hence reducing ecological footprints, once basic needs have been satisfied.

31.2.1 Basic Needs, Self-Determination, and Deliberation

"Basic needs" is one of the primary concepts that we see as the foundation of sustainable wellbeing. It aligns with the Brundtland definition of sustainable development as "meeting the needs of the current generation without compromising the needs of future generations" (Amiolemen et al., 2012, p. 6). The core process for meeting basic human needs requires a reconceptualisation of the idea of needs (Cruz et al., 2009), and especially, distinguishing needs from wants (Assiter & Noonan, 2007). To understand basic needs, we draw on Doyal and Gough's (1991) Universalist Theory of Human Needs (see also English (2010); Etzioni (1968); Moon (1991)). Doyal and Gough's essential premise is that all individuals, whatever their culture or the historical period in which they live, have certain basic needs in common that must be met in order for them to avoid harm, to participate in society, and to engage in critical reflection.

In his theory of Human Scale Development, Max-Neef (1992) argues that basic human needs are limited but universal, and begin with meeting material needs for biological thriving. If poverty and hunger are present, prosperity is not possible, as pointed out by Maslow as long ago as 1943 (Maslow, 1943). Once these have been met, Max-Neef identifies need satisfiers that are cultural and diverse and can be categorised according to how well they satisfy needs, ranging from completely failing to satisfy needs, through to satisfying a number of needs (called synergistic satisfiers). Max-Neef's theory is relevant for sustainable wellbeing because synergic satisfiers have a low ecological footprint and can be achieved by satisfying needs at a more local level (organic articulations, see Max-Neef, 1992, p. 197) than are currently promoted by economistic values, and are aimed at the core of human existence. Because economism is maintained by top-down processes, an advantage of Human Scale Development is that it aims to encourage development from the bottom up or the grass roots level.

Soper's (2007) work regarding alternative hedonism links to Max-Neef's (1992) concept of synergic satisfiers. It contends that the negative effects of over-consumption such as traffic congestion, pollution, stress levels, excessive working hours, and so on, are helping us re-think our sources of life satisfaction and what constitutes the good life (Alexander, 2013; Soper, 2007) Soper links a reduction of consumerism, such as via a reduction of working time to allow more time to be allocated for example to informal education. We see this developing as a result of the experience of the COVID-19 pandemic, which has provoked some deep soul-searching about what is important in life (Thompson, 2021).

Building on Self-determination Theory (SDT), which identifies relatedness, competence, and autonomy as vital psychological needs (Deci & Ryan, 2008), we simplify SDT to identify the concept of prosociality (equivalent to relatedness), and purpose and meaning (which potentially incorporates competence and autonomy) as vital basic non-material needs. We also include connection to nature as a third basic need, supported by research that shows a strong correlation with increased physical and mental health when people spend time in nature, and hence is important for sustainable wellbeing (Vries et al., 2003). One of the outcomes of the COVID-19 pandemic has been to illustrate, at a profound level, the human need for connection with the natural world (Young et al., 2021), which is also considered to assist with motivation to take environmental action (Koger, 2013). This may include concepts such as voluntary simplicity (Alexander, 2013), attachment to place (Kaltenborn & Williams, 2002), eco-localism (Curtis, 2003), and ecological literacy (ecoliteracy) (Smith, 2007).

Returning to the basic need of prosociality, one reason these skills are so vital is the importance of collective decision-making and deliberation for sustainability governance. Gracia (2016) contends that deliberation became a basic human need due to the evolutionary necessity for cooperation as the basis for survival. A dominant alternative to inclusive, genuinely democratic decision-making, as Beairsto (2012) notes, is leaving it to those who are most vehement, the loudest, the most powerful, and those with the most interest in shaping the rules for their own benefit. Beairsto goes further to contend that there are foundational decisions societies have to make about what is to be believed and what is to be valued. These not only determine who we become as individuals, but also shape the kind of society we create, and map out a useful process for consideration of the SDGs.

Whether or not deliberation is identified as a basic need, the significant benefits of deliberation for achieving the SDGs include, first, debating such concepts as the common good and the "good life" and increasing inclusive ownership and motivation to support the results of the deliberation. Second, it has the potential to decrease inequality and "power over." This is important, as governance must be accountable for the conditions experienced by the world's most disadvantaged people via deliberative mechanisms (Wisor, 2012). A third crucial benefit is to promote social learning, ideally towards changing worldviews towards the common good (Choi & Robertson, 2014). On the last point, Freeman (2000) contends that deliberation can be conceived as a way of spreading the norm of acting for the common good and of acting to contribute to the regeneration of socio-ecological support systems. This is supported by the "cognitive liberalization hypothesis," whereby contact with people with different values and worldviews has been shown to influence changes in values and worldviews, in particular to reduce prejudice (Hodson et al., 2018).

We contend that the more individuals are able to achieve greater prosociality, purpose and meaning, and connection to nature and deliberation in their everyday lives, the greater their sense of wellbeing. When this occurs, the individual is better able to support collective action, including deliberation on important societal issues and actions that reduce pressure on the environment. Although there may be doubts about deliberation being able to mitigate against the distorting effects of power, here we particularly emphasise the capacity of deliberation to change worldviews, to increase prosociality, purpose, and meaning, to increase pro-environmental values, and to build greater capacity both to address the current SDGs and gradually transform them to be more effective.

31.2.2 Sustainable Wellbeing and Education

Of the wide range and depth of concepts underpinning sustainable wellbeing that relate to the process of changing values and worldviews, above all, education from the micro to the macro level and across the lifespan, is central and critical to its achievement. Further, neuroscience is now able to point to environments most conducive to maintaining motivation for lifelong learning (Genge, 2001). Just as learning and education are key to sustainable development (Barth & Michelsen, 2013), they are also the foundational means of social development through the prosociality of deliberation, and hence of sustainable wellbeing. However, the corollary of economism, as Laininen (2019) notes, is that our education system is a prisoner of its history and worldview. We also concur with Brissett and Mitter (2017), that, like SDG3, SDG4 reflects a utilitarian view, whereby educational outcomes are based on the promoting economic growth, and that a radical change is needed to ensure educational models in particular support sustainable wellbeing rather than economic growth.

Just as wellbeing is an unconscious goal of all species, humans are hard-wired to learn in communities (Mündel & Schugurensky, 2008). However, there is a large body of literature that shows that this capacity is not built upon or addressed adequately throughout formal education (e.g. Sterling, 2010). In contrast to economism, where learning is essentially aimed at filling roles in the workforce, for Wals (2010), transformative social learning focuses on learning for simply being, as well as learning for knowing and for doing. Indeed Learning to Be is one of the four foundational pillars of education proposed by UNESCO (Charungkaittikul & Henschke, 2014). Regarding sustainable wellbeing, for Laininen (2019), education should focus on transformative learning for a sustainable future, which includes the importance of knowledge of how Earth's biophysical systems operate (e.g., Louv, 2008; Smith, 2007; Smith & Watson, 2020).

Educators have long recognised that learning is an active, social process, where new knowledge, principles, and concepts are attained through dialogue and interaction with others, and through experimentation and taking risks in psychologically safe environments (Halkett, 2010). Furthermore, levels of motivation and positive or negative emotional states can be critical to effective learning (Obradović & Armstrong-Carter, 2020). Although SDG4 focuses on formal education, we contend that changes to formal education must be accompanied by a transformed recognition of the importance of both formal and informal learning, and the increasing adoption of models that combine both.

A term that particularly resonates with the notion of transformative education is "lifewide learning," which complements lifelong learning, but also encapsulates the fact that individuals can learn at any time and any age, and in a wide range of environments (Reyes-Fournier, 2017). Here, Critical Place-based Pedagogy (Gruenewald, 2003; Häggström & Schmidt, 2021) is particularly relevant to sustainable wellbeing education, as it is based on an awareness of how human culture and ecological systems are interdependent, and the importance of place as a learning environment. This corresponds to lifedeep learning emphasising the necessity of challenging our values and worldviews (Davelaar, 2021).

31.2.3   Informal Education

Within the now voluminous writings on progressive and transformative education, a key idea relevant to sustainable wellbeing is the notion of informal education. Dewey (in Glasser, 2018) as long ago as 1899, proposed that education must be in accordance with the kind of society we want, and hence requires deep reflection on that question. Given that formal education does not typically engage with this except for areas within specialised (typically higher) education, informal education provides an opportunity to explore this vital question. This is particularly appropriate given that informal education includes experiential learning, lifelong, lifewide, and lifedeep learning; and viewed this way, formal education in some ways may be considered shallow in comparison.

Gaia Education (2021) notes that humans have a high level of motivation to form functional groups mainly because first, they fulfil important basic needs such as belonging (social affiliation), having supportive social relationships, and being able to influence others. Second, being part of a group allows goals to be achieved that individuals are unable to do alone, while facilitating creativity and innovation. Perhaps most compellingly, however, being part of any group where flourishing relationships have been developed, challenges the boundary between self and others, promoting a more collective consciousness (Gaia Education, 2021). Being part of a group in and of itself promotes the learning of inter-personal skills, promoting the influencing of values and worldviews.

Informal education is also important in that it provides a pathway and an alternative to the outdated industrial model of education that is tied to economism, but which remains the dominant form of much formal education today (Smith & Watson, 2018). Informal education has not been significantly co-opted by the dominant paradigm to the same extent as formal education and hence is one of the means by which prefigurative politics can develop. Hence, informal education is guided more by community needs and values than formal education.

Indeed, with lower levels of access to formal education in most countries of the Global South (The Human Journey, 2021), informal education is particularly important. Naidoo (2001) notes that practical participatory approaches are being used in many such countries to create lifelong community learning and community empowerment opportunities. Naidoo further notes that while poverty, apathy, and despair can be problematic, these can be addressed by lifelong community learning, which can be a source of social change and increase of health and wellbeing.

As argued above, the power of association is key to sustaining the motivation for lifelong learning (Smith, 2011). As Darling-Hammond et al. (2020) note, informal learning is generally voluntary and self-directed, linked to more open mindsets capable of thinking critically, laterally, and creatively.

31.3 Addressing Collective Capacity and Complex Social Problems: The Cradle Coast Academic Community of Practice

In this chapter we have shown how informal education includes experiential learning, lifelong, lifewide and lifedeep learning, and how formal education in some ways may be seen to be shallow in comparison. We theorise that to progress the SDGs and to achieve them fully, various modes of informal education need to accompany formal education to a greater degree. We contend along with many other authors (Arima, 2009; Sterling, 2010) that an enlightened version of education is in fact vital to underpin all the SDGs. Communities of Practice (CoPs) are one such example of enlightened education. An example of a CoP based within a university setting in Australia is the University of Tasmania's Cradle Coast Academic Community of Practice (CCACoP) to which this chapter's authors belong.

Wenger-Trayner and Wenger-Trayner (2015) define CoPs as "… groups of people who share a concern or a passion for something they do and learn how to do it better as they interact regularly" (p. 1). CoPs are further characterised by a particular combination of distinctive elements. The identity of a CoP is linked to the domain of interest, so that collective competence and peer learning in relation to the domain of interest is highly valued by group members, even if those external to the group may not recognise the group as having collective expertise (Wenger-Trayner & Wenger-Trayner, 2015). The community is built over time as members engage in information sharing, events, and activities to build knowledge and skills in relation to the domain of interest. It is the relationships, trust, and care that CoP members develop that form the basis of learning and capacity building, rather than through interactions based on hierarchy, positions, and titles that tend to characterise larger organisations. Members of CoPs are also characterised by being practitioners who develop a shared repertoire of "words, tools, ways of doing things, gestures, symbols, genres, actions or concepts" (Wenger, 1998, p. 83). For a CoP, sustained interaction is the foundation for shared practice, which has the purpose of addressing challenges and issues that arise in the domain of interest.

The passion, commitment, and collective knowledge of CoPs place them in a strong position to drive social change. As Botkin (2001) puts it, "[d]rawing on different members' expertise—and when combined with trust—they can be especially effective in dealing with complexity. The most lasting of them produce tangible results in their chosen domains, which further reinforces their effectiveness" (p. 81). The success in dealing with complexity is to a high degree due to the ability of CoPs to organise themselves, cross formal boundaries, and draw on interdisciplinary knowledge and connections. Complexity is a fundamental characteristic of the SDGs: more flexible ways of dealing with complexity via informal education are crucial. Although these key characteristics make CoPs efficient in driving social change and dealing with complexity, they can also "make them a challenge for traditional hierarchical organizations" (Wenger-Trayner & Wenger-Trayner, 2015, p. 4) due to the fluid and ever-changing nature of their networks.

The CCACoP comprises a group of academics and other staff members at the University of Tasmania's Cradle Coast Campus, located in the small regional town of Burnie in Tasmania's North-West. Members of this group are interested in working together across disciplinary boundaries to address the complex issue of creating sustainable innovation in teaching, learning, and research at a regional campus. Many CCACoP members are one of a few, or indeed the only, staff member in their disciplines on campus and many are part-time, casual, or have teaching-only positions. Because of geographical and professional distance, these staff members have limited access to professional development opportunities and other services available on the larger campuses of the University. The CCACoP provides a unique opportunity for individuals to work together across disciplines, titles, and positions, and contribute to key debates and issues. The informal and non-hierarchical nature of interaction within the CCACoP encourages authentic conversations, often with an element of playfulness, which leads to innovative strategies and solutions and is able to challenge the traditional and metro-centricity (Bunnell & Maringanti, 2010; Robinson, 2012) of university structures. This reflects a democratic process and the power of truly valuing a wide variety of voices and views, as theorised by Darling-Hammond et al. (2020).

Although the CCACoP has a Chair whose role is to coordinate opportunities for regular interaction, and knowledge sharing and to drive the agenda, the CoP's structure is informal and non-hierarchical. Members provide leadership in their various areas of expertise and readily share their knowledge with the group, leading to democratic discussion and decision-making. The fluid nature of the group ensures that new knowledge is introduced as new staff join the group, contributing to further development of individual and collective knowledge as well as of general staff and University capacity.

Just as interdisciplinarity is a strength of sustainability science (Kim & Oki, 2011), the CCACoP is comprised of members from a variety of disciplinary backgrounds; hence a key learning process is integrating knowledge from this diversity.

For example, through sustained interaction and collective competence, the CCACoP has facilitated learning and career development opportunities, workshops, teaching, learning and research seminars, and guest speakers. Providing these self-managed events addresses the complex issues of minimal professional, career, and leadership opportunities on a regional campus, and have led to various results such as publications across the disciplines and in many specialised areas (e.g., Schmidt, 2017; Smith & Krabbe, 2019), interdisciplinary research collaborations (for the most recent see Clayton et al., 2022), and monthly academic seminars (e.g., Hargreaves, 2022; Van Dam, 2022). In turn, these make a contribution to the University of Tasmania's broader strategic agendas of place-based teaching, learning, and research, and associated capacity building.

As a multidisciplinary group, the CCACoP is also well placed to engage with grassroots change and has extensively advocated for the provision of more course and unit options on campus, as well as an increase in staff, especially senior staff who can mentor other staff, provide opportunities for remote area students, and help to build research capacity. One example is the group's advocacy for the development of a new Humanities degree on campus (see e.g., CCACoP, 2018, 2019). Although the degree itself did not eventuate, the group's advocacy emphasised the importance of the University's agenda on place-based teaching, learning, and research. This has helped to highlight the need to focus on the right size and the sustainability of student and staff numbers rather than just economic growth. It has also highlighted a need to attract resources such as senior staff appointments and more course and unit options, which have now grown on campus. This demonstrates how the CCACoP has contributed to social change and produced tangible results in its domain of interest (Botkin, 2001; Wenger-Trayner & Wenger-Trayner, 2015).

With its non-hierarchical and collaborative structure, the CCACoP is an example of a learning community that provides a space where participants are able to reflect values that underpin broader sustainable developments rather than a narrow focus on economic growth. The learning that takes place within the CCACoP is essentially aimed at "learning for being" as well as learning for knowing and for doing (Wals, 2010). Sharing concerns and passions for "something they do and learn how to do it better as they interact regularly" (Wenger-Trayner & Wenger-Trayner, 2015, p. 1) and integrating knowledge have led to contributions to address some complex issues, which are characteristic of regional campuses in Australia, such as lack of opportunities for staff career development, research capacity, and leadership, as well as access to courses and degrees. As such, the CCACoP is an example of how informal learning in a caring environment is not only associated with increased individual wellbeing and capacity through opportunities to participate in meaningful interaction, collaboration, and learning (Jacobs et al., 1997; Scharmer, 2019), but also produces tangible results and contributes to overall University capacity.

The CCACoP provides an important example of how CoPs can complement formal education which, as we have argued above, is key to achieving sustainable wellbeing and hence to progress the SDGs. Hence, we believe that CoPs can provide a model for interested groups to come together to deliberate on the SDGs as they apply to their local communities and beyond, thus empowering individuals to understand, reflect on, and critique their situation and take action, rather than to sink into despair and hopelessness. The CoP can address issues at the heart of being able to take action towards the SDGs, including feeling we are not alone, and achieving the four pillars of the UNESCO "Education for the 21st Century" report (Delors, 2013), namely, learning to know, and learning to do, as well as the all-important learning to live together, and learning to be. Achieving sustainable wellbeing allows us to engage in all these four forms of learning, which are in turn vital for achieving the SDG's.

31.4 Conclusion

We recognise that the SDGs provide a useful framework with which to consider the dimensions and scope of sustainability. However, we find that the SDGs tend to focus on the outer manifestations of human capacities rather than exploring the inner worldviews that are necessary to transform development towards sustainable wellbeing. We highlight the importance of sustainable wellbeing, particularly its reliance on investment in education and health to promote human functioning, including supporting our capacity both to collaborate, and to assist the functioning of thriving ecological systems. CoPs, via informal education, are a powerful way of promoting the personal growth that is the core means of achieving sustainable wellbeing. This promotes human wisdom, which is limitless in its potential if allowed to flourish.

References

Alexander, S. (2013). Voluntary simplicity and the social reconstruction of law: Degrowth from the grassroots up. *Environmental Values, 22*(2), 287–308.

Amiolemen, S. O., Ologeh, I. O., & Ogidan, J. A. (2012). Climate change and sustainable development: The appropriate technology concept. *Journal of Sustainable Development, 5*(5), 50–53.

Arima, A. (2009). A plea for more education for sustainable development. *Sustainability Science, 4*(1), 3–5.

Ashley, R. K. (1983). The economic foundations of war. *International Studies Quarterly, 27*(4), 463–496.

Assiter, A., & Noonan, J. (2007). Human needs. *Journal of Critical Realism, 6*(2), 173–198.

Avelino, F. (2021). Theories of power and social change. Power contestations and their implications for research on social change and innovation. *Journal of Political Power, 14*(3), 425–448.

Bai, X., Leeuw, S. V. D., O'Brien, K., Berkhout, F., Biermanne, F., Brondiziof, E. S., Cudennec, C., Dearing, J., Duraiappah, A., Glaser, M., Revkin, A., Steffen, W., & Syvitski, J. (2016). Plausible and desirable futures in the Anthropocene: A new research agenda. *Global Environmental Change, 39*, 351–362.

Banks, J. A., Au, K. H., Ball, A. F., Bell, P., Gordon, E. W., Gutiérrez, K. D., Brice-Heath, S., Lee, C. D., Mahiri, J., Nasir, N., Valdes, G., & Zhou, M. (2007). *Learning in and out of school in diverse environments: Life-long, life-wide, and life-deep.* The LIFE Center (The Learning in Informal and Formal Environments Center) and the Center for Multicultural Education, University of Washington.

Barth, M., & Michelsen, G. (2013). Learning for change: An educational contribution to sustainability science. *Sustainability Science, 8*, 103–119.

Beairsto, B. (2012). *Deliberation—A basic skill for the future.* https://www.edcan.ca/articles/democratic-deliberation-a-basic-skill-for-the-future/#_ftn2.

Benatar, S., Upshur, R., & Gill, S. (2018). Understanding the relationship between ethics, neoliberalism and power as a step towards improving the health of people and our planet. *The Anthropocene Review, 5*(2), 155–176.

Bendell, J. (2018). Deep adaptation: A map for navigating climate tragedy. *IFLAS Occasional Paper 2.* https://mahb.stanford.edu/wp-content/uploads/2018/08/deepadaptation.pdf

Berry, T. (1999). *The great work: Our way into the future.* Bell Tower.

Boggs, C. (1977). Marxism, prefigurative communism, and the problem of workers' control. *Radical America, 11*(6), 3–39.

Botkin, J. (2001). Towards a wisdom society. In M. Jain, V. Miller, & S. Jain (Eds.), *Unfolding learning societies: Deepening the dialogues.* Shikshantar.

Boyden, S. (2004). *The biology of civilisation: Understanding human culture as a force in nature.* UNSW Press.

Boyer, P. (2018). *Minds make societies: How cognition explains the world humans create.* Yale University Press.

Brandt, B. (1995). *Whole life economics: Revaluing daily life.* New Society Publishers.

Brenner, S. L., Jones, J. P., Rutanen-Whaley, R. H., Parker, W., Flinn, M. V., & Muehlenbein, M. P. (2015). Evolutionary mismatch and chronic psychological stress. *Journal of Evolutionary Medicine, 3*, 1–11. https://doi.org/10.4303/jem/235885

Brissett, N., & Mitter, R. (2017). For function or transformation? A critical discourse analysis of education under the Sustainable Development Goals. *Journal for Critical Education Policy Studies, 15*(1), 181–204.

Bunnell, T., & Maringanti, A. (2010). Practising urban and regional research beyond metrocentricity. *International Journal of Urban and Regional Research, 34*(2), 415–420.

Charungkaittikul, S., & Henschke, J. A. (2014). Strategies for developing a sustainable learning society: An analysis of lifelong learning in Thailand. *International Review of Education, 60*, 499–522. https://doi.org/10.1007/s11159-11014-19444-y

Choi, T., & Robertson, P. J. (2014). Deliberation and decision in collaborative governance: A simulation of approaches to mitigate power imbalance. *Journal of Public Administration Research and Theory, 24*(2), 495–518. https://doi.org/10.1093/jopart/mut1003

Christie, D. J. (1997). Reducing direct and structural violence: The human needs theory. *Journal of Peace Psychology, 3*(4), 315–332.

Clayton, S., Guzys, D., Prior, S., & Schmidt, M. (2022). *Regional student experiences at the Cradle Coast Campus.* Research Project, University of Tasmania.

Cook-Greuter, S. R. (2004). Making the case for a developmental perspective. *Industrial and Commercial Training, 36*(7), 275–281. https://doi.org/10.1108/00197850410563902

Cornish, F., Haaken, J., Moskovitz, L., & Jackson, S. (2016). Rethinking prefigurative politics: Introduction to the special thematic section. *Journal of Social and Political Psychology, 4*(1), 114–127.

Costanza, R., Franco, C., Lawn, P., Talberth, J., Jackson, T., & Aylmer, C. (2013). Beyond GDP: Measuring and achieving global genuine progress. *Ecological Economics, 93*, 57–68.

Cradle Coast Academic Community of Practice. (2018). *Cascading conversations on our purpose: The view from the North West of Tasmania and the Cradle Coast campus.* University of Tasmania.

Cradle Coast Academic Community of Practice. (2019). *Cradle coast campus vision—Catalysing a sustainable region.* University of Tasmania.

Cruz, I., Stahel, A., & Max-Neef, M. (2009). Towards a systemic development approach: Building on the human-scale development paradigm. *Ecological Economics, 68*, 2021–2030.

Curtis, F. (2003). Eco-localism and sustainability. *Ecological Economics, 46*(1), 83–102.

Darling-Hammond, L., Flook, L., Cook-Harvey, C., Barron, B., & Osher, D. (2020). Implications for educational practice of the science of learning and development. *Applied Developmental Science, 24*(2), 97–140.

Davelaar, D. (2021). Transformation for sustainability: A deep leverage points approach. *Sustainability Science, 16*, 727–747.

Deci, E. L., & Ryan, R. M. (2008). Self-determination theory: A macrotheory of human motivation, development, and health. *Canadian Psychology, 49*(3), 182–185.

Delhey, J., & Dragolov, G. (2016). Happier together: Social cohesion and subjective wellbeing in Europe. *International Journal of Psychology, 51*(3), 163–176.

Delors, J. (2013). The treasure within: Learning to know, learning to do, learning to live together and learning to be. What is the value of that treasure 15 years after its publication? *International Review of Education, 59*, 319–330. https://doi.org/10.1007/s11159-11013-19350-11158

Doyal, L., & Gough, I. (1991). *A theory of human need.* Macmillan.

Easterlin, R. A. (2005). Diminishing marginal utility of income? Caveat emptor. *Social Indicators Research, 70*(3), 243–255.

Ehrlich, P., & Ehrlich, A. (2008). Too many people, too much consumption. *Yale Envrionment 360—Yale School of Forestry & Environmental Studies.* http://e360.yale.edu/feature/too_many_people_too_much_consumption/2041/

Eisenstein, C. (2011). *Sacred economics: Money, gift and society in the age of transition.* Evolver Editions.

English, M. (2010). For liberation or exploitation: Reviving the human needs debate. *Unrest Magazine.* https://www.academia.edu/10102463/For_Liberation_or_Exploitation_Reviving_the_human_needs_debate

Etzioni, A. (1968). Basic human needs, alienation and inauthenticity. *American Sociological Review, 33*(6), 870–885.

Freeman, S. (2000). Deliberative democracy: A sympathetic comment. *Philosophy & Public Affairs, 29*(4), 371–418.

Freistein, K., & Mahlert, B. (2016). The potential for tackling inequality in the Sustainable Development Goals. *Third World Quarterly, 37*(12), 2139–2155.

Freyenhagen, F. (2018). Critical theory and social pathology. In E. Hammer, A. Honneth, & P. Gordon (Eds.), *The Routledge companion to the Frankfurt School* (pp. 410–423). Routledge.

Fuchs, C. (2004). The antagonistic self-organization of modern society. *Studies in Political Economy, 73*, 183–209.

Gaia Education. (2021). *Social dimension.* https://www.gaiaeducation.org/

Genge, C. D. (2001). Nurturing: An alternative learning cosmology. In M. Jain, V. Miller, & S. Jain (Eds.), *Unfolding learning societies: Deepening the dialogues.* Shikshantar.

Giddens, A. (1991). *Modernity and self-identity: Self and society in the late modern age.* Polity Press.

Glasser, H. (2018). Toward robust foundations for sustainable wellbeing societies: Learning to change by changing how we learn. In J. W. Cook (Ed.), *Sustainability, human wellbeing, and the future of education* (pp. 31–89). Springer.

Göpel, M. (2016). *The Great mindshift: How a new economic paradigm and sustainability transformations go hand in hand.* Springer.

Grabs, J., Angen, N., Maschkowski, G., & Schäpke, N. (2016). Understanding role models for change: A multilevel analysis of success factors of grassroots initiatives for sustainable consumption. *Journal of Cleaner Production, 134*, 98–111. https://doi.org/10.1016/j.jclepro.2015.1010.1061

Gracia, D. (2016). Deliberation. In H. Have (Ed.), *Encyclopedia of global bioethics.* https://doi.org/10.1007/978-3-319-09483-0_135

Gray, K., & Manuel-Navarrete, D. (2021). Leveraging inner sustainability through cross-cultural learning: Evidence from a Quichua field school in Ecuador. *Sustainability Science, 16*, 1459–1473.

Gruenewald, D. A. (2003). The best of both worlds: A critical pedagogy of place. *Educational Researcher, 32*(4), 3–12.

Häggström, M., & Schmidt, C. (2021). Futures literacy—To belong, participate and act! An educational perspective. *Futures.* https://doi.org/10.1016/j.futures.2021.102813

Halkett, R. (2010). *The learning society.* Cisco Systems.

Hargreaves. S. (2022). *Exploring women's experiences of maternity service delivery in regional Tasmania: A descriptive qualitative study.* Unpublished Research Seminar, Cradle Coast Academic Community of Practice, University of Tasmania.

Hertwich, E. G., & Peters, G. (2009). Carbon footprint of nations: A global, trade-linked analysis. *Environmental Science & Technology, 43*(16), 6414–6420.

Hirvilammi, T., & Helne, T. (2014). Changing paradigms: A sketch for sustainable wellbeing and ecosocial policy. *Sustainability, 6*(4), 2160–2175.

Hodson, G., Crisp, R. J., Meleady, R., & Earle, M. (2018). Intergroup contact as an agent of cognitive liberalization. *Perspectives on Psychological Science, 13*(5), 523–548.

Hoggett, P. (2011). Climate change and the apocalyptic imagination. *Psychoanalysis, Culture & Society, 16*(3), 261–275.

Hsee, C. K., & Hastie, R. (2006). Decision and experience: Why don't we choose what makes us happy? *Trends in Cognitive Sciences, 10*(1), 31–37.

Ives, C. D., Freeth, R., & Fischer, J. (2020). Inside-out sustainability: The neglect of inner worlds. *Ambio, 49,* 208–217.

Jackson, T. (2009). *Prosperity without growth.* Sustainable Development Commission.

Jackson, W. A. (2005). Capabilities, culture and social structure. *Review of Social Economy, 63*(1), 249–267.

Jacobs, G., Macfarlane, R., & Asokan, N. (1997). *Comprehensive theory of social development.* International Center for Peace and Development. https://www.motherservice.org/node/100

Jordan, T. (2021). *Inner development goals: Background, method and the IDG framework.* https://static1.squarespace.com/static/600d80b3387b98582a60354a/t/61aa2f96dfd3fb39c4fc4283/1638543258249/211201_IDG_Report_Full.pdf

Kaltenborn, B. P., & Williams, D. R. (2002). The meaning of place: Attachments to Femundsmarka National Park, Norway, among tourists and locals. *Norwegian Journal of Geography, 56,* 189–198.

Kegan, R. (1994). *In over our heads: The mental demands of modern life.* Harvard University Press.

Kim, J., & Oki, T. (2011). Visioneering: An essential framework in sustainability science. *Sustainability Science, 6,* 247–251.

Koger, S. M. (2013). Psychological and behavioral aspects of sustainability. *Sustainability, 5*(7), 3006–3008.

Laininen, E. (2019). Transforming our worldview towards a sustainable future. In J. W. Cook (Ed.), *Sustainability, human wellbeing, and the future of education* (pp. 161–200). Palgrave McMillan.

Langford, M. (2016). Lost in transformation? The politics of the sustainable development goals. *Ethics & International Affairs, 30*(2), 167–176.

LifeWide Education UK. (n.d.). https://www.lifewideeducation.uk/

Logan, A. C., Jacka, F. N., & Prescott, S. L. (2016). Immune-microbiota interactions: Dysbiosis as a global health issue. *Current Allergy and Asthma Reports, 16*(2), Article 13. https://doi.org/10.1007/s11882-015-0590-5

Louv, R. (2008). *Last child in the woods.* Atlantic Books.

Marshall, P. (2009). *Positive psychology and constructivist developmental psychology: A theoretical enquiry into how a developmental stage conception might provide further insights into specific areas of positive psychology.* [Unpublished master's thesis]. University of East London.

Maslow, A. H. (1943). A theory of human motivation. *Psychological Review, 50*(4), 370–396.

Max-Neef, M. (1992). Development and human needs. In P. Ekins & M. Max-Neef (Eds.), *Real-life economics* (pp. 197–213). Routledge.

McKay, V. (2018). Literacy, lifelong learning and sustainable development. *Australian Journal of Adult Learning, 58*(3), 390–425.

Monkelbaan, J. (2019). *Governance for the Sustainable Development Goals*. Springer.

Moon, B. E. (1991). *The political economy of basic human needs*. Cornell University Press.

Mündel, K., & Schugurensky, D. (2008). Community based learning and civic engagement: Informal learning among adult volunteers in community organizations. *New Directions for Adult and Continuing Education, 118*, 49–60. https://doi.org/10.1002/ace.1295

Naidoo, S. (2001). Community empowerment through lifelong: Community learning in developing countries. In D. Aspin, J. Chapman, M. Hatton, & Y. Sawano (Eds.), *International handbook of lifelong learning* (pp. 713–732). Kluwer Academic Publishers.

Nelson, A., & Timmerman, F. (2011). Contract and converge. In A. Nelson & F. Timmerman (Eds.), *Life without money: Building fair and sustainable economies* (pp. 214–234). Pluto Press.

Obradović, J., & Armstrong-Carter, E. (2020). Addressing educational inequalities and promoting learning through studies of stress physiology in elementary school students. *Development and Psychopathology, 32*, 1899–1913.

Pettigrew, L. M., Maeseneer, J. D., Anderson, M.-I.P., Essuman, A., Kidd, M. R., & Haines, A. (2016). Primary health care and the Sustainable Development Goals. *The Lancet, 386*, 2119–2121.

Pouru-Mikkola, L., & Wilenius, M. (2021). Building individual futures capacity through transformative futures learning. *Futures*. https://doi.org/10.1016/j.futures.2021.102804

Pouw, N., & McGregor, A. (2014). An economics of wellbeing: What would economics look like if it were focused on human wellbeing? *Poverty and Inequality Research Cluster, IDS Working Paper, 2014*(436).

Prescott, S. L., & Logan, A. C. (2016). Transforming fife: A broad view of the developmental origins of health and disease concept from an ecological justice perspective. *International Journal of Environmental Research and Public Health, 13*(11). https://doi.org/10.3390/ijerph13111075

Prescott, S. L., & Logan, A. C. (2018). Larger than life: Injecting hope into the planetary health paradigm. *Challenges, 9*(13). https://doi.org/10.3390/challe9010013

Reyes-Fournier, E. (2017). Lifelong and lifewide learning. In E. Reyes-Fournier (Ed.), *Distance learning: Perspectives, outcomes and challenges* (pp. 1–15). Nova Science Publishers.

Sachs, J. D. (2012). From millennium development goals to Sustainable Development Goals. *Lancet, 379*, 2206–2211.

Scharmer, O. (2019). *Vertical literacy: Reimagining the 21st-century university*. https://medium.com/presencing-institute-blog/vertical-literacy-12-principles-for-reinventing-the-21st-century-university-39c2948192ee

Schmidt, M. (2017). No one cares in the city': How young people's gendered perceptions of the country and the city shape their educational decision making. *Australian and International Journal of Rural Education, 27*(3), 25–38.

Schumaker, J. (2001). T*he age of insanity: Modernity and mental health*. Praeger Publishers.

Slaughter, R. S. (2010). *The biggest wake up call in history*. Foresight International.

Smith, C. (2007). Education and society: The case for ecoliteracy. *Education and Society, 25*(1), 25–37.

Smith, C., & Krabbe, R. (2019). Towards a good Anthropocene for north-west Tasmania: Transforming the role of a regional university campus. *Social Alternatives, 38*(3), 67–75.

Smith, C., & Watson, J. (2018). STEM: Silver bullet for a viable future or just more flatland? *Journal of Futures Studies, 22*(4), 25–44.

Smith, C., & Watson, J. (2020). From streams to streaming: A critique of the influence of STEM on students' imagination for a sustainable future. *Journal of Applied Teaching and Learning, 3*(1), 21–29.

Smith, M. K. (2011). *Ivan Illich: Deschooling, conviviality and lifelong learning*. https://infed.org/mobi/ivan-illich-deschooling-conviviality-and-lifelong-learning/

Snyder, G. (2009). Home economics: Planting the seeds of a research agenda for the bioregional economy. http://dx.doi.org/10.2139/ssrn.1970210

Soper, K. (2007). Re-thinking the 'good life': The citizenship dimension of consumer disaffection with consumerism. *Journal of Consumer Culture, 7*(2), 205–229.

Sørensen, T., Kleiner, R., Ngo, P., Sørensen, A., & Bøe, N. (2013). From Sociocultural disintegration to community: Connectedness dimensions of local community concepts and their effects on psychological health of its residents. *Psychiatry Journal,* Article ID 872146.

Sterling, S. (Ed.). (2010). *Sustainability education: Perspectives and practice across higher education.* Taylor and Francis.

Swain, D. (2019). Not not but not yet: Present and future in prefigurative politics. *Political Studies, 67*(1), 47–62.

The Human Journey. (2021). *Education in the developing world.* https://humanjourney.us/health-and-education-in-the-modern-world/education-in-the-developing-world/

Thoits, P. A. (2010). Stress and health: Major findings and policy implications. *Journal of Health and Social Behavior, 51(S),* S41–S53.

Thompson, L. J. (2021). The adaptive moral challenge of COVID-19. *Mind & Society, 20*(2), 215–219.

Tooze, A. (2021). *Shutdown: How COVID shook the world's economy.* Viking.

Tröger, J., & Reese, G. (2021). Talkin' bout a revolution: An expert interview study exploring barriers and keys to engender change towards societal sufficiency orientation. *Sustainability Science, 16,* 827–840.

United Nations Economic Commission for Europe. (2012). *Learning for the future: Competences in education for sustainable development.* Steering Committee on Education for Sustainable Development.

Van Dam, P. (2022). *Avoiding hospital admissions using an innovative model of care.* Cradle Coast Academic Community of Practice, University of Tasmania: Unpublished Research Seminar.

Vare, P., & Scott, W. (2007). Learning for a change: Exploring the relationship between education and sustainable development. *Journal of Education for Sustainable Development, 1*(2), 191–198.

Vries, S. D., Verheij, R. A., Groenewegen, P. P., & Spreeuwenberg, P. (2003). Natural environments—Healthy environments? An exploratory analysis of the relationship between greenspace and health. *Environment and Planning A, 35,* 1717–1731.

Wals, A. E. J. (2010). Mirroring, Gestaltswitching and transformative social learning: Stepping stones for developing sustainability competence. *International Journal of Sustainability in Higher Education, 11*(4), 380–390. https://doi.org/10.1108/14676371011077595

Wamsler, C. (2020). Education for sustainability: Fostering a more conscious society and transformation towards sustainability. *International Journal of Sustainability in Higher Education, 21*(1), 112–130.

Wenger, E. (1998). *Communities of practice: Learning, meaning and identity.* Cambridge University Press.

Wenger-Trayner, E., & Wenger-Trayner, B. (2015). *Communities of practice: A brief introduction.* https://wenger-trayner.com/introduction-to-communities-of-practice/

Whiting, K., Konstantakos, L., Carrasco, A., & Carmon, L. G. (2018). Sustainable development, wellbeing and material consumption: A stoic perspective. *Sustainability, 10*(2), 474. https://doi.org/10.3390/su10020474

Wilber, K. (1996). *A brief history of everything.* Shambhala.

Wisor, S. (2012). After the MDGs: Citizen deliberation and the post-development framework. *Ethics & International Affairs, 26*(1), 113–133.

Witt, A. (2011). The rising culture and worldview of contemporary spirituality: A sociological study of potentials and pitfalls for sustainable development. *Ecological Economics, 70*(6), 1057–1065.

Witt, A. (2014). Rethinking sustainable development: Considering how different worldviews envision "development" and "quality of life." *Sustainability, 6,* 8310–8328. https://doi.org/10.3390/su6118310

Woiwode, C., Schäpke, N., Bina, O., Veciana, S., Kunze, I., Parodi, O., Schweizer-Ries, P., & Wamsler, C. (2021). Inner transformation to sustainability as a deep leverage point: Fostering new avenues for change through dialogue and reflection. *Sustainability Science, 16,* 841–858.

World Business Council for Sustainable Development. (2018). *Goodlife goals: The manual.* https://docs.wbcsd.org/2018/09/Good_Life_Goals/Manual.pdf

Young, N., Kadykalo, A. N., Beaudoin, C., Hackenburg, D. M., & Cooke, S. J. (2021). Is the Anthropause a useful symbol and metaphor for raising environmental awareness and promoting reform? *Environmental Conservation, 48,* 274–277.

Chapter 32
People, Pets and Art: A Model of Creative and Cultural Enterprise for Connecting Communities

Niklavs Rubenis, Meg Keating, Steven Carson, and Andy Terhell

32.1 Introduction

In this paper, we reflect on the broader frameworks of *The Pet Project*, a model of creative enterprise that aims to initiate, establish, and maintain a Community of Practice across regional Tasmania (Fig. 32.1). The primary strategy for our project is to develop a pedagogical model that not only advocates for creativity and culture, but also concurrently provides diverse participants access to mentoring, education, training, and resources.

The Pet Project advances four of the targets as outlined in the United Nations Sustainable Development Goal 4 (SDG) 4, "Quality Education" (Fig. 32.2). Several key areas of focus include bringing together different members of communities impacted by isolation, and more broadly, the pandemic, and providing educational opportunities that deploy arts-based methods in regional areas to those who have little or no connection with the university sector.

There are barriers that specifically prevent engagement with the University of Tasmania. Significantly, Tasmania has the lowest rates of literacy and numeracy

N. Rubenis (✉) · M. Keating · S. Carson
School of Creative Arts & Media, Centre for the Arts, College of Arts, Law and Education, University of Tasmania, Hunter Street, Hobart 7000, TAS, Australia
e-mail: niklavs.rubenis@utas.edu.au

M. Keating
e-mail: meg.keating@utas.edu.au

S. Carson
e-mail: steven.carson@utas.edu.au

A. Terhell
School of Creative Arts & Media, The Media School, College of Arts, Law and Education, University of Tasmania, Level 1/2 Salamanca Square, Battery Point 7004, TAS, Australia
e-mail: andrew.terhell@utas.edu.au

© The Author(s), under exclusive license to Springer Nature Singapore Pte Ltd. 2023   579
K. Beasy et al. (eds.), *Education and the UN Sustainable Development Goals*, Education for Sustainability 7,
https://doi.org/10.1007/978-981-99-3802-5_32

Fig. 32.1 Facilitating a community of practice and stakeholders

in Australia (Australian Bureau of Statistics, 2008; Denny et al., 2021; Tasmanian Government, Department of Education, 2019; Warner, 2021), as well as the lowest median income (Australian Bureau of Statistics, 2021a, 2021b). New student enrolment statistics for those attending the University of Tasmania report that 70% are "first in family" to go to university, and 5% are from remote areas (University of Tasmania, 2022). When coupled with data that claim approximately only 30% of Tasmanian secondary school leavers take up study at university one year out from school (Australian Bureau of Statistics, 2014), and with this engagement tapering off as the years progress, there lies a gap that can be bridged by training organisations to facilitate broader community engagement.

However, education and specifically art-based pedagogies that produce creative outcomes, as presented in this chapter, provide more than just a delivery of content —a range of social and cultural imperatives can also be built into training models. There is

	UNITED NATIONS SUSTAINABLE DEVELOPMENT GOAL 4: QUALITY EDUCATION	THE PET PROJECT
PRIMARY	4.3. By 2030, ensure equal access for all women and men to affordable and quality technical, vocational and tertiary education, including university	Development of a pedagogical model based on universal themes that is free for participation and brings community stakeholders together in a structured teaching and learning environment
	4.4. By 2030, substantially increase the number of youth and adults who have relevant skills, including technical and vocational skills, for employment, decent jobs and entrepreneurship	Focus on facilitating and maintaining communities of practice and social learning spaces that promote creative pedagogies as necessary for future skills and enterprise
SECONDARY	4.5. By 2030, eliminate gender disparities in education and ensure equal access to all levels of education and vocational training for the vulnerable, including persons with disabilities, indigenous peoples and children in vulnerable situations	Providing access to for those at different stages of life that is tailored training to different community locations and contexts, and sharing open access materials and resources
	4.7. By 2030, ensure that all learners acquire the knowledge and skills needed to promote sustainable development, including, among others, through education for sustainable development and sustainable lifestyles, human rights, gender equality, promotion of a culture of peace and non-violence, global citizenship and appreciation of cultural diversity and of culture's contribution to sustainable development	Showcasing how creative endeavours facilitate diverse perspectives in supportive environments underpinned by personal meaning/development as necessary for sustaining culture and sustainability

Fig. 32.2 United Nations SDG4 Targets vs. The Pet Project

increasing evidence of a need for the development of strategies that expand inclusivity and access to opportunities, particularly after the recent effects of COVID-19. There has been a dramatic negative impact on individual wellbeing[1] at a local level, particularly mental health, which has increased substantially since the onset of the pandemic (Australian Government Australian Institute of Health & Welfare, 2019; Lester et al., 2021). This is not an isolated trend, and extends nationally (Australian Government Australian Institute of Health & Welfare, 2022; Queensland Government, 2019), and globally (Xiong et al., 2020; World Health Organization, 2022b).

Therefore, a key aspect of *The Pet Project* is an emphasis on the repair of human relationships that have been challenged or severed through large- and small-scale community lock-down protocols, and isolation of people from family and community networks. Our approach is to facilitate recovery by celebrating the diversity of lived experience, knowledge, and stories; and to provide training, learning, skill development, opportunities, and ongoing support for a range of stakeholders (Fig. 32.1), in ways that are meaningful, tangible, and positive. We have focused on people and their relationship with pets because this is a universal, popular, and emotional theme which actively brings people together. Hands-on visual art workshops in painting pet portraiture facilitates this engagement, and further, coupled with semi-structured interviews alongside more traditional data collecting methods, a rich creative setting to engage the community is constructed. Also, to remove financial barriers, we do not charge a participation fee, and provide all necessary materials, equipment,

---

[1] It is worth noting that in this context of wellbeing we also use the term mental health which is defined by the *World Health Organization* as, "Health is a state of complete physical, mental and social wellbeing and not merely the absence of disease or infirmity" (2022a).

resources, and instruction. The University of Tasmania forms a state-wide institution comprising three regional campuses, one of which is rural. Hence, there lies an already-established network to leverage and deliver training programs outside of major centres and develop platforms that promote the value of creativity, imagination, and learning that can increase opportunities more in work and in life generally.

To begin our discussion of creative pedagogies and its links to sustainable development, we provide a brief background to *The Pet Project*. We then chart the development of communities of practice and the role of social learning spaces. In this section we discuss how intensive art workshops that include both general community members and established and emerging artists, can develop meaningful connections between people, and how this sets foundations for the human-centric approaches necessary for negotiating a world that is seemingly in perpetual crisis. One of the tenets of *The Pet Project* is relationships, as we recognise that for sustainability to genuinely exist, it must first begin with people and our connections with others. We then conclude with a discussion on what we have learnt. Here, we provide some reflections around the value of creative and cultural enterprise and its scalability in approaching complex societal problems, such as elements of wellbeing and accessibility. There exists a genuine exigency to develop alternative strategies that promote creative education as a primary strategy in building linkages within communities that include citizens, organisations, and other stakeholders as means to foster resilience, inclusivity, equity, and health imperatives. *The Pet Project* aims to address this.

32.2 Background

The Pet Project was established in Hobart, Tasmania in response to COVID-19 and its negative effects on social cohesion and the arts sector (to be discussed later in this chapter). It spawned from a conversation (among the authors) about how our lives had been impacted by the pandemic, and how it had shifted our perspectives on what we thought was most important to us. As we discussed and reflected on this, a common theme that emerged, surprisingly, was how crucial the relationships with our pets had been. We discussed how our human-animal relationships had changed, and potentially deepened, and the positive impact this had on personal wellbeing during lockdown and isolation. We considered that if we were interested and willing to deliberate on the relationships we have with our animals, then potentially, other members of the community might do so as well. From this conversation, *The Pet Project* was conceived with an aim to share and leverage the expertise of the project team (education, art, design, media, community development), and to bring diverse citizens together. Aside from local isolation, almost two years of restricted travel access into Tasmania from mainland Australian states and elsewhere had forced a separation of people from their communities and families (Humphries, 2021).

The Pet Project is also part of a larger project established by the University of Tasmania's Institute for Social Change, *The Tasmania Project*, which gathers information to give voice to individuals and groups to support "… good decisions made by and for the community" (Institute for Social Change, n.d.). Through surveys, interviews, and focus groups with Tasmanian residents, information is gathered and summarised as a resource for both the community and decision-makers. Together, these initiatives work with the community to inform policy and support long-term social and cultural planning (Institute for Social Change, n.d.).

32.3 Why Pets and Art?

Animal companionship features heavily in Tasmanian life. Tasmania has one of the highest rates of pet ownership per capita in Australia (Animal Health Alliance, 2013; Animal Medicines Australia, 2016; Newsmaker, 2015), perhaps in part because Tasmania is an isolated island state disconnected from mainland Australia. Pet companionship too has many positive health benefits—mental, physical, and social (Cleary et al., 2021; Hussein et al., 2021; RSPCA, 2020)—and pets connect people to each other. In difficult times such as the ongoing COVID-19 pandemic, it has been established that pets can play an important part in helping to maintain overall wellbeing (Damberg & Frömbling, 2021). Human-animal relationships also have a history that spans millennia (Germonpré et al., 2009; Perri et al., 2021), so in part, caring for an animal that is a pet is an inbuilt function of being human.

The representation of animals in visual art practices, such as painting, also has a long and deep history and a connection to human endeavour. Visual art, specifically, has a fundamental role in making tangible our stories, perceptions, realities, and understanding of the world, and as such, continues to play an important and popular role in the development of society's cultural fabric. Recently, in Australia, it was stated that 98% of the population is involved with the arts in some way (Australia Council for the Arts, 2020b). Participation in the arts is high and clearly very popular, as is animal companionship. Therefore, the combining of two popular themes establishes a universal anchor for bringing disparate community members together to engage with teaching and learning.

32.4 A Decimated Art Sector

Although participation in the arts might be high, funding is low. The statistic of art engagement as noted above, reflects the combined elements of those who engage with the arts and those who are employed in the sector (Australia Council for the Arts, 2020b). In Australia, and across the world, the pandemic has caused damaging social isolation and reduced community participation in the arts (Parliament of Australia, 2021a). It delivered economic blows to the creative sector, especially to those employed (Pacella et al., 2021; Pennington & Eltham, 2021), and now there is a long road to recovery (Watts, 2022). Tasmania has not been immune, experiencing severe economic downturn that has had detrimental socio-economic implications

(Tasmanian Government, 2020b). Specifically, regional communities are now met with long-term uncertainty and increased mental health issues, and artists, especially those working in regional Tasmania, have faced compromised travel, exhibition, sales, and employment opportunities (Tasmanian Government, 2020a).

Aside from economic concerns, there is a genuine need for creative experiences to be facilitated, as they aid in coping with uncertain times, a point acknowledged by the Federal Government (Parliament of Australia, 2021b). During the pandemic, although people were unable to engage with art-based mediums face-to-face, arts participation in fact increased over this period, primarily as a means of staying connected and as a mechanism to support overall individual wellbeing (Australia Council for the Arts, 2020a). This is a trend that extends globally, largely rolled out in key initiatives and projects throughout New Zealand, Canada, and the United Kingdom (Bennett et al., 2022). Yet, there is an inherent paradox here: although participation is high, arts funding typically does not fare well in government budgets (Benton, 2020; Reid, 2020), and more recently, disruptions from COVID-19 resulted in the tertiary sector disestablishing offerings within art school contexts (Rubenis & Nicol, 2021).

Accordingly, *The Pet Project* addresses a demand for public engagement with art practices, but also a need to provide direct employment for artists across regional Tasmania. Our project delivery model is structured in a way where University of Tasmania educators and researchers from the School of Creative Arts and Media, who work across art, design, and media disciplines, facilitate workshops that are delivered state-wide through paid partnerships with an established artist and an emerging artist in their respective communities. The established artist undertakes a stronger leadership or mentoring role in recognition of their experience or standing within the community, and the emerging artist, whilst also paid for their work, is afforded the opportunity to build skills as the mentee. Both established and emerging artists are mentored by the research team in workshop preparation, workshop delivery, strategies for engaging and building a positive learning experience for community participants, as well as being provided with ongoing support.

Fig. 32.3 The pet project pilot painting workshop participants in Hobart, 2020 (*Image Credit* Andy Terhell)

32.5   Pilot Program

The Pet Project was trialled as part of the Poochibald™ Art Prize 2020, a significant community open-call event on the Clarence City Council[2] creative calendar. The project team partnered with Clarence's Arts and Events[3] (Rosny Barn and School-house Gallery)[4] to provide a free workshop for community members to prepare a submission for the prize (Fig. 32.3).

Through an expression of interest advertised across the University of Tasmania and Clarence City Council, we received an overwhelming response. A wait list for the initial workshops had to be created, which indicated a clear need and want for open access to creative education and tuition. The combination of pets and art struck a chord. The success of the pilot program prompted additional workshops, and these were delivered with a clear intention to decentralise the delivery from Tasmania's

---

[2] The area that the council covers is rural, urban, and coastal. It is the biggest municipality in southern Tasmania. See City of Clarence's Strategic Plan 2021-2031 for more details: https://www.ccc.tas.gov.au/your-council/how-council-works/about-us/

[3] The School of Creative Arts and Media, which we fall under, has a Memorandum of Understanding in place with Clarence City Council.

[4] For more details see: https://www.ccc.tas.gov.au/community/culture-history/rosny-farm/

capital of Hobart to regional communities across the state. A unique aspect, however, of hosting some workshops on the university campus, allowed participants to experience a typical tertiary learning environment for the first time, in a safe, supportive, and inclusive environment. This is not always feasible in regional areas and hence, the delivery model/s were tailored to each region to replicate the setting and active nature of teaching and learning.

32.6 Communities of Practice and Narrative-Driven Pedagogies

Since the initial pilot, we have expanded the format to be inclusive of pets more broadly,[5] receiving funding to enable broadening of our organisational partnerships across the state, and refining our project model through ongoing reflection and feedback with participants and stakeholders.[6] The value of *The Pet Project* is that it is an educative experience in visual art and creative practice/enterprise that revolves around a transferal of knowledge, where reciprocal exchanges of concepts, ideas, influences, experiences, and even opportunities take place, as well as more practical elements such as materials, tools or techniques needed in creating work, being shared. This is a fundamental tactic in a creative pedagogical model and can be defined as a "Community of Practice", broadly explained as groups of people who come together with a shared interest (Wegner-Trayner & Wenger-Trayner, 2015). Similarly, notions of constructing "publics" are also useful in framing how a public (like a Community of Practice) can be built via a common concern or issue (DiSalvo, 2009). For our project, this manifests by linking one community, such as those interested in arts workshops, with other communities that consist of creative practitioners, educators, researchers, cultural and community organisations, and other stakeholders using the universality of pets as the anchor.

However, it is not just a common concern that might bring "publics" together; it is also through others effectively communicating those issues or concerns (DiSalvo, 2009, p. 51). The broader question for *The Pet Project* is how to repair social connections and cohesion, address wellbeing factors and understand what this might look like as a pedagogical model: one that provides skills, opportunities, and meaningful outcomes for people. Therefore, the project couples a common theme with arts-based approaches, surveys, and semi-structured interviews that invite personal storytelling,[7] as there are links between narrative-based community engagement

---

[5] Submissions have included dogs, cats, chickens, a frog and donkey, and rabbits to name a few.

[6] To date seven workshops have been completed with over 130 individual registrations from community members (excluding participation from project stakeholders and partner organisations) and other workshops are scheduled for 2022.

[7] Note that *The Pet Project* has ethics approval, project ID 23327.

and broader health imperatives. Strategies that promote the sharing of lived experience has been shown to improve emotional outcomes, mental health, and well-being (Harker Martin, 2020; Lusebrink, 2004). The results are better communication and cohesion in and among the community (Beauregard et al., 2020). Story-driven approaches support the time, as well as an opportunity, to reflect upon issues and experiences that hold personal meaning and relevance (Fraser & Al Aayah, 2011), and by encouraging creativity in a safe, inclusive, and supportive environment, individual self-expression can be explored as means to reconcile complex internal individual issues (Czamanski-Cohen & Weihs, 2016). Arts-based methodologies, such as painting workshops coupled with more traditional data gathering research, offer a powerful means to connect community-based activities together as a mechanism to transform thinking through sharing memories and activation and reactivation of emotion (Czamanski-Cohen & Weihs, 2016; Lane et al., 2015).

In this context, personal meaning and self-expression manifest by translating narratives, implied knowledge, and experience not easily communicable or translatable in words. This makes explicit, through representation and the art-making process, the transformation of feelings and emotion into consciousness (Czamanski-Cohen & Weihs, 2016). Human-centric and empathic perspectives that include personal, practical, and social meaning (Walker, 2014)[8] are important in expanding sustainability (Boro & Sankaran, 2018; Brown et al., 2019), because they place people first and foremost. Educational settings provide a window into—perhaps what is most important—the often-intangible yet positive effects and associations that happen between participants as the result of learning, and those peer-to-peer exchanges that are so vital in understanding perspectives and fostering learning environments. An approach like this has parallels with a "social learning space", an element within a Community of Practice that: (a) focuses on people and their participation; (b) allows participants to steer the learning; (c) establishes learning in reciprocal engagement including peer-to-peer, which then pushes the participants learning, and (d) places identity and meaning as fundamental to the process but is based on the care required for making a difference to their learning, and not necessarily the aptitude in social practices (Wegner-Trayner & Wegner-Trayner, 2020).

Strategies that engage community members in art practices are not a new concept (Madyaningrum & Sonn, 2011). They can, however, be a persuasive and successful method for establishing community connection and understanding (Borrup, 2006) that in turn has an impact on overall individual wellbeing (Gerber et al., 2018). Participation in art provides opportunities for the building of connections for individuals

---

[8] A holistic example of this approach is the "quadruple bottom line", expressed as a combination of personal meaning, practical meaning, social meaning, and economics (Walker, 2014). This framework takes the widely used "triple bottom line" of sustainability, defined as the convergence of social, environmental, and economic imperatives. The "quadruple bottom line" pushes economics to the background. Economics still exists in this framework—it must as we all have to live somehow— but it becomes solely a means to an end, not the main pursuit (2014, p. 42). This is an alternative shift from people being defined as "consumers" or "users" to more human defining factors such as that of being a "citizen" and a *being* that holds emotions—a person that operates within a community who has relationships with others—and one that is not defined as a unit of measure.

(community, artists, and industry partners) within local domains and the development of skills (for example: technical, creative, entrepreneurial), that empower participants to explore new experiences and new ways of thinking and being (Fancourt & Finn, 2019; Parkinson, 2018). This enhances adaptability during challenging times, opportunities to boost participants' confidence to express themselves creatively, and affirms individual/collective identity (Beauregard et al., 2020). A participant of our initial project pilot illustrated this point by stating, "A stark awakening for me to how socially isolated I had really been. It's a terrible time for us huggers. The workshop brightened my mood. I'm still talking about it" (Lisa, personal communication, September 21, 2020).

For *The Pet Project,* the aspects of community activation and access to quality education is underpinned by creativity and the role culture plays in the development of social cohesion, and these are core to the delivery of the workshops. It is aimed at including persons from different backgrounds regardless of status (educational, socio-economic, physical ability, cultural, gender identity) and brings them into a structured learning environment facilitated by social interaction and supported by university lecturers and professional, graduate, and semi-professional artists as tutors. It focuses on engaging people and promoting their creativity through the lens of their pet. All participants in the workshop receive direct one-on-one tuition from the project team in response to their individual needs and skill level. This develops a feedback loop and raises skill and confidence, and, because of the format of the workshop and the opportunity for participants to directly express and reflect on their experiences (art and creativity), meaning in the process is established. Wegner-Trayner and Wegner-Trayner suggest that "… social learning spaces are simpler, more pervasive structures than communities of practice" (2020, p. 32).

32.7   Artists

The engagement of local regional artists is fundamental to the social learning spaces we facilitate (Fig. 32.4). We enlist an established and emerging artist in each location to help facilitate the workshops. They are paid a rate as set out by national standards (National Association for the Visual Arts, n.d.), provided with all necessary resources and a teaching pack that outlines techniques to be covered as well as the general workshop format, and running sheet. Instructional videos are also provided. These resources are free, and can be adapted to a variety of teaching scenarios; the participating artist can adapt them to any scenario post-project (that is, we provide open access).

We understand it is not appropriate for us to maintain a community, but rather facilitate, encourage, and support individuals to build and grow Communities of Practice in ways that are relevant to them and their contexts. Therefore, the recognition of the skills, contribution and standing of the artists employed by *The Pet Project* within local areas must elevate the profiles of individual regional artists, and promote the contribution they play in cultural and social life, and in community learning. An

Fig. 32.4 Emerging artist Donnalee Young providing One-On-One tuition during a workshop held in 2021

aim has been to leave artists (and community) with new skills, networks, or opportunities that they can pursue once the project has been hosted in their specific region (Regional Arts Australia, 2019). We provide a mentoring program for the artists that links different skill sets together, and that further supports new networks and the development of professional and entrepreneurial skills. There are several touch points for the artists. Before the workshops, we hold an online session that brings the artists and project team together to discuss the workshops and resources, and to meet each other. This sets the scene for the workshop. During the workshop, artists are encouraged to demonstrate their skill sets in a short instructional demonstration, and to work one-on-one with participants, guiding and supporting their individual progress. At the conclusion of the workshop, artists are video interviewed to capture their initial experience and to gain feedback. A follow-up online discussion several months after the workshop is also held to ascertain how the workshop and resources have influenced their practice. Time between the workshop and follow-up allows space to reflect. Although the project only provides short-term renumeration for local artists, the intent is to cultivate longer-term entrepreneurial activities and employment in their local areas, to enhance access to resources, and to create an ongoing network of support (Regional Arts Australia).

Fig. 32.5 Examples of translating images into paintings. Basil by Cathy (left); Gabby by Bronwyn (centre); Luna by Tricia (right). Photographs courtesy of the participants (*Painting image credits* Meg Keating)

32.8   Workshop Format and Assessing Personal Impact

Our pedagogical model is delivered through a hands-on one-day intensive painting workshop that takes participants through the full process and the techniques required to take an image of their pet, and translates it as a painting onto a canvas. The structure and implementation of the workshop ensure that participants have a completed painting by the end of the workshop. A sense of accomplishment is paramount, and so too is the emphasis on participation and self-expression rather than virtuosic or masterful portraiture renderings of pets (Fig. 32.5).

The opportunity to try something new, and our straightforward approach, demystifies the processes of art making. There can be differences in defining creativity: from that of the "Big-C" of creativity, which might encapsulate famous artists, often from a Western perspective, and the notion of a singular creative genius, versus that of the "little-c", which focuses on the creative potential that everybody has (Kiernan et al., 2020). A presentation of how pets have been portrayed in art over time coupled with demonstrating techniques of painting, illustrates how art can be a means to foster expression and transform perception, emotion, relationships, and behaviours (Gerber et al., 2018). Confidence is built through simple techniques that support the participants to make early and significant progress in their creative works, as well as equip them with skills and resources to continue beyond the workshop.

Prior to enrolling, participants are informed they will be interviewed about their pet. Pre-workshop they are provided with participation information sheets and interview consent forms. During the workshop, participants are then video interviewed, and asked to describe their pet, its personality, and significance to them, as well as to contribute any stories about them. This footage documents the relationships people have with their pets, especially during COVID-19 and traumatic events, but it is also designed to provide an opportunity to reflect or express their feelings towards their pet which in turn, provides a deeper engagement with the actual creative process of painting.[9]

We recruit community participants in several ways: through partnerships with local councils and artist networks, cultural institutions, and health organisations.

_____

[9] Note that the video interview outputs are not the premise of this paper, however some examples can be viewed here: https://www.the-petproject.com/films.

Fig. 32.6 Community
participants are recruited
through a range of mediums
that promote outcomes from
previous workshops. Poster
design by Niklavs Rubenis
featuring the Painting
'Molly' by Cathy

Depending on the location, we use a combination of public posters, social media campaigns, and broader media support (Fig. 32.6).

Community members register their interest via an online expression of interest form and provide some basic information about themselves, such as why they would like to do the workshops and what they would like to capture in their pet's portrait. They also upload images of their pet, which we then prepare for the workshop. This begins initial correspondence from the team and starts to develop a relationship with the participants prior to the workshop beginning. We cap numbers between 15–20 participants per workshop, depending on location and available space (and COVID-19 restrictions). One experienced team member facilitates the workshops with the established and emerging artist as support, and the other team members video interview the participants. Hence, there is a high ratio of support for the participants.

To assess the success of our approach, we have adopted the positive psychology framework (Seligman & Csikszentmihalyi, 2000), which outlines five basic components: (a) Positive emotion—feelings of satisfaction, happiness, and comfort; (b)

Engagement—being invested and engrossed in activities; (c) Relationships—connections to other people; (d) Meaning—being connected to something bigger than individual needs; (e) Accomplishment—achievement and notions of success (Black Dog Institute, n.d.).

The data collected from a formal feedback participant survey, although only representative of a small sample (57), provide an indication that all five basic components are achieved through the workshops: 95% of participants stated they enjoyed the workshop; 96% would do it again; and 88% strongly agreed that they felt inspired throughout the day (positive emotion). Further, 89% rated the outcomes of the workshop as excellent, as did 87% in relation to the hands-on activities; 96% declared they would do it again even if offered in a different medium (engagement); 96% of participants agreed that the workshops helped them feel more connected to their community (relationships); and 94% felt comfortable during the semi-structured interview. The interview aims to allow participants a chance to reflect on their relationships with their pet which, as previously mentioned, adds layers of meaning that further influence the creative process (meaning). As well, 88% of participants also cited that the best outcome from the workshop was a finished painting (accomplishment); and furthermore, 81% of participants had never done a similar workshop. These statistics are beginning to indicate that there are positive benefits of art and creativity pedagogies that have been designed alongside the core elements of wellbeing.

32.9 Reflection and What We Have Learned for Now …

To create an engagement strategy that facilitates forms of post-pandemic recovery, this project combines a popular, if not universal, theme of animal companionship with art as a way of reaching community participants. Our intention has been to provide an opportunity to reflect on what animal companionship means individually and collectively as a way of engaging on an emotional level, and through these stories, establish a platform to celebrate a range of perspectives. Artistic endeavours centred upon pet companionship (past or present), transcends demographic or geographic boundaries, and this can provide a level playing field for broader long-term engagement and for building these communities through partnerships and relationships (Regional Arts Australia, 2019). These are valuable attributes. Art and the very act of being creative holds no boundaries, and does not yield right or wrong answers—anyone and everyone has the capacity to express, think, and learn through creative work.

32.10 SDG Goal 4 Target 4.3

We recognise that *The Pet Project* at this stage is a small-scale project. Although there is a focus on our locality of Tasmania, the project is applicable and scalable more broadly. The *Regional Engagement Guidelines* (Regional Arts Australia, 2019) state that for regional collaborations to build successful relationships, they need to be nurtured over several years, and that long-term engagement is key to the success of community building. Working with artists who belong to these communities, the project team has been able to tailor individual workshops and sessions to suit community needs. Understanding these needs has also required extra preparation and resources, which has resulted in the project starting small to achieve the outcomes. It is obvious that communities, Communities of Practice, and skills take time to build. The longer-term aim of this project is to build a networked community across Tasmania with our educational institute and our school as the core facilitator. Again, this will require sustained authentic work, but in part it is evidenced by the key stakeholders and supporters who recognise the project's value through their support.[10] We have had some success at our follow-up events for Hobart-based workshops, however, we did find that some of the most extraverted participants, surprisingly, were hesitant to attend these events. There are further strategies to explore so we can engage over the long term, as it is possible that these are the people that might need the community the most, but may have individual barriers to continue engagement.

32.11 SDG Goal 4 Target 4.4

The aim of training community artists and providing a guide/template for them to conduct their own workshops, although on a micro level, has indicated a level of self-sustainment through entrepreneurial activities. As noted above, we have re-visited some of the communities of participants with success such as exhibits and film screenings (Fig. 32.7), but in the regional workshops we have also encouraged artists to continue facilitating workshops independently and have received positive feedback. One participating established artist noted:

> … this opportunity was great in terms of giving me a bit more confidence and also the way it was laid out and the [team] indicated I could use the resources to potentially do my own workshops in the future will be really helpful.[11]

32.12 SDG Goal 4 Target 4.5

Working within communities is not without its inherent risks, particularly when equity, inclusion, and self-expression are core values. As an example, one regional workshop had several participants who were neurologically atypical. Managing the needs of all the workshop participants required additional preparation and support

---

[10] Excluding artists, we currently have 20 supporting organisations across Tasmania (cultural, art, health, and council).

[11] Post-workshop interview with established artist Josh Foley, March 25, 2022, at Devonport Regional Gallery.

Fig. 32.7 Public outcomes from the project include exhibition and film screenings to promote participants, artists, and stakeholders (*Image Credit* Andy Terhell)

Filmmakers Rebecca Thomson and Andy Terhell, with family dog Indi, have made a short film exploring the relationships between people and their pets.
Picture: Nikki Davis-Jones

PANDEMIC PETS TAKE A BOW WOW

JESSICA HOWARD

THE relationships forged between people and their four-legged friends during the COVID-19 lockdown in Hobart is the focus of a newly launched short film.

A partnership between the City of Hobart and the Tasmanian Museum and Art Gallery, the Hobart Current: Liberty exhibition features daily film screenings and art installations in public spaces across the city, encouraging people to reflect on the theme of liberty.

University of Tasmania school of creative arts and media associate lecturer Andy Terhell's three-minute film exploring the relationships between people and their pets during lockdown will play on a large scale outdoor public screen in Elizabeth St.

"Just after we came out of lockdown, we held a pizza workshop where about 15 people came along to paint pictures of their pets," Mr Terhell said.

"During the workshop, we interviewed participants about their relationship with their pets during lockdown. The film is about the stories they told us."

Other features of the program include works by 40 photographers, filmmakers and digital artists and a postcard exhibition where the public can draw, paint, sculpt, write or photograph their thoughts on the liberty theme on a postcard, which will then be displayed at the Waterside Pavilion.

from the community of artists. In this case, the local artists understood the context and behaviours of the participants and consequently helped to guide and support them in ways that the project team could not. This additional support included more one-on-one time and independent guiding of techniques, increased individual communication, and strong eye contact so that the participants felt engaged and connected to the instructions and processes of the workshop. The local artists were also able to remove the participants from the workshop and sit with them in a quiet moment when they felt overwhelmed or confronted. This occurred when the progress of their work was challenging to them, and they felt frustrated in not achieving the immediate results they desired. It has been important that all participants felt and could stay safe, which meant providing practical and emotional support during the workshop. What we have learnt from this experience is that it is important to have an emergency plan for participants if they become distressed or overwhelmed whilst expressing themselves through their painting. This has required a re-evaluation of our model, and that having community support from people with local knowledge can be very useful in understanding the individual needs of community members and their expectations, as well as the consideration of local politics.

Achieving success for the project has meant making sure that participants felt a sense of satisfaction, and had an outcome at the end of the day. The workshops have been planned so that all resources and techniques are simple, achievable, directly demonstrated by the facilitators, and freely available after the conclusion of the workshops.

Additionally, it is important that participants begin to apply paint immediately and do not labour over decisions such as which image to paint. This means many of the key decisions (such as composition and the initial drawing up of the image) are removed or simplified into very basic and achievable techniques. As part of the preparation of the workshop, images of participant's pets (which they uploaded online as part of the registration process) are prepared in advance of the workshop. This may seem like a minor detail, but being highly planned and prepared so participants can engage immediately with techniques and with each other, builds a far more inclusive and dynamic environment.

32.13 SDG Goal 4 Target 4.7

What we have discussed here is not a justification of why art is important. It is, however, significantly overlooked as a viable way of tackling complex issues in positive ways that, at the same time, introduces a range of new skills and links people together (Fig. 32.8). With respect to understanding art as an inherent human pursuit, it is worth noting that in many indigenous cultures across the world, there is no specific word for "art" (Mithlo, 2012; Sinclair, 2012). Art is implicit, a way of knowing, and not referred to as an isolated or exclusive activity as has been constructed by colonialism. Art is holistically entwined in "being", and hence a re-directive approach fosters art and creativity in ways that become part of how we live (and deal with living), not seen as something elitist or disconnected from publics, but rather the essence of being a human. In her interview, established artist Cheryl Rose remarked that "I am a very proud Aboriginal woman, descendant from Mannalargenna … art is healing, and so is our land … [our mob] do better being together—doing art, yarning, and telling our stories through art …" (Fig. 32.8).

Using a universal theme such as human-animal companionship binds people together in emotional ways. We note that the very act of being human and the relationships we form with other beings (human and/or animal) can form inclusive communities that can be resilient and supportive when faced with external factors beyond any one individual, or government, control. In the wake of traumatic scenarios

Fig. 32.8 Established artist Cheryl Rose providing instruction at Hive Tasmania, 2022 (*Image Credit* Andy Terhell)

such as the pandemic, promoting creativity and culture as a sustaining strategy that cares for relationships within communities, fosters resilience, inclusivity, equity, and overall health and sense of being—all of which are necessary components in moving towards increased sustainable futures.

References

Animal Health Alliance. (2013). *Pet ownership in Australia 2013.* https://animalmedicinesaustralia.org.au/wp-content/uploads/2019/10/AMA-Pet-Ownership-in-Australia-5-AUGUST-2013.pdf

Animal Medicines Australia. (2016). *Pet ownership in Australia 2016.* https://animalmedicinesaustralia.org.au/wp-content/uploads/2016/12/AMA_Pet-Ownership-in-Australia-2016-Report_sml.pdf

Australian Bureau of Statistics. (2008, June). *1307.6—Tasmanian state and regional indicators, June 2008.* Australian Bureau of Statistics. https://www.abs.gov.au/ausstats/abs@.nsf/lookup/1307.6feature+article1jun+2008#:~:text=Less%20than%20half%20(43.9%25),skills%20to%20understand%20and%20use

Australia Council for the Arts. (2020a). *Arts engagement during the COVID-19 pandemic.* https://australiacouncil.gov.au/wp-content/uploads/2021/07/omnibus-survey-results-arts-5eb50b49e163c-1.pdf

Australia Council for the Arts. (2020b). *Creating our future: Results of the national arts participation survey.* https://australiacouncil.gov.au/wp-content/uploads/2021/07/Creating-Our-Future-Results-of-the-National-Arts-Participation-Survey-PDF.pdf

Australian Bureau of Statistics. (2014, July). *Destinations and outcomes of Tasmanian year 12 graduates*. Australian Bureau of Statistics. https://www.abs.gov.au/AUSSTATS/abs@.nsf/Loo kup/4261.6Main+Features52006-2013

Australian Bureau of Statistics. (2021a). *Employee earnings: Weekly earnings of employees, including distribution of earnings and hourly earnings, by state, occupation, industry and quali-fications*. Australian Bureau of Statistics. https://www.abs.gov.au/statistics/labour/earnings-and-working-conditions/employee-earnings/latest-release

Australian Bureau of Statistics. (2021b). *Personal income in Australia: Regional data on the number of income earners, amounts received, and the distribution of income for the 2014–15 to 2018–19 financial years*. Australian Bureau of Statistics. https://www.abs.gov.au/statistics/labour/ear nings-and-working-conditions/personal-income-australia/latest-release

Australian Government Australian Institute of Health and Welfare. (2019). *Mental health services: In brief 2019*. https://www.aihw.gov.au/getmedia/f7395726-55e6-4e0a-9c1c-01f3ab 67c193/aihw-hse-228-in-brief.pdf.aspx?inline=true

Australian Government Australian Institute of Health and Welfare. (2022). *Mental health services in Australia*. https://www.aihw.gov.au/reports/mental-health-services/mental-health-services-in-australia/report-contents/mental-health-related-prescriptions

Beauregard, C., Tremblay, J., Pomerleau, J., Simard, M., Bourgeois-Guerin, E., Lyke, C., & Rousseau, C. (2020). Building communities in tense times: Fostering connectedness between cultures and generations through community arts. *American Journal of Community Psychology, 65*(3–4), 437–454. https://doi.org/10.1002/ajcp.12411

Bennett, J., Boydell, K., Davidson, J., & Hooker, C. (2022). *Arts, creativity and mental wellbeing: Research, practice and lived experience*. Australia Council for the Arts. https://australiacouncil.gov.au/wp-content/uploads/2022/04/Creativity-and-Wellbe ing-Summit-Discussion-Paper-3.pdf

Benton, P. (2020). *University cuts risk losing Australia's next generation of artists*. National Asso-ciation for the Visual Arts. https://visualarts.net.au/news-opinion/2020/university-cuts-risk-los ing-australias-next-generation-artists/

Black Dog Institute. (n.d.). *Wellbeing*. Black Dog Institute. https://www.blackdoginstitute.org.au/ resources-support/wellbeing/

Boro, R., & Sankaran, K. (2018). Empathy driving engaged sustainability in enterprises. In S. Dhiman & J. Marques (Eds.), *Handbook of engaged sustainability* (pp. 383–404). Springer. https://doi.org/10.1007/978-3-319-71312-0_20

Borrup, T. (2006). *The creative community builders handbook: How to transform communities using local assets, arts, and culture*. Fieldstone Alliance.

Brown, K., Adger, W. N., Devine-Wright, P., Anderies, J. M., Barr, S., Bousquet, F., Butler, C., Evans, L., Marshall, N., & Quinn, T. (2019). Empathy, place and identity interactions for sustainability. *Global Environmental Change, 56*, 11–17. https://doi.org/10.1016/j.gloenvcha.2019.03.003

Cleary, M., West, S., Visentin, D., Phipps, M., Westman, M., Vesk, K., & Kornhaber, R. (2021). The unbreakable bond: The mental health benefits and challenges of pet ownership for people experiencing homelessness. *Issues in Mental Health Nursing, 42*(8), 741–746. https://doi.org/ 10.1080/01612840.2020.1843096

Czamanski-Cohen, J., & Weihs, K. (2016). The bodymind model: A platform for studying the mechanisms of change induced by art therapy. *The Arts in Psychotherapy, 51*, 63–71. https:// doi.org/10.1016/j.aip.2016.08.006

Damberg, S., & Frömbling, L. (2021). Furry tales: Pet ownership's influence on subjective wellbeing during Covid-19 times. *Quality & Quantity: International Journal of Methodology, 2021*, 1–20. https://doi.org/10.1007/s11135-021-01303-7

Denny, L., Eslake, S., Jones, A., Martin, R., Mawad, R., Pritchard, A., & Rowan M. (2021). *A road map to a literate Tasmania*. https://cd15634f-1f19-4813-8142-fe3b6d00adcd.filesusr.com/ugd/ f6e09f_8b2f9c10e41541299b04c27b13ccefc3.pdf

DiSalvo, C. (2009). Design and the construction of publics. *Design Issues, 25*(1), 48–63.

Fancourt, D., & Finn, S. (2019). What is the evidence on the role of the arts in improving health and wellbeing? A scoping review. *Nordic Journal of Arts Culture and Health, 2*(01), 77–83. https://doi.org/10.18261/issn.2535-7913-2020-01-08

Fraser, K. D., & Al Aayah, F. (2011). Arts-based methods in health research: A systematic review of the literature. *Arts & Health, 3*(2), 110–145.

Gerber, N., Karolina, B., Potvin, N., & Blank, C. A. (2018). Arts-based research approaches to studying mechanisms of change in the creative arts therapies. *Frontiers in Psychology, 9.* https://doi.org/10.3389/fpsyg.2018.02076

Germonpré, M., Sablin, M. V., Stevens, R. E., Hedges, R. E. M., Hofreiter, M., Stiller, M., & Despré, V. R. (2009). Fossil dogs and wolves from Palaeolithic sites in Belgium, the Ukraine and Russia: Osteometry, ancient DNA and stable isotopes. *Journal of Archaeological Science, 36*(2), 473–490. https://doi.org/10.1016/j.jas.2008.09.033

Harker Martin, B. (2020). Brain research shows the arts promote mental health. *The Conversation.* https://theconversation.com/brain-research-shows-the-arts-promote-mental-health-136668

Humphries, A. (2021, December 15). *Tasmania open again after almost two years with its border shut due to COVID-19.* ABC News. https://www.abc.net.au/news/2021-12-15/tasmania-open-again-after-almost-two-years-shut-due-to-covid-19/100699854

Hussein, S. M., Soliman, W. S., & Khalifa, A. A. (2021). Benefits of pets' ownership, a review based on health perspectives. *Journal International Medicine and Emergency Research, 2*(1), 1–9.

Institute for Social Change. (n.d.). *The Tasmania Project.* The University of Tasmania. https://www.utas.edu.au/community-and-partners/the-tasmania-project

Kiernan, F., Davidson, J. W., & Oades, L. G. (2020). Researching creativity and wellbeing: Interdisciplinary perspectives. *International Journal of Wellbeing, 10*(5), 1–5. https://doi.org/10.5502/ijw.v10i5.1523

Lane, R., Ryan, D. L., Nadel, L., & Greenberg, L. (2015). Memory reconsolidation, emotional arousal, and the process of change in psychotherapy: New insights from brain science. *Behavioral and Brain Sciences, 38*(1).https://doi.org/10.1017/S0140525X14000041

Lester, L., Banham, R., Horton, E., Pisanu, N., Remund, A., Steel, R., Stoeckl, N., Sutton, G., & Tranter, B. (2021). *Report for the premier's economic and social recovery advisory committee: The Tasmania project wellbeing survey.* Institute for Social Change, University of Tasmania. https://www.pesrac.tas.gov.au/__data/assets/pdf_file/0018/283203/Wellbeing_Survey.pdf

Lusebrink, V. B. (2004). Art therapy and the brain: An attempt to understand the underlying processes of art expression in therapy. *Journal of the American Art Therapy Association, 21*(3), 125–135. https://doi.org/10.1080/07421656.2004.10129496

Madyaningrum, M., & Sonn, C. (2011). Exploring the meaning of participation in a community art project: A case study on the Seeming project. *Journal of Community and Applied Social Psychology, 21*(4), 358–370. https://doi.org/10.1002/casp.1079

Mithlo, N. M. (2012). No word for art in our language?: Old questions, new paradigms. *Special Issue: American Indian Curatorial Practice, 27*(1), 111–126. https://doi.org/10.1353/wic.2012.0005

National Association for the Visual Arts. (n.d.). *7.3 Schedule of fees for practitioners.* National Association for the Visual Arts. https://visualarts.net.au/code-of-practice/73-schedule-fees

Newsmaker. (2015). *Doggone it: Pet ownership in Australia.* https://www.newsmaker.com.au/news/35674/doggone-it-pet-ownership-in-australia#.YzwX4HbMI2w

Pacella, J., Luckman, S., & O'Connor, J. (2021). *Working paper—Keeping creative: Assessing the impact of the COVID-19 emergency on the art and cultural sector and responses to it by governments, cultural agencies and the sector.* https://www.unisa.edu.au/contentassets/33e97267a93046f1987edca85823e7b1/cp3-working-paper-01.pdf

Parkinson, C. (2018). Weapons of mass happiness: Social justice and health equity in the context of the arts. In N. Sunderland, N. Lewandowski, D. Bendrups & B.L. Bartleet (Eds.), *Music, Health and Wellbeing* (pp. 269–288). Palgrave. https://doi.org/10.1057/978-1-349-95284-7_14

Parliament of Australia. (2021a). *The impact of COVID-19 on the arts*. Parliament of Australia. https://www.aph.gov.au/Parliamentary_Business/Committees/House/Communica tions/Arts/Report/section?id=committees%2freportrep%2f024535%2f78295#footnote2target

Parliament of Australia. (2021b). *Sculpting a national cultural plan: Igniting a post-COVID economy for the arts*. https://parlinfo.aph.gov.au/parlInfo/download/committees/reportrep/024 535/toc_pdf/SculptingaNationalCulturalPlan.pdf;fileType=application%2Fpdf

Pennington, A., & Eltham, B. (2021). *Creativity in crisis: Rebooting Australia's arts and enter- tainment sector after COVID*. https://australiainstitute.org.au/wp-content/uploads/2021/07/Cre ativity_in_Crisis-_Rebooting_Australias_Arts___Entertainment_Sector_-_FINAL_-_26_July. pdf

Perri, A., Feuerborn, T., Frantz, L., Larson, G., Malhi, R., Meltzer, D., & Witt, K. (2021). Dog domestication and the dual dispersal of people and dogs into the Americas. *Anthropozoologica, 57*(1). https://doi.org/10.1073/pnas.2010083118

Queensland Government. (2019, February). *Understanding mental health*. Queensland Govern- ment. https://www.qld.gov.au/health/mental-health/understanding

Regional Arts Australia. (2019). *Collaborating with regional communities*. https://regionalarts.com. au/uploads/files/FINAL-Regional-Engagement-Guidelines-July-2019.pdf

Reid, L. (2020). *The arts sector is already suffering. This year's budget just pours salt on the wound*. National Association for the Visual Arts. https://visualarts.net.au/news-opinion/2020/ arts-sector-already-suffering/

RSPCA. (2020). *How many pets are there in Australia?* RSPCA. https://kb.rspca.org.au/knowle dge-base/how-many-pets-are-there-in-australia/

Rubenis, N., & Nicol, R. (2021). Crafted futures: New teaching, learning and research for craft in the Australian tertiary academy. In Q. Saad (Ed.) *Futuring Craft* (pp. 179–191). The Indian Ocean Triennial Australia IOTA21. https://indianoceancrafttriennial.com/wp-content/uploads/ 2021/12/IOTA21-conference-proceedings-3_compressed.pdf

Seligman, M. E. P., & Csikszentmihalyi, M. (2000). Positive psychology: An introduction. *American Psychologist, 55*(1), 5–14. https://doi.org/10.1037/0003-066X.55.1.5

Sinclair, B. E. (2012). PREFACE: itohtêwin (goal of journey). In B.E. Sinclair & D. Pellerier (Eds.), *We have to hear their voices: A research project on Aboriginal languages and art practice*. Canada Council for the Arts. https://canadacouncil.ca/research/research-library/2012/05/we- have-to-hear-their-voices

Tasmanian Government, Department of Education. (2019). *Literacy plan for action 2019–2022*. https://publicdocumentcentre.education.tas.gov.au/library/Shared%20Documents/ Literacy-Plan-for-Action-2019-2022.pdf

Tasmanian Government. (2020a). *Cultural & creative industries recovery strategy: 2020 and beyond*. https://www.stategrowth.tas.gov.au/__data/assets/pdf_file/0009/128691/SG0263_Cul tural_and_Creative_Recovery_Strategy_WCAG.PDF

Tasmanian Government. (2020b). *2020–21 Tasmanian Budget*. https://www.treasury.tas.gov.au/ budget-and-financial-management/2022-23-tasmanian-budget/budget-papers-archive/2020- 21-tasmanian-budget

University of Tasmania. (2022). *Student diversity dashboard data*. https://tableausp.utas.edu.au/#/ views/StudentDiversityDashboard/StudentProfile?:iid=2

Walker, S. (2014). *Designing sustainability: Making radical changes in a material world*. Taylor & Francis Group. https://doi.org/10.4324/9781315797328/designing-sustainability-stuart-walker

Warner, K. (2021). *Improving literacy and education standards in Tasmania*. Royal Society lecture delivered by her Excellency Professor the Honourable Kate Warner AC Governor of Tasmania, Tuesday 16 March, 2021. https://rst.org.au/wp-content/uploads/2021/03/Royal-Society-of-Tas mania-Lecture-by-Her-Excellency-March-2021.pdf

Watts, R. (2022, May). *Long term COVID impacts beset sector*. Arts Hub. https://www.art
shub.com.au/news/features/long-term-covid-impacts-beset-sector-2550423/?utm_source=Act
iveCampaign&utm_medium=email&utm_content=Sector+struggles+with+COVID+fallout%
2C+Greens+unveil+arts+policy+and+latest+jobs&utm_campaign=AHAU+Jobs+++Careers+
16+May+2022+-+newsletter

Wenger-Trayner, E., & Wenger-Trayner, B. (2015). *Introduction to communities of practice: A brief overview of the concept and its uses*. https://wenger-trayner.com/introduction-to-communities-of-practice/

Wenger-Trayner, E., & Wenger-Trayner, B. (2020). *Learning to make a difference: Value creation in social learning spaces*. Cambridge University Press. https://doi.org/10.1017/9781108677431

World Health Organization. (2022a). *Mental health: Strengthening our response*. World Health Organization. https://www.who.int/news-room/fact-sheets/detail/mental-health-strengthening-our-response

World Health Organization. (2022b). *COVID-19 pandemic triggers 25% increase in prevalence of anxiety and depression worldwide*. World Health Organization. https://www.who.int/news/item/02-03-2022b-covid-19-pandemic-triggers-25-increase-in-prevalence-of-anxiety-and-depression-worldwide

Xiong, J., Lipsitz, O., Nasri, F., Lui, L. M. W., Gill, H., Phan, L., Chen-Li, D., Iacobucci, M., Ho, R., Majeed, A., & McIntyre, R. S. (2020). Impact of COVID-19 pandemic on mental health in the general population: A systematic review. *Journal of Affective Disorders, 277*(December), 55–64. https://doi.org/10.1016/j.jad.2020.08.001

Chapter 33
Participatory Capacity Building for Sustainable Development: Community Skills Cafes

Sherridan Emery⊙**, Kim Beasy**⊙**, and Di Nailon**

33.1 Introduction

In its 2021 report, the Intergovernmental Panel on Climate Change (IPCC) emphasised the need to build more resilient communities, reiterating the call for "rapid, far-reaching and unprecedented changes in all aspects of society" (2018). The United Nations (UN) 2030 Agenda for Sustainable Development and its Sustainable Development Goals (SDGs), implore nations to "take the bold and transformative steps which are urgently needed to shift the world onto a sustainable and resilient path" (UN, n.d.a). Building community resilience (SDG11) was the focus of a project designed with and for the small community of Waverley in the northern regional city of Launceston in Tasmania, Australia.

This chapter takes up the challenge posed by Wendt (2021) of moving beyond innovative strategies to scale a project at a community level and create widespread community change beyond the discrete activities of a project. The aim was to effect a suburb-wide improvement in children's developmental outcomes by building capacity throughout the community for supporting young children's language development and physical health and wellbeing.

S. Emery (✉)
Peter Underwood Centre, University of Tasmania, Newnham Drive, Newnham, TAS 7248, Australia
e-mail: sherridan.emery@utas.edu.au

K. Beasy · D. Nailon
School of Education, College of Arts, Law and Education, University of Tasmania, Newnham Drive, Newnham, TAS 7248, Australia
e-mail: kim.beasy@utas.edu.au

D. Nailon
e-mail: diane.nailon@utas.edu.au

© The Author(s), under exclusive license to Springer Nature Singapore Pte Ltd. 2023   601
K. Beasy et al. (eds.), *Education and the UN Sustainable Development Goals*, Education for Sustainability 7,
https://doi.org/10.1007/978-981-99-3802-5_33

We discuss through a Theory of Change narrative, how the Waverley Community Skills Cafes (WCSC) project worked towards SDG11, to "make cities and human settlements inclusive, safe, resilient and sustainable," using an approach that emphasised SDG17 *Partnerships for the Goals*. In particular, we focus attention on Target 11.3, which states, "By 2030, enhance inclusive and sustainable urbanization and *capacity* (emphasis added) for participatory, integrated and sustainable human settlement planning and management in all countries" (https://sdgs.un.org/Goals/Goal11). Capacity building is central to Agenda 21 (UN, 1972), which has served as a key framing document for the SDGs. SDG11 has been informed by Chapter 7 of Agenda 21, entitled "Promoting Sustainable Human Settlement Development," which includes a focus on "Human resource development and capacity-building." By way of background, Chapter 7 states: "Capacity-building activities carried out by all countries … should go beyond the training of individuals and functional groups to include institutional arrangements, administrative routines, inter-agency linkages, information flows and consultative processes." (UN, 1972, para 25).

We drew inspiration from and responded to Agenda 21 Chapter 7 in conceptualising the WCSC goals. Further, the narrative shared herein exposes how community resilience as a core value was built into the conception, design, and implementation of the project. In sharing our Theory of Change, we detail the assumptions that were embedded in the project's logic and share the rationale behind the assumptions we identify; this could be considered the "literature review" of our chapter. The chapter is structured to allow for an unfolding of the project's story, and highlights activities or points of discussion that were significant to supporting the project in achieving its aims.

33.1.1   Sustainability Skills Cafes

WCSC was an adaptation of Sustainability Skills Cafes (SSCs), a concept that has been interpreted in locally relevant ways in numerous places (see, for example, Boyd and McNeill (2019) in Liverpool, UK, and Beasy et al. (2020) in Launceston, Australia). SSC projects promote intergenerational skill sharing in informal community settings through regular gatherings of people from a community who come together to engage in locally valued activities. In the northern Tasmanian region, SSCs have been led by Northern Early Years Group, a local Launceston-based association of education, health, local government, and social services providers. Recent SSCs included a 2018 project funded by the Launceston City Council (Emery et al., 2019) and a Skills 4 Kids Cafe project in 2019 with early childhood education and care provider, Northern Children's Network (Beasy et al., 2020). Similar to previous SSCs, the purpose of the WCSC was to bring together younger and older members of the community for sharing locally valued skills and building social connections. The intention was to extend existing successful programs offered within the local

Waverley Primary School, such as the kitchen garden program. Language acquisition and development were to be targeted through sharing stories with children and developing children's self-expression through creativity and play.

33.1.2 The Waverley Community Context

Waverley is a community in northern Tasmania with a population of 1500, including almost 400 families (Australian Bureau of Statistics [ABS], 2016). Of people aged 15 and over in Waverley, 24.1% reported having completed Year 10 as their highest level of educational attainment compared to 10.8% nationally (ABS, 2016), exemplifying the educational disadvantage that is widespread in the Waverley community. Waverley has limited infrastructure; the primary school and a general store form the main local services available. There is a picturesque lake and parkland adjacent to the school grounds. Intergenerational poverty and unemployment are features of the suburb, as well as limited availability of services in the immediate community, there is limited access to services in the nearby city of Launceston due to lack of transport options. An issue identified by Waverley school stakeholders was the limited opportunity for people in the Waverley community to encounter each other, due to the lack of infrastructure and spaces available to do so. This impacted the community resilience of the suburb, limiting the everyday social interactions that are an integral part of children's healthy development and social connection more broadly.

33.1.3 Scoping the Project

In 2019 Northern Early Years Group (NEYG) led the scoping of a project to support the Waverley community. In keeping with the ethos of SDG17, Partnership for the Goals, the project was developed in partnership with key stakeholders in the community including the school principal, school staff including a student networker; a non-government organisation that facilitated a parent committee at the school; and members of the Waverley community. The project scoping was informed by children's development indicators recorded by the Australian Early Development Census (AEDC), which showed that (i) physical and health development and (ii) children's language development were priority areas for Waverley (2018). Through conversations with project collaborators, the WCSC project outcomes were identified to support children's development in the nominated priority areas.

The aim of the project was to build the confidence and capacity of families and local community members to share skills with young children in a café-style social learning atmosphere. Fostering two-way learning was at the heart of the project. It was anticipated that this would be achieved through intergenerational relationships built around healthy food, physical activity, making and expressing in the arts, and story-telling and literary pursuits using various media. The exact nature of activities was undefined, as this was to be informed by community consultation, to identify interests, skills, and personal priorities of local people. The project set out to achieve regular co-designed community skills cafes, bringing older and younger members of the Waverley community together to build a stronger sense of community capacity for developing skills and improving children's outcomes on the two identified priority areas.

The project's Goals aligned with NEYG's own vision of making northern Tasmania a great place for children to grow up, which builds towards SDG11, in particular, "promoting human resource development and capacity-building for human settlements development" (UN, n.d.b). The model of project delivery, through a partnership between NEYG, the primary school, community members, and the non-government organisation drew upon SDG17, Partnership for the Goals.

The long-term outcomes identified in the project's funding application were to see:

- an increased sense of community capacity building in Waverley among younger and older residents, including a growing sense of efficacy in the Waverley community to target and support children's development through the understanding and use of AEDC indicators, beginning with physical health and language development.
- future AEDC data showing decreased levels of Waverley children's developmental vulnerability in the domains of physical health and wellbeing, and language and cognitive skills.
- ultimately, the community skills cafes aid in identifying gaps in provisions for children's healthy development in Waverley and help develop future collaborative responses by using the networks established through the project.

As we outline below, the COVID-19 pandemic and mandated lockdown requirements forced a reorientation in the implementation of the WCSC project. The lockdowns meant that the in-person skills cafes, which were initially a part of the project design, were no longer possible and new ways of meeting the project outcomes needed to be devised. We share this journey in the belief that the contemporary conditions of ecological system breakdown and climate crisis may result in many future projects needing to "pivot" or "adapt" to major rapid changes in circumstances. Sharing examples of how projects undertake such adaptation is important to maintaining progress, particularly in the area of supporting children's development and wellbeing.

33.2 Theory of Change—Development and Implementation

We now use a Theory of Change (ToC) to illuminate the ways that the Goals of the WCSC project were kept central to its design and delivery in the context of the COVID-19 pandemic and physical distancing mandates. Coined in the 1990s, the concept and approach currently known as ToC has historical roots in the field of theory-driven evaluation (Coryn et al., 2011). The approach emerged with an identified need in the field of evaluation for a way of understanding how and why an initiative works (Weiss, 1998). More recently, Wendt (2021) has argued that achieving the SDGs requires more than just innovative strategies. The impact has become central, as has the focus on desired outcomes and the change that is being sought. A ToC is commonly applied in the design stages of an initiative/project and is useful in guiding evaluation (Goldsworthy, 2021). ToC is defined by Reinholz and Andrews (2020, p. 3) as "a particular approach for making underlying assumptions in a change project explicit and using the desired outcomes of the project as a mechanism to guide project planning, implementation, and evaluation."

In the WCSC project, a ToC was used to make explicit the logics that guided how to get from project design to delivery, and ultimately to the achievement of outcomes. This was important due to there being multiple stakeholders, each with different priorities, needs, and interests in the project. In addition, a ToC provided benefits by making explicit the development of a shared vision with community stakeholders in the early stages of the project, and by formalising and valuing the tacit knowledges, experiences, and needs of the Waverley community (Funnell & Rogers, 2011). Together, outcomes from these actions went on to form the basis of activities that occurred in the project.

As Goldsworthy (2021) describes, there is no one way to document a ToC and in this chapter, we take a narrative approach to explaining how a ToC was enacted in the WCSC project. We detail the assumptions embedded in our ToC logics before outlining the activities that emerged through the project. Then in the discussion, we articulate the aspects of the project that we believe underpinned achieving the project outcomes.

33.2.1 Assumptions of Our Theory of Change

In developing a ToC for the project, it was important to articulate the assumptions that we had as a project team regarding the strategies we employed to deliver the project and achieve the aims. These assumptions were informed at times by our own beliefs and experiences, as well as by community development and leadership literature, and included assumptions about children's language acquisition, transparency in communication, and community development.

33.2.1.1 Children's Language Acquisition

In conceptualising the project, we assumed that one important way that children's language acquisition is supported is through everyday social interactions in the community. Our assumptions were drawn from Vygotsky's (1998) and Rogoff's (2003) sociocultural theories. Rogoff (2003) highlighted the importance of the social and cultural foundations of children's language learning. Vygotsky (1998) focused on the child's "social situation of development" (SSD), which he defined as "a system of relations between a child of a given age and social reality," with the home and other social settings, such as schools, being key locations of development (p. 199). Recent research also supports our assumption. For example, Hansen and Broekhuizen (2021) emphasise the role that a rich and varied language-learning environment can serve in children's language development.

Our awareness of structural barriers to language development, such as socio-economic status (Attig & Weinert, 2020), contributed to our focus on process contributors to language development in the form of providing resources to communities and community members to enable them to offer a wide range of verbal interactions with young children around activity-based skill sharing. Inherent to this assumption was the view that increasing the intergenerational interaction between younger and older members of the community would provide increased exposure to social interaction and therefore to language learning. In recognising this, we built the project around increasing opportunities for young and old community members to interact together, as a foundational way of promoting community resilience in keeping with SDG11. Likewise, the project assumed that by participating along-side others in these experiences there would be a growing understanding within the community of how children's language develops through play experiences in supportive environments—putting the tools of learning into the community's hands.

33.2.1.2 Transparency in Communications

We made the conscious decision in communicating the project to make the aims of the project and the background of the project visible: Waverley's children were considered vulnerable according to two key AEDC indicators. The decision was based on the premise that transparency when working in communities is important because it builds the foundations of respectful relationships and encourages all participants to communicate openly (Hutchison, 2020). As discussed by Pittaway et al. (2016) in their research with refugee communities, trust and organisational accountability and transparency were among the key characteristics identified in enabling the success of community development initiatives. We assumed therefore that being transparent about the project's objectives would increase awareness and motivate a community-wide response to supporting children's healthy development.

33.2.1.3 Community Development

Finally, we assumed that once the Waverley community began to interact, this would ripple out and create a self-perpetuating process of community building that would continue to deliver the long-term benefits envisaged. This assumption was based on Kenny's assertion that successful community development approaches are founded on the understanding that community members are experts in their own lives (Kenny, 2016). Our beliefs and working arrangements were based on the notion that community capacity building occurs through each individual's participation in social and cultural practices within communities (Dockery, 2010), particularly those practices underpinned by human rights, empowerment, and democratic processes (Kenny, 2016). We believed that people can be active agents in the development of their own communities. However, we also understood that token participation and disempowerment can limit people's opportunities and capacities to participate. The project began under a community-based work model (Australian Institute of Family Studies [AIFS], 2019) in which the people and organisations responsible for initiating the project identified broad aims, and agreed on operational strategies and entry-point community consultation initiatives. Over time, there was a transition to a community development model (AIFS, 2019), as the community members took the lead on identifying initiatives they were interested in undertaking and community issues they wanted to address that would be of value to young children's language learning and healthy development.

The assumption about the benefits of a transition to a community development model was based on a core value of the project's design, which aimed to see continued activities within Waverley beyond the funded project cycle. This connected with a further assumption of the project that the sustainability of the project would depend upon community uptake and involvement. Although starting out as a community-based work model, it was anticipated that it would need to shift to a community development model to sustain the project's outcomes.

33.3   Activities of the Project

In what follows we discuss activities that are intended to be illustrative rather than comprehensive and represent key moments within the project that highlight how community capacity building lay in the activities that unfolded. The ways in which these activities evolved were through negotiations between community and school stakeholders and are signposted throughout the retellings. In later sections, we discuss how social space was constituted differently by project stakeholders and how this was negotiated along the way.

33.3.1   Consultative and Participatory Processes

To ensure community capacity building through participants "doing for themselves" remained at the heart of our interactions, the project team worked closely with school and community stakeholders to develop a process of engaging the wider community that was authentic and true to the lived culture of the place. Therefore, the project began in October 2019 with a community conversation event held at the school, staged as a "welcome to Term 4 barbecue" for families. Barbecues, often referred to as "sausage sizzles," were a regular and much-enjoyed feature of the school to bring community members together.

The afternoon began with a student capacity-building workshop; inviting student leaders from Years 5 and 6 to take the lead in surveying their peers and family members about the types of skills they have and can share, and the types of skills they would like to learn. This consultation event was designed to inform the early directions of the project and was purposefully designed to be non-invasive and non-threatening. The student capacity building framework identified as fit for purpose was an adaptation of the "know, want, learn" (KWL) chart, commonly used in education settings to support learners to identify what they know, what they want to learn, and what they learned (Ogle, 1986). In the WCSC project, the "know, learn, teach" model was used to bring to the surface ideas for project activities from the community. This model allowed participants to identify skills that they either knew, wanted to learn, or could teach. Participants then engaged in a process of "dot democracy" (Diceman, 2010), given sticky dots to place next to any skills or abilities that they either knew, wanted to learn, or could teach. In this way, the activity was twofold: allowing people to actively identify and drive the skills for others to consider and to reflect on their own needs and wants.

The following reflection from a member of the project team (Sherridan) from the consultation event gives an insight into the ethos and early directions the project appeared set to follow.

> The project team recognised that they remained outsiders to the community they were entering and that at the heart of the project was the need to ensure participants were leading all processes. Therefore, it was organised with the principal to meet with some upper primary students with leadership qualities and preferably younger siblings, in the afternoon prior to the first community consultation event. A team member worked with students from the school on a process for engaging with adults and younger people in the consultation activity during the event. Students were up-skilled in the "know, learn, teach" activity, gaining a new appreciation for their own previously unrecognised or valued skills and abilities along the way (for example, how to count, fix bikes). During the sausage sizzle, students had conversations with the community and facilitated their participation in the activity.
>
> While the activity and the sausage sizzle were happening, activities were provided for young children as a means of showcasing some of the ways that sustainability skills can be facilitated during regular events. This included drumming, music making, painting, and some craft. More than 50 people attended, with similar numbers of children and adults actively engaging in the event (reflection on consultation event from NEYG volunteer).

Following the initial community consultation event, the project team undertook analysis of the dot democracy materials to understand the priorities and capabilities of the community and to determine how these could manifest in project activities.

33.4 Adapting Activities in Line with Project Aims

The COVID-19 pandemic outbreak in March 2020 initially brought this project, with its intentions for face-to-face community interaction, to a halt. However, in awareness of the need in the local Waverley community, the decision was taken by the project team to reorient the program to keep its benefits flowing. The following project activities exemplify how the project team responded in the face of rapidly changing circumstances.

33.4.1 Resource Packs

On the eve of the pandemic lockdown, the project funded "resource bags," which were put together for all children at the school. Each bag included games, learning resources, sporting equipment, and craft materials to provide additional opportunities for children to play and learn at home. The resource pack items were chosen with attention to the project outcomes including the development of physical- and health-related outcomes and children's language development.

The resource pack initiative was conceived by school stakeholders, with the rationale that it would meet a need among Waverley school children who would not have access to computers during lockdown. This became an important motivation for the school because the initial intention signalled by the Tasmanian Department of Education was for home learning to be facilitated via online platforms. With the assumption that many students would not have access to digital technologies at home, the school saw value in the provision of tactile and physical learning materials and resources. These resources focused on language acquisition and physical development.

33.4.2 Recipe Boxes

Recipe boxes with pantry basics, and fruit and vegetables, were provided to school families with children in the early years as an initiative of the WCSC project based on the idea that the cooking activities would help to provide a rich and varied language-learning environment (Hansen & Broekhuizen, 2021) at home for young children who were unable to attend school. Packs included recipes that families could cook together as a way for young children to learn about healthy foods and develop literacy skills with other family members. Families also interacted with the WCSC project's Facebook page by posting photographs of their children's engagement in cooking activities.

The recipe box initiative was conceived by the Community Project Officer in recognition of COVID-19 exacerbating food insecurity in the community. The initiative was supported by project stakeholders including the school. The popularity of the recipe boxes and recognition that they were a way for families to engage with children at home in their learning, led to the school adopting the initiative and embedding it within the school's curriculum at the end of the 2020 lockdown. The school continued to invest in sending home a series of recipe bags with ingredients for children to cook with their families.

33.4.3 Little Libraries

The project funded three Little Libraries (or "street libraries") placed on the front fences of residents in Waverley, once again with the focus on supporting children's language development. These libraries provided a collection of new books suitable for children in their early years. The libraries became an integral part of family walks within the community—a popular activity in other jurisdictions during lockdown (Baxter et al., 2020)—serving as a destination to borrow and return books (Fig. 33.1). The Little Libraries were conceived by the community in recognition that greater access to resources and activities was needed in their homes during lockdown. The school was also supportive of this initiative, recognising the benefits to young children having increased access to books to read or be read to by family members.

While the COVID-19 pandemic caused the project to reorient its activities to those that could be undertaken in home environments, focus remained on the central outcomes of supporting children's language development and physical health and wellbeing. Although the partners involved in the WCSC project supported the initial design and planning of school-community activities, community members increased their involvement and initiative as the project progressed and soon took over the leadership of planning and managing community activities and events when the lockdowns ended.

33.5 Discussion

In what follows, we explore how the design and implementation of the WCSC project responded to SDG11, facilitated through a school-community partnership approach, and explore how different project partners came together, relevant to SDG17. We discuss how a ToC provided a framework to support community capacity building and how negotiating social spaces in the school-community partnership was integral to project activity decision-making.

Fig. 33.1 WCSC little library (*Source* Sherridan Emery)

33.5.1 SDG11: Supporting Community Capacity Building Using a ToC

The WCSC project aligned with Target 11.3 in furthering "participatory, integrated and sustainable" capacity building. The aims of the project were informed by AEDC data indicating that in this place, some aspects of children's development required attention best served by community members themselves. The year-long WCSC project focused on capacity building within the Waverley community and was designed from the outset for a gradual uptake of community leadership over the term of the project (Fisher & Frey, 2013). Designing for sustainability beyond the project lifespan was done in recognition that too often projects that are "helicoptered in" to a community, end when funding ceases (Lindsey, 2013). This explicit intention formed part of our ToC for the project.

Applying ToC to underpin the project encouraged us to surface the assumptions that we (and all partners) brought to community capacity building. Identifying assumptions in the design stage helped to make visible risks and opportunities of the project (Goldsworthy, 2021). For instance, assumptions around community development, communication transparency, and ways of developing children's language, were reflected in the selection of project activities. Leveraging existing local capacity was a central focus of the project. In order to achieve this, roles were designed for local people with local presence and connections to Waverley. The selection of the Community Project Officer was an example of how this key principle was implemented. The project officer was a Waverley community member with strong social networks in the local community.

The project activities supported capacity building by investing in and building on the expertise already present within the community. For instance, the recipe boxes assumed that parents and carers were capable of supporting young children's literacy and language learning by cooking with their children at home. Community development approaches that adopt a strengths-based approach respect the dignity and wisdom of community members who are understood to be competent and knowledgeable (AIFS, 2019).

The project's focus on children's language development was further assisted by our ToC model. We moved beyond simply introducing innovative strategies, towards the crafting of a Waverley SDG "futures" orientation (Wendt, 2021). The Little Libraries initiative, which supported children's language learning via the provision of language learning resources (i.e., books), valued the capacity of parents and carers—and children themselves—to engage with the sharing of books. Little Libraries supported the vision of the project via the development of a Waverley community identity as "readers," with the intention that children would see the value placed on books and reading in their community (Merga & Mat Roni, 2018). It is our contention that Target 11.3, the "capacity for participatory, integrated and sustainable" approaches was evidenced in the ToC futures imagined by the Waverley community.

The initiatives introduced and led by Waverley community members aligned with Moll et al.'s (2013) notion of "funds of knowledge," whereby historically and culturally developed knowledge and skills that came from home environments reinforced the valuing of the role the family plays in children's learning. As community members took on leadership roles in planning and organising activities and events we perceived an emerging recognition of a growing community capacity for doing for themselves. This was not always smooth or seamless, because at times there were different views between people from the school and people from the community as to *who* should decide *what* initiatives would be funded by and undertaken in the project. This is discussed further in the next section, which focuses attention on negotiating social spaces in the project.

33.5.2   SDG17: Negotiating Social Spaces in School-Community Partnerships

This WCSC project was located at the nexus of school and community decision making as a project that involved both the formal education system and informal/

community education. Therefore, from the outset, this project focused on an often-overlooked space of school-community partnerships, where formal education system structures and community decision-making processes intersect. Negotiating the boundaries of these two different socio-spaces was necessary for the project, recognising that schools have their own structures and likewise, communities have their own processes and agendas. Both have different and sometimes competing needs and interests. For example, the school operates between particular hours, from Monday to Friday for most weeks of the year. Community, by contrast, is all hours of the day, every day of the year. At times, there was a need to calibrate between the priorities of people in the community and of people within the school.

Inter-agency partnerships facilitated this project to work across social spaces where there were differences in motivations, structures, processes, and priorities. The school was a legitimate and societally valid entity in the project partnership (a government institution), whereas the community was an unbounded, fluid, and unstructured project partner. The school came to the project with certain expectations regarding the level of decision-making power and oversight of project activities that it would have (Malen, 1994). A distributive leadership approach, defined as "leadership by expertise rather than leadership by role or years of experience" (Harris, 2014, para 5), was used in this project to mobilise both formal and informal leadership expertise in the school and in the community. This approach recognised the strengths that all project partners brought and generated opportunities for change and capacity for improvement. The partnerships assisted in fostering productive working relationships where both school and community members involved in the project were able to express what they valued and accommodated about each other. For instance, the community needed the school to administer funds, while the school needed the community to provide the human resource in delivering the agreed initiatives. The negotiations and organisational structure were instrumental in enabling the successes that occurred. Using a model of distributive leadership gave school, community and agency partners a seat at the table for decision-making, and valued equally the priorities and processes of all stakeholders. Although differences in the motivations and structures were explicit and observable in how the school and the community operated, less observable were the identity-spaces and negotiations that occurred throughout the project.

The social identities of project partners influenced their respective interpretations and constitutions of "community." In this project, how stakeholders identified themselves—as a school stakeholder or a community stakeholder—influenced how constitutions of community were formed (Beasy & Corbett, 2021). For example, when Resource Packs and Recipe Boxes were delivered to families whose children attended the school, it became apparent that "the school community" was not solely composed of families who lived in Waverley. Some families who attended the school lived in other more distant suburbs, and questions from the project team were raised about who constitutes "community" in the context of the WCSC project. In this instance the final decision was made in consultation with numerous stakeholders, embracing a spirit of generosity and inclusion. It was agreed that all students in the particular year group would receive the recipe boxes regardless of whether they lived outside the Waverley community.

The motivations of the respective school and community stakeholders at times appeared to differ. For example, when the Little Libraries and Resource Packs initiatives were developed, community members were motivated by the introduction of more resources and activities into homes to provide for all Waverley's young children. The school was similarly supportive, however, seemed motivated by the potential literacy outcomes that would be benchmarked by the school's and Australia's testing regime. Literacy is a central focus of schooling in Australia and one of the key pillars of assessment of school quality through the annual National Assessment Program—Literacy and Numeracy (NAPLAN) testing. Overall, it was felt that both school and community priorities were addressed through the Little Libraries and Resource Packs initiatives.

It is important to note that the partnership between the school and community that operated within the WCSC project enabled a capacity-building focus that differs from what Edwards and Evangelou (2019) describe as a competence-building focus. These authors express concern about interventions underpinned by "risk and resilience frameworks" (Little et al., 2004) that prioritise enhancing parent–child relationships and parents supporting children's developmental pathways, as a means of overcoming adversities in the home environment. They suggested that the focus on competence development trumps the focus on building secure relationships, and opportunities for children to develop their sense of self and agency may be compromised. Instead, the WCSC project's initiatives reflected sociocultural theories of learning (cf. Attig & Weinert, 2020; Hansen & Broekhuizen, 2021; Moll et al., 2013; Rogoff, 2003), which emphasise the fundamental role of social and cultural interaction in children's development. Accordingly, the focus of the project was providing resources and interactional opportunities, and trusting the community's capacity to support one another in their pursuit of enhancing young children's learning and development.

Creating partnerships to work towards the SDGs was central to building relationships across the social spaces that existed within this project. Throughout the project, Northern Early Years Group Tas Inc. operated as a conduit between institutional and community spaces, serving as a neutral and impartial party that was able to balance the interests of each of the stakeholders. Flexibility on both sides from the school and the community was needed regarding the boundaries of what constituted community and what constituted school. We noted that the different project activities benefited from the diverse project partners listening to each other's values, interests, and priorities.

33.6 Implications and Learnings

In the WCSC project, ToC allowed us to foreground the changes desired by Waverley community members. Given that COVID-19 had such a significant impact on this project, focusing on the changes the community wanted to see rather than the intended project deliverables, meant that we were able to be responsibly flexible to changing situations in timely ways. The pivoting of project activities was further assisted by the continued communication transparency of the project with stakeholders. As identified by Pittaway et al. (2016), transparency in community development initiatives builds trust in stakeholder relationships, and in this project, supported swift decision-making.

ToC was a useful framework in making explicit project assumptions and for ensuring the desired change of increasing community capacity was centralised through all project stages. However, there remain limitations in applying ToC to projects that rely on funding cycles. In this case, the WCSC project was funded for 12 months; the funds were acquitted and there was no requirement by the funders to revisit the project at a later date to consider its longer-term impact. Therefore, little opportunity exists in ascertaining whether the outcomes were achieved, particularly in a project such as this, which focused on children's language acquisition, physical health and wellbeing, and community capacity building. Flatau (2016) warns that changes such as these cannot typically be measured in the short term. An evaluation occurred immediately after the WCSC project was completed. We hold some optimism for longer-term outcomes as at that time community members spoke about how the community has never been so connected and vibrant (Emery et al., 2020). Following the conclusion of the project at the end of 2020, people in the Waverley community continued to produce a schedule of activities and were engaged in community development. Events that have taken place include Waverley Wallaby Picnics for families that attracted about 120 people, a Christmas event, and a fishing workshop for kids at Waverley Lake (Holmes, 2021). Additionally, the Waverley Community Cooperative, set up by the Community Project Officer of the WCSC not only provided food for residents in need during the height of COVID-19 lockdowns (McLennan, 2021) but also lobbied for and obtained funding for the establishment of a community garden in the suburb (Holmes, 2021). Although it is not suggested that these are outcomes of the WCSC project, they are an indicator of how the community advanced its own interests during and beyond the WCSC project.

33.7 Conclusion

Increasingly, schools and communities will need to work together to help deliver on the promise of the SDGs. The WCSC project outlined in this chapter demonstrates how one school-community partnership focused on children's healthy development and generated increased levels of community capacity building. The community capacity building that occurred in Waverley among younger and older residents contributed to a sense of efficacy in the Waverley community to support children's development. These outcomes aligned with SDG11 Sustainable Cities, and SDG17 Partnership for the Goals. The unexpected arrival of the COVID-19 pandemic led to a rapid reorientation of the WCSC; however, the project Goals and outcomes remained central to its implementation and the project was able to continue successfully through the uncertainty of lockdowns. Contemporary challenges, such as climate change and global pandemic outbreaks, are raising the need for human populations to be responsive to changing conditions (IPCC, 2021). The WCSC project met this need by modelling the flexibility of the ToC approach to community development.

References

Australian Bureau of Statistics. (2016). *2016 census quickstats Waverley.* https://quickstats.census data.abs.gov.au/census_services/getproduct/census/2016/quickstat/LGA18050

Australian Early Development Index. (2018). *Data explorer.* https://www.aedc.gov.au/data/data-explorer

Australian Institute of Family Studies. (2019). *Expert panel resource sheet.* https://aifs.gov.au/cfca/expert-panel-project/what-community-development

Attig, M., & Weinert, S. (2020). What impacts early language skills? Effects of social disparities and different process characteristics of the home learning environment in the first 2 years. *Frontiers in Psychology, 11*, Article 557751.

Baxter, J., Budinski, M., Carroll, M., & Hand, K. (2020). *Families in Australia survey: Life during COVID-19.* Australian Institute of Family Studies, Australian Government.

Beasy, K., & Corbett, M. (2021). What counts as sustainability? A sociospatial analysis. *Environmental Sociology, 7*(4), 327–337. https://doi.org/10.1080/23251042.2021.1913320

Beasy, K., Emery, S., Nailon, D., & Boyd, D. (2020). Enabling educators: Skills 4 kids cafes as professional learning. *Every Child, 26*(4), 20–21. https://doi.org/10.3316/informit.659737631 965539

Boyd, D., & McNeill, C. (2019). An intergenerational early childhood sustainable skills project. In *Intergenerational learning in practice* (pp. 205–220). Routledge.

Coryn, C. L. S., Noakes, L. A., Westine, C. D., & Schröter, D. C. (2011). A systematic review of theory-driven evaluation practice from 1990 to 2009. *American Journal of Evaluation, 32*(2), 199–226. https://doi.org/10.1177/1098214010389321

Diceman, J. (2010). *Dotmocracy handbook.* Version 2.2. https://dotmocracy.org/

Dockery, A. M. (2010). Culture and wellbeing: The case of Indigenous Australians. *Social Indicators Research, 99*(2), 315–332. https://doi.org/10.1007/s11205-010-9582-y

Edwards, A., & Evangelou, M. (2019). Easing transitions into school for children from socially excluded 'hard to reach' families: From risk and resilience to agency and demand. In M. Hedegaard & A. Edward (Eds.), *Support for children, young people and their carers in difficult transitions: Working in the zone of social concern* (pp. 115–130). Bloomsbury Academic.

Emery, S., Beasy, K., & Nailon, D. (2019). *Sustainability skills cafes: Funding acquittal and report.* Northern Early Years Group.

Emery, S., Watkins, D., & Northern Early Years Group. (2020). *Waverley community skills cafes project: Project summary and funding acquittal.* Northern Early Years Group.

Fisher, D., & Frey, N. (2013). *Better learning through structured teaching: A framework for the gradual release of responsibility.* Association for Supervision and Curriculum Development.

Flatau, P. (2016, November 7). Community organisations lack the funding and data to measure their impact. *The Conversation.* https://theconversation.com/community-organisations-lack-the-funding-and-data-to-measure-their-impact-68329

Funnell, S. C., & Rogers, P. J. (2011). *Purposeful program theory: Effective use of theories of change and logic models* (Vol. 31). Wiley.

Goldsworthy, K. (2021). *What is theory of change?* Australian Institute of Family Studies, Australian Government. https://aifs.gov.au/cfca/expert-panel-project/what-theory-change

Hansen, J. E., & Broekhuizen, M. L. (2021). Quality of the language-learning environment and vocabulary development in early childhood. *Scandinavian Journal of Educational Research, 65*(2), 302–317.

Harris, A. (2014, September 29). Distributed leadership. *Teacher.* https://www.teachermagazine. com/au_en/articles/distributed-leadership

Holmes, A. (2021, June 5). GroWaverley grows from humble beginnings, with funding to add a permanent presence for those in need. *The Examiner.* https://www.examiner.com.au/story/728 2354/as-need-grows-in-waverley-so-too-does-community-effort/

Hutchison, J. (2020, April 8). *Psychological safety and transparent communication at work: Strengthening collaboration and innovation.* [Video]. Zoom. https://worklife.msu.edu/events/ psychological-safety-and-transparent-communication-work-strengthening-collaboration-and

Intergovernmental Panel on Climate Change. (2018, October 8). *Summary for policy-makers of IPCC special report on global warming of 1.5°C approved by governments.* https://www.ipcc.ch/2018/10/08/summary-for-policymakers-of-ipcc-special-report-on-global-warming-of-1-5c-approved-by-governments/

Intergovernmental Panel on Climate Change. (2021). Summary for policymakers. In: *Climate change 2021: The physical science basis.* https://doi.org/10.1017/9781009157896.001

Kenny, S. (2016). Changing community development roles: The challenges of a globalising world. In R. Meade, M. Shaw, & S. Banks (Eds.), *Politics, power and community development* (pp. 47–64). Policy Press.

Lindsey, R. (2013). Exploring local hotspots and deserts: Investigating the local distribution of charitable resources. *Voluntary Sector Review, 4*(1), 95–116. https://doi.org/10.1332/204080 513X661563

Little, M., Ashford, N., & Morpeth, L. (2004). Research review: Risk and protection in the context of services for children in need. *Children and Family Social Work, 9*, 105–117.

Malen, B. (1994). 9. The micropolitics of education: Mapping the multiple dimensions of power relations in school polities. *Journal of Education Policy, 9*(5), 147–167. https://doi.org/10.1080/ 0268093940090513

McLennan, A. (2021, November 4). Launceston's community-run food co-op, GroWaverley, to shut, leaving hole in support for people doing it tough. *ABC News.* https://www.abc.net.au/ news/2021-11-04/tas-growaverley-food-charity-shuts-down/100590076

Merga, M. K., & Mat Roni, S. (2018). Children's perceptions of the importance and value of reading. *Australian Journal of Education, 62*(2), 135–153.

Moll, L. C., Soto-Santiago, S. L., & Schwartz, L. (2013). Funds of knowledge in changing communities. In B. Comber, K. Hall, L. Moll, & T. Cremin (Eds.), *International handbook of research on children's literacy, learning, and culture* (pp. 172–183). Wiley.

National Assessment Program—Literacy and Numeracy. https://nap.edu.au/naplan

Ogle, D. (1986). K-W-L: A teaching model that develops active reading of expository text. *The Reading Teacher, 39*(6), 564–570. https://www.jstor.org/stable/20199156

Pittaway, E., Bartolomei, L., & Doney, G. (2016). The glue that binds: An exploration of the way resettled refugee communities define and experience social capital. *Community Development Journal, 51*(3), 401–418. https://doi.org/10.1093/cdj/bsv023

Reinholz, D. L., & Andrews, T. C. (2020). Change theory and theory of change: What's the difference anyway? *International Journal of STEM Education, 7*(2), 1–12. https://doi.org/10.1186/s40594-020-0202-3

Rogoff, B. (2003). *The cultural nature of human development.* Oxford University Press.

United Nations. (1972). *Agenda 21. Chapter 7.* http://www.un-documents.net/a21-07.htm

United Nations. (n.d.a). *Transforming our world: The 2030 agenda for sustainable development.* https://sdgs.un.org/2030agenda

United Nations. (n.d.b). *Sustainable cities and human settlements.* https://sdgs.un.org/topics/sustai nable-cities-and-human-settlements

Vygotsky, L. S. (1998). The problem of age. In R. W. Rieber (Ed.), *The collected works of L. S. Vygotsky.* (Vol. 5), pp. 187–205. Plenum.

Weiss, C.H. (1998). *Methods for studying programs and policies* (2nd ed). Prentice.
Wendt, K. (2021). *Theories of change: Change leadership tools, models and applications for investing in sustainable development*. Springer.

Chapter 34
New Hope/*Omid Now* (امید نو): Supporting Afghan Women to Access Higher Education by Reimagining the Sustainable Development Goals

Barbara Kameniar, Gali Weiss, and Mursal Nazari

34.1 Introduction

Currently, Afghan women are deprived of their most basic human rights, including their right to education, work, freedom of movement without an Islamic Mahram (a close male of the family), their right to divorce, as well as many other status-based rights (Wenar, 2021). They cannot even choose what to wear. The Taliban's breathtaking restrictions on the one hand, coupled with the traditional and anti-woman views of many families, have made Afghanistan one of the most dangerous countries in the world for women (Georgetown Institute for Women, Peace and Security & Peace Research Institute Oslo, 2021). Afghanistan was ranked last across the three dimensions of security, justice, and inclusion on the Georgetown University Institute for Women, Peace, and Security 2021/2022 Index (Klugman et al., 2021). In Afghanistan, women are punished by institutions or families for assuming autonomy and defining themselves as human beings with human rights, and as persons worthy of moral consideration equal to that afforded to men.

The Sustainable Development Goals (SDGs) (United Nations [UN], 2015/2020) seek to address, among other things, circumstances such as those experienced by Afghan women. Adopted by the UN General Assembly in September 2015, the

B. Kameniar (✉)
School of Education, College of Arts, Law and Education, University of Tasmania, Churchill Ave, Hobart, TAS 7005, Australia
e-mail: b.kameniar@unimelb.edu.au

Melbourne Graduate School of Education, University of Melbourne, 234 Queensberry Street, Parkville, VIC 3010, Australia

G. Weiss · M. Nazari
Independent Scholar, Melbourne, Australia

© The Author(s), under exclusive license to Springer Nature Singapore Pte Ltd. 2023   619
K. Beasy et al. (eds.), *Education and the UN Sustainable Development Goals*, Education for Sustainability 7,
https://doi.org/10.1007/978-981-99-3802-5_34

SDGs built upon and expanded the eight Millennium Development Goals (MDGs), which had been adopted fifteen years earlier (Morton et al., 2017; Sachs, 2012). The scope of the SDGs is broader than that of the MDGs, not merely because the number of goals has expanded to incorporate concern about environmental degradation and climate change, and a more broadly conceived understanding of sustainability and poverty reduction, but also because the goals are intended to apply to all countries, not just "developing" countries (Duvic-Paoli, 2021; van der Heijden et al., 2015). It is this latter change in scope, as it applies to the education of Afghan women and the question this raises about who might have the responsibility to assist their access to higher education, why, and how, that we discuss in this chapter.

We examine the way in which a group of three women are working to ensure that young Afghan women of their generation are able to access higher education, an act of reflexive justice (Fraser, 2009) that signals a commitment to fighting not only to achieve gender equality and the empowerment of women and girls (SDG5) but also to ensure inclusive and equitable quality education, and the promotion of lifelong learning opportunities for all (SDG4). We commence with a brief discussion of the SDGs and the tension that lies in their broad acceptance of Westphalian assumptions of non-interference in the internal machinations of nation-states, and their recognition that sustainability and improvement across all aspects of life on Earth can occur only if all countries adopt the goals and commit to change. We argue that the tension created by the expansion of who might be the agent charged with securing the goals creates an opening for novel ways of addressing them. We then outline the theoretical framework we use to examine the approach taken up by this group of women. Importantly, the framework we engage speaks to actions beyond what might be included in normal approaches to justice, instead focusing on what has been called "social hope" and "reflexive justice" (Fraser, 2009).

We then provide a discussion of the background to New Hope/Omid Now (امید نو), the name given to the project. The section highlights how the origins of the project were forged more than a decade ago through an international art exchange project, a project that resonates with a vision of justice that is both feminist and reflexive. We then outline the individual aspects of the project, highlighting how the approach seeks to ensure not only that subalterns can speak (Spivak, 2003) but also that they are heard (Dutta, 2004). In particular, we highlight the way in which New Hope/ Omid Now (امید نو) works at the intersection between normal and abnormal justice to mobilise corrective strategies that change not only individual lives but institutional practices as well. We end by calling for a reconsideration of how the SDGs can be achieved through a social connection model of responsibility (Young, 2006, 2013), one that requires the engagement of state and transnational institutions alongside the work of individuals.

34.2 The Sustainable Development Goals: An Opening for Socially Connected Responsibility

The SDGs represent political aspirations at both a local and global level. However, having been adopted as a resolution, they remain aspirations. They carry no legal weight and are not normatively binding (Duvic-Paoli, 2021; van der Heijden et al., 2015). In spite of articulating the view that we live in a highly globalised world, the SDGs assert the right of individual states to develop policies and make laws applicable to their contexts. In doing so, they iterate a Westphalian view of maintenance of the integrity of individual nation-states and non-interference. Individual countries are said to have "primary responsibility for [design, implementation], follow-up and review" (UN, 2020) of environmental, social, political, health, and cultural justice practices within their own borders under a system that lacks specificity, and within an accountability mechanism that appears highly flexible and largely reliant on goodwill.

However, the SDGs also require states to consider the *implications* of their decisions beyond their borders. This more expansive understanding of attending to the effects of decisions made within discrete nation-states upon other states leads to a need to rethink what is meant by state responsibility. So too, the shift of responsibility for achieving the seventeen goals to *all* highlights the need for shared responsibility of a common planet, of addressing poverty and health, of ensuring girls' and women's equality and access to education and lifelong learning, and the interconnectedness of all human and non-human life on Earth.

We read the SDGs as requiring nations to take responsibility for a fairer and more sustainable world both within and *beyond* their borders. We also read the SDGs as providing support for the efforts of those who seek to take responsibility for injustices, who work within informal networks in the borderlands between autonomous action and institutional reliance, and who refuse quick, formal responses, instead, pointing out openings where others may not have done so. However, questions arise as to what we mean by responsibility and what the practical implications of such responsibility might look like.

34.2.1 Responsibility

Responsibility can be understood in a number of different ways. In their examination of the way in which "responsibility" is framed in the SDGs, Bexell and Jonsson (2017) propose an analytical framework that distinguishes between responsibility as cause (A did B causing C thereby making A responsible for C), responsibility as obligation (having caused C, A is now obligated to redress any harm that resulted from enacting B), and responsibility as accountability (someone has to answer for the way in which A carries out their obligations for the harms [C] that resulted from B; this can be A but can also be another agent). Although seeking to describe an expansive understanding of responsibility, one that captures the different and nuanced ways responsibility is used in the SDGs, their framework largely reflects what Iris Marion Young calls "liability models of responsibility" (Young, 2006, 2013).

According to Young, liability models tend to focus largely on isolating fault or blame so that individual agents or specific institutions can be held legally responsible. She argues that although this may be the case in circumstances where the immediate fault is clear, such a direct line of cause is seldom the case. Rather, in a fluid, interconnected, and globalised world where multiple agents have participated to larger or smaller degrees in harms, the search for a single responsible agent risks leaving no one accountable or attributing blame to those who may themselves be suffering under injustices. This is certainly the case regarding Afghan women and girls and the current denial of their right to access education beyond the age of 12. It is easy to isolate blame on the Taliban, their beliefs and practices, and indeed they are morally and practically responsible for the current state of women and girls' education in Afghanistan. However, the historic and contemporary circumstances that led to their current hold on power suggest others also share some responsibility (Baiza, 2013; Finnegan, 2020; Jamal, 2014).

Young also argues that liability models tend to judge the background conditions that may have resulted in harm as deviations from the norm, rather than as part of ongoing contributors to the harm that occurred. Under liability models, when some action results in harm (e.g., peace talks that excluded women and their rights contributed to the repression of Afghan girls and women and denial of their right to education and other freedoms) (Finnegan, 2020), it is understood to be the result of a contemporaneous event rather than broader background conditions. Attempts are then made to explain a current injustice as a discrete aberration, rather than an example of a pattern of failure in military, economic, and/or social interventions in poor nations by more powerful states (Baiza, 2013; Jamal, 2014).

Liability models are always backward-looking and therefore focus on what an actor or actors might be liable for in relation to a discrete, bounded event, understood to have deviated from normal moral practices, and now ended. Such an approach supports the identification of those who are "guilty" and works to absolve others of any responsibility in the future.

Finally, liability models tend to seek closure by requiring compensation be paid for past harms by agents who acted outside the bounds of what is morally acceptable. Again, we have seen this approach in Afghanistan where payments for "collateral damage to property, injury or loss of life" were paid to individuals or families (Hurst, 2016). The payments were intended to close the matter of civilian injuries, deaths, and loss of property, as though an egregious harm can be righted through recognition of liability for a single act and financial compensation alone.

For Young, liability models of responsibility are inadequate. She argues instead for a social connection model (SCM), one that seeks to examine the actions of all those who may have contributed to a wrong either directly or indirectly, calls into question background conditions, requires recognition that it is structures and processes that contribute to injustices and that therefore collective actions need to be undertaken to change structural and procedural issues that give rise to or enable injustice (Young, 2006).

Young also argues for the adoption of a shared approach to responsibility: one in which all people stand in solidarity *with* and *for* one another on matters of justice, particularly those matters with which they have some association or power to influence. For Young, solidarity is not a fixed mode of being together in the world but a future-focused orientation that requires negotiation. Solidarity she says, "must always be forged and reforged" (Young, 2013, p. 120). Because we have each participated in actions that have, even in a partial way, contributed to harm or injustice, we each have a responsibility to the planet and others. Following Derrida (1988) and Levinas (1979), Young suggests that merely through "speaking to another [we announce] a responsibility to others" (p. 119).

Three months after the Taliban takeover of Afghanistan, in November 2021, a small group of women in Australia decided to respond to Afghan women's call for help. The group named itself New Hope/Omid Now (امید نو). Although first set up to enact a practical and immediate response, its work and its subjects reflect the discursive aspects presented above.

New Hope/Omid Now (امید نو) emerged from an international art exchange project among Australian women artists and the *Organisation for the Promotion of Afghan Women's Capabilities* (OPAWC). OPAWC was established in Kabul in 2003 by a group of Afghan women who sought to ensure long-term and sustainable opportunities for women through the development of literacy, practical wage-earning skills, and health education.

Engaging in the art project exchanges, the Australian artists initially understood Afghan women's rights through the lens of Australian women's own understandings of women's rights, while open to differences in each other's situations. The major point of the forthcoming art projects was to provide a space for connectedness. In so doing, the Australian artists grew in their knowledge and identification with the Afghan participants, and thereby also grew in their sense of responsibility as Australians and as women, to do what they could to support progressing the rights of Afghan women. The Australian artist group's connections with the women of OPAWC, which came about in part because of the involvement of Australian armed forces in the country, "announced" their responsibility to the women of OPAWC.

Under a simple liability model, both the art projects and New Hope/Omid Now (امید نو) would be able to claim they had no responsibility for what was happening to the people of Afghanistan. However, reflecting Young's (2006) SCM, they recognised their connectedness to Afghans. They saw this as a matter of justice.

In the next section, we outline a theoretical framework drawn from the work of political philosopher, critical theorist, and feminist Nancy Fraser. This framework provides a tool for describing and explaining the work of New Hope/Omid Now (امید نو).

34.3   Theoretical Framing

Fraser argues that the traditional "way in which we think about justice is changing" (Warriner, 2013) and must continue to change. In particular, she argues that *who* we imagine as the subjects of justice, *what* we think is the content of justice, and *how* we frame and resolve disputes about justice, must be re-imagined so that justice reflects a more complex and protean world than that perceived by traditional political theorists who have hitherto assumed a model focused on issues of economic distribution within geographically bounded nation-states.

Fraser refers to traditional ways of framing justice as "normal justice" (Fraser, 2009). Under normal justice the *who* or subject of justice is (more likely than not) an individual, one whose proximal relationship within the citizenry of a politically bounded territory has established them as being entitled to equal concern within that state. Therefore, theoretically at least, all citizens within a given state are understood to have interests and concerns that require equal consideration. Justice within this framing means arbitrating among demands from, and obligations to, different disadvantaged groups in regard to the distribution of resources. Practically, however, maldistribution of resources and the misrecognition and misrepresentation of marginalised groups can be commonplace because ideas of a common citizenry are often located within a narrow polity. Even so, under normal justice, one's identity as a citizen entitles one to forms of consideration that differ from and exceed those of the non-citizen.

The *what* of normal justice are the claims individual citizens make regarding the provision of personal entitlements that have been denied, or to ensure redress for any harms that have been endured. Such claims tend to be those that focus on matters related to property or to the distribution of material resources. "Justice" under this framing is seen largely as "distributive justice"—what should be distributed equitably? As positive entitlements, one might argue for equal access to medical treatment, access to education, access to adequate food, the right to a "living wage", shelter, etc. When framed in the negative one might argue that under normal justice citizens should be free from ignorance, free from poverty, or free from having their goods taken without due compensation. In either the positive or negative framings (Berlin, 1969/2002), the *what* of normal justice is primarily focused on the distribution of resources and, within a capitalist context, the maintenance of ownership of property.

Under normal justice, the *how,* or "grammar of justice" (Fraser, 2009), is first to be found at the local level—injustices should ideally be resolved without the need for formal institutions or procedures. As normal justice focuses on the individual, it is individuals who should, in the first instance, seek justice regarding the distribution of resources from one another. However, when local efforts fail, justice can be found with the agents and agencies of the state. State agencies such as courts are often occupied by powerful private elites and their agents. Such occupants are charged with making decisions with limited consultation and implementing decisions without question. When the state intervenes to resolve conflicts, the justice meted out is asserted to be impartial and consistent, even while it may be neither. Contestation of such justice is discouraged as state institutions are seen as the rightful bodies of rational law (Fraser, 2009).

Fraser argues that the assumptions underpinning "normal justice" are inadequate because we live in "abnormal times" where the imagined boundedness of the nation-state no longer applies, thereby rendering the guidance of traditional agents and agencies incapable of meeting the demands of a more complex world (Fraser, 2009; Klugman et al., 2021). Resources and people flow across traditional boundaries in ways, and at speeds, that "shake" the grammar of normal justice. In abnormal times, the *who, what,* and *how* of justice are deeply contested. Marginalised individuals and groups internal and external to bounded nation-states demand more than the redistribution of resources. They also require cultural recognition, reciprocal respect, political representation, and support for aims defined by them, rather than imposed upon them.

For Fraser, identifying the *who* of justice in abnormal times requires justice to be reframed as "participatory parity", a state in which social arrangements "permit all to participate as peers in social life" (Fraser, 2009, p. 60). Importantly, peers should be afforded equal consideration. Justice can only be attained when hitherto marginalised, occluded, or disadvantaged individuals, groups, or categories of persons are able to be "full partners in social interaction" (p. 60). Like the SDGs' concern that countries must attend to the impact of their actions on those beyond their borders, and Young's (2006) SCM of responsibility, Fraser's concern for participatory parity goes beyond those within bounded nation-states to include "all those who are subject to a given governance structure" (Fraser; Warriner, 2013). She calls this the "all-subjected principle" (Fraser, p. 65), the idea that anyone impacted by a particular structure of governance has moral standing in relation to that structure and should therefore be afforded moral consideration by agents of those structures.

When considering the *what* or the substance of abnormal justice Fraser proposes a three-dimensional approach: (1) an economic dimension (redistribution, the focus of normal justice and maintained under abnormal justice), (2) a cultural dimension (recognition of difference and equality of status), and (3) a political dimension (representation, including full participation in political community). These are multiple aims that "must be pursued simultaneously in struggles for social justice" (Fraser, 1997, p. 129), even while there are tensions among them (Young, 1997). Fraser acknowledges there may be other dimensions to justice that have not yet been defined, a particularly salient observation given that she expanded her own understanding of justice from one centred on distribution and recognition (Fraser, 1995), to one that included representation. This shift reflected the changing demands of subordinated persons and groups, first for a share of resources, then for recognition and equality of status, and more recently for representation (Fraser, 2009). While injustice persists, other dimensions not included in those described may emerge and require a response.

So too, the *how* of justice in abnormal times requires a shift away from monological responses to disputes and injustices that proceed solely from powerful nations or elites. Abnormal times require the grammar of justice to be dialogical. And it must be truly democratic through the inclusion of all those who are subjected to the specific structure of governance under discussion. It must embrace contestation, incorporate fair procedures, and seek to resolve matters discursively (Fraser, 2009). Such an approach could occur at "grassroots" levels among the population, thereby exerting power from below. However, just because a particular claim or response emerges from below, it does not mean it will always and everywhere be just. Fraser argues that in abnormal times the *how* of justice must be both dialogical and institutional, incorporating all-subjected along with institutional processes and responses.

However, she warns that even this approach is insufficient because old injustices can be renormalised, new injustices instituted, and a "new normal" established and settled. Instead, she argues for "reflexive justice", an approach that signals "a genre of theorizing that works at two levels at once: entertaining urgent claims on behalf of the disadvantaged, while also parsing the meta-disagreements that are interlaced with them" (Fraser, 2009, p.73). Such an approach requires "tacking back and forth" between individuals and institutions, normal and abnormal approaches to justice, refusing to be captured by either approach, but working towards justice through engaging the openings within both. This is the approach taken by New Hope/Omid Now (امید نو). Below we provide a brief outline of the history and context of the project before utilising Fraser's framework to describe and explain the approach.

34.4 Background

New Hope/Omid Now (امید نو) has its origins in an international art exchange project entitled *Unfolding Projects* that was led by Melbourne artist, feminist, and scholar Gali Weiss. Commencing in 2009 *Unfolding Projects* has drawn together over 20 Australian women artists and 60 Afghan women artists, curators, teachers, and students of OPAWC to work on two collaborative art projects over a period of 11 years: (1) The artists' books project, completed 2010, documented in *Two Trees* (Weiss et al., 2013); and (2) The Handkerchief Project, completed 2018, documented in *Making Marks* (Weiss & Kameniar, 2020). Each collaboration commenced in Australia with the hope of connecting women artists in Australia with women in Afghanistan as a gesture of openness, friendship, and solidarity. Each collaboration reflected an intention to continue a conversation about women's and girls' rights to education, to respect, to freedom, to political representation, and to economic independence. Each was also designed to continue to raise awareness of the situation of women in Afghanistan, of Australia's continued military presence there and to remind Afghan women that they had not been forgotten. The sale of the artworks and subsequent books also assisted in raising money to support OPAWC's work among some of the poorest women in Afghanistan.

Mursal Nazari was the most recent director of OPAWC with whom Gali Weiss and Barbara Kameniar had worked, in varying ways, on *Making Marks*. When Kabul fell to the Taliban in August 2021, Mursal fled Afghanistan with her family. They found refuge in Australia, where they currently reside, and have been granted permanent

Humanitarian visas. In the chaos that ensued, the hasty withdrawal of Western troops and the re-entry of the Taliban, schools and universities closed. OPAWC also closed and many of the women who had worked there dispersed across the country or fled. Women's rights activists were among the first group of people to be targeted. In a conversation between Gali and Mursal about how to best continue to support the women of Afghanistan under the new order, the idea of New Hope/Omid Now (امید نو) was born.

34.5   "New Hope"/Omid Now (امید نو)

New Hope/Omid Now (امید نو) was formed to support a need expressed by Afghan women. The small and ambitious enterprise is committed to seeking justice for the women of Afghanistan through what these women see as a direction—higher education.

The project's aim is to assist as many Afghan women as possible to continue to access higher education either within Afghanistan, within Australia, or within a third country, such as India, Bangladesh, or Turkey. Below, Mursal takes up her voice as an Afghan woman to explain:

> When the Taliban took power in the late 1990s, and the first wave of poverty in Afghanistan commenced, many families in Kabul and the provinces sold underage girls and infant girls so they could buy food. How is it that girls can be reduced to a commodity? Even when people are hungry, why do they choose to sell their daughters? As an Afghan girl, I saw all these tragedies with my eyes and felt such pain within my heart. Since childhood my biggest goal in life has been to help women, especially in the field of education and literacy.

> Since mid-August 2021 when the Taliban re-established themselves as rulers, we are witnessing such tragedies again. While the women of my country remain under torture, I do not feel free, even here in Australia.

> Acting against women is one of the most common attributes of Islamic fundamentalism. Islamic fundamentalists know how powerful women are, and they know that it is in the hands of women that their destruction lies. So, they try to keep women uneducated and illiterate. This was clear in the first minutes of their coming to power. They closed the doors of the schools and universities on girls. And they have deprived women access to all social, political, economic, and cultural activities.

> Although women were always marginalised in Afghanistan's male-patriarchal society and are the first victims of oppressive wars and traditional family views, they have shown heroism in various historical contexts.

> In the most recent case, we can point out the women protesting in recent months, who, despite the rule of the throbbing atmosphere, still took courage and took to the streets for their human demands.

> I believe that one of the ways to get rid of the current situation in Afghanistan and reach a free and peaceful Afghanistan is to raise women's knowledge and awareness. So far, we do not know of any country that has achieved prosperity without the active presence of women. The progress of a country can be measured by the economic, social, and political status of women in that society. Therefore, it is my duty to use the smallest opportunities to help the women in my country. (Mursal Nazari)

For Mursal and other Afghans, ensuring an educated populace (one that is inclusive of women at all levels of education and power, and in all fields of employment) is vital to the future of the nation.

Since the first fall of the Taliban in 2001, significant gains had been made across all levels of Afghan society, even while the country remained one of the poorest in the world (World Bank, 2020). Gains at the legislative level included the enshrinement of equal rights for men and women in the 2004 Constitution, and the 2009 *Law on Elimination of Violence against Women (EVAW)* that criminalised violence against women, a move that signalled publicly, if not so much practically (Hakimi, 2020), that discrimination and violence along gender lines would not be tolerated.

Even so, on the 2020 Human Development Index, Afghanistan remained ranked below other South Asian countries on the majority of indicators (although improving faster than other nations). Among the grouping, Afghanistan came last on the Gender Development Index and was only just in front of Pakistan on the Education Index (UN, 2020). However, according to data outlined in a 2021 UNESCO report, enrolments across all levels of education increased tenfold, from about one million students being enrolled in some form of education in 2001, to approximately ten million by 2018 (UNESCO, 2021). Of those enrolled in 2018, close to 40% were girls and women. The female literacy rate almost doubled between 2007 and 2018. By 2018 around 25% of all university places were taken up by women. Over 90,000 women were engaged in some form of higher education prior to the fall of Kabul in 2021 (UNESCO, 2021).

These changes help to explain why after the initial shock of the fall of Kabul had lifted, the Taliban encountered strong resistance from many women and girls in Kabul and some of the regions. As Borshchevskaya observed, "…many women now see themselves as part of a 'new' generation that has the right to shape its own destiny". She cites a young girl, who confronted a Taliban soldier, saying "I am from a new generation… I want to go to school" (Borshchevskaya, 2021).

The perseverance of women for a future through the active presence of women is evident in their networks of collective responsibility. When street protests were violently stopped, protest campaigns were held in homes and on social media as acts of strength, solidarity, and defiance (Rukhshana Media, 2022). When schooling for girls shut down, hidden schools were set up "to circumvent Taliban's ban on girls [sic] education" (Sharifi, 2022). One of the most common statements in Afghan women's communications to New Hope/Omid Now (امید نو) is that in seeking tertiary education, they wish to lead their country to a better future (Weiss, 2022).

34.5.1 Why Higher Education?

Education is a human right. Continuity of education is vital to effective learning and the development of expertise. This is recognised within the SDGs with their emphasis on lifelong learning (Elfert, 2019; UN, 2020). Consistent, high-quality educational experiences support the development and wellbeing of not only individuals but also the state. This means that not only is higher education important for individual women, but it also is important to the future of Afghanistan too.

In the following section, we report on the *who, what,* and *how* of the reflexive justice approach taken up by New Hope/Omid Now (امید نو) to help ensure that the current generation of young Afghan women continues to access quality higher education.

34.6 Ensuring Education for a Generation of Afghan Women—A Reflexive Justice Approach

34.6.1 Who?

For New Hope/Omid Now (امید نو) all women in Afghanistan are understood to be the subjects of justice. Whether from the regions or the cities, whether poor or wealthy, and with no regard to their ethnic, tribal, or family background, concern has only been whether a woman wants to access higher education and is unable to do so because of a lack of finances or a lack of access. In an era where universal access to basic primary education (MDG) is no longer considered adequate, it is a matter of "participatory parity" that Afghan girls and women be able to engage in lifelong learning (SDG) and where possible, access higher education.

Utilising a "snow-balling" methodology through established networks, New Hope/Omid Now (امید نو) identified four distinct groups of young Afghan women (late teens to mid-twenties) requiring support to access studies in higher education:

1. Women who were already in higher education within Afghanistan or were about to commence higher education when the Taliban took power and who wished to continue to access higher education within Afghanistan—*Remain.*
2. Afghan women who were already undertaking higher degrees outside Afghanistan in countries other than Australia when Kabul fell and who wished to continue their studies but were no longer able to do so because their families could not afford to pay for their education—*Established Outside.*
3. Women within Afghanistan who may or may not have already commenced higher degrees and who wish to participate in higher education outside Afghanistan—*Outside New.*
4. Afghan women in Australia who want to access higher education, particularly those who already have a degree and would like to undertake post-graduate studies—*Within Australia.*

34.6.2   What?

The substance of the New Hope/Omid Now (اميد نو) response varies according to the needs of each woman and her individual circumstances. Even so, the need for an economic response has been immediately apparent for all (economic dimension), as is the need to have their status as persons worthy of moral consideration and equal respect acknowledged (cultural dimension). In addition to these general cultural claims, it is vital that each woman be recognised as autonomous, intelligent, capable of succeeding in higher education, and in most cases, supported by family to pursue their studies and chosen careers. Misrecognition of Afghan women as always already victims does not do justice to the many strong and determined women within the country. Likewise, there is a powerful need to provide a forum for the thoughts, desires, and ambitions of these women (political dimension).

In addition to requiring funds for tuition and living, the *Remain* group asserts the need for recognition and equality of status with male students undertaking the same courses. Many women continue to attend classes in Afghanistan, regardless of how limited they are, because they want to learn. They also continue as a form of resistance. Their ongoing presence refutes and refuses the misrecognition of them by the fundamentalists. Women students have told us of those who have stopped attending their university because of the low standard of instruction, while others attend despite this as a form of action, so that a lack of significant attendance will not be used as a rationale to exclude women altogether from universities. The women's participation is dangerous but insistent.

The *Established Outside* group requires funds to continue to study in universities in Turkey and India (the two countries where women were identified as requiring support). As tertiary students unable to return to Afghanistan due to fear of persecution, and without their families in Afghanistan able to continue their financial support, they require a just response which includes acknowledgement of their circumstances, a willingness to hear their wish to continue, and continuation of their visas so they can complete their studies.

The *Outside New* group represents a group of women who believe, for reasons of safety and/or access to education, that they cannot remain within Afghanistan. In addition to financial support, they require access to higher education institutions within South Asian Association for Regional Cooperation countries where tuition fees are affordable, or within stable states like Australia where institutions understand the needs of the women and the moral responsibility due to them. As with the *Remain* group, the *Outside New* group requires recognition of their strengths and capabilities, so they are granted access to universities. The universities require knowledge of their allocated foreign language, usually English, which many women in Afghanistan do not have, and hence they require academic language learning as part of their offered studies. They also need student visas, a challenge that requires host states to recognise each woman as more than a citizen of a state ruled by the Taliban. Each woman is a discreet human person, worthy of consideration in her own right, regardless of the state from which she comes.

Afghan women who fled to Australia after August 2021 (*Within Australia* group) and who wish to continue or to advance their studies require recognition of the status of their prior studies, recognition of prior experience, a willingness of higher education institutions to provide support and allow time for language development, as well as fee waivers.

The *what* of justice as it pertains to the women with whom New Hope/Omid Now (امید نو) works is more complex than what is outlined above. However, the list indicates a few of the material requirements that support educational justice for these women.

34.6.3   How?

During the fall of Kabul in August 2021, Gali and Barbara worked to assist Mursal and her family to acquire a visa for Australia. They then joined with a third woman to help support Mursal and her family to flee Afghanistan. During the process of acquiring the visas and eventually escaping the country, it became clear that mono-logical approaches to visa applications and safe passage outside Afghanistan were inadequate. Not only were official governmental channels cumbersome and slow, but also, the sheer number of applications meant government departments were overwhelmed. Added to this was the chaos of the evacuation of the Australian military, nationals, and visa holders from Kabul airport and the terror that ensued once the Taliban took control. Such abnormal times demanded dialogical and reflexive approaches, approaches that built on existing informal networks and forged new ones. The success of Mursal's escape in September 2021 framed the informal, networked, dialogical, and reflexive approach taken up by New Hope/Omid Now (امید نو).

The approach of New Hope/Omid Now (امید نو) towards the women being supported is to have as much direct communication as possible with them. This includes connections with their sponsors. New Hope/Omid Now (امید نو) is not a funding venture alone. It is a supporting enterprise, in which support includes connections and exchanges, listening and sharing, through emails, phone apps, and video calls, in English and Dari with Mursal as a translator. Both from the art projects and Mursal's journey of escape, the group has learnt that *accompaniment* is crucial to understanding and morale, resulting in a deeper sense of shared responsibility.

Women in the *Remain* group have been supported to continue their study through funds that cover the cost of tuition and modest living. The money for this group comes from the sale of the *Making Marks* handkerchief artworks to the *Australian War Memorial* and is sent via informal networks.

Two of the three *Established Outside* women were attending university in India and one was attending university in Turkey before the Taliban takeover in August 2021. Friends and networks of the two Australian members of New Hope/Omid Now (امید نو) offered to support each of the women by paying for their university fees. In the case of the two women in India, they are also supported with a living allowance. In each case, tuition fees have been paid directly to the university by the people who have offered support. Although New Hope/Omid Now (امید نو) does not handle any of the money, sponsors are supported to manage the complex banking issues that arise through such transfers and sponsors are invited to speak to the young women whose education they are supporting.

For the women who wish to study outside Afghanistan (*Outside New*) finding places in universities and acquiring student visas has been challenging. New Hope/ Omid Now (امید نو) has approached the task by "tacking back and forth" (Fraser, 2009) among individuals, informal networks, and institutions. In India, this has involved identifying appropriate universities, speaking to institutional personnel ranging from admission officers to Chancellors, and seeking support for applications. At the time of writing, no additional women have gained access to a university in India. Difficulties in acquiring a student visa to study in India may be contributing to a general reluctance among the universities to accept Afghan women, in spite of guarantees their fees will be paid.

With the support of New Hope/Omid Now (امید نو) four women submitted applications to the Asian University for Women (AUW) in Bangladesh, three were accepted into the university, and are studying at the AUW. Additionally, the AUW offered a significant number of scholarships specifically for Afghan women, subject to visa approvals.

In Australia, two universities quickly indicated support for Afghan women through New Hope/Omid Now (امید نو), with one university offering three scholarships and the second university offering four scholarships and substantial stipends. Four Afghan women are currently studying in Melbourne as a result of a partnership among New Hope/Omid Now (نو امید), Hawthorn-Melbourne English Language Centre, Trinity College, and The University of Melbourne. Negotiations continue regarding the types of "packages" that might be offered to Afghan women in other Australian institutions. Securing a student visa is often the most challenging part of the enterprise. It requires considerable negotiation because visas are seldom granted under the conditions being proposed—students coming from "failed" states without significant financial resources who are committed to learning and then returning to their people. Discussions with government departments and ministers demand a capacity to assist them in envisioning new and more just processes for those who are rendered subaltern and those who wish to support them.

34.7 Final Remarks

New Hope is built on "old Hope", when opportunities for education and acknowledgement of women's rights opened up in Afghanistan after 2001, mobilised by Western infiltration and aims. During the following 20-year period, women's aims for independence and gender equality grew within a struggle for full acceptance of their rights. While that period of struggle saw inaction and corruption by formal legal systems towards the protection of women and their claims of abuse (Human Rights Watch, 2021), it also saw a resistance to women's injustices through an evolving justice process with professional women workers, from police officers to judges

(Khan, 2014). Systems of justice and organised protections that were supported globally and locally have now been destroyed and repression of women is the current authority.

Education is the new resistance to repression. It is not resistance as a "fight" but as reflexive empowerment. Now that many women are at a point of confidence with their natural rights and abilities, they wish to use their rights to education no matter what the risks—whether in their "prisons" of home or despite the limitations imposed on them at public institutions—as an act of resistance that is also an action for the future of their country.

That is what seems to be motivating their hopes for studying further—to contribute knowledge to others. It is not only a contribution of knowledge but also a modelling for the continuing generations of women, that women can exist, function, and grow both themselves and their people despite the authority's attempts to absent them.

New Hope/Omid Now (امید نو) understands responsibility as a social connection and understands the group's connections to women in Afghanistan as a call to morally just action. In doing so, we take seriously the aspirations of the SDGs and the call for us all to be responsible. New Hope/Omid Now (امید نو) operates in the borderlands between autonomous action and institutional dependency, understanding the limits of both. It builds and relies upon informal networks of people who refuse to submit to institutional responses that fail to ameliorate injustices and instead are able to creatively imagine "other ways" of achieving justice. New Hope/Omid Now (امید نو) is optimistic and future-oriented, understanding that although life in Afghanistan is currently highly oppressive, things will change. The continuation of women's education will ensure change can come more quickly, and when it does, women will have the skills and knowledge to ensure they are able to take their place as leaders within a more just Afghanistan.

We end with the words of Mursal:

> The New Hope/Omid Now (امید نو) project literally opened the door of hope to 30 Afghan girls, with all their aspirations, who were confined to the four walls of the house when the Taliban terrorist group came.

> A number of these girls have experienced many big problems at a young age. And they've lost their best things and loves due to war, migration, and poverty during the last 30 years. And it's the biggest happiness for them to hear that there are some people very far from them who are trying to support them. They are in a terrible situation and they are defenceless. They feel that the UN has forgotten about them. So, any small support, even a letter or a short message, can keep their hope alive.

> I warmly shake the beloved hands of my friends and the wonderful people around me who, with their support and human efforts, are changing the lives of a few of the girls in my homeland.

References

Baiza, Y. (2013). *Education in Afghanistan: Developments, influences and legacies since 1901.* Routledge.

Berlin, I. (1969/2002). Two concepts of liberty. In *Four essays on liberty*. Oxford University Press.

Bexell, M., & Jönsson, K. (2017, January). Responsibility and the United Nations' sustainable development goals. *Forum for Development Studies, 44*(1), 13–29.

Borshchevskaya, A. (2021, December 1). The Taliban remain the same, but society has changed. A new generation of Afghan women resisting a return to the Middle Ages. *The Insider*. https://theins.ru/en/opinion/anna-borshchevskaya/246753

Derrida, J. (1988). The politics of friendship. *The Journal of Philosophy, 85*(11), 632–644.

Dutta, N. (2004). The face of the other: Terror and the return of binarism. *Interventions, 6*(3), 431–450.

Duvic-Paoli, L. A. (2021). From aspirational politics to soft law? Exploring the international legal effects of sustainable development Goal 7 on affordable and clean energy. *Melbourne Journal of International Law, 22*(1), 1–23.

Elfert, M. (2019). Lifelong learning in Sustainable Development Goal 4: What does it mean for UNESCO's rights-based approach to adult learning and education? *International Review of Education, 65*(4), 537–556.

Finnegan, C. (2020, February 26). Pompeo: US, Taliban deal 'historic opportunity for peace,' but women's rights up to Afghans. *ABC News*. https://abcnews.go.com/Politics/pompeo-us-taliban-deal-historic-opportunity-peace-womens/story?id=69202161

Fraser, N. (1995, July 1). From redistribution to recognition? Dilemmas of justice in a 'post-socialist' age. *New Left Review,* (212), 68. https://www.proquest.com/scholarly-journals/redistribution-recognition-dilemmas-justice-post/docview/1301909778/se-2?accountid=12372

Fraser, N. (1997, May 1). A rejoinder to Iris Young. *New Left Review,* (223), 126. https://www.proquest.com/scholarly-journals/rejoinder-iris-young/docview/1301912874/se-2?accountid=12372

Fraser, N. (2009). *Scales of justice: Reimagining political space in a globalizing world*. Columbia University Press.

Hakimi, M. J. (2020). Elusive justice: Reflections on the tenth anniversary of Afghanistan's law on elimination of violence against women. *Northwestern University Journal of International Human Rights, 18*, 52. https://www.idlo.int/sites/default/files/IDLO_Afghan%20Legal%20Professionals%20summary.pdf

Human Rights Watch. (2021). *'I thought our life might get better': Implementing Afghanistan's elimination of violence against women law*. https://www.hrw.org/sites/default/files/media_2021/07/afghanistan0821_web.pdf

Hurst, D. (2016, January 13). Australia pays $207,000 compensation to 2,800 Afghans over six years. *The Guardian*. https://www.theguardian.com/world/2016/jan/13/australia-pays-207000-compensation-to-2800-afghans-over-six-years

Jamal, A. (2014). Men's perception of women's role and girls' education among Pashtun tribes of Pakistan: A qualitative Delphi study. *Cultural and Pedagogical Inquiry, 6*(2), 17–34.

Khan, I. (2014). *Out of the shadows, onto the bench: Women in Afghanistan's justice sector*. International Development Law Organisation. https://www.idlo.int/sites/default/files/IDLO_Afghan%20Legal%20Professionals%20summary.pdf

Klugman, J., Kovacevic, M., Gottschalk, M., Ortiz, E., Diaz, J., Thebo, V., Raj-Silverman, I., Zhao, J., Aas Rustad, S., Negash, S., & Borchgrevink, K. (2021). *Women, Peace, and Security Index 2021/22: Tracking sustainable peace through inclusion, justice, and security for women*. Georgetown Institute for Women, Peace and Security, and Peace Research Institute Oslo Centre on Gender, Peace and Security. https://www.prio.org/publications/12900

Levinas, E. (1979). *Totality and infinity: An essay on exteriority* (Vol. 1). Springer Science & Business Media.

Morton, S., Pencheon, D., & Squires, N. (2017). Sustainable Development Goals (SDGs), and their implementation: A national global framework for health, development and equity needs a systems approach at every level. *British Medical Bulletin, 124*(1), 81–90. https://doi.org/10.1093/bmb/ldx031

Rukhshana Media. (2022, February 23). *Afghan women call on the Taliban to release detained activists.* https://rukhshana.com/en/afghan-women-call-on-the-taliban-to-release-detained-activists

Sachs, J. D. (2012). From millennium development goals to sustainable development goals. *The Lancet, 379*(9832), 2206–2211.

Sharifi, A. (2022, May 21). Female protestor opened a secret school to circumvent Taliban's ban on girls' education. *Rukhshana Media.* https://rukhshana.com/en/female-protester-opened-a-secret-school-to-circumvent-talibans-ban-on-girls-education

Spivak, G. C. (2003). Can the subaltern speak? *Die Philosophin, 14*(27), 42–58.

United Nations. (2015/2020). *Transforming our world: The 2030 Agenda for Sustainable Development.*

United Nations Development Programme (UNDP). (2020). Human Development Report 2020. The Next Frontier: Human Development and the anthropocene briefing note for countries on the 2020 Human Development Report: Lesotho. https://hdr.undp.org/sites/default/files/Country-Profiles/AFG.pdf

United Nations Educational, Scientific, and Cultural Organization. (2021). *The right to education: What's at stake in Afghanistan? A 20 year review.* https://en.unesco.org/sites/default/files/afghanistan_v11.pdf

van der Heijden, K., Suter, S., & Bouyé, M. (2015, July 8). *Sustainable development goals: From rhetoric to reality.* World Resources Institute. https://www.wri.org/insights/sustainable-development-goals-rhetoric-reality

Warriner, J. (2013). Review of the book scales of justice: Reimagining political space in a global world. *Hypatia, 28*(1), 222–225.

Weiss, G. (2022). *Afghanistan now! A woman's perspective.* https://galiweiss.wixsite.com/making-marks-book/blog

Weiss, G., & Kameniar, B. (2020). *Making marks: Australia and Afghanistan.* Vivid Publishing.

Weiss, G., Kameniar, B., & Tomczak, M. (2013). *Two trees: Australian artists' books to Afghanistan and back.* Vivid Publishing.

Wenar, L. (2021). Rights. In E. N. Zalta (Ed.), *The Stanford encyclopedia of philosophy.* https://plato.stanford.edu/archives/spr2021/entries/rights/

World Bank. (2020). World Bank national accounts data, and OECD National Accounts data files. *GNI per capita, Atlas method (Current US$).* https://data.worldbank.org/indicator/NY.GNP.PCAP.CD

Young, I. M. (1997, March 1). Unruly categories: A critique of Nancy Fraser's dual systems theory. *New Left Review,* (222), 147. https://www.proquest.com/scholarly-journals/unruly-categories-critique-nancy-frasers-dual/docview/1301912752/se-2?accountid=12372

Young, I. M. (2006). Responsibility and global justice: A social connection model. *Social Philosophy and Policy, 23*(1), 102–130.

Young, I. M. (2013). *Responsibility for justice.* Oxford University Press.

Chapter 35
Platforms of Skills Ecosystems: A Lifelong Learning System Model in Which TVET Can Lead Local Communities to Achieve the Sustainable Development Goals

Filippo Del Ninno and Giovanni Crisonà

Abstract A group of European stakeholders founded the Skillman Network for the development of skills in Advanced Manufacturing (Skillman) in 2014, bringing together industry leaders, research institutes, and vocational education and training providers, including Fiat Chrysler Automobiles, the National Research Council (CNR), various universities, and large companies such as Jaguar Land Rover and Scandinavian Airlines System.

35.1 Introduction

A group of European stakeholders founded the Skillman Network for the development of skills in Advanced Manufacturing (Skillman) in 2014, bringing together industry leaders, research institutes, and vocational education and training providers, including Fiat Chrysler Automobiles, the National Research Council (CNR[1]), various universities, and large companies such as Jaguar Land Rover and Scandinavian Airlines System. The network provides the basis for a concept, the Skillman Global platforms of Centres of Vocational Excellence (CoVEs.eu) (Crisonà, 2019), an environment in which members jointly apply the concepts of the United Nations (UN) Sustainable Development Goals (SDGs) (UN Department of Economic and Social Affairs, 2022), towards excellence in vocational education and training, looking to

---

[1] The National Research Council (CNR) is the largest public research institution in Italy, the only one under the Research Ministry.

F. Del Ninno
European Training Foundation, Viale Settimio Severo 65, 10133, Torino, Italy

G. Crisonà (✉)
Skillman.eu, Via Puccini 80, 51100, Pistoia, Italy

637

provide an inclusive approach to excellence in technical and vocational education and training (TVET).

The Skillman network is currently represented in over 95 countries and has over 700 members. The network's various initiatives include a multi-year debate that brings together ideas and initiatives at the annual Skillman International Forum (SIF). The Forum was recently complemented by another think tank platform, the Alliance Summit (AS). This has created a preliminary stage where the network, in collaboration with the European Training Foundation of the European Union (EU) Commission, has gathered high level stakeholders to identify the groundwork for its annual debate on the future of education.

The previous forum, SIF 2021 (Skillman Secretariat, 2021b), brought together education leaders and stakeholders from around the world to discuss the concepts of the SDGs and analyse the key trends and challenges for human capital development in advanced manufacturing. The AS 2022 (Skillman Secretariat, 2022a), held in April, was a full week of presentations and discussions that provided a wealth of inspiration. The authors, together with a group of Human Capital Development (HCD) specialists, participated in the AS 2022 (Skillman Secretariat, 2022a), analysing the results of SIF 2021 (Skillman Secretariat, 2021b), grouping concepts and identifying common idea patterns to lay the foundation for SIF 2022 (Skillman Secretariat, 2022b).

This chapter summarises these findings and highlights some of the key links that exist between Skillman strategies for the future of education and the SDGs. It aims to present the main aspects that the Skillman Network promotes for the implementation of the SDG principles for excellence in TVET. This involves a system that values international cooperation and assesses the level of excellence as a collective outcome of members forming local skills ecosystems, rather than assessing the success of individual TVET providers acting as an elite.

35.2   SDGs Principles for Excellence in TVET

The model for Centres of Vocational Excellence circulating among the Skillman members (Crisonà, 2019) includes the idea of sharing sustainability and ethical values across countries. Implementing this idea requires a comprehensive mix of complementary participating organisations that represent TVET, and also industry leaders and many other stakeholders acting, at a local community level, as local skills ecosystems that allow them to develop a culture of achievement and excellence, which fosters innovation and generate new knowledge for sustainable development (Joshi et al., 2019). This model aims to foster strong transnational multi-stakeholder collaboration with the belief that "excellence" in TVET is a result of a joint strategy to strengthen vocations and/or interdependence among stakeholders.

In 2021, as part of its Global CoVEs.eu initiative (Crisonà, 2019), the Skillman network launched the idea of an inclusive approach to excellence in TVET, which was aligned with the principles of the SDGs, requiring the promotion of strong transnational cooperation (Crisonà, 2021a). This holistic and inclusive concept of

TVET addresses a variety of SDGs. The most obvious is SDG4 (Quality Education). The objective of this SDG, "equitable quality education and promotion of Lifelong Learning opportunities for all," is the basis of the reflection carried out in the context of Global CoVEs.eu initiative (Crisonà, 2019; United Nations Education, Scientific and Cultural Organisation Institute for Lifelong Learning, 2016). However, the innovative approach also indirectly addresses three additional SDGs. These are the following.

- SDG1 (no poverty) aims at ending poverty in all its forms everywhere. Reviewing the concept of excellence and moving the focus from exclusivity and competition to inclusivity and equity, transforms vocational education and training from a mere tool to meet labour market needs, into a key factor for the growth of society. The innovation does not lie in allocating TVET the role of providing basic qualifications to lower educated segments of the population (this has already been the case in many countries). The new radical approach tries to move from the setting up of policies and mechanisms to provide basic skills, to the ambitious idea that TVET should provide the necessary key competencies to everybody, allowing the entire population to grow into excellence in their job within a real Lifelong Learning path.
- SDG8 (decent work and economic growth) is also an objective that is impacted by the new approach proposed by the Global CoVE.eu initiative (Crisonà, 2019). The local skills ecosystems, based on strong connections among all key stakeholders, provide the most fertile ground for policies related to support for entrepreneurship, the creation of decent jobs, and formalisation and growth of micro-, small-, and medium-sized enterprises.
- SDG10 (reduce inequalities within and among countries) is addressed by multiple core elements of the Global CoVEs.eu initiative (Crisonà, 2019) approach. Within countries, the new approach clearly focuses on the increasing opportunity for social growth and reduction of inequalities, as addressed before. In relation to the issue of inequalities among countries, the strong transnational multi-stakeholder collaboration promoted by the new approach aims at providing an international dimension to the issue of equality.
- SDG13 (take urgent action to combat climate change and its impacts) and SDG15 (protect, restore, and promote sustainable use of terrestrial ecosystems, sustainably manage forests, combat desertification, and halt and reverse land degradation and halt biodiversity loss) are both addressed by the Skillman Skills Ecosystems, which promote skills and human and institutional capacities on climate change and the transition to a green economy that respects the environment and is based on the principles of sustainable growth.

Given this framework, and the question of what challenges local communities face in achieving the SDGs through an approach where TVET leads the local skills ecosystem, the authors reflect on the meaning of excellence in TVET, referring to some of the key components that Skillman members have built into their CoVEs (n.d.) model:

- Economist David Finegold (1999) suggests that there are four elements required to create and sustain high-skills ecosystems: a catalyst, nourishment, a supportive host environment, and a high level of mutual interdependence.
- The EU Commission launched its plan, Partnerships for Excellence, aimed to support the constitution of CoVEs during 2021–2027.
- Skillman Global CoVEs.eu (Crisonà, 2019) is a model designed to set a transnational platform of skills ecosystems joined by Regional Authorities and Ministries of TVET, aimed to embed ethical values in education and training.

As part of the SIF debates, the network began to define its concept of "excellence" in TVET as the result of a common strategy that can strengthen individual capacities and/or the interdependent capacities of networked TVET providers and companies.

One of the other themes of SIF 2021 (Skillman Secretariat, 2021b) was "sharing is caring," a concept adopted to stimulate TVET providers and industry initiatives to find and implement a common pathway to vocational excellence for innovation and to sustainable competitiveness in advanced manufacturing.

This vision for a solidarity-based stakeholder relationship also includes and promotes the acquisition of green, digital, and ethical skills for all, for inclusive and sustainable development without gender discrimination (SDG5) and ensuring decent work for all (SDG8).

The main principles that the authors have identified behind this model, and that are also functional to the achievement of the SDGs, in relation to the next sections are:

- a strong ethical commitment that is the base for creating solid local skills ecosystems and the propellent for an effective international collaboration among them on environmental, social, and societal challenges;
- deployment of an effective skills foresight exercise, linked to the need for designing future societies through new and updated curricula and fine credentials;
- valorisation of existing experiences, linked to a "sharing is caring" approach to knowledge, that aim to fight inequalities and support fair transformations and social inclusion;
- assessment of excellence in TVET with a systematic approach, and strong connections with existing tools, that are related to identify and promote the best practices and examples of how the Lifelong Learning system can work and provide decision-makers with the right recommendations for the future.

35.3   Strong Ethical Commitment to International Cooperation for the Implementation of the SDGs

Such an inclusive approach to excellence in TVET, aimed at advancing the implementation of the SDGs, sees a compelling mandate in supporting international cooperation among TVET providers. This approach consists of mutual improvement and finding joint responses to unmet needs and new phenomena. The debate among the

Skillman members has assigned a value to the international dimensions and identified specific activities aimed at enabling upward convergence by:

- facilitating networking and exchanges of good practices at international level, supporting the move up the value chain of TVET excellence;
- bringing together partners that are at different stages of TVET excellence development and that have different characteristics;
- implementing assessments aimed to identify areas for international collaboration, peer learning international activities, and transnational training.

The ideas about internationalisation of TVET to achieve the goal of implementing the SDGs aim to connect members across countries and promote an international vision of future-proof TVET through vibrant multi-stakeholder collaboration. This internationalisation strategy also envisages promoting the mobility of CoVEs' leaders, staff, and learners, and provides for collaborative partnerships, strategic linkages, strong and lasting relationships, and transnational joint curriculum development.

From the authors' perspective, one of the most important approaches that this strategy could envisage is a cross-sectoral skills development activity, which values a joint analysis of future skills needs involving TVET providers and companies, with their territorial components, as well as international stakeholders and industry leaders. This scenario expects an ongoing exercise that includes technological scouting, providing a living vision for the skills of the future, and including a systemic perspective on technological trends that identifies the sectoral skills needs of a particular socio-economic system.

The active involvement of the connected organisations in this process, engaging all actors in a CoVEs' ecosystem, is fundamental to enhancing the international capacity of each component to innovate on a transnational basis and acting as drivers of excellence, to adapt skills rapidly to provide for evolving local needs.

35.4 Other TVET Potential in Relation to the SDGs

35.4.1 Internationalisation: Micro-Credentials, Digital, and Alternative Credentials

In order to create local skills ecosystems that also impact the recognition of qualifications, the authors see the need to adopt a tailored approach to learning in order to individualise and personalise learning and training opportunities with a particular focus on micro-credentials, and a shift from paper-based certificates to digitally signed credentials.

In this area, there is an ongoing dialogue between the Skillman Secretariat and the ENIC—NARIC (European Network of Information Centres in the European Region—National Academic Recognition Information Centres in the European

Union) network (Crisonà, 2021b), a well-known and recognised organisation in the field of accreditation in education. The two partners are jointly reflecting on how to meet the existing need for international reference standards (Chakroun & Keevy, 2018), by developing a strategy for micro-credentials in the field of advanced manufacturing to meet the growing needs of the labour market for graduates and professionals, who need to be able to acquire and demonstrate state-of-the-art knowledge, skills, and competencies quickly.

The approach of the Skillman CoVEs is to consider micro-credentials as the basis for a common system of international recognition. This aspect makes it necessary to strengthen the capacity of TVET skills ecosystems to move from National Qualification Frameworks to international recognition frameworks, by linking learning outcomes to micro-credentials that are valid within and beyond national borders.

As the authors believe that paper-based certificates need to be replaced by digitally signed certificates, it is also necessary to support local communities with systems that promote their ability to release digital certificates, such as the new Europass tool (EU, n.d.), which provides a legal framework that has the same legal value as paper-based certificates.

As learning credentials and transferability also mean better opportunities for learner and worker mobility, the international dimension of the local skills ecosystems must also include the improvement of their capacity to send and receive learners with international standards for different types of on-site and virtual mobility placements, study visits, study abroad periods, etc.

35.4.2   Curricula and Requirements for Digital Skills

Hazelkorn and Edwards (2019) state that:

> Across the EU, 90% of future jobs will require some level of digital skills, yet 44% of EU people do not have basic digital skills, and 24% of the working age population do not have upper secondary education ... At the same time, 40% of European businesses can't find appropriate people to work for them ... Sixty-five percent of children entering primary school today will work in occupations that don't currently exist ... (p.8).

According to the study prepared by Ecors and the Danish Technological Institute for the DG Communications Networks, Content & Technology of the European Commission in 2017, digital skills are increasingly important in all job profiles in the labour market (Curtarelli et al., 2017). They are also relevant to support the transition to a circular and greener economy, to meet the emerging occupational demand for green skills and sustainable development.

According to the authors, a valuable feature of the CoVEs.eu (Crisonà, 2019) model is the capacity to identify and keep up-to-date information on what skills are needed and when. This can help to develop the right and timely actions needed to overcome the obstacles resulting from the current and future mismatch among digital skills, supply, and demand, because if one goes beyond the basic skills that are essential to enter the digital world, one enters a labyrinth of enormous proportions.

To this end, we need to establish a continuous skills anticipation exercise at sectoral, central, and territorial levels. This will involve actors of the smart speciali-sation platform (European Commission S3P-Industry, n.d.), in a skills analysis that is not only oriented towards general requirements but also linked to territorial needs, in order to make it possible to develop curricula and teaching methods concretely linked to the rapid and continuous development of digital technologies.

By promoting Goal 8.3 of the SDGs, "… development-oriented policies that support productive activities, decent job creation, entrepreneurship, creativity and innovation" (Joshi et al., 2019, para. 8.3), it is necessary to recognise the crucial role of digital skills for employability, and full participation in society, by embedding all these concepts in foundational pillars of education systems (Goals 4.3 and 4.4). It also requires focusing on the design of specific learning outcomes that include at least skills related to coding, Internet of Things (IoT), robotics, Big Data, cloud technolo-gies, advanced human–machine interfaces, advanced automation, and virtual and augmented reality.

The above pillars are crucial in the CoVEs model for citizens' and especially workers' access to digital skills, and they are also the preconditions for the transition to Industry 4.0^2 paradigms in order to "enhance scientific research … [and] upgrade the technological capabilities of industrial sectors in all countries" (Joshi et al., 2019, para. 9.5). By promoting workers' full access to digital skills, the CoVEs model supports "… domestic technology development, research and innovation" (Joshi et al., para. 9.b) and promotes significant "… access to information and communica-tions technology" (Joshi et al., para. 9.b). Finally, the crucial role of digital skills for employability and full participation in society promoted as a cornerstone for teaching and reducing the digital divide and provides an opportunity to influence government and policy levels with clear and actionable goals.

The new paradigm that incorporates digital skills as key competencies of any profession and unites the interests of people, communities, businesses, and organisa-tions, must be used in the development of curricula, career guidance services, skills development, training, and retraining, in order to work towards making digital skills an integral part of all further actions by local communities engaged in the skills ecosystem. This paradigm will fully support SDG8 to promote "sustained, inclu-sive and sustainable economic growth, full and productive employment and decent work for all" (Joshi et al., 2019, para. 8), and ensure that local skills ecosystems also contribute to supporting SDG target 8.3 (Joshi et al., para. 8.3), in particular, by promoting bottom-up innovation capacity in productive activities.

These cornerstones include the adoption of appropriate methodological training solutions to embed ICT-based learning tools and environments into curricula. Methodological guidance is needed for the effective integration of digital learning methods, such as virtual or augmented reality, augmented, extended and mixed reality, validated adaptive microlearning (combination of technology and machine learning, person-centred approach to Lifelong Learning), gamification of learning, and deep encoding, etc.

---

[2] Sometimes referred to as the 4th Industrial Revolution

Taking all these aspects into account when developing training methods and curricula, also means that there needs to be a strong focus on teacher qualification systems, in line with the targets of SDG 4.c (Joshi et al., 2019, para. 4.c). Indeed, local CoVEs need to deliver concrete results to stimulate a debate on the need for digital skills, and on the strategies necessary for the digital transformation of services and economic sectors, by focusing on both infrastructure and skills.

35.4.3 Green Skills

The Skillman Skills Ecosystems intervention model aims at improving "… education, awareness-raising and human and institutional capacity on climate change mitigation, adaptation, impact reduction and early warning" (Joshi et al., 2019, para. 13.3), by recognising the need for a commitment to support the transition to a green economy, and an inclusive and smart society, where access to opportunity for all, competitiveness, and respect for the environment, are the key guiding principles for growth.

How can this commitment be implemented by local Skills Ecosystems?

> We are facing unprecedented challenges—social, economic and environmental—driven by accelerating globalisation and a faster rate of technological developments. At the same time, those forces are providing us new opportunities for human advancement. Schools and VET providers are asked to prepare youngsters for jobs that have not yet been created, for technologies that have not yet been invented, to solve problems that have not yet been anticipated. (Organisation for Economic Co-operation and Development, 2020, p. 9)

In this context, the ability to anticipate local market trends, and the evolution of skills needs in conjunction with global trends, are key advantages for local communities, which can act as local sensors of an interconnected network of skills ecosystems, by providing shared knowledge and taking interlinked initiatives. By being anchored in the territory, this system has all the necessary conditions to guide principles such as sustainable production, green innovation, green economy, sustainability, circular economy, etc., and can represent these concepts in an international dimension that guides design and development under the principles of the SDGs.

The focus on environmental protection should, therefore, be the overarching approach for all actions taken by local skills ecosystems to integrate the greening of VET into their cornerstones. This approach can refer, in particular, to the development and implementation of green learning units, curricula, green training and learning opportunities, and career guidance services, and requires solutions to equip the workforce with technical skills, knowledge, values, and attitudes to develop and support sustainable social, economic, and environmental outcomes in business, industry, and the community. Applied to the advanced manufacturing sector, which is Skillman's main focus, it includes the skills to investigate and design solutions in response to real-world challenges such as those relating to clean and abundant drinking water, food supply issues, and renewable energy.

35.4.4 Twin Transformations and Social Inclusion

Reflections on the Skillman ecosystem model show a strong commitment by stakeholders in supporting the innovation of TVET systems to increase their responsiveness to emerging global challenges to "reduce inequality within and among countries" (Joshi et al., 2019, para. 10). The attention to the digitalisation of production processes in advanced manufacturing, and the increasing need for digital skills among the different target groups and actors (people, communities, companies, and organisations) stimulate the debate on the design of revised or new solutions, especially in terms of curriculum development and updating, career guidance services, joint upskilling and re-skilling actions, and further training.

Particular attention is given to the importance of curriculum co-design, adopting an approach that also aims to provide leadership to the process itself, in order to promote a shared vision of the future based on mutual understanding and cooperation among local skills ecosystems. The idea behind this approach is in line with promoting SDG4: "to ensure inclusive and equitable quality education and promote Lifelong Learning opportunities for all" (Joshi et al., 2019, para. 4). It requires finding an appropriate way to introduce ethical skills in advanced manufacturing, including measures that help address inclusion and diversity.

It also promotes the adoption of shared values such as respect for life, equality, gender equality and non-discrimination, and social inclusion and integration of people with special needs/fewer opportunities, through innovative and integrated approaches. In this direction, social inclusion is a prerequisite for the development of a more just, equal, and sustainable economy, as explained in the ethical campaign that Skillman launched in 2021. It states that

> ethical principles for education should not only inspire strategic action plans and systemic change, but also … [enable] the recognition and integration of ethical competencies … [into] new and revised curricula in order to achieve an inclusive and peaceful society capable of achieving all the … SDGs. (Skillman Secretariat, 2021a)

The challenge for local communities, which act as skills ecosystems, is therefore to open up vocational education and training to all, regardless of regional location, gender, ethnicity, age, and social or economic status.

Accordingly, it is essential to guide a multi-stakeholder collaboration to transform TVET systems, "future-proof" them, and redesign existing curricula to promote both "Skills for Life" and "Skills for Work." The ethical Skillman campaign looks at TVET excellence in an inclusive dimension where it is:

- not just a high-quality level of training and education;
- not a matter for the elites and not something that belongs to elites;
- not a status or a level, but an organisational dimension linked to the TVET community as a whole, giving results at an aggregate dimension that goes behind the education and that addresses the whole society;
- something that implies an enlarged, more comprehensive, and inclusive conceptualisation of skills provision; something that addresses innovation, pedagogy,

social justice, Lifelong Learning, transversal skills, and organisational and continuing professional learning and community needs;

- a sustainable goal for a large aggregate of subjects aiming at the upward levelling of their performance, and not at a destructive competition to the exclusion of others; and
- a reason to look at a holistic and homeostatic approach to education that makes all parties in need of working together, increasing the attractiveness of TVET (Skillman Secretariat, 2021a).

35.5   High-Level Decision-Makers Strategic Recommendations for the Future

During the AS 2022 (Skillman Secretariat, 2022a), the authors discussed and identified, with the group of High-Level Decision-Makers, four main areas that could be analysed and developed to promote an "inclusive approach to excellence in TVET." These four elements were considered by the stakeholders, as Strategic Recommendations for the future of education, and for promoting a larger debate during SIF 2022 (Skillman Secretariat, 2022b):

1. Revising what a Lifelong Learning system should prioritise. This aspect refers to all UN SDGs goals, but in particular, to Goal 4 (Joshi et al., 2019, para. 4).
2. How should a Lifelong Learning system work? (Is there an ideal pathway?). This aspect is in relation to SDGs 4, 8, and 9 (Joshi et al., paras. 4, 8, 9).
3. What megatrends are influencing the Lifelong Learning system? This aspect highlights relations with SDGs 1 (poverty), 2 (sustainable agriculture), 3 (health/covid), 6 (water), 7 (energy), 13 (climate change), 15 (desertification), and 16 (peace) (Joshi et al., paras. 1, 2, 3, 6, 7, 13, 15, 16).
4. What partnerships and alliances can support the Lifelong Learning system? This aspect is in relation to SDG17 (Joshi et al., paras. 17.6–17.9).

35.5.1   Revising What a Lifelong Learning System Should Prioritise—Identifying Key Competencies

There is a worldwide shared agreement that humanity is facing a paradigm shift from initial education systems to Lifelong Learning systems. The group of High-Level Decision-Makers are convinced that people should be provided with the necessary competencies to be able to upskill and navigate evolving careers for their whole lives. Europe has spent significant resources in developing frameworks conceptualising key competencies and life competencies, e.g., Lifecomp (Sala et al., 2020), Entrecomp (Bacigalupo et al., 2016), and Digicomp (Vuorikari et al., 2022).

At the same time, the decision-makers have not been bold enough to bring real change to how the education systems structure initial education. Most systems are still based on early and rigid student tracking, which mimics the current structure of the labour market, linking qualifications to existing occupations, and pre-determining what place in society children will have as soon as they are 12 or 13 years old. There are policies and tools (e.g., educational pathways, upskilling opportunities, and validation of informal and nonformal learning) that have been developed to reduce this effect and provide opportunities for individuals for upgrading their qualifications. But the reality is that education systems do not put enough effort into providing all students with the key competencies that are the real drivers for Lifelong Learning. The priority remains subject-based study and learning outcomes on which students are assessed to specific standards of knowledge and expertise. The education system is aware that students possess different key competencies, but instead of addressing this unbalance, it uses it to track them in different study programmes.

There is only one reason for reversing the current logic, and making a stronger effort in providing students with comparable key competencies. It is idealistic and refers to providing real equitable education and "at least comparable" opportunities for all students. There might be some political bias here. The economy does generate a continuous evolution of occupations, which makes the current objective of education of providing qualifications relevant for the labour market, outdated. Continuous upskilling is becoming inevitable in all sectors. If we do not provide students with the key competencies necessary to engage in it, the skills gap will continue to be a significant mark of the European labour market. A European Commission study (Temussi, 2022) found that there were more than 1 million unmet job offers in 2021. Evidence demonstrates that below tertiary educational attainment, people just do not engage in continuing training.

Especially in initial education, key competencies should become a priority, not only in terms of how the labour market works, but rather, in terms of what our society does or, to some extent, does not do. It is a package of key competencies linked to active citizenship. The group of High-Level Decision-Makers pointed out one as an example: in a world of infinite information, the capacity of individuals to assess the sources and become unbiased and active members of society is becoming an essential trait for democracies.

35.6 How Should a Lifelong Learning System Work? (Is There an Ideal Pathway?)

The shift from traditional educational systems centred on rigid initial education processes, to real Lifelong Learning systems started long ago. As mentioned before, several reforms have been introduced to incentivise continuing training, recognition of non-formal learning, and transparency of qualifications systems. The recommendation in the short term, is to continue with reforms that build on these achievements and focus on improving the effectiveness of existing educational systems. As stakeholders have bought into these reforms, teachers have gone through extensive training, and countries have all developed different cases of best practice that they are willing to share.

The first new trend is the development of pedagogical approaches that allow students to develop strong transversal and key competencies, while addressing complex problems. A good example is the adoption of transdisciplinary programmes. The second trend, which further contributes to the creation of a real flexible Life-long Learning system, is the joint development of micro-credentials and individual learning accounts. As with many other educational reforms, these two have been conceptualised within the European Commission, but they can be easily integrated into national systems, thanks to the substantial efforts made in developing transparent educational systems with learning outcomes-based qualifications.

The recommendation to key stakeholders for the long term is to be bolder. The development of key competencies and citizenship competencies should slowly become the priority for education systems, reducing or postponing to late cycles the focus on labour market occupations. There is a limit to what students can absorb in their compulsory education. The attempt to introduce key competencies in existing curricula in many countries has created a conflict with the extension of subject-based content that students can reasonably absorb. Years of experience in integrating key competencies in education will solve many of these conundrums, but in the end, if countries aim to establish real and effective Lifelong Learning systems, the priority should be given to key competencies. This will require a deep revision of how a society conceives initial education and initial qualifications, as well as what will be the role of teachers. But the progress many countries are making, and the willingness to share experiences and build on each other's best practices, make this vision less utopian than it may appear at first glance.

35.6.1 What Megatrends Are Influencing the Lifelong Learning System?

There are a number of megatrends that affect the continuous reforms of education systems. The first that was highlighted by the AS 2022 (Skillman Secretariat, 2022a) participants, is de-globalisation and/or re-globalisation. The COVID-19 pandemic and the Ukraine international crisis have put into question the globalisation model that has been dominant since the 1990s. Both macro events are forcing countries and companies to reflect on the sustainability of an industrial production model based on extreme outsourcing and delocalisation. Lifelong Learning systems will inevitably have to monitor how a revision of the current industrial model will affect human capital development needs, and adapt their services. From a more long-term perspective, Lifelong Learning systems should have the ambition of strengthening democratic values through the creation of strong citizenship competencies and values, with the final aim of eliminating any support for armed resolutions of international crises.

The second megatrend is the green revolution. Awareness has finally moved up from pioneers to the whole political, industrial, and economic world. Changes are coming fast, and the pace will only increase with time. In Europe, governments, and the EU, in particular, are using their powers of setting standards to force industry and civil society to embrace change. Lifelong Learning systems are trying to cope with the revolution, but it is clear that more than initial education is needed to continue the education component of Lifelong Learning systems that will fill the growing skills gap created by the green revolution.

The third megatrend highlighted is the digital revolution, and its impact on what digital competencies students should learn through education, and how they can use digital teaching and learning processes to acquire qualifications more effectively. Also, in this case, a continuing education provision should be enforced to address any skills gap in the population that was born before the digital revolution. The pandemic not only caused huge challenges to education provision but also forced countries to realise the potential of the digital revolution for education.

The last two megatrends identified by the AS 2022 (Skillman Secretariat, 2022a) participants refer to endogenous changes in Lifelong Learning that have been forced by the aforementioned exogenous trends. The first of these is the pressing need to make educational planning more flexible towards the evolving needs of the labour market, as well as students' lifelong careers. The current initial education systems, in particular, are still based on the twentieth-century foundations and contain governance and administrative provisions that become barriers that too often overcome political will to reform. The second is the process of creating flexible and combined qualifications (e.g. economics and art), supported by solid key competencies arming individuals for a flexible and unforeseeable future.

35.7 What Partnerships and Alliances Can Support the Lifelong Learning System?

35.7.1 Cross-Country Networks/Partnerships

Over the last 30 years, educational providers in Europe have greatly increased their networking activities at sub-national, national, and international levels. Higher education institutions started earlier, benefiting from the boost of the Erasmus Program (n.d.), now 35 years old. The trend has now expanded to all educational providers, with the focus slowly moving from initial education to the broader Lifelong Learning dimension.

The factors behind this process have not changed; on the contrary, they have strengthened the trend and expanded it to a wider range of providers and educational levels. Converging policy reforms in most EU countries (e.g., the increased operational and financial autonomy of educational providers), a bonanza of opportunities for partnering and learning across 29 different countries, and a very supportive financial framework, have made Europe *the* international case of best practice in the area of cross-country networks and partnerships.

One of the most interesting aspects of this trend is that the process of moving from a non-competitive environment (typical of compulsory public education in Europe) to a competitive one (for money, for students), determined an increase in the establishment of cross-country networks and partnerships. This atypical link between competition and cooperation is mainly due to the nature of the educational sector, and the strong will of the EU for exploiting the strengths and complementarities of the different systems. In the last few years, two developments have been observed. The first is geographical expansion. As mentioned before, the EU has been the strongest driver behind the process of inter-institutional cooperation in education, generating a huge networking volume among EU institutions; however, more and more, these networks have outgrown the old continent in all directions. EU institutions have interiorised the value of peer learning and continuous development and started to look to other countries for different models of excellence. On the other hand, the EU's bustling cooperation environment has become a beacon for many countries and their educational institutions. Pressure for joining networks from Africa, for example, has become stronger over recent years, and most networks have willingly welcomed the new members. Partnerships like Skillman have become effective worldwide networks.

The second trend is the growth of cooperation of TVET providers, in particular, the Centres of Excellence (European Training Foundation, 2020). This trend is bringing two key innovations: an additional attention to different forms of learning (non-formal, informal learning, adult learning, etc.) and a stronger involvement in the world of work.

35.8   Moving to 2030 Driven by Education Systems

The ideas presented here are the outcome of the interaction among Skillman members over the last years, and in the last AS (Skillman Secretariat, 2022a). The value of information-sharing and knowledge co-creation is the key aspect that this chapter wishes to highlight.

The authors would like to use the arguments discussed in this chapter as a basis for a lively debate during the next SIF 2022 (Skillman Secretariat, 2022b), and to stimulate further reflection and consideration on the future of education in general, in the belief that the best way to find answers is to ask the right questions.

The authors believe that education should have an important cross-cutting role in achieving the SDGs. Education is a key tool to achieve the changes needed to address effectively the biggest challenges in society. Designing a vision for education in 2030 cannot be as simple as it was before the pandemic, and before the invasion of Ukraine. Megatrends and universal concerns are changing dramatically the way we look at the future. The objectives of education should be revised. Providing the skills and competencies that a fast-evolving labour market requires, cannot be education's sole or main purpose. The development of green consciousness and active citizenship can no longer be taken for granted, they must be operationalised and assessed. The same is true for the development of a real Lifelong Learning system, where students are provided with the necessary key competencies to grow throughout their lives and careers. The authors do not see this as an idealistic afflatus; they see this as a real and only viable solution to the challenges and megatrends identified in the chapter. The authors see the role of TVET as a catalyst for the creation of local skills ecosystems, in which to embed their new vision of education. The local dimension is crucial, because it helps the creation of real and strong networks among different stakeholders.

Reviewing the objective of education for the twenty-first century requires a seismic systemic change and cannot be implemented in a conflicted environment with actors pulling in different directions or engaging only when it fits their interests. The creation of cohesive partnerships, where commitment and purpose are shared, is the only way to achieve sustainable change, exemplified by the targets of SDG17.

At a first glance, TVET may not be expected to be the first education sector to embrace the proposed evolution. Indeed, in the medium to long term, this new approach should start from primary education and even earlier. However, TVET is the sector that is more connected to our society and world of work. It is the first sector that becomes obsolete if it fails to adapt to evolving challenges. It is the sector where stakeholders' cooperation is stronger and continuous. It is natural for the TVET sector to pioneer this new approach.

In summary, there are many challenges that local communities need to address in order to achieve the SDGs through an approach where TVET leads the local skills ecosystem. They need to work to move in the direction presented here, by focusing their attention on issues such as designing and managing learning pathways that are open to all; by designing micro-credentials, digital and alternative credentials, digital and green skills; by inclusion, avoiding inequality within and between countries: by promoting understanding and collaboration between skills ecosystems and prioritising and focusing on megatrends.

The challenges identified in this chapter are intended to stimulate debate among citizens who care about the future of education and the participants in the SIF 2022 (Skillman Secretariat, 2021b). This is not only about available solutions and ideas for better education but also about the implementation of principles that will determine the future of education, the future of society and by responsibility towards the community of educators.

References

Bacigalupo, M., Kampylis, P., Punie, Y., & Van den Brande, G. (2016). *EntreComp: The entrepreneurship competence framework.* Publication Office of the European Union. https://doi.org/10.2791/593884

Chakroun, B., & Keevy, J. (2018). *Digital credentialing: Implications for the recognition of learning across borders*. United Nations Education, Scientific and Cultural Organisation. https://unesdoc. unesco.org/ark:/48223/pf0000264428

Crisonà, G. (2019). *Global CoVEs—The future of TVET/TVET in the future*. Skillman.eu. https:// docs.google.com/document/d/1jIkP35ajS0HdXOVrWXtmVYACAH2NoiogoH3Bt9noS9k/ edit

Crisonà, G. (2021a). *Workplace-based training in the European Union and the experience of Skillman*. In S. Ra, S. Jagannathan, & R. Maclean (Eds.), Powering a learning society during an age of disruption (pp. 241–257). Springer. https://doi.org/10.1007/978-981-16-0983-1_17

Crisonà, G. (2021b). *ENIC—NARIC pledges future of alliance*. https://youtube/BEXhwHEaGNA? t=31023

Curtarelli, M., Gualtieri, V., Shater Jannati, M., & Donlevy, V. (2017). *ICT for work: Digital skills in the workplace: Final report*. European Union. https://doi.org/10.2759/498467

ENIC—NARIC network. https://www.enic-naric.net/

Erasmus Programme. (n.d.). https://www.erasmusprogramme.com/post/what-is-the-erasmus-pro gramme

European Commission S3P-Industry. (n.d.). *Industrial modernisation*. http://tiny.cc/qlizuz

European Union. (n.d.). *Europass digital credentials*. https://europa.eu/europass/en/europass-dig ital-credentials

European Training Foundation. (2020). *Centres of vocational excellence an engine for vocational education and training development: An international study*. https://doi.org/10.2816/771725

Finegold, D. (1999). Creating self-sustaining, high-skill ecosystems. *Oxford Review of Economic Policy, 15*(1), 60–81. https://doi.org/10.1093/oxrep/15.1.60

Hazelkorn, E., & Edwards, J. (2019). *Skills and smart specialisation: The role of vocational education and training in smart specialisation strategies*. https://op.europa.eu/publication/manifesta tion_identifier/PUB_KJNA29875ENN

Joshi, A., Gonzalez Morales, L., Szymon, K., & Helton, A. (2019). *A knowledge organization system for the United Nations Sustainable Development Goals*. http://metadata.un.org/sdg

Organisation for Economic Co-operation and Development. (2020). What students learn matters: Towards a 21st century curriculum. *OECD Publishing*. https://doi.org/10.1787/d86d4d9a-en

Sala, A., Punie, Y., Garkov, V., & Cabrera, M. (2020). *LifeComp: The European framework for personal, social and learning to learn key competence*. European Commission, & Joint Research Centre. Publication office of the European Union. https://doi.org/10.2760/302967

Skillman Secretariat. (2021a). *Redefining the future of learning*. Skillman.eu. https://skillman.eu/ ethical-campaign-to-redefine-the-future-of-learning

Skillman Secretariat. (2021b). *Skillman international forum 2021b*. Skillman.eu. https://skillman. eu/sif2021

Skillman Secretariat. (2022a). *Alliance summit 2022a*. Skillman.eu. https://skillman.eu/as2022

Skillman Secretariat. (2022b). *Skillman international forum 2022b*. Skillman.eu. https://skillman. eu/sif2022

Temussi, M. (2022). *Alliance summit 2022—Presentation within the session: Ideas on strategies to develop products and opportunities within the TVET alliance* [Speech/video recording]. https:// learn.skillman.eu/course/view.php?id=137

Vuorikari, R., Kluzer, S., & Punie, Y. (2022). *DigComp 2.2, The digital competence framework for citizens. With new examples of knowledge, skills and attitudes*. European Commission, Joint Research Centre. Publication office of the European Union. https://op.europa.eu/publication/ manifestation_identifier/PUB_KJNA31006ENN

United Nations Department of Economic and Social Affairs. (2022). *Sustainable development*. Sdgs.un.org

United Nations Education, Scientific and Cultural Organisation. Institute for Lifelong Learning. (2016). *Conceptions and realities of lifelong learning*. UNESCO. https://unesdoc.unesco.org/ ark:/48223/pf0000245626

Part VII
Moving the Sustainable Development Goals Forward: Alternative Perspectives

Chapter 36
The Sustainable Development Goals and STEM Education: Paradoxes and Reframings

Mellita Jones and Caroline Smith

Abstract The United Nations Sustainable Development Goals (SDGs) are the successor to the Millennium Development Goals (MDGs, 2015)—eight international development goals for the year 2015, which were established after the United Nations (UN) Millennium Summit (UN, 2000).

36.1 Introduction

The United Nations Sustainable Development Goals (SDGs) are the successor to the Millennium Development Goals (MDGs, 2015)—eight international development goals for the year 2015, which were established after the United Nations (UN) Millennium Summit (UN, 2000). However, it remains debatable whether the MDGs achieved anything like they set out to accomplish, and in fact Vandemoortele (2018), a co-architect of the MDGs, has gone as far as commenting that they achieved little more than "[p]rogress for better-off people, regress for the planet" (p. 85).

Of course, the hope is that lessons have been learned and the SDGs will be more effective than their predecessors. At their heart is a plan of action for people, prosperity, planet, partnership, and peace (UN Sustainable Development Group, n.d.). These "5Ps" are to be achieved by identifying and addressing 17 Goals relating to areas of development needs. These areas have been drawn from the wickedly entwined global crises of environmental degradation, climate change, gross inequities, and poverty, both within and between countries across the world—the so-called "permacrises" or "polycrises" of our time (Bendell, 2022; Tooze, 2021).

M. Jones
Faculty of Arts and Education, National School of Education, Australian Catholic University, Ballarat, VIC, Australia
e-mail: mellita.jones@acu.edu.au

C. Smith (✉)
School of Education, College of Arts, Law and Education, University of Tasmania, Burnie, TAS, Australia
e-mail: caroline.smith1@utas.edu.au

655

Education is widely seen as a key pathway to achieving the SDGs—indeed it has a goal in its own right (SDG4)—and within education, science and technology are regarded as integral to achieving many areas of the SDG agenda. However, we argue that science and technology in their latest iteration as STEM (Science, Technology, Engineering, Mathematics) contribute paradoxically both to exacerbating the global crises and to having the potential to help address many of these complex issues.

As other chapters in this volume have explored, much of current formal education is underpinned by a particular Western ideology, neoliberalism, as are the SDGs themselves (Bendell, 2022). This ideology has created a contradiction that makes achievement of the SDGs' purportedly balanced approach to addressing social, economic, and environmental needs, fraught with difficulties. We explore this contradiction by briefly examining the rise of the SDGs from their roots in colonialism and show that this parallels the roles of science and technology in the industrialisation of Western society. We highlight the links between these constructs and the development agenda and mass education. We consider the impact of the now overarching neoliberal ideology that permeates STEM education and point out how, in its current framing, STEM education is not well positioned to take the sustainability agenda forward. We conclude the chapter by considering an alternative framework for how STEM education could (and we believe, should) be reframed towards a more socially just orientation that might better achieve the "5Ps" outcomes of the Goals in a manner that is truly sustainable.

36.2 Background: The Rise of the Development Agenda

Within government and Non-Government Organisations (NGO) circles, the SDGs have been adopted as the main pathway for considering sustainability at the global scale, and are being referred to, acted and reported on to varying degrees across nations and their jurisdictions (e.g., United Nations SDG Monitoring and Reporting Toolkit for UN Country Teams, 2018; United Nations Sustainable Development Group, n.d.). They have tended to be accepted as aspirational, despite having arisen from the nefarious, intertwined history of decolonisation and industrialisation, and are entrenched within a neoliberal ideology (Bendell, 2022; Carter & Smith, Chapter 3, this volume), that is perpetuated through mass education (Reid, 2019).

Conceptually and in its rhetorical use, the *development* construct is heavily contested (e.g. McGillivray, 2016). Kingsbury (2016) aligns development with those "outside the industrialized world [as they] attempt to improve their conditions of life through material and social means" (p. 14)—conditions that are enjoyed in Global North countries due to advances in industrialisation. Kingsbury's development notion parallels the SDGs, which also focus on economic and social inequities experienced by the world's least developed countries (UN, 2015), and are, as such, largely framed as re-orientating the life conditions in the world of the poor Global South towards those of the affluent Global North.

Historically, the rise of the development agenda arose during the period of mass European decolonisation in the latter half of the twentieth century, which saw the transition of colonial states (designated "developing countries") to so-called "independence" (Desai, 2017). Economic drivers, alongside recognition of the extreme human rights violations from ongoing global and regional conflicts, were the impetus for change. This led to the beginnings of the mass withdrawal of European colonial powers from colonised countries, where indigenous populations had been denied the ability to define their own capacity-building and governance (Hira, 2012).

As part of their withdrawal, the colonial powers felt a (nascent) responsibility to provide development support in the transition to independence, while, in some cases, at the same time insisting on crippling financial reparations, such as in the case of India (Chakrabarti & Patnaik, 2018). However, this anti-emancipatory agenda largely ignored indigenous populations' histories, cultures, and desires; rather, it exhorted them to aspire to an essentially Western worldview through the growing influence of late-stage capitalism, known as neoliberalism. Development plans were imposed on newly independent economies that encouraged their participation in global trade, enabled by advances in transport and communication, mediated by science, technology, industrialisation, and financialisaton (Desai, 2017; Rostow, 1991).

"Development" was couched in a rhetoric of aid and assistance, but the reality for many former colonies was that it was tainted by the underlying agendas of their former colonial powers, who asserted new forms of power and influence that essentially maintained or even increased dependence—an outcome largely enabled by the scientific and technological advancements underpinning industrialisation (Desai, 2017). For example, most newly independent, decolonised countries had agrarian economies, in contrast to the industrialised economies of the former colonial powers (Desai), due to a lack of access to evolving modern science and technology (Rostow, 1991). This permitted a trade dependency to develop whereby the agrarian countries would provide primary products, usually for labour costs set by industrialised countries that far undermined their worth (Desai), to the former colonial powers whose technology could expedite processing and manufacturing. The agrarian countries would then buy back the value-added industrial goods, and what is more, they were required to pay for them in the hard currencies of the colonial powers, thus setting up a new form of economic dependency. Industrial goods were (and are) highly priced compared with primary products, which decreased in value as more producers entered the market throughout the period of decolonisation. This, coupled with the requirements to re-finance development assistance "start-up" loans (with interest), which neophyte nation states could ill-afford, has kept the previous colonisers entrenched in positions of power (Beihami & Meifa, 2014; Desai). As Klieman predicted as early as 1976, "[t]he period following the Second World War witnessed the final liquidation of colonial empires. It is sometimes argued, however, that the trade patterns imposed under colonialism may continue to exist long after the termination of direct colonial rule" (p. 460).

The inevitable defaults on loans instigated a "Third World" debt crisis. In response, Western nations established economic policies to assist developing nations to meet loan repayments, and to exhort them to compete better in the burgeoning global "free" market. This economic policy, borne out of the 1989 Washington Consensus (Irwin & Ward, 2021), saw further loans provided to meet the debt, but which came with conditions of structural adjustment (Desai, 2017). This forced many struggling post-colonial governments to alter their economic practices to align with the free market agendas of the lending institutions (i.e., the World Bank, the International Monetary Fund (IMF), the United States Department of the Treasury—conglomerates of the wealthy Global North).

In addition, equipment, expertise, and necessary resources for development projects were required to be obtained from the industrialised donor countries, meaning that funds flowed back to them rather than supporting local investment and resourcing. When machinery and other equipment break down, there is often not the expertise locally to repair or replace them once a project has terminated, because of lack of training of local people and a lack of equipment. Often this is addressed by the hiring of expatriate workers ("expats") and importing of industrial machinery and goods (often of an obsolete standard in the industrialised countries) from the techno-logically advancing donor countries to provide equipment and expertise, rather than providing training for local people to enable them to take over the projects. These practices further exacerbate the already uneven economic relationship.

Moreover, rather than equalising the market to increase their capacity to partic-ipate in global trade, large, well-established Global North companies were able to become transnational, ultimately squeezing out smaller competitors. This saw the control of the global market by private companies, a form of unfettered capi-talism, where increasingly, government intervention was minimised, if not dispensed with altogether. This uneven pattern of development amplified the rise of neoliber-alism, an ideology that "cultivate[s] individualistic, competitive, acquisitive, and entrepreneurial behaviours" (Carter, 2017, p. 3) and a prevailing discourse of "growth" and "catch up" (Fine, 2013). That the SDGs are located within the same economic framework is deeply problematic, begging the question as to how they will be able to achieve economic and social equity. This again points to the contradiction that seems to be contained within SDG8, which calls for "[p]romot(ing) sustained, inclusive and sustainable economic growth, full and productive employment and decent work for all" (United Nations Department of Economic and Social Affairs (n.d.); see also Adelman, 2018; Bendell, 2022).

36.2.1   *Neoliberal Influences on Development*

Neoliberalism is "an extreme form of unregulated capitalism" (Ife, 2016, p. 20), promoting free trade, individualism, self-interest, competition, consumerism, and a culture of blaming the poor as not being able to help themselves (Fitzsimons, 2017; Ife, 2016). Its globalised, free-market ideology exacerbates the relative inability of countries of the Global South to compete in free-market trade, even as they are compelled to do so by the forces described above (Jamrozik, 2009). Hence, they become even more indebted to institutions like the IMF and World Bank, and dependent on "development aid." Neither institution, in their current forms, is noted for enabling emancipatory outcomes (Toomey, 2009). As such, economic and social inequities are perpetuated rather than reduced, and as Ledwith (2011) contends, the world is at the mercy of a "western worldview that is unhealthily preoccupied with …[a] profit imperative [that] is both undermining human wellbeing and destroying the planet" (p. 2). Globalisation has made the neoliberal agenda almost ubiquitous (McKay, 2016), with many countries unable to compete and with limited opportunity to develop their economies otherwise. China is the obvious exception, managing to engage in high levels of economic growth through what Harvey (2005) terms "a particular kind of market economy that increasingly incorporates neoliberal elements interdigitated with authoritarian centralized control" (p. 120).

For many, this worldview has entrenched the view that economic growth and competition are signs of progress, and acquisition of material goods is a measure of success (Rostow, 1991; Smith & Watson, 2018). The triumph of neoliberalism in the Global South is seen by its power brokers as a positive sign of development. The SDGs themselves refer to "sustained economic growth" (UN, 2015, p. 2; UN Sustainable Development Group, n.d.), a notion that has given rise to a number of critiques of the Goals (e.g., Adelman, 2018; Bendell, 2022; Eisenmenger et al., 2020). A key argument is that continued growth is clearly an unsustainable proposition for a planet straining under the demand for its natural resources, which are a requirement for the industrialisation needed to underpin economic growth in the Global North. Such ubiquitous notions of progress, which relate to consumer-driven value, not only threaten ecological systems, but also preserve the conditions where the wealthy are increasingly able to access further wealth and opportunities at the expense of the poor (Dutta, 2011). Hence, not only are cultures' and peoples' wellbeing undermined by this form of "development," but environmental sustainability is impacted by colonising and industrial development practices. By encouraging inappropriate consumerism and treating colonised countries' natural resources as commodities to be exploited, the impacts on Earth's fragile ecosystems are further compromised (Fine, 2013; Ledwith, 2011). Nowhere was this more clearly seen than the impact on the Amazon rainforest and its indigenous peoples through land clearing for soy production to feed livestock in the Global North, which peaked during the 2000s. Thankfully, global outrage and protest have, at least for now, placed a moratorium on this activity (Greenpeace, 2016), though similar destructive exploits are still being carried out in many other parts of the world. Earth's natural resources continue to be depleted at an unsustainable rate, waste continues to pile up, and formerly biodiverse ecosystems are on the brink of collapse or have collapsed already (Ripple et al., 2020). Ecosystem destruction and harvesting of wild species is also considered the likely underlying cause of the latest zoonotic COVID-19 pandemic (Lawler et al., 2021).

These exploitative impacts on the people of the Global South and their ecosystems have been made possible by advances in science and technology, which have enabled industrialisation and mass production. This continues to have a substantial reliance on burning fossil fuels as energy sources, directly leading to the current climate emergency. At the same time, gaps in living standards and quality of life outcomes have been exacerbated both within and between countries, as growthism drives wealth creation for the few at the expense of the many (Wilkinson & Pickett, 2010). This is also driven in part by another, newer face of science and technology, the so-called 4th Industrial Revolution ("IR4"), mediated by the "Big Tech" companies through the development of cyber-physical systems (Davies, 2017). These are the automated or augmented systems based on Artificial Intelligence (AI), such as robots, intelligent buildings, implantable medical devices, self-driving cars and planes, and so on. AI also provides the means for increased online surveillance and data theft, as well as persuasion to engage in endless consumption through relentless influencing, mediated by online algorithms (Zuboff, 2019).

Although some of these advances undoubtedly provide an improved quality of life for those who have the means to afford them, it remains of great concern that the main drivers behind IR4 are a very small, exclusive cohort of mainly Generation Y white men, operating from Silicon Valley (Walsh, 2022). IR4 is now increasingly associated with the projected world-wide technology-driven displacement of 85 million people from their employment within the next few years (World Economic Forum, 2020). Whilst new employment trajectories will also be created, the World Economic Forum's (2020) *Future of Jobs* survey shows that the nature of this displacement will be in jobs that require lower skills and levels of education, whilst the growing digitally based workforce will demand higher skills and qualifications, and hence an increasingly educated, yet smaller, workforce. Consequently, IR4 is set to widen already existing disparities both within and between countries, as the advanced economies leapfrog those parts of the world that continue to struggle with access to their most basic of needs, such as clean water, food, sanitation, and security (Davies, 2017). This directly impacts SDG 1 (No Poverty), SDG 2 (Zero Hunger), SDG5 (Gender Equality), and SDG8 (Decent Work and Economic Growth), as well as all others indirectly. These social inequities are a consequence of unabated neoliberal capitalism, driven by a profit imperative, and made possible by and dependent on advances in science and technology as key enablers. They are critically problematic because they ignore the voices, values, and worldviews of the vast majority of the world's people who have been denied any meaningful input into the shaping and bringing forth of this brave new world (Walsh).

These are among the key crises the SDGs are supposed to address, but their many inbuilt contradictions make it difficult. SDG4, "Ensure inclusive and equitable quality education and promote lifelong learning opportunities for all," implies that education has the power to bring about a more sustainable future. However, many education systems are themselves bound by the same neoliberal drivers identified above. Indeed, education that is underpinned by neoliberal ideology could be considered to be largely responsible for perpetuating the conditions that counteract the notion of sustainable development and global equity, as its curriculum has (and continues to be) almost exclusively preoccupied with employment outcomes, defined and encouraged to support economic growth and competition between nations. To examine this notion further, we now turn a closer eye to the rise of mass education and the place of science and technology within it.

36.2.2 The Neoliberal Shaping of Education

Widely recognised as a fundamental human right, education should be a "good thing." However, education can equally reify inequity. As Russell and Bajaj (2015) indicate, "curriculum and schooling are oriented to different notions of what it means to be an ideal citizen" (p. 94); and since the 1970s, governments that control education through prescribed curricula and associated funding (Purcell, 2012; Reid, 2019), have sought to sustain neoliberalism as their ideology. Thus, notions of economic growth and competition are promoted and valued above concerns for social justice and sustainability, and government-controlled, mass education ensures these ideals are promulgated throughout society.

The need for mass education has its genealogy in advances in the science and technology that brought forth and accelerated the rise of the European industrial revolution in the seventeenth century, powered by the ability to mass-extract fossil fuels, firstly coal, and then oil and gas. This revolution enabled the production of machines and factories, which replaced much of manual labour, and heralded the beginning of mass production. People with basic literacy and numeracy skills were needed to operate the machines, while others required further education to develop managerial and engineering processes (Becker & Woessmann, 2019). Later, the discovery and mass supply of electricity was to transform lives and living standards of those in countries positioned to invest in these products of science and technology. These advances saw the rapid growth in the economies of the Global North that became industrialised, dubbed "developed" in reference to their strong, industrialised economies. This trajectory culminated in the stage of late capitalism known as neoliberalism, discussed above.

The advances experienced over the past two centuries are inextricably linked to advances in the harnessing of science and technology to economic growth, not only in increased productivity, but also in health outcomes and access to information and communication technologies. These gains in standard of living in an increasingly globalised world have been coupled with an increase in life expectancy, though this is now declining after 69 years of uninterrupted growth from 1950 to 2019 (Heuveline, 2022). Although their benefits cannot be denied, these outcomes tend to be reserved for those living in Global North. Moreover, their impact on Earth's ecosystems is largely ignored and even promoted through an acritical education system rooted in the driving forces of neoliberalism.

As Tait (2019) articulates, education is the means through which the cogs of society are turned. As a result, as Jones (2017) notes, "the status quo citizenship demanded by a neoliberal, industrial society [is] supported by school systems" (p. 503). Indeed, decades of commentary agree, reflecting the power of education to reproduce existing entrenched socio-economic structures and systems (e.g., Bourdieu, 1984, 2004; Freire, 1972; Illich, 2000; Russell, 2009).

Although mass education arose out of a combination of religious, economic, and political influences, it remains surprising that, despite geographic, religious, cultural, social, resource, and population size differences, it is structured, organised, and idealised in ways that are remarkably similar throughout the world, demonstrating the ubiquity of the globalised, neoliberal education agenda (Boli et al., 1985; Reid, 2019). Within education, neoliberalism is essentially a political ideology whereby the state has been able to reduce overt control over certain aspects of society (such as family life, child rearing, and the market) but has still been able to maintain influence over the lives of its citizens through schooling. Through schooling, governments are able to exercise *covert* control: shaping citizens to align with the broader governmental agenda (Tait, 2019). Tait describes mass education as "a form of social regulation … based upon an increasing focus on individuality, … where the school subtly conforms to the requirements of the state" (p. 84).

It is through control of schooling, especially through the curriculum, that particular behaviours and worldviews are forged to align with those of the dominant ideologies of the day (Boli et al., 1985). This means, as Apple (1991) argues, that the writing and endorsing of curriculum is a deeply political activity that determines both *what* and *whose* knowledge is taught. Under neoliberalism there is, through the mediation of the market, immense pressure to meet the goals of business and industry, whose successes are defined in terms of Gross Domestic Product (GDP). In most countries, schools must adopt their government's prescribed curriculum in order to be registered and receive government funding, and outcomes are controlled through government-administered standardised testing of both students and pre-service teachers (see Paglayan, 2021).

In Australia, for example, the neoliberal environment has seen school students subjected to the National Assessment Program – Literacy and Numeracy (NAPLAN) testing (Australian Curriculum, Assessment and Reporting Authority [ACARA], 2022b), and the Program for International Student Assessment (PISA) (Organisation for Economic Development [OECD], n.d.). These enable "league tables" to compare schools, and international comparisons between countries to be created. Reid (2019) argues that "[im]proved NAPLAN results have become the purpose of education … targets are set, the curriculum is narrowed further and teachers teach to the test" (p. 41). Similarly, pre-service teachers must undertake the Literacy and Numeracy Test for Initial Teacher Education Students (LANTITE) (Australian Council for Educational Research, 2022), with ongoing disputes as to whether results should be tied to funding (e.g., Anderson & Boyle, 2015). Many education systems have thus become instrumental and culpable in programming societal thinking and behaviour (Bourdieu, 1984; Purcell, 2012; Russell & Bajaj, 2015; Sklair, 2012). In these ways, education not only works against equitable consumption and distribution of wealth and resources, but also compromises cultural diversity, especially in those countries and cultures that identify more strongly with collectivism than individualism (Ledwith, 2011; Wagler, 2009).

In spite of the damage both to Western and post-colonial societies, the Western paradigm of neoliberalism continues both to be promoted and perceived largely as aspirational. Ledwith (2011) describes current forms of education as "moralising ideology in which 'greed' is replaced with 'enterprise' in the political lexicon, and the cultivation of 'national unity' … disguised the active reinforcement of social divisions" (p. 17). Given the critical role of science and technology in industrialisation that has enabled many of these outcomes, any efforts to address the issues and work towards more equitable and sustainable goals, must involve a (re)examination of science and technology in education.

36.3   Science, Technology, Engineering, and Mathematics (STEM) Education and the SDGs

As discussed earlier, the world we live in is one where science and technology have been paramount in forging the political, social, and economic structures of some of the richest nations for more than two centuries. At the same time, the divide between rich and poor is widening (Wilkinson & Pickett, 2010) and ecosystems and biodiversity continue to be depleted. Surely then, we urgently need to ask difficult questions about the purpose that science and technology education should be serving, and to question whether, in their current iteration—STEM—they are able to contribute to alleviating the complex polycrises that the SDGs seek to address.

Currently, in most education systems, STEM education is championed as being of critical importance to an individual's workforce readiness and a country's economic productivity (Australian Government Office of the Chief Scientist, 2016; United Kingdom House of Commons, 2018; United States National Science and Technology Council (NSTC) 2018; and for protecting security (NSTC). Clearly, STEM education is critical for understanding and meeting a number of the SDGs directly (e.g., Good Health and Wellbeing (SDG3); Clean Sanitation and Water (SDG6); Affordable and Clean Energy (SDG7); Climate Action (SDG13); Life below Water (SDG14); and Life on Land (SDG15), as well as all the others indirectly. However, as argued above, a default neoliberal ideology drives the STEM education agenda (Bencze & Carter, 2019; Smith & Watson, 2018), perpetuating the unexamined and contradictory contribution of science and technological advancement to the very dysfunctional complex of wicked issues that STEM is called upon to address. In fact, the OECD (2018) notes that "unless steered with a purpose, the rapid advance of science and technology may widen inequities, exacerbate social fragmentation and accelerate resource depletion" (p. 3).

The political climate of Global North, preoccupied with maintaining ongoing economic advantage in the global free market, has largely framed STEM education in terms of the knowledge and skills perceived as needed for the twenty-first century (OECD, 2018). Thus, STEM education has become contextualised and placed in the service of the production of technological-focussed outcomes that drive knowledge-based, growthist economies further (Bencze & Carter, 2019; Educación & Ng, 2019; Marginson, et al., 2013; Sjöström & Eilks, 2019; Smith & Watson, 2019; Tytler & Self, 2020). It is clear that STEM education needs to be aware and take far greater consideration of the many undesirable outcomes associated with gearing science and technology towards employment. Also concerning is the more recent trend that promotes a purely technological approach to resolving issues to do with climate change to the exclusion of all else, including considering alternative approaches to the otherwise culpable consumer-driven lifestyle associated with neoliberal capitalism that is so entrenched in the Global North.

Although the term "STEM" itself is quite recent, dating back to around 2005 (Loewus, 2015), STEM-related curricula since World War 2 have been explicitly focussed on knowledge and skills that support economic growth and globalisation through consumerism and its affiliated profit-driven activity. Smith and Watson (2019), in discussing STEM-based curricula over the last few decades, note that:

> the chemistry curriculum was heavy with industrial processes, whereas mathematics was the mathematics of engineering and science — algebra, trigonometry, and calculus — rather than of accounting, statistics, and economics. Once the structure of DNA was understood, genetics, the precursor to biotechnology, became a major focus in biology education, whereas the focus in botany education shifted away from taxonomy and towards plant growth physiology and the importance of plant growth hormones in horticulture. Agriculture education focused on pesticides, inorganic fertilisers, intensification of production and later, genetic modification of crops, rather than on sustainable agriculture and maintaining the soil microbiome. (p. 5)

At the same time, STEM curriculum is largely devoid of consideration of the sociocultural issues afflicting a world heavily impacted by science and technology, i.e., the ethics of how science and technology are used, who benefits from them, and who has the power to decide their use. The rise of STEM education has also seen a concomitant shift from the more social and culturally based Education for Sustainable Development (ESD) towards more technologically based solutions as education's main way of addressing sustainability (Davies, 2017; Smith & Watson, 2019). Smith and Watson remind us that education that explicitly addressed environmental issues (i.e., ESD/Education for Sustainability [EfS])[1] was itself not properly recognised until the Tbilisi Declaration of 1977 (Global Development Research Center (GDRC), 1977). While ESD/EfS had its day in the sun during the 1990s and 2000s, today it has waned in influence and been relegated (in the Australian curriculum at least), to being a "cross-curriculum priority" (ACARA, 2022a), potentially (and often) allowing it to be ignored in schools (Smith & Watson, 2019). For Smith and Watson (2020), given the relegation of ESD, the rise of STEM as a framework for considering sustainability with its narrow focus on technological futures has led to a critically dangerous narrowing of students' ability to imagine flourishing futures beyond the technological.

Based in same ideology and systems that are increasing the divide between rich and poor (Reid, 2019), education systems the world over are exacerbating the inequities and conditions that the SDGs seek to address. Thus, any progress to alleviate poverty and inequity, and repair a degraded planet seems increasingly difficult if these current education systems persist. With others (e.g., Folke et al., 2021; Raworth, 2017), we argue that there are ways in which science and technology can be instrumental in promoting human flourishing that do not entirely depend on hi-tech and growthist solutions, but also include socio-cultural and ecological dimensions.

[1] Although often used interchangeably, ESD and EfS are ideologically different, see Sterling (2001) for a full discussion.

36.4 A Reconceptualised STEM Education for the "5Ps"—People, Prosperity, Planet, Partnership, and Peace

Although education in the main has been aligned with the values and worldviews of the dominant power brokers, this nexus can be challenged and broken. Rather than merely being the servant of the prevailing ideology, as Ledwith (2011) notes, education has the potential to raise awareness and empower people to "question their reality" (p. 3). Reid (2019) agrees; although acknowledging that "it is difficult to dislodge neoliberalism in education" (p. 49), he notes that there are many examples of educators resisting and working around policy impositions. There is still a residual of the "critical consciousness" famously espoused by Freire (1972) amongst educators, who continue to challenge prevailing hegemony and enable more emancipatory outcomes. The polycrises of today provide fertile ground and impetus for raising educators' consciousness towards a better future. As Purcell (2012) claims,

> such a level of consciousness can be achieved through a process of identifying ... generative themes and facilitating people through a reflection–vision–planning–action process to reinterpret their view of both themselves and the world, and to identify objectives for change. (p. 268)

The view that environmental problems can be solved with more technology and better management is merely one more neoliberal myth (Bendell, 2022; Smith & Watson, 2018). Nothing is more naïve than the eco-modern view that a shift to renewable energy from fossil fuels is all that is required, then we can go about business as usual. On the contrary, further damage will be done to fragile environments because of rising demand for the raw materials needed to create renewable energy systems and continued economic growth. The very fact that technological advancement is seen as the answer to a flourishing future reminds us of the title of Audre Lorde's (1984) famous essay entitled, "The master's tools will never dismantle the master's house."

With regard to science education in particular, Roberts (2007) proposed that there are essentially two "Visions" in how it is expressed. Vision I is concerned with the unproblematised teaching of canonical knowledge and skills—the traditional products and processes of science itself, presenting them predominantly from a reductionist, factual "right or wrong" perspective. However, as Apple (1991) notes, all curriculum is political, and Vision I merely masks the imprint of neoliberalism in its projection of science as an objective set of knowledge and skills, without the need to ask, "whose knowledge, whose skills, for what purpose, who benefits, and at what costs?".

Vision II is concerned with the more messy and often controversial socially critical, ideological, and ethical concerns linked more overtly to the way science and technology inform and play out in society. This Vision is reflected in Bourdieu's (2004) essays on the social conditions in which science is developed and portrayed in order to continue to claim its objectivity. Given this messiness, Vision II perspectives have long had difficulty obtaining traction in science curricula, and at best, they may be perceived as an afterthought or add-on rather than a framework for teaching. However, Vision II approaches have the potential to address outcomes aligned with those of the SDGs with their increased focus on science for active citizenship (Hodson, 2010). Hodson specifically argues for Vision II socio-scientific issues to be addressed through what he terms "civic scientific literacy [which] comprises the knowledge, skills, attitudes, and values necessary for making decisions on matters such as energy policy, use of natural resources, environmental protection, and moral-ethical issues raised by technological innovations" (p. 197).

Given the role of science and technology in the production of uneven industrialisation and financialisaton, and the widening poverty gaps between the Global North and Global South (as well as within countries themselves), ecosystem destruction, biodiversity loss, and the climate crisis, there are strong arguments for STEM education to be reconceptualised well beyond Vision II. This would see a shift to curriculum that engages students in learning about and being overtly activist, in addressing issues of socio-scientific concern including human responsibility for the flourishing of all life on earth. Hence, it would play a key role in forging a sustainable future as promoted by the SDGs. If nothing else, it must heed the voices of young people who, terrified of a climate-damaged future and inspired by the young activist Greta Thunberg, are calling for climate science and its impacts to be foregrounded in a re-imagined science and technology education (Brett & Ayre, Chapter 25, this volume; Shah, 2021).

Responding to Hodson (2010), a number of scholars have recently articulated a Vision III of science education—one that moves towards socio-political activism, with aspirations of "emancipation and socio-ecojustice" (Sjöström & Eilks, 2019, p. 67). With others (e.g., Bencze, 2017; Bencze & Carter, 2011; Levinson, 2018; Simonneaux, 2014), they argue for a science and technology curriculum embedded in contexts that expose, question, and propose solutions and action on socially acute applications and topics of science and technology that are otherwise being approached in ways that undermine the wellbeing of individuals, societies, and nature.

Further, the question remains whether the term "STEM" itself is part of the problem. Carter (personal communication, July 10th, 2022) argues that the very essence of STEM education encodes neoliberalism, and that the term "science and technology education" is the better one if new conceptualisations are to be considered. Whether the term "STEM" is retained or replaced, education in the sciences and technology needs to be interdisciplinary, critical, and contextualised within sociopolitical, real-world applications, grounded and appropriate, and placed at the service of the flourishing for the "5Ps."

36.5   The Role of Teachers

Despite the natural synergies between many STEM-related topics in curriculum that could be approached through Vision II and III perspectives that would better enable the SDGs to be addressed, teachers and pre-service teachers receive little background and professional learning in how to shape curriculum towards these more sophisticated, integrated, messy and controversial contexts and applications (United Nations Oficina Internacional de Educación & Ng, 2019). Even given the rhetoric of the importance of STEM for advancing the knowledge economies of the Western world, most initial teacher education courses, government standardised testing, and subsequently, school professional development programs and curriculum timetables, continue to prioritise literacy and numeracy (and/or English and mathematics) in terms of time, resources, and professional learning (OECD, 2020).

Given this lack of education in Vision III perspectives, it is not surprising that there exists some resistance to a more socially oriented and activist form of STEM education. Firstly, the current limited integration across the STEM curriculum areas (Marginson et al., 2013; Tytler & Self, 2020) restricts the exploration of socio-scientific issues that are interdisciplinary in nature (Levinson, 2018; United Nations Oficina Internacional de Educación & Ng). Secondly, teachers themselves may resist actively engaging in what could be considered controversial areas, perhaps out of fear of reprisal from other staff and/or parents (e.g., Jones, 2017), or because they believe the topics are too complex (Levinson, 2018), or inappropriate for school-based learning (Forgasz et al., 2015; Pountney, 2021).

36.6   Conclusion

We have argued that a long history of colonialisation, neo-colonialism and neolib-eral agendas underpin the framing of the SDGs, rendering them inherently para-doxical and contradictory in their quest to forge a flourishing future. A critical education that challenges neoliberal hegemony has the potential to promote soli-darity and address global inequity within a more inclusive, eco-socio-political, and action-focussed framework, as advanced by the SDGs' "5Ps"—people, prosperity, planet, partnership, and peace. As Apple (1991) pointed out over 20 years ago, "rather than an educational system and a society based on selfish norms of individual profit, consumption, and advancement at all costs, we must be guided by a more cooperative and democratic ethic" (p. 42).

We believe it is important that educators recognise these framings and the role of education, and in particular, STEM education, play in either perpetuating or ignoring global world issues, so that progress towards the underlying principles of the SDGs can be better realised. Curriculum that seeks to critique as well as to address the goals of the SDGs needs to confront the bloated lifestyles that the Global North and increasingly others have somewhat blindly accepted and still desire. It also needs to seek actively to turn them around into more equitable lives and attitudes. This requires a shift in the social and political mindsets of those in the Global North, where unity needs to replace nationalism, equality needs to replace power, eco-social justice needs to replace capitalism, and sustainability and flourishing need to replace growthism. Only through such a shift will we be able to overcome the continuing legacy of colonialism within the classroom (Tait, 2017).

Currently, discourses about the drivers of STEM education and the global issues to which advances in science and technology are inextricably tied—health, poverty, food security, and of course, climate change—remain unproblematised, poorly understood, and ill-addressed in education and school curricula. Vision I approaches still determine and dominate STEM curricula, whether by default or intention, and hence continue to support and drive economic growth within a colonial and neoliberal framing (Bencze et al., 2020; Simonneaux, 2014). As such, STEM education in its current form has little chance of moving us towards a flourishing future.

Given the state of the world, and in the light of the SDGs, the time is right to make bold moves towards a Vision III science and technology/STEM education that addresses the very issues caused by its unexamined application in the past. A long history of inaction on climate demonstrates that providing information is not enough to engender change. Instead, we need to support the young activists who recognise that their lives and futures are directly impacted by climate change and are calling for curriculum change (Pountney, 2021). This means overtly engaging in an activist education couched in the skills and knowledges that will help achieve SDGs, as promoted by Vision III approaches. Doing so is not only necessary for growing empathy and care for human beings around the world, but also critical to working to repair and generate flourishing environments on Earth that future generations of all species are able to inhabit and enjoy.

There is much work to be done to move towards this eco-social justice agenda in STEM education. It requires a move from its technoscience focus to engage students with the wider human experience of connection with one another and with nature. In particular, science needs to be given its prominent place in the lives of young people as a means to re-imagine a future beyond technology, rather than being complicit in the narrowing of their imaginations (Smith & Watson, 2020). STEM education is potentially a powerful space for this to occur, given its inextricable link to industrialisation, health outcomes, and the plethora of environmental conditions that are reflected in the SDGs. Educators need to be brave. We need to reject the colonial and neoliberal influences that are entrenched in STEM and reflect on and embrace contexts that pave new pathways towards a future that is able to create real peace and prosperity for people and planet.

References

Adelman, S. (2018). The sustainable development goals, anthropocentrism and neoliberalism. In D. French & L. Kotzé (Eds.), *Sustainable development goals: Law, theory and implementation* (pp. 15–40). Edward Elgar.

Anderson, J., & Boyle, C. (2015). NAPLAN data and school funding: A dangerous link. *The Conversation.* https://theconversation.com/naplan-data-and-school-funding-a-dangerous-link46021#:~:text=As%20a%20result%2C%20tying%20educational,from%20particular%20cohorts%20of%20students

Apple, M. (1991). Global crises, social justice, and teacher education. *Journal of Teacher Education, 62*(2), 222–234.

Australian Council for Educational Research. (2022). *Literacy and numeracy test for initial teacher education students.* http://www.teacheredtest.acer.edu.au

Australian Curriculum, Assessment and Reporting Authority. (2022a). *Cross-curriculum priorities.* https://v9.australiancurriculum.edu.au/f-10-curriculum/f-10-curriculum-overview/cross-curriculum-priorities

Australian Curriculum, Assessment and Reporting Authority. (2022b). *NAP: National assessment program.* http://www.nap.edu.au

Australian Government. Office of the Chief Scientist. (2016). *Australia's STEM workforce: Science, technology, engineering and mathematics.* https://www.chiefscientist.gov.au/2016/03/report-australias-stem-workforce

Becker, S. O., & Woessman, L. (2019). Education and socioeconomic development during the industrialization. In C. Diebolt & M. Haupert (Eds.), *Handbook of cliometrics* (pp. 253–273). Springer.

Bencze, L. (Ed.). (2017). *Science and technology education promoting wellbeing for individuals, societies and environments: STEPWISE.* Springer.

Bencze, J. L., & Carter, L. (2011). Globalizing students acting for the common good. *Journal of Research in Science Teaching, 48*(6), 648–669. https://doi.org/10.1002/tea.20419

Bencze, J. L., & Carter, L. (2019, September 4–7). *STEM education in right wing populist contexts.* Paper presentation. Society for the Social Studies of Science Annual Conference.

Bencze, J. L., Pouliout, C., Pedretti, E., Simonneaux, L., Simonneaux, J., & Zeidler, D. (2020). SAQ, SSI and STSE education: Defending and extending "science-in-context." *Cultural Studies of Science Education, 15*(3), 825–851.

Bendell, J. (2022). Replacing sustainable development: Potential frameworks for international cooperation in an era of increasing crises and disasters. *Sustainability 14*, 8185. https://doi.org/10.3390/su14138185

Bihami, H., & Meifa, F. (2014). The effects of decolonization in Africa. *World Scientific News, 3*, 16–21.

Boli, J., Ramirez, F. O., & Meyer, J. W. (1985). Explaining the origins and expansion of mass education. *Comparative Education Review, 29*(2), 145–170.

Bourdieu, P. (1984). *Distinction: A social critique of the judgment of taste.* Routledge.

Bourdieu, P. (2004). *Science of science and reflexivity.* Polity.

Brett, P., & Ayre, I. *They're preparing you for how life is at the moment, not how to change how life is at the moment: Tasmanian secondary students' experiences of education for sustainability.* This volume.

Carter, L. (2017). Neoliberalism and STEM education: Some Australian policy discourse. *Canadian Journal of Science Mathematics and Technology Education, 17*(4), 247–257. https://doi.org/10.1080/14926156.2017.1380868

Carter, L., & Smith, C. *The United Nations sustainable development goals in a neoliberal world.* This volume.

Chakrabarti, S., & Patnaik, U. (Eds.). (2018). *Agrarian and other histories: Essays for Binay Bhushan Chaudhury.* Tulika Books.

Davies, I. (2017). Education for a better world: The struggle for social justice in the twenty-first century. In S. Choo, D. Sawch, A. Villanueva, & R. Vinz (Eds.), *Educating for the 21st century: Policies and practices from around the world* (pp. 131–145). Springer.

Desai, R. (2017). Theories of development. In P. Haslam, J. Schafer, & P. Beaudet (Eds.), *Introduction to international development: Approaches, actors and issues* (3rd ed., pp. 43–64). Oxford University Press.

Dutta, M. (2011). *Communicating social change: Structure, culture, and agency*. Routledge.

Educación, U.O., & Ng, S. B. (2019). *Exploring STEM competences for the 21st century*. United Nations Educational, Scientific and Cultural Organization. https://www.semanticscholar.org/paper/Exploring-STEM-competences-for-the-21st-century-Educaci%C3%B3n-Ng/55f1bff79642ca16d1054ef78f16cbb2b1b83234

Eisenmenger, N., Pichler, M., Krenmayr, N., Noll, D., Plank, B., Schalmann, E., Wandl, M.-T., & Gringich, S. (2020). The sustainable development goals prioritize economic growth over sustainable resource use: A critical reflection on the SDGs from a socio-ecological perspective. *Sustainability Science, 15*, 1101–1110. https://doi.org/10.1007/s11625-020-00813-x

Fine, B. (2013). Beyond the developmental state: An introduction. In B. Fine, J. Saraswati, & D. Tavasci (Eds.), *Beyond the developmental state: Industrial policy into the twenty-first century* (pp. 1–32). Pluto Press.

Fitzsimons, P. (2017). Human capital theory and education. In M. A. Peters (Ed.), *Encyclopedia of educational philosophy and theory*. Springer. https://doi.org/10.1007/978-981-287-588-4_331

Folke, C., Polasky, S., Rockström, J., & Walker, B. H. (2021). Our future in the Anthropocene biosphere. *Ambio, 50*, 834–869. https://doi.org/10.1007/s13280-021-01544-8

Forgasz, H., Bleazy, J., & Sawatzki, C. (2015). Ethics and the challenges for inclusive mathematics teaching. In A. Bishop, H. Tan, & T. Barkatsas (Eds.), *Diversity in mathematics education* (pp. 147–165). Springer.

Freire, P. (1972). *Pedagogy of the oppressed*. Penguin.

Global Development Research Center. (1977). *Tbilisi Declaration*. https://www.gdrc.org/uem/ee/tbilisi.html

Greenpeace. (2016). *10 years ago the Amazon was being bulldozed for soy—then everything changed*. https://www.greenpeace.org/usa/victories/amazon-rainforest-deforestation-soy-moratorium-success/

Harvey, D. (2005). Neoliberalism 'with Chinese characteristics'. In D. Harvey (Ed.), *A brief history of neoliberalism* (pp. 120–151). Oxford. https://doi.org/10.1093/oso/9780199283262.003.0009

Heuveline, P. (2022). Global and national declines in life expectancy: An end-of-2021 assessment. *Population Development Review, 48*(1), 31–50. https://doi.org/10.1111/padr.12477

Hira, A. (2012). State of the state: Does the state have a role in development? In P. Beaudet, P. A. Haslam, & J. Schafer (Eds.), *Introduction to international development; approaches, actors, and issues* (2nd ed., pp. 45–67). Oxford University Press.

Hodson, D. (2010). Science education as a call to action. *Canadian Journal of Science, Mathematics and Technology Education, 10*(3), 197–206.

Ife, J. (2016). *Community development in an uncertain world: Vision, analysis and practice*. Cambridge University Press.

Illich, I. (2000). *Deschooling society*. Marion Boyars.

Irwin, D. A., & Ward, O. (2021, September 8). What is the "Washington consensus?" *Peterson Institute for International Economics*. https://www.piie.com/blogs/realtime-economic-issues-watch/what-washington-consensus

Jamrozik, A. (2009). *Social policy in the post-welfare state. Australian society in a changing world* (3rd ed.). Pearson.

Jones, M. (2017). "Preach or teach?" A journey to becoming STEPWISE. In J. L. Bencze (Ed.), *Science and technology education promoting wellbeing for individuals, societies and environments* (pp. 503–522). Springer.

Kingsbury, D. (2016). Introduction. In D. Kingsbury, J. McKay, J. Hunt, M. McGillivray, & M. Clarke (Eds.), *International development: Issues and challenges* (3rd ed., pp. 1–20). Palgrave.

Lawler, O., Allen, H., Baxter, P., Castagnino, R., Tor, M., Daan, L., Hungerford, J., Karmacharya, D., Lloyd, T., Lopez-Jara, M., Massie, G., Novera, J., Rogers, A., & Kark, S. (2021). The COVID-19 pandemic is intricately linked to biodiversity loss and ecosystem health. *The Lancet Planetary Health, 5*(11), e840–e850.

Ledwith, M. (2011). *Community development: A critical approach* (2nd ed.). Policy Press.

Levinson, R. (2018). Realising the school science curriculum. *The Curriculum Journal, 29*(4), 522–537.

Loewus, L. (2015, April 2). When did science education become STEM? *Education Week.* https://www.edweek.org/teaching-learning/when-did-science-education-become-stem/2015/04

Lorde, A. (1984). *The master's tools will never dismantle the master's house. Essay.* Essays and Speeches. Crossing Press.

Marginson, S., Tytler, R., Freeman, B., & Roberts, K. (2013). *STEM - country comparisons: International comparisons of science, technology, engineering and mathematics (STEM) education. Final report.* Australian Council of Learned Academies, https://dro.deakin.edu.au/eserv/DU:30059041/tytler-stemcountry-2013.pdf

McGillivray, M. (2016). What is development? In D. Kingsbury, J. McKay, J. Hunt, M. McGillivray, & M. Clarke (Eds.), *International development: Issues and challenges* (3rd ed., pp. 21–49). Palgrave.

McKay, J. (2016). The economics of development. In D. Kingsbury, J. McKay, J. Hunt, M. McGillivray, & M. Clarke (Eds.), *International development: Issues and challenges* (3rd ed., pp. 78–107). Palgrave.

Millennium Development Goals. (2015). *We can end poverty.* https://www.un.org/millenniumgoals/news.shtml

Organisation for Economic Co-operation and Development. (n.d.). *PISA: Programme for international student assessment.* http://www.oecd.org/pisa

Organisation for Economic Co-operation and Development. (2018). *The future of education and skills: Education 2030—the future we want.* https://www.oecd.org/education/2030project/contact/E2030_Position_Paper_(05.04.2018).pdf

Organisation for Economic Co-operation and Development. (2020). *Curriculum overload: A way forward.* OECD Publishing. https://doi.org/10.1787/3081ceca-en

Paglayan, A. (2021). The non-democratic roots of mass education: Evidence from 200 years. *American Political Science Review, 115*(1), 179–198.

Pountney, R. (2021). The activist curriculum & global climate change education: Interruption, intervention or integration? International perspectives on the curriculum. *BERA Research Intelligence, 148*, 26–27. http://shura.shu.ac.uk/29188/14/Pountney-ActivistCurriculumGlobal%28VoR%29.pdf

Purcell, R. (2012). Community development and everyday life. *Community Development Journal, 47*(2), 266–281.

Raworth, K. (2017). *Doughnut economics: Seven ways to think like a 21st-century economist.* Random House Business.

Reid, A. (2019). *Changing Australian education.* Allen & Unwin.

Ripple, W., Wolf, C., Newsome, T., Barnard, P., & Moomaw, W. (2020). World scientists' warning of a climate emergency. *BioScience, 70*(1), 8–12.

Roberts, D. (2007). Scientific literacy, science literacy. In N. Lederman & S. Abell (Eds.), *Handbook of research on science education* (Vol. II, pp. 729–780). Taylor & Francis.

Rostow, W. W. (1991). *The stages of economic growth: A non-communist manifesto* (3rd ed.). Cambridge University Press.

Russell, B. (2009). *Education and the social order.* Taylor & Francis. (Original work published 1932).

Russell, S., & Bajaj, M. (2015). Schools, citizens and the nation state. In T. McCowan & E. Unterhalter (Eds.), *Education and international development: An introduction* (pp. 93–109). Bloomsbury.

Shah, K. (2021, April 6). Greta Thunberg's amazing year meeting the world's climate scientists. *New Scientist.* https://www.newscientist.com/article/2273634-greta-thunbergs-amazing-year-meeting-the-worlds-climate-scientists/

Simonneaux, L. (2014). From promoting the techno-sciences to activism—A variety of objectives involved in the teaching of SSIs. In L. Bencze & S. Alsop (Eds.), *Activist science and technology education* (pp. 99–111). Springer.

Sjöström, J., & Eilks, I. (2019). Reconsidering different visions of scientific literacy and science education based on the concept of *Bildung.* In Y. Dori, Z. Mevarech, & D. Baker (Eds.), *Cognition, metacognition, and culture in STEM education* (pp. 65–88). Springer.

Sklair, L. (2012). Culture-ideology of consumerism. *The Wiley-Blackwell Encyclopedia of Globalization.* https://doi.org/10.1002/9780470670590.wbeog099

Smith, C., & Watson, J. (2018). STEM: Silver bullet for a viable future or just more flatland? *Journal of Futures Studies, 22*(4), 25–44.

Smith, C., & Watson, J. (2019). Does the rise of STEM education mean the demise of sustainability education? *Australian Journal of Environmental Education, 35*(1), 1–11.

Smith, C., & Watson, J. (2020). From streams to streaming: A critique of the influence of STEM on students' imagination for a sustainable future. *Journal of Applied Teaching and Learning, 3*(1), 21–29.

Sterling, S. (2001). *Sustainable education: Re-visioning learning and change.* Schumacher Briefings Book 6.

Tait, G. (2017). *Schooling and society.* Cambridge University Press.

Tait, G. (2019). *Making sense of mass education* (3rd ed.). Cambridge University Press.

Toomey, A. (2009). Empowerment and disempowerment in community development practice: Eight roles practitioners play. *Community Development Journal, 46*(2), 181–195.

Tooze, A. (2021). *Shutdown: How COVID shook the world's economy.* Viking.

Tytler, R., & Self, J. (2020). *Designing a contemporary STEM curriculum.* United Nations Educational, Scientific and Cultural Orgainsation International Bureau of Education. https://unesdoc.unesco.org/ark:/48223/pf0000374146

United Kingdom House of Commons. (2018). *Delivering STEM skills for the economy. Forty-seventh report of session 2017–19* (HC691). https://publications.parliament.uk/pa/cm201719/cmselect/cmpubacc/691/691.pdf

United Nations. (2015). *Transforming our world: The 2030 agenda for sustainable development.* UN General Assembly, Report A/res/70/1. https://undocs.org/A/RES/70/1

United Nations. (2000). *Millennium Summit.* https://www.un.org/en/conferences/environment/new york2000

United Nations Department of Economic and Social Affairs. (n.d.). *Sustainable development Goals.* https://sdgs.un.org/goals/goal8

United Nations Sustainable Development Group. (n.d.). *The 5Ps of the SDGs: People, planet, prosperity, peace and partnership.* https://unsdg.un.org/latest/videos/5ps-sdgs-people-planet-prosperity-peace-and-partnership United Nations.

United States National Science and Technology Council (2018). *Charting a course for success: America's strategy for STEM education.* Executive Office of the President of the United States.

Vandemoortele, J. (2018). From simple-minded MDGs to muddle-headed SDGs. *Development Studies Research, 5*(1), 83–89. https://doi.org/10.1080/21665095.2018.1479647

Wagler, R. (2009). Foucault, the consumer culture and environmental degradation. *Ethics, Place & Environment, 12*(3), 331–336.

Walsh, T. (2022). *Machines behaving badly: The morality of AI.* La Trobe University Press.

Wilkinson, R., & Pickett, K. (2010). *The spirit level: Why equality is better for everyone.* Penguin.

World Economic Forum. (2020). *The future of jobs report 2020. World Economic Forum.* http://www3.weforum.org/docs/WEF_Future_of_Jobs_2020.pdf

Zuboff, S. (2019). *The age of surveillance capitalism.* Profile Books.

Chapter 37
Towards the Sustainable Development Goals: Building Capacity for Action via a Participation Income

Robin Krabbe

Abstract One view of the trajectory of human evolution is that it has involved greater and greater levels of cooperation to tackle the problems with which humanity is presented (Stewart, Bio Systems 198, 2020).

37.1 Introduction

One view of the trajectory of human evolution is that it has involved greater and greater levels of cooperation to tackle the problems with which humanity is presented (Stewart, 2020). Greater levels of cooperation have helped technological development, and both have tackled the scarcity of material resources, the economic problem that humanity has addressed since the Agricultural Revolution some 10,000 years ago (Raskin et al., 2002). We now, however, have environmental limits, arguably replacing economic problems as the major challenge for humanity and needing further expansion of levels of cooperation (Giddens, 1991). This requires utilising our full potential, both individually and collectively (Laininen, 2019), and involving both social (Jacobs et al., 1997) and human development (Pradhan & Sanyal, 2011). The discourse on the Sustainable Development Goals (SDGs) increasingly recognises this need for deep cultural change from the micro- to the macro-level (Riedy, 2003).

There is much to be admired about the intent of the SDGs in attempting to correct the level of crises in late modernity (Wisor, 2012). In spanning concern for people, planet, and prosperity, the goals are comprehensive in their scope. However, a linking of prosperity with economic growth is a major shortcoming. As stated by Mahbub (in Lawrence, 2017), the real wealth of a nation is its people, and development must

R. Krabbe (✉)
School of Social Sciences, College of Arts, Law and Education, University of Tasmania, Burnie, TAS, Australia
e-mail: robin.krabbe@utas.edu.au; rkrabbe@westnet.com.au

Live Well Tasmania Coordinator, Wynyard, TAS, Australia

© The Author(s), under exclusive license to Springer Nature Singapore Pte Ltd. 2023   673
K. Beasy et al. (eds.), *Education and the UN Sustainable Development Goals*, Education for Sustainability 7,
https://doi.org/10.1007/978-981-99-3802-5_37

be aimed at creating an enabling environment for people to live healthy, creative, and meaningful lives. The pursuit of material and financial wealth obscures this quest. As Maiteny (2003) notes, non-material forms of wealth are crucial for both addressing ecological overshoot and increasing human wellbeing and development. Above all however, as Mnguni (2010) suggests, meaningful co-existence, interpreted here as being based on prosociality, purpose, and meaning, is a key approach to increasing collective action towards engaging with the SDGs.

More broadly, this chapter identifies a number of factors considered crucial to progressing sustainable development. These include the need to reduce the environmental impact of our footprint, and the need to build the conditions in which basic needs are met, and in which we and the larger Earth community can thrive. It all begins with enabling functional relationships, and in particular, includes the need to change the world of work, which is currently driven by the breakdown of the model of income generation, under- or unemployment, and the rise of precarious and alienating work. Underpinning this is an urgent need for a form of democracy that promotes prosociality that provides humans with a sense of purpose and meaning.

Addressing these factors requires collective action which is based on meaningful co-existence. A major barrier to collective action and meaningful co-existence is a relational failure. Neoliberalism and its antecedents can, above all, be seen as responsible for relational failure (Layton, 2010), defined here as a failure to protect and promote the social relationships that are so crucial for creating and maintaining eco-social responsibility. The evolution of governance systems that are hierarchical, exploitative, and polarising (Walters, 2010) is a major contributor to relational failure. Hence, transformation in how we relate to each other and to the environment is paramount. Indeed, transformation is increasingly called for with regard to the SDGs (Sachs et al., 2019; Witt, 2013), but there is much less discussion of how to achieve it. This chapter identifies, in seven sections, a pathway towards transformation to increase collective action to engage with the SDGs, by highlighting two basic human needs, culminating in a discussion of the policy of Participation Income to provide a significant foundation to achieve these broader actions towards sustainable development.

To make the case that a focus on (1) prosociality, (2) purpose and meaning, and (3) the implementation of a Participation Income, is an effective way to advance the SDGs, firstly, a concept of humans as wary cooperators is discussed. Secondly, based on this concept, sustainability is then highlighted as a vital opportunity for redirecting humanity towards a more scientific-based foundation for surviving and thriving. The third section argues that, as an ultrasocial species, all human endeavour ultimately depends on the quality of relationships. Achieving the SDGs in particular, depends on our ability to collaborate, hence prosociality is a key skill. The fourth section identifies purpose and meaning as the second vital human need to help to build sustainable societies. The fifth section briefly outlines a need to transform work beyond SDG8 (decent work and economic growth), as an important option for achieving purpose and meaning. The sixth section discusses the role of deliberation in addressing the SDGs, which leads to the final section that discusses Participation Income. This is proposed as having the potential to promote sustainability, particularly by promoting prosociality, purpose and meaning, and deliberation. The conclusion summarises the case for a Participation Income to progress the SDGs via greater individual and collective capacity.

37.2 Wary Cooperation

The key argument underpinning this chapter is that both to progress the SDGs in the short term, and to transform them in the longer term, human capacities for collective action, and addressing in particular, a problematic reliance on consumerism as a source of meaning (Kaza, 2000), need to be strengthened. Later, it is argued that prosociality, purpose and meaning, and deliberation are all effective ways of improving systemic responses to unsustainable development.

This section first analyses the literature on human nature, identifying a useful conceptualisation of humans as wary cooperators (Smith, 2006). Wary cooperation encapsulates a view of human nature as being challenged by a need to balance two basic tendencies: self-interest and other-interest. The beginning assumption is that humans will tend to privilege their own interests above that of society; however, they are also hard-wired to cooperate (Richerson et al., 2003). Wary cooperation encapsulates this view of human nature. Firstly, the greater the stress placed on people, and secondly, the less the investment in helping people build inner resources to deal with stress, the greater the wariness and the less the cooperation (Schneiderman et al., 2005).

According to Smith (2006), as wary cooperators, humans are very sensitive to the actions of other people and to others' perceptions of themselves. In general, people seek to be perceived as worthy and willing to contribute to the group, but they are also highly sensitive to any perceived free-riding of others, that is, being taken advantage of. Wary cooperators follow two basic rules in social interaction: cooperate with ingroup members who also cooperate, and punish those who do not cooperate (Smith). Modern society provides substantial opportunities for free-riding, and, as Smith notes, people will often not cooperate if they think there are a substantial number of other people who are not cooperating. It is important therefore, for institutions to provide confidence that free-riding is being monitored and minimised. An important role of institutions is to regulate and control such human instincts (Peltz, 2005) for the common good in lieu of any human inability to do so, particularly after generations of maladaptive environments for self-control (Rees, 2010). This point is reviewed later when Participation Income is discussed.

Smith (2006) also notes, crucially, that the temptation for selfish behaviour is particularly strong in those at the higher end of the social dominance hierarchy, because power and status increase opportunities for individual gain (for example, by shaping the rules and influencing politics and other institutions to their advantage). This is another crucial point in the argument for a move towards deliberative democracy. Because sustainability is, above all, a problem of human behaviour (Davelaar,

2021), how we conceptualise human nature is important. The next section discusses the significance of sustainability and the SDGs for the deepest aspects of the human condition.

37.3 Sustainability and the SDGs

One reason why sustainability is important is because it forces us to question our values and our lifestyles. Relatedly, sustainability provides a unique and arguably the ultimate opportunity to re-organise human co-existence (Zabel, 2005) to meet basic human needs. For Mnguni (2010), the significance of sustainability is its core focus on the quest for meaningful co-existence—both co-existence between people and co-existence between people and the greater Earth community through ecological systems. This involves building capacity for "psychological maturity and integration" (Mnguni, p. 117), versus the current trend of a level of immaturity amplified by a promotion of rights over responsibilities, and consumption versus other more eco-social sources of life satisfaction (Küng, 2005).

This chapter also draws on work by Fukuda-Parr and Muchhala (2020), who contend that sustainable development requires two central elements. The first is the promotion of values regarding reducing consumption, and the second is reconfiguring production systems according to environmental limits. This aligns with the literature on sustainable production and consumption (Tukker et al., 2008), and with SDG12 (responsible consumption and production). Blesh et al. (2019) add to the debate regarding ecological production systems, by highlighting the effectiveness of approaches to achieving zero hunger (SDG2) that are place-based, adaptive, and participatory, both in the Global South and North.

In terms of the capacity of the SDGs to progress towards an expanded triple bottom line (economic, social, and environmental) version of sustainability, on the one hand, they represent a great achievement in advancing the global conversation about people, planet, and prosperity (Jönsson, 2017). The focus on meeting basic needs is a particularly strong element of the SDGs (Pogge & Sengupta, 2015). On the other hand however, the inclusion of the aim of economic growth is a major shortcoming which undermines the ability of the goals to have a sufficient impact (Hickel, 2019). The overwhelming research showing that firstly, beyond a certain level, material goods do not lead to increased wellbeing (Eckersley, 2000), and secondly, that our ecological systems cannot support current levels of consumption, let alone higher levels, is not reflected in the SDGs (Dasgupta et al., 2021). Indeed, SDG8 calls for further economic growth.

There is substantial evidence that there are sufficient levels of material goods being produced in most parts of the world: however, it is its distribution that is highly unequal, leaving many without adequate levels of resources, while others have rates of consumption well above what appears to be sufficient for wellbeing (Whiting et al., 2018). As Laruffa et al. (2021) note, a post-productivist approach of providing income support and public services to meet basic needs, instead of focusing on wage labour productivity and economic growth, is an urgent priority.

Two basic needs are identified here in particular, which, when satisfied, can increase both individual and collective capacity towards achieving the SDGs. These are prosociality and purpose and meaning. Prosociality and more broadly, the significance of cooperative relationships for achieving societal goals such as the SDGs, are discussed next.

37.4 Why Are Relationships so Important to All Human Endeavour, in Particular the SDGs?

The main premise of this chapter is that collection action, involving cooperation from the micro to the macro scale, is vital for making progress on the SDGs. According to Rothstein and Stolle (2002), along with Ostrom (2000), the most fundamental problem in every organisation and society more generally, is trust, in terms of the willingness of people to cooperate with each other. Trust and cooperation then, are at the core of sustainable development. There is currently a crisis of trust, contributed to, as Rothstein and Uslaner (2005) note, by inequality: trust decreases when there is a failure of those with more resources to reallocate them to those who have less.

More broadly, supportive social relationships are a key aspect of human survival and thriving. There are two main arguments supporting this position. The first is the basic human need to belong to a supportive social group (ideally based on face-to-face relationships), and that human health suffers if we are not able to give and receive social support (Barbour et al., 2010; Umberson & Montez, 2010; Umberson et al., 2010; Way, 2013). The second is that our capacity to act collectively is crucial for solving our current problems (Fung & Wright, 2001), and specifically for achieving the SDGs (Monkelbaan, 2019). Division of labour (Turchin & Gavrilets, 2009) and the distribution of knowledge (Adler & Heckscher, 2005), are both significant sources of wealth, however, obviously cooperation is needed to reap their benefits.

A corollary is that our capacity to learn and adapt—crucial capacities given the current challenges we face—is highly correlated to how capable we are of giving and receiving social support; however, stress from the perception of a lack of social support can reduce the allocation of cognitive resources for the purpose of learning (Crum et al., 2017). Relational failure (Layton, 2010) is a major source of stress, exacerbated by competitive market relationships, and is a major barrier to collective action. Hence, prosociality and social relationships are important for individual wellbeing and collective action. We now turn to the second main life domain that has been identified as important for wellbeing of purpose and meaning.

37.5 Purpose and Meaning

There are a number of points that have been made, firstly, about the centrality of purpose and meaning to human wellbeing, and secondly, that consumerism and lack of meaningful work are obstacles to achieving greater purpose and meaning. Giddens (1991) contends that meaning is so important that its lack underpins all the dilemmas of human existence. He points to routine activities (like work), as well as basic trust, as being important for sustaining meaning.

For Maiteny (2000) a key aspect of achieving sustainable behaviours and wellbeing in general is the striving for meaning and life satisfaction. He contends that physical survival is not sufficient for overall health and that we have a persistent addiction-like striving for something beyond survival (Maiteny, 2011). Maiteny (2003) also notes that regarding the debate about whether a materialistic or a non-materialistic approach is more effective in gaining meaning, that over history in almost all cultures, the latter has dominated. He further states that as far as can be known, our current culture is the first in the history of human evolution where materialism has dominated as an attempt to gain meaning. However, Maiteny (2011) notes that dissatisfaction with consumerism (see also Soper, 2007) has become evident in recent times, encapsulated by the post-materialist literature (Inglehart, 2018).

The search for meaning is highlighted in the eudemonic version of wellbeing. For example, Wong (2014) defines meaning as serving something bigger than oneself. Emmons (2003) contends that a meaningful life must include transcending self-interest to serve the common good. Meaningful work is identified as a significant way of achieving meaning in life, while Mayseless and Keren (2014) contend that work, potentially at least, provides one of the major opportunities for mastery, exploration, and life satisfaction. Lips-Wiersma and Morris (2009) identify four elements of meaningful work: a sense of unity with others, a perception that one's work benefits others, it expresses non-materialistic values, and it provides the opportunity to develop and build character. The next section considers some of the literature on how modern conceptions of work often fail to provide these goods and are often more meaningless than meaningful.

37.6 The Need to Transform Work Beyond SDG8

One of the aims of SDG8 is to achieve full and productive employment and decent work for all (Rai et al., 2019). Its sub-goals include ending forced labour, modern slavery, and human trafficking—all very important aspects of human rights and vital for human wellbeing. However, as Frey (2017) notes, the SDGs assume that work is the central means of reducing poverty (SDG1). For example, Frey and MacNaughton (2016) note that the International Labour Organization (ILO) has focused on ending poverty, and identifies decent work as the most effective way to avoid it occurring. Alston (2019) identifies the ILO as one of the few organisations that has campaigned for ending poverty as a human right versus an economic right, and that the ILO has documented its recommendations for a social protection floor for all. The United Nations Development Programme (UNDP) contends that only about 50% of workers globally were in formal waged or salaried employment in 2014, with more than 1.5 billion workers relying on informal and precarious employment (in Frey, 2017). They also estimate that 204 million people worldwide, including 74 million young people, were unemployed in 2015 (Frey).

All of these figures are reflected in the estimate of over 3 billion people, as of November 2021, who are living on less than US $5.50 per day (Suckling et al., 2021). Relying on work for economic security is deeply problematic in late modernity. Work in the modern era can be seen to have three main roles: the basis for producing goods and services, the source of earning income, and providing non-material benefits such as purpose and meaning to increase wellbeing (Hines, 2019). Hines notes, however, that we tend to conflate them and assume that they all must emanate from the same source, i.e. from wage labour or its equivalent.

For Macarov (1996), the corollary of the importance of work is that the need to provide jobs is one of the most urgent tasks of government, and is "the reason they use various schemes and subterfuges to try to reduce or conceal unemployment" (p. 194). His basic point is that society does not need, and cannot provide, employment for all, and is decreasingly able to do so, particularly as automation increases. Macarov contends that a substantial effort goes into trying to create jobs, divide jobs, maintain meaningless jobs, and obscure the real extent of un- and underemployment. As Wisman (2002) notes, modern societies accept a significant level of permanent unemployment to reduce inflation, and avoid perceived costs of ensuring full employment, despite its high costs for both individuals and society. He contends that tolerating unemployment is morally wrong and socio-economically irrational. He further points to the myriad ways that work is not meaningful to workers and that many have the sense that the work they do is not seen as important or valued. Likewise, Thompson (2015) found that 70% of Americans are disengaged from their work, indicating a serious failure of modern cultures to satisfy needs for purpose and meaning via employment.

Macarov (1996) adds to the debate by proposing that there is a substantial ambivalence towards paid employment, evidence of which includes that universal unemployment "benefits" are set at a rate well below the average wage, which is linked to the assumption that many people would choose not to work if they were paid an unconditional liveable wage. Unfortunately to the extent that work is seen as a disutility (Carr-Hill & Lintott, 2002), this view is likely to have a long shadow, in terms of not being easy to overcome.

In addition to often being perceived as a disutility, some forms of work are not institutionally valued. Avis (2021) points out how the health crisis, exacerbated by the COVID-19 pandemic, has promoted a re-acknowledgement of what should be considered highly valuable labour, aligning with feminist economists (Power, 2004) on the importance of a vital set of social skills: caring for others, raising children, maintaining households and broader communities, and sustaining connections more generally. A reconceptualisation of work would place much more value on these reproductive activities. The extent to which work needs to be transformed beyond SDG8 requires input from citizens, experts, and policymakers—the realm of deliberative decision-making, as discussed in the next section.

37.7 Deliberation and the SDGs

McKenzie (2021) contends that conventional models of policymaking are inadequate for formulating the SDGs, with deliberative democracy (DD) models having potential to improve SDG policies. Certainly SDG16 (peace, justice, and strong institutions) itself does not aspire to a vision of vastly more participation by citizens in decision-making. A crucial aspect of DD is the bringing together of citizens, experts, and policymakers in all relevant areas, such as initial consultation, the generation of ideas, policy design, and evaluation. Two examples of deliberative democracy models that McKenzie (2021) provides are citizens' juries and national conversations, both of which are aimed at increasing citizens' understanding of policy issues and allowing citizen input into policymaking.

Pelletier et al. (1999) note three specific benefits of participatory/deliberative democracy and decision-making. The first is that it increases the knowledge base for decision-making, and hence can result in better decisions. Secondly, it can increase the motivation of those involved to participate, by generating a greater sense of ownership. Thirdly, increased legitimacy of decisions can result from the knowledge that the broader society, beyond privileged elites, has the opportunity to have input. Laurian (2009) notes a link between public participation, or deliberation, and increased social capital. This is particularly the case for participation processes that are based on transparency, mutual respect, social learning, and trust, and lead to robust outcomes. A fourth major benefit is the capacity of deliberation to change worldviews (Gough, 2021). This is particularly important, because consumerism is so entrenched in providing meaning for many people's lives, while the attempt to reduce our ecological footprint is such a politically fraught and super-wicked problem.

Although the formal education system would appear to be the direct means by which to promote deliberation, and increase prosociality, and purpose and meaning, the level of inertia and number of institutional barriers to the necessary transformation in our formal education systems are currently formidable (O'Brien & Sygna, 2013). There are, however a large number of concepts emerging that challenge the traditional banking system of education that serves neoliberalism (Misiaszek, 2018). For example, ecopedagogies, drawing on critical pedagogies, advocate for a more holistic and ecological educational model that highlights the human potential and the interdependence of social, economic, and ecological wellbeing (Esteva et al., 2005). For Misiaszek (2018), one important role of ecopedagogy, of particular relevance to this chapter, is highlighting the tendency of neoliberal discourses to promote a view of an inverse relationship between the health of the environment and people's ability to make a living. This is particularly problematic given the need to reduce our impact on the planet through reduced growth.

A further connection with ecopedagogy is implied in the eco-social work advocated for in the next section, whereby experiential learning afforded by a Participation Income is a highly effective way of promoting the linkages among social, economic, and ecological wellbeing. The Participation Income and the eco-social work it can enable is discussed next.

37.8 From Unconditional Basic Income to a Conditional Participation Income

The topic of Basic Income is being increasingly discussed in an environment where automation is predicted to take anywhere between 20 and 78% of jobs in most economies over the next decades (Chessell, 2018). Basic Income has been proposed as a solution, particularly to address the resulting potentially high unemployment problem. The most discussed form of Basic Income is Universal Basic Income, which is an unconditional, generally subsistence level regular payment made by governments to all citizens, predominantly to ensure a level of economic security for all (Nieswandt, 2020). It crucially provides a Social Protection Floor, as advocated in SDG1, target 1.3 (Alston, 2019).

A Basic Income preserves market-orientated economies by, for example, allowing supplementation without any penalty via employment, savings, and investment (Gilbert et al., 2018). There are many other variations, such as a Job Guarantee, including a Climate Change Job Guarantee (Foster, 2021), and an Employer of Last Resort (Wisman, 2002). There have already been trials conducted on Basic Income, and many others are being planned or are currently taking place (Gilbert et al., 2018), in both the Global South and North.

To strengthen the base for a form of Basic Income, and a frequent argument against automation having a serious impact on jobs, is that the experience in the past has been that new markets have always been created to replace the jobs lost to automation (Vermeulen et al., 2018). Environmental sustainability, however, excludes relying on material consumption to support employment; if anything, sustainable development requires a reduction in employment and the associated resources involved in the production of goods and services that do not add to health and wellbeing (Spangenberg, 2014).

Christensen (2008) nicely sums up the potential of Basic Income, which he proposes can be seen as "a global story about sustainable development and the good society", as "a great story about the development of democracy, citizenship and the welfare state", as "a couple of small stories about the problems of the welfare state (unemployment, clientisation, gender inequality)", and "as a number of technical stories about simplification and rationalisation of the system of transfer payments"

(p. 137). Indeed, evidence from previous Basic Income-oriented experiments indicates the potential for Basic Income to increase all five psychological indicators of a healthy society: agency, security, connection, meaning, and trust (Griffin et al., 2017).

Basic Income has been particularly relevant for countries of the Global South due to their potential for reducing poverty (SDG1) (Hasdell, 2020). From a trial in Namibia, Basic Income certainly does appear to be promising in this regard. Jauch (2015) found that after a 2004 trial with Basic Income, not only did poverty decrease (by 39%), but also, there was improved nutrition (25% decrease of underweight children), improved school attendance (increase of 42%), reduced dropout rates (by 40%), and reduced rates of crime (by 42%).

Some literature tends to identify Basic Income as a solution to an inadequate welfare system (Alston, 2019), however this chapter proposes in addition, the importance of a Participation Income (PI) as a means of building capacity for the provision of eco-social services, which will both help to regenerate social systems as well as ecological systems. PI is defined as an income paid to all citizens in exchange for engaging in an activity deemed useful for society (Pérez-Muñoz, 2016). Laruffa et al.'s (2021) promotion of co-production in managing a PI accords with the more general advocating of capacity building and affirmation of agency.

Recently, there have been two contributions in particular that have discussed PI as a means of promoting individual and collective capacity via eco-social policy. First, given the need to reduce our ecological footprint, Pérez-Muñoz (2016) notes that a PI is particularly useful in rewarding socially useful activities that we often perform for free, that is, a PI can explicitly promote the provision of eco-social services, while a Basic Income will not necessarily mobilise people to participate in providing eco-social services. The second contribution comes from Laruffa et al. (2021), who make similar points, but also discuss the concept of co-production, whereby a PI can be much more appealing when people have an opportunity to participate in the details and design of activities that would count as participation. This is a particularly strong element of PI which is not present in discussions on Basic Income, that is, the affirmation of agency and the promotion of active participation, of trust, and of deliberation. Laruffa et al. go on to discuss the seeming contradiction of aiming for empowerment but using the threat of sanctions to force compliance. They propose that the quality of the participation options, enhanced by being co-created with participants, could increase intrinsic motivation and decrease the need for sanctions.

Recalling the concept of wary cooperation, the main argument that a conditional PI would be more effective than an unconditional Basic Income, is based on the literature on the basic social dilemma, whereby, as Stewart (2014) argues, free-riding must be prevented to ensure sufficient levels of cooperation. The literature on neoliberal subjectivity (Layton, 2010), whereby the individualistic neoliberal worldview becomes internalised, helps to explain why free-riding is an issue in all late modern societies, both "developed" and "developing". Kasper and Mulder (2015), for example, highlight problematic levels of cooperation in Tanzania, following an increase of neoliberal policies.

Unconditional Basic Income (UBI) is extolled by some as creating real freedom for everyone (Widerquist, 2001); however, it should be approached with caution. Although human nature is conceived here as being based on wary cooperation, the uncertainty and insecurity of modern life has exacerbated a sense of wariness of volunteering for the common good, as required under a UBI. Indeed, the large volume of literature on neoliberal subjectivity points to the deep embeddedness of norms that contribute to a failure to advance sustainable development (Layton, 2014). Our values and worldviews have become adapted to a culture of asocial individualism, therefore maladapted in terms of our ability for collective action. The corollary is as, Pearson et al. (2016) contend, that climate change is caused by the collective actions of individuals and groups motivated by short-term gains that have resulted in long-term collective harm. Here, the same dynamic supports the argument for a conditional income. Pérez-Muñoz (2018) adds to the argument on conditionality, stating that the voluntary actions of those receiving a Basic Income are unlikely to be sufficient to address unmet social needs. She contends that a centralised process is likely to be required that promotes, coordinates, and monitors participation. Likewise, literature on the difficulty of attracting volunteers supports the argument that a Basic Income is unlikely to generate the level of participation required for the regeneration of social and ecological systems required for sustainability. For example, Hallett et al. (2020), in their survey of 6749 people, identified four main constructs as explaining the failure to volunteer: inertia, self-interest, anxiety, and lack of knowledge, with the first two as the most influential. They contend that prosociality is highly correlated to volunteering, but again, a culture of individualism tends to mitigate against prosociality.

The intention here is not to cast late modern humans as irretrievably selfish, but rather, to point to the evidence that certain socioeconomic conditions generate a level of selfishness (Kitayama & Salvador, 2017). As Atkinson and Jacquet (2022) state, the failure to address climate change is not so much a problem of a universal and fixed human nature, but rather it relates to culturally evolved values, norms, institutions, and technologies. Therefore, although there has been increasing discussion of a UBI as a means of advancing the SDGs, particularly SDG1 "no poverty" (Alston, 2019), this chapter makes the case that a conditional payment, with its much greater focus on both "inner development" and eco-social policy, would be much more effective at promoting a substantial number of the SDGs (for example SDGs 1, 2, 3, 4, 5, and 8) than an unconditional Basic Income.

Turning to examples of the activities that could be counted as participation, in their concept of a Community Development Job Guarantee, Mitchell et al. (2003) identify urban renewal projects, community and caring work, and environmental schemes such as reforestation and regenerative agriculture, as worthwhile activities to build community capacity. As previously mentioned, flourishing ecological production systems are vital to achieve sustainable development, while Blesh et al. (2019) point to place-based, adaptive, and participative initiatives to build capacity. Likewise, Laruffa et al. (2021) propose a re-thinking of work based on a recognition of the importance of care, proposing that a PI can help care for people and planet. Mitchell et al. point out that this type of work is labour intensive but requires minimal capital equipment and training.

There is a significant body of literature highlighting the social and ecological benefits of these types of activities, in particular, their capacity to increase prosociality, and purpose and meaning (Seyfang et al., 2010). For example, Illich's (1975) concept of conviviality captures the sense of the value of self-motivated endeavour beyond paid employment. Similarly, the literature on voluntary simplicity encapsulates alternative conceptualisations of the "good life", involving, as Alexander (2013) notes, a re-substitution of social relations, community engagement, creative activity, home-based production, and self-development, for the materialist sources of life satisfaction currently being relied on. As Nørgård (2013) notes, we gain direct satisfaction from many of the activities we engage in on a voluntary basis, compared with the current dominant economy, where any lack of intrinsic satisfaction is (theoretically) assumed to be compensated for by consumption of material goods.

The specific tasks involved in taking care of people and planet are best defined through democratic deliberation. This deliberation would, in particular, replace capitalist and market determination of what counts as valuable work (Laruffa et al., 2021). McGann and Murphy (2021) also note the importance, via PI, of a shift from a focus on people's (in)ability to work, to the approach of investing in people's skills, abilities, and opportunities. To emphasise the importance of a model of PI that relies on co-creation, Laruffa et al. alert us to the problem of defining participation either too narrowly, or too broadly, and/or that the process is insufficiently transparent: co-creation via deliberation at the local level is identified as the solution.

Finally, a common argument against any form of Basic Income is its affordability in terms of financial feasibility. Three ideas with regard to addressing this are first, Modern Monetary Theory, involving the government effectively printing money to increase appropriate economic activity (Mitchell et al., 2003; Thomas, 2020), which occurred in particular during the early days of COVID-19 in many countries (Johnson & Roberto, 2020); second, taxes on the rich, and third, a robot tax (Pulkka, 2017). It is beyond the scope of this chapter to explore further the financial feasibility of a PI; however again, public deliberation is likely to be vital to gaining legitimacy and support for the solution to funding a PI. COVID-19 has shown that governments can manage to provide large amounts of money when they need (or choose) to, particularly in response to fears about economic decline (Prabhakar, 2020).

37.9   Conclusion

This chapter contends that greater individual and collective capacity is required to achieve the SDGs in the short term, and to work towards transforming them to a post-productivist, more eco-social model in the long term. Increasing prosociality, purpose and meaning, and deliberation are identified as significant ways of improving individual capacity to work towards the regeneration of a social and ecological system crucial to sustainable development. The need to transform work, to go well beyond

SDG8, is a particularly important rationale for major economic transformation via a PI. PI is a conditional model of Basic Income; conditionality is advocated, firstly, because it is more politically feasible, and secondly, because it is likely to be much more effective in promoting the cultural transformation to post-productivist, eco-social systems. A PI is based on a view of humans as having the potential for sustainable behaviours, but that long-term cultural transformation is required for this to occur.

References

Adler, P. S., & Heckscher, C. (2005). Towards collaborative community. In P. S. Adler & C. Heckscher (Eds.), *The firm as a collaborative community: Reconstructing trust in the knowledge economy* (pp. 11–105). Oxford University Press.

Alexander, S. (2013). Voluntary simplicity and the social reconstruction of law: Degrowth from the grassroots up. *Environmental Values, 22*(2), 287–308.

Alston, P. (2019). Universal basic income as a social rights–based antidote to growing economic insecurity. In K. G. Young (Ed.), *The future of economic and social rights.* Cambridge University Press.

Atkinson, Q. D., & Jacquet, J. (2022). Challenging the idea that humans are not designed to solve climate change. *Perspectives on Psychological Science, 17*(3), 619–630. https://doi.org/10.1177/17456916211018454

Avis, J. (2021). Beyond neo-liberalism a new settlement—Three crises and post-secondary education. *Journal for Critical Education Policy Studies, 19*(1), 158–183.

Barbour, V., Clark, J., Jones, S., & Veitch, E. (2010). Social relationships are key to health, and to health policy. *PLOS Medicine, 7*(8), e1000334.

Blesh, J., Hoey, L., D., Jones, A., Friedmann, H., & Perfecto, I. (2019). Development pathways toward "zero hunger". *World Development, 118*, 1–14. https://doi.org/10.1016/j.worlddev.2019.1002.1004.

Carr-Hill, R., & Lintott, J. (2002). *Consumption, jobs and the environment.* Palgrave Macmillan.

Chessell, D. (2018). The jobless economy in a post-work society: How automation will transform the labor market. *Psychosociological Issues in Human Resource Management, 6*(2), 74–79.

Christensen, E. (2008). *The heretical political discourse - a discourse analysis of the Danish debate on basic income.* Aalborg University Press.

Crum, A. J., Akinola, M., Martin, A., & Fath, S. (2017). The role of stress mindset in shaping cognitive, emotional, and physiological responses to challenging and threatening stress. *Anxiety, Stress & Coping, 30*(4), 379–395.

Dasgupta, P., Dasgupta, A., & Barrett, S. (2021). Population, ecological footprint, and the sustainable development goals. *Environment and Resource Economics*, 1–14. https://doi.org/10.1007/s10640-021-00595-5

Davelaar, D. (2021). Transformation for sustainability: A deep leverage points approach. *Sustainability Science, 16*, 727–747.

Eckersley, R. (2000). The mixed blessings of material progress: Diminishing returns in the pursuit of happiness. *Journal of Happiness Studies, 1*(3), 267–292.

Emmons, R. A. (2003). Personal goals, life meaning, and virtue: Wellsprings of a positive life. In C. L. M. Keyes & J. Haidt (Eds.), *Flourishing: Positive psychology and the life well-lived* (pp. 105–128). American Psychological Association.

Esteva, G., Prakash, M. S., & Stuchul, D. L. (2005). From a pedagogy for liberation to liberation from pedagogy. In C. A. Bowers & F. Apffel-Marglin (Eds.), *Rethinking Freire: Globalization and the environmental crisis* (pp. 13–30). Lawrence Erlbaum Associates.

Foster, J. (2021). *Why we need a climate jobs guarantee.* https://overland.org.au/2021/10/why-we-need-a-climate-jobs-guarantee/

Frey, D. F. (2017). Economic growth, full employment and decent work: The means and ends in SDG 8. *The International Journal of Human Rights, 21*(8), 1164–1184.

Frey, D. F., & MacNaughton, G. (2016, April-June). A human rights lens on full employment and decent work in the 2030 sustainable development agenda. *Journal of Workplace Rights,* 1–13. https://doi.org/10.1177/2158244016649580

Fukuda-Parr, S., & Muchhala, B. (2020). The Southern origins of sustainable development goals: Ideas, actors, aspirations. *World Development, 126.* https://doi.org/10.1016/j.worlddev.2019.104706.

Fung, A., & Wright, E. O. (2001). Deepening democracy: Innovations in empowered participatory governance. *Politics & Society, 29*(1), 5–41.

Giddens, A. (1991). *Modernity and self-identity: Self and society in the late modern age.* Polity Press.

Gilbert, R., Murphy, N. A., Stepka, A., Barrett, M., & Worku, D. (2018). Would a basic income guarantee reduce the motivation to work? An analysis of labor responses in 16 trial programs. *Basic Income Studies, 13*(2), https://doi.org/10.1515/bis-2018-0011

Gough, I. (2021). Two scenarios for sustainable selfare: A framework for an eco-social contract. *Social Policy & Society, 21,* 460–472. https://doi.org/10.1017/S1474746421000701

Griffin, V., Zlotowitz, S., McLoughlin, E., & Kagan, C. (2017). Universal basic income: A psychological impact assessment. *Educational Psychology Research and Practice, 3*(1), 86–111.

Hallett, R. J., Mullen, N. K., Tideswell, A. E., Haake, S. J., Graney, M., & Hurley, M. V. (2020). Community event sustainability: Why don't people volunteer? *Voluntary Sector Review, 11*(2), 137–167.

Hasdell, R. (2020). *What we know about universal basic income: A cross-synthesis of reviews.* Basic Income Lab. http://basicincome.stanford.edu/uploads/Umbrella%20Review%20BI_final.pdf

Hickel, J. (2019). The contradiction of the sustainable development goals: Growth versus ecology on a finite planet. *Sustainable Development, 27,* 873–884.

Hines, A. (2019). Getting ready for a post-work future. *Foresight and STI Governance, 13*(1), 19–30.

Illich, I. (1975). *Tools for conviviality.* Fontana.

Inglehart, R. (2018). *Cultural evolution: People's motivations are changing, and reshaping the world.* Cambridge University Press.

Jacobs, G., Macfarlane, R., & Asokan, N. (1997). *Comprehensive theory of social development.* International Center for Peace and Development.

Jauch, H. (2015). The rise and fall of the basic income grant campaign: Lessons from Namibia. *Global Labour Journal, 6*(3), 336–350.

Johnson, A. F., & Roberto, K. J. (2020). The COVID-19 pandemic: Time for a universal basic income? *Public Administration and Development, 40*(4), 232–235.

Jönsson, M. B. K. (2017). Responsibility and the United Nations' sustainable development goals. *Forum for Development Studies, 44*(1), 13–29.

Kasper, C., & Mulder, M. B. (2015). Who helps and why? Cooperative Networks in Mpimbwe. *Current Anthropology, 56*(5), 701–732.

Kaza, S. (2000). Overcoming the grip of consumerism. *Buddhist-Christian Studies, 20,* 23–42.

Kitayama, S., & Salvador, C. E. (2017). Culture embrained: Going beyond the nature-nurture dichotomy. *Perspectives Psychological Science, 12*(5), 841–854. https://doi.org/10.1177/1745691617707317

Küng, H. (2005). *Global ethic and human responsibilities.* Submitted to the high-level expert group meeting on "Human rights and human responsibilities in the age of terrorism", Santa Clara University. http://www.scu.edu/ethics/practicing/focusareas/globalethics/laughlin-lectures/global-ethic-human-responsibility.html

Laininen, E. (2019). Transforming our worldview towards a sustainable future. In J. W. Cook (Ed.), *Sustainability, human wellbeing, and the future of education* (pp. 161–200). Palgrave McMillan.

Laruffa, F., McGann, M., & Murphy, M. P. (2021). Enabling participation income for an eco-social state. *Social Policy & Society*. https://doi.org/10.1017/S1474746421000750

Laurian, L. (2009). Trust in planning: Theoretical and practical considerations for participatory and deliberative planning. *Planning Theory & Practice, 10*(3), 369–391.

Lawrence, J. E. S. (2017). A missing link in Gloss et al. ("From handmaidens to POSH humanitarians"). *Industrial and Organizational Psychology, 10*(3), 407–410.

Layton, L. (2010). Irrational exuberance: Neoliberal subjectivity and the perversion of truth. *Subjectivity, 3*, 303–322.

Layton, L. (2014). Some psychic effects of neoliberalism: Narcissism, disavowal, perversion. *Psychoanalysis, Culture & Society, 19*, 161–178.

Lips-Wiersma, M., & Morris, L. (2009). Discriminating between "meaningful work" and the "management of meaning." *Journal of Business Ethics, 88*, 491–511.

Macarov, D. (1996). The employment of new ends: Planning for permanent unemployment. *Annals of the American Academy of Political and Social Science, 544*(March), 191–202.

Maiteny, P. (2000). Psychodynamics of meaning and action for a sustainable future. *Futures, 32*, 339–360.

Maiteny, P. (2003). Psychological and cultural dynamics of sustainable human systems. In F. Parra-Luna (Ed.), *Systems science and cybernetics, in encyclopedia of life support systems*. UNESCO.

Maiteny, P. (2011). Longing to be human: Evolving ourselves in healing the earth. In M. J. Rust & N. Totton (Eds.), *Vital signs: Psychological responses to ecological crisis* (pp. 69–82). Karnac.

Mayseless, O., & Keren, E. (2014). Finding a meaningful life as a developmental task in emerging adulthood: The domains of love and work across cultures. *Emerging Adulthood, 2*(1), 63–73.

McGann, M., & Murphy, M. P. (2021). Income support in an eco-social state: The case for participation income. *Social Policy & Society*. https://doi.org/10.1017/S1474746421000397

McKenzie, K. (2021). How to increase the likelihood of making the sustainable development goals a reality: An enhanced model of deliberative democracy and the role for psychologists within it. In M. MacLachlan & J. McVeigh (Eds.), *Macropsychology*. Springer.

Misiaszek, G. (2018). *Educating the global environmental citizen: Understanding ecopedagogy in local and global contexts*. Routledge.

Mitchell, W., Cowling, S., & Watts, M. (2003). *A community development job guarantee*. Centre of Full Employment and Equity. http://e1.newcastle.edu.au/coffee/docs/policy_reports/CDJG.pdf

Mnguni, P. (2010). Anxiety and defense in sustainability. *Psychoanalysis, Culture & Society, 15*, 117–135.

Monkelbaan, J. (2019). *Governance for the sustainable development goals*. Springer.

Nieswandt, K. (2020). Automation, basic income and merit. In K. G. Breen & J. P. Deranty (Eds.), *Whither work? The politics and ethics of contemporary work* (pp. 102–119). Routledge.

Nørgård, J. S. (2013). Happy degrowth through more amateur economy. *Journal of Cleaner Production, 38*, 61–70.

O'Brien, K., & Sygna, L. (2013). Responding to climate change: The three spheres of transformation. In *Proceedings of transformation in a changing climate* (pp. 16–23). University of Oslo.

Ostrom, E. (2000). Collective action and the evolution of social norms. *The Journal of Economic Perspectives, 14*(3), 137–158.

Pearson, A. R., Schuldt, J. P., & Romero-Canyas, R. (2016). Social climate science: A new vista for psychological science. *Perspectives on Psychological Science, 11*(5), 632–650. https://doi.org/10.1177/1745691616639726

Pelletier, D., Kraak, V., McCullum, C., Uusitalo, U., & Rich, R. (1999). The shaping of collective values through deliberative democracy: An empirical study from New York's North Country. *Policy Sciences, 32*(103–131).

Peltz, R. (2005). The manic society. *Psychoanalytic Dialogues, 15*(3), 347–366.

Pérez-Muñoz, C. (2016). A defence of participation income. *Journal of Public Policy, 36*(2), 169–193.

Pérez-Muñoz, C. (2018). Participation income and the provision of socially valuable activities. *The Political Quarterly, 89*(2), 268–272.

Pogge, T., & Sengupta, M. (2015). The sustainable development goals: A plan for building a better world? *Journal of Global Ethics, 11*(1), 56–64.

Power, M. (2004). Social provisioning as a starting point for feminist economics. *Feminist Economics, 10*(3), 3–19.

Prabhakar, R. (2020). Universal basic income and COVID-19. *IPPR Progressive Review, 27*(1), 105–113.

Pradhan, R. P., & Sanyal, G. S. (2011). Good governance and human development: Evidence from Indian states. *Journal of Social and Development Science, 1*(1), 1–8.

Pulkka, V.-V. (2017). A free lunch with robots—Can a basic income stabilise the digital economy? *Transfer: European Review of Labour and Research, 23*(3), 295–311. http://doi.org/10.1177/1024258917708704

Rai, S. M., Brown, B. D., & Ruwanpura, K. N. (2019). SDG 8: Decent work and economic growth—A gendered analysis. *World Development, 113*, 368-380.

Raskin, P., Banuri, T., Gallopín, G., Gutman, P., Hammond, A., Kates, R., & Swart, R. (2002). Great transition: The promise and lure of the times ahead. *A report of the Global Scenario Group, SEI PoleStar Series Report no. 10,* http://www.sei.se

Rees, W. (2010). What's blocking sustainability? Human nature, cognition, and denial. *Sustainability: Science, Practice, & Policy 6*(2), 13–25.

Richerson, P. J., Boyd, R. T., & Henrich, J. (2003). *Cultural evolution of human cooperation.* MIT Press.

Riedy, C. (2003). A deeper and wider understanding of sustainable development. *Ecopolitics. XIV conference: Greening sustainability,* Victoria.

Rothstein, B., & Stolle, D. (2002). How political institutions create and destroy social capital: An institutional theory of generalized trust. *Paper prepared for the 98th Meeting of the American Political Science Association in Boston, MA.*

Rothstein, B., & Uslaner, E. M. (2005). All for all: Equality, corruption and social trust. *World Politics, 58*(1), 41–72.

Sachs, J. D., Schmidt-Traub, G., & Mazzucato, M. (2019). Six transformations to achieve the Sustainable Development Goals. *Nature Sustainability, 2*, 805–814.

Schneiderman, N., Ironson, G., & Siegel, S. D. (2005). Stress and health: Psychological, behavioral, and biological determinants. *Annual Review of Clinical Psychology, 1*, 607–628.

Seyfang, G., Smith, A., & Longhurst, N. (2010). Grassroots innovations for sustainable development: A new research agenda. *Economic Sociology - the European Electronic Newsletter, 12*(1), 1–5.

Smith, K. B. (2006). Representational altruism: The wary cooperator as authoritative decision maker. *American Journal of Political Science, 50*(4), 1013–1022.

Soper, K. (2007). Re-thinking the "good life": The citizenship dimension of consumer disaffection with consumerism. *Journal of Consumer Culture, 7*(2), 205–229.

Spangenberg, J. H. (2014). Institutional change for strong sustainable consumption: Sustainable consumption and the degrowth economy. *Sustainability: Science, Practice and Policy, 10*(1), 62–77.

Stewart, J. E. (2014). The direction of evolution: The rise of cooperative organization. *Bio Systems, 123*, 27–36.

Stewart, J. E. (2020). Towards a general theory of the major cooperative evolutionary transitions. *Biosystems, 198.* https://doi.org/10.1016/j.biosystems.2020.104237

Suckling, E., Christensen, Z., & Walton, D. (2021). Poverty trends: Global, regional and national. *Development Initiatives,* https://www.devinit.org/resources/poverty-trends-global-regional-and-national/#note-LdT0zfnCl

Thomas, A. (2020). Full employment, unconditional basic income and the Keynesian critique of rentier capitalism. *Basic Income Studies 15*(1). https://doi.org/10.1515/bis-2019-0015

Thompson, D. (2015, July/August). A world without work. *The Atlantic.* https://www.theatlantic.com/magazine/archive/2015/07/world-without-work/395294/

Tukker, A., Emmert, S., Charter, M., Vezzoli, C., Sto, E., Andersen, M. M., Geerken, T., Tischner, U., & Lahlou, S. (2008). Fostering change to sustainable consumption and production: An evidence based view. *Journal of Cleaner Production, 16*, 1218–1225.

Turchin, P., & Gavrilets, S. (2009). Evolution of complex hierarchical societies. *Social Evolution & History, 8*(2), 167–198.

Umberson, D., Crosnoe, R., & Reczek, C. (2010). Social relationships and health behavior across life course. *Annual Review Sociology, 36*, 139–157.

Umberson, D., & Montez, J. K. (2010). Social relationships and health: A flashpoint for health policy. *Journal of Health and Social Behavior, 51*(S), S54–S66.

Vermeulen, B., Kesselhut, J., Pyka, A., & Saviotti, P. P. (2018). The impact of automation on employment: Just the usual structural change? *Sustainability, 10*(5), https://doi.org/10.3390/su10051661

Walters, S. (2010). The planet will not survive if it's not a learning planet: Sustainable development within learning through life. *International Journal of Lifelong Education, 29*(4), 427–436.

Way, B. M. (2013). Social relationships and public health: A social neuroscience perspective focusing on the opioid system. In P. A. Hall (Ed.), *Social neuroscience and public health* (pp. 163–177). Springer.

Whiting, K., Konstantakos, L., Carrasco, A., & Carmon, L. G. (2018). Sustainable development, wellbeing and material consumption: A stoic perspective. *Sustainability, 10*(2), 474, https://doi.org/10.3390/su10020474-

Widerquist, K. (2001). Perspectives on the guaranteed income, Part II. *Journal of Economic Issues, 35*(4), 1019–1030.

Wisman, J. D. (2002). The moral imperative and social rationality of government-guaranteed employment and reskilling. *Review of Social Economy, 63*(2), 269–289.

Wisor, S. (2012). After the MDGs: Citizen deliberation and the post-development framework. *Ethics & International Affairs, 26*(1), 113–133.

Witt, A. H. (2013). *Worldviews and the transformation to sustainable societies: An exploration of the cultural and psychological dimensions of our global environmental challenges.* Doctoral thesis, VU University.

Wong, P. T. P. (2014). Viktor Frankl's meaning seeking model and positive psychology. In A. Batthyany & P. Russo-Netzer (Eds.), *Meaning in existential and positive psychology* (pp. 149–184). Springer.

Zabel, H. U. (2005). A model of human behaviour for sustainability. *International Journal of Social Economics, 32*(8), 717–734. https://doi.org/10.1108/03068290510608228

Chapter 38
For an Education that Contributes to Heal the World: The Role of Buddhist Education

Marie-Laure Mimoun-Sorel

38.1 Introduction

By who we are individually, collectively, and generationally, by the way we perceive ourselves and our surroundings, but also by the way we react, create, and educate, we have contributed to the suffering of today's world. Rabhi (2011) emphasises that it may seem incongruous to believe that the choice of a tomato, a chicken, or a piece of clothing, the attention we pay to the people we meet every day, or the choice of our management systems in our workplaces, can change the direction of humanity. And yet, it is this sum of small choices, stimulated by a consumerist and productivist vision of the world, that has brought us to where we are.

However, the actual state of the world is still mainly discussed and analysed from a perspective where the predominant techno-economic conception privileges calculation as a way of knowing human realities (growth rates, GDP, surveys, etc.), whereas suffering and joy, unhappiness and happiness, and love and hate, are incalculable. Thus, it is not only our ignorance, but also our knowledge that blinds us (Morin, 2020a). The very type of data we gather contributes to restraining us from reaching our sustainable goals.

For years, we have known that re-evaluations of priorities must be done, and all sorts of reconciliations and conciliations have to be made in order to engage in a process of restoration of our world. We know that our mode of living needs to be reorganised according to a way of thinking and doing that considers both the wellbeing of human beings and the entirety of Nature (Mimoun-Sorel, 2016; Morin, 2003; Rabhi, 2010). What we seem to miss in trying to achieve our sustainability goals is our collective mobilisation. We do not feel concerned with this mobilisation for a sustainable future because, in our criteria for success in life, wisdom is not considered

M.-L. Mimoun-Sorel (✉)
Hoa Nghiem Buddhist College, Springvale South, VIC 3172, Australia
e-mail: mlsmet@comcen.com.au

K. Beasy et al. (eds.), *Education and the UN Sustainable Development Goals*, Education for Sustainability 7,
https://doi.org/10.1007/978-981-99-3802-5_38

the ultimate achievement. Therefore, we do not look for wisdom as a priority and criterion for finding and applying solutions for future generations. Reconnecting with the nature of wisdom and the level of consciousness it implies should be seen as the ultimate purpose of education to regenerate the humanity within us and put it into action.

As there is an emergency to engage with the 2030 Sustainable Development Goals (SDGs) (United Nations, n.d.b), after scanning the roots of our suffering world and the essential learning for our time, this chapter relates the possibility of fulfilling the realisation of SDG Goal 4, relating to Quality Education from a Buddhist perspective. The example of the Hoa Nghiem Buddhist College (HNBC) approach shows that education for wisdom is the ultimate educational achievement that will lead to the realisation of all other SDGs (United Nations, n.d.a), as intentions and actions in every context are driven by the desire to find wise solutions for individuals, communities, and nature in its entirety. As a model for wisdom education, we consider the HNBC Systemic Learning Approach, which incorporates the four dimensions of *Learning to Be* for sustainable living in the twenty-first century (Delors, 1996; Mimoun-Sorel, 2011). These four dimensions are Learning to Be *Wise*, Learning to Learn *Holistically*, Learning to Do *Ethically,* and Learning to Live *Together,* as well as the implementation of biomimicry thinking (Benyus, 2002). They are the foundation of all aspects of the HNBC curriculum, playing an important part in the development of our quality of being, in order to fulfil the 17 SDGs and contribute to healing the world.

38.1.1 Commenting on a Suffering World

The 17 SDGs are the almost inevitable result of decades of humans and Nature suffering, because of the way we are, learn, do things, and live together. It often happens that when we are immersed for too long in a suffering state, we compensate with "distractions" to such a point that we do not even realise our state of ill-being, and do not even make the connection with its effects. For example, as we are caught in our economic system of infinite growth, we do not see or do not want to see that the machine for producing the GDP of nations needs a human being who is a consumer, consumed, and ignorant (Rabhi, 2019). It is what we have become.

We are caught up in the complexity of a system that we have created and that we can no longer control. We are dominated by the model we have set up, which frees itself from human determination to establish and follow its own logic, despite the goodwill to reorientate our thinking, our actions, and our destiny. Due to our frenzy of consumption, we have become servants, more or less aware, of the mechanisms we have created (Rabhi, 2019). We have become products destined to serve economic growth (Hamilton, 2003; Morin, 2020a). By giving priority to over-developing our own personal comfort, we are increasingly losing our humanity, which means our capacity to feel our interconnection with others and the whole living world. However, the humanity within us endows us with the responsibility to care for our habitat and its inhabitants. By damaging our earthly ecosystem from which we owe our living, we do not realise that we are losing our freedom to exist, and we are increasingly losing our humanity and the dignified choices that it engenders. We are losing our awareness of being, and being part of life, to the detriment of having, of always having to have more to fill the void of not feeling connected to life and its cycles (Mimoun-Sorel, 2011).

38.1.2   The Quantitative Drift: Consumerism as a Pain Killer

Consumerism is the idea that increasing the consumption of goods and services purchased in the market is always a desirable goal, and that a person's wellbeing and happiness depend fundamentally on obtaining consumer goods and material possessions. Environmental problems are frequently associated with consumerism to the extent that consumer goods industries, and the direct effects of consumption, produce environmental impacts. These can include pollution by producing industries, resource depletion due to widespread, conspicuous consumption, and problems with waste disposal from excess consumer goods and packaging. Consumerism is often criticised on psychological grounds. It is blamed for increased status anxiety, where people increase their consumption to deal with the stress associated with social status (Rabhi, 2019).

Productivity at all costs has led to the creation of a dominant model of society that measures its success only by output, i.e. the quantitative, to the detriment of the qualitative, i.e. the human and Nature. Earth is now not recognised as our living ecosystem on which our survival depends, as land to produce food, but instead, to "grow" money. Rabhi (2021) underlines that one of the principles of a democracy is the possibility to make choices. If we have to follow the technological race at all costs, we are no longer in a democracy, but in a technocracy. The consumerist society has conditioned us to seek something that is always more than we already have, and places us in a constant illusory temporality every time we pronounce the phrases "when I get that." As a result of our greed, the land is no longer for producing food, but for spitting out money (Capra, 1982; Gangadean, 2006; Hanh, 2012; Morin, 2020a; Rabhi, 2010).

This mindset expresses the stigma of being continuously outside of ourselves and therefore, fragile. We dream; we imagine. We think that we think freely, but we lose contact with the real. Being disconnected from our humanity means that we do not understand our essential needs to survive as individuals, members of communities, and members of human species, among other species. Therefore, we become ignorant and biologically, we inflict suffering on Nature; but what we do not realise is that we also inflict it on ourselves. Our ignorance makes us become irresponsible human beings. We are lost in illusionary freedom, and we suffer, usually without being aware that we suffer, because what we gain from the consumerist society is a very powerful pain killer. Our whole beings are disconnected from what makes us alive: Nature and life itself, with their wise sustainable knowledge to keep life alive.

The planetary crisis caused by the COVID-19 coronavirus highlights that the community of destiny of all humans is inseparably linked with the bio-ecological destiny of planet Earth. At the same time, it intensifies the crisis of humanity, which fails to constitute itself as humanity (Capra, 2003; Morin, 2020a). However, here, now in front of us, the 17 SDGs provide us with a framework that helps to raise our awareness of the interconnected priorities from which we might choose, as global citizens, to engage our responsibility, and develop our expertise and willingness in doing our part to achieve one goal or another, at our own level.

38.1.3 Moderation to Change Our Community of Destiny

One of the most concrete and simple ways for Western populations to achieve these goals is to practise moderation (Benyus, 2002; Capra, 2014; Elgin, 1993; Hanh, 2012; Rabhi, 2011). Moderation means adjusting the indispensable and the necessary and reducing the superfluous. As long as we do not reduce the superfluous, we will continue to be victims of our bulimia, because the human being is manipulated to be insatiable with the ingrained illusion that "having" will make us happier. A human being, who is set up with the idea that he or she never has enough, is what the money-makers want. If the human being is satiable, it is all over for the latter (Rabhi, 2019). There is still something to be found that would generate a general mobilisation to practice moderation: something that would come from individual and collective choice to live in moderation, before the forces of Nature push us over the edge with an unquestionable authority that robs us of free will.

The quest for moderation appears to be necessary to enable a sustainable future. The initiation to moderation is a source of joy, because it makes satisfaction more accessible, abolishing the frustration produced by the ever-increasing demand for more and more, constantly maintained by a pernicious advertising talent, from which all children should be protected. Furthermore, with the pressure for "everything, right away," it means the end of that desire to which patience gives so much flavour and value (Morin, 2020b; Rabhi, 2011).

We have to learn the major lesson on moderation that every ecosystem on Earth demonstrates every day. Moderation is a natural and spontaneous attitude when we have understood that we belong to the Earth. Unfortunately, the majority of us still does not see that the community of destiny of all humans is inseparable from the bio-ecological destiny of the planet Earth (Morin, 2020a). To comprehend the complexity of what is at stake to keep us alive, it has become imperative to reconnect to our intrinsic interconnectedness to the living world. Being aware of this natural systemic process of interconnectedness, which is also a unifying force for the diversity of life's expression, brings us back to humility. This indispensable humility is an essential key to realising that we are not here to dominate Nature but to understand, love, and care for her (Capra, 2003).

At the same time this humility towards the grandeur of Nature is emerging, and it becomes urgent to make reforms to heal the world by keeping the notion of interconnectedness in mind. These would not be about budget cuts, but reforms of civilisation, of society, linked to reforms of life. It would combine the contradictory terms: "globalisation" (for everything that is about cooperation) and "de-globalisation" (to establish an autonomous food and health system and save the land from desertification); "growth" (of the economy of essential needs, of sustainability, of agriculture) and "de-growth" (of industrial agriculture and breeding, of the economy of the frivolous, of the illusory, and of the disposable); "development" (of everything that produces wellbeing, health, and responsible freedom) and "envelopment" (in community solidarity) (Morin, 2020b). These reforms of living only can be accomplished from our deep understanding of the benefits of moderation for our survival and the humility in front of Nature, and finally to learn from her. They would contribute to transforming our bulimic consumption to fill our inner emptiness into the conscious intention to engage in the 17 SDGs for an active participation and a meaningful life. At the educational level, priority will have to be given to a quality education that will enable students to understand deeply the interconnected challenges of our time, and the quality of being needed to participate in healing the world to make it sustainable.

38.1.4 What Has to Be Learned to Heal the World?

In order to contribute to healing the world, we need to be aware of and learn about two primordial aspects, from a fundamental perspective, as Earthlings. The first is to learn what it means to be born as an Earth species (Benyus, 2002; Morin, 2003; Rabhi, 2011). The second is to learn the quality of being necessary to live sustainably on Earth (Mimoun-Sorel, 2011; Morin, 2020b). We have to learn to be Indigenous to planet Earth.

While we are the children of our biological parents, we are also all equally Earthlings. Human beings on Earth are the result of local and global ecosystems, designed by Nature and composed of biotic and abiotic elements, that overtime gave birth to different species, including ours. In our reductive consciousness, we have made a great error in ignoring, for the majority of us, that our primary identity is that of all, being indigenous to planet Earth (Mimoun-Sorel, 2011). The Cambridge dictionary (n.d.) defines the word *indigenous* as "the people who originally lived in a place, rather than people who moved there from somewhere else." As human beings, we have originally lived on Earth, we have not moved here from somewhere else in the galaxy. In terms of our inherent and fundamental identity as indigenous to planet Earth and as social beings, this knowledge of our common indigeneity could provide us with a common ground from which we have the innate potential to produce unity of view, understanding, and solidarity among us all, regarding our survival as a species. Understanding that we are all part of planet Earth is the key to mobilising the world for a sustainable future. It reconnects us to our interconnectedness with the whole living world as taught in the *Ubuntu* tradition: I am because you are, and I exist because you exist (Bolden, 2014). It is an acknowledgement that is relevant to all species and connects them all to the inherent survival force that drives us all. Naturally, this is followed by an awareness of our community of earthly destiny, which urges us to play our part in avoiding damage or destruction to the ecosystems in which we live. It encourages us to practice moderation, which naturally contributes to our progress towards achieving the SDGs.

38.2 Our Triple Human Identity and Inter-being Nature

Being aware of our indigenous identity, we can better address the triple aspect of our human identity that makes us who we are, both in our uniqueness and in our commonality. Our triple identity is made up of who we are as individuals, as members of our communities, and as members of the human species among other species (Morin, 2001). Each aspect of our triple identity nourishes the development of the others. Becoming aware of it is a gift to ourselves, that of being well-equipped for our first steps towards a wisdom approach in our lives. This awareness that our identity is more than just individual or communitarian would help to avoid the development of our tyranny towards each other, either at the individual or communitarian level, or to serve the benefit of the human species at the expense of other species. Knowing and respecting our triple identity engenders our integrity of being and living on Earth.

Learning about our intrinsic triple identity helps understanding our interconnectedness with other human beings and communities as well with as living species, and to become accountable for maintaining their wellbeing. The Buddhist monk and peace activist Thich Nhat Hanh has translated this interconnectedness as a process of "inter-being." Hanh (2012) writes: "How we view the world affects everything within it. When we do harm to the environment, we do harm to ourselves … The ecosystem and we humans are not two different things. When we kill the ecosystem, we're killing ourselves. We *are* the ecosystem. …. We are the planet" (p. 76). Hanh advocates that we are only here because the planet is here. Our mineral and animal ancestors are still there within us, deeply in our cells. Knowing our inter-being nature makes us realise that all species, including ours, are inevitably embarked in a common destiny. What is done on one side of the Earth will have repercussions on the other side. Our triple identity embedded in our inter-being nature has the potential to awaken our sense of responsibility to take actions for a sustainable life on Earth. Once re-connected to our inter-being nature, we develop a systemic comprehension of our present world context and therefore, an understanding of the importance of SDG17: Partnerships for all the other sustainable development goals.

38.2.1   Nature of a Sustainable Life on Earth

To be born on Earth and to be able to keep living on it, it is essential to know how life creates conditions conducive to living on our limited planet. Life on Earth has survived and thrived by adapting to the limits and boundaries of Earth's planetary context—what we might call "Earth's Operating System" (Benyus, 2002). Our earthly context has particular characteristics, which means that, for example, the amount of water is limited. We are also constrained by gravity and the Earth's ecological and chemical cycles. This dynamic equilibrium responds to the fluctuating states of constant change within this earthly context. The problem we have had for decades is that we are constantly plundering and polluting the Earth. The damage is such that it will take years for the Earth to recover, while living species no longer have the conditions necessary to adapt to a context that is depriving them of the vital minimum. To keep the dynamic equilibrium essential to life on Earth, nine living principles have to be respected. We should learn and respect that Nature runs on sunlight, uses only the energy it needs, adapts form to function, recycles natural materials, rewards cooperation, relies on diversity, requires local expertise, curbs excesses from within, and exploits the power of boundaries (Benyus). As a human species, we should learn to apply these principles in the way we organise our lives and in the way we create technologies to serve life on Earth. Biomimicry thinking is one way of achieving this and has begun to be implemented to solve various sustainable global and local problems (AskNature, 2022).

38.3   Biomimicry: Reconnecting with the Wisdom of Nature

For more than a century, industrial civilisation has distracted us from the sustainability seen in living organisms gracefully orchestrated over the long term, by what we could call the wisdom of Nature. It is in this respect that recently, the idea of biomimicry (Benyus, 2002) represents a major paradigm shift in our relationship with the biosphere. Biomimicry constitutes a great advance regarding our confidence in a possible sustainable future on Earth as a way of thinking and as a methodology. Studying, experiencing, and acknowledging the mastery of Nature from its 3.8 billion years of regeneration and sustainable knowledge, Benyus spread the concept of Biomimicry in 2002 through the launch of her book titled "Biomimicry: Innovation inspired by Nature." Since then, through multiple conferences, articles, and websites such as *Biomimicry Institute* and *Biomimicry 3.8,* she has promoted Biomimicry as a natural foundation: as a way of thinking, organising, and making a sustainable future.

Benyus (2002) emphasises that Biomimicry is innovation inspired by Nature, arguing that in a society accustomed to dominating or "perfecting" Nature, this reverent imitation is a fundamentally new approach that is akin to a revolution. However, as the opposite of the Industrial Revolution, the Biomimicry Revolution inaugurates an age founded not on what we can extract or plunder from Nature, but on what we can actually learn from it. Biomimicry is essentially a process of taking a design challenge, then identifying an ecosystem that has already resolved that challenge, and literally attempting to mimic what we have learned from it while respecting life principles (see above). With the Biomimicry paradigm, it is not only about learning *about* Nature but also learning *from* Nature, as it has been mastering sustainable knowledge for billions of years.

38.4   Nature Bears All the Solutions Within Itself

Biomimicry is intrinsically relevant to each of the 17 SDGs in terms of its purpose and methodology. For example, looking at the way the structure and material of a spider web can capture, transport, and store a good amount of water from condensation from the air, has inspired very simple and cheap water-harvesting devices to collect water from clouds, such as mesh billboards used in the Moroccan mountains. In a more sophisticated way, but from the same biological strategy developed by spiders to design their webs, a system has been created for local water capture and storage for greenhouses in urban settings (AskNature, 2022). In these examples, Biomimicry technology responds to Goal 6 of the SDGs: Clean Water and Sanitation. Another example, inspired by the way fish can reduce energy losses from swimming in a school, vertical axis wind turbines are placed close together so that individual turbines can capture downstream airflow produced by the neighbouring turbines. This technique reduces the total area required for the turbines, while increasing energy production by up to 10 times. This Nature-inspired innovation addresses Goal 7: Affordable and Clean Energy. Numerous examples of sustainable innovations mimicking Nature can be found on the AskNature.org website, which shows how Biomimicry technology supports the achievement of the 2030 Sustainable Development Goals.

When we start to look, Benyus (2002) tells us that the answers to our questions are everywhere in Nature; we just need to change the lens with which we see the world. Through the exponential development of Biomimicry, Nature-based design and solutions offer endless expertise in biological strategies. Biologists, architects, engineers, builders, policymakers, researchers of all sorts, economists, entrepreneurs, and others can be inspired to work together on common ground to support our common sustainable destiny. With a Biomimicry approach, we not only learn from Nature's wisdom, but also heal ourselves—and this planet—in the process.

38.5   Quality of Being for a Sustainable World

After learning what it means to be born on Earth, the second aspect to participate in healing the world is to learn the quality of being necessary to live sustainably. Once we have understood the importance of realising that Earth has limited resources, it is essential to be initiated only to use what we need to live in moderation. In order to act this way, we need to develop humility from which we will understand that Nature has been a master of sustainable knowledge for 3.8 billion years, and that we should learn from it (Benyus, 2002). To make it work, we must value and acknowledge collaboration, solidarity, and mobilisation, instead of competition that only serves individualistic purposes (Capra, 2014).

It is encouraging to see that a new humility is also emerging from Biomimicry practice, one that, for example, turns an ordinary tree into a model for specialists in architecture, materials strength, fluid circulation, or energy management: a humility that is doubled by a fascination for complexity mastered without any conscious intervention. With humility also comes the feeling of reconnection to our inter-being nature, that which makes us attentive to the know-how of the spider in the corner of the window or to the seedlings in the cellars. This interconnectedness with the living world allows us to move constantly back and forth between our sense of belonging to the great family tree of life, to our more familiar sense of belonging to the human species, and finally, to the core of our personhood, with our awareness of a unique individuality (Chapelle, 2015).

38.6   Wisdom as a Life Purpose

The American Psychological Association (n.d.) defines wisdom as involving the integration of knowledge, experience, and deep understanding, as well as a tolerance for the uncertainties of life. The process of wisdom in decision-making requires an awareness of how things unfold over time, which gives a sense of balance. People demonstrating qualities of wisdom show a clear vision in regard to the possibilities to solve life's problems, and a certain composure in the face of difficult decisions. Intelligence may be needed for wisdom, but it is by no means sufficient; an ability to see the big picture, a sense of perspective, intellectual humility, and considerable self-examination also contribute to its development. Furthermore, wisdom requires a systemic understanding of how everyone plays their part at different levels of inter-connection and complexity, in order to contribute to the whole. Knowing what constitutes wisdom and better understanding its process will help propagate this natural, direct, and efficient human remedy that has the power to heal the world. Education to Wisdom should be the cornerstone and purpose of education before anything else. It would increasingly promote a wise choice of an art of living based on individual and collective self-limitation to support sustainability on Earth. Only individual change through the awakening of consciousness and a path towards wisdom will save us, as well as the humanity in us (Rabhi, 2011).

Buddhist practice has a long history of exploring the mindsets and thoughts that hinder the development of wisdom. *Buddhi* is a Sanskrit term derived from the root, *budh*, which means "to know" or "to be awake." Therefore, *Buddhi* refers to intellect and wisdom from a comprehensive vision of the real, allowing full understanding and decision-making. *Buddhi* is a clear and lucid thought, which connects true causes and effects, and highlights unfolding events in a rigorous way (Desjardins, 2010). Considerable awareness is therefore needed to be lucid and avoid deviance, leading to misunderstanding as well as systematic internal and external misconceptions and therefore, suffering. An essential knowledge to acquire is that, in most cases, we do not see situations as they are: we see them as our mind interprets them.

In the real world, if we run very fast without looking and our leg hits a table, it hurts in a neutral way. In our interpretation, it not only hurts, but above all, the table should not be in "my way" and that's it. "Blaming the table" is a common reaction; however, it is from that simple kind of thought that our desire to dominate others and Nature is born. We take it personally that "the table" should not be in "our way," and little by little, this erroneous perception of the real misleads our full conception and understanding of the world that surrounds us. The thought of systematically removing what disturbs us in our personal landscape has contributed to our need to conquer Nature as well as other human beings and species. The desire for something other than what is, and against which we can do nothing, is limitless. Driven by desire or fear of missing out, our minds enter into endless battles of compensation and conquests, until we reach the destruction of our planet and before that, all the creatures that live on it.

38.6.1 Education to Wisdom at Hoa Nghiem Buddhist College

In its approach to education, Hoa Nghiem Buddhist College (HNBC) is deeply committed to cultivating reverence for life and Nature and, to this end, to promoting an education of wisdom. HNBC is one of just a few Buddhist schools in Australia. The author of this chapter has the role of educational leader in this college, which was co-founded by the Most Venerable Thich Thien Tam and Venerable Thich Phuoc Uyen (principal of the school) in 2015. The aim and priority of this educational environment is the development of students' wisdom through all aspects of their learning areas, based on the pillar of *Learning to Be* in the 21st Century (Delors, 1996; Mimoun-Sorel, 2011). Another aspect of Thich Thien Tam and Thich Phuoc Uyen's intention in establishing the school was to support the education of children from families who have experienced hardship, by providing them with the environment, resources, and learning to overcome the transgenerational suffering that usually comes from the trauma, for example, from the long-term effects of the Vietnam War. In this respect, the creation of HNBC aligns with what is called *"engaged Buddhism"* by Thich Nath Hanh, the internationally known Vietnamese Buddhist monk and spiritual leader. *"Engaged Buddhism* means that mindfulness is practised wherever we are, whatever we are doing, at any time" (Hanh, 2012, p. 3). Complementary to contemplative moments, this immersed-in-the-world practice intends to lessen the suffering of people in the communities and is actively committed to participate in preserving all forms of life on Earth.

The school reflects and implements the Buddhist practices of compassion and kindness that contribute daily to the experience and understanding of mental and emotional processes leading to greater inner peace and wisdom for new generations of children. Wisdom has been increasingly understood by families and students as the main purpose of learning which will be implemented throughout students' schooling, and subsequently in any career and life choices they will make. Within her role of promoting the cultivation of wisdom in each student and teacher, as well as shaping the school's management and curriculum models, Tu My Nguyen (Venerable Thich Phuoc Uyen) designed and introduced—in collaboration with the educational leader—a very comprehensive Systemic Learning Approach (see Fig. 38.1) to prepare students for the complexity and challenges of our time, such as the ones expressed in the 17 SDGs.

As discussed above, HNBC has embarked on the development of a culture of thinking and doing that promotes a Systemic Learning Approach encompassing

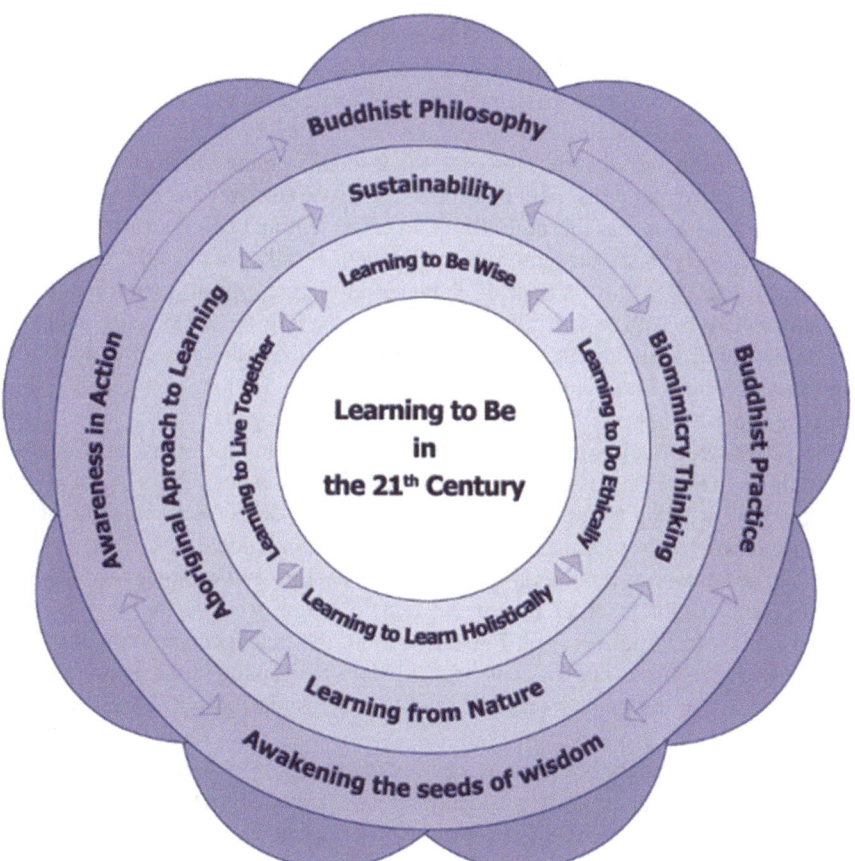

Fig. 38.1 Systemic learning approach at Hoa Nghiem Buddhist College

Buddhist philosophy and practice, as well as Biomimicry thinking and technology, to offer the views and possibilities of a sustainable future to the new generations. While the Australian state of Victoria's curriculum provides the framework (Victorian Curriculum and Assessment Authority, n.d.), HNBC enacts it beyond the boundaries of the curriculum so that students become better connected to life, and confident to bring their learning, insights, talents, and humanity to the world. The HNBC Systemic Learning Approach also encompasses all four essential pillars/dimensions for *Learning to Be in the twenty-first century,* which were recommended by UNESCO (Delors, 1996) and re-evaluated and redefined through the research of Mimoun-Sorel (2011) and in collaboration with HNBC, expressed as: Learning to Be *Wise*, Learning to Learn *Holistically*, Learning to Do *Ethically,* and Learning to Live *Together*.

38.7 Buddhist Philosophy and Practice

From Buddhist philosophy, HNBC students learn that as soon as we are born on Earth, our Nature as humans—as well as the Nature of all living things—is automatically stamped by three marks of existence that will lead us to wisdom when we fully embrace them. The first is that in the course of life, everyone will experience ill-being and suffering of all sorts. However, the Buddhist practice advocates that there is a learning and experiential path that shows the way to recover and connect to inner peace. The second is that life on Earth is impermanent and being aware of it helps us to live serenely in the present moment, as well as fully embrace the uncertainty inherent in life. The third is that all elements in Nature and in human nature are interconnected as well as interdependent: understanding the inter-being nature of life on Earth brings lucidity to approach the real, and therefore, inner freedom from any conditioning. These three marks of existence in the Buddhist philosophy align with the above definition of wisdom by Western psychologists.

At HNBC, meditation practice and its breathing techniques play an important role. It aims to increase self-awareness, which will develop inner peace, clear vision, and therefore wisdom to approach and understand any decision-making and action processes involved in solving life's problems, on an individual or collective level. Buddhist practice also requires a rigorous introspection and awareness to develop lucidity and insight in order to see the real in which we live to provide accurate responses to life challenges. For this reason, the management team, teachers, and students practise awareness and seek wisdom by looking and listening deeply, engaging fully in the present moment, and taking responsibility for their thoughts and actions.

The Buddhist practice is a learning journey requiring the same inquiring mind that students use to investigate any topic in any subject. It challenges them not to take any concept or truth for granted, but to question, observe, and experiment with Buddhist principles and daily life experiences, just as they practise in the fields of science and philosophy. These introspective, open-minded, and open-hearted practices help them, first to see clearly in themselves, then in others. It provides the skill to let go of the feeling of frustration and anger that usually biases understanding as it makes us blind to the common good as well as our common humanity.

38.8 Nature as a Model and Mentor

Looking at Nature as a model and a mentor, HNBC promotes the development of a culture of thinking that prioritises reverence for life, and where Biomimicry thinking and practice play a primordial role, as it gives hope to the new generations. Despite the catastrophic state of the world, HNBC is convinced that we have the possibility to do things differently to address the 17 SDGs, and therefore preserve life on Earth. To operate closer to Nature's sustainable model, HNBC took into consideration Capra's suggestion (2003) that we shift our perception and perspective as follows:

- Shifting from object to *relationship*: developing the HNBC programme as a systemic learning approach; moving away from teaching only on account of disciplines where students become objects of the learning industry;
- Shifting from objective knowledge to *contextual knowledge*: prioritising wisdom as it always refers to local and/or global contexts to find solutions to problems;
- Shifting from structure to *process*: HNBC's management process consists in evolving organically, based on individuals' quality of being, their ability to be in the present moment, and their wisdom to adapt to changing priorities. This organic process enhances the confidence and potential of both students and teachers in approaching diverse learning experiences and challenges in constantly changing contexts. This approach requires that everyone involved understands and embraces that they play a unique role in the functioning, evolution, and sustainability of the whole school, just as an ecosystem does.

At HNBC, implementing Biomimicry thinking in all aspects of our learning by going beyond the curriculum and wondering "how does Nature solve this problem?" is about valuing Nature for what we can learn, not what we can extract, harvest, or domesticate. Benyus (2002) argues that in this process, we also learn about ourselves, our purpose, and our connection to each other, as well to as Earth as our home. Being inspired by Nature's wisdom contributes to healing ourselves, and this planet, in the process. Through Biomimicry thinking and practice, students discover that for all the challenges we face, Nature has a solution. While inquiring, they realise that what we have to do is not only change the lens with which we see the world, but also develop an empathetic and interconnected understanding of how life operates and, in the end, how we fit into it. Combined with the learning of our inter-being nature, students understand that their life challenges will be to create products, processes, and systems—new ways of living—that will solve our greatest design challenges sustainably, and in solidarity with all life on Earth. As they feel and see that they have the possibility to play a concrete role in shaping their future, students gain confidence in themselves and in their communities.

Through land-based learning approaches, students develop advocacy for Nature. They experience a sense of honouring the Earth and paying respect to its faculty to regenerate itself in the face of challenges from environmental hardships over the past 3.8 billion years. With the practice of "Awareness in Action," they perceive that growing a vegetable garden is not just about growing vegetables, it is about learning to marvel at the mystery of life. At the level of their wellbeing, while connecting with Nature, its ecosystems and wonders, they experience that cultivating natural and simple contentment frees them from frustration. Thanks to their reconnection to Nature and the development of their thinking and being towards life in terms of sustainability, students notice and learn that happiness is not found, it is made. One of the important teachings of Buddhist practice is that happiness does not depend on what we lack, but on how we use what we have (Desjardins, 2010; Hanh, 2012).

HNBC students' reconnection with Nature, her ecosystems and wonders, is particularly experienced and visible during the numerous school Nature camps they attend every year. During the last one-week winter camp at Wilson Promontory (in the state of Victoria), Year 5 and 6 students practised a silent walking meditation for one and a half hours on a beach at 7 a.m. One of the educational purposes of this silent walking meditation was for the students to pay attention to their own noise pollution in order to have the minimum impact on Nature and feel totally immersed in her. The alternating inhalation and exhalation of their lungs gave rhythm to their bare feet, which they placed delicately on the sandy ground as if they were softly "kissing" the Earth.

This practice allowed them to experience being an integral part of Nature while they tried to disturb her as little as possible. Focused on their steps and breathing while being mindful, they connected to Nature with all their senses. Embracing the practice, they developed the awareness of belonging to Nature, they experienced the inter-being relationship with the surrounding elements and creatures, which was a gigantic step regarding the development of their awareness. This practice improved the students' quality of being and presence in Nature. They began to develop the skills of deep listening, as well as humility, which are the roots of wisdom in Buddhist practice.

Later, during an evening silent meditation walk in a clearing, while demonstrating reverence through breathing, mindset, and movement, for a while, an emu seemed confident to choose to follow students at the back of the silent single file they were forming to avoid disturbing the kangaroos around them. The emu was not threatened by their silent and respectful presence. Students felt the joy of having attracted a companion from another species that seemed to enjoy their company spontaneously as if it were one of them. While honouring the Earth through their quality of being and presence, once again students experienced the inter-being relationship with Nature. At that precise moment, they did not learn about Nature. They became Nature, blending completely into her.

As mentioned earlier, most students come from a difficult background, where life at home is often challenging. The most common way to express their frustration towards life is likely to be to tap their feet, use rough movements and a loud voice, or even initiate a confrontation with others. What these students experience in their families does not predispose them to develop inner peace; rather the opposite. Therefore, when Dylan (a Year 5 student) said "I'm sorry to have disturbed you" to a plant because he touched it with his walking stick while climbing a mountain, or when he insisted the class do a meditation to pay respect for the lives of two dead seals found on the beach, the impact of the transformative Buddhist education and healing process could be seen.

From the Buddhist approach, with wisdom and reverence for life in mind and heart, HNBC students develop an ability to tune to Nature's rhythm. In doing so, Nature becomes a support to heal the children while they experience the powerful inter-being relationship with their natural surroundings. In return, like Dylan spontaneously showed, students participate in caring for and healing the Earth, above all by preserving her from harm. Then, the hope is that the diligence they show to Nature is naturally applied to their peers and community.

HNBC education plays a role in developing students' awareness of the 17 SDGs, while encouraging them to feel and experience their interconnection and interdependence with the living world. Students are encouraged to imagine how to make their future possible alongside their human friends, their big cousins the beluga and the orca, their little cousins the daisies, and their ancestors, the bacteria. In doing so, it develops their sensitivity to see and gather around the immense beauty of the natural objects of art and co-creation that they still see around them in Nature, and recognise them as holders of sustainable knowledge, from which they will draw inspiration through Biomimicry thinking and science. With an open mind and heart, the HNBC educational team takes every opportunity to prioritise a deeper understanding of the meaning and practice of wisdom to serve "reverence for life," for all life on Earth. Every day in their classrooms, students honour the Earth by understanding that wisdom is also found in every ecosystem. Each day they practise respect and humility towards Nature by wondering, "How does Nature solve this problem?" Nature becomes their reference and model of resilience, creativity, and ingenuity, from which they draw resources for imagining and developing sustainable solutions to participate in the healing of the world they have inherited.

38.9   Conclusion

Nature is inherently authoritarian towards us Earthlings. Unlike when diplomats are sent to try to resolve tensions, conflicts, or wars between states in different parts of the world, we cannot sit at a negotiating table and try to reason with Nature when she is on the rampage. In terms of climate change, once a tipping point of chaos is reached, it will be a point of no return because the forces of Nature will be even more uncontrollable (Lazslo, 2006). To try to minimise Nature's powerful reactions to the constraints we have imposed on her over the years, our first responsibility is to adapt to her rhythms, which will allow her to continue in a sustainable way. To do this, we must work with her as other species do. The Earth is our living home, and it dictates to us how to live according to the laws of its ecosystems. We have ignored her for too long, and in the near future all creatures and species will pay the consequences, unless we play our part as wise Earthlings, aware of the power of moderation for a sustainable future, and urgently engage with the 17 SDGs at our level of expertise and in our daily lives.

Aware of the inter-being relationship between earthly creatures and all natural elements, HNBC educates students in the quality of being and wisdom that are needed to respond to the ecological emergencies of our time. Ultimately, the hope is that it will help students to develop a natural predisposition to moderation in their lives in order to fulfil their triple identity, not exclusively as individuals, but also as members of their communities, and as members of the human species among other species. Such awareness is a guarantee that everything will be done to approach and achieve the SDGs in a systemic way, as wisdom always takes into consideration not only all contexts, but also their interrelationships in order to elaborate equitable and sustainable solutions.

Given the very small size of HNBC, it is a daring gamble to believe that a handful of students will help save the living world from a dramatic common destiny. In response to this suspicious thought, Tu My Nguyen, principal of HNBC, claims that it is a daring gamble that it would be insane not to risk. She points out that in any case, everything is to be gained, if only to live at peace with our consciousness, knowing that as educators we have done our part generously, far beyond what is required. We are exercising our responsibility towards new generations and letting our inner wisdom express *the insurrection of our consciousness* (Mimoun-Sorel, 2016) to participate spontaneously in all possible healing processes, every day at our humble level as educators. Nguyen insists that it is an invaluable privilege to be able to encourage students to pursue "reverence for life" and wisdom as their main goals and achievements in life.

References

American Psychological Association. (n.d.). *APA Dictionary of Psychology.* https://dictionary.apa.org/wisdom
Ask Nature. (2022). https://asknature.org/
Benyus, J. (2002). *Biomimicry: Innovation inspired by nature.* Perennial. Biomimicry Institute. https://biomimicry.org/
Bolden, R. (2014). Ubuntu. In D. Coghlan & M. Brydon-Miller (Eds.), *The SAGE Encyclopedia of Action Research* (pp. 8801–8802). SAGE.
Cambridge Dictionary. (n.d.). https://dictionary.cambridge.org/
Capra, F. (1982). *The turning point.* Simon & Schuster.
Capra, F. (2003). *The hidden connections.* Flamingo.
Capra, F. (2014). *The systems view of life: A unifying vision.* Cambridge University Press.
Chapelle, G. (2015). *Le vivant comme modèle* [The living as a model]. Albin Michel.
Delors, J. (1996). *Learning to be: The treasure within.* UNESCO.
Desjardins, A. (2010). *Les chemins de la sagesse* [The paths of wisdom]. Editions de la Table Ronde.
Elgin, D. (1993). *Awakening earth: Exploring the evolution of human culture and consciousness.* Morrow.

Gangadean, A. (2006). A planetary crisis of consciousness: From ego-based cultures to a sustainable global world. *Kosmos: An Integral Approach to Global Awakening, V*, 37–39.

Hamilton, C. (2003). *Growth fetish*. Griffin Press.

Hanh, N. (2012). *Good citizens: Creating enlightened society*. Parallax Press.

Lazslo, E. (2006). *The chaos point. The world at the crossroads*. Piaktus.

Mimoun-Sorel, M.-L. (2011). *Learning to be in the 21st century: Meanings and needs. A transdisciplinary approach*. [Doctoral dissertation, Australian Catholic University, Melbourne, Australia].

Mimoun-Sorel, M.-L. (2016). Adopting a transdisciplinary attitude in the classroom, to create a viable future. *Journal of Future Studies, 20*(3), 21–34.

Morin, E. (2001). *Seven complex lessons in education for the future*. UNESCO.

Morin, E. (2003). *Eduquer pour l'ère planétaire: La pensée complexe comme Méthode d'apprentissage dans l'erreur et l'incertitude humaines*. [Educating for the global age: Complex thinking as a method of learning in human error and uncertainty]. Balland.

Morin, E. (2020a). *Changeons de voie: Les leçons du coronavirus*. [Changing path: Lessons from the coronavirus]. Denoël.

Morin, E. (2020b). *Un festival d'incertitudes*. [A festival of uncertainty]. Editions Gallimard.

Rabhi, P. (2010). *Vers la sobriété heureuse* [Toward happy sobriety]. Babel.

Rabhi, P. (2011). *Manifeste Pour La Terre Et L'Humanisme* [Manifesto for the Earth And Humanism]. Babel.

Rabhi, P. (2019). *Mieux vivre sans croissance* [Living better without growth]. Presse du Chatelet.

Rabhi, P. (2021). *L'humain au risque de l'intelligene artificielle* [The human at risk of artificial intelligence]. Presse du Chatelet.

United Nations. (n.d.a). *Department of economic and social affairs. Sustainable development. Do you know all the 17 SDGs?* https://sdgs.un.org/goals

United Nations. (n.d.b). *Transforming our world: The 2030 agenda for sustainable development.* https://sdgs.un.org/2030agenda

Victorian Curriculum and Assessment Authority. (n.d.). *The Victorian Curriculum F-10.* https://victoriancurriculum.vcaa.vic.edu.au/

Chapter 39
Ethical and Spiritual Values for Transformative Sustainable Development: The Earth Charter Vision

Richard M. Clugston and Peter Blaze Corcoran

39.1 Introduction

The first pillar is the Charter of the United Nations, which regulates the relations among states and thus sets the rules for their behavior in order to secure peace and stability. The second pillar is the Universal Declaration of Human Rights, which regulates the relations between states and individuals, and guarantees to all citizens a set of rights which their respective governments should provide. The importance of these two documents cannot be overestimated. But it has become obvious that another document is missing, one which would regulate the relations among states, individuals, and nature by defining the human duties towards the environment. In my opinion, the Earth Charter should fill this void, acquire equal status, and become the third pillar supporting the peaceful development of the modern world. (Gorbachev, 2005, p. 10)

Analyzing and reflecting upon the importance of the United Nations Sustainable Development Goals (SDGs), and the slow progress toward achieving them, the need for ethical and spiritual values in the development process becomes clear. Such values

R. M. Clugston
The Association of University Leaders for a Sustainable Future, St. Paul, MN 55104, USA

Member, Earth Charter International Council, San Jose, Costa Rica

P. B. Corcoran (✉)
Environmental Studies and Environmental Education, Florida Gulf Coast University, Fort Myers, FL, USA

Earth Charter Center for Education for Sustainable Development, University for Peace, San Jose, Costa Rica

Senior Advisor for Faith and Ecology, Unity Earth, Melbourne, VIC, Australia

Adjunct Professor of Environmental and Sustainability Education, University of the Sunshine Coast, Maroochydore, QLD, Australia

K. Beasy et al. (eds.), *Education and the UN Sustainable Development Goals*, Education for Sustainability 7,
https://doi.org/10.1007/978-981-99-3802-5_39

709

are of particular importance in creating a firm foundation for realizing the transformative potential of future sustainable development efforts. The ethical principles of the *Earth Charter* (Earth Charter Commission, 2000) can guide policymakers and educators in these efforts. The core values of the *Earth Charter* can add vital missing elements of ethics that speak to cultural and ecological diversity, indigenous wisdom, human rights, and the rights of nature.

The *Earth Charter* represented a milestone in the postmodern era of global documents and people's movements. It resulted from years-long research and consultation. In the words of Maurice Strong, this was "a process designed to produce a people's *Earth Charter* to manifest the commitment of people to a set of principles designed to ensure the security and sustainability of life on Earth" (Strong, 2005, p. 11). From the drafting process, to the launch at the Peace Palace in The Hague, to the ongoing process of endorsement and implementation, the *Earth Charter* has represented the aspirations of the global community for an ethics of sustainability. The hope has been that such a set of principles can guide development in harmony with the Earth's ecosystems. The *Earth Charter* is of significant educational value. It provides a vision of possibility in a world imperiled by human failure to live within the limits of the natural systems that support life on Earth as it has been known.

> As Brendan Mackey, [former] Director of Education for the Earth Charter ... has written, the core values of the Earth Charter "are life affirming, promote human dignity, advance environmental protection and social and economic justice, and respect cultural and ecological diversity, and integrity" ... They are an excellent place to begin. They represent serious intellectual and cultural efforts to chart a course toward global responsibility and global sustainability. How globalisation is managed will determine the quality of life on Earth. Institutions of higher education, in particular, have a moral obligation to examine critical globalisation and seek to move it in a direction that is humane, just, and sustainable. The Earth Charter provides an ethical framework for this urgent task. (Corcoran, 2002, p. 79)

Fernández-Herrería and Martínez-Rodríguez (2020) describe the *Earth Charter* as a "new vision" that can "place us in that state of consciousness" required to create a world that works for all. The *Earth Charter Preamble* states, "we are one human family and one Earth community with a common destiny." This *Earth Charter* "Community of Life model, as a new worldview," cultivates what these authors call a "global biophilic consciousness ... an extended self that affirms its identity in union with all humans, and moreover, with all living beings, with the entire Community of Life" (2020, p. 601). Completed in 2000, the *Earth Charter*'s *biophilic* ethics was ahead of its time, but its time seems to be now. Increasingly, there is a great awakening to the need for ethical and spiritual values for transformative sustainable development.

39.2   Historical Perspective: The Earth Charter[1]

> The United Nations is an ideal, and it remains so. Its charter articulates its vision "to practice tolerance and live together in peace with one another as good neighbors, and to unite our strength to maintain international peace and security" … In this same way, the Earth Charter is an ideal. It is a visionary document that creates a template for ecological consciousness around the world, rooted in local actions. It asks us to embrace the planet while taking care of our own backyards. (Williams, 2008, p. xiii)

Thirty-five years ago, a call was issued for "new norms for state and interstate behaviour needed to maintain livelihoods and life on our shared planet" (World Commission on Environment and Development [WCED], 1987, p. 273). The WCED, chaired by Gro Harlem Brundtland, wrote in *Our Common Future*, "there is now a need to consolidate and extend relevant legal principles in a new charter to guide state behaviour in the transition to sustainable development" (1987, p. 33). The WCED was convinced "that the security, wellbeing, and very survival of the planet depend on such changes, now" (1987, p. 27). In the lead-up to the 1992 Rio United Nations Conference on Environment and Development (UNCED), both the delegations of the UN member states and nongovernmental organizations worked on a draft *Earth Charter* that would consolidate and even reach beyond existing agreements and conventions for sustainable development. The hope for this *Earth Charter* was that it would provide an ethical foundation upon which the UNCED agreements, called Agenda 21, could be based.

Although many new priorities for environmentally responsible development emerged from the Rio Earth Summit, as it came to be called, an *Earth Charter* did not. The ethical demands embodied in the draft *Earth Charter* were beyond the scope of the negotiators, and the "Rio Declaration" replaced it. Yet, because of the Summit, some governments and many nongovernmental organizations came to recognize the paramount importance of creating a document that outlined common principles for meeting the challenges of our increasingly interconnected world. In addition, the Rio Earth Summit provided a foundation for the emergence of a participatory worldwide process of building consensus on shared ethical values. According to Mirian Vilela, longtime Executive Director of Earth Charter International, the 1992 Rio Earth Summit, the end of the Cold War, and the progress of communication technology were key elements that marked the beginning of a new era in the development of such a global document.

The failure of intergovernmental negotiations to draft a new charter at the 1992 Rio Earth Summit allowed for the emergence of broader involvement of civil society in this project. Significantly, the shift from exclusively governmental involvement to civil society involvement also enabled the drafting process to benefit from diverse input from the international community and from various soft law agreements reached at the many UN summits held over the decade of the 1990s. In 1994, after nongovernmental members from nineteen countries developed an initial draft that was based on work completed at the Rio Earth Summit, the creation of an *Earth Charter*, as it

---

[1] The full text of The *Earth Charter* is included as an Appendix to this chapter.

had come to be known, shifted fully to a civil society project under the leadership of Maurice F. Strong, who had chaired the Rio conference and was Chair of the Earth Council, and Mikhail Gorbachev, who was President of Green Cross International.

From 1994 to 2000, extensive research, consultation, and drafting took place throughout the world. The Earth Charter Initiative has involved the most open and participatory consultation process ever conducted in connection with the drafting of an international document. Tens of thousands of individuals and hundreds of organizations from all regions of the world, from different cultures, and from diverse sectors of society participated. The *Earth Charter* was shaped by experts, government and civil society leaders, students, and representatives from indigenous groups and grassroots communities. In late 1996, the Earth Council formed an Earth Charter Commission—a distinguished group of leaders from many sectors, cultures, and regions of the world.

In March 2000, the Earth Charter Commission officially adopted the *Earth Charter* at UNESCO in Paris, and it was launched at the Peace Palace in The Hague three months later. The story of the creation of the *Earth Charter* is dramatic and inspiring. In some ways, the most amazing thing about the *Earth Charter* is that it exists at all, given the challenges of working across the many divides that characterize the world—Northern and Southern hemispheres, faith traditions, political perspectives, and generations. The Preamble of the *Earth Charter* briefly describes the cosmological and ecological situation and the major challenges and choices facing humanity. There follow sixteen main principles, which are divided into four parts. Each part contains four main principles with a number of supporting principles that elaborate the meaning of the main principles. The principles in the *Charter* are formulations of fundamental ethical guidelines and major strategies. The *Charter* does not attempt to describe the mechanisms and instruments required to implement its principles. This is a task for other international legal instruments and for national and local sustainable development plans.

Speaking to its substance, Chair of the Drafting Committee, Steven C. Rockefeller, has stated,

> The *Earth Charter* is centrally concerned with the transition to sustainable ways of living and sustainable human development. The four major themes of the *Earth Charter* are expressed in its four parts: Part I, Respect and Care for the Community of Life; Part II, Ecological Integrity; Part III, Social and Economic Justice; and Part IV, Democracy, Nonviolence, and Peace. The *Earth Charter* vision reflects the conviction that caring for people and caring for Earth are two interrelated dimensions of one great task. It supports the view that economic institutions and activities should promote equitable human development and should value and protect Earth's ecological systems and the many services they provide. The *Earth Charter* is both a people-centered and ecosystem-centered document. Recognizing that our environmental, economic, social, political, and spiritual challenges are interdependent, the *Earth Charter* provides an integrated framework for thinking about and addressing these issues. The result is a fresh, broad conception of what constitutes a sustainable society and sustainable development.[2]

---

[2] Parts of the account of the early history of *The Earth Charter* have been published elsewhere, including Corcoran and Wohlpart, *A Voice for Earth: American Writers Respond to the Earth Charter* (2008). These accounts also rely on the writing of others, especially Steven C. Rockefeller, to whom we are indebted for their insight.

The *Earth Charter* guides us toward a deeper and more complete vision of what sustainability really requires. Its main principles and supporting principles provide a framework for sustainable development, or "good globalization," developed through a broadly inclusive and participatory consultation process. Since the *Earth Charter* was completed in 2000, Earth Charter International has focused on having the governments represented at the United Nations acknowledge the contribution of the *Earth Charter* and translate its principles into action. Major efforts involved working with the Commission on Sustainable Development (CSD), The World Summit on Sustainable Development (2002), and with UN agencies (e.g., UNESCO, UN Environmental Program [UNEP], UN Development Program [UNDP]) to endorse the *Earth Charter* and adopt policies consistent with its principles. UNESCO did recognize the *Earth Charter* as an important framework for education for sustainable development. Some language from the *Earth Charter* was incorporated in the Johannesburg Declaration—the outcome document of the 2002 UN World Summit on Sustainable Development (2002).

In 2000, the UN adopted the eight Millennium Development Goals (MDGs) with targets, indicators, and a timeline for their accomplishment in 2015. After more than a decade of annual meetings convened by the CSD at UN Headquarters in New York to assess progress on the implementation of Agenda 21, "summit fatigue" set in. The 9/11 terrorist attack shifted governmental and UN priorities. Other than working on the MDGs, there was little focus on sustainable development policy during the 2000s.

During this time, Earth Charter International continued to develop a civil society initiative. It was recognized that the UN would not endorse a document that did not evolve from a UN process. Nevertheless, Earth Charter International continued to engage with UN agencies regarding the value added of ethical and spiritual values in sustainable development. In 2009, Brazil and Colombia took the lead in promoting the need for fundamental, transformative change, acknowledging the interconnectedness of our global challenges and the need to adopt a new development agenda that prioritized social and ecological wellbeing as well as economic sufficiency. Brazil hosted the UN Conference on Sustainable Development (called Rio+20) in 2012. The Outcome Document of this conference called for the development of the Sustainable Development Goals (SDGs), to begin in force after the MDGs expired in 2015 (United Nations Conference on Sustainable Development, Rio+20, 2012). These SDGs would incorporate the unfinished business of the MDGs, and add new goals that would address economic, ecological, and governance issues that the MDGs did not address. From 2012 to 2015, the representatives of the UN member states, in consultation with major groups from the private sector and civil society, drafted the new SDGs and their targets to be reached by 2030.

39.3 Transforming Our World: The 2030 Agenda for Sustainable Development

In September 2015, the 193 UN member states adopted "Transforming our World: the 2030 Agenda for Sustainable Development" with 17 SDGs and 169 targets (UN, 2015). This Agenda 2030 seeks to create a world that works for all and one that leaves no one behind. To accomplish this transformation, business as usual is not an option.

The 17 SDGs fall into three general categories:

1. Providing for everyone's basic needs: eliminating poverty and ensuring food security, good health and education, water and sanitation, energy, gender equality, and decent work for all (SDGs 1 to 8).
2. Protecting ecological integrity: combating climate change; protecting, restoring, and sustainably using terrestrial and ocean ecosystems (SDGs 13, 14, and 15).
3. Strengthening enabling mechanisms: increasing economic (Gross Domestic Product, GDP) growth and sustainable (green) infrastructure; reducing inequality; promoting sustainable production and consumption as well as good governance and effective global partnerships (the remaining SDGs).

From 2016 to 2030, nations were voluntarily implemented the policies spelled out in Agenda 2030 and reported on their progress each year at the High-Level Political Forum (HLPF) at UN Headquarters in New York City. As of 2021, 177 member states had reported. In the 2019 UN SDG review, most concluded that inadequate progress was being made in implementing the SDGs, especially in eliminating poverty and providing a social safety net for the poor and vulnerable. Biodiversity loss and climate change were increasing. Resurgent nationalism and authoritarianism were increasing violations of basic human rights. More refugees and migrants were on the move. Nations were withdrawing from multilateral cooperation. The COVID-19 pandemic has exacerbated many negative trends. Our beginning recovery is K-shaped, meaning the already privileged are gaining more wealth (and vaccinations), and the poor and marginalized are experiencing a decline in income, health, and food security. The pandemic has highlighted the inequitable distribution of resources and opportunities, as well as the lack of preparedness for global crises, including climate change.

39.4 A Comparative Analysis of the *Earth Charter* Principles and the Sustainable Development Goals

The *Earth Charter* articulates a set of 16 major principles and 61 supporting principles. There is considerable overlap between these principles and the 17 goals and 169 targets of Agenda 2030. In addition to its goals and targets, Agenda 2030 has 244 indicators that provide quantitative measures for how the targets are to be accomplished by 2030. The *Earth Charter*'s principles are general guidelines, and the document does not provide specific indicators or timelines (Zubialde, 2014).

Agenda 2030 emphasizes the importance of sustained economic growth for realizing its goals and targets, and it emphasizes that this economic growth must be "inclusive," benefitting all people, and "sustainable," meaning preserving and enhancing ecological integrity. Central to Agenda 2030 is moving people out of poverty and providing for everyone's basic needs while not degrading Earth's ecological systems (terrestrial, oceanic, and atmospheric). For the past decade, the UN has promoted the triple bottom line of economic, social, and environmental wellbeing—the three pillars of sustainable development—but little progress has been made in developing a new bottom line for development other than GDP.

The *Earth Charter* emphasizes that in order to create a world that works for all, transformative change will need to be based on shared ethics and spiritual values. An emphasis on economic growth alone will not be able to bring about the changes needed in our lifestyles, institutional practices, and development policies. As Earth Charter International's input into Rio+20's outcome document stated:

> A shared vision of ethical and spiritual values is necessary to inspire and guide cooperative action for change. Shared values awaken a sense of common purpose and build community spirit. In an increasingly interdependent world, achieving the environmental, economic, and social goals associated with sustainability requires worldwide collaboration, and cooperation is not possible without shared values and a sense of common purpose. The vision of a sustainable future as an inclusive social and ecological ideal that is good, right, and just is what is needed to inspire strong commitment and drive change.
>
> The emergence throughout the world of a new ethical and spiritual consciousness that supports the transition to a just, sustainable, and peaceful world is one of the most promising developments of the last sixty years. The ethical and spiritual values associated with this new consciousness have been given expression in many intergovernmental and civil society declarations such as the Universal Declaration of Human Rights, the World Charter for Nature, the Rio Declaration, and the *Earth Charter*. The *Earth Charter* identifies the basic spiritual challenge that the world community must address if it is to make the transition to strong sustainability when it states: We must realize that when basic needs have been met, human development is primarily about being more, not having more.
>
> This guideline is, of course, entirely consistent with the teachings of all the world's great wisdom traditions. The values associated with human rights, cultural diversity, social and economic justice, a culture of peace, intergenerational responsibility, and respect and care for the greater community of life, are all part of what "being more" means in the 21st century. In addition, the *Earth Charter* recognizes the importance of reverence for the mystery of being, compassion, love, hope, and the joyful celebration of life. "Being more" in the spirit of these values and ideals is the only sure path to a sustainable world. (Rockefeller, in Clugston, 2016, pp. 164–165)

39.5 The *Earth Charter*'s Potential Contributions to Deepening and Implementing the SDGs

Based on this emerging ethical and spiritual consciousness, the *Earth Charter* calls for respect and care for the community of life, thus the development agenda would need to care for all members of the more-than-human Earth community, as well as future generations. The *Earth Charter*'s emphasis on "being more" leads to a set of recommendations for bringing these *Earth Charter* emphases more fully into the SDGs, thereby increasing their potential for transformative change.[3]

Four recommendations are described below. Each recommendation is based on an *Earth Charter* principle, which is quoted. Under each of these principles, its corresponding SDG is quoted, and the following text elaborates on the implications of each principle for rethinking each SDG's focus.

39.5.1 Recommendation One: Earth Charter Principle 12.b. "Affirm the Right of Indigenous Peoples to Their Spirituality, Knowledge, Lands, and Resources and to Their Related Practice of Sustainable Livelihoods."

The SDGs do not recognize the important contributions of indigenous and other spiritual and ecological communities as guiding "best practices" for sustainable development, thus, no SDG is quoted. However, a major *Earth Charter* priority is recognizing, protecting, and learning from communities and cultures that demonstrate how to live with respect and care for the whole community of life and future generations. These are societies that care for creation, for Mother Earth, "recognizing that all beings are interdependent and every form of life has value regardless of its worth to human beings" (Earth Charter Principle 1.a.).

Indigenous communities are the original caretakers of ecological systems and their cultures do emphasize "being more," not "having more." Today, many indigenous communities are still living in harmony with nature. Unfortunately, the thrust of economic development has displaced, and is still displacing, these peoples from their land, bringing large-scale deforestation, mining, hunting, and grazing into their territories, undermining their ecocultural integrity. Such displacement is rationalized by assumptions that indigenous communities are impoverished and need to be integrated into the mainstream of our materialistic culture.

Some major objectives for *Earth Charter* Recommendation One come from the proposal for a Framework Law of Mother Earth, drafted by Bolivia's main social movements in November 2010, and passed in 2012 (Grantham Research Institute

---

[3] The content of these recommendations has, in part, been adapted from Earth Charter International's input into Rio+20, see (Clugston et al., 2011.).

on Climate Change and the Environment, 2012). This framework provides a new development model focused on living in harmony with nature, called "Vivir Bien, Living Well." It emphasizes respecting indigenous worldviews as a guiding framework for development, guaranteeing the informed consent of native, indigenous, and campesino peoples in development projects that affect their territories and ways of life.

39.5.2   Recommendation Two: Earth Charter Principle 9: "Eradicate Poverty as an Ethical, Social, and Environmental Imperative."

39.5.2.1   SDG1: "End Poverty in All Its Forms Everywhere."

The *Earth Charter* asks us to rethink our understanding of poverty. A broader, sustainable livelihoods approach to poverty alleviation is necessary. Eradicating absolute poverty requires providing social protection floors to meet everyone's basic needs. Though this often requires increasing income for the poorest to buy necessary goods and services, reducing poverty is primarily about providing rich social and ecological environments in which individuals and communities can thrive, enabling sustainable livelihoods, which need not be heavily monetized. Earning $1.25 a day instead of no dollars a day may not be progress if it involves moving people from a rural village with clean air and water, sufficient local food, and strong bonds of intergenerational caring, to a big city slum with none of these.

The shift to being more, not having more, after basic needs are met requires the development agenda actively to discourage overconsumption. Consumerism is based on economics that encourage the acquisition of ever more goods and services. Advertising is about convincing individuals that they do not have enough, thus increasing a sense of relative poverty even in those that have more than enough. In Agenda 2030/ SDGs there is no critique of increasing economic growth by increasing overconsumption—no mention that one must choose to live in ways that support the flourishing of all. Many spiritual communities and eco-communities prioritize caring for creation/ the natural world, and provide examples of emphasizing being more, not having more.

39.5.3 Recommendation Three: Earth Charter Principle 10: "Ensure that Economic Activities and Institutions at All Levels Promote Human Development in an Equitable and Sustainable Manner."

39.5.3.1 SDG8: "Promote Sustained, Inclusive and Sustainable Economic Growth, Full and Productive Employment and Decent Work for All."

Agenda 2030 assumes that for transformative change to occur, there needs to be ever-increasing economic growth as measured by a country's GDP. SDG8 does affirm that this growth in GDP will need to be inclusive, by benefiting all people, as well as sustainable, through protecting and restoring the ecological systems that are the foundations of human wellbeing.

An analysis of Agenda 2030 in the *Jacobin* magazine states,

> The core of [Agenda 2030's] program for development and poverty reduction relies precisely on the old model of industrial growth—ever-increasing levels of extraction, production, and consumption. In fact, an entire goal, Goal 8, is devoted to growth, specifically export-oriented growth, in keeping with existing neoliberal models. This is the mortal flaw at the heart of the SDGs. True, Goal 8 is peppered with progressive-sounding qualifications: the growth should be inclusive, should promote full employment and decent work, and we should endeavor to decouple growth from environmental degradation. But these qualifications are vague, and the real message that shines through is that GDP growth is all that ultimately matters. (Hickel, 2016, para. 9)

Although Agenda 2030 recognizes the need for "measurements of progress on sustainable development that complement GDP" (Target 169), it fails to provide any new indicators that would provide metrics for a new bottom line that integrates the three concerns of sustainable development: economic, social, and ecological wellbeing (profit, people, and planet). Thus, short-term GDP growth still remains the bottom line for development policy.

Fortunately, many countries, cities, and communities are developing or have established alternative measures for their development. These measures integrate social and ecological wellbeing (or well-living) and concern for future generations, as well as economic sufficiency into new metrics of progress. Examples include Buen Vivir (Bolivia, etc.), Gross National Happiness (Bhutan), Genuine Prosperity (Thailand), and a wide range of genuine progress indicators. UN agencies are working on a Genuine Wealth Index, which describes well the tasks involved in creating alternative indicators (United Nations Environment Programme, 2018).

A central and urgent task for transformative change is to draw on these development alternatives to create new metrics for measuring progress, and to mainstream these metrics, replacing (or complementing) GDP in mainstream economic discourse. Such new economics will require internalizing social and environmental costs in pricing goods and services, eliminating perverse subsidies, and shifting to sustainable production and consumption (SDG12).

In addition to the economic, social, and environmental pillars that need to be integrated into a new "bottom line" for development, Steven C. Rockefeller (2010) argues that "there is a fourth pillar: the global, ethical, and spiritual consciousness that is awakening in civil society around the world … This global ethical consciousness is in truth the first pillar of a sustainable way of life, because it involves the internalization of the values of sustainable human development and provides the inspiration and motivation to act, as well as essential guidance regarding the path to genuine sustainability." Recognizing the urgent need for new indicators that measure social and ecological wellbeing, Earth Charter International is developing an Earth Charter Index for Planetary Wellbeing, combining indicators that measure a county's progress in realizing the principles of the four major pillars of the *Earth Charter*.

39.5.4 Recommendation Four: Earth Charter Principle 4: "Secure Earth's Bounty and Beauty for Future Generations," and Earth Charter Principle 1: "Respect Earth and Life in All Its Diversity."

39.5.4.1 SDG16: "Promote Peaceful and Inclusive Societies for Sustainable Development, Provide Access to Justice for All and Build Effective, Accountable and Inclusive Institutions at All Levels."

Certainly, many of the targets listed in SDG16 are necessary, but not sufficient, to create a world that works for all. The *Earth Charter*'s definition of inclusive societies would also include members of the more-than-human Earth community, as well as future generations. To represent the interests of these voiceless members, the following two objectives are recommended as priorities for inclusive institutions.

Objective One: Express responsibility to future generations by establishing Ombudspersons for Future Generations at global, national, and local levels. As defined by the Brundtland Commission Report (World Commission on Environment and Development, 1987), sustainable development requires that the needs of the present must be met without compromising the ability of future generations to meet their own needs, within the limits imposed by the capacity of the biosphere to absorb the effects of human activities. Yet no progress has been made in the last 35 years toward realizing this responsibility. Short-termism rules, and in current economics the future is discounted. Ombudspersons representing the interests of future generations in policy settings are a key step in realizing this enduring priority for sustainable development.

In addition, the interests of future generations can in part be insured by implementing the precautionary principle as adopted in the Rio Declaration and the UN Framework Convention on Climate Change, among other international agreements.

Principle 6 of the *Earth Charter* states, "Prevent harm as the best method of environmental protection and, when knowledge is limited, apply a precautionary approach" (Earth Charter Commission, 2000, para. 8).

Objective Two: Adopt mechanisms of trusteeship for global common goods on behalf of all peoples, the greater community of life, and future generations. Global common goods include obligations for maintaining the integrity of planetary boundaries and the ecological wellbeing of all, overseeing markets to ensure that they are protective of non-market common goods, and ensuring impartiality between all interests—individual, civil society, corporate, and national.

The notion of an international institution exercising a trusteeship function is not new. Indeed, under the auspices of the UN, a Trusteeship Council was enacted to act on behalf of states transitioning from colonization to independence. This Trusteeship Council was mandated to speak for the yet-to-be state entities that had no legal standing or representation. The Trusteeship Council acted on behalf of entities that were not legally recognized. An obvious parallel can be drawn between the functioning of this Council and a global trusteeship function over global common goods on behalf of all peoples, the greater community of life, and future generations.

39.6   Education for Sustainable Development and for Global Citizenship Inspired by the Earth Charter

Values that are life-affirming and ethics that promote intergenerational equity are essential to the continuation of life on Earth. Everything that can be done to bring values of sustainability to education at all levels must be done. Education for Sustainable Development (ESD) was a major and neglected, priority of the 1992 Earth Summit's Agenda 21. Tasked with coordinating the UN Decade of Education for Sustainable Development (UN DESD), UNESCO's efforts to promote ESD through formal educational institutions, as well as many nonformal and media-based education and advertising enterprises, made an important contribution. However, universal access to quality education, let alone ESD, for both boys and girls, even at the primary level, is an elusive goal. The shift to a sustainable society is deeply dependent on the educational system, and such education should address the material, social, and spiritual dimensions of human development. In its strongest sense, education must provide the space for value-based sustainable learning (Clugston, 2016, p. 167).

SDG4, "Ensure inclusive and equitable quality education and promote life-long learning opportunities for all" is strong, but needs to be achieved in a values context. Earth Charter Principle 14 is helpful in this regard. It states the need to:

Integrate into formal education and life-long learning the knowledge, values, and skills needed for a sustainable way of life:

a. Provide all, especially children and youth, with educational opportunities that empower them to contribute actively to sustainable development.

b. Promote the contribution of the arts and humanities as well as the sciences in sustainability education.

c. Enhance the role of the mass media in raising awareness of ecological and social challenges.

d. Recognize the importance of moral and spiritual education for sustainable living.

A major focus of Earth Charter International is advancing Education for Sustainable Development based on the Earth Charter. A wealth of educational resources are available at earthcharter.org. The 2020 publication, *Earth Charter, Education and the Sustainable Development Goal 4.7: Research, Experiences and Reflections*, provides many examples of how the *Earth Charter* is being used to enable this SDG target to be realized (Vilela & Jimenez, 2020).

The following is an example of learning outcomes inspired by the *Earth Charter*'s values and principles. Education for Sustainable Development would enable all to:

a. Engage deeply and effectively in contemplative practices that awaken us to the mystery of being, and to our vocations where our deepest passions meet the real needs of the world.

b. Experience our interconnectedness and interdependence with the whole living world—appreciating diverse cultures, all animals, the cycles of life, and the unfolding cosmos.

c. Feel, and act from, compassionate concern for others, doing no harm, reaching out to assist all beings.

d. Live in ways that all can live, consuming no more than one's fair share of Earth's bounty—choosing products and services (e.g., food, energy, transportation, housing) that are ecologically sound, socially just, and economically viable (e.g., local, fair trade, organic, carbon and pollution neutral, humane).

e. Act to shift policies to support a just and sustainable future by voting, lobbying, and participating in political decision-making at all levels to promote policies to better care for future generations and the whole community of life, e.g., creating better measures of genuine progress than GDP, internalizing social and environmental costs in pricing goods and services, eliminating perverse subsidies, and creating ombudspersons and trusteeship structures at all governmental levels to effectively represent the interests of all members of the life community, current and future (Clugston, 2016, pp. 168–169).

These core values in action are especially valuable as education is ever-increasingly challenged by social and environmental problems. Consider the crisis of youth climate anxiety. We find ourselves in a civilizational crisis. David Wallace-Wells (2019) reminded us that all the conditions that produced our civilization are behind us. We are on new and shifting ground.

A recent study by Hickman et al. (2021) titled "Young People's Voices on Climate Anxiety, Governmental Betrayal and Moral Injury: A Global Phenomenon," shows how deep the crisis of climate concern among youth is. The authors conclude:

Distress about climate change is associated with young people perceiving that they have no future, that humanity is doomed, that governments are failing to respond adequately, and with feelings of betrayal and abandonment by governments and adults. These are chronic stressors which will have significant long-lasting and incremental implications on the mental health of children and young people. The failure of governments to adequately address climate change and the impact on younger generations, potentially constitutes moral injury. Nations must respond to protect the mental health of children and young people by engaging in ethical, collective, policy-based action against climate change. (Hickman et al., 2021, p. e864)

Educators and education policymakers face a dual crisis with regard to climate. Authors of the study say, "failure of governments to prevent harm from climate change could this be argued to be a failure of ethical responsibility to care leading to moral injury" (Hickman et al., 2021, p. e864). The response of education can be informed by the hopeful and sound vision of a sustainable future provided by *Earth Charter* principles.

To respond to the multiple threats of climate change, climate anxiety, and environmental degradation; to drive positive social change; to create a sense of global citizenship, urgent action is required. Education, training, and social learning, if fully oriented to an ethics of sustainability, can improve knowledge of paths to resilience, instill values, shift attitudes, and change harmful lifestyles and social practices. We believe *Earth Charter* principles can add considerable value to this process.

39.7   Conclusion

The current Anthropocene is an age characterized by violence against nature and by environmental injustice of enormous magnitude—and most often directed at the world's poorest people. The impact of anthropogenic climate change and the climate anxiety that it has evoked have created a civilizational crisis. Daily, we see evidence of systemic destruction of the natural and social systems upon which we have depended for life on Earth as we have known it. The conditions that produced civilization as we have known it no longer exist. Natural and social systems are in agony. We hear what Leonardo Boff has called "the cry of the Earth and the cry of the poor." As Pope Francis and many others have stated, we have not heeded the wisdom of the *Earth Charter*. Pope Francis (2015) has written in *Laudato Si,*

> The Earth Charter asked us to leave behind a period of self-destruction and make a new start, but we have not as yet developed a universal awareness needed to achieve this. Here, I would echo that courageous challenge: 'As never before in history, common destiny beckons us to seek a new beginning... Let ours be a time remembered for the awakening of a new reverence for life, the firm resolve to achieve sustainability, the quickening of the struggle for justice and peace, and the joyful celebration of life'. (Francis, 2015, para. 207)

In citing one of the most stirring passages of "The Way Forward" in the *Earth Charter*, Pope Francis calls us to the ethical and spiritual challenges we must meet for "a new beginning." May the *Earth Charter* provide a foundation for this transformation. It has often been said that the *Earth Charter* was ahead of its time. May its time be now!

Appendix: The Earth Charter

Preamble

We stand at a critical moment in Earth's history, a time when humanity must choose its future. As the world becomes increasingly interdependent and fragile, the future at once holds great peril and great promise. To move forward we must recognize that in the midst of a magnificent diversity of cultures and life forms we are one human family and one Earth community with a common destiny. We must join together to bring forth a sustainable global society founded on respect for nature, universal human rights, economic justice, and a culture of peace. Toward this end, it is imperative that we, the peoples of Earth, declare our responsibility to one another, to the greater community of life, and to future generations.

Earth, Our Home

Humanity is part of a vast evolving universe. Earth, our home, is alive with a unique community of life. The forces of nature make existence a demanding and uncertain adventure, but Earth has provided the conditions essential to life's evolution. The resilience of the community of life and the wellbeing of humanity depend upon preserving a healthy biosphere with all its ecological systems, a rich variety of plants and animals, fertile soils, pure waters, and clean air. The global environment with its finite resources is a common concern of all peoples. The protection of Earth's vitality, diversity, and beauty is a sacred trust.

The Global Situation

The dominant patterns of production and consumption are causing environmental devastation, the depletion of resources, and a massive extinction of species. Communities are being undermined. The benefits of development are not shared equitably and the gap between rich and poor is widening. Injustice, poverty, ignorance, and violent conflict are widespread and the cause of great suffering. An unprecedented rise in human population has overburdened ecological and social systems. The foundations of global security are threatened. These trends are perilous—but not inevitable.

The Challenges Ahead

The choice is ours: form a global partnership to care for Earth and one another or risk the destruction of ourselves and the diversity of life. Fundamental changes are needed in our values, institutions, and ways of living. We must realize that when basic needs have been met, human development is primarily about being more, not having more. We have the knowledge and technology to provide for all and to reduce our impacts on the environment. The emergence of a global civil society is creating new opportunities to build a democratic and humane world. Our environmental, economic, political, social, and spiritual challenges are interconnected, and together we can forge inclusive solutions.

Universal Responsibility

To realize these aspirations, we must decide to live with a sense of universal responsibility, identifying ourselves with the whole Earth community as well as our local communities. We are at once citizens of different nations and of one world in which the local and global are linked. Everyone shares responsibility for the present and future wellbeing of the human family and the larger living world. The spirit of human solidarity and kinship with all life is strengthened when we live with reverence for the mystery of being, gratitude for the gift of life, and humility regarding the human place in nature.

We urgently need a shared vision of basic values to provide an ethical foundation for the emerging world community. Therefore, together in hope we affirm the following interdependent principles for a sustainable way of life as a common standard by which the conduct of all individuals, organizations, businesses, governments, and transnational institutions is to be guided and assessed.

Principles

I. Respect and Care for the Community of Life

1. Respect Earth and life in all its diversity.

    a. Recognize that all beings are interdependent and every form of life has value regardless of its worth to human beings.
    b. Affirm faith in the inherent dignity of all human beings and in the intellectual, artistic, ethical, and spiritual potential of humanity.

2. Care for the community of life with understanding, compassion, and love.

    a. Accept that with the right to own, manage, and use natural resources comes the duty to prevent environmental harm and to protect the rights of people.

    b. Affirm that with increased freedom, knowledge, and power comes increased responsibility to promote the common good.

3. Build democratic societies that are just, participatory, sustainable, and peaceful.

    a. Ensure that communities at all levels guarantee human rights and fundamental freedoms and provide everyone an opportunity to realize his or her full potential.

    b. Promote social and economic justice, enabling all to achieve a secure and meaningful livelihood that is ecologically responsible.

4. Secure Earth's bounty and beauty for present and future generations.

    a. Recognize that the freedom of action of each generation is qualified by the needs of future generations.

    b. Transmit to future generations values, traditions, and institutions that support the long-term flourishing of Earth's human and ecological communities. In order to fulfill these four broad commitments, it is necessary to:

II. Ecological Integrity

5. Protect and restore the integrity of Earth's ecological systems, with special concern for biological diversity and the natural processes that sustain life.

    a. Adopt at all levels of sustainable development plans and regulations that make environmental conservation and rehabilitation integral to all development initiatives.

    b. Establish and safeguard viable nature and biosphere reserves, including wild lands and marine areas, to protect Earth's life support systems, maintain biodiversity, and preserve our natural heritage.

    c. Promote the recovery of endangered species and ecosystems.

    d. Control and eradicate non-native or genetically modified organisms harmful to native species and the environment, and prevent the introduction of such harmful organisms.

    e. Manage the use of renewable resources such as water, soil, forest products, and marine life in ways that do not exceed rates of regeneration and that protect the health of ecosystems.

    f. Manage the extraction and use of non-renewable resources such as minerals and fossil fuels in ways that minimize depletion and cause no serious environmental damage.

6. Prevent harm as the best method of environmental protection and, when knowledge is limited, apply a precautionary approach.

   a. Take action to avoid the possibility of serious or irreversible environmental harm even when scientific knowledge is incomplete or inconclusive.

   b. Place the burden of proof on those who argue that a proposed activity will not cause significant harm, and make the responsible parties liable for environmental harm.

   c. Ensure that decision-making addresses the cumulative, long-term, indirect, long distance, and global consequences of human activities.

   d. Prevent pollution of any part of the environment and allow no build-up of radioactive, toxic, or other hazardous substances.

   e. Avoid military activities damaging the environment.

7. Adopt patterns of production, consumption, and reproduction that safeguard Earth's regenerative capacities, human rights, and community wellbeing.

   a. Reduce, reuse, and recycle the materials used in production and consumption systems, and ensure that residual waste can be assimilated by ecological systems.

   b. Act with restraint and efficiency when using energy, and rely increasingly on renewable energy sources such as solar and wind.

   c. Promote the development, adoption, and equitable transfer of environmentally sound technologies.

   d. Internalize the full environmental and social costs of goods and services in the selling price, and enable consumers to identify products that meet the highest social and environmental standards.

   e. Ensure universal access to health care that fosters reproductive health and responsible reproduction.

   f. Adopt lifestyles that emphasize the quality of life and material sufficiency in a finite world.

8. Advance the study of ecological sustainability and promote the open exchange and wide application of the knowledge acquired.

   a. Support international scientific and technical cooperation on sustainability, with special attention to the needs of developing nations.

   b. Recognize and preserve the traditional knowledge and spiritual wisdom in all cultures that contribute to environmental protection and human wellbeing.

   c. Ensure that information of vital importance to human health and environmental protection, including genetic information, remains available in the public domain.

III. Social and Economic Justice

9. Eradicate poverty as an ethical, social, and environmental imperative.

   a. Guarantee the right to potable water, clean air, food security, uncontaminated soil, shelter, and safe sanitation, allocating the national and international resources required.
   b. Empower every human being with the education and resources to secure a sustainable livelihood, and provide social security and safety nets for those who are unable to support themselves.
   c. Recognize the ignored, protect the vulnerable, serve those who suffer, and enable them to develop their capacities and to pursue their aspirations.

10. Ensure that economic activities and institutions at all levels promote human development in an equitable and sustainable manner.

   a. Promote the equitable distribution of wealth within nations and among nations.
   b. Enhance the intellectual, financial, technical, and social resources of developing nations, and relieve them of onerous international debt.
   c. Ensure that all trade supports sustainable resource use, environmental protection, and progressive labor standards.
   d. Require multinational corporations and international financial organizations to act transparently in the public good, and hold them accountable for the consequences of their activities.

11. Affirm gender equality and equity as prerequisites to sustainable development and ensure universal access to education, health care, and economic opportunity.

   a. Secure the human rights of women and girls and end all violence against them.
   b. Promote the active participation of women in all aspects of economic, political, civil, social, and cultural life as full and equal partners, decision-makers, leaders, and beneficiaries.
   c. Strengthen families and ensure the safety and loving nurture of all family members.

12. Uphold the right of all, without discrimination, to a natural and social environment supportive of human dignity, bodily health, and spiritual wellbeing, with special attention to the rights of indigenous peoples and minorities.

   a. Eliminate discrimination in all its forms, such as that based on race, color, sex, sexual orientation, religion, language, and national, ethnic, or social origin.
   b. Affirm the right of indigenous peoples to their spirituality, knowledge, lands, and resources and to their related practice of sustainable livelihoods.
   c. Honor and support the young people of our communities, enabling them to fulfill their essential role in creating sustainable societies.
   d. Protect and restore outstanding places of cultural and spiritual significance.

IV. Democracy, Nonviolence, and Peace

13. Strengthen democratic institutions at all levels, and provide transparency and accountability in governance, inclusive participation in decision-making, and access to justice.

    a. Uphold the right of everyone to receive clear and timely information on environmental matters and all development plans and activities which are likely to affect them or in which they have an interest.
    b. Support local, regional, and global civil society, and promote the meaningful participation of all interested individuals and organizations in decision-making.
    c. Protect the rights to freedom of opinion, expression, peaceful assembly, association, and dissent.
    d. Institute effective and efficient access to administrative and independent judicial procedures, including remedies and redress for environmental harm and the threat of such harm.
    e. Eliminate corruption in all public and private institutions.
    f. Strengthen local communities, enabling them to care for their environments, and assign environmental responsibilities to the levels of government where they can be carried out most effectively.

14. Integrate into formal education and life-long learning the knowledge, values, and skills needed for a sustainable way of life.

    a. Provide all, especially children and youth, with educational opportunities that empower them to contribute actively to sustainable development.
    b. Promote the contribution of the arts and humanities as well as the sciences in sustainability education.
    c. Enhance the role of the mass media in raising awareness of ecological and social challenges.
    d. Recognize the importance of moral and spiritual education for sustainable living.

15. Treat all living beings with respect and consideration.

    a. Prevent cruelty to animals kept in human societies and protect them from suffering.
    b. Protect wild animals from methods of hunting, trapping, and fishing that cause extreme, prolonged, or avoidable suffering.
    c. Avoid or eliminate to the full extent possible the taking or destruction of non-targeted species.

16. Promote a culture of tolerance, nonviolence, and peace.

    a. Encourage and support mutual understanding, solidarity, and cooperation among all peoples and within and among nations.

    b. Implement comprehensive strategies to prevent violent conflict and use collaborative problem-solving to manage and resolve environmental conflicts and other disputes.

    c. Demilitarize national security systems to the level of a non-provocative defense posture, and convert military resources to peaceful purposes, including ecological restoration.

    d. Eliminate nuclear, biological, and toxic weapons and other weapons of mass destruction.

    e. Ensure that the use of orbital and outer space supports environmental protection and peace.

    f. Recognize that peace is the wholeness created by right relationships with oneself, other persons, other cultures, other life, Earth, and the larger whole of which all are a part.

The Way Forward

As never before in history, common destiny beckons us to seek a new beginning. Such renewal is the promise of these Earth Charter principles. To fulfill this promise, we must commit ourselves to adopt and promote the values and objectives of the Charter.

This requires a change of mind and heart. It requires a new sense of global interdependence and universal responsibility. We must imaginatively develop and apply the vision of a sustainable way of life locally, nationally, regionally, and globally. Our cultural diversity is a precious heritage and different cultures will find their own distinctive ways to realize the vision. We must deepen and expand the global dialogue that generated the Earth Charter, for we have much to learn from the ongoing collaborative search for truth and wisdom.

Life often involves tensions between important values. This can mean difficult choices. However, we must find ways to harmonize diversity with unity, the exercise of freedom with the common good, short-term objectives with long-term goals. Every individual, family, organization, and community has a vital role to play. The arts, sciences, religions, educational institutions, media, businesses, nongovernmental organizations, and governments are all called to offer creative leadership. The partnership of government, civil society, and business is essential for effective governance.

In order to build a sustainable global community, the nations of the world must renew their commitment to the United Nations, fulfill their obligations under existing international agreements, and support the implementation of Earth Charter principles with an international legally binding instrument on the environment and development.

Let ours be a time remembered for the awakening of a new reverence for life, the firm resolve to achieve sustainability, the quickening of the struggle for justice and peace, and the joyful celebration of life.

References

Clugston, R. (2016). The Earth Charter, spirituality and sustainable development. *Journal of Oriental Studies, 26*, 155–170.

Clugston, R., Lubbers R., Mackey B, Rockefeller S., Roerink A., & Vilela, M. (2011). *Earth Charter International recommendations for the zero draft of the UNCSD (Rio+20) outcome document.* Compilation document. UNCSD Website. http://www.uncsd2012.org/rio+20/index.php

Corcoran, P. B. (2002). The values of the Earth Charter in education for sustainable development. *Australian Journal of Environmental Education, 18*, 77–80.

Corcoran, P. B., & Wohlpart, A. J. (Eds.). (2008). *A voice for Earth: American writers respond to the Earth Charter.* University of Georgia Press.

Earth Charter Commission. (2000). *The Earth Charter.* Resource Document. https://earthcharter.org/wp-content/uploads/2020/03/echarter_english.pdf?x62355

Fernández-Herrería, A., & Martínez-Rodríguez, F. M. (2020). Planetary ethics beyond neoliberalism: the Earth Charter's "Community of Life." In H. Hosseini, J. Goodman, S. Motta, and B. Gills. (Eds.), *The Routledge handbook of transformative global studies* (pp. 273–286). Routledge.

Francis. (2015, May 24). Encyclical *Letter Laudato Si' of the Holy Father Frances on care of our Common Home.* https://www.vatican.va/content/francesco/en/encyclicals/documents/papa-francesco_20150524_enciclica-laudato-si.html

Gorbachev, M. (2005) Preface: The third pillar of sustainable development. In P. B. Corcoran (Ed.), *The Earth Charter in action: toward a sustainable world.* (pp. 9–10). Royal Tropical Institute (KIT).

Grantham Research Institute on Climate Change and the Environment. (2012). *Climate Change Laws of the World database: The Mother Earth law and integral development to live well, law no 300.* https://www.climate-laws.org/

Hickel, J. (2016, August 8). The problem with saving the world. *Jacobin.*

Hickman, C., Marks, E., Pihkala, P., Clayton, S., Lewandowshi, E., Mayall, E. E., Wray, B., Mellor, C. & van Susteren, L. (2021). *Young People's Voices on Climate Anxiety, Governmental Betrayal and Moral Injury: A Global Phenomenon* [Unpublished manuscript]. University of Bath.

Rockefeller, S. C. (2010). *Challenges and opportunities facing the Earth Charter initiative.* [Unpublished Keynote Address, Ahmedabad, India]. https://earthcharter.org/wp-content/assets/virtual-library2/images/uploads/Speech_by_steven_rockofeller.pdf

Strong, M. (2005) Preface: A people's Earth Charter. In P. B. Corcoran (Ed.), *The Earth Charter in action: Toward a sustainable world* (pp. 11–12). Royal Tropical Institute (KIT).

United Nations (2015). *Transforming our world: The 2030 agenda for sustainable development.* Resource document. United Nations. https://sustainabledevelopment.un.org/post2015/transformingourworld

United Nations Conference on Sustainable Development, Rio+20. (2012). *Rio+20 outcome document.* Resource Document. United Nations. https://sustainabledevelopment.un.org/rio20/futurewewant

United Nations Environment Programme (2018). *Inclusive wealth report 2018.* Resource Document. United Nations. https://www.unep.org/resources/inclusive-wealth-report-2018

United Nations World Summit on Sustainable Development. (2002). *Report of the world summit on sustainable development, Johannesburg Summit.* Resource Document. United Nations. https://sustainabledevelopment.un.org/milesstones/wssd

Vilela, M., & Jiménez, A. (Eds.) (2020). *Earth Charter, education and the Sustainable Development Goal 4.7: Research, experiences and reflections.* ©UPEACE Press in collaboration with Earth Charter International.

Wallace-Wells, D. (2019). *The uninhabitable earth.* Penguin.

Williams, T. T. (2008). Foreword: Taking the globe to our bosom. In P. B. Corcoran & A. J. Wohlpart (Eds.), *A voice for Earth: American writers respond to the Earth Charter.* University of Georgia Press.

World Commission on Environmental and Development. (1987). *Our common future.* Oxford University Press.

Zubialde, A. (2014). *Comparison between the new Sustainable Development Goals and the ethical principles of the Earth Charter.* https://biencommunchartedelaterre.wordpress.com/2015/06/29/comparison-between-the-new-sustainable-development-goals-and-the-ethical-principles-of-the-earth-charter/

Chapter 40
The Closing Challenge for a Flourishing and Sustainable Future

Kim Beasy, Caroline Smith, and Jane Watson

The purpose of this book is to add to the increasing body of literature recognising that education is, and must, in its praxis, be at the heart of all the Sustainable Development Goals (SDGs): a key vehicle through which the concepts and practices needed to address the goals can be progressed. As we enter the third decade of the twenty-first century, we have a clear understanding of the wicked and complex polycrises regarding the health of life on our planet. Continuing in the direction of unsustainable exploitation of people and nature is no longer an option if life is to have a flourishing future. There is also now a general global recognition of what we need to do, through our decisions, policies, and actions, to halt decline and enable this flourishing.

The United Nations 2030 Agenda, through the vehicle of the SDGs, represents the most far-reaching effort to date by the global community, to guide the world towards a more sustainable future. Although they are described in 17 goals and address different aspects of the global geo-biophysical and social system, the SDGs are highly interconnected. For example, access to clean water is an essential component of health, sanitation, biodiversity, and agriculture (SDGs 6, 14, and 15), while

K. Beasy (✉)
School of Education, College of Arts, Law and Education, University of Tasmania, Launceston, TAS 7248, Australia
e-mail: kim.beasy@utas.edu.au

Centre for Marine Socioecology, University of Tasmania, Hobart, TAS, Australia

C. Smith
School of Education, College of Arts, Law and Education, University of Tasmania, Burnie, TAS 7320, Australia
e-mail: caroline.smith1@utas.edu.au

J. Watson
School of Education, College of Arts, Law and Education, University of Tasmania, Hobart, TAS 7005, Australia
e-mail: jane.watson@utas.edu.au

malnutrition cannot be tackled without engaging with agriculture, the food industry, health, and of course, education (SDGs 2, 3, 4, and 10). It is also clear that the goals themselves are far from perfect, and for many, continue to reflect the dominant western neoliberal growthist worldview that has created them (see Chapters 3, 19, 36, and 39). As well, many gaps in their formulation, coverage, and targets still remain, in particular, the inner, spiritual dimension (as discussed in Chapters 37, 38, and 39), Indigenous voices (see Chapters 5, 6, and 39) and, we would also add, voices from the LBTQI+ community across the planet. However, the SDGs are currently the dominant international pathway whereby nations are engaging in their moves towards sustainability, and as such, it is important that the global education community is aware of and engages with them fully. Indeed, whichever way the goals are read, critiqued, and employed, one thing is clear: education can, and needs to, play a critically important role. Agenda 2030 challenges us to make the biggest paradigm shift in our history, requiring systemic transformational development through the need for trans-disciplinary and holistic approaches. Without such a paradigm shift, there is limited ability to turn our efforts towards creating a flourishing world. This shift particularly applies to our education systems.

This does not mean that nothing is being done through education, and indeed, great strides have been made on many fronts. For decades, educators and institutions across the world have been responding to the challenge of sustainability in their own particular contexts. For decades, the big questions have been asked of education, such as: "what is the purpose of education in today's world?"; "what does an education that responds to a climate-constrained and resource and ecosystems-depleted world, with a massive and increasing divide between rich and poor, look like?"; "what sort of learning is needed and how do we create the conditions to enable it?"; and, "what pedagogies and curricula support movement towards sustainability?" As a global community interested in the role of education in forging a flourishing future for all, however, we still have a very long way to go. It remains remarkable that, in the twenty-first century, too many schools are not vastly different from the institutions of the nineteenth century, where same-age students sit at their desks while a single teacher exposits from the front, teaching from a centralised curriculum. Indeed, educational systems are particularly resistant to change, and a number of authors have provided in-depth analyses of why this is the case. Apart from addressing global inequities, there also remains the need to challenge the innate beliefs of those involved in education at all levels; some of this will involve costs for those of us who have more than we need, who believe we have inalienable rights to Earth's resources, and who continue to ignore our environmental impacts.

If we are to move towards a flourishing future, as a collective, we need to be open to letting go of some of our old ways or, in some cases, re-engaging with others. To *do* differently, we must be given opportunities to *read* differently, *learn* differently, and *understand* differently. We would argue—and believe is evidenced through this collection—that education is at the heart of the journey of *being* different to enable flourishing. We have drawn together a diversity of perspectives, spanning the full range of educational contexts—purposively—to break down sectoral divides and challenge constitutions of education and how it is, and ought to be done. We have intentionally highlighted how working towards SDGs is best achieved through contextually relevant and locally grounded practice, though we have worked to ensure that the learnings from each chapter present guiding principles translatable across contexts. We contend that it is often through chance reading and engaging with materials, knowledge, and practice that may lay beyond our regular grasp, that we often garner new insights and find the inspiration needed to take that first step towards *being* different. We find that the materials in this book have inspired us to do just this; we hope you may do so too.

We have used the phrase "Education for Sustainability" (EfS) in its broadest sense to encompass the understandings, skills, attitudes, values, and actions, as well as opportunities, that are needed in the paradigm shift towards a flourishing future. This is recognised within the SDGs themselves; SDG4 has determined that education is a human right in itself. From its very basic premise—that all children have a right to education—the SDGs recognise that this is critical if we are to work towards a flourishing future. Target 4.1 states that "by 2030, all girls and boys must be able to complete free, equitable and quality primary and secondary education leading to relevant and effective learning outcomes" (see Chapter 4). The sad fact remains, however, that many children are still denied an education, and that education is still not fully accessible to many girls and women, or those with disabilities (see Chapters 12, 23, and 34), thus denying them the opportunity to have a voice in their communities (as described in SDG5). In too many places, education contributes to, rather than reduces, inequality. This remains a serious impediment to EfS in the broadest sense.

Even where education is available, context and conditions are critical. Those wondering where their next meal is coming from, or are caught in the horror of war, are in a very different position in being able to act, from those who have the means to influence their communities and leadership. Those who are labouring under oppressive regimes may have access to schooling, but are not in a position to challenge authority, or are severely repressed if they attempt to do so. As well, there are far too many international development projects where simplistic, short-term solutions to complex educational problems fail to deliver lasting, systemic, and transformational change. Schools might be built in regions of the Global South by well-meaning donors, only to find there are not sufficient teachers to staff them, or resources to run them properly. Teachers from rural areas may be trained, only to leave for the city or overseas where they have greater opportunities.

The broad diversity of work contained in this volume showcases some of the many ways in which EfS can be considered and approached in relation to the SDGs, through scholarship on histories, philosophies, concepts, and practices. Clearly, EfS does not only refer to formal schooling. It refers more broadly to life-long learning, from informal, family and community-based education, to university, the TVET sector and beyond, in order to develop a consciousness and mindset that are reflected in the way we think and act for a flourishing future. It also considers the important interconnections between all of these educational forms. In the beginning part, we aim to provide readers with background to the SDGs in general, so that educators can understand and be aware of the deeper structures that permeate them, and reflect on them critically in order to inform thinking and develop practice around what needs to be considered when engaging with them. With this understanding, educators can use the SDGs as a tool through which to work towards flourishing futures in more nuanced ways that are relevant to their own particular contexts. The SDGs span all contexts from local to global, acknowledging that resources and capacities for change vary widely. Thus, the remaining parts of the book explore a range of innovative thinking and practices from across the globe: success stories and lessons learned, as well as challenges still to be overcome.

A particularly strong message of this book is the critically important role of universities as models of sustainable practice in their management, as well as research, teaching, and community engagement, through collaborating and partnering at all levels from local to global. There is great need for more research in particular areas, e.g., navigating systemic challenges, collaboration across sectors, and appropriate, holistic sustainability-focussed curricula and pedagogies based around the principles of EfS. Universities need to continue to position themselves as accessible educational thought and practice leaders, stepping outside normal professional roles and boundaries, and breaking from traditional siloes to focus on the inter- and transdisciplinary approaches needed to solve the complex, wicked problem of sustainability. By engaging with all 17 SDGs, universities are well-placed to work with their communities to tackle the challenges at hand, and to position themselves as key drivers for achieving them. Several chapters (e.g., Chapters 14 to 16) describe ways in which this is being addressed. It is heartening to see this aspect is now becoming entrenched globally, with the Times Higher Education Impact Rankings now assessing all universities against the SDGs, as well as other measures such as the STARS rating system, described in Chapter 17.

Through focussing on the myriad ways in which education can engage with the interconnectedness of the SDGs, we hope that this book has demonstrated that education is at the heart of understanding, critiquing, and working with all the Goals. The final SDG, SDG17, "Partnerships for the Goals," calls upon us to form partnerships, alliances, and collaborations across the life span, with life-long and life-wide education central to creating and enabling such partnerships. Finally, we hope that this book is able to provide inspiration, challenge, and provocation, as well as solace, and especially, hope, to readers in their own contexts, journeys, and places, who wish to make our Earthly home a better place for all through the powerful medium of education. Our goal, indeed our dream, through the many small actions of all of us, is that education takes its rightful place in embracing and creating a more inclusive, Earth-centred perspective, and flourishing future for all life on Earth.

Index

A

Ableism, 429
  ableist, 69, 151
Abnormal justice, 620, 625
Aboriginal and Torres Strait Islanders, 18,
    19, 66, 73–75, 83–85, 96
  Aboriginal and Torres Strait Islanders
    students, 414
Aboriginal elders, 88, 417
Aboriginal history, 417
Aboriginality, 90
Aboriginal Land Council, 87, 90
Aboriginal Protected Areas, 93
Aboriginal rights, 68, 89
Aboriginal sovereignty, 68, 73, 89, 91, 92
Aboriginal Sovereign Warrior Woman, 70
Academe
  academia, 30, 68, 509
  academic stepping stones, 420
  academic vocabulary, 526–529, 533,
    535
Acceptance of difference and individuality,
    419
Access to education, 232, 428, 431, 497,
    514, 621, 624, 630, 727
Action research, 529
Active Healthy Kids Global Alliance, 475
Active learning approaches, 466
Active transportation, 480, 481
ACTS (Australasian Campuses Towards
    Sustainability), 289
Adaptation, 106, 259–263, 266, 270–272,
    275, 281, 287, 291, 321, 342, 400,
    401, 404, 446, 452, 549, 559, 602,
    604, 608, 644

Addressing inequality, 415
Adult learning, 650
Advanced and leadership training, 438
Advanced automation, 643
Advanced human-machine interfaces, 643
Advanced manufacturing, 8, 637, 638, 640,
    642, 644, 645
Advocacy, 43, 72, 120, 121, 339, 346–353,
    375, 392, 404, 430, 433, 438, 571,
    704
AEDC data, 604, 611
AEDC indicators, 604, 606
Afghanistan, 619, 622, 623, 626–633
  Afghan women, 8, 619, 620, 622, 623,
    626–632
After-school strategies, 481
Agenda 21, 602, 711, 713, 720
Agrarian economies, 657
Agriculture
  agricultural production, 170, 175, 551
  Agricultural Revolution, 673
  agriculture farming robot, 381
Alliance Summit (AS), 638
AMEE Consensus Statement, 342
American Psychological Association, 699
Angola, 495
Animal companionship, 583, 592, 595
Anthropocene, 3, 343, 460, 722
Anthropocentrism, 111, 469
Anthropogenic climate change, 288, 396,
    722
Anthropogenic ecosystems, 338
Anti-discrimination legislation, 435
Apartheid, 70

Architecture, 106, 111, 112, 320–323, 327,
    328, 699
Art
    art-based pedagogies, 580
    art exchange, 620, 623, 626
    art making, 590
    art practices, 583, 584, 587
    art projects, 623, 626, 631
    arts and crafts, 318, 320, 322, 327, 328
    arts-based, 579, 580, 584, 586
    arts-based methodologies, 587
    arts-based methods, 8, 579
    arts funding, 584
    arts participation, 584
    arts sector, 582
    art universities, 316, 318–321
    art workshops, 581, 582, 586
Artificial intelligence (AI), 109, 315, 660
Artists, 67, 267, 324, 328, 582, 584,
    588–591, 593–595, 623, 626
Asian Development Bank (ADB), 173
Asphalt, 385
Associated Schools Project (ASP), 13–15
Association for the Advancement of
    Sustainability in Higher Education
    (AASHE), 290, 298
At-risk individuals, 477
Attention Deficit Hyperactivity Disorder
    (ADHD), 413, 414, 418, 420, 430,
    436
Australia, 3, 12, 14–20, 23, 24, 58, 66, 67,
    73, 74, 76, 83–89, 93, 107, 108, 110,
    114–117, 120, 136, 142, 245, 256,
    260, 263, 267, 271, 282, 284–287,
    309, 377, 397, 400–402, 411, 413,
    414, 419, 421, 432–436, 446, 447,
    449, 459–463, 475, 476, 481, 510,
    529, 545, 547, 548, 550, 553, 569,
    571, 580, 583, 584, 589, 592, 601,
    602, 614, 623, 626, 627, 629–632,
    662, 700
Australian Academy of Science, 16
Australian Bureau of Statistics (ABS), 414,
    546, 580, 603
Australian Conservation Foundation, 18
Australian Curriculum Assessment and
    Reporting Authority [ACARA], 18,
    413, 414, 447, 461, 462, 478, 543,
    545, 550, 551, 662, 664
Australian Early Development Census
    (AEDC), 603, 604, 606, 611
Australian First Nations, 399
Australian Geography Curriculum, 550

Australian Government Department of
    Foreign Affairs and Trade (DFAT),
    432, 548
Australian Institute for Teaching and
    School Leadership, 411, 412
Australian Law Schools Standards
    Committee, 116
Australian Mathematics Curriculum, 543,
    551
Australian Science Curriculum, 550
Australian subnational climate change
    policy, 271
Australian Sustainable Schools Initiative,
    462
Austria, 494
Authoritarianism, 29, 37, 714
Autism, 430
Autism Spectrum Disorder (ASD), 417, 420
Automation, 375, 679, 681
Awareness in Action, 704
Axiological, 94
    axiomatic truths, 31

B

Bangladesh, 397, 399, 402, 627, 632
Barcelona Declaration, 376
Basic human needs, 561, 563, 565, 674, 676
    basic needs, 501, 562, 565, 568, 674,
    676, 677, 714, 715, 717, 724
Basic human rights, 619, 714
Basic Income, 681–685
Basic primary education, 629
Basic skills, 153, 542, 639, 642
Basic vocabulary, 526
Behaviour agreement, 417, 418
Benefits, 37, 50, 51, 54, 66, 68, 71, 73, 75,
    89, 93, 95, 96, 108, 109, 117, 122,
    142, 147, 161, 174, 176, 179, 207,
    218, 224, 281, 289, 304, 307, 340,
    341, 348, 349, 356, 394, 421, 436,
    453, 455, 468, 473–476, 478, 492,
    500, 509, 511, 517, 519, 550, 566,
    583, 592, 605–607, 609, 610, 661,
    664, 665, 677–680, 684, 695, 696,
    711, 723
Bicultural heritage, 22
Biodiverse
    biodiversity, 3, 4, 16, 17, 20, 30, 42, 72,
    75, 86, 93, 94, 106, 108, 111, 112,
    139, 170, 175, 306, 307, 355, 549,
    550, 663, 725, 733
    biodiversity loss, 3, 17, 110, 121, 353,
    526, 549, 550, 560, 639, 666, 714

biodiversity restoration, 87
Biofiltration, 385
Biogas Production, 386
Biomass, 291, 336
Biomimicry, 692, 697–699, 702, 703, 705
    Biomimicry Revolution, 697
Biosphere, 335, 337, 338, 697, 719, 723,
    725
Blackcurious, 67
    Blackcuriousity, 63
Blak country, 93
Blaks, 65–68, 75, 89, 90, 93, 94, 96
Blaq, 66, 70, 71, 85, 86, 89
Blue Economy Cooperative Research
    Centre, 310
Blueprint for a climate-positive Tasmania,
    272
Body image, 482, 483
Boehm 3 Test, 532
Boston University, 285
Bottom-up approaches, 515
Brazil, 15, 40, 132, 713
Bristol University, 283
Britain, 33
    British Government, 92
Brundtland, G., 4, 11, 31, 43, 377, 565,
    711, 719
Buddhi
    Buddhism, 9
    Buddhist, 692, 696, 699–702, 704, 705
    Buddhist education, 705
Building back better initiative, 493
Building relationships, 614
Bulgaria, 494
Bullying, 419
Bureaucracy, 68, 325, 333
Bushfire damage, 266
    bushfires, 3, 16, 110, 272, 287, 349, 549

C
Calgary University, 320
Canada, 116, 120, 136, 225, 476, 480, 494,
    584
Canmore Declaration, 342
Capacity building, 24, 93, 227, 318, 569,
    571, 602, 604, 606–608, 610–612,
    614, 615, 657, 682
Capitalism, 31, 34, 35, 38, 44, 96, 111, 141,
    563, 657, 658, 660, 661, 664, 668
    capitalist, 30, 142, 624, 684
Carbon accounting, 283, 284
Carbon colonialism, 288

Carbon credits, 284
Carbon-free transport, 282
Carbon neutral, 282, 287–289, 308, 309
Carbon offsets, 288, 289, 291
Careful lesson planning, 420
Caring for country, 73, 74, 93, 94
Census at School project, 546
Centre for Marine Socioecology, 310
Centre for Renewable Energy and Power
    Systems (CREPS), 310
Centres of Excellence, 650
Centres of Vocational Excellence, 637, 638
Certification, 188, 308, 309
Change agents, 132, 133, 140, 249, 296,
    355
Charge small mobile devices, 381
Charter of the United Nations, 709
Check and connect, 417
Child development, 531
Child mortality, 4, 31
Children's developmental outcomes
    children's healthy development, 603,
        604, 606, 607, 615
    children's language development, 601,
        603, 606, 609, 610, 612
China, 23, 36, 39, 132, 216, 659
Circular and greener economy, 642
    circular economy, 287, 290, 383, 491,
        644
Citizenship, 64, 172, 175, 176, 178, 223,
    224, 226, 227, 236, 238, 452, 647,
    651, 661, 666, 681
    citizenship competences, 648
Civic scientific literacy, 666
    civility, 64
Clarence City Council, 585
Classroom management, 197, 412, 415,
    416, 419–421
    classroom management practices, 412,
        415, 416
Classroom-ready teachers, 411
Climate action, 11, 14, 31, 74, 84, 112, 171,
    259–262, 267, 269, 273, 279–283,
    285–287, 289–291, 305, 308, 310,
    379, 382, 386, 387, 404, 445, 448,
    449, 452, 455, 469, 540, 663
    climate action leadership, 263, 280, 287
Climate anxiety, 446, 460, 721, 722
Climate café, 347
Climate change, 3, 7, 11, 12, 15–23, 29–31,
    40, 43, 64, 106, 109, 110, 114, 120,
    121, 139–141, 169–171, 174–176,
    179–181, 259–273, 275, 279–282,

287, 289, 291, 308, 310, 315,
   319–321, 327, 331, 336, 341, 349,
   351, 353, 354, 376, 392–405,
   445–456, 459–461, 511, 540, 547,
   549–551, 553, 559, 616, 620, 639,
   644, 646, 655, 664, 668, 683, 705,
   714, 721, 722
climate change education, 18, 21, 23,
   392, 403, 446–448, 455
climate change pedagogy, 268, 274
Climate Connection initiative, 23
Climate crisis, 7, 11, 42, 279, 282, 291,
   446, 604, 666
Climate-damaging emissions, 281
Climate decision making, 260, 263
Climate emergency, 283, 309, 459, 560, 660
Climate Futures, 266, 271, 272, 276, 287,
   309, 446
Climate-induced migration, 392–394,
   396–400, 402–405
   climate-migration-development nexus,
   392
Climate justice, 44, 268, 282, 392, 400,
   404, 405
Climate knowledges, 261
Climate leadership, 260, 262, 280, 282,
   283, 291
Climate literacy, 260–263, 267–269, 271,
   273–275, 392, 446–449, 452, 454,
   455
   climate literacy learning, 268, 270, 455
Climate modelling, 260, 271, 272
Climate positive, 291
Climate problem, 261, 446
Climate-related projects, 308
Climate science, 12, 20, 42, 260–262, 266,
   268, 271–276, 280, 291, 392, 446,
   449, 666
Climate sustainable food culture, 287
Climate thought leadership, 260
Clinical focus, 350
Closing the Gap, 74, 84
Cloud technologies, 643
Co-creation, 650, 684, 705
Co-curricular HPE Strategies, 480
Co-designed community skills cafes, 604
Cognitive function, 477
   cognitive functioning, 474
   cognitive skills, 561, 604
Collaboration, 16, 23, 45, 72, 120, 138,
   171, 173, 199, 231, 251, 272, 273,
   289, 300, 305, 307, 308, 342, 353,
   354, 356, 357, 392, 394, 396, 397,

399, 402, 405, 495, 509, 514–516,
   518, 519, 571, 593, 626, 638–641,
   645, 651, 699, 701, 702, 715, 736
collaboration and quality education, 514
collaborative learning models, 508
Collective action, 20, 290, 567, 622, 674,
   675, 677, 683
Colonialisation
   colonialism, 31, 35, 64, 69, 88, 95, 111,
      224, 595, 656, 657, 668
   neo-colonialism, 70, 667
Colonial powers, 355, 657
Colonisation, 33, 63–66, 74, 76, 83, 85, 86,
   91, 92, 94, 355
Colonising, 63, 65–67, 70, 76, 83, 90, 91,
   96, 281, 659
Commission on Sustainable Development
   (CSD), 713
Commitment to Sustainable Practices of
   Higher Education Institution, 393
Commodification, 69, 316, 318
Commonwealth Climate Active, 309
Communities of Practice (CoPs), 569, 582,
   588, 593
Community activation, 588
Community-based, 8, 13, 19, 587, 607, 735
   community-based climate literacy, 261
Community building, 593, 606
Community capacity, 604, 612, 615, 683
   community capacity building, 604, 606,
      607, 610, 611, 615
Community change, 601
Community consultation, 604, 607, 608
Community development, 582, 605, 606,
   611, 612, 615, 616
Community Development Job Guarantee,
   683
Community development model, 607
Community engagement, 318, 319, 321,
   326, 333, 580, 586, 684, 736
   community engagement strategies, 492
Community garden, 615
Community learning, 569, 588
Community needs, 569, 593, 646
Community of life, 45, 710, 712, 715, 716,
   720, 721, 723, 724
Community of Practice, 8, 307, 354, 500,
   501, 560, 579, 586, 587
Community participation, 75, 583
Community resilience, 601–603, 606
Community stakeholders, 181, 605, 607,
   614
Community understanding, 263, 271, 273

Competence building
competencies, 116, 119, 120, 143, 179,
180, 189, 194, 227, 228, 231, 238,
261, 342, 346, 347, 349, 351–353,
377, 391, 404, 418, 420, 492, 496,
515, 519, 540, 541, 639, 642, 643,
645–649, 651
Concept-construction, 528
conceptions, 34, 511, 678
conceptual knowledge, 530
conceptual play, 531, 533, 534
Concord Consortiums CODAP, 551
Conference of the Parties (COP), 11, 12,
30, 170, 569, 570, 572
Consciousness, 68, 519, 561, 568, 587,
651, 665, 692, 695, 699, 706, 710,
715, 716, 719, 735
Conservation, 13, 15, 21, 41–43, 67, 75, 86,
93, 110, 111, 170, 175, 326, 450,
453, 465, 725
Consumer
consumerism, 8, 69, 108, 111, 115, 317,
318, 321, 339, 566, 658, 659, 664,
675, 678, 680, 693, 717
consumerist, 691, 693
consumption, 12, 30, 32, 45, 67, 69, 84,
96, 107, 109, 261, 285, 288, 304, 340,
375, 468, 492, 500, 551, 563, 565,
660, 662, 667, 676, 681, 684, 692,
693, 695, 714, 718, 723, 726
responsible consumption, 379, 381,
383, 384, 387, 676
Contemporary global issues, 469
Content-driven model of genre-based
education, 508
Contextual knowledge, 350, 703
Conventional Transactions, 61
Convention on the Rights of the Child, 51,
150
Conviviality, 684
Cool Food Pledge, 288
Co-operation, 4, 13, 14, 18, 20, 23, 24, 148,
178, 186, 188, 282, 324, 437, 483,
519, 566, 638, 640, 645, 650
Cooperative learning, 14, 479
COP26, 12, 16, 21, 44, 170, 450, 454
Corporate environmentalism, 42
Corporatism, 31
Corrective strategies, 418, 620
Council of Australian Law Deans (CALD),
115–117
Covenant University, 285

COVID-19, 235, 257, 336, 357, 399, 495,
581, 582, 584, 590, 591, 609, 614,
615, 684, 694
pandemic, 13, 16, 21, 152, 162,
235–238, 248, 255, 263, 493, 540,
566, 583, 604, 609, 610, 615, 648,
659, 679, 714
Cradle Coast Academic Community of
Practice (CCACoP), 569–571
Creative education, 585
creative learning processes and
outcomes, 394
creative pedagogies, 582
Critical appraisal of health information, 501
Critical literacy, 511, 513
Critical mathematics education, 539
Critical pedagogies, 142, 680
Critical Place-based Pedagogy, 568
Critical thinking, 45, 136, 142, 143, 176,
385, 392, 397, 448, 449, 452, 454,
468, 513, 543
Cross-country networks, 650
Cross-curricular priority
cross-curriculum priority(ies), 18, 461,
664
Cross-disciplinary peer network, 393
Cross-sectoral integration, 501
Crowded curriculum, 388, 419, 421
Crypto currencies, 109
Cultural artefacts, 218
Cultural boundaries, 218
Cultural discourse, 208, 215
Cultural diversity, 74, 133, 170, 172, 186,
460, 662, 715, 729
Cultural enterprise, 582
Cultural heritage, 11, 13–15, 17–19, 21, 23,
24, 266
Cultural identity, 14, 21, 212–214
Cultural imperialism, 74, 96
Cultural practices, 246, 606
Cultural values, 203, 209, 214
Culture, 14, 15, 21, 22, 24, 40, 67, 74, 85,
89, 91, 96, 133, 134, 171, 172, 177,
181, 207, 296, 299, 304, 306, 318,
321, 339, 405, 416, 417, 419, 460,
461, 469, 499, 510, 511, 515, 516,
560, 564, 565, 568, 579, 588, 596,
607, 638, 658, 678, 683, 701, 703,
715, 716, 723, 728
Culture of respect, 419
Culture, values, beliefs, 203, 560
Curious Climate Schools, 287, 447,
449–455

Curricula, 7, 13, 18, 20, 31, 115–117, 119,
        136, 137, 149, 155, 162, 171, 179,
        180, 262, 300, 305, 318, 320, 321,
        328, 335, 336, 339, 343, 344, 347,
        348, 352–354, 376, 388, 392, 446,
        454, 469, 479, 507, 510, 539, 548,
        640, 643–645, 648, 661, 664, 665,
        668, 734, 736
    curricular HPE Strategies, 479
Curriculum, 13, 18, 19, 22, 40, 116, 134,
        136, 143, 148, 153, 171–175,
        178–181, 186, 187, 189, 198, 204,
        205, 208, 218, 224, 225, 227, 229,
        231, 232, 262, 287, 315–317, 321,
        327, 328, 333, 341, 348, 349, 352,
        353, 355–357, 377, 388, 392, 394,
        405, 416, 420, 421, 431, 436, 447,
        448, 451, 454, 455, 459, 460, 462,
        466, 469, 479, 497, 509, 528, 534,
        535, 545, 550, 553, 554, 610, 645,
        660–662, 664–668, 692, 701–703,
        734
    curriculum development, 173, 180, 343,
        347, 349, 353, 641, 645
Cycle of oppression, 438

D
Danish Technological Institute for the DG
        Communications Networks,
        Content & Technology, 642
Data, 13, 21, 135, 141, 149–151, 153,
        156–158, 162, 171, 172, 176, 191,
        193, 208, 224, 226, 229, 234–236,
        263, 266–268, 272, 297, 301, 304,
        307, 309, 316, 397, 435, 460, 463,
        464, 468, 469, 474, 530–532, 534,
        539, 541–543, 545–551, 553, 580,
        581, 587, 592, 628, 660, 691
    Big Data, 643
    data mining, 29
Deakin University, 285
Decade of Education for Sustainable
        Development [DESD], 526
Decarbonisation, 268, 286, 289
Decision-making strategies, 479
Declaration of the Alma-Ata, 337
Decolonisation, 64, 86, 656, 657
    decolonising, 63, 64, 71, 85, 88, 96
    decolonising methodologies, 70, 89
Deep adaptation, 559
De-escalation, 419
Deficit construction, 39
Defining health, 337

De-globalisation, 648, 695
De-growth, 695
Deliberation, 566, 567, 674, 675, 680, 682,
        684
Deliberative democracy (DD), 675, 680
Democracy, 29, 36, 56, 172, 175, 176, 647,
        674, 681, 693
    democratic processes, 607
Department of Agriculture, Water, and
        Environment (DAWE), 16, 17
Depletion of fish, 336
Depoliticisation, 30
Derisking, 44
Designers, 180, 245, 254, 257
Design project, 379–381, 384
Design thinking, 246, 249, 251–253, 255,
        257
Development, 17–19, 21–24, 30–33, 36–38,
        42–44, 51, 54, 62, 64, 71, 74, 76, 86,
        89, 95, 96, 107–114, 133, 134,
        136–139, 142, 147, 148, 151, 161,
        163, 169, 170, 172, 174–176,
        178–180, 186–191, 203, 207, 223,
        224, 226–228, 234, 236, 238, 245,
        246, 267, 271, 273, 279, 291, 296,
        297, 299, 305, 315, 317, 320, 324,
        326, 328, 337, 346, 348–350, 353,
        354, 357, 375–382, 385, 388,
        391–395, 398, 399, 405, 420, 427,
        428, 433–435, 437, 438, 446–449,
        455, 460, 467, 475, 476, 478–481,
        484, 491–499, 501, 502, 507–509,
        513–515, 518–520, 525, 526, 528,
        530, 532, 533, 540, 560, 561, 564,
        565, 567, 570–572, 581–583, 588,
        589, 602–607, 609, 612, 614, 615,
        623, 628, 631, 632, 637, 638,
        640–645, 648, 650, 651, 655–660,
        667, 673–677, 681, 683, 684, 692,
        695, 696, 698–701, 703, 704,
        709–713, 715–720, 723–729, 734,
        735
    development agenda, 43, 73, 93–96,
        356, 656, 657, 713, 716, 717
Developmental vulnerability, 604
Diet, 288, 453
Digital and design technology, 545
Digital economy, 227
Digitalization, 139, 645
Digitally signed credentials, 641
Digital revolution, 649
Digital skills, 642–645

Digital technologies, 235, 237, 238, 609, 643
Dimensions of sustainability, 9, 246, 377
Disability(ies)
    disability awareness, 429, 437
    Disability Discrimination Act (DDA), 434, 435
    disability legislation, 428
    Disability Standards for Education (DSE), 434, 435
    Disabled People's Organisations, 433, 437
Disadvantaged students, 140, 421, 527
Discomfort, 70, 88, 91, 352, 404
Discourse, 6, 30, 32, 34, 69, 70, 75, 85, 133, 135, 139, 142, 143, 203, 206, 208, 209, 215, 218, 261, 316, 341, 463, 507, 515, 528, 540, 658, 668, 673, 680, 718
Discrimination, 39, 64, 69, 70, 75, 150, 204, 207, 208, 215, 224, 247, 249, 414, 429, 431, 434–436, 438, 477, 628, 640, 727
    discriminatory attitudes, 204
Discursive power, 208
Disease care paradigm, 342
Disempowerment, 607
Disengaged and disruptive behaviour, 413
Disengagement in schools, 414
Displacement, 64, 392, 660, 716
Dispossession, 64
Disruptive practitioners, 107
Distributive justice, 624
Distributive leadership, 613
Diverse language and cultural backgrounds, 412, 414, 421
Diversification, 138
Diversity, 6, 22, 117, 170, 174, 176, 180, 181, 225, 305, 307, 316, 393, 394, 396, 400, 419, 430, 431, 465, 515, 516, 550, 570, 581, 645, 694, 697, 723–725, 729, 734, 735
Divesting from Fossil Fuels, 285
Documenting Sustainability, 299
Dog-walking programs, 483
Dot democracy, 608
Doughnut economics, 351, 356
    doughnut economics model, 246, 343
Dreaming, 95
Drinking water, 74, 84, 174, 187, 195, 197, 644
D Stages, 253
Dyslexia, 430, 436

Dyspraxia, 436

E
Early childhood, 6, 15, 225, 526–528, 535, 602
Early school leaving, 414, 415
Earth Charter
    Earth Charter Australia, 18
    Earth Charter Commission, 710, 712, 720
    Earth Charter Index for Planetary Wellbeing, 719
Earth community, 3, 4, 674, 676, 710, 716, 719, 723, 724
Earth Council, 712
Earth Summits, 4, 5, 43, 711, 720
Easterlin Paradox, 563
Eastern philosophy, 177
Eco-anxiety, 270, 347, 401
Eco-art, 319, 320, 328
Eco Club, 171, 174
Eco-friendly industry, 382
Ecological
    ecological consciousness, 711
    ecological crisis, 560
    ecological diversity, 710
    ecological educational model, 680
    ecological footprint, 462, 465, 564, 565, 680, 682
    ecological integrity, 113, 714, 715
    ecologically oriented learning, 469
    ecological overshoot, 674
    Ecological Society of Australia, 17
    ecological system breakdown, 604
    ecological systems, 561, 564, 568, 572, 659, 676, 682, 683, 712, 715, 716, 718, 723, 725, 726
Ecology, 19
Economic
    economic dependency, 657
    economic development, 18, 19, 140, 716
    economic growth, 5, 32, 42, 43, 45, 64, 86, 109, 112, 113, 121, 142, 148, 280, 315, 317, 339, 340, 387, 500, 560, 562, 563, 567, 571, 639, 643, 658–661, 664, 665, 668, 673, 674, 676, 677, 692, 715, 717, 718
    economic independence, 626
    economic justice, 710, 715, 723, 725
    economic prosperity, 32, 203
    economic system, 317, 461, 563, 692
Economism, 560, 562–565, 567, 568

Ecopedagogy(ies), 680, 681

Ecors, 642

Eco-social justice, 8, 668

Eco-social responsibility, 674

Eco-social work, 681

Eco-sociological model, 338

Ecosystem, 4, 16, 21, 49–51, 75, 87, 132,
  255, 266, 338, 341, 357, 459, 526,
  530, 638–645, 651, 659, 661, 663,
  693, 694, 696, 698, 703–705, 710,
  712, 714, 725, 734
  ecosystem destruction, 659, 666

Ecosystemic, 49
  ecosystems, 4, 16, 21, 49–51, 75, 87,
    132, 255, 266, 338, 341, 357, 459,
    526, 530, 638–645, 651, 659, 661,
    663, 666, 693–696, 698, 703–705,
    710, 712, 714, 725, 734

Education, 4–9, 11–15, 18–24, 30–33, 35,
  44, 45, 50–54, 61, 62, 69, 105–108,
  111, 112, 114–121, 133, 134,
  136–138, 140–143, 147–153, 155,
  156, 161–163, 169–177, 179–181,
  185–190, 192–199, 203, 204, 207,
  223–229, 234–238, 249, 256,
  260–263, 270, 273, 282, 283, 287,
  305, 306, 308, 310, 317, 318, 324,
  328, 333, 335, 337–339, 342–344,
  346, 348–353, 355, 357, 376, 387,
  388, 392–394, 404, 411, 414–416,
  420, 421, 427–438, 446–449, 454,
  459–463, 469, 477–479, 481, 492,
  495–501, 507–511, 513–519,
  526–528, 534, 535, 539–541, 545,
  553, 560, 562, 566–570, 572, 579,
  580, 582, 588, 602, 608, 619, 620,
  622, 623, 626–629, 632, 633,
  637–640, 642–651, 656, 660–668,
  680, 692, 695, 699, 700, 705, 713,
  714, 720–722, 727, 728, 733–736

Educational attainment, 147, 204, 207, 223,
  496, 501, 603, 647

Educational disadvantage, 413, 603

Educational discourse, 203, 204, 208

Educational experiences, 415, 448, 514,
  628

Educational reform, 648

Education for Sustainability Community of
  Practice, 307, 354

Education for sustainability (EfS), 8, 19,
  21, 32, 45, 118, 174–176, 179, 181,
  287, 307, 319, 354, 411, 460–465,
  469, 509, 514, 516, 664, 735, 736

Challenges for EfS, 461
State of EfS in Australia, 462

Education for Sustainable Development
  (ESD), 13, 18, 32, 176, 186, 318,
  391, 515, 519, 520, 526, 541, 664,
  720, 721

*Education for Sustainable Development
  Goals*
  Learning Objectives, 540

Education for the 21st Century, 572

Education for wisdom, 692

Education Index, 628

Education system, 6, 7, 135, 152, 174, 196,
  225, 432, 434, 438, 511, 518, 567,
  612, 647, 661, 662, 664, 680, 734

Electrical and electronics, 377, 384

Electrical power engineering, 383, 384

Embedding sustainability, 117, 134, 299,
  304, 305, 376

Emissions offsets, 284

Emissions Reduction Strategic Plan, 309

Emotional health, 413

Emotional literacy, 392

Emotional outcomes, 587

Emotional responses, 392, 402, 454

Emotional wellbeing, 73, 448

Empiricism, 33

Employer of Last Resort, 681

Employment-focused skills, 508

Empowerment, 92, 179, 205, 467, 477, 508,
  511, 569, 607, 620, 633, 682
  empowerment of women and girls
    (SDG5), 620

Enabling mechanisms, 714

Enbesat, 328, 333

Endangered species, 16, 17, 19, 330, 725

Energy reduction and generation, 285

Energy supply safety, 383

Engineered farming, 381

Engineering
  engineering design, 375, 380, 383
  engineering design practice, 378, 379
  engineering education, 376
  Engineers Australia, 375–377
  Engineers without Borders, 379

English as a Foreign Language (EFL), 8,
  507, 514, 515

English proficiency, 189, 192

ENIC–NARIC, 641

Enlightenment, 32, 469

Enslavement, 70

Entry to practice engineering degree, 376

Environment

environmental awareness, 39, 177, 316, 318, 327, 328
environmental conceptualisations of sustainability, 464
environmental degradation, 108, 121, 175, 315, 620, 655, 718, 722
environmental education programmes, 11
Environmental Engineering, 378, 383
environmental impact statement, 383
environmental injustice, 722
environmental justice, 346, 351
environmental limits, 338, 673, 676
environmental problems, 32, 42, 141, 315, 395, 665, 693, 721
Environmental Protection Agency (EPA), 39, 285
environmental refugees, 392
environmental standards, 35, 726
environmental stewardship, 111, 262
Environment Protection and Biodiversity Protection Act (EPBC Act), 16, 17
Epistemic injustice, 68
Epistemic violence, 94
Epistemological, 94, 340, 354
epistemologies, 38, 65, 173, 469
Epochal history, 38
EPortfolio, 379, 384
Equality, 32, 72, 74, 84, 206, 249, 376, 427, 430, 498, 500, 510, 621, 625, 630, 639
equitable, 5, 14, 50, 64, 73, 76, 106, 109, 111, 113, 114, 138, 143, 147, 148, 150, 155, 156, 162, 185, 186, 203, 266, 411, 412, 421, 437, 476, 477, 497, 500, 527–529, 540, 550, 562, 620, 645, 647, 660, 662, 663, 668, 706, 712, 720, 726, 727, 735
gender equality, 3, 4, 132, 133, 148, 203, 204, 387, 460, 499, 501, 620, 632, 645, 714, 727
Equality and Human Rights Commission (EHRC), 432
Equal opportunities, 207, 479, 499, 508
Equity, 35, 113, 114, 137, 143, 174, 179, 204, 205, 218, 223, 224, 227, 228, 235–238, 302, 303, 337, 338, 396, 412, 420, 427, 435, 437, 493–495, 509, 511, 514, 593, 596, 639, 658, 660, 720, 727
equity of education, 514
Erasmus Program, 649

Establishment man, 6, 63, 65–68, 70, 73, 75, 76, 83, 85, 89–94, 96
Ethical and spiritual values, 709, 710, 713, 715
Ethical understanding, 528
Ethical work practice, 379
Ethnic discrimination, 69
EU Commission, 640
Eudemonic, 678
Europass, 642
Europe, 33, 69, 134, 142, 646, 649, 650
European decolonisation, 657
European industrial revolution, 661
European Union (EU) Commission, 638
Excellence discourse, 133, 135, 141–143
Expected behaviours, 416
Extinction, 90, 328, 336, 723

F
Failed states, 632
Fair play, 483
fairness, 109, 153, 224, 477
Families, 12, 86, 136, 137, 151, 153, 174, 205, 226, 247, 248, 303, 417, 428, 492, 497, 498, 500, 527, 535, 547, 582, 603, 607, 609, 610, 613, 615, 619, 622, 627, 629, 630, 700, 701, 705, 727
Farmbot, 381
Faux-wokeness, 63, 66–69, 71–74, 76, 83, 89, 91–94, 96
Feedback loops, 251, 588
Female literacy rate, 207, 628
Fiat Chrysler Automobiles, 637
Fiji, 14, 23
Finite planet, 32, 562, 563
First Nations Voices, 84
First Peoples, 73, 74, 87, 88, 97
First-order learning, 519
Fisheries, 22, 453
Five stages of design, 251
Flourishing, 3–6, 22, 31, 45, 49–51, 54, 106, 107, 111, 121, 392, 465, 560–562, 564, 568, 664–668, 683, 717, 725, 733–736
Fluid Mechanics, 378, 382
Focus group interviews, 171, 463
Food insecurity, 170, 609
Food on campus, 288
Food supply issues, 644
Forest Schools, 528, 534
Formal and informal leadership

formal education, 8, 50, 173, 225, 261, 447, 567–569, 571, 656, 720, 728
formal education system, 613, 680
Fossil Free UC, 286
Fossil Free UTAS, 308, 309
Fossil fuel industries, 12, 281, 286, 291
Fossil fuels, 12, 17, 42, 281, 285–287, 309, 339, 350, 384, 551, 659, 661, 665, 725
Foucauldian approach, 38
   Foucauldian perspective, 208
   Foucault, 36, 38, 208
Four pillars, 405, 572
Fourth Industrial Revolution, 643, 660
Framework for Action on Climate Change, 271
Framework Law of Mother Earth, 716
Framing problems, 249
Freedom, 31, 33–36, 39, 40, 53, 56–59, 62, 546, 547, 551, 561, 619, 622, 626, 683, 693, 695, 702, 725, 728, 729
Free-market ideology, 658
Frustrations, 403, 404, 460, 466, 694, 703, 704
Fundamental Movement Skills (FMS), 479
Funds of knowledge, 612
Future generations, 4, 7, 22, 32, 45, 114, 132, 170, 177, 265, 270, 467, 491, 498, 565, 668, 692, 716, 718–721, 723, 725

G
Game-based approaches, 479
Gender
   gender-based discrimination, 147, 204
   gender-based inequity, 204
   gender bias, 205, 477
   Gender Development Index, 628
   gendered inequality, 155
   gendered racial oppression, 85
   gender identities, 203–206, 208, 209, 218
   gender roles, 205, 206, 218
   gender stereotypes, 7, 204, 205
Genealogy, 5, 6, 31, 32, 44, 661
General learning theory, 544
Genocide, 64
Genre and social justice, 509
Genre-based teaching, 508–511, 513, 514, 519
Genre fluency, 510
Genres of power and dominance, 519

Genuine Wealth Index, 718
Geography and Environment, 393, 395
Geography of hegemonic exclusion, 74
Georgetown University Institute for Women, Peace and Security 2021/2022 Index, 619
Germany, 36, 494, 497
Ghana, 133, 135–139, 141, 142, 150, 494
Girls, 7, 132, 148, 152, 162, 188, 203, 204, 207–209, 218, 247, 386, 477, 479, 481–484, 508, 621, 622, 626–629, 633, 720, 727, 735
   girls' physical activity levels, 482
   girls' sports uniform, 482
Global average temperatures, 281
Global citizens, 22, 51, 320, 446, 541, 694
   global citizenship, 11, 14, 133, 455, 460, 722
   global citizenship education, 18
Global Climate Change Week, 290, 310
Global Climate Coalition (GCC), 42, 43
Global ecosystems, 336, 695
Global Financial Crisis (GFC), 40, 43
Global Geographies of Change, 393, 394, 395
Global Initiative on Education and HIV and AIDS (EDUCAIDS), 495
Globalisation
   globalised citizenship, 507
Global mindset, 509
Global North, 65, 69, 70, 73, 76, 86, 90, 94–96, 108, 281, 397, 399–401, 405, 430, 559, 562, 564, 656, 658, 659, 661, 663, 664, 666–668, 676, 681
Global (North) Health Systems, 341
Global South, 4, 44, 69, 76, 86, 87, 90, 94, 96, 108, 134, 397, 399, 401, 403, 559, 562, 569, 656, 658, 659, 666, 676, 681, 682, 735
Global Tobacco Industry, 351
Global warming, 16, 23, 169, 281, 459, 467, 543, 544, 551
Go Fossil Free, 308
Good Health and Wellbeing and Quality Education, 496
Good Life Goals, 561
Governance
   governance for health, 492
   governance framework, 111, 304
   governance regimes, 108, 113, 114, 121
   governance systems, 107, 108, 118, 674
Governmentality, 38
Government policy, 149, 262

Gradual Release of Responsibility, 508, 509, 514, 516, 517
Gratitude, 172, 176–178, 724
Great Barrier Reef, 16, 17, 19
Green Areas, 385
Green capitalism, 31
Green colonialism, 64
Green consciousness, 651
Green crime, 69
Green economy, 140, 639, 644
Green focus on ecology, 461
Green Gown Awards Australasia, 287, 308
Greenhouse emissions, 12, 17, 22, 24
Greenhouse gas (GHG), 43, 549
    greenhouse gas (GHG) emissions, 12, 42, 109, 265, 281, 283, 284, 287–289, 309, 341, 459, 549, 553, 560, 563
Green Impact, 290
Greening of Universities, 20
Green innovation, 644
Green Power Partnership, 285
Green Report Card, 20
Green revolution, 649
Green skills, 642, 651
Greenwashing, 41, 42, 280, 290, 291
Greta Thunberg, 460, 540, 554, 666
Gross Domestic Product (GDP), 39, 113, 139, 148, 186, 199, 252, 289, 339, 662, 691, 692, 714, 715, 718, 721
Gross National Happiness (Bhutan), Genuine Prosperity (Thailand), 718
Group work, 394, 509, 515–518
Growth, 5, 30, 35, 42, 43, 45, 64, 65, 86, 111–113, 121, 142, 148, 149, 152, 153, 280, 290, 307, 315, 317, 324, 339, 340, 387, 414, 427, 475, 500, 528, 560–565, 567, 571, 572, 639, 643, 644, 650, 658–661, 664, 665, 668, 673, 674, 676, 677, 681, 691, 692, 695, 714, 715, 717, 718
    growthism, 660, 668

H
Habitat loss, 17
Harvard University, 317
Healing, 85, 94, 95, 419, 595, 692, 695, 698, 703, 705, 706
Health
    Health and Physical Education, 474
    health and wellbeing, 11, 70, 74, 84, 148, 256, 301, 339, 341, 343, 387, 476, 477, 484, 495, 498, 501, 562, 564, 569, 601, 604, 610, 615, 681

healthcare, 337, 339–342, 346, 350, 355, 493, 494, 499
health crisis, 16, 679
health curricula, 335, 336, 344, 348, 353
health education, 8, 13, 342, 343, 350, 492, 495, 497, 499, 500, 623
health for all, 337, 338, 341, 477
health-harming messaging, 500
health imperatives, 582, 587
health inequities, 492, 493, 499
HealthLit4Kids, 497
health literacy, 8, 492, 494, 495, 497
health outcomes, 428, 495, 496, 498, 500, 501, 562, 661, 668
health professional education, 335, 337–339, 342, 346, 348, 349, 352, 353, 355, 357
health promotion strategy, 493
health risks, 492, 493, 499
healthy choices, 492
healthy food, physical activity, 603
healthy lifestyles, 494
healthy lives, 478, 493, 562
Hegemony, 63, 65, 69–71, 89, 96, 208, 218, 665, 667
Heteronormative, 89
Higher education, 7, 8, 13, 115, 132–138, 140–143, 260–262, 268, 279, 287, 289–291, 296–298, 301, 310, 319, 343, 352, 356, 384, 412, 435, 507, 526, 620, 627–631, 710
High Level Political Forum (HLPF), 187
Historicity, 32, 44
History, 5, 6, 15, 18, 33, 38, 39, 71, 73, 87, 88, 115, 162, 173, 223, 224, 322, 323, 346, 415, 445, 453, 462, 545, 560, 567, 583, 626, 656, 657, 667, 668, 678, 699, 712, 722, 723, 729, 734, 735
Hoa Nghiem Buddhist College (HNBC), 692, 700–706
Hobart, 92, 272, 287, 582, 586, 593
Home automation systems, 381
Home learning, 609
Human-animal relationships, 582, 583
Human capital, 142, 223, 226, 474
    human capital development, 476, 638, 648
    human capital theory, 223
Human-centred design, 379
Human-centric approaches, 582
Human cognition, 38

Human development, 95, 203, 484,
    560–562, 673, 712, 715, 719, 720,
    724, 727
Human evolution, 673, 678
Human flourishing, 5, 31, 50, 664
Human Gap, 559
Human health, 335, 337, 357, 476, 564,
    677, 726
Humanist and inclusive approach, 415, 416
Humanistic behaviour management, 419
Humanitarian engineering, 379, 380
Human migration, 7, 397
Human population, 543, 559, 616, 723
Human resource development, 602, 604
Human rights, 14, 31, 35, 36, 40, 51, 69,
    71, 72, 106, 133, 176, 179, 180, 428,
    431–433, 460, 607, 619, 628, 657,
    661, 678, 679, 710, 715, 723,
    725–727, 735
  human rights discourses, 69
Human Scale Development, 565
Human selfishness, 468
Human settlement, 41, 602, 604
Hydroelectricity, 266, 271, 468

I
Iceberg model, 249, 251, 351
Identity bias, 392
Ideological weaponising, 67
Ideology, 32, 38, 45, 68, 206, 261,
    338–340, 344, 355, 429, 656, 658,
    660–665
Imagination, 38, 50, 74, 483, 535, 565, 582,
    668
Impact ranking, 141, 260, 736
Impairment, 414, 427, 429, 430
Imperial project, 74
  imperialism, 34, 35
Incheon Declaration, 169, 460
Inclusion, 20, 22, 112, 141, 153, 180, 245,
    296, 303–305, 349, 376, 384, 417,
    427, 430, 436–438, 477–479, 499,
    508, 513, 531, 593, 613, 619, 626,
    640, 645, 651, 676
  inclusive, 5, 11, 14, 15, 24, 31, 45, 50,
    54, 61, 71, 72, 106, 138, 147–150,
    174, 185, 266, 300, 320, 328, 343,
    351, 357, 412, 415, 416, 421,
    427–431, 433, 434, 436–438, 481,
    483, 499, 519, 527, 540, 562, 566,
    586, 587, 595, 602, 620, 628, 638,
    640, 643–646, 658, 660, 667, 713,
    715, 718–720, 724, 728, 736

  inclusiveness, 187, 419, 507
Inclusive and equitable quality education,
    5, 14, 50, 147, 185, 266, 412, 437,
    496, 527, 562, 620, 645, 660, 720
Inclusive economic growth, 31, 500
Inclusive education, 14, 54, 415, 428–431,
    434, 436–438
Inclusive institutions, 106, 719
Inclusive mainstream education, 434
Increasing student engagement, 415
Index of Community Socio-Educational
    Advantage (ICSEA), 413
India, 40, 176, 187, 627, 630–632, 657
Indigenous
  Indigenous communities, 74, 84, 87, 94,
    176, 256, 716
  indigenous cultures, 6, 15, 19, 21, 23,
    174, 595
  Indigenous Peoples, 17, 24, 64, 67, 69,
    71–76, 84, 86, 87, 89, 90, 92, 94–96,
    114, 355, 659, 727
  Indigenous perspectives, 267
  indigenous populations, 657
  Indigenous research, 88
  Indigenous traditional knowledge, 73
  indigenous wisdom, 710
Individual differences, 415, 416, 420
Individualism, 33, 35, 113, 339, 469, 658,
    662, 683
Industrial growth, 718
Industrialisation, 64, 86, 656, 657, 659,
    662, 666, 668
Industrial Revolution, 34, 453, 563, 697
Industrial-scale microgrid, 285
Industry, 12, 16, 17, 20, 41–43, 69, 88, 108,
    109, 114, 138, 139, 247, 256, 263,
    266, 267, 271, 274, 281, 286, 315,
    317, 319, 323, 324, 326, 341, 351,
    379–388, 453, 500, 549, 588, 637,
    638, 640, 641, 643, 644, 649, 662,
    693, 703, 734
  Industry 4.0, 643
Industry specific climate data, 267
Inequality(ies), 3, 11, 29–31, 34, 35, 37, 40,
    69, 74, 84, 109, 110, 121, 141, 142,
    147, 148, 155, 156, 162, 181, 203,
    204, 218, 224, 226, 227, 235, 236,
    245, 336, 339, 357, 387, 404, 405,
    415, 421, 430, 432, 433, 493, 495,
    498–501, 508, 509, 519, 541, 562,
    566, 639, 640, 645, 651, 677, 681,
    714, 735
  Inequality in Australian Schools, 412

Informal learning, 8, 568, 569, 571, 650
Informal training, 191
Information and communication technology
    (ICT), 188, 224, 227–238, 527, 643
    ICT devices, 229, 230, 234–237
Infrastructure, 33, 39, 44, 69, 114, 148,
    170, 187, 188, 227, 234, 272, 285,
    291, 306, 307, 331, 376, 380–382,
    385–387, 429, 477, 491, 603, 644,
    714
Initial teacher education, 171, 179, 411,
    436, 667
    initial teacher training, 438
Injustice, 35, 68, 315, 335, 342, 353, 400,
    402, 403, 405, 621–625
Inner Development Goals, 561
In-service training, 438
Institute for Social Change, 582, 583
Insufficient training, 196
Integrating diverse knowledge domains,
    394
Inter-agency partnerships, 613
Inter-being, 696, 699, 702–706
Interconnectedness, 251, 338, 621,
    694–696, 699, 713, 721, 736
Interdisciplinary academic inquiry, 306
Interdisciplinary knowledge, 570
Intergenerational, 113, 114, 720
    intergenerational inequalities, 498
    intergenerational interaction, 606
    intergenerational poverty, 499, 603
    intergenerational relationships, 603
    intergenerational responsibility, 715
Intergenerational skill, 602
Intergovernmental Oceanographic
    Commission (IOC), 12
Intergovernmental Panel on Climate
    Change (IPCC), 11, 16, 42, 84, 110,
    260, 276, 281, 287, 445, 451, 553,
    601, 616
Intergovernmental Science-Policy Platform
    on Biodiversity and Ecosystem
    Services (IPBES), 110
International Covenant on Civil and
    Political Rights, 432
International Covenant on Economic,
    Social and Cultural Rights, 432
International Energy Agency (IEA), 11, 281
International English Language Testing
    System (IELTS), 512, 513
International human rights, 428, 432
Internationalisation, 507, 641

International Labour Organization (ILO),
    226, 383, 385, 678, 679
International law scholarship, 113
International Monetary Fund (IMF), 35, 39,
    658, 659
International recognition frameworks, 642
International students, 414
International Union for Health Promotion
    and Education, 495
International Universities Climate Alliance,
    289
Internet of Things (IoT), 643
Interpersonal communication, 191
Interrelationships, 112, 140, 175, 235, 706
Intersex, 72
Intragenerational, 113, 114
InVIVO Planetary Health, 337
Iran, 7, 316–318, 321, 323, 327, 328
Islamic fundamentalism, 627
Islamic Mahram, 619
Isolation, 476, 501, 579, 581–583
Italy, 494, 637
IUCN Red List, 72

J
Jaguar Land Rover, 637
Japan, 252, 508, 512, 515, 517
Job Guarantee, 681
Joint United Nations Programme on HIV/
    AIDS, 495
Justice, 44, 45, 68, 75, 84, 88, 106, 109,
    112, 117, 137, 141, 175–177, 180,
    181, 224, 256, 262, 280, 291, 337,
    341, 343, 346, 351, 376, 387, 392,
    400, 404, 405, 433, 461, 465,
    507–511, 517, 519, 564, 619–621,
    623–627, 629–633, 646, 661, 668,
    680, 710, 712, 715, 722, 723, 725,
    728, 729
    justice-forward frameworks, 405

K
Keynesianism, 36
Khosravi leather factory, 323
Kinship, 70, 85, 89, 724
Kiribati, 23
Kitchen garden program, 603
Knowledge economy, 141, 142, 233
Knowledge sharing, 13, 518, 570

L
Lack of agency, 59, 60, 173, 467
Lack of empowerment, 467
Lahore College for Women University, 186
Laissez faire, 34–37
Land-based learning, 704
Land rights, 68, 89
Language
    language acquisition, 603, 605, 609, 615
    language barrier, 7, 191
    language development, 189, 191, 192,
        530, 601, 603, 604, 606, 609, 610,
        612, 631, 632
    language learning, 605–607, 612, 630
    language-learning environment, 606,
        609
Late modernity, 673, 679
Late-stage capitalism, 657
Launceston, 309, 385, 601–603
    Launceston City Council, 602
Law on Elimination of Violence against
    Women (EVAW), 628
Laws, 6, 16, 21, 31, 33, 37, 51, 52, 54–57,
    61, 96, 105–122, 282, 287, 428, 429,
    431, 435, 436, 499, 508, 621, 625,
    705, 711
Law students, 105, 114, 117, 118
Lawyers, 105, 106, 109, 115–117, 121, 450
Leadership, 22, 141, 171, 181, 188, 189,
    191, 197, 251, 260, 262, 263, 268,
    270, 273, 280, 282, 284, 287, 288,
    290, 291, 298, 301–304, 306,
    308–310, 316–319, 321, 326, 331,
    341, 346, 352–354, 356, 357, 394,
    438, 502, 561, 570, 571, 584, 605,
    608, 610–612, 645, 712, 729, 735
    leadership and governance, 297, 299
    Leadership in Energy and
        Environmental Design, 327
League of Nations, 39
Learner-centred environment, 394
Learners with disabilities, 428
Learning
    learning communities, 270, 560, 571
    learning disabilities, 412–414, 420, 421,
        428, 430, 436
    Learning in Future Environments
        (LiFE), 296
    Learning to Be, 567, 692, 700, 702
    Learning to Be Wise, 692, 702
    Learning to Do *Ethically*, 692, 702
    Learning to Learn *Holistically*, 692, 702
    Learning to Live *Together*, 692, 702

Least developed countries, 148, 508, 656
Legal education, 105–108, 111, 114–121
    legal educators, 106, 107, 118, 121, 122
    leverage points, 249, 346
Leviathan, 33, 34, 39
Liability models, 622, 623
    liability models of responsibility, 622
Liberal democratic, 31, 40
Liberalism, 6, 29, 31–36, 38, 57
Life course approach, 493
Lifedeep learning, 560, 568, 569
Life expectancy, 74, 84, 315, 411, 493, 661
Lifelong learning, 20, 270, 494, 528, 560,
    567–569, 621, 628, 629, 639, 646,
    648, 649, 651
    lifelong learning opportunities, 5, 50,
        147, 185, 259, 266, 412, 437, 527,
        562, 620, 639, 645, 660
    lifelong physical activity engagement,
        483, 484
Life on Earth, 3, 5, 20, 31, 559, 620, 621,
    666, 696, 697, 700, 702, 703, 705,
    710, 720, 722, 736
Lifespan, 475, 476, 483, 567, 611
Lifestyle choices, 339
Lifewide, 560, 568, 569
    lifewide learning, 568
Lifeworld, 96, 316
Limited cognisance, 465
Literacy, 8, 150, 155, 187, 188, 197,
    260–263, 267–269, 273, 274, 327,
    392, 404, 447, 449, 452, 454, 461,
    494, 496, 497, 507, 508, 513, 516,
    543, 548, 550, 553, 566, 579, 609,
    612, 614, 623, 627, 628, 661, 667
    Literacy and Numeracy Test for Initial
        Teacher Education Students
        (LANTITE), 662
    literacy levels, 207, 494
Litter-free surroundings, 464
Little Libraries, 610, 612, 614
Living lab, 306
Local communities, 24, 170, 176, 181, 255,
    273, 317, 379, 481, 493, 572, 603,
    612, 638, 639, 642–645, 651, 724,
    728
Local government, 149, 173, 266, 272, 309,
    602
Local skills ecosystems, 638–645, 651
Lockdown, 153, 582, 604, 609, 610, 615,
    616
    lockdown restrictions, 255
Locomotion skills, 479

Longevity, 336
Loose parts play, 483
Low-appeal and high-appeal activities, 420
Low-carbon design, 285
Low hanging fruit, 301
Low-income countries, 23, 148, 498
Lunch programs, 227
Lutruwita, 6, 63, 64, 67, 68, 70, 83, 85–88, 90–94

M
Maladaptiveness, 563
Manufacturing Chemists Association, 41
Maori, 21
Marginalised communities, 110, 392, 399
    marginalised groups, 137, 174, 224, 434, 624
    marginalized populations, 68
Marine debris, 468
Marine Science, 453
Marton's general learning theory, 550
Marxist approach, 38
Mass education, 147, 656, 660–662
Materialism, 678
Maternal mortality, 336
Mathematics
    mathematical skills, 539, 542
    Mathematics Curriculum, 550
    mathematics education, 539
Matriarchy, 70, 71
Matthew Effect, 527, 534
Meaning, 38, 67, 71, 135, 176, 271, 455, 509, 510, 515, 526, 532, 548, 561–563, 566, 567, 587, 588, 592, 639, 658, 674, 675, 677–680, 682, 684, 705, 712, 714, 715, 735
Meaningful work, 678
Measuring Societal Impact: Climate Change in Tasmania, 262, 267
Media literacy, 497
Mediator of health, 492
Medicalised model of disability, 427
Medical technologies, 335
Megatrends, 646, 648–651
Mental health, 270, 417, 427, 446, 449, 452, 473, 477, 493, 562–564, 566, 581, 584, 587, 722
Mentoring, 196, 198, 307, 381, 579, 584, 589
Mercantilist, 34
Meritocracy, 40
Methodological training, 643

Methodologies, 32, 70, 89, 150, 172, 188, 191, 224, 251, 378, 529, 587, 629, 697, 698
Methods, 8, 37, 71, 72, 171, 188, 189, 191–193, 195–197, 228, 246, 249, 254, 284, 316, 321, 380, 381, 385, 418, 437, 448, 463, 479, 501, 509, 529, 540, 542, 546, 547, 551, 581, 587, 643, 644, 720, 725, 728
Mexico, 495, 551
Microbiology, 349
Micro-credentials, 274, 641, 642, 648, 651
Microplastics in the Ocean, 385
Millennium Development Goals (MDGs), 4, 71, 135, 246, 620, 655, 713
Mind-body-spirit connections, 355
Ministry of Science, Research and Technology (MSRT), 317, 321, 331
Minority groups, 176, 499
Misconceptions, 261, 700
Mismatched discourse, 341
Mission integrator, 296, 302, 303
Mitigate environmental harm, 265
Mobile kayaking device, 380
Mock international summit, 393
Mode of reason, 115
Modern Monetary Theory, 684
Moldova, 495
Moral agency, 58, 59
Moral imperative, 51, 61
Moral obligation, 6, 54, 55, 283, 710
Moral principle, 55, 56, 60
Moral status, 51, 53, 58–61
Multiple perspectives, 463
Murdoch University, 393

N
Narrative approach, 605
Narrative-based community engagement, 586
National Aeronautics and Space Administration (NASA), 551
    NASA Global Land and Ocean Temperature Anomalies January-December, 551
National Assessment Program-Literacy and Numeracy (NAPLAN), 18, 614, 662
National Disability Insurance Agency, 434
    National Disability Insurance Scheme, 433
National Environment Development Association (NEDA), 42

Nationalism, 35, 668, 714
Nationally Consistent Collection of Data
    (NCCD), 435
National Qualification Framework, 642
National Research Council, 548, 637
Nation-state, 34, 39, 84, 281, 296, 401, 620,
    621, 624, 625
Native Title, 75, 87, 88
Natural law theory, 55
Natural rights, 56, 633
Nature, 21, 24, 33, 34, 37, 44, 61, 67, 69,
    74, 75, 87, 106, 109–111, 113, 114,
    120, 177, 191, 229, 246, 249, 251,
    253, 255, 257, 264, 320, 322, 336,
    343, 346, 351, 354, 376, 381, 382,
    385, 386, 394, 431, 434–436, 448,
    449, 455, 461, 465, 466, 469, 474,
    498, 516, 528, 532, 535, 541, 545,
    547, 566, 567, 570, 586, 603, 650,
    660, 666–668, 675, 676, 683,
    692–700, 702–705, 709, 710, 716,
    717, 722–725, 733
Nature-based design, 698
Negative behaviour, 416
Neo-colonialism, 70, 667
Neoliberal
    neoliberal economies, 316, 317
    neoliberal forces, 117, 119
    neoliberal ideology, 338–340, 656, 660,
    663
    Neoliberal Thought Collective (NTC),
    38
Neoliberalism, 6, 8, 29–33, 35–41, 43, 45,
    115, 339, 656–659, 661, 662, 665,
    666, 674, 680
Nepal, 6, 169–180
Net zero, 44, 271, 284, 288, 289, 291
Neurodevelopmental difficulties, 430
Neurodiversity, 430
Neurologically atypical, 593
Neuroscience, 567
Neurotransmitters, 382
New Hope/Omid Now (امید نو), 620, 623,
    626–633
New Zealand, 3, 14, 15, 20–24, 132, 188,
    584
Next Generation Science Standards, 548
NGO advocacy, 433
Nigeria, 285
Niue, 23
No excuse approach, 418
Non-communicable diseases (NCDs), 473,
    475, 477, 495, 498, 500

Non-curricular HPE Strategies, 480
Non-formal learning, 647
Non-public universities, 317
Normal justice, 624, 625
Norms, 18, 21, 69, 71, 107, 111, 120, 142,
    177, 181, 205, 207, 209, 218, 378,
    400, 401, 417, 435, 508, 540, 566,
    622, 667, 683, 711
Northern Children's Network, 602
Northern Early Years Group (NEYG),
    602–604, 608, 614
Norway, 15
Numeracy, 136, 150, 155, 188, 397, 461,
    494, 496, 501, 579, 661, 667

O
Object control, 479
Oceania, 21
Offsetting, 284, 288, 289
Open-ended, project inquiries, 466
Optional Protocol, 431
Oral language, 525
Ordoliberals, 37, 38
Organisation for Economic Co-operation
    and Development (OECD), 148,
    493, 494, 497, 644, 662, 663, 667
    OECD countries, 17
Organisation for the Promotion of Afghan
    Women's Capabilities (OPAWC),
    623, 626, 627
Organizational legitimacy, 142
Ottawa Charter for Health Promotion, 337
Our common future, 4, 11, 23, 24, 31, 43,
    711
Outdoor environments, 530
Overcrowded curriculum, 19, 461, 469
Overseas Development Aid (ODA), 23

P
Pacific, 3, 14, 16, 20–24, 74, 134
    Pacific Island Forum, 20
    Pacific Islands, 23
Pakistan, 7, 176, 186, 187, 189, 190, 194,
    196–199, 204–209, 218, 628
Palawa, 65, 69–71, 85–87, 90–93
Papua New Guinea, 23
Paradigm, 37, 44, 71, 75, 118, 121, 315,
    341, 350, 352, 355, 405, 431, 469,
    560, 564, 568, 643, 646, 662, 697,
    698, 734, 735
Paris Agreement, 11, 12, 43, 106, 111, 279,
    284, 288, 447

Participation, 7, 8, 39, 69, 72, 75, 84, 94,
    113, 138, 143, 147, 175, 205, 218,
    224, 227, 236, 251, 304, 305, 319,
    320, 331, 414, 420, 421, 428, 429,
    437, 438, 447, 455, 473–475, 477,
    478, 480–484, 501, 511, 581, 583,
    584, 586, 587, 590, 606–608, 625,
    630, 643, 657, 680, 682–684, 695,
    727, 728
Participation Income (PI), 674, 675,
    681–685
Participatory parity, 625, 629
Partnership for the Goals, 387, 603, 604,
    615
Partnership in Statistics for Development in
    the 21st Century, 541
Partnerships, 30, 41, 43, 72, 247, 255, 289,
    291, 297, 300, 308, 346, 353, 357,
    379, 428, 433, 462, 481, 501, 584,
    586, 590, 592, 603, 604, 610,
    613–615, 641, 646, 650, 651, 655,
    667, 696, 714, 724, 729, 736
    Partnerships and Engagement, 300
    Partnerships for Excellence, 640
Passive styles of learning, 519
Paternalistic, 84
Pathophysiology, 340, 349, 351
Patriarchal, 65, 91, 92, 95, 204–207, 627
Peace, 4, 30, 33, 51, 75, 106, 112, 133, 186,
    337, 433, 460, 622, 646, 655, 667,
    668, 680, 696, 701, 702, 705, 706,
    709, 711, 715, 722, 723, 728, 729
Pedagogical approaches
    pedagogical intervention, 171
    pedagogical model, 508, 516, 517, 579,
    586, 590
    pedagogical skills, 188, 189
    pedagogical training, 455
Pedagogical Content Knowledge (PCK),
    189, 191–193, 197, 228
Pedagogies, 31, 116, 179, 189, 193, 197,
    270, 305, 336, 341, 349, 350, 352,
    355, 392, 393, 414, 437, 438, 461,
    469, 508, 514, 519, 568, 580, 582,
    592, 645, 734, 736
Peer collaboration, 394
Peer-to-peer exchanges, 587
Pennsylvania State University, 283
People power, 24
People, prosperity, planet, partnership, and
    peace, 655, 667
Performance making, 392, 400, 401, 405
Performative, 66, 68, 71, 401

Permacrises, 655
Personal action plan for sustainability, 352
Personal agency, 515
Personal storytelling, 586
Persons with disability, 427
Persuasive genres, 509, 512
Persuasive texts, 510, 511, 515
Pet companionship, 592
    pets, 8, 35, 581–583, 585, 586, 590, 595
Pharmaceuticals, 341
Photo elicitation interviews, 464
Physical activity, 473–484, 495, 603
Physical-activity-related engagement, 483
Physical and health development, 603
Physical design of the classroom, 417
Physical education, 477–479, 481, 483
Physical facilities, 187, 188
Physical fitness, 413
Physical health, 601, 604, 610, 615
Physiocratic, 34
Pirate kayaker, 380
Place-based education, 463, 515
Planetary crisis, 694
Planetary health, 7, 335–338, 340–344,
    346, 348, 349, 352–354, 356, 357,
    564
Planetary health curricula, 336, 344, 348,
    353
Planetary Health Education Framework
    (PHEF), 342, 343
Planetary levels, 49
Planetary resources, 35
Plastic bottle recycling device, 381
Play, 7, 13, 15, 19, 20, 23, 24, 45, 52, 86,
    113, 118, 132, 133, 170, 173, 175,
    177, 180, 189, 193, 206, 261, 262,
    266, 302, 316, 375, 392, 396–399,
    401, 402, 421, 430, 475, 478,
    482–484, 499, 508, 528, 530–534,
    583, 588, 603, 606, 609, 665–667,
    696, 702, 703, 706, 729, 734
    play-based learning, 528, 533
Plutocracy, 40
Policy enactment, 438
Policymakers, 132, 147, 172, 173, 176,
    226, 237, 238, 260, 261, 315, 438,
    460, 494, 680, 698, 710, 722
Political identity, 68
Political ideology, 429, 662
Political representation, 625, 626
Pollution, 3, 12, 17, 20, 42, 108, 170, 174,
    175, 315, 319, 328, 330, 331, 336,

341, 351, 383, 465, 467, 551, 565, 693, 704, 721, 726
Polycrises, 559, 655, 663, 665, 733
Poochibald™ Art Prize 2020, 585
Population health, 492, 493, 499
Portraiture, 581, 590
Positive behaviour, 416
Positive interactions in the classroom, 416
Positive psychology framework, 591
Post-colonial societies, 662
Post-pandemic recovery, 592
Post-secondary education, 227, 263
Post structuralist, 205, 208
Post-truth, 108, 553
Poverty, 4, 11, 30, 31, 35, 64, 65, 69, 70, 89, 113, 119, 121, 132, 136, 137, 140, 143, 148, 152, 153, 224–226, 235–237, 245, 247, 249, 315, 336, 353, 379, 387, 428, 433, 500, 501, 508, 525, 541, 562, 565, 569, 621, 624, 627, 633, 639, 646, 655, 664, 666, 668, 678, 679, 682, 683, 714, 715, 717, 718, 723, 727
    poverty reduction, 620, 718
Power differential, 419, 420
Powerlessness, 173, 401, 452, 467
Power relations, 96, 208
Power Systems, 378, 383, 388
Practical wisdom, 50, 51
Practice of Statistics, 8, 540–548, 550, 553, 554
Precautionary principle, 19, 113, 719
Prefigurative politics, 564, 565, 569
Preservice educators, 497
    pre-service teacher education, 7, 428
    pre-service teachers, 7, 229, 411, 412, 415, 507, 662, 667
Primary intervention, 497
Printed turbine, 381
Privilege, 38, 65, 69, 76, 96, 137, 143, 340, 675, 706
Problem-based approach, 394
Problem framing space, 253
Problem-posing, 142, 350, 545
Problem solving, 251, 255, 479
Problem-solving tools, 247
Procurement policy, 301
Productive classroom, 421
Productive group work, 515
Productivity, 661, 663, 677, 693
Professional competencies, 194

Professional development, 22, 24, 148, 163, 188–190, 227, 234, 388, 395, 438, 447, 455, 481, 497, 570, 667
Professional learning, 171, 180, 646, 667
Program for International Student Assessment (PISA), 662
Project-based learning, 419
Promote student participation, 420
Prosociality, 566, 567, 674, 675, 677, 680, 683, 684
Protestantism, 34
Psychosocial challenges, 153
Public engagement, 320, 584
Public health, 36, 473
Public survey, 263, 266
Public universities, 284, 317
Purpose, 15, 55, 92, 116, 117, 119, 135, 171, 206, 226, 283, 286, 305, 317, 337, 339, 347, 352, 355, 377, 392, 393, 427, 430, 447, 454, 497, 510–514, 544, 545, 561, 566, 567, 570, 602, 608, 651, 662, 663, 665, 674, 675, 677–680, 684, 692, 698, 699, 701, 703, 704, 715, 729, 733, 734

Q
Qatar, 475
Qawwam, 206
Qualified teachers, 148, 150, 156, 157, 161, 162, 186, 188, 189, 198, 508
Qualitative interviews, 464
Qualitative survey, 463
Quality education, 5, 6, 11, 14, 15, 22, 50, 51, 112, 147, 153, 155, 156, 161, 163, 171, 175, 185–190, 192, 193, 195–199, 223, 224, 235–238, 266, 333, 387, 411, 412, 421, 427, 430, 432, 437, 469, 479, 498, 501, 519, 527, 528, 535, 562, 588, 620, 639, 645, 660, 695, 720
Quality of life, 281, 562, 565, 660, 710, 726
Queer Indigenous Standpoint Theory, 70, 71, 89, 90
    queer theories, 89
Quran, 206

R
Race to Zero, 289, 309
Racial discrimination, 39, 64, 69
    racism, 35, 40, 68, 69, 75, 84, 85, 88, 91, 96, 414

racist, 65, 69, 90

Reading, 38, 135, 148, 155, 179, 192, 246, 251, 404, 501, 507, 511, 517, 525, 527, 533, 612, 735

Reality-rhetoric gap in relation to EfS, 463

Real-life learning, 420

Real-World Strategies and Solutions, 245, 246, 255, 257

Recipe boxes, 609, 610, 612, 614

Reconciliation, 68, 90, 92, 114, 691

Recycling, 19, 42, 265, 290, 302, 304, 321, 323, 325, 380, 381, 383, 465, 534, 535

Reduce inequality, 84, 501, 508, 645

Reducing traffic volumes, 477

Reflexive justice, 620, 626, 629

Reflexivity, 392

Reforestation, 683

Refugee background, 414

Refugee status designation, 393

Regenerative agriculture, 683

Regenerative education, 118

Re-globalisation, 648

Relational failure, 674, 677

Relationality, 95, 338

Relationships, 52, 53, 61, 62, 87, 93–95, 118–120, 136, 138, 139, 171, 173, 177, 249, 253, 266, 267, 306, 324, 339, 346, 355, 396, 398, 399, 401, 402, 414, 416, 419, 421, 430, 496, 501, 510, 518, 540, 541, 546, 547, 551, 561, 563, 568, 569, 581–583, 587, 590–593, 595, 596, 603, 606, 613–615, 624, 640, 641, 658, 674, 677, 680, 697, 703–706, 729

Religious belief, 212, 215

Religious identity, 209, 212, 213, 218

Religious (Islamic) teachings, 205

Renaissance, 32, 33

Renewable energy, 12, 64, 140, 281, 282, 284, 287, 289, 308, 309, 323, 382–384, 388, 491, 551, 644, 665, 726

Renewable and Sustainable Energy, 378, 384

renewable energy technologies, 17, 323

Representation of animals, 583

Researchism policy, 318

Resilience, 38, 64, 107, 139, 170, 236, 256, 272, 320, 347, 348, 582, 596, 705, 722, 723

Resilient Australia Award, 309

resilient communities, 22, 601

Resource depletion, 663, 693

Resource-related barriers, 193

Resource stewardship, 346

Responsibility, 12, 14, 15, 18, 31, 36, 41, 45, 57, 59, 62, 85, 94, 97, 109, 113, 116, 137, 175, 177, 181, 199, 206, 207, 216–218, 245, 255, 265, 269, 270, 279, 281, 289, 302, 315, 317, 320, 339, 341, 342, 356, 357, 397, 399, 401, 411, 452, 468, 479, 499, 517, 528, 561, 620–623, 625, 628, 630, 631, 633, 651, 657, 666, 676, 692, 694, 696, 702, 705, 706, 710, 719, 722–725, 728, 729

responsibility as cause, 621

responsibility as obligation, 621

Retention, 147, 152, 162, 303, 413, 417

Retrofitting, 285, 291

Riawunna, 306

Rights

Rights, Education, and Protection (REAP) project, 434

rights-holders, 51, 53, 55, 57, 61

rights of indigenous peoples, 18, 86, 727

rights of nature, 710

rights to education, 53, 626, 633

Right wing populist (RWP) movements, 40

Rinotex, 324, 325

Rio Declaration on Environment and Development

Rio+20, 393, 713, 715, 716

Rio summit, 43

Rio United Nations Conference on Environment and Development 1992 (UNCED), 711

Risk and resilience frameworks, 614

RMIT University, 245, 246

Robotics, 643

Role model, 138, 280, 282, 289, 346, 415, 454

Role of schools, 478

Rule-making, 109, 119

S

Samoa, 14, 23

Scaffolding, 517, 518

Scandinavian Airlines System, 637

School

community decision-making, 613

school-community partnership, 610, 613, 615

school completion rates, 413

school culture, 22, 171, 172, 181
school environment, 187, 188, 416, 431, 535
school fees, 151, 227
schooling, 7, 54, 148, 151, 224, 226, 227, 234, 411, 412, 414–416, 419–421, 435, 455, 459, 529, 614, 628, 661, 662, 701, 735
school leadership, 171, 188, 189, 191, 194, 197
school prizes, 419
School Strike 4 Climate Action (SS4C), 540
school uniforms, 481
Science and technology, 656, 657, 659–666, 668
Science and technology education, 663, 666, 668
Science education, 417, 665, 666
Science, Technology, Engineering and Mathematics (STEM), 8, 138, 229, 526, 528, 529, 534, 535, 656, 663, 664, 666–668
Scientific skills, 526
Scientism, 469
SDG 1, 113, 136, 137, 140, 148, 247, 379, 428, 493, 501, 639, 660, 678, 681–683, 717
SDG2, 250, 493, 676
SDG3, 8, 70, 84, 148, 351, 427, 428, 474, 475, 478–481, 483, 484, 493–495, 562, 567, 663
SDG4
  Goal 4.3, 643
  SDG4 Target 4.5, 593
  SDG4 Target 4.7, 133, 595
  Target 4.7, 32, 170, 273, 540
SDG5, 8, 114, 132, 148, 203, 205, 208, 218, 247, 248, 428, 474, 481–484, 499, 620, 640, 660, 735
SDG6, 74, 84, 663
SDG7, 353, 663
SDG8, 148, 428, 493, 639, 640, 643, 658, 660, 674, 676, 678, 680, 685, 718
  Goal 8.3, 643
SDG9, 148
SDG10, 8, 74, 84, 95, 148, 224, 236, 428, 430, 432, 433, 477, 493, 507, 508, 541, 639
SDG11, 171, 247, 248, 252, 254, 272, 601, 602, 604, 606, 610, 615
SDG12, 676, 718

SDG13, 7, 8, 43, 75, 84, 106, 112, 171, 247, 248, 259, 260, 262, 266, 274, 279, 283, 284, 305, 308, 310, 349, 392, 405, 541, 546, 548, 549, 553, 639, 663
SDG14, 111, 112, 529, 535, 663
SDG15, 72, 75, 87, 111, 112, 171, 529, 535, 639, 663
SDG16, 75, 106, 148, 224, 236, 430, 433, 680, 719
SDG17, 346, 433, 602–604, 610, 615, 646, 651, 696, 736
SDGs 1, 2, 3, 4, 5, 683
SDGs 2, 3, 4, & 10, 734
SDGs 4, 8, and 9, 646
SDGs 6, 14, & 15, 733
Sea level rise, 109, 110, 121, 401
Secondary education, 6, 18, 147–152, 155, 156, 162, 172, 173, 176, 226, 463, 477, 517, 642, 735
  secondary schools, 149, 152, 153, 156, 171, 174, 225, 227, 228, 462, 463, 469, 510
  secondary students, 234, 460
Second-order learning, 519
Security, 30, 35, 40, 132, 140, 149, 619, 660, 663, 668, 679, 681, 682, 710, 711, 714, 723, 727, 729
Self-determination Theory (SDT), 566
Self-expression, 587, 590, 593, 603
Semi-structured interviews, 190, 263, 581, 586
Sense of belonging, 95, 415–417, 420, 421, 528, 699
Sense of competence, 415
Sensory overload, 417
Shadow Report, 433
Shanghai Declaration on Health Promotion, 492, 494
Shared visions, 249, 356, 605, 645, 715, 724
Shortage of qualified teachers, 188
Silent Spring, 41
Singapore, 510
Skillman Global, 637
  Skillman International Forum, 638
  Skillman Network, 637, 638
Skills
  Skills 4 Kids Cafe, 602
  skills ecosystem, 638–645, 651
  Skills for Life, 645
  Skills for Work, 645
  skills gap, 647, 649

Social
social actions for health, 495
social capital, 153, 680
social cohesion, 484, 582, 586, 588
social connection, 586, 602, 603, 620,
633
social connection model (SCM), 622,
623, 625
social development, 31, 223, 226, 337,
494, 561, 567
social disadvantage, 224, 236
social equality, 32, 510
social equity, 137, 143, 179, 509, 658
social growth, 639
social hope, 620
social impacts, 4, 351
social inclusion, 640, 645
social interaction, 420, 588, 603, 605,
606, 625, 675
social isolation, 476, 583
social justice, 45, 68, 84, 137, 141,
175–177, 180, 224, 262, 280, 337,
461, 465, 507–511, 517, 519, 625,
646, 661
social learning, 107, 118, 515, 564, 566,
567, 582, 587, 588, 603, 680, 722
social meaning, 587
social model of disability, 427, 429,
430, 436
social networks, 476, 492, 612
social norms, 142, 207, 218
social pathology, 563
social protection floor, 679, 681, 717
social relationships, 119, 568, 674, 677
social science, 135, 175, 268, 282, 287,
318, 347, 394, 453, 545
social situation of development, 605
social space, 607, 610, 612–614
social systems, 561, 682, 722, 723
societal impact, 263
societal testbed for sustainability, 283
Socio-cultural barriers, 152
Sociocultural theory, 517, 605
sociocultural theories of learning, 614
Socio-ecological approach to health, 337
Socio-ecological systems, 106, 561
Socio-economically disadvantaged
individuals, 498
Socio-economic implications, 583
Socio-economic status (SES), 137, 143,
152, 256, 303, 413, 420, 421,
525–529, 535, 606

Socio-economic systems, 110, 560, 561,
563
Socio-emotional, 152
Socio-political, 53, 73, 108, 114, 396, 666,
667
Socio-political change, 108
Socio-scientific issues, 666, 667
Solidarity, 14, 270, 282, 376, 400, 454,
623, 626, 628, 640, 667, 695, 699,
703, 724, 728
Solomon Islands, 14, 23, 256, 397, 399, 402
Solution space, 253
South Africa, 132, 188
South America, 3
South Asian Association for Regional
Cooperation, 630
Sovereignty, 63, 66–68, 73, 75, 84, 87–97
Spain, 494
Spiritual
spiritual consciousness, 715, 716, 719
spiritual dimensions, 720
spiritual values, 709, 710, 713, 715
Sporting Schools, 481
Staff performance frameworks, 305
Standard of living, 337, 565, 661
State Emergency Service, 266, 267
State of California, 282
State responsibility, 41, 621
Statistical literacy, 541, 543, 548, 550, 553
Statistics, 149, 156, 207, 414, 415,
539–541, 543, 545, 547, 548, 551,
553, 580, 592, 664
Statistics education, 539, 540, 545
Stockholm Declaration, 41, 43
Story-driven approaches, 587
Story-telling, 603
Strategic Framework for Sustainability,
296, 298, 299
Strong institutions, 75, 106, 181, 387, 430,
433, 680
Structural barriers to language
development, 606
Structuration Theory, 564
Structured learning environment, 588
Student
capacity, 227, 608
student capacity building framework,
608
student-centred learning, 142, 508, 518,
519
student learning outcome, 191, 192, 195
student retention, 152, 303

students from diverse language and
  cultural backgrounds, 412, 414, 421
students from lower socio-economic
  backgrounds, 137, 412, 413, 417
students with learning disabilities, 412,
  413
student-teacher ratio, 195, 196
Subaltern, 620, 632
Subjective quality of beauty, 464
Subjugation, 64, 96
Sudan, 132
Suffering, 30, 110, 429, 459, 622, 691–693,
  700, 702, 723, 728
Summer camp, 480
Survey, 197, 228, 229, 234, 236, 254, 263,
  264, 266, 268, 269, 377, 449, 460,
  462, 467, 478, 482, 544, 547, 592,
  660, 683
Survivalism, 560
Sustainability
  Sustainability Committee, 287, 303,
    306, 307
  sustainability governance, 566
  Sustainability Induction Module, 290,
    305
  Sustainability Integration Program for
    Students (SIPS), 305–308, 310
  sustainability-linked content, 180
  sustainability literacy, 327, 507
  sustainability maturity scale, 299, 310
  Sustainability Mission Integrator, 302,
    303
  Sustainability of Design, 379
  Sustainability Skills Cafes (SSCs), 602
  Sustainability Teaching Award, 320
  Sustainability, Tracking, Assessment &
    Rating System (STARS), 7, 132, 290,
    296–306, 308, 310, 356, 736
  Sustainability Wheel of Fortune, 354
Sustainable
  sustainable aesthetics, 319
  Sustainable Campus Index (SCI), 290
  sustainable development, 5, 7, 13, 14,
    18, 19, 21–24, 31–33, 42–44, 51, 62,
    64, 76, 93–96, 111–113, 133, 134,
    137, 138, 142, 151, 169–171, 174,
    175, 178–180, 186, 187, 224, 236,
    238, 273, 279, 291, 296, 297, 324,
    337, 354, 356, 357, 375–377, 379,
    388, 391, 392, 398, 399, 405, 428,
    446, 455, 460, 467, 476, 478, 479,
    491–495, 498, 501, 507, 514, 515,
    519, 526, 540, 560, 561, 565, 567,
  571, 582, 638, 640, 642, 660, 674,
  676, 677, 681, 683, 696, 710–713,
  715, 716, 718–720, 725, 727, 728
sustainable education, 6, 62, 514
sustainable futures, 357, 515, 516, 528,
  596
sustainable growth, 639
sustainable human settlement, 602
sustainable pedagogy, 508
sustainable production, 644, 676, 714,
  718
Sustainable Schools, 19, 462
sustainable societies, 176, 509, 561,
  674, 712, 720, 727
sustainable university, 295–297, 302,
  306, 310
sustainable water management, 383
sustainable wellbeing, 560, 562,
  564–568, 571, 572
Sustainable Development Goals (SDGs),
  4–9, 11–13, 17, 30–35, 37, 38, 41,
  43–45, 50–53, 63, 65–67, 69–74, 76,
  83–87, 89, 90, 92–96, 106, 107,
  111–116, 118, 119, 121, 132–138,
  140–143, 147, 148, 170–174, 176,
  178, 180, 181, 186, 197, 198, 203,
  204, 224, 226, 236, 245–247, 249,
  255, 257, 259, 273, 280–284, 287,
  291, 296–299, 304–306, 310, 316,
  318–322, 326, 327, 331, 333, 335,
  337, 338, 342, 343, 349, 351, 354,
  356, 376, 379–386, 388, 391, 400,
  401, 405, 411, 412, 427, 428, 432,
  434, 436, 446, 455, 460, 461, 465,
  469, 470, 474–476, 491–494, 496,
  501, 507, 508, 519, 526–529, 534,
  535, 540, 541, 548, 553, 560–562,
  566, 567, 569–572, 601, 605, 614,
  619–621, 625, 633, 637–641,
  643–646, 650, 651, 655, 656,
  658–660, 663, 664, 666–668,
  673–678, 680, 683, 684, 692, 694,
  696, 698, 701, 703, 705, 706, 709,
  713, 714, 716–718, 733–736
Sustainable Development Solutions
  Network (SDSN), 318
Syllabus, 189, 192, 194, 197, 349
Synergistic satisfiers, 565
System
  systemic design, 245–247, 249, 251,
    252, 254–257
  systemic functional linguistics, 509
  systemic global dysfunction, 118

systemic inequalities, 415
Systemic Learning Approach, 692,
    701–703
systemic racism, 68, 69
systems mapping, 251, 255
systems of oppression, 68
systems thinking, 45, 246, 249, 251,
    252, 257, 346, 349, 351, 354, 392, 514

T
Tabriz Islamic Art University, 316, 321,
    322, 324, 331, 333
Tacit knowledges, 605
Taliban, 619, 622, 623, 626–631, 633
Tasmania
    Tasmanian Aboriginal Centre, 90
    Tasmanian Climate Change Office
        (TCCO), 267, 271
    Tasmanian Department of Education,
        609
    Tasmanian Parks and Wildlife Service,
        266
    Tasmanian Policy Exchange, 272
    Tasmanian public, 263
Tbilisi Declaration, 32, 664
Teacher
    teacher professional development, 163,
        481
    teacher qualification systems, 644
    teacher-student relationships, 416
    teacher training, 148, 149, 180, 189,
        198, 427, 438, 517
Teacher education, 7, 13, 18, 22, 171, 172,
    175, 179, 181, 186, 188, 189, 198,
    427, 428, 436–438, 667
    teacher education institutions, 427
Teaching, Learning and Research, 22, 571
Teaching methods, 189, 191–193, 195–197,
    437, 643
Teamwork skills, 394
Technical, creative, entrepreneurial, 588
Technocracy, 693
Technological
    technological challenge, 560
    technological change, 231, 338, 469
    technological development, 36, 108,
        560, 644, 673
    technological era, 189
    Technological Knowledge (TK),
        228–230
    Technological Pedagogical Content
        Knowledge (TPACK), 228, 229, 231

Technological scouting, 641
Technology Development and Transfer
    Centre (TDTC), 138, 139
Technoscientific concepts, 560
Tertiary educational attainment, 647
Tertiary learning environment, 586
Thematic analysis, 135, 191, 208, 449, 464
Theory-driven evaluation, 604
Theory of Change (ToC), 8, 602, 604, 605,
    610–612, 614–616
Theory U, 561
Third-order learning, 519
Third Way, 37, 39
Third World debt crisis, 657
Threatened species, 17, 75
Time in nature, 348, 566
Times Higher Education Impact Rankings,
    260, 736
Times Impact Ratings, 20
Tinkerplots, 546, 548, 551, 552
Tobacco industry, 351, 500
Tobago, 7, 223–229, 234–238
Tokelau, 23
Tokyo Olympic games, 482
Traditional educational systems, 461, 647
Training, 19, 22, 24, 105, 106, 117, 120,
    138, 140, 142, 148, 149, 156, 171,
    175, 180, 186–191, 194–198, 226,
    321, 322, 324, 341, 348, 355, 427,
    430, 431, 434–436, 447, 455, 480,
    517, 579–582, 593, 602, 637,
    639–641, 644, 645, 647, 648, 658,
    684, 722
    training-related barriers, 194
Transdisciplinary coalitions, 356
Transdisciplinary programs, 648
Transformationist, 178
Transformative educational experiences
    transformative learning experiences,
        392, 400
    transformative pedagogy, 336, 350, 352,
        438
    transformative potential, 262, 350–352,
        710
Transnational cooperation, 638
Transnational institutions, 620, 724
Transnational multi-stakeholder
    collaboration, 638, 639
Transversal, 646, 648
Trauma-affected students, 414, 417, 419
Trawlwoolway, 85
Treaty, 37, 43, 63, 68, 69, 83–85, 90–93,
    96, 431–433

Trinidad, 7, 223–229, 234–238
Triple bottom line, 587, 676, 715
Triple identity, 696, 706
Tropical diseases, 336
Truth-telling, 84, 85, 90–93
Turbines, 382, 466, 698
Turkey, 627, 630, 631
Two-way conversation, 464
Two-way learning, 603

U
Ubuntu, 695
Uganda, 6, 148–153, 155, 156, 161–163
Ukraine, 29, 30, 648, 650
Uluru Statement from the Heart, 74, 75, 84
Uncertainty, 12, 115, 245, 246, 466,
     539–541, 543, 546, 550, 551, 553,
     584, 616, 683, 699, 702
UN Decade of Education for Sustainable
     Development (UN DESD), 32, 117,
     720
Undergraduate education, 317
Unemployment, 40, 226, 562, 603, 674,
     679, 681
UN Environmental Program [UNEP], 3, 11,
     87, 281, 713
Unfolding Projects, 626
UN General Assembly (UNGA), 246, 619
UniSuper, 286
United Kingdom (UK), 37, 40, 142, 252,
     283, 284, 343, 353, 401, 475, 476,
     478, 560, 584, 602
United Nations Conference on Sustainable
     Development, Rio+20, 2012, 393,
     713
United Nations Conference on the Human
     Environment, 460
United Nations Development Programme
     (UNDP), 13, 628, 679
United Nations Economic Commission for
     Europe, 561
United Nations Educational, Scientific and
     Cultural Organization (UNESCO),
     11–15, 18–21, 23, 24, 32, 50, 51, 53,
     134, 148, 150, 152, 155, 157, 158,
     162, 169, 173, 174, 176, 177, 186,
     224, 226, 227, 236, 260, 261, 460,
     475, 476, 478, 479, 483, 484, 495,
     509, 514, 515, 540, 541, 548, 567,
     572, 628, 702, 712, 713, 720
United Nations Framework Convention on
     Climate Change (UNFCCC), 11, 43,
     111, 112, 281, 540, 719

United Nations High Commissioner for
     Refugees, 393
United Nations (UN), 4, 5, 30, 51, 69, 71,
     72, 76, 87, 113, 132, 140, 142, 147,
     150, 196, 203, 261, 281, 296, 337,
     377, 398, 427, 446, 460, 473, 493,
     507, 527, 601, 619, 633, 637, 655,
     656, 692, 711, 713, 729
United Nations (UN) 2030 Agenda for
     Sustainable Development, 30, 71,
     86, 317, 427, 493, 601, 714
United Nations (UN) Millennium Summit,
     655
United States Department of the Treasury,
     658
United States (US), 12, 31, 37, 39–43, 70,
     188, 282, 285, 286, 289, 418, 475,
     476, 494, 510, 548, 679
Universal and mobile water filter, 381
Universal Basic Income, 681
Universal Declaration of Human Rights
     (UDHR), 150, 432, 436, 709, 715
Universal health coverage, 499, 562
Universalist Theory of Human Needs, 565
Universities, 6, 7, 12, 15, 17, 20, 115–117,
     132–134, 136–143, 148, 225, 229,
     245, 246, 255, 256, 259, 260,
     262–268, 270–273, 279, 280,
     282–291, 296, 297, 308, 309,
     315–318, 321, 326, 327, 331, 393,
     430, 508, 516, 519, 627, 630, 632,
     637, 736
University College London (ULC), 284
University culture, 318, 321
University-government relationships, 272
University Impact Rankings, 132
University of Cadiz, 412
University of California Berkley, 286
University of Gothenburg, 283
University of Maryland (UMD), 288
University of Melbourne, 284, 291
University of New South Wales (UNSW),
     284, 393
University of Queensland (UQ), 17, 285
University of Tasmania, 171, 190, 260, 262,
     276, 286, 287, 290, 295, 296, 310,
     356, 376, 377, 380, 386, 388, 393,
     450, 570, 571, 579, 580, 582, 584,
     585
University of Wollongong, 393
University Science Translation for Societal
     Impact, 274
University teaching, 267, 268

UN SDG Tasmania network, 307
UN Secretary General, 281
Unsustainability, 31, 32, 45, 108, 109, 113,
    181, 461, 515, 560
Unsustainable development, 110, 317, 320,
    675
Urban renewal, 683
Urban Water Metabolism, 385
Urdu, 193, 204, 208, 209, 213

V
Value-based sustainable learning, 720
Values, 5, 15, 21, 31, 32, 40, 45, 51, 56, 75,
    85, 96, 107, 108, 111, 112, 115, 117,
    120, 170–173, 176–178, 204, 205,
    209, 233, 247, 249, 263, 306, 317,
    339, 342, 343, 351, 352, 355, 357,
    377, 399, 400, 412, 420, 432, 437,
    447, 461, 477, 483, 526, 540, 542,
    547, 560, 561, 565–569, 571, 593,
    614, 638, 640, 641, 644, 645, 648,
    660, 665, 666, 676, 678, 683,
    709–711, 715, 719–722, 724, 725,
    728, 729, 735
Van Dieman's Land, 92
Variability, 37, 542, 547
Variation, 161, 510, 541, 542, 544–548,
    550, 551, 553, 681
Vietnam, 495
Virtual and augmented reality, 643
Visual art, 581, 583, 586
Vivir Bien (Living Well), 717
Vocabulary, 8, 177, 191, 193, 525–535
Vocational and technical education, 138,
    147, 638
Vocational Education and Training
    (TVET), 8, 225, 638–642, 645, 646,
    650, 651, 735
Vocational opportunities, 420, 527
Voice of country, 63, 83
Voluntary simplicity, 566, 684

W
Walking school bus, 481
Wary cooperation, 675, 682, 683
Washington Consensus, 44, 658
Waste disposal, 170, 174, 284, 693
Wastewater treatment, 383, 384
Water pollution, 175, 326, 341
Water treatment, 324, 384
Waverley Community Skills Cafes
    (WCSC), 602–605, 608–616

Waverley Primary School, 603
Wealth inequality, 336, 339
Weaponisation, 89
Wellbeing, 11, 45, 70, 71, 73, 74, 84, 86,
    95, 113, 115, 140, 148, 169, 203,
    223, 226, 236, 256, 301, 337–339,
    341, 343, 387, 412, 427, 445, 448,
    465, 476, 477, 484, 492–495, 498,
    501, 560, 562–568, 571, 572,
    581–584, 586, 587, 592, 604, 610,
    615, 628, 659, 666, 674, 676–681,
    691, 693, 696, 704, 711, 713, 715,
    718–720, 723, 724, 726, 727
Western democracy, 56
Western ideology, 656
Western worldview, 657, 659
Westphalian worldview, 76
White Australian, 74, 88
White male hegemony, 63
Whiteness, 63, 83, 85
White possession, 63, 67, 75, 76, 83, 89,
    91, 92, 94–96
    White possessiveness, 68, 76, 88, 89
White saviours, 68
White supremacy, 70
Wicked problem, 31, 114, 245, 247, 249,
    392, 398, 403–405, 452, 680, 736
Wilderness Society, 18
Wildlife, 41, 170
Wilson Promontory, 704
Windfarm project, 382
Wisdom, 9, 50, 51, 85, 499, 572, 612, 691,
    692, 696–706, 715, 726, 729
Women, 7, 34, 65, 70, 85–87, 92, 132, 137,
    138, 203–209, 213–218, 247, 248,
    254, 386, 474, 477, 482, 484, 495,
    499, 508, 619–623, 626–633, 727,
    735
    women's education, 633
    women's rights, 623, 627, 632
Work packages, 147
Workplace practice, 303
World's best practice, 300
World Bank, 35, 39, 110, 142, 173, 174,
    195, 225, 226, 628, 658, 659
World Business Council for Sustainable
    Development, 561
World Commission on Environment and
    Development [WCED], 11, 31, 711,
    719
World Economic Forum, 660
World Federation of Engineering
    Organisation, 376

World Health Organization (WHO), 13,
    335–337, 428, 436, 473–475, 484,
    492–494, 497–502, 581
World Heritage, 13–15
    World Heritage Area, 272
World Heritage Convention, 11, 13, 14, 18,
    20, 23
World Heritage sites, 13, 16, 17, 20, 21, 23
World Summit on Sustainable
    Development (2002), 713
Worldviews, 45, 76, 111, 118, 176, 246,
    339, 350–352, 355, 400, 519,
    560–562, 566–568, 572, 657, 659,

660, 662, 665, 680, 682, 683, 710,
    717, 734
World War 2, 664

Y
Young children's language development,
    601
Youth climate anxiety, 721
Youth unemployment, 226, 228

Z
Zeitenwende, 29, 30, 33